SOCIOLOGY OF ORGANIZATIONS

SOCIOLOGY OF ORGANIZATIONS

Structures and Relationships

Editors

Mary Godwyn
Babson College

Jody Hoffer Gittell
Brandeis University

SAGE | PINE FORGE

Los Angeles | London | New Delhi
Singapore | Washington DC

Los Angeles | London | New Delhi
Singapore | Washington DC

FOR INFORMATION:

Pine Forge Press

An Imprint of SAGE Publications, Inc.

2455 Teller Road

Thousand Oaks, California 91320

E-mail: order@sagepub.com

SAGE Publications Ltd.

1 Oliver's Yard

55 City Road

London, EC1Y 1SP

United Kingdom

SAGE Publications India Pvt. Ltd.

B 1/I 1 Mohan Cooperative Industrial Area

Mathura Road, New Delhi 110 044

India

SAGE Publications Asia-Pacific Pte. Ltd.

33 Pekin Street #02-01

Far East Square

Singapore 048763

Acquisitions Editor: David Repetto

Editorial Assistant: Maggie Stanley

Production Editor: Astrid Virding

Copy Editor: Melinda Masson

Typesetter: Hurix Systems Pvt. Ltd.

Proofreader: Sally M. Scott

Indexer: Diggs Publication Services

Cover Designers: Anupama Krishnan and Candice Harman

Marketing Manager: Erica DeLuca

Permissions Editor: Karen Ehrmann

Printed in the United States of America.

Library of Congress Cataloging-in-Publication Data

Godwyn, Mary.
Sociology of organizations : structures and relationships /
Mary Godwyn, Jody Hoffer Gittell.
p. cm.
Includes bibliographical references and index.
ISBN 978-1-4129-9195-7 (cloth) -- ISBN 978-1-4129-9196-4 (pbk.)

I. Gittell, Jody Hoffer. II. Title.

HM786.G63 2012

302.3'5--dc22   2011006598

This book is printed on acid-free paper.

11 12 13 14 15 10 9 8 7 6 5 4 3 2 1

CONTENTS

Acknowledgments   x

Introduction   xi

PART I: THE RELATIONAL ORGANIZATIONAL FORM   **1**

1. Business as an Integrative Unity   7
   Mary Parker Follett

2. Mechanistic and Organic Systems of Management   14
   Tom Burns and G. M. Stalker

3. Markets, Bureaucracies, and Clans   19
   William G. Ouchi

4. Neither Market Nor Hierarchy: Network Forms of Organization   30
   Walter W. Powell

5. Organizational Social Capital and Employment Practices   41
   Carrie R. Leana and Harry J. Van Buren III

6. Doing Your Job *and* Helping Your Friends: Universalistic Norms About
   Obligations to Particular Others in Networks   53
   Carol A. Heimer

7. Social Exchange and Micro Social Order   60
   Edward J. Lawler, Shane R. Thye, and Jeongkoo Yoon

PART II: THE BUREAUCRATIC ORGANIZATIONAL FORM   **73**

8. Bureaucracy   79
   Max Weber

9. Co-ordination   84
   Mary Parker Follett

10. The Horizontal Dimension in Bureaucracy   87
     Henry A. Landsberger

11. The Social Embeddedness of Labor Markets and Cognitive Processes   94
     Michael J. Piore

12. Defining the Post-Bureaucratic Type   98
     Charles Heckscher

13. Two Types of Bureaucracy: Enabling and Coercive   107
     Paul S. Adler and Brian Borys

14. Organized Dissonance: Feminist Bureaucracy as Hybrid Form   119
     Karen Lee Ashcraft

PART III: THE COORDINATION OF WORK   **127**

15. The Process of Control   133
     Mary Parker Follett

16. The Division of Work   139
     James G. March and Herbert A. Simon

17. Organization Design: An Information Processing View   146
     Jay R. Galbraith

18. Input Uncertainty and Organizational Coordination
in Hospital Emergency Units   163
     Linda Argote

19. Collective Mind in Organizations: Heedful Interrelating on Flight Decks   173
     Karl E. Weick and Karlene H. Roberts

20. Coordination in Fast-Response Organizations   186
     Samer Faraj and Yan Xiao

21. A Relational Model of How High-Performance Work Systems Work   205
     Jody Hoffer Gittell, Rob Seidner, and Julian Wimbush

PART IV: AUTONOMY AND CONTROL   **227**

22. Fundamentals of Scientific Management   233
     Frederick Winslow Taylor

23. The Basis of Authority   241
     Mary Parker Follett

24. Theory Y: The Integration of Individual and Organizational Goals   248
     Douglas McGregor

25. Toward an Economic Model of the Japanese Firm   254
     Masahiko Aoki

26. Work Organization, Technology, and Performance
   in Customer Service and Sales   267
      Rosemary Batt

27. Connective Leadership: Female Leadership Styles
   in the 21st-Century Workplace   279
      Jean Lipman-Blumen

28. Trust and Influence in Combat: An Interdependence Model   294
      Patrick J. Sweeney, Vaida Thompson, and Hart Blanton

PART V: ORGANIZATIONAL CULTURE   303

29. What Is Culture?   311
      Edgar H. Schein

30. The Organizational Culture War Games:
   A Struggle for Intellectual Dominance   315
      Joanne Martin and Peter Frost

31. Moral Economy and Cultural Work   337
      Mark Banks

32. Representing Blue: Representative Bureaucracy and Racial
   Profiling in the Latino Community   349
      Vicky M. Wilkins and Brian N. Williams

33. "This Place Makes Me Proud to Be a Woman": Theoretical
   Explanations for Success in Entrepreneurship Education
   for Low-Income Women   364
      Mary Godwyn

34. Hospitals as Cultures of Entrapment:
   A Re-Analysis of the Bristol Royal Infirmary   381
      Karl E. Weick and Kathleen M. Sutcliffe

35. Representative Bureaucracy and Policy Tools: Ethnicity,
   Student Discipline, and Representation in Public Schools   390
      Christine H. Roch, David W. Pitts, and Ignacio Navarro

PART VI: ORGANIZATIONAL CONFLICT   409

36. Capital: A Critique of Political Economy   415
      Karl Marx

37. Constructive Conflict   417
      Mary Parker Follett

38. Organizational Conflict: Concepts, and Models   427
      Louis R. Pondy

39. Marx, Globalization and Alienation: Received
and Underappreciated Wisdoms   440
W. Peter Archibald

40. Racial Inequality in the Workplace: How Critical
Management Studies Can Inform Current Approaches   448
Brenda Johnson

41. Mythicizing and Reification in Entrepreneurial Discourse:
Ideology-Critique of Entrepreneurial Studies   457
John O. Ogbor

PART VII: DIVERSITY WITHIN ORGANIZATIONS   **471**

42. Women's Careers in Static and Dynamic Organizations   477
Elin Kvande and Bente Rasmussen

43. "We Have to Make a MANagement Decision":
Challenger and the Dysfunctions of Corporate Masculinity   492
Mark Maier

44. Just One of the Guys? How Transmen Make Gender Visible at Work   510
Kristen Schilt

45. The Emperor Has No Clothes: Rewriting "Race in Organizations"   527
Stella M. Nkomo

46. The Colonizing Consciousness and Representations of the Other:
A Postcolonial Critique of the Discourse of Oil   546
Anshuman Prasad

47. The Disclosure Dilemma for Gay Men and Lesbians:
"Coming Out" at Work   563
Kristin H. Griffith and Michelle R. Hebl

48. Identification of the Characteristics of Work Environments and
Employers Open to Hiring and Accommodating People With Disabilities   577
Dennis Gilbride, Robert Stensrud, David Vandergoot, and Kristie Golden

PART VIII: ORGANIZATIONAL LEARNING AND CHANGE   **587**

49. Single-Loop and Double-Loop Models in Research on Decision Making   595
Chris Argyris

50. The Iron Cage Revisited: Institutional Isomorphism and
Collective Rationality in Organization Fields   605
Paul J. DiMaggio and Walter W. Powell

51. Organizational Learning   616
Barbara Levitt and James G. March

52. The Local and Variegated Nature of Learning in Organizations:
A Group-Level Perspective   631
     Amy C. Edmondson

53. Practical Pushing: Creating Discursive Space in Organizational Narratives   641
     Joyce K. Fletcher, Lotte Bailyn, and Stacy Blake Beard

54. Operating Room: Relational Spaces and Microinstitutional Change in Surgery   649
     Katherine C. Kellogg

PART IX: NEW TECHNOLOGY, SOCIAL MEDIA, AND EMERGING COMMUNITIES   **661**

55. Constructions and Reconstructions of Self in Virtual Reality:
Playing in the MUDs   667
     Sherry Turkle

56. Link, Search, Interact: The Co-Evolution of NGOs and Interactive Technology   676
     Jonathan Bach and David Stark

57. Tweeting the Night Away: Using Twitter to Enhance Social Presence   687
     Joanna C. Dunlap and Patrick R. Lowenthal

58. E-mail in Government: Not Post-Bureaucratic but
Late-Bureaucratic Organizations   696
     Albert Jacob Meijer

59. Online Dating in Japan: A Test of Social Information Processing Theory   711
     James Farrer and Jeff Gavin

60. Online Organization of the LGBT Community in Singapore   720
     Joe Phua

Index   729

About the Editors   739

ACKNOWLEDGMENTS

The editors thank the editorial staff at Pine Forge Press/Sage Publications, Inc., especially David Repetto, who believed in our vision for this volume, and Maggie Stanley, Astrid Virding, and Melinda Masson, who so adeptly guided us through the publishing process. We thank Peter Conrad for the introduction upon which our authorship collaboration was built and the reviewers who provided us with valuable comments: Barbara Arrighi, William Canak, Chikwendu Christian, Jason Combs, Maria Dixon, Scott Dolan, Qingwen Dong, David Edens, Samuel Gilmore, Erin Hatton, Shoon Lio, Dan Morgan, Eric Neuman, Peter Nowak, A. Olu Oyinlade, Susan Pfefferle, Rene Rios, Masoud Shadnam, Joshua Woods, and Cory Young.

Mary Godwyn would like to thank her family and dedicate this book to them: Phil, Sam, Graham, Emily, and Henry—you give me so much happiness.

Jody Hoffer Gittell would also like to thank her family—Ross, Rose, and Grace—for their constant love and companionship. She dedicates this book to Marilyn Jacobs Gittell, inspiration and role model to many, for introducing her to the work of Mary Parker Follett.

INTRODUCTION

W. Lloyd Warner, an Australian anthropologist, argued that "we [know] more about tribal societies than we [do] about our own" modern society (Collins 1994:214). Warner was referring to the tendency to interpret contemporary, technologically sophisticated societies as being held together by their secular and rational characteristics. This tendency is evident in the dominance of the rational perspective in the sociology of organizations and in organization studies. Modern societies differ from tribal ones because they are characterized by bureaucratic order and populated by a multiplicity of diverse, complex, and stratified groups. However, the emphasis on rational theories overlooks the fact that all societies, whether tribal or modern, are held together by mutual identification and powerful emotional attachments that are created and reinforced through rituals. One of Warner's most famous students, Erving Goffman, carefully chronicled the microinteractions that occur in modern societies. Goffman's *Interaction Ritual* (1967) and *The Presentation of Self in Everyday Life* (1959) reveal some of the underlying social rituals that often remain taken for granted and invisible, especially to those who enact them every day.

In fact, one of the fundamental insights of sociology is that society has a *nonrational basis*. Randall Collins (1992) writes that what distinguishes sociology from most other disciplines is the understanding "that the human power of reasoning is based on nonrational foundations, and that human society is held together not by rational agreements but by deeper emotional processes that produce social bonds of trust among particular kinds of people" (p. vi). From this perspective, bureaucracies are not an expression of an ahistorical rational order serendipitously discovered in the modern age. Instead, rational bureaucracies are a type of social organization that achieves solidarity and trust through a set of specific relationships and distinctive rituals that characterize many formal organizations in modern societies. Similarly, the sociological view finds that none of the general categories that exist in human thought, such as space, time, and number, are universal, atemporal, or separate from human existence. Though these categories transcend any given individual, they arise from and change according to the social context.

Sociology developed in response to radical upheaval in the social order. Political transformations were marked by the breakdown of feudal systems and the rise of modern states and representative republics. Urbanization and industrialization provided dramatic geographic and economic shifts. Using multiple theoretical paradigms, sociologists tend to analyze and challenge the official, traditional and commonsense description of social order; they provide "non-obvious" explanations of how the social world operates (Collins 1992). Consequently, sociology has evolved as a multi-causal, "problem-oriented" discipline that tends to engage in critical and reflexive examination (Levin 1994:14). Reflexivity is the ability of an individual or group of people to study themselves; as George

Herbert Mead (1934) put it, "This characteristic is represented in the word 'self' which is reflexive, and indicates that which can be both subject and object" (p. 136). Critical and reflexive examination includes studying our beliefs, theories, and worldviews: not only by testing them empirically, but by exploring their social significance—what they say about us as people, how these beliefs make us *feel,* and how they contribute to our sense of self-identity and solidarity with specific others. Sociological paradigms are worldviews founded on sets of basic assumptions about humanity—whether people are fundamentally cooperative and similar or naturally competitive and different, driven by individual self-interest or governed by their interactions with others. Inevitably, these assumptions guide our perceptions and inform our preferences for certain theories and practices.

A central theme of this volume, then, is to question what has become the theoretical orthodoxy in the sociology of organizations. In order to provide a reflexive analysis we go beyond the traditional emphasis on the rational paradigm and draw upon all four sociological traditions: rationalism, interactionism, conflict theory, and functionalism. These four paradigms provide a basis to examine and identify each author's theoretical assumptions and to situate articles within the larger sociological perspective. At the same time, we also acknowledge that the complex insights offered by many of the authors featured here, including the two we highlight as founders of organization studies—Mary Parker Follett and Max Weber—demonstrate how these paradigms can overlap, complement, and contradict each other.

This anthology not only provides classical perspectives; it also explores contemporary developments in sociological theory and organization studies. We include articles on formal, bureaucratic organizations and those that discuss voluntary and nontraditional ones like nongovernmental organizations and nonprofits. We explore the creation of informal and spontaneous organizations as a response to the decline in fixed social identities and the emergence of a fluid and increasingly pluralistic sense of self and community. To that end, we include articles that represent the most recent advancements in organizational structure and theory due to the influence of new technology, such as online communities organized around gaming, social media, and political activism.

The remainder of this introduction explains the four sociological paradigms. We reflect on their strengths and weaknesses and encourage discussions about how these perspectives are often adopted (or rejected) not only because of their explanatory capability or theoretical rigor, but also on the basis of convention, group values, power dynamics, and social bonds. Modern societies, though diverse, complex, and stratified, are built upon nonrational foundations just as tribal societies are, and like tribal people, members of modern societies have their own rituals of trust and social solidarity.

THE FOUR SOCIOLOGICAL PARADIGMS: EXPLANATION AND APPLICATION

Our abbreviated treatment of the four sociological paradigms is intended as an introduction to this volume rather than a comprehensive theoretical and historical grounding in the discipline of sociology. As mentioned, the perspectives are rationalism, interactionism, conflict theory, and functionalism.

The Rational Paradigm

Rational theories interpret organizations as instruments to achieve goals that would be difficult or impossible for separate individuals to accomplish on their own (Handel 2003a:2). Included under this rubric are rational choice theory, exchange theory, and the rational-bureaucratic perspective. Rational choice and exchange theories have their intellectual roots in the idea of the social contract—that is, the idea that societies were formed by individuals who calculated that their chances of survival would be advanced by joining together in a group. Historically, rational choice and exchange theories have been associated more with economics than with sociology. These theories define individuals as rational agents who routinely use instrumental (means-end) calculations to determine and act upon their own best interest. Often this interest is assumed to be material and monetary. Sociology is "a view of human behavior that focuses on the *pattern of relationships among individuals* rather than solely on the individuals themselves" (Levin 1994:9, emphasis added), but since rational choice examines the calculation of individual self-interest, some have argued that it is not a sociological theory. Therefore, rational choice has been embraced at times by some sociologists, but has also been roundly criticized and rejected by others.

Weber's rational-bureaucratic perspective represents the current theoretical orthodoxy in the sociology of organizations, and many scholars use his account in *Economy and Society* ([1924] 1978) as the initial point of intellectual engagement. Rational-bureaucratic order is a replicable legitimacy grounded in the abstraction of the office rather than in any given individual administrator; in Weber's words, bureaucracy is "the established impersonal order" ([1924] 1978:215). Inherent in the rational-bureaucratic perspective is the idea of "legitimate domination" (Weber [1924] 1978:212). This legitimate domination establishes a hierarchy, enforced by "formal legality" (Weber [1924] 1978:216), and this hierarchy is in turn responsible for the efficient and coordinated production that characterizes organizations in modern industrial and postindustrial societies.

Weber's ([1924] 1978) concept of rational-bureaucratic legitimacy seems to suggest that rational theories are the most direct and uncomplicated of the four sociological paradigms. The emphasis on instrumental means-end calculation, the idea of decisions structured to maximize benefit and minimize costs, and the assumption of an impersonal, nonemotional, and therefore objective basis for organizational structure implies a logical integrity and resonates with the cultural assumptions of modern societies to such a degree that these ideas seem familiar and commonsensical. Additional support for rational legitimacy comes from the obvious shortcomings of the other types of authority Weber discusses: traditional and charismatic. Traditional authority emphasizes habit, convention, and established beliefs, all anathema to notions of individualism, progress, and mobility. Charismatic authority, the adoration of a specific heroic individual, focuses on emotional rather than cognitive assessment, is unique and nonreplicable, and therefore cannot be systematized. Rather than usher in

modernity, traditional and charismatic authority evoke characteristics of antiquity.

Though seemingly straightforward and transparent, rational theories have complications that warrant consideration. As will be discussed in more detail, the term *rational* has multiple meanings, both in ordinary language and in sociology. Often defined in modern societies as reasonable, unbiased, sane, logical, and sound, *rational* has a very positive connotation. Of course, the terms *irrational* and *nonrational* are condemnatory in direct proportion that *rational* is commendatory. Therefore, rational theories have their own merit, but they are also imbued with social values and serve as significant cultural emblems for societies and organizations that seek to be identified as modern.

Additionally, Weber's ([1924] 1978) account of rational bureaucracy is often interpreted as an endorsement of bureaucracy as the "ideal" process to which modern organizations should conform. He is credited with the view that bureaucracy is "technically superior," "a pillar of modern society," and "the most efficient form of organization" (Handel 2003b:5). And yet, it is important to remember that Weber was deeply conflicted about the rise of rationalism. Though it is true he oriented his sociology around historical comparisons and understood rational authority and bureaucratic method to be characteristic of modernity, he was much less an enthusiastic endorser of rationality and bureaucracy than is commonly represented. Moreover, Weber embraced the idea that history and development are riddled with complexity that often transcends any one theoretical framework. He rejected the simpler, linear explanations of progress popular in the natural sciences in favor of applying multicausal theories. Nevertheless, Weber recognized that even multi-causal theories only partially capture the nearly limitless particulars of human experience and at best demonstrate mild predictive ability.

Before discussing Weber's reflections on the problems of rationality, it is worth briefly expounding on his concept of "ideal type." To make sociological sense of historical particulars, Weber ([1925] 1946) created the notion of ideal type to describe an abstraction, an analytical construct that reflects patterns of behaviors and beliefs that characterize particular groups. Because ideal types are grounded in social reality, they are not stagnant but shift over time to reflect changes in social relationships and social meaning. Therefore, the bureaucratic order that Weber set forth is an *abstraction* of actual bureaucracies, and the rational-bureaucratic legitimacy Weber attributes to modern organizations can be interpreted as less an endorsement of this authority as ultimately "superior," and more a description of its legitimacy in the context of modern economic structures and social values.

As mentioned earlier, Weber had serious concerns about rational-bureaucratic legitimacy. One was that *rational* is a contested term. Weber ([1904] 1958) writes,

It is a question of the specific and peculiar rationalism of Western culture. Now by this term very different things may be understood . . . there is, for example, rationalization of mystical contemplation, that is of an attitude which, viewed from other departments of life, is specifically irrational, just as much as there are rationalizations of economic life, of technique, of scientific research, of military training, of law and administration. Furthermore, each one of these fields may be rationalized in terms of very different ultimate values and ends, and what is rational from one point of view may well be irrational from another. (P. 26)

Given the various definitions and meanings of *rational*, Weber (Kalberg 1980) created a typology to capture what he saw as two different, and opposing, kinds of rationality. Functional, or formal, rationality is associated with bureaucracies and is most like instrumentality: It is the means-end calculation of how a result can be quickly and efficiently achieved. Substantive (also called substantial) rationality is holistic, reticular, and value-driven rather than results-driven; substantive rationality recognizes the interdependency of a wide range of objectives and perspectives. Richard Munch (1994) writes, "Formal rationality is limited to specific causal knowledge about specific means-end relationships and to the realization of a specific end and one substantial value. Substantive rationality has to include many substantial values; it has to

look at the whole world as something that should be made better" (pp. 174–75).

Karl Mannheim further developed the distinction between these types of rationality by highlighting their opposition; he argued that functional rationality "tends to drive out substantive rationality" (Collins 1992:5). Collins (1992) describes the process:

The same procedures can be *functionally* rational but lead to *substantially* irrational results. A bureaucracy consists of a network of specialists, who are concerned only with the most efficient means to achieve a particular goal. Just what these goals are is someone else's business, not theirs. That is why a bureaucracy can prove so frustrating for people who have to deal with it . . . And this is not just a failure on the part of the individuals involved; it is the very rationality of the organization that results in the inability of bureaucrats to see the overall ends they are meeting or failing to meet. (P. 5)

For Weber, rationalism represented the uniform, linear, and (ideally) meritocratic processes that were upheld by legal mandates and therefore distanced from impulse, sentiment, and social status. However, mechanistic formalization also represents the deterioration of substantive, conscious reflection on the far-reaching ramifications of action and responsibility; it ignores the mutable boundaries of interconnected systems and the mutual feedback loops between individuals and institutions. Weber ([1904] 1958) bitterly lamented the de-emphasis of the nonrational, spiritual origin of capitalism and the seemingly inexorable rationalization and bureaucratization that has come to define this economic system and its influence on social interactions:

For this last stage of this cultural development, it might truly be said: "Specialists without spirit, sensualists without heart; this nullity imagines that it has attained a level of civilization never before achieved." (Pp. 181–82)

Weber's concept of rational-bureaucratic authority, or at least a narrow interpretation of this concept, lends itself as a justification for the vertical hierarchy, domination, and narrow focus on profit-generation that has come to characterize corporations in modern capitalistic societies. In fact, Weber's emphasis on the *impersonal* aspect of rational bureaucracy, the separation of personal property from organizational property, can be used to claim that business organizations constitute a separate sphere that is not governed by the same processes or considerations as other social spheres. Weber ([1904] 1958) writes,

[There is a] separation of workplace, office of business in general and the private dwelling, of firm and name, of business capital and private wealth, the tendency to make of the business a *corpus mysticum* (at least in the case of corporate property). (P. 276)

A major element in rational-bureaucratic processes, then, is the separation of spheres into household/personal on the one hand, and business/impersonal on the other. This schism provides the rationale to claim that these two spheres—Jürgen Habermas (1989) refers to them as the lifeworld and the system—operate on oppositional premises: the lifeworld on cooperation, ethics, and community values; the system on instrumental and strategic reason, self-interest, and avarice. Habermas (1989) writes:

As we shall see, modern societies attain a level of system differentiation at which increasingly autonomous organizations are connected with one another via delinguistified media of communication: these systemic mechanisms—for example, money—steer a social intercourse that has been largely disconnected from norms and values, above all in those subsystems of purposive rational economic and administration action that, on Weber's diagnosis, have become independent of their moral-political foundations. (P. 189)

Many scholars in organization studies cite Weber as the lead architect of the field, and, despite his deep ambivalence, typically draw on his authority to assert that bureaucracy is the superior organizational form. However, at most, Weber ([1904] 1958) saw bureaucracy as emblematic of a stage of cultural development associated with a particular population, and a stage he felt could well lead to "purely mundane passions" and "mechanized petrification, embellished with a sort of convulsive self-importance" (p. 182). Moreover, many misinterpret

Weber's *ideal type* of bureaucracy to mean the *practical reality* of bureaucracy. By capitalizing on the positive connotations of the term *rational*, these misinterpretations actively ignore the unplanned and unrecognized inefficiencies of real bureaucracies. These inefficiencies are often a result of the failure of the ideal type of rational-bureaucratic form to account for the inevitability of personal relationships, boredom with and alienation from work, the refusal to follow rules and orders, and resentment of the hierarchy. Rosabeth Moss Kanter (1977) writes,

The requirements for a perfectly technically "rational" bureaucracy that never has to rely on the personal discretion of a single individual can never be met: complete knowledge of all cause-effect relationships plus control over all of the relevant variables. Thus sources of uncertainty that are inherent in human institutions mean that some degree of reliance on individual persons must always be present. It is ironic that in those most impersonal of institutions the essential communal problem of trust remains. For wherever there is uncertainty, *someone* (or some group) must decide, and thus, there must be personal discretion. And discretion raises not technical but human, social, and even communal questions: trust, and its origins in loyalty, commitment, and mutual understanding based on the sharing of values. (Pp. 48–49)

The Interactionist Paradigm

In contrast to the rational paradigm where organizations are seen as instruments to achieve goals, interactionists view organizations from a relational perspective—as associations that provide members with a sense of connection and meaning. This perspective understands organizations to be a set of ongoing interactions and emerging relationships wherein people negotiate and construct understandings of reality and identity. Interactionism, which has its roots in philosophical pragmatism, includes symbolic interaction, social psychology, interpretative sociology, ethnomethodology, and dramaturgy. The interactionist paradigm is distinct from the structuralism of Durkheimian functionalism and the materialism of Marx's conflict theory. However, this perspective has been fluid enough to, at times, use elements of conflict theory, especially in the field of deviance, and elements of functionalism, especially with regard to the relationship between microinteractions and group solidarity. For our purposes here, the common elements among interactionist perspectives are a qualitative approach that stresses the subjective experiences of actors; a focus on symbols (including language) as they contribute to emerging, negotiated reality; and the idea that there is no presocial self, but a self that is continually constructed through interactions with others. Of the connections between self and other, individual and group, Mary Parker Follett (1918) writes,

> I find my expression of the whole-idea, the whole-will, through my group life . . . The group must always dictate the modes of activity for the individual . . . The seeing of self as, with all other selves, creating, demands a new attitude and a new activity . . . the fallacy of self-and-others fades away and there is only self-in-and-through-others, only others so firmly rooted in the self and so fruitfully growing there that sundering is impossible. We must now enter upon modes of living commensurate with this thought. (Pp. 7–8)

In *The New State* (1918), Mary Parker Follett's relational approach to the sociology of organizations predates the rational approach emphasized in Weber ([1924] 1978). Much as Weber is often cited as the progenitor of the rational paradigm in the sociology of organizations, Follett is arguably the founder of the interactionist approach. Writing in the early 1900s, Follett ([1924] 1995) posits that reality is created through a circular response at all levels of interaction:

> In human relations, as I have said, this is obvious: I never react to you but to you-plus-me; or to be more accurate, it is I-plus-you reacting to you-plus-me. "I" can never influence "you" because you have already influenced me; that is, in the very process of meeting, by the very process of meeting, we both become something different. (P. 42)

Follett's strong identification with philosophical pragmatism, her idea of negotiated and emerging reality, and her denial of dualism generally, but especially dualism between subject and object and individual and society, form the basis of the interactionist perspective. For Follett, social interactions reflect not the passive stability of underlying structures, as the functionalist paradigm holds, but rather active, dynamic processes.

This mutuality of self, central to Follett's interactionist perspective and evident later in the work of Mead and Goffman, serves as the basis for her rejection of hierarchy and domination, and her embrace of a different mode of achieving control in organizations. Moreover, Follett's denial of dualism explains how a noncoercive and progressive integration of ideas can be reached on an organizational level. She therefore embraces conflict and conflict resolution as creative and constructive forces in organizations.

Unlike the rational paradigm, Follett's interactionism does not allow for such a separation between spheres wherein one sphere, the organizational sphere characterized by rational-bureaucratic legitimacy, is largely divorced from social norms and values. In fact, central themes in her work are relatedness and integration. Ansell (2009) writes, "A *relational ontology* is one in which social entities are to be understood in terms of their relationships rather than in terms of their inherent (essential) characteristics. Follett's work is thoroughly *relational* in its approach to the Organizational phenomena" (p. 471). Follett (1918) unites workers and managers, self and society, subject and object: She does not choose between entities; she focuses on the relation that connects them:

> We see now that the process of the many becoming one is not a metaphysical or mystical idea; psychological analysis shows us how we can at the same moment be the self and the other, it shows how we can be forever apart and forever united. It is by the group process that the transfiguration of the external into the spiritual takes place, that is, that what seems a series becomes a whole. The essence of society is difference, related difference. (P. 33)

Whereas the bureaucratic form can be used to reinforce hierarchal and rigid power structures, Follett's philosophy of organizations calls for mutuality and egalitarianism.

Though Weber is associated with the rational perspective, his scholarship is also associated with conflict theory and interactionism. He earns his interactionist credentials because his antipositivist *verstehen* approach stresses the subjectivity of both the researcher and the participants. In this approach, to gather understanding of any given social circumstance, the researcher must see the situation from the actors' point of view. Because of the emphasis on the subjective view of actors and the mutual construction of self, the interactionist paradigm is characterized by qualitative rather than quantitative research—that is, textual rather than numerical data. Though Weber ([1904] 1958) used this methodology in his macrosociology, for instance to understand how aesthetic Protestantism influenced the development of capitalism, the *verstehen* approach became key in the development of methodologies in the microinteractionist traditions, such as participant observation, ethnomethodology, ethnography, and dramaturgy. William Levin (1994) writes about the differences between qualitative and quantitative methodologies:

> In the natural sciences, the measurement of objects, including their behavior and relationship to one another, is overwhelmingly quantitative. That is, researchers use numerical evaluations such as weight in grams, velocity in meters per second, length in centimeters, and energy in joules. This is an effective approach, because there seems to be a stable, physical reality in the natural world that yields consistent measurement results . . . and that does not seem to mind the process at all. Of course, rocks, electrons, and red blood cells have no consciousness with which to respond to the measurement they undergo. But people do. (P. 66)

And although not all interactionists would agree, Levin (1994) claims that "the symbolic interactionists argue that the methods of the natural sciences have virtually no application to the study of human behavior" (p. 51). In fact, Herbert Blumer, author of *Symbolic Interactionism: Perspective and Method* (1969), argues passionately against quantitative methods as failing to capture the unique aspects of social life. According to Blumer, questionnaires and surveys are inadequate tools because they do not gather data on how people behave in their everyday lives; they gather data on how people answer questionnaires and surveys. The belief that human social interactions cannot be understood quantitatively is, of course, open to challenge. Many scholars in organization studies who pursue an interactionist perspective now use perceptual measures and tools of network analysis to quantify and measure the nature of social interactions.

The strengths of interactionism, including the centrality of subjectivity, the concept of the circular self, and the insistence that "society is not a structure, but a process" (Collins 1994:262), are, according to its critics, also the weaknesses of this paradigm. Critics assert that the emphasis on subjectivity produces qualitative data that might lack rigor and cannot be generalized or replicated.

The Conflict Paradigm

Both functionalism and conflict theory are used to investigate organizations as vehicles for social order and social control. However, whereas functional theories assume system stability through consensus and cooperation, conflict theories focus on the competition among members and the power dynamics within and among organizations. Therefore, this perspective analyzes conflicts of interest and understands organizations as tools that benefit some people at the expense of others. Essential to conflict theory is the importance of diverse perspectives and the mandate that multiple views, causalities, and theories are recognized, with special concern given to issues of social justice, equal representation, and fair treatment. Conflict theories tend to represent the perspectives of those who are not well served by organizations, and these theories are therefore associated with liberation movements and radical change. The motivation behind this perspective is to critique and improve social systems, not just explain or describe them. The goal is progress and emancipation—the intent is to reduce and resist systems of domination and expand the scope of freedom and autonomy. Feminist theory, critical theory, postcolonial theory, race theory, queer theory, cultural studies, ecological theory, and environmental studies all fall under the rubric of critique; all are oriented toward agency and self-reflection, and all influence the way the self is experienced, expressed, and represented in the social.

Karl Marx is most often cited as the classical conflict theorist in sociology—and for good reason. Marx's theory on social class and his concepts of alienation, ideology, false consciousness, and objectification have informed the political, economic, and social impact of conflict theory from the nineteenth through the twenty-first centuries. Yet, most sociologists also situate Weber in the conflict paradigm, and some argue that he provided the intellectual, if not the political, fundamentals of conflict theory. Collins (1994) writes, "Weber deserves to be named as the individual who set off modern conflict sociology" (p. 92), and "his multidimensionality made him fundamentally a conflict theorist . . . Weber not only saw that there are multiple spheres, but also that there is a struggle for domination going on inside each one" (p. 85).

By the same token, Follett is also a conflict theorist. She, too, appreciated the multidimensionality and contending voices that inform social interaction. However, unlike the focus on exploitation usually associated with conflict theory, there is optimism in her belief that not only can conflicts be equitably resolved; they can also help produce creativity and cooperation. Rooted in philosophical pragmatism, Follett's ([1924] 1995) ideal of "integration" transcends and improves upon the basic dualism—domination and subordination—in conflict theory:

> Integration means finding a third way which will include both what A wishes and what B wishes, a way in which neither side has had to sacrifice anything . . . and the extraordinarily interesting thing about this is that the third way means progress. In domination you stay where you are. In compromise likewise you deal with no new values. By integration something new has emerged, the third way, something beyond either-or . . . Hence, difference can be constructive rather than destructive if we know what to do with it. It may be a sign of health, a prophecy of progress. (Pp. 188–90)

Moreover, Follett (1918) glorifies diversity, and admonishes against the tendency to confuse difference with animosity and consensus with happiness:

> Give *your* difference, welcome *my* difference, unify *all* difference in the larger whole—such is the law of growth. The unifying of difference is the eternal process of life—the creative synthesis, the highest act of creation, the atonement . . . And throughout our participation in the group process we must be ever on our guard that we do not confuse differences and antagonisms, that diversity does not arouse hostility . . . If my friend and I are always trying to find the things on which we agree, what is the use of meeting? Because the consciousness of agreement makes us happy? . . . Someone ought to write an essay on the dangers to the soul of congeniality. Pleasant little glows of feelings can never be fanned into the fire which becomes the driving force of progress. (Pp. 40–41)

Follett stops short, however, of saying that conflict is functional in the same way that theorists like Lewis Coser (1956) claim that conflict contributes to the social order. Blending conflict theory with functionalism, Coser proposed that under the right circumstances, social conflict can *increase* group solidarity by providing an outside threat, acting as a release valve, or clarifying norms. Though Coser's theory uses the idea of conflict, he views conflict primarily as adding to the stability of social groups rather than contributing to social change. Therefore, Coser's theory is still conservative-leaning rather than change-inducing, and more consistent with a functional perspective than with conflict theory.

Conflict theorists generally see two possible outcomes of conflict: A winner emerges and dominates others, or no winner emerges and there is a tense balance of power until one does. In theory, there is the overarching progressive dialectical process commonly described as thesis, antithesis, and synthesis; however, in practical application, the stalemate of domination and subordination is a central assumption. Just as functionalism assumes consensus and cooperation, the conflict paradigm assumes disagreement and competition as fundamental to human nature and social interaction. Therefore, conflict theory does not have a clear definition of what constitutes synthesis or explicit examples of positive and equitable resolutions of conflict.

In fact, both Marx and Weber employ the concept of ideology wherein the powerful promote their own interests through belief systems that legitimize their domination of others (MacLeod 2009:114). Marx's concept of ideology includes *false consciousness,* which is the idea that subordinated populations agree with cultural values and partake in social conventions only because they are unaware of how these norms are controlled by the dominant members of society. Therefore, false consciousness is the unwitting participation in one's own subordination. Though false consciousness is undeniably an insightful and compelling concept, given the assumption of domination and subordination, and the lack of a coherent definition of fair and equitable conflict resolution, any and all agreement can be attributed to false consciousness. In this way, false consciousness is not falsifiable or refutable. That is to say, since the conflict paradigm assumes domination and subordination, and ideology dictates that subordinated populations are unaware of their own exploitation, no consent that issues from subordinated populations can ever escape the suspicion of being the result of false consciousness. Therefore, there are no verifiably fair agreements—no way to know if synthesis, rather than manipulation and exploitation, has transpired.

Follett ([1924] 1995) improves on this situation considerably because she eschews the dualistic construction of domination and subordination and carefully describes the third way of integration wherein multiple perspectives are reconciled while each maintains its own integrity. In her concept of the circular process, each perspective necessarily influences the others and creates a practical synthesis, which in Marx's conflict theory remains merely theoretical. Therefore, Follett provides a basis wherein conflict can potentially be constructive for all parties involved. However, rather than viewing conflict as contributing to the conservation of the system, as functionalists have, she suggests that creative, non-coercive change can result.

The Functionalist Paradigm

The functionalist paradigm, also commonly referred to as the consensus paradigm or as sociological positivism, tends to understand organizations as constructive, cooperative, and stable systems based on the agreement or consensus of members. Therefore, this perspective emphasizes what is working well and tacitly assumes the point of view of those who benefit from the organizational structure and objectives. Because functionalism regards organizations as benign, advantageous, and beneficial, it is a relatively conservative theory that does not tend to prescribe or anticipate change.

Functionalism has been used in both social and natural sciences; historically, the functionalist approach in sociology has attempted to follow the scientific method used in natural sciences. That is to say, functionalists look for replicable causes that can be generalized and systematically compared between and among groups. Levin (1994) writes that functionalism "focuses on the identification of positive functions in society, assuming that society naturally tends toward equilibrium or balance" (p. 91).

Functionalism, then, can be compared to the type of investigation common to ethology. When ethologists observe animals, there is an assumption that patterns of behavior exist because they are necessary for survival and group coherence. Ethologists do not endeavor to bring new social order or moral conscience to the animals they study. They do not manipulate male sea horses away from taking care of their young or suggest to gorillas that they are spending too much time grooming each other and might want to do a bit more foraging. Whether ethologists observe violent or caretaking behavior, hierarchies or egalitarianism, they assume functionality and then attempt to generate a testable theory that reflects that assumption and predicts future behavior. (The accuracy of the observations is another subject, and of course perceptions are influenced by assumptions.) This is consistent with the functionalist paradigm in sociology.

For instance, Herbert Gans (1972) theorizes that poverty, one of the greatest human ills, actually serves many positive social functions, such as creating a population desperate enough to take the most undesirable jobs and extending the value of goods by maintaining a market for used and damaged products. Finding functionality in behavior does not necessarily imply an endorsement (Levin

1994:90). In fact, functionalists like Gans argue that strategies for social change are most successful when they recognize and offer alternatives to the functionality of current systems. Given the search for functionality in some of the most problematic and deplorable human behaviors such as war, murder, and rape, one strength of functionalism is that it uncovers what Collins (1992) calls "non-obvious" explanations for social phenomena and, therefore, can make key contributions to solving social ills.

Moreover, Durkheim ([1893] 1964), a classical functionalist, arguably provided the most comprehensive account of the mechanisms of social structure and social cohesion. He was also a vociferous critic of the idea that social groups, including organizations, are held together by rational contracts. His argument that social groups are founded on a nonrational basis of trust and solidarity was fundamental to establishing the discipline of sociology. Those organizations with high solidarity, loyalty, and trust are referred to as having "strong cultures." We will explore this notion further in the section on "organizational culture."

Though it has notable strengths, functionalism also has significant weaknesses. It does not ordinarily deliver a critique of injustice or inequality—functional accounts assume both contribute to stability in various ways. For instance, Kingsley Davis and Wilbert Moore (1945) famously claimed that inequality is a social mechanism that functions to ensure that the most valuable individuals in society are directed to the most socially significant positions. In addition to the fact that functionalism does little to challenge social injustice, it also has logical flaws. First, it has the drawback of being a circular theory: Functions are postulated based on existent social processes and institutions; functions are also used to explain the existence of these same processes and institutions. Additionally, functionalism has teleological issues: It seems to suggest an institution or process emerged due to the very function that it was destined to fulfill. Nevertheless, some of the weaknesses of functionalism contribute to providing its most powerful and counterintuitive insights; therefore it remains a central sociological perspective.

FUNDAMENTAL CHALLENGES THAT ORGANIZATIONS FACE: COORDINATION, CONTROL, AND CONFLICT

These four sociological paradigms have informed the ways that organizations are understood. (See Table I.1 for a brief overview of these paradigms.) In particular, these paradigms shape how we understand and address the problems that organizations face. This anthology is framed around three of the most fundamental of these problems: coordination, control, and conflict. Organizations are challenged to achieve coordination and control in the face of conflict. *Coordination,* according to Follett ([1924] 1995), is the "reciprocal relating of all the factors in a situation," which she identifies as the first fundamental principle of organization (p. 214). For some time, organizational scholars have portrayed coordination as a relatively mechanistic information processing problem, but more recently scholars have returned to Follett's interactionist perspective on coordination as a fundamentally relational process of social construction.

Control is the alignment of behavior with a particular set of goals or interests. The problem of control can be solved by organizations in a way that is consistent with and reinforces the coordination of work, or in a way that undermines it. For example, if workers are assigned to carry out interdependent activities but are *also* assigned to report to different managers in different departments with competing objectives, then control may be achieved at the expense of coordination. Many of the shortcomings of bureaucracy and the resulting attempts to create postbureaucratic alternatives can be seen as arising from this so-called paradox of coordination and control.

Conflict can be seen as the breakdown of alignment due to opposing goals or interests. The opposing goals or interests that give rise to conflict are often created by organizations themselves. For example, workers may be assigned to departments with competing goals and yet be engaged in activities that require coordination with each other, or they may be required to compete for recognition, promotion, and other rewards in processes that are neither transparent nor equitable. But the opposing interests that drive conflict can also arise from more fundamental inequalities in the larger society that are simply re-created and reinforced by organizations. Karl Marx (1886) argued that gender, race, and socioeconomic class inequalities are created in organizations through unequal ownership of the means of production and through the relations of production. In either event, conflict has the potential to undermine both coordination and control, though as Follett ([1924] 1995) argues conflict can also serve as a force for creativity, innovation, and change.

This anthology is organized into nine parts. In Part I, we introduce the relational organizational form, characterized primarily by webs of

Table I.1   A Brief Overview of the Four Sociological Paradigms

RATIONALIST	*INTERACTIONIST*
Some Early Theorists: Thomas Hobbes Jean-Jacques Rousseau Max Weber	Some Early Theorists: Mary Parker Follett Max Weber George Herbert Mead Herbert Blumer Erving Goffman
Assumptions: People are largely rational, free, self-governing agents who make their decisions strategically based on a short-term cost-benefit analysis, rather than considerations of the public good, solidarity with others, reputation, or emotional attachments. To the degree these other considerations come into play, they are deemed "nonrational."	*Assumptions:* Reality is constructed through human interaction as people negotiate agreement on the meaning of the situations in which they are involved. Human identity itself is social and contextual in that people are changed by their interactions with one another.
Observations: This paradigm is an outgrowth of social contract theory. This perspective assumes that people join groups based on calculations of self-interest rather than a sense of solidarity. Because it begins with the individual as the unit of analysis, this paradigm is more consistent with the underlying intellectual principles of economic theory and behaviorist psychology than with sociology. Its strength is predicting individual decisions in a market context. Its weakness is that it cannot explain altruistic behavior, solidarity, identity formation, or why people routinely and knowingly act against their own self-interest and sacrifice themselves for the group or for a greater cause.	*Observations:* The strength of this paradigm is its ability to examine the development of self and subjectivity within a social context. It theorizes about how people make sense of their individual subjective experience in the shared, objective world. Social reality mediates these two worlds and helps determine how people understand what is real. Interactionism is antipositivistic. The weakness and the strength of the paradigm is its emphasis on subjectivity, including the subjective position of the researcher, the respondents, and those interpreting the qualitative data. The lack of scientific method and quantifiable results often means that qualitative research cannot be replicated.
Associated Theories and Concepts: Rational choice, exchange theory, functional rationality, instrumental rationality, cost-benefit analysis.	*Associated Theories and Concepts:* Taking the role of the other and the generalized other, play and game, the Me and the I, dramaturgy, qualitative methods, participant observation, ethnomethodology, *verstehen.*

CONFLICT	FUNCTIONALIST
Some Early Theorists: Karl Marx Mary Parker Follett C. Wright Mills Max Weber	Some Early Theorists: Emile Durkheim Talcott Parsons Robert Merton

CONFLICT

Some Early Theorists:
Karl Marx
Mary Parker Follett
C. Wright Mills
Max Weber

Assumptions:

Power and material resources are unevenly distributed, and competition for both dictates social order and social change. One group gains power over another in the competition for scarce resources, creating the potential for injustice.

Observations:

The strengths of this paradigm are the critical examination of injustice, analyzing social structures, and promoting social change. Conflict theory can also explain solidarity in that close-knit subgroups gather strength to counter their enemies. It does not explain agreement or consensus well except to attribute them to false consciousness or to intragroup solidarity against an external threat. Conflict theory promotes change through a critique of current conditions and therefore tends to represent those who are subordinated. It is associated with Marxism, critical theory, feminist theory, postmodernism, poststructuralism, queer theory, and postcolonial theory.

Associated Theories and Concepts:

Workers' consciousness (solidarity), false consciousness, alienation, resistance, ideology, objectification.

FUNCTIONALIST

Some Early Theorists:
Emile Durkheim
Talcott Parsons
Robert Merton

Assumptions:

Social structures and behaviors contribute to the coherence, stability, and survival of the group.

Observations:

This paradigm is also known as consensus theory or sociological positivism. It focuses on how and why social structures obtain and endure. Strengths include nonobvious theories, such as the functionality of war or crime and the most developed typology of group solidarity. Functionalism's main shortcoming is that it does little to theorize about or challenge social injustice. Problems such as racism, sexism, and poverty are often explained as providing stability and coherence to the social system. Change is often interpreted as destabilizing and therefore disadvantageous. Because functionalism tends to assume the current social arrangements are necessary for the survival of the group, it is generally considered to be a conservative perspective. Consequently, functionalist theories typically appeal to those for whom the system works well.

Associated Theories and Concepts:

Anomie, solidarity (organic, mechanical, precontractual), rituals, manifest and latent functions, the net aggregate of functions.

horizontal relationships, and in Part II, we introduce the bureaucratic organizational form, characterized primarily by formalized structures that support vertical relationships. The bureaucratic organizational form is typically associated with the rational paradigm, while the relational organizational form is often associated with the interactionist paradigm. We introduce critiques of each form, and invite readers to consider how the strengths of each might address the weaknesses of the other.

Part III, "The Coordination of Work," and Part IV, "Autonomy and Control," focus explicitly on the problems of *coordination* and *control,* and alternative ways that these problems are resolved in organizations. Part V, "Organizational Culture," explores the reciprocal influence between the larger social culture and cultures in specific organizations and examines the creation and manipulation of organizational culture through rituals intended to produce trust and solidarity.

In Part VI, "Organizational Conflict," we explicitly address *conflict* as emerging from organizational processes, as deeply rooted in the class structures of society, and as a creative force for change. Part VII, "Diversity within Organizations," explores the inclusion and exclusion of diverse populations in workplace organizations. Part VIII, "Organizational Learning and Change," integrates two disparate literatures—organizational learning, which tends to take a more micro focus on the interpersonal dynamics within organizations, and organizational change, which tends to take a more macro focus on organizations responding to their environments. We conclude in Part IX by exploring a new organizational form—virtual or online communities. In so doing, we seek to understand whether this new organizational form employs novel approaches to achieving coordination and control in the face of conflict and, if so, whether these novel approaches might yield new insights into the sociology of organizations.

Throughout this volume, we continue to explore the sociological paradigms that inform how organizations are understood to solve the problems of coordination, control, and conflict. In so doing, we seek to remind the reader that sociology does not have a single dominant paradigm. It remains a multicausal, problem-oriented discipline that recognizes the remarkable complexity of social behavior. Because our social world is outside of us but also part of us, it can be a most elusive, confounding, and unsettling subject of study. The dominance of the rational theories in organization studies is commonly presumed, yet the theoretical underpinnings and assumptions associated with the study of organizations often remain unstated. Such unstated assumptions are inconsistent with the reflexivity of the sociological perspective. Therefore, in this volume, we focus on accomplishing three things: offering a wider and historically accurate portrait of the diversity of sociological theories and their application to organization studies; providing readings that reflect a variety of ways that new technology affects methods of organizing and types of organizations; and including readings that examine a range of both formal and informal structures, and both established and impromptu interactions.

In the service of transparency, we offer an analytical introduction to each section that situates readings within the range of theoretical paradigms. While we acknowledge the influence of the four sociological paradigms, including attempts to synthesize rational and interactionist paradigms and to blend conflict and functionalist paradigms, we provide articles that demonstrate the growing diversity of theoretical perspectives beyond all of these. We also recognize a range of authors from around the globe, and restore Mary Parker Follett to her rightful place as a foundational thinker in the sociology of organizations. Our hope is that this volume will be lively and provocative, theoretically rigorous, disciplinarily informed, and representative of the heterogeneity within organization studies.

REFERENCES

Ansell, Christopher. 2009. "Mary Parker Follett and Pragmatist Organization." Pp. 464–485 in *The Oxford Handbook of Sociology and Organization Studies: Classical Foundations*, edited by Paul Adler. Oxford, England: Oxford University Press.

Blumer, Herbert. 1969. *Symbolic Interactionism: Perspective and Method*. Berkeley: University of California Press.

Collins, Randall. 1992. *Sociological Insight: An Introduction to Non-Obvious Sociology*. 2nd ed. New York: Oxford University Press.

———. 1994. *Four Sociological Traditions*. New York: Oxford University Press.

Coser, Lewis. 1956. *Functions of Social Conflict*. New York: Free Press.

Davis, Kingsley, and Wilbert Moore. 1945. "Some Principles of Stratification." *American Sociological Review* 10:242–49.

Durkheim. Emile. [1893] 1964. *The Division of Labor in Society*. New York: Free Press.

Follett, Mary Parker. 1918. *The New State: Group Organization, the Solution of Popular Government*. London: Longmans, Green, and Co.

———. [1924] 1995. "Relating: The Circular Response." In *Mary Parker Follett—Prophet of Management: A Celebration of Writings from the 1920s,* edited by Pauline Graham. Cambridge, MA: Harvard Business School Press. Reprinted from *Creative Experience* (New York: Longmans, Green, 1924), Chapters 3 and 4.

———. [1925] 1949. "Constructive Conflict." Pp. 30–49 in *Dynamic Administration: The Collected Papers of Mary Parker Follett*, edited by Henry C. Metcalf and L. Urwick. New York: Harper and Brothers Publishers.

———. 1949a. "Coordination." Pp. 61–76 in *Freedom and Co-ordination: Lectures in Business Organization by Mary Parker Follett*, edited by L. Urwick. London: Management Publications Trust, Ltd.

———. 1949b. "The Process of Control." Pp. 77–89 in *Freedom and Co-ordination: Lectures in Business Organization by Mary Parker Follett*, edited by L. Urwick. London: Management Publications Trust, Ltd.

Gans, Herbert. 1972. "The Positive Functions of Poverty." *American Journal of Sociology* 78(September):275–89.

Goffman, Erving. 1959. *The Presentation of Self in Everyday Life*. New York: Anchor Books.

———. 1967. *Interaction Ritual: Essays on Face-to-Face Behavior*. New York: Pantheon Books.

Habermas, Jürgen. 1989. "The Uncoupling of System and Lifeworld." Pp. 188–228 in *Jürgen Habermas on Society and Politics: A Reader*, edited by Steven Seidman. Boston: Beacon Press.

Handel, Michael. 2003a. "Introduction." Pp. 1–4 in *The Sociology of Organizations*. Thousand Oaks, CA: Sage.

———. 2003b. "Organizations as Rational Systems I: Classical Theories of Bureaucracy and Administration." Pp. 5–16 in *The Sociology of Organizations*. Thousand Oaks, CA: Sage.

Kalberg, Stephen. 1980. "Max Weber's Types of Rationality." *American Journal of Sociology* 85:1145–79.

Kanter, Rosabeth Moss. 1977. *Men and Women of the Corporation*. New York: Basic Books.

Levin, William. 1994. *Sociological Ideas*. 4th ed. Belmont, CA: Wadsworth Publishing Company.

MacLeod, Jay. 2009. *Ain't No Makin' It*. 3rd ed. Boulder, CO: Westview Press.

Marx, Karl. 1886. *Capital: A Critique of Political Economy*. Volume 1. New York: International Publishers.

Mead, George Herbert. 1934. *Mind, Self, and Society: From the Standpoint of a Social Behaviorist*, edited by Charles W. Morris. Chicago: University of Chicago Press.

Munch, Richard. 1994. *Sociological Theory from the 1850s to the 1920s*. Chicago: Nelson-Hall.

Weber, Max. [1904] 1958. *The Protestant Ethic and the Spirit of Capitalism*. Translated by Talcott Parsons. Introduction by Anthony Giddens. New York: Charles Scribner's Sons.

———. [1924] 1978. *Economy and Society: An Outline of Interpretative Sociology,* edited by Guenther Roth and Claus Wittich. Berkeley: University of California Press.

———. [1925] 1946. *Max Weber: Essays in Sociology,* edited and translated by Hans H. Gerth and C. Wright Mills. New York: Oxford University Press.

PART I

THE RELATIONAL ORGANIZATIONAL FORM

AN INTRODUCTION TO THE RELATIONAL ORGANIZATIONAL FORM

The relational organizational form—also known as the clan-based or network organizational form—starts with the notion that people are fundamentally social beings, and that our identities and understanding of the world around us are formed through our interactions with others. The relational organizational form thus reflects the interactionist paradigm. Mary Parker Follett (1918) offers one of the earliest formulations of this organizational form, starting with a relational view of human identity:

> We have long been trying to understand the relation of the individual to society; we are only just beginning to see that there is no "individual," that there is no "society" . . . The old psychology was based on the isolated individual as the unit, on the assumption that a man thinks, feels and judges independently. Now that we know that there is no such thing as a separate ego, *that individuals are created by reciprocal interplay*, our whole study of psychology is being transformed. (P. 19, emphasis added)

In "Business as an Integrative Unity," excerpted in this section, Follett ([1925] 1942) extends her relational perspective from the interpersonal to the organizational:

> It seems to me that the first test of business administration, of industrial organization, should be whether you have a business with all its parts so co-ordinated, so moving together in their closely knit and adjusting activities, so linking, interlocking, interrelating, that they make a working unit—that is, not a congeries of separate pieces, but what I have called a functional whole or integrative unity. (P. 71)

She argues further that through reciprocal relating, participants who work in different functions are able to see their own part in relation to the whole, giving them a more holistic understanding of their own task and thus a greater ability to work together as a whole. This continual interaction between part and whole carried out through interpersonal exchanges therefore enables higher levels of organizational performance. Contrary to Weber ([1924] 1978), Follett argues in effect that the relational form is the better way to achieve efficiency and effectiveness.

Since Follett, organizational theorists have continued to develop our understanding of the relational organizational form. In an excerpt from their classic book *The Management of Innovation*, included in this section, Tom Burns and G. M. Stalker ([1961] 1995) define the relational or organic organizational form as one that relies on "the adjustment and continual re-definition of individual tasks through interaction with others," "a network structure of control, authority, and communication," and "a lateral rather than a vertical direction of communication through the organization, communication between people of different rank, also, resembling consultation rather than command" (p. 121). They contrast this organic form to the mechanistic form that is characterized by "the specialized differentiation of functional tasks into which the problems and tasks facing the concern as a whole are broken down"; "hierarchic structure of control, authority and communication"; and "a tendency for interaction between members of the concern to be vertical, i.e., between superior and subordinate" (Burns and Stalker [1961] 1995:120). They argue further that the two systems represent a polarity, not a dichotomy, and that many intermediate stages can be observed to exist between these extremities. Most important, neither system nor organizational form is superior to the other in their view; rather these "two management systems represent for us the two polar extremities of the forms which such systems can take when they are *adapted to a specific rate of technical and commercial change*" (Burns and Stalker [1961] 1995:119, emphasis added), where the organic form is well adapted to conditions of rapid change and the mechanistic form is well adapted to conditions of high stability, an idea we will return to later in Part VIII, "Organizational Learning and Change."

Burns and Stalker's ([1961] 1995) distinction between the organic and the mechanistic organizational forms is reminiscent of Durkheim's ([1893] 1997) distinction between organic and mechanistic solidarity, where organic solidarity is made possible by the high levels of role differentiation in modern society, which create high levels of interdependence. Consistent with Follett but in contrast to Weber, Durkheim ([1893] 1997) predicts modern society's evolution toward the relational rather than the bureaucratic organizational form as a natural consequence of differentiation and specialization.

Other theorists contrast the relational organizational form to bureaucracies and markets as alternative ways to solve the challenges of coordination and control. In an article included in this section, William Ouchi (1980) argues that markets are the best solution when outcomes are easily measured and goals are highly differentiated, that bureaucracies are the best solution when outcomes are somewhat easily measured and goals are somewhat shared, and that clan-based organizations are the best solution when outcomes are not easily measured but goals are strongly shared. Ouchi argues furthermore that high levels of goal congruity or alignment are *required* for the existence of the relational or "clan-based" organizational form, and that these high levels of goal congruity can be achieved through the socialization of members to accept unquestioningly the goals of the organization. Note that Ouchi's notion of a relational organizational form based on unquestioning acceptance of organizational goals stands in stark contrast to Follett and others. In another article included in this section, Walter Powell (1990) argues that the relational or "network" organizational form is distinguished from markets and bureaucracies by its reliance on relationships of reciprocity. By contrast, markets rely on individually negotiated contracts, and bureaucracies rely on hierarchical control. The network organizational form is neither completely spontaneous, like markets, nor prescribed, like bureaucracies, but instead is based on emergent patterns of reciprocity. Connecting to social capital theory (e.g., Adler and Kwon 2002; Leana and Van Buren 1999; Nahapiet and Ghoshal 1998), the relational organizational form can be understood as a type of organization that fosters and benefits from the development of social capital—relationships that are resources for social action—among its participants.

In sum, the relational organizational form is characterized by three primary features. First, it is based primarily on horizontal, reciprocal relationships rather than vertical, unidirectional relationships, resulting in high levels of information-processing capacity or communication richness. Second, relationships in the relational organizational form are emergent, spontaneous, and informal, not deliberately created or prescribed through formal organizational structures. Because communication channels are emergent rather than prescribed, participants can create them as needed to get work done. Third, relationships in the relational organizational form tend to be personal, built on close ties among individual participants based on common experiences they have shared. The interpersonal nature of these relationships increases the potential for participant engagement, bonding, loyalty, and trust.

Due to this reliance on horizontal, emergent, personal relationships, the relational organizational form is expected to have distinctive performance advantages relative to markets and bureaucracies. According to Powell (1990),

> Networks are particularly apt for circumstances in which there is a need for efficient, reliable information. The most useful information is rarely that which flows down the formal chain of command in an organization, or that which can be inferred from shifting price signals. Rather it is that which is obtained from someone whom you have dealt with in the past and found to be reliable. You trust best information that comes from someone you know well . . . Information passed through networks is "thicker" than information obtained in the "market" and "freer" than communicated in a hierarchy . . . The open ended, relational features of networks, with their relative absence of explicit quid pro quo behavior, greatly enhance the ability to transmit and learn new knowledge and skills. (P. 304)

Likewise, social capital theorists have explored the performance benefits that accrue to organizations with high levels of social capital (Adler and Kwon 2002; Leana and Van Buren 1999; Nahapiet and Ghoshal 1998), including knowledge creation, knowledge transfer, and the coordination of work.

The relational organizational form also has some disadvantages. Max Weber (1920) argued that organizations built on personal ties are particularly vulnerable to the abuse of power, to favoritism, and to inefficiencies that arise from behaviors that are driven by the need to curry personal favor rather than by the need to accomplish organizational goals. Furthermore, Jody Hoffer Gittell and Leigh Weiss (2004) argued that personal ties will not necessarily emerge at the critical junctures where they are most needed for coordinating work because they tend to emerge among those who are similar, due to the existence of occupational cultures (Van Maanen and Barley 1984), functional thought worlds (Dougherty 1992), and communities of practice (Faraj and Sproull 2000). The patterns that are expected to emerge in the relational organizational form therefore share some of the same weakness as the patterns found in traditional bureaucracies. In both, the movement of information is likely to be found predominantly within functions, rather than across functions where it is crucial for the successful coordination of work. The reliance on personal relationships also limits the interchangeability of participants. One participant cannot easily substitute for another participant because the personal ties that are needed to get work done are embedded in specific individuals. The relational organizational form is therefore particularly vulnerable to participant turnover and to the temporary absence of specific individuals, making scheduling flexibility, including work/life balance, challenging to achieve. While scheduling flexibility is limited in the bureaucratic organizational form by the principle of standardized treatment, it is limited in the relational form by the lack of participant interchangeability.

In addition, the larger and more geographically dispersed an organization becomes, the less feasible it is for coordination to be achieved through personal work relationships due to the difficulty of forming and preserving personal relationships with more people and across greater distances. The relational organizational form is therefore less scalable (Bigley and Roberts 2001) and more vulnerable to geographic dispersion (Carlson and Zmud 1999) than the bureaucratic organizational form, whose impersonal relationships are designed for interchangeability, scalability, and geographic dispersion.

Perhaps the greatest weakness of the relational organizational form, as conceptualized thus far, is the shortage of insights about how organizations can reinforce, support, and sustain the horizontal relationships that are fundamental to their operation. It is commonly accepted that the horizontal relationships that define the relational organizational form are not designed—rather they emerge from the common experiences of organizational participants. As a result, theorists have tended to see little room for prescribed or formal structures of any kind in the relational organizational form and have tended instead to see structures as emerging from the informal relationships themselves (Krackhardt and Brass 1994). William Ouchi (1980) addresses this question by arguing that participants must be socialized from the start into accepting the organization's goals without question, thus enabling the organization to achieve control without hierarchy or contracts. Karl Weick (1995) views organizations as patterns of intersubjectivity and states that the fundamental challenge faced by organizations is to sustain those patterns of intersubjectivity over time as people are replaced. Organizations, he argues, are entities that move continuously between intersubjectivity and generic subjectivity, and they must find a way to bridge between them because the shared meanings that enable coordinated action are first created through intimate intersubjectivity but then sustained and generalized to the organization and over time through generic intersubjectivity.

> It is precisely the quality of susceptibility of an interaction to replacement and substitution of the interactants that is an important defining property of organizations. If the capability to make mutually reinforcing interpretations is lost when people are replaced, then neither organization nor sense-making persist. (Weick 1995:73)

Carol Heimer (1992) argues that the personal nature of relationships in the relational organizational form need not be a limitation. While sociologists since Talcott Parsons have tended to elevate universalistic organizational relationships above particularistic or personal organizational relationships, she argues that this view is based on an unnecessary dichotomy. The key for an effective network organization is instead to *apply universalistic principles to the treatment of particular individuals*. Heimer argues that this is also the solution to the dichotomy that Carol Gilligan (1982) observed between the norms of rights or equal treatment that tend to be central to male development and the norms of caring or responsibility that tend to be central to female development: Norms of equal treatment can be applied to taking responsibility for particular individuals. Similarly, Edward Lawler, Shane Thye, and Jeongkoo Yoon (2008) argue that person-to-person ties can become generalized into person-to-group ties over time, thus generating universal or group obligations from interpersonal obligations. Though the Lawler et al. solution is in effect the reverse of the Heimer solution, both seek to combine the advantages of the personal ties found in the relational organizational form with the advantages of scalability found in the bureaucratic organizational form.

Notably, however, not one of these authors explains how universal principles can evolve from interpersonal obligations or general subjectivity to interpersonal subjectivity except through repeated interactions over time, which suggests limitations to the scalability, replicability, and interchangeability of these relationships. Carrie Leana and Harry Van Buren (1999) come closer by articulating formal structures that enable the formation of organizational social capital, identifying organizational practices such as employment security and reciprocity. Interestingly, these practices are about keeping people in place long enough to allow habits and beliefs to become normative, which works against scalability, replicability, and interchangeability. But they do note in passing that rules and procedures can be used to define horizontal ties in terms of positions rather than people, as in the bureaucratic organizational forms (Leana and Van Buren 1999). Further work remains to be done regarding structures that can reinforce, support, and sustain the horizontal ties that are core to the relational organizational form, in order to address the limitations of this otherwise promising concept.

QUESTIONS FOR DISCUSSION

1. What are the most significant advantages and disadvantages of the relational organizational form, in your assessment? Explain.
2. Are there circumstances under which the relational organizational form would work well, relative to other circumstances? Explain.
3. How would you design an organization that addresses the negative attributes of the relational organizational form without losing its positive attributes?

SUGGESTIONS FOR FURTHER READING

Fletcher, Joyce. 1999. *Disappearing Acts: Gender, Power and Relational Practice at Work.* Cambridge, MA: MIT Press.

Heckscher, Charles, and Paul Adler. 2006. *The Firm as a Collaborative Community: Reconstructing Trust in the Knowledge Economy.* Oxford, England: Oxford University Press.

Vogus, Timothy. 2006. "What Is It About Relationships? A Behavioral Theory of Social Capital and Performance." *Labor and Employment Relations Proceedings* 58:164–73.

REFERENCES

Adler, Paul, and Seok-Woo Kwon. 2002. "Social Capital: Prospects for a New Concept." *Academy of Management Review*, 27(1):17–40.

Bigley, G. A., and Karlene Roberts. 2001. "The Incident Command System: High Reliability Organizing for Complex and Volatile Task Environments." *Academy of Management Journal*, 44(6):1281–299.

Burns, Tom, and G. M. Stalker. [1961] 1995. "Mechanistic and Organic Systems of Management." Pp. 96–125 in *The Management of Innovation*. Oxford, England: Oxford University Press.

Carlson, J. R., and R. W. Zmud. 1999. "Channel Expansion Theory and the Experiential Nature of Media Richness Perceptions." *Academy of Management Journal*, 42(2):153–70.

Dougherty, Deborah. 1992. "Interpretive Barriers to Successful Product Innovation in Large Firms." *Organization Science*, 3(2):179–202.

Durkheim, Emile. [1893] 1997. *The Division of Labor in Society*. New York: The Free Press.

Faraj, Samer, and Lee Sproull. 2000. "Coordinating Expertise in Software Development Teams." *Management Science*, 46(12):1554–568.

Follett, Mary Parker. 1918. "The Group and the New Psychology." Pp. 19–23 in *The New State: Group Organization, the Solution of Popular Government*. London: Longmans, Green.

———. [1925] 1942. "Business as an Integrative Unity." Pp. 71–94 in *Dynamic Administration: The Collected Papers of Mary Parker Follett*, edited by Henry C. Metcalf and L. Urwick. New York: Harper and Brothers Publishers.

Gilligan, Carol. 1982. *In a Different Voice: Psychological Theory and Women's Development*. Cambridge, MA: Harvard University Press.

Gittell, Jody Hoffer, and Leigh Weiss. 2004. "Coordination Networks Within and Across Organizations: A Multi-Level Framework." *Journal of Management Studies*, 41(1):127–53.

Heimer, Carol. 1992. "Doing Your Job and Helping Your Friends: Universalistic Norms About Obligations to Particular Others." Pp. 165–188 in *Networks and Organizations: Structure, Form and Action*, edited by Nitin Nohria and Robert Eccles. Boston: Harvard Business School Press.

Krackhardt, David, and Daniel Brass. 1994. "Intraorganizational Networks: The Micro Side." Pp. 207–229 in *Advances in Social Network Analysis: Research in the Social and Behavioral Sciences*, edited by Stanley Wasserman and Joseph Galaskiewicz. Beverly Hills, CA: Sage.

Lawler, Edward J., Shane R. Thye, and Jeongkoo Yoon. 2008. "Social Exchange and Micro Social Order." *American Sociological Review*, 73(4):519–42.

Leana, Carrie, and Harry Van Buren. 1999. "Organizational Social Capital and Employment Practices." *Academy of Management Review*, 24:538–55.

Nahapiet, Janice, and Sumantra Ghoshal. 1998. "Social Capital, Intellectual Capital and the Organizational Advantage." *Academy of Management Review*, 23(2):242–66.

Ouchi, William G. 1980. "Markets, Bureaucracies and Clans." *Administrative Science Quarterly*, 25:129–41.

Powell, Walter. 1990. "Neither Market Nor Hierarchy: Network Forms of Organization." *Research in Organizational Behavior*, 12:295–336. Greenwich, CT: JAI Press.

Van Maanen, John, and Stephen Barley. 1984. "Occupational Communities: Culture and Control in Organizations." *Research in Organizational Behavior*, 6:287–365.

Weber, Max. [1924] 1978. "Bureaucracy." Pp. 956–1005 in *Economy and Society: An Outline of Interpretive Sociology*. Volume 2. Berkeley: University of California Press.

Weick, Karl. 1995. *Sensemaking in Organizations*. Thousand Oaks, CA: Sage.

1

BUSINESS AS AN INTEGRATIVE UNITY[1]

MARY PARKER FOLLETT

A man said to me once, a man working on a salary as the head of a department in a factory, "I'm no wage-earner, working so many hours a day; if I wake up at midnight and have an idea that might benefit the factory, it belongs to the factory." His implication was that the wage-earner would not feel this. Can business reach its maximum of efficiency and service unless it is so organized that the wage-earner does feel this?

But the subject we are considering, that of integrative unity, goes far beyond the question of the worker's place in industry. It seems to me that the first test of business administration, of industrial organization, should be whether you have a business with all its parts so co-ordinated, so moving together in their closely knit and adjusting activities, so linking, interlocking, interrelating, that they make a working *unit*—that is, not a congeries of separate pieces, but what I have called a functional whole or integrative unity. I have taken these phrases from Kempf, the psychobiologist. They seem to me to represent one of the most profound of philosophical and psychological principles, and one which helps us very materially in working out practical methods of business organization. For this principle applies to the relation of men, the relation of services, the relation of departments, the last of which I have found one of the weakest points in the businesses which I have studied. How are we to get an integrative unity? How are we to know when we have it? What tests are there which will show us when we are approaching it? . . .

This is the problem in business administration: how can a business be so organized that workers, managers, owners, feel a collective responsibility? The advantages of creating a sense of individual responsibility have long been noted as one of the cardinal principles of business administration, and many have leaned toward employee representation because they thought it was developing this. Some say in the language of the old maxim: Responsibility sobers. Or as one young manager said to me of his workmen, "They don't have so many darn fool ideas now." The idea of a collective responsibility, however, has been neither fully accepted nor the methods of obtaining it worked out.

I think myself that collective responsibility should begin with group responsibility, that a form of departmental organization which includes the workers is the most effective method for unifying a business. In one business, where there is a strong feeling on the part of the managers that the worker should be given responsibility to his full capacity, group responsibility is encouraged wherever possible. For instance, the chauffeurs asked for shorter hours. They were given a fifty-four hour week with overtime, and the chairman and secretary of the chauffeur group, acting for the group, assumed the responsibility for each man giving an honest week's work. We see the next step in collective responsibility, interdepartmental relations, in a store where, for instance, the elevator force has meetings at which are considered how the elevator force can help the store superintendent, how it can help the charge office, the advertising office, the information bureau, the mail order department, etc. Such steps are, of course, mere beginnings in the solving of what seems to me the crux of business administration, the relation of departments, of functions, however you wish to put it. Any study of business as an integrative unity should, I think, make this problem its chief concern.

An understanding of this principle of integrative unity which we are considering will keep us not only from a false individualism, but also from a false altruism. For instance, if we dislike many of the old ways of hiring and firing which often left too much to the mere whim of the foreman, we sometimes say that we dislike these methods because they are not fair to the workman, but the truth is that we do not change these methods in order to benefit the workman only, but because the change will benefit the business as a whole. Or take the necessity of regularizing employment so that seasonal or so-called "cyclical" fluctuations will be reduced. This need should not be taken up solely as a grievance of labour, for there is loss in overhead as well as loss to the employees. Again, the arbitrator should arbitrate for the institution. This should go without saying, but a union girl asked, "Is he pro-labour?" You can be *for* labour without being *against* capital; you can be for the institution.

When you have made your employees feel that they are in some sense partners in the business, they do not improve the quality of their work, save waste in time and material, because of the Golden Rule, but because their interests are the same as yours. Over and over again in the past we have heard it said to workmen, "If this were your material, you wouldn't waste it," and over and over again that

admonition fails. We find, however, that when there is some feeling in a plant, more or less developed, that that business is a working unit, we find then that the workman is more careful of material, that he saves time in lost motions, in talking over annoyances, that he helps the new hand by explaining things to him, that he helps the fellow working at his side by calling attention to the end of a roll on the machine, etc. This is the Golden Rule taken behaviouristically. It is, by the way, the Golden Rule taken idealistically, too, for a functional whole is a much higher conception than our old notion of the Golden Rule.

Before we leave the subject of joint responsibility, I should like to consider the matter of how far it should go. We might base our discussion of this on a case which came up in Wisconsin some years ago. After the workmen's compensation law was passed in Wisconsin, a case in dispute came before the Industrial Commission for decision. A teamster got drunk in his employer's time, fell off his wagon and was killed. His widow petitioned for the amount of indemnity to be paid by the employer and won. The Supreme Court sustained the decision and later the Legislature sustained their opinion by making the law more explicit. Professor Commons tells us that back of the overt reasoning in this case there was the feeling of group responsibility. "On the former legal theory of individual responsibility," he says, "these decisions could not be justified. Only on a theory of partnership or solidarity of interest can they find justification. Employer and employee are engaged in a common enterprise. They jointly assume the risks and share the burdens and the benefits of the enterprise. More than that they share each other's frailties." I cannot see the matter wholly in this light, but a principle recently and soberly embodied in the law of one of our states is worth consideration.

I want to add one word more in regard to this conception of joint responsibility, joint control, and that is to point out that what we are considering is not at all the same as the conception of reciprocity so often advocated. I disagree with Professor Commons that "loyalty is an expectation of reciprocity." Our obligations, our responsibilities, our loyalty, should be, as we said of obedience in the previous lecture, to a functional unity of which we are a part. Robert Valentine said: "Employers should stop talking about the loyalty of their employees until they are ready to make an equal noise talking about their loyalty to employees." This was well worth saying, but if Mr. Valentine were here to-day he would say, I think, that this is a rather crude way of looking at the matter compared with our present conception of loyalty as part of the process of creating business unities.

Joint loyalty, then, joint responsibility, are very different conceptions when considered as an inter-weaving of obligations and when considered as a reciprocity of obligations. I wish you would make a note of this fallacy wherever you find it, in your reading or in your observation of business adminis-tration. For instance, Mr. Leiserson asks: "Does the company desire to do justice as the company sees it, or is the employer ready to administer justice to his employees as they understand justice?" But why should Mr. Leiserson think the latter any bet-ter than the former? It seems to me that it is just as true in regard to the standards for the conduct of business as it is for control, responsibility, loyalty, that standards, too, must be jointly developed. And the immediate moral of that is that the organization of the plant should be such as to make this possible.

THE REDISTRIBUTION OF FUNCTION

The first test of any part of business organization and administration should be, I think: how far does this make for integrative unity? Take the question often discussed, and sometimes made a practical issue, whether foremen should belong to unions. The arguments in this discussion are not based on the theory of integrative unity, but on the theory of sides, controversial sides. Indeed perhaps no one subject could throw more light on this subject than the foreman's position, and if there had been time I had intended to give a section to that. If, however, we have not time for this or many other interest-ing questions, there is one point I wish to speak of, and that is that managing itself is an interpenetrat-ing matter, that the distinction between those who manage and those who are managed is somewhat fading. We are on the way, it seems to me, to a dif-ferent analysis of services from that which we now have. This is the most valuable suggestion, I think, in a very valuable paper read by Mr. Dennison to the Taylor Society. Mr. Tawney has also shown us that no sharp division can be drawn between management and labour, and that the line between them fluctuates widely from industry to industry with the nature of the work carried on. "There are certain occupations in which an absolute separa-tion between the planning and the performance of the work is, for technical reasons, impracticable. A group of miners who are cutting and filling coal are 'working' hard enough. But very little coal will be cut . . . unless they display some of the qualities of scientific knowledge, prevision and initiative which are usually associated with the word 'man-agement.' What is true of miners is true, in different degrees, of men on a building job, or in the transport trades. They must exercise considerable discretion in their work because, unless they do, the work does not get done, and no amount of supervision can compensate for the absence of discretion." That is a sentence worth remembering—no amount of super-vision can compensate for the absence of discretion.

We can all see daily the truth of the statement that not all the managing is done by the manage-ment, that workers are sometimes managing. I can see this clearly in my household; if my cook plans my meals as well as cooks them, she does some of the managing of my household. It is claimed that the plan of the Baltimore and Ohio, of bi-weekly conferences between managers and employees in the workshops, has produced the following results: reduction in labour turnover; routes of carrying material shortened and made easier; fuller and more regular operation made possible; the average delays per week behind schedule reduced; monthly materi-als per employee reduced; and the work of repairs greatly facilitated as well as the quality improved— the problem of getting a steady flow of adequate material was solved and certain difficulties in the tool-room which wasted time were straightened out. This is all part of the service of managing. But even when the workmen's managerial capacity is not tested so far as this, there is usually room for some. Whenever labour uses its judgment in plan-ning, that perhaps is managing. If the worker is given a task and allowed to decide *how* he will do it, that perhaps is managing. It would not be pos-sible to carry on a business if the workers did not do some managing.

There are two ways, however, of looking at this matter of managing ability among the workmen. One executive says: "We wanted to get any managing ability there was, from counter, stock-room, truck delivery or wherever, into the management. We wanted it for ourselves as well as to help the people advance." This is certainly sound business sense, but then in addition to this, it seems to me that there is another attitude to be taken. It should be recognized that almost everyone has some managing ability, even if it be very little, and opportunity should be given each man to exercise what he has on his actual job. If all on the managerial force have— as, of course, they have—initiative, creative imagination, organizing and executive ability, there are many workmen who are not entirely lacking in these qualities. We want to make use of what they have.

If the job of every workman were analysed so that each could understand what opportunities he had for managing, that might have both a direct and an indirect influence on production. Indirect because this might greatly increase the workman's self-respect and pride in his work, which is so necessary for the best results. A workman who had sat on a good many conference committees said to me, with dignity and pride: "When I am on that committee I am the equal of anyone; of course when I go back to my work I am just a workman, but while I am on that committee I am the equal of the President himself." I told that to the President and he said: "He must be made to feel that all the time." Yes, but the difficulty is how. I wish you would consider that. Perhaps one way would be so to analyse each man's work that he would realize that he had some managing to do as well as the President.

To be sure, the awards for suggestions given in so many plants now are a recognition that the workman has managing ability. This recognition is, however, not yet sufficiently widespread. The post-office workers of England have repeatedly claimed that they have made suggestions for the improvement of the service which have been turned down. In a group of Derbyshire miners one man rose and said, "There isn't a man in this room who hasn't time and again made suggestions and been told that he was paid to work and not to think."

Whenever the trade unions show managing capacity, I think they do more for their cause than by any other of their activities. When the Amalgamated worked out a plan of employee insurance, when a few years ago the Photo-Engravers Union of New York drew up a new price-list, submitted it to their employers and won its acceptance, they went far beyond the function of unions as defence organizations.

In England we have several examples of plans from the workers actually making possible the continuation of production, as in the case of the British Westinghouse employees when the managers were thinking of closing down the foundry on account of the high cost of production. The fact that workers themselves have in many instances treated the disputed points between employers and employees as problems rather than matters of rights is a hopeful sign that the workers' demand for share in control is not a mere gesture for "power," that they feel in themselves managing capacity.

If the worker's job ought to be analysed to see what part of it is managing, so the managers' jobs should be analysed to see if to any part of those the workers could contribute anything. It may be found that even in those activities which have been considered exclusively the functions of the managers, as correlating the selling and production departments, the buying of material and equipment, the control of the flow of material through the plant so that there will be no congestion—even to these the worker can make some contribution. . . .

VARIOUS FACTORS AND RELATIONSHIPS UNDERLYING FUNCTIONAL UNITY

I have had time to give only hints of what I mean by functional unity in business. Let me emphasize a few points even if I can do so by scarcely more than headings. First, the interdependence of all the activities involved is clearly evident. There really is not such a thing, strictly speaking, as a departmental problem; there is hardly a problem, more-over, which can be considered purely one of production or distribution. The parts of modern business are so intricately interwoven that the worker, in order to have an intelligent opinion in regard to even his own problems, has not only to know something of processes, of equipment, has not only to consider the effect of the introduction of new machinery and the training of the worker; he should also understand the connection between the production and the commercial side, should know something of the effectiveness of the sales organization—misguided sales or purchasing policies may ruin a business. There are many now who think the worker should study unit costs, but he cannot understand low unit costs, can he, without knowing something of the terms of securing credit which help to determine unit costs? More-over, I think some knowledge of the general business and trade policy—adjustment of supply and demand, prospective contracts, even the opening of new markets—would make the opinion of the worker on production processes more valuable.

While the necessity of team-work between the departments is recognized by everyone, the methods for obtaining it are not yet sufficiently worked out, and the matter is sometimes a little blurred by the fact that different departments are working at different things at any one moment. The manufacture of cigars is almost a continuous process because cigars have to be fresh, but the buying of the tobacco has to be concentrated in short periods in spring and summer. The signing of contracts for delivery takes place at a different time from the manufacture of the product. This, however, does not change our problem; it merely makes it a more intricate one.

Besides all these relations which I have named, there is the newer one of production manager and personnel director, an important and often very delicate matter. As one Works Manager said, "Why is this young man of thirty-two supposed to know more of human nature than I at fifty-eight?" We are sometimes told how necessary it is that these two should "get on" together, but *you* all know that unless the personnel director does a good deal more than "get on" with Works Manager or Manufacturing Committee, he will not be of the greatest usefulness to his firm. In fact one of the things I feel most strongly about business administration as it exists to-day is that until we find some better way of uniting technical and so-called psychological problems than we have at present, we are far from efficient business administration.

Another necessary unifying we have not considered is the relation of the main firm to its branches—branch banks, branch stores, or a number of plants operating under one management. Many

problems would meet us here, but we can use the same principles in trying to solve them.

In concluding my necessarily meagre treatment of what I have called integrative unity, I should say that the efficiency of many plants is lowered by an imperfectly worked out system of co-ordination of parts. In some instances what co-ordination there is depends chiefly on the ability of certain heads to get on together; their willingness to consult each other depends too often on mere chance qualities or conditions—perhaps whether certain men commute by the same train! An adequate system of co-ordination has not yet, so far as I know, been worked out for business administration.

It is impossible, however, to work most effectively at co-ordination until you have made up your mind where you stand philosophically in regard to the relation of parts to the whole. We have spoken of the relation of departments—sales and production, advertising and financial—to each other, but the most profound truth that philosophy has ever given us concerns not only the relation of parts, but the relation of parts to the whole, not to a stationary whole, but to a whole a-making. What does this mean in business? It means that the sales department, for instance, should have some principle by which to test the relation of a sales policy to general policy. Books on management sometimes tell us that the production manager should subordinate departmental policy to business policy. I do not agree with this. In the *Bulletin of the Taylor Society* for February, 1924, it is stated that "any department head should recognize organization policies as more vital than his own." I wonder why more "vital"? Or I have seen it stated that department heads should realize that general policy is more "important" than departmental policy. He should not, because it is not, any more than the United States is more important than New York, and I am no states-righter either. Co-ordinate manufacture and sales? Certainly, also work out the relation between manufacturing and general policy and between sales and general policy, always remembering that general policy is, or should be, no more important, but that all the time manufacturing and sales policies are contributing to general policy. The production manager should not subordinate departmental policy to business policy; he should contribute it, and he should see that it is a contributable policy. That is the chief test of the production manager, whether his policy is a contributable policy.

I should like to say parenthetically that in order to consider this subject in one paper, we are leaving out many questions. Perhaps to secure independence of outside capital is necessary to functional unity, but such questions would carry us too far afield.

THE ADMINISTRATOR AS INTEGRATOR OF THE INTERESTS OF ALL PARTIES CONCERNED

So far we have been looking only at the unifying of a single plant in its many relations. We have left out of consideration the question of unifying a whole industry, although obviously that is very important. Many shortline railroads cannot pay if considered separately. In a number of industries, profits as a whole could make reasonable return on that industry as a whole. If the industry were considered as a whole, the so-called marginal plants might be kept going. Again, wages cannot be set by one plant; the tendency is toward equalization in the same trade over considerable areas. This applies also to hours of work. Moreover, it is the whole industry which should take into consideration the demand for its product; one plant cannot, to the greatest advantage, organize its production in relation to the demand. This is part of the problem of unemployment. The selling agencies throughout an industry should have some connection if production is to be regularized.

I need not speak at any length of how much competing firms have in common and the many instances we have of the increasing recognition of that, as in the case of the two rival Ohio firms which arranged for transfer from one plant to another for promotional purposes. (I am aware that the radicals would say that was probably a move against the consumer, but I do not want to go into that now.) The Joint Council of Electrical Contractors and Electrical Workers made an arrangement in New York in 1919 or 1920 for the exchange of skilled workers, and set up an employment bureau. It was thought at the time that statistics on cost of living, etc., could be pooled, wages and working conditions standardized, and the flow of labour to some extent controlled. The stated object of the National Industrial Council movement of England was increasing uniformity in labour standards *by industries*.

And beyond all this, beyond the matter of the unifying of single plants, beyond even the unifying of all the plants in the same industry, there is still another way of looking at business unity which should be one of the chief concerns of the business administrator. He sees the three classes: (1) workers, including industrial and managerial workers, (2) consumers, and (3) investors. The chief job of business is to find a method for integrating the interests of these three classes. I have said nothing of the consumer, because there has not been time, but when we find employers and employees uniting against the consumer to secure higher prices, tariff regulations or other preferential advantages, when we are told that the cotton industry in England will always, in case of anticipated government interference, respond to the call of "Lancashire against London," then we see how important is this branch of our subject.

Just as the *relation* of jobs is a part of job analysis, just as the *relation* of departments is a part of scientific management, so a study of all these relations just mentioned should be a part of the study of business administration. I wish it were not so often assumed that the subject of personnel relations in industry applies only to employers and employees. The manager has to get credit from the bankers, make dividends for the stockholders, and he has to deal with his competitors. To be more exact, the manager has relations with (1) bankers, (2) stockholders, (3) co-managers and directors, (4) wage-earners, (5) competitors, (6) the people from whom he buys, (7) customers.

The business man has probably the opportunity to-day of making one of the largest contributions to society that has ever been made, a demonstration of the possibility of collective creativeness. Many writers tell us that we are living in a barren age and deplore this as a sign of our degeneration. These writers look to the periods of creative energy in the past and find there their Leonardos and their Dantes; they then look around to-day and, seeing no Leonardos nor Dantes, deplore the unproductiveness of our modern civilization. Such people make the mistake of connecting creativeness always and inevitably with individuals. They do not see that we are now at the beginning of a period of creative energy, but that instead of being the individual creativeness of the past which gave us our artists and our poets, we may now enter on a period of collective creativeness if we have the imagination to see its potentialities, its reach, its ultimate significance, above all if we are willing patiently to work out the method.

In the field of politics we see little to encourage us; but in the League of Nations, in the co-operatives, above all in business administration, we see an appreciation emerging, not in words but in deeds, of what collective creativeness might mean to the world. Much of our theoretical writing accepts without analysis time-honoured phrases and notions, treats as fundamental ideas the crude, primitive attempts to get at democracy by rule of thumb. The world has long been fumbling for democracy, but has not yet grasped its essential and basic idea. Business and industrial organization is, I believe, on the verge of making large contributions to something far more important than democracy, democracy in its more superficial meaning—to the development of integrative unity. Business cannot serve its maximum degree of usefulness to the community, cannot perform the service which it has, tacitly, *bound* itself to perform, unless it seeks an enlarged understanding of the practical methods of unifying business organization.

NOTE

1. This paper was presented in January, 1925.

SOURCE: Follett, Mary Parker. 1942. Excerpt from "Business as an Integrative Unity." Pp. 71–94 in *Dynamic Administration: The Collected Papers of Mary Parker Follett.* New York: Harper and Brothers.

2

MECHANISTIC AND ORGANIC SYSTEMS OF MANAGEMENT

TOM BURNS AND G. M. STALKER

We are now at the point at which we may set down the outline of the two management systems which represent for us the two polar extremities of the forms which such systems can take when they are adapted to a specific rate of technical and commercial change. The case we have tried to establish from the literature, as from our research experience exhibited in the last chapter, is that the different forms assumed by a working organization do exist objectively and are not merely interpretations offered by observers of different schools.

Both types represent a 'rational' form of organization, in that they may both, in our experience, be explicitly and deliberately created and maintained to exploit the human resources of a concern in the most efficient manner feasible in the circumstances of the concern. Not surprisingly, however, each exhibits characteristics which have been hitherto associated with different kinds of interpretation. For it is our contention that empirical findings have usually been classified according to sociological ideology rather than according to the functional specificity of the working organization to its task and the conditions confronting it.

We have tried to argue that these are two formally contrasted forms of management system. These we shall call the mechanistic and organic forms.

A *mechanistic* management system is appropriate to stable conditions. It is characterized by:

(a) the specialized differentiation of functional tasks into which the problems and tasks facing the concern as a whole are broken down;

(b) the abstract nature of each individual task, which is pursued with techniques and purposes more or less distinct from those of the concern as a whole; i.e., the functionaries tend to pursue the technical improvement of means, rather than the accomplishment of the ends of the concern;

(c) the reconciliation, for each level in the hierarchy, of these distinct performances by the immediate superiors, who are also, in turn, responsible for seeing that each is relevant in his own special part of the main task;

(d) the precise definition of rights and obligations and technical methods attached to each functional role;

(e) the translation of rights and obligations and methods into the responsibilities of a functional position;

(f) hierarchic structure of control, authority and communication;

(g) a reinforcement of the hierarchic structure by the location of knowledge of actualities exclusively at the top of the hierarchy, where the final reconciliation of distinct tasks and assessment of relevance is made;[1]

(*h*) a tendency for interaction between members of the concern to be vertical, i.e., between superior and subordinate;

(*i*) a tendency for operations and working behaviour to be governed by the instructions and decisions issued by superiors;

(*j*) insistence on loyalty to the concern and obedience to superiors as a condition of membership;

(*k*) a greater importance and prestige attaching to internal (local) than to general (cosmopolitan) knowledge, experience, and skill.

The *organic* form is appropriate to changing conditions, which give rise constantly to fresh problems and unforeseen requirements for action which cannot be broken down or distributed automatically arising from the functional roles defined within a hierarchic structure. It is characterized by:

(*a*) the contributive nature of special knowledge and experience to the common task of the concern;

(*b*) the 'realistic' nature of the individual task, which is seen as set by the total situation of the concern;

(*c*) the adjustment and continual re-definition of individual tasks through interaction with others;

(*d*) the shedding of 'responsibility' as a limited field of rights, obligations and methods. (Problems may not be posted upwards, downwards or sideways as being someone's else's responsibility);

(*e*) the spread of commitment to the concern beyond any technical definition;

(*f*) a network structure of control, authority, and communication. The sanctions which apply to the individual's conduct in his working role derive more from presumed community of interest with the rest of the working organization in the survival and growth of the firm, and less from a contractual relationship between himself and a non-personal corporation, represented for him by an immediate superior;

(*g*) omniscience no longer imputed to the head of the concern; knowledge about the technical or commercial nature of the here and now task may be located anywhere in the network; this location becoming the *ad hoc* centre of control authority and communication;

(*h*) a lateral rather than a vertical direction of communication through the organization, communication between people of different rank, also, resembling consultation rather than command;

(*i*) a content of communication which consists of information and advice rather than instructions and decisions;

(*j*) commitment to the concern's tasks and to the 'technological ethos' of material progress and expansion is more highly valued than loyalty and obedience;

(*k*) importance and prestige attach to affiliations and expertise valid in the industrial and technical and commercial milieux external to the firm.

One important corollary to be attached to this account is that while organic systems are not hierarchic in the same sense as are mechanistic, they remain stratified. Positions are differentiated according to seniority—i.e., greater expertise. The lead in joint decisions is frequently taken by seniors, but it is an essential presumption of the organic system that the lead, i.e. 'authority,' is taken by whoever shows himself most informed and capable, i.e., the 'best authority.' The location of authority is settled by consensus.

A second observation is that the area of commitment to the concern—the extent to which the individual yields himself as a resource to be used by the working organization—is far more extensive in organic than in mechanistic systems. Commitment, in fact, is expected to approach that of the professional scientist to his work, and frequently does. One further consequence of this is that it becomes far less feasible to distinguish 'informal' from 'formal' organization.

Thirdly, the emptying out of significance from the hierarchic command system, by which co-operation is ensured and which serves to monitor the working organization under a mechanistic system, is countered by the development of shared beliefs about the values and goals of the concern. The growth and accretion of institutionalized values, beliefs, and conduct, in the form of commitments, ideology, and manners, around an image of the concern in its industrial and commercial setting make good the loss of formal structure.

Finally, the two forms of system represent a polarity, not a dichotomy; there are, as we have tried to show, intermediate stages between the extremities empirically known to us. Also, the relation of one form to the other is elastic, so that a concern oscillating between relative stability and relative change may also oscillate between the two forms. A concern may (and frequently does) operate with a management system which includes both types.

The organic form, by departing from the familiar clarity and fixity of the hierarchic structure, is often experienced by the individual manager as an uneasy, embarrassed, or chronically anxious quest for knowledge about what he should be doing, or what is expected of him, and similar apprehensiveness about what others are doing. Indeed, as we shall see later, this kind of response is necessary if the organic form of organization is to work effectively. Understandably, such anxiety finds expression in resentment when the apparent confusion besetting him is not explained. In these situations, all managers some of the time, and many managers all the time, yearn for more definition and structure.

On the other hand, some managers recognize a rationale of non-definition, a reasoned basis for the practice of those successful firms in which designation of status, function, and line of responsibility and authority has been vague or even avoided.

The desire for more definition is often in effect a wish to have the limits of one's task more neatly defined—to know what and when one doesn't have to bother about as much as to know what one does have to. It follows that the more definition is given, the more omniscient the management must be, so that no functions are left wholly or partly undischarged, no person is overburdened with undelegated responsibility, or left without the authority to do his job properly. To do this, to have all the separate functions attached to individual roles fitting together and comprehensively, to have communication between persons constantly maintained on a level adequate to the needs of each functional role, requires rules or traditions of behaviour proved over a long time and an equally fixed, stable task.

The omniscience which may then be credited to the head of the concern is expressed throughout its body through the lines of command, extending in a clear, explicitly titled hierarchy of officers and subordinates.

The whole mechanistic form is instinct with this twofold principle of definition and dependence which acts as the frame within which action is conceived and carried out. It works, unconsciously, almost in the smallest minutiae of daily activity. 'How late is late?' The answer to this question is not to be found in the rule book, but in the superior. Late is when the boss thinks it is late. Is he the kind of man who thinks 8.00 is the time, and 8.01 is late? Does he think that 8.15 is all right occasionally if it is not a regular thing? Does he think that everyone should be allowed a 5-minutes grace after 8.00 but after that they are late?

Settling questions about how a person's job is to be done in this way is nevertheless simple, direct, and economical of effort. We shall, in a later chapter, examine more fully the nature of the protection and freedom (in other respects than his job) which this affords the individual.

One other feature of mechanistic organization needs emphasis. It is a necessary condition of its operation that the individual 'works on his own,' functionally isolated; he 'knows his job,' he is 'responsible for seeing it's done.' He works at a job which is in a sense artificially abstracted from the realities of the situation the concern is dealing with, the accountant 'dealing with the costs side,' the works manager 'pushing production,' and so on. As this works out in practice, the rest of the organization becomes part of the problem situation the individual has to deal with in order to perform successfully; i.e., difficulties and problems arising from work or information which has been handed over the 'responsibility barrier' between two jobs or departments are regarded as 'really' the responsibility of the person from whom they were received. As a design engineer put in, 'When you get designers handing over designs completely to production, it's "their responsibility" now. And you get tennis games played with the responsibility for anything that goes wrong. What happens is that you're constantly getting unsuspected faults arising from characteristics which you didn't think important in the design. If you get to hear of these through a sales person, or a production person, or somebody to whom the design was handed over to in the dim past, then, instead of being a design problem, it's an annoyance caused by that particular person, who can't do his own job—because you'd thought you were finished with that one, and you're on to something else now.'

When the assumptions of the form of organization make for preoccupation with specialized tasks, the chances of career success, or of greater influence, depend rather on the relative importance which may be attached to each special function by the superior whose task it is to reconcile and control a number of them. And, indeed, to press the claims of one's job or department for a bigger share of the firm's resources is in many cases regarded as a mark of initiative, of effectiveness, and even of 'loyalty to the firm's interests.' The state of affairs thus engendered squares with the role of the superior, the man who can see the wood instead of just the trees, and gives it the reinforcement of the aloof detachment belonging to a court of appeal. The ordinary relationship prevailing between individual managers 'in charge of' different functions is one of rivalry, a rivalry which may be rendered innocuous to the persons involved by personal friendship or the norms of sociability, but which turns discussion about the situations which constitute the real problems of the concern—how to make products more cheaply, how to sell more, how to allocate resources, whether to curtail activity in one sector, whether to risk expansion in another, and so on—into an arena of conflicting interests.

The distinctive feature of the second, organic system is the pervasiveness of the working organization as an institution. In concrete terms, this makes itself felt in a preparedness to combine with others in serving the general aims of the concern. Proportionately to the rate and extent of change, the less can the omniscience appropriate to command organizations be ascribed to the head of the organization; for executives, and even operatives, in a changing firm it is always theirs to reason why. Furthermore, the less definition can be given to status, roles, and modes of communication, the more do the activities of each member of the organization become determined by the real tasks of the firm as he sees them than by instruction and routine. The

individual's job ceases to be self-contained; the only way in which 'his' job can be done is by his participating continually with others in the solution of problems which are real to the firm, and put in a language of requirements and activities meaningful to them all. Such methods of working put much heavier demands on the individual. The ways in which these demands are met, or countered, will be enumerated and discussed in Part Three.

We have endeavoured to stress the appropriateness of each system to its own specific set of conditions. Equally, we desire to avoid the suggestion that either system is superior under all circumstances to the other. In particular, nothing in our experience justifies the assumption that mechanistic systems should be superseded by organic in conditions of stability.[2] The beginning of administrative wisdom is the awareness that there is no one optimum type of management system.

NOTES

1. This functional attribute of the head of a concern often takes on a clearly expressive aspect. It is common enough for concerns to instruct all people with whom they deal to address correspondence to the firm (i.e., to its formal head) and for all outgoing letters and orders to be signed by the head of the concern. Similarly, the printed letter heading used by Government departments carries instructions for the replies to be addressed to the Secretary, etc. These instructions are not always taken seriously, either by members of the organization or their correspondents, but in one company this practice was insisted upon and was taken to somewhat unusual lengths; *all* correspondence was delivered to the managing director, who would thereafter distribute excerpts to members of the staff, synthesizing their replies into the letter of reply which he eventually sent. Telephone communication was also controlled by limiting the numbers of extensions, and by monitoring incoming and outgoing calls.

2. A recent instance of this assumption is contained in H. A. Shepard's paper addressed to the Symposium on the Direction of Research Establishments, 1956. There is much evidence to suggest that the optimal use of human resources in industrial organizations requires a different set of conditions, assumptions, and skills from those traditionally present in industry. Over the past twenty-five years, some new orientations have emerged from organizational experiments, observations and inventions. The new orientations depart radically from doctrines

associated with "Scientific Management" and traditional bureaucratic patterns.

'The central emphases in this development are as follows:

1. Wide participation in decision-making, rather than centralized decision-making.

2. The face-to-face group, rather than the individual, as the basic unit of organization.

3. Mutual confidence, rather than authority, as the integrative force in organization.

4. The supervisor as the agent for maintaining intra-group and intergroup communication, rather than as the agent of higher authority.

5. Growth of members of the organization to greater responsibility, rather than external control of the member's performance or their tasks.'

SOURCE: Burns, Tom, and G. M. Stalker. [1961] 1995. Excerpt from "Mechanistic and Organic Systems of Management." Pp. 119–125 in *The Management of Innovation*. Oxford, England: Oxford University Press.

3

Markets, Bureaucracies, and Clans

William G. Ouchi

Evaluating organizations according to an efficiency criterion would make it possible to predict the form organizations will take under certain conditions. Organization theory has not developed such a criterion because it has lacked a conceptual scheme capable of describing organizational efficiency in sufficiently microsopic terms. The transactions cost approach provides such a framework because it allows us to identify the conditions which give rise to the costs of mediating exchanges between individuals: goal incongruence and performance ambiguity. Different combinations of these causes distinguish three basic mechanisms of mediation or control: markets, which are efficient when performance ambiguity is low and goal incongruence is high; bureaucracies, which are efficient when both goal incongruence and performance ambiguity are moderately high; and clans, which are efficient when goal incongruence is low and performance ambiguity is high.[1]

The Nature of Organizations

What is an organization, and why do organizations exist? Many of us would answer this question by referring to Barnard's (1968) technological imperative, which argues that a formal organization will arise when technological conditions demand physical power, speed, endurance, mechanical adaptation, or continuity beyond the capacity of a single individual (1968: 27–28). Yet when the stone is too large or the production facility too complex for a single person, what is called for is cooperation, and cooperation need not take the form of a formal organization. Indeed, grain farmers who need a large grain elevator do not form corporations which take over the farms and make the farmers into employees; instead, they form a cooperative to own and operate the elevator.

Others would refer to March and Simon's (1958) argument that an organization will exist so long as it can offer its members inducements which exceed the contributions it asks of them. While this position explains the conditions under which an organization may continue to exist, it does not explain how an organization can create a whole which is so much greater than the sum of its parts that it can give them more than they contribute.

Most of us, however, would refer to Blau and Scott's (1962) definition of a formal organization as a purposive aggregation of individuals who exert concerted effort toward a common and explicitly recognized goal. Yet we can hardly accept this definition whole, suspecting as Simon (1945: 257–278) has that individuals within organizations rarely have a common understanding of goals.

Another point of view on the question of why organizations exist began with an inquiry by Coase (1937) and has recently been developed by Williamson (1975). In this view, an organization such as a corporation exists because it can mediate economic transactions between its members at lower costs than a market mechanism can. Under certain conditions, markets are more efficient because they can mediate without paying the costs of managers, accountants, or personnel departments. Under other conditions, however, a market mechanism becomes so cumbersome that it is less efficient than a bureaucracy. This transactions cost approach explicitly regards efficiency as the fundamental element in determining the nature of organizations.

Markets, Bureacracies, and Clans

Transactions costs are a solution to the problem of cooperation in the realm of economic activity. From the perspective of Mayo (1945) and Barnard (1968), the fundamental problem of cooperation stems from the fact that individuals have only partially overlapping goals. Left to their own devices, they pursue incongruent objectives and their efforts are uncoordinated. Any collectivity which has an economic goal must then find a means to control diverse individuals efficiently.

Many helpful ideas have flowed from this definition of the problem of cooperation. Some (e.g., Etzioni, 1965; Weick, 1969) have emphasized the tension between individual autonomy and collective interests which must attend cooperative action, while others (e.g., Simon, 1945) have emphasized the impossibility of achieving a completely cooperative effort. Our interest is in the efficiency with which transactions are carried out between individuals who are engaged in cooperative action.

Cooperative action necessarily involves interdependence between individuals. This interdependence calls for a transaction or exchange in which each individual gives something of value (for example, labor) and receives something of value (for example, money) in return. In a market relationship, the transaction takes place between the two parties and is mediated by a price mechanism in which the existence of a competitive market reassures both parties that the terms of exchange are equitable. In a bureaucratic relationship, each party contributes labor to a corporate body which mediates the relationship by placing a value on each contribution and then compensating it fairly. The perception of equity in this case depends upon a social agreement that the bureaucratic hierarchy has the legitimate authority to provide this mediation. In either case, individuals must regard the transaction as equitable: it must meet the standards of reciprocity which Gouldner (1961) has described as a universal requirement for collective life.

It is this demand for equity which brings on transactions costs. A transactions cost is any activity which is engaged in to satisfy each party to an exchange that the value given and received is in accord with his or her expectations.

Transactions costs arise principally when it is difficult to determine the value of the goods or service. Such difficulties can arise from the underlying nature of the goods or service or from a lack of trust between the parties. When a company is being sold by one corporation to another corporation, for example, it may not be unambiguously clear what the true value of that company is. If firms similar to the company are frequently bought and sold, and if those transactions occur under competitive conditions, then the market process will be accepted as a legitimate estimator of the true value. But if the company is unique, and there is only one potential buyer, then market forces are absent. How will the buyer and seller determine a fair price? They may call upon a third party to estimate the value of the company. Each party may in addition call upon other experts who will assist them in evaluating both the value of the company and the adequacy of the judgment of the third party. Each side may also require an extensive and complete contract which will describe exactly what is being bought and sold. Each of these activities is costly, and all of them are regarded here as transactions costs: they are necessary to create a perception of equity among all parties to the transaction.

This same argument applies to transactions in which a service, such as the labor of an individual, is the object of exchange. If one individual sells his or her services to another, it may be difficult to assess the true value of that labor. In particular, if the labor is to be used in an interdependent technology, one which requires teamwork, it may be difficult to assess the value contributed by one worker as opposed to another, since their joint efforts yield a single outcome in this case, or in a case where it is likely that task requirements will change, then the auditing and complex contracting required to create the perception of equity can become unbearably costly.

We have identified two principal mechanisms for mediating these transactions: a market and a bureaucracy. These alternatives have received the greatest attention from organization theorists (e.g., Barnard, 1968; Weber, 1968) and economists (e.g., Coase, 1937; Arrow, 1974). However, the paradigm also suggests a third mechanism: If the objectives of individuals are congruent (not mutually exclusive), then the conditions of reciprocity and equity can be met quite differently.

Both Barnard and Mayo pointed out that organizations are difficult to operate because their members do not share a selfless devotion to the same objectives. Mayo (1945) argued that organizations operated more efficiently in preindustrial times, when members typically served an apprenticeship during which they were socialized into accepting the objectives of the craft or organization. Barnard (1968: 42–43) posed the problem thus:

> A formal system of cooperation requires an objective, a purpose, an aim. . . . It is important to note the complete distinction between the aim of a cooperative effort and that of an individual. Even in the case where a man enlists the aid of other men to do something which he cannot do alone, such as moving a stone, the objective ceases to be personal.

While Barnard, like Arrow, views markets and bureaucracies as the basic mechanisms for achieving the continued cooperation of these individuals, he also allowed (1968: 141) for the possibility of reducing the incongruence of goals in a manner consistent with Mayo's view of the preindustrial organization:

An organization can secure the efforts necessary to its existence, then, either by the objective inducement it provides or by changing states of mind. It seems to me improbable that any organization can exist as a practical matter which does not employ both methods in combination.

If the socialization of individuals into an organization is complete, then the basis of reciprocity can be changed. For example, Japanese firms rely to a great extent upon hiring inexperienced workers, socializing them to accept the company's goals as their own, and compensating them according to length of service, number of dependents, and other nonperformance criteria (see Abegglen, 1958; Dore, 1973; Nakane, 1973). It is not necessary for these organizations to measure performance to control or direct their employees, since the employees' natural (socialized) inclination is to do what is best for the firm. It is also unnecessary to derive explicit, verifiable measures of value added, since rewards are distributed according to nonperformance-related criteria which are relatively inexpensive to determine (length of service and number of dependents can be ascertained at relatively low costs). Thus, industrial organizations can, in some instances, rely to a great extent on socialization as the principal mechanism of mediation or control, and this "clan" form ("clan" conforms to Durkheim's meaning of an organic association which resembles a kin network but may not include blood relations, 1933: 175) can be very efficient in mediating transactions between interdependent individuals.

Markets, bureaucracies, and clans are therefore three distinct mechanisms which may be present in differing degrees, in any real organization.[2] Our next objective is to specify the conditions under which the requirements of each form are most efficiently satisfied.

THE MARKET FAILURES FRAMEWORK

We can approach this question most effectively by examining the markets and hierarchies approach provided by Williamson (1975), which builds upon earlier statements of the problem by Coase (1937) and others (for a more detailed description of the functioning of each mechanism, see Ouchi, 1979).

Market transactions, or exchanges, consist of contractual relationships. Each exchange is governed by one of three types of contractual relations, all of which can be specified completely. That is, because each party is bound only to deliver that which is specified, the contract must specify who must deliver what under every possible state of nature. The simplest form of contract is the "spot" or "sales" contract. This is what occurs when you walk up to a candy counter, ask for a candy bar, and pay the amount the salesperson asks. In such a transaction, all obligations are fulfilled on the spot. However, the spot market contract is, by definition, incapable of dealing with future transactions, and most exchange relationships involve long-term obligations.

A common device for dealing with the future is the "contingent claims contract," a document that specifies all the obligations of each party to an exchange, contingent upon all possible future states of nature. However, given a future that is either complex or uncertain, the bounded rationality of individuals makes it impossible to specify such a contract completely. Leaving such a contract incompletely specified is an alternative, but one that will succeed only if each party can trust the other to interpret the uncertain future in a manner that is acceptable to him. Thus, given uncertainty, bounded rationality, and opportunism, contingent claims contracting will fail.

Instead of trying to anticipate the future in a giant, once-and-for-all contract, why not employ a series of contracts, each one written for a short period within which future events can confidently be foreseen? The problem with such "sequential spot contracting" is that in many exchange relationships, the goods or services exchanged are unique, and the supplier requires specialized knowledge of how to supply the customer best and most efficiently. The supplier acquires this knowledge over time and in doing so gains a "first mover advantage," which enables him to bid more effectively on subsequent contracts than any potential competitor can. Knowing this, potential competitors will not waste their time bidding, thus producing a situation of "small numbers bargaining" or bilateral monopoly, in which there is

only one buyer and seller. Under this condition, competitive pressures are absent, and each party will opportunistically claim higher costs or poor quality, whichever is in his or her interest. In order to maintain such an exchange, each party will have to go to considerable expense to audit the costs or performance of the other. If these transactions costs are too high, the market relationship will fail due to the confluence of opportunism with small numbers bargaining, even though the limitations of uncertainty and bounded rationality have been overcome.

Thus, under some conditions no completely contractual market relationship is feasible. Table 3.1 summarizes the conditions which lead to market failure. According to the paradigm, no one of the four conditions can produce market failure, but almost any pairing of them will do so.

The idea of market failure is an analytical device. Economists do not agree on a specific set of conditions that constitute the failure of a market; indeed one point of view argues that even monopolistic conditions may be competitive. However, the idea of market failure as expressed by Williamson (1975) is useful as a conceptual framework within which to compare the strengths of markets as opposed to bureaucracies. The technique is to contend that all transactions can be mediated entirely by market relations, and then ask what conditions will cause some of these market mechanisms to fail and be replaced by bureaucratic mechanisms. In this sense, every bureaucratic organization constitutes an example of market failure.

The bureaucratic organization has two principal advantages over the market relationship. First, it uses the employment relation, which is an incomplete contract. In accepting an employment relation, a worker agrees to receive wages in exchange for submitting to the legitimate right of the organization to appoint superior officers who can (1) direct the work activities of the employee from day to day (within some domain or zone of indifference), thus overcoming the problem of dealing with the future all at once and (2) closely monitor the employee's performance, thus minimizing the problem of opportunism.

Table 3.1   The Market Failures Framework*

Human factors	Environmental factors
Bounded rationality	Uncertainty/Complexity
Opportunism	Small numbers

*Adapted from Williamson (1975: 40).

Second, the bureaucratic organization can create an atmosphere of trust between employees much more readily than a market can between the parties to an exchange. Because members of an organization assume some commonality of purpose, because they learn that long-term relationships will reward good performance and punish poor performance, they develop some goal congruence. This reduces their opportunistic tendencies and thus the need to monitor their performance.

Bureaucracies are also characterized by an emphasis on technical expertise which provides some skill training and some socialization into craft or professional standards. Professionals within a bureaucratic setting thus combine a primary affiliation to a professional body with a career orientation, which increases the sense of affiliation or solidarity with the employer and further reduces goal incongruence.[3]

In summary, the market failures framework argues that markets fail when the costs of completing transactions become unbearable. At that point, the inefficiencies of bureaucratic organization will be preferred to the relatively greater costs of market organization, and exchange relationships move from one domain into the other.

Consider one example. The 10,000 individuals who comprise the workforce of a steel mill could be individual entrepreneurs whose interpersonal transactions are mediated entirely through a network of market or contractual relationships. Each of them could also have a market relation with yet another combine which owned the capital equipment and facilities necessary to produce steel. Yet steel mills are typically bureaucratic in form and each worker is in an employment, not market, relation with the corporation. Market forces have failed because the determination of value contributed by one worker is highly ambiguous in the integrated steelmaking process, which makes the transactions cost attendant upon maintaining a market too high.

EXTENDING THE MARKET FAILURES FRAMEWORK: CLANS

Bureaucracies can fail when the ambiguity of performance evaluation becomes significantly greater than that which brings about market failure. A bureaucratic organization operates fundamentally according to a system of hierarchical surveillance, evaluation, and direction. In such a system, each superior must have a set of standards to which he can compare behavior or output in order to provide control. These standards only indicate the value of an output approximately, and are subject to idiosyncratic interpretation. People perceive them as equitable only as long as they believe that they contain a reasonable amount of performance information. When tasks become highly unique, completely integrated, or ambiguous for other reasons, then even bureaucratic mechanisms fail. Under these conditions, it becomes impossible to evaluate externally the value added by any individual. Any standard which is applied will be by definition arbitrary and therefore inequitable.

If we adopt the view that transactions costs arise from equity considerations, then we can interpret Table 3.1 in a different light. Simon's work on the employment relation (1957: 183–195) shows that Table 3.1 contains some redundancy. He emphasized that under an employment contract, the employer pays a worker a premium over the "spot" price for any piece of work. From the point of view of the worker, this "risk premium" compensates him for the likelihood that he will be asked to perform duties which are significantly more distasteful to him than those which are implied in the employment contract. The uncertainty surrounding the likelihood of such tasks and the expectation that the employer will or will not ask them determines the size of the risk premium. If the employee agreed with all the employer's objectives, which is equivalent to completely trusting the employer never to request a distasteful task, then the risk premium would be zero.

The employment relation is relatively efficient when the measurement of performance is ambiguous but the employer's goals are not. In an employment relation, each employee depends on the employer to distribute rewards equitably; if employees do not trust the employer to do so, they will demand contractual protections such as union representation and the transactions cost will rise.

Thus, the critical element in the efficiency of market versus employment relations has to do with (1) the ambiguity of the measurement of individual performance, and (2) the congruence of the employees' and employer's goals. We can now reformulate the transactions cost problem as follows: in order to mediate transactions efficiently, any organizational form must reduce either the ambiguity of performance evaluation or the goal incongruence between parties. Put this way, market relations are efficient when there is little ambiguity over performance, so the parties can tolerate relatively high levels of opportunism or goal incongruence. And bureaucratic relations are efficient when both performance ambiguity and goal incongruence are moderately high.

What form of mediation succeeds by minimizing goal incongruence and tolerating high levels of ambiguity in performance evaluation? Clearly, it is one which embodies a strong form of the employment relation as defined by Simon (1945), which is a relationship in which the risk premium is minimized. The answer is what we have referred to as the clan, which is the obverse of the market relation since it achieves efficiency under the opposite conditions: high performance ambiguity and low opportunism.

Perhaps the clearest exposition of the clan form appears in what Durkheim (1933: 365) refers to as the case of organic solidarity and its contrast with contractual relations:

> For organic solidarity to exist, it is not enough that there be a system of organs necessary to one another, which in a general way feel solidarity, but it is also necessary that the way in which they should come together, if not in every kind of meeting, at least in circumstances which most frequently occur, be predetermined. . . . Otherwise, at every moment new conflicts would have to be equilibrated. . . . It will be said that there are contracts. But, first of all, social relations are not capable of assuming this juridical form. . . . A contract is not self-sufficient, but supposes a regulation which is as extensive and complicated as contractual life itself. . . . A contract is only a truce, and very precarious, it suspends hostilities only for a time.

The solidarity to which Durkheim refers contemplates the union of objectives between individuals which stems from their necessary dependence upon one another. In this sense, any occupational group which has organic solidarity may be considered a clan. Thus, a profession, a labor union, or a corporation may be a clan, and the professionalized bureaucracy may be understood as a response to the joint need for efficient transactions within professions (clan) and between professions (bureaucracy). Goal congruity as a central mechanism of control in organizations also appears repeatedly in Barnard:

> The most intangible and subtle of incentives is that which I have called the condition of communion. . . . It is the feeling of personal comfort in social relations that is sometimes called solidarity, social integration. . . . The need for communion is a basis of informal organization that is essential to the operation of every formal organization (1968: 148; see also pp. 89, 152, 169, 273).

Descriptions of organizations which display a high degree of goal congruence, typically through relatively complete socialization brought about through high inclusion (Etzioni, 1965), are also found in Lipset, Trow, and Coleman (1956: 79–80), Argyris (1964: 10, 175), Selznick (1966), and Clark (1970). In each case, the authors describe the organization as one in which it is difficult to determine individual performance. However, such organizations are not "loosely coupled" nor are they "organized anarchies" simply because they lack market and bureaucratic mechanisms. A clan, as Durkheim points out, provides great regularity of relations and may in fact be more directive than the other, more explicit mechanisms. That clans display a high degree of discipline is emphasized by Kanter (1972) in her study of Utopian communities, some of which were successful businesses such as Oneida and Amana. According to Kanter, this discipline was not achieved through contractualism or surveillance but through an extreme form of the belief that individual interests are best served by a complete immersion of each individual in the interests of the whole (1972: 41).

More recently, Ouchi and Jaeger (1978) and Ouchi and Johnson (1978) have reported on modern industrial organizations which closely resemble the clan form. In these organizations, a variety of social mechanisms reduces differences between individual and organizational goals and produces a strong sense of community (see also Van Maanen, 1975; Katz, 1978). Where individual and organizational interests overlap to this extent, opportunism is unlikely and equity in rewards can be achieved at a relatively low transactions cost. Moreover, these organizations are typically in technologically advanced or closely integrated industries, where teamwork is common, technologies change often, and therefore individual performance is highly ambiguous.

When a bureaucracy fails, then due to excessively ambiguous performance evaluation, the sole form of mediation remaining is the clan, which relies upon creating goal congruence. Although clans may employ a system of legitimate authority (often the traditional rather than the rational-legal form), they differ fundamentally from bureaucracies in that they do not require explicit auditing and evaluation. Performance evaluation takes place instead through the kind of subtle reading of signals that is possible among intimate coworkers but which cannot be translated into explicit, verifiable measures. This means that there is sufficient information in a clan to promote learning and effective production, but that information cannot withstand the scrutiny of contractual relations. Thus, any tendency toward opportunism will be destructive, because the close auditing and hard contracting necessary to combat it are not possible in a clan.

If performance evaluation is so ambiguous and goals so incongruent that a clan fails, what then? We can only speculate, but it seems that this final cell may be the case discussed by Meyer and Rowan (1977) in which control is purely ceremonial and symbolic. School systems, like other organizations, do employ a variety of mechanisms. Yet if there is no effective mechanism of mediation between individuals, the perception of equity may be purely superstitious, based on a broad, community-based acceptance of the legitimacy of the institution.

MARKETS, BUREACRACIES, AND CLANS: AN OVERVIEW

Having distinguished three mechanisms of intermediation, we can now summarize them and attempt to set out the general conditions under which each form will mediate transactions between individuals most efficiently. Table 3.2 discriminates markets, bureaucracies, and clans along two dimensions: their underlying normative and informational requirements.

Normative requirements refer to the basic social agreements that all members of the transactional network must share if the network is to function efficiently, without undue costs of performance auditing or monitoring. A norm of reciprocity, according to Gouldner (1961), is one of only two social agreements that have been found to be universal among societies across time and cultures (the other is the incest taboo). If no such norm were widely shared, then a potential trader would have to consume so much energy in setting the contractural terms of exchange in advance and in auditing the performance of the other party afterwards that the potential transaction would cost too much. Under such conditions, a division of labor is unthinkable and social existence impossible. Therefore, a norm of reciprocity underlies all exchange mechanisms.

A norm of legitimate authority is critical for two reasons. As discussed above, it permits the assignment of organizational superiors who can, on an ad hoc basis, specify the work assignments of subordinates, thus obviating the need for a contingent claims employment contract which would be

Table 3.2 An Organizational Failures Framework

Mode of control	Normative requirements	Informational requirements
Market	Reciprocity	Prices
Bureaucracy	Reciprocity	Rules
	Legitimate authority	
Clan	Reciprocity	Traditions
	Legitimate authority	
	Common values and beliefs	

either so complex as to be infeasible or so simple as to be too confining or else incomplete. Legitimate authority also permits organizational superiors to audit the performance of subordinates more closely than is possible within a market relationship. In a bureaucracy, legitimate authority will commonly take the "rational/legal" form, whereas in a clan it may take the "traditional" form (see Blau and Scott, 1962: 27–38). Legitimate authority is not ordinarily created within the organization but is maintained by other institutions such as the church or the educational system (Weber, 1947; Blau and Scott, 1962; Barnard, 1968: 161–184). While the legitimacy of a particular organization may be greater or smaller as a result of its managerial practices, it is fundamentally maintained within a society generally.

Common values and beliefs provide the harmony of interests that erase the possibility of opportunistic behavior. If all members of the organization have been exposed to an apprenticeship or other socialization period, then they will share personal goals that are compatible with the goals of the organization. In this condition, auditing of performance is unnecessary except for educational purposes, since no member will attempt to depart from organizational goals.

A norm of reciprocity is universal, legitimate authority is accepted, though in varying degree, in most formal organizations, and common values and beliefs are relatively rare in formal organizations. Etzioni (1965) has described this last form of control as being common only to "total organizations" such as the military and mental hospitals, and Light (1972) describes its role in ethnically bound exchange relationships. However, we have also noted that a partially complete form of socialization, accompanied by market or bureaucratic mechanisms, may be effective across a wider range of organizations. Mayo (1945) contended that instability of employment, which upsets the long socialization period necessary, is the chief enemy of the development of this form of control.

The informational prerequisites of each form of control are prices, rules, and traditions. Prices are a highly sophisticated form of information for decision making. However, correct prices are difficult to arrive at, particularly when technological interdependence, novelty, or other forms of ambiguity obscure the boundary between tasks or individuals. Rules, by comparison, are relatively crude informational devices. A rule is specific to a problem, and therefore it takes a large number of rules to control organizational responses. A decision maker must know the structure of the rules in order to apply the correct one in any given situation. Moreover, an organization can never specify a set of rules that will cover all possible contingencies. Instead, it specifies a smaller set of rules which cover routine decisions, and refers exceptions up the hierarchy where policymakers can invent rules as needed. As Galbraith (1973) has pointed out, under conditions of uncertainty or complexity the number of exceptions becomes so great that the hierarchy becomes overloaded and the quality of decision making suffers.

Traditions are implicit rather than explicit rules that govern behavior. Because traditions are not specified, they are not easily accessible, and a new member will not be able to function effectively until he or she has spent a number of years learning them (Van Maanen and Schein, 1978). In terms of the precision of the performance evaluation they permit, traditions may be the crudest informational prerequisite, since they are ordinarily stated in a general way which must be interpreted in a particular situation. On the other hand, the set of traditions in a formal organization may produce a unified, although implicit philosophy or point of view, functionally equivalent to a theory about how that organization should work. A member who grasps such an essential theory can deduce from it an appropriate rule to govern any possible decision, thus producing a very elegant and complete form of control. Alternatively, a disruption of the socialization process will inhibit the passing on of traditions and bring about organizational inefficiency.

SOME CONCLUDING THOUGHTS

Under conditions of extreme uncertainty and opportunism, transactions cost may rise. Indeed, Denison (1978) has observed that net productivity declined in the United States between 1965 and 1975 due to changes in "the industrial and human environment within which business must operate" (1978:21). According to Denison, output per unit of input has declined for two reasons: 78 percent of the decline is due to increased costs of air, water, and safety on the job, and the remaining 22 percent is attributable to increased needs for surveillance of potentially dishonest employees, customers, contractors, and thieves. The resources put into improvements in air, water, and safety are not a net loss to society although they may reduce corporate profitability. The increased need for surveillance in business, however, may represent the fact that the cost of monitoring transactions has risen. Mayo (1945) might have predicted this change as an inevitable result of the instability which accompanies industrialization. In our framework, we could advance the following explanation: exchange relationships are generally subject to so much informational ambiguity that they can never be governed completely by markets. Consequently, they have been supplemented through cultural, clan mechanisms. As instability, heterogeneity, and mobility have intensified in the United States, however, the effectiveness of these cultural mechanisms has been vitiated and bureaucratic mechanisms of surveillance and control have increased. Although bureaucratic surveillance may be the optimal strategy under present social conditions, it is nonetheless true that the United States is devoting more of its resources to transactional matters than it did ten years ago, and that represents a net decline in its welfare.

The degree of uncertainty and opportunism that characterize American society may be such that no mechanisms of control ever function very well. We have already observed that the conditions necessary for a pure market, bureaucracy, or clan are rare. Even a combination of these control mechanisms may be insufficient in many cases, however. In organizations using new technologies or in the public sector, the rate of change, instability of employment, or ambiguity of performance evaluation may simply overwhelm all rational control attempts.

In these cases, exchange becomes institutionalized. Meyer and Rowan's (1977) central thesis is that school systems, by their nature, evade any form of rational control. They have no effective price mechanism, no effective bureaucratic control, and no internally consistent cultures (see also Meyer et al., 1978). Thus school systems (as distinguished from education, which need not be done by large organizations) continue to grow and survive because

the objectives which they are believed to pursue have been accepted as necessary by society. Since rational control is not feasible within the school, no one knows whether it is actually pursuing these goals, but an institutionalized organization (the church is another example) need not give evidence of performance (see also Ouchi, 1977: 97–98).

All work organizations are institutionalized in the sense that fundamental purposes of all viable organizations must mesh at least somewhat with broad social values (Parsons and Shils, 1951). This institutionalization permits organizations to survive even under conditions that severely limit their capacity for rational control. Ultimately, organizational failure occurs only when society deems the basic objectives of the organization unworthy of continued support.

What is an organization? An organization, in our sense, is any stable pattern of transactions between individuals or aggregations of individuals. Our framework can thus be applied to the analysis of relationships between individuals or between subunits within a corporation, or to transactions between firms in an economy. Why do organizations exist? In our sense, all patterned transactions are organized, and thus all stable exchanges in a society are organized. When we ask "why do organizations exist," we usually mean to ask "why do bureaucratic organizations exist," and the answer is clear. Bureaucratic organizations exist because, under certain specifiable conditions, they are the most efficient means for an equitable mediation of transactions between parties. In a similar manner, market and clan organizations exist because each of them, under certain conditions, offers the lowest transactions cost.

Notes

1. I am indebted to many colleagues for their constructive criticisms of this paper, particularly to Chris Argyris, Peter Blau, Larry Cummings, Charles Horngren, Joanne Martin, John Meyer, Jerry Porras, Edgar Schein, W. Richard Scott, Arnold Tannenbaum, Richard Walton, and Oliver Williamson.

2. In the broader language necessary to encompass both economics and organization theory, an organization may be thought of as any stable pattern of transactions.

In this definition, a market is as much an organization as is a bureaucracy or a clan. The only requirement is that, for the purposes of this discussion, we maintain a clear distinction between the idea of "bureaucracy" and the idea of "organization." Bureaucracy as used here refers specifically to the Weberian model, while organization refers to any stable pattern of transactions between individuals or aggregations of individuals.

3. Despite these desirable properties, the bureaucratic type has continually been under attack and revision. As Williamson points out, the move from U-form (functional) to M-form (divisional) organization among many large firms has been motivated by a desire to simulate a capital market within a bureaucratic framework because of its superior efficiency. By regrouping the parts of the organization, it is possible to create subentities that are sufficiently autonomous to permit precise measurement and the determination of an effective price mechanism. Although each division may still operate internally as a bureaucracy, the economies which accrue from this partial market solution are often large, offsetting the diseconomies of functional redundancy which often accompany the separation of the organization into divisions.

REFERENCES

Abegglen, James C.
    1958 The Japanese Factory Aspects of Its Social Organization. Glencoe. Il: Free Press.
Argyris, Chris
    1964 Integrating the Individual and the Organization. New York: Wiley.
Arrow, Kenneth J.
    1974 The Limits of Organization. New York: Norton.
Barnard, Chester I.
    1968 The Functions of the Executive, 30th anniversary ed. Cambridge: Harvard.
Blau, Peter M., and W. Richard Scott
    1962 Formal Organizations. San Francisco: Scott, Foreman.
Clark, Burton R.
    1970 The Distinctive College: Antioch, Reed, and Swarthmore. Chicago: Aldine.
Coase, R. H.
    1937 "The nature of the firm." Economica, new series, 4: 386–405.
Denison, Edward F.
    1978 Effects of Selected Changes in the Institutional and Human Environment upon Output Per Unit of Input. Brookings General Series Reprint #335. Washington: Brookings.

Dore, Ronald
    1973 British Factory–Japanese Factory. Berkeley: University of California.
Durkheim, Emile
    1933 The Division of Labor in Society. G. Simpson, trans. New York: Free Press.
Etzioni, Amitai
    1965 "Organizational control structure." In James G. March (ed.), Handbook of Organizations: 650–677. Chicago: Rand McNally.
Galbraith, Jay
    1973 Designing Complex Organizations. Reading, MA: Addison-Wesley.
Gouldner, Alvin W.
    1961 "The norm of reciprocity." American Sociological Review, 25: 161–179.
Kanter, Rosabeth Moss
    1972 Commitment and Community. Cambridge: Harvard.
Katz, Ralph
    1978 "Job longevity as a situational factor in job satisfaction." Administrative Science Quarterly, 23: 204–223.
Light, Ivan H.
    1972 Ethnic Enterprise in America. Berkeley: University of California.
Lipset, Seymour M., Martin A. Trow, and James S. Coleman
    1956 Union Democracy. Glencoe, Il: Free Press.
March, James G., and Herbert A. Simon
    1958 Organizations. New York: Wiley.
Mayo, Elton
    1945 The Social Problems of an Industrial Civilization. Boston: Division of Research, Graduate School of Business Administration, Harvard University.
Meyer, John W., and Brian Rowan
    1977 "Institutionalized organizations: Formal structure as myth and ceremony." American Journal of Sociology, 83: 340–363.
Meyer, John W., W. Richard Scott, Sally Cole, and Jo-Ann K. Intili
    1978 "Instructional dissensus and institutional consensus in schools." In Marshall W. Meyer and Associates (eds.), Environments and Organizations: 233–263. San Francisco: Jossey-Bass.
Nakane, Chie
    1973 Japanese Society, rev. ed. Middlesex, England: Penguin.
Ouchi, William G.
    1977 "The relationship between organizational structure and organizational control." Administrative Science Quarterly, 22: 95–113.

1979 "A conceptual framework for the design of organizational control mechanisms." Management Science, 25: 833–848.

Ouchi, William G., and Alfred M. Jaeger
1978 "Type 2 organization: Stability in the midst of mobility." Academy of Management Review, 3: 305–314.

Ouchi, William G., and Jerry B. Johnson
1978 "Types of organizational control and their relationship to emotional well-being." Administrative Sconce Quarterly, 23: 293–317.

Parsons, Talcott, and Edward A. Shils
1951 "Values, motives, and systems of action." In Talcott Parsons and Edward A Shils (eds.), Toward a General Theory of Action: 47–275. Cambridge: Harvard.

Selznick, Philip
1966 TVA and the Grass Roots (orig. ed., 1949). New York: Harper Torchbooks.

Simon, Herbert A.
1945 Administrative Behavior. New York: Free Press.
1957 Models of Man. New York: Wiley.

Van Maanen, John
1975 "Police socialization: A longitudinal examination of job attitudes in an urban police department." Administrative Science Quarterly, 20: 207–228.

Van Maanen, John, and Edgar H. Schein
1978 "Toward a theory of organizational socialization." Manuscript. Sloan School of Industrial Administration. Massachusetts Institute of Technology.

Weber, Max
1947 The Theory of Social and Economic Organization (orig. ed. 1925). A. M. Henderson and T. Parsons, trans. New York: Free Press.
1968 Economy and Society (orig. ed., 1925). G. Roth and C. Wittich, eds. New York: Bedminster Press.

Weick, Karl E.
1969 The Social Psychology of Organizing. Reading, MA: Addison-Wesley.

Williamson, O. E.
1975 Markets and Hierarchies: Analysis and Antitrust Implications. New York: Free Press.

SOURCE: Ouchi, William G. 1980. "Markets, Bureaucracies, and Clans." *Administrative Science Quarterly* 25:129–41.

4

NEITHER MARKET NOR HIERARCHY

Network Forms of Organization

WALTER W. POWELL

In recent years, there has been a considerable amount of research on organizational practices and arrangements that are network-like in form. This diverse literature shares a common focus on lateral or horizontal patterns of exchange, interdependent flows of resources, and reciprocal lines of communication. Yet this rich vein of work has had much impact on students of organizational behavior. This is not particularly surprising, given the many divergent strands of this work. One would need to have followed the fields of international business, technology strategy, industrial relations, organizational sociology, and the new institutional economics, as well as interdisciplinary work on such themes as cooperation, the embeddedness of economic life in social structure, and the proliferation of small business units to have kept abreast. The purpose of this chapter is to render this literature more accessible to scholars in the organizational behavior field. I do so by arguing that relational or network forms of organization are a clearly identifiable and viable form of economic exchange under certain specifiable circumstances.

I begin by discussing why the familiar market-hierarchy continuum does not do justice to the notion of network forms of organization. I then contrast three modes of organization—market, hierarchy, and network—and stress the salient features of each. The logic of network forms is explored systematically in order to demonstrate how networks differ from other forms. I cull the literature in a number of social science and management fields and provide examples of a wide range of organizational arrangements that can be characterized as networks. This review affords considerable insight into the etiology of network forms, and allows me to develop a number of empirically disconfirmable arguments about the circumstances that give rise to networks and allow them to proliferate. I close with some thoughts on the research agenda that follows from these arguments.

MARKETS AND FIRMS

In his classical article on the nature of the firm, the economist Ronald Coase (1937) conceived of the firm as a governance structure, breaking with orthodox accounts of the firm as a "black box" production function. Coase's key insight was that firms and markets were alternative means for organizing similar kinds of transactions. This provocative paper, however, lay fallow, so to speak, for nearly four decades, until it was picked up by Williamson and other proponents of transaction costs economics in the 1970s. This work took seriously the notion that organizational form matters a great deal, and in so doing moved the economics of organization much closer to the fields of law, organization theory, and business history.

The core of Williamson's (1975; 1985) argument is that transactions that involve uncertainty about their outcome, that recur frequently and require substantial "transaction-specific investments"—of money, time or energy that cannot be easily transferred—are more likely to take place within hierarchically organized firms. Exchanges that are straightforward, non-repetitive and require no transaction-specific investments will take place across a market interface. Hence, transactions are moved out of markets into hierarchies as knowledge specific to the transaction (asset specificity) builds up. When this occurs, the inefficiencies of bureaucratic organization will be preferred to the relatively greater costs of market transactions. There are two reasons for this: (1) bounded rationality—the inability of economic actors to write contracts that cover all possible contingencies; when transactions are internalized, there is little need to anticipate such contingencies since they can be handled within the firm's "governance structure"; and (2) "opportunism"—the rational pursuit by economic actors of their own advantage, with every means at their disposal, including guile and deceit; opportunism is mitigated by authority relations and by the stronger identification that parties presumably have when they are joined under a common roof.

This dichotomous view of markets and hierarchies (Williamson, 1975) sees firms as separate from markets or more broadly, the larger societal context. Outside boundaries of firms are competitors, while inside managers exercise authority and curb opportunistic behavior. This notion of sharp firm boundaries was not just an academic view. A good deal of management practice as well as antitrust law shared the belief that, in Richardson's (1972) colorful language, firms are "islands of planned co-ordination in a sea of market relations."

But just as many economists have come to view firms as governance structures, and are providing new insights into the organization of the employment relationship and the multidivisional firm (to cite only two examples), firms appear to be changing in significant ways and forms of relational contracting appear to have assumed much greater importance. Firms are blurring their established boundaries and engaging in forms of collaboration that resemble neither the familiar alternative of arms' length market contracting nor the former ideal of vertical integration.

Some scholars respond to these changes by arguing that economic changes can be arrayed in a continuum-like fashion with discrete market transactions located at one end and the highly centralized firm at the other. In between these poles, we find various intermediate or hybrid forms of organization.[1] Moving from the market pole, where prices capture all the relevant information necessary for exchange, we find putting-out systems, various kinds of repeated trading, quasi-firms, and subcontracting arrangements; toward the hierarchy pole, franchising, joint ventures, decentralized profit centers, and matrix management are located.

Is this continuum view satisfactory? Can transaction costs logic meet the task of explaining this rich array of alternative forms? Williamson clearly thinks that it can. Shifting gears somewhat, he remarks that he is "now persuaded that transactions in the middle range are much more common" than he previously recognized (Williamson, 1985, p. 83).[2] But, he avers, the distribution of transactions are such that the tails of this continuum from market to hierarchy are "thick."

I do not share the belief that the bulk of economic exchange fits comfortably at either of the poles of the market-hierarchy continuum. The legal theorist Ian Macneil (1985, p. 485) also disputes this view, arguing that, "discrete exchange can play only a very limited and specialized function in any economy."[3] Moreover, although I was earlier of the view that nonmarket, nonhierarchical forms represented hybrid modes (Powell, 1987), I now find that this mixed mode or intermediate notion is not particularly helpful. It is historically inaccurate, overly static, and it detracts from our ability to explain many forms of collaboration that are viable means of exchange.[4]

The view that transactions are distributed at points along a continuum implies that markets are the starting point, the elemental form of exchange out of which other methods evolve. Such a view is, obviously, a distortion of historical and anthropological evidence. As Moses Finley (1973) tells us so well, there was no market in the modern sense of the term in the classical world, only money in the nature of free booty and treasure trove. Nor did markets spring full blown with the Industrial Revolution. Economic units emerged from the dense webs of political, religious and social affiliations that had enveloped economic activity for centuries. Agnew (1986) documents that the word *market* [italics added] first enters the English language during the twelfth century to refer to specific locations where provisions and livestock were sold. The markets of medieval England had a highly personal, symbolic, and hierarchical flavor. E.P. Thompson (1971) used the term "the moral economy" to characterize the intricate pattern of symbolic and statutory expectations that surrounded the eighteenth century marketplace. It was not until the latter part of the eighteenth century that among the British educated classes the term *market* [italics added] became separated from a physical and social space and came to imply a boundless and timeless phenomenon of buying and selling (Agnew, 1986).[5]

By the same token, hierarchies do not represent an evolutionary end-point of economic development. A long view of business history would suggest that firms with strictly defined boundaries and highly centralized operations are quite atypical.[6] The history of modern commerce, whether told by Braudel, Polanyi, Pollard, or Wallerstein, is a story of family businesses, guilds, cartels, and extended trading companies—all enterprises with loose and highly permeable boundaries.

Recent work on the growth of small firms also casts doubt on the utility of a continuum view of economic exchange. Larson (1988) and Lorenzoni and Omati (1988) draw similar portraits from very different settings—high tech start-ups in the United States and craft-based firms in Northern Italy—which do not follow the standard model of small firms developing internally through an incremental and linear process. Instead, they suggest an entirely different model of externally-driven growth in which preexisting networks of relationships enable small firms to gain an established foothold almost overnight. These networks serve as conduits to provide small firms with the capacity to meet resource and functional needs.[7]

The idea that economic exchanges can be usefully arrayed along a continuum is thus too quiescent and mechanical. It fails to capture the complex realities of exchange.[8] The continuum view also misconstrues patterns of economic development and blinds us to the role played by reciprocity and collaboration as alternative governance mechanisms. By sticking to the twin pillars of markets and hierarchies, our attention is deflected from a diversity of organizational designs that are neither fish nor fowl, nor some mongrel hybrid, but a distinctly different form.

To be sure, there are a number of social scientists who question whether the distinction between market and hierarchy is particularly useful in the first place.[9] They contend that no sharp demarcation exists and that the argument is more a matter of academic pigeon-holing than of substantive operational differences. These analysts are united, however, more by their dislike of stylized models of economic exchange than by any shared alternative perspective.

One group of critics emphasizes the embeddedness of economics in social and cultural forces. Markets, in this view, are structured by a complex of local, ethnic, and trading cultures, and by varying regimes of state regulation (Gordon, 1985). Historians and sociologists contend that the market is not an amoral self-subsistent institution, but a cultural and social construction (Agnew, 1986; Reddy, 1984; Zelizer, 1988).[10] Others maintain that markets cannot be insulated from social structure because differential social access results in information asymmetries, as well as bottlenecks, thus providing some parties with considerable benefits and leaving others disadvantaged (Granovetter, 1985; White, 1981).

Another chorus of skeptics point to the intermingling of various forms of exchange. (See Bradach & Eccles, 1989, for a good review of this literature.) Stinchcombe (1985) shows that there are strong elements of hierarchy and domination in written contracts. Goldberg (1980, p. 338) notes that many market exchanges have been replaced by interorganizational collaborations. He contends that much economic activity "takes place within long-term, complex, multiparty contractual (or contract-like) relationships; behavior is in various degrees sheltered from market forces." Similarly, much of the observed behavior in hierarchical firms seems unrelated to either top management directives or the logic of vertical integration. For example, a firm's relationships with its law, consulting, accounting, and banking firms may be much more enduring and personal than its employment relationship with even its most senior employees.[11] The introduction of market processes into the firm also appears to be widespread. Eccles (1985) observes that large firms commonly rely on such market-like methods as transfer pricing and performance-based compensation schemes, while Eccles and Crane (1987) report that dual reporting relationships, internal competition, and compensation based on services provided to clients are the current norm in investment banking.

Markets, Hierarchies, and Networks

I have a good deal of sympathy regarding the view that economic exchange is embedded in a particular social structural context. Yet it is also the case that certain forms of exchange are more social—that is, more dependent on relationships, mutual interests, and reputation—as well as less guided by a formal structure of authority. My aim is to identify a coherent set of factors that make it meaningful to talk about networks as a distinctive form of coordinating economic activity. We can then employ these ideas to generate arguments about the frequency, durability, and limitations of networks.

When the items exchanged between buyers and sellers possess qualities that are not easily measured, and the relations are so long-term and recurrent that it is difficult to speak of the parties as separate entities, can we still regard this as a market exchange? When the entangling of obligation and reputation reaches a point that the actions of the parties are interdependent, but there is no common ownership or legal framework, do we not need a new conceptual tool kit to describe and analyze this relationship? Surely this patterned exchange looks more like a marriage than a one-night stand, but there is no marriage license, no common household, no pooling of assets. In the language I employ below, such an arrangement is neither a market transaction nor a hierarchical governance structure, but a separate, different mode of exchange, one with its own logic, a network.

Table 4.1   Stylized Comparison of Forms of Economic Organization

| Key Features | *Forms* | | |
	Market	*Hierarchy*	*Network*
Normative Basis	Contract—Property rights	Employment relationship	Complementary strengths
Means of Communication	Prices	Routines	Relational
Methods of Conflict Resolution	Haggling—Resort to courts for enforcement	Administrative fiat—Supervision	Norm of reciprocity—Reputational concerns
Degree of Flexibility	High	Low	Medium
Amount of Commitment Among the Parties	Low	Medium to High	Medium to High
Tone or Climate	Precision and/or suspicion	Formal, bureaucratic	Open-ended, mutual benefits
Actor Preferences or Choices	Independent	Dependent	Interdependent
Mixing of Forms	Repeat transactions (Geertz, 1978)	Informal organization (Dalton, 1957)	Status hierarchies
	Contracts as hierarchical documents (Stinchcombe, 1985)	Market-like features: profit centers, transfer pricing (Eccles, 1985)	Multiple partners Formal rules

Many firms are no longer structured like medieval kingdoms, walled off and protected from hostile outside forces. Instead, we find companies involved in an intricate latticework of collaborative ventures with other firms, most of whom are ostensibly competitors. The dense ties that bind the auto and biotechnology industries, discussed below, cannot be easily explained by saying that these firms are engaged in market transactions for some factors of production, or by suggesting that the biotechnology business is embedded in the international community of science. At what point is it more accurate to characterize these alliances as networks rather than as joint ventures among hierarchical firms?

We need fresh insights into these kinds of arrangements. Whether they are new forms of exchange that have recently emerged or age-old practices that have gained new prominence (more on the etiology of networks below), they are not satisfactorily explained by existing approaches. Markets, hierarchies, and networks are pieces of a larger puzzle that is the economy. The properties of the parts of this system are defined by the kinds of interaction that takes place among them. The behaviors and interests of individual actors are shaped by these patterns of interaction. Stylized models of markets, hierarchies, and networks are not perfectly descriptive of economic reality, but they enable us to make progress in understanding the extraordinary diversity of economic arrangements found in the industrial world today.

Table 4.1 represents a first cut at summarizing some of the key differences among markets, hierarchies, and networks. In market transactions the benefits to be exchanged are clearly specified, no trust is required, and agreements are bolstered by the power of legal sanction. Network forms of exchange, however, entail indefinite, sequential transactions within the context of a general pattern of interaction. Sanctions are typically normative rather than legal. The value of the goods to be exchanged in markets are much more important than the relationship itself; when relations do matter, they are frequently defined as if they were commodities. In hierarchies, communication occurs in the context of the employment contract. Relationships matter and previous interactions shape current ones, but the patterns and context of intraorganizational exchange are most strongly shaped by one's position within the formal hierarchical structure of authority.

The philosophy that undergirds exchange also contrasts sharply across forms. In markets the standard strategy is to drive the hardest possible bargain in the immediate exchange. In networks, the preferred option is often one of creating indebtedness and reliance over the long haul. Each approach thus devalues the other: prosperous market traders would be viewed as petty and untrustworthy shysters in networks, while successful participants in networks who carried those practices into competitive markets would be viewed as naive and foolish. Within hierarchies, communication and exchange is shaped by concerns with career mobility—in this sense, exchange is bound up with considerations of personal advancement. At the same time, intra-organizational communication takes place among parties who generally know one another, have a history of previous interactions, and possess a good deal of firm-specific knowledge, [and] thus there is considerable interdependence among the parties. In a market context, it is clear to everyone concerned when a debt has been discharged, but such matters are not nearly as obvious in networks or hierarchies.

Markets, as described by economic theory, are a spontaneous coordination mechanism that imparts rationality and consistency to the self-interested actions of individuals and firms. One need not go as far as Polanyi (1957) did, when he argued that market transactions are characterized by an "attitude involving a distinctive antagonistic relationship between the partners," but it is clear that market exchanges typically entail limited personal involvement. "A contract connects two people only at the edges of their personalities" (Walzer, 1983, p. 83). The market is open to all comers, but while it brings people together, it does not establish strong bonds of altruistic attachments. The participants in a market transaction are free of any future commitments. The stereotypical competitive market is the paradigm of individually self-interested, noncooperative, unconstrained social interaction. As such, markets have powerful incentive effects for they are the arena [in] which each party can fulfill its own internally defined needs and goals.

Markets offer choice, flexibility, and opportunity. They are a remarkable device for fast, simple communication. No one need rely on someone else for direction, [as] prices alone determine production and exchange. Because individual behavior is not dictated by a supervising agent, no organ of system-wide governance or control is necessary. Markets are a form of noncoercive organization, [and] they have coordinating but not integrative effects. As Hayek (1945) suggested, market coordination is the result of human actions but not of human design.

Prices are a simplifying mechanism, [and] consequently they are unsuccessful at capturing the intricacies of idiosyncratic, complex, and dynamic exchange. As a result, markets are a poor device for learning and the transfer of technological know-how. In a stylized perfect market, information is freely available, alternative buyers or sellers are easy to come by, and there are no carry-over effects from one transaction to another. But as exchanges become more frequent and complex, the costs of conducting and monitoring them increase, giving rise to the need for other methods of structuring exchange.

Organization, or hierarchy, arises when the boundaries of a firm expand to internalize transactions and resource flows that were previously conducted in the marketplace. The visible hand of management supplants the invisible hand of the market in coordinating supply and demand. Within a hierarchy, individual employees operate under a regime of administrative procedures and work roles defined by higher level supervisors. Management divides up tasks and positions and establishes an authoritative system of order. Because tasks are often quite specialized, work activities are highly interdependent. The large vertically-integrated firm is thus an eminently social institution, with its own routines, expectations, and detailed knowledge.

A hierarchical structure—clear departmental boundaries, clean lines of authority, detailed reporting mechanisms, and formal decision making procedures—is particularly well-suited for mass production and distribution. The requirements of high volume, high speed operations demand the constant attention of a managerial team. The strength of hierarchical organization, then, is its reliability—its capacity for producing large numbers of goods or services of a given quality repeatedly—and its accountability—its ability to document how resources have been used (DiMaggio & Powell,

1983; Hannan & Freeman, 1984). But when hierarchical forms are confronted by sharp fluctuations in demand and unanticipated changes, their liabilities are exposed.

Networks are "lighter on their feet" than hierarchies. In network modes of resource allocation, transactions occur neither through discrete exchanges nor by administrative fiat, but through networks of individuals engaged in reciprocal, preferential, mutually supportive actions. Networks can be complex: they involve neither the explicit criteria of the market, nor the familiar paternalism of the hierarchy. [The] basic assumption of network relationships is that one party is dependent on resources controlled by another, and that there are gains to be had by the pooling of resources.[12] In essence, the parties to a network agree to forego the right to pursue their own interests at the expense of others.

In network forms of resource allocation, individual units exist not by themselves, but in relation to other units. These relationships take considerable effort to establish and sustain, [and] thus they constrain both partners' ability to adapt to changing circumstances. As networks evolve, it becomes more economically sensible to exercise voice rather than exit. Benefits and burdens come to be shared. Expectations are not frozen, but change as circumstances dictate. A mutual orientation—knowledge which the parties assume each has about the other and upon which they draw in communication and problem solving—is established. In short, complementarity and accommodation are the cornerstones of successful production networks. As Macneil (1985) has suggested, the "entangling strings" of reputation, friendship, interdependence, and altruism become integral parts of the relationship.

Networks are particularly apt for circumstances in which there is a need for efficient, reliable information. The most useful information is rarely that which flows down the formal chain of command in an organization, or that which can be inferred from shifting price signals. Rather, it is that which is obtained from someone whom you have dealt with in the past and found to be reliable. You trust best information that comes from someone you know well. Kaneko and Imai (1987) suggest that information passed through networks is "thicker" than information obtained in the market, and "freer" than communicated in a hierarchy. Networks, then, are especially useful for the exchange of commodities whose value is not easily measured. Such qualitative matters as know-how, technological capability, a particular approach or style of production, a spirit of innovation or experimentation, or a philosophy of zero defects are very hard to place a price tag on. They are not easily traded in markets nor communicated through a corporate hierarchy. The open-ended, relational features of networks, with their relative absence of explicit quid pro quo behavior, greatly enhance the ability to transmit and learn new knowledge and skills.

Reciprocity is central to discussions of network forms of organization. Unfortunately it is a rather ambiguous concept, used in different ways by various social science disciplines. One key point of contention concerns whether reciprocity entails exchanges of roughly equivalent value in a strictly delimited sequence of whether it involves a much less precise definition of equivalence, one that emphasizes indebtedness and obligation. Game theoretic treatments of reciprocity by scholars in political science and economics tend to emphasize equivalence. Axelrod (1984) stresses that reciprocal action implies returning ill for ill as well as good for good. As Keohane (1986) notes, the literature in international relations "emphatically" associates reciprocity with equivalence of benefits.[13] As a result, these scholars take a view of reciprocity that is entirely consistent with the pursuit of self-interest.

Sociological and anthropological analyses of reciprocity are commonly couched in the language of indebtedness. In this view, a measure of imbalance sustains the partnership, compelling another meeting (Sahlins, 1972). Obligation is a means through which parties remain connected to one another. Calling attention to the need for equivalence might well undermine and devalue the relationship.[14] To be sure, sociologists have long emphasized that reciprocity implies conditional action (Gouldner, 1960). The question is whether there is a relatively immediate assessment or whether "the books are kept open," in the interests of continuing satisfactory results. This perspective also takes a different tack on the issue of self-interest. In his classic work *The Gift*, Marcel Mauss (1967 [1925]) attempted to show that the obligations to give, to receive, and

to return were not to be understood simply with respect to rational calculations, but fundamentally in terms of underlying cultural tenets that provide objects with their meaning and significance, and provide a basis for understanding the implications of their passage from one person to another. Anthropological and sociological approaches, then, tend to focus more on the normative standards that sustain exchange; game theoretic treatments emphasize how individual interests are enhanced through cooperation.

Social scientists do agree, however, that reciprocity is enhanced by taking a long-term perspective. Security and stability encourage the search for new ways of accomplishing tasks, promote learning and the exchange of information, and engender trust. Axelrod's (1984) notion of "the shadow of the future"—the more the immediate payoff facing players is shaped by future expectations—points to a broadened conception of self-interest. Cooperation thus emerges out of mutual interests and behavior is based on standards that no one individual can determine alone. Trust is thereby generated. Trust is, as Arrow (1974) has noted, a remarkably efficient lubricant to economic exchange. In trusting another party, one treats as certain those aspects of life which modernity rendered uncertain (Luhmann, 1979). Trust reduces complex realities far more quickly and economically than prediction, authority, or bargaining.

It is inaccurate, however, to characterize networks solely in terms of collaboration and concord. Each point of contact in a network can be a source of conflict as well as harmony. Recall that the term *alliance* [italics added] comes from the literature of international relations where it describes relations among nation states in an anarchic world. Keohane (1986) has stressed that processes of reciprocity or cooperation in no way "insulate practitioners from considerations of power." Networks also commonly involve aspects of dependency and particularism.[15] By establishing enduring patterns of repeat trading, networks restrict access. Opportunities are thus foreclosed to newcomers, either intentionally or more subtly through such barriers as unwritten rules or informal codes of conduct. In practice, subcontracting networks and research partnerships influence who competes with whom, thereby dictating the adoption of a particular technology and making it much harder for unaffiliated parties to join the fray. As a result of these inherent complications, most potential partners approach the idea of participating in a network with trepidation. In the various examples presented below, all of the parties to network forms of exchange have lost some of their ability to dictate their own future and are increasingly dependent on the activities of others.

Illustrative Cases of Network Forms

It is time to add some flesh to these stylized models. Substantive details enable us to see how these abstractions operate in economic life. I provide examples of networks from a diversity of industries, ranging from highly traditional sectors to the most technologically advanced ones. These disparate examples share some important commonalities. They all involve intricate, multifaceted, durable relationships in which horizontal forms of exchange are paramount. My argument is based on the Simmelian notion that similar patterns of exchange are likely to entail similar behavioral consequences, no matter what the substantive context.

I begin this section with craft industries, a setting where network forms have long been dominant. I turn next to a discussion of industrial districts, where network forms have made a resurgence. I then move to high technology fields; here, networks are a much more novel phenomenon. They are being established for strategic purposes because neither market nor hierarchical forms have delivered the goods. Networks, in this case, are very much associated with the early stages of product life cycles. I conclude with the case of vertical disaggregation, where networks represent an effort to introduce collaboration into well-established contexts in which trust and cooperation have long been absent. The logic is to move from arenas in which networks are common and easy to form to settings where they are developed almost as a last resort.

NOTES

1. See Koenig and Thietart (1988) on intermediate forms in the aerospace industry, Thorelli (1986) on industrial marketing networks, Eccles and White (1986) on transfer pricing, and Powell (1987) on hybrid forms in craft and high technology industries.

2. This recognition of intermediate forms has not, however, been accompanied by much in the way of concerted analysis. *The Economic Institutions of Capitalism* may include relational contracting in its subtitle, but the index lists a scant four pages of references to the topic. Similarly, Riordan and Williamson (1985) emphasize polar firm and market choices throughout their analysis, and then acknowledge in their last paragraph that "hybrid modes of organization are much more important than had hitherto been realized."

3. Transaction costs reasoning borrows freely from legal scholars, such as Macaulay and Macneil, who are noted for the development of ideas regarding relational contracting. Gordon (1985), however, questions whether this assimilation is satisfactory, noting that the price of success by economists is the "exclusion of the very elements of contract relations to which Macneil and Macaulay have given most prominence: culture, politics, and power" (p. 575).

4. Transaction cost logic involves the comparison of discrete structural alternatives, [and] typically the comparison that is made is that between market and hierarchy. The problem I have with this analysis is that in many cases where transaction cost reasoning predicts internalization; we find other kinds of governance structures, particularly networks. But one can read Williamson (1985) in a different manner, ignoring the argument about the predominance of markets and hierarchies, and focus instead on the highly important role of credible commitments. The book discusses a marvelous array of mechanisms for creating mutually reliant and self-enforcing agreements, if one conceives of production as a chain of activities in which value is added (Porter, 1985), the question is thus posed: which activities does a firm choose to perform internally and which activities are either downplayed or "farmed out" to members of a network who presumably can carry them out more effectively, due to benefits of specialization, focus, or size (see Jarillo, 1988 for an extended discussion of this network value chain). When production is viewed in this manner, Williamson's arguments about credible commitments are quite useful in assessing what kinds of network agreements are likely to prove durable.

5. This does not mean that market forces were of little consequences before the eighteenth century. Braudel (1982) argues that economic history is the story of slowly-evolving mixtures of institutional forms. He suggests that we can speak of a market economy when the prices in a given area appear to fluctuate in unison, a phenomenon that has occurred since ancient times. But this does not imply that transactions between individuals were of a discrete, impersonal nature.

6. I owe this observation to comments made by Jim Robins.

7. What is remarkable about the firms in these two studies is how explicitly the entrepreneurs follow a "network" strategy, intentionally eschewing internalization for such crucial and recurrent activities as manufacturing, sales, and research and development.

8. On this point, Macneil (1985, p. 496) suggests that "the transaction costs approach is far too unrelational a starting point in analyzing" relational forms of exchange. Richardson (1972, p. 884) provides an apt example of these densely connected forms of exchange: "Firm A, . . . is a joint subsidiary of firms B and C, has technical agreements with D and B, subcontracts work to F, is in marketing association with G—and so on. So complex and ramified are these arrangements, indeed, that the skills of a genealogist rather than an economist might often seem appropriate for their disentanglement."

9. Bob Eccles and Mark Granovetter have repeatedly made this point to me in personal communications, insisting that all forms of exchange contain elements of networks, markets, and hierarchies. Since they are smarter than me, I should listen to them. Nevertheless, I hope to show that there is merit in thinking of networks as an empirically identifiable governance structure.

10. This line of work is both novel and promising, but it has yet to demonstrate how social ties and cultural patterns transform economic exchange in a systematic fashion; nor do we as yet have any clear cut notions about how cultural or historical factors create or introduce comparative variations in economic life. The focus, thus far, has been more on the intriguing question of how are economic motives culturally constructed.

11. Some economists (Alchian and Demsetz, 1972; Klein, 1983) go so far as to regard the firm as merely a set of explicit and implicit contracts among owners of different factors of production.

12. Many other scholars have their own definitions. Jarillo (1988, p. 32) defines strategic networks as "long-term, purposeful arrangements among distinct but related for-profit organizations that allow those firms in them to gain or sustain competitive advantage vis-à-vis their competitors outside the network." Kaneko and Imai (1987) conceive of networks as a particular form of multi-faceted, inter-organizational relationships through which new information is generated. Johanson and Mattsson (1987) regard networks as a method of dividing labor such that firms are highly dependent upon one another. Coordination is not achieved through hierarchy or markets, but through the interaction and mutual obligation of the firms in the network. Gerlach (1990) suggests that alliances among Japanese firms are an important institutional alternative that links Japanese firms to one another in ways that are fundamentally different from U.S. business practices. Alliances, in his view, are coherent networks of rule-ordered exchange, based on the mutual return of obligations among parties bound in durable relationships.

I find these various definitions very helpful, but also limited. They all describe networks as a form of dense interorganizational relationships. But networks can also evolve out of personal ties, or market relationships among various parties. Many of the arrangements discussed below, commonly found in the publishing, fashion, computer software, construction, and entertainment businesses, are among individuals, independent production teams, or very small business units. Thus, my conception of networks is closer to Macneil's (1978; 1985) ideas about relational contracts than to the above views.

13. In an illuminating essay, Keohane (1986, p. 8) defines reciprocity as exchanges of roughly equivalent values in which the actions of each party are contingent on the prior actions of the others in such a way that good is returned for good, and bad for bad.

14. For example, successful reciprocal ties in scholarly book publishing—between authors and editors or between editors in competing houses—were highly implicit, of long-standing duration, and not strictly balanced (Powell, 1985). It was widely believed that the open-ended quality of the relationship meant that the goods being exchanged—advice, recommendations, or manuscripts—were more valuable and reliable.

15. Parties are, of course, free to exit from a network. But the difficulty of abandoning a relationship around which a unit or a company has structured its operations and expectations can keep a party locked into a relationship that it experiences as unsatisfactory. This problem of domination in networks obviously lends itself to transaction costs discussions of credible commitments.

REFERENCES

Agnew, J. (1986). *Worlds Apart: The market and the theater in anglo-American thought, 1550–1750*. New York: Cambridge University Press.

Alchian, A., & Demsetz, H. (1972). Production, information costs, and economic organization. *American Economic Review, 62,* 5, 777–795.

Arrow, K. (1974). *The limits of organization*. New York: Norton.

Axelrod, R. (1984). *The evolution of cooperation*. New York: Basic Books.

Bradach, J.L., & Eccles, R.G. (1989). Markets versus hierarchies: From ideal types to plural forms. *Annual Review of Sociology, 15,* 97–118.

Braudel, F. (1982). *The wheels of commerce.* New York: Harper and Row.

Coase, R. (1937). The nature of the firm. *Economica, 4,* 386–405.

Cole, R. (1985). The macropolitics of organizational change: A comparative analysis of the spread of small-group activities. *Administrative Science Quarterly, 30,* 560–585.

Contractor, F.J. & Lorange, P. (1988). *Cooperative strategies in international business.* Lexington, MA: Lexington Books.

Dalton, M. (1957). *Men who manage.* New York: Wiley.

DiMaggio, P., & Powell, W.W. (1983). The iron cage revisited: Institutional isomorphism and collective rationality in organizational fields. *American Sociological Review, 48,* 147–160.

Dorfman, N. (1983). Route 128: TV development of a regional high-tech economy. *Research Policy, 12,* 299–316.

Eccles, R. (1981). The quasifirm in the construction industry. *Journal of Economic Behavior and Organization, 2,* 335–357.

Eccles, R. (1985). *The transfer pricing problem: A theory for practice.* Lexington, MA: Lexington Books.

Eccles, R.G., & Crane, D. (1987). Managing through networks in investment banking. *California Management Review, 30(1),* 176–195.

Eccles, Robert G., & Harrison C. White. (1986). "Firm and market interfaces of profit center control." Pp. 203–220 in *Approaches to social theory,* ed. by S. Lindenberg, J.S. Coleman, and S. Novak. New York: Russell Sage.

Finley, M. (1973). *The ancient economy.* Berkeley: University of California Press.

Friar, J., & Horwitch, M. (1985). "The emergence of technology strategy: A new dimension of strategic management." *Technology in Society* 7(2/3), pp. 143–178.

Geertz, C. (1978). The bazaar economy: Information and search in peasant marketing. *American Economic Review, 68(2),* 28–32.

Gerlach, M.L. (1990). *Alliances and the social organization of Japanese business.* Berkeley: University of California Press.

Goldberg, V.P. (1980). Relational exchange: Economics and complex contracts. *American Behavioral Scientist, 23(3),* 337–352.

Gordon, R.W. (1985). Macaulay, Macneil, and the discovery of solidarity and power in contract law. *Wisconsin Law Review, 3,* 565–580.

Gouldner, A. (1960). The norm of reciprocity: A preliminary statement. *American Sociological Review, 25,* pp. 161–178.

Graham, M. (1985). Corporate research and development: The latest transformation. *Technology in Society, 7(2/3),* 179–196.

Granovetter, M. (1985). Economic action and social structure: A theory of embeddedness. *American Journal of Sociology, 91(3),* 481–510.

Hamilton, W.F. (1985). Corporate strategies for managing emerging technologies. *Technology in Society, 7(2/3),* 197–212.

Hannan, M., & Freeman, J.H. (1984). Structural inertia and organizational change. *American Sociological Review, 49,* 149–164.

Hayek, F. (1945). The use of knowledge in society. *American Economic Review, 35,* 519–530.

Jarillo, J.-C. (1988). On strategic networks. *Strategic Management Journal, 9,* 31–41.

Johanson, J., & Mattson, L.-G. (1987). Interorganizational relations in industrial systems: A network approach compared with the transaction-cost approach. *International Studies of Management and Organization, 18(1),* 34–48.

Kaneko, I., & Imai, K. (1987). A network view of the firm. Paper presented at 1st Hitotsubashi-Stanford conference.

Keohane, R. (1986). Reciprocity in international relations. *International Organization, 40(1),* 1–27.

Klein, B. (1983). Contracting costs and residual claims: The separation of ownership and control. *Journal of Law and Economics, 26,* 367–374.

Koenig, C., & Thietart, R.A. (1988). Managers, engineers and government. *Technology in Society, 10,* 45–69.

Larson, A. (1988). Cooperative alliances: A study of entrepreneurship. Ph.D. dissertation. Harvard Business School.

Lorenzoni, G., & Omati, O. (1988). Constellations of firms and new ventures. *Journal of Business Venturing, 3,* 41–57.

Luhmann, N. (1979). *Trust and power.* New York: Wiley.

Macneil, I. (1978). Contracts: Adjustment of long-term economic relations under classical, neoclassical, and relational contract law. *Northwestern University Law Review, 72(6),* 854–905.

Macneil, I. (1985). Relational contract: What we do and do not know. *Wisconsin Law Review, 3,* 483–526.

Mauss, M. (1967, 1925). *The gift.* New York: Norton.

Ouchi, W.G., & Bolton, M.K. (1988). The logic of joint research and development. *California Management Review, 30(3),* 9–33.

Peck, M.J. (1986). Joint R&D: The case of microelectronics and computer technology corporation. *Research Policy, 75,* 219–231.

Polanyi, K. (1957). *The great transformation.* Boston: Beacon.

Porter, M. (1985). *Competitive advantage.* New York: Free Press.

Powell, W.W. (1985). *Getting into print: The decision making process in scholarly publishing.* Chicago: University of Chicago Press.

Powell, W.W. (1987). Hybrid organizational arrangements: New form or transitional development? *California Management Review, 30(1),* 67–87.

Reddy, W.M. (1984). *The rise of market culture.* New York: Cambridge University Press.

Richardson, G.B. (1972). The organization of industry. *Economic Journal, 82,* 883–896.

Riordan, M.H., & Williamson, O.E. (1985). Asset specificity and economic organization. *International Journal of Industrial Organization, 3,* 365–378.

Sahlins, M. (1972). *Stone age economics.* Chicago: Aldine.

Stinchcombe, A. (1985). Contracts as hierarchical documents. Pp. 121–171 in A. Stinchcombe & C. Heimer, *Organization theory and project management.* Oslo: Norwegian University Press.

Thompson, E.P. (1971). The moral economy of the English crowd in the eighteenth century. *Past and Present,* 50, 78–98.

Thorelli, H.B. (1986). Networks: Between markets and hierarchies. *Strategic Management Journal,* 7, 37–51.

Walzer, M. (1983). *Spheres of justice.* New York: Basic Books.

White, H.C. (1981). Where do markets come from? *American Journal of Sociology,* 87, 517–547.

Williamson, O.E. (1975). *Markets and hierarchies: Analysis and antitrust implications.* New York: Free Press.

Williamson, O.E. (1985). *The economic institutions of capitalism.* New York: Free Press.

Zelizer, V. (1988). Beyond the polemics of the market: Establishing a theoretical and empirical agenda. Paper presented at conference on Economy and Society, University of California–Santa Barbara.

SOURCE: Powell, Walter W. 1990. Excerpt from "Neither Market Nor Hierarchy: Network Forms of Organization." *Research in Organizational Behavior* 12: 295 -336. Used by permission of JAI Press, Greenwich, CT.

5

ORGANIZATIONAL SOCIAL CAPITAL AND EMPLOYMENT PRACTICES

CARRIE R. LEANA AND HARRY J. VAN BUREN III

The term *social capital* has received considerable recent attention from scholars in a variety of fields. Social capital is broadly defined as an asset that inheres in social relations and networks. Beyond this general definition, researchers have used the term in competing and sometimes contradictory ways. Scholars have described social capital as an attribute of individual actors who realize advantages owing to their relative status (e.g., Useem & Karabel, 1986) or location (e.g., Burt, 1997) in a group. On a macro level, scholars have described social capital as an attribute of communities (e.g., Putnam, 1993a), nations (e.g., Fukuyama, 1995), and industry networks (e.g., Walker, Kogut, & Shan, 1997). As an organizational phenomenon, social capital has received comparatively less attention, although recently Nahapiet and Ghoshal (1998) have described mechanisms by which social capital can facilitate the intellectual capability of firms.

We develop here a construct that we label *organizational social capital*. We define this as a resource reflecting the character of social relations within the firm. *Organizational social capital* is realized through members' levels of collective goal orientation and shared trust, which create value by facilitating successful collective action. Organizational social capital is an asset that can benefit both the organization (e.g., creating value for shareholders) and its members (e.g., enhancing employee skills).

In describing organizational social capital, we define members as individuals who have an employment relationship with the firm. These need not be traditional employees, in the sense of being full-time, permanent staff. But membership does not include outside individuals or other organizations with whom the firm transacts or forms alliances, such as suppliers, customers, or even competitors. Members are individuals who have an employment relationship with the firm, be it as temporary, contingent, or core workers.

In this article we discuss employment practices as primary mechanisms by which organizational social capital is fostered or discouraged within the firm. Employment practices can provide an effective means of managing organizational social capital, thus extracting its value for the organization and its members. We (1) describe organizational social capital, (2) propose a model of its components and consequences, and (3) discuss the role of employment practices in shaping organizational social capital. To ground our model in the existing social capital literature, we begin our discussion with a description of social capital and the different ways researchers have conceptualized it.

THE MANY FACES OF SOCIAL CAPITAL

Social capital is broadly described by researchers as an asset embedded in relationships—of individuals, communities, networks, or societies (Burt, 1997; Coleman, 1990; Nahapiet & Ghoshal, 1998; Walker et al., 1997). As with other kinds of capital, such as plant and equipment (physical capital) and knowledge and technical ability (human capital), more is generally seen as better than less. Scholars generally regard social capital, like other forms of capital, as an asset that must be managed appropriately if its value is to be realized. Unlike other kinds of capital, social capital cannot be traded on an open market; rather, it is a form of capital that can change as relationships and rewards change over time, and it disappears when the relations cease to exist. It has also been treated generally as a moral resource (Hirschman, 1984), the supply of which increases rather than decreases with use.

Despite these similarities in the ways in which researchers have described social capital, there are deep and fundamental differences in the various treatments. Three in particular—level of analysis, normative implications, and primacy of benefits—distinguish the various conceptualizations of social capital.

Distinctions Based on Level of Analysis

Researchers differ in the level of analysis they use in describing social capital; it has been described as an attribute of nations or geographic regions (Fukuyama, 1995), communities (Putnam, 1993b), individual networks (Burt, 1992a), firms in their interactions with other firms (Baker, 1990), and individual actors (Belliveau, O'Reilly, & Wade, 1996; Portes & Sensenbrenner, 1993). In some usages entire countries or geographic regions can

leverage their social capital to expedite economic development (Fukuyama, 1995). In other usages social capital is not an aspect of a region, nation, or society but is an asset individuals can accrue and spend over the course of a career (Useem & Karabel, 1986). Alternatively, Burt (1997) defines social capital explicitly in terms of the locational characteristics of individual actors and their capacities to be unique transmitters of information. Social capital thus crosses several levels of analysis and has been described using both a macro and a micro lens.

Distinctions Based on Normative Implications

Researchers also vary with regard to the normative aspects of social capital implicit in their theories. Social network researchers, for example, assume Granovetter's (1973, 1985) position that individuals best develop social capital by pursuing numerous and strategically positioned "weak ties" with others. Burt (1992b, 1997) describes social capital in terms of "brokerage opportunities" within a social system, whereby individuals who are able to bridge gaps between otherwise disconnected others (i.e., fill "structural holes") enhance their stores of social capital. Lin, Ensel, and Vaughn (1981) suggest that a job seeker's personal resources (initially family background, but later educational and career achievements) interact with his or her use of weak ties to affect occupational status. Writers like Fukuyama (1995), conversely, implicitly argue for the value of "strong ties" among individuals within cohesive and bounded social networks or communities. Coleman (1990) also notes the importance of a closed system in maintaining social capital. Thus, different approaches to social capital alternatively stress density, redundancy, or efficiency in social interactions and, in this regard, vary in terms of their implicit normative recommendations for building social capital.

Distinctions Based on Primary Versus Secondary Benefits

A third, and related, distinction among definitions of social capital concerns the benefits of social capital and how they are distributed across a social unit. Although in all models individuals can benefit from the presence of social capital, there are differences in how direct those benefits are. Coleman (1990) and Fukuyama (1995) stress the "public goods" aspect of social capital, assuming that a society or group that is strong in it secondarily confers benefits to the individual. In contrast, network theorists like Burt (1997) and such researchers as Belliveau et al. (1996) and Lin et al. (1981) stress the ways in which individuals benefit directly from their own levels of social capital. To these researchers, social capital is implicitly an asset that individuals can "spend" to better their own situations. Thus, social capital is not a public good, widely distributed across a social unit or network, but, rather, is a private good—one that varies depending on individual position and positioning strategies.

Burt (1997) documents the differential benefits of social capital to individuals based on their network strategies. Belliveau et al. (1996) make an even stronger argument for the individual as the primary beneficiary of social capital. Here, social capital is distributed unevenly, even within a relatively homogeneous sample (in this case CEOs), based on educational experiences and social affiliations.

Patterns in the Treatments of Social Capital

Two patterns emerge in the various definitions of social capital. The first includes researchers who emphasize what one may describe as the *public goods* facets of social capital. These researchers

tend to study the phenomenon at the macro or meso level and emphasize the secondary nature of individual benefits. They see social capital as an attribute of a social unit, rather than an individual actor, and the individual benefits from its presence or suffers from its absence in a secondary way. Moreover, the "payoff" from individuals' acts to enhance social capital directly accrues to the social unit as a whole and only indirectly back to the individual (Asefa & Huang, 1994; Fukuyama, 1995; Putnam, 1993b); thus, according to Coleman (1988), social capital is noticed most readily in its absence.

The alternative approach is a *private goods* model of social capital. Some private goods treatments of social capital focus explicitly on the individual and his or her accrued social assets, such as prestige, educational credentials, and social clubs (e.g., Belliveau et al., 1996; Useem & Karabel, 1986). Also included here are network researchers like Burt (1992b, 1997), who stress individual advantages to forming particular types of social networks. The private goods model has been applied at the individual (e.g., Belliveau et al., 1996), group (e.g., Krackhardt, 1990), and even organizational and industry (e.g., Gulati, 1995; Walker et al., 1997) levels of analysis, but the focus in terms of outcomes is always on the individual person or unit and the types of social arrangements and strategies that can work to his, her, or its private benefit. In this regard, one can describe private goods models as operating at the individual level, at least in terms of outcomes.[1] We summarize these distinctions between public and private goods models in Table 5.1.

Table 5.1   Distinctions Between Public and Private Goods Models of Social Capital

Attribute	Social Capital As:	
	Public Good	Private Good
Level of analysis	Macro and meso (social unit)	Micro (individual)
Benefit to individual	Indirect	Direct
Benefit to collective	Direct	Incidental
Necessary ties	Resilient	Fragile
Individual incentives	Weak or moderate (function of indirect benefits assessment)	Strong

AN ORGANIZATIONAL MODEL OF SOCIAL CAPITAL

Our concern here is with social capital as an attribute of organizations. We have defined organizational social capital as a resource reflecting the character of social relations within the organization, realized through members' levels of collective goal orientation and shared trust. Our unit of analysis is the organization and our focus largely on the public goods facets of social capital. Therefore, we examine macrolevel and mesolevel constructs, such as shared identity and collective action. At the same time, we incorporate the individual (and the corresponding private goods) facets of social capital into our discussion of specific components, such as trust and network ties. As noted by Coleman (1990) and Nahapiet and Ghoshal (1998), social capital is a resource that is jointly owned, rather than controlled by any one individual or entity. Thus, our model of organizational social capital must necessarily include the perspectives (and interests) of both the organization as a whole and its individual members and, in this way, incorporate aspects of the private goods model of social capital, along with the public goods approach.

Public and private goods models of social capital might initially appear irreconcilable because they operate from different assumptions about individuals and organizations. We take up this issue in depth later in our discussion, but we wish to emphasize here that the two need not be in conflict if properly managed. For example, newly formed organizations must create organizational social capital where none exists. If individuals within such organizations operate solely according to a private goods model of social capital, it is unlikely that the organization will be able to build a sufficient stock of social capital to make successful collective action possible. However, if individuals act in ways that enhance organizational social capital, secondary benefits will accrue to them as well. As we later describe, encouraging an optimal balance between individual interests and the interests of the collective can be shaped by employment practices.

The give-and-take aspects of private and public goods models of social capital have been observed not just in relationships between firms and employees but also in relationships among firms. Walker et al. (1997) found that in an industry's early history, social capital among firms is low and yet necessary for developing the kinds of cooperative relationships that create positive externalities for the entire industry. Cooperation among firms within an industry increases the stability and technical knowledge of all of its members—benefiting all firms within it and, thus, each individual firm as well. Despite economic analyses suggesting that freeriding would prevent such cooperative behavior, Walker et al. (1997) found evidence that refutes such divergence between public and private goods approaches.

This line of reasoning suggests that the benefits—and, thus, the value—of organizational social capital must accrue to the organization and its members. In this way organizational social capital differs from financial and physical capital, for example, which are unambiguously owned by the organization. Human capital is an attribute of individuals, although the organization can contribute to and profit from it. But organizational social capital—if it is to be useful in facilitating collective action—should be understood as jointly owned by the organization and its members. Rational individuals or firms would not be expected to engage in social capital-enhancing acts without any expectation of benefit, even if such benefits are both indirect and distant. Moreover, such benefits do not have to be realized solely in the form of extrinsic rewards like compensation; they also can be intrinsic, appealing to the individual's sense of personal accomplishment and development. But in order for organizational social capital to be sustained, the benefits that accrue from its "use" should be realized by the organization and its members.

COMPONENTS OF ORGANIZATIONAL SOCIAL CAPITAL

Thus far, we have identified organizational social capital as an attribute of the collective, rather than the sum of individuals' social connections. Social capital is a by-product of other organizational activities (Coleman, 1990) that is nevertheless integral to the success of collective action (Nahapiet & Ghoshal, 1998). We also have stated that individual social capital-enhancing acts benefit the collective directly and the individual more indirectly. In this section we describe the primary components of organizational social capital.

Associability

The first component of organizational social capital is associability, which we define as the willingness and ability of participants in an organization to subordinate individual goals and associated actions to collective goals and actions. The relevance of social interactions to economic matters has long been studied by political scientists and sociologists. From Tocqueville (1945) to Banfield (1958), to more recent writers like Putnam (1993a, 1995) and Sable (1993), scholars have shown considerable interest in the issues of how and why individuals pursue private goals through participation in a collective.

The opposite of associability might be Banfield's *amoral familialism*, which he defines as a decision rule to "maximize the material, short-run advantage of the nuclear family, [and] assume that all others will do likewise" (1958: 82). The residents of Banfield's subject of study—the town of Montegranato—were unable to agree on collective goals because each family had different goals inconsistent with any other family's; moreover, they would have been unable to effect common goals, even if they were able to agree upon them. The familial ties of Montegranesi made it impossible for them to associate meaningfully with anyone outside the family.

But why associability, as opposed to sociability? The propensity to socialize may be largely universal, but the ability to do so for the achievement of a collective purpose is not. The phenomenon of social loafing (Harkins, 1987; Karau & Williams, 1993; Latane, Williams, & Harkins, 1979) or freeriding (Kerr, 1993) is well known as an explanation of why group productivity losses occur. In social loafing the problem is not that the group's members are social misfits—unable to communicate with one another (i.e., unsociable or antisocial). Rather, the group's members are unable to establish the relationships, norms, or systems for holding one another accountable and, thus, ensuring effort.

Associability, therefore, requires something more than sociability. It also requires more than simply

interdependence (i.e., orderly transacting), where individuals "together make up a whole because each contributes something and receives something from the whole" (Thompson, 1967: 6). Associability combines elements of sociability (the ability to interact socially with others) with a willingness to subordinate individual desires to group objectives. Thus, associability can be better compared to the concept of collectivism, which has been examined as both a characteristic of individuals (e.g., Wagner, 1995) and, more important to our discussion, of organizations, groups, and cultures (e.g., Hofstede, 1980; Ouchi, 1980; Triandis, Bontempo, Villareal, Asai, & Lucci, 1988). A collectivistic culture is characterized by cooperation among members and an emphasis on the welfare of the group. As summarized by Early, "An essential element of a collectivistic society is that individuals will subordinate their personal interests to the goals of their collective, or in-group, those with whom a person works and identifies" (1989:567–568). Conversely, "In an individualistic culture, emphasis is placed on self-sufficiency and control" (Early, 1989: 568).

We propose that groups strong in associability will exhibit collectivist tendencies—a prerequisite to a generalized ability to agree upon collective goals. Collective goals provide a basis for evaluation, while also serving as a set of implicit norms that guide individual and collective behavior (Guzzo & Shea, 1992; Harkins & Szymanski, 1989). Even after agreeing upon a set of collective goals, however, the social unit must be able to effect those goals through collective action. Work must be divided and coordinated among members in a way that ensures that collective goals are achieved. Thus, associability is both task centered and goal driven.

The collective action problem animates much (if not most) of the academic and practitioner work in management theory and practice. Organizations exist as means of resolving the collective action problem, as Coase (1937) recognized. The ability to engage in collective action thus focuses the sociability of an organization's members.

Associability, therefore, is the willingness and the *ability* of individuals to define collective goals that are then enacted collectively. Associability has both an affective component (e.g., collectivist feelings) and a skill-based component (e.g., ability to coordinate activities). But one's willingness to participate in collective action is partially dependent on the belief that individual efforts benefiting the whole directly will also benefit the individual indirectly—an issue we take up in the next section.

Trust

The second component of organizational social capital is *trust*—a concept that has been the subject of much recent study in management and related literature (see, for example, Gambetta, 1988; Korsgaard, Brewer, & Hanna, 1996; Kramer & Tyler, 1996; Mayer, Davis, & Schoorman, 1995; McAllister, 1995; Ring, 1996; Rousseau, Sitkin, Burt, & Camerer, 1998). Within an organizational context, research has been complicated by the fact that trust is both an antecedent to and a result of successful collective action. Trust is necessary for people to work together on common projects, even if only to the extent that all parties believe they will be compensated in full and on time. But trust is also a by-product of successful collective action; workgroups that successfully complete a project are likely to exhibit higher trust, which makes further and more complex collaborative efforts possible.

Fragile versus resilient trust. Researchers have defined trust in many different ways, but they generally agree that it requires a willingness to be vulnerable (Rousseau et al., 1998). Some observers consider trust in terms of a risk-reward relationship (Mayer et al., 1995; Ring & Van de Ven, 1992; Sable, 1993; Williamson, 1993) that requires the results of collaboration to be sufficient and predictable. If one believes that a person or organization is predictable, at least for a single transaction, then contracting is possible if the potential rewards are sufficient (McAllister, 1995; Scully & Preuss, 1996).

This conceptualization of trust is termed *fragile trust*, which is based on perceptions of the immediate likelihood of rewards (Ring, 1996; Ring & Van de Ven, 1992). Tyler and DeGoey (1996) label this *instrumental trust,* and Rousseau (1995) refers to this as *transacting* (rather than forming relationships). Transactions built on fragile trust often are governed by formal, contractual means. Fragile trust does not

survive the occasional transaction in which benefits and costs are not equilibrated.

In addition to fragile trust, Ring and Van de Ven (1992) have developed the concept of *resilient trust*,[2] which is based on stronger and more numerous links between the organization and its members. Resilient trust can survive the occasional transaction in which benefits and costs are not equilibrated. Such trust is not calculative but is based rather on experience with the other parties and/or beliefs about their moral integrity. Norms and values are the glue that holds together communities in which resilient trust is extant (Banfield, 1958; Etzioni, 1988; Fort, 1996; Granovetter, 1985; Ouchi, 1980; Sable, 1993). If fragile trust is concerned with developing a workable *strategy* of reciprocity, resilient trust rests upon ongoing reciprocity norms.

Dyadic versus generalized trust. Thus far, we have drawn our discussion from the literature on what may be described as *dyadic trust*: trust between two parties who have direct knowledge of one another. There is a different perspective on trust, however, that relies less on direct knowledge and more on affiliation or reputation. In his discussion of social capital, Putnam (1993b) describes a kind of impersonal or indirect trust that does not rest with knowledge of particular individuals but rather [rests] with norms and behaviors that are generalized to others in the social unit as a whole. Thus, an individual may be trusted—and may even be the beneficiary of resilient trust—without the other party having much personal knowledge of or interaction with him or her. This generalized trust, according to Putnam, characterizes systems with strong social capital.

As Granovetter (1985) has noted, economic theories that assume fragile, dyadic exchanges provide an under-socialized model of human action that does not take into account how actors are embedded in social systems. One component of embeddedness is the extent to which trust is resilient rather than fragile; an equally important component is the degree to which individuals may trust one another without much direct information and/or previous interaction, simply by virtue of being in the same social system. Ties do not have to be dense in order to be resilient but, instead, may be weak in the frequency of interaction but made strong through association. The presence of resilient, weak ties, in fact, may strengthen the social capital within a system because it enhances interaction across subunits and thus connects the system as a whole (Granovetter, 1973).

As summarized by Putnam, "Ironically . . . strong interpersonal ties (like kinship and intimate friendship) are less important than weak ties (like acquaintanceship and shared membership in secondary associations) in sustaining community cohesion and collective action" (1993b: 175). Thus, organizations strong in social capital will exhibit resilient trust, even among individuals connected generally rather than personally. Organizations weak in social capital, conversely, will be characterized by fragile trust (if any), even among individuals who directly and frequently interact.

Summary of Components of Organizational Social Capital

We have described two components of organizational social capital, each with its own set of attributes. Strong associability in the form of both the willingness and the ability to engage in collective action is the first. Second, trust is a key element of organizational social capital. Our model suggests that some level of each element is necessary for a firm to have organizational social capital.

Without some degree of associability, even the most trusting employees will be unable to realize the benefits of organizational social capital, since they cannot agree upon or coordinate their common activities. Associability without some level of trust, however, seems largely impossible in an organization where membership is voluntary. That trust need not rise to a relational level or be generalized throughout the organization, but without some level of trust, goals are unlikely to be either agreed upon or attained. Therefore, both associability and trust are necessary for organizational social capital to exist. We now turn our attention to employment practices as mechanisms to permit and encourage organizational social capital and thus extract its value.

MANAGING ORGANIZATIONAL SOCIAL CAPITAL THROUGH EMPLOYMENT PRACTICES

Organizational social capital and the relationships among individuals within a firm are supported and perhaps most defined by the organization's employment practices. Organizational social capital, therefore, provides a perspective from which to analyze the efficacy of such popular practices as downsizing and contingent employment that have been argued to be, among other things, detrimental to the formation and maintenance of relationships in the workplace (see, for example, Leana, 1996). The effects of such human resource practices as compensation and selection on organizational-level outcomes also can be analyzed in terms of their effects on organizational social capital.

Strong and stable relationships are one way to build and to maintain organizational social capital, but there are substitutes for such relationships that might facilitate organizational social capital as well. In this section we discuss three possible ways in which social capital can be built and maintained through employment practices: (1) stable relationships among organizational members, (2) organizational reciprocity norms, and (3) bureaucracy and specified roles.

The first two approaches are complementary, rather than competing; indeed, many studies of high-performance work processes emphasize the need for "bundling" various employment practices for successful implementation (e.g., Ichniowski & Shaw, 1995). At the same time, there are instances where one approach (e.g., specified roles) can substitute for another (e.g., stable relationships) in creating and maintaining at least a minimal level of organizational social capital. Particular human resource practices like selection and compensation affect the stock of organizational social capital, and we incorporate them into our discussion. Finally, there are challenges associated with managing both public (organizational) and private (individual) social capital for organizational benefit, and we conclude this section with a discussion of these issues.

Stability in Employment Relationships

The most obvious way in which organizations build social capital is through the relationships that exist among their members. Organizations wishing to enhance their stores of social capital can do so through employment practices that promote stability among members and flexibility in how employees are deployed *within* these stable relationships.

A strong social capital model of employment supports high-performance work (Ichniowski, Kochan, Levine, Olson, & Strauss, 1996) and includes investments in training, job security, and collaborative work and learning. These practices are meant to build relational contracts (Rousseau, 1995), both between employee and employer and among coworkers within an organization.

Because organizational social capital is built over time but can be destroyed quickly by such trust-breaking behavior as contract violation, a long-term rather than short-term orientation in employment relationships is stressed. Clearly, practices like downsizing and the regular use of temporary employees may undermine the ability of individuals to form meaningful relationships at work and therefore retard organizational social capital. Practices like compensation and selection systems also affect organizational social capital. Economic theorists recognize that wage levels affect job turnover—for example, an "efficiency wage" that is higher than the market-clearing rate is a means of reducing turnover and increasing worker commitment (Campbell, 1994; Ritter & Taylor, 1997). In efficiency wage models scholars often analyze employee turnover in terms of the costs associated with hiring and retraining (and perhaps also with the loss of individual human capital); with such models researchers could consider the effects of efficiency wages on organizational social capital as well.

Compensation policies can affect organizational social capital in ways other than turnover. Campbell, Campbell, and Chia (1998) observe that compensation policies that reward individual achievement may be inappropriate in environments where team production occurs (see also Bok, 1995). Compensation policies based on group performance might lead to social loafing or diminution of individual effort (Latane, Williams, & Harkins, 1979), but they might also encourage behaviors and beliefs consistent with organizational social capital development—like shared knowledge and collective goal orientation—which, as we argue in the next section, might be used to the organization's advantage.

Human resource practices that focus exclusively on gathering individual human capital fail to take into account the social embeddedness of individual contribution (Nahapiet & Ghoshal, 1998) and the vulnerability of organizations in such hiring

decisions (Bigley & Pearce, 1998). Human resource practices that simultaneously encourage stable job tenure and reinforce associability and trust might well yield better organizational-level results than those observed in systems that focus exclusively on individual contributions (Frank & Cook, 1995).

Organizational Reciprocity Norms

Coleman (1990) and Coleman and Hoffer (1987) emphasize the important role of ideology and norms in creating and maintaining social capital. Here, the governing factor is not the stability of the relationships among the particular individuals involved but, rather, the overarching philosophy and corresponding norms within which different individuals enact that philosophy. Coleman and Hoffer (1987) report that children in religiously affiliated schools, for example, have lower dropout rates than do children enrolled in public or other private schools, in part because of the ideology and corresponding norms that make inattention to individual students unacceptable. In a business context, General Electric has developed an organizational culture in which shared commitment is built not necessarily through stable individual relationships but, rather, through an overarching organizational philosophy that emphasizes teamwork, shared learning, and collective high-performance work (Byrne, 1998). Thus, norms rather than interpersonal interactions can build and sustain organizational social capital.

One way in which organizational social capital can be built over time is by the organization selecting and rewarding people it trusts to share its values and goals (Bigley & Pearce, 1998; McKnight, Cummings, & Chervany, 1998). The literature on socialization suggests that values and ways of working collectively are communicated to new members, socializing them and shaping their perceptions and job-related behavior (Louise, 1980). Similarly, promotion practices can affect organizational norms (and, by extension, organizational social capital) in two ways: (1) promotion decisions send a signal to organizational members about the kinds of activities and habits of practice that are valued by the organization and (2) the direct effect of the promoted employee's ability to affect the actions of future subordinates. Our point here is not to minimize the importance of human capital when making human resource decisions but, rather, to suggest that employment practices like selection and promotion can support—and, indeed, if they are to be effective, must support—the social context of the organization as well.

Bureaucracy and Specified Roles

A third way of managing social capital is to circumvent the need for stable relationships among individuals by developing rules and procedures that define social structure in terms of positions rather than people. As Coleman notes, "The social invention of organizations having positions rather than persons as elements of the structure has provided one form of social capital that can maintain stability in the face of instability of individuals" (1990: 320). Thus, one of the classic rationales for bureaucracy—depersonalization of positions (Weber, 1947)—can substitute for relationship- and norm-based social capital: positions can be so highly specified and structured that qualified individuals are largely interchangeable.

Educational credentials and professional certifications serve a signaling function that identifies the feasible set of qualified individuals for particular roles (Spence, 1973). Thus, a hospital surgical group can function interdependently without its members having extensive experience working together, as long as each role is specified and each individual is certified to competently perform his or her role. Here, employment practices do not emphasize stability in the employment of particular individuals or, necessarily, the fostering of strong norms; rather, stability is provided through specialized roles and specified procedures for monitoring individual compliance with those roles. However, this strategy is arguably less effective than it once was, as many firms face environments less predictable and thus less hospitable to bureaucratic approaches to organizing (see Heckscher, 1994, for a discussion of the "postbureaucratic organization").

Balancing Individual and Organizational Social Capital

Earlier, we differentiated between public (collective) and private (individual) goods aspects of social capital. There is a growing literature suggesting that individually held social capital benefits not just the individual holding it but the organization employing such an individual as well. Burt (1997), for example, observes that managers who bridge "structural holes" and, in doing so, increase their personal stores of social capital can benefit their firms as well through their enhanced abilities to search for and to find information that can resolve organizational problems (see also Stincombe, 1990). The manager who is "plugged in" through his or her intrafirm network can not only expect to be more influential but also more useful to an organization through his or her ability to pull together resources to solve problems (Krackhardt, 1990). In this way employment practices that select, encourage, and retain such individuals are rational for the organization (Frank & Cook, 1995).

At the same time, such practices present other sorts of vulnerabilities for the organization. For example, there is no guarantee that the manager with a well-developed intrafirm network will use it (and the concomitant information the network provides) to support organizational objectives. Further, while structural holes generally are good for those individuals whose networks span them, the existence of structural holes within the firm may signal that some kinds of information are shared inefficiently and/or are not widely available. Looking at structural holes from an organizational perspective, we see that a network rich in them may represent a fractured organization unable to work effectively toward a commonly shared goal.[3] At best, such an organization is replete with principal-agent problems that require management's attention to monitoring and incentive schemes.

The optimal amount of each kind of social capital—individual and organizational—will obviously vary based on an organization's context, but here we note: (1) it is often necessary to take conscious steps to balance the two; (2) as a public good, the value of organizational social capital is not as immediate to the individual; and (3) employment practices shape the levels of social capital held by the individual and the firm. These points are probably best illustrated by considering compensation practices.

An emerging trend in compensation within U.S. firms is the enormous returns to private capital accruing disproportionately to select individuals. Just as sports franchises try to put together winning teams by acquiring a star player, many organizations pay large sums to add or to keep a few key members who are believed to have skills and connections essential to the organization's success. Thus, we commonly find a wide disparity in wages between those at the top versus the bottom of many firms that is justified by this "winner-take-all" strategy (Frank & Cook, 1995), which depends almost exclusively on individual's potential human capital contributions to organizational success (Bok, 1995).

The organizational social capital model suggests a contrary view. High pay to a few members of the organization may reduce perceived equity and, thus, the kinds of social behaviors that support collective action. Therefore, the presence of significant pay differentials among employees may undermine cooperative behavior within the organization as a whole. The challenge facing organizations is to select and to reward individuals whose skills are valued while also paying attention to the effect that such compensation has on the trust, associability, and reciprocity norms of the larger collective. The organizational social capital model surfaces such dilemmas and offers a wider lens for examining human resource practices and their effect on organizational-level outcomes.

NOTES

1. Although network researchers acknowledge the joint ownership of social capital by the parties to a relationship rather than a single individual, they focus largely, nonetheless, on individual person or unit outcomes (see, for example, Burt, 1997).

2. Resilient trust also has been labeled *relational trust* (Scully & Preuss, 1996; Tyler & DeGoey, 1996), *deep trust* (Hirschman, 1984), and *knowledge-* and/ or *identification-based trust* (Lewicki & Bunker, 1996; Sheppard & Tuchinsky, 1996).

3. But as more people in an organization fill structural holes, the value of such a strategy to the *individual* declines (Burt, 1997).

REFERENCES

Asefa, S., & Huang, W. 1994. *Human capital and economic development*. Kalamazoo, MI: Upjohn Institute.

Baker, W. E. 1990. Market networks and corporate behavior. *American Journal of Sociology,* 96: 589–625.

Banfield, E. 1958. *The moral basis of a backward society.* New York: Free Press.

Belliveau, M., O'Reilly, C., & Wade, J. 1996. Social capital at the top: Effects of social similarity and status on CEO compensation. *Academy of Management Journal,* 39: 1568–1593.

Bigley, G., & Pearce, J. 1998. Straining for shared meaning in organizational science: Problems of trust and distrust. *Academy of Management Review,* 23: 405–421.

Bok, D. C. 1995. *The cost of talent.* New York: Free Press.

Burt, R. S. 1992a. *Structural holes.* Cambridge, MA: Harvard University Press.

Burt, R. S. 1992b. The social structure of competition. In N. Nohria & R. Eccles (Eds.), *Networks and organizations: Structure, form, and action*: 57–91. Boston: Harvard Business School Press.

Burt, R S. 1997. The contingent value of social capital. *Administrative Science Quarterly,* 42: 339–365.

Byrne, J. 1998. Jack: A close-up look at how America's #1 manager runs GE. *Business Week,* June 8: 90–95, 98, 99, 102, 104–106.

Campbell, C. M. 1994. Wage change and the quit behavior of workers: Implications for efficiency wage theory. *Southern Economic Review,* 61: 133–148.

Campbell, D. J., Campbell, C. M., & Chia, H. 1998. Merit pay, performance appraisal, and individual motivation: An analysis and alternative. *Human Resource Management,* 37: 131–146.

Coase, R. 1937. The nature of the firm. *Economica,* 4: 386–405.

Coleman, J. 1988. Social capital in the creation of human capital. *American Journal of Sociology,* 94: S95–S120.

Coleman, J. 1990. *Foundations of social theory.* Cambridge, MA: Harvard University Press.

Coleman, J., & Hoffer, T. 1987. *Public and private high schools: The impact of communities.* New York: Basic Books.

Early, C. 1989. Social loafing and collectivism: A comparison of the United States and the People's Republic of China. *Administrative Science Quarterly,* 34: 565–581.

Etzioni, A. 1988. *The moral dimensions: Toward a new economics.* New York: Free Press.

Fort, T. L. 1996. Business as a mediating institution. *Business Ethics Quarterly,* 6: 149–164.

Frank, R., & Cook, P. 1995. *The winner-take-all society.* New York: Free Press.

Fukuyama, F. 1995. Trust: *The social virtues and the creation of prosperity.* New York: Free Press.

Gambetta, D. 1988. *Trust: Making and breaking cooperative relations.* New York: Blackwell.

Granovetter, M. 1973. *The strength of weak ties. American Journal of Sociology,* 78: 1360–1380.

Granovetter, M. 1985. Economic action and social structure: The problem of embeddedness. *American Journal of Sociology,* 91: 481–510.

Gulati, R. 1995. Social structure and alliance formation patterns: A longitudinal analysis. *Administrative Science Quarterly,* 40: 619–652.

Guzzo, R., & Shea, G. 1992. Group performance and intergroup relations in organizations. In M. D. Dunnette & L. Hough (Eds.), *Handbook of industrial and organizational psychology* (2nd ed.), vol. 3: 269–313. Palo Alto, CA: Annual Reviews.

Harkins, S. 1987. Social loafing and social facilitation. *Journal of Experimental and Social Psychology,* 23: 1–18.

Harkins, S., & Szymanski, K. 1989. Social loafing and social facilitation. *Journal of Personality and Social Psychology,* 56: 934–941.

Heckscher, C. 1994. Defining the post-bureaucratic type. In C. Heckscher & A. Donnellon (Eds.), *The post-bureaucratic organization: New perspectives on organizational change:* 14–62. Thousand Oaks, CA: Sage.

Hirschman, A. O. 1984. Against parsimony: Three easy ways of complicating some categories of economic discourse. *American Economic Review,* 74(May): 89–96.

Hofstede, G. 1980. *Culture's consequences: international differences in work-related values.* Beverly Hills, CA: Sage.

Ichniowski, C., Kochan, T., Levine, D., Olson, C., & Strauss, G. 1996. What works at work: Overview and assessment. *Industrial Relations,* 35: 299–333.

Ichniowski, C., & Shaw, K. 1995. Old dogs and new tricks: Determinants of the adoption of productivity-enhancing work practices. In M. Baily, P. Reiss, & C. Winston (Eds.), *Brookings papers on economic activity:* 1–65. Washington, DC: Brookings Institute.

Karau, S., & Williams, K. 1993. Social loafing: A meta-analytic review and theoretical integration. *Journal of Personality and Social Psychology,* 65: 681–706.

Kerr, N. L. 1993. Motivation losses in small groups: A social dilemma analysis. *Journal of Personality and Social Psychology,* 45: 819—828.

Korsgaard, M., Brewer, M., & Hanna, B. 1996. Collective trust and collective action: The decision to trust as a social decision. In R. Kramer & T. Tyler (Eds.), *Trust in organizations: Foundations of theory and research:* 357–389. Thousand Oaks, CA: Sage.

Krackhardt, D. 1990. Assessing the political landscape: Structure, cognition, and power in organizations. *Administrative Science Quarterly,* 35: 342–369.

Kramer, R., & Tyler, T. 1996. *Trust in organizations: Frontiers of theory and research.* Thousand Oaks, CA: Sage.

Latane, B., Williams, K., & Harkins, S. 1979. Many hands make light work: The causes and consequences of social loafing. *Journal of Personality and Social Psychology,* 37: 822–832.

Leana, C. 1996. Downsizing's downside. *The Chicago Tribune Magazine,* April 14: 14–16, 18.

Lewicki, R., & Bunker, B. B. 1996. Developing and maintaining trust in work relationships. In R. Kramer & T. Tyler (Eds.), *Trust in organizations: Foundations of theory and research:* 114–139. Thousand Oaks, CA: Sage.

Lin, N., Ensel, W., & Vaughn, W. 1981. Social resources and strength of ties: Structural factors in occupational status attainment. *American Sociological Review,* 46: 393–405.

Louise, M. 1980. Surprise and sense making: What newcomers experience in entering unfamiliar organizational settings. *Administrative Science Quarterly,* 25: 226–251.

Mayer, R., Davis, J., & Schoorman, F. 1995. An integrative model of organizational trust. *Academy of Management Review,* 20: 709–734.

McAllister, D. 1995. Affect- and cognition-based trust as a foundation for interpersonal trust in organizations. *Academy of Management Journal,* 38: 24–59.

McKnight, D., Cummings, L., & Chervany, N. 1998. Initial trust formation in new organizational relationships. *Academy of Management Review,* 23: 473–490.

Nahapiet, J., & Ghoshal, S. 1998. Social capital, intellectual capital, and the organizational advantage. *Academy of Management Review,* 23: 242–266.

Ouchi, W. 1980. Markets, bureaucracies, and clans. *Administrative Science Quarterly,* 25: 129–141.

Portes, A., & Sensenbrenner, J. 1993. Embeddedness and immigration: Notes on the social determinants of economic action. *American Journal of Sociology,* 98: 1320–1350.

Putnam, R. 1993a. The prosperous community: Social capital and public life. *The American Prospect,* 13: 35–42.

Putnam, R. 1993b. *Making democracy work: Civic traditions in modern Italy.* Princeton, NJ: Princeton University Press.

Putnam, R. 1995. Bowling alone: America's declining social capital. *Journal of Democracy,* 6: 65–78.

Ring, P. 1996. Fragile and resilient trust and their roles in economic exchange. *Business & Society,* 35: 148–175.

Ring, P., & Van de Ven, A. 1992. Structuring cooperative relationships between organizations. *Strategic Management Journal,* 13: 483–498.

Ritter, J., & Taylor, L. 1997. Economic models of employee motivation. *Federal Reserve Bank of St. Louis Review,* 79: 3–21.

Rousseau, D. 1995. *Psychological contracts in organizations.* Thousand Oaks, CA: Sage.

Rousseau, D., Sitkin, S., Burt, R., & Camerer, C. 1998. Not so different after all: A cross-discipline view of trust. *Academy of Management Review,* 23: 393–404.

Sable, C. 1993. Studied trust: Building new forms of cooperation in a volatile society. In R. Swedberg (Ed.), *Explorations in economic sociology:* 104–144. Thousand Oaks, CA: Sage.

Scully, M., & Preuss. G. 1996. *Two faces of trust: The roles of calculative and relational trust in work transformation.* Working paper No. 3923–96. Massachusetts Institute of Technology, Cambridge, MA.

Sheppard, B., & Tuchinsky, M. 1996. Micro-OB and network organizations. In R. Kramer & T. Tyler (Eds.), *Trust in organizations: Foundations of theory and research*: 140–165. Thousand Oaks, CA: Sage.

Spence, M. 1973. Job market signaling. *Quarterly Journal of Economics,* 87: 355–374.

Stincombe, A. 1990. *Information and organizations.* Berkeley, CA: University of California Press.

Thompson, J. D. 1967. Organizations in action: Social science bases of administrative theory. New York: McGraw-Hill.

Tocqueville, A. 1945. *Democracy in America* (vols. 1 & 2). New York: Vintage Books.

Triandis, H., Bontempo, R., Villareal, M., Asai, M., & Lucci, N. 1988. Individualism and collectivism: Cross-cultural perspectives on self-in group relationships. *Journal of Personality and Social Psychology,* 54: 323–338.

Tyler, T., & DeGoey, P. 1996. Trust in organizational authorities: The influence of motive attributions on willingness to accept decisions. In R. Kramer & T. Tyler (Eds.), *Trust in organizations: Foundations of theory and research:* 331–356. Thousand Oaks, CA: Sage.

Useem, M., & Karabel, J. 1986. Pathways to top corporate management. *American Sociological Review,* 44: 184–200.

Wagner, J. 1995. Studies of individualism-collectivism: Effects of cooperation in groups. *Academy of Management Journal,* 38: 152–172.

Walker, G., Kogut, B., & Shan, W. 1997. Social capital, structural holes, and the formation of an industry network. *Organizational Science,* 8: 109–125.

Weber, M. 1947. *The theory of social and economic organization.* New York: Oxford University Press.

Williamson, O. 1993. Calculativeness, trust, and economic organization. *Journal of Law and Economics,* 34: 453–500.

SOURCE: Leana, Carrie R. and Harry J. Van Buren III. 1999. Excerpt from "Organizational Social Capital and Employment Practices." *Academy of Management Review,* 24:538–48.

6

DOING YOUR JOB *AND* HELPING YOUR FRIENDS

Universalistic Norms About Obligations to Particular Others in Networks

CAROL A. HEIMER

UNIVERSALISM AND PARTICULARISM

I have heard it said of Talcott Parsons that he was "so universalistic that he wouldn't help a friend." Despite sociologists' views that organizations are built on the norm of universalism, I will argue that actually, organizational life is as much about helping your friends as about behaving universalistically. The point is that if members of an organization are to serve their clients well, they must in some cases become their friends (this is probably a bit of an overstatement) in order to know what the clients need; if members of an organization are to decide whom they can trust as coworkers, they have to become friends with the coworkers; and if members of an organization are to develop skills that are crucial to an organization, they must be confident of the organization's loyalty to them.[1] Relations are among named individuals who know one another as particular others and not just as generalized actors playing broadly defined roles. When actors play out their general roles, these roles are meaningful only

in the context of the loyalty they feel to one another and the knowledge they have of one another's needs, quirks, and whims. In short, my argument is that Parsons has left us with a false dichotomy since only by "helping friends" can anyone ever do business. To formulate it with less paradox, almost every relation to a category of people such as fellow workers or clients actually consists of a series of actions that at any particular time and place are directed to a particular named individual. The universalistic norms then require that one do what a series of particular individuals need or want, as well as deserve, at a given time.

But often the peculiarities of the individuals figure prominently in each interaction, and as a consequence of those interactions ties develop between named individuals. Through these networks built on particularistic ties, organizations reach their universalistic ends. For example, scholars serve the universalism of science by hearing or reading and commenting on a paper by a particular person at a particular time. Their obligations under the norms are to that person and his or her scholarly work. If they discharge their obligations well, a link in a scientific network is formed, tying them all together.

In this paper I discuss when universalism without network ties to particular others is counterproductive for organizations. I argue first that the work of Parsons and Shils (1951) falls short as a *description* of what goes on in organizations, and especially in their relations with network partners, largely because networks are structured less by universalism than by the obligations of network partners to one another. These obligations are simultaneously obligations to perform tasks in a universalistic way and obligations to behave responsibly in one's relations to particular network partners. By asking who is responsible for what and to whom, what organizations and individuals do to increase the likelihood of responsible behavior, and where pressures for universalism and for particularism come from, we can address this paradox that norms simultaneously require universalistic and particularistic behavior and uncover some of the strategies network partners use for meeting these theoretically conflicting but actually often mutually supportive demands.

Mark Granovetter (1992) argues that "economic activity . . . occurs in networks of personal relations" and that people "try actively to *prevent* economic and noneconomic aspects of their lives from being separated." My argument parallels his, though we start from different places and have different aims. Granovetter's quarrel is primarily with economists and sociologists studying economic life. Granovetter aims to show that economic life is not really distinct from family life (or religious life or whatever); because it is embedded in the rest of social life, economic life is never governed solely by economic motives or universalistic rules. My quarrel is with theorists writing about normative systems. My argument is that those who contend that organizations are (and should be) governed by universalistic rules are wrong because life in organizations and networks necessarily entails obligations to concrete others that can be met responsibly only by adopting a particularistic orientation. At the core of both arguments, then, is Granovetter's claim that "the mere *fact* of attachment to others may modify economic action."

Finally, I argue that Carol Gilligan's (1982) work on the contrast between an ethic of care and an ethic of rights fits neatly the distinction between universalism and particularism and enriches the argument here because it is in essence an argument about the kind of morality that really governs network relations. An ethic of care is often demanded in organizations. The key to all of these arguments is that universalistic norms generate responsibilities to particular others as named nodes in a functioning network.

This paper is concerned with the general question of the conditions under which the fundamental opposition between universalism and particularism breaks down, the roles in which the requirement to be universalistic is at odds with responsible behavior, and how the tension between those two requirements is resolved. At least six issues are of interest here:

1. The rules that grow up in bureaucracies tend to be rules about universalism, about how to deal with categories of people or types of relationships rather than about the need to take account of individual differences, idiosyncratic characteristics, or unusual circumstances. Why do we tend to have such an imbalance, with explicit rules about universalism but silence about particularism?

2. We recognize that it is sometimes *irresponsible* to be too universalistic and that when the circumstances of a job require particularism, that particularism may well not be of the suspect sort of favoring one's friends and family. Can we say anything about the conditions under which responsible particularism will be especially important?

3. It is hard to distinguish between "bad" and "good" particularism, and so difficult to legislate particularism. In contrast, it is easy to tell the difference between universalism and particularism and so to legislate that people should behave universalistically. Because of this there may be a tendency for organizations concerned with justice to err on the side of universalism.

4. Particularism is an expensive virtue compared with universalism because it requires tracking individuals rather than categories and requires long relationships, extensive record keeping, and the like, all of which are expensive.

5. We can say *where* tensions about particularism will be located (teaching, any kind of people processing, any place where adjustments to individual specifications are required and so where condensed communication born of repeat interactions is important, situations in which there are ombudsmen), and what kinds of occupations will be ones in which techniques for being universalistically particularistic will grow up.

6. Some of the central debates about careers in modern organizations revolve around the question of how to be particularistic and how *not* to be particularistic (mentorship, which many value, is about particularism, but so are some forms of sexual harassment, and those anxious to avoid sexual harassment may avoid the close relationships that are required for effective mentoring).

The classic statements about the contrast between universalism and particularism come from Max Weber's (1978) writings about legal formalism, the process of rationalization, and the driving forces behind the codification of law,[2] and from Talcott Parsons' work on the pattern variables.[3] Parsons and Shils argue:

> In confronting any situation, the actor faces the dilemma whether to treat the objects in the situation in accordance with a general norm covering *all* objects in that class or whether to treat them in accordance with their standing in some particular relationship to him or his collectivity, independently of the objects' subsumibility under a general norm (1951:81).

Though Parsons and Shils here emphasize the relationship between two actors, I would argue that particularism need not entail judgments made in the light of what kind of relationship one actor has with another, but only information that one actor has about another as a result of a joint history. That is, the distinction I have in mind has as much to do with considering the other's biography, whether or not one figures prominently in that biography, as with considering one's relation to the other. So particularism involves two things: considering a person "in the round" rather than just as a member of a category, and considering a person in the context of his or her relationships to oneself and to others in a network. These two aspects of particularism are not entirely separable, of course, since the information needed to evaluate a person in the round typically comes from having a tie to that person.

My argument will be that all universalistic category systems must have a distinction analogous to the distinction between rating and underwriting in insurance. Rating tells how a category of risks is to be treated. Underwriting classifies individual risks into those categories by evaluating the risk in the round. Just as in insurance the treatment of an individual is modified over time as the insurer's experience with him or her accumulates ("experience rating"), eventually placing the individual into his or her unique category, so network partners start with a general rule about how to treat one another and modify that rule in the light of their developing understanding of each other. Only the most rigid bureaucracies treat their interaction partners truly universalistically, and even in those situations only a few unimportant or powerless interaction partners are treated that way.

UNIVERSALISM AND BUREACRACY

One virtue of bureaucracies is that they create order and predictability by producing rules that regulate the treatment of particular categories of people.[4] The rules tell members of categories how they should conduct themselves and how they can expect to be treated if they conduct themselves according to the rules. Rules give people obligations—to come to work on a fixed schedule, to perform various tasks, to treat all customers equally, not to judge family members by more relaxed standards, for a few examples. But rules also give people rights—to expect that other people will do their own work, for example, and to anticipate advances in salary and rank if they meet certain criteria. Most bureaucratic rules are also universalistic; all persons occupying a particular category have the same or similar obligations, will be judged by the same standards, and have the same rights. The universalistic orientation of bureaucratic rules is not accidental. Without universalism it would be difficult to form the categories to which rules apply, and the rules would not do nearly as much to increase the predictability of organizational life.

When organizations and occupations are not governed by universalistic orientations, we find two characteristic difficulties, one associated with obligations and the other with rights. When, for instance, workers' obligations to customers are not defined universalistically, workers may treat customers erratically. And when workers' rights are not defined universalistically, workers may have difficulty claiming promotions that they deserve (see Kanter 1977 and Heimer 1986 on careers of clerical workers). Without some standard against which to chart their progress, an assumption that anyone who meets a standard should be rewarded accordingly, and some way to demonstrate that they have the skills and experience required for a higher-level position, employees who have lower-status characteristics or who occupy lower-status positions may find it especially difficult to claim that they should receive promotions. Neckerman and Kirschenman (1991) make a similar point about the hiring of minority workers. They find that black applicants are more likely to be hired by employers who use (universalistic) skills tests as part of their recruitment process rather than by those who rely only on more subjective assessments.

But the predictability and order associated with universalism have their down side, of course. One difficulty is that job descriptions, a hallmark of the universalism of bureaucracy, go hand in hand with people insisting, "That's not my job!" Precise job descriptions often are too narrow, either because they do not include the full range of tasks associated with a given occupation or because they fail to take into account the full range of variation in customers and clients. Because clients vary, precise job descriptions are hard to write for occupations that entail interactions with other people. Thus it is difficult to write job descriptions for, or to "script" (scripts are really a form of job description) what Leidner (1988) calls "interactive service work." Leidner argues that employers of interactive service workers may try to transform their workers by teaching them appropriate attitudes and interactional styles when the work itself cannot be scripted because of variations in the customers. That is, employers try to reduce variation by standardizing their employees, as they cannot standardize their customers or clients. When interactive service work

can be scripted (e.g., at McDonald's), some customers are irritated at being treated too universalistically. "Suggestive selling" is one example. Being asked if they want apple pie after stating clearly that all they want are french fries causes anger in some.

The second difficulty with universalism comes when organizations fail to accommodate the variation in those who have careers in the organization. All workers do not learn at the same pace, so a year of experience may make one worker ready to move on to more complex tasks while another worker needs an additional year of apprenticeship. Although one might write a general norm about "merit" at the end of an apprenticeship in that job, in the practical case that norm comes down to treating Wendy differently from Nicki. How the advantages of universalistic treatment of workers will need to be traded off against particularism will depend on how narrow the specifications are in any given line of work, and whether the "true" requirements (e.g., being able to perform some task rather than "having a year of experience") can be written in an easily administered universalistic rule. Educational programs that require students to proceed lockstep through them entail considerable cost to students who are too dull or too bright for the program. Loosely coupled educational organizations (Weick 1976) may sacrifice fewer students even though they must sacrifice the efficiency of universalism. Organizations that process people (especially, perhaps, those that process minds and personalities rather than bodies) necessarily deal in unstandardized parts and therefore need to relax their universalism. . . .

PARTICULARISM AND ORGANIZATIONAL NETWORKS

While relationships between interaction partners are governed by universalistic rules, one ordinarily expects that over the duration of a relationship those rules will be bent a bit to accommodate the needs of particular interaction partners. This will happen partly through the formation of categories and general rules to take into account the characteristics and needs of those partners, partly through the introduction of modifications of general rules to accommodate interaction partners, and partly by one actor turning a blind eye to a favored partner's minor violations. In networks of interactions, the universalistic rules of the official system are tempered by the particularism that grows up in relationships between organizations and between the members of one organization and the members of another.

A network is distinguished from the yellow pages by the particularism in the ties among the organizations. If long-standing clients of a law firm were treated like strangers walking in off the street, or if the users of IBM computers were given service that failed to take into account the history of their troubles or the goodwill built up over a long relationship, organizations would not succeed in making these clients into long-term members of their network. The lore surrounding the care and feeding of important network members suggests that particularism plays a fundamental role in organizational networks. That goodwill appears as an accounting category further supports my point, and shows that particularism is considered a legitimate part of organizational life by a group of people who make their living policing the universalism of others' expenditures.[5]

We have previously failed to see that universalism by itself is an unworkable principle, because particularism inevitably enters as category systems are refined and applied to individuals. But this particularism continues to be held in check by the requirement that particularistic treatment be justified on universalistic grounds through the formulation of a general rule showing which one-member category this actor belongs to and how members of that category should in general be treated. In the same way that insurers justify individual rates, particularism in organizational networks is made consistent with the universalistic principles of bureaucracies through demonstrating the connection between individual cases and general categories.

To overstate the point, organizations are islands of universalism in a particularistic sea. Within an organization one must employ the rules of the organization to justify one's claim on universalistic grounds. In relations with outsiders these rules do not apply. One can claim that one's product is superior, that one's students or protégés are the best and most deserving, and that one's organization has the best service record without having to provide a full and balanced consideration of the alternatives. A person giving a reference for a job applicant does not ordinarily ask detailed questions about the competition before giving an evaluation of his or her candidate. The reason for this is that all universalistic treatment has to be delivered ultimately to particular named other people, people with whom we have networks of continuing relations. Ignoring that continuity and particularity of networks in organizations renders universalism impotent.

PARTICULARISM, RESPONSIBILITY, AND THE ETHIC OF CARE AND RELATIONSHIPS

In this section I discuss the connection between particularism, responsibility, and relationships. My point is that responsible behavior is necessarily partly particularistic and necessarily about relationships.

The difference between a rule- or justice-oriented system of ethics and a care-oriented system has been hotly discussed in social science circles in recent years (Held 1990, Gilligan 1982, Gilligan et al. 1988, Mansbridge 1990a and 1990b, Ruddick 1980). The argument that Gilligan and others make has two parts: first, that there are two distinct orientations to moral dimensions, what they call a "justice orientation" and what they call a "care orientation"; and second, that men are more likely to have a justice orientation, whereas women are more likely to have a care orientation. Gilligan and Attanucci explain the distinction this way:

> The distinction made here between a justice and a care orientation pertains to the ways in which moral problems are conceived and reflects different dimensions of human relationships that give rise to moral concern. A justice perspective draws attention to problems of inequality and oppression and holds up an ideal of reciprocity and equal respect. A care perspective draws attention to problems of detachment or abandonment and holds up an ideal of attention and response to need. Two moral injunctions—not to treat others unfairly and not to turn away from someone in need—capture these different concerns. From a developmental standpoint, inequality and attachment are universal human experiences; all children are born into a situation of inequality and no child survives in the absence of some kind of adult attachment. The two

dimensions of equality and attachment characterize all forms of human relationship, and all relationships can be described in both sets of terms—as unequal or equal and as attached or detached. Since everyone has been vulnerable both to oppression and to abandonment, two moral visions—one of justice and one of care—recur in human experience (1988:73–74).

Whether or not there is a connection between gender and this distinction is immaterial here; what is important is that an ethical system in which behavior is judged by a standard of care rather than a standard of justice is one in which judgments are based on the relationships between people, on particularistic grounds, rather than on the application of a single rule to everyone.

Elsewhere I have argued that taking responsibility entails accepting contingency (Heimer 1986). Responsible behavior then entails providing different things under different circumstances, collecting enough information to know what the other party needs and so what one is obliged to supply, and accepting that one's own welfare varies with what one is required to provide or do for the other party. Many contracts are written so that what exactly is required of the parties varies with the circumstances. When the norm or contract says a fiduciary or professional must adapt to what a person needs (or, in some cases, wants), then the contingencies that determine needs give particular individuals, those with bad luck, superior claims; conversely, these same contingencies increase the obligations of those meeting the needs. Thus one is responsible to meet the demands of those who can make legitimate claims under the contingencies of the contract. If one is obliged to care for some person or to supply some good to another organization "come hell or high water," then taking responsibility means adjusting one's tasks so that one can still fulfill one's obligations. Of course responsibility is more onerous when there is a lot of hell and high water.

Mansbridge (1990a and 1990b) argues that there are costs to "gratuitous gendering," to harnessing an idea too tightly to gender, so that for instance one might exaggerate the empirical connection between some phenomenon and gender or neglect the nongendered arguments for an idea. Here I am constructing a nongendered argument for something

that has been discussed up to this point mainly in the light of its alleged connection to gender. The ethic of care can be defended by the argument I have been making for particularism. And then much of the argument of this paper can be restated in the following form: Many things cannot get done in organizations without networks governed by an ethic of care. An ethic of care means the creation of particularistic obligation to others in the network. Responsible response to uncertain environments and to the needs they generate often requires such a network tied together by an ethic of care, and so requires disinterested particularistic norms.

Notes

1. When organizational takeovers become common, we would expect workers to be less willing to invest in organization-specific human capital precisely because the particularistic relation between worker and employer is undermined. Workers are treated then as factors of production rather than as friends.

2. Weber argues that the rationalizing tendencies he is describing "were not part of any articulate and unambiguous policy on the part of the wielders of power" (809) but instead came from the need for rational administration (and so were driven more by the administrators) and from pressure from powerful interest groups (such as the bourgeois classes). Law was rationalized on formal rather than substantive grounds, became more universal (that is, the law of the land began to prevail over special laws applying to different status groups), and was increasingly likely to be codified. Codification, Weber argues, was especially likely to be favored by "those who had hitherto suffered most from the lack of an unambiguously fixed and generally accessible set of norms, i.e., of norms that would allow checking up on the administration of justice" (849). This argument that disadvantaged groups such as the peasantry would be eager to have laws codified is especially interesting given contemporary arguments that legal codes necessarily disadvantage the powerless since they are written to take account of the interests and experiences of those in power. Presumably no codes are worse than codes written by the powerful, which in turn are worse than codes written to take full account of difference.

Weber also discusses anti-formalist tendencies in modern law, including legal decisions made "in the light of concrete evaluations rather than in accordance with formal norms" (886; generally, 882–889).

3. See, especially, Weber 1978:815–819, 848–852, 880–895, and 973–980; Parsons and Shils 1951:76–88. For a defense of universalism because of its relation to equality, see Berlin 1969.

4. Interestingly, Weber argues that "very recent legal developments have brought an increasing particularism within the legal system" (1978:880) since though commercial law may not be status group law (and so particularistic on those grounds) it is *class* law (and so particularistic on different grounds). These particularistic laws, he argues, are the result of occupational differentiation and pressure from commercial and industrial groups. Weber also identifies a second cause of this increasing particularism, which is more important for the argument being made here. He argues that commercial and industrial groups have wished to "eliminate the formalities of normal legal procedure for the sake of a settlement that would be both expeditious and better adapted to the concrete case. In practice, this trend signifies a weakening of legal formalism out of considerations of substantive expediency . . ." (882).

5. Weber notes that the law tends to be rigorously formalistic "as far as it is required for security to do business," but becomes "informal for the sake of business goodwill where this is required by the logical interpretation of the intention of the parties or by the 'good usage' of business intercourse, interpreted as some 'ethical minimum'" (1978:894).

References

Berlin, Isaiah. (1956) 1969. "Equality." In William T. Blackstone, ed., *The Concept of Equality.* Minneapolis: Burgess, pp. 14–34.

Gilligan, Carol. 1982. *In a Different Voice: Psychological Theory and Women's Development.* Cambridge, MA: Harvard University Press.

Gilligan, Carol, and Jane Attanucci. 1988. "Two Moral Orientations." In Carol Gilligan, Janie Victoria Ward, and Jill MacLean Taylor, eds., *Mapping the Moral Domain.* Cambridge, MA: Harvard University Press.

Gilligan, Carol, Janie Victoria Ward, and Jill MacLean Taylor, eds. 1988. *Mapping the Moral Domain.* Cambridge, MA: Harvard University Press.

Granovetter, Mark. 1992. "Problems of Explanation in Economic Sociology." In Nitin Nohria and Robert Eccles, eds., *Networks and Organizations: Structure, Form and Action,* pp. 25–56. Boston: Harvard Business School Press.

Heimer, Carol A. 1986. "On Taking Responsibility." Unpublished draft. Department of Sociology, Northwestern University.

Held, Virginia. 1990. "Mothering versus Contract." In Jane J. Mansbridge, ed., *Beyond Self-interest.* Chicago: University of Chicago Press, pp. 287–304.

Kanter, Rosabeth Moss. 1977. *Men and Women of the Corporation.* New York: Basic Books.

Leidner, Robin L. 1988. *Working on People: The Routinization of Interactive Service-Work.* Unpublished Ph.D. dissertation. Northwestern University.

Mansbridge, Jane J. 1990a. "Feminism and Democracy." *The American Prospect* 1(1):126–139.

———. 1990b. "'Difference' as a Feminist Political Strategy." Unpublished paper, Northwestern University.

Neckerman, Kathryn M., and Joleen Kirschenman. 1991. "Hiring Strategies, Racial Bias, and Inner City Workers." Chicago: Department of Sociology, University of Chicago. (Revision of paper presented at the annual meetings of the American Sociological Association, August 1990.)

Parsons, Talcott, and Edward A. Shils. 1951. "Categories of the Orientation and Organization of Action." In T. Parsons and E. A. Shils, eds., *Toward a General Theory of Action.* New York: Harper and Row, pp. 53–109.

Ruddick, Sara. 1980. "Maternal Thinking." *Feminist Studies* 6(3):343–367.

Weber, Max. 1946. 1978. *Economy and Society.* Guenther Roth and Claus Wittich, eds. Berkeley: University of California Press.

Weick, Karl. 1976. "Educational Organizations as Loosely Coupled Systems." *Administrative Science Quarterly* 21 (March): 1–19.

SOURCE: Heimer, Carol A. 1992. Excerpt from "Doing Your Job *and* Helping Your Friends: Universalistic Norms About Obligations to Particular Others." Pp. 143–48 and 157–64 in *Networks and Organizations: Structure, Form and Action.* Boston: Harvard Business School Press.

7

SOCIAL EXCHANGE AND MICRO SOCIAL ORDER

EDWARD J. LAWLER, SHANE R. THYE, AND JEONGKOO YOON

It is generally understood that social structures pattern and shape social interaction and also that social interactions can generate, repro- duce, and sometimes alter social structures (e.g., Emerson 1981; Giddens 1984; Stryker 1980; Turner 1978). When structures promote repeated interac- tions among the same individuals, people tend to form enduring relations or group affiliations (e.g., Emerson 1972a, 1972b; Homans 1950). If enduring relations or affiliations form, the social units that frame or make possible these relations— small groups, organizations, or communities—may become objects or realities for actors (Berger and Luckmann 1967). It is plausible that people develop ties to social units, as they interact with each other, and that these ties are a separable, independent force, distinct from the ties people have to each other (e.g., see Mead 1934; Parsons 1951; Tajfel and Turner 1986). In this article, we ask how and when social exchange processes generate person-to-unit ties that reflect micro social order. The *affect theory of social exchange* (Lawler 2001) guides our theo- retical and empirical analysis.

The distinction between person-to-person and person-to-social unit ties has broad-reaching impli- cations for micro social order. Individuals may be bound to each other primarily by their interper- sonal ties (e.g., friends, associates, or colleagues) or they may be conjoined primarily by some com- mon tie to a social unit (e.g., its mission, values, or identity-affirming features). Parsons (1951) argues that theorizing the problem of social order involves an analysis of person-to-person and person-to-society ties as analytically distinct phenomena, a view traced to Durkheim ([1893] 1997). This distinction is also evident in Giddens's (1984) structuration theory, Collins's (2004) theory of interaction ritual chains, and contemporary theories of economy and society (Swedberg 2003). Moreover, the two kinds of ties thematically appear in theories of collective action (Benford and Snow 2000; Brewer and Gardner 1996; Prentice, Miller, and Lightdale 1994), embeddedness in economic transactions (Granovetter 1985, 1992; Uzzi and Lancaster 2004), and structural cohesive- ness and equivalence (Burt 1978; Moody and White 2003). In more general terms, person-to-unit ties are one aspect of the classic self-collectivity or indi- vidual/society dichotomy that has historically framed sociological theories of order.

We approach the problem of social order in this article from a social exchange perspective (see Cook and Emerson 1978; Ekeh 1974; Homans

1950; Lawler, Thye, and Yoon 2000; Molm 2003a). Our analysis begins with an *exchange network,* defined as a set of possible or potential ties that limit and constrain who may exchange and interact with whom. A *social exchange* occurs when two actors give something of value to one another and receive something of value in return (Emerson 1972a, 1972b; Wilier and Anderson 1981). The outcome of interest is the *micro social order* that emerges from the patterns of interaction or exchange produced by the network. Micro social orders can be construed as emergent social units with group-like properties (e.g., see Lawler 2002; Lawler and Thye 1999); they can transform a network, crosscut groups or organizations, or be subdivisions within a larger social structure. The concept of a micro social order is implicit in theorizing that falls under the broad umbrella of "microsociology" (Scheff 1990; Stolte, Fine, and Cook 2001). Our purpose here is to theorize and empirically examine how and when micro social order develops among a set of actors who have structural ties to one another.

We define a *micro social order* as a recurrent or repetitive pattern of activity (interaction, transaction, exchange) among two or more actors with four attendant dimensions: (1) actors exchange with or orient their behavior toward members of the social unit, (2) they experience global emotions from those interactions, (3) actors come to perceive they are a social unit, and (4) over time, individuals develop affective attachments to the larger social unit (Lawler 2002). This concept of micro order interweaves collectively-oriented behavior (i.e., interactions with members or the group), positive affect (i.e., global emotions and affective attachments to the unit), and group perceptions (i.e., a sense of unity or cohesion). In these terms, a network becomes a micro social order to the degree that it generates recurrent patterns of exchange, a sense of network cohesion, and positive feelings directed at the actors and the overarching network. Together, these behavioral, emotional, and cognitive conditions imply that actors define themselves with reference to a larger social unit and are willing to act on its behalf. Micro social orders involve the development of a self-to-collectivity relationship.

The *affect theory of social exchange* (Lawler 2001) indicates that the structure of social exchange bears on the degree that micro social orders are likely to emerge from exchange processes. One important structural dimension is the connection between the giving behaviors in the transaction. Business or economic transactions tend to be contractual, negotiated, and explicit; the giving behaviors are closely connected and tit-for-tat. Exchanges in friendship relations tend to be implicit and occur over unspecified time periods; they lack the explicit, tit-for-tat character of business transactions. Collective action involves person-to-collective transactions wherein a jointly-produced good generates benefits for those who contribute to its production. Public goods dilemmas and informal employer-employee contracts tend to fit this pattern. Finally, the structural connections between giving behaviors may allow actors to only give and receive from different others within a larger group or social structure (Bearman 1997; Malinowski 1922). Social exchange theorists have conceptualized these exchange structures as four *forms of exchange* referred to, respectively, as negotiated, reciprocal, productive, and generalized (Ekeh 1974; Emerson 1981; Lawler 2001; Molm 1994). Our theory hypothesizes that these forms of exchange differ in their capacity to produce micro social order.

Beyond social exchange theory there are a wide range of approaches that address some version of the stability and micro social order problem. Rational choice theories emphasize the role of monitoring, norms, and sanctions to redress the tension between individual and collective interests (Coleman 1990; Hechter 1987; Nee and Ingram 1998). Norms and sanctions emerge because of "externalities" produced by the widespread pursuit of individual self-interest. Social constructionist theories stress the consensual meanings and interpretations that emerge endogenously among actors who engage in regular or repeated interactions (Berger and Luckmann 1967; Goffman 1959). Such meanings can "objectify" relations or groups, making them "realities" for actors. Identity theories emphasize how social interactions create and sustain shared self-other definitions associated with structural roles, social categories, and group affiliations (Burke 1991; Hogg 2004; Stryker 1980). Social exchange theories emphasize the role of trust and commitment in stabilizing relations (Cook, Hardin, and Levi 2005; Kollock 1994; Molm 2003a, 2003b). Although rational choice, social constructionist, identity, and social exchange theories approach the self-collectivity relationship in varied ways, they have overlapping and convergent themes. The affect theory of social exchange (Lawler 2001) interweaves elements from each approach to incorporate an actor who experiences emotion or affect from exchange.

Emotions are generally defined as positive or negative evaluative states with physiological, neurological, and cognitive features (Damasio 1999; Izard 1991; Kemper 1978). Our theorizing draws from work in psychology, sociology, and neuroscience. From psychology, emotions entail both a response to a stimulus (e.g., exchange with another) and a stimulus that itself produces cognitive work (Clore, Schwarz, and Conway 1994; Izard 1991). From sociology, cognitive work involves interpreting the meaning of emotions felt in the context of relationships, situational norms, and self-other definitions (see Hochschild 1979; Kemper 1978; Smith-Lovin and Heise 1988; Thoits 1989). From neurobiology (Damasio 1999; LeDoux 1996), emotions induce organism-wide neurological effects that generate a rudimentary awareness of a self-collectivity connection.[1] Drawing on these literatures, everyday feelings from repeated interactions may foster the development of sentiments (positive or negative) about a social unit, and it is important to understand the conditions under which this is likely to occur.

BACKGROUND: RELATIONAL DIMENSIONS OF EXCHANGE

Social exchange theories conceive of relationships in purely instrumental and transactional terms. A basic tenet of social exchange theory is that individuals form and maintain a relationship as long as the benefits from that relationship exceed those available elsewhere (Emerson 1972a, 1972b; Molm and Cook 1995; Wilier 1999). By implication, better offers or greater individual profits from alternatives break apart existing relations. This tenet is one reason that issues of power, reward allocation, and distributive justice have been central to the exchange-theoretic landscape. The exchange-network tradition, in particular, has focused on how network structures produce power gradients and stratification when the payoffs from exchange benefit some individuals at the expense of others (Cook et al. 1983; Emerson 1972a, 1972b; Markovsky, Wilier, and Patton 1988; Skvoretz and Lovaglia 1995; Stolte and Emerson 1977; Thye 2000a; Thye, Lovaglia, and Markovsky 1997; Wilier 1999). The relational aspect of social exchange is tied to the fact that structures tend to generate repeated exchanges among the same actors. Emerson (1972b) portrays this as a key difference between social and economic exchange.

There are two general approaches to the relational aspect of social exchange. Emerson (1972b; see also Homans 1961) adopts an "individualistic" approach whereas Ekeh (1974; see also Malinowski 1922; Levi-Strauss 1969) offers a "collectivist" viewpoint. The individualistic approach starts with actors in a simple network structure who have rational-choice or behavioral incentives to exchange. Few, if any, assumptions are made about a larger group or social unit. Here, micro orders are emergent and necessarily tenuous as they are tied to individual self interest. Relations develop and prevail only to the degree that the incentives to exchange, preferences of actors, and structures of opportunity are stable. Relations as such emerge out of individualist conditions. In contrast, the collectivist approach assumes a larger social unit or group affiliation. Social exchanges as such are embedded within and reflect a cultural or normative order or framework (see Bearman 1997; Ekeh 1974). Here exchange takes on a more symbolic or expressive character and is driven by the cultural beliefs or norms of the larger social unit. In sum, the individualistic perspective draws attention to the exchange processes through which micro orders develop and are sustained, while the collectivist account emphasizes how exogenous conditions—structural or cultural—promote cooperation and minimize opportunism (see also Fukuyama 1995).

The affect theory of social exchange (Lawler 2001) further develops and bridges the individualist and collective approaches. It starts with and assumes an individualistic context but then shows how actors develop a collective affiliation and affective ties.

Our approach differs from other social exchange approaches in several ways (for reviews, see Lawler and Thye 2006; Thye, Yoon, and Lawler 2002). First, we argue that in social exchange there are social constructionist and identity processes that alter the foundation of relationships and groups, essentially transforming them from transactional (instrumental) to relational (expressive) entities. Second, we assert that this transformation is most likely when structures lead the same actors to interact or exchange repeatedly over time, a condition that is generally assumed in much of social exchange theory (Emerson 1981; Wilier 1999). Third, the mechanism through which this occurs is emotional or affective. We posit, and have found empirically, that solving an exchange problem is an accomplishment that produces positive emotions (see Lawler et al. 2000; Lawler and Yoon 1996); and under some conditions, actors associate these emotions with their relational or group affiliation (Lawler and Yoon 1996, 1998; Lawler et al. 2000).

The relational consequences of repeated exchanges are most thoroughly documented in research on commitment in exchange relations (e.g., Kollock 1994). *Commitment* is generally defined as the tendency of actors to stay with and continue to exchange with those they have exchanged with in the past (Kollock 1994; Lawler and Yoon 1996; Molm, Takahashi, and Peterson 2000). Research reveals greater rates of commitment when actors face high uncertainty or risk (Kollock 1994; Molm, Peterson, and Takahashi 1999) and also when they have equal power or high mutual power and dependence (Lawler and Yoon 1996). There are two analytically-distinct interpretations for the emergence of commitment in social exchange: trust and affect. The *trust* interpretation asserts that individuals develop stable, ongoing relations in response to high risk and uncertainty (see Cook 2005; Kollock 1994; Molm 1994, 2003a). From this perspective, commitment is a strategy to reduce uncertainty in an unstable environment and trust is the "glue" that binds together relations and groups (see also Fukuyama 1995; Yamagishi and Yamagishi 1994). The *affect* explanation contends that actors develop more stable, cohesive relations and groups if and when exchanges generate positive feelings that actors associate with the social unit (i.e., relation or group). Recent evidence suggests that uncertainty reduction and affect are "dual processes" that operate in parallel to promote stable, cohesive, ongoing exchange relations (see Lawler et al. 2000; Yoon and Thye 2000). We focus here on the role of affect.

The *theory of relational cohesion* (Lawler and Yoon 1996) was the first to draw attention to the role of affect in social exchange (see also Lawler and Thye 1999). The central argument is that relations with more equal power-dependence and greater mutual dependence produce more frequent exchange between pairs of actors in a network and this leads to relational commitments. These effects are indirect and operate through an endogenous causal chain: (1) more frequent exchange generates more positive feelings; (2) more positive feelings generate a perception of the exchange relation as a unifying (cohesive) force; and (3) greater perceived cohesion promotes commitment behavior (see Lawler and Yoon 1996, 1998). Research has consistently supported this *exchange-to-emotion-to-cohesion* chain and also affirmed that power dependence effects on relational commitments occur indirectly, through this process (Lawler and Yoon 1993, 1996, 1998; Lawler, Thye, and Yoon 2000, 2006). The *affect theory of social exchange* (Lawler 2001, 2002, 2006) addresses questions and issues that are complementary to relational cohesion theory, focusing not on conditions of power, but on determinants of social order across the forms of exchange. One question examined in the current research is whether the relational-cohesion process mediates the effects of forms of exchange on micro social orders.

THE AFFECT THEORY OF SOCIAL EXCHANGE

The *affect theory of social exchange* posits that the *task jointness* of the exchange or activity determines whether actors perceive the social unit as a source of their individual emotions or feelings. Actors attribute their individually-felt emotions to their relations or groups if the task is high in jointness; whereas if the task is low in jointness they attribute the emotions to their own or another's behavior. Jointness varies along both objective and subjective dimensions. For example, a manager may objectively structure the tasks of a work group to be highly interwoven. The jointness of other tasks may depend less on objective conditions and more on the subjective framing of the task. To illustrate, consider childrearing by two parents or partners. If parental responsibilities are subjectively defined to be loose and overlapping, rather than divided precisely, "parenting" should foster a greater sense of joint responsibility. The key point is that both objective and subjective conditions are important.

The theory makes a sharp distinction between global emotions that are immediately felt and specific emotions that emerge from subsequent interpretations of global emotions or feelings. This distinction is based primarily on Weiner's (1986) attribution theory of emotion, but it also dovetails with Damasio's (1999) notion that "feeling feelings" make salient that one is being affected in some way. Global emotions are involuntarily felt as a result of exchange or other social interaction. Feeling up/down, good/bad, or pleasure/displeasure are common examples. Specific emotions are associated with, or directed at, particular social objects such as self, other, or a social unit. Examples include pride in self and gratitude toward the other, shame in self and anger toward the other, and affective attachments or detachments from a social unit. In the theory, the specific emotions directed at self, other, or a social unit emerge as actors experience and interpret the sources of their global feelings. The theory's conceptual framework for these emotions is provided in Table 7.1. Theory and research in psychology indicates that people tend to attribute positive events (success) to themselves and negative events (failures) to others or the situation (Jones and Davis 1965; Kelley 1967; Mezulis et al. 2004). The implication is that individuals, even those engaged in a joint task, will be more inclined to attribute group success to their own efforts and feel greater pride in self rather than gratitude toward the other. In the case of task failure, the predominant emotion would be anger toward one or more others rather than shame toward one's self. These self-serving attributions suggest that it is difficult for repeated exchanges to generate positive sentiments about relations or groups. The *affect theory of social exchange* takes this as a challenge and specifies conditions under which social-unit attributions of

Table 7.1 Emotions Directed at Each Object

	Valence of Emotion	
Social Object	Positive	Negative
Task	Pleasantness	Unpleasantness
Self	Pride	Shame
Other	Gratitude	Anger
Social Unit	Affective Attachment	Affective Detachment

NOTE: Reprinted from *An Affect Theory of Social Exchange* (Lawler 2001).

emotion will overcome or mitigate self-serving biases to produce person-to-unit attachments.

Specifically, the theory asserts there are structural (objective) and cognitive (subjective) conditions that determine when global emotions are attributed to social units. The primary structural condition is the degree that each individual's contributions to task success (or failure) are separable (distinguishable) or nonseparable (indistinguishable). This comparison is informed by Williamson's (1985) trenchant analysis of work conditions and governance structures. He argues that relational-team governance structures are common where work structures make it difficult to distinguish individual contributions, thus generating a sense of collective responsibility. One implication is that specialized or independent roles in a work setting make salient individual responsibility; whereas collaborative or overlapping roles make salient shared or collective responsibility. For our purposes, this implies that structures of collective responsibility yield greater coordination or, in our terms, successful social exchange. Adopting these notions from Williamson (1985), the affect theory characterizes the objective structural condition as the *nonseparability* of task behaviors and contributions.

The subjective dimension of jointness is the degree that the exchange task promotes a sense of *shared responsibility* for success or failure at exchange. If social exchange generates a sense of shared responsibility, actors are more likely to interpret their individual feelings as jointly produced in concert with others and thus attribute those feelings to social units. To illustrate, if employees in a work team perceive a shared responsibility for team success, positive feelings from doing the task are more likely to generate affective attachments to the team. On the other hand, if members share in the responsibility for team failure, the resulting negative feelings are likely to generate affective detachments from the group. Given this logic, there are two core propositions of the theory (Lawler 2001):

Proposition 1: The greater the nonseparability of task activities and outcomes, the greater the perception of shared responsibility.

Proposition 2: The greater the perception of shared responsibility for success or failure at a joint task, the more inclined actors are to attribute the global emotions to social units (relations, networks, or groups).

These propositions constitute a causal chain wherein nonseparability of task activity generates perceived shared responsibility and, in turn, shared responsibility produces social unit attributions of emotions (i.e., affective attachments). A theoretical link can be drawn between this causal sequence and that of relational cohesion theory. These two theories specify parallel yet interrelated processes. Whereas the affect theory theorizes the consequences of task nonseparability, the theory of relational cohesion theorizes the effects of total and relative power in the relation. All these factors capture and reflect types of interdependence that should yield greater exchange frequency. Nonseparability, as Williamson implies, involves more task interdependence, which enhances task coordination, reduces the cost of monitoring others, and yields a heightened sense of collective responsibility. High total and equal relative power, as documented in relational cohesion theory, entail greater outcome interdependence, which directly promotes concession making due to the profits at stake. Taken together, the overall implication is that task nonseparability should generate perceptions of shared responsibility *and* also activate the relational cohesion process linking exchange frequency-to-emotion-to-cohesion. In this article, we empirically examine the link between the two theories by testing whether the relational-cohesion process mediates the effects of forms of exchange on affective attachments to the unit.

To conclude, the strongest affective ties to the social unit occur when the structure of exchange

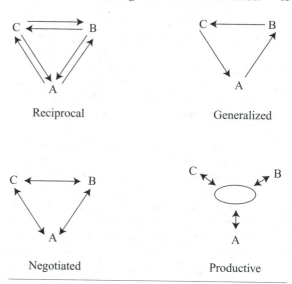

Figure 7.1   Diagram of Four Forms of Social Exchange

entails high nonseparability and fosters a high sense of shared responsibility. Theoretically, these propositions are applicable to any structural condition that generates variation in the objective (nonseparability) or subjective (shared responsibility) conditions. We next apply these principles to the four forms of social exchange illustrated in Figure 7.1.

Productive exchange involves a jointly-produced collective good wherein people unilaterally provide benefits to the group and receive benefit from it. Interdependence is high, yet there are coordination problems that need to be solved to generate the common good and allocate collective benefits. This implies an "assurance game" in which the largest payoffs are from mutual cooperation (Kollock 1998). Prototypes include a business partnership, coauthoring scholars, or a homeowners' association working together to solve a community problem. In each case, individual agents cannot accomplish the desired outcome alone but stand to reap significant benefits from cooperation. Actors make individual contributions but these are interwoven in the joint products of their behavior. The affect theory asserts that nonseparability and perceptions of shared responsibility should be higher here than in other forms of exchange. The tendency to attribute emotions to the social unit (the network or group) should also be strongest in a productive exchange environment.

Direct exchange occurs when two or more actors give directly to one another over time. There are two forms: negotiated and reciprocal. *Negotiated* exchange involves bargaining over the terms of an agreement. Through this process, actors develop a contractual agreement that allows them to provide benefits to one another (e.g., a salary for work or a price for a product).

Agreements emerge from a process that entails offers, counteroffers, and mutual concessions. Actors' contributions to exchange—their offers and concessions—are distinguishable, but there is a joint result produced by the explicit agreement on terms of the trade. The jointness of the exchange should be salient in negotiated exchange, and the sense of shared responsibility for the result should be relatively high, though lower than that found in productive exchange. Thus, nonseparability and shared responsibility should result in global emotions being attributed in part to the social unit, but somewhat attenuated relative to productive exchange.

Reciprocal exchange is similar to negotiated exchange, except that giving and receiving are sequential, unilateral acts separated by time and provided without explicit expectations of reciprocity. Patterns of reciprocity can emerge over time, however, if actors make their giving contingent on the prior giving by the other (see Molm et al. 1999). If A receives a unilateral benefit from B, A may feel obligated to provide benefits in return to B; and if A gives unilateral benefits to B, A may come to expect that B will later reciprocate (Gouldner 1960). Giving advice to a fellow employee, providing favors to a roommate, and inviting colleagues to dinner are acts that may initiate or become part of reciprocal exchanges. A major issue for actors in reciprocal exchange is risk or trust, that is, whether actors anticipate or expect reciprocal cooperative behavior from others (Molm 2003a, 2003b). Given that each act of giving is distinct, however, the jointness of exchange is not as explicit or salient as in productive or negotiated exchange. The degree of nonseparability and sense of shared responsibility, therefore, should be lower here.

Generalized exchange is an indirect form of exchange that entails three or more actors who can give to (and receive from) one other, but here, givers and receivers are not matched in pairs. In an organization, a structure of generalized reciprocity among different departments exists if a department provides information to one other department but receives information from a different department. Other common examples involve acts of generalized reciprocity such as helping a stranded motorist or opening a door for a stranger. Like productive exchange, a structure of generalized exchange fosters high levels of interdependence and makes coordination a significant problem. Unlike productive exchange, giving behaviors are highly separable; and, all things being equal, acts of giving benefit are unlikely to generate much sense of shared responsibility. Thus, based on the affect theory, generalized exchange poses important obstacles to micro social order.[2]

To conclude, applying core propositions of the theory produces four general predictions for forms of exchange, as follows:

Hypothesis 1: Productive exchange generates stronger perceptions of shared responsibility and stronger global emotions than do direct or generalized exchange.

Hypothesis 2: Direct exchange produces stronger perceptions of shared responsibility and stronger global emotions than does generalized exchange.

Hypothesis 3: Within direct forms of exchange, negotiated exchange produces stronger perceptions of shared responsibility and stronger global emotions than does reciprocal exchange.

Hypothesis 4: The strength of a micro social order is ordered as follows across forms of social exchange: productive > [negotiated > reciprocal] > generalized.

Hypothesis 4 has a number of subcomponents that correspond to the four dimensions of micro social order. It predicts the ordering of (1) frequency of exchange, (2) global positive feelings about the exchanges, (3) perceptions of network cohesion, and (4) affective attachments about the social unit across the four forms of exchange. The experiment to follow tests the impact of the forms of exchange on these dimensions of micro order.

Other theoretical traditions predict different orderings among some of the forms of social exchange based on issues of risk, the expressive value of reciprocity, and trust (Ekeh 1974; Molm 2003a, 2003b). Molm and colleagues (2003a, 2003b; Molm, Collett, and Schaefer 2007) predict and demonstrate empirically that reciprocal exchange fosters more commitment and stronger positive feelings about exchange partners (Molm et al. 1999; Molm et al. 2000) than does negotiated exchange. This suggests the opposite ordering for negotiated and reciprocal exchange (Hypothesis 3). Molm and colleagues also theorize that reciprocal exchange involves greater risk of nonreciprocity and more expressive value than negotiated exchange due to the latter's explicit, binding character. As a result, giving behavior in reciprocal exchange is interpreted more positively by partners than giving in negotiated exchanges. Molm's logic further suggests that because generalized exchange involves indirect, rather than direct, reciprocity, it generates the highest levels of expressive value (Molm et al. 2007). As such, she predicts that generalized exchange will produce even stronger positive feelings and commitments than both negotiated and reciprocal exchange (see Molm 2003a). The collectivist approach of Ekeh (1974) and the individualist approach of Molm (2003a, 2003b) both theorize that trust is higher in generalized than in direct exchange. Our research considers these alternatives in the context of the first simultaneous examination of all four forms of exchange identified in the exchange tradition.[3]

Specific Emotions Toward Self and Other

Based on Propositions 1 and 2, objective task jointness and the sense of shared responsibility determine whether social-unit or self-serving attributions are likely to emerge. This has implications for specific emotions directed at self and others. To the degree that individuals engage in social-unit rather than self-serving attributions, they should feel *both* pride in self and gratitude toward the other, following successful social exchange. That is, gratitude toward the other does not reduce the sense of pride in self, or vice versa. By comparison, if actors engage in self-serving attributions, they attribute positive results to their own efforts and pride

toward self and gratitude toward others will thus be inversely related. Therefore, the forms of social exchange that promote stronger micro social orders should also generate more pride and more gratitude.

The case of negative emotions is more complex. On one hand, as with positive emotions, when individuals fail to exchange and engage in social-unit attributions both anger (toward the other) and shame (toward the self) should be mitigated as the focus is on the social unit. Given the theory, this would lead us to conclude that negative emotions will be less likely to emerge within forms of exchange high on objective task jointness. On the other hand if individuals engage in self-serving attributions, failures to exchange should generate anger toward the other but not shame toward the self. This would suggest that the mean level of anger will be greater than the mean level of shame. Overall, the theory suggests that the forms of exchange should reveal the following order for the specific emotions directed at self and other:

Hypothesis 5: The ordering of positive emotions directed at self (pride) and other (gratitude) across the forms of exchange should correspond with the ordering of objective task jointness: productive > [negotiated > reciprocal] > generalized.

Hypothesis 6: The ordering of negative emotions directed at self (shame) and other (anger) across the forms of exchange should be the inverse of the ordering of objective task jointness: generalized > [reciprocal > negotiated] > productive.

Mediating Processes

The linkages between structure, interaction, and outcome are defining characteristics of exchange theories. A key issue is whether structures have direct or indirect effects on outcomes. Whereas Emerson (1972a, 1972b) and others (Wilier 1999; Markovsky et al. 1988) emphasize the direct effects of structure on outcomes, recent work reveals a shift in emphasis toward the mediating effects for structure. This is most clearly shown in research on commitment (Kollock 1994; Lawler and Yoon 1996; Molm et al. 1999) that emphasizes the mediating roles of uncertainty reduction, trust, risk, and affect. Emotional mediation is central to the theory of relational cohesion, given its focus on the indirect effects of structural power on relational commitments through this causal chain: exchange frequency $\longrightarrow$ positive emotions $\longrightarrow$ cohesion (Lawler and Yoon 1996; Thye et al. 2002). We propose that objective task nonseparability unleashes the endogenous process of relational cohesion theory, thereby strengthening affective attachments to social units. This is based on the supposition that objective task jointness promotes more frequent exchange by promoting coordination and a sense of collective responsibility. In turn, frequent exchange fosters more global positive feelings about the exchange tasks, as well as a greater sense of cohesion at the network level. Cohesion at the network level makes the network itself a relevant social object and possible target for affective sentiments. Thus, as a complement to Hypotheses 1 to 4, we test whether the endogenous relational-cohesion process mediates the impact of forms of social exchange on affective attachments, as follows:

Hypothesis 7: The effects of forms of exchange on affective attachments are mediated by the exchange-to-emotion-to-cohesion process, specified by relational-cohesion theory.

To summarize, this article conducts the first explicit test of the affect theory of social exchange (Lawler 2001) simultaneously comparing the four forms of social exchange identified by exchange theorists (Ekeh 1974; Emerson 1972b; Lawler 2001; Molm 1994). In basic terms, the theory identifies structural (task nonseparability) and cognitive (perceptions of shared responsibility) dimensions under which social exchange generates emergent micro social orders at the collective or group level. Applied to the forms of exchange, the theory predicts that productive exchange will generate the strongest micro orders and generalized exchange the weakest, while the two forms of direct exchange (negotiated and reciprocal) will fall in between.

NOTES

1. The organism-wide neurological effects mean that when an actor feels good he feels good all over; when an actor feels bad he feels bad all over. These effects are due to chemical secretions—such as dopamine, epinephrine, and oxytocin—that stem from different regions of the brain. Damasio (1999, 2001) indicates that these neurological secretions generate the "feeling of feelings" and suggests these are the foundation for consciousness, that is, a sense of the self juxtaposed to the external objects or events. For such reasons, neurological processes may promote awareness of or attention to social unit affiliations that are part of the context within which emotions occur.

2. Ekeh (1974) categorizes what we term productive and generalized under the same rubric (generalized) on the grounds that these are both collective forms involving high interdependence (see also Yamagishi and Cook 1993). While we acknowledge and accept Ekeh's (1974) observation, the affect theory of social exchange suggests that different degrees of shared responsibility render these qualitatively different.

3. We do not claim a competitive test vis-à-vis the formulations of Ekeh (1974) or Molm (2003a). This study is designed to test implications of the shared-responsibility logic of the affect theory, examining micro social order across all four forms of exchange simultaneously. We assume somewhat different initial conditions (i.e., exchange partners need not exclude connected others) relative to these authors, and as such, we see our approach and those of Ekeh (1974) and Molm (2003a) as complementary.

REFERENCES

Bearman, Peter. 1997. "Generalized Exchange." *American Journal of Sociology* 102(5): 1383–1415.

Benford, Robert D. and David A. Snow. 2000. "Framing Processes and Social Movements: An Overview and Assessment." *Annual Review of Sociology* 26:611–39.

Berger, Peter and Thomas Luckmann. 1967. *Social Construction of Reality.* New York: Anchor Books.

Brewer, Marilynn B. and Wendi Gardner. 1996. "Who is this 'We'? Levels of Collective Identity and Self Representations. *Journal of Personality and Social Psychology* 71(1):83–93.

Burke, Peter J. 1991. "Identity Processes and Social Stress." *American Sociological Review* 56(6):836–49.

Burt, Ronald S. 1978. "Cohesion Versus Structural Equivalence as a Basis for Network Subgroups." *Sociological Methods & Research* 7(2):189–212.

Clore, Gerald L., Norbert Schwarz, and Michael Conway. 1994. "Affective Causes and Consequences of Social Information Processing." Pp. 323–417 in *Handbook of Social Cognition.* Vol. 1, edited by R. S. Wyer and T. K. Srull. Hillsdale, NJ: Erlbaum.

Coleman, James S. 1990. *Foundations of Social Theory.* Cambridge, MA: Harvard University Press.

Collins, Randall. 2004. *Interaction Ritual Chains.* Princeton, NJ: Princeton University Press.

Cook, Karen S. 2005. "Networks, Norms, and Trust: The Social Psychology of Social Capital." *Social Psychology Quarterly* 68(1):4–14.

Cook, Karen S. and Richard M. Emerson. 1978. "Power, Equity and Commitment in Exchange Networks." *American Sociological Review* 43(5):721–39.

Cook, Karen S., Richard M. Emerson, Mary R. Gillmore, and Toshio Yamagishi. 1983. "The Distribution of Power in Exchange Networks: Theory and Experimental Results." *American Journal of Sociology* 89(2):275–305.

Cook, Karen S., Russell Hardin, and Margaret Levi. 2005. *Cooperation Without Trust?* New York: Russell Sage Foundation.

Damasio, Antonio R. 1999. *The Feeling of What Happens: Body and Emotion in the Making of Consciousness.* New York: Harcourt Brace.

———. 2001. "Fundamental Feelings." *Nature* 413:781.

Durkheim, Emile. [1893] 1997. *The Division of Labor in Society.* New York: Free Press.

Ekeh, Peter. 1974. *Social Exchange Theory.* Cambridge, MA: Harvard University Press.

Emerson, Richard M. 1972a. "Exchange Theory Part I: A Psychological Basis for Social Exchange." Pp. 38–57 in *Sociological Theories in Progress,* edited by J. Berger, M. Zelditch Jr., and B. Anderson. Boston, MA: Houghton-Mifflin.

———. 1972b. "Exchange Theory Part II: Exchange Relations and Networks." Pp. 58–87 in *Sociological Theories in Progress,* edited by J. Berger, M. Zelditch Jr., and B. Anderson. Boston, MA: Houghton-Mifflin.

———. 1981. "Social Exchange Theory." Pp. 30–65 in *Social Psychology: Sociological Perspectives,* edited by M. Rosenberg and R. H. Turner. New York: Basic Books.

Fukuyama, Francis. 1995. *Trust: The Social Virtues and the Creation of Prosperity.* New York: Free Press.

Giddens, Anthony. 1984. *The Constitution of Society: Outline of the Theory of Structuration.* Berkeley, CA: University of California Press.

Goffman, Irving. 1959. *The Presentation of Self in Everyday Life.* New York: Doubleday.

Gouldner, Alvin W. 1960. "The Norm of Reciprocity: A Preliminary Statement." *American Sociological Review* 25(2):161–78.

Granovetter, Mark. 1985. "Economic Action and Social Structure: The Problem of Embeddedness." *American Journal of Sociology* 91:482–510.

———. 1992. "Problems of Explanation in Economic Sociology." Pp. 25–56 in *Networks and Organizations: Structure, Form and Action,* edited by Nitin Nohria and Robert Eccles. Boston, MA: Harvard Business School Press.

Hechter, Michael. 1987. *Principles of Group Solidarity.* Berkeley, CA: University of California Press.

Heise, David R. 1979. *Understanding Events: Affect and the Construction of Social Action.* New York: Cambridge University Press.

Hochschild, Arlie Russell. 1979. "Emotion Work, Feeling Rules, and Social Structure." *American Journal of Sociology* 85(3):551–75.

Hogg, Michael A. 2004. "Social Categorization, Depersonalization, and Group Behavior." Pp. 202–31 in *Self and Social Identity,* edited by M. B. Brewer and M. Hewstone. Malden, MA: Blackwell Publishers.

Homans, George Caspar. 1950. *The Human Group.* New Brunswick, NJ: Transaction Publishers.

———. 1961. *Social Behavior: Its Elementary Forms.* New York: Harcourt, Brace & World.

Izard, Carroll E. 1991. *The Psychology of Emotions.* New York: Plenum Press.

Jones, Edward E. and Keith E. Davis. 1965. "From Acts to Dispositions: The Attribution Process in Person Perception." Pp. 219–66 in *Advances in Experimental Social Psychology,* Vol. 2, edited by L. Berkowitz. New York: Academic Press.

Kelley, Harold H. 1967. "Attribution Theory in Social Psychology." Pp. 220–66 in *Nebraska Symposium on Motivation,* Vol. 15, edited by D. Levine. Lincoln, NE: University of Nebraska Press.

Kemper, Theodore D. 1978. *A Social Interactional Theory of Emotions.* New York: Wiley.

Kollock, Peter. 1994. "The Emergence of Exchange Structures: An Experimental Study of Uncertainty, Commitment, and Trust." *American Journal of Sociology* 100(2):313–5.

———. 1998. "Social Dilemmas: The Anatomy of Cooperation." *Annual Review of Sociology* 24:183–214.

———. 2001. "An Affect Theory of Social Exchange." *American Journal of Sociology* 107(2): 321–52.

———. 2002. "Micro Social Orders." *Social Psychology Quarterly* 65(1):4–17.

———. 2006. "Exchange, Affect, and Group Relations." Pp. 177–202 in *George C. Homans: History, Theory, and Method,* edited by A. J. Trevino. Boulder, CO: Paradigm Publishers.

Lawler, Edward J. and Shane R. Thye. 1999. "Bringing Emotions into Social Exchange Theory." *Annual Review of Sociology* 25:217–44.

———. 2006. "Social Exchange Theory of Emotions." Pp. 295–320 in *Handbook of the Sociology of Emotions,* edited by J. E. Stets and J. H. Turner. New York: Springer.

Lawler, Edward J., Shane R. Thye, and Jeongkoo Yoon. 2000. "Emotion and Group Cohesion in Productive Exchange." *American Journal of Sociology* 106(3):616–57.

———. 2006. "Commitment in Structurally Enabled and Induced Exchange Relations." *Social Psychology Quarterly* 69(2): 183–200.

Lawler, Edward J. and Jeongkoo Yoon. 1993. "Power and the Emergence of Commitment Behavior in Negotiated Exchange." *American Sociological Review* 58(4):465–81.

———. 1996. "Commitment in Exchange Relations: Test of a Theory of Relational Cohesion." *American Sociological Review* 61(1):89–108.

———. 1998. "Network Structure and Emotion in Exchange Relations." *American Sociological Review* 63(6):871–94.

LeDoux. Joseph E. 1996. *The Emotional Brain: The Mysterious Underpinnings of Emotional Life.* New York: Simon & Schuster.

Levi-Strauss, Claude. 1969. *The Elementary Structures of Kinship.* Boston, MA: Beacon Press.

Malinowski, Bronislaw. 1922. *Argonauts of the Western Pacific: An Account of Native Enterprise and Adventure in the Archipelagoes of Melanesian New Guinea.* London, UK: Routledge.

Markovsky, Barry, David Wilier, and Travis Patton. 1988. "Power Relations in Exchange Networks." *American Sociological Review* 53(2):220–36.

Mead, George Herbert. 1934. *Mind, Self and Society.* Chicago, IL: University of Chicago Press.

Mezulis, Amy, Lyn Y. Abramson, Janet S. Hyde, and Benjamin L. Hankin. 2004. "Is There a Universal Positivity Bias in Attributions? A Meta-Analytic Review of Individual, Developmental, and Cultural Differences in the Self-Serving Attributional Bias." *Psychological Bulletin* 130(5):711–47.

Molm, Linda D. 1994. "Dependence and Risk: Transforming the Structure of Social Exchange." *Social Psychology Quarterly* 57(3):163–76.

———. 2003a. "Theoretical Comparisons of Forms of Exchange." *Sociological Theory* 21(1):1–17.

———. 2003b. "Power, Trust, and Fairness: Comparisons of Negotiated and Reciprocal Exchange." Pp. 31–66 in *Advances in Group Processes: Power and Status,* Vol. 20, edited by S. R. Thye and J. Skvoretz. Oxford, UK: Elsevier.

Molm, Linda D., Jessica L. Collett, and David R. Schaefer. 2007. "Building Solidarity through Generalized Exchange: A Theory of Reciprocity." *American Journal of Sociology* 113(1):205–42.

Molm, Linda D. and Karen S. Cook. 1995. "Social Exchange and Exchange Networks." Pp. 209–35 in *Sociological Perspectives on Social Psychology,* edited by K. S. Cook, G. A. Fine, and J. S. House. Boston, MA: Allyn and Bacon.

Molm, Linda D., Gretchen Peterson, and Nobuyuki Takahashi. 1999. "Power in Negotiated and Reciprocal Exchange." *American Sociological Review* 64(6):876–90.

Molm, Linda D., Nobuyuki Takahashi, and Gretchen Peterson. 2000. "Risk and Trust in Social Exchange: An Experimental Test of a Classical Proposition." *American Journal of Sociology* 105(5):1396–1427.

Moody, James and Douglas R. White. 2003. "Structural Cohesion and Embeddedness: A Hierarchical Concept of Social Groups. *American Sociological Review* 68(1):103–27.

Nee, Victor and Paul Ingram. 1998. "Embeddedness and Beyond: Institutions, Exchange, and Social Structure." Pp. 19–45 in *New Institutionalism in Sociology,* edited by M. C. Brinton and V. Nee. New York: Russell Sage Foundation.

Parsons, Talcott. 1951. *The Social System.* Glencoe, IL: Free Press.

Prentice, Deborah A., Dale T. Miller, and Jenifer R. Lightdale. 1994. "Asymmetries in Attachments to Groups and to Their Members: Distinguishing Between Common-Identity and Common-Bond Groups." *Personality and Social Psychology Bulletin* 20(5):484–93.

Scheff, Thomas J. 1990. *Microsociology: Discourse, Emotion and Social Structure.* Chicago, IL: University of Chicago Press.

Skvoretz, John and Michael J. Lovaglia. 1995. "Who Exchanges with Whom: Structural Determinants of Exchange Frequency in Negotiated Exchange Networks." *Social Psychology Quarterly* 58(3):163–77.

Smith-Lovin, Lynn and David R. Heise, eds. 1988. *Analyzing Social Interaction: Advances in Affect Control Theory.* New York: Gordon and Breach Science Publishers.

Stolte, John and Richard M. Emerson. 1977. "Structural Inequality: Position and Power in Network Structures." Pp. 117–38 in *Behavioral Theory in Sociology,* edited by R. L. Hamblin and J. H. Kunkel. New Brunswick, NJ: Transaction Books.

Stolte, John, Gary Alan Fine, and Karen S. Cook. 2001. "Sociological Miniaturism: Seeing the Big through the Small in Social Psychology. *Annual Review of Sociology* 27:387–413.

Stryker, Sheldon. 1980. *Symbolic Interactionism: A Social Structural Version.* Menlo Park, CA: Benjamin/ Cummings Publisher.

Swedberg, Richard. 2003. *Principles of Economic Sociology.* Princeton, NJ: Princeton University Press.

Tajfel, Henri and John C. Turner. 1986. "The Social Identity Theory of Intergroup Behavior." Pp. 7–24 in *Psychology of Intergroup Relations,* edited by S. Worchel and W. G. Austin. Chicago, IL: Nelson-Hall.

Thoits, Peggy A. 1989. "The Sociology of Emotions." *Annual Review of Sociology* 15:317–42.

Thye, Shane R. 2000. "A Status Value Theory of Power in Exchange Relations." *American Sociological Review* 65:407–32.

Thye, Shane R., Michael J. Lovaglia, and Barry Markovsky. 1997. "Responses to Social Exchange and Social Exclusion in Networks." *Social Forces* 75(3):1031–47.

Thye, Shane R., Jeongkoo Yoon, and Edward J. Lawler. 2002. "The Theory of Relational Cohesion: Review of a Research Program." Pp 89–102 in *Advances in Group Process,* Vol. 19, edited by S. R. Thye and E. J. Lawler. Oxford, UK: Elsevier.

Uzzi, Brian and Ryon Lancaster. 2004. "Embeddedness and Price Formation in the Corporate Law Market." *American Sociological Review* 69(3):319–44.

Weiner, Bernhard. 1986. *An Attributional Theory of Motivation and Emotion.* New York: Springer.

Wilier, David. 1999. *Network Exchange Theory.* Westport, CT: Praeger Publisher.

Wilier, David and Bo Anderson. 1981. *Networks, Exchange and Coercion: The Elementary Theory and Its Applications.* New York: Elsevier.

Williamson, Oliver E. 1985. *The Economic Institutions of Capitalism: Firms, Markets, Relational Contracting.* New York: Free Press.

Yamagishi, Toshio and Karen S. Cook. 1993. "Generalized Exchange and Social Dilemmas." *Social Psychology Quarterly* 56(4):235–48.

Yamagishi, Toshio and Midori Yamagishi. 1994. "Trust and Commitment in the United States and Japan." *Motivation and Emotion* 18(2):129–66.

Yoon, Jeongkoo and Shane R. Thye. 2000. "Supervisor Support in the Work Place: Legitimacy and Positive Affectivity." *Journal of Social Psychology* 140(3):295–316.

SOURCE: Lawler, Edward J., Shane R. Thye, and Jeongkoo Yoon. 2008. Excerpt from "Social Exchange and Micro Social Order." *American Sociological Review,* 73(4):519–28.

PART II

THE BUREAUCRATIC ORGANIZATIONAL FORM

AN INTRODUCTION TO THE BUREAUCRATIC ORGANIZATIONAL FORM

The bureaucratic organizational form is designed to segment workers into areas of functional specialization, shaping their communication and even their thought processes into narrow areas of expertise. Information moves within functional stovepipes and is integrated primarily at the top, while those on the front line work with some autonomy but only within their area of expertise (Weber 1920). According to Weber, the bureaucratic form is characterized by (1) formal rules, (2) functional specialization, (3) hierarchy without domination, and (4) professionalism.

The advantages of the bureaucratic organizational form are fundamental, in Weber's view. Bureaucracy's emphasis on formal rules is a substantial improvement over despotism and other organic organizational forms in which work is carried out through personal favor. Bureaucracy in its ideal form equalizes all whom it serves by acting without regard for the individual person, offering instead a depersonalized application of rules to situations. Second, through functional specialization, bureaucracy leverages the power of the division of labor as conceptualized by Karl Marx (1886) and Frederick Winslow Taylor (1911), though as we see below, Marx also analyzes the negative attributes of functional specialization. According to Weber (1920), "Bureaucratic apparatus . . . rests upon expert training, a functional specialization of work, and an attitude set of habitual virtuosity in the mastery of single yet methodically integrated functions" (p. 988). To protect functional specialization and to accommodate the bounded rationality or limited information processing capacity of human actors, the bureaucratic organizational form deliberately limits horizontal connections across roles (March and Simon 1958), instead achieving coordination at the top of the organization and through structural means—that is, by prestructuring task execution and inserting coordination demands into the structures (Williamson 1975).

Hierarchy without domination is the third principle of bureaucracy. While hierarchy offers the advantage of unified control to facilitate the achievement of organizational goals, the lack of domination means that at the same time, each level of the hierarchy is intended to have its own jurisdiction and power based on competence. Hierarchy without domination, referred to elsewhere by Weber ([1924] 1978:212) as "legitimate domination," means that a subordinate who reports to the person in the hierarchy above does so within the parameters of the job, and not at the personal will or whim of the superior. Professionalism, the fourth and final principle of bureaucracy, offers the advantage of workers who are obligated to and governed by the requirements of their roles, rather than personal considerations, linking back to the first principle of decisions driven by formal rules and the third principle of hierarchy without domination. While recognizing shortcomings of bureaucracy in his other writings, namely the depersonalization and the potential alienation that stems from it, Weber (1920) predicts that bureaucracy would be an enduring organizational form due to its ability to get things done:

> Once fully established, bureaucracy is among those social structures which are the hardest to destroy [because] bureaucracy is the means of transforming social action into rationally organized action. (P. 987)

The most profound critique of bureaucracy is offered by Mary Parker Follett. In a lecture first delivered in the 1920s, she notes the failure of bureaucracy to systematically foster horizontal interrelationships and notes that, as a result, effective coordination often depends on whether people in different departments would by chance have personal relationships with each other:

> In the businesses I have studied, the greatest weakness is in the relation of departments. The efficiency of many plants is lowered by an imperfectly worked out system of coordination. In some cases all the coordination there is depends on the degree of friendliness between the heads of departments, on whether they are willing to consult; sometimes it depends on the mere chance of two men coming up to town on the same train every morning. (Follett 1949:61)

Follett (1949) argues further that the functional division of responsibility overshadows the sense that all participants are responsible for the whole. Referring issues up the chain of command for resolution is not sufficient because that solution ignores the process of reciprocal relating through which humans come to understand and act effectively upon the world around them. "When you have a purely up and down the line system of management . . . you lose all the advantage of the first-hand contact, that backwards and forwards, that process of reciprocal modification" (Follett 1949:76).

Others recognize this shortcoming of bureaucracy—referring to it as the loss of the gains from cooperation—and note other inefficiencies as well, including limits to the managerial span of attention and the difficulty of evaluating activities that are organized by function (Barnard 1938; March and Simon 1958; Taylor 1911). In particular, March and Simon (1958) argue that bureaucracy is vulnerable to subgoal optimization, which occurs when participants strive to achieve narrow functional goals at the expense of the organization's overarching goals. Still, these writers argue that the disadvantages of bureaucracy are outweighed by its advantages, namely the ability to coordinate work at the highest levels of the organization to achieve control and unity of purpose.

Later theorists made a contingency argument: While the bureaucratic organizational form works well under some conditions, it works poorly under the conditions that increasingly characterize modern life. In particular, they argued, bureaucratic structures work well when the environment is slow moving and predictable, but in environments that are uncertain, ambiguous, or complex, bureaucratic segmentation hampers the flexible, timely responses that are needed. Bureaucracies thus become vulnerable when speed is required, or when a holistic perspective on the work process is required. From this concern came a renewed attention to formalizing lateral relations in organizations (Landsberger 1961; Lawrence and Lorsch 1967). Henry Landsberger (1961) notes the critical importance of horizontal ties between managers at all levels in industrial organizations, not just for engaging in "politics," but for getting work done in a highly interdependent, fast-moving environment, and critiques Weber for overlooking these horizontal ties:

> It is interesting to speculate why Max Weber, conscious though he was of functional specialization as an essential characteristic of bureaucracy, showed so little interest in the relation between functions. By creating an image of organizations as consisting primarily of vertical relationships, he unwittingly set the course for subsequent investigators. (P. 308)

Landsberger speculates that it was Weber's focus on government bureaucracies, a setting in which the traditional bureaucratic form could still be effective, that caused him to overlook the importance of horizontal ties.

Landsberger (1961) sought a compromise solution that would enable bureaucracy to be more effective in fast-moving industrial settings with interdependent work flows across functions. This solution would formalize horizontal ties between managers at multiple levels of the organization, incorporating cross-functional coordination into their job descriptions, without fundamentally challenging the bureaucratic organizational form. Consistent with this conception, the matrix organization emerged in the 1960s and '70s (Davis and Lawrence 1977; Galbraith 1972). The matrix form achieves cross-functional coordination at lower levels of the organization than in a traditional bureaucracy, through project teams, in areas of the organization that require a high degree of responsiveness to the environment (Davis and Lawrence 1977). Consistent with Landsberger's (1961) conception, however, matrices did not involve frontline employees but rather were confined to professionals and middle managers.

By leaving out frontline employees, this modified bureaucratic form does not address Follett's (1949) critique that bureaucracy's fundamental flaw is to disrupt the intersubjective cognitive process through which workers gain their understanding of a situation and their ability to respond holistically to it. Michael Piore's (1993) critique of bureaucracy captures the spirit of Follett's concerns:

> The division of productive activity among institutions involves the partitioning of wholes into a set of separate elements or parts. . . . One can argue that the organizational principles involved in Taylorism and Fordism have pushed us even further in this regard . . . From the cognitive perspective, the problem is that [the division of labor] limits the hermeneutic process, the cycle back and forth between parts and wholes, through which cognitive structures evolve. . . . The fragmentation of work . . . reduces particular jobs to such a small number of elements that the worker needs no abstract framework at all to understand the job. . . . Knowledge understood in this way does not lend itself to cognitive evolution. If one looks at innovations in business practice and the critique of existing organizational structures within the management literature, the thrust is in precisely the opposite direction. The attempt is to break down barriers between different organizations and within organizations between distinct divisions and departments, and encourage direct, rich and textured communication. (P. 16)

Similarly, Charles Heckscher (1994) critiques bureaucracy for its segmentation of work such that (1) intelligence is wasted, (2) people are required to go outside the formal structure to get their jobs done, and (3) informal networks emerge but tend to take the form of one-on-one personal relationships that are not sufficiently reliable for getting work done. Echoing Follett (1949), Heckscher (1994) envisions a postbureaucratic alternative to address these weaknesses:

> The master concept is an organization in which everyone takes responsibility for the success of the whole. If that happens, then the basic notion of regulating relationships among people by separating them into specific functions must be abandoned. The problem is to create a system in which people can enter into relations that are determined by problems rather than predetermined by the structure . . . Because of the crucial role of back and forth dialogue rather than one way communication, I will call it the interactive type. (P. 24)

This so-called "interactive type" clearly suggests the relational organizational form that we explored in the previous section. But Marx and others have suggested that the lack of horizontal ties between frontline workers is not easily corrected within the capitalist economic system. In particular, they argue that the segmentation of work is necessary in the capitalist context to keep workers divided, unable to organize, and subservient to the interests of capital (Edwards 1979; Marx 1886).

As we address the limitations of bureaucracy, however, Paul Adler and Brian Borys (1996) warn us not to overlook its strengths. In particular, they point to the potential benefits of bureaucratic formalization. "In what we call the enabling type of formalization, procedures provide organizational memory that captures lessons learned from experience" (Adler and Borys 1996:69). More radically,

> Enabling procedures provide users with visibility into the processes they regulate by explicating its key components and by codifying best practice routines. They provide users with an understanding of the underlying theory of the process by clarifying the rationale of the rules . . . [Although tasks are specialized and partitioned] procedures are designed to afford [workers] an understanding of where their tasks fit into the whole. (Adler and Borys 1996:72)

Clearly, this is not always true of formalized procedures, which often take the form of job-specific rules that fail to provide visibility into the larger work process. Still, Adler and Borys (1996) caution us to evaluate formalized procedures carefully and distinguish between those that are enabling and those that are not. In a similar vein, Karen Ashcraft (2001) explores a hybrid organizational form—feminist bureaucracy—that balances bureaucratic control with a more collectivist model of control:

> Viewing bureaucracy as a structural expression of male dominance, feminist theorists have long promoted collectivism . . . Yet feminist practitioners have found this form impossible to sustain . . . Some compromise has emerged with the rise of feminist bureaucracies that blend hierarchical and egalitarian models of power. (P. 1301)

In sum, the disagreement among organizational theorists is not whether the bureaucratic organizational form tends to foster vertical flows of information at the expense of horizontal flows. That analysis is widely accepted. The central disagreement is whether and under what conditions the advantages of this organizational form outweigh the disadvantages. There is also a disagreement about the consequences of minimizing horizontal flows—does it merely slow down the organization's response to its environment, due to the time required to refer issues upwards for coordination, or does the lack of horizontal flows hamper cognitive processes such that workers are unable to envision the larger process of which they are part, hindering their understanding and their ability to act effectively? Finally, we are reminded to ask whether there is an organizational form that can address these negative attributes of bureaucracy without losing its enabling attributes.

QUESTIONS FOR DISCUSSION

1. What are the key differences between the relational and bureaucratic organizational forms, in your view? How do they compare to markets as a way of organizing activity?
2. Describe the advantages and disadvantages of the bureaucratic organizational form relative to the relational organizational form.
3. How would you create an organization that combines at least some of the advantages of both the bureaucratic and relational organizational forms?

SUGGESTIONS FOR FURTHER READING

Heckscher, Charles, and Anne Donnellon. 1994. *The Post-Bureaucratic Organization: New Perspectives on Organizational Change.* Thousand Oaks, CA: Sage.

Meyer, John W., and Brian Rowen. 1977. "Institutionalized Organizations: Formal Structure as Myth and Ceremony." *American Journal of Sociology,* 83:340–63.

Oliver, A. L., and K. Montgomery. 2000. "Creating a Hybrid Organizational Form from Parental Blueprints: The Emergence and Evolution of Knowledge Firms." *Human Relations,* 53:33–56.

Rousseau, Denise. 1978. "Characteristics of Departments, Positions and Individuals: Contexts for Attitudes and Behavior." *Administrative Science Quarterly,* 23:521–40.

REFERENCES

Adler, Paul, and Brian Borys. 1996. "Two Types of Bureaucracy: Enabling and Coercive." *Administrative Science Quarterly,* 41:61–89.

Ashcraft, Karen. 2001. "Organized Dissonance: Feminist Bureaucracy as Hybrid Form." *Academy of Management Journal,* 44(6):1301–322.

Barnard, Chester. 1938. *Functions of the Executive.* Cambridge, MA: Harvard University Press.

Davis, Steve, and Paul Lawrence. 1977. *Matrix.* Reading, MA: Addison-Wesley.

Edwards, Richard. 1979. *Contested Terrain: The Transformation of the Workplace in the 20th Century.* New York: Basic Books.

Follett, Mary Parker. 1949. "Coordination." Pp. 61–76 in *Freedom and Co-ordination: Lectures in Business Organization by Mary Parker Follett,* edited by L. Urwick. London: Management Publications Trust, Ltd.

Galbraith, Jay. 1972. "Organization Design: An Information Processing View." Pp. 49–74 in *Organization Planning: Cases and Concepts.* Homewood, IL: Richard D. Irwin.

Heckscher, Charles. 1994. "Defining the Post-Bureaucratic Type." Pp. 14–62 in *The Post-Bureaucratic Organization.* Thousand Oaks, CA: Sage.

Landsberger, Henry. 1961. "The Horizontal Dimension in Bureaucracy." *Administrative Science Quarterly,* 6(3):299–332.

Lawrence, Paul, and Jay Lorsch. 1967. *Organization and Environment: Managing Differentiation and Integration.* Boston: Graduate School of Business Administration, Harvard University.

March, James, and Herbert Simon. 1958. *Organizations.* New York: Wiley.

Marx, Karl. 1886. *Capital: A Critique of Political Economy.* Volume 1, pp. 348–360. New York: International Publishers.

Piore, Michael. 1993. "The Social Embeddedness of Labor Markets and Cognitive Processes." *Labour,* 7(3):3–18.

Taylor, Frederick Winslow. 1911. *Scientific Management.* New York: Harper and Row.

Weber, Max. 1920. "Bureaucracy." Pp. 956–1005 in *Economy and Society: An Outline of Interpretive Sociology.* Volume 2. Berkeley: University of California Press.

———. [1924] 1978. *Economy and Society: An Outline of Interpretative Sociology,* edited by Guenther Roth and Claus Wittich. Berkeley: University of California Press.

Williamson, O. 1975. *Markets and Hierarchies: Analysis and Anti-trust Implications.* New York: The Free Press.

8

BUREAUCRACY

MAX WEBER

CHARACTERISTICS OF MODERN BUREAUCRACY

Modern officialdom functions in the following manner:

I. There is the principle of official *jurisdictional areas,* which are generally ordered by rules, that is, by laws or administrative regulations. This means:

(1) The regular activities required for the purposes of the bureaucratically governed structure are assigned as official duties.

(2) The authority to give the commands required for the discharge of these duties is distributed in a stable way and is strictly delimited by rules concerning the coercive means, physical, sacerdotal, or otherwise, which may be placed at the disposal of officials.

(3) Methodical provision is made for the regular and continuous fulfillment of these duties and for the exercise of the corresponding rights; only persons who qualify under general rules are employed.

In the sphere of the state these three elements constitute a bureaucratic *agency,* in the sphere of the private economy they constitute a bureaucratic *enterprise.* Bureaucracy, thus understood, is fully developed in political and ecclesiastical communities only in the modern state, and in the private economy only in the most advanced institutions of capitalism. Permanent agencies, with fixed jurisdiction, are not the historical rule but rather the exception. This is even true of large political structures such as those of the ancient Orient, the Germanic and Mongolian empires of conquest, and of many feudal states. In all these cases, the ruler executes the most important measures through personal trustees, table-companions, or court-servants. Their commissions and powers are not precisely delimited and are temporarily called into being for each case.

II. The principles of *office hierarchy* and of channels of appeal (*Instanzenzug*) stipulate a clearly established system of super- and subordination in which there is a supervision of the lower offices by the higher ones. Such a system offers the governed the possibility of appealing, in a precisely regulated manner, the decision of a lower office to the corresponding superior authority. With the full development of the bureaucratic type, the office hierarchy is *monocratically* organized. The principle of hierarchical office authority is found in all bureaucratic structures: in state and ecclesiastical structures as well as in large party organizations and private enterprises. It does not matter for the character of bureaucracy whether its authority is called "private" or "public."

When the principle of jurisdictional "competency" is fully carried through, hierarchical subordination—at least in public office—does not mean that the "higher" authority is authorized simply to take over the business of the "lower." Indeed, the opposite is the rule; once an office has been set up, a new incumbent will always be appointed if a vacancy occurs.

III. The management of the modern office is based upon written documents (the "files"), which are preserved in their original or draft form, and upon a staff of subaltern officials and scribes of all sorts. The body of officials working in an agency along with the respective apparatus of material implements and the files makes up *a bureau* (in private enterprise often called the "counting house," *Kontor).*

In principle, the modern organization of the civil service separates the bureau from the private domicile of the official and, in general, segregates official activity from the sphere of private life. Public monies and equipment are divorced from the private property of the official. This condition is everywhere the product of a long development. Nowadays, it is found in public as well as in private enterprises: in the latter, the principle extends even to the entrepreneur at the top. In principle, the *Kontor* (office) is separated from the household, business from private correspondence, and business assets from private wealth. The more consistently the modern type of business management has been carried through, the more are these separations the case. The beginnings of this process are to be found as early as the Middle Ages.

It is the peculiarity of the modern entrepreneur that he conducts himself as the "first official" of his enterprise, in the very same way in which the ruler of a specifically modern bureaucratic state [Frederick II of Prussia] spoke of himself as "the first servant" of the state. The idea that the bureau activities of the state are intrinsically different in character from the management of private offices is a continental European notion and, by way of contrast, is totally foreign to the American way.

IV. Office management, at least all specialized office management—and such management is distinctly modern—usually presupposes thorough training in a field of specialization. This, too, holds increasingly for the modern executive and employee of a private enterprise, just as it does for the state officials.

V. When the office is fully developed, official activity demands the *full working capacity* of the official, irrespective of the fact that the length of his obligatory working hours in the bureau may be limited. In the normal case, this too is only the product of a long development, in the public as well as in the private office. Formerly the normal state of affairs was the reverse. Official business was discharged as a secondary activity.

VI. The management of the office follows general *rules,* which are more or less stable, more or less exhaustive, and which can be learned. Knowledge of these rules represents a special technical expertise which the officials possess. It involves jurisprudence, administrative or business management.

The reduction of modern office management to rules is deeply embedded in its very nature. The theory of modern public administration, for instance, assumes that the authority to order certain matters by decree—which has been legally granted to an agency—does not entitle the agency to regulate the matter by individual commands given for each case, but only to regulate the matter abstractly. This stands in extreme contrast to the regulation of all relationships through individual privileges and bestowals of favor, which, as we shall see, is absolutely dominant in patrimonialism, at least in so far as such relationships are not fixed by sacred tradition. . . .

The Technical Superiority of Bureaucratic Organization Over Administration by Notables

The decisive reason for the advance of bureaucratic organization has always been its purely *technical* superiority over any other form of organization. The fully developed bureaucratic apparatus compares with other organizations exactly as does the machine with the non-mechanical modes of production. Precision, speed, unambiguity, knowledge of the files, continuity, discretion, unity, strict subordination, reduction of friction and of material and personal casts—these are raised to the optimum point in the strictly bureaucratic administration, and especially in its monocratic form. As compared with all collegiate, honorific, and avocational forms of administration, trained bureaucracy is superior on all these points. And as far as complicated tasks are concerned, paid bureaucratic work is not only more precise but, in the last analysis, it is often cheaper than even formally unremunerated honorific service.

Honorific arrangements make administrative work a subsidiary activity: an avocation and, for this reason alone, honorific service normally functions more slowly. Being less bound to schemata and more formless, it is less precise and less unified than bureaucratic administration, also because it is less dependent upon superiors. Because the establishment and exploitation of the apparatus of subordinate officials and clerical services are almost unavoidably less economical, honorific service is less continuous than bureaucratic and frequently quite expensive. This is especially the case if one thinks not only of the money costs to the public treasury—costs which bureaucratic administration, in comparison with administration by notables, usually increases—but also of the frequent economic losses of the governed caused by delays and lack of precision. Permanent administration by notables is normally feasible only where official business can be satisfactorily transacted as an avocation. With the qualitative increase of tasks the administration has to face, administration by notables reaches its limits—today even in England. Work organized by collegiate bodies, on the other hand, causes friction and delay and requires compromises between colliding interests and views. The administration, therefore, runs less precisely and is more independent of superiors; hence, it is less unified and slower. All advances of the Prussian administrative organization, for example, have been and will in the future be advances of the bureaucratic, and especially of the monocratic, principle.

Today, it is primarily the capitalist market economy which demands that the official business of public administration be discharged precisely, unambiguously, continuously, and with as much speed as possible. Normally, the very large modern capitalist enterprises are themselves unequalled models of strict bureaucratic organization. Business management throughout rests on increasing precision, steadiness, and, above all, speed of operations. This, in turn, is determined by the peculiar nature of the modern means of communication, including, among other things, the news service of the press. The extraordinary increase in the speed by which public announcements, as well as economic and political facts, are transmitted exerts a steady and sharp pressure in the direction of speeding up the tempo of administrative reaction towards various situations. The optimum of such reaction time is normally attained only by a strictly bureaucratic organization. (The fact that the bureaucratic apparatus also can, and indeed does, create certain definite impediments for the discharge of business in a manner best adapted to the individuality of each case does not belong into the present context.)

Bureaucratization offers above all the optimum possibility for carrying through the principle of specializing administrative functions according to purely objective considerations. Individual performances are allocated to functionaries who have specialized training and who by constant practice increase their expertise. "Objective" discharge of business primarily means a discharge of business according to *calculable rules* and "without regard for persons."

"Without regard for persons," however, is also the watchword of the market and, in general, of all pursuits of naked economic interests. Consistent bureaucratic domination means the leveling of "status honor." Hence, if the principle of the free market is not at the same time restricted, it means the universal domination of the "class situation." That this consequence of bureaucratic domination has not set in everywhere proportional to the extent of bureaucratization is due to the differences between possible principles by which polities may supply their requirements. However, the second element mentioned, calculable rules, is the most important one for modern bureaucracy. The peculiarity of modern culture, and specifically of its technical and economic basis, demands this very "calculability" of results. When fully developed, bureaucracy also stands, in a specific sense, under the principle of *sine ira et studio*. Bureaucracy develops the more perfectly, the more it is "dehumanized," the more completely it succeeds in eliminating from official business love, hatred, and all purely personal, irrational, and emotional elements which escape calculation. This is appraised as its special virtue by capitalism.

The more complicated and specialized modern culture becomes, the more its external supporting apparatus demands the personally detached and strictly objective expert, in lieu of the lord of older social structures who was moved by personal sympathy and favor, by grace and gratitude. Bureaucracy offers the attitudes demanded by the external apparatus of modern culture in the most favorable combination. In particular, only bureaucracy has established the foundation for the administration of a rational law conceptually systematized on the basis of "statutes" such as the later Roman Empire first created with a high degree of technical perfection. During the Middle Ages, the reception of this [Roman] law coincided with the bureaucratization of legal administration. The advance of the rationally trained expert displaced the old trial procedure which was bound to tradition or to irrational presuppositions. . . .

Bureaucratic Objectivity, Raison D'État and Popular Will

It is perfectly true that "matter-of-factness" and "expertness" are not necessarily identical with the rule of general and abstract norms. Indeed, this does not even hold in the case of the modern administration of justice. The idea of a "law without gaps" is, of course, under vigorous attack. The conception of the modern judge as an automaton into which legal documents and fees are stuffed at the top in order that it may spill forth the verdict at the bottom along with the reasons, read mechanically from codified paragraphs—this conception is angrily rejected, perhaps because a certain approximation to this type would precisely be implied by a consistent bureaucratization of justice. Thus even in the field of law-finding there are areas in which the bureaucratic judge is directly held to "individualizing" procedures by the legislator.

For the field of administrative activity proper, that is, for all state activities that fall outside the field of law creation and court procedure, one has become accustomed to claims for the freedom and the paramountcy of individual circumstances. General norms are held to play primarily a negative role, as barriers to the official's positive and "creative" activity which should never be regulated. The bearing of this thesis may be disregarded here. Decisive is that this "freely" creative administration (and possibly judicature) would not constitute a realm of *free*, arbitrary action and discretion, of *personally* motivated favor and valuation, such as we shall find to be the case among pre-bureaucratic forms. The rule and the rational pursuit of "objective" purposes, as well as devotion to these, would always constitute the norm of conduct. Precisely those views which most strongly glorify the "creative" discretion of the official accept, as the ultimate and highest lodestar for his behavior in public administration, the specifically modern and strictly "objective" idea of *raison d'état*. Of course, the sure instincts of the bureaucracy for the conditions of maintaining its *own* power in the home state (and through it, in opposition to other states) are inseparably fused with this canonization of the abstract and "objective" idea of "reasons of state." Most of the time, only the power interests of the bureaucracy give a concretely exploitable content to this by no means unambiguous ideal: in dubious cases, it is always these interests which tip the balance. We cannot discuss this further here. The only decisive point for us is that in principle a system of rationally debatable "reasons" stands behind every act of bureaucratic administration, namely, either subsumption under norms, or a weighing of ends and means.

In this context, too, the attitude of all "democratic" currents, in the sense of currents that would minimize "domination," is necessarily ambiguous. "Equality before the law" and the demand for legal guarantees against arbitrariness demand a formal and rational "objectivity" of administration, as opposed to the personal discretion flowing from the "grace" of the old patrimonial domination. If, however, an "ethos"—not to speak of other impulses—takes hold of the masses on some individual question, its postulates of *substantive* justice, oriented toward some concrete instance and person, will unavoidably collide with the formalism and the rule-bound and cool "matter-of-factness" of bureaucratic administration. Emotions must in that case reject what reason demands.

The propertyless masses especially are not served by the formal "equality before the law" and the "calculable" adjudication and administration demanded by bourgeois interests. Naturally, in their eyes justice and administration should serve to equalize their economic and social life-opportunities in the face of the propertied classes. Justice and administration can fulfill this function only if they assume a character that is informal because "ethical" with respect to substantive content (*Kadi*-justice). Not only any sort of "popular justice"—which usually does not ask for reasons and norms—but also any intensive influence on the administration by so-called "public opinion"—that is, concerted action born of irrational "sentiments" and usually staged or directed by party bosses or the press—thwarts the rational course of justice just as strongly, and under certain circumstances far more so, as the "star chamber proceedings *(Kabinettsjustiz)* of absolute rulers used to be able to do. . . .

THE OBJECTIVE AND SUBJECTIVE BASES OF BUREAUCRATIC PERPETUITY

Once fully established, bureaucracy is among those social structures which are the hardest to destroy. Bureaucracy is *the* means of transforming social action into rationally organized action. Therefore, as an instrument of rationally organizing authority relations, bureaucracy was and is a power instrument of the first order for one who controls the bureaucratic apparatus. Under otherwise equal conditions, rationally organized and directed action *(Gesellschaftshandeln)* is superior to every kind of collective behavior *(Massenhandeln)* and also social action *(Gemeinschaftshandeln)* opposing it. Where administration has been completely bureaucratized, the resulting system of domination is practically indestructible.

The individual bureaucrat cannot squirm out of the apparatus into which he has been harnessed. In contrast to the "notable" performing administrative tasks as a honorific duty or as a subsidiary occupation (avocation), the professional bureaucrat is chained to his activity in his entire economic and ideological existence. In the great majority of cases he is only a small cog in a ceaselessly moving mechanism which prescribes to him an essentially fixed route of march. The official is entrusted with specialized tasks, and normally the mechanism cannot be put into motion or arrested by him, but only from the very top. The individual bureaucrat is, above all, forged to the common interest of all the functionaries in the perpetuation of the apparatus and the persistence of its rationally organized domination.

The ruled, for their part, cannot dispense with or replace the bureaucratic apparatus once it exists, for it rests upon expert training, a functional specialization of work, and an attitude set on habitual virtuosity in the mastery of single yet methodically integrated functions. If the apparatus stops working, or if its work is interrupted by force, chaos results, which it is difficult to master by improvised replacements from among the governed. This holds for public administration as well as for private economic management. Increasingly the material fate of the masses depends upon the continuous and correct functioning of the ever more bureaucratic organizations of private capitalism, and the idea of eliminating them becomes more and more utopian.

SOURCE: FROM MAX WEBER: Translated by H. H. Gerth & C. Wright Mills (1958): pp. 196–198; 214–216; 224–228. Total 8 pages © 1946, 1956, 1973 by H. H. Gerth and C. Wright Mills "by Permission of Oxford University Press, Inc."

9

CO-ORDINATION

MARY PARKER FOLLETT

I have said that we find responsibility for management shot all through a business, that we find some degree of authority all along the line, that leadership can be exercised by many people besides the top executive. All this is now being increasingly recognised, and the crux of business organisation is how to join these varied responsibilities, these scattered authorities, these different kinds of leadership. For a business, to be a going concern, must be unified. The fair test of business administration, of industrial organisation, is whether you have a business with all its parts so co-ordinated, so moving together in their closely knit and adjusting activities, so linking, interlocking, inter-relating, that they make a working unit, not a congerie of separate pieces. In the businesses I have studied, the greatest weakness is in the relation of departments. The efficiency of many plants is lowered by an imperfectly worked-out system of co-ordination. In some cases all the co-ordination there is depends on the degree of friendliness existing between the heads of department, on whether they are willing to consult; sometimes it depends on the mere chance of two men coming up to town on the same train every morning.

I spoke to you last week of a recent conference here in London of Works Managers and Sales Managers. The object of the conference was to discuss ways in which Works Managers and Sales Managers could work more closely together. We heard a great deal about the lack of co-operation between them. We heard a great deal of the necessity of understanding each other's problems, that the production department should know more of customers' demands, why they liked one product, why they complained of another; that the sales department, on the other hand, should know more of the difficulties of production, the difficulty, for instance, of producing what the customer wants within the price the customer is willing to pay. And so on. Many instances were given of the way in which Sales Managers and Works Managers could help each other by a greater understanding of each other's work. We heard that neither side should lead, that they should work together, that they should make a team.

I thought this one of the best conferences I had ever attended. I thought it was bound to do a lot of good. But one thought persisted uppermost in my mind all day and just at the end of the afternoon one man voiced this thought when he rose and said: "But surely co-ordination is a problem of management." There was no discussion of this point and quite rightly. These were Works Managers and Sales Managers and they were considering how, as industry is generally organised, they could co-operate more effectively. But surely it is obvious that many of the capital suggestions made at that Conference, suggestions for voluntary co-operation, were things that could be required of the sales and production department. Two men thought it desirable that the heads of these departments should lunch together frequently. One trembles to think of the success of industry depending on such a mere chance as that. Surely regular meetings between production department and sales department could be required at which they could inform each other of all the things which were mentioned at this conference as essential each should know of the other.

And indeed a good many companies are considering co-ordination a question of management and organisation, and the problem is met in different ways. In some cases regular meetings between departments is required. Some companies have a co-ordinating department whose special function it is to bring into closer relation the work of the various departments. Some have a planning department which serves also as a co-ordinating agency. A department of sales research, separate from the selling department as such, may act as a link with production. Research as to future lines of production must necessarily be linked up with sales research. The merchandise department to a certain extent links production and sales. And so on. I give these merely as illustrations. If I were to describe to you all the ways in which co-ordination is being effected in industry that would be a talk on organisation, and, besides the fact that that would take all winter, it is not what I have undertaken to do. I have, therefore, chosen three things which seem to me to make for the greater unity of an enterprise. I might express this more forcefully and say that I think they embody the fundamental principle of unity.

One, which I consider a very important trend in business management, is a system of cross-functioning between the different departments. Let me take, as providing an example of this trend, the Telephone Company of which I have already spoken to you, although of course there are many other companies which would do equally well for illustration. Here we find the four departments—traffic, engineering, commercial and plant—conferring with one another and all together. These conferences are often informal but they are expected of all officials. Each department is expected to get in touch with certain

others. The district traffic manager asks the wire chief from the plant department to talk some matter over with him, or if it is a commercial matter, he calls in the commercial manager of that district, or if it is a question of blue prints or costs, he asks the engineering department if they will send a man over. They may settle it among themselves. If not, the district traffic manager puts the matter up to the superintendent of the traffic department. The superintendent of the traffic department may consult the superintendent of the plant or the commercial department.

Here, you see, we have a combination of going both across the line and up the line. When one of the exchanges was cut in two (such questions come up every day, I mention this only because it occurred while I was making my investigation), the question came up whether to cut thirty-five a day or five hundred in a blanket order one night. This affected all four departments—traffic, engineering, commercial and plant. They agreed after discussion on the blanket order. If they had disagreed they would have taken it up to the general superintendent of each department—up the line, note. Then the four superintendents would have consulted, now across the line. If they had agreed the matter would have ended there. If not it would have had to go to the General Manager—up the line.

This combination of across and up exists, as I have said, in many plants today. Many businesses are now organised in such a way that you do not have an ascending and descending ladder of authority. You have a degree of cross-functioning, of inter-relation of departments, which means a horizontal rather than a vertical authority. That means in this case that a problem which occurs at X which concerns Y does not have to be taken up the line from X and then taken down the line to Y.

A telephone company sells service rather than a product, but you can have the same cross-functioning anywhere. If you have it in a company which both manufactures and sells a product, instead of all that the selling department knows of customers' demands going up the line to the general manager and then going down the line from him to the manufacturing department, and the problem of the manufacturing department going up the line to the general manager and then from him down the line to the sales department, instead of this you can have a system of cross-relations which gives opportunity for direct contact between Sales Manager and Production Manager. Where you have this direct contact there is much less chance of misunderstanding, [and] there is opportunity of explaining problems and difficulties each to the other. This seems to me very important. Direct contact of the responsible people concerned is, indeed, one of the four vital principles of organisation which I shall speak of later.

I should like to say incidentally that where we see a horizontal rather than a vertical authority, we have another proof of what I said two weeks ago, namely that we are now finding in business practice less of that kind of authority which puts one man over another. We have conferences of parallel heads.

But there are companies who get this horizontal authority, as I have called it, by another method.

These companies think that the methods which I have been describing to you, where each man decides for himself when he needs to discuss a matter with another, is not sufficient for the steadily continuous binding together of the different parts of a business. These companies, therefore, have a system of committees composed of men who have closely related problems who meet regularly to discuss these problems. I do not, however, propose to consider the question of committees in industry here, [as] it is too large and too controversial a subject. I mention them because they are a form of cross-functioning, and cross-functioning was one of the ways of unifying a business of which I wished to speak to you.

SOURCE: Follett, Mary Parker. 1949. Excerpt from "Co-ordination." Pp. 61–65 in *Freedom and Co-ordination: Lectures in Business Organization*. London: Management Publications Trust.

10

THE HORIZONTAL DIMENSION IN BUREAUCRACY

HENRY A. LANDSBERGER

The purpose of the paper is threefold. First, it is to plead that greater attention be paid—both in the form of empirical investigations and through more conceptualization—to the horizontal dimension of bureaucracy. Horizontal relationships are those whose functions are not primarily the passing down of orders or the passing up of information and whose nature and characteristics are not primarily determined by the fact that one actor is superior to the other in the organization's hierarchy. The function of horizontal relationships is to facilitate the solution of problems arising from division of labor, and their nature and characteristics are determined by the participants having different organizational subgoals but interdependent activities that need to intermesh.

Second, we wish to suggest that in these horizontal relationships, conflict and disagreement may be frequent, inevitable, and at times useful to the organization. Some conflict at least stems from dilemmas facing the organization—problems "out there," in reality, and the organization may benefit from having all sides of a problem clearly argued by some group within it. If it is true that the problem is a reality problem, then similarly placed organizations will face the same dilemmas and should be subject to the same controversies regardless of local politics and personalities. We shall present empirical evidence to show that this is indeed the case.

Finally, we suggest that the exploration of these dilemmas and reality problems requires the collection of research data quite different from those most frequently utilized in studies of organizations. Moreover, analyzing the effects of these factors requires that the researcher understand the organization's technical processes, accounting procedures, marketing and competitive problems, and so forth; research methods and theories of general behavioral science are not enough.

Vertical authority relationships may perhaps be understood without knowledge of reality factors, though this, too, is questionable. There has of late been increasing interest in reality factors determining leadership patterns.[1] In addition, leaders have been exhorted to be more "reality centered"[2] and to "manage by objective."[3] This is an implicit recognition that problems of vertical authority, too, may be matters of dealing more with objective reality than with subjective psychology. In any case, understanding of horizontal relationships, molded as they are by the division of labor, requires that the investigator grasp the real nature of that "labor" and the obstacles it must overcome.

LITERATURE OF HORIZONTAL RELATIONSHIPS

The neglect[4] of horizontal relationships in organizations and the failure to deal with them in terms of formal organizational functions is revealed by a glance at the literature. Writers who have used what Gouldner calls the "natural system model of organizational analysis"[5] have, by definition, focused on the informal aspects of behavior in organizations, whether discussing vertical or horizontal relationships. The natural-system theorists view organizations as little communities. Intergroup, e.g., management-worker, relationships are determined primarily by whether the groups concerned have similar values and expectations and by their relative status in the larger community. Work problems play a part in determining intergroup relations, but more as a trigger for these other determinants than in their own right.

The most thorough of all studies of horizontal relationships has, in fact, been undertaken from this particular point of view—Melville Dalton's *Men Who Manage.*[6] The impression left by Dalton's subtle and many-faceted investigation is that while the interdepartmental conflicts which he so vividly describes may have a positive function for the organization, this is unintended and accidental. Horizontal relationships in general, and interdepartmental conflict in particular, are to be understood primarily as the result of intense personal ambitions and rivalries and as the result also of clique struggles between groups whose membership is determined not so much by departmental membership as by criteria such as religion and age, criteria that are irrelevant from the formal organization's point of view. Organizational problems serve as convenient issues but are of secondary importance.

While our position will be the opposite of Dalton's, we do not deny that the forces he discusses are always present to some extent. We do, however, wish to establish organizational dilemmas as of equal importance in causing interdepartmental conflicts or, more broadly, as determinants of horizontal relationships in general.

It should be noted that the incidence and type of Dalton's informal factors (e.g., personality characteristics, education) are largely random, relative to the organizational level of analysis. Those with a particular status may be in one department in one organization and in another department (or widely dispersed) in another organization. This makes it difficult to integrate variables of this kind systematically into a theory of organization and of interdepartmental relations. If, however, the determinants of horizontal relationships are to be found in the nature of organizations themselves—as we believe they are—it should be easier to deal with them systematically.

Those who have approached organizations not from the informal point of view, but with a "rational" model of analysis in mind,[7] focusing on such formal processes as planning, authorizing, co-ordinating, and so on, have not contributed greatly to the understanding of horizontal relationships, whether they have followed the sociological writings of Max Weber or the traditional school of administrative theory typified by Urwick.[8] While writers of these two schools have realized that the horizontal division of labor, or technical specialization, is a prime characteristic of organizations, they have in fact avoided direct exploration of the relationships which such specialization involves.

They have not studied these horizontal relationships intensively per se, but have assimilated them into a problem of vertical relationships between superior and several subordinates, as Dubin has.[9] Again we do not deny that such reference upward occurs, and that such co-ordination is indeed a function of superior authority. We wish rather to encourage an addition to our knowledge of organizational processes by pointing out that much happens *before* such reference upward occurs and that these preliminaries should be of interest to students of organization. Indeed, very frequently, there is no reference upward, since the need to bring in a superior as arbiter is obviated by existing rules, by mutual agreement after discussion, or by agreement after bargaining where the rules permit it and their vagueness necessitates it.

Writers with "rational" models have avoided dealing with horizontal relationships by focusing on the role of the staff specialist. His activities are described either as advisory to his horizontal equal on the "line," or as advisory to a superior (thus once again assimilating the problem into the framework of a vertical, superior-subordinate relationship). Even as a description of the specialist's way of relating himself to the rest of the organization, the "advisory" label is inadequate, and there has been increasing dissatisfaction with it;[10] for the specialist's contribution must be more than advice if his area is critically involved. Hence, as most writers have pointed out, the lawyer has the ultimate decision in legal matters and the scientist in scientific feasibility, and so on.

A more serious deficiency in this formulation is that it segregates the specialist away from the daily or yearly flow of operations. There are, in many organizations, flows which routinely involve persons from different functional provinces at a roughly equal level. Such a flow has generally been briefly recognized as existing at the hardware stage in the manufacturing process; that is, at its lowest level. It has been regarded as exceptional, and those who have dealt with it have not seen it as a general phenomenon existing at all levels of the organization. This emphasis is found in Bakke in his discussion of "functional specification" as one of the five bonds of organization;[11] in the Tavistock group's emphasis on the "socio-technical production system";[12] and, more recently, in Sayles's analysis of interdependent work groups.[13] Dubin, for example, says that "the flow of commands and orders between jobs at the same level is a less common, though clearly recognized circumstance, as when the hooker directs the crane operator to hoist away. . . ."[14] Likewise Schneider, while recognizing that the line type of organization relates people both in a superior-subordinate (vertical) fashion *and* in terms of doing a specific task (horizontally), illustrates this in terms only of blue-collar operations.[15] Significantly, Schneider also explores this relationship not in itself but only in terms of its significance for a co-ordinating type of authority.

One of the very few empirical studies in this area sees horizontal communications determined by hardware technology,[16] and focuses on communication between first-line supervisors of blue-collar personnel. Simpson's ultimate theoretical interest is on the determinants of superior-subordinate relationships.[17] He sees their frequency determined by the complexity of technology and thus leaves the frequency of horizontal interactions as a residual category.

A REFORMULATION

My own position is, first, that there is frequently a routine work flow horizontally across the organization, which may be just as important and as frequent as any flow of authoritative orders up and down the organization. Second, this flow is not confined to the lowest organizational level. Third, these flows, lying on top of each other, so to speak, may be relatively independent and qualitatively different from each other. A higher-level manager may admittedly spend some of his time arbitrating between subordinates, but at least as important is the time he spends in solving with colleagues roughly at his own level problems appropriate to his own level.

As one goes higher in the hierarchy, each type of problem is dealt with from a longer and longer time perspective.[18] In addition to differences in time perspective, the kinds of problems dealt with at each level change qualitatively. Talcott Parsons has emphasized in his latest writings these qualitative breaks in the managerial chain, calling the lowest "technical," the middle "managerial," and the broadest "institutional." Occasionally, there may be a fourth, even broader level, the "societal." Organizations have to solve problems at the first three of these levels, and their managerial hierarchy is generally set up to do so.[19]

The existence of horizontal work flows at all levels can be seen most vividly in industrial organizations, where the concept of staff specialist cannot possibly cover the relationship between the various departments. A typical system may work as follows. The sales department will have to check with production scheduling (via sales liaison) on the delivery date to be given an important customer for a large order he wishes to place. Production scheduling may then have to check with stock control for availability of parts, with purchasing if bought-out parts or materials are needed, with industrial engineering if special equipment is necessary, and with design if the customer has requested special features. In each instance, the process of "checking" may turn into one of attempting to get commitments.[20]

During production (broadly defined to include design and purchasing) there may also be horizontal exchanges concerning progress. The customer may, for example, ask for a different delivery date, for cancellation of the order outright, redestination, new features, and so on. In short, there is a constant stream of horizontal interaction necessitated by reality requirements. While some of the interaction may be quite routine, some of it may go beyond the standard procedure because the situation is in some way unusual. In that case, unusual efforts are required to collect information, evaluate it, and arrive at decisions. In addition there will be—even at the middle management level—consultation about the formulation of long-range plans: what the market situation looks like for the next three or six months, whether certain productive capacity is likely to be available soon, and so on.

Nor is this kind of horizontal relationship confined to manufacturing or even to industry. Circuits of horizontal interaction, one on top of another, each solving problems at the level appropriate to it, exist in any organization where functions need to intermesh. It is not only that, to handle a certain patient who is in the hospital, the X-ray, surgical, and anaesthetic departments need to be in horizontal contact. This is only the equivalent of technological integration in the plant within the production department of the factory. Such interaction gives rise to its share of human relations problems, but no major functional policy problems are likely to be involved for the organization. The real equivalent would be the kind of issues that arise between a patient who needs a certain kind of treatment, the hospital's intake department, the "technical" departments of the hospital (treatment scheduling, drugs), the hospital's accounting department, and so forth.[21]

As in the case of the industrial organization, the horizontal circuit also exists at a higher authority level, where the hospital concerns itself with long-range problems: whether it is getting an appropriate mix of patients; what trends in diseases (i.e., market trends) portend for it (e.g., the virtual elimination of the need for long-term treatment of tuberculosis); what the implications of technological changes are (e.g., the requirements for more and more expensive equipment); and so on. Most major changes will undoubtedly be decided upon under the direction of a final, vertical, authority which has co-ordinating responsibility. But others need not be. Even when the final decision is officially that of a higher authority, this may be no more than formalization of a decision that has grown largely out of horizontal interchanges whose nature and determinants are worth analysis in their own right.

It is interesting to speculate why Max Weber, conscious though he was of functional specialization as an essential characteristic of bureaucracy, showed so little interest in the relation between functions.[22] By creating an image of organizations as consisting primarily of vertical relationships, he unwittingly set the course for subsequent investigators. It may well be that, because of his concern for freedom and political authority, he was primarily interested in government bureaucracies. Their work—at least at the time when Weber wrote—had consisted of interpreting general rules formulated at the top. There may have been less, and there may still be less, horizontal "work flow" required by the "technology" to achieve the organization's goal in government as compared with industry. In fact, the extent to which organizations differ in this requirement is a dimension which should be analyzed.

We shall now suggest some concepts which might be used in the description of these relationships, to be followed by an analysis of the forces underlying them and determining their nature.

DESCRIPTIVE CONCEPTS

As a first approximation to a description of some of the characteristics of horizontal relationships we suggest that concepts used to describe vertical relationships be employed to describe horizontal relationships on a *mutatis mutandis* basis. We suggest, in particular, that the whole concept of *authority* and its many subsidiary concepts be applied systematically to horizontal relationships with suggestive modifications.

For example, decisions of vertical authority have to be *legitimated* to facilitate acceptance, and this is done (1) through belief in the individual competence of the incumbent, (2) on the basis of organizational logic, and (3) on the basis of pure fiat. This combination often mixes poorly.[23]

So, too, in the case of functional divisions. The purchasing department may have the authority to state that production cannot expand beyond a certain point since it is impossible to obtain the necessary materials. It has the authority (1) through fiat because the rules say the department may decide this, (2) because presumably those in the purchasing department are in a better position to make this kind of decision than others since they specialize in it, and (3) because the people in the department are presumably competent enough as individuals to have obtained the very best delivery dates possible. (Simon, Smithburg, and Thompson refer to this as "authority of confidence."[24])

Our opinion is that horizontal authority is more strongly supported than vertical authority by organizational logic, and is less dependent on arbitrary fiat. It seems less specious to accept that the purchasing department knows best about minimum delivery dates for sheet steel than it is to accept a superior's decision about a problem with which the subordinate may be in closer contact.

Various concepts first developed in relation to vertical authority also apply to horizontal authority. First, the rules allocating authority to make decisions, *institutionalization,* have the same psychological function horizontally as they do vertically. They *depersonalize* the order and thus protect the ego of those to whom it is issued.[25] Second, rules exist to cover routine cases so that decisions do not have to be made (precedents, standing orders, etc.). Hence, decisions are confined to exceptional situations, just as in the case of vertical authority, where the principle of management by exception is a useful one. In the horizontal context, too, routinization protects the ego of those who would otherwise be continually ordered about.

How frequently exceptions arise in horizontal relationships depends, first, on how the system is structured. In the case of vertical authority, there is much checking upwards if decision-making spheres are *(a)* poorly defined, *(b)* narrowly defined, and *(c)* if the style of supervision is close. In the case of horizontal authority, the frequency of checking also depends on these three factors. If, for example, there are frequent changes in design because of the nature of the product (computers during the last few years are an example), there may be frequent orders emanating from the design department for changes

in materials to be bought, specifications to be given to customers, and so on.

Further, it has long been noted that in the case of superior-subordinate relationships, there is *mutual dependence,* unequal though it may be.[26] This is true of horizontal relationships. The production department of a manufacturing organization is, of course, dependent on the sales department for its very existence, but the sales department in its turn can be hampered by the faulty operation of the production department. This mutual dependence is based on the fact that various functions are essential since they are linked to real processes needed by the organization to attain its goal. Some functions, however, are more essential than others, and the essential function will be more depended on than dependent, just as in the case of vertical authority the subordinate is more dependent on the superior than vice versa.

The difference between this kind of mutual dependence and its vertical parallel is first that there is likely to be more equality in the mutual dependence of two departments than between superior and subordinate. Secondly the dependence, like horizontal relationships as a whole, is more like a network in which many points are interconnected and hence interdependent, and not a single line.

Just as there is a top and a bottom in the line of vertical relationships, however, so in horizontal relationships there is usually a starting point and an end, though this is not as marked. In the case of routine production, sales is the starting point and production, or dispatch, the end. Purchasing and personnel are the end points of feeder systems acquiring the personnel and materials necessary for production. They are, perhaps, to be thought of as "staff" to the horizontal line, slotting in at different stages of it as is customary of staff in vertical relationships. Where routine production and sales are not involved, for example, the introduction of new designs and processes, it is these departments that are at the head of the chain, and production once again at the end. Just as in the case of vertical authority, where those doing the initiating have higher job satisfaction than those for whom they initiate, so in the case of horizontal relations, there is some evidence to show that those at the head of the chain have more satisfaction than those who come second, third, fourth, and so on in the line of division of labor.[27]

Under the general heading of authority, the concept of *anticipation*[28] also has a parallel in the horizontal context. Just as a subordinate will seek to outguess his superior to avoid having to ask for and be given orders, so horizontal departments will outguess each other rather than ask for instructions. The sales department will avoid asking other departments (production, design) for the "impossible" since it can guess the answer in advance and does not want to be given a "no"—any more than a subordinate does. Like a subordinate, however, the sales department may in fact tell the customer a white lie: that its hands are tied, in this instance not by the boss, but by "the factory."

The man-in-the-middle situation in which every vertical authority finds itself[29] also has its counterpart. Every vertical authority has to mediate between pressures from below and from above. With respect to horizontal relations, some positions may have a similar problem of dual loyalty, particularly at the ends of the line. The salesman at one end and the purchasing department or personnel department at the other are not infrequently suspected of loyalties outside the organization. In this they parallel the first-line supervisor at one end and the president at the other. Between the sales department at one end of the horizontal chain and the purchasing department at the other end there is no one who does not believe he is a crucial mediator, the only one capable of seeing "both points of view" and the "entire picture." Sales liaison people, for example, are prone to this kind of feeling, and with much justification, as are persons in production scheduling. Generally, there is both satisfaction and some stress associated with this kind of mediation and the process of adjusting pressures from two sides to each other.

A final similarity between horizontal relations and vertical ones—and with some definite differences—is that both authority and responsibilities for functions may be evenly or unevenly divided. In the case of the line of vertical authority, authority and responsibility may be highly concentrated, usually at the top, or it may be evenly spread. Tannenbaum and his associates have highlighted this idea for vertical authority in proposing a "control graph."[30] Fashions, the traditions of the organization, and various informal factors may play their part in the shape and location of the control graph. But reality factors are by no means

without effect, as witness the prediction by Leavitt and Whisler that technological factors—information technology—will lead to centralization at the top, regardless of any managerial philosophies currently in vogue.[31]

Notes

1. See, for example, Edward A. Fleishman, Edwin F. Harris, and Harold E. Burtt, *Leadership and Supervision in Industry* (Bureau of Educational Research Monograph No. 33; Columbus, 1955). In the final chapter of this monograph, "Leadership Behavior, Morale, and Efficiency," the authors point out how heavily supervisory patterns seem to be influenced by technological pressures (line production versus nonproduction).

2. Chris Argyris, *Personality and Organization* (New York, 1957).

3. Peter F. Drucker, *The Practice of Management* (New York, 1954).

4. The work of Herbert A. Simon and his associates is the major exception to this statement. See, in particular chs. vii–xiv in Herbert A. Simon, Donald W. Smithburg, and Victor A. Thompson, *Public Administration* (New York, 1950). The discussion in these chapters is, however, chiefly in terms of staff groups and in terms of competing agencies, and not in terms of regular work flows across departments in a single organization which is emphasized in this paper. Chapters v and vi of James G. March and Herbert A. Simon's *Organizations* (New York, 1958) also deal extensively with horizontal conflict, but emphasize perceptual and information flow as determinants of the intensity of conflict. We shall emphasize the nature of realistic dilemmas in the environment, as determinants of the *content* of conflicts, similar for similarly placed organizations. We therefore intend to add to, rather than to differ with, Simon's ideas.

5. Alvin W. Gouldner, "Organization Analysis," in Robert K. Merton, Leonard Broom, and Leonard S. Cottrell, eds., *Sociology Today: Problems and Prospects* (New York, 1959), ch. xviii, pp. 400–428, especially pp. 404 ff.

6. Melville Dalton, *Men Who Manage: Fusion of Feeling and Theory in Administration* (New York, 1959). See esp. chs. iii, iv, "Power Struggles in the Line," and "Relations between Staff and Line," pp. 18–109.

7. Gouldner, *op. cit.*

8. Most writers today do not, of course, confine themselves to one of these approaches, but blend not only Weber and the traditionalists, but the ideas of the natural system theorists as well. See, for example, Robert Dubin, *The World of*

Work: Industrial Society and Human Relations (Englewood Cliffs, N. J., 1958), as well as Wilbert Moore, *Industrial Relations and the Social Order* (New York, 1951).

9. Dubin, *op. cit,* pp. 380 ff.

10. Louis A. Allen, *Management and Organization* (New York, 1958). See also William F. Whyte, *Men at Work* (Chicago, 1961); and Simon, Smithburg, and Thompson, in "Are Overhead Units Advisory?" *op. cit.,* p. 284. They also refer to the "complex process of decision" that in public agencies may precede "the approval and even the drafting" of an order in a public agency, and to "non-hierarchical channels of authority" (p. 188). The general idea of horizontal authority goes back to Chester I. Barnard and to Mary Parker Follett's concern with the "authority of ideas." There has, however, been comparatively little systematic application to the horizontal dimension of the many subconcepts associated with vertical authority, as we attempt here.

11. E. Wight Bakke, *Bonds of Organization* (New York, 1950).

12. A. T. M. Wilson, Contrasting Socio-technical Production Systems, *The Manager,* 23(1955), 1–8.

13. Leonard R. Sayles, *The Behavior of Industrial Work Groups* (New York, 1958).

14. Dubin, *op. cit.,* p. 44.

15. Eugene V. Schneider, *Industrial Sociology: The Social Relations of Industry and Community* (New York, 1957), p. 81.

16. Richard L. Simpson, Vertical and Horizontal Communication in Organizations, *Administrative Science Quarterly,* 4 (1959), 188–196.

17. *Loc. cit.,* pp. 195–196.

18. For a perceptive discussion of organizational level and length of time perspective, see Elliott Jaques, *Measurement of Responsibility* (London, 1956).

19. Talcott Parsons, "Some Ingredients of a General Theory of Formal Organization," ch. iii, in Andrew W. Halpin, ed., *Administrative Theory in Education* (Chicago, 1958), pp. 40–72.

20. This is a typical list: in any one organization, sales-liaison, or dispatch, may be a subdivision of the sales department; in another, stock control may be a part of purchasing; in a third, production scheduling may come under production. The significance of these variations—and of changes over time in any one organization—are discussed in a later section.

21. At the same time that the patient—as Parsons has pointed out—is a customer, he is also the product of the hospital; he is the purchaser of the improved body or mind which he hopes to enjoy. This applies also to the student who purchases his own intellectual improvement.

22. Max Weber, "Bureaucracy," in H. H. Gerth and C. Wright Mills, eds., *From Max Weber: Essays in Sociology* (New York, 1946), ch. viii, pp. 196–224.

23. Gouldner, *op. cit.,* pp. 413 ff.

24. *Op. cit.,* p. 189.

25. Chester I. Barnard, "Functions of Status Systems in Formal Organizations," in Robert Dubin, ed., *Human Relations in Administration* (Englewood Cliffs, N. J., 1951), pp. 225–267. There is little in this book which deals with leadership, authority, power, and decision making that cannot be reformulated to shed light on horizontal relationships instead of the vertical relationships to which they supposedly exclusively apply.

26. Philip Selznick, "The Leader as Agent of the Led," in Dubin, *op. cit.,* pp. 249–253.

27. Personal communication from Professor Andrew Schultz, College of Engineering. Cornell University.

28. The concept is C. J. Friedrich's, quoted by Herbert A. Simon in his chapter "Authority" in Dubin, *op. cit.,* p. 192.

29. Fritz J. Roethlisberger, The Foreman: Master and Victim of Double Talk, *Harvard Business Review,* 23 (1945), 285–294.

30. See, for example, Arnold S. Tannenbaum, The Distribution of Control in Formal Organizations, *Social Forces,* 136 (1957), 44–50.

31. J. Leavitt and Thomas L. Whisler, Management in the 1980's, *Harvard Business Review,* 36 (1958), 41 ff.

SOURCE: Landsberger, Henry A. 1961. Excerpt from "The Horizontal Dimension in Bureaucracy." *Administrative Science Quarterly,* 6(3):299–312.

11

THE SOCIAL EMBEDDEDNESS OF LABOR MARKETS AND COGNITIVE PROCESSES

MICHAEL J. PIORE

I want to talk about the relationship between the economy and the society and, in that context, about how we understand and interpret economic institutions. This is not a new subject for me; indeed, those of you who know my work will recognize that I talk about it all the time. But there are several reasons for turning to this topic anew at the present juncture. One of these is the process of economic integration which is, or at least has been up to now, taking place in Western Europe. We are facing the prospect of a similar process in North America initiated by the free trade agreement between Canada, Mexico and the United States which has just been negotiated. These processes are bringing societies, with distinct cultures, social structures, and particular institutions into intimate contact with each other which many believe will end by merging social forms and requiring institutional conformity, and we need to know if this is the case and, if so, how it will happen. Second, the efforts of the former Communist countries in Eastern Europe to create market economies poses similar questions about the social and institutional preconditions of capitalism: will market-oriented firms emerge

naturally and spontaneously once the restraints upon private activity are removed, or are there certain institutional prerequisites for this process to occur? Can productive institutions which were created to operate in a planned economy be converted to operate effectively in a private system, or must they be scrapped and replaced? Third, in my own country, we find ourselves in intense competition with Japan, and to a lesser extent with Europe: managers, and a number of business analysts and scholars, believe that we are handicapped in this competition by the internal social and organizational structure of our economic institutions, and many companies have been attempting to adopt structural innovations modeled on those of other nations, and yet economists have a weak vocabulary for talking about these suppositions, let alone evaluating their plausibility and the public policies which might be associated with them. Fourth, the discipline of economics, partly in response to these practical questions, partly as a result of its own internal intellectual dynamic has become increasingly interested in international difference in institutional forms and in a theory which would explain them. In micro-economics, this interest is direct and explicit, spawning what is widely termed the new institutional economics. It is perhaps less obvious in macro-economics, but it is nonetheless evident in the revival of growth theory and the concern about alternative growth paths and regional economies. . . .

How might one integrate the insights of cognitive theory into conventional economics? At one level, the two theories are complementary. Cognitive structure is a precondition of rationality. In this sense, the behavior assumed in conventional theory is a subset of the broader behavioral theory generated by cognitive psychology. The behavior associated with the generation, conservation, and adjustment of cognitive structure is *arational or prerational.*

Clearly, there are a set of problems which conventional theory has been unable to address and for which cognitive theory promises a resolution. For labor economists, the most obvious of these is the "free rider" problem, the commitment of individuals to institutions and groups which cannot be explained by narrow self-interest, especially that of trade unions. For unions, the question is how to obtain enough of a commitment to maintain a dues-paying base and mount a credible strike threat when the benefits of union gains cannot be limited to those who participate and when the contribution of any single individual is too small to affect the outcome. For us, as analysts, the question is why unions are ever able to resolve this problem without some form of coercion. The answer which cognitive theory suggests is that, under some circumstances, individual commitment to the organization is the commitment in Kuhn's [1970] experiment to the deck of cards; it provides the context for our grasp on reality.

Cognitive theory must also provide the clues to explain that substantial portion of economic growth which cannot be explained in terms of the accumulation of resources or the efficiency with which they are used. We call that residual technological change. The term generically means the generation of new ideas and that is exactly what cognitive psychology as a theory is about.

But the fundamental question is whether the implications of cognitive theory can be confined to a set of problems which conventional theory does not address. In other words, can the domain of economic theory be partitioned in a neat and simple way so that conventional theory is preserved and we can continue to believe the stories which it tells about how to organize economic activity?

The structure of conventional theory, at least until recently, seemed to lend itself to this solution. The economy is conceived as a set of islands connected to each other through a market system. The islands are generally assumed to have their own information processing structures. But one could equally well assume that those structures are not given and that instead they evolve in time through some kind of process. So long as that process is independent of the process through which the islands communicate with each other, economists are not necessarily obligated to investigate it. One way in which that investigation could be avoided is simply to cede it to another discipline. The more elegant way—in terms of our claim to tell an important and complete story—is natural selection, to argue that the competitive market ensures an efficient evolutionary process for the society as a whole, whatever goes on in individual firms.

This approach no longer seems so satisfactory. Or, at least, we have increasingly violated the boundaries which it defines. One reason is that it is not so clear that the economy evolves through natural selection. We do not know exactly how much of the adjustment process is borne by changes within institutions and how much by the redistribution of activity among them, but one suspects that quite a bit takes place through internal adjustments. But we are ever more interested in internal adjustment because we are ever less indifferent to the distribution of the adjustment burden, and ever more concerned with facilitating internal adjustment, however much of the burden of adjustment they bear. In part, this must be because now more economists see their careers linked to business schools which, after all, are charged with managing the internal affairs of enterprises, not the relationships between them. But it is also because the concerns with which I initially tried to motivate this paper, i.e. the increasing economic integration of distinct cultural units and social entities within larger regional and international economies makes those with particular cultural attachments—which are basic to the human condition—care more and more about their survival. In any case, the discipline has clearly moved to break down the boundaries which institutions used to constitute for the application of individual maximizing models. We have failed in this process to say why those boundaries, which *we* are no longer willing to respect, exist in the first place, but I will not belabor this point.

However, if one thinks that cognitive structures and their ability to evolve over time are at stake, one can question whether the market model is satisfactory for understanding not only the internal operations of an institution, but also the relationship between institutions. It could well be that cognitive structures can most effectively evolve through the direct interaction of people who are separated in distinct institutions, that, in other words, for the dynamic evolution involved in economic growth, communication across institutions cannot be confined to price signals. The hermeneutic process suggests that this is indeed the case. The division of productive activity among institutions involves the partitioning of wholes into a set of separate elements or parts. If the nature of institutional barriers is such that we then restrict communication among the people responsible for the way in which the different parts are performed, we have broken the hermeneutic circle. In my own country, at least, one can argue that the organizational principles involved in Taylorism and Fordism have pushed us even further in this regard. They have led us to divide the internal structure of large organizations into a series of functionally distinct divisions as well. These divisions are not related to each other through a market but largely because there are not enough units performing any one function to create competition; there is, in the words of Oliver Williamson, a small numbers problem. But given the way in which activity is partitioned, the communications problem would otherwise lend itself to a market solution. As a result, the prevailing structure *does* lend itself to precisely the kind of organizational prescriptions which one gets from an economic theory which attempts to abstract the basic principles of a market and then simulate them with large organizations.

The tendencies have been still further exaggerated by other organization developments. One of these is professionalization, a process which anchors the division of labor of a given historical moment in a set of corporatist institutions outside the enterprises. Again, from the conventional perspective, the problem with this structure is that it forestalls competition. This diagnosis leads to remedies which simulate market incentives. But from the cognitive perspective, the problem is that it limits the hermeneutic process, the cycle back and forth between parts and wholes, through which cognitive structures evolve. And a simulated market solution, which depends upon stable categories to which price signals can be assigned, will maintain this effect.

The fragmentation of work can be taken as a further exaggeration of these same tendencies. It reduces particular jobs to such a small number of elements that the worker needs no abstract framework at all to understand the job. It can simply be memorized as a sequence of operations. Even job enlargement in this context comes to mean a multiplication in the repertoires of memorized operations. These repertoires can then be cued by price signals. They thus lend themselves to a simulated market mechanism. But knowledge understood in this way does not lend itself to cognitive evolution.

If one looks at innovations in business practice and the critique of existing organizational structures within the management literature, the thrust is in precisely the opposite direction. The attempt is to break down barriers between different organizations and within organizations between distinct divisions and departments, and encourage direct, rich and textured communication. Manufacturers are moving to reduce the number of subcontractors and the competition that occurs between them and develop close collaborative relations with those who remain. There is a movement to eliminate the in-process inventories which insulate subcontractors from their customers and different operations from each other in the internal production process, forcing people who previously operated at arm's length to confront coordination problems directly and resolve them cooperatively. Product development is shifting from a sequential organization to parallel engineering by teams. Large corporations are being restructured in the form of networks and matrices which involve the continual repositioning of different components and a renegotiation of lines of authority and patterns of communication.

These changes are being modeled on Japanese organizational innovations or production networks of central Italy and southern Germany which are reminiscent of Marshallian industrial districts. Whether these new organizational forms, or even the models upon which they are built, actually do resemble the forms prevailing in Japan or in Europe is debatable. What is significant is that they seem to be drawn from societies without the kind of institutionalized division of labor which we have created in the United States. And they seem to operate on the basis of principles which are very different than those upon which economic theory is built. What we need is not to apply market models to internal organizational problems but to apply the principles which might distinguish an institution internally to the way in which institutions interrelate with each other across their boundaries. We need, this would imply, not to extend the realm of conventional theory but to narrow it, indeed possibly to replace it in exactly those dimensions of economic organization in which it seems most relevant and most secure.

REFERENCE

Kuhn T. S. (1970) *The Structure of Scientific Revolutions,* Chicago: University of Chicago Press.

SOURCE: Piore, Michael J. 1993. Excerpt from "The Social Embeddedness of Labor Markets and Cognitive Processes." *Labour*, 7(3):3, 14–18.

12

DEFINING THE POST-BUREAUCRATIC TYPE

CHARLES HECKSCHER

THE LIMITS OF BUREAUCRACY

It is not easy to take even the first step in this analysis, which is to understand the limitations of the bureaucratic form. Engulfed by the current wave of criticism, we tend to forget its historically demonstrated strengths. Most critics, moreover, make a crucial mistake: They fail to distinguish which aspects of these problems are results of *badly managed* bureaucracy, and which are *inherent* in the model. For if the main issues are of the first type, then the solution is to tighten up the traditional systems—to "clean up" the bureaucracy. If, however, they are of the second type, the solution is a much more complex transformation.

The concept of bureaucracy has been so heavily treated in both popular and academic literature that only the highlights need be sketched. The major concepts articulated by Weber are the same ones still used by most managers in their conscious planning: rationality, accountability, and hierarchy.

For Weber, perhaps the central concept was the differentiation of person from *office:* That is, jobs were defined by the needs of the organization rather than by the people in them. This was one of the most important breaks with prior tradition, when nonbureaucratic tax collectors, for example, had the job as a personal possession and defined it according to their own interests.

Thus the key to bureaucracy is the rational definition of offices. In order to guarantee the functioning of the organization, each piece has to be clearly specified in terms of its duties and methods. The more complete the specification, the more confident the leaders can be that their orders will be interpreted correctly, rather than being distorted by personal interests.

The principal boundary or point of conflict in the early growth of bureaucracy was with "communal" systems dependent on personal relationships; in the business world these included partnerships, federations, and craft networks.[1] Except for isolated niches, bureaucracy won the battle hands down. It was far superior in organizing large numbers of people in a goal-directed effort.

The Red Herring of Badly Managed Bureaucracy

As the triumph of bureaucracy has been consolidated, there have emerged many "failures of the first type"—organizations that are badly managed. It is, for example, common for a successful bureaucracy to become complacent and lose its focus on the mechanisms that got it to its position of dominance. A *good* bureaucracy is not fat: It establishes positions through a careful analysis of tasks to be performed. It is not soft: It has strong control systems that establish goals and reward performance in achieving them. And it is not necessarily inflexible: It can respond rapidly to demands from the top. These principles are built into the classic theories of bureaucratic management and have always been manifest in successful large companies.

When a company succeeds too well, however, and pressure from the environment diminishes, its focus may become dulled. General Motors, under the leadership of Alfred Sloan in the 1920s and 1930s, was a model of a good bureaucracy, tightly managed through clear objectives and measurements. Later, with lack of real competition, it added fat and lost its ability to evaluate. These problems do not require great inventiveness to fix.

But this type of bureaucratic dysfunction is a major source of confusion and distraction. When one evaluates an organization as ineffective, there are two choices: to better enforce the bureaucratic pattern, or to seek another one altogether. Many of the efforts at "de-bureaucratization" are in fact nothing but efforts to get rid of the fat and waste of a badly managed system and return to the pure, clear model.

In order to justify the highly uncertain search for something entirely new, it must be clear that the problems of bureaucracy are more fundamental than this—that they are inherent even in *well-managed* systems.

The Fundamental Problem of Bureaucratic Segmentation

There is such an inherent and fundamental limitation of bureaucracy, one that derives from its very foundation in the specification of offices: That is that *people are responsible only for their own jobs.* The point of the system is that it divides work up into chunks and holds individuals accountable for different pieces. If they move beyond their specific realms, or seek to communicate outside of their appointed channels, they cause trouble: they confuse lines of responsibility and authority. The paradigm of a bureaucrat's attitude—a *good* one as well as a bad one—is, "That's not my job"; and

in the traditional organization, anyone who tries to break this bond will be *told*, "That's not your job." Improving bureaucratic management only makes this *more* true. Segmentation of responsibility is vital to the massive effectiveness of the structure.

This segmentation brings with it, however, a set of undesirable consequences.

The Waste of Intelligence

The first is that it systematically limits the use of intelligence by employees: The system uses only a small fraction of the capacity of its members.

The slotting of people into predefined offices would make full sense if, and only if, individuals were so matched to jobs by training and aptitude that the job used all their abilities.[2] But this is logically improbable, and by now it is clear that it is empirically false. Whenever employees, at whatever level, have been involved in decision making beyond the limits of the usual job descriptions, they have proved capable of developing improvements that their superiors could never do alone. This is the source of the success of Quality Circles and other shop floor participation groups: these have their limitations, but they *always* produce gains unforeseen by the industrial engineers whose "office" it is to maximize their effectiveness.

An essential assumption of bureaucracy is that the top managers can get into their heads all the necessary information to make the best possible decisions about the whole system; then the head can delegate pieces of implementation to people who are not so gifted. The top layer has a fundamentally different nature from the rest of the organization: It is the only place where the substantive questions of direction and strategy can be considered. All other levels deal only with implementation. In Weber's terms, this is a locus of charisma in the otherwise rational organization.

The alternative view is that strategy is best developed through a social process of discussion that uses the full intelligence of all. On purely logical grounds, it seems irrefutable that a successful mobilization of multiple intelligence will outdo any individual, no matter how smart. The issue then becomes an empirical one: Can such a system be made to work without falling into chaos?

The Formal-Informal Split

The second consequence of bureaucratic segmentation is a failure effectively to control the "informal" organization. The formal links of the bureaucratic structure are too impoverished to support the real work of organizations; if everyone really followed the rules, if everyone really went through the boss to work out relations with their peers, the system would grind to a halt. Indeed, unions have long demonstrated the effectiveness of the tactic of "working to rule"—following the formal structure of the organization to a T, which is even more devastating than a strike.

Therefore, a whole set of informal systems and relationships is essential if a bureaucracy is to work at all. But these informal systems are "hidden," as it were, from the control systems, comprising the ambiguous realm of "politics." These dynamics often do work in support of the organization, as has been convincingly demonstrated in the case of blue-collar work: The development and application of "working knowledge" even in assembly-line operations is necessary to smooth functioning, and not even the tightest bureaucratic controls can make it unnecessary.[3] At the professional and managerial levels of organizations, where the need for cooperation and the difficulty of control are much higher, the political realm is still more critical.[4]

In other cases, of course, "politics" works against the organization. At the blue-collar level it can become organized rate-setting or "soldiering"; among managers and professionals it can turn into empire-building and private deal-making. Such patterns are remarkably impervious to bureaucratic control. The famous management theorist Frederick Taylor devoted his life to stamping out "soldiering" by taking rational bureaucracy to new levels—trying to specify tasks so exactly, and enforce them so strongly, that the informal organization would be destroyed. He succeeded in driving the rate-setting practices further underground, but he never succeeded in eliminating them: they remain a major feature of factory work to this day. Efforts to rationalize away white-collar politics have met with no greater success.

The art of "leadership" in a bureaucracy is largely a matter of understanding these subterranean processes—"how things really work around here"—and turn them toward support of collective goals. Nevertheless, this domain—the world of lateral connections beyond a single manager's authority—remains detached from the control systems of bureaucracy. There is little formal attempt to structure informal "politics"; compared to the steady development and learning about bureaucratic structures, this realm remains stunted, with little cumulative learning.

Even in the most favorable cases, under the best leadership, lateral politics are systematically limited: They do not maximally contribute to the functioning of the organization:

1. They are built from personal contacts and are dependent on accidents of friendship and personal trust. Thus they do not necessarily involve those with knowledge relevant to a decision; the political network follows paths defined by other, more personal criteria.

2. They generally function only in homogeneous groups, ones in which the members can easily trust each other because of their similarity; this is the source of exclusive "old-boys' networks." One of the great problems in integrating minority groups is that they disrupt the personal links that make organizational cooperation possible, thus pushing the structure toward more formal and "bureaucratic" systems.

3. The informal networks are built from series of one-to-one relationships; the building of *group* associations outside the hierarchy is viewed as especially threatening. People may view themselves as part of a category—"the programmers," "the old-timers," and so on—but they do not act in a concerted manner. Thus, achieving a coherent team effort across bureaucratic boundaries is extremely difficult.

4. When conflict among different groupings does emerge, as in the case study described by Pettigrew (1973), there are few mechanisms for resolving the dispute. Because the groupings themselves are unacknowledged by the formal organization, there is no way to discuss the differences. The conflict remains a matter of water-cooler conversation rather than open dialogue, and it is dealt with through backroom maneuvering and horse-trading.

5. When there are differences in view between levels of the hierarchy, a vicious cycle of power and resistance is easily set up. Middle managers, for

example, often disagree with the dictates of the top: sometimes this is for "good" reasons (they know important things that the top does not) and sometimes for "bad" (they are resisting changes that might disrupt their domains). But in either case, it is difficult to overcome the misunderstanding.

The Crudeness of Organization Change

The third limitation of even the best bureaucracies concerns their pattern of change and adaptation: They do not effectively manage processes over time.

The common claim that bureaucracy is inflexible cannot be entirely accepted: One of the great successes of the structure was that, unlike traditional craft systems, it was able to respond quickly to changing commands from the top. And the differentiation of a strategic level of management, one of Alfred Sloan's major innovations, made it more possible than before to separate long-term issues from the daily pressures of operational management. Yet there remains a clumsiness about the process of change that has become increasingly visible in recent years.

Bureaucracies tend to evolve not smoothly, but in fits and starts: Periods of routine are punctuated by intense periods of revolution from above. This results, again, primarily from the segmented structure: By design, only the top of the organization has a full picture of the whole plan of change. Those lower down see only the pieces that they are "assigned"; they are unable to adapt smoothly to the inevitable shifts in relations to other parts of the organization and have to refer problems for formal resolution to their bosses. This results in a tremendous grinding of the gears.

Another way of putting this is that, as we have seen, management operates primarily through formal structure; change therefore almost always involves "restructuring." And restructuring—the shifting of job responsibilities and offices—is always a highly painful and disruptive process. The possibility of smoother, more gradual evolution is limited by the formalism of the system.[5]

The limitation of vision to the top further means that change in a bureaucracy is entwined with the charisma of top leaders, who necessarily have a very limited time in office to realize their aspirations. Thus the pacing and timing of change is forced into an artificially narrow range of possibilities.

Finally, the rigidity of the segmental structure typically results in a tendency toward inertia and *gradual degeneration over time,* which can only be countered by sudden and dramatic "shaking-up" from above. The reasons for this degeneration are several:

1. Rules tend to accumulate: Whenever a mistake is made, a rule is made to prevent its recurrence; but there is no process for undoing it again.

2. Operational responsibility tends to drift upward for much the same reason: When mistakes are made, higher levels take over direct review of that domain. Then there is no clear point or reason within the bureaucratic logic to push it down again.

3. Rules become "sanctified" rather than a means to an end. In bureaucracy, after all, people are *supposed* to be responsible for the rules but neutral with regard to the whole. The psychological tendency to identify with one's responsibility therefore leads to the emotional attachment to bureaucratic rules rather than to the wider goals.[6]

These dynamics, accumulating slowly, inevitably bring out the worst aspects of bureaucracy and bury the best. Then what happens is a "restructuring": the top levels see the irrationalities and try to re-balance the system. Bureaucracy therefore tends to move in fits and starts, accumulating little dysfunctions until it is reorganized and shaken from top to bottom.

There is a growing sense that effective organization change has its own dynamic, a process that cannot simply follow strategic shifts and that is longer and subtler than can be managed by any single leader. It is generated from the insights of many people trying to improve the whole, and it accumulates, is it were, over long periods. Dramatic moments of "revolutionary" transformation are only a small piece of it, and often are not the most effective way to bring about change.[7] If this is true—and there is much reason to believe it is—the bureaucratic structures are not the most effective ones for managing the process.

The Post-Bureaucratic Model

The Ideal Type

This definition of the weaknesses of bureaucracy brings the desired change into focus. The master concept is *an organization in which everyone takes responsibility for the success of the whole.* If that happens, then the basic notion of regulating relations among people by *separating* them into specific, predefined functions must be abandoned. The problem is to create a system in which people can enter into relations that are determined by problems rather than predetermined by the structure. Thus, organization control must center not on the management of tasks but the management of relationships; in effect, "politics" must be brought into the open.

This suggests a positive name to replace *post-bureaucratic:* Because of the crucial role of back-and-forth dialogue rather than one-way communication or command, I will call it the *interactive* type.[8] The set of mechanisms that drew our attention in the introduction all have to do with achieving effective organized action without the "prop" of a positional framework to predetermine the key relations: they are essentially structures that develop *informed consensus* rather than relying on hierarchy and authority. Examples of such mechanisms in industry include all kinds of consensus-based committees: task forces, product development teams, and problem-solving groups. These involve all those concerned with a given issue in discussion, gathering of information, and development of agreement.

In order to accomplish this basic shift, we can derive—both from theory and from the admittedly incomplete examples—the following conceptual description:

1. In bureaucracies, consensus of a kind is created through acquiescence to authority, rules, or traditions. In the post-bureaucratic form it is created through institutionalized dialogue.[9]

2. Dialogue is defined by the use of influence rather than power: That is, people affect decisions based on their ability to persuade rather than their ability to command.[10] The ability to persuade is based on a number of factors, including knowledge of the issue, commitment to shared goals, and proven past effectiveness. It is not, however, based significantly on official position. Relations of influence can and do form a hierarchy: some people are more persuasive than others. Thus this system is not in any strict sense "egalitarian." But the influence hierarchy is not embedded in permanent offices, and is to a far greater degree than bureaucracy based on the consent of, and the perceptions of, other members of the organization.

3. Influence depends initially on trust—on the belief by all members that others are seeking mutual benefit rather than maximizing personal gain. Without this basic trust, persuasion is impossible, because everyone assumes that others are trying to "put one over" on them. A system stressing influence must have a higher level of internal trust than one based on command and power. The major source of this kind of trust is interdependence: an understanding that the fortunes of all depend on combining the performances of all. Specifically, in a business, it derives from an understanding of the ways in which different parts of the organization contribute to the accomplishment of the overall strategy.

4. Because interdependence around strategy is the key integrator, there is a strong emphasis on organizational *mission.* The trend has been to focus on what the company actually seeks to achieve rather than on universalistic statements of values. It is often hard for an outsider to understand what all the effort is about: Most mission statements seem remarkably innocuous. They say something about improving quality and cutting costs, and something about the kind of business the company is in—rarely anything surprising. But the mission plays a crucial integrating role in an organization that relies less heavily on job definitions and rules. Employees need to understand the key objectives in depth in order to coordinate their actions intelligently "on the fly."

5. In order to link individual contributions to the mission, there is widespread sharing of information about corporate strategy, and an attempt to make conscious the connection between individual jobs and the mission of the whole. This enables individuals to break free of the boundaries of their "defined" jobs and to think creatively and cooperatively about improvements in performance. In the past decade, companies have greatly increased the dissemination of information about systemwide performance, even to blue-collar employees. A decade ago very few companies gave productivity data to blue-collar employees; now it is common. And even at the present day, in my own research, I have found most middle managers struggling to cope with the flood of new information about strategy and mission that they have been asked to absorb. Information technology has greatly facilitated the dissemination of information. Since computer networks tend to be quite open, this information often flows not just from the top down but is criticized and added to from the bottom up.

This process increases the *credibility* of the data being shared.

6. The focus on mission must be supplemented by guidelines for action: these, however, take the form of *principles* rather than rules. The difference is that principles are more abstract, expressing the *reasons behind* the rules that are typical of bureaucracy. The use of principles carries a major advantage and a major danger. The advantage is that principles allow for flexibility and intelligent response to changing circumstances: People are asked to think about the reasons for constraints on their actions, rather than rigidly following procedures. The danger is that this flexibility can be intentionally or unintentionally abused, threatening the integration of the system. The dangers are reduced by two mechanisms: the creation of trust, derived especially from a clear understanding of the interdependence among all; and by periodic reviews and discussions of the principles to be sure that they accurately capture what is needed and have not been distorted. Post-bureaucratic organizations spend a great deal of time developing and reviewing principles of action.

7. Because of the fluidity of influence relations by comparison to offices and authority, decision-making processes must be frequently reconstructed; they cannot be directly "read" from an organization chart. The choice of "who to go to" is determined by the nature of the problem, not by the positions of those initially raising it. Thus, processes are needed for *deciding how to decide*—what might be called "meta-decision-making" mechanisms. In a number of companies there are cross-functional and perhaps cross-level committees that sort issues and try to develop appropriate processes for each of them. To choose a single example: At a Shell plant in Canada, issues that cannot be dealt with by individual teams of workers go to a "team norm review board" composed of operators, union officials, and managers; this committee then establishes a way of resolving the problem—they may, for example, set up a sub-committee, or a series of meetings of the affected groups, or call for additional information from inside or outside, or some combination of these tactics.

8. Though relationships of trust are a critical ingredient in these systems, these are not the warm *gemeinschaft* solidarities of traditional communities, or even of the communal version of bureaucracy. Relationships in such a system are formalized and specialized to a high degree: it is a matter of "knowing who to go to" for a particular problem or issue, rather than a matter of building a stable network of friendship relations. Thus influence relations are wider and more diverse, but also shallower and more specific, than those of traditional "community."[11] Managers in systems moving toward a more interactive form often report a sense of loneliness and isolation, in comparison to the "old days" of communal bureaucracy.[12] Information systems have also facilitated the building of temporary networks. It is now possible in some companies for managers to put out a general message asking for help on a given project, or to collect a list of people who have knowledge and experience in the area: they can maintain contacts with people whom they never meet face to face.

9. In order for a system of influence to function, there must be ways of verifying and publicizing reputations. There must, therefore, be unusually thorough and open processes of association and peer evaluation, so that people get a relatively detailed view of each others' strengths and weaknesses. Perhaps the best example of such systems in industry is in investment banking: in many such firms people work in a wide variety of peer teams and are constantly involved in mutual evaluation.[13]

10. A post-bureaucratic system is relatively open at the boundaries. A critical manifestation of this is career patterns: Unlike the situation in large bureaucracies, there is no expectation that employees will spend their entire careers in one organization. There is far more tolerance for outsiders coming in and for insiders going out. This ingredient of the pattern has recently caused great distress in the closed communities of the corporate management. The competitive pressures of the 1980s have caused widespread managerial layoffs for the first time, and simultaneously the speed of technical innovation has required increased hiring of outsiders. Both these developments have threatened the "family" atmosphere that has fostered unity and cooperation in the past. A second aspect of "openness" is the growth of alliances and joint ventures among different firms. These have been growing explosively in recent years even among firms, such as AT&T or IBM, which have had a long tradition of "going it alone."

11. The problem of equity acquires some new wrinkles. In a bureaucratic system, the main touchstone is always objectivity and equality of treatment: Thus,

there is a constant effort to devise rules for treatment of employees, and to minimize the element of personal judgment. In a post-bureaucratic order there is first of all an effort to reduce rules, and concomitantly an increased pressure to recognize the variety of individual performances. This is a major point of tension in many innovating companies at the moment. It is likely that the solution involves the development *of public standards* of performance, openly discussed and often negotiated with individual employees, against which they will be measured; this is an apparently increasingly common approach to compensation.

12. Time is structured in a distinctly different way from a bureaucracy. In the latter, decisions are made with an expectation of permanence: "This is the right way of doing things." Review processes occur at regular intervals, usually annually in a budgeting process, as a way of checking that things are functioning as they should—but not with the anticipation of making fundamental changes. Thus, structural change in bureaucracy comes as something of a surprise, as a dramatic "break" in the flow of events. A post-bureaucratic system, by contrast, builds in an expectation of constant change, and it therefore attaches time frames to its actions. One element in structuring a process is to determine checkpoints for reviewing progress and for making corrections, and establishing a time period for reevaluating the basic direction and principles of the effort. These time periods are not necessarily keyed to the annual budget cycle: They may be much shorter or much longer, depending on the nature of the task. This flexibility of time is essential to adaptiveness because the perception of a problem depends on putting it in the right time frame. If one focuses—as most managers do—on the issues that must be dealt with in the next week, one will simply never recognize the existence of issues that have a longer "cycle time"; and of course the reverse is equally true. The ability to manage varying time frames is a major advantage of the post-bureaucratic system.

Notes

1. See Chandler (1977, 1981, 1988); Daems (1980); Lazonick (1987); Shorter (1973).

2. In a rather bizarre turn of logic, Elliott Jaques's 1990 defense of bureaucracy comes to just such a conclusion. He argues that different levels of good bureaucracies are marked by different time horizons—the higher up in the organization, the longer the view. Then he argues that there are different types of people who, it so happens, have innate capacities to handle just these different time horizons. The first assertion has a lot of evidence behind it, but the second does not.

3. On the importance of "working knowledge" and informal cooperation among blue-collar workers, see Mathewson (1931); Kaboolian (1991); Kusterer (1978).

4. On informal vs. formal organization, see for example Whyte (1956); Kanter (1977); Rubin (1976); Selznick (1949); Krackhardt (1991); Deinard and Friedman (1990); Blau (1963); Manning (1977); Blankenship (1977), ch. 10; Walton and Hackman (1985); Weir (1973); Alvarez (1991).

5. Henry Mintzberg's (with Raisinghani and Théorêt) study (1976) of change processes notes that "political" shifts, involving this kind of restructuring of offices, brings many efforts to grief.

6. The classic analysis of this dynamic of bureaucratic personality is Merton (1940). See also Veblen (1904).

7. On the inadequacy of the top-down description of planning, see for example Burgelman (1983); Pattee (1973); Golden (1990); Mintzberg and McHugh (1985); Hayes (1986).

8. Others have the term *interactive* in ways related to this—most especially the firm Interaction Associates, which is one of the more advanced consulting groups in this area, and Russ Ackoff (1981), whose concept of "interactive planning" is very consistent with the direction of the chapter.

9. The concept of "dialogue" in this analysis owes much to Habermas's concept of "ideal speech." It is, however, considerably more concrete and less ideal; the types of consensus and discussion found in even the most "advanced" forms of associational organization are far from fully undistorted communication. See Habermas (1991).

10. See Parsons (1969), ch. 14 and ch. 15.

11. A recent literature originating with Granovetter (1973) has uncovered the importance of "weak ties"—relations that are not communal and exclusive, but open and more shallow—in holding networks together.

12. A number of theorists have in different ways made a distinction between "personal trust"—the traditional friendship or family relationship—and "system trust," which is a depersonalized faith in the functioning of a larger order. (See, e.g., Luhmann, 1979; Silver, 1985; Zucker, 1986; Shapiro, 1987.) I am here adding a third category: a form of one that is *personal,* in the sense that it is specific to a given individual, and yet *specific* rather than diffuse. A major component of post-bureaucratic

organization is a network of relationships based on specific performances and abilities, rather than on friendship; people one can "work with" on particular projects rather than "live with." The closest concept in the literature that I am familiar with is, as mentioned earlier, Granovetter's (1973) notion of "weak ties"—though these are perhaps weaker than I mean!

13. See Eccles and Crane (1987).

REFERENCES

Ackoff, R. L. (1981). *Creating the corporate future: Plan or be planned for.* New York: Wiley.

Alvarez, J. L. A. (1991). *The international diffusion and institutionalization of the new entrepreneurship movement: A study in the sociology of organizational knowledge.* Cambridge, MA: Ph.D. dissertation in Organizational Behavior.

Blankenship, R. L. (Ed.). (1977). *Colleagues in organization: The social construction of professional work.* New York: Wiley.

Blau, P. M. (1963). *The dynamics of bureaucracy.* Chicago. IL: University of Chicago Press.

Burgelman, R. A. (1983). A process model of internal corporate venturing in the diversified major firm. *Administrative Science Quarterly, 28,* 223–224.

Chandler, A. D., Jr. (1977). *The visible hand: The managerial revolution in American business.* Cambridge, MA: Harvard University Press.

Chandler, A. D., Jr. (1981). Historical determinants of managerial hierarchies: A response to Perrow. In A. H. Van de Van & W. F. Joyce (Eds.), *Perspectives on organization design and behavior.* New York: Wiley. [Reprinted in Chandler (1988)]

Chandler, A. D., Jr. (1988). *The essential Alfred Chandler: Essays toward a historical theory of big business.* Boston: Harvard Business School Press.

Daems, H. (1980). The rise of the modern industrial enterprise: A new perspective. In A. D. Chandler & H. Daems (Eds.), *Managerial hierarchies: Comparative perspectives on the rite of modern industrial enterprises* (pp. 203–223). Cambridge, MA: Harvard University Press.

Deinard, C., & Friedman, R. (1990). *Black caucus groups at Xerox Corporation (A) and (B).* Boston, MA: Harvard Business School.

Eccles, R. G., & Crane, D. B. (1987, Fall). Managing through networks in investment banking. *California Management Review, 30*(1), 176–195.

Golden, O. (1990). Innovation in public sector human services programs: The implications of innovation by "groping along." *Journal of Policy Analysis and Management, 9*(2), 219–248.

Granovetter, M. S. (1973). The strength of weak ties. *American Journal of Sociology, 78*(6), 1360–1380.

Habermas, J. (1991). *Communication and the evolution of society.* Translated and with an introduction by Thomas McCarthy. Cambridge, UK: Polity Press.

Hayes, R. H. (1986, April 20). Why strategic planning goes awry. *New York Times.*

Jaques, E. (1990, January–February). In praise of hierarchy. *Harvard Business Review,* pp. 127–33.

Kaboolian, L. (1991). *How is effort determined?* Mimeo. Harvard Kennedy School of Government, Cambridge.

Kanter, R. M. (1977). *Men and women of the corporation.* New York: Basic Books.

Krackhardt, D. (1991, February). *Does informal structure make a difference? The relationship between social networks and bank branch performance.* Mimeo. Harvard University.

Kusterer, K. C. (1978). *Know-how on the job: The important working knowledge of 'unskilled' workers.* Boulder, CO: Westview Press.

Lazonick, W. (1987). *Organization capability and technological change in comparative perspective.* Mimeo, draft.

Luhmann, N. (1979). *Trust and power.* New York: Wiley. (Orig. German eds. in 1973 and 1975.)

Manning, P. K. (1977). Rules, colleagues, and situationally justified actions. In R. L. Blankenship (Ed.), *Colleagues in organization: The social construction of professional work* (ch. 10). New York: Wiley.

Mathewson, S. B. (1931). *Restriction of output among unorganized workers.* New York: Viking.

Merton, R. K. (1940). Bureaucratic structure and personality. *Social Forces, 17,* 560–568.

Mintzberg, H., & McHugh, A. (1985). Strategy formation in an adhocracy. *Administrative Science Quarterly, 30,* 160–197.

Mintzberg, H., Raisinghani, D., & Théorêt, A. (1976, June). The structure of "unstructured" decision processes. *Administrative Science Quarterly, 21,* 246–275.

Parsons, T. (1969). *Politics and social structure.* New York: The Free Press.

Pattee, H. H. (1973). *Hierarchy theory: The challenge of complex systems.* New York: George Braziller.

Pettigrew, A. M. (1973). *The politics of organizational decision-making.* London: Tavistock.

Rubin, L. B. (1976). *Worlds of pain: Life in the working-class family.* New York: Basic Books.

Selznick, P. (1949). *TVA and the grass roots: A study in the sociology of formal organizations.* Berkeley, CA: University of California Press.

Shapiro, S. P. (1987, November). The social control of impersonal trust. *American Journal of Sociology, 93*(3), 623–658.

Shorter, E. (1973). The history of work in the West: An overview. In E. Shorter (Ed.), *Work and community in the West* (ch. 1). New York: Harper & Row.

Silver, A. (1985). "Trust" in social and political theory. In Suttles, G. D. & Zald, M. N. (Eds.), *The challenge of social control* (ch. 4). Norwood, NJ: Ablex.

Veblen, T. (1904). *The theory of business enterprise.* New York: Scribner's.

Walton, R. E., & Hackman, J. R. (1985, July). *Implications of management strategy for groups in organizations.* Harvard Business School working paper.

Weir, S. (1973). The informal work group. In A. Lynd & S. Lynd (Eds.), *Rank & file: Personal histories by working-class organizers* (pp. 177–200). Boston, MA: Beacon Press.

Whyte, W. H., Jr. (1956). *The organization man.* New York: Simon & Schuster.

Zucker, L. G. (1986). Production of trust: Institutional sources of economic structure, 1840–1920. *Research in Organizational Behavior, 8,* 53–111.

SOURCE: Heckscher, Charles. 1994. Excerpt from "Defining the Post-Bureaucratic Type." Pp. 18–28 in *The Post-Bureaucratic Organization.* Thousand Oaks, CA: Sage.

13

TWO TYPES OF BUREAUCRACY

Enabling and Coercive

PAUL S. ADLER AND BRYAN BORYS

Organizational research presents two conflicting views of the human, or attitudinal, outcomes of bureaucracy. According to the negative view, the bureaucratic form of organization stifles creativity, fosters dissatisfaction, and demotivates employees. According to the positive view, it provides needed guidance and clarifies responsibilities, thereby easing role stress and helping individuals be and feel more effective. This article develops a partial reconciliation of these two views with a new conceptual model.

There is a practical need for some theoretical reconciliation. Notwithstanding the burgeoning literature on the demise of the bureaucratic form of organization (e.g., Dumaine, 1991; Heckscher and Donnellon, 1994), surveys show that the vast majority of employees work in establishments with extensive formal procedures: over 74 percent have written job descriptions, and 80 percent have rules and procedures manuals (Marsden, Cook, and Knoke, 1994). Managers of such organizations are pulled in contradictory directions by conflicting recommendations. Lawler (1994) highlighted the tensions between the recommendations of total quality management (TQM) and employee involvement (EI) currently offered practitioners. TQM's emphasis

on work process codification seems to contradict EI's focus on increasing employee discretion, a contradiction similar to that between the "lean" and "team" approaches described by Applebaum and Batt (1994). The conflict between these approaches is particularly visible in the debate over appropriate organizational and job designs in repetitive operations such as auto assembly (e.g., Womack, Jones, and Roos, 1990; Berggren, 1992; Adler and Cole, 1993). Similar debates concern the organization of far less repetitive activities such as software development (Cusumano, 1991; Lecht, 1991; Soat, 1991). These debates reflect contradictory assessments of the core features of the bureaucratic form—workflow formalization, specialization, and hierarchy.

We seek to identify and reconcile the valid elements of these assessments. We focus on workflow formalization and reserve for the conclusion some thoughts on how our analysis can be extended to encompass other dimensions of bureaucracy. Formalization—the extent of written rules, procedures, and instructions— is a central feature of Weber's bureaucratic ideal type and an extensively researched dimension of organizational structure (Pugh and Hickson, 1976; Mintzberg, 1979). This research, however, has started often from conflicting theoretical premises and resulted in conflicting empirical findings. We argue that this divergence reflects the fact that while research to date has focused on the impact of different degrees of formalization, it has paid insufficient attention to different types of formalization. If we interpret formalization as an organizational technology, we can draw inspiration from recent research on the design of equipment technology to differentiate two generic types of formalization—formalization designed to enable employees to master their tasks, and formalization designed to coerce effort and compliance from employees. The attitudinal outcomes are likely very different.

FORMALIZATION

Research on the attitudinal effects of formalization has generated contradictory assessments. The basic divergence can be traced back to what many commentators, starting with Parsons (1947: 58), believe to be a profound ambiguity in Weber's analysis. Weber (1947: 339) identified two very different sources of authority in bureaucracies: "incumbency in a legally defined office" and "the exercise of control on the basis of knowledge." Gouldner (1954: 22–23) believed that Weber "thought of bureaucracy as a Janus-faced organization, looking two ways at once," since on the one hand, "it was administration based on discipline," and, on the other, "an individual obeys because the rule of order is felt to be the best known method of realizing some goal." Subsequent research on the functions and effects of bureaucracy has split correspondingly, with one branch focused on its power to enforce compliance from employees assumed to be recalcitrant or irresponsible and the other branch focused on bureaucracy's technical efficiency.[1]

Negative Assessments

The coercive function of bureaucracy is highlighted if one assumes that all organization is essentially coercive because organization entails an abrogation of individual autonomy. In employing organizations, the centrality of bureaucracy's coercive function is further emphasized by the economists' standard assumption that work is a disutility. Such assumptions seem to underlie Mintzberg's (1979) assertion that formalized work procedures in "machine bureaucracies" must be imposed on employees by staff experts. The coercive function can also be posited on a less psychological and more sociopolitical foundation: neo-Marxists such as Clawson (1980) have argued that the asymmetries of power and divergence of economic interests in capitalist firms inevitably turn formalization into a coercive mechanism.

Types of Bureaucracy

Negative assessments of formalization's effects on employees' well-being abound. Rousseau (1978) studied several departments in an electronics firm and a radio station and found formalization (written rules and procedures governing employee activities) positively related to absences, propensity to leave, physical and psychological stress, and negatively related to innovation and job satisfaction. In studies of social service workers, Arches (1991) found formalization negatively associated with job satisfaction, and Kakabadse (1986) found formalization of tasks and work processes positively associated with feelings of powerlessness and self-estrangement. Bonjean and Grimes (1970) found formalization of procedures and rules positively related to self-estrangement, anomie, and a general measure of alienation for a sample of blue-collar workers.

Much of the human resource management literature is consistent with this negative assessment. In Walton's (1985: 38) "new commitment" model of HRM, for example, coordination and control are "based more on shared goals, values, and traditions," in contrast to the "traditional control model," which relies on "rules and procedures." Walton assumed that rules and procedures substitute for, rather than complement or encourage, employee commitment. The main alternatives to a coercive, command-and-control method of management are ones that are low on bureaucracy and formalization scales—organizational forms characterized variously as antibureaucratic (Bennis and Slater, 1968), as organic rather than mechanistic (Burns and Stalker, 1961), and associated with a Theory Y rather than Theory X management style (McGregor, 1960).

If formalization undermines employees' commitment and fosters dissatisfaction, it follows that it also limits innovation, since employees in formalized settings have little motivation to contribute to the complex nonroutine tasks that constitute innovation. Burns and Stalker (1961), Thompson (1965), and Bennis (1966) are emblematic of a large literature arguing that bureaucracy is an ineffective form of organization for dealing with innovation, change, and environmental complexity. Refining this global assessment, others have argued that bureaucracies do well in the implementation of innovations but poorly in the generation of innovations (Pierce and Delbecq, 1977; Zaltman, Duncan, and Holbek, 1973). Much of the literature on the sociology of scientists and engineers asserts that employees in these occupations typically aspire to high levels of autonomy in their work and that bureaucratic formalization undermines their commitment and innovation effectiveness (Kornhauser, 1962; Ritti, 1971; Bailyn, 1985; Raelin, 1985).

Positive Assessments

A second, more positive stream of research highlights the technical function of bureaucracy. Here the assumption is that work can be fulfilling, rather than a disutility, and that organization can be experienced as a cooperative endeavor rather than as an abrogation of autonomy. If employees see at least some overlap between their goals and those of the organization as a whole, they might also welcome the potential contribution of formalization to efficiency. Under these assumptions, employees will embrace formal work procedures that are appropriately designed and implemented. Well-designed procedures would facilitate task performance and thus augment employees' pride of workmanship (Deming, 1986). Invoking or implying assumptions such as these, many writers in the operations management field, such as Deming (1986) and Schonberger (1986), have endorsed formalized systems such as statistical quality control and total quality management.

Role stress theory provides one possible underlying mechanism for a positive relationship between formalization and attitudinal outcomes (Kahn et al., 1964). Numerous studies in this vein have shown that formalization reduces role conflict and ambiguity, thereby increasing work satisfaction and

reducing feelings of alienation and stress (for a review, see Jackson and Schuler, 1985). In their study of technical professionals, Organ and Greene (1981) found that the negative correlation of formalization (of standard practices, job descriptions, and policies) with role ambiguity more than offset a positive correlation with role conflict; on balance, formalization reduced feelings of alienation. Podsakoff, Williams, and Todor (1986) replicated this study for both a broader sample of professionals and for a sample of nonprofessional employees, finding that in both groups formalization reduced both role conflict and role ambiguity and thereby reduced alienation. In their study of supervisors in data processing and manufacturing, Nicholson and Goh (1983) found that formalization of tasks and work processes was negatively correlated with role conflict and role ambiguity in both samples, although the relationships were stronger for the manufacturing sample than for the data processing sample. In his study of auditing professionals, Senatra (1980) found that formalization of rules and procedures reduced role conflict even more than it reduced role ambiguity.

Other research that does not explicitly invoke role stress as the mediating variable has generated results that lean in the same, positive direction. Michaels et al. (1988) found formalization of work activities positively associated with commitment and negatively associated with alienation among industrial salespeople. Snizek and Bullard (1983) found formalization of work procedures positively related to job satisfaction among forest rangers. Stevens, Diedriks, and Philipsen (1992) found formalization of work activities positively related to satisfaction among physicians. Maslach and Pines (1978) and Pines and Maslach (1980) found that in more structured daycare programs employees experienced less emotional exhaustion.

Even the frequently asserted negative impact of formalization on innovativeness is not uncontested. In the meta-analysis reported by Damanpour (1991), the commonly hypothesized negative relationship between innovation and formalization held for most studies of service and not-for-profit organizations and for innovations of higher scope, but the preponderance of the evidence pointed to a positive, not negative, correlation between formalization and innovation in manufacturing and for-profit organizations and for both product and process innovations. Procedures appear to facilitate innovation when they capture lessons of prior experience and when they help coordinate larger-scale projects (e.g., Craig, 1995). Scientists and engineers might prefer less formalization ceteris paribus, but if the use of such procedures to formalize the more routine parts of their task set enhances their effectiveness and their subjective self-efficacy (Bandura, 1977), they could be expected to embrace formalization.

Contingency Theory's Contribution and Limits

The divergent assessments of formalization could be resolved if it could be shown that each holds under different circumstances. Contingency theorists (Thompson, 1967; Lawrence and Lorsch, 1967; Galbraith, 1977) have taken a step in this direction by arguing that many of the previously cited models of the relationship between formalization and attitudinal outcomes are misspecified, since they control for the characteristics of neither the tasks nor the employees. The addition of these variables, we argue, clarifies but does not resolve the debate.

According to contingency theory, negative attitudinal outcomes attributed to formalization are often due to a misalignment of task requirements and organization/job design. Employees will react positively both when high levels of formalization are associated with routine tasks and when low levels of formalization are associated with nonroutine tasks. If, however, work is too formalized for the task at hand—if there are too many procedures too rigidly applied—all the outcomes invoked by the critics of formalization should be expected. The lack of autonomy and control will create feelings of dissatisfaction and demotivation. Contingency theorists have been less forthcoming about processes underlying the attitudinal effects of underformalization, but Morse and Lorsch (1970) suggested that underformalization will impair employees' sense of competence.

Unfortunately, relatively few studies have sought to control for task routineness directly, and the results of these studies are often inconclusive if only for technical reasons such as collinearity among variables (e.g., Pennings, 1975; Dewar and Werbel,

1979). With perhaps the sole exception of Engel (1969), researchers have not followed the advice of James and Jones (1976) and tested directly the hypothesis that attitudinal outcomes exhibit a curvilinear relationship to the degree of formalization for a given level of task routineness.

While empirical tests of better specified models would certainly be valuable, the contingency-theoretic account does not resolve the central theoretical issue of the controversy. It is easy enough for the critics of formalization to agree that most employees will feel relatively more satisfied performing nonroutine tasks under conditions of low formalization. The critics can also agree that the underformalization of very routine tasks will generate strain. But the critics disagree with the argument that employees will feel positively about performing routine tasks under conditions of high formalization. This, they would argue, presumes a very high degree of goal congruence between employees and employers, a condition that the critics believe rarely obtains. For mainstream theories of organizational power (e.g., Cyert and March, 1963; Pfeffer, 1981), goal congruence is highly unlikely, since in an open system there is no mechanism to guarantee that the goals defined by a dominant coalition will be consistent with the goals of other groups in the organization. For neo-Marxists, a divergence of goals reflects an inevitable contradiction of class interests (e.g., Braverman, 1974; Edwards, 1979; Clawson, 1980).

Contingency theorists have also argued that poor employee selection is often to blame for negative outcomes attributed to formalization. If organizations performing routine tasks select employees who have only an instrumental attitude to work and manifest only low growth-needs strength, such employees will not react negatively to the extensive formalization and Theory X style of management that such tasks call for (Hackman and Oldham, 1980; Bowen and Lawler, 1992). With this argument, however, contingency theory comes close to capitulating to the critics' position, because it assumes that at best, employee selection might neutralize strong negative attitudinal outcomes. Contingency theory is essentially pessimistic in its assessment of formalization insofar as it predicts that with the appropriate employee selection, high levels of formalization in the performance of routine tasks will lead to employee motivation and commitment levels that are at best weakly positive.

TWO TYPES OF FORMALIZATION: ENABLING AND COERCIVE

Something is missing from these accounts: Surely employees' attitudes to formalization depend on the attributes of the type of formalization with which they are confronted. Organizational researchers have noted that people particularly resent what they consider "bad" rules, while "good" rules are taken for granted and rarely noticed (Perrow, 1986: 24). The variable proportion of good to bad procedures across organizations might help account for the fact that studies of formalization typically explain only a small proportion of its attitudinal impacts, reflecting the fact that employee attitudes differ considerably across organizations with comparably high levels of formalization—even in cases in which task routineness is high. Organizational theory has had little to say, however, about the criteria that shape subordinates' assessments of rules as "good" or "bad." To the extent that such a distinction is made in the literature, it is as untheorized common sense. The primary thrust of this paper is to develop a useful theory of how employees distinguish good from bad rules.

Gouldner's (1954) contrast of three different patterns of bureaucracy is a possible starting point. A pattern Gouldner called representative bureaucracy obtains when rules serve the interests of both managers and workers (e.g., safety rules). A pattern of punishment-centered bureaucracy prevails when rules serve as a means of legitimating one party's right to sanction the other in areas of conflict (e.g., rules against taking company property for personal use). And in the mock bureaucracy pattern, rules are ignored by both parties (e.g., no-smoking rules in the 1950s).

Institutionalization theory has given new impetus to research on the mock bureaucracy type (e.g., Meyer and Rowan, 1977), but the other two types are not well delineated in the available theory. In Gouldner's analysis, whether a particular rule fits the punishment, representative, or mock pattern depends on the constellation of interests in the rules'

application domain: For example, if a rule governs issues in which conflict of interest obtains, it will be punishment-centered. But this insight provides little guidance for more concrete analysis, since the causal link is often the reverse of that envisaged by Gouldner: Whether in a given organization a given rule domain is conflictual depends in part on the nature of the rule at work in that context. We therefore need to understand the distinctive features of the different types of rules and to understand what distinguishes how these types are formulated and implemented. Studies of technology provide a useful guide for how to specify different types of formalization. Not only do such studies speak directly to how features, design, and implementation influence work practices, but students of technology have confronted issues similar to those surrounding the effects of bureaucracy. . . .

Formulating Enabling or Coercive Procedures

In the deskilling logic, equipment design is left to the technical experts. There is little to be gained by involving technically untrained users in the design process, and such involvement risks politicizing the process. This is the more traditional approach. Salzman (1992) reviewed over 100 U.S. books on equipment design and 100 textbooks used in U.S. engineering design courses and found not one discussion of the possible advantages of user involvement in designing systems. If, however, the rationale underlying design is usability, the design process will be managed very differently. The literature on the usability assurance process suggests four key process imperatives well illustrated in the Xerox case: an early and continual focus on users, an integrated view of the various aspects of usability, early and continual user testing, and an iterative design process that allows for progressive improvement (Gould, 1988). User involvement in the design of equipment can be an important mechanism for both building a subjective sense of "buy-in" and improving the technical quality of the system (Corbett, Rasmussen, and Rauner, 1991; Leonard-Barton and Sinha, 1993; Ives and Olson, 1984).

Such lessons carry over to the design of formal procedures. The literature on participative decision making suggests that at least in some conditions, employee participation improves morale and performance (Cotton et al., 1988, 1990; Leana, Locke, and Schweiger, 1990). Depending on the relevance of the procedures to the employee, and assuming that the employees are given the appropriate training and resources, employee involvement in the formulation of procedures is likely to have a positive effect on both attitudinal and technical outcomes. If, as in the scenario hypothesized by Mintzberg (1979), staff analysts formulate procedures in distrustful isolation from line employees, it is not surprising that those employees resist the resulting system. At NUMMI [New United Motor Manufacturing, Inc.], workers develop standardized work procedures themselves. According to a worker at NUMMI who had previously worked at a General Motors facility on the same site:

> The GM system [of job design] relied on authority. People with rank—the managers—ruled regardless of their competence or the validity of what they were saying. . . . At NUMMI, rank doesn't mean a damn thing—standardized work means that we all work out the objectively best way to do the job, and everyone does it that way. I might make some minor adjustments because of my height, for example, but I follow the procedure we've laid out because it makes sense . . . Management has delegated responsibility to the people who do the work and that gives workers a sense of pride in their jobs. (Adler, 1993: 145)

Implementation for Enablement vs. Coercion

A long tradition of research has attempted to formulate robust generalizations about the impact of new technologies, assuming that when organizations implement a new technology they adapt their structure to use it effectively (see reviews in Gerwin, 1981; Scott, 1990; Adler, 1992). Other authors have challenged what they see as an implicit technological determinism in this research stream. These critics have argued that the implementation of a given technology has no determinate effects on organizational or attitudinal outcomes because technological change is primarily an opportunity for various social forces to play out another round in their rivalry. The thrust of this indeterminacy thesis is reinforced by research showing that implementation is typically accompanied by modifications that

adapt the technology to local technical and social conditions (Sahal, 1981; Leonard-Barton and Sinha, 1993). A plausible middle ground was charted by Corbett (1992), who argued that some technologies, and some aspects of any given technology, are less organizationally constraining and more technically malleable than others; he therefore characterized the nature of the impact of technology on work organization as "soft determinism."

This determinism is in general softer for organizational technologies than for equipment. One of the differences between equipment technology and organizational technology is that the former is typically imported into the organization—through purchase from a supplier, for example—while the latter is typically developed internally. Whereas equipment suppliers typically sell to a range of customers and thus design their products to fit a generic user profile, the procedure design process and the procedure's features are typically shaped by the specific implementation context right from the outset. And even if the procedure design team tries to change the broader organization by taking a new, enabling orientation, a procedure designed with an enabling intent and embodying enabling features can be implemented coercively. In one company we studied, a comprehensive tracking and reporting system was designed to render more transparent the engineering change process. After several months and under pressure to improve the timeliness with which engineering changes were processed, some managers began using it coercively to cajole their own department's engineers and to disparage managers from other rival departments. The senior manager intervened, fearful that the coercive use would lead to covert game playing: "We have to ensure that these procedures are used as tools, not weapons."

Scattered prior research suggests some characteristics of the implementation contexts likely to preserve and enhance the enabling potential of formalized procedures. Weber's (1978, v.2: 968) discussion of bureaucracy in *Economy and Society* identifies some:

> According to experience, the relative optimum for the success and maintenance of a rigorous mechanization of the bureaucratic apparatus is offered by an assured salary connected with the opportunity of a career that

is not dependent upon mere accident and arbitrariness. Taut discipline and control which at the same time have consideration for the official's sense of honor, and the development of prestige sentiments of the status group as well as the possibility of public criticism also work in the same direction. With all this, the bureaucratic apparatus functions more assuredly than does legal enslavement of functionaries.

Blau's (1955) discussion of adjustive development updates and refines Weber's characterization. He defined adjustive development as the emergence of practices that solve incipient operational problems, practices developed by employees in the course of their work that were not deliberately instituted by superiors. Such adjustive development was the hallmark of an effective bureaucracy. He identified five prerequisites for it: a minimum of employment security, a professional orientation toward the performance of duties, established work groups that command the allegiance of their members, the absence of basic conflict between work group and management, and organizational needs that are experienced as disturbing. These features all seem strikingly salient in organizations such as NUMMI that make extensive use of enabling formalization to support the process of adjustive development they call continuous improvement or *kaizen.*

The analysis of such organizations (Adler, 1993) suggests that to Blau's list of preconditions, we might add employee voice (to ensure that the absence of conflict is not merely passive acquiescence), employee skills (to ensure that employees can respond effectively to disturbances), and process control (to ensure a concrete foundation for improvement efforts).

Blau's notion of adjustive development also points to the importance of flexibility in the implementation context as distinct from the flexibility of the procedures themselves. His point is reinforced by Gaines and Jermier's (1983) finding that formalization of tasks and work processes correlated only weakly with emotional exhaustion among police officers and support personnel, but management's flexibility in interpreting the procedures was a strong predictor of officers' exhaustion.

Flexibility in changing the procedures is also important. Coercive procedures, like coercive equipment designs, are difficult to change, because users have neither the knowledge nor the incentive to facilitate change and because designers and users will interpret changes as risks to the established power balance. In the U.S., Big Three auto assembly plants avoid changing line speeds because every time they do so, industrial engineers need to recalibrate every workstation and foremen need to renegotiate work requirements with every worker. By contrast, Toyota plants in Japan change line speed every month as a function of the sales forecast, and they use these changes as opportunities to mobilize the whole workforce to revise their standardized work sheets.

A Typology of Organizations

Distinguishing between enabling and coercive types of formalization seems potentially fruitful as a way to theorize the difference between good and bad procedures as experienced by employees. They are likely to have different features, and these features are more likely to emerge through different design processes. To preserve and augment their enabling or coercive potential, they need to be implemented in different organizational contexts.

The enabling versus coercive distinction suggests that we can characterize organizations along two dimensions: type and degree of formalization. The type of formalization can be conceptualized in the terms we have just identified. The degree of formalization can be conceptualized in the now-conventional terms of the Aston group (Pugh and Hickson, 1976) or Hall (1963), as the extent of formalized rules governing work behavior and the extent to which they are enforced. This two-dimensional framework implies that formalization's attitudinal outcomes depend both on the fit of the degree of formalization with the routineness of the task, as argued in contingency theory, and on the type of formalization. Positive attitudinal outcomes, we submit, can be expected in organizations with a high or low degree of (technically required) formalization as long as the type of formalization is enabling. Negative outcomes are to be expected in organizations with a high or low degree of (technically required) formalization whenever the type of formalization is coercive.

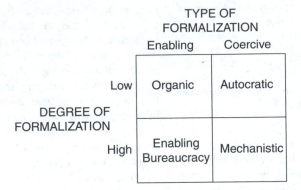

Figure 13.1   A typology of organizations

Figure 13.1 summarizes the resulting typology of organizations, with, on one dimension, the degree of formalization that is required by the routineness of the task and, on the other dimension, the type of formalization. We have simplified the representation by dichotomizing both dimensions. In reality, of course, both the degree and the type of formalization are continuous variables. Between coercion and enablement lie those types of formalization that fit Barnard's (1938) notion of a "zone of indifference," in which formalizations arouse neither positive nor negative responses.

In this representation, the conventional contrast between organic/nonbureaucratic and mechanistic/bureaucratic organizations appears as the relationship between two cells on a diagonal. Many of the asserted negative attitudinal effects of the bureaucratic and mechanistic form now appear as the result of a specifically coercive type of organization. The other diagonal contrasts the enabling-bureaucratic and the autocratic forms of organization. The former is the model we cull from the NUMMI case. The latter corresponds to the model of simple control described by Edwards (1979) and can be found in despotic as well as paternalistic variants (Burawoy, 1985: ch. 2).

This two-dimensional design matrix overcomes two problems with the conventional, one-dimensional contrast of organic and mechanistic/bureaucratic forms of organization. First, in the context of routine tasks, the conventional contrast assumes that formalization is at best a necessary evil and that organizations must reduce formalization—and forgo the associated efficiencies—to achieve high motivation and satisfaction levels. The empirical research reviewed above shows that this negative assessment of formalization's attitudinal impact is not a viable generalization. The high formalization row of the matrix shows that organizations undertaking very routine tasks can engender high or low levels of motivation and satisfaction depending on the type of formalization. The conventional contrast embodies the pessimistic "metaphysical pathos" denounced by Gouldner (1955)—an unsubstantiated feeling that bureaucracy's efficiency necessarily comes at the expense of employee well-being.

The second advantage of this expanded typology is that it renders intelligible changes we observe in less routine operations, in particular, professional, knowledge-intensive, innovative organizations that are under competitive pressure to reduce costs, increase timeliness, and improve quality. Positions in such organizations typically involve a mix of routine and nonroutine tasks. The conventional view suggests that such mixed situations create an organization design dilemma because the routine parts cannot be managed in a mechanistic, coercive, and bureaucratic way at the same time and for the same employees as the nonroutine parts are managed in an organic and empowering way. The motivational underpinnings for employees and the requisite attitudes and behavior for managers are incompatible, like oil and water (Heckscher, 1994: 45). Closer analysis of effective innovators shows that this dilemma is a figment of our impoverished theoretical imagination. Cusumano (1991) documented apparently successful efforts to turn software development into a factory-like process without alienating the software developers. At Toshiba's Fuchu Works software factory, for example, development methodologies are extensively formalized and standardized, and projects are tracked daily for performance with respect to targets of cost, output, and software reuse ratios. Similarly, Jelinek and Schoonhoven (1993) analyzed several U.S. electronics firms and showed that some make extensive use of highly systematic procedures and detailed formalized disciplines in their strategic management and product development processes. While in one case (Texas Instruments in the early 1980s) this formalization went awry and became coercive and alienating (1993: 80–83). in several other cases (such as Motorola), equally high levels of formalization supported high levels of commitment and innovation.

The enabling column in the organization design matrix permits us to understand such hybrids. Once routine and nonroutine tasks are both managed in an enabling way, the organization can become effectively ambidextrous (Duncan, 1976; McDonough and Leifer, 1983). In organizations such as Toshiba, and Motorola, jobs effectively mix organic and enabling-bureaucratic features, allowing employees to switch easily between routine and nonroutine tasks. The innovation goals of these organizations are supported by their enabling-organic features while their efficiency and control requirements are supported by the collaborative, shared control afforded by their enabling-bureaucratic features. Even organizations whose core tasks are essentially routine, like NUMMI, can use the same ambidextrous approach—varying, of course, the relative proportion—to enable workers to switch between production tasks and quality-circle activity.

The key flaws underlying the conventional view are twofold, one psychological and the other sociological. The psychological flaw lies in the conventional dichotomization of motivation into extrinsic and intrinsic. Assuming such a dichotomy, contingency theorists join many of the critics of formalization and are led down the following chain of logic: First, in organizations with high levels of formalization, work does not afford the levels of task identity and autonomy required for intrinsic motivation; second, such organizations must therefore rely on purely extrinsic motivation based on threats and rewards; and third, to avoid strongly negative employee responses, these organizations should recruit employees with low growth-needs strength and an instrumental attitude to work. We challenge the second step. Ryan and Connell (1989) showed that intrinsic and extrinsic are merely two poles of a spectrum characterizing varying degrees of internalization of values. There are at least two intermediate points: "introjections," based on avoidance of guilt or search for approval, and "identification," based on an internalization both of goals and of the discipline necessary to reach them. An enabling type of formalization is one that encourages motivation based on identification. Ryan and Connell cited education research suggesting that the identified form of motivation has positive effects very similar to those of intrinsic motivation in improving conceptual learning and recall, reducing anxiety, encouraging more positive and less negative coping with failure, and improving task performance.

The sociological flaw in the conventional view lies in its view of organizational goals. In our discussion of the divergent assessments of formalization found in prior research, we indicated this divergence was rooted in different conceptions of the origins and functions of organization as cooperative endeavor or negation of individual autonomy. But these different views apply in different situations. When the organization's goals diverge from those of employees, the enabling type of formalization is unavailable. Among other reasons for this is that the psychological conditions for identification are absent. When organizational goals are salient to the employees, employees no longer experience formal procedures for routine work as a negation of individual autonomy but as a valuable means to a desired end. Goal congruence is thus a critical contingency.

Note

1. A third, institutionalist branch focuses on the purely symbolic functions of bureaucracy signaling submission to cultural norms of rationality, but because this branch

has little to say about bureaucracy's effects on employees, we leave it aside.

REFERENCES

Adler, Paul S. (ed.) 1992 Technology and the Future of Work. New York: Oxford University Press.

Adler, Paul S. 1993 "The 'learning bureaucracy'; New United Motors Manufacturing incorporated." In Barry M. Staw and Larry L. Cummings (eds.), Research in Organizational Behavior, 15: 111–194. Greenwich, CT: JAI Press.

Adler, Paul S., and Robert E. Cole 1993 "Designed for learning: A tale of two auto plants." Sloan Management Review, 34(3): 85–94.

Applebaum, Eileen, and Rosemary Batt 1994 The New American Workplace Transforming Work Systems in the United Slates. Ithaca, NY: ILR Press.

Arches, J. 1991 "Social structure, burnout, and job satisfaction." Social Work, 36(3): 202–206.

Bailyn, Lotte 1985 "Autonomy in the R&D lab." Human Resource Management, 24(2): 129–146.

Bandura, A. 1977 "Self-efficacy: Toward a unifying theory of behavioral change." Psychology Review, 54: 191–215.

Barnard, Chester I. 1938 The Functions of the Executive. Cambridge, MA: Harvard University Press.

Bennis, Warren G. 1966 Changing Organizations. New York: McGraw-Hill.

Bennis, Warren G., and Philip E. Slater 1968 The Temporary Society. New York: Harper and Row.

Berggren, Christian 1992 Alternatives to Lean Production: Work Organization in the Swedish Auto Industry. Ithaca, NY: ILR Press.

Blau, Peter M. 1955 The Dynamics of Bureaucracy. Chicago: University of Chicago Press.

Bonjean, Charles M., and Michael D. Grimes 1970 "Bureaucracy and alienation: A dimensional approach." Social Forces, 48: 365–373.

Bowen, David E., and Edward E. Lawler III 1992 "The empowerment of service workers: What, why, how and when." Sloan Management Review, 33(3): 31–40.

Braverman, Harry 1974 Labor and Monopoly Capital. New York: Monthly Review Books.

Burawoy, Michael 1985 The Politics of Production. London: Verso.

Burns, Tom, and George M. Stalker 1961 The Management of Innovation. London: Tavistock.

Clawson, Daniel 1980 Bureaucracy and the Labor Process. New York: Monthly Review Press.

Corbett, J. Martin 1992 "Work at the interface: Advanced manufacturing technology and job design." In Paul S. Adler and Terry A. Winograd (eds.), Usability: Turning Technologies into Tools: 133–163. New York: Oxford University Press.

Corbett, J. Martin, L. Rasmussen, and F. Rauner 1991 Crossing the Border: The Social and Engineering Design of Computer Integrated Manufacturing Systems. Springer-Verlag, London.

Cotton, John L., David A. Vollrath, Kirk L. Froggatt, Mark L. Lengnick-Hall, and Kenneth R. Jennings 1988 "Employee participation: Diverse forms and different outcomes." Academy of Management Review, 13: 8–22.

Cotton, John L., David A. Vollrath, Mark L. Lengnick-Hall, and Kirk L. Froggatt 1990 "Fact: The form of participation does matter: A rebuttal to Leana, Locke, and Schweiger." Academy of Management Review, 15: 147–153.

Craig, Tim 1995 "Achieving innovation through bureaucracy: Lessons from the Japanese brewing industry." California Management Review, 38(1): 8–36.

Cusumano, Michael A. 1991 Japan's Software Factories. New York: Oxford University Press.

Cyert, Richard M., and James G. March 1963 A Behavioral Theory of the Firm. Englewood Cliffs, NJ: Prentice-Hall.

Damanpour, Fariborz 1991 "Organizational innovation." Academy of Management Journal, 34: 555–591.

Deming, W. E. 1986 Out of the Crisis. Cambridge, MA: MIT Center for Advanced Engineering Study.

Dewar, Robert, and James Werbel 1979 "Universalistic and contingency predictions of employee satisfaction and conflict." Administrative Science Quarterly, 24: 426–446.

Dumaine, Brian 1991 "The bureaucracy busters." Fortune, June 17: 36–50.

Edwards, Richard 1979 Contested Terrain. New York: Basic Books.

Engel, Gloria V. 1969 "The effect of bureaucracy on the professional autonomy of the physician." Journal of Health and Social Behavior, 10: 30–41.

Gaines, Jeannie, and John M. Jermier 1983 "Emotional exhaustion in a high-stress organization." Academy of Management Journal, 26: 567–586.

Galbraith, Jay R. 1977 Organization Design. Reading, MA: Addison-Wesley.

Gerwin, Donald 1981 "Relationship between structure and technology." In Paul C. Nystrom and William H. Starbuck (eds.), Handbook of Organizational Design, 2: 3–38. London: Oxford University Press.

Gould, John D. 1988 "How to design usable systems." In M. Helander (ed.), Handbook of Human-Computer

Interaction: 757–789. Amsterdam: North-Holland/ Elsevier.

Gouldner, Alvin W. 1954 Patterns of Industrial Bureaucracy. New York: Free Press.

Gouldner, Alvin W. 1955 "Metaphysical pathos and the theory of bureaucracy." American Political Science Review, 49: 496–507.

Hackman, J. Richard, and Greg R. Oldham 1980 Work Redesign. Reading, MA: Addison-Wesley.

Hall, Richard H. 1963 "The concept of bureaucracy: An empirical assessment." American Journal of Sociology, 69: 32–40.

Heckscher, Charles 1994 "Defining the post-bureaucratic type." In C. Heckscher and A. Donnellon (eds.), The Post-bureaucratic Organization: New Perspectives on Organizational Change: 14–62. Thousand Oaks, CA: Sage.

Heckscher, Charles, and Anne Donnellon (eds.) 1994 The Post-bureaucratic Organization: New Perspectives on Organizational Change. Thousand Oaks, CA: Sage.

Ives, Blake, and Margrethe H. Olson 1984 "User involvement and MIS research: A review of research." Management Science, 30: 586–603.

Jackson, Susan E., and Randall S. Schuler 1985 "A meta-analysis and conceptual critique of research on role ambiguity and role conflict in work settings." Organizational Behavior and Human Decision Processes, 36: 17–78.

James, Lawrence R., and Allen P. Jones 1976 "Organizational structure." Organizational Behavior and Human Performance, 16: 74–113.

Jelinek, Mariann, and Claudia Bird Schoonhoven 1993 The Innovation Marathon. San Francisco: Jossey-Bass.

Kahn, Robert L., Donald M. Wolfe, Robert P. Quinn, J. Diedrick Snoek, and Robert A. Rosenthal 1964 Organizational Stress. New York: Wiley.

Kakabadse, Andrew 1986 "Organizational alienation and job climate." Small Group Behavior, 17: 458–471.

Kornhauser, William 1962 Scientists in Industry: Conflict and Accommodation. Berkeley: University of California Press.

Kornhauser, William 1994 "Total quality management and employee involvement: Are they compatible?" Academy of Management Executive, 8(1): 68–76.

Lawrence, Paul R., and Jay W. Lorsch 1967 Organization and Environment: Managing Differentiation and Integration. Boston: Harvard University Graduate School of Business Administration.

Leana, Carrie R., Edward A. Locke, and David M. Schweiger 1990 "Fact and fiction in analyzing research on participative decision making: A critique of Cotton, Vollrath, Froggatt, Lengnick-Hall, and Jennings." Academy of Management Review, 15: 137–146.

Lecht, Charles P. 1991 "Japan's software threat: A U.S.-made paper tiger." Computerworld, April 8: 25.

Leonard-Barton, Dorothy, and Deepak Sinha 1993 "Developer-user interaction and user satisfaction in internal technology transfer." Academy of Management Journal, 36: 1125–1139.

Marsden, Peter V., Cynthia R. Cook, and David Knoke 1994 "Measuring organizational structures and environments." American Behavioral Scientist, 37: 891–910.

Maslach, C., and A. Pines 1978 "The burn-out syndrome in the day-care setting." Child Care Quarterly, 6: 100–113.

McDonough, Edward F., III, and Richard Leifer 1983 "Using simultaneous structures to cope with uncertainty." Academy of Management Journal, 26: 727 735.

McGregor, Douglas 1960 The Human Side of Enterprise. New York: McGraw-Hill.

Meyer, John W., and Brian Rowan 1977 "Institutionalized organizations: Formal structure as myth and ceremony." American Journal of Sociology, 83: 340–363.

Michaels, Ronald E., William L. Cron, Alan J. Dubinsky, and Erich A. Joachimsthaler 1988 "Influence of formalization on the organizational commitment and work alienation of salespeople and industrial buyers." Journal of Marketing Research, 25: 376–383.

Mintzberg, Henry 1979 The Structuring of Organizations. Englewood Cliffs, NJ: Prentice-Hall.

Morse, John J., and Jay W. Lorsch 1970 "Beyond Theory Y." Harvard Business Review, May–June: 61–68.

Nicholson, Peter J., Jr., and Swee C. Goh 1983 "The relationship of organization structure and interpersonal attitudes to role conflict and ambiguity in different work environments." Academy of Management Journal, 26: 148–155.

Organ, Dennis W., and Charles N. Greene 1981 "The effects of formalization on professional involvement: A compensatory process approach." Administrative Science Quarterly, 26: 237–252.

Parsons, Talcott 1947 "Introduction." In Max Weber, The Theory of Social and Economic Organization: 3–86. Glencoe, IL: Free Press.

Pennings, Johannes M. 1975 "The relevance of the structural-contingency model for organizational effectiveness." Administrative Science Quarterly, 20: 393–410.

Perrow, Charles 1986 Complex Organizations: A Critical Essay. 3rd ed. New York: Random House.

Pfeffer, Jeffrey 1981 Power in Organizations. Marshfield, MA: Pitman.

Pierce, John L., and Andre L. Delbecq 1977 "Organization structure, individual attributes, and innovation." Academy of Management Review, 2: 27–37.

Pines, A., and C. Maslach 1980 "Combating staff burnout in a day care center: A case study." Child Care Quarterly, 9: 5–16.

Podsakoff, Philip M., Larry J. Williams, and William T. Todor 1986 "Effects of organizational formalization on alienation of professionals and nonprofessionals." Academy of Management Journal, 29: 820–831.

Pugh, D. S., and D. J. Hickson 1976 Organizational Structure and Its Context: The Aston Program. Lexington, MA: D.C. Heath.

Raelin, Joseph A. 1985 "The basis for the professional's resistance to managerial control." Human Resource Management, 24(2): 147–175.

Ritti, R. R. 1971 The Engineer in the Industrial Corporation. New York: Columbia University Press.

Rousseau, Denise M. 1978 "Characteristics of departments, positions and individuals: Contexts for attitudes and behavior." Administrative Science Quarterly, 23: 521–540.

Ryan, R. M., and J. P. Connell 1989 "Perceived locus of causality and internalization: Examining reasons for acting in two domains." Journal of Personality and Social Psychology, 57: 749–761.

Sahal, D. 1981 Patterns of Technological Innovation. Reading, MA: Addison-Wesley.

Salzman, Harold 1992 "Skill-based design: Productivity, learning and organizational effectiveness." In Paul S. Adler and Terry A. Winograd (eds.), Usability: Turning Technologies into Tools: 66–95. New York: Oxford University Press.

Schonberger, R. I. 1986 World Class Manufacturing. New York: Free Press.

Scott, W. Richard 1990 "Technology and structure: An organization-level perspective." In Paul S. Goodman, Lee S. Sproull, and Associates, Technology and Organizations: 109–143. San Francisco: Jossey-Bass.

Senatra, Phillip T. 1980 "Role conflict, role ambiguity, and organizational climate in a public accounting firm." Accounting Review, 55: 594–603.

Snizek, William E., and Jerri Hayes Bullard 1983 "Perception of bureaucracy and changing job satisfaction: A longitudinal analysis." Organizational Behavior and Human Performance, 32: 275–287.

Soat, John 1991 "Software factories." Information Week, July 22: 22–28

Stevens, Fred, Joseph Diedriks, and Hans Philipsen 1992 "Physician satisfaction, professional characteristics, and behavior formalization in hospitals." Social Science and Medicine, 35(3): 295–303.

Thompson, James D. 1967 Organizations in Action. New York: McGraw-Hill.

Thompson, Victor A. 1965 "Bureaucracy and innovation." Administrative Science Quarterly, 10: 1–20.

Walton, Richard E. 1985 "Toward a strategy of eliciting employee commitment based on policies of mutuality." In Richard E. Walton and Paul R. Lawrence (eds.), HRM Trends and Challenges: 119–218. Boston: Harvard Business School Press.

Weber, Max 1947 The Theory of Social and Economic Organization. Glencoe, IL: Free Press.

Weber, Max 1978 Economy and Society. Berkeley, CA: University of California Press.

Womack, James, Dan T. Jones, and Daniel Roos 1990 The Machine That Changed the World. New York: Rawson Associates/Macrnillan.

Zaltman, Gerald, Robert Duncan, and Jonny Holbek 1973 Innovations and Organizations. New York: Wiley.

SOURCE: Adler, Paul S., and Brian Borys. 1996. Excerpt from "Two Types of Bureaucracy: Enabling and Coercive." *Administrative Science Quarterly*, 41:61–67, 75–80.

14

ORGANIZED DISSONANCE

Feminist Bureaucracy as Hybrid Form

KAREN LEE ASHCRAFT

It has become commonplace to brand the present as an era of fragmentation, swift change, and decentralized control. Such pressures can strain and crack bureaucratic foundations, generating keen interest in other forms of organized action (Heckscher & Applegate, 1994; Heydebrand, 1989; Putnam, 1997). Scholars from varied camps have joined the search for alternatives to bureaucracy. Some management scholars have explored hybrid forms that adapt to modern environmental pressures to achieve competitive advantage (e.g., Borys & Jemison, 1989; Powell, 1987, 1990). Others have pursued alternatives that increase organization member control to improve quality of work life (e.g., Cheney, 1999; Deetz, 1992). I seek to demonstrate how a feminist perspective can link these diverse literatures and enrich understanding of organizational forms. Specifically, a feminist lens reveals a novel hybrid I term "organized dissonance," which disrupts dominant assumptions regarding rationality, power, and forms of organization.

Although feminists have played a vital role in the political and conceptual development of alternatives to bureaucracy (Martin, 1990; Rodriguez, 1988), their experiments with organizational form remain on the margins of scholarship. Rarely have management scholars considered how feminist practice informs organization theory (for an exception, see Martin, Knopoff, and Beckman [1998]). Even feminist management critics seldom speak of the abundant literature on feminist organizations (for exceptions, see Martin [1993] and Mumby [1996]). These silences seem especially curious, given the rise of feminist critique in management theory (e.g., Calas & Smircich, 1996; Mills & Tancred-Sheriff, 1992) and the pragmatic response feminist organizations may well represent. Nonetheless, the question remains open: Can feminism offer fresh alternatives to management studies?

Viewing bureaucracy as a structural expression of male dominance, feminist theorists have long promoted collectivism (e.g., Ahrens, 1980; Ferguson, 1984). Yet feminist practitioners have found this form impossible to sustain (e.g., Murray, 1988; Seccombe-Eastland, 1988). Some compromise has emerged with the rise of feminist bureaucracies that blend hierarchical and egalitarian models of power (e.g., Eisenstein, 1995; Gottfried & Weiss, 1994). I argue that this shift has produced a unique hybrid, organized dissonance, which defies the logic of mainstream management theory by embracing the strategic, ironic union of antagonistic elements.

(RE)DRAFTING DISSONANCE: THEORIZING FROM FEMINIST ORGANIZATION

Power Versus Performance: Counterbureaucratic Empowerment Meets Postbureaucratic Hybrid

Alternatives to bureaucracy attract lively scholarly debate (Heckscher & Donnellon, 1994; Heydebrand, 1989), in part because bureaucratic habits persist despite awareness that they are ill-suited to complex, fast-paced environments (e.g., Barker, 1993; Kelley & Harrison, 1992). This essay most directly informs two research traditions with disparate critiques of bureaucracy.

First, "counterbureaucratic" arguments stem from critical management theory and reflect emancipatory motives. In this view, bureaucracy inherently maximizes the power of few at the expense of many, at profound ethical and practical cost (e.g., Fischer & Sirianni, 1984). Scholars in this tradition turn to democratic, collectivist, and other participatory forms designed to enable empowerment, generally defined as equality and enhanced control over work life (e.g., Cheney, 1995, 1999; Deetz, 1992; Mansbridge, 1973; Newman, 1980; Rothschild-Whitt, 1976). These forms are loosely guided by value rationality, a view in which empowered community is a worthy goal in itself, financial performance aside (Rothschild-Whitt, 1979; Weber, 1968). With some exceptions (e.g., Deetz, 1995; Sirianni, 1984), scholars in this area endorse a near blanket rebuff of bureaucratic power.

In contrast, a more mainstream strand of scholarship faults bureaucracy for outdated rigidity, *not* innate malice. This work addresses hybrid forms thought to improve firm performance amid the pressures of postbureaucratic times, examining calculated blonds of governance structures like those found in mergers, acquisitions, joint ventures, network forms, and "knowledge firms" (e.g., Bahrami, 1992; Borys & Jemison, 1989; Bradach & Eccles, 1989; Oliver & Montgomery, 2000; Powell, 1987, 1990; Steier, 1998). Although these hybrid forms revise bureaucratic methods and may even entail empowerment tactics (e.g., Drucker, 1988; Gittleman, Horrigan, & Joyce, 1998), the literature implies that they retain bureaucracy's instrumental rationality, whereby organization is chiefly a means to a competitive edge (Weber, 1968).

To date, these areas of study remain separate and seem unlikely allies, since their respective interests in power and performance are presumed to conflict. Though largely unnoticed, a parallel line of research integrates these disparate motives: feminist organization studies. Like most work on alternative forms, work on feminist organizations is pervaded by two questions: What features distinguish the form? and, To what extent is it a viable alternative?

The Novelty Question: Feminist Organization as Counterbureaucratic Empowerment

As with most alternative forms, scholars devote much discussion to traits that differentiate feminist organization. For over 30 years, they have overwhelmingly depicted it as antithetical to bureaucracy (e.g., Ahrens, 1980; Buzzanell et al., 1997; Cassel, 1977; Ferguson, 1984; Lugones & Spelman, 1987; Maguire & Mohtar, 1994; Martin et al., 1998; Rodriguez, 1988).[1] Historically, feminists have maintained that bureaucracy is a structural manifestation of male domination—that the form's defining features endorse the subordination of women and feminized others and so preserve oppressive gender relations (Ferguson, 1984). For instance, the bureaucratic canons of rationality and hierarchy privilege "professionals" (i.e., strategic, objective, managerial workers who suppress private needs) and exclude or devalue workers aligned with emotionality, sexuality, and other "irrational" matters (Acker, 1990; Ashcraft, 1999; Pringle, 1989). In short, feminists have long objected to the kind of power relations that bureaucracy engenders; thus, their search for gender justice and better business has required an alternative organizational form (Ianello, 1992).

Feminist organization generally promotes empowerment through (1) personal development of self-reliance and (2) egalitarian group relations (Reinelt, 1994). Individual power is viewed as an antecedent and outcome of genuinely collective power, but any use of influence that elevates some over others becomes illegitimate. Typically, feminist organization is found in women-centered missions, feminist health care agencies, rape crisis centers, domestic violence shelters, bookstores, banks, and other smaller non- and for-profit organizations. Although typically collectivism feminist organization also includes careful efforts to attend to private issues in organizational life (Martin et al., 1998). For example, "bounded emotionality" (Mumby & Putnam, 1992), a feminist pattern of work relations, fosters caring community by inviting expression of spontaneous, emergent work feelings. Simultaneously, members negotiate flexible feeling rules that limit sharing as needed to preserve functional relations. Several empirical studies illustrate this feminist alternative to bureaucratic impersonality (Ashcraft, 2000; Gayle, 1994; Martin et al., 1998; Morgen, 1994).

The Viability Question: Performance Problems and the Shift to a Feminist-Bureaucratic Hybrid

A second question that drives research on alternative organizational forms stresses viability, or the extent to which alternatives are feasible, productive, and sustainable. As Putnam observed, "Even though these new forms invoke patterns and social arrangements that differ from bureaucratic structures, the verdict is still out as to whether they are genuine alternatives" (1997:131). The troubled history of feminist organization vividly illustrates why "the verdict is still out."

Countless studies have documented a disabling contradiction between the ideals of feminist empowerment and the demands of practice (e.g., Morgen, 1990; Pahl, 1985; Seccombe-Eastland, 1988). For example, environmental pressures related to funding and community alliances have eroded the radical politics of feminist nonprofits (Ahrens, 1980; Mueller, 1995; Reinelt, 1994). Needs for efficiency, growth, competition, and other resource dependencies spur the growth of formal hierarchy, which structurally undermines egalitarianism (Maguire & Mohtar, 1994; Murray, 1988; Riger, 1994; Pfeffer & Salancik, 1978; Staggenborg, 1988). Further, as members' cultural habits play out, potent informal power structures emerge (Freeman, 1972–73; Morgen, 1988; Ristock, 1990). Embarrassment over the tendency of feminist organizations to reproduce bureaucracy may explain why some feminist management scholars seem reticent regarding the feminist form (Acker, 1990; Calas & Smircich, 1996). But for other scholars, the same empirical tendency is an honorable marriage, not a dirty secret.

Recently, several authors have begun to address hybrid feminist forms as such (Ashcraft, 2000; Eisenstein, 1995; Gottfried & Weiss, 1994; Leidner, 1991; Martin et al., 1998; Mayer, 1995; Reinelt, 1995; Riger, 1994). They seek compound structures "not premised on a principled hostility to all aspects of bureaucracy and market exchange" (Sirianni, 1984: 484). In particular, feminist-bureaucratic hybrids are marked by the merger of hierarchical and egalitarian modes of power. This odd union complicates the traditional feminist account of legitimate uses of power, as it evokes the irony that some individuals can exercise power over others to promote equality. Therefore, despite considerable success at achieving practical goals (e.g., Eisenstein, 1995; Staggenborg, 1988), feminist bureaucracy has its own—and no less acute—vulnerabilities. If antagonism to bureaucracy distinguishes feminist organization, what unique features can it claim when it allies with the enemy? If appropriate power is defined in opposition to bureaucratic power, how can a hybrid empower? Given bureaucracy's deep institutionalization, will such an alliance inevitably further dilute the feminist form? Put simply, in what sense is feminist bureaucracy a genuine alternative? . . .

The Implications of Organized Dissonance: Present Challenges, Future Directions

The primary contribution of this article is that it surfaces dissonance as a class of hybrid organization. Organized dissonance adds more than emotionality to rationality; it uproots the entrenched assumption that rational organization needs consistency or even its pursuit. In a word, it shakes faith in unity of direction, in "one head with one plan" (Fayol, 1949). Several management scholars have begun to explore the organizational manifestation and management of irony and paradox (e.g., Filby & Willmott, 1988; Hatch, 1997; Meyers & Garrett, 1993; Putnam, 1986, 1992; Stohl, 1995; Trethewey, 1999; Westenholz, 1993). With *strategic* incongruity as its guiding premise, the dissonance model extends such work to capture the case of organizations that employ incompatible forms to meet conflicting objectives and demands. Consequently, organized dissonance enables a radical shift in perspective: it allows one to engage contradiction as *deliberate* dialectical tension. Mary Parker Follett presaged this view in her enduring words on constructive conflict: "Instead of condemning it, we should set it to work for us. . . . The music of the violin we get by friction. . . . So in business, too, we have to know when to try to eliminate friction and when to try to capitalize it. . . . Integration involves invention, and the clever thing is to recognize this and not to let one's thinking stay within the boundaries of two alternatives which are mutually exclusive" (cited in Graham, 1995: 68, 70). Such a shift can dramatically alter one's approach to organizational forms and, specifically, to alternatives to bureaucracy.

For example, current research on postbureaucratic hybrids submits a catalogue of motives for combining forms, such as pooling resources, diversifying, increasing access to technologies, and mediating markets and hierarchies (e.g., Bahrami, 1992; Borys & Jemison, 1989; Powell, 1987, 1990). Organized dissonance supplies a new motive—accomplishing paradoxical goals—that disturbs the ideal of a hybrid as a harmonious fusion in the service of one purpose. Future research can generate a typology of other dissonant hybrids and build knowledge of ways to use friction between partnered forms to offset their respective pitfalls (ways, for instance, to maintain personalized client service amid massive growth and standardization).

The counterbureaucratic empowerment literature also needs this shift. Buzzanell and colleagues argued that as long as scholars and practitioners talk in terms of "oppositions rather than tensions, we, as researchers and as organizational members, envision the bridge between 'sides' as insurmountable, all-or-nothing propositions. These perceptions contribute to our difficulty in creating and sustaining democratic processes within corporate and alternative organizations" (1997: 304). As noted earlier, critical theories of alternatives to bureaucracy rarely address hybrid empowerment (Sirianni, 1984). As in the traditional feminist view, the assumption appears to be that bureaucracy will eventually overwhelm alternatives (e.g., Barker, 1993). Organized dissonance is a rejection of a hero versus villain account of alternative versus bureaucratic forms, a proposal that cautious pairing with the "enemy" might better enable social change (Ashcraft, 2000; Martin, 1987; Reinelt, 1995). By integrating the study of organization member empowerment with that of hybrid forms, the dissonant model merges the quest for empowerment with that for improved performance (Alvesson & Willmott, 1992; Sirianni, 1984). Simultaneously, it forsakes the tacit premise in much mainstream management work that empowerment is chiefly a means to profitability or is, at best, secondary to that end (Fletcher, 1994). In sum, organized dissonance discards the notion that the only way to manage competing goals is to subordinate one to the other.

In addition, organized dissonance flags the significance of the structure-practice relationship for the study of organizational forms. Much current research continues to privilege a priori structures over process and/or to disparage practice through the lens of idealized conceptual models (Bahrami, 1992; Gottfried & Weiss, 1994; Kanter & Zurcher, 1973; Martin, 1990). Putnam proposed that "rather than classifying new organizational forms as networks or modular corporations, we might examine the discursive practices that form alliances, the institutional texts that mediate social interaction, and the paradoxes and tensions that arise from enacting oppositional forms" (1997: 131). I undertook such a project by examining how members produced an alternative to bureaucracy in practice. In the model of organized dissonance proposed here, form is an ongoing accomplishment, constructed as formal arrangements are enacted and acted upon in practice (Barley & Tolbert, 1997). Further, similar structures play out differently, practice can undermine structure, and structural tensions take shape and get managed in practice.

Finally, organized dissonance alters traditional relationship boundary debates. Typically, researchers consider the relationship between a hybrid and its environment or between its partners and the hybrid (Borys & Jemison, 1989; Oliver & Montgomery, 2000). Organized dissonance calls attention to the partner-environment relationship. In the case of a feminist-bureaucratic hybrid, imbalanced institutional influence between partners (feminism and bureaucracy) can compromise sustainability. For example, as a nonprofit dependent on external funding, interagency cooperation, and free labor, SAFE exhibited acute concern for alliances with patrons, businesses, law enforcement and educational groups, and volunteers. These relationships impelled the institutionalization of bureaucracy at SAFE. But the weaker partner, the feminist form of organization, is not inexorably doomed (Child, 1997; Pfeffer, 1992). The SAFE case suggests at least three resources members can marshal to boost it: the mission/nature of the work, regional and organizational culture (Taylor, 1999), and alliances with sister agencies. Here, domestic violence work bred members who were adept at talking about gender and power. SAFE's distaste for bureaucratic authority and penchant for self-reflection came easily in a regional culture friendly to egalitarian and therapeutic themes; the area was known for its odd blend of antiestablishment, "new age" discourse and staggering wealth. Reportedly, SAFE began as a feminist collective, which embedded egalitarian ideology in the organization's culture. Finally, the national battered women's movement linked shelters around the United States in a network of financial and media support.

Studies of larger, for-profit dissonant hybrids could inform the partner-environment relationship by probing distinct resource contexts and attendant dialectical tensions. Empirical study of bureaucracies that attempt grafts of counterbureaucratic forms might be an interesting point of departure. Such work would reverse the case of this essay and test the capacity of the radical perspective shift it suggests. For instance, many have described how corporate empowerment programs become distorted and diluted (e.g., Barker, 1993; Deetz, 1992; Stohl, 1995; Stohl & Cheney, 1999); the dissonant model should help allay this trend. The study of more mainstream cases of organized dissonance would also refine the model, particularly its sensitivity to such contextual factors as an organization's history or base form.

My analysis tempers optimism. Despite the appeal of the message that irony begets innovation, the SAFE case is a vivid reminder of the constraints and costs of lived tension. Certainly, fine lines divide strategic incongruity, delusions of unfettered agency, and crippling binds. Additional research is needed

to determine which dialectical tensions are more critical or immobilizing and if, when, how, and why alternative practices mitigate bureaucratic excess. Dissonance can be reframed as a strategic choice, without embracing all forms of incongruity or neglecting the limits of member agency (Child, 1997).

Can organized dissonance stand as a genuine alternative? Whatever the verdict, contemporary feminist practice brings dissonant forms into relief and common assumptions into question. It compels researchers to imagine productive organization founded on incongruity and conflict. However thorny and precarious, organized dissonance hints at the potential to use the fragmentation and dissensus of our time to induce social change.

NOTE

1. Martin's work (e.g., 1987, 1990, 1993) provides a notable exception, as do the recent studies of feminist hybrids cited in the next section. Otherwise, bureaucratic feminist communities have customarily been (1) discussed in terms other than organizational form, (2) treated as institutionalized political action, or (3) criticized in light of the pure feminist form.

REFERENCES

Acker, J. 1990. Hierarchies, jobs, bodies: A theory of gendered organizations. *Gender & Society*, 4: 139–158.

Ahrens, L. 1980. Battered women's refuges: Feminist cooperatives vs. social service institutions. *Radical America*, 14(3): 41–47.

Alvesson, M., & Willmott, H. 1992. On the idea of emancipation in management and organization studies. *Academy of Management Review*, 17: 432–464.

Ashcraft, K. L. 1999. Managing maternity leave: A qualitative analysis of temporary executive succession. *Administrative Science Quarterly*, 44: 40–80.

Ashcraft, K. L. 2000. Empowering "professional" relationships: Organizational communication meets feminist practice. *Management Communication Quarterly*, 13: 347–392.

Bahrami, H. 1992. The emerging flexible organization: Perspectives from Silicon Valley. *California Management Review*, 34(4): 33–52.

Barker, J. R. 1993. Tightening the iron cage: Concertive control in self-managing teams. *Administrative Science Quarterly*, 38: 408–437.

Barley, S. R., & Tolbert, P. S. 1997. Institutionalization and structuration: Studying the links between action and institution. *Organization Studies,* 18: 93–117.

Borys, B., & Jemison, D. B. 1989. Hybrid arrangements as strategic alliances: Theoretical issues in organizational combinations. *Academy of Management Review,* 14: 234–249.

Bradach, J. L., & Eccles, R. G. 1989. Price, authority, and trust: From ideal types to plural forms. In W. R. Scott & J. Blake (Eds.), *Annual review of sociology,* vol. 15: 97–118. Palo Alto, CA: Annual Reviews.

Burns, T., & Stalker, G. M. 1961. *The management of innovation.* London: Tavistock.

Buzzanell. P., Ellingson, L., Silvio, C., Pasch, V., Dale, B., Mauro, G., Smith, E., Weir, N., & Martin, C. 1997. Leadership processes in alternative organizations: Invitational and dramaturgical leadership. *Communication Studies,* 48: 285–310.

Calas, M., & Smircich, L. 1993. Dangerous liaisons: The "feminine-in-management" meets "globalization." *Business Horizons,* 36(2): 71–81.

Calas, M., & Smircich, L. 1996. From "the woman's" point of view: Feminist approaches to organization studies. In S. R. Clegg, C. Hardy, & W. R. Nord (Eds.), *Handbook of organization studies:* 218–257. Thousand Oaks, CA: Sage.

Cassel, J. 1977. *A group called women: Sisterhood and symbolism in the women's movement.* New York: David McKay.

Champy, J. 1995. *Reengineering management: The mandate for new leadership.* New York: Harper-Business.

Cheney, G. 1995. Democracy in the workplace: Theory and practice from the perspective of communication. *Journal of Applied Communication Research,* 23: 167–200.

Cheney, G. 1999. *Values at work: Employee participation meets market pressure at Mondragon.* Ithaca, NY: ILR Press.

Child, J. 1997. Strategic choice in the analysis of action, structure, organizations and environment: Retrospect and prospect. *Organization Studies,* 18: 43–76.

Conger, J. A. 1989. Leadership: The art of empowering others. *Academy of Management Executive,* 2(1): 17–21.

Crom, M. 1998. The leader as servant. *Training,* 35(7): 6.

Deetz, S. 1992. *Democracy in an age of corporate colonization: Developments in communication and the politics of everyday life.* Albany: State University of New York Press.

Deetz, S. 1995. *Transforming communication, transforming business: Building responsive and responsible workplaces.* Cresskill, NJ: Hampton.

Drucker, P. 1988. The coming of the new organization. *Harvard Business Review,* 88(1): 45–53.

Eisenstein, H. 1995. The Australian femocratic experiment: A feminist case for bureaucracy. In M. M. Ferree & P. Y. Martin (Eds.), *Feminist organizations: Harvest of the new women's movement:* 69–83. Philadelphia: Temple University Press.

Fayol, H. 1949. *General and industrial management* (C. Storrs, trans.). London: Sir Isaac Putnam.

Ferguson, K. 1984. *The feminist case against bureaucracy.* Philadelphia: Temple University Press.

Filby, I., & Willmott, H. 1988. Ideologies and contradictions in a public relations department: The seduction and impotence of living myth. *Organization Studies,* 9: 335–349.

Fischer, F., & Sirianni, C. (Eds.). 1984. *Critical studies in organization and bureaucracy.* Philadelphia: Temple University Press.

Fisher, K. 1993. *Leading self-directed work teams.* New York: McGraw-Hill.

Fletcher, 1994. Castrating the female advantage: Feminist standpoint research and management science. *Journal of Management Inquiry,* 3: 74–82.

Freeman, J. 1972–73. The tyranny of structurelessness. *Berkeley Journal of Sociology,* 17: 151–164.

Galbraith, J. R. 1973. *Designing complex organizations.* Reading, MA: Addison-Wesley.

Gayle, B. M. 1994. Bounded emotionality in two all-female organizations: A feminist analysis. *Women's Studies in Communication,* 17(2): 1–19.

Gittleman, M., Horrigan, M., & Joyce, M. 1998. "Flexible" workplace practices: Evidence from a nationally representative survey. *Industrial and Labor Relations Review,* 52: 99–115.

Gottfried, H., & Weiss, P. 1994. A compound feminist organization: Purdue University's Council on the Status of Women. *Women & Politics,* 14(2): 23–44.

Graham, P. (Ed.). 1995. *Mary Parker Follett: Prophet of management.* Boston: Harvard Business School Press.

Hatch, M. J. 1997. Irony and the social construction of contradiction in the humor of a management team. *Organization Science,* 8: 275–288.

Heckscher, C., & Applegate, L. M. 1994. Introduction. In C. Heckscher & A. Donnellon (Eds.), *The post-bureaucratic organization: New perspectives on organizational change:* 1–13. Thousand Oaks, CA: Sage.

Heckscher, C., & Donnellon, A. (Eds.). 1994. *The post-bureaucratic organization: New perspectives on organizational change.* Thousand Oaks, CA: Sage.

Heydebrand, W. V. 1989. New organizational forms. *Work and Occupations,* 16: 323–357.

Ianello, K. P. 1992. *Decisions without hierarchy: Feminist interventions in organization theory and practice.* New York: Routledge.

Kanter, R. M., & Zurcher, L. A. 1973. Concluding statement: Evaluating alternatives and alternative valuing. *Journal of Applied Behavioral Science,* 9: 381–397.

Kelley, M. R., & Harrison, B. 1992. Unions, technology, and labor-management cooperation. In L. Mishel & P. B. Voos (Eds.), *Unions and economic competitiveness:* 247–286. New York: M. E. Sharpe.

Lawrence, P. R., & Lorsch, W. 1967. *Organization and environment: Managing differentiation and integration.* Boston: Graduate School of Business Administration, Harvard University.

Leidner, R. 1991. Stretching the boundaries of liberalism: Democratic innovation in a feminist organization. *Signs,* 16: 263–289.

Lugones, M. C., & Spelman, E. V. 1987. Competition, compassion, and community: Models for a feminist ethos. In V. Miner & H. E. Longino (Eds.), *Competition: A feminist taboo?* 234–247. New York: Feminist Press.

Maguire, M., & Mohtar, L. F. 1994. Performance and the celebration of a subaltern counterpublic. *Text and Performance Quarterly,* 14: 238–252.

Mansbridge, J. J. 1973. Time, emotion, and inequality: Three problems of participatory groups. *Journal of Applied Behavioral Science,* 9: 351–367.

Martin, J., Knopoff, K., & Beckman, C. 1998. An alternative to bureaucratic impersonality and emotional labor: Bounded emotionality at The Body Shop. *Administrative Science Quarterly,* 43: 429–469.

Martin, P. Y. 1987. A commentary on *The feminist case against bureaucracy* by Kathy Ferguson. *Women's Studies International Forum,* 10: 543–548.

Martin, P. Y. 1990. Rethinking feminist organizations. *Gender & Society,* 4: 182–206.

Martin, P. Y. 1993. Feminist practice in organizations: Implications for management. In E. A. Fagenson (Ed.), *Women in management: Trends, issues, and challenges in managerial diversity:* 274–296. Newbury Park, CA: Sage.

Mayer, A. M. 1995. *Feminism-in-practice: Implications for feminist theory.* Paper presented at the 1995 annual meeting of the International Communication Association.

Meyers, R. A., & Garrett, D. E. 1993. Contradictions, values, and organizational argument. In C. Conrad (Ed.), *The ethical nexus:* 149–170. Norwood, NJ: Ablex.

Mills, A. J., & Tancred-Sheriff, P. (Eds.). 1992. *Gendering organizational analysis.* Newbury Park, CA: Sage.

Morgen, S. 1988. The dream of diversity, the dilemma of difference: Race and class contradictions in a feminist health clinic. In J. Sole (Ed.), *Anthropology for the nineties:* 370–380. New York: Free Press.

Morgen, S. 1990. Contradictions in feminist practice: Individualism and collectivism in a feminist health center. In C. Calhoun (Ed.), *Comparative social research supplement 1:* 9–59. Greenwich, CT: JAI Press.

Morgen, S. 1994. Personalizing personnel decisions in feminist organizational theory and practice. *Human Relations,* 47: 665–684.

Mueller, C. 1995. The organizational basis of conflict in contemporary feminism. In M. M. Ferree & P. Y. Martin (Eds.), *Feminist organizations: Harvest of the new women's movement:* 263–275. Philadelphia: Temple University Press.

Mumby, D. K. 1996. Feminism, postmodernism, and organizational communication studies: A critical reading. *Management Communication Quarterly,* 9: 259–295.

Mumby, D. K., & Putnam, L. L. 1992. The politics of emotion: A feminist reading of bounded rationality. *Academy of Management Review,* 17: 465–486.

Murray, S. B. 1988. The unhappy marriage of theory and practice: An analysis of a battered women's shelter. *NWSA Journal,* 1(1): 75–92.

Newman, K. 1980. Incipient bureaucracy: The development of hierarchies in egalitarian organizations. In G. M. Britan & R. Cohen (Eds.), *Hierarchy & society:* 143–163. Philadelphia: Institute for the Study of Human Issues.

Oliver, A. L., & Montgomery, K. 2000. Creating a hybrid organizational form from parental blueprints: The emergence and evolution of knowledge firms. *Human Relations,* 53: 33–56.

Pahl, J. 1985. Refuges for battered women: Ideology and action. *Feminist Review,* 19(March): 25–43.

Pfeffer, J. 1992. *Managing with power: Politics and influence in organizations.* Boston: Harvard Business School.

Pfeffer, J., & Salancik, G. R. 1978. *The external control of organizations: A resource dependence perspective.* New York: Harper & Row.

Powell, W. W. 1987. Hybrid organizational arrangements: New form or transitional development? *California Management Review,* 30(1): 67–87.

Powell, W. W. 1990. Neither market nor hierarchy: Network forms of organization. In B. M. Staw & L. L. Cummings (Eds.), *Research in organizational behavior,* vol. 12: 295–336. Greenwich, CT: JAI Press.

Pringle, R. 1989. Bureaucracy, rationality, and sexuality: The case of secretaries. In J. Hearn, D. Sheppard, P.

Tancred-Sheriff, & G. Burrell (Eds.), *The sexuality of organization:* 158–177. Newbury Park, CA: Sage.

Putnam, L. L. 1986. Contradictions and paradoxes in organizations. In L. Thayer (Ed.), *Organization communication: Emerging perspectives:* 151–167. Norwood, NJ: Ablex.

Putnam, L. L. 1992. Embedded metaphors and organizational ironies as research tools. In P. J. Frost & R. E. Stablein (Eds.), *Doing exemplary research:* 105–110. Newbury Park, CA: Sage.

Putnam, L. L. 1997. Organizational communication in the 21st century: Informal discussion with M. Scott Poole, L. L. Putnam, and D. R. Seibold. *Management Communication Quarterly,* 11: 127–138.

Reinelt, C. 1994. Fostering empowerment, building community: The challenge for state-funded feminist organizations. *Human Relations,* 47: 685–705.

Reinelt, C. 1995. Moving onto the terrain of the state: The battered women's movement and the politics of engagement. In M. M. Ferree & P. Y. Martin (Eds.), *Feminist organizations: Harvest of the new women's movement:* 84–104. Philadelphia: Temple University Press.

Riger, S. 1994. Challenges of success: Stages of growth in feminist organizations. *Feminist Studies,* 20: 275–300.

Ristock, J. L. 1990. Canadian feminist social service collectives: Caring and contradictions. In L. Albrecht & R. M. Brewer (Eds.), *Bridges of power: Women's multicultural alliances:* 172–181. Philadelphia: New Society Publishers.

Rodriguez, N. M. 1988. Transcending bureaucracy: Feminist politics at a shelter for battered women. *Gender & Society,* 2: 214–227.

Rothschild-Whitt, J. 1976. Conditions facilitating participatory-democratic organizations. *Sociological Inquiry,* 46(2): 75–86.

Rothschild-Whitt, J. 1979. The collectivist organization: An alternative to rational-bureaucratic models. *American Sociological Review,* 44: 509–527.

Seccombe-Eastland, L. 1988. Ideology, contradiction, and change in a feminist bookstore. In B. Bate & A. Taylor (Eds.), *Women communicating: Studies of women's talk:* 251–276. Norwood, NJ: Ablex.

Sirianni, C. 1984. Participation, opportunity, and equality: Toward a pluralist organizational model. In. F. Fischer & C. Sirianni (Eds.), *Critical studies in organization and bureaucracy:* 482–503. Philadelphia: Temple University Press.

Staggenborg, S. 1988. The consequences of professionalization and formalization in the prochoice movement. *American Sociological Review,* 53: 585–606.

Steier, L. 1998. Confounding market and hierarchy in venture capital governance: The Canadian immigrant investor program. *Journal of Management Studies,* 35: 511–535.

Stohl, C. 1995. Paradoxes of participation. In R. Cesaria & P. Shockley-Zabalak (Eds.), *Organizzazioni e commuincazione [Organizations and communication]:* 199–215. Rome: Servizio Italiano Publicazioni Internazionali.

Stohl, C, & Cheney, G. 1999. *Participatory processes/ paradoxical practices.* Paper presented at the annual meeting of the International Communication Association, San Francisco.

Taylor, B. C. 1999. Browsing the culture: Membership and intertextuality at a Mormon bookstore. *Studies in Cultures, Organizations, and Societies,* 5(1): 61–95.

Trethewey, A. 1999. Isn't it ironic: Using irony to explore the contradictions of organizational life. *Western Journal of Communication,* 63: 140–167.

Weber, M. 1968. *Economy and society* [G. Roth & C. Wittich, Eds.]. New York: Bedminster.

Westenholz, A. 1993. Paradoxical thinking and change in the frames of reference. *Organization Studies,* 14: 37–58.

SOURCE: Ashcraft, Karen Lee. 2001. Excerpt from "Organized Dissonance: Feminist Bureaucracy as Hybrid Form." *Academy of Management Journal,* 44(6):1301–304, 1314–322.

PART III

THE COORDINATION OF WORK

AN INTRODUCTION TO THE COORDINATION OF WORK

Coordination can be defined most simply as the management of interdependence between tasks or activities (Malone and Crowston 1994). Coordination is arguably one of the central challenges that organizations must address, along with control and the management of conflict. But there are different ways to solve the problem of coordination. In the relational organizational form, coordination is achieved through horizontal networks of relationships that connect people throughout the organization at every level including the front line. In the bureaucratic organizational form, by contrast, coordination is achieved primarily at the top of a vertical hierarchy in order to preserve the specialization and focus of each functional area, and perhaps to prevent an organized challenge from a potentially hostile workforce. This difference in how coordination is achieved is one of the primary differences between the relational and bureaucratic organizational forms.

Mary Parker Follett is the earliest scholar we have found who portrays coordination as a relational process. In a lecture first given in the 1920s, Follett (1949) argues that coordination is a relational process that is fundamental to the functioning of organizations:

Four fundamental principles of organisation are:

(1) Co-ordination as the reciprocal relating of all the factors in a situation.
(2) Co-ordination by direct contact of the responsible people concerned.
(3) Co-ordination in the early stages.
(4) Co-ordination as a continuing process.

My first principle, coordination as the reciprocal relating of all factors in a situation, shows us just what this process of coordination actually is, shows us the nature of unity. . . . This sort of reciprocal relating, this interpenetration of every part by every other part and again by every other part as it has been permeated by all, should be the goal of all attempts at coordination, a goal, of course, never wholly reached. (P. 78)

Follett (1949) distinguishes further between achieving coordination as an *additive total* versus achieving coordination as a *relational total,* arguing that this distinction plays a role in the social sciences similar to the role played by Einstein's theory of relativity in the natural sciences. The process of coordination is not one of adding up all the factors in a situation but rather one of understanding their interpenetration or interdependence.

Follett (1949) is arguing in essence that effective coordination requires systems thinking, a sharing and integration of knowledge itself. Because coordination occurs through the integration of knowledge, and because that integrated knowledge then informs action, Follett contends that coordination should occur *throughout* the organization, not just at the level of top management. In effect, she is arguing that coordination must occur throughout the organization in order to enable control to be distributed throughout the organization, a point we return to in Part IV, "Autonomy and Control." This requirement runs counter to the structure and logic of the bureaucratic organizational form, where coordination is exercised primarily at the level of top management, keeping frontline workers largely divided and uninformed of the larger picture, thus limiting their ability to share in the process of leadership and control.

By contrast, the scholars who followed Follett tended to focus on the conditions that increase the need for relational forms of coordination with a view toward *minimizing* those conditions. When levels of uncertainty and interdependence are low, coordination can be achieved at relatively low cost through programming or routines, but when levels of uncertainty or interdependence are high, coordination must be achieved instead through feedback or direct interaction among the participants. These relational forms of coordination are akin to the coordination Follett (1949) wrote about, but rather than exploring how to facilitate relational forms of coordination, organizational scholars focused on minimizing the conditions that would require them. As James March and Herbert Simon (1958) point out,

> Interdependence does not itself cause difficulties if the pattern of interdependence is fixed and stable. For in this case, each subprogram can be designed to take account of all the other subprograms with which it interacts. Difficulties arise only if program execution rests on contingencies that cannot be predicted perfectly in advance. In this case, coordinating activity is required to secure agreement about the estimates that will be used as the basis for action, or to provide information to each subprogram unit about the relevant activities of the others. (P. 180)

In order to reduce the perceived challenges of these relational forms of coordination, March and Simon (1958) identify ways to buffer organizations from uncertainty and minimize interdependence.

James Thompson (1967) describes relational forms of coordination as "mutual adjustment"—a process of adjusting all factors of the situation to each other—similar to Follett's (1949) definition of coordination. But like March and Simon (1958), Thompson (1967) argues that relational forms of coordination are prohibitively difficult and can be avoided except under the condition of "reciprocal task interdependence" where the outcome of one activity affects the performance of another activity *and vice versa,* a condition that Follett (1949) argues is always essentially present.

The dominant approach by organizational scholars after Follett was therefore to identify the conditions that favored the relational form of coordination and then seek ways to *minimize* those conditions, enabling the survival of a more mechanistic, bureaucratic way of coordinating work that they assumed to be simpler and more cost-effective. To minimize the need for relational coordination, organizations were advised to build buffer inventories—work-in-process inventories that enable each task to proceed relatively independently from other tasks, and that enable each task to be relatively robust to unpredicted changes that might occur in other task areas or in the external environment. These buffers enable the bureaucratic form of coordination—based on routines, supervision, preplanning, and standardization—to endure, minimizing the need for direct horizontal relationships among participants throughout the organization.

In the 1970s and '80s, a range of innovations emerged to address the challenge of coordinating work in an increasingly fast-moving, unpredictable environment, many of them placing an emphasis on achieving coordination directly between frontline employees. If frontline employees are strategically positioned at the interface between the organization and a fast-moving environment rather than simply operatives who respond to orders from above, then coordination should occur at this interface as well as at higher levels of the organization. Jay Galbraith (1972) proposes an information-processing theory of coordination, in effect formalizing the contingency model of coordination put forward by March and Simon (1958), but shifting the weight of attention toward feedback-mechanisms that can support relational forms of coordination. Michael Tushman and David Nadler (1978) further elaborate these feedback-coordinating mechanisms, while Linda Argote (1982) demonstrates the increasing usefulness of feedback-coordinating mechanisms (such as meetings) and the decreasing usefulness of programmed coordinating mechanisms (such as protocols) under conditions of uncertainty.

In contrast to earlier theories that present formal structures as an alternative to relational forms of coordination, protocols can facilitate relational coordination; however, their ability to do so depends on their design. As Paul Adler and Brian Borys (1996) argue in their article (see Chapter 13),

> Enabling procedures provide users with visibility into the processes they regulate by explicating key components and by codifying best practice routines. They provide users with an understanding of the underlying theory of the process by clarifying the rationale of the rules. . . . [Although tasks are specialized and partitioned] procedures are designed to afford [workers] an understanding of where their tasks fit into the whole. (P. 72)

This argument is further supported by Samer Faraj and Yin Xiao (2006), who show that both epistemic (protocols) and dialogic (joint sense-making, protocol breaking) coordination practices contribute to successful outcomes in dynamic, time-constrained settings with a low tolerance for error. Likewise Jody Hoffer Gittell (2002) finds that both feedback and programmed coordination mechanisms can support the development of relational coordination. She argues that cross-boundary protocols that provide workers with a mental map of how tasks are connected to the overall process and enable them to develop a sense of shared goals and mutual respect with each other serve to increase relational coordination.

Relational forms of coordination have been more fully developed in recent years, drawing upon insights from interactionism (Follett 1949; Mead 1934) and collective sense-making (Weick 1995). Karl Weick (1995) argues that coordination occurs through the development of mutually reinforcing interpretations among participants, enabled by a process of collective sense-making. The notion of coordination as collective mind is further developed by Karl Weick and Karlene Roberts (1993) in a study of heedful interrelating on flight decks, demonstrating that collective mind and heedful interrelating enable reliable performance to be achieved under demanding conditions. Shared cognitions are also at the heart of expertise coordination as proposed by Samer Faraj and Lee Sproull

(2000). Expanding beyond shared cognitions, Ryan Quinn and Jane Dutton (2005) and John Paul Stephens (2010) explore the emotional dynamics of relational coordination.

In the final paper included in this section, Jody Hoffer Gittell, Rob Seidner, and Julian Wimbush (2010) integrate the cognitive and emotional dimensions of relationships, proposing that relational coordination is carried out through relationships of shared goals and mutual respect, as well as shared knowledge. Building on Beth Bechky (2006), they propose that this broader concept of relational coordination can be achieved through role-based relationships, not just interpersonal relationships, thus reducing limits to sustainability and replicability. Moreover, they propose, the formal organizational practices found in high-performance work systems can be redesigned to foster these role-based relationships among workers, which can facilitate the coordination of work and promote the quality and efficiency outcomes associated with improved coordination. The relational approach to coordination is therefore poised to integrate bureaucratic organizational features along with relational organizational features, drawing upon both the rationalist and interactionist paradigms.

QUESTIONS FOR DISCUSSION

1. What does coordination look like when it is a relational process? What does it look like when it is a mechanistic or bureaucratic process?
2. What are the advantages of carrying out coordination in a relational way? Disadvantages?
3. What are the advantages of carrying out coordination in a bureaucratic way? Disadvantages?
4. How might you combine the advantages of relational and bureaucratic approaches to coordination?

SUGGESTIONS FOR FURTHER READING

Crowston, Kevin and Eva Kammerer. 1998. "Coordination and Collective Mind in Software Requirements Development." *IBM Systems Journal,* 372:227–45.

Gittell, Jody Hoffer. 2011. "New Directions for Relational Coordination Theory." Pp. 74–94 in *Oxford Handbook of Positive Organizational Scholarship,* edited by Kim Cameron and Gretchen Spreitzer. Oxford: Oxford University Press.

Wageman, Ruth. 1995. "Interdependence and Group Effectiveness." *Administrative Science Quarterly,* 40:145–80.

REFERENCES

Adler, Paul S. and Brian Borys. 1996. "Two Types of Bureaucracy: Enabling and Coercive." *Administrative Science Quarterly,* 41:61–89.

Argote, Linda. 1982. "Input Uncertainty and Organizational Coordination in Hospital Emergency Units." *Administrative Science Quarterly,* 27:420–34.

Bechky, Beth. 2006. "Gaffers, Gofers and Grips: Role-Based Coordination in Temporary Organizations." *Organization Science,* 17(1):3–21.

Faraj, Samer and Lee Sproull. 2000. "Coordinating Expertise in Software Development Teams." *Management Science,* 46(12):1554–68.

Faraj, Samer and Yin Xiao. 2006. "Coordination in Fast Response Organizations." *Management Science,* 52(8):1155–69.

Follett, Mary Parker. 1949. "The Process of Control." Pp. 77–89 in *Freedom and Co-ordination: Lectures in Business Organization by Mary Parker Follett,* edited by L. Urwick. London: Management Publications Trust, Ltd.

Galbraith, Jay. 1972. "Organization Design: An Information Processing View." Pp. 49–74 in *Organization Planning: Cases and Concepts.* Homewood, IL: Richard D. Irwin.

Gittell, Jody Hoffer. 2002. "Coordinating Mechanisms in Care Provider Groups: Relational Coordination as a Mediator and Input Uncertainty as a Moderator of Performance Effects." *Management Science,* 48(11):1408–426.

Gittell, Jody Hoffer, Rob Seidner, and Julian Wimbush. 2010. "A Relational Model of How High-Performance Work Systems Work." *Organization Science,* 21(2):490–506.

Lawrence, Paul and Jay Lorsch. 1967. *Organization and Environment: Managing Differentiation and Integration.* Boston: Graduate School of Business Administration, Harvard University.

Malone, Thomas and Kevin Crowston. 1994. "The Interdisciplinary Study of Coordination." *Computing Surveys,* 26(1):87–119.

March, James and Herbert Simon. 1958. *Organizations.* New York: Wiley.

Mead, George Herbert. 1934. *Mind, Self, and Society: From the Standpoint of a Social Behaviorist,* edited by Charles W. Morris. Chicago: University of Chicago Press.

Quinn, Ryan and Jane E. Dutton. 2005. "Coordination as Energy-in-Conversation." *Academy of Management Review,* 30(1):36–57.

Stephens, J. P. 2010. *Towards a Psychology of Coordination: Exploring Feeling and Focus in the Individual and Group in Music-Making.* Unpublished doctoral dissertation, University of Michigan–Ann Arbor.

Thompson, James. 1967. *Organizations in Action: Social Science Bases of Administrative Theory.* New York: McGraw-Hill.

Tushman, Michael and David Nadler. 1978. "Information Processing as an Integrating Concept in Organizational Design." *Academy of Management Review,* 3:613–24.

Weick, Karl. 1995. *Sensemaking in Organizations.* Thousand Oaks, CA: Sage.

Weick, Karl and Karlene Roberts. 1993. "Collective Mind in Organizations: Heedful Interrelating on Flight Decks." *Administrative Science Quarterly,* 38:357–81.

15

THE PROCESS OF CONTROL

MARY PARKER FOLLETT

Four fundamental principles of organisation are:

(1) Co-ordination as the reciprocal relating of all the factors in a situation.

(2) Co-ordination by direct contact of the responsible people concerned.

(3) Co-ordination in the early stages.

(4) Co-ordination as a continuing process.

My first principle, co-ordination as the reciprocal relating of all the factors in a situation, shows us just what this process of co-ordination actually is, shows us the nature of unity. We have considered unity, but I want to penetrate further into its meaning. We have seen the process by which any two people may combine their different kinds of knowledge and experience. I compared it to a game of tennis. Let us now take more than two. There usually are more than two concerned in any decision. Take four heads of departments. You cannot envisage accurately what happens between them by thinking of A as adjusting himself to B and to C and to D. A adjusts himself to B and also to a B influenced by C and to a B influenced by D and to a B influenced by A himself. Again he adjusts himself to C and also to a C influenced by B and to a C influenced by D and to a C influenced by A himself—and so on. One

could work it out mathematically. This sort of reciprocal relating, this interpenetration of every part by every other part and again by every other part as it has been permeated by all, should be the goal of all attempts at co-ordination, a goal, of course, never wholly reached.

You will understand that I am simplifying when I speak of A, B, C and D adjusting themselves to one another. They are of course at the same time adjusting themselves to every other factor in the situation. Or it would be more accurate to say that all the factors in the situation are going through this process of reciprocal relating.

If anyone finds this principle difficult to accept, I would suggest that it is a principle which he has already accepted in regard to facts. Any fact gains its significance through its relation to all the other facts pertaining to the situation. For instance, if you have increased sales, you are not too pleased until you find out whether there has been an increased sales cost. If there has been, or one out of proportion to sales, your satisfaction disappears. Merchandising shows you this principle at work. For merchandising is not merely a bringing together of designing, engineering, manufacturing and sales departments, [but] it is these in their total relativity.

This may seem a rather clumsy phrase, *total relativity* [italics added], but I am trying to express a total which shall include all the factors in a situation not as an additional total but as a relational total—a total where each part has been permeated by every other part.

The possible examples from business management of the working of this fundamental principle are innumerable. Take a situation made by credit conditions, customers' demand, output facilities and workers' attitude. They all together constitute a certain situation, but they constitute that situation through their relation to one another. They don't form a total situation merely by existing side by side.

It is necessary to emphasize this because while it is customary nowadays to speak of "the total situation"—you find that phrase often in articles on business management—that phrase, *total situation* [italics added], means to many people merely that we must be sure to get all the factors into our problem. But that is by no means enough for us to do, [and] we have to see these factors [with] each one affecting every one of the others.

Many examples of this come to mind at once. Take an instance of a social worker. She is dealing with a girl of a difficult temperament, who has a nagging stepmother, is working at a job for which she is not fitted, and has evening recreations of not the most wholesome character. It is obvious that here you have a situation, a whole, made up not of its parts but of the interacting of the parts. Perhaps it is because the girl is working at something she is not interested in that makes her seek over-excitement in the evening. And so on. The most successful social worker is not the one who deals with these separately, but [the one] who sees them in relation to one another.

This is the first requirement of statesmanship. We shall get no control over economic conditions until we have statesmen who can meet this requirement. American life is stagnant at present for lack of any such statesman. Here we say Buy British, but then the foreigner will not be able to buy our goods if we do not buy of him, and where are we then? I do not say we shouldn't Buy British. I do not know; personally I have been doing so. I say only that we shall get no grip on our economic affairs until we acquire a greater capacity than we seem to have at present for understanding how economic factors affect one another at every point.

I am talking in all this of the nature of a unity. This, which is a matter of everyday experience to business men in their problems of co-ordinating, happens to be considered by some scientists the most important thing in present scientific thinking. The most interesting thing in the world to me is the correspondence between progressive business thinking and certain recent developments in the thinking of scientists and philosophers. Such biologists as J. B. S. Haldane, such philosophers as Whitehead, such physiologists as Sherrington, are telling us that the essential nature of a unity is discovered not alone by a study of its separate elements, but also by observing how these elements interact.

I could give you many examples from the sciences. I am going to take a moment to give you one, although it may seem far from my subject, simply to bring home to you this remarkable correspondence in thinking in such entirely different fields. I found this in an article in a Journal of Zoology—a very different subject from business management! The article was on the local distribution of wild mice, and the whole point of the article was that this distribution, while controlled by food and water supply, by nesting material, by climatic conditions, and by antagonism between species, while controlled by these, was controlled by them only as they were related to one another, that the behaviour of the wild mice was governed by an environmental complex, that it was not influenced by these various factors one by one.

I thought this expression, "environmental complex," strikingly like what I have been trying to say to you in describing the nature of unities, very much like what I called a relational total as distinct from an additional total. And business men, as I have said, see this every day. The ablest business man, or social worker, or statesman, the ablest worker in any field, looks at an "environmental complex," sees the solution of his problem depending on the interacting of the elements of that complex.

This seems to me a principle of the utmost importance for industry or for any joint endeavour. This seems to me as important a principle for the social sciences as Einstein's theory of relativity has been for the natural sciences. They are both, it may be noticed in passing, concerned with relativity. I believe that the principle of relativity in the realm of social theory will displace as many of our old ideas in the social sciences as Einstein's has in the natural sciences. And I think it greatly to the honour of progressive business thinking that it is taking a lead here—a lead which I am sure must be followed eventually by statesmen, national and international.

Before I leave this point, let me call particularly to your attention that this reciprocal relating, co-ordinating, unifying, is a process which does not require sacrifice on the part of the individual. The fallacy that the individual must give up his individuality for the sake of the whole is one of the most pervasive, the most insidious, fallacies I know. It crops up again and again in one place after another. In some of the businesses I have studied, I have been told that the head of a department should subordinate the good of his department to the good of the whole undertaking. But of course he should do no such thing. His departmental point of view is needed in the whole. It must indeed be reconciled with all the other points of view in the business, but it must not be abandoned. Just as we have been told by an eminent authority in international matters that men should not de-nationalise themselves but internationalise themselves, so I should say to the heads of departments that they should not de-departmentalise themselves but inter-departmentalise themselves. In other words, departmental policy should be an integral part of what is known as "general policy." General policy is not an imaginary "whole," an air-plant, [but] it is the interweaving of many policies. Whether we are talking of the individual man, or individual department, the word should never be *sacrifice*, [and] it should always be *contribution* [italics added]. We want every possible contribution to the whole.

My second principle was co-ordination by direct contact of the responsible people concerned. We saw last week that in some industrial plants, control is exercised through cross relations between heads of departments instead of up and down the line through the chief executive. This seems sensible as these are the people closest to the matter in hand. Moreover, if my first principle was right, if the process of co-ordination is one of interpenetration, it is obvious that it cannot be imposed by an outside body. It is essentially, basically, by its very nature, a process of auto-controlled activity. It is the same as with

the individual. We know that every individual has many warring tendencies inside himself. We know that the effectiveness of an individual, his success in life, depends largely on these various tendencies, impulses, desires, being adjusted to one another, being made into one harmonious whole. Yet no one can issue a fiat by which I am adjusted, [and] I can only be helped to adjust myself. It is the same with a group, with a group of executives for instance. Here too the process is one of self-adjustment. This being so, it is essential that they should have the opportunity for direct contact.

My third principle was co-ordination in the early stages. This means that the direct contact must begin in the earliest stages of the process. We see how this works in the co-relation of policies in a business. If the heads of departments confront each other with finished policies, agreement will be found difficult. Of course they then begin to "play politics," or that is often the tendency. But if these heads meet while they are forming their policies, meet and discuss the questions involved, a successful co-relation is far more likely to be reached. Their thinking has not become crystallized. They can still modify one another. I should say that one of the fundamental ideas for business management is that the making of decisions and the co-relating of decisions should be one process. You cannot, with the greatest degree of success for your undertaking, make policy forming and policy adjusting two separate processes. Policy adjusting cannot begin after the separate policies have been completed.

I speak of the co-relation of departmental policies, yet the principle of early stages should, I believe, begin to be operative far earlier than with the heads of departments—with heads of sub-divisions, with foremen, and, where you have union-management co-operation, with the workers themselves. In the union-management plan of the Baltimore & Ohio Railroad, the adjustment of trade unions and management begins down in the lowest shop committees. We see this also in the Canadian railways. The same principle should guide us where we have shop stewards or employee representatives on committees. That is, we shouldn't put to these representatives of the workers finished plans in order merely to get their consent. We should bring them into the game while the plan is still in a formative stage. If we do not, one or two things is likely to happen, both bad: either we shall get a rubber-stamp consent and thus lose what they might contribute to the problem in question, or else we shall find ourselves with a fight on our hands—an open fight or discontent seething underneath.

I do not mean by this that I think workers should be consulted on all questions, only on those on which they are competent to have some opinion. To that extent I think they should have a share in management. If control is the process of the inter-functioning of the parts, if the most perfect control is where we have the inter-functioning of all the parts, then I think the workers should have a share, not from any vague idea of democracy, not because of their "rights," but simply because if you leave out one element in a situation you will have just that much less control. It has been found that piece-rates cannot be wholly decided by an expert, that the question of fatigue cannot be wholly decided by psychologists, that the cost of living cannot be wholly decided by statisticians. And so on.

And it is because of this conception of control which I have been giving you that I cannot believe in "workers' control" as advocated by some in the Labour Party. I think managers and workers should share in a joint control.

These two principles, direct contact and early stages—I have given you three principles now, reciprocal relating, direct contact and early stages— these last two, direct contact and early stages, which I have seen in operation in some of our industries, governed some of the Allied co-operation during the War, and are vigorously advocated by Sir Arthur Salter in his *Allied Shipping Control.* He thinks that adjustments between nations should be made not through their Foreign Offices, but between those who exercise responsible authority in the matters concerned, that is, between departmental ministers. This corresponds, you see, to what I have said of the cross-relations between departments in a business. And in regard to the principle of early stages, Sir Arthur shows us most convincingly that a genuine international policy cannot be evolved by first for-mulating your national policy and then presenting it as a finished product to confront the policies of other nations. For the only process, he tells us, by which completed policies can be adjusted is that of

bargaining and compromise; if you want integration, he says, the process of the interpenetration of poli-cies must begin before they are completed, while they are still in the formative stage.

It seems to me extraordinarily significant that we should find these principles recognised in such different fields as those of business management and international relations. It means that our ablest thinkers, men who are at the same time thinkers and doers, have found a way of making collective control collective self-control. That is a phrase used by Sir Arthur Salter and I think it a remarkably good one—*collective self-control* [italics added].

My fourth principle was co-ordination as a con-tinuous process. Just as I think that co-ordination cannot be enforced on us, that it must be a self-activity, just as I think it must begin in the earliest stages, so I think it must go on all the time. I do not think that the various people concerned should meet to try to unite only when difficulties arise. I think that continuous machinery for this purpose should be provided.

One reason for this is that there is then a greater incentive to discover the principles which can serve as guides for future similar cases. If we make some classification of problems, then when a fresh one arises we can see the points in which that resembles a certain class of case, and we can ask "Have we evolved any principles for dealing with cases of this kind?" One of the interesting things about the League of Nations as one watches its work at Geneva, is that many in the Secretariat are trying deliberately to discover the principles underlying the decisions made in order that they may be taken as precedents in similar cases arising later. A mem-ber of the political section of the Secretariat said to me: "Our treatment of every question is two-fold:

(1) An attempt to solve the immediate problem;

(2) The attempt to discover root causes to help our work the future."

Another advantage of continuous machinery for co-ordination is that then the line is not broken from planning to activity and from activity to further planning. A mistake we often tend to make is that the world stands still while we are going through a certain adjustment. And it does not. Facts change,

[and] we must keep up with the facts; keeping up with the facts changes the facts. In other words, the process of adjustment changes the things to be adjusted. If you want an illustration of this, consider the financial and economic adjustments between nations. When one financial adjustment is made, that means only that we have a fresh financial problem on our hands, [or that] the adjustment has made a new situation which means a new problem. We pass from situation to situation. It is a fallacy to think that we can solve problems—in any final sense. The belief that we can do so is a drag upon our thinking. What we need is some process for meeting problems. When we think we have solved one, well, by the very process of solving, new elements or forces come into the situation and you have a new problem on your hands to be solved. When this happens men are often discouraged. I wonder why; it is our strength and our hope. We do not want any system that holds us enmeshed within itself.

In order, however, to get the fullest benefit of continuous machinery for co-ordinating, in order to utilise our experience, get the advantage of precedents, be able to formulate principles, we must learn how to classify our experience. I do not think any satisfactory method for that has yet been worked out. I was present once at a meeting of heads of departments in a large shop, and heard one of these heads say in regard to a case they were discussing, "We had a problem like this two or three years ago. Does anyone remember how we treated that?" No one did! We talk much about learning from experience, but we cannot do that unless we

(1) observe our experience,

(2) keep records of our experience, and

(3) organise our experience, that is, relate one bit to another.

Unrelated experience is of little use to us; we can never make wise decisions from isolated bits, only as we see the parts in relation to one another.

I have given four principles of organisation. These principles show the basis of control, show the process of control, show that control is a process. They show us control as self-generated through a process of the interweaving of the parts. The degree of co-relation is the measure of control; the more complete the reciprocal adjusting, the more complete the control.

We find this principle also in the sciences. I said a few moments ago that scientists are finding that the nature of the unities they deal with is governed by a certain principle and that that is the same principle which we find in the co-ordinations that appear in the running of a business. I want now to go further and say that both scientists and business men find that this principle of unity is the principle of control, that is, that organisation is control.

Biologists tell us that the organising activity of the organism is the directing activity, that the organism gets its power of self-direction through being an organism, that is, through the functional relating of its parts.

On the physiological level, control means co-ordination. I cannot get up in the morning, I cannot walk downstairs without that co-ordination of muscles which is control. The athlete has more of that co-ordination than I have and therefore has more control than I have.

On the personal level I gain more and more control over myself as I co-ordinate my various tendencies.

This is just what we have found in business. Let me remind you how often we have noticed this even in the few illustrations I have had time to give you in these talks. We have seen that if the price of a certain article has to be lowered, the situation will not be controlled by the production manager's solution of the problem, or by the sales manager's. The situation will be controlled when these two men, and the others concerned, unite their different points of view. We saw that if the personnel manager tries to force his opinion of a worker on the foreman, or the foreman tries to force his opinion on the personnel manager, the situation will not be controlled.

The question of the debt to America will find no satisfactory solution if either America tries to force her will on England or England tries to force her will on America. We shall have control of the situation only if England and America are able to unite their different points of view, only if we can find what I have called in these talks an integration. A writer in the *Observer* last Sunday spoke of the divergence between English and American opinion on the debt question, but added that there were indications that we might yet be able to get the hyphen back into Anglo-American opinion. That expresses wittily and concisely what I have taken two hours to say to you. His hyphen is a symbol of my integration. If instead of an English opinion and an American opinion, we can get an Anglo-American opinion, that unity will mean control of the situation.

I come now to my conclusion. We aim at co-ordination in industry because we know that through unity an enterprise generates its own driving force. And this self-generated control does not coerce. But I do not think that this kind of control is sufficiently understood. Everyone knows that our period of *laissez-faire* is over, but socialists wish to give us in its place state control and they mean by that state coercion—we find again and again in their pamphlets the words *force, coerce* [italics added]. Those using these words are making the fatal mistake, I believe, of thinking that the opposite of *laissez-faire* is coercion. And it is not. The opposite of *laissez-faire* is co-ordination.

Others who do not believe in state control are urging National Planning Boards of experts to co-ordinate industry. If these boards were to be composed of the heads of industry or their representatives, we might hope to have the kind of self-adjusting, of self-correlating, which I have been describing to you, but I have not seen any plan which allows for this process. Therefore I do not believe that as at present conceived they will bring us any appreciable degree of co-ordination. The policies of our different industrial and economic organisations will have to be adjusted to one another by changes not imposed by an outside authority, but voluntarily undertaken, no, not exactly undertaken, but spontaneously brought about by the process of integration. In order for this to be done, the Planning Boards will have to be composed of the heads of the

industries themselves, of course with expert economists on the Board as well. I think the consideration of Planning Boards a splendid step in the right direction. I am only hoping that before we establish such Boards we shall see that both their composition and their functions are in line with the more progressive thinking on organisation.

The period of *laissez-faire* is indeed over, but I do not think we want to put in its place a forcibly controlled society, whether it be controlled by the state of the socialists or the experts of a planning board. The aim and the process of the organisation of government, of industry, of international relations, should be, I think, a control not imposed from without the regular functioning of society, but one which is a co-ordinating of all those functions, that is, a collective self-control.

If then you accept my definition of control as a self-generating process, as the interweaving experience of all those who are performing a functional part of the activity under consideration, does not that constitute an imperative? Are we not every one of us bound to take some part consciously in this process? Today we are slaves to the chaos in which we are living. To get our affairs in hand, to feel a grip on them, to become free, we must learn, and practise, I am sure, the methods of collective control. To this task we can all devote ourselves. At the same time that we are selling goods or making goods, or whatever we are doing, we can be working in harmony with this fundamental law of life. We can be aware that by this method control is in our power.

SOURCE: Follett, Mary Parker. 1949. "The Process of Control." Pp. 77–89 in *Freedom and Co-ordination: Lectures in Business Organization by Mary Parker Follett*, edited by L. Urwick. London: Management Publications Trust, Ltd.

16

THE DIVISION OF WORK

JAMES G. MARCH AND HERBERT A. SIMON

Insofar as tasks are highly programmed, the division of work is a problem of efficient allocation of activities among individuals and among organizational units. However, we need to make two distinctions that tend to be overlooked in the classical theory: First, there is a problem of specialization among organizational units. There is no reason to suppose that both sets of problems have the same answers or that the same general principles apply to both. Second, the division of work that is most effective for the performance of relatively programmed tasks need not be the same as that which is most effective for the performance of relatively unprogrammed tasks. In the present discussion, we shall be concerned primarily with programmed tasks.

The economies of individual specialization arise principally from opportunities for using programs repetitively. To develop in a person the capacity to carry out a particular program requires an investment in training. In automatic operations, there is an analogous capital investment in machinery capable of carrying out the program. In the case of a computing machine, a substantial part of this investment actually consists of the cost of programming the machine for the particular operations in question. In all of these cases there are economics to be derived, *ceteris paribus,* from assigning the work so as to minimize this investment cost per unit of program execution.

Programs that are built into machines or acquired by humans usually take the form of generalized means—skills or processing capacities that can be used in executing a wide variety of tasks. Typing skill, for example, is a skill of transforming any manuscript into type-written form, and typing occurs as a subprogram in a wide range of programs. Similarly, a drill press is a bundle of capacities for drilling holes; the program can be called into play whenever the fabrication of some product requires holes to be drilled.

This rather obvious point underlies the central problem in specializing highly programmed activities. Consider an organization that performs a large number of tasks, each consisting of the fabrication of a product. If we analyze the fabrication process into subprograms, we find that it becomes economical to arrange the work so that there will be specialized means (machines and trained employees) for performing some of these subprograms. But since a number of these specialties will be required for the manufacture of each product, we create in this way considerable interdependence and need for coordination among them. The greater the *specialization by subprograms* (process specialization), the greater the *interdependencies among organizational subunits.*

Interdependence does not by itself cause difficulty if the pattern of interdependence is stable and fixed. For in this case, each subprogram can be designed to take account of all the other subprograms with which it interacts. Difficulties arise only if program execution rests on contingencies that cannot be predicted perfectly in advance. In this case, coordinating activity is required to secure agreement about the estimates that will be used as the basis for action, or to provide information to each subprogram unit about the relevant activities of the others. Hence, we arrive at the proposition that the more repetitive and predictable the situation, the greater the *tolerance for interdependence.* Conversely, the greater the elements of variability and contingency, the greater is the burden of coordinating activities that are specialized by process (MacMahon, Millet, and Ogden, 1941).

Thus, we predict that process specialization will be carried furthest in stable environments, and that under rapidly changing circumstances specialization will be sacrificed to secure greater self-containment of separate programs. A second prediction is that organizations, in order to permit a greater degree of process specialization, will devise means for increasing stability and predictability of the environment.

Three important devices come under this heading. All of these devices may be regarded as instances of the more general practice of standardization—of reducing the infinite number of things in the world, potential and actual—to a moderate number of well-defined varieties. The greater the *standardization of the situation*, the greater the tolerance for subunit interdependencies.

The first step in almost all major manufacturing sequences that lead from natural raw materials to finished goods is refining. In steel manufacture, a complex of natural materials—ores, coke, and flux—is reduced to a relatively homogeneous, standard material—pig iron. In the natural textile industries, fibers are transformed into threads of uniform size, strength, and elasticity by carding and spinning processes. In all such cases, the complexity of subsequent manufacturing processes and their contingency on raw materials is reduced by transforming highly variable natural materials into much more homogeneous semimanufactured products. After homogeneity has been attained, subsequent steps in the manufacturing process may again produce

great variety in the product—alloy steels in the first example, dyed fabrics in the second. But it is often difficult and expensive to program this subsequent elaboration unless the processing begins with a simple, homogeneous material of known properties.

A second important device for dealing with the interdependencies created by specialization is the use of interchangeable parts. When the fit of two parts is assured by setting minimum and maximum size limits, the interdependency between the units that make them is decreased and the burden of coordination partly removed.

Third, the need for coordinated timing between successive process steps is reduced by holding buffer inventories. If process A precedes process B in the manufacture of some item, then the effect of variations in the rate of process A upon process B can be largely removed by maintaining an inventory of products on which process A has been completed.

Even with such devices, the need for coordination typically remains. The most common device for securing coordination among subprograms where there is a high degree of process specialization is scheduling. A schedule is simply a plan, established in advance, that determines what tasks will be handled and when. It may have greater or less detail, greater or less precision. The *type of coordination* used in the organization is a function of the extent to which the situation is standardized. To the extent that contingencies arise, not anticipated in the schedule, coordination requires communication to give notice of deviations from planned or predicted conditions, or to give instructions for changes in activity to adjust to these deviations. We may label coordination based on pre-established schedules *coordination by plan,* and coordination that involves transmission of new information *coordination by feedback.* The more stable and predictable the situation, the greater the reliance on coordination by plan; the more variable and unpredictable the situation, the greater the reliance on coordination by feedback.

Insofar as coordination is programmed and the range of situations sufficiently circumscribed, we would not expect any particularly close relation between the coordinative mechanisms and the formal organizational hierarchy. That is to say, scheduling information and feedback information required for coordination are not usually communicated through hierarchical channels. Hierarchy may be important in establishing and legitimizing programs, but the communication involved in the execution of highly programmed activities does not generally follow the "lines of command" (Bakke, 1950).

In addition, from the standpoint of any particular organization, specialization and the structure of subprograms is as much sociological as it is technological. The organization depends to a great extent upon the training that employees bring to it—training acquired by apprenticeship or in schools. Hence the boundaries of specialization of individual jobs tend to be determined by the structure of trades and professions in the broader social environment.

Communication

On the basis of the foregoing analysis, we may classify the occasions for communication as follows:

1. Communication for nonprogrammed activity. This is a catchall category that will need further analysis later.

2. Communication to initiate and establish programs, including day-to-day adjustment or "coordination" of programs.

3. Communication to provide data for application of strategies (i.e., required for the execution of programs).

4. Communication to evoke programs (i.e., communications that serve as "stimuli").

5. Communication to provide information on the results of activities.

The distinction between the first two categories and the last three is the familiar distinction between communication relating to procedural matters and communication relating to substantive content.

Empirical evidence for the distinction among the last three categories was obtained from a study of the use of accounting data by operating departments in manufacturing concerns. It was found that accounting information was used at various executive levels to answer three different kinds of questions: (a) Problem-solving questions: Which course of action is better? This corresponds to our

category three. (b) Attention-directing questions: What problems shall I look into? This corresponds to category four. (c) Score-card questions: How well am I (or is he) doing? This corresponds to category five. Some of the accounting information was also used in connection with less programmed activity (Simon, Guetzkow, Kozmetsky, and Tyndall, 1954). We will consider this point below.

Communication and Coordination

The capacity of an organization to maintain a complex, highly interdependent pattern of activity is limited in part by its capacity to handle the communication required for coordination. The greater the *efficiency of communication* within the organization, the greater the tolerance for interdependence. The problem has both quantitative and qualitative aspects.

As we noted earlier, it is possible under some conditions to reduce the volume of communication required from day-to-day by substituting coordination by plan for coordination by feedback. By virtue of this substitution, organizations can tolerate very complex interrelations among their component parts in the performance of repetitive activities. The coordination of parts is incorporated in the program when it is established, and the need for continuing communication is correspondingly reduced. Each specific situation, as it arises, is largely covered by the standard operating procedure.

A different method for increasing the organisation's tolerance for interdependence is to increase the efficiency of communication by making it possible to communicate large amounts of information with relatively few symbols. An obvious example is the blueprint, which provides a common plan stated in extreme detail. The blueprint employs a carefully defined, highly developed "language" or set of symbolic and verbal conventions. Because of this standardized language, it can convey large quantities of information. The same attention to standardization of language is seen in accounting systems and other reporting systems that employ numerical data.

Accounting definitions and blueprint conventions are examples of a still more general phenomenon: technical languages, whose symbols have definite and common meanings to the members of an organization. Prominent in these technical languages are categories for classifying situations and events.

The role of unambiguous technical terms in permitting coordination by feedback is shown by the Christie-Luce-Macy experiments (Macy, Christie, and Luce, 1953) with "noisy marbles" in the Bavelas network. Participants in the experiment were given some colored marbles, and they were required to discover what color was held by all of them. Control groups were given marbles that had solid colors like "red," "yellow," etc. Experimental groups were given streaked marbles whose colorings did not correspond in any simple way to color designations in common language. Comparison of the performance of the control with the experimental groups showed (a) that the latter were much hindered by the lack of adequate technical vocabulary, and (b) that their performance became comparable to that of the control groups only when they succeeded in inventing such a vocabulary and securing its acceptance throughout the group.

Classification schemes are of particular significance for the program-evoking aspects of communication. When an event occurs that calls for some kind of organization response, the question is asked, in one form or other: "What *kind* of event is this?" The organization has available a repertory of programs, so that once the event has been classified the appropriate program can be executed without further ado. We can make this process more specific with a pair of examples.

The oil gauge on the dashboard of an automobile is an example of the use of classification in program-evoking. For most drivers, the oil pressure is either "all right" or "low." In the first case, no action is taken; in the second case a remedial program is initiated (e.g., taking the automobile to a repair shop). Some auto manufacturers have substituted a red light, which turns on when the oil pressure is not in the proper range, for the traditional gauge. This example also illustrates how substituting standards of satisfactory performance for criteria of optimization simplifies communication.

Similarly, inspection activities often involve dichotomous decisions. In those cases, the choice is not usually between evoking a program or not evoking one (action or inaction), but between different programs. Thus, if the item being inspected meets the standards, one program is evoked (it is passed on for further processing); if it fails to meet standards, another program is evoked (scrapping, or reworking, as the case may be).

One reason that classifying is so economical of communication is that most of the coordination can be preprogrammed; the organization has a repertory of responses to stimuli, and it only needs to know what kind of stimulus it is confronted with in order to execute an elaborate program. On the other hand, if the communication system could handle a more complete description of the program-evoking event, and if the action part of the organization had the capacity to develop programs on the spot to meet present needs, no doubt one could conceive tailor-made programs that would be more accurately adapted to each separate situation than are the preprogrammed responses.

Here again the normative or adaptive problem of organization design is one of balance. If its model of reality is not to be so complex as to paralyze it, the organization must develop radical simplifications of its responses. One such simplification is to have (a) a repertory of standard responses, (b) a classification of program-evoking situations, (c) a set of rules to determine what is the appropriate response for each class of situations. The balance of economies and efficiencies here is exactly the same as it is in all cases of standardization. Note that what we have described in an organizational framework is quite comparable to discrimination learning in individuals. In the individual case, as in the organizational, there is a close relationship between the categories used in the cognitive code and the operational decision rules (Whorf, 1956).

In our culture, language is well developed for describing and communicating about concrete objects. The blueprint has already been mentioned as an important technical device for this purpose. Language is also very effective in communicating about things that can be classified and named, even if they are intangible. Thus, when there are standard repertories of programs, it is easy to refer to them.

On the other hand, it is extremely difficult to communicate about intangible objects and nonstandardized objects. Hence, the heaviest burdens are placed on the communications system by the less structured aspects of the organization's tasks, particularly by activity directed toward the explanation of problems that are not yet well defined. This difference in communication difficulty has important implications for the organization of nonprogrammed activities.

Where the available means of communication are primitive—relative to the communication needs—so will be the system of coordination. There will tend to be less self-containment of organizational units and a greater reliance on coordination through communication the greater the efficiency of communication. This relation may sometimes be obscured by the fact that pressure toward coordination (e.g., under conditions of rapid change) may compel attempts at feedback coordination even though available communication is inefficient. It should also be noted that self-containment decreases and interdependencies increase the likelihood of developing an efficient communication code.

The Absorption of Uncertainty

The use of classification schemes in communication has further consequences, some of which go back to our earlier discussion of perception and identification. The technical vocabulary and classification schemes in an organization provide a set of concepts that can be used in analyzing and in communicating about its problems. Anything that is easily described and discussed in terms of these concepts can be communicated readily in the organization; anything that does not fit the system of concepts is communicated only with difficulty. Hence, the world tends to be perceived by the organization members in terms of the particular concepts that are reflected in the organization's vocabulary. The particular categories and schemes of classification it employs are reified, and become, for members of the organization, attributes of the world rather than mere conventions (Blau, 1955).

The reification of the organization's conceptual scheme is particularly noticeable in *uncertainty absorption*. Uncertainty absorption takes place when inferences are drawn from a body of evidence and the inferences, instead of the evidence itself, are then communicated. The successive editing steps that transform data obtained from a set of questionnaires into printed statistical tables provide a simple example of uncertainty absorption.

Through the process of uncertainty absorption, the recipient of a communication is severely limited in his ability to judge its correctness. Although there may be various tests of apparent validity, internal consistency, and consistency with other communications, the recipient must, by and large, repose his confidence in the editing process that has taken place, and, if he accepts the communication at all, accept it pretty much as it stands. To the extent that he can interpret it, his interpretation must be based primarily on his confidence in the source and his knowledge of the biases to which the source is subject, rather than on a direct examination of the evidence.

By virtue of specialization, most information enters an organization at highly specific points. Direct perception of production processes is limited largely to employees in a particular operation on the production floor. Direct perception of customer attitudes is limited largely to salesmen. Direct evidence of the performance of personnel is restricted largely to immediate supervisors, colleagues, and subordinates.

In all of these cases, the person who summarizes and assesses his own direct perceptions and transmits them to the rest of the organization becomes an important source of informational premises for organizational action. The "facts" he communicates can be disbelieved, but they can only rarely be checked. Hence, by the very nature and limits of the communication system, a great deal of discretion and influence is exercised by those persons who are in direct contact with some part of the "reality" that is of concern to the organization. Both the amount and the *locus of uncertainty absorption* affect the *influence structure of the organization*.

Because of this, uncertainty absorption is frequently used, consciously and unconsciously, as a technique for acquiring and exercising power. In a culture where direct contradiction of assertions of fact is not approved, an individual who is willing to make assertions, particularly about matters that do not contradict the direct perceptions of others, can frequently get these assertions accepted as premises of decision.

We can cite a number of more or less "obvious" variables that affect the absorption of uncertainty. The more complex the data that are perceived and the less adequate the organization's language, the closer to the source of the information will the uncertainty absorption take place, and the greater will be the amount of summarizing at each step of transmission. The locus of absorption will tend to be a function of such variables as: (a) the needs of the recipient for raw as against summarized information (depending upon the kinds of data used in selecting the appropriate program), (b) the need for correction of biases in the transmitter, (c) the distribution of technical competence for interpreting and summarizing raw data, and (d) the need for comparing data from two or more sources in order to interpret it.

The way in which uncertainty is absorbed has important consequences for coordination among organizational units. In business organizations, expected sales are relevant to decisions in many parts of the organization: purchasing decisions, production decisions, investment decisions, and many others. But if each organizational unit were permitted to make its own forecast of sales, there might be a wide range of such estimates with consequent inconsistencies among the decisions made by different departments—the purchasing department, for example, buying raw materials that the production department does not expect to process. It may be important in cases of this kind to make an *official* forecast and to use this official forecast as the basis for action throughout the organization.

Where it is important that all parts of an organization act on the same premises, and where different individuals may draw different conclusions from the raw evidence, a formal uncertainty absorption point will be established, and the inferences drawn at that point will have official status in the organization as "legitimate" estimates. The greater the need for coordination in the organization, the greater the *use of legitimized "facts."*

The Communication Network

Associated with each program is a set of information flows that communicate the stimuli and data required to evoke and execute the program. Generally this communication traverses definite channels, either by formal plan or by the gradual development of informal programs. Information and stimuli move from sources to points of decision; instructions move from points of decision to points of action; information of results moves from points of action to points of decision and control.

Rational organization design would call for the arrangement of these channels so as to minimize the communication burden. But insofar as the points of origin of information and the points of action are determined in advance, the only mobile element is the point of decision. Whatever may be the position in the organization holding the formal authority to legitimize the decision, to a considerable extent the effective discretion is exercised at the points of uncertainty absorption.

In large organizations, specialization of communication functions will be reflected in the division of work itself. Among the specialized communication units we find are (a) units specializing in the actual physical transmission of communications: a telephone and teletype unit, messenger group, or the like; (b) units specializing in recording and report preparation: bookkeeping and other record-keeping units; (c) units specializing in the acquisition of raw information, usually referred to as intelligence units, sometimes as research units; (d) units specializing in the provision of technical premises for decision: research units, technical specialists; (e) units specializing in the interpretation of policy and organizational goals, a function usually not much separated from the main stem of the hierarchy; and (f) units specializing in the retention of information: files, archives units.

In part, communication channels are deliberately and consciously planned in the course of programming. In part, they develop through usage. We will make two hypotheses about such development. First, the greater the communication efficiency of the channel, the greater the *communication channel usage.* The possession by two persons, or two organization units, of a common, efficient language facilitates communication. Thus, links between members of a common profession tend to be used in the communication system. Similarly, other determinants of language compatibility—ethnic background, education, age, experience—will affect what channels are used in the organization.

Second, channel usage tends to be self-reinforcing. When a channel is frequently used for one purpose, its use for other unrelated purposes is encouraged. In particular, formal hierarchical channels tend to become general-purpose channels to be used whenever no special-purpose channel or informal channel exists or is known to the communicator. The self-reinforcing character of channel usage is particularly strong if it brings individuals into face-to-face contact. In this case (the Homans hypothesis) informal communication, much of it social in character, develops side-by-side with task-oriented formal communication, and the use of the channel for either kind of communication tends to reinforce its use for the other.

In part, the communication network is planned; in part, it grows up in response to the need for specific kinds of communication; in part, it develops in response to the social functions of communication. At any given stage in its development, its gradual change is much influenced by the pattern that has already become established. Hence, although the structure of the network will be considerably influenced by the structure of the organization's task, it will not be completely determined by the latter.

Once a pattern of communication channels has become established, this pattern will have an important influence on decision-making processes, and particularly upon nonprogrammed activity. We next indicate briefly the nature of this influence.

The existing pattern of communication will determine the relative frequency with which particular members of the organization will encounter particular stimuli, or kinds of stimuli, in their search processes. For example, a research and development unit that has frequent communication with sales engineers and infrequent communication with persons engaged in fundamental research will live in a different environment of new product ideas than a research and development unit that has the opposite communication pattern.

The communication pattern will determine how frequently and forcefully particular consequences of action are brought to the attention of the actor. The degree of specialization, for example, between design engineers, on the one hand, and installation and service engineers, on the other, will have an important influence on the amount of awareness of the former as to the effectiveness of their designs.

From our previous propositions concerning time pressure effects, we would predict that the pattern of communication would have a greater influence on nonprogrammed activities carried out with deadlines and under time pressure than upon activities that involve relatively slow and deliberate processes of decision. For, given sufficient time, if particular information is available anywhere in an organization, its relevance to any particular decision is likely to be noticed. Where decisions are made relatively rapidly, however, only the information that is locally available is likely to be brought to bear. We see here another reason why specialization (in this case specialization with respect to possession of information) is tolerated to a greater degree under "steady-state" conditions than when the organization is adapting to a rapidly changing environment.

REFERENCES

Bakke, E.W. (1950). *Bonds of Organization*. New York.

Blau, P.M. (1955). *The Dynamics of Bureaucracy*. Chicago.

MacMahon, A.W., J.D. Millett, and G. Ogden (1941). *The Administration of Federal Work Relief*. Chicago.

Macy, J., Jr., L.S. Christie, and R.D. Luce (1953). Coding noise in a task-oriented group. *Journal of Abnormal and Social Psychology*, 48: 401–9.

Simon, H.A., H. Guetzkow, G. Kozmetsky, & G. Tyndall (1954). *Centralization vs. Decentralization in Organizing the Controller's Department*. New York: The Controllership Foundation.

Whorf, B.L. (1956). *Language, Thought, and Reality*. New York.

SOURCE: Excerpt (pp. 179–90) from *Organizations*, 2nd Edition, by James G. March and Herbert A. Simon. Copyright 1972. Reproduced with permission of Blackwell Publishing Ltd.

17

ORGANIZATION DESIGN

An Information Processing View

JAY R. GALBRAITH

TASK PREDICTABILITY AND INFORMATION PROCESSING

The relationship between task predictability and organization form is probably like many social science relations in that there are multiple and interacting influences. One explanation was put forth and tested by Lawrence and Lorsch. Their concept of differentiation implies that as tasks vary in predictability, the attitudes of the task performers vary in systematic ways. For example, the predictable task requires personalities with low tolerance for ambiguity while unpredictable tasks require high tolerances. In addition, there is another reason which is more highly related to the overall configuration of the organization. This reason is also suggested by Lawrence and Lorsch.

The basic proposition is that the greater the uncertainty of the task, the greater the amount of information that has to be processed during the execution of the task. If the task is well understood prior to performing it, much of the activity can be preplanned. If it is not understood, then during the actual task execution more knowledge is learned which leads to changes in resource allocations, schedules, and priorities. All these changes require information

processing during task performance. Therefore the greater the *task uncertainty*, the greater the *amount of information* that must be processed in order to insure effective performance. From this proposition it follows that variations in organizational forms are variations in the ability to process varying amounts of information.

The relation must be stated more explicitly and developed further if it is to be useful in further theory development. What has been hypothesized so far can be stated in functional form

$$I = f(u) \tag{1}$$

where

I = the amount of information that must be processed to insure effective performance.

u = degree of uncertainty concerning the task requirements such as resources needed, time to complete, etc.

Another factor influencing the amount of information to be processed is the size of the organization. The greater the size, the greater the amount of information. But there are other factors which are related to size. For a given size firm, more information must be processed if there are many occupations represented than if there are few. Similarly for a given size firm, the greater the number of products the more information must be processed. Thus it is the *number of elements relevant for decision making* that influences the amount of information to be processed. The functional form now becomes

$$I = f(u, N) \qquad (2)$$

where

N = number of elements relevant for decision making such as number of departments, number of occupational specialties, clients, products, etc.

As it stands, equation (2) is still incomplete. The reason is that uncertainty is a necessary but not a sufficient condition to guarantee the need for communication during task execution. The other necessary condition is some degree of *interrelatedness or interdependence* among the elements. That is, the behavior in one department must directly affect the goal accomplishment of another. Then as one unit learns more about its task it cannot unilaterally change schedules and priorities. It must communicate with other units that would be affected by a schedule change and resolve the decision in the best interest of the collective.

There is considerable variation in the amount of interdependence in organizations. The kinds of variation can be illustrated by considering a large research and development laboratory employing some 500 scientists and engineers. Further assume that there are 250 projects all of which are pursuing the state-of-the-art. Thus we have a large number of elements and high task uncertainty. However, there is little need for communication. All the projects are small and not directly connected to other projects. Therefore a schedule delay or a design change does not directly affect other design groups. The only source of interdependence is that the design groups share the same pool of resources—men, facilities, ideas, and money. But once the initial resource allocations are made, the only necessary communication between design groups is to pass on new ideas (Allen, 1969). This type of interdependence has been termed as *pooled* (Thompson, 1967, pp. 54–55).

If the nature of the projects is changed from 250 small independent projects to two large projects, a different pattern of interdependence arises. The large projects will require sequential designs. That is, a device is first designed to determine how much power it will require. After it is complete, then the design of

the power source can take place. Under these conditions, a problem encountered in the design of the device will directly affect the group working on the design of the power source. The greater the number of problems the greater the amount of communication that must take place to jointly resolve problems.

The second example describes a situation which is more complex and requires greater amounts of information processing. The second example has all the problems that were described in the first example. There must be budget and facilities allocations made under conditions of uncertainty. There must be a flow of new ideas among the technical specialties. But in addition, the second example requires information processing and decision making to regulate the schedule of sequential activities. This is because there is greater interdependence in the second example.

The interdependence or interrelatedness of the design groups can be increased above what is described in the second example by the degree to which "design optimization" is pursued. Optimization means that a highly efficient device is desired and any change in the design of one of the components requires redesign of some others.

This can be illustrated by an automobile engine and body. The handling qualities of a car depend on the weight of the engine. The engine compartment can hold only a certain size of engine with its accessories. The drive shaft and differential can handle only a limited amount of torque. Changes in the weight, size, or output of the engine may necessitate changes in the body of the automobile. These interrelations and many others must be taken into account in the design of an automobile.

Actually, in the case of the passenger automobile there is a good deal of flexibility with regard to the body-engine match. The engine compartment is usually large, the parts of the suspension are easily changed, and the drive shaft probably has plenty of excess torque-carrying capability. Engines of a variety of shapes and sizes are frequently placed in the same body. But this need not be the case. In high performance automobiles, the size of the engine compartment is frequently sharply constrained by aerodynamics considerations. There may be efforts to lighten the whole automobile by making the parts of the drive system and body as light as possible, given the required strengths. In such a situation, the flexibility in the size, shape, and performance of the engine placed in the body is sharply reduced or eliminated (Glennan, 1967).

Thus the high performance auto is a highly inter-related system while the passenger car is a flexible, loosely coupled system. The same is true of the organizational subunits which must design these systems. Any change in engine design for the high performance car must be communicated to the group designing the body so that an optimal fit is still achieved after the change. This is less true for the passenger car. Therefore the organization designing the high performance car must be capable of handling the information flows described in examples one and two for budgets, ideas, and schedules and also those for all the design-redesign decisions deriving from the interrelated design. The amount of information that must be processed increases as the amount of interdependence increases.

The functional equation now becomes

$$I = f(U, N, C) \tag{3}$$

where

C = amount of connectedness or interdependence among the elements that are necessary for decision making.

While it is too early to completely specify equation (3), some hypotheses can be made concerning its general form. First, it is probable that the amount of information is a monotonically increasing function of the independent variables (e.g., $\delta I/\delta U \geq 0$). Second, at some point the function increases at a decreasing rate (e.g., $\delta^2 I/\delta U^2 \leq 0$). Both functions in Figure 17.1 are consistent with this hypothesis.

The most significant property of equation (3) is that in analysis of variance terms, the interactive effect dominates the independent effects. This was illustrated with the first example of the research and development laboratory that was characterized by many small projects, a high degree of uncertainty, and large size. There was little need for communication because the subunits were not interdependent. Similarly, the automobile assembly line is characterized by large size and a high degree of interdependence. However there is little need for communication since the predictability of the task allows most of the activity to be specified in advance of task execution. Therefore it is hypothesized that it is the interaction between the three variables which will account for the amount of information to be processed. It follows that the interaction effect will primarily account for variations in organizational forms. The most complex form occurs for tasks that are highly uncertain, highly interdependent, and large in size. The aerospace programs are good examples of such complex tasks. At the other extreme, the simplest form of large organization is one with a predictable and loosely coupled task. The distinguishing feature between the simple and complex structure is the capability to process large amounts of information. The remainder of the paper presents a model which describes the mechanisms that simple organizations adopt to increase their information processing capacities.

AN INFORMATION PROCESSING MODEL OF ORGANIZATION

In this section an organization design model is developed. The model attempts to explain how simple organizations increase their information processing capacities to become complex organizations. The model is based on the assumption that in order to be effective, the information processing capacity of an organization must be equal to the information processing requirements of the task. The information processing requirements are determined by equation (3).

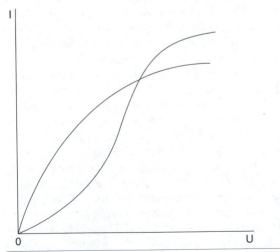

Figure 17.1 Information Processing as a Function of Task Uncertainty Holding Connectedness and Size Constant

In order to develop the model of organizational forms with various information processing capacities, assume there is a large organization with a highly interdependent set of activities. Further assume the subtasks are differentiated and make use of a functional specialization. The problem now facing the organization is to obtain an integrated pattern of behavior across all of the interdependent subunits. The magnitude of the integration problem depends on the amount of information that has to be processed in order to coordinate the interdependent subunits. In the situation just described, the amount of information varies with the uncertainty of the task. For the purpose of exposition, assume first that the task is predictable and then increases in uncertainty. As the uncertainty increases, the amount of information will increase. As the amount of information increases, the example organization will adopt integrating mechanisms which are hypothesized to increase its information processing capabilities. Let us begin with a predictable task and the simplest forms of integration mechanisms. Figure 17.2 will serve as the representation of the formal authority structure of the example organization.

Rules and Programs

The simplest method of coordinating interdependent departments is to specify the behaviors in advance of their execution (March and Simon, 1958, chap. 6). The organization's employees are taught the job-related situations with which they will be faced and the behaviors appropriate to those situations. Then as situations arise daily, the employees act out behaviors appropriate to the situations. If everyone adopts the appropriate behavior, the resultant aggregate response is integrated or coordinated.

The primary virtue of rules is that they eliminate the need for further communication among the subunits. If an organization has hundreds of employees, they cannot all communicate with each other in order to guarantee coordinated action. To the extent that the job-related situations can be anticipated in advance and rules derived for them, then integrated activity is guaranteed without communication. However, rules have a limited range of usefulness. To the extent that rules are limited, the organization must rely on additional integration mechanisms.

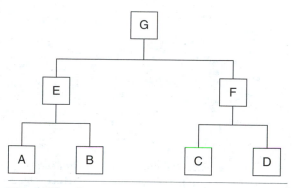

Figure 17.2   Representation of Formal Authority Structure

Hierarchy of Authority

The use of rules is limited in the amount of complexity that can be handled. For tasks with multiple job-related situations, the number of rules necessary to coordinate interdependent behavior becomes too large to learn. At this point the formal hierarchy of authority is employed on an exception basis. That is, the recurring job situations are programmed with rules while the infrequent situations are referred to higher levels in the hierarchy. If all the interdependencies are to be considered, the exception should rise in the hierarchy to the first position where a shared superior exists for all affected subunits. For example, if department A (see Figure 17.2) encounters an exceptional situation which also affects department D, the situation should rise to G for resolution. The combination of rules for repetitive situations and upward referral in the hierarchy for exceptional situations guarantees an integrated or coordinated organizational response to the situations faced by the organization. The combination is effective as long as the number of exceptional situations remains within the capacity of the hierarchy to process them. As the task uncertainty increases, the hierarchy gets overloaded and additional mechanisms are needed.

Planning

As the uncertainty of the organization's task increases, coordination increasingly takes place by specifying outputs, goals, or targets. Instead of specifying specific behaviors to be enacted, the organization undertakes processes to set goals to be achieved and the employees select behaviors which lead to goal accomplishment. Planning reduces the amount of information processing in the hierarchy

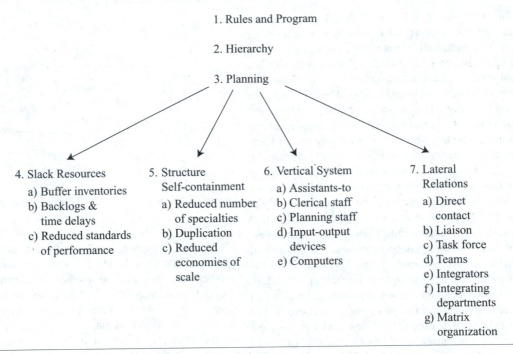

1. Rules and Program

2. Hierarchy

3. Planning

4. Slack Resources
   a) Buffer inventories
   b) Backlogs &
      time delays
   c) Reduced standards
      of performance

5. Structure
   Self-containment
   a) Reduced number
      of specialties
   b) Duplication
   c) Reduced
      economies of
      scale

6. Vertical System
   a) Assistants-to
   b) Clerical staff
   c) Planning staff
   d) Input-output
      devices
   e) Computers

7. Lateral
   Relations
   a) Direct
      contact
   b) Liaison
   c) Task force
   d) Teams
   e) Integrators
   f) Integrating
      departments
   g) Matrix
      organization

Figure 17.3   Alternative Organization Responses to Increased Task Uncertainty

by increasing the amount of discretion exercised at lower levels. Like the use of rules, planning achieves integrated action and also eliminates the need for continuous communication among interdependent subunits.

An example of the way goals are used can be demonstrated by considering the design group responsible for an aircraft wing structure. The group's interdependence with other design groups is handled by technical specifications elaborating the points of attachment, forces transmitted at these points, centers of gravity, etc. The group also has a set of targets (not to be exceeded) for weight, design man-hours to be used, and a completion date. They are given minimum stress specifications below which they cannot design. The group then designs the structures and assemblies which combine to form the wing. They need not communicate with any other design group on work-related matters if they and the interdependent groups are able to operate within the planned targets.

The ability of design groups to operate within the planned targets depends on two factors: The first is the degree to which the task is understood and predictable. This is necessary in order to determine the nature of the interdependence and elaborate meaningful subgoals. The other factor is the complexity of the pattern of interdependence. If there are multiple linkages between numerous subunits, then a complicated model is needed in order to compute the magnitude of the subgoals. For example, job shop scheduling is a difficult problem not because the task is uncertain but because the model needed for subgoal elaboration is computationally infeasible. The result caused by both uncertainty and complexity is the same. In the process of task execution the subunit must violate some of the planned targets unless additional decisions are made. In the case of uncertainty, targets are missed because they were based on incomplete knowledge. For complexity, targets are missed because known factors had to be ignored when determining the goals.

The violation of planned targets usually requires additional decision making and hence additional information processing. The additional information processing takes place through the hierarchy in the same manner as rule exceptions were handled.

Problems are handled on an exception basis. They are raised into higher levels of the hierarchy for resolution. The problem rises to the first level where a shared superior exists for all affected subunits. A decision is made, and the new targets are communicated to the subunits. In this manner the behavior of the interdependent subunits remains integrated.

In summary, the organization adopts integrating mechanisms which keep the amount of information processing within its capacity to process information. These mechanisms are adopted *in addition to* not *instead of* the previous mechanisms. Therefore, if an organization is using planning processes then it is also using the hierarchy and rules. The examples used so far have exaggerated the mechanistic behavior of the organization in order to highlight the information processing aspects of organization behavior. The mechanistic model which has been described so far uses only vertical information flows. It is doubtful that any real organization operates this way. But the mechanistic model serves as a base from which alternative organization designs can evolve.

The ability of an organization to successfully utilize coordination by planning, hierarchy, and rules depends on the combination of the frequency of exceptions and the capacity of the hierarchy to handle them. As the task uncertainty increases, the number of exceptions increases until the hierarchy is overloaded again. Therefore the organization must again take organization design action. It can proceed in two ways: First, it can take action to eliminate the need for processing information and therefore reduce the number of exceptions referred up the hierarchy. Second, the organization can take action to increase its capacity to handle more information. The two methods for reducing the need for information and the two methods for increasing processing capacity are shown schematically in Figure 17.3. In the next sections each of these methods and the costs and benefits will be discussed individually. In reality, the organization will balance the use of each of these methods. It is the choice of balance that determines the organizational form.

Slack Resources

As the number of exceptions begins to overload the hierarchy, one response is to increase the target levels so that fewer exceptions occur. For the example of the wing design group, an increase in the completion date of several weeks will significantly reduce the likelihood that an exception will occur. Therefore completion dates can be extended until the number of exceptions that occurs is within the existing information processing capacity of the organization. This has been the practice in solving job shop scheduling problems (Pounds, 1963). Job shops quote delivery times that are long enough to keep the scheduling problem within the computational and information processing limits of the organization.

Similarly the budget targets or the technical specifications can be relaxed. The degree of design optimization can be reduced thereby creating a flexible design. For manufacturing operations, buffer inventories can be added between sequential operations. All of these examples have a similar effect. They represent the use of slack resources to reduce the amount of interdependence between subunits (March and Simon, 1958; Cyert and March, 1963). With reference to equation (3) the amount of information that has to be processed is reduced by reducing interdependence. This keeps the required amount of information within the capacity of the organization to process it. It follows that the greater the uncertainty, the greater the additional inventory or schedule delay necessary to maintain the balance between information required and capacity to process it.

The strategy of using slack resources has its costs. Relaxing budget targets has the obvious cost of requiring more budget. Increasing the time to completion date has the effect of delaying the customer. Inventories require the investment of capital funds which could be used elsewhere. Reduction of design optimization reduces the performance of the article being designed. Whether slack resources are used to reduce information or not depends on the cost relative to the cost of other alternatives. As technologies and environments vary so will the cost of the use of slack resources.

Authority Structure

The second method for reducing the amount of information is to modify the formal authority structure. The direction of the modification is toward

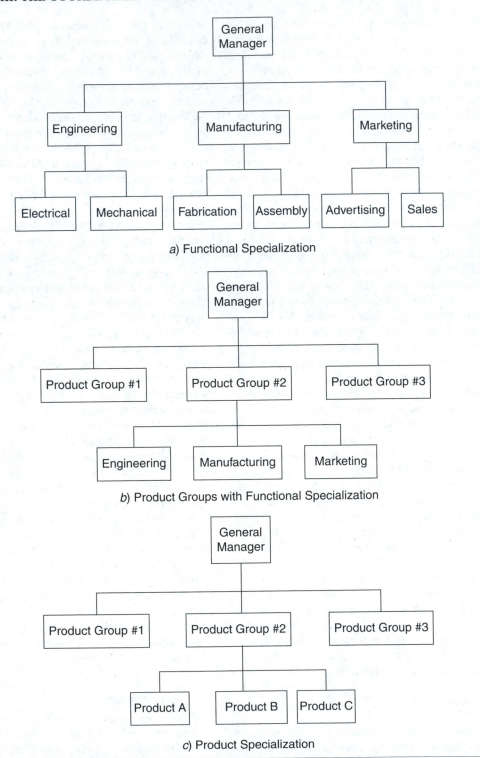

a) Functional Specialization

b) Product Groups with Functional Specialization

c) Product Specialization

Figure 17.4 Formal Authority Structure Respresenting High Interdependence (*a*) to High Independence or Self-Containment (*c*)

greater self-containment of the units which must communicate (i.e., those which are most interdependent) (March and Simon, 1958, pp. 158–61; Thompson, 1967, chap. 5). The effect of such a change is to break up one large problem into several smaller independent subproblems. The total amount of information processing and decision making needed to coordinate the smaller independent subunits is less than that needed to coordinate the large integrated unit. An example will help illustrate why this is so.

It was assumed earlier that the example organization had a high degree of interdependence because it was functionally specialized. Figure 17.4 (*a*) shows a functionally specialized manufacturing firm. In this form, joint problems involving mechanical-fabrication, or assembly-sales, etc., must rise to the general manager for a decision. If there are many new products being introduced, these joint problems arise frequently and overload the general manager. One response is to change the authority structure to one of three identical product groups which are functionally specialized. This form is represented in Figure 17.4 (*b*).

The form in Figure 17.4 (*b*) self-contains the interdependent units. It reduces the amount of information processing by reducing the number of levels through which joint decision problems must pass. The information processing is reduced by bringing the decision-making power down to where the information exists. In addition, the product group form multiplies the number of people making trade-off decisions concerning engineering, manufacturing, and marketing. If the rate of change of market activities is great enough, the three product group executives will be overloaded. In this case the self-containment can be carried lower in the organization as illustrated by Figure 17.4 (*c*). This brings decision making lower in the organization and multiplies the number of the decision makers considering the interdependent activities.

Thus, the greater the task uncertainty, the lower the level in the hierarchy at which self-containment will occur. This means the organization's response to increased task uncertainty is to decentralize or to increase the decision-making influence of the lower levels. The integration is maintained in spite of the fact that decisions are made with only local knowledge. The local knowledge is sufficient to encompass all interactions due to the self-containment of the authority structure.

Like the use of slack resources, changes to the authority structure will create costs for the organization. The first kind is a loss of economies of scale of manufacturing equipment. In Figure 17.4 (*a*) the organization needs only one large machine, in (*b*) it needs three smaller machines, and finally in (*c*) it needs nine machines. In each case the cost of the machines for the same processing capacity is greater. The other cost is associated with either a loss of expertise or duplication depending on the organization's response. In a functional engineering organization there can be two electrical engineers—one electromechanical and one electronics. If the structure is changed to two product groups, two electrical engineers are still needed but will be required to generalize across electromechanical and electronics applications. (This assumes that more knowledge is required to generalize across disciplines than across products.) If a high level of expertise is necessary, the organization can maintain one electromechanical and one electronics engineer for each product group. But now there is duplication involved. Four engineers are required instead of two. Despite these costs, the organization may reduce specialization because it is believed to be less costly than customer delay or inventory carrying costs. Likewise manpower duplication in capital intensive operations may be an insignificant cost. Also for very large operations self-containment may not reduce specialization to the point where it is costly.

Vertical Information Systems

The first pure strategy of increasing the capacity of an organization to process information is to operate directly on the vertical, formal information system. The purpose of the action is to reduce the number of exceptions flowing up the hierarchy. This can be accomplished by reducing the plan-replan cycle. Thus by making up schedules more often, the number of missed due dates can be decreased (Carroll, 1966; Galbraith, 1968).

The reason a reduction in the plan-replan cycle reduces exceptions is that every plan begins to decay in usefulness immediately after it is conceived. The longer one operates with a plan the less useful it is. The greater the task uncertainty, the greater the rate of decay. Thus to maintain a given level of plan usefulness, the decision frequency must be greater, the greater the task uncertainty. A highly predictable plant can be scheduled once a month. Therefore about every four weeks the status of all jobs in all departments is updated and a new schedule is generated. This serves to guide operations for the next four weeks. In another shop where there are frequent engineering changes, absenteeism, and machine breakdowns, the same schedule effectiveness is maintained by weekly updates and rescheduling. In this case there is four times the amount of information processing and decision making at planning times. But it does keep the number of exceptions to a minimum between schedule changes.

This is a more efficient way to operate since it is more economical in terms of managerial time, delays resulting from exception handling, and time devoted to information collection. That is, if one large planning effort is made every week, less decision-making resources are consumed than if 10 exceptions resulted in 10 small planning changes.

The additional information processing and decision making is achieved at the cost of adding assistants-to, by adding scheduling staffs, and by adding clerical personnel. Also with an advantage of approximately 100,000 to 1, computers are used in place of manual processing of quantitative information. Computers are combined with various forms of input-output devices to provide access to data. All of these devices increase the capacity to process more information. The cost of these devices is to be balanced against loss of economies of scale, customer delay costs, and inventory carrying costs. The experience with computers in job shops has shown that their application has reduced slack resources by reducing the average time to complete an order (Buffa, 1968, chap. 12).

Lateral Relationships

The second way to increase the capacity of the organization to process greater amounts of information is to establish lateral relations and undertake joint decisions (Landsberger, 1961; Strauss, 1962; Dutton, Walton, and Fitch, 1966; Simpson, 1959). These lateral relations can take many forms. It is hypothesized that the form and extent of the relations is directly related to the predictability of the task. In order to develop the different forms let us move from certain to highly uncertain tasks. It is also hypothesized that the lateral forms are cumulative. That is, each form is adopted and added to the previous forms. They are not a substitute for other lateral forms.

a) Direct Contact. The simplest and least costly form of lateral relationship is direct contact between managers affected by a problem. For example, refer to Figure 17.2. If department A is about to overrun its schedule on an item which goes next to department D, the manager of A could refer the problem upward to C for resolution. G would decide who would work overtime or suggest some other solution. Alternatively, A could contact D directly and they could reach a mutually agreeable joint decision. To the extent that problems can be resolved in this manner, then the number of exceptions flowing up and down the hierarchy is reduced. The top managers are left free for only those decisions that cannot be solved by direct contact between managers.

The problem that arises when direct contact is used is that an entirely new set of behaviors is required from the managers. They must now be able to behave cooperatively and to be able to reach joint decisions with peers without an authority relationship. This requires a reward system designed to facilitate the kinds of behaviors necessary to meet the information processing requirements of the task (Zander and Wolfe, 1964). It also requires skills and techniques for conflict resolution (Lawrence and Lorsch, 1967, chaps. 3 and 5).

b) Liaison Roles. When the volume of contacts between any two departments grows, it becomes economical to set up a specialized role to handle this communication. Liaison men are typical examples of specialized roles designed to facilitate communication between two interdependent departments and to bypass the long lines of communication involved in upward referral. Liaison roles arise at lower and middle levels of management.

c) Task Forces. Direct contact and liaison roles, like the integration mechanisms before them, have a limited range of usefulness. They work when two managers or functions are involved. When problems arise involving seven or eight departments, the decision-making capacity of direct contacts is exceeded. Then these problems must be referred upward. For uncertain, interdependent tasks such situations arise frequently. Task forces are a form of horizontal contact which is designed for problems of multiple departments.

The task force is made up of representatives from each of the affected departments. Some are full-time members; others may be part-time. The task force is a temporary group. It exists only as long as the problem remains. When a solution is reached, each participant returns to his normal tasks.

To the extent that they are successful, task forces remove problems from higher levels of the hierarchy. The decisions are made at lower levels in the organization. In order to guarantee integration, a group problem-solving approach is taken. Each affected summit contributes a member and therefore provides the information necessary to judge the impact on all units. Task forces also require the same cooperative forms of behavior mentioned for direct contact (Likert, 1967, chap. 10).

d) Teams. As tasks become less predictable, more problems arise during the act of execution. At some point, the combined use of rules, plans, direct contact, task forces, and upward referral are no longer adequate to the task of maintaining integration. The delays in decisions become long, lines of communication become extended, and top managers are forced to spend more time on day-to-day operations. The next response is to use group problem solving on a more permanent basis. Thus

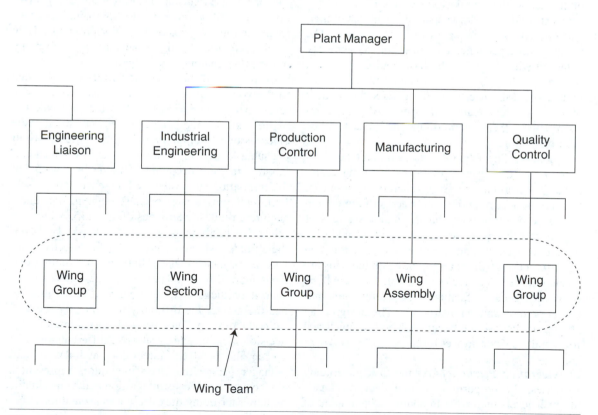

Figure 17.5   Wing Team Overlaid on a Functional Structure

teams are formed around frequently occurring problems. These teams meet daily or weekly to discuss problems affecting the group. They solve all the problems which require commitments that they are capable of making. Larger problems are referred upward.

Teams can be formed at various levels. Actually an entire hierarchy of teams could be designed. The designs of team structures present the same kind of departmentalization problems that are involved in the design of the formal hierarchy of authority. They could be formed around common customers, clients, geographic regions, functions, processes, products, or projects, whichever is appropriate. If the hierarchy of authority is based on common functions such as engineering, production, and marketing, the teams could be formed around products with representatives from each function. Thus the teams involve design decisions concerning the basis of the team, the composition of membership, the levels at which they are to operate, the extent of their discretion, and the frequency of their meetings. The pattern interdependence and basis for the authority structure will determine the basis and composition of membership. It is also hypothesized that the greater the task uncertainty the greater the number of levels at which teams will operate, the more frequent will be their meetings, and the greater will be their discretion.

An interesting example of teams can be illustrated by an aerospace firm's manufacturing operations. The formal authority structure is based on common functions and is illustrated in Figure 17.5. Teams were formed around the major sections of the aircraft that were being produced. In addition, the groups were physically located around common aircraft sections. All groups working on the wing are located in the same area of the plant. Thus the basis of physical location facilitates the lateral communication process and team structure. The design is an attempt to achieve the benefits of both a functional form and a task or project form.

e) Integrating Personnel. As the task uncertainty increases, the proportion of total decisions made at lower levels increases. In addition the amount of discretion increases. At this point the organization becomes concerned about the quality of decisions made at lower levels through group processes. It is desired that these joint decisions be made from the perspective of the general manager. However, the general manager cannot personally check or participate in all decisions. A compromise is to create a number of roles which represent the general manager's perspective. These are called integrating roles (Lawrence and Lorsch, 1967, chap. 3). They carry labels such as product managers, project managers, brand managers, and materials managers. These managers do not supervise any of the actual work but are responsible for integration of the interdependent subunits which are not directly integrated with an authority relationship. The integrators generally acquire power through a direct reporting relationship to the general manager.

It is the function of the integrators to bring the general manager perspective to bear on joint decision problems arising at lower levels in the organization. They will do this by acting as chairmen of task forces and teams considering joint problems. They act as secretaries for the groups and perform many of the group maintenance functions.

In one sense the integrator's role emerges due to the volume of joint decisions reached at lower levels. The volume is related to the predictability of the task. In another sense the integrator's role emerges due to *differences* in the predictability of the subtasks performed by managers who must collaborate in joint decisions. This is the concept of differentiation suggested by Lawrence and Lorsch. Differentiation arises because subunit managers acquire attitudes and modes of operation which are related to predictability of the subtask. However, the attitudes which are necessary for effective subtask performance make collaboration on joint decisions more difficult. The greater the differences in subtask predictability, the greater the differentiation and the greater the difficulty in achieving successful collaboration. Thus for a given volume of joint decision making, the greater the differentiation the greater the need for integrators and the general manager perspective. The integrators represent a device which achieves integration between subunits without sacrificing the differences needed for effective subtask performance.

f) Integrating Departments. As the uncertainty of the organization's task increases further, larger numbers of decisions of consequence are reached at low levels. As the differences between the predictability of subunits tasks increase, the greater the difficulty in reaching joint decisions on these problems. Therefore in order to make the role of the integrator more effective, the organization increases the power of the integrator. The power is increased in several ways. First, the integrator receives subordinates to aid him in carrying out the function. Collectively they form an integrating department.

A second and major change is the reporting of information around the integrator's duties. The usual reporting system for a functional organization shown in Figure 17.4 (*a*) is to report actual data versus budget for each function. If the integrators are product managers, then the information system reports product costs and profits in addition to functional information. In this way the teams and integrators have information for decision making and an ability to get feedback to see how well they have done.

The third change is to give the integrator a voice in the budgeting process. Therefore any change in engineering's budget on product No. 1 will require the approval of the product manager on product No. 1. The product manager may not approve a request for overtime funds for engineering because it would be cheaper to wait and have manufacturing work overtime to get the new product back on schedule. This is what is meant by the general manager's perspective.

g) Matrix Organization. The final step in the utilization of lateral relationships is the establishment of a matrix organization. The matrix represents another increase in the amount of influence that the integrating department has on the decision-making process. More power or influence is required when a greater amount of decision making is carried on at lower levels in the hierarchy. The increased decision making is a response to increased task uncertainty. That is, in order to handle the required increase in information processing and decision making, more decisions are made at lower levels. This maintains a balance between the information processing requirements of the task and capacity of the organization

to process information. The increased power of the integrator is to enable him to maintain the quality of low-level joint decisions.

The matrix organization represents a complete commitment to joint problem solving and shared responsibility. The other lateral relations all utilize joint decision making and shared responsibility but not to the degree that a pure matrix organization does. In this paper a pure matrix organization differs from the previous lateral forms in two ways: First, at some level in the organization, a *dual authority* relationship exists. In Figure 17.6, an organization chart illustrates the formal authority relationships in a typical aerospace firm. In this case one man is both the technical specialty department manager and the subproject manager. While there are other variations, the main feature is the dual reporting relationships in a typical aerospace firm. In this case one man is both the technical specialty department manager and the subproject manager. While there are other variations, the main feature is the dual reporting relationship. This feature distinguishes the matrix from the use of integrating departments. The matrix uses integrating departments but with a dual authority relationship in addition.

The other feature of the matrix is a reasonable *balance of power* between the two bases of organizing the work. With respect to Figure 17.6, this means that reasonable power balances are desired between the technical specialty managers and the project managers. While equal power is an unattainable razor's edge, the power differences are much smaller than the differences in the previous lateral forms. The power balance is obtained and maintained in several ways. The addition of the dual authority relation helps establish the power balance. Also the project manager gets the budget for the project and buys service from the technical specialties. The technical specialties also get funds for work which is not for any specific project. The formal authority structure and the funds allocation process are used to control the power balance.

The reason a power balance is desired is that the decisions and preferred solutions to problems cannot be predicted in advance. Rather than have solutions biased toward the stronger of the

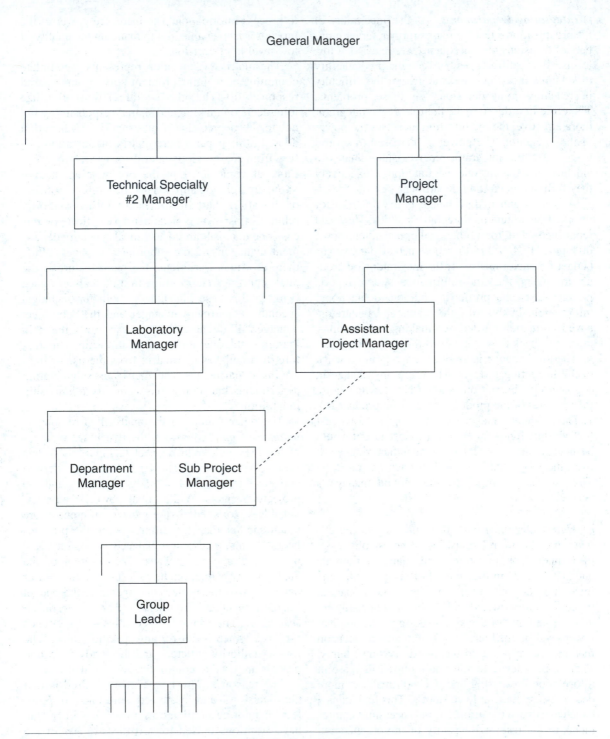

Figure 17.6   Formal Authority Structure of Matrix Organization

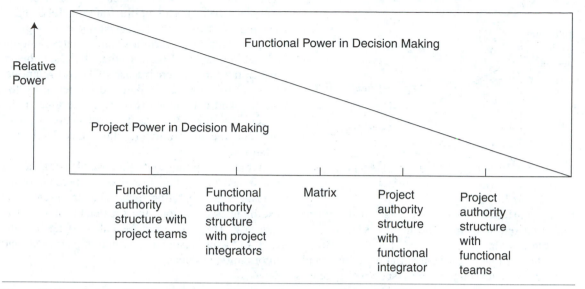

Figure 17.7   Relative Decision Power as a Function of the Authority Structure

Table 17.1

	Plastic	*Food*	*Containers*
Percentage new product in last 10 years	20	10	0
Differentiation	10.7	8.0	5.7
Integrating device	Rules	Rules	Rules
	Hierarchy	Hierarchy	Hierarchy
	Planning	Planning	Planning
	Direct contact	Direct contact	Direct contact
	Team at 3 levels	Task forces	
	Integrating department	Integrators	
Percent integrators/Managers	22	17	0

SOURCE: Adapted from Paul R. Lawrence and Jay W. Lorsch, *Organization and Environment* (Boston, Mass.: Division of Research, Harvard Business School, 1967), pp. 86–138; and Jay W. Lorsch and Paul R. Lawrence, "Environmental Factors and Organization Integration," paper read at the Annual Meeting of the American Sociological Association, August 27, 1968, Boston, Mass.

technical specialty or project manager, a balance is maintained. This means the realities of the problem at hand will determine the preferred solution if the joint decision making is effective. Of course this does not mean that power differences do not arise. Personality factors alone would introduce differences. In addition environmental changes will affect the power balance. In the aerospace industry the technical specialties had more power in the early 1960s due to the missile gap crisis and a lag in the space race. Then a balance occurred with the addition of incentive contracts and PERT-Cost techniques. Now in the context of the Proxmire Senate hearings and cost problems on the C-5A aircraft, the project managers have more influence on decisions. These power shifts

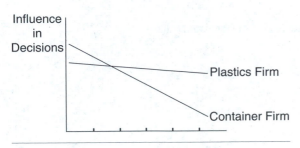

Figure 17.8   Influence Graph Showing Influence in Decisions by level

have occurred without any change to the formal reporting relationships. The matrix is thus a very flexible design.

If the volume of consequential decisions made from the project manager's perspective increases still further, the matrix would be abandoned and the authority structure changed to a project form. However, the functional managers would now perform the integrating roles. Therefore no new categories are needed. As a matter of fact there is continuum of relative power differences between technical specialty managers and projects. The relative power or influence on decisions is affected by the authority structure, the information system, and the flow of budget dollars. Figure 17.7 shows this continuum of *relative* power differences and how it is affected by the authority structure.

Thus the use of lateral relations represents a method of decentralizing or making decisions at low levels in the hierarchy. Like self-containment, the greater the task uncertainty, the lower the level of decision making. However in order to prevent the making of decisions which affect global goals with only local information, group problem solving is used. In this way all departments pool their local information thereby providing sufficient information to reach a decision affecting global goals. This puts a premium on cooperative behavior, conflict resolution, and joint problem solving.

The work of Lawrence and Lorsch is highly consistent with the assertions concerning lateral relations (Lawrence and Lorsch, 1967; Lorsch and Lawrence, 1968). This is illustrated in Table 17.1. The plastics firm has the greatest rate of new product introduction (uncertainty) and greatest amount of differentiation. Likewise the plastics industry makes the most extensive use of lateral relations. Figure 17.8 shows the pattern of influence for the plastics and container firms. Thus the greater the uncertainty the lower the level of decision making, and the integration is maintained by lateral relations.

Table 17.1 points out the cost of using lateral relation. The plastics firm has 22 percent of its managers in integrating roles. Thus the greater use of lateral relations the greater the managerial intensity. This cost must be balanced against the cost of slack resources, structure variation and information systems.

SUMMARY

Several explanatory statements are needed before summarizing. First, a word of caution is required. All of the above statements are hypotheses. They require testing. The text of the paper makes assertions only for the convenience of eliminating the frequent use of the phrase "it is hypothesized that . . ." Second, almost all of the propositions have appeared before in various forms. What this paper has tried to do is to put them into a logically consistent framework based on concepts suggested from empirical research.

This paper was based on the premise that certainty of the task is a primary independent variable which distinguishes between the appropriateness of alternative organization forms. The premise was derived from the empirical research performed in the last few years. What is missing in this empirical research is an explanation of why uncertainty should affect organization forms. The model presented here gives a partial explanation of why this is so. The basic explanation was that task uncertainty required information processing during the execution of the task. The effect of uncertainty was hypothesized to be moderated by the interdependence between subtasks and the number of elements (such as number of employees, number of specialties, etc.) relevant for decision making. The result is summarized by equation 3.

The other premise of the paper is that in order to be effective, an organization must design a structure which is capable of processing the amount of information required by the task. The organization can take action either to reduce the amount of information required or to increase the capacity of the structure to process more information. It was hypothesized that the organization can reduce the amount of information by adding slack resources which in turn reduces interdependence between subtasks. This strategy maintains a centralized decision-making process as long as slack is added as uncertainty increases. The other way the organization reduces the amount of information to be processed is to change the authority structure to a more self-contained form. This also reduces interdependence between subtasks. However, it brings the decision-making power down to where the information exists. Therefore the response is decentralization.

The first strategy to increase the capacity of the organization to process more information is [to] reduce the time between successive planning sessions. This requires more information flowing to update the status of files. The change occurs in the formal, sometimes mechanical, information system. It brings information up to the decision makers and results in centralization of decisions. The other response is to use lateral relations between interdependent subunits. It brings decision making lower in the organization and therefore results in decentralization. In order to use decentralized decision making in the presence of interdependence, joint decision making is used.

In reality various combinations of these strategies will be used depending on the relative costs involved. In another paper, the author describes a case study in which an organization is faced with these design choices (Galbraith, 1970).

The implication of this paper for future research is that the research designs must be more complex. The need is for greater control of the interacting variables which affect the information processing characteristics of an organization.

REFERENCES

Allen, Thomas. "Information Flows in Research and Development Laboratories," *Administrative Science Quarterly,* March 1969, pp. 12–20.

Buffa, Elwood. *Production-Inventory Systems.* Homewood, Ill.: Richard D. Irwin, Inc., 1968.

Carroll, Donald. "On the Structure of Operational Control Systems" in *Operations Research and the Design of Management Information Systems* (ed. John Pierce), pp. 391–415. New York: Technical Association of the Pulp and Paper Industry, 1966.

Cyert, Richard, and March, James. *The Behavioral Theory of the Firm.* Englewood Cliffs, N.J.: Prentice-Hall, Inc., 1963.

Dutton, J., Walton, Richard, and Fitch, H. "A Study of Conflict in the Process, Structure and Attitudes of Lateral Relationships" in *Some Theories of Organization.* Eds. Albert H. Rubenstein and Chadwick J. Haberstroh. Rev. ed. Homewood, Ill.: Richard D. Irwin, Inc., 1966.

Galbraith, Jay. "Achieving Integration through Information Systems," *Proceedings of the Academy of Management,* December 1968.

———. "Environmental and Technological Determinants of Organization Design: A Case Study" in *Studies in Organization Design.* Eds. Jay W. Lorsch and Paul K. Lawrence. Homewood, Ill.: Richard D. Irwin, Inc., 1970.

Glennan, Thomas. "Issues in the Choice of Development Policies" in Marschak, Glennan, and Summers, *Strategy for R&D,* pp. 13–48. New York: Springer-Verlag Inc., 1967.

Landsberger, H. A. "The Horizontal Dimension in a Bureaucracy," *Administrative Science Quarterly,* 1961, pp. 298–332.

Lawrence, Paul R., and Lorsch, Jay W. *Organization and Environment.* Boston, Mass.: Division of Research, Harvard Business School, 1967.

Likert, Rensis. *The Human Organization.* New York: McGraw-Hill Book Co., Inc., 1967.

Lorsch, Jay W., and Lawrence, Paul R. "Environmental Factors and Organization Integration." Paper read at the Annual Meeting of the American Sociological Association, August 27, 1968, Boston, Mass.

March, James, and Simon, Herbert. *Organizations.* New York: John Wiley & Sons, Inc., 1958.

Pounds, William. "The Scheduling Environment" in *Industrial Scheduling.* Eds. Mirth and Thompson. Englewood Cliffs, N.J.: Prentice-Hall, Inc., 1963.

Simpson, R. L. "Vertical and Horizontal Communication in Organization," *Administrative Science Quarterly,* 1959, pp. 188–96.

Strauss, George. "Tactics of Lateral Relationship," *Administrative Science Quarterly,* 1962, pp. 161–86.

Thompson, James. *Organizations in Action.* New York: McGraw-Hill Book Co., Inc., 1967.

Zander, Alvin, and Wolfe, Donald. "Administrative Rewards and Coordination among Committee Members," *Administrative Science Quarterly,* June 1964, pp. 50–69.

SOURCE: Galbraith, Jay R. 1972. Excerpt from "Organization Design: An Information Processing View." Pp. 52–74 in *Organization Planning: Cases and Concepts.* Homewood, IL: Richard D. Irwin.

18

INPUT UNCERTAINTY AND ORGANIZATIONAL COORDINATION IN HOSPITAL EMERGENCY UNITS

LINDA ARGOTE

Theoretical and empirical work in organizational behavior has shifted from the premise that there is one best way to organize, to the view that the best way to organize depends on various contingencies. Examples of contingencies thought to be critical for the functioning of organizations include the rate of technical change in their environments (Burns and Stalker, 1966), the uncertainty of their environments (Lawrence and Lorsch, 1967; Duncan, 1972), and the manageability of the tasks that they perform (Mohr, 1971).

While there is considerable agreement about the importance of these contingencies, the specification of exactly what the contingencies are and how they relate to organizational problem solving, structure, and effectiveness is less clear. The concept of uncertainty, however, often recurs in discussions of organizations as the critical contingency with which organizations must deal in order to be effective (e.g., Thompson, 1967; Galbraith, 1973).

There are almost as many definitions of uncertainty as there are treatments of the subject. But the majority of the definitions commonly describe one characteristic of uncertainty, namely, incomplete information. Incomplete information makes it difficult to predict the future states of many factors associated with an organization's environment or tasks. Accordingly, it is difficult to plan or to fully specify organizational activities in advance.

The sources of uncertainty for organizations are varied. For example, organizations may lack information about the availability of raw materials, about the preferences of their customers, or about the technologies they use. Most organizations probably experience some uncertainty about these and other factors. Yet, if we are to make progress in understanding how uncertainty affects organizations, we must first specify which particular source of uncertainty we are studying. Differences in the degree to which organizations experience that particular source of uncertainty can then be related to differences in their problem-solving capability, structure, and effectiveness.

This study focused on hospital emergency units, which experience a high degree of uncertainty in their day-to-day operations.

The source of uncertainty most critical in emergency units is their patient inputs, input uncertainty. Accordingly, this study focused on input uncertainty and explored how it relates to various means of coordination and to certain criteria of the effectiveness of hospital emergency units. Specifically, two research questions were addressed: (1) Does input uncertainty relate to the use of various means of coordination? (2) Are the relationships between various means of coordination and organizational effectiveness criteria affected by input uncertainty? That is, are certain means of coordination more or less appropriate depending, in part, on the uncertainty experienced by the units?

BACKGROUND

Previous research on uncertainty in organizations (e.g., Lawrence and Lorsch, 1967; Mohr, 1971; Duncan, 1973) has generally examined either task or environmental uncertainty in relation to organizational structure and effectiveness. The evidence indicates that task uncertainty is related to organizational structure (e.g., Mohr, 1971; Van de Ven, Delbecq and Koenig, 1976; McCulloch, 1978). For example, Van de Ven, Delbecq, and Koenig (1976) found that as task uncertainty increased, organizational use of programs and rules to achieve coordination decreased and organizational reliance on personal, horizontal channels of communication increased. The effects of task uncertainty on relationships between organizational structure and effectiveness are less clear. McCulloch (1978) reported that screening of inputs and monitoring of behavior were more positively related to organizational effectiveness under conditions of high task uncertainty than under conditions of low task uncertainty. On the other hand, Mohr (1971) did not find any differences in effectiveness between organizations whose structures were "consonant" with their tasks, e.g., high participation and low task manageability, and organizations whose structures were "dissonant" with their tasks.

Findings on the relationships between environmental uncertainty and organizational structure are conflicting. Several researchers (e.g., Lawrence and Lorsch, 1967; Duncan, 1973) found that increases in environmental uncertainty were associated with a loosening of the structure of organizational subunits. Conversely, other researchers (e.g., Huber, O'Connell,

and Cummings, 1975; Bourgeois, McAllister, and Mitchell, 1978) found that increases in environmental uncertainty were associated with a tightening of organizational structures. In addition, Pennings (1975) found a general lack of relationship between environmental uncertainty and organizational structure. The effects of environmental uncertainty on relationships between organizational structure and organizational effectiveness are also not clear. Lawrence and Lorsch (1967) and Duncan (1973) found that organizational effectiveness was contingent at least in part on achieving a fit or consonance between the requirements of an organization's environment and its structure. However, Pennings (1975) generally did not find that environmental uncertainty affected relationships between organizational structure and effectiveness.

The disparate research findings may be due to several things. Different conceptual and measurement approaches to uncertainty have been used in the different studies, and the specification of exactly what is meant by uncertainty has often been vague. The reliability and validity problems that Tosi, Aldag, and Storey (1973) and Downey, Hellriegel, and Slocum (1975) found with the measures used in certain studies probably derive in part from these definitional problems. In addition to these definitional problems, the theory linking uncertainty to dimensions of organizational structure and the processes underlying the creation of that linkage have been left largely unspecified.

UNCERTAINTY IN HOSPITAL EMERGENCY UNITS

Hospital emergency units face much uncertainty in the course of their work. There is uncertainty about what is wrong with particular patients and about appropriate treatment methods. There is also uncertainty about the overall composition of patient inputs, such as the number of patients in various conditions. The concept "input uncertainty" is developed here to refer to this last type of uncertainty. This concept draws on work done in the areas of cybernetics and information theory (e.g., Wiener, 1948; Shannon and Weaver, 1949; Miller, 1953; Attneave, 1959) in which uncertainty is expressed as a function of the number of choices or alternatives in a given situation, e.g., patient conditions, and of the probability of various alternatives occurring.

According to information theory, uncertainty is greatest when the alternatives are many and are equally likely to occur. Information reduces uncertainty by making one alternative more likely than the others. As an example of how this approach could be applied, consider the uncertainty associated with patient conditions in two hospital emergency units. In one unit, about 16 different patient conditions are seen, on the average, in a given time period, and the conditions are about equally likely to occur. In the other unit, a quarter of the unit's patients have colds or respiratory problems that could have been handled in a doctor's office, and the other three-quarters of the patient load falls into six conditions that occur about equally often. The uncertainty in the latter unit, where there are fewer alternatives and one alternative is more likely than the others, is less than the uncertainty in the former unit where there are many alternatives that are equally likely to occur.

This conceptual approach to uncertainty makes sense, given that emergency units vary in the type and range of patient conditions they see. For example, some units specialize in the treatment of particular kinds of patients such as those with severe burns or high-risk infants, others see a wide range of patient conditions, and still others serve primarily as walk-in clinics for patients who do not have a regular doctor.

The concept of input uncertainty bridges the somewhat artificial distinction between environmental and task-related uncertainty. Input uncertainty stems from the external environment with which the various units are in continuous contact, yet it has an immediate impact on the tasks that the units perform. Input uncertainty is a specific type of uncertainty. Its specificity enables us to move from diffuse characterizations of an organization's environment or task to more precise descriptions of the uncertainty characterizing a particular element of an organization's task environment. In addition, input uncertainty is likely to have approximately the same meaning across respondents in various units.

Coordination and Effectiveness

Research has been done on the conditions under which various coordination means are used in organizations (e.g., Van de Ven, Delbecq, and Koenig, 1976). Research has also been done on how means of coordination relate to criteria of organizational effectiveness (e.g., Georgopoulos and Mann, 1962; Longest, 1974). This study examines how means of coordination relate to organizational effectiveness criteria under conditions of high and low input uncertainty.

Organizational coordination. Coordination is one of the major problems an organization must face and solve in order to be effective (March and Simon, 1958; Georgopoulos, 1972). Coordination involves fitting together the activities of organization members, and the need for it arises from the interdependent nature of the activities that organization members perform. Coordination can be achieved through a variety of means, and several typologies of coordination methods have been advanced (e.g., March and Simon, 1958; Thompson, 1967). The one that is used here is the categorization of coordination methods into programmed and nonprogrammed means. This categorization was developed by Georgopoulos and Mann (1962) and elaborated in Georgopoulos and Cooke (1979).

The basic distinction between programmed and nonprogrammed coordination centers around the extent to which activities can be specified in advance. In programmed coordination, the activities of organization members are dictated by plans, programs, and relationships specified in advance by the organization. Programmed means of achieving coordination used in this study are rules, scheduled meetings, and authority arrangements. In nonprogrammed coordination, activities are not specified in advance by the organization, but rather are worked out on the spot by organization members. The organization only specifies desired ends. The nonprogrammed means of coordination studied here include autonomy of organization members, general policies of the units, and mutual adjustment among the members involved.

Clearly, it becomes increasingly difficult for an emergency unit to specify activities in advance as the uncertainty characterizing the unit's patient inputs increases. An emergency unit could, in principle, identify a priori potential patient conditions and could specify appropriate responses. If there are few conditions, organization members can learn and apply the prespecified plan of action for each condition. Alternatively, if there are many conditions, but only a few occur regularly, organization members can learn and apply the prespecified response for those conditions that occur frequently. When a less frequently observed condition arises, the member can consult with a supervisor to determine the prespecified response. As the number of frequently observed patient conditions increases, however, the demands that a programmed system of coordination place on the organization and on individual organization members increase. The organization is required to develop an elaborate repertoire of prespecified responses to deal with the increased number of frequently observed conditions. Individual organization members are required to learn how to identify a greater number of conditions and are required to learn a larger set of prespecified responses and learn how and when to apply them. Nonprogrammed means of coordination, which involve on-the-spot sharing of information among organization members, are an effective way of limiting the increased demands associated with increased uncertainty. The organization does not require as elaborate a repertoire of prespecified responses to achieve coordination, since individual organization members work out responses on the spot. A given individual can rely to some extent on expertise and information possessed by others in developing appropriate responses.

The demands on coordination discussed above lead us to expect two relationships. The first is that when uncertainty is low, emergency units will rely on programmed means such as rules and authority arrangements to achieve coordination. The units could also rely on nonprogrammed means of coordination when uncertainty is low. However, nonprogrammed coordination is likely to be less effective than programmed coordination under conditions of low uncertainty, since in nonprogrammed coordination, activities are worked out on the spot by organization members. This takes time and can delay treatment of emergency patients. To the extent that patient conditions recur, time spent working out how to deal with the condition each time it recurs is wasted.

The second is that when uncertainty is high, emergency units will rely on nonprogrammed means of coordination. The units could also attempt to use programmed means of coordination under conditions of high uncertainty. However, relying on programmed means of coordination when uncertainty is high is likely to be less effective, because of the increased demands placed on individual organization members by programmed means of coordination under conditions of high uncertainty and because of the increased difficulty of anticipating and specifying appropriate responses for large numbers of frequently observed patient conditions.

Organizational effectiveness. The conceptual approach to organizational effectiveness used in this study draws on the approach of the Hospital Emergency Services project (Georgopoulos, 1978; Georgopoulos and Cooke, 1979) of which this study was a part. In that project, organizational effectiveness was seen as a joint function of the clinical, economic, and social efficiency of the emergency units. Since this study focused on the uncertainty characterizing emergency unit patient inputs, clinical efficiency was chosen as the most appropriate criterion of effectiveness.

Clinical efficiency involves the quality of care and of staff performance from a patient's entry into an emergency unit to the patient's exit from the unit (Georgopoulos et al., 1977). Thus, clinical efficiency represents how a patient is handled along an emergency unit's input-transformation-output work cycle. Three measures of clinical efficiency were used in this study: the promptness of care, the quality of nursing care, and the quality of medical care.

The promptness-of-care measure represents how efficiently units handle the "input" phase of their work cycle. This phase includes the entry and initial screening of emergency unit patients. The two quality-of-care measures reflect how well the units handle the "transformation" or "throughput" phase of their work cycle. This phase includes the assessment, diagnosis, and treatment of patients' conditions.

A measure representing how well the units handle the output phase of their work cycle was not included. In this phase, patients are prepared for discharge and are then released from the units. This phase is not thought to be particularly sensitive to variations in input uncertainty, since there is little residual input uncertainty by the time patients get to this phase.

Hypotheses

The following hypotheses specify the expected relationships among input uncertainty, organizational coordination, and effectiveness.

Hypothesis 1a. The higher the input uncertainty, the less programmed means, including rules, scheduled meetings, and authority arrangements, will be used to achieve coordination in the units.

Hypothesis 1b. The higher the input uncertainty, the more nonprogrammed means, including autonomy of the staff, policies of the units, and mutual adjustment among the staff, will be used to achieve coordination in the units.

Hypothesis 2a. Programmed means of coordination will make a greater contribution to organizational effectiveness under conditions of low uncertainty than under conditions of high uncertainty.

Hypothesis 2b. Nonprogrammed means of coordination will make a greater contribution to organizational effectiveness under conditions of high uncertainty than under conditions of low uncertainty.

Hypotheses 2a and 2b specify which method of coordination is expected to be appropriate when uncertainty is low and which method is expected to be appropriate when uncertainty is high. Hypotheses 1a and 1b specify how uncertainty is expected to relate to the use of methods of coordination. Tests of these two sets of hypotheses provide information about whether emergency units are actually using the coordination method appropriate for the type of inputs they receive. . . .

RESULTS

Relationships Between Input Uncertainty and Organizational Coordination

We tested hypotheses 1a and 1b through Pearson product-moment correlations. Since all of the hypotheses specified the direction of the expected relationships, one-tailed tests were used.

Hypothesis 1a, that increases in input uncertainty would be associated with decreases in the use of programmed means to achieve coordination, was supported only with respect to the use of authority arrangements. That is, as input uncertainty increased, the use of authority to achieve coordination decreased ($r = -.53$, $p > .01$). No support was provided for hypothesis 1b, that increases in input uncertainty would be associated with increases in the use of nonprogrammed means of coordination.

Correlations between input uncertainty and means of coordination were computed holding several contextual variables constant. A pattern virtually identical to that reported previously was found when analyses were done controlling for hospital size, emergency unit patient volume, and the number of medical specialties at the units.

Effects of Input Uncertainty on Relationships Between Means of Coordination and Organizational Effectiveness Criteria

Results showing how input uncertainty affects relationships between the means of achieving coordination and organizational effectiveness criteria are presented in Table 18.1 (results of the moderated regressions) and Table 18.2 (results of the subgroup analyses).

In moderated regression, two regressions are run for each relationship. In one regression, input uncertainty and the use of a particular means of coordination were entered as predictors of the effectiveness criterion. In the other regression, the interaction, i.e., cross product of input uncertainty and the coordination means was entered in addition to the main effects. A test (Kerlinger and Pedhazur, 1973) was performed to see whether the addition of the interaction term resulted in a significant increment in the percent of variance explained in the criterion variable over that already explained by the main effect terms.

In the subgroup analyses, the sample was split at the median into groups of high and low uncertainty. Correlations between the use of means of coordination and the effectiveness criteria were computed separately for each subgroup. These correlations were then tested to see if they were significantly different from one another.

Table 18.1   Effects of Input Uncertainty on Relationships Between Means of Coordination and Criteria of Effectiveness ($N = 30$)

Means of organizational coordination	R^2 Main effects	R^2 Main and interaction effects	F-ratio of R^2 increment
Promptness of care			
Programmed			
Rules	.20*	.34**	5.54**
Scheduled meetings	.19*	.19	0.23
Authority	.14	.24*	3.32*
Nonprogrammed			
Autonomy of the staff	.18*	.33**	6.07**
Policies of the unit	.14	.27**	4.67**
Mutual adjustment	.14	.20	2.09
Quality of medical care			
Programmed			
Rules	.01	.17	4.88**
Scheduled meetings	.04	.06	0.50
Authority	.02	.24*	7.55**
Nonprogrammed			
Autonomy of the staff	.01	.15	4.38**
Policies of the unit	.01	.12	3.40*
Mutual adjustment	.02	.03	0.11
Quality of nursing care			
Programmed			
Rules	.10	.14	1.15
Scheduled meetings	.11	.11	0.06
Authority	.10	.17	2.22
Nonprogrammed			
Autonomy of the staff	.09	.13	1.25
Policies of the unit	.02	.10	2.53
Mutual adjustment	.10	.11	0.26

*$p < .10$; **$p < .05$

These analyses are two slightly different tests of the hypotheses. The moderated regression analysis makes use of the continuous nature of the uncertainty variable and tests how each increment in input uncertainty and each increment in the use of means of coordination combine to explain the effectiveness criterion. The subgroup analysis splits the uncertainty variable at the median and then shows relationships between the use of means of coordination and effectiveness for units below and units above the median in uncertainty. Given the lack of information about the exact functional form of the underlying relationship among variables, moderated regression and subgroup analysis were used as complementary tests of the hypotheses.

As can be seen from the tables, input uncertainty affected relationships between the use of means of coordination and organizational effectiveness criteria as predicted by hypotheses 2a and 2b. That is, programmed means of coordination made a greater contribution to organizational effectiveness when uncertainty was low than when it was high. Conversely, nonprogrammed means of coordination made a greater contribution to organizational effectiveness when uncertainty was high than when it was low.

When the effectiveness measure was the promptness of care, as shown in Table 18.1, all three programmed means of coordination related to the promptness of care measure as predicted by

Table 18.2   Correlations Between Means of Coordination and Criteria of Effectiveness for High and Low Input Uncertainty Subgroups

| | Input uncertainty | | |
Means of organizational coordination	High (N = 15)	Low (N = 15)	Z*
Promptness of care			
Programmed			
Rules	−.50**	.10	−1.60*
Scheduled meetings	−.33	−.22	−0.29
Authority	−.22	.34	−1.41*
Nonprogrammed			
Autonomy of the staff	.44**	−.12	1.45*
Policies of the unit	.13	−.49**	1.62*
Mutual adjustment	.26	−.13	0.97
Quality of medical care			
Programmed			
Rules	−.18	.48**	−1.74**
Scheduled meetings	.16	.24	−0.21
Authority	−.27	.39*	−1.69**
Nonprogrammed			
Autonomy of the staff	.21	−.23	1.11
Policies of the unit	.22	−.35*	1.45*
Mutual adjustment	.20	−.37*	1.47*
Quality of nursing care			
Programmed			
Rules	.31	.32	−0.01
Scheduled meetings	.23	.33	−0.28
Authority	.19	.31	−0.30
Nonprogrammed			
Autonomy of the staff	.57**	−.01	1.59*
Policies of the unit	.24	−.30	1.33*
Mutual adjustment	.05	−.43*	1.26

*$p < .10$; **$p < .05$

NOTE: Positive Z scores indicate that the correlations between various means of coordination and the effectiveness criteria were greater under conditions of high input uncertainty than under conditions of low input uncertainty. Conversely, negative Z scores indicate that the correlations were greater under conditions of low, than under conditions of high input uncertainty.

hypothesis 2a. Two of the three relationships were significant. In particular, the inclusion of an input uncertainty-by-rules interaction term increased the variance explained in the promptness of care from 20 to 34 percent ($F = 5.54$, $df = 1/26$, $p > .05$). The inclusion of an uncertainty-by-authority interaction term increased the explained variance from 14 to 24 percent ($F = 3.32$, $df = 1/26$, $p > .10$). The coefficients of all the interaction terms were negative, as predicted.[1] The subgroup analyses (Table 18.2) were consistent with the findings

of the moderated regressions. They indicated that correlations between programmed means of coordination and promptness of care were greater under conditions of low than under conditions of high uncertainty.

The three nonprogrammed means of coordination also related to the promptness of care measure as predicted; that is, the coefficients of all the interaction terms were positive. Two of these relationships were significant. Specifically, the inclusion of an uncertainty-by-autonomy interaction term and the inclusion of an uncertainty-by-policies interaction term both significantly increased the variance explained in this effectiveness measure. The subgroup analyses yielded similar results. They indicated that correlations between nonprogrammed means of coordination and the promptness of care were greater under conditions of high uncertainty than under conditions of low uncertainty.

A similar pattern emerged when the effectiveness measure was the quality of medical care. Input uncertainty affected relationships between all three programmed means of coordination and the quality of medical care as was predicted. The coefficients of all the interaction terms were negative. The uncertainty-by-rules interaction term and the uncertainty-by-authority interaction term were both significant. As predicted by hypothesis 2a, the subgroup analyses indicated that correlations between programmed means of coordination and the quality of medical care were greater under conditions of low, than under conditions of high uncertainty.

Input uncertainty also influenced relationships between nonprogrammed means of coordination and the quality of medical care as predicted by hypothesis 2b; the coefficients of all the interaction terms were positive. The autonomy and policies relationships were both significant. Subgroup analyses indicated that relationships between nonprogrammed means of coordination and the quality of medical care were greater when uncertainty was high than when it was low, giving further support to hypothesis 2b.

The pattern of results obtained with the nursing-care measure of effectiveness was similar to that obtained with the other two effectiveness measures. However, fewer relationships were significant.

The general pattern of the results presented in Tables 18.1 and 18.2 provides strong support for the influence of input uncertainty on relationships between the means of coordination and organizational effectiveness criteria. In particular, the coefficients of the interaction terms from the moderated regression analyses had the predicted sign in all cases. Further, in all instances correlations between programmed means of coordination and the effectiveness criteria were greater when uncertainty was low than when it was high. Conversely, correlations between nonprogrammed means of coordination and the effectiveness criteria were greater when uncertainty was high than when it was low.

The subgroup analyses discussed above tested the difference between correlation coefficients obtained in the high and low uncertainty subgroups. The correlation coefficients themselves are worth examining. In particular, as can be seen from Table 18.2, when uncertainty was low, correlations between certain programmed means of coordination and the effectiveness criteria were positive and significant. On the other hand, the use of certain nonprogrammed means of coordination was negatively associated with effectiveness criteria when uncertainty was low. The pattern was reversed when uncertainty was high. This suggests that the use of particular coordination means can increase or decrease the effectiveness of the units, depending on the degree of uncertainty they face.

DISCUSSION

Several steps were taken to rule out alternative explanations of these findings. First, data from different respondent groups and from different methods, such as interviews and questionnaires, were used to minimize problems of spuriousness and respondent source bias. Second, multiple measures of organizational effectiveness were used. The similarity of the pattern of results obtained with the different measures provides support for the hypotheses. Third, correlations were computed between uncertainty and means of coordination holding several contextual variables, such as hospital size, constant.

A problem encountered in this study was the relatively low between-group variance of several coordination measures. This problem clearly was not fatal, since statistically significant results were obtained in spite of the low variance that characterized several of the measures. However, further work needs to be done on the conceptualization and measurement of means of achieving coordination in organizations.

The conceptual and measurement approach to uncertainty used here has several advantages over previous approaches. Because the measure is specific, it is likely to have the same meaning across respondents at the various units. Further, it is a measure of uncertainty as it comes into the organization and is relatively unconfounded by factors internal to the organization. Nonetheless, the measure is perceptual. Future research using this approach would benefit by including measures of uncertainty based on the actual numbers of patients in various conditions. This is no trivial undertaking, as it involves the collection of data on patient diagnoses over a significant interval of time and the categorization of the diagnoses into patient-condition categories by experts such as emergency unit physicians. A measure based on objective data would be useful, however, in further validating the perceptual measure and, more generally, in exploring the relationship between objective and subjective uncertainty.

While the results from the cross-sectional data used here are consistent with the hypothesized causal sequence, they do not establish causality. Longitudinal research and research in more controlled settings would be helpful in establishing further support for the causal sequence outlined here.

CONCLUSION

This study provides empirical evidence about how organizations achieve coordination and how they could achieve better coordination to increase their effectiveness. These data suggest that the use of programmed means of coordination is most appropriate in emergency units experiencing low uncertainty, while the use of nonprogrammed means of coordination is most appropriate in emergency units experiencing high uncertainty. The criteria of appropriateness used here are clinical ones, namely, the efficiency with which patients are processed and the quality of nursing and medical care they receive. Further research is needed on how uncertainty interacts with means of coordination in determining other criteria of organizational effectiveness. For example, is a similar pattern of results obtained when social or economic criteria of effectiveness are used?

There is compelling evidence that the appropriateness of methods of coordination depends on the uncertainty characterizing an organization's inputs. Yet there is little evidence that the actual methods used to coordinate units depends on input uncertainty, suggesting that emergency units are not using the coordination methods appropriate for the type of inputs they receive. Two reasons may account for the failure to use appropriate coordination methods. First, as mentioned previously, the criteria of

effectiveness used here are clinical ones. Emergency units might be using coordination methods appropriate for other effectiveness criteria.

Alternatively, emergency units may receive inadequate feedback about the effectiveness of various coordination methods. Thus, the units may not possess information about which methods of coordination are appropriate for the type of inputs they receive. Analyses of uncertainty in other types of organizations and the consideration of additional criteria of organizational effectiveness would help tease apart these alternative explanations of the apparent failure of the units to use appropriate methods.

Several avenues of research, beyond the scope of this study, would increase our understanding of uncertainty in organizations. One question is how other sources of uncertainty, such as uncertainty about treatment methods, relate to input uncertainty, organizational coordination, and effectiveness. Further elaboration of the model of how organizations choose means of coordination would be helpful, as would analyses of how individuals deal with uncertainty in organizational settings.

This study underscores the importance organizational theorists (e.g., Thompson, 1967; Katz and Kahn, 1978; Weick, 1979) place on uncertainty in organizations. Uncertainty does have an effect on the effectiveness of hospital emergency units, and it appears to be a key variable in understanding organizations in general.

NOTE

1. To save space, the coefficients of the interaction terms are not shown in Table 18.1. The significance level for the coefficients is identical to the significance level for the R^2 increment.

REFERENCES

Attneave, Fred
    1959 Applications of Information Theory to Psychology. New York: Holt, Rinehart and Winston.
Bourgeois, L. J., III, Daniel W. McAllister, and Terence R. Mitchell
    1978 "The effects of different organizational environments upon decisions about organizational structure." Academy of Management Journal, 21: 508–514.

Burns, Tom, and G. M. Stalker
1966 The Management of Innovation, 2d ed. London: Tavistock.

Downey, H. Kirk, Don Hellriegel, and John W. Slocum, Jr.
1975 "Environmental uncertainty: The construct and its application." Administrative Science Quarterly, 20: 613–629.

Duncan, Robert B.
1972 "Characteristics of organizational environments and perceived environmental uncertainty." Administrative Science Quarterly, 17: 313–327.
1973 "Multiple decision making structures in adapting to environmental uncertainty: The impact on organizational effectiveness." Human Relations, 26: 273–291.

Galbraith, Jay
1973 Designing Complex Organizations. Reading, MA: Addison-Wesley.

Georgopoulos, Basil S.
1972 "The hospital as an organization and problem-solving system." In Basil S. Georgopoulos (ed.), Organizational Research on Health Institutions: 9–48. Ann Arbor, MI: University of Michigan, Institute for Social Research.
1978 "An open-system approach to evaluating the effectiveness of hospital emergency departments." Emergency Medical Services, 7: 118–129.

Georgopoulos, Basil S., and Robert A. Cooke
1979 Conceptual-Theoretical Framework for the Study of Hospital Emergency Services. Ann Arbor, MI: University of Michigan, Institute for Social Research.

Georgopoulos, Basil S., Robert A. Cooke, Linda Argote, and Lorraine M. Uhlaner
1977 Clinical Efficiency: Preliminary Working Statement. Ann Arbor, MI: University of Michigan, Institute for Social Research.

Georgopoulos, Basil S., and Floyd C. Mann
1962 The Community General Hospital. New York: Macmillan.

Huber, George P., Michael O'Connell, and Larry L. Cummings
1975 "Perceived environmental uncertainty: Effects of information and structure." Academy of Management Journal, 18: 725–740.

Katz, Daniel, and Robert L. Kahn
1978 The Social Psychology of Organizations, 2d ed. New York: Wiley.

Kerlinger, Fred N., and Elazar J. Pedhazur
1973 Multiple Regression in Behavior Research. New York: Holt, Rinehart and Winston.

Lawrence, Paul R., and Jay W. Lorsch
1967 "Differentiation and integration in complex organizations." Administrative Science Quarterly, 12: 1–47.

Longest, B. B.
1974 "Relationships between coordination, efficiency, and quality of care in general hospitals." Hospital Administration, 19: 65–86.

March, James G., and Herbert A. Simon
1958 Organizations. New York: Wiley.

McCulloch, Donna
1978 "The structure and performance of institutional review boards: A contingency perspective." Unpublished Ph.D. dissertation, Psychology Department, University of Michigan.

Miller, George A.
1953 "What is information measurement?" American Psychologist, 8: 3–11.

Mohr, Lawrence B.
1971 "Organizational technology and organizational structure." Administrative Science Quarterly, 16: 444–459.

Pennings, Johannes M.
1975 "The relevance of the structural-contingency model for organizational effectiveness." Administrative Science Quarterly, 20: 393–410.

Shannon, Claude E., and Warren Weaver
1949 The Mathematical Theory of Communication. Urbana, IL: University of Illinois Press.

Thompson, James D.
1967 Organizations in Action. New York: McGraw-Hill.

Tosi, Henry, Ramon Aldag, and Ronald Storey
1973 "On the measurement of the environment: An assessment of the Lawrence and Lorsch environmental uncertainty questionnaire." Administrative Science Quarterly, 18: 27–36.

Van de Ven, Andrew H., Andre L. Delbecq, and Richard Koenig, Jr.
1976 "Determinants of coordination modes within organizations." American Sociological Review, 41: 322–338.

Weick, Karl E.
1979 The Social Psychology of Organizing, 2d ed. Reading, MA: Addison-Wesley.

Wiener, Norbert
1948 Cybernetics. New York: Wiley.

SOURCE: Argote, Linda. 1981. Excerpt from "Input Uncertainty and Organizational Coordination in Hospital Emergency Units." *Administrative Science Quarterly*, 27:420–25, 428–34.

19

COLLECTIVE MIND IN ORGANIZATIONS

Heedful Interrelating on Flight Decks

KARL E. WEICK AND KARLENE H. ROBERTS

Some organizations require nearly error-free operations all the time because otherwise they are capable of experiencing catastrophes. One such organization is an aircraft carrier, which an informant in Rochlin, LaPorte, and Roberts' (1987: 78) study described as follows:

> . . . imagine that it's a busy day, and you shrink San Francisco Airport to only one short runway and one ramp and one gate. Make planes take off and land at the same time, at half the present time interval, rock the runway from side to side, and require that everyone who leaves in the morning returns that same day. Make sure the equipment is so close to the edge of the envelope that it's fragile. Then turn off the radar to avoid detection, impose strict controls on radios, fuel the aircraft in place with their engines running, put an enemy in the air, and scatter live bombs and rockets around. Now wet the whole thing down with sea water and oil, and man it with 20-year-olds, half of whom have never seen an airplane close-up. Oh and by the way, try not to kill anyone.

Even though carriers represent "a million accidents waiting to happen" (Wilson, 1986: 21), almost none of them do. Here, we examine why not. The explanation we wish to explore is that organizations concerned with reliability enact aggregate mental processes that are more fully developed than those found in organizations concerned with efficiency. By fully developed mental processes, we mean that organizations preoccupied with reliability may spend more time and effort organizing for controlled information processing (Schneider and Shiffrin, 1977), mindful attention (Langer, 1989), and heedful action (Ryle, 1949). These intensified efforts enable people to understand more of the complexity they face, which then enables them to respond with fewer errors. Reliable systems are smart systems.

Before we can test this line of reasoning we need to develop a language of organizational mind that enables us to describe collective mental processes in organizations. In developing it, we move back and forth between concepts of mind and details of reliable performance in flight operations on a modern super carrier.[1] We use flight operations to illustrate organizational mind for a number of reasons: The technology is relatively simple, the coordination among activities is explicit and visible, the socialization is continuous, agents working alone have less grasp of the entire system than they do when working together, the system is constructed of interdependent know-how, teams of people think on their feet and do the "right thing" in novel situations, and the consequences of any lapse in attention are swift and disabling. Because our efforts to understand deck operations got us thinking about the possibility that performance is mediated by collective mental processes, we use these operations to illustrate that thinking, but the processes of mind we discuss are presumed to be inherent in all organizations. What may vary across organizations is the felt need to develop these processes to more advanced levels.

THE IDEA OF GROUP MIND

Discussions of collective mental processes have been rare, despite the fact that people claim to be studying "social" cognition (e.g., Schneider, 1991). The preoccupation with individual cognition has left organizational theorists ill-equipped to do much more with the so-called cognitive revolution than apply it to organizational concerns, one brain at a time. There are a few exceptions, however, and we introduce our own discussion of collective mind with a brief review of three recent attempts to engage the topic of group mind.

Wegner and his associates (Wegner, Giuliano, and Hertel, 1985; Wegner, 1987; Wegner, Erber, and Raymond, 1991) suggested that group mind may take the form of cognitive interdependence focused around memory processes. They argued that people in close relationships enact a single transactive memory system, complete with differentiated responsibility for remembering different portions of common experience. People know the locations rather than the details of common events and rely on one another to contribute missing details that cue their own retrieval. Transactive memory systems are integrated and differentiated structures in the sense that connected individuals often hold related information in different locations. When people trade lower-order, detailed, disparate information, they often discover higher-order themes, generalizations, and ideas that subsume these details. It is these integrations of disparate inputs that seem to embody

the "magical transformation" that group mind theorists sought to understand (Wegner, Giuliano, and Hertel, 1985: 268). The important point Wegner contributes to our understanding of collective mental processes is that group mind is *not* indexed by within-group similarity of attitudes, understanding, or language, nor can it be understood without close attention to communications processes among group members (Wegner, Giuliano, and Hertel, 1985: 254–255). Both of these lessons will be evident in our reformulation.

Work in artificial intelligence provides the backdrop for two additional attempts to conceptualize group mind: Sandelands and Stablein's (1987) description of organizations as mental entities capable of thought and Hutchins' (1990, 1991) description of organizations as distributed information-processing systems. The relevant ideas are associated with theories of "connectionism," embodied in so-called "neural networks." Despite claims that their work is grounded in the brain's microanatomy, connectionists repeatedly refer to "neurological plausibility" (Quinlan, 1991: 41), "neuron-like units" (Churchland, 1992: 32), "brain-style processing" (Rumelhart, 1992: 69), or "neural inspiration" (Boden, 1990: 18). This qualification is warranted because the "neural" networks examined by connectionists are simply computational models that involve synchronous parallel processing among many interrelated unreliable and/or simple processing units (Quinlan, 1991: 40). The basic idea is that knowledge in very large networks of very simple processing units resides in patterns of connections, not in individuated local symbols. As Boden (1990: 14) explained, any "unit's activity is regulated by the activity of neighboring units, connected to it by inhibitory or excitatory links whose strength can vary according to design and/or learning." Thus, any one unit can represent several different concepts, and the same concept in a different context may activate a slightly different network of units.

Connectionism by itself, however, is a shaky basis on which to erect a theory of organizational mind. The framework remains grounded in a device that models a single, relatively tightly coupled actor as opposed to a loosely coupled system of multiple actors, such as an organization. Connectionists have difficulty simulating emotion and motivation

(Dreyfus and Dreyfus, 1990), as well as every-day thought and reasoning (Rumelhart, 1992). In computational models there is no turnover of units akin to that found in organizations, where units are replaced or moved to other locations. And the inputs connectionists investigate are relatively simple items such as numerals, words, or phrases, with the outputs being more or less accurate renderings of these inputs (e.g., Elman, 1992). This contrasts with organizational researchers who pay more attention to complex inputs, such as traditional competitors who make overtures to cooperate, and to outputs that consist of action as well as thought.

What connectionism contributes to organizational theory is the insight that complex patterns can be encoded by patterns of activation and inhibition among simple units, if those units are richly connected. This means that relatively simple actors may be able to apprehend complex inputs if they are organized in ways that resemble neural networks. Connectionists also raise the possibility that mind is "located" in connections and the weights put on them rather than in entities. Thus, to understand mind is to be attentive to process, relating, and method, as well as to structures and content.

Sandelands and Stablein (1987: 139–141) found parallels between the organization of neurons in the brain and the organization of activities in organizations. They used this parallel to argue that connected activities encode concepts and ideas in organizations much like connected neurons encode concepts and ideas in brains. Ideas encoded in behaviors appear to interact in ways that suggest operations of intelligent processing. These parallels are consistent with the idea that organizations are minds. The important lessons from Sandelands and Stablein's analysis are that connections between behaviors, rather than people, may be the crucial "locus" for mind and that intelligence is to be found in patterns of behavior rather than in individual knowledge.

Hutchins (1990, 1991: 289) has used connectionist networks, such as the "constraint satisfaction network," to model how interpretations based on distributed cognitions are formed. These simulations are part of a larger inquiry into how teams coordinate action (Hutchins, 1990) and the extent to which distributed processing amplifies or counteracts errors that form in individual units. Hutchins'

analysis suggests that systems maintain the flexible, robust action associated with mindful performance if individuals have overlapping rather than mutually exclusive task knowledge. Overlapping knowledge allows for redundant representation that enables people to take responsibility for all parts of the process to which they can make a contribution (Hutchins, 1990: 210).

The potential fit between connectionist imagery and organizational concepts can be inferred from Hutchins' (1990: 209) description of coordination by mutual constraint in naval navigation teams:

> [The] sequence of action to be taken [in group performance] need not be explicitly represented anywhere in the system. If participants know how to coordinate their activities with the technologies and people with which they interact, the global structure of the task performance will emerge from the local interactions of the members. The structure of the activities of the group is determined by a set of local computations rather than by the implementation of the sort of global plan that appears in the solo performer's procedure. In the team situation, a set of behavioral dependencies are set up. These dependencies shape the behavior pattern of the group.

The lessons we use from Hutchins' work include the importance of redundant representation, the emergence of global structure from local interactions, and behavioral dependencies as the substrate of distributed processing.

Our own attempt to describe group mind has been informed by these three sources but is based on a different set of assumptions. We pay more attention to the form of connections than to the strength of connections and more attention to mind as activity than to mind as entity. To make this shift in emphasis clear, we avoid the phrases "group mind" and "organizational mind" in favor of the phrase "collective mind." The word "collective," unlike the words "group" or "organization," refers to individuals who act as if they are a group. People who act as if they are a group interrelate their actions with more or less care, and focusing on the way this interrelating is done reveals collective mental processes that differ in their degree of development. Our focus is at once on individuals and the collective, since only individuals can contribute to a collective mind, but a collective mind is distinct from an individual mind because it inheres in the pattern of interrelated activities among many people.

We begin the discussion of collective mind by following the lead of Ryle (1949) and developing the concept of mind as a disposition to act with heed. We then follow the lead of Asch (1952) and develop the concept of collective interrelating as contributing, representing, and subordinating, and illustrate these activities with examples from carrier operations. We next combine the notions of heed and interrelating into the concept of collective mind as heedful interrelating and suggest social processes that may account for variations in heedful interrelating. Finally, we describe three examples of heedful interrelating, two from carrier operations and one from the laboratory, and present an extended example of heedless interrelating that resulted in a $38-million accident.

MIND AS DISPOSITION TO HEED

"Mind" is a noun similar to nouns like *faith*, *hope*, *charity*, *role*, and *culture* [italics added]. "Mind" is not the name of a person, place, or thing but, rather, is a dispositional term that denotes a propensity to act in a certain manner or style. As Ryle (1949: 51) said,

The statement "the mind is its own place," as theorists might construe it, is not true, for the mind is not even a metaphorical "place." On the contrary, the chessboard, the platform, the scholar's desk, the judge's bench, the lorry-driver's seat, the studio and the football field are among its places. These are where people work and play stupidly or intelligently.

That mind is actualized in patterns of behavior that can range from stupid to intelligent can be seen in the example Ryle (1949: 33) used of a clown who trips and stumbles just as clumsy people do. What's different is that "he trips and stumbles on purpose and after much rehearsal and at the golden moment and where the children can see him and so as not to hurt himself." When a clown trips artfully, people applaud the style of the action, the fact that tripping is done with care, judgment, wit, and appreciation of the mood of the spectators. In short, the tripping is done with heed. Heed is not itself a behavior but

it refers to the way behaviors such as tripping, falling, and recovering are assembled. Artful tripping is called heedful, not so much because the tripping involves action preceded by thought but because the behaviors patterned into the action of tripping suggest to the observer qualities such as "noticing, taking care, attending, applying one's mind, concentrating, putting one's heart into something, thinking what one is doing, alertness, interest, intentness, studying, and trying" (Ryle, 1949: 136). These inferences, based on the style of the action, are called "heed concepts" and support the conclusion that the behaviors were combined intelligently rather than stupidly.

The word "heed" captures an important set of qualities of mind that elude the more stark vocabulary of cognition. These nuances of heed are especially appropriate to our interest in systems preoccupied with failure-free performance. People act heedfully when they act more or less carefully, critically, consistently, purposefully, attentively, studiously, vigilantly, conscientiously, pertinaciously (Ryle, 1949: 151). Heed adverbs attach qualities of mind directly to performances, as in the description, "the airboss monitored the pilot's growing load of tasks attentively." Notice that the statement does not say that the airboss was doing two things, monitoring and also checking to be sure that the monitoring was done carefully. Instead, the statement asserts that, having been coached to monitor carefully, his present monitoring reflects this style. Mind is in the monitoring itself, not in some separate episode of theorizing about monitoring.

Heedful performance is not the same thing as habitual performance. In habitual action, each performance is a replica of its predecessor, whereas in heedful performance, each action is modified by its predecessor (Ryle, 1949: 42). In heedful performance, the agent is still learning. Furthermore, heedful performance is the outcome of training and experience that weave together thinking, feeling, and willing. Habitual performance is the outcome of drill and repetition.

When heed declines, performance is said to be heedless, careless, unmindful, thoughtless, unconcerned, indifferent. Heedless performance suggests a failure of intelligence rather than a failure of knowledge. It is a failure to see, to take note of, to be attentive to. Heedless performance is not about ignorance, cognition (Lyons, 1980: 57), and facts. It is about stupidity, competence, and know-how. Thus, mind refers to stretches of human behavior that exhibit qualities of intellect and character (Ryle, 1949: 126).

Group as Interrelated Activity

Ryle's ideas focus on individual mind. To extend his ideas to groups, we first have to specify the crucial performances in groups that could reflect a disposition to heed. To pinpoint these crucial performances, we derive four defining properties of group performance from Asch's (1952: 251–255) discussion of "mutually shared fields" and illustrate these properties with carrier examples.[2]

The first defining property of group performance is that individuals create the social forces of group life when they act as if there were such forces. As Asch (1952: 251) explained it,

> We must see group phenomena as both *the product and condition* of actions of individuals. . . . There are no forces between individuals as organisms; yet to all intents and purposes they act as if there were, and they actually create social forces. Group action achieves the kind of result that would be understandable if all participants were acting under the direction of a single organizing center. No such center exists; between individuals is a hiatus, which nevertheless, they succeed in overcoming with surprising effectiveness.

An example from carriers occurs during flight operations. The men in the tower (Air Department) monitor and give instructions to incoming and departing aircraft. Simultaneously, the men on the landing signal officers' platform do the same thing. They are backed up by the men in Air Operations who monitor and instruct aircraft at some distance from the ship. From the aviator's viewpoint, he receives integrated information about his current status and future behavior from an integrated source when, in reality, the several sources are relatively independent of one another and located in different parts of the ship.

The second defining property of group performance is that when people act as if there are social forces, they construct their actions (contribute) while envisaging a social system of joint actions (represent), and interrelate that constructed action with the system that is envisaged (subordinate). Asch (1952: 251–252) explained this as follows:

> There are group actions that are possible only when each participant has a representation that includes the actions of others and their relations. The respective actions converge relevantly, assist and supplement each other only when the joint situation is represented in each and when the representations are structurally similar. Only when these conditions are given can individuals subordinate themselves to the requirements of joint action. These representations and the actions that they initiate/bring group facts into existence and produce the phenomenal solidity of group process.

The simultaneous envisaging and interrelating that create a system occur when a pilot taxies onto the catapult for launching, is attached to it, and advances his engines to full power. Even though pilots have to rely on the catapult crew, they remain vigilant to see if representations are similar. Pilots keep asking themselves questions like, "Does it feel right?" or "Is the rhythm wrong?" The referent for the question, "Does *it* feel right?" however, is not the aircraft but the joint situation to which he has subordinated himself. If a person on the deck signals the pilot to reduce his engines from full power, he won't do so until someone stands in front of the plane, directly over the catapult, and signals for a reduction in power. Only then is the pilot reasonably certain that the joint situation has changed. He now trusts that the catapult won't be triggered suddenly and fling his underpowered aircraft into a person and then into the ocean.

The third defining property of group performance is that contributing, representing, and subordinating create a joint situation of interrelations among activities, which Asch (1952: 252) referred to as a system:

> When these conditions are given we have a social system or a process of a definite form that embraces the actions of a number of individuals. Such a system does not reside in the individuals taken separately, though each individual contributes to it; nor does it reside outside them; it is present in the interrelations between the activities of individuals.

An example from carriers is a pilot landing an aircraft on a deck. This is not a solitary act. A pilot doesn't really land; he is "recovered." And recovery is a set of interrelated activities among air traffic controllers, landing signal officers, the control tower, navigators, deck hands, the helmsman driving the ship, etc. As the recovery of a single aircraft nears completion in the form of a successful trap, nine to ten people on the landing signal officer's platform, up to 15 more people in the tower, and two to three more people on the bridge observe the recovery and can wave the aircraft off if there is a problem. While this can be understood as an example of redundancy, it can also be interpreted as activities that can be interrelated more or less adequately, depending on the care with which contributing, representing, and subordinating are done.

The fourth and final defining properly of group performance suggested by Asch is that the effects produced by a pattern of interrelated activities vary as a function of the style (e.g., heedful-heedless) as well as the strength (e.g., loose-tight) with which the activities are tied together. This is suggested by the statement that, in a system of interrelated activities, individuals can work with, for, or against each other:

> The form the interrelated actions take—on a team or in an office—is a datum of precisely the same kind as any other fact. One could say that all the facts of the system can be expressed as the sum of the actions of individuals. The statement is misleading, however, if one fails to add that the individuals would not be capable of these particular actions unless they were responding to (or envisaging the possibility of) the system. Once the process described is in motion it is no longer the individual "as such" who determines its direction, nor the group acting upon the individual as an external force, but individuals working with, for, or against each other. (Asch, 1952: 252)

It is these varying forms of interrelation that embody collective mind. An example of interrelating on carriers can be seen when ordnance is loaded onto an aircraft and its safety mechanisms are removed. If there is a sudden change of mission, the live ordnance must be disarmed, removed, and replaced by other ordnance that is now activated, all of this under enormous time pressure. These interrelated activities, even though tightly coupled, can become more or less dangerous depending on how the interrelating is done.

In one incident observed, senior officers kept changing the schedule of the next day's flight events through the night, which necessitated a repeated change in ordnance up to the moment the day launches began. A petty officer changing bombs underneath an aircraft, where the pilot couldn't see him, lost a leg when the pilot moved the 36,000-pound aircraft over him. The petty officer should have tied the plane down before going underneath to change the load but failed to do so because there was insufficient time, a situation created by continual indecision at the top. Thus, the senior officers share the blame for this accident because they should have resolved their indecision in ways that were more mindful of the demands it placed on the system.

Although Asch argued that interrelated activities are the essence of groups, he said little about how these interrelations occur or how they vary over time. Instead, he treated interrelations as a variable and interrelating as a constant. If we treat interrelations as a variable and interrelating as a process, this suggests a way to conceptualize collective mind.

HEEDFUL INTERRELATING AS COLLECTIVE MIND

The insights of Ryle and Asch can be combined into a concept of collective mind if we argue that dispositions toward heed are expressed in actions that construct interrelating. Contributing, representing, and subordinating, actions that form a distinct pattern external to any given individual, become the medium through which collective mind is manifest. Variations in heedful interrelating correspond to variations in collective mind and comprehension.

We assume, as Follett (1924: 146–153) did, that mind begins with actions, which we refer to here as contributions. The contributions of any one individual begin to actualize collective mind to the degree that heedful representation and heedful subordination define those contributions. A heedful contribution enacts collective mind as it begins to converge with, supplement, assist, and become defined in relation to the imagined requirements of joint action presumed to flow from some social activity system.

Similar conduct flows from other contributing individuals in the activity system toward others imagined to be in that system. These separate efforts vary in the heedfulness with which they interrelate, and these variations form a pattern. Since the object of these activities ("the envisaged system," to use Asch's phrase) is itself being constituted as these activities become more or less interrelated, the emergent properties of this object are not contained fully in the representation of any one person nor are they finalized at any moment in time. A single emergent property may appear in more than one representation, but seldom in all. And different properties are shared in common by different subsets of people. Asch seems to have had this distributed representation of the envisaged system in mind when he referred to "structurally similar representations." This pattern of distributed representation explains the transindividual quality of collective mind. Portions of the envisaged system are known to all, but all of it is known to none.

The collective mind is "located" in the process of interrelating just as the individual mind for Ryle was "located" in the activities of lorry driving, chess playing, or article writing. Collective mind exists potentially as a kind of capacity in an ongoing activity stream and emerges in the style with which activities are interrelated. These patterns of interrelating are as close to a physical substrate for collective mind as we are likely to find. There is nothing mystical about all this. Collective mind is manifest when individuals construct mutually shared fields. The collective mind that emerges during the interrelating of an activity system is more developed and more capable of intelligent action the more heedfully that interrelating is done.

A crude way to represent the development of a collective mind is by means of a matrix in which the rows are people and the columns are either the larger activities of contributing, representing, and subordinating, or their component behaviors (e.g., converging with, assisting, or supplementing). Initially, the cell entries can be a simple "yes" or "no." "Yes" means a person performs that action heedfully; "no" means the action is done heedlessly. The more "yeses" in the matrix, the more developed the collective mind.

We portray collective mind in terms of method rather than content, structuring rather than structure,

connecting rather than connections. Interrelations are not given but are constructed and reconstructed continually by individuals (Blumer, 1969: 110) through the ongoing activities of contributing, representing, and subordinating. Although these activities are done by individuals, their referent is a socially structured field. Individual activities are shaped by this envisioned field and are meaningless apart from it. When people make efforts to interrelate, these efforts can range from heedful to heedless. The more heed reflected in a pattern of interrelations, the more developed the collective mind and the greater the capability to comprehend unexpected events that evolve rapidly in unexpected ways. When we say that a collective mind "comprehends" unexpected events, we mean that heedful interrelating connects sufficient individual know-how to meet situational demands. For organizations concerned with reliability, those demands often consist of unexpected, nonsequential interactions among small failures that are hard to see and hard to believe. These incomprehensible failures often build quickly into catastrophes (Perrow, 1984: 7–12, 22, 78, 88).

An increase in heedful interrelating can prevent or correct these failures of comprehension in at least three ways. First, longer stretches of time can be connected, as when more know-how is brought forward from the past and is elaborated into new contributions and representations that extrapolate farther into the future. Second, comprehension can be improved if more activities are connected, such as when interrelations span earlier and later stages of task sequences. And third, comprehension can be increased if more levels of experience are connected, as when newcomers who take nothing for granted interrelate more often with old-timers who think they have seen it all. Each of these three changes makes the pattern of interrelations more complex and better able to sense and regulate the complexity created by unexpected events. A system that is tied together more densely across time, activities, and experience comprehends more of what is occurring because the scope of heedful action reaches into more places. When heed is spread across more activities and more connections, there should be more understanding and fewer errors. A collective mind that becomes more comprehensive, comprehends more.

Variations in Heed

If collective mind is embodied in the interrelating of social activities, and if collective mind is developed more or less fully depending on the amount of heedfulness with which that interrelating is done, we must address the issue of what accounts for variations in heed. We suspect the answer lies in Mead's (1934: 186) insight that mind is "the individual importation of social process." We understand the phrase "social process" to mean a set of ongoing interactions in a social activity system from which participants continually extract a changing sense of self-interrelation and then re-enact that sense back into the system. This ongoing interaction process is recapitulated in individual lives and continues despite the replacement of people.

Mead stressed the reality of recapitulation, as did others. Ryle (1949: 27), for example, observed that "this trick of talking to oneself in silence is acquired neither quickly nor without effort; and it is a necessary condition to our acquiring it that we should have previously learned to talk intelligently aloud and have heard and understood other people doing so. Keeping our thoughts to ourselves is a sophisticated accomplishment." Asch (1952: 257) described the relationship between the individual and the group as the only part-whole relation in nature "that depends on recapitulation of the structure of the whole in the part." The same point is made by Morgan (1986) and Hutchins (1990: 211), using the more recent imagery of holograms: System capacities that are relevant for the functioning of the whole are built into its parts. In each of these renderings, social processes are the prior resources from which individual mind, self, and action are fashioned (Mead, 1934: 191–192). This means that collective mind precedes the individual mind and that heedful interrelating foreshadows heedful contributing.

Patterns of heedful interrelating in ongoing social processes may be internalized and recapitulated by individuals more or less adequately as they move in and out of the system. If heedful interrelating is visible, rewarded, modeled, discussed, and preserved in vivid stories, there is a good chance that newcomers will learn this style of responding, will incorporate it into their definition of who they are in the system, and will reaffirm and perhaps even augment this style as they act. To illustrate, Walsh and Ungson (1991: 60) defined organization as a "network of intersubjectively shared meanings that are sustained through the development and use of a common language and everyday social interactions." Among the shared meanings and language on carriers we heard these four assertions: (1) If it's not written down you can do it; (2) Look for clouds in every silver lining; (3) Most positions on this deck were brought in blood; and (4) Never get into something you can't get out of. Each of these guidelines, if practiced openly, represents an image of heedful interrelating that can be internalized and acted back into the system. If such guidelines are neglected, ignored, or mocked, however, interrelating still goes on, but it is done with indifference and carelessness.

Whether heedful images survive or die depends importantly on interactions among those who differ in their experience with the system. While these interactions have been the focus of preliminary discussions of communities of practice (e.g., Lave and Wenger, 1991: 98–100) involving apprentices and experts, we highlight a neglected portion of the process, namely, the effects of socialization on the insiders doing the socializing (Sutton and Louis, 1987).

When experienced insiders answer the questions of inexperienced newcomers, the insiders themselves are often resocialized. This is significant because it may remind insiders how to act heedfully and how to talk about heedful action. Newcomers are often a pretext for insiders to reconstruct what they knew but forgot. Heedful know-how becomes more salient and more differentiated when insiders see what they say to newcomers and discover that they thought more thoughts than they thought they did.

Whether collective mind gets renewed during resocialization may be determined largely by the candor and narrative skills of insiders and the attentiveness of newcomers. Candid insiders who use memorable stories to describe failures as well as successes, their doubts as well as their certainties, and what works as well as what fails, help newcomers infer dispositions of heed and carelessness. Insiders who narrate richly also often remind themselves of forgotten details when they reconstruct a previous event. And these reminders increase the substance of mind because they increase the number of examples of heed in work.

Narrative skills (Bruner, 1986; Weick and Browning, 1986; Orr, 1990) are important for collective mind because stories organize know-how, tacit knowledge, nuance, sequence, multiple causation, means-end relations, and consequences into a memorable plot. The ease with which a single story integrates diverse themes of heed in action foreshadows the capability of individuals to do the same. A coherent story of heed is mind writ small. And a repertoire of war stories, which grows larger through the memorable exercise of heed in novel settings, is mind writ large.

The quality of collective mind is heavily dependent on the way insiders interact with newcomers (e.g., Van Maanen, 1976). If insiders are taciturn, indifferent, preoccupied, available only in stylized performances, less than candid, or simply not available at all, newcomers are in danger of acting without heed because they have only banal conversations to internalize. They have learned little about heedful interdependence. When these newcomers act and try to anticipate the contributions of others, their actions will be stupid, and mistakes will happen. These mistakes may represent small failures that produce learning (Sitkin, 1992). More ominous is the possibility that these mistakes may also represent a weakening of system capacity for heedful responding. When there is a loss of particulars about how heed can be expressed in representation and subordination, reliable performance suffers. As seasoned people become more peripheral to socialization, there should be a higher incidence of serious accidents.

We have dwelt on insider participation simply because this participation is a conspicuous phenomenon that allows us to describe collective mind, but anything that changes the ongoing interaction (e.g., preoccupation with personalities rather than with the task) can also change the capability of that interaction to preserve and convey dispositions of heed. Those changes in turn should affect the quality of mind, the likelihood of comprehension, and the incidence of error. . . .

The Conceptualization of Topics in Organizational Theory

Our analysis of collective mind and heedful interrelating throws new light on several topics in organizational theory, including organizational types, the measurement of performance, and normal accidents.

The concept of mind may be an important tool in comparative analysis. LaPorte and Consolini (1991) argued that high-reliability organizations such as aircraft carriers differ in many ways from organizations usually portrayed in organizational theory as (for convenience) high-efficiency organizations. Typical efficiency organizations practice incremental decision making, their errors do not have a lethal edge, they use simple low-hazard technologies, they are governed by single rather than multilayered authority systems, they are more often in the private than the public sector, they are not preoccupied with perfection, their operations are carried on at one level of intensity, they experience few nasty surprises, and they can rely on computation or judgment as decision strategies (Thompson and Tuden, 1959) but seldom need to employ both at the same time. LaPorte and Consolini (1991: 19) concluded that existing organizational theory is inadequate to understand systems in which the "consequences and costs associated with major failures in some technical operations are greater than the value of the lessons learned from them."

Our analysis suggests that most of these differences can be subsumed under the generalization that high-efficiency organizations have simpler minds than do high-reliability organizations. If dispositions toward individual and collective heed were increased in most organizations in conjunction with increases in task-related interdependence and flexibility in the sequencing of tasks, then we would expect these organizations to act more like high-reliability systems. Changes of precisely this kind seem to be inherent in recent interventions to improve total quality management (e.g., U.S. General Accounting Office, 1991).

Our point is simply that confounded in many comparisons among organizations that differ on conspicuous grounds, such as structure and technology, are less conspicuous but potentially more powerful differences in the capability for collective mind. A smart system does the right thing regardless of its structure and regardless of whether the environment is stable or turbulent. We suspect that organic systems, because of their capacity to reconfigure themselves temporarily into more mechanistic structures, have more fully developed minds than do mechanistic systems.

We also suspect that newer organizational forms, such as networks (Powell, 1990), self-designing systems (Hedberg, Nystrom, and Starbuck, 1976), cognitive oligopolies (Porac, Thomas, and Baden-Fuller, 1989: 413), and interpretation systems (Daft and Weick, 1984) have more capacity for mind than do M forms, U forms, and matrix forms. But all of these conjectures, which flow from the idea of collective mind, require that we pay as much attention to social processes and microdynamics as we now pay to the statics of structure, strategy, and demographics.

The concept of mind also suggests a view of performance that complements concepts such as activities (Homans, 1950), the active task (Dornbusch and Scott, 1975), task structure (Hackman, 1990: 10), group task design (Hackman, 1987), and production functions (McGrath, 1990). It adds to all of these a concern with the style or manner of performance. Not only can performance be high or low, productive or unproductive, or adequate or inadequate, it can also be heedful or heedless. Heedful performance might or might not be judged productive, depending on how productivity is defined.

Most important, the concept of mind allows us to talk about careful versus careless performance, not just performance that is productive or unproductive. This shift makes it easier to talk about performance in systems in which the next careless error may be the last trial. The language of care is more suited to systems concerned with reliability than is the language of efficiency.

Much of the interest in organizations that are vulnerable to catastrophic accidents can be traced to Perrow's (1981) initial analysis of Three Mile Island, followed by his expansion of this analysis into other industries (Perrow, 1984). In the expanded analysis, Perrow suggested that technologies that are both tightly coupled and interactively complex are the most dangerous, because small events can escalate rapidly into a catastrophe. Nuclear aircraft carriers such as those we have studied are especially prone to normal accidents (see Perrow, 1984: 97) because they comprise not one but several tightly coupled, interactively complex technologies. These include jet aircraft, nuclear weapons carried

on aircraft, nuclear weapons stored on board the ship, and nuclear reactors used to power the ship. Furthermore, the marine navigation system and the air traffic control system on a ship are tightly coupled technologies, although they are slightly less complex than the nuclear technologies.

Despite their high potential for normal accidents, carriers are relatively safe. Our analysis suggests that one of the reasons carriers are safe is because of, not in spite of, tight coupling. Our analysis raises the possibility that technological tight coupling is dangerous in the presence of interactive complexity, unless it is mediated by a mutually shared field that is well developed. This mutually shared field, built from heedful interrelating, is itself tightly coupled, but this tight coupling is social rather than technical. We suspect that normal accidents represent a breakdown of social processes and comprehension rather than a failure of technology. Inadequate comprehension can be traced to flawed mind rather than flawed equipment.

The Conceptualization of Practice

The mindset for practice implicit in the preceding analysis has little room for heroic, autonomous individuals. A well-developed organization mind, capable of reliable performance is thoroughly social. It is built of ongoing interrelating and dense interrelations. Thus, interpersonal skills are not a luxury in high-reliability systems. They are a necessity. These skills enable people to represent and subordinate themselves to communities of practice. As people move toward individualism and fewer interconnections, organization mind is simplified and soon becomes indistinguishable from individual mind. With this change comes heightened vulnerability to accidents. Cockpit crews that function as individuals rather than teams show this rapid breakdown in ability to understand what is happening (Orlady and Foushee, 1987). Sustained success in coping with emergency conditions seems to occur when the activities of the crew are more fully interrelated and when members' contributions, representations, and subordination create a pattern of joint action. The chronic fear in high-reliability systems that events will prove to be incomprehensible (Perrow, 1984) may be a realistic fear only when social skills are underdeveloped. With more development of social skills goes more development of organization mind and heightened understanding of environments.

A different way to state the point that mind is dependent on social skills is to argue that it is easier for systems to lose mind than to gain it. A culture that encourages individualism, survival of the fittest, macho heroics, and can-do reactions will often neglect heedful practice of representation and subordination. Without representation and subordination, comprehension reverts to one brain at a time. No matter how visionary or smart or forward-looking or aggressive that one brain may be, it is no match for conditions of interactive complexity. Cooperation is imperative for the development of mind.

Reliable performance may require a well-developed collective mind in the form of a complex, attentive system tied together by trust. That prescription sounds simple enough. Nevertheless, conventional understanding seems to favor a different configuration: a simple, automatic system tied together by suspicion and redundancy. The latter scenario makes sense in a world in which individuals can comprehend what is going on. But when individual comprehension proves inadequate, one of the few remaining sources of comprehension is social entities. Variation in the development of these entities may spell the difference between prosperity and disaster.

Notes

1. Unless otherwise cited, aircraft carrier examples are drawn from field observation notes of air operations and interviews aboard Nimitz class carriers made by the second author and others over a five-year period. Researchers spent from four days to three weeks aboard the carriers at any one time. They usually made observations from different vantage points during the evolutions of various events. Observations were entered into computer systems and later compared across observers and across organizational members for clarity of meaning. Examples are also drawn from quarterly workshop discussions with senior officers from those carriers over the two years. The primary observational research methodology was to triangulate observations made by three faculty researchers, as suggested by Glaser and Strauss (1967) and Eisenhardt (1989). The methodology is more fully discussed in Roberts, Stout, and Halpern (1993). Paper-and-pencil

data were also collected and are discussed elsewhere (Roberts, Rousseau, and LaPorte, 1993). That research was supported by Office of Naval Research contract #N-00014–86-k-0312 and National Science Foundation grant #F7–08046.

2. We could just as easily have used Blumer's (1969: 78–79) discussion of "the mutual alignment of action."

3. There is a limit to heedfulness, given the number and skill of participants, and on this night this ship was at that limit. The system was overloaded, and the situation was one that managers of high-technology weapons systems worry about all the time. They call it OBE (overcome by events). Given perhaps only minor differences in the situation, the outcomes might have been different in the situation, for example, had the carrier air group commander come to the tower (which he often does), he would have added yet another set of eyes and ears, with their attendant skills. Perhaps he could have monitored one aspect of the situation while the boss and mini boss took charge of others, and the situation would have been a more heedful one. Had the squadron representative in the tower been a pilot, he might have searched through his own repertoire of things that can go wrong and helped the F-14's pilot calm down and solve his problem, increasing the heedfulness of the situation.

References

Asch, Solomon E. 1952 Social Psychology. Englewood Cliffs, NJ: Prentice-Hall.

Blumer, Herbert 1969 Symbolic interaction. Berkeley: University of California Press.

Boden, Margaret A. 1990 "Introduction." In Margaret A. Boden (ed.), The Philosophy of Artificial Intelligence: 1–21. New York: Oxford University Press.

Bruner, Jerome 1986 Actual Minds, Possible Worlds. Cambridge, MA: Harvard University Press.

Churchland, Paul M. 1992 "A deeper unity: Some Feyerabendian themes in neurocomputational form." In Steven Davis (ed.), Connectionism: Theory and Practice: 30–50. New York: Oxford University Press.

Daft, Richard, and Karl E. Weick 1984 "Toward a model of organizations as interpretation systems." Academy of Management Review, 9: 284–295.

Dornbusch, Sandford M., and W. Richard Scott 1975 Evaluation and the Exercise of Authority. San Francisco: Jossey-Bass.

Dreyfus, Hubert L., and Stuart E. Dreyfus 1990 "Making a mind versus modeling the brain: Artificial intelligence back at a branch point." In Margaret A. Boden (ed.), The Philosophy of Artificial Intelligence: 309–333. New York: Oxford University Press.

Eisenhardt, Kathleen M. 1989 "Building theories from case study research." Academy of Management Review, 14: 532–550.

Elman, Jeffrey L. 1992 "Grammatical structure and distributed representations." In Steven Davis (ed.), Connectionism: Theory and Practice: 138–178. New York: Oxford University Press.

Follett, Mary Parker 1924 Creative Experience. New York: Longmans, Green.

Glaser, Barney, and Anselm L. Strauss 1967 The Discovery of Grounded Theory: Strategies for Qualitative Research. Chicago: Aldine.

Hackman, J. Richard 1987 "The design of work teams." In Jay Lorsch (ed.), Handbook of Organizational Behavior: 315–342. Englewood Cliffs, NJ: Prentice-Hall.

Hackman, J. Richard (ed.) 1990 Groups That Work (and Those That Don't). San Francisco: Jossey-Bass.

Hedberg, Bo L. T., Paul C. Nystrom, and William H. Starbuck 1976 "Camping on seesaws: Prescriptions for a self-designing organization." Administrative Science Quarterly, 21: 41–65.

Homans, George C. 1950 The Human Group. New York: Harcourt.

Hutchins, Edwin 1990 "The technology of team navigation." In Jolene Galegher, Robert E. Kraut, and Carmen Egido (eds.), Intellectual Teamwork: 191–220. Hillsdale, NJ: Erlbaum.

1991 "The social organization of distributed cognition." In Lauren B. Resnick, John M. Levine, and Stephanie D. Teasley (eds.), Perspectives on Socially Shared Cognition: 283–307. Washington, DC: American Psychological Association.

Langer, Eleanor J. 1989 "Minding matters: The consequences of mindlessness-mindfulness." In Leonard Berkowitz (ed.), Advances in Experimental Social Psychology, 22: 137–173. New York: Academic Press.

LaPorte, Todd R., and Paula M. Consolini 1991 "Working in practice but not in theory: Theoretical challenges of high-reliability organizations." Journal of Public Administration Research and Theory, 1: 19–47.

Lave, Jean, and Etienne Wenger 1991 Situated Learning: Legitimate Peripheral Participation. New York: Cambridge University Press.

Lyons, William 1980 Gilbert Ryle: An Introduction to His Philosophy. Atlantic Highlands, NJ: Humanities Press.

McGrath, Joseph E. 1990 "Time matters in groups." In Jolene Galegher, Robert E. Kraut, and Carmen Egido (eds.), Intellectual Teamwork: 23–61. Hillsdale, NJ: Erlbaum.

Mead, George Herbert 1934 Mind, Self, and Society. Chicago: University of Chicago Press.

Morgan, Gareth 1986 Images of Organization. Beverly Hills, CA: Sage.

Orlady, Harry W., and H. Clayton Foushee 1987 Cockpit Resource Management Training. Springfield, VA: National Technical Information Service (N87–22634).

Orr, Julian E. 1990 "Sharing knowledge, celebrating identity: Community memory in a service culture." In David Middleton and Derek Edwards (eds.), Collective Remembering: 169–189. Newbury Park, CA: Sage.

Perrow, Charles 1981 "The President's Commission and the normal accident." In D. Sills, C. Wolf, and V. Shelanski (eds.), The Accident at Three Mile Island: The Human Dimensions: 173–184. Boulder, CO: Westview Press.

Perrow, Charles 1984 Normal Accidents. New York: Basic Books.

Porac, Joseph F., Howard Thomas, and Charles Baden-Fuller 1989 "Competitive groups as cognitive communities: The case of Scottish knitwear manufacturers." Journal of Management Studies, 26: 397–416.

Powell, Walter W. 1990 "Neither market nor hierarchy: Network forms of organization." In Barry M. Staw and Larry L. Cummings (eds.), Research in Organizational Behavior, 12: 295–336. Greenwich, CT: JAI Press.

Quinlan, Phillip 1991 Connectionism and Psychology. Chicago: University of Chicago Press.

Roberts, Karlene H., Denise M. Rousseau, and Todd R. LaPorte 1993 "The culture of high reliability: Quantitative and qualitative assessment aboard nuclear powered aircraft carriers." Journal of High Technology Management Research (in press).

Roberts, Karlene H., Susan Stout, and Jennifer J. Halpern 1993 "Decision dynamics in two high reliability military organizations." Management Science (in press).

Rochlin, Gene I., Todd R. LaPorte, and Karlene H. Roberts 1987 "The self-designing high-reliability organization: Aircraft carrier flight operations at sea." Naval War College Review, 40(4): 76–90.

Rumelhart, David E. 1992 "Towards a microstructural account of human reasoning." In Steven Davis (ed.), Connectionism: Theory and Practice: 69–83. New York: Oxford University Press.

Ryle, Gilbert 1949 The Concept of Mind. Chicago: University of Chicago Press.

Sandelands, Lloyd E., and Ralph E. Stablein 1987 "The concept of organization mind." In Samuel Bacharach and Nancy DiTomaso (eds.), Research in the Sociology of Organizations, 5: 135–161. Greenwich, CT: JAI Press.

Schneider, David J. 1991 "Social cognition." In Lyman W. Porter and Mark R. Rosenzweig (eds.), Annual Review of Psychology, 42: 527–561. Palo Alto, CA: Annual Reviews.

Schneider, W., and R. M. Shiffrin 1977 "Controlled and automatic human information processing: I. Detection, search and attention." Psychological Review, 84: 1–66.

Sitkin, Sim 1992 "Learning through failure: The strategy of small losses." In Barry Staw and Larry Cummings (eds.), Research in Organizational Behavior, 14: 231–266. Greenwich, CT: JAI Press.

Sutton, Robert I., and Meryl R. Louis 1987 "How selecting and socializing newcomers influences insiders." Human Resource Management, 26: 347–361.

Thompson, James D., and Arthur Tuden 1959 "Strategies, structures, and processes of organizational decision." In James D. Thompson (ed.), Comparative Studies in Organization: 195–216. Pittsburgh: University of Pittsburgh Press.

U.S. General Accounting Office 1991 Management Practices: U.S. Companies Improve Performance through Quality Efforts. Document GAO/NSIAD-91–190. Washington, DC: U.S. Government Printing Office.

Van Maanen, John 1976 "Breaking in: Socialization to work." In Robert Dubin (ed.), Handbook of Work, Organization and Society: 67–130. Chicago: Rand McNally.

Walsh, James P., and Gerardo R. Ungson 1991 "Organizational memory." Academy of Management Review, 16: 57–91.

Wegner, Daniel M. 1987 "Transactive memory: A contemporary analysis of the group mind." In Brian Mullen and George R. Goethals (eds.), Theories of Group Behavior: 185–208. New York: Springer-Verlag.

Wegner, Daniel M., Ralph Erber, and Paula Raymond 1991 "Transactive memory in close relationships." Journal of Personality and Social Psychology, 61: 923–929.

Wegner, Daniel M., Toni Giuliano, and Paula T. Hertel 1985 "Cognitive interdependence in close relationships." In William J. Ickes (ed.), Compatible and Incompatible Relationships: 253–276. New York: Springer-Verlag.

Weick, Karl E., and Larry Browning 1986 "Arguments and narration in organizational communication." Journal of Management, 12: 243–259.

Wilson, G. C. 1986 Supercarrier. New York: Macmillan.

SOURCE: Weick, Karl E., and Karlene H. Roberts. 1993. Excerpt from "Collective Mind in Organizations: Heedful Interrelating on Flight Decks." *Administrative Science Quarterly*, 38:357–68, 376–81.

20

COORDINATION IN FAST-RESPONSE ORGANIZATIONS

SAMER FARAJ AND YAN XIAO

INTRODUCTION

Coordination has been at the center of organization theory ever since March and Simon (1958) suggested that work in organizations could be coordinated through pre-specified programs or mutual adjustment. This long dominant view is based on the information processing model wherein increasing task demands must be matched to structures capable of higher information processing (Daft and Lengel 1986, Galbraith 1977, Thompson 1967). Studies of coordination in settings as varied as office work units (Van de Ven, Delbecq and Koenig 1976), hospital emergency departments (Argote 1982), R&D teams (Keller 1994), and accounting audit teams (Gupta, Dirsmith and Fogarty 1994) have substantiated the core idea that matching increased task uncertainty to less formal modes of coordination leads to better performance.

The importance of coordination is increasing as organizations become reliant on interdisciplinary teams of specialists and distributed operations using communication technology (Child and McGrath 2001, DeSanctis and Monge 1999). More and more organizations face highly volatile environments often characterized by dynamism, and discontinuous change (Bourgeois and Eisenhardt

1989, Brown and Eisenhardt 1997). Further, as knowledge work in organizations principally takes place in work groups, coordination is less dependent on structural arrangements and more contingent on knowledge integration (Argote 1999). A gap exists between the traditional view of coordination as structural arrangements and coordination as an unfolding process of linked know-how and inter-related actions. Work groups themselves have traditionally been portrayed as coordination mechanisms (e.g. Galbraith 1977, Van de Ven, et al. 1976) rather than settings where complex and interdependent work gets performed.

In this paper, we focus on the collective performance aspect of coordination and emphasize the temporal unfolding and situated nature of coordinative action. The question addressed in this paper is: how is knowledge work coordinated in organizations that must operate essentially error free in high-velocity decision-making environments? We call organizations that face such operating conditions fast-response organizations. Such organizations develop structures and risk mitigation processes that allow them to function reliably under the most demanding of circumstances (Grabowski and Roberts 1999, Weick, Sutcliffe and Obstfeld 1999). While much has been learned about the unique structures, decision making, and culture of fast-response organizations, little research has addressed their specific coordination mechanisms and practices.

Based on an 18-month-long investigation of a leading trauma center, this paper explores how coordination of knowledge work occurs in a fast-response organization. Previous models of this type of coordination have emphasized the management of resources (e.g., resources. technology, personnel) through well-understood administrative coordination mechanisms (e.g., task assignment, resource allocation, input integration) (Malone and Crowston 1994, March and Simon 1958, Thompson 1967, Van de Ven, et al. 1976). Using a practice lens (Brown and Duguid 2001, Orlikowski 2000), we suggest that in settings where work is contextualized and non-routine, traditional models of coordination are insufficient to explain coordination as it occurs in practice. First, because expertise is distributed and work highly contextualized, expertise coordination is required to manage knowledge and skill interdependencies. Second, to avoid error, and to ensure that the patient remains on a recovering trajectory, fast-response cross boundary coordination practices are enacted. Because of the epistemic distance between specialists organized in communities of practice, these last coordination practices magnify knowledge differences and are partly contentious. An explanation of how expertise is coordinated and how coordination practices unfold in a fast-response setting is the core contribution of this article.

REFRAMING COORDINATION

At its core, coordination is about the integration of organizational work under conditions of task interdependence and uncertainty. Early theories of coordination focused on the need to balance differentiation among organizational units, with integration achieved through coordination mechanisms (Galbraith 1977, Lawrence and Lorsch 1967, Thompson 1967). The information processing paradigm provides a common theme for prior research on coordination. Each coordination mechanism is endowed with a specific information processing capability and must be matched to the information processing demands of the environment or to needs generated by the interdependence of work units.

Not surprisingly, previous models have emphasized the mode of coordination based on the assumption that certain modes are richer or more interactive, and can therefore provide higher information processing capacity. As a result, research findings have emphasized the distinction between formal and informal modes of coordination, along with the need for the latter in uncertain environments. Coordination has accordingly been measured along various modal continua; for example, by program or feedback (March and Simon 1958), impersonal vs. mutual adjustment (Van de Ven, et al. 1976), formal vs. informal (Kraut and Streeter 1995), programmed vs. non-programmed (Argote 1982).

More recently, Malone and colleagues (Malone and Crowston 1994, Malone, et al. 1999) developed a coordination theory that emphasizes the management of interdependencies among resources and activities. By characterizing various interdependencies and focusing on the process level, a variety of coordination mechanisms can be identified and applied. These mechanisms can be used as building blocks to solve coordination problems in organizations or to design novel organization processes. A strength of coordination theory is its recognition of the complexity of interdependencies in organizational work. However, it shares with the information processing view the assumption that the environment is predictable enough to characterize existing interdependencies and that pre-defined mechanisms can be designed for various contingencies.

In knowledge work, several related factors suggest the need to reconceptualize coordination. First, it may be just as important to focus on the content of coordination (what is being coordinated) as on the mode of coordination. Traditional coordination theory emphasizes the *how* (i.e., the mode) of coordination as opposed to the *what* (content) and *when* (circumstances) of coordination. This distinction becomes increasingly important in complex knowledge work where there is less reliance on formal structure, interdependence is changing, and work is primarily performed in teams. In fact, complex knowledge work requires the application of specialized skills and knowledge in a timely manner, thus raising difficult coordination issues in dynamic and time-constrained environments (Faraj and Sproull 2000, Gittell 2002).

Second, the traditional concept of interdependence as a property of existing linkages between organizational units is of limited use in work settings already organized in teams, where individual cooperation is essential. Thompson's (1967) highly influential but simple typology of interdependencies may be useful to describe necessary inter-unit or inter-organizational linkages. However, it assumes that pre-determined work patterns accurately reflect requisite interdependencies and thus is a less compelling frame for explicating interdependent knowledge work performed in interdisciplinary teams.

Third, coordination theories have limited applicability in organizations that face a high-velocity environment and must also operate essentially error free. Contrary to the tenets of coordination theories, in such settings the empirical record shows that formal modes of coordination do not melt away in favor of more improvised ways of coordinating. To the contrary, the dilemma of coordination in such settings is that on the one hand there is a need for tight structuring, formal coordination, and hierarchical decision making in order to ensure a clear division of responsibilities, prompt decision processes, and timely action; but on the other hand, because of the need for rapid action and the uncertain environment, there is a competing need to rely on flexible structures, on-the-spot decision-making, and informal coordination modes. Thus, such organizations paradoxically emphasize both formal and improvised coordination mechanisms (e.g., Bigley and Roberts 2001, Brown and Eisenhardt 1997, Weick and Roberts 1993).

Finally, the coordination of knowledge work may introduce contingencies and intersubjectivities that are asunder to the information processing capacity of a coordination mode. For instance, knowledge work increasingly involves specialists embedded in different epistemic communities of practice (COP) where individuals bring with them significant differences in problem conceptualizations and speak different (technical) languages. One implication is that coordination at the boundary may require reconciliation and transformation of knowledge (Bechky 2003) and thus involve the COPs themselves (Brown and Duguid 2001). Further, knowledge tends to be embedded in localized work practice and difficult to decontextualize (Brown and Duguid 2001, Lave 1988). Thus, because of differences in perspectives and interests, it becomes necessary to provide support for cross-boundary knowledge transformation (Carlile 2002).

We propose a reorientation of knowledge coordination away from pre-identified interdependencies and modes of coordination. This reframing is necessary and timely due to the growing recognition that routine coordination (in the sense of recognizable and repetitive patterns) cannot be specified in sufficient detail to be carried out and is thus insufficient to coordinate complex knowledge work (Brown and Duguid 2001, Feldman and Pentland 2003). We suggest that for environments where knowledge work is interdisciplinary and highly contextualized, the relevant lens is one of practice. Practices emerge from an ongoing stream of activities and are enacted through the contextualized actions of individuals (Orlikowski 2000). These practices are driven by a practical logic, that is, a recognition of novel task demands, emergent situations, and the unpredictability of evolving action. Bourdieu (1990: 12) defines practices as generative formulas reflecting the *"modus operandi"* (manner of working) in contrast to the *"opus operatum"* (finished work). These practices are characterized by "an uncertainty and fuzziness resulting from the fact that they have as their principle not a set of conscious, constant rules, but practical schemes, opaque to their possessors, varying according to the logic of the situation." Finally, a practice view breaks with perspectives that overemphasize the role of rules and structures at the expense of actors in explaining work activities. It emphasizes the contextualized engagement of actors and their capacity to make "practical and normative judgment among alternative possible trajectories of action" (Emirbayer and Mische 1998).

Based on a practice view, we suggest the following definition of coordination: a temporally unfolding and contextualized process of input regulation and interaction articulation to realize a collective performance. Two important points follow. First, the definition emphasizes the temporal unfolding and contextually situated nature of work processes. It recognizes that coordinated actions are enacted within a specific context, among a specific set of actors, and following a history of previous actions and interactions that necessarily constrain future action. Second, following Strauss (1993), we emphasize trajectories to describe sequences of actions toward a goal with an emphasis on contingencies and interactions among actors. Trajectories differ from routines in their emphasis on progression toward a goal and attention to deviation from that goal. Routines merely emphasize sequences of steps and thus are difficult to specify in work situations characterized by novelty, unpredictability, and ever-changing combination of tasks, actors, and resources. Trajectories emphasize both the unfolding of action as well as the interactions that shape it. A trajectory-centric view of coordination recognizes the stochastic aspect of unfolding events and the possibility that certain combinations of inputs or interactions can lead to trajectories leading to dreadful outcomes—the Apollo 13 "Houston, we have a problem" scenario. In such moments, coordination is more about dealing with the "situation" than about formal organizational arrangements.

In this paper, we report on a study of coordination in a leading trauma center. Trauma centers are representative of organizational entities that are faced with unpredictable environmental demands—complex sets of technologies, high coordination loads, and the paradoxical need to achieve high reliability while maintaining efficient operations. Trauma victims require intensive and immediate care to aggressively stabilize the patient in the first hour, known as the "golden hour," in order to forestall complications and multi-organ failures later. A trauma center has little control over its input environment (the kind, number, and timing of patients being brought in) and must organize its staff and resources effectively to provide the best medical care to any number of arriving victims. The primary goal is patient stabilization and initiating a *treatment trajectory*—a temporally unfolding sequence of events, actions, and interactions—aimed at ensuring patient medical recovery.

We found that coordination in a trauma setting entails two specific practices. First, there is heavy reliance on *expertise coordination processes* to facilitate the management of skill and knowledge interdependencies in a dynamic and highly situated context. Second, when "situations" arise, i.e.

when a patient is at risk or already on a deteriorating trajectory, intervention is necessary irrespective of specialization, formal role, and reputation. We call these time critical cross-boundary responses to treatment trajectories degradation *dialogic coordination practices*. Such practices occur infrequently but are highly significant due to the possibility of medical error and disastrous outcome. They are often contentious because of unclear cause-effect relationships and because they involve players with different viewpoints and epistemologies. The rest of the paper describes our field study and discusses our findings.

METHODOLOGY

Site

The study site, Trauma Center (TC), is a leading trauma center located in an urban setting in the Mid-Atlantic region. It was one of the first trauma centers in the country and has pioneered some of the key advances in trauma medicine. The center considers itself "the world leader in research in trauma medicine" and trains "250 residents and fellows, scores of medical students, and hundreds of nurses, paramedics, and advanced practitioners per year" (Resident's Manual 2001). TC is self-contained in a six-story building that is physically co-located next to the medical school and its hospital. TC operates a number of specialized subunits, including the 10-bay Trauma Resuscitation Unit (TRU), an Operating Room (OR) area with six separate rooms, a Post Anesthesia Care Unit (PACU), and in-patient ward (82 beds). All supporting functions such as X-rays, Computerized Axial Tomography (CAT) scans, a hyperbaric chamber, and clinical laboratories are located within the building. According to the state health agency, the center has 6,000 admissions per year and is designated as the primary adult trauma center for a metropolitan area of about 2 million people. This trauma center has a complement of approximately 250 specialists including surgeons, anesthesiologists, medical residents, nurses, and associated support staff.

We chose TC as a site for three important reasons. First, the site is widely recognized as one of the leading trauma centers in the country. As several interviewees noted with pride, most other trauma centers are modeled on this one and more trauma specialists have trained at this center than at any other in the country. Second, as the primary Level-1 center of a large urban area, TC faces a complex environment and a high volume of admissions. Third, part of our research team had a long history of research in this setting, so that site personnel were familiar with members of the research team, trusted them, and were open to speaking frankly to them. However, researchers from a different university performed the interviews and observations in order to create a psychological buffer and because of concern about history—important considerations when covering sensitive organizational issues.

Data Collection

We began our investigation aiming to understand the interplay of formal and improvised coordination processes but open to alternative frames. We focused our questions during the semi-structured interviews on various aspects of coordination, organizing, teamwork, and failures of coordination. As other constructs emerged, we embraced them with an open mind and frequently revisited our interviewing protocol. For example, we initially looked for evidence of "coordination failures." However, most respondents could not easily relate to this focus. One charge nurse responded, "We basically don't have coordination failures: we don't allow it." Based on the evidence emerging from the setting we continuously compared data and theory to gain a deeper understanding of the phenomena (Glaser and Strauss 1967, Strauss and Corbin 1990), and shifted our focus to coordination practices.

We collected data over a period of 11 months between December 1999 and October 2000. We used multiple investigators and a mixture of data collection methods in order to develop complementary insight, achieve theoretical triangulation, and enhance confidence in our findings (Eisenhardt 1989). These methods included review of archival records, observation, shadowing, and in-depth interviews. Additional follow-up interviews were performed in order to answer any remaining

questions, or if the initial interview had been cut short due to logistical considerations, such as an interviewee's need to respond to an emergency. During the first three months, we observed TC operations intensively and shadowed some key personnel in order to immerse ourselves in the setting and deepen our understanding of procedures. During the next stage, we intensified our interviews with representatives of every specialty. The research team then analyzed findings and explored emergent theoretical themes. In the final stage of data collection, we performed some follow-up interviews that focused specifically on coordinative actions and interactions resulting from problematic treatment trajectories.

Overall, we observed patient admissions and treatment for a total of 140 hours (with an average session lasting 3.1 hours). We shadowed nine key personnel in five roles for a total of 28 hours and recorded all their interactions and behaviors. We conducted 56 in-depth interviews and 15 short complementary interviews. Interviews lasted from 20 minutes to 1.5 hours, averaging approximately 45 minutes. The interviews were transcribed and checked for accuracy. Based on successive reviews of the observation, shadowing, and interview data, we arrived at a set of recurring themes.

FINDINGS

We start with a description of the environment and associated uncertainties under which the trauma center operates. Then we describe two categories of coordination practices that ensure effective work outcomes. The first category, which we call *expertise coordination practices,* represents processes that make it possible to manage knowledge and skill interdependencies. These processes bring about fast-response, superior reconfiguration, efficient knowledge sharing, and expertise vetting. Second, because of the rapidly unfolding tempo of treatment and the stochastic nature of the treatment trajectory, *dialogic coordination practices* are used as contextually and temporally situated responses to occasional trajectory deviation, errors, and general threats to the patient. These dialogic coordination practices are

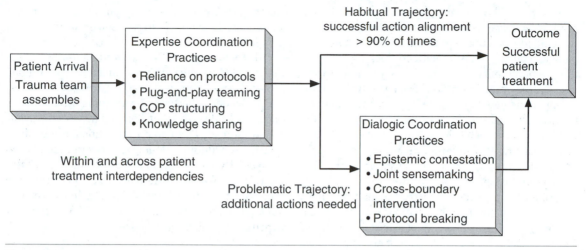

Figure 20.1   Coordination-Focused Model of Trauma Patient Treatment

crucial for ensuring effective coordination but often require contentious interactions across communities of practice. Figure 20.1 presents a coordination-focused model of patient treatment and describes the circumstances under which dialogic coordination practices are called for.

Input Uncertainty

The trauma center receives a large range of trauma injuries. The main categories include penetration trauma (e.g., a gunshot or knife wound) and multi-system trauma patients (e.g., from car crashes and falls). In addition, the center receives patients requiring hyperbaric oxygen therapy (diving accidents, carbon monoxide poisoning) as well as a variety of less frequent injuries. At any point in the day, it is impossible to predict what the workload will be like. By design, the center needs to be able to handle sudden peaks in demand such as when a multiple motor vehicle crash produces a large number of admissions at the same time. The demand is not completely random. Traffic rush hours and summer holiday nights generate more admissions.

For the staff, input uncertainty means long periods of waiting without an admission followed by sudden bursts of activity with multiple admissions over a short period of time. As an X-ray technician reported, "I've gone a full shift without getting admissions and also my worst case scenario . . . It

was a Friday night, we got 11 admissions in forty-five minutes."

Because incoming patients differ in their injury type and severity, the TC experiences high levels of input uncertainty (Argote 1982). Using Perrow's (1970) organizational analysis framework, variability of input is high (each patient is different) and analyzability is low (treatment cannot be pre-specified and must be customized). Patients in critical condition are routed to TC with just minutes of warning and treatment must be provided upon arrival. The TC has no control over the number of patients arriving, or their timing and medical conditions.

The treatment process has some uniquely demanding characteristics. TC staff has to establish a diagnosis within minutes and initiate a treatment plan before moving on to the next admission. Because exams are often rushed, the treatment process retains a stochastic quality (Weick 1990). In complicated cases, medical treatment is often described as an educated guess based on limited clues (Gawande 2002). Critical information about the patient (medical history or allergies) is often unavailable (unconscious patient) or unreliable (semiconscious patients). Thus, in its haste to establish a diagnosis, the TC team may miss factors (e.g., internal bleeding, allergy, previous injury/illness) that can interact in unexpected ways with the evolving treatment.

Another characteristic of the process is the need to manage complex interdependencies both within and across patient treatments. Working on a patient requires finely tuned activities and interactions among nurses, surgeons, and anesthesiologists. Some of the interdependence is sequential; for example, the patient needs to be anesthetized before the surgeon can perform a surgical intervention. However, the stochastic nature of the treatment process can rapidly impose a reciprocal interdependence (Thompson 1967). For example, depending on how the patient is reacting to surgery, the anesthesiologist may need to intervene multiple times during surgery. At the same time, the team must treat all admitted patients and cannot afford the luxury of focusing exclusively on one patient at a time. Thus, cross-patient interdependence is also a core characteristic of the process.

Because medical expertise is highly specialized and the patient conditions TC faces are very diverse, a necessary organizing principle is that teams must incorporate differentiated expertise.[1] TC's core technology can be summarized as a combination of differentiated expertise (the various specialists) and complex interactions (during treatment). Because the timing of disasters and accidents cannot be planned, TC must organize itself to provide superior care at any time of day and no matter how many patients have already been admitted. Keeping the facility open and trauma teams available on a 24/7 basis is extremely costly during down times. The staffing dilemma is to have the smallest team possible that will not be overwhelmed by the peaks in demand.

Expertise Coordination Practices

We found evidence of well-developed coordination of expertise practices. Because medical expertise is distributed among the various members of the team, there is a need for team-level processes that support shared cognition and information sharing. Expertise coordination refers to processes that manage knowledge and skill interdependencies (Faraj and Sproull 2000). Expertise coordination processes are important for the team because they facilitate the development of a common mental model of patient condition and treatment options. Such processes

also enhance performance by ensuring that crucial knowledge is available to those who need it when they need it.

We found four expertise coordination processes that seemed to enhance performance. First, trauma protocols streamline work and reduce process uncertainty. Second, plug-and-play teaming arrangements allow flexibility to meet contingencies with available personnel. Third, many operational responsibilities for scheduling, training and control are carried by specialty-based communities of practice (COP). Fourth, knowledge externalization processes are relied on to reduce information sharing problems. Table 20.1 presents evidence in support of the four expertise coordination practices.

Reliance on protocols. A trauma protocol can be viewed as a specification of care procedures integrated within a decision-making flow chart that specifies the treatment of a specific patient condition. Organizationally, it represents a standard operating procedure where roles, decision points, and event sequences are specified. For example, the ABC (Airway-Breathing-Circulation) protocol lays out the specific steps to be taken to ensure that a patient has no obstruction along the airways, is breathing properly, and has effective blood circulation. Protocols serve as organizationally sanctioned standards for best practices. Trauma protocols build on consensus among experts based on reliable experience.

While routines have generally been portrayed as repetitive and stable performance programs (March and Simon 1958, Nelson and Winter 1982), we found that the trauma protocols serve important coordinative functions even under the most demanding of circumstances in the TC setting. Protocols can be viewed as proven ways to structure interactions and manage the basic resource and expertise interdependencies that emerge around the treatment of a patient. A protocol details what needs to be done, by whom, and in what order, as well as stipulating various actions based on recognized contingencies. Task ambiguity is reduced as everyone knows what needs to be done. Role ambiguity is reduced because roles and actions appropriate to each person and specialty are pre-defined. Decision making is enhanced because the protocol provides

Table 20.1   Evidence of Expertise Coordination Practices

Reliance on protocol	*Plug-and-play teaming*	*Communities of practice*	*Knowledge externalization*
Interdependence managed: Within patient across specialization	*Interdependence managed:* Within specialty across patient	*Interdependence managed:* Within specialty organizing, identity, and participation	*Interdependence managed:* Admission and inter-caregiver knowledge dependencies
"[Talking about residents] they do have their medical degrees, and hopefully the nurses will work collaboratively with them in how to take care of the patient but there are certain protocols and certain things that we do because of the level of expectation that we should not miss any injuries at the world famous shock trauma center." [charge nurse] "To try and get folks to sing from the same hymnal as much as possible, is really the key to good organization. Once we decide to do it a certain way and we [the attendings] sit in a room and we'll go, 'Well, you know, we decided.' They're written as policies, for the most part. It depends on how big a deal it is, but we actually do have treatment care plans and books that say: "Here's how to do protocol X." [attending surgeon] "We actually teach a lot of residents in terms of procedure wise here in the TRU, specifically. [...] they come in and say: OK I want this lab, etc. But you know we have a protocol here and I show them this is what we do as soon as somebody comes in." [nurse]	"So if you have a multiple accident and have three patients coming in, you don't have the benefit of the full team. For our team, it's fairly automatic to split up an upper and a higher, you don't want to leave 2 interns admitting a sick patient, you want to put a third year and a first year or a second year and a third year." [chief resident] An attending anesthesiologist in the middle of an operation in the OR is paged to the TRU due to a new arrival. He leaves his assistant [a resident] to continue the operation. Ten minutes later, he returns to finish the operation. [observation] Then as I was walking out [of the operating room], there is another page that a policeman had been injured in a motor vehicle crash, has an ETA of 2 minutes. But I was due to start the case in Room 4 at that point. When the admission came I said: "John [another anesthesiologist], you've got to do this admission for me, I'll start the operating room case." [attending anesthesiologist]	"I don't want to say we make our own rules, but we govern ourselves a lot, we police ourselves. We don't need someone from three floors up in a suit that's sitting here and making sure we dot our i's and cross our t's." [nurse] "Surgery residents want to operate, emergency medicine residents want to 'do stuff.' If we let the residents at the patient, we would kill them with the procedure. They want a particular experience, but his [the attending] goal is to educate them to appreciate injury as a mechanism for illness." [attending surgeon] "You can go to the operating room five minutes after you meet somebody and you don't know what kind of skill they have even though they say they're a fourth year or fifth year, you don't know if they have any ability at all to stop bleeding, or can handle a knife or a needle. Because some people at a fifth year level function as a third year level somewhere else just depending on the quality of their training." [attending surgeon]	"Most of the time the information that the surgeon wants is the same as the information that the nurses want is the same information that I want. So if the team leader or the nurse is extracting information from the patient, I'm listening and so is everyone else." [nurse anesthetist] [During a busy time] nurse at end of his shift follows the charge nurse updating her with his key information as she moves around performing tasks. [observation] [About lack of knowledge sharing] "it's never a good feeling, but I think the thing to do is not to get upset about it, instead look back at what happened. Who didn't tell whom what, were you busy doing something else and that's why you missed it?" [surgery fellow] "It's important, that turnover of information to the person who is leaving, getting that forward knowledge that they have. All of the knowledge accumulated in the last 12 hours is conveyed." [attending anesthesiologist]

easy-to-follow decision heuristics based on best practices. Finally, because a protocol has beginning and end points and outcome measures, status results can easily be analyzed and communicated to others who have not yet been involved in the treatment.

The strong emphasis on mastering and using treatment protocols at TC may be due to two principal reasons. First, protocols generate a shared cognitive framework of the task, its temporal progression and what constitutes appropriate patient responses. Because TC team members have learned the various protocols, when they are to be used, and how they fit into the overall plan of resuscitation, teamwork becomes implicit and the need to communicate is reduced—an important advantage in times of stress. Second, because TC is a teaching institution that yearly trains hundreds of medical personnel, the use of protocols controls for the variation in expertise among trauma team members. While the TRU core staff is made up of highly experienced attending physicians, nurses, and technicians, medical residents also participate extensively in the medical care. These are individuals who hold an M.D. but are still training in trauma medicine. New residents are expected to quickly learn all 51 protocols used at TC.[2] There is a strong consensus that using protocols helps achieve positive patient results.

Plug-and-play teaming. A trauma team is made up of approximately 15 to 20 people including an attending surgeon (formal leader), a surgery fellow (second in charge but still training), three to five residents (M.D.s specializing in emergency medicine or surgery), two to four medical students, an attending anesthesiologist, two to three trauma nurses, the OR charge nurse (for patients needing immediate surgery), and two technicians. There are three separate teams to ensure 24-hour coverage. Similarly to members of temporary work teams in other fields, such as aircraft cockpit crews, individuals on trauma teams do not underscore their trauma team identity. Instead, they view their disciplinary group (e.g., anesthesia, surgery, nursing) as the team that matters.

In other words, temporary action teams form around patients. Such a team can function regardless of which member of a given specialty serves on it, as long as the requisite expertise is adequate. For example, an attending surgeon may be able to leave the completion of a simple surgical procedure to an experienced resident in order to focus on an incoming admission that requires advanced expertise. The surgeons thus acted interchangeably, yet team processes and performance seemed unaffected, since both of these specialists were highly experienced.

Another interesting aspect of team formation under pressure is the ability of a given group to split up and create two functioning subunits when the situation requires it. This process can frequently be observed in surgery, which is often the most time-consuming trauma activity. We observed situations wherein the trauma team was operating on a patient when one or more new admissions arrived. The surgeons on the team quickly divided up into two surgery groups possessing roughly comparable expertise, with the rest of the disciplines on the trauma team following suit. The result was that each new team had the needed variety of expertise, and could start working on a different patient in parallel. This process can be further repeated if necessary. When the crisis passes, the team returns to its original form.

The reliance on role-based ad-hoc teaming, and the ease with which teams subdivided and reconstituted themselves, leads us to apply the label of "plug-and-play" teaming to these unique flexible teaming arrangements. We view plug-and-play teaming as a coordination process enacted to cope with time-critical task demands and input uncertainty. It is an efficient and flexible way to manage across-patient knowledge and skill interdependencies that emerge as new patients are brought in.

Communities of practice. We learned from our interviews, shadowing, and observations that most participants saw the ad-hoc teams that formed and re-formed around each patient as only temporary occasions for joint action. The key organizational entity that governs these medical providers' lives is the specialty community of practice they belong to, of which there are three main ones: surgery, anesthesiology, and nursing. Contrary to our expectation that the dynamic environment would force flexible and interdisciplinary structures on TC, we found that the specialty communities played a major role in organizing and coordinating TC operations. We found that communities of practice support work coordination at the trauma center level by managing staffing interdependencies and internally managing the participation (learning) process.

The traditional medical disciplinary divisions within TC are well established and clearly recognized. Each anesthesiologist, surgeon, nurse, and specialist knows his or her role in patient treatment and generally respects these epistemological lines of demarcation. Each discipline has its own hierarchy and, within reason, sets its own policies and manages its own schedule. The COPs structure themselves in shifts in such a way as to cover operations 24 hours a day, seven days a week. The scheduling task is complex because team members have to be scheduled not only for the on-call team but also for the second-call (backup) team. The schedule is planned a month in advance and it is the sole responsibility of each COP to set its schedule. Individuals are in turn responsible for negotiating coverage of their slots if they are unable to make their shift. This specialty-based mode of scheduling organizing reduces the need for overall managerial intervention and centralized planning. As a nurse reported with pride, the COP structure is cherished: "The [nursing] unit is run by the nurses from scheduling to discipline to evaluations: nurses run the place."

An advantage of the COP structure is that each specialty can manage the complex processes needed to train new members while ensuring patient outcomes. Incoming patient conditions differ drastically from one admission to the next, so that less experienced staff may suddenly need to call on people with a higher level of expertise. The COP structure provides flexible coordination and control processes for its members, allowing them to go beyond anything that can be specified in a set of organizational rules or medical routines such as the trauma protocols. One set of emergent processes integrates and trains peripheral members of the community. For example, residents (who are already physicians) are eager to practice their skills and may often overestimate their ability to handle complex cases.

In order to safeguard patients, core members of the key medical communities (e.g., surgery) have developed immediate coaching and supervision heuristics and a healthy skepticism regarding the talent at hand. There is a specific ability-based control structure. The attending surgeon (or "attending," usually a professor) is the highest authority. "It is on his credit card," a resident explained, indicating where ultimate responsibility lies. Since the attending is often busy caring for multiple patients (sometimes in different care units), there is a control process that clearly specifies how responsibility devolves within the team: When the attending is not present, the fellow who is apprenticing to become an attending is in charge. The residents and students have their own pecking order based on seniority. This leads to a layered responsibility system. Each person is responsible for those more junior than him or her. This system provides significant operational flexibility as the attending physician and the fellow may have multiple demands on their time outside the TRU.

Because medical error is potentially fatal, training of new physicians is tightly monitored. As a chief resident said, "You tend to watch them more carefully before you trust them with more responsibility or you test them with responsibility to find out how good they are . . . I allow him only to do that which I trust him to." This self-policing of each individual by senior members of the COP reduces the need for the organization to rely on formal behavior controls for each specialty (such as who can do what procedure). It also facilitates trauma team coordination, because other members are able to quickly size up a new person's ability by observing how much trust and responsibility senior specialty members place in that person.

Knowledge sharing. The high velocity environment at TC requires the generation and sharing of large amounts of knowledge. At admission, the whole team needs to learn about the patient's injury mechanism, how they fared during transport, medical history, and related conditions. Whether a patient was injured in a motor vehicle rollover or suffered from smoke inhalation has immediate implications for how the bay is to be prepared and whether to call in additional specialists. Once the treatment is underway, significant new information is generated from the examination, monitoring devices, and lab results. The team builds on the data to discuss alternative treatment plans and reevaluate the diagnosis several times within a brief period. Ensuring that knowledge is shared prevents errors of omission, faulty cognitions, and individual actions based on partial information.

A great deal of the knowledge sharing is verbal and face-to-face. The medics delivering a patient to the TRU are required to call out loud the key facts of the case in front of the team. Another process that occurred frequently is an attending-led "conference," mostly occurring near the bay where the patient is being treated, where the team members share the technical information in their possession and pool their knowledge about how the treatment is proceeding. Finally, during shift change, a lot of information accumulated over the previous shift must be shared. An anesthesiologist stressed the need for a full debriefing: "It's important, that turnover of information from the person who is leaving, getting that forward knowledge that they have."

All team members pay close attention to the overall information flow and extract those items that may affect their own functioning, since any new piece of information could have a major impact on the evolving treatment plan. Furthermore, depending on the patient load, the attending or fellow who was working on the patient may be called away on a moment's notice and any team member should able to step in without needing to be brought up to speed. But sometimes during stressful situations, team members may forget to share knowledge or report some important piece of information. Because of the importance of knowledge sharing for evolving treatment plans, team leaders take such lapses very seriously. As a surgery fellow notes:

> Everyone from the top down needs to have some idea of the things that are going on, and if things don't flow all the way up, what happens is the next day or whenever, it suddenly comes up that, oh, the patient had this done yesterday, and you're like, I didn't know about that!

Ensuring that knowledge-sharing processes are well maintained is one of the most difficult aspects of expertise coordination. Technological solutions provide redundancy but cannot replace the human element. The system only works well when people invest the time to share what they know. As one attending anesthesiologist noted: "There are various gradations of redundancy in the communications; but despite all of that, many times neither the trauma attending nor the nurse actually communicates anything."

Dialogic Coordination Practices

The expertise coordination processes discussed so far ensure expertise integration and flexible teamwork under conditions of multiple concurrent interdependencies driven by patient condition variability and overall patient load. However, coordination requires more than smooth integration of individual actions to ensure patient outcomes. As the treatment process unfolds, new interdependencies are generated and new paths and possibilities are created, not all of which are positive from a patient outcome perspective. Like some organizational work processes, such as R&D work, trauma medicine is an inherently stochastic process that cannot be fully elucidated and controlled. Diagnoses can sometimes be little more than educated guesses and errors are frequent (e.g., Gawande 2002). In the high pressure setting of TC the combination of severely injured trauma victims needing immediate intervention and highly motivated but inexperienced doctors in training can be especially risky.

In this section, we extend previous definitions of coordination to reflect some unique practices that occasionally take place and are crucial to ensuring coordination success and patient safety. In our fast paced setting, we find it necessary to highlight the continuous interactions, joint sensemaking, common responsibility, and cross-boundary interventions that are so important for saving patients. The term *dialogic*—as opposed to *monologic* [italics added]—recognizes differences and emphasizes the existence of epistemic boundaries, different understandings of events, and the existence of boundary objects (e.g., the diagnosis or the treatment plan). A dialogic approach to coordination is the recognition that action, communication, and cognition are essentially relational and highly situated. We use the concept of trajectory (Bourdieu 1990, Strauss 1993) to recognize that treatment progressions are not always linear or positive. The idea of a treatment trajectory emphasizes the dual nature of the treatment process. On one hand, it is a recognizable course of action that typically moves the patient from a state of trauma admission to a state of successful treatment. On the other hand, the treatment trajectory is partially stochastic, unpredictable, and affected by patient condition as well as team actions,

Table 20.2   Evidence of Dialogic Coordination Practices

Epistemic contestation	*Joint sensemaking*	*Cross boundary intervention*	*Protocol breaking*
Trigger: Different beliefs among different specialties as to which treatment step is required	*Trigger:* Patient is not responding to treatment in line with diagnosis	*Trigger:* Safety of patient is compromised by actions of a team member	*Trigger:* Following the protocol negatively slows down treatment
"There are times when the surgeon wants to perform an operation, and the anesthesiologist doesn't want to compromise the patient's health. You can't put this patient out, he's too sick for the drugs, then the attending surgeon has to figure out whether they are going to do at all, and sometimes they are at odds, and sometimes the anesthesiologist won't, 'we are not giving this patient anesthesia.'" [nurse anesthesiologist] "If the resident is pushing for something that really seems outrageous to the nurse, that they'll say. "Well this is what you've asked us to do and this is what we're supposed to do and these are the consequences.'" [technician] "I have seen it all, I have seen attendings [physicians] yelling at each other, screaming at each other, and I have seen intelligent discussions, negotiations." [nurse anesthesiologist]	"In highly uncertain states of affairs, you see a lot more communication occurring at a higher level in the team structure, so you'll see the attending level group discussing what they think the problem is, and each group of experts at the attending level will be chipping in with what they think (...) we may ask someone else to "just quickly take a look at this patient,' have they 'any thoughts about this?'" [anesthesiologist] [Describing a difficult case] "They say 'Yeah, but here, look at it!' OK, you do it [surgical intervention] and then just what should happen according to every textbook known to man, doesn't happen and you're like, argh! Patients don't follow textbooks." [attending surgeon] "The way we cope with [mysteriously deteriorating patients] is to consult with our colleagues; to vocalize more freely about what we think about the possibilities; to consult at the highest level of the organization with those who might have more experience, or might have seen cases or something like it before." [attending anesthesiologist]	[Talking about nurses] "So if they pick something up and they tell me they're concerned or if they disagree with the resident, chances are I'll go along with the nursing decision rather than my second year resident. Because, you know. I'm throwing 20 years vs. two years or a few months of trauma experience." [attending surgeon] "We actually have to like say, 'Do you want this test done? Do you want that test done?' We nurses are pretty assertive in terms of getting things going. I'm not putting the doctors down but they're thinking of something else. So lots of times we do ask them, prod them to do this test." [nurse] "In circumstances where we see someone doing something which isn't right, for example, not being appropriately gowned and gloved to do a surgical procedure, or if we see someone contaminate their sterile field, their gloves, or their gown, we tell them—we don't let them proceed with the process and contaminate the wound." [attending anesthesiologist]	"For example, you see that at least the experienced person sees, that the issue is not ABC but is FGH, you can, in the hands of the experienced person, skip the ABC, go to FGH, and then cover the ABC just as a double-check after you dealt with what you think is the critical problem that the patient has." [attending anesthesiologist] [Talking about pressured situations] "Obviously different patients require different things and so, sometimes we bypass or make a cookbook out of it, you know. We pick out whatever is appropriate to that patient and then go on from there. But, yes, there is a set of guidelines to follow." [nurse] "Another example is of putting a central line and auto transfusion of blood because they hadn't gotten the cross-match blood for the patient. There was this huge amount of blood coming out of the patient's chest, we could just re-circulate it back into the patient's circulation." [anesthesiologist]

interactions, and contingencies. Treatment steps (and missteps) can limit later options, generate new dependencies, and launch a patient on a different trajectory. For example, a patient whose health is degrading requires different coordination interactions than a patient who is responding well to treatment. Thus, from a coordination perspective, it is important to distinguish between habitual trajectories and problematic ones.

A habitual trajectory is a sequence of actions and interactions that moves the patient steadily toward successful treatment as per expectation. A problematic trajectory, defined as a deviation onto a path hazardous to the patient, is often driven by a novel event, an unexpected realization, or disconcerting information that challenges participants' mental models. Because in fast-response settings, time is short, stakes are high, alternative responses are suddenly required without the benefit of complete analysis or planning. Novel events in trauma settings include: a patient deteriorating badly contrary to treatment protocol and medical expectation; or a novice surgeon attempting to perform a surgical intervention that other actors feel may needlessly endanger the patient.

A dialogic coordination practice differs from more general expertise coordination processes in that it is highly situated in the specifics of the unfolding event, is urgent and staked, and occurs at the boundary between communities of practice. Because cognition is distributed, responsibility is shared, and epistemic differences present, interactions can be contentious and conflict laden. Much is at stake: reputations, group interests, epistemological claims, and occasionally blame apportioning.

We identify four kinds of coordination practices: epistemic contestation, joint sensemaking, cross-boundary intervention, and protocol breaking. Table 20.2 provides detailed evidence and description of triggers for dialogic coordination practices.

Epistemic contestation. The interactions between COPs during a resuscitation can sometimes be touchy, since opinions may differ as to the patient's condition and what must be done at the moment. Boundary work requires the ability to see perspectives developed by people immersed in a different

community of knowing (Boland and Tenkasi 1995, Star and Griesemer 1989). Often, particular disciplinary foci lead to differences in opinion regarding what steps to take next in treating the patient. For example, a surgeon is likely to want to perform surgery quickly. To do so, he or she needs the anesthesiologist to anesthetize the patient. But the anesthesiologist is sometimes concerned about the overall state of the patient's health and the danger posed by putting an unstable, severely injured patient under anesthesia. This can lead to differences of opinion. As an attending surgeon says:

> Typical case is I'm the attending trauma surgeon and there's an attending anesthesiologist. I think the patient should be intubated and the anesthesiologist doesn't. So who outranks? Sometimes it goes by the level of seniority. Who has been there longer? Or it goes by who's more aggressive about standing firm, or the interpersonal relationship between the two.

There is general consensus in trauma centers as to which medical interventions belong to which disciplinary communities. Separation of roles and responsibilities is medically, legally, and historically long standing. As an attending anesthesiologist exclaimed: "The responsibility of the airway is the anesthesiology team: responsibility of the belly issue is the surgical team." However, some medical cases fall on the boundary and generate an epistemic tussle among specialties. The existence of this tension is not usually emphasized and is kept under control by the attending physicians. Several times, individuals shared with us the story of a dispute between a surgeon and an anesthesiologist regarding the proper treatment of a patient in a New York hospital that degenerated into a fistfight. The story carries two messages: the epistemological contestation is serious; however, things would never be allowed to go that far at TC.

Joint sensemaking. In some cases, patients do not respond well to the given treatment plan and their condition deteriorates. An attending surgeon says: "No matter how much you say about what should happen, patients do not follow textbooks, they don't follow all the rules." The fact that patients sometimes do not react according to diagnosis and treatment is well recognized in emergency medicine (Gawande 2002). The reasons may be multiple but primarily have to do with incomplete diagnoses or emergent complications. When it becomes clear that the patient has shifted to a problematic trajectory, disciplinary boundaries that seem so rigid in "normal" cases suddenly melt away. A process of joint sensemaking begins with the team and spirals up the hierarchy as more experienced doctors are pulled in to help solve the puzzle. An anesthesiologist describes it as a process where everyone chips in: "[We pull in experts] and discuss a very brief scenario, we let other people know what we are thinking, and get their opinion as to what they think is reasonable in this state of affairs."

During joint sensemaking, significant negotiation of meaning takes place, regardless of COP boundaries. Other specialists are sought to confirm the reading of the patient condition (did we miss anything?) and to ultimately to warrant the correctness of the steps taken (we did the right thing). Having expert others join the conference increases the chance of having someone recognize a rare condition. It also facilitates difficult interventions where high levels of skills are required at the boundary of specialties (e.g., anesthesia and surgery). The practice is emergent and specific to the patient at hand. During such events, when time-critical cross-disciplinary decision making has to occur, the specialization-based boundaries are temporarily discarded and replaced by an emergent dialogue intended to generate a new collective understanding of the patient.

Cross-boundary intervention. A cross-boundary intervention occurs when the safety of a patient is compromised, or is about to be compromised, by the actions of a team member. For example, we observed that when a surgeon inadvertently contaminated his gloves, a nurse drew his attention to that fact and prodded him to replace them. These practices are emergent because specific actions cannot be specified or pre-defined ahead of time. Because the expertise level of many staff members is so high, it is possible for people in the non-focal disciplines to know when things are not going right and to take action. The actions can take the form of reminders, such as when a nurse reminds a resident to do a task or when an anesthesiologist tells the surgeon that he

has breached the sterile field. The actions can also be indirect: nurses feel that their role includes warning the attending surgeon when his residents are engaging in actions that in their opinion endanger the patient. These are not formal mechanisms, but emergent coordination practices that ensure either that operations are error-free, or that if an error does occur, the relevant personnel take immediate action. For example, several attending surgeons actively rely on nurses to provide warning about possibly dangerous behavior by surgery residents. An attending surgeon explains:

> Our trauma nurses here are probably better than anybody's. Because they've just been doing it for so long. So if they pick something up and they tell me they're concerned. . . . If they disagree with the resident, chances are I'll go along with the nursing decision rather than my second year resident. Because, you know, I'm throwing 20 years [of experience] versus two years or a few months of trauma experience.

With experience, specialists recognize the value of the complementary perspective provided by others on the team. An attending surgeon grudgingly recognized the value of others stepping in on his turf: "In a sense, [the anesthesiologist] they are probably policing me; saying: 'Hey, I don't think this guy is stable. You need to just get his blood pressure up.' And the nursing does the same thing." Nonetheless, the interactions can be contentious, since no individual likes to be told that he or she is putting a patient's life in danger. One attending surgeon actually disagreed with the majority opinion and felt that residents were too frequently the victims of sarcasm and abuse by nurses: "The relationship between nurses and physicians can be stressful. Sometimes they don't accept the kind of decision where the intern says that I am the doctor." Nonetheless, the value of cross-boundary checking and intervention is universally recognized as crucial for patient safety.

Protocol breaking. Breaching a trauma treatment protocol is a risky step that is sometimes undertaken in an emergency situation when following the protocol would take too much time and thus delay a crucial intervention. Medically, it is a judgment call that goes against the evidence-based best practices that have been incorporated in the protocol. A missed or delayed treatment step may result in further harm to the patient. The doctor who violates the protocol in error faces an inquiry and is no longer protected under the commonly accepted norms of medicine. A serious medical error can have major repercussions on a medical career. In addition, if the patient's family learns about the error, there is possibility of legal liability.

Still, there are often compelling medical reasons to violate protocol. For example, an anesthesiologist said that protocol calls for gunshot victims to come in with a C-spine (neck) collar to ensure that the neck is not injured. But the collar makes it difficult to manage the airways. Therefore:

> If there was an urgent need to intubate the patient and I was having difficulty, I would just take the collar off. I wouldn't bother with maintaining that sort of strict requirement of keeping the collar on, because I know that the instance of neck injuries is probably less than 1%. Whereas the harm associated with managing the airway incorrectly is much greater than the risk to the neck of having neurological deficits.

From a coordination perspective, protocol violation upsets work plans, roles, and expectations. The team has to accept the break in protocol and reorganize its actions and interactions to support it on the fly. For all these reasons, protocol is seldom broken without the approval or involvement of senior team members such as an attending or a fellow.

DISCUSSION

Using a combination of observation, archival, and interview techniques, we have identified coordination practices that permit a trauma center to operate reliably and effectively in the face of inordinate input and task uncertainty. Principally, we have argued that the combination of expertise specialization, overlapping interdependencies, and a rapid tempo requires organizational members to enact new coordinative responses. We have identified two interrelated dimensions that are critical for effective coordination in a fast-response setting. First, expertise coordination practices such as COP structuring and knowledge externalization make it

possible to manage various intra- and inter-patient dependencies. These practices effectively reduce the need for formal structural coordination or arrangements while guaranteeing that the right expertise is brought to bear during patient treatment. Second, dialogic coordination practices operate as timely and situated responses to unexpected developments and failing patient trajectories. Because ensuring patient safety is an overarching goal, these latter practices are potentially contentious and operate in the space between COPs. By describing specific coordination practices, this study increases the understanding of how complex and highly interdependent work can effectively be coordinated.

Recent research has attempted to extend coordination models beyond the traditional focus on modalities and structures and their contingent relationship with the environment. For example, recent investigation of coordination in design and manufacturing activities has resulted in the development of more complex taxonomies of coordination mechanisms (Adler 1995). Other researchers have focused on the detailed specification of dependencies in processes and the generation of libraries of coordination methods (Malone and Crowston 1994, Malone, et al. 1999). Our findings point to the limitations of approaches emphasizing the development of pre-specified coordination methods. In environments characterized by distributed expertise, high uncertainty, and variable interdependence, coordination needs may not be easily specifiable. Our findings provide support for relational conceptualizations of coordination as an emergent phenomenon highly dependent on the quality of the relationships across functions and individuals (Gittell 2002) and on the presence of transactive memory processes (Faraj and Sproull 2000, Liang, Moreland and Argote 1995).

Our findings also point to a broader divide in coordination research. Much of the power of traditional coordination models resides in their information processing basis and their focus on the design issues surrounding work unit differentiation and integration. This design-centric view with its emphasis on rules, structures, and modalities of coordination is less useful for studying knowledge work. However, as we have seen in our trauma setting, these response mechanisms are ineffective when the organization is faced with novel equivocal situations coupled with the potential for disaster. To be effective, such organizations need to accept a certain amount of cross-boundary contention in return for the immediate and flexible response provided by dialogic coordination practices. These practices are highly situated, emergent, and contextualized and thus cannot be pre-specified the way traditional coordination mechanisms can be. Thus, recent efforts based on an information processing view to develop typologies of coordination mechanisms (e.g., Malone, et al. 1999) may be too formal to allow organizations to mount an effective response to events characterized by urgency, novelty, surprise, and different interpretations.

Our practice-oriented view of coordination challenges the implicit focus on rules and structure that has guided most of coordination research. Recently, some researchers have emphasized the enabling view of bureaucratic structures (Adler and Borys 1996), while others have conceived of structures as flexible scaffolds for dynamic improvisation (Bigley and Roberts 2001, Brown and Eisenhardt 1997, Moorman and Miner 1998). However, our findings regarding dialogic coordination practices and their contested nature point to the limitations of a structuralist view of coordination. In the same way that an organizational routine may unfold differently each time because it cannot be fully specified (Feldman and Pentland 2003), coordination will vary each time. Independent of espoused rules and programs, there will always be an element of *bricolage* reflecting the necessity of patching together working solutions with the knowledge and resources at hand (Weick 1993). Actors and the generative schemes that propel their actions under pressure make up an important component of coordination's *"modus operandi"* (Bourdieu 1990, Emirbayer and Mische 1998). Thus, coordination practices cannot be specified by the organization in the same way that administrative and expertise coordination processes can be articulated.

Organizations that are hospitable to dialogic coordination practices recognize the stochastic nature of trajectories, expect appropriate reaction to novelty, and accept the contentious nature of cross-boundary intervention. In short, a practice view provides a richer and more balanced view of coordination as it is actually practiced. This practice-based rethinking of coordination builds and complements parallel research on the related topics of work practices (Orlikowski 2002), organizational routines (Feldman and Pentland 2003), learning (Lave 1988), and innovation (Brown and Duguid 2001).

Our findings about the ways in which COPs play important coordination roles enrich the growing literature on COPs' role in organizing knowledge work (Brown and Duguid 2001, Orr 1996, Wenger 1998). Not only are the specialty-based COPs used for regulating within-specialty learning and participation, [but] they are also used to manage key knowledge interdependencies, generate schedules and plans, and negotiate boundary-over-boundary objects (such as the diagnosis). This reduces the overall coordination load on the organization by allowing those with local knowledge to take on this role and thus free scarce managerial attention and resources. The results also support the contentions of several researchers that interacting communities of practice are effective prisms through which to view complex interdisciplinary technical work (e.g., Boland and Tenkasi 1995).

Recently, Brown and Duguid (2001: 208) have suggested that coordination of organizational knowledge is likely to be more challenging than coordination of routine work, principally because the "elements to be coordinated are not just individuals but communities and the practices they foster." As we found in our investigation of coordination at the boundary, significant epistemic differences exist and must be recognized. As the dialogic practices enacted in response to problematic trajectories show, the epistemic differences reflect different perspectives or priorities and cannot be bridged through better knowledge exchange. This is why they are often contentious and require joint sensemaking and complicated decision making. This finding confirms important recent findings about the importance of common ground (Bechky 2003) and the need for negotiation and transformation across boundaries (Carlile 2002) for effective knowledge transfer.

The situated and emergent nature of coordination does not imply that practices are completely unique and novel. On one hand, they vary according to the logic of the situation and the actors present. On the other hand, as seen in our categorization of dialogic coordination, they follow a recognizable logic and are only partially improvised. This tension between familiarity and uniqueness of response is at the core of a practice view of work (Orlikowski 2002). While we have identified four core dialogic practices surrounding trauma care, these are not constant and may evolve in response to a change in the actors or the environment. They differ from informal coordination because they involve the intersection of multiple epistemologies. They also involve an element of *bricolage*. In turn, they demand reinterpretation and realignment of cognition and action (Mische and White 1998). They are distinctly intersubjective and require accommodation, trust, and respect.

At the most basic level, dialogic coordination practices are reactions aimed at rectifying failing performance trajectories. Their dialogic nature is based on the need to cross epistemic boundaries, disregard hierarchies, and publicly challenge a teammate's "expert" judgment. That is why they are fraught with danger to the actors, the patient, and the team processes. They are also essential from a performance perspective because without them coordination is likely to become stylized and formal or to fall apart completely. Much recent work on high-reliability organizing stresses aspects of safety culture and mindfulness that are consonant with the promotion of dialogic coordination (Grabowski and Roberts 1999, Weick, et al. 1999). Creating the space for such practices is difficult. Stakes are high: errors can easily damage professional reputations or injure patients. Sustaining dialogic practices requires organizational leadership and structures that create a safe haven where mistakes can be admitted with little loss of face (Edmondson 1999). This requires efforts at bringing together different communities of practice and making sure various members respect and accept the value of the alternative epistemology to the situation and the patient (Boland and Tenkasi 1995).

This study has limitations that must be recognized and addressed in future work. First, the theoretical framework of coordination in fast-response organizations is based on the insight gained from a single site and thus may be limited. Our primary goal was to understand in great detail how a leading trauma center develops and uses coordination practices, and therefore there was an inevitable trade-off between sample breadth and depth of immersion. Future research is needed to corroborate the extent to which our model is generalizable to other fast-response environments in medical as well as non-medical settings. Second, our study did not address the link between the various coordination practices and organizational performance. Because our focus was on the detailed understanding of coordination practices in one setting, we cannot establish causality between the coordination practices we observed and TC's performance profile. Third, because of the situated nature of the coordination practices that allow the TC to operate flexibly and reliably, future research is needed to specify which coordination practices operate in other settings, and thus to identify theoretical boundary conditions.

CONCLUSION

Organizational knowledge researchers have suggested that practice is central to understanding work and have called for a deeper understanding of complex organizational work processes (Brown and Duguid 2001, Carlile 2002, Feldman and Pentland 2003, Orlikowski 2002). The research reported here focuses on knowledge work coordination and thus represents an effort to answer this call. Our findings from our in-depth investigation of a fast-response organization indicate that coordination practices are highly emergent and cannot necessarily be pre-specified. Expertise coordination practices are needed to manage evolving skill and knowledge interdependencies during treatment of a single patient and between treatment of different patients. Dialogic coordination practices are necessary because much of the coordination occurs at the boundary of epistemological communities and involves cross-boundary interventions, leading to contention and contestation. Future studies of knowledge coordination may benefit from a deeper investigation of both the expertise coordination practices and the dialogic coordination at the boundary.

NOTES

1. Narrow specialists (e.g., ophthalmologic surgeons) are available on an on-call basis.

2. Protocols are described in great detail in a 185-page book that is mandatory reading for new personnel.

REFERENCES

Adler, P. S., "Interdepartmental interdependence and coordination: the case of the design/manufacturing interface," *Organization Science,* 6, 2 (1995), 147–167.

Adler, P. S. and B. Borys, "Two types of bureaucracy: enabling and coercive," *Administrative Science Quarterly,* 41 (1996), 61–89.

Argote, L., "Input uncertainty and organizational coordination in hospital emergency units," *Administrative Science Quarterly,* 27 (1982), 420–434.

Argote, L., *Organizational learning: creating, retaining and transferring knowledge,* Kluwer Academic Publishers, Boston, 1999.

Bechky, B., "Sharing meaning across occupational communities: the transformation of understanding on a production floor," *Organization Science,* 14, 3 (2003), 312–330.

Bigley, G. A. and K. H. Roberts, "The incident command system: high reliability organizing for complex and volatile task environments," *Academy of Management Journal,* 44, 6 (2001), 1281–1300.

Boland, R. J. and R. V. Tenkasi, "Perspective making and perspective taking in communities of knowing," *Organization Science, 6,* 4 (1995), 350–372.

Bourdieu, P., *The logic of practice,* Stanford University Press, Stanford: CA, 1990.

Bourgeois, L. J. and K. M. Eisenhardt, "Strategic decision processes in high velocity environments: four case studies in the microcomputer industry," *Management Science,* 34, 7 (1989), 816–835.

Brown, J. S. and P. Duguid, "Knowledge and organization: a social-practice perspective," *Organization Science,* 12, 2 (2001), 198–213.

Brown, S. L. and K. Eisenhardt, "The art of continuous change: linking complexity theory and time-paced evolutions in relentlessly shifting organizations," *Administrative Science Quarterly,* 42 (1997), 1–34.

Carlile, P. R., "A pragmatic view of knowledge and boundaries: boundary object in new product development," *Organization Science,* 13, 4 (2002), 442–455.

Child, J. and R. G. McGrath, "Organizations unfettered: organizational form in an information-intensive economy," *Academy of Management Journal,* 44, 6 (2001), 1135–1148.

Daft, R. L. and R. H. Lengel, "Organizational information requirements, media richness and structural design," *Management Science,* 32, 5 (1986), 355–366.

DeSanctis, G. and P. Monge, "Communication processes for virtual organizations," *Organization Science,* 10, 6 (1999), 693–703.

Edmondson, A. C., "Psychological safety and learning behavior in work teams," *Administrative Science Quarterly,* 44, 4 (1999), 350–383.

Eisenhardt, K., "Building Theory from Case Study Research," *Academy of Management Review,* 14, 4 (1989), 532–550.

Emirbayer, M. and A. Mische, "What is agency?" *American Journal of Sociology,* 103, 4 (1998), 962–1023.

Faraj, S. and L. Sproull, "Coordinating expertise in software development teams," *Management Science,* 46, 12 (2000), 1554–1568.

Feldman, M. S. and B. T. Pentland, "Reconceptualizing organizational routines as a source of flexibility and change," *Administrative Science Quarterly,* 48 (2003), 94–118.

Galbraith, J. R., *Organization design,* Addison-Wesley, Reading, MA, 1977.

Gawande, A., *Complications: a surgeon's notes on an imperfect science,* Henry Holt and Company, New York, 2002.

Gittell, J. H., "Coordinating mechanisms in care provider groups: relational coordination as a mediator and input uncertainty as a moderator of performance effects," *Management Science,* 48, 11 (2002), 1408–1426.

Glaser, B. and A. Strauss, *The Discovery of Grounded Theory,* Aldine, Chicago, 1967.

Grabowski, M. and K. H. Roberts, "Risk mitigation in virtual organizations," *Organization Science,* 10, 6 (1999), 704–721.

Gupta, P. P., M. W. Dirsmith and T. J. Fogarty, "Coordination and control in a government agency: Contingency and institutional theory perspectives on GAO audits," *Administrative Science Quarterly,* 39, 2 (1994), 264–284.

Keller, R. T., "Technology-information processing fit and the performance of R&D project groups: a test of contingency theory," *Academy of Management Journal,* 37, 1 (1994), 167–179.

Kraut, R. E. and L. A. Streeter, "Coordination in software development," *Communications of the ACM,* 38, 3 (1995), 69–81.

Lave, J., *Cognition in Practice,* Cambridge University Press, Cambridge, UK, 1988.

Lawrence, P. R. and J. W. Lorsch, *Organization and Environment,* Harvard Business School Press, Boston, 1967.

Liang, D. W., R. Moreland and L. Argote, "Group versus individual training and group performance: the mediating role of transactive memory," *Personality and Social Psychology Bulletin,* 21, 4 (1995), 384–393.

Malone, T. W. and K. Crowston, "The interdisciplinary study of coordination," *Computing Surveys,* 26, 1 (1994), 87–119.

Malone, T. W., K. Crowston, J. Lee, B. Pentland, C. Dellarocas, G. Wyner, J. Quimby, C. S. Osborn, A. Bernstein, G. Herman, M. Klein and E. O'Donnell, "Tools for inventing organizations: Toward a handbook of organizational processes," *Management Science,* 45, 3 (1999), 425–443.

March, J. G. and H. A. Simon, *Organizations,* Wiley, New York, 1958.

Mische, A. and H. White, "Between conversation and situation—public switching dynamics across network domains," *Social Research,* 65, 3 (1998), 695–724.

Moorman, C. and A. S. Miner, "Organizational improvisation and organizational memory," *Academy of Management Review,* 23 (1998), 698–723.

Nelson, R. R. and S. G. Winter, *An Evolutionary Theory of Economic Change,* Belknap Press, Cambridge, MA, 1982.

Orlikowski, W. J., "Using technology and constituting structures: a practice lens for studying technology in organizations," *Organization Science,* 11, 4 (2000), 404–428.

Orlikowski, W. J., "Knowing in practice: enacting a collective capability in distributed organizing," *Organization Science,* 13, 3 (2002), 249–273.

Orr, J., *Talking About Machines: An Ethnography of a Modern Job,* ILR Press, Ithaca, NY, 1996.

Perrow, C. A., *Organizational Analysis: A Sociological View,* Brooks/Cole Publishing, Monterey, CA, 1970.

Resident's Manual, *University Shock Trauma Center,* 2001.

Star, S. L. and J. R. Griesemer, "Institutional ecology, 'translations' and boundary objects: amateurs and professionals in Berkeley's museum of vertebrate zoology, 1907–39," *Social Studies of Science,* 19 (1989), 387–420.

Strauss, A. and J. Corbin, *Basics of Qualitative Research: Grounded Theory Procedures and Techniques,* Sage Publications, Newbury Park, CA, 1990.

Strauss, A. L., *Continual permutations of action,* Aldyne de Gruyter, New York, 1993.

Thompson, J. D., *Organizations in Action,* McGraw-Hill, New York, 1967.

Van de Ven, A. H., A. L. Delbecq and R. Koenig, "Determinants of coordination mode within organizations," *American Sociological Review,* 41, 2 (1976), 322–338.

Weick, K. and K. H. Roberts, "Collective mind in organizations: Heedful interrelating on flight decks," *Administrative Science Quarterly,* 8 (1993), 357–381.

Weick, K. E., "Technology as equivoque: Sensemaking in new technologies," in P. S. Goodman, L. E. Sproull and Associates (Ed.), *Technology and Organizations,* Jossey-Bass, San Francisco, 1990, 1–44.

Weick, K. E., "The collapse of sensemaking in organizations: The Maim Gulch disaster," *Administrative Science Quarterly,* 38, 4 (1993), 628–652.

Weick, K. E., K. M. Sutcliffe and D. Obstfeld, "Organizing for high reliability: processes of collective mindfulness," *Research in organizational behavior,* 21 (1999), 81–123.

Wenger, E., *Communities of practice: Learning, meaning, and identity,* Cambridge University Press, Cambridge, UK, 1998.

SOURCE: Faraj, Samer, and Yan Xiao. 2006. Excerpt from "Coordination in Fast Response Organizations." *Management Science,* 52(8):1155–69.

21

A Relational Model of How High-Performance Work Systems Work

Jody Hoffer Gittell, Rob Seidner, and Julian Wimbush

Introduction

One of the core principles of strategic human resource management is that organizational performance is influenced by the way employees are managed. In support of this argument, certain sets of human resource practices have been found to improve employee effectiveness and to predict higher levels of organizational performance (Bailey et al. 2001, Ramsey et al. 2000; see also reviews by Becker and Gerhart 1996, Ichniowski et al. 1996). Researchers have documented the impact of human resource practices on efficiency outcomes such as worker productivity (Arthur 1994, Bartel 1994, Datta et al. 2005, Koch and McGrath 1996) and equipment reliability (Ichniowski et al. 1997, Youndt et al. 1996), on quality outcomes such as manufacturing quality (MacDuffie 1995) and patient mortality (West et al. 2002), and on business growth (Bartel 2004) and financial performance (e.g., Collins and Smith 2006, Delery and Doty 1996, Huselid 1995, Wright et al. 2006). Human resource practices have also been found to explain performance differences among steel-finishing lines (Ichniowski et al. 1997),

call centers (Batt 1999), airlines (Gittell 2001), banks (Richard and Johnson 2004), and high-tech firms (Collins and Clark 2003), though some studies have found no performance differences associated with human resource practices (e.g., Cappelli and Neumark 2001).

Multiple labels have been applied to this basic argument, including high-performance work systems, high-commitment work systems, high-involvement work systems, and high-performance human resource management. Despite these different labels, their common thread is that organizations can achieve high performance by adopting practices that recognize and leverage employees' ability to create value. Though some disagreement remains among researchers, it is generally agreed that these practices include selection, training, mentoring, incentives, and knowledge-sharing mechanisms (Horgan and Muhlau 2006) and that these practices are most effective when they are implemented in bundles because of their combined effects on performance (Batt 1999, Dunlop and Weil 1996, Ichniowski et al. 1997, Laursen 2002, MacDuffie 1995).

There is less agreement, however, regarding the causal mechanisms through which high-performance work systems influence performance outcomes. The two dominant arguments are based on human capital and skill on the one hand, and motivation and commitment on the other. In addition, there is an emerging view that employee-employee relationships constitute a third causal mechanism through which high-performance work systems influence performance outcomes (Delery and Shaw 2001). Rather than focusing primarily on the knowledge and skills of employees or on the commitment of employees to their organization, this third view focuses on *relationships between employees* as the primary causal mechanism that connects high-performance work systems and performance outcomes (e.g., Collins and Clark 2003, Collins and Smith 2006).

In this paper we adopt this third view and propose a model of high-performance work systems in which each component practice reaches across multiple functions to engage employees in a coordinated effort. All the high-performance work practices identified in this study are focused on building employee-employee relationships. We argue that these high-performance work practices contribute to performance by supporting the development of relational coordination, a mutually reinforcing web of communication and relationships carried out for the purpose of task integration (Gittell 2002b).

We test our model with multilevel data from a nine-hospital study of patient care that includes administrator interviews to measure work practices, care provider surveys to measure relational coordination, and patient surveys to measure patient outcomes. We explore the effects of these high-performance work practices on quality and efficiency outcomes for patients and the mediation of these effects through relational coordination among care providers. Hospitals are notorious for operating with well-defined silos that engender turf battles between them. We expect that relational coordination will be critical for achieving desired performance outcomes in this setting due to the high levels of task interdependence, uncertainty, and time constraints found there (Gittell 2000). We expect these high-performance work practices will foster relational coordination, thus bridging the boundaries between the distinct professions that are responsible for carrying out the work.

HUMAN CAPITAL AND COMMITMENT MODELS OF HOW HIGH-PERFORMANCE WORK SYSTEMS WORK

Models of high-performance work systems often draw on human capital theory, whose central implication is that human resource practices can improve organizational performance by increasing the knowledge and skills of employees (Becker 1975). To be successful, firms must invest in and maintain the workforce just as they invest in and maintain the capital infrastructure. Researchers have found that companies can achieve sustained performance advantages by leveraging the knowledge of their employees. High-performance work systems can foster the development of human capital in the form of firm-specific idiosyncratic skills (Gibbert 2006), creating a performance advantage for organizations (Fried and Hisrich 1994, MacMillan et al. 1987, Tyebjee and Bruno 1984) through processes such as increased employee problem solving (Snell and Dean 1992) and improved customization by employees in service industries (Batt 2002).

Others have argued that in addition to building the knowledge and skills of employees, high-performance work systems also enhance the motivation and commitment of employees. Commitment-based human resource practices create an organizational climate that motivates employees to act in the best interest of the organization, thus enhancing performance (Appelbaum et al. 2000, Arthur 1992, Osterman 1988, Rousseau 1995). A key argument in this literature is that human resource practices build a psychological contract by signaling an employer's commitment to a long-term relationship, in turn yielding a long-term commitment from the employee (Tsui et al. 1997). Consistent with this argument, studies have found that particular work practices are associated with higher levels of commitment (e.g., Tsui et al. 1997, Whitener 2001) and that commitment in turn is positively associated with performance. In particular, Bowen and Ostroff (2004) provide arguments suggesting that motivation and discretionary effort underlie the association between human resource practices and performance and are triggered by a strong human resource system. Note that the human capital and commitment pathways are not mutually exclusive. Although research and theory often focus on one or the other, some theorists have argued that high-performance work systems can contribute to performance through both pathways (e.g., Appelbaum et al. 2000).

Relational Models of How High-Performance Work Systems Work

Relationships among employees have also been theorized to play a role in achieving high levels of organizational performance. Some scholars have made this argument by drawing on the concept of organizational social capital, a type of social capital that exists in and can be developed by organizations as a distinctive organizational capability and source of competitive advantage (Leana and Van Buren 1999, Nahapiet and Ghoshal 1998). Organizational social capital has been shown to improve performance by enabling employees to access the resources that are embedded within a given network and by facilitating the transfer and sharing of knowledge (Levin and Cross 2004, Tsai and Ghoshal 1998).

Other theorists have argued that employee-employee relationships are important for coordinating work (Adler et al. 2008, Faraj and Sproull 2000, Gittell 2000), based on the argument that coordination is the management of task interdependence (Malone and Crowston 1994) and therefore fundamentally a relational process (Bechky 2006, Faraj and Sproull 2000, Gittell 2002b, Weick and Roberts 1993). One of these relational perspectives—relational coordination—identifies specific dimensions of relationships that are integral to the coordination of work. According to the theory of relational coordination, coordination that occurs through frequent, high-quality communication supported by relationships of shared goals, shared knowledge, and mutual respect enables organizations to better achieve their desired outcomes (Gittell 2006). Defined as "a mutually reinforcing process of interaction between communication and relationships carried out for the purpose of task integration" (Gittell 2002a, p. 301), relational coordination is a type of employee-employee relationship that is particularly relevant for coordinating work that is highly interdependent, uncertain, and time-constrained.

Substantial progress has been made toward identifying the work practices through which organizations influence the development of employee-employee relationships. Leana and Van Buren (1999) argue that stable employment relationships and reciprocity norms facilitate the formation of social capital among employees. Evans and Davis (2005) argue that work practices such as selective staffing, self-managed teams, decentralized decision making, extensive training, flexible job assignments, open communication, and performance-contingent compensation influence multiple dimensions of an organization's social structure, including the development of bridging ties, norms of reciprocity, shared mental models, role making, and organizational citizenship behavior.

Gittell (2000) argues that work practices such as cross-functional selection, cross-functional conflict resolution, cross-functional performance measurement, flexible job design, and cross-functional boundary spanner roles can foster the development of relational coordination. These work practices were shown to predict significantly higher levels of relational coordination among airline employees from 12 distinct functions who were engaged in the flight departure process, though their impact on performance was not explored.

Similarly, Gant et al. (2002) show that on steel-finishing lines with high-performance work systems, defined as selection, training, incentive pay, job design, problem-solving teams, and extensive labor/management communication, production employees have denser communication networks with each other and that these steel-finishing lines also exhibit higher performance, measured in terms of fewer delays and higher yields. They argue that these human resource practices influence performance outcomes because they influence the social networks of production employees. Their results suggest that social networks may mediate the link between work practices and outcomes, though mediation was not demonstrated.

Collins and Clark (2003) have provided one of the best empirical tests to date of the argument that human resource practices influence outcomes through their impact on relationships among employees. They argue that the social networks of top management teams enhance a firm's information-processing capability and that human resource practices, including mentoring, incentives, and performance appraisals, can be designed to encourage the development of these social networks. They then demonstrate that the impact of these high-performance work practices on firm performance is mediated by the strength of firms' top management team social networks. More recently, Vogus (2006) has argued that high-performance work practices such as selection, training, performance appraisal, performance-based rewards, and job security contribute to high-quality interactions and mindfulness by signaling to employees the importance of relationships. Vogus continues by postulating that these high-quality interactions contribute to higher-quality outcomes for hospital patients. Empirical tests of this model demonstrated mediation.

Though the types of employee-employee relationships explored in these studies are varied, including relational coordination (Gittell 2000), social networks (Collins and Clark 2003, Gant et al. 2002), social capital (Evans and Davis 2005, Leana and Van Buren 1999), and mindful interacting (Vogus 2006), these studies suggest that high-performance work practices can enhance performance through the pathway of employee-employee relationships.

Theory Building

The work practices found in the studies described above resemble in many ways the work practices found in the earlier high-performance work systems literature—they include selection, training, performance measurement, rewards, knowledge-sharing mechanisms, and so on. But they differ in an important way. Although the work practices found in these studies have the potential to influence employee skills and commitment, they are focused primarily on strengthening relationships between employees. This understanding of high-performance work practices therefore responds implicitly to an argument by post-bureaucracy theorists that traditional work practices often create divisions between employees even when relationships are critically important due to the need for coordination (Heckscher 1994, Piore 1993). According to Piore (1993, p. 15), the bureaucratic organizational practices that have become widespread through the rise of Taylorism "have

pushed us to restrict communication among the people responsible for the way in which the different parts are performed." Heckscher (1994, p. 24) envisions a postbureaucratic, interactive organizational form in which "everyone takes responsibility for the success of the whole" and in which "workers need to understand the key objectives in depth in order to coordinate their actions intelligently 'on the fly.'"

High-Performance Work Practices as Predictors of Relational Coordination. Rather than rejecting the role of formal work practices as the postbureaucratic literature has tended to do, we argue that formal work practices can be redesigned to foster the employee-employee relationships through which work is effectively coordinated "on the fly." High-performance work practices can serve to overcome the silos of bureaucratic organizations by connecting employees directly with each other to enable them to coordinate their work. We focus here on six high-performance work practices—cross-functional selection, cross-functional conflict resolution, cross-functional performance measurement, cross-functional rewards, cross-functional meetings, and cross-functional boundary spanners—and their impact on relational coordination, reflected in the frequency, timeliness, accuracy, and problem-solving nature of communication among employees and the degree to which their relationships are characterized by shared goals, shared knowledge, and mutual respect.

Selection has long been recognized as a powerful way to achieve fit between a prospective employee and a job (Lawrence and Lorsch 1968). Though selection traditionally focused on skills, other attributes such as personality traits (Day and Silverman 1989), organizational fit (Kwiatkowski 2003), and teamwork ability (Cappelli and Rogovsky 1994) are also relevant to job performance. In the context of highly interdependent work, selection for cross-functional teamwork is expected to be particularly relevant and has been found to affect coordination across functional boundaries (Gittell 2000), in particular strengthening the mutual respect dimension of relational coordination.

Conflicts are likely to occur in the presence of high levels of task interdependence and/or diversity—including functional diversity—among participants (Pelled et al. 1999, Walton and Dutton

1967). Conflicts have been found to improve performance when they take place in a group that values task-related conflict; however, unresolved conflicts undermine relationships and hinder performance over time (Jehn 1995). Cross-functional *conflict resolution* can play a constructive role by providing a way to articulate and accommodate multiple points of view, each with the potential to add value to the work process. Consistent with this argument, conflict resolution has been found to provide opportunities for building a shared understanding of the work process among participants, thereby strengthening the relationships through which coordination is carried out (Gittell 2000, Mareschal 2003), in particular strengthening the shared knowledge and mutual respect dimensions of relational coordination.

Traditional *performance measurement* practices assign accountability for outcomes to individuals or functions, despite the task interdependencies that often make outcomes the responsibility of a larger group. This focus on individual or functional accountability encourages subgoal optimization (March and Simon 1958), whereas cross-functional accountability encourages workers to adopt a broader perspective and to focus on problem solving rather than the assignment of blame (Chenhall 2005, Deming 1986, Locke and Latham 1990). Performance measurement practices that focus on problem solving have been found to strengthen working relationships, while the reactive assignment of blame has been found to undermine those relationships (Edmondson 1996). In particular, these cross-functional performance measurement practices strengthen the shared goals and problem-solving communication dimensions of relational coordination.

Likewise, *rewards* have traditionally been tied to individual or functional outcomes, thereby encouraging subgoal optimization at the expense of organizational outcomes. Employees engaged in interdependent tasks are most likely to coordinate their tasks effectively if their rewards are also interdependent (Wageman and Baker 1997). But because rewards are often put in place without a clear understanding of how they are expected to work, misalignment is common. Research indicates that more individualized rewards are associated with lower levels of integration across units, whereas shared rewards have been found to support coordination and goal commitment among parties involved in the same work process (Guthrie and Hollensbe 2004, Zenger and Hesterly 1997). In particular, cross-functional rewards strengthen the shared goals dimension of relational coordination.

Meetings are a coordinating mechanism that fosters real time coordination, incorporating information as it becomes available (Argote 1982). Meetings give participants the opportunity to coordinate their tasks interactively, on the spot. Face-to-face interactions are expected to have particular relevance for assuring effective communication because of their high bandwidth, their immediacy, and their ability to build connections among participants through the use of nonverbal cues (Goffman 1961, Nohria and Eccles 1992). While informal meetings are sometimes argued to be more effective than formal meetings (Mangrum et al. 2001), formal meetings may be needed to connect participants who work in distinct functions. In particular, cross-functional meetings strengthen the accuracy of communication as well as the shared goals and shared knowledge dimensions of relational coordination.

Boundary spanners are staff members whose primary task is to integrate the work of other people around a project, process, or customer (Galbraith 1995, Lawrence and Lorsch 1968). Because boundary spanners enable new information to be incorporated on an ongoing basis, they are typically used when tasks cannot be fully programmed in advance. Because they build understanding between areas of functional expertise, they are expected to add value when existing boundaries are highly divisive (Galbraith 1995, Mohrman 1993). In particular, cross-functional boundary spanners strengthen the frequency and timeliness of communication as well as the shared knowledge dimensions of relational coordination.

In summary, the high-performance work practices described above are expected to foster relational coordination, which is reflected in the frequency, timeliness, accuracy, and problem-solving nature of communication among employees and the degree to which their relationships are characterized by shared goals, shared knowledge, and mutual respect. We know from previous research that "firms can improve performance either by increasing the number of practices they employ within the system or by using the practices in an AR system in a more comprehensive and widespread manner" (Youndt et al. 1996, p. 849). Relational coordination therefore depends not only on the adoption of high-performance work practices, but also on the intensity of their adoption and the degree to which they reach across all relevant employee functions. Our concept of high-performance work practices therefore reflects (1) the number of work practices that are adopted, (2) the intensity of their adoption, and (3) the degree to which they reach across all relevant employee functions, together summarized as the *strength* of high-performance work practices.

Hypothesis 1. *The strength of high-performance work practices positively predicts relational coordination among employees.*

High-Performance Work Practices and Relational Coordination as Predictors of Quality and Efficiency Performance. Through their impact on relational coordination, high-performance work practices are expected to improve quality and efficiency performance for organizations. Previous research has shown how relationships of shared goals, shared knowledge, and mutual respect enabled employees from different functions to coordinate work by supporting frequent, timely, problem-solving communication among them (Gittell 2006). Relational coordination is expected to result in fewer missed signals between employees with different areas of functional expertise, due to the information-processing capacity that is created through shared goals, shared knowledge, and mutual respect. Relational coordination enables more consistent communication and a reduction in the probability of errors, leading to *higher-quality* outcomes. Because high-performance work practices strengthen relational coordination among employees, we expect the association between high-performance work practices and quality outcomes to be mediated by relational coordination.

Hypothesis 2. *The association between high-performance work practices and quality outcomes is mediated by relational coordination among employees.*

In the same way, high-performance work practices are also expected to improve efficiency outcomes for organizations. Because relational coordination results in fewer missed signals between employees, it is expected to reduce the time that is wasted carrying out redundant communication, searching for missing information, and waiting to hear from coworkers. Relational coordination thus enables organizational resources—including staff, facilities, and equipment—to be utilized more productively, leading to more *efficient* outcomes such as faster turnaround times and shorter throughput times. Because high-performance work practices strengthen relational coordination among employees, we expect the association between high-performance work practices and efficiency outcomes to be mediated by relational coordination.

Hypothesis 3. *The association between high-performance work practices and efficiency outcomes is mediated by relational coordination among employees.*

Together, these hypotheses serve as the basis for a relational model of how high-performance work systems work.

METHODS

Setting

To test these hypotheses, a study of patient care was conducted using a convenience sample of nine major urban hospitals. Previous studies have shown that coordination between care providers is positively related to both quality and efficiency. Specifically, coordination is associated with provider-perceived (Argote 1982) and patient-perceived quality of care (Gittell 2000), and with reduced lengths of hospital stay (Gittell et al. 2000, Shortell et al. 1994). However, the contribution of high-performance work practices to these outcomes and to the coordination of care has not been explored. We chose a work process for which outcomes were well understood and readily measured—surgical care for joint replacement patients. We selected nine orthopedics units, each located in a different hospital that performed relatively large numbers of joint replacements. In each orthopedics unit, there was a group of care providers—including physicians, nurses, physical therapists, case managers, and social workers—who were responsible for providing care to joint replacement patients over a six-month study period.

Data Sources

Data from the participating orthopedics units included administrator interviews, a care provider survey, a patient survey, and patient hospitalization records. Administrator interviews were used to measure high-performance work practices at the unit level. The care provider survey was used to measure relational coordination at the level of individual care providers. Patient surveys and hospitalization records were used to measure outcomes at the level of individual patients. To measure high-performance work practices, front-line administrators were interviewed in each orthopedics department, including at least one physician, nurse, physical therapist, social worker, and case manager. For each unit, unstructured interviews and observations were conducted in person at the time of the initial site visits, followed up by more systematic structured telephone interviews after the site visits. The interview protocol that we developed based on our first stage of interviews and observations was used as a guide for our second stage of interviews.

To measure relational coordination, surveys were mailed to all eligible care providers in the nine orthopedics units who had responsibilities for joint replacement patients during the study period in five core functions: physicians, nurses, physical therapists, social workers, and case managers. A unit administrator designated by the chief of orthopedics identified all eligible care providers in each unit. The administrator received written guidelines as to whom should be included (all providers from the above five functions who were directly or indirectly involved with providing care for joint replacement patients). Surveys were mailed to all eligible care providers initially during the second month of the study period, with one repeat mailing during the study period for nonrespondents. Responses were received from 338 of 666 providers for an overall provider response rate of 51%.

To measure patient outcomes, the patient survey was adapted from a validated instrument that is widely used to assess the quality of care in health care settings (Cleary et al. 1991). We received responses to 878 of 1,367 questionnaires sent to patients in the target population—patients with a diagnosis of osteoporosis who received primary unilateral hip or knee replacement in one of the nine hospitals during the six-month study period—for a response rate of 64%. In addition, hospital administrators provided hospitalization records for each patient. These records were used to determine length of stay for each patient and to extract information regarding patient characteristics to use as control variables in models of quality and efficiency outcomes. Of the 878 survey respondents, 69 were dropped because they failed to meet one or more conditions of the study (primary unilateral hip or knee replacement with a diagnosis of osteoporosis), leaving 809 viable respondents. Of these, all 809 respondents had full data available for the variables taken from the hospitalization records (age, race, gender, surgical type, length of stay), but some had missing data on the patient survey variables. The number of respondents with complete responses for the quality outcome models was $n = 588$ and for the efficiency outcome models was $n = 599$. Testing for missing data bias, we found that respondents who were excluded from our final models were older, more likely to be female, and had lower levels of preoperative functioning, but that they did not differ significantly on any of the other variables in our models, including quality of care or length of stay.

High-Performance Work Practices

High-performance work practices included in this study were cross-functional selection, cross-functional conflict resolution, cross-functional performance measurement, cross-functional rewards, cross-functional team meetings, and cross-functional boundary spanners. Descriptive data for these work practices are shown in Table 21.1.

Selection was measured by asking administrators in each orthopedics unit about selection criteria for physicians, nurses, and physical therapists, probing as to whether cross-functional teamwork ability was considered an important selection criterion. This variable was coded from 0 to 2 for each of these three workgroups, 0 indicating that cross-functional teamwork ability was not considered, 1 indicating

Table 21.1   High-Performance Work Practices and Relational Coordination

	Factor loading	Range	Mean	SD	No. of observations
Cross-functional selection					
Physicians selected for cross-functional teamwork	0.701	0–2	0.44	0.88	9
Nurses selected for cross-functional teamwork	0.760	0–2	0.44	0.73	9
Physical therapists selected for cross-functional teamwork	0.570	0–2	0.67	0.88	9
Cross-functional conflict resolution					
Physician access to cross-functional process	0.916	0–1	0.44	0.53	9
Nurse access to cross-functional process	0.700	0–1	0.22	0.44	9
Physical therapists access to cross-functional process	0.438	0–1	0.33	0.50	9
Cross-functional performance measurement					
Cross-functional approach to quality measurement	0.544	1–5	3.33	1.41	9
Problem-solving approach to quality measurement	0.729	1–5	2.78	1.39	9
Cross-functional approach to efficiency measurement[a]		1–5	2.56	1.88	9
Problem-solving approach to efficiency measurement	0.834	1–5	3.00	1.58	9
Cross-functional rewards					
Physicians rewarded for cross-functional teamwork	0.438	0–3	0.22	0.67	9
Nurses rewarded for cross-functional teamwork	0.560	0–2	0.56	0.88	9
Physical therapists rewarded for cross-functional teamwork	0.803	0–2	1.11	1.05	9
Cross-functional meetings					
Nurses included in physician rounds	0.548	0–2	1.33	0.87	9
Physical therapists included in physician rounds	0.691	0–2	0.56	0.88	9
Case managers included in physician rounds	0.677	0–2	0.67	0.87	9
Physicians included in nursing rounds[a]	−0.210	0–2	0.78	0.44	9
Physical therapists included in nursing rounds[a]	−0.112	0–2	1.44	0.73	9
Case manager included in nursing rounds	0.642	0–2	1.33	1	9
Cross-functional boundary spanners					
Case manager caseload	−0.740	6.7–40	26.30	10.80	9
Case manager discharge planning role	0.515	0–1	0.89	0.33	9
Case manager coordination role[a]	0.368	0–1	0.44	0.53	9
Primary nursing model	0.746	−1	0.56	0.53	9
High-performance work practices index ($\alpha = 0.93$)					
Relational coordination					
Shared goals	0.629	1–5	4.21	0.61	331
Shared knowledge	0.629	1–5	3.93	0.59	333
Mutual respect	0.659	1–5	3.81	0.59	327
Frequency of communication	0.566	1–5	3.84	0.73	334
Timeliness of communication	0.782	1–5	4.08	0.62	334
Accuracy of communication	0.796	1–5	4.23	0.62	333
Problem-solving focus of communication	0.796	1–5	4.05	0.46	320
Relational coordination index ($\alpha = 0.86$)					

NOTES: Work practices, $N = 9$ hospital units. Variables coded from interviews with administrators. Relational coordination, $N = 336$ care providers. Variables coded from survey of care providers.

[a] These four items were dropped from the high-performance work practices index because of weak factor loadings.

that it was considered to some extent, and 2 indicating that it was a consistent criterion for selection.

Conflict resolution was measured by asking about conflict-resolution processes. Questions probed as to whether any formal cross-functional conflict resolution process was in place for physicians, nurses, or physical therapists. This variable was coded 0 or 1 for physicians, nurses, and physical therapists; 0 indicated that the workgroup had no access to a formal cross-functional conflict resolution process and 1 indicated that the workgroup did have access.

Performance measurement was measured by asking about the quality-assurance process and the utilization review process in each hospital, probing as to whether each of these processes were largely focused on identifying the single function that was responsible for a quality or utilization problem or whether the approach was more cross-functional. Responses were coded on a 5-point scale, where 1 = highly functional, 2 = fairly functional, 3 = equally functional/cross-functional, 4 = fairly cross-functional, and 5 = highly cross-functional. Questions also probed interviewees as to whether these two performance-measurement processes were reactive (focused on affixing blame) or proactive (focused on problem solving). Responses were coded on a 5-point scale: 1 = highly reactive, 2 = fairly reactive, 3 = equally reactive/proactive, 4 = fairly proactive, and 5 = highly proactive.

Rewards were measured by asking about the criteria for rewards for physicians, nurses, and physical therapists, probing as to whether rewards were based purely on individual performance or whether they were based on some cross-functional performance criteria as well. This variable was coded from 0 to 2. For nurses and physical therapists, 0 indicated no performance-based rewards, 1 indicated individual rewards only, and 2 indicated some cross-functional team rewards. For physicians, 0 indicated individual rewards only, 1 indicated surplus sharing with the hospital (potential for sharing positive financial outcomes), and 2 indicated risk sharing with the hospital (potential for sharing both positive and negative financial outcomes).

Meetings were measured by asking key informants about participation in physician rounds and nursing rounds, probing to find out which functional groups participated in those rounds and the consistency of their participation. Rounds are the primary form of meeting used for coordinating patient care. These variables were coded on a 0–2 scale, with 0 indicating that the functional group did not participate in the rounds, 1 indicating that they participated sometimes, and 2 indicating that they participated usually or always.

Boundary spanner was measured by asking about the caseload and roles of the case managers who worked with joint replacement patients and whether the primary nursing model was in place on that unit (i.e., the practice of assigning one nurse to assume primary responsibility for a patient throughout his or her stay and to serve as a point person for coordinating that patient's care). Caseload, the number of patients for whom case managers were typically responsible at a time, was measured as a continuous variable, ranging across hospitals from 6.7 to 40. Each of the case manager roles—leadership of rounds and planning for patient discharge—was coded as 0 or 1, with 0 indicating that the role was not expected and 1 indicating that it was expected of case managers. Primary nursing was coded as 1 if the model was in place and 0 if not.

Because these six work practices were correlated with one another, forming a "bundle" of work practices, we combined the above measures into an index of high-performance work practices. Exploratory factor analysis suggested that these high-performance work practices can be characterized fairly well as a single factor. Nineteen of the original 23 items had factor 1 loadings greater than 0.40 and were retained; see Table 21.1 for factor loadings. Four items with loadings less than 0.40 were dropped, including cross-functional approach to utilization review (1 item), participation in nursing rounds (2 items), and coordination role for case managers (1 item). The eigenvalue for factor 1 was 8.53, and the eigenvalue for factor 2 was 3.08. Checking for cross-loadings, we found that 6 of the 19 variables in the high-performance work practices index also loaded onto factor 2 with loadings of 0.40 or higher. If we drop these six items from our high-performance work practices, our regression results remain virtually the same, with no changes in the significance level of our key independent variables and no change in the significance of mediation as measured by the Sobel test. We therefore elected to retain all 19 items.

All items in the high-performance work practices index had item-to-total correlation scores of 0.40 or greater, suggesting that our index meets standards for convergent validity. An additive scaling method was used in which each item that loaded onto factor 1 with loading of 0.40 or more was standardized with a mean of 0 and a standard deviation of 1 so that each item in the high-performance work practices index was equally weighted. A joint test for skewness and kurtosis indicated that normal distribution of the high-performance work practices index could not be rejected (chi square 2.01, prob(chi square) = 0.3654). Cronbach's alpha for the high-performance work practices index was 0.93, suggesting that this construct has a high level of reliability.

We selected an additive rather than a multiplicative approach for aggregating high-performance work practices into an index because the additive approach is more comprehensive, withstands missing human resource practices, and reflects the entire gestalt (Becker and Gerhart 1996, Delery 1998, Youndt et al. 1996). Moreover, additive models assume each practice is equally important within the index, an appropriate assumption for our study given that we have offered no hypotheses that indicate otherwise. A multiplicative approach is more appropriate when the practices together are expected to add up to more than the sum of the individual practices because of their fit with each other. Although this may be the case with the high-performance work practices presented here, the theoretical construct as developed thus far does not include explicit arguments regarding fit. As with other types of high-performance work practices, organizations can improve performance either by increasing the number of work practices they employ within the system or by using the practices within the system in a more comprehensive and widespread manner, for example, by extending their reach to cover a wider array of employee functions.

Table 21.1 shows that the high-performance work practices in this study do not cover all employee functions in an equally comprehensive way. We can see that physicians are less likely than nurses and therapists to be included in high-performance work practices. Our subsequent analyses therefore account for differences between functions.

Relational Coordination

Relational coordination was measured using the survey of care providers. Seven questions reflected the dimensions of relational coordination: the frequency of communication among care providers; the timeliness and accuracy of communication; the problem-solving nature of communication; and the degree to which relationships are characterized by shared goals, shared knowledge, and mutual respect.

Respondents from each of the functions believed to be most central to the care of joint replacement patients—physicians, residents, nurses, physical therapists, case managers, and social workers—were asked to answer each of the following questions with respect to each of the other functions.

- How frequently do you communicate with each of groups about the status of joint replacement patients? (1 = never, 2 = rarely, 3 = occasionally, 4 = often, 5 = constantly)
- Do people in these groups communicate with you in a timely way about the status of joint replacement patients? (1 = never, 2 = rarely, 3 = occasionally, 4 = often, 5 = always)
- Do people in these groups communicate with you accurately about the status of joint replacement patients? (1 = never, 2 = rarely, 3 = occasionally, 4 = often, 5 = always)
- When an error has been made regarding joint replacement patients, do people in these groups blame others rather than sharing responsibility? (1 = never, 2 = rarely, 3 = occasionally, 4 = often, 5 = always)
- To what extent do people in these groups share your goals for the care of joint replacement patients? (1 = not at all, 2 = a little, 3 = some, 4 = a lot, 5 = completely)
- How much do people in these groups know about the work you do with joint replacement patients? (1 = nothing, 2 = little, 3 = some, 4 = a lot, 5 = everything)
- How much do people in these groups respect you and the work you do with joint replacement patients? (1 = not at all, 2 = a little, 3 = some, 4 = a lot, 5 = completely)

Exploratory factor analysis suggested that relational coordination is best characterized as a single factor. See Table 21.1 for factor loadings. The eigenvalue for this factor was 3.41, and the eigenvalue for factor 2 was 0.55.

An additive scaling method was used in which each item was standardized with a mean of 0 and a standard deviation of 1 so that each item was equally weighted. Cronbach's alpha was 0.86, suggesting that this construct has a high level of reliability. No items were dropped due to weak factor loadings, and no cross-loadings greater than 0.40 were found. Furthermore, all items had item-to-total correlation scores of 0.40 or greater. We conclude that the relational coordination index meets standards for reliability and convergent validity.

Using one-way analysis of variance, significant cross-unit differences in relational coordination were found—$F(8,327) = 5.32$, $p < 0.001$—as well as significant cross-functional differences in relational coordination—$F(5,330) = 2.89$, $p < 0.05$. When unit-level and function-level differences were considered jointly, unit-level differences remained significant—$F(8,322) = 4.51$, $p < 0.001$—and function-level differences became insignificant—$F(5,322) = 1.75$, $p = 0.12$. To further assess treating relational coordination as a unit-level construct, we computed intraclass correlations ICC(1) and ICC(2). ICC(1) is the proportion of total variance explained by unit membership with values ranging from −1 to +1 and values between 0.05 and 0.30 being most typical. This number provides an estimate of the reliability of a single respondent's assessment of the unit mean. ICC(2) provides an overall estimate of the reliability of unit means, with values equal to or above 0.70 being acceptable. For relational coordination, ICC(1) = 0.25 and ICC(2) = 0.81. We concluded that relational coordination performs well on both forms of intraclass correlation. Taken together, these results are consistent with treating relational coordination as a unit-level construct.

Performance Outcomes

Performance outcomes for this study included both the quality and efficiency of patient care. Hospitals have been striving to improve the quality of care as perceived by patients (Cleary et al. 1991). All hospitals in this study had been conducting patient surveys for years, but differences between their surveys required them to adopt a new survey for this study. We used a single item measure of patient-perceived quality of care ("Overall, how would you rate the care you received at the hospital?"), measured on a five-point Likert-type scale, consistent with other studies that have used single-item measures of patient-perceived quality of care (Ware and Hays 1988, Young et al. 2000, Rohrer and Wilkinson 2008). Responses were coded as 1 = poor, 2 = fair, 3 = good, 4 = very good, and 5 = excellent.

Hospitals have also been striving to improve the efficiency of care by reducing the lengths of patient stays. Length of stay is the number of inpatient days of care used by a given patient. Days of inpatient care are a resource that external payers are intent on reducing. This study therefore uses the length of hospital stay as a measure of the efficiency of care for each individual patient, controlling for the patient characteristics that are believed to necessitate longer lengths of stay (described below). Length of stay was calculated from hospital records for each patient as the number of whole days between the date of admission and the date of discharge.

Control Variables

For Predicting Relational Coordination. Control variables for predicting relational coordination include dummy variables that indicate the functional identity of the care provider respondent, given that different functions are expected to engage differently in relational coordination due to the differences in their professional identities and their differential coverage by high-performance work practices. Ideally, control variables would also include demographic characteristics such as tenure and gender that might influence care provider engagement in relational coordination; however, these variables were not included on the survey. We included the total number of joint replacements conducted by each unit in the six-month period prior to the study period to control for possible learning effects (Luft 1990) that could improve relational coordination between the functions involved in patient care.

For Predicting Quality and Efficiency Outcomes.
Control variables for predicting quality and efficiency outcomes were selected to adjust for factors that have been shown in the health care literature to affect quality of care and length of stay for joint replacement patients. Control variables included the following patient characteristics: age, comorbidities, psychological well-being, preoperative status, surgical procedure (hip versus knee), marital status, race, and gender.

Patient age was determined from hospital records. Older patients were expected to require longer hospital lengths of stay. Preoperative clinical status was assessed in the patient survey using the pain and functioning elements of the WOMAC. Patients with lower preoperative status were expected to require longer lengths of stay. Comorbidities were assessed in the patient survey with a series of questions asking patients whether they suffered from heart disease, high blood pressure, diabetes, ulcer or stomach disease, kidney disease, anemia or other blood disease, cancer, depression, or back pain (Katz et al. 1996). Individual patients with a greater number of comorbid conditions were expected to require longer hospital lengths of stay.

Surgical procedure was measured through procedure code in the hospital record and was either a hip or a knee replacement. Knee replacements were expected to require longer lengths of stay than hips, due to greater difficulty of achieving postoperative mobility.

Psychological well-being was assessed in the patient survey using the mental health component of the SF-36 (Stewart et al. 1988). Patients with higher levels of psychological well-being were expected to report receiving higher quality of care: psychological theory suggests that people with high levels of positive affect tend to perceive experiences in a more favorable light. Patient gender, race, and marital status were determined through the patient survey and were included because some studies have found demographic influences on health care outcomes.

Data Analyses

To test Hypothesis 1, we regressed relational coordination ($n = 336$ care providers in 9 units) on the high-performance work practices index ($n = 9$ units), controlling for the functional identity of the care provider respondents (with "nurse" as the omitted respondent category) and for the volume of joint replacements conducted on the unit in the six-month period prior to the study.

To test Hypothesis 2, we regressed quality outcomes ($n = 588$ patients in 9 units) on the high-performance work practices index ($n = 9$ units), controlling for the patient characteristics expected to affect these outcomes, as well as the volume of joint replacements conducted on the unit in the six-month period prior to the study; we then aggregated relational coordination to the unit level ($n = 9$ units) and entered it along with the high-performance work practices index ($n = 9$ units) into the above equation for quality outcomes ($n = 588$ patients in 9 units).

To test Hypothesis 3, we regressed efficiency outcomes ($n = 599$ patients in 9 units) on the high-performance work practices index ($n = 9$ units), controlling for the patient characteristics expected to affect these outcomes, as well as the volume of joint replacements conducted by the unit in the six-month period prior to the study. We then aggregated relational coordination to the unit level ($n = 9$ units) and entered it along with the high-performance work practices index ($n = 9$ units) into the above equation for efficiency outcomes ($n = 599$ patients in 9 units).

We therefore test mediation in this study across multiple levels of analysis, consistent with previous studies of relational coordination (e.g., Gittell 2001, 2002b). Given its status as a multilevel theory that operates across multiple levels of analysis, relational coordination is particularly amenable to testing mediation across levels. If the coefficient on high-performance work practices becomes insignificant when relational coordination is added to the outcomes equations, this result can be taken to suggest that relational coordination mediates between high-performance work practices and outcomes, or in other words that high-performance work practices influence outcomes through their effect on relational coordination. We used the Sobel test to determine whether the association between high-performance work practices and outcomes is reduced significantly when controlling for relational coordination, then drew on the critical values recommended by MacKinnon et al. (2002) to determine whether the results for quality and efficiency outcomes supported mediation.

For all the above analyses, random effects modeling was used to adjust standard errors for the multilevel nature of the data, accounting for non-independence of the error terms (Raudenbush and Bryk 1992). To determine the days of hospital stay associated with a change in relational coordination, we conducted a Poisson random effects regression on the length of stay model.

FINDINGS

Descriptive data and intercorrelations between key variables are reported in Table 21.2 in aggregate form, and broken out by individual hospital unit. Due to the high correlation found between high-performance work practices and relational coordination, we tested for multicollinearity in the outcomes models that include both high-performance work practices and relational coordination as independent variables by examining variance inflation factors. Evidence of multicollinearity exists if (1) the largest variance inflation factor is greater than 10, or (2) the mean value of all the variance inflation factors is considerably larger than 1, where 4.02 is given as an example of a variance inflation factor that is not considerably larger than 1 (Chatterjee and Price 1991). We found that the variance inflation factors for the quality of care model ranged from 1.06 to 8.45, with an average variance inflation factor of 2.46; for the length of stay model they ranged from 1.06 to 8.50, with an average variance inflation factor of 2.47. Comparing our results to the Chatterjee and Price criteria, we conclude that multicollinearity is not likely to be a substantial problem in our models.

High-Performance Work Practices and Relational Coordination

Hypothesis 1 test results are reported in Table 21.3. The results show that high-performance work practices are positively associated with relational coordination ($r = 0.31$, $p < 0.001$). The physician respondent dummy variable was negative and significant ($r = -0.16$, $p < 0.001$), suggesting that physicians were significantly less engaged in relational coordination than nurses. The other dummy variables were not significant, suggesting that residents, physical therapists, case managers, and social workers did not differ significantly from nurses in their engagement in relational coordination.

The estimated effect of high-performance work practices on relational coordination is statistically significant and moderately large. The standardized coefficient of 0.31 on high-performance work practices suggests that for a hospital at the mean level of relational coordination, a one-point change in high-performance work practices would correspond to a 31 percent change in relational coordination. Because the primary explanatory variable—high-performance work practices—is measured at the unit level, the equations explain relatively little within-unit variation in relational coordination ($R^2 = 0.07$), but they explain a large percentage of between-unit variation in relational coordination ($R^2 = 0.90$). These results support our argument that high-performance work practices positively predict relational coordination (Hypothesis 1).

High-Performance Work Practices, Relational Coordination, and Quality Outcomes

Results from testing Hypothesis 2 are shown in Table 21.4, columns 1–3. Results indicate that high-performance work practices are associated with higher quality of care ($r = 0.38$, $p < 0.001$) (column 1). When relational coordination is aggregated to the unit level and included in the equation (column 3), relational coordination is associated with higher quality of care ($r = 1.93$, $p = 0.041$), and the coefficient on high-performance work practices becomes insignificant, suggesting mediation.

Again, the estimated effects are statistically significant and moderately large to large. The nonstandardized coefficient of 0.38 on high-performance work practices suggests that for a hospital at the mean level of quality, a one-point change in high-performance work practices would correspond to a 0.38-point change in patient-perceived quality of care. The coefficient of 1.93 on relational coordination suggests that for a hospital at the mean level of quality, a one-point change in relational coordination would correspond to a 1.93-point change in patient-perceived quality of care. Because the primary explanatory variables—high-performance work practices and relational coordination—are measured at the unit level, the equations explain little within-unit variation in quality of care ($R^2 = 0.05$), but they explain a large percentage of between-unit variation in quality

Table 21.2 Descriptive Data and Correlations

	No. of observations	Range	MMean (S.D.)	1. High performance work practices	2. Relational coordination	3. Quality of care	Hospitals								
							1	2	3	4	5	6	7	8	9
1. High-performance work practices	9	−0.95–0.83	0 (0.66)	—			−0.95 n (n=1)	−0.54 n (n=1)	−0.28 n (n=1)	00.75 n (n=1)	00.83 n (n=1)	00.82 n (n=1)	00.12 n (n=1)	−0.32 n (n=1)	−0.42 (n=1)
2. Relational coordination	3336	−3.30–1.61	0 (0.73)	−0.92** (0.000)	—		−0.19 (0.84) (n=52)	−0.27 (0.84) (n=51)	−0.17 (0.54) (n=33)	00.35 (0.64) (n=40)	00.12 (0.52) (n=15)	00.56 (0.66) (n=27)	−0.04 (0.86) (n=33)	00.14 (0.61) (n=39)	−0.02 (0.58) (n=46)
3. Quality of care	7788	1–5	44.01 (1.01)	0.74* (0.023)	0.78* (0.013)	—	33.62 (1.11) (n=108)	33.68 (1.08) (n=90)	44.08 (0.99) (n=123)	44.43 (0.70) (n=134)	44.19 (0.96) (n=64)	44.08 (1.04) (n=63)	33.98 (0.94) (n=93)	44.24 (0.85) (n=68)	33.62 (1.19) (n=45)
4. Length of stay	8809	2–35	55.11 (2.13)	−0.68** (0.045)	−0.80** (0.009)	−0.17*** (0.000)	55.57 (2.06) (n=109)	55.80 (2.39) (n=93)	55.90 (1.74) (n=125)	44.44 (1.46) (n=135)	44.17 (1.33) (n=65)	44.37 (3.94) (n=67)	55.60 (1.92) (n=97)	44.30 (1.00) (n=70)	44.98 (1.51) (n=48)

$*p < 0.05$; $**p < 0.01$; $***p < 0.001$.

Table 21.3   Impact of High-Performance Work Practices on Relational Coordination

	Relational Coordination
High-performance work practices	0.31***
	(0.000)
Physician respondent	–0.16***
	(0.000)
Resident respondent	–0.02
	(0.613)
Physical therapist respondent	0.07+
	(0.091)
Case manager respondent	0.04
	(0.300)
Social worker respondent	–0.07+
	(0.095)
Surgical volume	–0.03
	(0.386)
Constant	0.03
	(0.450)
Within-unit R^2	0.07
Between-unit R^2	0.90
No. of observations	336

NOTES: Unit of analysis is care provider (physicians, residents, nurses, physical therapists, social workers, and case managers) assigned to work with joint replacement patients ($n = 336$). Nurse respondent is the omitted category. Random effects regression is used to account for clustering of care providers by hospital unit ($n = 9$). High-performance work practices and surgical volume are entered at the hospital unit level ($n = 9$). All coefficients are standardized.

$+p < 0.10$; $*p < 0.05$; $**p < 0.01$; $***p < 0.001$.

high-performance work practices are associated with shorter lengths of stay ($r = -0.16$, $p = 0.001$). When relational coordination is aggregated to the unit level and included in the equation (column 6), relational coordination is associated with shorter lengths of stay ($r = -1.19$. $p = 0.005$); the coefficient on high-performance work practices becomes insignificant, again suggesting mediation.

The coefficient of –0.16 on high-performance work practices suggests that a one-point increase in high-performance work practices is associated with a 0.16-day reduction in patient length of stay. The coefficient of –1.19 on relational coordination suggests that a one-point increase in relational coordination is associated with a 1.2-day reduction in patient length of stay. Among U.S. hospitals, the median for the average charge per day was $4,357 in 2006 *(Medicare Cost Reports* 2006), or $4,803 in 2008, adjusted for annual health care cost increases of 4.5% in 2007 and 5.5% in 2008. So a one-point increase in relational coordination is associated with $5,764 ($4,803/day * 1.2 days) in average cost savings for each joint replacement patient served. Results of the Sobel test suggest that the association between high-performance work practices and length of stay is significantly mediated by relational coordination ($z^1 = 2.40$, $p < 0.01$). Together, these results suggest that high-performance work practices predict efficiency outcomes and that they do so by strengthening relational coordination among employees in different functions (Hypothesis 3). See Figure 21.1 for a summary of all results.

of care ($R^2 = 0.73$ for the most complete model). Results of the Sobel test suggest that the association between high-performance work practices and quality of care is significantly mediated by relational coordination ($z^1 = 1.87$. $p < 0.01$). Together, these results suggest that high-performance work practices predict quality outcomes and that they do so by strengthening relational coordination among employees in different functions (Hypothesis 2).

High-Performance Work Practices, Relational Coordination, and Efficiency Outcomes

Results from testing Hypothesis 3 are shown in columns 4–6 of Table 21.4. Findings indicate that

Discussion

In this paper we explored a relational pathway through which high-performance work systems were predicted to contribute to performance outcomes. We proposed that high-performance work practices can enhance organizational performance by encouraging the development of relational coordination between employees who perform distinct functions—in contrast to traditional bureaucratic work practices that divide and separate employees and in contrast to other types of high-performance work practices that focus primarily on the development of employee skills and commitment. High-performance work practices that focus only on

Table 21.4   Impact of High-Performance Work Practices and Relational Coordination on Quality and Efficiency Outcomes

	Patient-perceived quality of care			Patient length of stay		
	1a	1b	1c	2a	2b	2c
High-performance work practices	0.38***		0.00	−0.16**		0.08
	(0.000)		(0.993)	(0.001)		(0.367)
Relational coordination		1.94***	1.93*		−0.84***	−1.19**
		(0.000)	(0.041)		(0.000)	(0.005)
Patient age	0.00	0.00	0.00	−0.00	−0.00	−0.00
	(0.888)	(0.904)	(0.904)	(0.642)	(0.621)	(0.611)
Preoperative functioning	−0.00	−0.00	−0.00	0.00	0.00	0.00
	(0.853)	(0.773)	(0.774)	(0.435)	(0.438)	(0.419)
Comorbidities	0.05	0.06	0.06	0.03⁺	0.03⁺	0.03⁺
	(0.119)	(0.103)	(0.104)	(0.091)	(0.084)	(0.081)
Surgery type (hip = 1)	0.22**	0.23**	0.23**	−0.01	−0.01	−0.01
	(0.009)	(0.005)	(0.005)	(0.843)	(0.776)	(0.709)
Psychological well-being	0.15**	0.15**	0.15**	−0.04⁺	−0.04⁺	−0.04⁺
	(0.001)	(0.001)	(0.001)	(0.063)	(0.071)	(0.082)
Marital status (married = 1)	0.12	0.14	0.14	0.00	0.00	−0.00
	(0.165)	(0.127)	(0.128)	(0.942)	(0.982)	(0.998)
Gender (female = 1)	−0.07	−0.07	−0.07	0.03	0.03	0.05
	(0.391)	(0.442)	(0.415)	(0.450)	(0.486)	(0.202)
Race (black = 1)	0.13	0.13	0.13	0.02	0.02	0.02
	(0.472)	(0.469)	(0.445)	(0.757)	(0.789)	(0.771)
Surgical volume	0.00⁺	0.00⁺	0.00⁺	0.00*	0.00*	0.00*
	(0.088)	(0.081)	(0.081)	(0.046)	(0.030)	(0.038)
Constant	3.07***	−4.81***	−4.78***	1.53***	4.96***	6.38***
	(0.000)	(0.000)	(0.000)	(0.000)	(0.000)	(0.000)
Within-unit R^2	0.05	0.05	0.05	NA	NA	NA
Between-unit R^2	0.64	0.73	0.73	NA	NA	NA
Chi square	NA	NA	NA	0.0022	0.0000	0.0000
No. of observations	588	588	588	599	599	599

NOTES: Unit of analysis is the joint replacement patient ($n = 588$ for quality of care, $n = 599$ for length of stay). Random effects regression is used to account for clustering of patients by hospital unit ($n = 9$). High-performance work practices, relational coordination, and surgical volume are entered at the hospital unit level ($n = 9$).
⁺$p < 0.10$; *$p < 0.105$; **$p < 0.01$; ***$p < 0.001$.

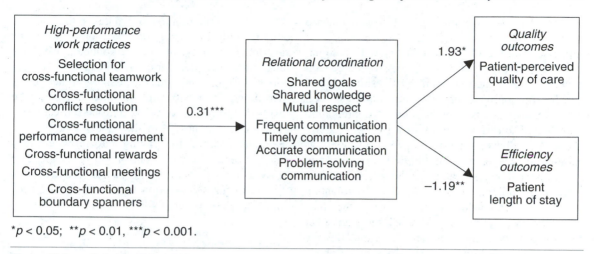

*p < 0.05; **p < 0.01, ***p < 0.001.

Figure 21.1   Relational Model of How High-Performance Work Systems Work

employee skills and commitment are not expected, on their own, to yield the coordinated, synergistic behaviors that are needed to achieve the highest levels of performance in interdependent work settings.

Contributions

This study has made two key contributions. First, we have linked the high-performance work systems literature to post-bureaucracy theory by articulating the potentially positive role of formal work practices. Post-bureaucracy theorists (e.g., Heckscher 1994, Piore 1993) argue that the networks needed for getting work done tend to emerge informally and that formal organizational practices, traditionally designed to segment and divide employees from their counterparts in different functions, serve more as obstacles than facilitators of these networks. Along with other recent work (Collins and Clark 2003, Gant et al. 2002, Leana and Van Buren 1999, Vogus 2006), our study provides a countervailing argument that formal practices are not necessarily obstacles and can indeed be designed to encourage the development of relationships between employees in different functions, producing significant performance advantages for organizations. Of the existing research on high-performance work systems, Collins and Clark's (2003) study is the most similar to ours. Like us, Collins and Clark conceptualize

relationships as mediators between human resource practices and performance. Despite that similarity, our work differs from that of Collins and Clark both theoretically and methodologically. Theoretically, we focus on relationships between employees in different functions rather than on business relationships more generally. Furthermore, our theory building is focused at the level of production or service delivery rather than of relationships among top managers, because of our interest in the coordination of work. Methodologically, we differ from Collins and Clark by using multiple data sets to test our hypotheses. Collins and Clark interviewed CEOs to determine human resource practices, social networks, and performance, thus introducing the potential for biases that can arise when relying on a single source of data; in contrast, we interviewed front-line managers to determine human resource practices, surveyed direct service workers to measure relational coordination, and examined customer data to determine performance outcomes. Because of these theoretical and methodological differences from previous work, our study uniquely demonstrates how formal work practices play an important role in producing high performance in multidisciplinary work groups that are engaged in interdependent work.

A second contribution of this study is that we articulate a novel relational pathway through which high-performance work practices contribute to performance. We have argued that high-performance work practices can contribute to performance by supporting the development of relational coordination, "a mutually reinforcing process of interaction between communication and relationships carried out for the purpose of task integration" (Gittell 2002a, p. 301). Like the role-based coordination found in Thompson (1967) and Bechky (2006), and like role-based relationships more generally as explored by Meyerson et al. (1996) in their work on swift trust and by Klein and coauthors (2006) in their work on de-individualization, relational coordination focuses on relationships between roles rather than individual role inhabitants. Although there are other relational perspectives on coordination (Bechky 2006, Faraj and Sproull 2000, Weick and Roberts 1993), the theory of relational coordination is unique in identifying specific dimensions of relationships that are integral to the coordination of interdependent work, while focusing on the development of these relationships between roles rather than individuals. By showing that relational coordination constitutes a pathway between high-performance work practices and outcomes, our study provides a new relational model of how high-performance work systems work.

Limitations

Despite its contributions and strengths, this study is limited in several ways. First, this study is limited by the use of interviews rather than survey instruments to measure work practices, rendering the results less amenable to replication because of the time-consuming process of conducting interviews and constructing variables. Second, our data are limited by the lack of measures for individual skill and commitment. We have counterbalanced this omission by arguing that individual skill and commitment are not sufficient to yield the coordinated, synergistic behaviors needed to achieve the highest levels of performance in interdependent work settings. Although this study has identified a unique and important mechanism—relational coordination—through which high-performance work systems work in such settings, we recommend that future studies explore the interplay among skill, commitment, and relational coordination.

A third limitation of our data is the lack of employee-level control variables other than the functional identity of the respondent. We have fairly extensive demographic information for our patient respondents but no demographics other than functional identity for the care providers who responded to our survey. The omission of care provider demographics from the model that predicts relational coordination among care providers may result in omitted variable bias. Finally, our focus on cross-functional relationships pays less attention to the within-function relationships that have also been shown to be important (Vogus 2006).

Future Research

Next steps in theory development should include the development of high-performance work system models that include all three causal mechanisms—skills, commitment, and employee-employee relationships. Others have begun to take steps in this direction. Smith et al. (2005) developed a model that explores the contribution of human capital and social capital to perceived knowledge-creation capability in technology firms, based on the argument that one without the other is not very useful. Leana and Pil (2006) developed and tested a similar model in the context of public schools. But to our knowledge, no one has yet explored the high-performance work systems that would support the development of skills, commitment, and employee-employee relationships. We believe that the next frontier for theories of high-performance work systems is the design of work systems that explicitly support the development of all three pathways, and we hope that this paper, by further explicating the relational path through which high-performance work systems work, will serve as a building block in that direction.

CONCLUSION

In conclusion, this study suggests that adopting high-performance work practices to foster relational coordination constitutes one viable path for improved organizational performance. But organizations have other options when choosing paths for improving performance. What are the relative advantages of the relational approach explored here? Relational coordination enables employees to more effectively coordinate their work with each other, thus pushing out the production possibilities frontier to achieve higher-quality outcomes while using resources more efficiently—for example, as we found here, enabling hospital workers to achieve better patient-perceived quality of care along with shorter patient lengths of stay. Relational coordination and the high-performance work practices that support its development are therefore particularly relevant in industries that must maintain or improve quality outcomes while responding to cost pressures. In an increasingly competitive economy, nearly all industries are likely to face this dual challenge.

Second, unlike relationships that are based on personal ties, the relationships found in relational coordination are based instead on ties between roles. The high-performance work practices explored in this paper are expected to foster relationships of shared goals, shared knowledge, and mutual respect among employees whose work is interdependent, with or without the presence of personal ties. This feature allows for the interchangeability of employees, allowing employees to come and go without missing a beat, an important consideration for organizations that strive to achieve high levels of performance while allowing employees the scheduling flexibility to meet their outside commitments. Role-based relationships may require greater organizational investments to foster than personal ties—for example, designing cross-functional boundary spanner roles and cross-functional performance measurement systems versus hosting after-work parties—but they are also more robust to staffing changes that occur over time. High-performance work systems that foster these role-based relationships may therefore provide organizations with a relatively sustainable source of competitive advantage.

REFERENCES

Adler, P., S. Kwon, C. Heckscher. 2008. Professional work: The emergence of collaborative community. *Organ. Sci.* **19**(2) 359–376.

Appelbaum, E., T. Bailey, P. Berg, A. L. Kalleberg. 2000. *Manufacturing Advantage: Why High-Performance Work Systems Pay Off.* ILR Press, Ithaca, NY.

Argote, L. 1982. Input uncertainty and organization coordination in hospital emergency units. *Admin. Sci. Quart.* **27** 420–134.

Arthur, J. B. 1992. The link between business strategy and industrial relations systems in American steel mini-mills. *Indust. Labor Rel. Rev.* **45** 488–506.

Arthur, J. B. 1994. Effects of human resource systems on manufacturing performance and turnover. *Acad. Management J.* **37** 670–687.

Bailey, T., P. Berg, C. Sandy. 2001. The effect of high-performance work practices on employee earnings in the steel, apparel, and medical electronics and imaging industries. *Indust. Labor Rel. Rev.* **54** 525–544.

Bartel, A. P. 1994. Productivity gains from the implementation of employee training programs. *Indust. Rel.* **33** 411–425.

Bartel, A. P. 2004. Human resource management and performance outcomes: Evidence from retail banking. *Indust. Labor Rel. Rev.* **57** 181–203.

Batt, R. 1999. Work design, technology and performance in customer service and sales. *Indust. Labor Rel. Rev.* **52** 539–564.

Batt, R. 2002. Managing customer services: Human resource practices, quit rates, and sales growth. *Acad. Management J.* **45** 587–598.

Bechky, B. A. 2006. Gaffer, gofers, and grips: Role-based coordination in temporary organizations. *Organ. Sci.* **17**(1) 3–21.

Becker, B., B. Gerhart. 1996. The impact of human resource management on organizational performance: Progress and prospects. *Acad. Management J.* **39**(4) 779–801.

Becker, G. S. 1975. *Human Capital.* Columbia University Press, New York.

Bowen, D. E., C. Ostroff. 2004. Understanding HRM-firm performance linkages: The role of the "strength" of the HRM system. *Acad. Management Rev.* **29** 203–221.

Cappelli, P., D. Neumark. 2001. Do high performance work practices improve establishment level outcomes? *Indust. Labor Rel. Rev.* **54** 737–775.

Cappelli, P., N. Rogovsky. 1994. New work systems and skill requirements. *Internal Labour Rev.* **133**(2) 205–220.

Chatterjee, S., B. Price. 1991. *Regression Analysis by Example.* John Wiley and Sons, New York.

Chenhall, R. H. 2005. Integrative strategic performance measurement systems, strategic alignment of manufacturing, learning and strategic outcomes. *Account. Organ. Soc.* **30**(5) 395–422.

Cleary, P. D., S. Edgman-Levitan, M. Roberts, T. W. Moloney, W. Mullen, J. D. Walker. 1991. Patients evaluate their hospital care: A national survey. *Health Affairs* **10** 254–267.

Collins, C. J., K. Clark. 2003. Strategic human resource practices, top management team social networks, and firm performance. *Acad. Management J.* **46** 740–751.

Collins, C., K. Smith. 2006. Knowledge exchange and combination: The role of human resource practices in the performance of high-technology firms. *Acad. Management J.* **49**(3) 544–560.

Datta, D. K., J. P. Guthrie, P. M. Wright. 2005. HRM and labor productivity: Does industry matter? *Acad. Management J.* **48**(1) 135–145.

Day, D., S. Silverman. 1989. Personality and job performance: Evidence of incremental validity. *Personnel Psych.* **42**(1) 25–36.

Delery, J. E. 1998. Issues of fit in strategic human resource management: Implications for research. *Human Resource Management Rev.* **8**(3) 289–310.

Delery, J. E., D. H. Doty. 1996. Modes of theorizing in strategic human resource management: Tests of universalistic, contingency, and configurational performance predictions. *Acad. Management J.* **39**(4) 802–835.

Delery, J. E., J. D. Shaw. 2001. The strategic management of people in work organizations: Review, synthesis and extension. G. R. Ferris, ed. *Research in Personnel and Human Resource Management,* Vol. 20. JAI Press, Greenwich, CT, 165–197.

Deming, J. E. 1986. *Out of the Crisis.* MIT University Press, Cambridge, MA.

Dunlop, J. T., D. Weil. 1996. Diffusion and performance of modular production in the U.S. apparel industry. *Indust. Rel.* **35**(3) 334–355.

Edmondson, A. 1996. Learning from mistakes is easier said than done: Group and organizational influences on the detection and correction of human error. *J. Appl. Behav. Sci.* **32**(1) 5–32.

Evans, W. R., W. D. Davis. 2005. High-performance work systems and organizational performance: The mediating role of internal social structure. *J. Management* **31** 758–775.

Faraj, S., L. Sproull. 2000. Coordinating expertise in software development teams. *Management Sci.* **46**(12) 1554–1568.

Fried, V. H., R. D. Hisrich. 1994. Toward a model of venture capital investment decision-making. *Financial Management* **23**(3) 28–37.

Galbraith, J. 1995. *Competing with Flexible Lateral Organizations.* Addison-Wesley, Reading, MA.

Gant, J., C. Ichniowski, K. Shaw. 2002. Social capital and organizational change in high-involvement and traditional work organizations. *J. Econom. Management Start.* **11** 289–328.

Gibbert, M. 2006. Generalizing about uniqueness: An essay on an apparent paradox in the resource-based view. *J. Management Inq.* **15** 124–134.

Gittell, J. H. 2000. Organizing work to support relational coordination. *Internat. J. Human Resource Management* **11** 517–539.

Gittell, J. H. 2001. Supervisory span, relational coordination and flight departure performance: A reassessment of post-bureaucracy theory. *Organ. Sci.* **12**(4) 467–482.

Gittell, J. H. 2002a. Relationships between service providers and their impact on customers. *J. Service Res.* **4**(4) 299–311.

Gittell, J. H. 2002b. Coordinating mechanisms in care provider groups: Relational coordination as a mediator and input uncertainty as a moderator of performance effects. *Management Sci.* **48**(11) 1408–1426.

Gittell, J. H. 2006. Relational coordination: Coordinating work through relationships of shared goals, shared knowledge and mutual respect. O. Kyriakidou, M. Ozbilgin, eds. *Relational Perspectives in Organizational Studies: A Research Companion.* Edward Elgar Publishers, Cheltenham, UK, 74–94.

Gittell, J. H., K. Fairfield, B. Bierbaum, R. Jackson, M. Kelly, R. Laskin, S. Lipson, J. Siliski, T. Thornhill, J. Zuckerman. 2000. Impact of relational coordination on quality of care, postoperative pain and functioning, and length of stay: A nine-hospital study of surgical patients. *Medical Care* **38**(8) 807–819.

Goffman, E. 1961. *Encounters.* Bobbs Merrill, Indianapolis.

Guthrie, J. P., E. C. Hollensbe. 2004. Group incentives and performance: A study of spontaneous goal setting, goal choice, and commitment. *J. Management* **30**(2) 263–285.

Heckscher, C. 1994. Defining the post-bureaucratic type. C. Heckscher, A. Donnellon, eds. *The Post-Bureaucratic Organization.* Sage Publications, Thousand Oaks, CA.

Horgan, J., P. Muhlau. 2006. Human resource systems and employee performance in Ireland and the Netherlands: A test of the complementarity hypothesis. *Internat. J. Human Resource Management* **17** 414–439.

Huselid, M. 1995. The impact of human resource management on turnover, productivity and corporate financial performance. *Acad. Management J.* **38** 635–672.

Ichniowski, C., K. Shaw, G. Prennushi. 1997. The effects of human resource practices on manufacturing performance: A study of steel finishing lines. *Amer. Econom. Rev.* **87** 291–313.

Ichniowski, C., T. Kochan, D. Levine, C. Olsen, G. Strauss. 1996. What works at work: Overview and assessment. *Indust. Rel.* **35** 299–333.

Jehn, K. A. 1995. A multi-method examination of the benefits and detriments of intra group conflict. *Admin. Sci. Quart.* **40**(2) 256–282.

Katz, J. N., L. C. Chang, O. Sangha, A. H. Fossel, D. W. Bates. 1996. Can comorbidity be measured by questionnaire rather than medical record review? *Medical Care* **34**(1) 73–84.

Klein, K. J., J. C. Ziegert, A. P. Knight, Y. Xiao. 2006. Dynamic delegation: Shared, hierarchical and deindividualized leadership in extreme action teams. *Admin. Sci. Quart* **51**(4) 590–621.

Koch, M. J., R. G. McGrath. 1996. Improving labor productivity: Human resource management policies do matter. *Start. Management J.* **17**(5) 335–354.

Kwiatkowski, K. 2003. Trends in organizations and selection. *J. Managerial Psych.* **18**(5) 382–395.

Laursen, K. 2002. The importance of sectoral differences in the application of complementary HRM practices for innovation performance. *Internat. J. Econom. Bus.* **9**(1) 139–156.

Lawrence, P. R., J. W. Lorsch. 1968. *Organization and Environment: Managing Differentiation and Integration.* Graduate School of Business Administration, Harvard University, Boston.

Leana, C. R., F. Pil. 2006. Social capital and organizational performance: Evidence from urban public schools. *Organ. Sci.* **17**(3) 353–366.

Leana, C. R., H. J. Van Buren. 1999. Organizational social capital and employment practices. *Acad. Management Rev.* **24** 538–555.

Levin, D. Z., R. Cross. 2004. The strength of weak ties you can trust: The mediating role of trust in effective knowledge transfer. *Management Sci.* **50**(11) 1477–1490.

Locke, E., G. Latham. 1990. *A Theory of Goal Setting and Task Performance.* Prentice, Englewood, NJ.

Luft, H. S. 1990. *Hospital Volume, Physician Volume and Patient Outcomes: Assessing the Evidence.* Health Administration Press, Ann Arbor, MI.

MacDuffie, J. 1995. Human resource bundles and manufacturing performance: Organizational logic and flexible production systems in the world auto industry. *Indust. Labor Rel. Rev* **48** 173–188.

MacKinnon, D. P., C. M. Lockwood. J. M. Hoffman, S. G. West, V. Sheets. 2002. A comparison of methods to test mediation and other intervening variable effects. *Psych. Methods* **7** 83–104.

MacMillan, I. C., L. Zemann, P. N. Subhanarasimha. 1987. Criteria distinguishing successful from unsuccessful ventures in the venture screening process. *J. Bus. Venturing* **2** 123–138.

Malone, T., K. Crowston. 1994. The interdisciplinary study of coordination. *Comput. Surveys* **26**(1) 87–119.

Mangrum, F. G., M. S. Fairley, D. Weider. 2001. Informal problem-solving in the technology-mediated workplace. *J. Bus. Comm.* **38**(3) 315–336.

Mareschal, P. M. 2003. Solving problems and transforming relationships: The bifocal approach to mediation. *Amer. Rev. Public Admin.* **33**(4) 423–449.

March, J. G., H. A. Simon. 1958. *Organizations.* Wiley, New York.

Medicare Cost Reports. 2006. Cleverley Associates, Worthington, OH, http://www.cleverleyassociates.com.

Meyerson, D., K. E. Weick, R. Kramer. 1996. Swift trust and temporary groups. R. Kramer, T. R. Tyler, eds. *Trust in Organizations: Frontiers of Theory and Research.* Sage Publications, Thousand Oaks, CA, 166–195.

Mohrman, S. A. 1993. Integrating roles and structure in the lateral organization. J. R. Galbraith, E. E. Lawler, III, eds. *Organizing for the Future: The New Logic for Managing Complex Organizations.* Jossey-Bass, San Francisco, 109–141.

Nahapiet, J., S. Ghoshal. 1998. Social capital, intellectual capital and the organizational advantage. *Acad. Management Rev.* **232** 242–266.

Nohria, N., R. G. Eccles. 1992. Face-to-face: Making network organizations work. N. Nohria, R. G. Eccles, eds. *Networks and Organizations.* Harvard Business School Press, Boston.

Osterman, P. 1988. *Employment Futures.* Oxford University Press, New York.

Pelled, L. H., K. M. Eisenhardt, K. R. Xin. 1999. Exploring the black box: An analysis of work group diversity, conflict and performance. *Admin. Sci. Quart.* **44** 1–28.

Piore, M. 1993. The social embeddedness of labor markets and cognitive processes. *Labour* **7**(3) 3–18.

Ramsey, H., D. Scholarios, B. Harley. 2000. Employees and high-performance work systems: Testing inside the black box. *British J. Indust. Rel.* **38** 501–532.

Raudenbush, S. W., A. S. Bryk. 1992. *Hierarchical Linear Models: Applications and Data Analysis Methods.* Sage Publications, Newbury Park, CA.

Richard, O. C., N. B. Johnson. 2004. High performance work practices and human resource management effectiveness: Substitutes or complements? *J. Bus. Strat.* **21**(2) 133–148.

Rohrer, J. E., J. Wilkinson. 2008. Physical limitations and perceived quality of care among family medicine patients. *Clinical Rehab.* **22** 283–287.

Rousseau, D. M. 1995. *Psychological Contracts in Organizations: Understanding Written and Unwritten Agreements.* Sage Publications, Thousand Oaks, CA.

Shortell, S. M, J. E. Zimmerman, D. M. Rousseau, R. R. Gillies, D. P. Wagner, E. A. Draper, W A. Knaus, J. Duffy. 1994. The performance of intensive care units: Does good management make a difference? *Medical Care* **32**(5) 508–525.

Smith, K. G., C. J. Collins, K. D. Clark. 2005. Existing knowledge, knowledge creation capability, and the rate of new product introduction in high-technology firms. *Acad. Management J.* **48**(2) 346–357.

Snell, S. A., J. W Dean. 1992. Integrated manufacturing and human resource management: A human capital perspective. *Acad. Management J.* **35** 467–504.

Stewart, A. L., R. D. Hays, J. E. Ware, Jr. 1988. The MOS short-form general health survey: Reliability and validity in a patient population. *Medical Care* **26**(7) 724–735.

Thompson, J. D. 1967. *Organizations in Action.* McGraw-Hill, New York.

Tsai, W., S. Ghoshal. 1998. Social capital and value creation: The role of intrafirm networks. *Acad. Management J.* **41** 464–476.

Tsui, A. S., J. L. Pearce, L. V. Porter, Tripoli. 1997. Alternative approaches to the employee-organization relationship: Does investment in employees pay off? *Acad. Management J.* **40**(5) 1089–1121.

Tyebjee, T. T., A. V. Bruno. 1984. A model of venture capitalist investment activity. *Management Sci.* **30** 1051–1066.

Vogus, T. 2006. What is it about relationships? A behavioral theory of social capital and performance. *Labor Emp. Rel. Proc.* **58** 164–173.

Wageman, R., G. Baker. 1997. Incentives and cooperation: The joint effects of task and reward interdependence on group performance. *J. Organ. Behav.* **8**(2) 139–158.

Walton, R., J. Dutton. 1967. The management of interdepartmental conflict: A model and review. *Admin. Sci. Quart.* **14**(1) 73–83.

Ware, J. E., R. D. Hays. 1988. Methods for measuring patient satisfaction. *Medical Care* **26**(4) 393–402.

Weick, K. E., K. Roberts. 1993. Collective mind in organizations: Heedful interrelating on flight decks. *Admin. Sci. Quart.* **38** 357–381.

West, M., C. Borrill, J. Dawson, J. Scully, M. Carter, S. Anelay, M. Patterson, J. Waring. 2002. The link between the management of employees and patient mortality in acute hospitals. *Internat. J. Human Resource Management* **13** 1299–1311.

Whitener, E. M. 2001. Do "high commitment" human resource practices affect employee commitment? A cross-level analysis using hierarchical linear modeling. *J. Management* **27**(5) 515–535.

Wright, P. M., T. M. Gardner, L. Moynihan. 2006. Impact of HR practices on the performance of business units. *Human Resource Management J.* **13**(3) 21–36.

Youndt, M. A., S. Snell, J. W. Dean, Jr., D. P. Lepak. 1996. Human resource management, manufacturing strategy, and firm performance. *Acad. Management J.* **39**(4) 836–866.

Young, G., M. Meterko, K. Desai. 2000. Patient satisfaction with hospital care. *Medical Care* **38**(3) 325–334.

Zenger, T. R., W. S. Hesterly. 1997. The disaggregation of corporations: Selective intervention, high-powered incentives, and molecular units. *Organ. Sci.* **8**(3) 209–222.

SOURCE: Gittell, Jody Hoffer, Rob Seidner, and Julian Wimbush. 2010. "A Relational Model of How High-Performance Work Systems Work." *Organization Science*, 21(2):490–506.

PART IV

Autonomy and Control

An Introduction to Autonomy and Control

Control can be described as alignment among organizational participants. In the bureaucratic organizational form, control is achieved through hierarchy or more specifically through "hierarchy without domination" or "legitimate domination," meaning that a realm of autonomy exists within the confines of a worker's job description, protected by formal rules from domination (Weber [1924] 1978). According to Weber, this characteristic of the bureaucratic organizational form distinguishes it from the despotic organizational form in which leaders have the ability to dominate their subordinates more or less absolutely due to the lack of protection from formal rules and procedures. More recent theories of "street-level bureaucracy" support the notion that frontline workers in bureaucratic organizations have a realm of autonomy within the confines of their job descriptions, though one could argue that their effective use of this autonomy is limited by their lack of understanding of the whole due to their position in the hierarchy and in the division of labor. This realm of autonomy enables proactive behaviors such as actions taken on behalf of the customer (despite the inconsistency of individualized treatment with bureaucratic principles), as well as defensive behaviors such as blaming, territorialism, and the withholding of work effort.

In his treatise on scientific management, excerpted in this section, Frederick Winslow Taylor (1911) reacts against this realm of autonomy, arguing that it leads to "soldiering" or the withholding of work effort by workers. While Karl Marx (1886) argues that the withholding of work effort is the expected response to a fundamental conflict of interest between workers and their managers, Taylor argues that this conflict of interest is "a fallacious idea." Workers "still firmly believe, as their fathers did before them, that it is against their best interests for each man to turn out each day as much work as possible. Under this fallacious idea a large proportion of the workmen of both countries each day deliberately work slowly so as to curtail the output" (Taylor 1911:17). The withholding of work effort is further enabled by managers' lack of knowledge of the work process: "It is the *ignorance of employers* as to the proper time in which work of various kinds should be done [that] makes it for the interest of the workman to 'soldier'" (Taylor 1911:18, emphasis in original). A third reason for soldiering, he argues, is the workers' own lack of knowledge about how to best accomplish the work. Taylor (1911) thus argues for a scientific approach to the work process, with improved knowledge of how best to accomplish work but with this knowledge held by managers rather than workers:

> To work according to scientific laws, the management must take over and perform much of the work which is now left to the men; almost every act of the workman should be preceded by one or more preparatory acts of the management which enable him to do his work better and quicker than he otherwise could. (P. 26)

Michael Lipsky's (1980) theory of street-level bureaucracy supports the idea that frontline workers in bureaucratic organizations do indeed have a realm of autonomy granting them some discretion within the confines of their job descriptions. This realm of autonomy can be used for nonsanctioned behaviors such as the withholding of work effort or "soldiering," consistent with Taylor's (1911) observations. It can also be used for nonsanctioned behaviors such as actions taken on behalf of particular clients—nonsanctioned due to the inconsistency of individualized treatment with bureaucratic principles. In either case, effective use of this autonomy is limited by workers' lack of understanding of the whole due to their subordinate position in the hierarchy and their narrow role in the division of labor.

In a series of lectures given in the 1920s, Mary Parker Follett (1949c) provides a contrasting perspective on control, arguing that organizations should seek control that is not coercive but rather "a coordinating of all functions, that is, a collective self-control" (p. 89). To achieve this collective self-control requires a form of leadership that is shared or distributed throughout the organization rather than concentrated in a few positions. Follett (1949b) observes some organizations in which "we find responsibility for management shot all through a business [and] some degree of authority all along the line [such that] leadership can be exercised by many people besides the top executive" (p. 61). The best approach, she argues, is not to vest authority in one person over another based on his or her position in the hierarchy, but rather to recognize authority in each position based on the knowledge associated with it—and, more important, to vest each person with the knowledge of how the work is done and how his or her work connects to the whole. She quotes the president of a company as saying,

> The kind of management we are aiming at is management with authority all down the line, as contrasted with management by edict from a central source. We are trying to teach our men what their jobs are, what the underlying principles of these jobs are, and then we are trying to get them to exercise the authority of their job with the idea that they shall use their brains, their discretion, having in mind these fundamental principles. We teach people what their job is, and then insist that they shall exercise the authority and responsibility which goes with that job instead of relying on the fellow above them. (Follett 1949a:40)

Follett's (1949a) notion of shared control stands in stark contrast to Taylor's (1911) call to shrink the realm of autonomy of the worker by vesting managers rather than workers with knowledge of the underlying principles of the work. While Taylor's approach places scientific systems knowledge in the hands of managers to the exclusion of workers, Follett's approach aims to place that knowledge into the hands of all participants.

Consistent with Follett's (1949a) view of workers, Douglas McGregor (1960) proposed Theory Y of human behavior in contrast to the dominant Theory X, in a chapter included in this section. Theory X assumes that work is a disutility, that shirking is to be expected, and that the job of management is therefore to elicit work effort from recalcitrant workers. Theory Y assumes instead that work is a self-rewarding human activity and that the job of management is to provide the conditions that enable work to be experienced as intrinsically motivating. McGregor (1960) argues that "the capacity to exercise a relatively high degree of imagination, ingenuity and creativity in the solution of organizational problems is widely, not narrowly, distributed in the population [but] under the conditions of modern industrial life, the intellectual potentialities of the average human being are only partially utilized" (pp. 47–48). The primary way to enact Theory Y, according to McGregor (1960), is to rely on integration and self-control rather than on external direction and control:

> The principle of integration demands that both the organization's and the individual's needs be recognized . . . The assumptions of Theory Y imply that unless integration is achieved the organization will suffer. The objectives of the organization are not achieved best by the unilateral administration of promotions, because this form of management by direction and control will not create the commitment which would make available the full resources of those affected. The lesser motivation, the lesser resulting degree of self-direction and self-control, will more than offset the gains obtained by unilateral decisions "for the good of the organization." (Pp. 51–52)

Furthermore this relational approach to control requires supervisors to spend more time engaging in discussions with workers about the goals of the organization, and about the best ways to achieve those goals, suggesting that getting rid of supervisors is an overly simplistic and even counterproductive way to achieve the goal of worker empowerment (Gittell 2001).

Contemporary economic theorists continue to hold the assumptions associated with Theory X, namely that work is a disutility and that shirking is to be expected. In their view, hierarchy is often the most efficient organizational design, due to its ability to solve the problem of control in an efficient way (e.g., Jensen and Meckling 1976; Williamson 1985). According to the dominant principal/agent theory of the firm, incentives must be aligned so as to avoid shirking and malfeasance not only by workers but also by managers against the interests of owners. These theorists represent a rationalist perspective on control. Representing the conflict perspective on control, neo-Weberian and neo-Marxist theorists have also accepted Theory X, not as fundamental to human nature but rather as an expected outgrowth of the conflict of interest between workers and managers (Edwards 1979; Gouldner 1954; Merton 1957; Stone 1976). They see bureaucracy as designed to divide and conquer a hostile workforce that, if allowed to collaborate, would collaborate against the interests of the firm's owners, perhaps by sabotaging production and demanding a greater share of the proceeds. Bureaucracy in effect sacrifices the gains from horizontal coordination in order to keep workers in a weakened position.

Masahiko Aoki (1990), along with other organizational economists (Leibenstein 1987; Milgrom and Roberts 1992), recognizes and attempts to address the apparent trade-off between vertical control and horizontal coordination. Based on his observation of management practices in Japanese firms, Aoki (1990) argues in an article included in this section that this apparent trade-off, taken for granted by the principal/agent theory of the firm, can be overcome by achieving vertical control in a way that is consistent with horizontal coordination:

> Comparatively speaking, Japanese firms tend to be less hierarchical in the coordination mode, while they rely upon rank hierarchies in their incentive system . . . In the Japanese firm,

management may feel secure in delegating tasks of coordination to lower levels where relevant on-site information is available, because employees are aware that they are being evaluated by their own long term contribution to organizational goals. Thus they are induced to comply with management authority without explicitly hierarchical direction over daily operation . . . *Organizational goals themselves may need to be adjusted in response to employees' voices.* In this way, a sense of joint effort is created so that employees' active cooperation in horizontal coordination may be elicited. This amounts to a set of mutual vertical commitments in which management recognizes the interests of employees and, in return, employees exert greater effort. Internal promotion and the representation of employee interests in top management decisions are important aspects of a system of vertical control which does not undermine horizontal coordination. (P. 14, emphasis added)

Rather than dividing and conquering the workforce, keeping workers focused on their own isolated tasks, the alternative is to make mutual vertical commitments with workers, thus enabling managers to foster shared knowledge and direct horizontal coordination among workers without fear that workers will use this knowledge to sabotage production, though they may demand a greater share of the proceeds. In effect, Aoki (1990) suggests that the solution is to achieve worker commitment to the organization's goals by recognizing the interests of workers, consistent with the principle of control through integration proposed by McGregor (1960). Both McGregor's and Aoki's solutions are consistent with, though perhaps not as radical and far-reaching as, Follett's (1949a) proposal to distribute leadership throughout the organization, enabling coordination and control to be exercised by each organizational participant based on the knowledge associated with his or her own job, and the knowledge of how that job contributes to the larger whole.

These ideas have been further developed by subsequent organizational theorists. Some have explored the organizational conditions for achieving worker participation. In an article excerpted in this section, Rosemary Batt (1999) compares Tayloristic work practices with participatory, high-involvement work practices, and assesses the performance outcomes associated with these different ways of organizing work. Jay Carson, Paul Tesluk, and Jennifer Marrone (2007) explore the role of supervisory support and a shared sense of purpose for achieving widespread participation among team members, and the associated performance benefits. Others have explored leadership behaviors that are conducive to achieving empowerment in others. Typically contrasted with directive or autocratic leadership, empowering leadership behaviors have been given different labels over the years, including *democratic leadership*, *participatory leadership*, and *transformational leadership* (Denhardt and Campbell 2006). A common insight is that leadership is a form of social influence that can be exercised by anyone regardless of formal position, and that can be used either to inhibit or to inspire leadership behaviors in others. Another common insight is that formal leaders are most effective when they can inspire others to engage in the responsibilities of leadership, rather than attempting to carry out all leadership responsibilities on their own.

Leaders can also exercise relational control by seeking to build connections among others based on a common set of goals. According to Jean Lipman-Blumen (1992),

Connective leadership derives its label from its character of connecting individuals not only to their own tasks and ego drives, but also to those of the group and community that depend upon the accomplishment of mutual goals. It is leadership that connects individuals to others and to others' goals, using a broad spectrum of behavioral strategies. It is leadership that "proceeds from a premise of connection" (Gilligan, 1982) and a recognition of networks of relationships that bind society in a web of mutual responsibilities. It shares responsibilities, takes unthreatened pride in the accomplishments of colleagues and protégés, and experiences success without the compulsion to outdo others. (P. 184)

In an article excerpted for this section, Lipman-Blumen (1992) argues that connective leadership comes more naturally to women because they are socialized from an early age to take responsibility for creating and maintaining connection among others. Consistent with this argument, Joyce Fletcher (1999) shows that women are more likely to engage in relational practices in the workplace. She also shows that although these relational practices are instrumental for achieving desired outcomes, they are often "disappeared" and unrecognized while the individual heroic efforts (more often performed by men) that are less conducive to achieving desired outcomes are rewarded instead. We conclude this section with an article by Patrick Sweeney, Vaida Thompson, and Hart Blanton (2009), which explores relational leadership behaviors in a male-dominated military context, inviting a debate about whether leadership behaviors are associated with gender—or not.

QUESTIONS FOR DISCUSSION

1. Describe the differences between a relational and bureaucratic approach to control. What are the advantages and disadvantages of each approach?
2. How do organizations influence the way that control is carried out? How do individuals and their backgrounds influence the way that control is carried out? How does the larger society influence the way that control is carried out?
3. In your experience, are women more likely to take a relational approach to control, relative to men? Explain what you have observed, and provide a theoretical explanation.

SUGGESTIONS FOR FURTHER READING

Battistelli, Fabrizio and Giuseppe Ricotta. 2005. "The Rhetoric of Management Control in Italian Cities: Constructing New Meanings of Public Action." *Administration & Society,* 36:661–87.

Herbst, P. G. 1976. "Non-Hierarchical Forms of Organization." *Acta Sociologica,* 19(1):65–75.

Spreitzer, Gretchen, Suzanne C. de Janasz, and Robert E. Quinn. 1999. "Empowered to Lead: The Role of Psychological Control in Leadership." *Journal of Organizational Behavior,* 20:511–26.

REFERENCES

Aoki, Masahiko. 1990. "Toward an Economic Model of the Japanese Firm." *Journal of Economic Literature,* 28:1–27.

Batt, Rosemary. 1999. "Work Organization, Technology and Performance in Customer Service and Sales." *Industrial and Labor Relations Review,* 52:539–64.

Carson, J. B., Paul E. Tesluk, and Jennifer A. Marrone. 2007. "Shared Leadership in Teams: An Investigation of Antecedent Conditions and Performance." *Academy of Management Journal,* 50(5):1217–34.

Denhardt, Janet B. and Kelly B. Campbell. 2006. "The Role of Democratic Values in Transformational Leadership." *Administration & Society,* 38:556–72.

Edwards, Richard. 1979. *Contested Terrain: The Transformation of the Workplace in the Twentieth Century.* New York: Basic Books.

Fletcher, Joyce. 1999. *Disappearing Acts: Gender, Power, and Relational Practice at Work.* Cambridge, MA: MIT Press.

Follett, Mary Parker. 1949a. "The Basis of Authority." Pp. 34–46 in *Freedom and Co-ordination: Lectures in Business Organization by Mary Parker Follett,* edited by L. Urwick. London: Management Publications Trust, Ltd.

———. 1949b. "Coordination." Pp. 61–76 in *Freedom and Co-ordination: Lectures in Business Organization by Mary Parker Follett,* edited by L. Urwick. London: Management Publications Trust, Ltd.

———. 1949c. "The Process of Control." Pp. 77–89 in *Freedom and Co-ordination: Lectures in Business Organization by Mary Parker Follett,* edited by L. Urwick. London: Management Publications Trust, Ltd.

Gilligan, Carol. 1982. *In a Different Voice: Psychological Theory and Women's Development.* Cambridge, MA: Harvard University Press.

Gittell, J. H. 2001. "Supervisory Span, Relational Coordination and Flight Departure Performance: A Reassessment of Post-Bureaucracy Theory." *Organization Science,* 12(4):467–82.

Gouldner, Abner. 1954. *Patterns of Industrial Bureaucracy.* Glencoe, IL: Free Press.

Jensen, Michael and William Meckling. 1976. "Theory of the Firm: Managerial Behavior, Agency Costs and Ownership Structure." *Journal of Financial Economics,* 3(4):305–60.

Leibenstein, Harvey. 1987. *Inside the Firm: The Inefficiencies of Hierarchy.* Boston: Harvard University Press.

Lipman-Blumen, Jean. 1992. "Connective Leadership: Female Leadership Styles in the 21st Century Workplace." *Sociological Perspectives,* 35(1):183–203.

Lipsky, M. 1980. *Street-Level Bureaucracy: Dilemmas of the Individual in Public Service.* New York: Russell Sage Foundation.

Marx, Karl. 1886. *Capital: A Critique of Political Economy.* New York: International Publishers.

McGregor, Douglas. 1960. *The Human Side of Enterprise.* New York: McGraw-Hill.

Merton, Robert. 1957. *Social Theory and Social Structure.* Glencoe, IL: Free Press.

Milgrom, Paul and John Roberts. 1992. *Economics, Organization and Management.* Englewood Cliffs, NJ: Prentice Hall.

Stone, Katherine. 1976. "The Origins of Job Structure in the Steel Industry." *Review of Radical Political Economy,* 6(2):113–73.

Sweeney, Patrick, Vaida Thompson, and Hart Blanton. 2009. "Trust and Influence in Combat: An Interdependence Model." *Journal of Applied Social Psychology,* 39(1):235–64.

Taylor, Frederick Winslow. 1911. *Scientific Management.* New York: Harper and Row.

Weber, Max. [1924] 1978. "Bureaucracy." Pp. 956–1005 in *Economy and Society: An Outline of Interpretive Sociology.* Volume 2. Berkeley: University of California Press.

Williamson, Oliver. 1985. *The Economic Institutions of Capitalism.* New York: Free Press.

22

FUNDAMENTALS OF SCIENTIFIC MANAGEMENT

FREDERICK WINSLOW TAYLOR

The principal object of management should be to secure the maximum prosperity for the employer, coupled with the maximum prosperity for each employé.

The words "maximum prosperity" are used, in their broad sense, to mean not only large dividends for the company or owner, but the development of every branch of the business to its highest state of excellence, so that the prosperity may be permanent.

In the same way maximum prosperity for each employé means not only higher wages than are usually received by men of his class, but, of more importance still, it also means the development of each man to his state of maximum efficiency, so that he may be able to do, generally speaking, the highest grade of work for which his natural abilities fit him, and it further means giving him, when possible, this class of work to do.

It would seem to be so self-evident that maximum prosperity for the employer, coupled with maximum prosperity for the employé, ought to be the two leading objects of management, that even to state this fact should be unnecessary. And yet there is no question that, throughout the industrial world, a large part of the organization of employers, as well as employés, is for war rather than for peace, and that perhaps the majority on either side do not believe that it is possible so to arrange their mutual relations that their interests become identical.

The majority of these men believe that the fundamental interests of employés and employers are necessarily antagonistic. Scientific management, on the contrary, has for its very foundation the firm conviction that the true interests of the two are one and the same; that prosperity for the employer cannot exist through a long term of years unless it is accompanied by prosperity for the employé, and *vice versa;* and that it is possible to give the workman what he most wants—high wages—and the employer what he wants—a low labor cost—for his manufactures.

It is hoped that some at least of those who do not sympathize with each of these objects may be led to modify their views; that some employers, whose attitude toward their workmen has been that of trying to get the largest amount of work out of them for the smallest possible wages, may be led to see that a more liberal policy toward their men will pay them better; and that some of those workmen who begrudge a fair and even a large profit to their employers, and who feel that all of the fruits of their labor should belong to them, and that those for whom they work and the capital invested in the business are entitled to little or nothing, may be led to modify these views.

No one can be found who will deny that in the case of any single individual the greatest prosperity can exist only when that individual has reached his highest state of efficiency; that is, when he is turning out his largest daily output.

The truth of this fact is also perfectly clear in the case of two men working together. To illustrate: if you and your workman have become so skilful that you and he together are making two pairs of shoes in a day, while your competitor and his workman are making only one pair, it is clear that after selling your two pairs of shoes you can pay your workman much higher wages than your competitor who produces only one pair of shoes is able to pay his man, and that there will still be enough money left over for you to have a larger profit than your competitor.

In the case of a more complicated manufacturing establishment, it should also be perfectly clear that the greatest permanent prosperity for the workman, coupled with the greatest prosperity for the employer, can be brought about only when the work of the establishment is done with the smallest combined expenditure of human effort, plus nature's resources, plus the cost for the use of capital in the shape of machines, buildings, etc. Or, to state the same thing in a different way: that the greatest prosperity can exist only as the result of the greatest possible productivity of the men and machines of the establishment—that is, when each man and each machine are turning out the largest possible output; because unless your men and your machines are daily turning out more work than others around you, it is clear that competition will prevent your paying higher wages to your workmen than are paid to those of your competitor. And what is true as to the possibility of paying high wages in the case of two companies competing close beside one another is also true as to whole districts of the country and even as to nations which are in competition. In a word, that maximum prosperity can exist only as the result of maximum productivity. Later in this paper illustrations will be given of several companies which are earning large dividends and at the same time paying from 30 per cent, to 100 per cent, higher wages to their men than are paid to similar men immediately around them, and with whose employers they are in competition. These illustrations will cover different types of work, from the most elementary to the most complicated.

If the above reasoning is correct, it follows that the most important object of both the workmen and the management should be the training and development of each individual in the establishment, so that he can do (at his fastest pace and with the maximum of efficiency) the highest class of work for which his natural abilities fit him.

These principles appear to be so self-evident that many men may think it almost childish to state them. Let us, however, turn to the facts, as they actually exist in this country and in England. The English and American peoples are the greatest sportsmen in the world. Whenever an American workman plays baseball, or an English workman plays cricket, it is safe to say that he strains every nerve to secure victory for his side. He does his very best to make the largest possible number of runs. The universal sentiment is so strong that any man who fails to give out all there is in him in sport is branded as a "quitter," and treated with contempt by those who are around him.

When the same workman returns to work on the following day, instead of using every effort to turn out the largest possible amount of work, in a majority of the cases this man deliberately plans to do as little as he safely can—to turn out far less work than he is well able to do—in many instances to do not more than one-third to one-half of a proper day's work. And in fact if he were to do his best to turn out his largest possible day's work, he would be abused by his fellow-workers for so doing, even more than if he had proved himself a "quitter" in sport. Underworking, that is, deliberately working slowly so as to avoid doing a full day's work, "soldiering," as it is called in this country, "hanging it out," as it is called in England, "ca canae," as it is called in Scotland, is almost universal in industrial establishments, and prevails also to a large extent in the building trades; and the writer asserts without fear of contradiction that this constitutes the greatest evil with which the working-people of both England and America are now afflicted.

It will be shown later in this paper that doing away with slow working and "soldiering" in all its forms and so arranging the relations between employer and employé that each workman will work to his very best advantage and at his best speed, accompanied by the intimate cooperation with the management and the help (which the workman should receive) from the management, would result on the average in nearly doubling the output of each man and each machine. What other reforms, among those which are being discussed by these two nations, could do as much toward promoting prosperity, toward the diminution of poverty, and the alleviation of suffering? America and England have been recently agitated over such subjects as the tariff, the control of the large corporations on the one hand, and of hereditary power on the other hand, and over various more or less socialistic proposals for taxation, etc. On these subjects both peoples have been profoundly stirred, and yet hardly a voice has been raised to call attention to this vastly greater and more important subject of "soldiering," which directly and powerfully affects the wages, the prosperity, and the life of almost every working-man, and also quite as much the prosperity of every industrial establishment in the nation.

The elimination of "soldiering" and of the several causes of slow working would so lower the cost of production that both our home and foreign markets would be greatly enlarged, and we could compete on more than even terms with our rivals. It would remove one of the fundamental causes for dull times, for lack of employment, and for poverty, and therefore would have a more permanent and far-reaching effect upon these misfortunes than any of the curative remedies that are now being used to soften their consequences. It would insure higher wages and make shorter working hours and better working and home conditions possible.

Why is it, then, in the face of the self-evident fact that maximum prosperity can exist only as the result of the determined effort of each workman to turn out each day his largest possible day's work, that the great majority of our men are deliberately doing just the opposite, and that even when the men have the best of intentions their work is in most cases far from efficient?

There are three causes for this condition, which may be briefly summarized as:

First. The fallacy, which has from time immemorial been almost universal among workmen, that a material increase in the output of each man or each machine in the trade would result in the end in throwing a large number of men out of work.

Second. The defective systems of management which are in common use, and which make it necessary for each workman to soldier, or work slowly, in order that he may protect his own best interests.

Third. The inefficient rule-of-thumb methods, which are still almost universal in all trades, and in practising which our workmen waste a large part of their effort.

This paper will attempt to show the enormous gains which would result from the substitution by our workmen of scientific for rule-of-thumb methods.

To explain a little more fully these three causes:

First. The great majority of workmen still believe that if they were to work at their best speed they would be doing a great injustice to the whole trade by throwing a lot of men out of work, and yet the history of the development of each trade shows that each improvement, whether it be the invention of a new machine or the introduction of a better method, which results in increasing the productive capacity of the men in the trade and cheapening the costs, instead of throwing men out of work make in the end work for more men.

The cheapening of any article in common use almost immediately results in a largely increased demand for that article. Take the case of shoes, for instance. The introduction of machinery for doing every element of the work which was formerly done by hand has resulted in making shoes at a fraction of their former labor cost, and in selling them so cheap that now almost every man, woman, and child in the working-classes buys one or two pairs of shoes per year, and wears shoes all the time, whereas formerly each workman bought perhaps one pair of shoes every five years, and went barefoot most of the time, wearing shoes only as a luxury or as a matter of the sternest necessity. In spite of the enormously increased output of shoes per workman, which has come with shoe machinery, the demand for shoes has so increased that there are relatively more men working in the shoe industry now than ever before.

The workmen in almost every trade have before them an object lesson of this kind, and yet, because they are ignorant of the history of their own trade even, they still firmly believe, as their fathers did before them, that it is against their best interests for each man to turn out each day as much work as possible.

Under this fallacious idea a large proportion of the workmen of both countries each day deliberately work slowly so as to curtail the output. Almost every labor union has made, or is contemplating making, rules which have for their object curtailing the output of their members, and those men who have the greatest influence with the working-people, the labor leaders as well as many people with philanthropic feelings who are helping them, are daily spreading this fallacy and at the same time telling them that they are overworked.

A great deal has been and is being constantly said about "sweat-shop" work and conditions. The writer has great sympathy with those who are overworked, but on the whole a greater sympathy for those who are *under paid.* For every individual, however, who is overworked, there are a hundred who intentionally underwork—greatly underwork—every day of their lives, and who for this reason deliberately aid in establishing those conditions which in the end inevitably result in low wages. And yet hardly a single voice is being raised in an endeavor to correct this evil.

As engineers and managers, we are more intimately acquainted with these facts than any other class in the community, and are therefore best fitted to lead in a movement to combat this fallacious idea by educating not only the workmen but the whole of the country as to the true facts. And yet we are practically doing nothing in this direction, and are leaving this field entirely in the hands of the labor agitators (many of whom are misinformed and misguided), and of sentimentalists who are ignorant as to actual working conditions.

Second. As to the second cause for soldiering— the relations which exist between employers and employés under almost all of the systems of management which are in common use—it is impossible in a few words to make it clear to one not familiar with this problem why it is that the *ignorance of employers* as to the proper time in which work of various kinds should be done makes it for the interest of the workman to "soldier."

The writer therefore quotes herewith from a paper read before The American Society of Mechanical Engineers, in June, 1903, entitled "Shop Management," which it is hoped will explain fully this cause for soldiering:

"This loafing or soldiering proceeds from two causes. First, from the natural instinct and tendency of men to take it easy, which may be called natural soldiering. Second, from more intricate second thought and reasoning caused by their relations with other men, which may be called systematic soldiering.

"There is no question that the tendency of the average man (in all walks of life) is toward working at a slow, easy gait, and that it is only after a good deal of thought and observation on his part or as a result of example, conscience, or external pressure that he takes a more rapid pace.

"There are, of course, men of unusual energy, vitality, and ambition who naturally choose the fastest gait, who set up their own standards, and who work hard, even though it may be against their best interests. But these few uncommon men only serve by forming a contrast to emphasize the tendency of the average.

"This common tendency to 'take it easy' is greatly increased by bringing a number of men together on similar work and at a uniform standard rate of pay by the day.

"Under this plan the better men gradually but surely slow down their gait to that of the poorest and least efficient. When a naturally energetic man works for a few days beside a lazy one, the logic of the situation is unanswerable. 'Why should I work hard when that lazy fellow gets the same pay that I do and does only half as much work?'

"A careful time study of men working under these conditions will disclose facts which are ludicrous as well as pitiable.

"To illustrate: The writer has timed a naturally energetic workman who, while going and coming from work, would walk at a speed of from three to four miles per hour, and not infrequently trot home after a day's work. On arriving at his work he would immediately slow down to a speed of about one mile an hour. When, for example, wheeling a loaded wheelbarrow, he would go at a good fast pace even up hill in order to be as short a time as possible under load, and immediately on the return walk slow down to a mile an hour, improving every opportunity for delay short of actually sitting down. In order to be sure not to do more than his lazy neighbor, he would actually tire himself in his employer, who, when his attention was called to this state of things, answered: 'Well, I can keep them from sitting down, but the devil can't make them get a move on while they are at work.'

"The natural laziness of men is serious, but by far the greatest evil from which both workmen and employers are suffering is the *systematic soldiering* which is almost universal under all of the ordinary schemes of management and which results from a careful study on the part of the workmen of what will promote their best interests.

"The writer was much interested recently in hearing one small but experienced golf caddy boy of twelve explaining to a green caddy, who had shown special energy and interest, the necessity of going slow and lagging behind his man when he came up to the ball, showing him that since they were paid by the hour, the faster they went the less money they got, and finally telling him that if he went too fast the other boys would give him a licking.

"This represents a type of *systematic soldiering* which is not, however, very serious, since it is done with the knowledge of the employer, who can quite easily break it up if he wishes.

"The greater part of the *systematic soldiering*, however, is done by the men with the deliberate object of keeping their employers ignorant of how fast work can be done.

"So universal is soldiering for this purpose that hardly a competent workman can be found in a large establishment, whether he works by the day or on piece work, contract work, or under any of the ordinary systems, who does not devote a considerable part of his time to studying just how slow he can work and still convince his employer that he is going at a good pace.

"The causes for this are, briefly, that practically all employers determine upon a maximum sum which they feel it is right for each of their classes of employees to earn per day, whether their men work by the day or piece.

"Each workman soon finds out about what this figure is for his particular case, and he also realizes that when his employer is convinced that a man is capable of doing more work than he has done, he will find sooner or later some way of compelling him to do it with little or no increase of pay.

"Employers derive their knowledge of how much of a given class of work can be done in a day from either their own experience, which has frequently grown hazy with age, from casual and unsystematic observation of their men, or at best from records which are kept, showing the quickest time in which each job has been done. In many cases the employer will feel almost certain that a given job can be done faster than it has been, but he rarely cares to take the drastic measures necessary to force men to do it in the quickest time, unless he has an actual record proving conclusively how fast the work can be done.

"It evidently becomes for each man's interest, then, to see that no job is done faster than it has been in the past. The younger and less experienced men are taught this by their elders, and all possible persuasion and social pressure is brought to bear upon the greedy and selfish men to keep them from making new records which result in temporarily increasing their wages, while all those who come after them are made to work harder for the same old pay.

"Under the best day work of the ordinary type, when accurate records are kept of the amount of work done by each man and of his efficiency, and when each man's wages are raised as he improves, and those who fail to rise to a certain standard are discharged and a fresh supply of carefully selected men are given work in their places, both the natural loafing and systematic soldiering can be largely broken up. This can only be done, however, when the men are thoroughly convinced that there is no intention of establishing piece work even in the remote future, and it is next to impossible to make men believe this when the work is of such a nature that they believe piece work to be practicable. In most cases their fear of making a record which will be used as a basis for piece work will cause them to soldier as much as they dare.

"It is, however, under piece work that the art of systematic soldiering is thoroughly developed; after a workman has had the price per piece of the work he is doing lowered two or three times as a result of his having worked harder and increased his output, he is likely entirely to lose sight of his employer's side of the case and become imbued with a grim determination to have no more cuts if soldiering can prevent it. Unfortunately for the character of the workman, soldiering involves a deliberate attempt to mislead and deceive his employer, and thus upright and straightforward workmen are compelled to become more or less hypocritical. The employer is soon looked upon as an antagonist, if not an enemy, and the mutual confidence which should exist between a leader and his men, the enthusiasm, the feeling that they are all working for the same end and will share in the results is entirely lacking.

"The feeling of antagonism under the ordinary piece-work system becomes in many cases so marked on the part of the men that any proposition made by their employers, however reasonable, is looked upon with suspicion, and soldiering becomes such a fixed habit that men will frequently take pains to restrict the product of machines which they are running when even a large increase in output would involve no more work on their part."

Third. As to the third cause for slow work, considerable space will later in this paper be devoted to illustrating the great gain, both to employers and employés, which results from the substitution of scientific for rule-of-thumb methods in even the smallest details of the work of every trade. The enormous saving of time and therefore increase in the output which it is possible to effect through eliminating unnecessary motions and substituting fast for slow and inefficient motions for the men working in any of our trades can be fully realized only after one has personally seen the improvement which results from a thorough motion and time study, made by a competent man.

To explain briefly: owing to the fact that the workmen in all of our trades have been taught the details of their work by observation of those immediately around them, there are many different ways in common use for doing the same thing, perhaps forty, fifty, or a hundred ways of doing each act in each trade, and for the same reason there is a great variety in the implements used for each class of work. Now, among the various methods and implements used in each element of each trade there is always one method and one implement which is quicker and better than any of the rest. And this one best method and best implement can only be discovered or developed through a scientific study and analysis of all of the methods and implements in use, together with accurate, minute, motion and time study. This involves the gradual substitution of science for rule of thumb throughout the mechanic arts.

This paper will show that the underlying philosophy of all of the old systems of management in common use makes it imperative that each workman shall be left with the final responsibility for doing his job practically as he thinks best, with comparatively little help and advice from the management. And it will also show that because of this isolation of workmen, it is in most cases impossible for the men working under these systems to do their work in accordance with the rules and laws of a science or art, even where one exists.

The writer asserts as a general principle (and he proposes to give illustrations tending to prove the fact later in this paper) that in almost all of the mechanic arts the science which underlies each act of each workman is so great and amounts to so much that the workman who is best suited to actually doing the work is incapable of fully understanding this science, without the guidance and help of those who are working with him or over him, either through lack of education or through insufficient mental capacity. In order that the work may be done in accordance with scientific laws, it is necessary that there shall be a far more equal division of the responsibility between the management and the workmen than exists under any of the ordinary types of management. Those in the management whose duty it is to develop this science should also guide and help the workman in working under it, and should assume a much larger share of the responsibility for results than under usual conditions is assumed by the management.

The body of this paper will make it clear that, to work according to scientific laws, the management must take over and perform much of the work which is now left to the men; almost every act of the workman should be preceded by one or more preparatory acts of the management which enable him to do his work better and quicker than he otherwise could. And each man should daily be taught by and receive the most friendly help from those who are over him, instead of being, at the one extreme, driven or coerced by his bosses, and at the other left to his own unaided devices.

This close, intimate, personal cooperation between the management and the men is of the essence of modern scientific or task management.

It will be shown by a series of practical illustrations that, through this friendly cooperation, namely, through sharing equally in every day's burden, all of the great obstacles (above described) to obtaining the maximum output for each man and each machine in the establishment are swept away. The 30 per cent, to 100 per cent, increase in wages which the workmen are able to earn beyond what they receive under the old type of management, coupled with the daily intimate shoulder to shoulder contact with the management, entirely removes all cause for soldiering. And in a few years, under this system, the workmen have before them the object lesson of seeing that a great increase in the output per man results in giving employment to more men, instead of throwing men out of work, thus completely eradicating the fallacy that a larger output for each man will throw other men out of work.

It is the writer's judgment, then, that while much can be done and should be done by writing and talking toward educating not only workmen, but all classes in the community, as to the importance of obtaining the maximum output of each man and each machine, it is only through the adoption of modern scientific management that this great problem can be finally solved. Probably most of the readers of this paper will say that all of this is mere theory. On the contrary, the theory, or philosophy, of scientific management is just beginning to be understood, whereas the management itself has been a gradual evolution, extending over a period of nearly thirty years. And during this time the employés of one company after another, including a large range and diversity of industries, have gradually changed from the ordinary to the scientific type of management. At least 50,000 workmen in the United States

are now employed under this system; and they are receiving from 30 per cent, to 100 per cent, higher wages daily than are paid to men of similar caliber with whom they are surrounded, while the companies employing them are more prosperous than ever before. In these companies the output, per man and per machine, has on an average been doubled. During all these years there has never been a single strike among the men working under this system. In place of the suspicious watchfulness and the more or less open warfare which characterizes the ordinary types of management, there is universally friendly cooperation between the management and the men.

Several papers have been written, describing the expedients which have been adopted and the details which have been developed under scientific management and the steps to be taken in changing from the ordinary to the scientific type. But unfortunately most of the readers of these papers have mistaken the mechanism for the true essence. Scientific management fundamentally consists of certain broad general principles, a certain philosophy, which can be applied in many ways, and a description of what any one man or men may believe to be the best mechanism for applying these general principles should in no way be confused with the principles themselves.

It is not here claimed that any single panacea exists for all of the troubles of the working-people or of employers. As long as some people are born lazy or inefficient, and others are born greedy and brutal, as long as vice and crime are with us, just so long will a certain amount of poverty, misery, and unhappiness be with us also. No system of management, no single expedient within the control of any man or any set of men can insure continuous prosperity to either workmen or employers. Prosperity depends upon so many factors entirely beyond the control of any one set of men, any state, or even any one country, that certain periods will inevitably come when both sides must suffer, more or less. It is claimed, however, that under scientific management the intermediate periods will be far more prosperous, far happier, and more free from discord and dissension. And also, that the periods will be fewer, shorter and the suffering less. And this will be particularly true in any one town, any one section of the country, or any one state which first substitutes the principles of scientific management for the rule of thumb.

That these principles are certain to come into general use practically throughout the civilized world, sooner or later, the writer is profoundly convinced, and the sooner they come the better for all the people.

SOURCE: Taylor, Frederick Winslow. 1911. "Fundamentals of Scientific Management." Pp. 9–29 in *Scientific Management*. New York: Harper and Row.

23

THE BASIS OF AUTHORITY

MARY PARKER FOLLETT

We have considered the question of order-giving. That obviously is only an aspect of the subject of authority. All through books on business administration you find the word *authority* [italics added] constantly used. We hear of supreme authority, of ultimate authority, of final authority. We hear of the delegation of authority, of the division of authority, of the limit of authority. These expressions are current phrases in the business world. But it seems to me that some of these expressions are a survival of former days. And are consequently misleading. For they do not describe business as conducted today in many plants. Business practice has gone ahead of business theory, business practice has gone ahead of business language.

In the best managed plants today there is a tendency for each man to have the authority which goes with his particular job rather than that inhering in a particular position in a hierarchy. The most fundamental idea in business today, that which is permeating our whole thinking and business organisation, is that of function. Research and scientific study are coming more and more to determine function. And we are coming more and more to think that a man should have just as much, no more and no less, authority as goes with his function or task. People often talk about the limit of authority when it would be better to speak of the definition of task.

When each man's function is defined by scientific research, when the form of organisation is such that he has the authority which belongs to his function, we automatically get rid of that kind of authority which puts one man "over" another because he is higher up on the page in an organisation chart. I know a man in a factory who is superintendent of a department which includes a number of sub-departments. He tells me that in many cases he says to the head of a sub-department, that is, to a man in a subordinate position to his own, "With your permission I shall do so and so." This is a decided reversal of the usual method, is it not? In the old hierarchy of position, the head of the sub-department would be "under" the superintendent of the department, the "lower" would take orders from the "higher." But this man recognised that authority should go with knowledge and experience, that that is where obedience is due no matter whether it is up the line or down the line. Where knowledge and experience are located, there, he says, you have the key man of the situation. If this has begun to be recognised in business practice, we have here the fore-runner of some pretty drastic changes in our thinking on business management.

I was having a talk a little while ago with the head of a large corporation. His telephone bell rang. He took up the receiver and said in answer to some question, "My secretary decides that, she knows much more about it than I do." Just the other day the head of a big organisation here in London came to one of his heads of departments, this woman told me, and said, "I've come for my orders." She was much amused, but this wasn't a pleasantry on his part. It was simply a recognition that she knew more about the matter in hand than he did.

Perhaps sometime it may seem advisable to get rid of the words "over" and "under." We find a growing dislike to these words in many places. A few years ago my nurse in hospital said to me, "Did you notice that nurse in the operating room? Didn't she look black?" I innocently said, "Perhaps one of the surgeons had reprimanded her for something." To which my nurse replied, "Why, he couldn't. The doctors are not over us. They have their work and we have ours." Now while it is not true that a doctor cannot reprimand a nurse for a mistake, while a doctor certainly has the right to expect his directions in regard to a patient to be obeyed, yet on speaking of this occurrence to several doctors, I was told that there is a growing tendency, on the part of nurses to consider that they are following the standards of their profession rather than merely obeying orders from someone over them. And these doctors said that while this attitude obviously has drawbacks, there may be a good side to it, for it may indicate on the part of the nurses a greater pride in their profession, a greater interest in their work, and a willingness to take responsibility. This should be a matter of further observation, I think, before we form an opinion.

The testimony before the Coal Commission a few years ago threw much light on this question. We heard there stated explicitly the dislike of being "under some one," the dislike of the feeling of "subordination," the dislike of being "at the will of another." One man said: "It's all right to work with anyone: what is disagreeable is to feel too distinctly that you are working under anyone."

This objection to being under we find among executives as well as among the rank and file. A business man here in London talking to me of two of his executives said: "Mr. A. will take instructions from Mr. B. but will not admit that he is under him." Well, perhaps that is all right. I don't know that it makes us under a person to take instructions from him. We are all of us, as a matter of fact, taking instructions from people all the time. I take instructions from my plumber, my electrician, but I am not under them. Or perhaps I am in a sense and to an extent.

I say that executives as well as workers object to being under anyone. I have found among chief executives an objection to being over others and a feeling that these words *over* and *under* are unfortunate [italics added]. One general manager said to me, "I don't know whether I'm at the head or the bottom and I wish there were some way of making out a chart that didn't put the general manager at the top." Another general manager tells me that he thinks the use of the terms "higher," "superior," in an organisation is unwise, that a meaning is attached to them which they ought not to have. The head of a large business in the north of England told me that one of the things which was retarding the unification of his plant was this feeling of over and under. The head of another English firm said to me, "I don't like all this over and under talk. I have a lot of able executives all doing their work well. My work is different from theirs, but I don't see why I should be considered over them."

I think one difficulty about this matter, one reason why people object so strongly to being "under" others, is that there has been too much pomp attached to the idea of being over someone, of giving orders. I am convinced that we have to change our thinking very radically in this respect. I am convinced that any feeling of exaltation because we have people under us should be conquered, for I am sure that if we enjoy being over people, there will be something in our manner which will make them dislike being under us. And often there is not sufficient ground for any feeling of superiority. Indeed, if I give instructions to someone who knows less about a matter than I do, he probably knows more than I about some other matter. I know more about the composition of menus than my cook, but she knows more about cooking and the management of the kitchen range. So we can all be over and under at the same time.

There is an amusing story of a teacher who went into a new school. There were certain rules in regard to the disposal of small pieces of chalk, of erasers that needed cleaning, and so on, but she disregarded these rules as she had been in a school where there were no rules for such matters. In a little while she was taken to task by the caretaker of the building who remarked that evidently she wasn't used to working under a caretaker. She was, naturally, much amused, but perhaps she was under him in regard to leftover pieces of chalk.

I know a lady who had one maid for the work of her little summer cottage. One summer she was very tired mentally and decided that instead of the maid she would engage someone to run her cottage for her, and she took one of the students from a college which taught household economics. This girl obviously couldn't do the planning and buying and all the work too, so the lady did part of the work. She had the physical exercise and the mental rest she needed, and was only too pleased to be told what to do by the household economics girl.

In the conduct of business there have been many changes in recent years which have tended to make them feel less pompous about being over others. I heard a man at the head of a factory in the West of England say, "You can call me General Manager, but any kid can come along with a chit and I have to do what it says." The most marked difference in this respect we find among foremen. I remember the wife of a foreman who said with pride, "John has seventy in his department that he's boss over." There is much now that is hastening the disappearance of that phrase, notably newer methods of dismissal. When employment managers were first introduced into a business, the foremen were almost invariably jealous. One of the duties of the employment manager is, as you know, to hire and dismiss, of course with the concurrence of the foreman, but the foreman thought that this took away from their authority. They had to be led to see that it is merely a division of duties, just as one of the general manager's jobs is often nowadays given to some specialist engaged to do that particular thing. Moreover, when dismissals are made after consultation between foreman and employment manager, or between foreman, employment manager and psychologist, that is, when it is decided that a man has not the qualifications for a particular job, such dismissals may come in time to be looked at in the same way as when a doctor says a man's heart is too weak for a certain kind of work. That decision does not mean that the doctor is over anyone. It is only capricious firing, firing that is

unfounded, that makes a man over another, and that kind of firing is disappearing. One of the differences between the old-time foreman and the present is that the former was thinking in terms of his authority; he thought he could not keep up his dignity before his men unless he had this thing he called authority. Many foremen today are learning to think in terms of responsibility for definite tasks.

Indeed there are many indications in the present reorganisation of industry that we are beginning to rid ourselves of the over and under idea, that we are coming to a different conception of authority, many indications that there is an increasing tendency to let the job itself, rather than the position occupied in a hierarchy, dictate the kind and amount of authority. An incident in my own experience brought this vividly home to me. One morning in America I wanted to telephone a certain bank. I could not get them. I tried repeatedly without success. I knew of course that the switchboard of a large bank was not dead at the busiest time of the day. I therefore tried by calling first one official of the telephone company and then another, to see if someone couldn't get that number for me. I did at length get the bank, but before the incident was closed, I learned a good deal about the organisation of that Telephone Company. For one thing each official seemed to be thinking more in terms of his job than of his position. The first thing that struck my attention was the minor importance of hierarchy of each. This was rather a good joke on me. For, forgetting all my beautiful theories, all my preaching against one man having power over another, forgetting all this, the mental habits of a life-time asserted themselves without my being aware of it, and I started out on a hunt for someone in authority over another. When the operator didn't get my number I called the chief operator, then I called the exchange manager because I thought he was over the chief operator. I then asked for a superintendent because I thought he was over the exchange manager. But I found that the officials of the Telephone Company did not seem to be thinking in those terms. When I said to the superintendent: "Are you over the exchange manager?" he replied in rather bewildered tones, "No, I'm not over him." When in the afternoon a superintendent who wished to investigate the matter rang me up, the first thing I said to him was "Are you over the superintendent I talked with this morning?" He replied, "Oh, no, I'm not over him." You see, in spite of all my principles, I was so used to the old way of thinking that I couldn't adjust myself quickly to a different way of thinking. I wanted someone who had the authority to boss, so I kept straight on in this search for someone above others instead of asking: "What particular job is this?"

And later on (for the President of the Company, when he found I was studying organisation, asked me to investigate theirs) later on I found that this lack of emphasis of hierarchy of rank went right through the whole organisation. There was either no position which as such carried with it the right to boss, or else no-one took advantage of such a position. Everyone seemed to be thinking not so much in terms of to whom he was responsible as for what he was responsible—a much healthier attitude of mind.

When I finally had a talk with the President, part of what he said is I think worth quoting in full. "The kind of management we are aiming at," he said, "is management with authority all down the line, as contrasted with management by edict from a central source. We are trying to teach our men what their jobs are, what the underlying principle of these jobs are, and then we are trying to get them to exercise the authority of their job with the idea that they shall use their brains, their discretion, having in mind these fundamental principles. We teach people what their job is, and then insist that they shall exercise the authority and responsibility which goes with that job instead of relying on the fellow above them."

In many companies we find this emphasis on the job rather than on the hierarchy of position. For one thing, as management is becoming more and more specialised, the policies and methods of a department tend more and more to rest on that department's special body of knowledge. We find authority with the head of a department or with an expert or with a staff official. The despatch clerk has more authority in despatching work than the general manager. The balance of stores clerk, as he is called in some places, will tell the purchasing agent when to act, although the purchasing agent is above him in the official scale.

Moreover, some firms have planning departments, and these, it is obvious, lessen arbitrary authority.

Again, all that I said of the order being found by research, of executives or workers being asked to co-operate in the forming of rules for the job—all this takes away from arbitrary authority.

Moreover, we are not now drawing the line so sharply as formerly between those who manage and those who are managed. A close analysis of jobs shows us many which occupy a place at the bottom of the organisation chart which yet contain some degree of management, which carry with them some degree of authority. That is, there is authority all down the line: the driver of a delivery van has authority as he decides on the order of deliveries.

Instead then of "supreme control," "ultimate authority," we might perhaps think of cumulative control, cumulative authority.

What has been keeping us back in our thinking on this subject is, I think, what I have called elsewhere the fallacy of finals. The final moment in a process may be the most striking, the most dramatic, but it may not be any more important than all the other moments. What we have to recognise about authority is that it is a process. To recognise this gives us a thoroughly realistic view of our subject. The old theory of authority I call unrealistic because it tends to ignore the process by which authority is generated. Perhaps it will help us to destroy the illusion of final authority if we consider for a moment executive decisions, if we ask ourselves where a decision really comes from.

It is often supposed that the administrative head receives facts from his heads of departments and that then from the facts thus gained he makes his decisions, constructs his policies. But it is a matter of everyday experience to top executives that their heads of departments pass up to them more than mere facts. They give interpretations of facts, the conclusions they have drawn from these facts, yes, and often judgments too, so that they contribute very largely to final authority, supreme control.

The various experts too, the staff officials, the planning department—all these give more than mere facts. The planning department, to be sure, is still so much of a novelty that there are many different ideas as to its place in the plant. It may be asked for only statistical information. For instance, in the case of a decision pending for the sales department, it may be asked only for a record of past sales with analyses in regard to volume, localities, and so on. Usually, however, it is asked for more than this, for the probable future development of certain localities, what the future demand will probably be, the probable effect of the raising of price. By the time this has all been passed up to the head, this decision is already largely pre-determined.

Hence, while the board of directors or executive committees may be theoretically the governing body, practically, as many of our large businesses are now organised and operated, before their decisions are made there has already taken place much of the process of which these decisions are but a last step.

Moreover, both as to conclusions and judgments handed up from executives it is often not possible for the chief executive or the board of directors to reject them. For these conclusions and judgments are already, to a certain extent, woven into the pattern, and in such a way that it would be impossible to get them out.

For instance, suppose the question comes up in a board of directors or executive committee in a factory whether a psychologist shall be engaged. Much has gone on before that question comes up. It has been felt desirable by many to have better tests for hiring, promoting and dismissing, to have studies in fatigue, and so on. But there has been at the same time many other influences at work.

The foremen perhaps think that their methods of testing applicants are sufficient, the older men among the upper executives may oppose what they call "new-fangled" notions, the workers may think that fatigue studies will tend only to more work being required of them, and so on. It is obvious, is it not, that the decision in regard to engaging a psychologist will be the cumulative result of all these interacting influences. The decision will be a moment pregnant with much experience, with many emotions, with many interests. When you hear someone say that there are not so many one-man decisions in scientifically managed plants as in others, they do not mean necessarily that the decisions in those plants are made by committees, but rather that the decisions are part of a process of interacting influence made possible by the form of organisation, and the interacting influences gather force until comes the moment which we call the decision. The

fallacy of finals has too long blinded us to the true nature of decisions.

In summary of this matter I think we may say that so much goes to contribute to executive decisions before the part which the executive head takes in them, that the conception of final authority is losing its force in the present organisation of business. And this is as true of other executives as of the head. Here, too, final decisions have the form and the force which they have accumulated. I have seen an executive seem a little self-important over a decision he had made when it had really come to him ready made.

I do not of course want to imply that there is no such thing as final authority. There are some questions which have to be decided by the head alone. Moreover, the head must decide when there is disagreement between executives which these executives cannot manage to deal with themselves. I am not denying the existence of final authority. I am speaking only against its over-emphasis, against ignoring the fact that decisions are usually reached through a process. The growth of a decision, the accumulation of authority, not the final step, is what we need most to study.

What I have wanted to try to make clear is that authority is not something from the top which filters down to those below. I hoped it would help us to understand this if we considered how decisions were really made. There is something else which may help us to understand this very important point, and that is the relation of departmental policy to general policy.

In books on business management we sometimes find this sentence, "General policy dictates departmental policies." But when the Board of Directors want to decide on a general policy, have they not to take into consideration the policy of the sales department, of the manufacturing department, the views of the financial department and of those dealing with the human element, the personnel department? You will find that general policy is made up of all the departmental policies. Is it then wrong to say that general policy dictates departmental policy? No, because after general policy is formulated by the Board of Directors or Executive Committee, then the various departments have to see that their various policies conform to it. The flow goes both ways.

They contribute to general policy and then they must conform to general policy. They follow what they have helped to construct. But this latter part is what we forget when we say that general policy dictates departmental policies. We forget that general policy is not an air plant, but has its roots in all that is going on in the business.

Mr. Gerard Swope, President of the General Electric, told me, "It is the greatest mistake to think that a business is run from the President's chair, that there is constantly flowing out of my office a stream of directions. In fact the flow is just the other way. I sit all day in my office and receive my upper executives who come to me with plans and suggestions for my acceptance." I said, "What then is the need of you? What is your particular job?" He had his answer to that all ready, but I am not going to give it to you until later in our talks when we consider the function of the chief executive more particularly. All that I am calling your attention to now is the flow from executives up to the General Manager. I do not say that the General Manager's consent is not important. It is very important, but it is only one part of the process.

The whole science of business management today tends to be based on the linking of one part with another, on the contribution of some narrower aspect of the work to a broader aspect. When I am told that sales planning is but a division of business planning, when I am told that sales research is only part of a broader function which might be designated commercial research, then I say that we have got out of the region of finals and absolutes, that we are going beyond our old notion of supreme authority.

If we accept the statement that authority is a process, we find that the phrase *delegation of authority* [italics added] is a little misleading. What is the fallacy here? Suppose we consider what actually happens when we wish to start a new business. We probably call in an expert organiser to organise it. One executive is given authority over one thing, another over something else. When I say "is given" I do not mean that the expert gives it, but that the form of organisation decides the matter. The form of organisation decides what authority the general manager shall have. Therefore we do not talk about the delegation of authority, because that would

seem to imply that someone had the right to all the authority, but that for purposes of convenience he delegated some of it.

It becomes still more obvious that this is not true if you consider the creation of new functions. The head of a large concern told me that he knew nothing about merchandising and must therefore engage a merchandise manager. Obviously he was not giving up any of his authority, but a certain amount of authority would belong to that job.

It is just the same with the separation of functions as with the creation of new ones. For instance, in a small bank the head in addition to his other duties, looks after the new business. As the business of the bank increases, a separate man is given responsibility for new business: exchange, deposits, credit loans, and so on. Here we see very clearly that the separation of function does not mean the delegation of authority. Authority follows the function. When one man had the job he had the authority. When the job went to someone else, the authority went with it. Authority belongs to the job and stays with the job.

We have been confused in theory on this point because we have never got over the eighteenth-century way of thinking when men were always thinking about their rights. And so we have gone at this subject from the angle of rights, tried to see what authority belonged by right to certain people. But this has only been in theory. In practice it all works out quite naturally. For instance, to take another illustration from banking, the head of a branch bank may decide on small loans, while large loans may have to go up to the executive committee. This is not because the matter of large loans belongs by "right" to the executive committee, but because it is recognised that the combined judgment of executive committee and the head of the branch bank is probably better than that of either alone.

That we are beginning now to get away from the notion of rights, that we are beginning to think more and more in terms of the job, is why I call the treatment of authority I am presenting to you a realistic one. We are beginning in business management to rid ourselves of many theories, abstract notions, mere clichés, of conceptions which have become meaningless, and nowhere is this more marked than in the case of my subject this evening. For we are trying to think out the form of organisation whereby authority may go with three things: knowledge, experience, and the skill to apply that knowledge and experience.

It is perhaps due to the fact that arbitrary authority, the authority of mere position, is diminishing, more than to anything else, that business management is approaching a science.

To sum up: all this question of decisions, of responsibility, of authority has been made, I think, too personal. The important thing about a decision is not who makes it but what gets into it. The important thing about responsibility is not to whom you are responsible, but for what you are responsible. The important thing about authority is that real authority and official authority shall coincide.

You will see by this time that I believe in authority. Those writers who think people should rebel against authority seem to me to have a wholly wrong idea of the matter. Submission to authority does not imply, as these writers seem to think, a lack of freedom. On the contrary, it is by an understanding of the laws which govern the process by which authority is generated that we gain our freedom, freedom in any true sense of the word. For authority, genuine authority, is the outcome of our common life. It does not come from separating people, from dividing them into two classes, those who command and those who obey. It comes from the intermingling of all, of my work fitting into yours and yours into mine, and from that intermingling of forces a power being created which will control those forces. Authority is a self-generating process. To learn more of that process, the process of control, is what we all think the world today most needs.

SOURCE: Follett, Mary Parker. 1949. "The Basis of Authority." Pp. 34–46 *Freedom and Co-ordination: Lectures in Business Organization by Mary Parker Follett*. London: Management Publications Trust, Ltd.

24

THEORY Y

The Integration of Individual and Organizational Goals

DOUGLAS MCGREGOR

To some, the preceding analysis will appear unduly harsh. Have we not made major modifications in the management of the human resources of industry during the past quarter century? Have we not recognized the importance of people and made vitally significant changes in managerial strategy as a consequence? Do the developments since the twenties in personnel administration and labor relations add up to nothing?

There is no question that important progress has been made in the past two or three decades. During this period the human side of enterprise has become a major preoccupation of management. A tremendous number of policies, programs, and practices which were virtually unknown thirty years ago have become commonplace. The lot of the industrial employee—be he worker, professional, or executive—has improved to a degree which could hardly have been imagined by his counterpart of the nineteen twenties. Management has adopted generally a far more humanitarian set of values; it has successfully striven to give more equitable and more generous treatment to its employees. It has significantly reduced economic hardships, eliminated the more extreme forms of industrial warfare, provided

a generally safe and pleasant working environment, *but it has done all these things without changing its fundamental theory of management.* There are exceptions here and there, and they are important; nevertheless, the assumptions of Theory X remain predominant throughout our economy.

Management was subjected to severe pressures during the Great Depression of the thirties. The wave of public antagonism, the open warfare accompanying the unionization of the mass production industries, the general reaction against authoritarianism, the legislation of the New Deal produced a wide "pendulum swing." However, the changes in policy and practice which took place during that and the next decade were primarily adjustments to the increased power of organized labor and to the pressures of public opinion.

Some of the movement was away from "hard" and toward "soft" management, but it was short-lived, and for good reasons. It has become clear that many of the initial strategic interpretations accompanying the "human relations approach" were as naive as those which characterized the early stages of progressive education. We have now discovered that there is no answer in the simple removal of control—that abdication is not a workable alternative to authoritarianism. We have learned that there is no direct correlation between employee satisfaction and productivity. We recognize today that "industrial democracy" cannot consist in permitting everyone to decide everything, that industrial health does not flow automatically from the elimination of dissatisfaction, disagreement, or even open conflict. Peace is not synonymous with organizational health; socially responsible management is not coextensive with permissive management.

Now that management has regained its earlier prestige and power, it has become obvious that the trend toward "soft" management was a temporary and relatively superficial reaction rather than a general modification of fundamental assumptions or basic strategy. Moreover, while the progress we have made in the past quarter century is substantial, it has reached the point of diminishing returns. The tactical possibilities within conventional managerial strategies have been pretty completely exploited, and significant new developments will be unlikely without major modifications in theory.

The Assumptions of Theory Y

There have been few dramatic break-throughs in social science theory like those which have occurred in the physical sciences during the past half century. Nevertheless, the accumulation of knowledge about human behavior in many specialized fields has made possible the formulation of a number of generalizations which provide a modest beginning for new theory with respect to the management of human resources. Some of these assumptions, which will hereafter be referred to as Theory Y, are as follows:

1. *The expenditure of physical and mental effort in work is as natural as play or rest.* The average human being does not inherently dislike work. Depending upon controllable conditions, work may be a source of satisfaction (and will be voluntarily performed) or a source of punishment (and will be avoided if possible).

2. *External control and the threat of punishment are not the only means for bringing about effort toward organizational objectives. Man will exercise self-direction and self-control in the service of objectives to which he is committed.*

3. *Commitment to objectives is a function of the rewards associated with their achievement.* The most significant of such rewards, e.g., the satisfaction of ego and self-actualization needs, can be direct products of effort directed toward organizational objectives.

4. *The average human being learns, under proper conditions, not only to accept but to seek responsibility.* Avoidance of responsibility, lack of ambition, and emphasis on security are generally consequences of experience, not inherent human characteristics.

5. *The capacity to exercise a relatively high degree of imagination, ingenuity, and creativity in the solution of organizational problems is widely, not narrowly, distributed in the population.*

6. *Under the conditions of modern industrial life, the intellectual potentialities of the average human being are only partially utilized.*

These assumptions involve sharply different implications for managerial strategy than do those of Theory X. They are dynamic rather than static: They indicate the possibility of human growth and development; they stress the necessity for selective adaptation rather than for a single absolute form of control. They are not framed in terms of the least common denominator of the factory hand, but in terms of a resource which has substantial potentialities.

Above all, the assumptions of Theory Y point up the fact that the limits on human collaboration in the organizational setting are not limits of human nature but of management's ingenuity in discovering how to realize the potential represented by its human resources. Theory X offers management an easy rationalization for ineffective organizational performance: It is due to the nature of the human resources with which we must work. Theory Y, on the other hand, places the problems squarely in the lap of management. If employees are lazy, indifferent, unwilling to take responsibility, intransigent, uncreative, uncooperative, Theory Y implies that the causes lie in management's methods of organization and control.

The assumptions of Theory Y are not finally validated. Nevertheless, they are far more consistent with existing knowledge in the social sciences than are the assumptions of Theory X. They will undoubtedly be refined, elaborated, modified as further research accumulates, but they are unlikely to be completely contradicted.

On the surface, these assumptions may not seem particularly difficult to accept. Carrying their implications into practice, however, is not easy. They challenge a number of deeply ingrained managerial habits of thought and action.

The Principle of Integration

The central principle of organization which derives from Theory X is that of direction and control through the exercise of authority—what has been called "the scalar principle." The central principle which derives from Theory Y is that of integration: the creation of conditions such that the members of the organization can achieve their own goals *best* by directing their efforts toward the success of the enterprise. These two principles have profoundly different implications with respect to the task of managing human resources, but the scalar principle is so firmly built into managerial attitudes that the implications of the principle of integration are not easy to perceive.

Someone once said that fish discover water last. The "psychological environment" of industrial management—like water for fish—is so much a part of organizational life that we are unaware of it. Certain characteristics of our society, and of organizational life within it, are so completely established, so pervasive, that we cannot conceive of their being otherwise. As a result, a great many policies and practices and decisions and relationships could only be—it seems—what they are.

Among these pervasive characteristics of organizational life in the United States today is a managerial attitude (stemming from Theory X) toward membership in the industrial organization. It is assumed almost without question that organizational requirements take precedence over the needs of individual members. Basically, the employment agreement is that in return for the rewards which are offered, the individual will accept external direction and control. The very idea of integration and self-control is foreign to our way of thinking about the employment relationship. The tendency, therefore, is either to reject it out of hand (as socialistic, or anarchistic, or inconsistent with human nature) or to twist it unconsciously until it fits existing conceptions.

The concept of integration and self-control carries the implication that the organization will be more effective in achieving its economic objectives if adjustments are made, in significant ways, to the needs and goals of its members.

A district manager in a large, geographically decentralized company is notified that he is being promoted to a policy level position at headquarters. It is a big promotion with a large salary increase. His role in the organization will be a much more powerful one, and he will be associated with the major executives of the firm.

The headquarters group who selected him for this position have carefully considered a number of possible candidates. This man stands out among them in a way which makes him the natural choice. His performance has been under observation for some time, and there is little question that he possesses the necessary qualifications, not only for this opening but for an even higher position. There is genuine satisfaction that such an outstanding candidate is available.

The man is appalled. He doesn't want the job. His goal, as he expresses it, is to be the "best damned district manager in the company." He enjoys his direct associations with operating people in the field, and he doesn't want a policy level job. He and his wife enjoy the kind of life they have created in a small city, and they dislike actively both the living conditions and the social obligations of the headquarters city.

He expresses his feelings as strongly as he can, but his objections are brushed aside. The organization's needs are such that his refusal to accept the promotion would be unthinkable. His superiors say to themselves that of course when he has settled in to the new job, he will recognize that it was the right thing. And so he makes the move.

Two years later he is in an even higher position in the company's headquarters organization, and there is talk that he will probably be the executive vice-president before long. Privately he expresses considerable unhappiness and dissatisfaction. He (and his wife) would "give anything" to be back in the situation he left two years ago.

Within the context of the pervasive assumptions of Theory X, promotions and transfers in large numbers are made by unilateral decision.

The requirements of the organization are given priority automatically and almost without question. If the individual's personal goals are considered at all, it is assumed that the rewards of salary and position will satisfy him. Should an individual actually refuse such a move without a compelling reason, such as health or a severe family crisis, he would be considered to have jeopardized his future because of this "selfish" attitude. It is rare indeed for management to give the individual the opportunity to be a genuine and active partner in such a decision, even though it may affect his most important personal goals. Yet the implications following from Theory Y are that the organization is likely to suffer if it ignores these personal needs and goals. In making unilateral decisions with respect to promotion, management is failing to utilize its human resources in the most effective way.

The principle of integration demands that both the organization's and the individual's needs be recognized. Of course, when there is a sincere joint effort to find it, an integrative solution which meets the needs of the individual *and* the organization is a frequent outcome. But not always—and this is the point at which Theory Y begins to appear unrealistic. It collides head on with pervasive attitudes associated with management by direction and control.

The assumptions of Theory Y imply that unless integration is achieved *the organization will suffer.* The objectives of the organization are *not* achieved best by the unilateral administration of promotions, because this form of management by direction and control will not create the commitment which would make available the full resources of those affected. The lesser motivation, the lesser resulting degree of self-direction and self-control are costs which, when added up for many instances over time, will more than offset the gains obtained by unilateral decisions "for the good of the organization."

One other example will perhaps clarify further the sharply different implications of Theory X and Theory Y.

It could be argued that management is already giving a great deal of attention to the principle of integration through its efforts in the field of economic education. Many millions of dollars and much ingenuity have been expended in attempts to persuade employees that their welfare is intimately connected with the success of the free enterprise system and of their own companies. The idea that they can achieve their own goals best by directing their effort toward the objectives of the organization has been explored and developed and communicated in every possible way. Is this not evidence that management is already committed to the principle of integration?

The answer is a definite no. These managerial efforts, with rare exceptions, reflect clearly the influence of the assumptions of Theory X. The central message is an exhortation to the industrial employee to work hard and follow orders in order to protect his job and his standard of living. Much has been achieved, it says, by our established way of running industry, and much more could be achieved if employees would adapt themselves *to management's definition* of what is required. Behind these exhortations lies the expectation that of course the requirements of the organization and its economic success must have priority over the needs of the individual.

Naturally, integration means working together for the success of the enterprise so we all may share in the resulting rewards. But management's implicit assumption is that working together means adjusting to the requirements of the organization *as management perceives them.* In terms of existing views, it seems inconceivable that individuals, seeking their own goals, would further the ends of the enterprise. On the contrary, this would lead to anarchy, chaos, irreconcilable conflicts of self-interest, lack of responsibility, inability to make decisions, and failure to carry out those that were made.

All these consequences, and other worse ones, *would* be inevitable unless conditions could be created such that the members of the organization perceived that they could achieve their own goals *best* by directing their efforts toward the success of the enterprise. If the assumptions of Theory Y are valid, the practical question is whether, and to what extent, such conditions can be created. To that question the balance of this volume is addressed.

The Application of Theory Y

In the physical sciences there are many theoretical phenomena which cannot be achieved in practice. Absolute zero and a perfect vacuum are examples. Others, such as nuclear power, jet aircraft, and human space flight, are recognized theoretically to be possible long before they become feasible. This fact does not make theory less useful. If it were not for our theoretical convictions, we would not even be attempting to develop the means for human flight into space today. In fact, were it not for the development of physical science theory during the past century and a half, we would still be depending upon the horse and buggy and the sailing vessel for transportation. Virtually all significant technological developments wait on the formulation of relevant theory.

Similarly, in the management of the human resources of industry, the assumptions and theories about human nature at any given time limit innovation. Possibilities are not recognized, innovating efforts are not undertaken, until theoretical conceptions lay a groundwork for them. Assumptions like those of Theory X permit us to conceive of certain possible ways of organizing and directing human effort, *but not others.* Assumptions like those of Theory Y open up a range of possibilities for new managerial policies and practices. As in the case of the development of new physical science theory, some of these possibilities are not immediately feasible, and others may forever remain unattainable. They may be too costly, or it may be that we simply cannot discover how to create the necessary "hardware."

There is substantial evidence for the statement that the potentialities of the average human being are far above those which we typically realize in industry today. If our assumptions are like those of Theory X, we will not even recognize the existence of these potentialities and there will be no reason to devote time, effort, or money to discovering how to realize them. If, however, we accept assumptions like those of Theory Y, we will be challenged to innovate, to discover new ways of organizing and directing human effort, even though we recognize that the perfect organization, like the perfect vacuum, is practically out of reach.

We need not be overwhelmed by the dimensions of the managerial task implied by Theory Y. To be sure, a large mass production operation in which the workers have been organized by a militant and hostile union faces management with problems which appear at present to be insurmountable with respect to the application of the principle of integration. It may be decades before sufficient knowledge will have accumulated to make such an application feasible. Applications of Theory Y will have to be tested initially in more limited ways and under more favorable circumstances. However, a number of applications of Theory Y *in managing managers and professional people* are possible today. Within the managerial hierarchy, the assumptions can be tested and refined, techniques can be invented and skill acquired in their use. As knowledge accumulates, some of the problems of application at the worker level in large organizations may appear less baffling than they do at present

Perfect integration of organizational requirements and individual goals and needs is, of course, not a realistic objective. In adopting this principle, we seek that degree of integration in which the individual can achieve his goals *best* by directing his efforts toward the success of the organization. "Best" means that this alternative will be more attractive than the many others available to him: indifference, irresponsibility, minimal compliance, hostility, sabotage. It means that he will continuously be encouraged to develop and utilize voluntarily his capacities, his knowledge, his skill, his ingenuity in ways which contribute to the success of the enterprise.[1]

Acceptance of Theory Y does not imply abdication, or "soft" management, or "permissiveness." As was indicated above, such notions stem from the acceptance of authority as the *single* means of managerial control, and from attempts to minimize its negative consequences. Theory Y assumes that people will exercise self-direction and self-control in the achievement of organizational objectives *to the degree that they are committed to those objectives.* If that commitment is small, only a slight degree of self-direction and self-control will be likely, and a substantial amount of external influence will be necessary. If it is large, many conventional external controls will be relatively superfluous, and to some extent self-defeating. Managerial policies and practices materially affect this degree of commitment.

Authority is an inappropriate means for obtaining commitment to objectives. Other forms of influence—help in achieving integration, for example—are required for this purpose. Theory Y points to the possibility of lessening the emphasis on external forms of control to the degree that commitment to organizational objectives can be achieved. Its underlying assumptions emphasize the capacity of human beings for self-control, and the consequent possibility of greater managerial reliance on other means of influence. Nevertheless, it is clear that authority *is* an appropriate means for control under certain circumstances—particularly where genuine commitment to objectives cannot be achieved. The assumptions of Theory Y do not deny the appropriateness of authority, but they do deny that it is appropriate for all purposes and under all circumstances.

Many statements have been made to the effect that we have acquired today the know-how to cope with virtually any technological problems which may arise, and that the major industrial advances of the next half century will occur on the human side of enterprise. Such advances, however, are improbable so long as management continues to organize and direct and control its human resources on the basis of assumptions—tacit or explicit—like those of Theory X. Genuine innovation, in contrast to a refurbishing and patching of present managerial strategies, requires first the acceptance of less limiting assumptions about the nature of the human resources we seek to control, and second the readiness to adapt selectively to the implications contained in those new assumptions. Theory Y is an invitation to innovation.

NOTE

1. A recent, highly significant study of the sources of job satisfaction and dissatisfaction among managerial and professional people suggests that these opportunities for "self-actualization" are the essential requirements of both job satisfaction and high performance. The researchers find that "the wants of employees divide into two groups. One group revolves around the need to develop in one's occupation as a source of personal growth. The second

group operates as an essential base to the first and is associated with fair treatment in compensation, supervision, working conditions, and administrative practices. *The fulfillment of the needs of the second group does not motivate the individual to high levels of job satisfaction and . . . to extra performance on the job.* All we can expect from satisfying [this second group of needs] is the prevention of dissatisfaction and poor job performance." Frederick Herzberg, Bernard Mausner, and Barbara Bloch Snyderman, *The Motivation to Work.* New York: John Wiley & Sons, Inc., 1959, pp. 114–115. (Italics mine.)

REFERENCES

Brown, J. A. C., *The Social Psychology of Industry.* Baltimore: Penguin Books, Inc., 1954.

Cordiner, Ralph J., *New Frontiers for Professional Managers.* New York: McGraw-Hill Book Company, Inc., 1956.

Dubin, Robert, *The World of Work: Industrial Society and Human Relations.* Englewood Cliffs, N.J.: Prentice-Hall, Inc., 1958.

Friedmann, Georges, *Industrial Society: The Emergence of the Human Problems of Automation.* Glencoe, Ill.: Free Press, 1955.

Herzberg, Frederick, Bernard Mausner, and Barbara Bloch Snyderman, *The Motivation to Work.* New York: John Wiley & Sons, Inc., 1959.

Krech, David, and Richard S. Crutchfield, *Theory and Problems of Social Psychology.* New York: McGraw-Hill Book Company, Inc., 1948.

Leavitt, Harold J., *Managerial Psychology.* Chicago: University of Chicago Press, 1958.

McMurry, Robert N., "The Case for Benevolent Autocracy," *Harvard Business Review,* vol. 36, no. 1 (January–February), 1958.

Rice, A. K., *Productivity and Social Organizations: The Ahmedabad Experiment.* London: Tavistock Publications, Ltd., 1958.

Stagner, Ross, *The Psychology of Industrial Conflict.* New York: John Wiley & Sons, Inc., 1956.

SOURCE: McGregor, Douglas. 1960. "Theory Y: The Integration of Individual and Organizational Goals." Pp. 45–57 in *The Human Side of Enterprise.* New York: McGraw-Hill.

25

TOWARD AN ECONOMIC MODEL OF THE JAPANESE FIRM

MASAHIKO AOKI

HORIZONTAL COORDINATION

A key to an understanding of Japan's industrial performance can be found in the ability of firms in certain industries to coordinate their operating activities flexibly and quickly in response to changing market conditions and to changes in other factors in the industrial environment, as well as to emergent technical and technological exigencies. Representative Japanese firms have cultivated an ability for rapid response by developing an internal scheme in which emergent information is utilized effectively on-site and in which operating activities are coordinated among related operating units on the basis of information sharing. In this section, I first illustrate this claim with three examples drawn from operating practices in the automobile and steel industries and from R&D activities in manufacturing industry generally. I then characterize generic aspects of these and other examples as a mechanism of horizontal coordination that stand in contrast with the more familiar mechanism of hierarchical coordination. I summarize some results of a comparative analysis of the relative information efficiency of the two coordination mechanisms; and finally I discuss their implications for understanding and interpreting Japanese industrial performance.

I am aware that any attempt to draw general propositions from specific examples runs the risk of small sample bias. But the following examples are drawn from many observations made recently in the course of plant visits and interviews with engineers and managers, and I am reasonably confident that they represent widespread and generic elements of Japanese practice.[1] Also I believe that the significance of the comparative analysis to follow is very hard to grasp without breaking open the economists' black box of the production function and gaining a concrete image of how firms operate without a rigid hierarchical order. . . .

Theory and Interpretations

These examples of industrial practices in Japan suggest that the coordination mode that operates within representative Japanese firms differs from the traditional modeling of organizational hierarchies—the *H-mode*: Let us now try to identify the fundamental differences between the two modes by focusing on a few important factors and examine how the relative cost efficiencies of the two can differ in various environments. Doing this, one is bound to commit the sin of oversimplification. But the point here is to make it clear that the cost function of the firm is not exogenously and solely determined by an engineer's blueprint; it also depends on organizational and human factors. I shall, therefore, venture to offer a sharp theoretical formulation of non-hierarchical coordination and then interpret its performance characteristics in the context of the Japanese economy.

The H-mode has two essential features: (1) the hierarchical separation between planning and implemental operation and (2) the emphasis on the economies of specialization. That is, planning, such as for production scheduling, manufacturing process control, and commodity development is entrusted to an office at the top level of each function (e.g., the production planning office, the engineering office, the development laboratory) which is supposed to have specialized prior knowledge (on markets, engineering know how, etc.). Let us call this planning *prior planning*. Prior planning is fixed for a certain period of time and implemented by operating units of the lower levels (e.g., workshops, plant), each of which is assigned a hierarchically decomposed special operational function. Any random event during the implementation period may be coped with by a priori devices (e.g., buffer inventories, troubleshooting specialists such as relief-men and mechanics), and new knowledge that emerges may be used only for the next round of planning by the higher office.

Consider an alternative mode reflecting aspects of Japanese firms—let us call it the *J-mode,* which has two main features: (1) the horizontal coordination among operating units based on (2) the sharing of ex post on-site information (learned results). That is, prior planning sets only the indicative framework of operation. As new information becomes available to operating units during the implementation period (e.g., customers orders at dealers, quality defect problems that become apparent at a workshop, engineering problems associated with development of a new product that become evident only at the plant site), prior plans may be modified. But in order for on-site information to be utilized in a way that is consistent with the organizational goal, adaptation must be coordinated among interrelated operating units.

In the J-mode, on-site information may be better utilized for the realization of organizational goals (more formally, one may say that the J-mode can generate information value by the use of ex post information). Such a gain, of course, is not costless. In the J-mode, economies of specialization of operational activities are sacrificed, for some portion of time and effort of the operating units needs to be diverted for acquiring new information (i.e., learning) as well as for communicating and bargaining with each other for coordination. Such costs may be reduced by the development of information technology: hardware, software, and humanware. Therefore, the comparative advantage of the H-mode and the J-mode depends on such factors as the learning ability of personnel, the ease of communication among operating units, and the degree of economies of specialization with regard to the variety and volatility of market demand. Aoki (1986, 1989) and Itoh (1987) (see also Jacques Cremer 1989) examined the advantages and disadvantages of the two modes and came up with the following noteworthy proposition: When environments for planning (e.g., markets, engineering process, development opportunity) are stable, learning at the operational level may not add much information value to prior planning, and the sacrifice of economies of specialization in operational activities may not be worthwhile. On the other hand, if environments are extremely volatile or uncertain, decentralized adaptation to environmental changes may yield highly unstable results. In both these two contrasting cases, the H-mode may be superior in achieving the organizational goal. In the intermediate situation, however, where external environments are continually changing but not too drastically, the J-mode is superior. In this case, the information value created by learning and horizontal coordination at the operational level may more than compensate for the loss of efficiency due to the sacrifice of operational specialization.

This result is consistent with the often-stated suggestion that the hierarchical mode of coordination based on a highly developed specialization scheme, which prevailed in the American steel and auto industries until the late 1960s, lost its advantage in the face of product variation and weakening oligopolistic control (Michael Piore and Charles Sabel 1984). Economies of specialization may be exploited more favorably for the stable and large-scale production of standardized commodities, but not for the small- and medium-batch production of varieties of products in a high-volume assembly process where thousands of independent steps must be coordinated. These markets are precisely the ones where Japanese manufacturers exhibit strong competitive capabilities; however, "in simpler processes, such as a foundry, where perhaps thirty operational steps are required, the Japanese advantage is slight, and sometimes non existent" (Abegglen and Stalk 1985, p. 61).

These propositions are consistent with the observation that Japanese manufacturers have shown relative strength in process innovation, as exemplified in the steel industry, to which intense interactions between engineers in the development laboratory and engineers, and even workers, at the factory site may contribute (Edwin Mansfield 1988). On the other hand, Japanese manufacturers have not shown a conspicuous advantage in highly uncertain innovations involving new conceptualizations of market potential and highly specialized scientific approaches. Nor have they acquired a competitive edge in industries where there is customized production of newly *designed* products, such as in the aerospace industry (David Mowery and Rosenberg 1985).

It is obvious that greater efficacy of communications and learning at the operational level tends to favor the J-mode relative to the H-mode in a large and perhaps growing sector of industry. It is interesting to note, in this connection, that the J-mode of horizontal coordination based on shared learning at the factory site has emerged and developed in the last two decades or so by relying on highly qualified and diligent blue-collar workers who have formed the core of the work team. They were mainly recruited directly out of high schools in the 1950s and early 1960s when the share of male persons who found employment right after junior high school was still as high as 45 to 25 percent depending on business cycle conditions (currently less than 4 percent). Now that the economic obstacles for qualified and motivated youths to advance to higher education have been virtually removed, a serious challenge facing representative manufacturing firms in Japan today is to recruit highly qualified blue-collar workers.

The J-mode as practiced by Japanese firms has one feature in common with advanced Western firms

as exemplified by the American computer manufacturer described in example (3), that is, *knowledge sharing* among various organizational units. The subtle difference is, however, that in the case of the American manufacturer knowledge sharing is formally instituted based on explicit documentation through the computerized network system and other technological means. In the Japanese case, by contrast, knowledge sharing and the horizontal coordination based on it are often informal and based on verbal communications (even tacit understanding), although here too there is increasing use of the computer network system as indicated by the integrated marketing-manufacturing network system of the auto manufacturer described in example (1). Such undocumented communications may generate information value by the finer use of on-site information that is too subtle or cumbersome to document usefully. But the efficacy of face-to-face communications is limited by geographical proximity. (It may be recalled that the research laboratories of Japanese manufacturers are often located at the factory site. The need for geographical proximity also may explain why there is such a high concentration of business activity in Tokyo.) Also, the ethnic homogeneity of the Japanese domestic factory may have been a crucial factor for the development and effectiveness of the J-mode (Aoki 1988a, ch. 7). Further, the dual functions of performing an operating task and learning-communicating-bargaining in contributing to smooth horizontal coordination may require intense effort on the part of blue-collar workers. It is clear that all these factors are now subject to serious challenge. On one hand, Japanese firms are expanding their activities globally to an ever increasing degree and, on the other hand, their ability to recruit qualified blue-collar workers willing to carry out intense work on the shop floor is becoming problematical as a result of recently acquired affluence.

THE HIERARCHY OF RANKS

Having examined the coordination mode of the Japanese firm, we now turn to its incentive system to see how the characteristics of these two aspects of Japanese firms are related to each other. We begin by listing some factors required for the efficient and effective operation of the J-mode that may have important bearings on the nature of the incentive system at Japanese firms.

1. In the H-mode, operating tasks are separated from the coordinating task and divided into specific functions. Operating skills valued in this mode are therefore specialized skills. In the J-mode, however, operating units are expected to be engaged in mutually coordinating their tasks as well. Exclusive attention to the efficient performance of a particular operating task in isolation may not contribute to overall efficiency (i.e., the generation of information value made possible through efficient horizontal coordination based on information sharing) and may not be appreciated much. In addition to skills in particular operating tasks, the ability to communicate and work together with peers and others with different functions is required. (Recall the role of the engineer in the integrated process control office in the steel industry in example (2) in last section.)

2. As suggested by example (1) in the previous section, smooth adaptation of production scheduling to emergent customer demands through horizontal coordination requires each operating unit to be capable of responding to needed changes quickly (e.g., in jigs and tools) and of coping independently with somewhat unusual problems (e.g., breakdown of a machine, quality defect of an in-process product). Otherwise, smooth operation may be disrupted. Workers in the final assembly line are entitled to stop the line whenever they see problems that would justify doing so. The problem is handled on the spot, possibly with the help of neighboring workers, subforemen, and so on, but not by calling in outside specialists such as mechanists. The integration of operating skill with autonomous problem-solving capability can be assured only when the worker has a good understanding of the relevant work process as a whole, rather than only a certain aspect of it. Such general understanding in turn may be nurtured by making the worker familiar with many related aspects of the work process. This is a point that Kazuo Koike has rightly emphasized in a series of influential papers (Koike 1984, 1988, 1989).

3. In examples (2) and (3) in the last section, it was pointed out that the practice of job rotation of engineers among different engineering offices as well as between engineering jobs and supervisory jobs at the factory facilitates the knowledge sharing needed for horizontal coordination among different phases of engineering and development processes. For similar and other purposes, white-collar workers on the lifetime career track (and sometimes even blue-collar workers) are rotated among various jobs in different offices and workshops every few years. Such rotation familiarizes workers with various jobs and enhances their ability to process and communicate information needed for the efficient operation of the J-mode. Regular rotation also prevents workers from identifying themselves strongly with the interests of specific jobs, workshops, plants, and offices so that the development and assertion of local interests inconsistent with the organizational goal are restrained.

These factors point to two important needs: (1) the design of incentives not tightly related to a specific job category, but that motivate wide-ranging job experience among employees; and (2) the development of a personnel office that administers such incentives and is also responsible for personnel posting, including interjurisdictional rotations, with an eye to the firm's long-run organizational goals.

As for the first, Japanese firms have developed rank hierarchies as a primary incentive device, which Aoki (1988a, ch. 2) describes in some detail (also see Ronald Dore 1973 for a classical description). The essential idea may be summarized as follows. There are usually separate rank hierarchies for blue-collar workers, white-collar workers, and engineers, as well as one for the supervisory and managerial employees above them. Each rank carries a certain level of pay, but not a specific job. Therefore employees in the same rank may be doing different jobs. For instance, an engineer at the integrated process control office, an engineer at development laboratory, and an engineer at the plant site may well be in the same rank and receive identical pay (possibly with minor allowances for particular jobs). New entrants to the firm who are just out of school are placed at appropriate ranks in the nonmanagerial rank hierarchies determined by their years of education.

After entry at an identical starting point for a certain educational credential, employees compete for promotion in rank throughout their careers. The criteria for promotion are years of service and merit, with the latter not specifically related to particular jobs but to broadly defined problem-solving abilities, communication skills, and so on. The speed of promotion for all employees is the same early in their careers, however, as young employees are consider to be in training and their aptitude for the firm's specific implementation of the J-mode is being tested. Differences in speed of promotion among employees becomes more apparent, however, in midcareer (say, after employees reach their mid-30s). So, the fast flyer among blue-collar workers may reach the top rank in his later 30s (and proceed to supervisory ranks afterward), while the slow mover may reach the top rank only a year before mandatory retirement at age 60. Promotion criteria become stricter particularly for white-collar employee as his career advances and if an employee does not exhibit continual progress he or she may be separated in mid to late career, although an honorable exit is usually arranged by the employing firm by posting the employee in a less promising quasi-outside job at a minor subsidiary or other related firm. Thus the mystifying notion of "lifetime" employment and the "seniority" system tells only half of the truth. Also it may be noted that in the late 1980s, the personnel departments of some large Japanese firms have begun official recruiting of midcareer specialists and skilled workers from other firms as the shortage of such staff has become more pronounced.

The ways in which rank hierarchy works as an incentive, that is, the ways in which it copes with the problems of moral hazard (the possibility of employees' shirking in the absence of proper monitoring), adverse selection (the difficulty of hiring the right workers, whose qualifications cannot be known with certainty prior to employment), and the provision of motivation for wide-ranging firm-specific learning and teamwork can be rigorously analyzed in the light of recent development of the incentive literature, and the theories proposed may be tested (see Aoki 1988a, ch. 3 for the theoretical analysis of Japanese employment practices and the relevant literature). From the theoretical point of view, one point should be stressed here: The existence of a credible threat of discharge when the employee does not meet the criteria for continual promotion plays an important role in enabling the rank hierarchy to operate as an effective incentive to curb shirking. A discharge in midcareer may point to some negative attributes of the discharged so that he or she may not be able to gain equivalent rank outside, when information about him or her is not perfect. So an employee must compare short-run gains from shirking with potential losses in wealth due

to discharge and consequent demotion. As stated above, in fact, "lifetime" employment and "seniority" advancement are not automatic. Otherwise, they would not be effective as incentives.

Theoretical analysis (e.g., Bentley MacLeod and James Malcomson 1986) shows, however, that actual dismissal as a disciplinary measure seldom needs to be observed, insofar as the rank-hierarchy system operates well as an effective monitoring mechanism. Also, the possibility of promotion gives employees a positive incentive to learn within the context of their employing firms, and the potential loss of seniority and of retirement compensation related to duration of employment discourages the midcareer exit of trained employees. As a result, the duration of employment tends to be relatively long for Japanese workers (e.g., Hashimoto and Raisian 1985; Mincer and Higuchi 1988). But, how much of the seniority rise in employee''s income is due to learning achievement and consequent productivity increase (which is explained by human capital theory) and how much to "bonding" for diligence (which is explained by monitoring theory) is still to be empirically settled.

In order to administer rank hierarchies, Japanese firms have developed the personnel department as an important institution. This department has full control of the recruitment of new employees for career tracks out of school, designs and runs rank hierarchies (pay scale and promotion criteria), and rotates white-collar workers with an eye to the wider interests of the organization. (The rotation of blue-collar workers may be delegated to a subsection of a personnel department at the plant level.) Since the personnel department potentially has excessive power because of its control of promotion and rotation, managers of the department are usually themselves subject to rotation. To avoid demoralizing employees by unfair treatment, the criteria for promotion and rotation are designed to be as objective as possible. Also the supervisory assessment of an employee by multiple supervisors through the rotation of the employee and supervisors may make actual personnel decisions consistent with "public opinion" within the firm. Yet mistakes and personal complaints, reasonable and unreasonable, are unavoidable. But protest by "exit" is costly; hence the enterprise union, the institution through which employees can "voice" their complaints and grievances, has developed as a counterpart to the personnel department.

The enterprise union covers all regular employees, blue-collar and white. It does not negotiate about "the" wage rate for each job category; it does negotiate about the base pay for the bottom rank, pay differentials among ranks, and the admissible range regarding the speed of promotion. Within the negotiated agreement, however, the personnel department has discretion over the ranking and job assignments of employees. One of the important roles of the enterprise union is to absorb employees' grievances about personnel decisions and to monitor the fairness of the personnel administration of the firm. It is not accidental that unions take an enterprise-based form at Japanese firms rather than that of industrial or craft unionism as in those economies where workers' careers are more oriented to a broader market rather than to the individual firm (Aoki 1984a, part 3; Koike 1984; Shirai 1984).

Thus there seems to be an interesting asymmetry between typical Western firms and typical Japanese firms regarding ways that incentive and coordination modes are interrelated. In the Japanese firm, rank hierarchy is used as a primary incentive device, while the coordination mode is less hierarchical. In contrast, the Western firm combines a relatively more hierarchical approach to coordination with the relatively decentralized market approach to incentives (i.e., clear employment contracts relating specific jobs to competitive wages may be written). In the Japanese firm, management may feel secure in delegating tasks of coordination to lower levels where relevant on-site information is available, because employees are aware that they are being evaluated by their own long-term contributions to organizational goals. Thus they are induced to comply with management authority without explicit hierarchical direction over daily operation. On the other hand, in the societal environment where more individualistic values prevail, management authority is not automatically assured within the firm organization and needs to be asserted by a contractually agreed, hierarchical structure of decision making.

Keeping in mind that the alleged asymmetry is an overly simplified stylization,[2] let us dare to summarize it in the following manner;

The First Duality Principle: In order for firms to be internally integrative and organizationally effective, either their coordination or their incentive mode needs to be hierarchical, but not both. Comparatively speaking, Japanese firms tend to be less hierarchical in the coordination mode, while they rely upon rank hierarchies in their incentive system. . . .

DUAL CONTROL OVER CORPORATE MANAGEMENT DECISION

In this section I discuss questions concerning the goals and purposes of Japanese management. We have seen in the last section that Japanese management is relatively independent of external financial control in making corporate decisions. This freedom, however, exists only so long as a satisfactory state of profits is maintained. Should that state be seriously compromised, the external power of the main bank, which stands in the background, will be exercised. This substantial, if constrained, freedom of Japanese management poses a question: Is the conventional profit-maximizing objective itself routinely qualified by an admixture of other goals? Does it apply only as a subsidiary constraint on the pursuit of other goals? Some influential economists argue in that way, for example, Komiya, who advances the hypothesis, as a first approximation, that a Japanese firm "chooses the amount of output and the amounts of labor and capital inputs so as to maximize income per employee . . . after the payment of a fixed share of profits to stockholders" (1989, p. 115).

Such a presumption essentially boils down to the model of a worker-controlled firm that postulates the maximization of income per worker since the profit motive is assumed not to have any direct impact on the decisions of corporate management. I predict, however, that it will be difficult to sustain such a hypothesis, if its implications for corporate behavior are empirically tested. For example, the hypothesis implies that to protect the interests of incumbent employees the growth rate of the worker-controlled firm would be slower than that of a profit-maximizing firm (Anthony Atkinson 1973), an unlikely situation in Japanese firms.

On the other hand, there are reasons to believe that employees as a group constitute assets specific and internal to the firm. We have seen that Japanese firms rely upon a system of horizontal coordination in which employees at the operational level actively participate. Also I have argued that the information-processing and communicative abilities of participating employees are nurtured largely through learning by doing in the context of a firm-specific coordination network. Such abilities cannot be acquired in ready-made form prior to membership in the network and their values cannot be thoroughly realized in isolation from it. In other words, skills effective for the creation of information value in the context of horizontal coordination may not be classifiable along well-defined job categories, for which market contracts transferable between firms can be unambiguously written. One may reason then that employees of Japanese firms as a group become assets specific to the internal network and that rewards for them are internally determinable (subject to possible external constraints) and payable out of the value generated by the network net of costs due to the training of employees, the sacrifice of economies of specialization, and so on.

If so, however, the following hypothetical question may be raised from another angle: Why do employees not purchase the physical assets necessary to maintain the network through debts and replicate the network, guaranteeing to themselves its whole value? In short, why would an employee-controlled firm not be created? This question arises not only out of intellectual curiosity alone, for some authors do argue that Japanese firms are in effect managed on behalf of their employees. Yet there are reasons that make it difficult for employees to control their firms explicitly and entirely. One is the obvious limitation of the availability of finance for the purpose of creating the employee-controlled firm. It may be recalled that monitoring by the main bank is particularly effective because of its dual position as a major creditor and a main stockholder. Since potential creditors are excluded from equity ownership of the employee-controlled firm, however, they may not feel as secure in providing credit and reluctant to do so.

Further, to convince all employees to move to the new "clone" firm, they must agree on how to divide up the value appropriated by the firm. This division involves costs of collective choice which may be prohibitively high, specifically when the employees are not homogeneous. Also, George Mailath and Andrew Postlewaite (1988) argued that if there are intangible gains that employees get from the firm (as distinguished from the network as such) and that they cannot each verify, they may be induced to exaggerate their reservation wages (that is, the wage at which they would move to the proposed clone firm) and that an attempt to induce truthful revelation may make a proposal for a new viable employee-controlled firm untenable. This would be especially true when the size of the network becomes very large. Such private reservation wages, for example, may take the following forms. The performances of employees of the Japanese firm are evaluated and rewarded in the long run by the elaborate and admittedly impartial personnel administration system crystallized in the hierarchy of ranks, and this may provide to workers the long-run security and the sense of fair treatment they desire. It does not seem obvious, however, how the egalitarian idea of the employee-controlled firm and the centralized management of hierarchy of ranks can be made mutually compatible. Also, the loss of the main bank's services in monitoring management may impose costs of monitoring management on each employee in terms of time, effort, and resources. Such costs may be private information.

The discussion in the preceding two paragraphs is admittedly hypothetical, but it may help us understand that the impact of financial control over Japanese firms cannot be neglected entirely even if employees are network-specific assets. A portion of the value created by the network thus accrues to financial investors who supply finance and monitor management. On the other hand, if employees' reward cannot be entirely determined by external market competition, but is negotiated internally, employees, too, would be interested in how corporate decisions are made. Corporate decisions would have an impact on workers' short-term and long-term positions in the rank hierarchies that define their lifetime earnings. Employees are not only interested, they are also able to exercise influence on corporate decisions. When employees are promoted to be executive managers, their motives may well remain mixed and contain a carry-over from their longer careers as employees in the lower ranks. It is true that, as executive managers, they must give attention to profit making in order to maintain their own position and autonomy. Yet they may retain a degree of identification with the interests of employees and a degree of freedom to support them.

Further, for financial interests as well, it may be reasonable to leave open the possibility of mutually beneficial exchange between the levels of employees' earnings and effort, on one hand, and the direction of corporate decision making, on the other. For example, employees may be willing to trade off current earnings and expend more effort for higher job security, which may also raise the profit level. Further, such exchange may help preserve the network-specific assets as well, which would be mutually beneficial in the long run. Therefore, we propose the following hypothesis, making its behavioral implications subject to future empirical testing.

The Third Duality Principle. The corporate management decisions of Japanese firms are subject to the dual control (influence) of financial interests (ownership) and employees' interests rather than to unilateral control in the interests of ownership.

It may be noted that this proposition departs not only from the usual neoclassical presupposition, but also from the "share system" view of Martin Weitzman (1984), although Weitzman claims that the Japanese economy is "the only industrial economy in the world with anything remotely resembling a share system" (p. 76). The essential difference lies in the fact that in the model I propose, not only distributive shares but also corporate decision making is implicitly or explicitly subject to "sharing." In Weitzman's theoretical design, only the share parameter defining the division of value-added between profit and workers' earnings is subject to bilateral agreement. After such agreement, corporate decision making, such as on the size of employment, is the prerogative of management who are driven exclusively by the profit motive.

If the marginal return from a worker is diminishing, yet the share parameter is fixed ex ante at less than one, income per worker is ever diminishing as the size of employment increases. On the other hand, when marginal returns are positive, management is induced to expand the size of employment.

I find it unrealistic to imagine that unions (at least the Japanese enterprise union) fail to recognize the subsequent outcome of agreeing with the Weitzman's share contract, namely that they lose control over remuneration per worker. I would maintain that the hypothesis of dual control by financial and employees' interests over corporate decision making is a more reasonable one, once the network specificity of employees' skills is accepted.

Questions to be asked next are as follows: How do firms behave under dual control? Is there any qualitative or quantitative difference between the implications of dual control and unilateral ownership control in how firms are run? How is dual control exercised? What role do management and employees each play?

First we note that employees as a group can withdraw cooperation in horizontal coordination if they feel that they are not treated "fairly" by management in pecuniary rewards and corporate decision making. On the other hand, the main bank as the major creditor cum stockholder can threaten management with the discipline of bank takeover if a sufficient level of profits over time is not assured.[3] Further, management's social prestige and autonomy are enhanced if the managed firm stands higher in corporate profit ranking. We may therefore suppose that the distribution of a firm's revenue between employees' earnings and profits reflects either the relative bargaining power of the enterprise union vis-à-vis management acting in the interests of profits or the notion of fairness by management.[4] Further, let us imagine that management strikes a balance between employees' interests and financial interests in making corporate policy. Finally, suppose that, to the degree that employees trust management corporate policy making to be fair, they supply more effort in operating activities and horizontal coordination than would be expected under the competitive wage system (i.e., more effort than maximizing "individual" labor surplus obtained by equating the marginal value disutility of effort with the wage rate).

Such mutual commitments by management and the employees are expected to yield a Pareto superior outcome under the assumption of network specificity of human assets.[5] The following are some of their behavioral implications, in which the "stockholder-controlled" firm refers to a firm that maximizes the stock value (the present value of a stream of future profits) of the firm under the competitive wage system.

1. The dually controlled firm pursues a higher growth rate (or somewhat more loosely speaking, tends to have a longer horizon) in investment decision making than the stockholder-controlled firm facing the same level of employees' current earnings, because the former takes into account employees' extra benefits from the growth of the firm in the form of enhanced future promotion possibilities in their rank hierarchies (Aoki 1988a, pp. 164–66).

2. The dually controlled firm sets the amount of employment at the level at which the marginal value product of an additional worker is equal to a worker's earnings minus the marginal rate of an implicit unemployment insurance premium. Thus if the employees' fear of unemployment is positive, the dually controlled firm provides a higher degree of job security than the stockholder-controlled firm (Aoki 1988a, pp. 174–76).

3. In order to protect the interests of incumbent employees, the dually controlled firm tends to limit the expansion of the work force relative to the growth of value-added by spinning off relatively labor-intensive activities to relatively lower wage subsidiaries or outside suppliers,[6] as well as leaning more toward capital-intensive technology than the stockholder-controlled firm (Aoki 1988a, pp. 166–74; Hajime Miyazaki 1984).

4. If the implicit unemployment insurance premium payable by employees is high, the dually controlled firm chooses work sharing rather than layoffs as a first response to bad business conditions (Aoki 1988a, pp. 176–81).

5. The dually controlled firm seeks innovative opportunities by developing an in-house knowledge base rather than pursuing breakthrough innovation requiring an entirely new organization of its research and development team (Aoki 1988a, pp. 237–52; Aoki and Rosenberg 1989).

Theoretically speaking, the dually controlled firm may be viewed as a mixture of the conventional neoclassical model (the N-model) of the stockholder-controlled firm and the model of the worker-controlled firm (the W-model) in the manner of Domar-Ward (Aoki 1984a, ch. 5). It is well known that the worker-controlled firm tends to limit the size of the labor force in order to increase the probability of job security in comparison to the conventional N-model (Miyazaki 1984). The behavioral characteristics of the W-model may help us understand propositions (2) through (4) intuitively. Proposition (1) appears to run counter to this characteristic, but note that this proposition is stated in comparison to a firm that chooses a growth rate solely to maximize its stock price after having made its wage bargain. Efficiency requires the conjoint decision of wage rate *and* growth rate when employees become assets internal to the network, because employees may be willing to forgo the current earnings level for future benefits made possible by promotion in the rank hierarchy. Proposition (5) may be understood by considering that engineers and researchers who have firm-specific knowledge are constituent members of the dually controlled firm.

The characterizations above may seem to imply that employees are the only beneficiaries of the dually controlled firm. But this is not so. As employees in the dually controlled firm may be induced to trade off the level of current earnings, make investment in training, and commit to the higher level of effort for those benefits indicated above, the profit level is expected to rise as well. In other words, once employees become network-specific assets, mutual commitments of employees and management would yield a Pareto superior outcome.

Concluding Remarks

In preceding sections, I described a model of a Japanese firm based on stylized facts, the essence of which is summarized in the three Duality Principles. This model—the J-model—is in many respects different from models of the firm constructed by Western economists. Archibald described the current state of the theory of the firm in his contribution to *The New Palgrave: A Dictionary of Economics:* "It is doubtful if there is yet general agreement among economists on the subject matter designated by 'theory of the firm,' on, that is, the scope and purpose of the part of economics so titled" (1987, p. 357). It would be fair to say, however, that agency theory is currently one of the most influential theories on the firm, especially among Anglo-American theoretical economists.

According to this theory, the firm is conceived as a "nexus of (agency) contracts" (Michael Jensen and William Meckling 1976). In an agency contract, the entity called the principal delegates decision making for realizing its own objective to the agent who may have superior on-site information, but different preferences. The principal tries to control the latter's action by the design of an appropriate incentive contract. The ultimate principal of the firm is its owner, or the stockholders in the context of the modern corporate firm, and its agent is management. Management is then conceived to operate hierarchically through a chain of incentive contracts, with management of the higher level acting as the surrogate for the ultimate principal and that of the lower level as the agents of higher-level management. At the bottom of the hierarchy, management controls operating employees through incentive contracts.

An agency contract may be written in many ways, but its design is conditioned by outside markets in one important way: the principal cannot induce the agent to enter a contractual relation unless the principal guarantees the agent at least the level of its reservation utility determined by outside opportunities. Finally, the stockholders' rights to control management are market-transferable so that the "bidding" among investors will ultimately lead to the maximization of firm's value subject to the inevitable costs incurred in the chain of agency contracts ("the agency loss").

Thus the essential factors of the agency model of the firm are summarized as: (1) hierarchical decomposition of control originating at stockholders (H-mode); (2) market-conditioned incentive contracting; and (3) the control of the management decision according to the value maximization criterion. Compare these with the three Duality Principles for the J-model. Between them, clear differences are evident. Why are there the differences? Is that because the J-model is culturally unique and useful only as a tool for a microanalytic understanding of the Japanese economy?

One of reasons why many Anglo-American economists are comfortable with the agency model as the "model of the firm" and why I am presenting the J-model as a tool for understanding the workings of the Japanese economy is doubtless that there

are differences in the ways that firms are run in the West and in Japan and that the models reflect some aspects of those real differences. But, are these differences absolute? Are they more important than the possible commonality that may not be taken into account by either of the models? If there is a convergent trend between the West and Japan, does it not mean that the J-model and the agency model represent only prototypes to be absorbed into a more general hybrid model of the firm?

The primitive comparative analysis of the H-mode versus the J-mode of coordination indicated that the relative efficiency of these two prototype models depends on various environmental parameters such as defining the nature and volatility of consumer demands, the degree of market concentration, the technology involved in the production process, and possibly government regulation. Therefore if only efficiency matters (and if relevant government regulations are alike across national economies), we would observe different coordination patterns across markets. In spite of the increasing globalization of markets the fact that we have been observing a relatively similar coordination mode within each economy, but relatively dissimilar patterns in the West and Japan, may have to do with historical, cultural, and regulation factors. As indicated just before the description of the first Duality Principle, the maintenance of organizational integrity in the context of individualistic values in the West (particularly in North America) may have necessitated contractual agreement on the more hierarchical structuring of internal coordination. On the other hand, in Japan, respect for differentiated status by attributes (sex, age, seniority, family background, etc.) and level of training has been a dominant traditional social value. A superior in Japan may therefore be more comfortable in delegating actual decision making to his subordinate. Also within a small group, horizontal coordination rather than clear job demarcation tends to emerge spontaneously in Japan, possibly because of the collective memory of the traditional agrarian customs and values (Aoki 1988b).

Having admitted that there are some cultural and historical traits in the ways that firms operate in each economy and that the efficiency criterion is not the only factor shaping the ways that firms are run, however, I would maintain that there is an important element of conscious design in viable business organizations. For example, small group dynamism per se, to which cultural anthropologists attribute the role of a driving force in Japanese organization (e.g., Chie Nakane 1970), cannot be effective in the context of large organizations. A coherent, self-centered group may develop and assert its own interests at the sacrifice of organization goals. Managements of Japanese firms have taken pains to combat such tendencies by consciously designing intergroup co-ordinational mechanisms (the *kanban* system is but one example), shifting the emphasis from seniority to merit acquired by experience as a promotion criterion. They have transformed the seniority-oriented rank hierarchies into forms compatible with an organization-wide competitive drive, and so on. The sharing of rents and the commitment to employees' interests in corporate policy making are no longer considered an expression of paternalistic benevolence of the management or owner, but can be regarded as a means to elicit employees' cooperation and diligence. Many elements of the J-model should now be regarded as serious objects of economic-analysis, particularly in view of Japanese industrial and technological challenges on the global scale.

As indicated in preceding sections, the relative merits of horizontal versus hierarchical coordination, market-oriented incentive contracting versus rank hierarchy, bank-oriented versus market-oriented financial control are not yet so clear-cut, however, and comparative analysis dealing with such issues has only just begun. Meanwhile, there is a greater tendency toward a convergence of organizational form and practice because of the strong force of natural selection operating through international market competition as well as deregulation within and across national boundaries.[7] Phenomena similar to some aspects of the J-model have emerged in the West spontaneously or as a result of conscious design, while some elements of the agency and other contractual modeling are becoming ever more visible in Japan. From this angle, the J-model may provide a new analytical insight into the working of newly emergent—or latent—phenomena in the Western economy. And similarly, the agency model may be helpful for understanding some aspects of Japanese organization. But, in the future the J-model is perhaps fated to be subsumed under the yet to be developed general theory of the firm, and so is the agency model.

NOTES

1. Between September 1987 and August 1989, I interviewed managers and engineers of about 50 Japanese manufacturing firms and banks. In particular, I conducted intensive studies, which included plant visits, of the following firms: Nippon Steel Corporation, Matsushita Electric Industrial Co., Ltd., Sony Corporation, Honda Motor Co., Ltd., Toyota Motor Corporation, Omron Tateisi Electronics Co., Kyowa Hakko Kogyo Co., Ltd., Tonen Corporation, IBM Japan, Ltd., Kajima Corporation, Ohbayashi Corporation, Toray Corporation, the Sumitomo Bank, Ltd., and the Sanwa Bank, Ltd. A small portion of interview records have been published in Aoki, Koike, and Iwao Nakatani (1989).1.

2. Organizational practices usually attributed to "Japanese management," such as life-time employment (actually long-term employment), internal career advancement based on seniority and merit, the rotation of personnel over jobs and broader job assignment, bonuses, have also been widely observed with respect to the personnel administration of white-collar employees of many "well-run" Western firms for quite some time (e.g., Fred Foulkes 1980). Koike (1984) even described the position of blue-collar workers in Japanese firms, albeit somewhat controversially, as "the white collarization of blue-collar workers."

3. Strictly speaking, there is a question as to whether there is any conflict of interest between the main bank as a creditor cum stockholder and the individual stockholders. This problem is investigated in Aoki (1984b; 1988, pp. 127–38) within the framework of a miniature general financial equilibrium model incorporating features of taxes and financial regulation in Japan. This analysis indicates that the bank prefers its portfolio company to rely more on debt financing than on equity financing than individual stockholders would do and that the conflict has been resolved in favor of the bank, although less so since the mid-1970s.

4. If the management's notion of fairness is represented by Nash's formulation of symmetry in his axiomatic approach to bargaining (Nash 1950), on one hand, and if the relative bargaining power of the union is measured in terms of "boldness" as formulated in cooperative game theory, the distributive outcomes predicted by the two approaches are identical (see Aoki 1984a, ch. 5).

5. Let us imagine as a thought experiment that management formulates corporate policy by weighting the policy optimal to the representative employee and the policy optimal to long-run profit making (i.e., the present

value of the future stream of profits), with weights being given by each distributive share in firm-specific quasi rent. I call this policy making the "weighting rule" (Aoki 1984a, pp. 74–80). Further, assume that the employees supply the level of effort that maximizes "collective" value surplus by equating the marginal value utility of effort with the marginal value product (not the wage rate). When the utility function of the profit claimant and that of representative employee are both the "constant pure boldness type" in the sense defined in Aoki (1984a, pp. 74–77), this idealized constellation of mutual commitments can be proven to yield the outcome known as the generalized Nash bargaining solution, with weights given by distributive shares (see Aoki 1984a, ch. 6; 1988, ch. 5 for a proof). As is well known, the Nash bargaining solution is the only one outcome that satisfies the set of axioms that John Nash (1950) imposed on the efficient and "fair" (symmetric) arbitration to fulfill. Also, the recent development of game theory showed that, under certain conditions, an equilibrium of a noncooperative two-person bargaining game, known as the "perfect sub-game equilibrium," exhibits qualitatively equivalent characteristics with the generalized Nash bargaining solution (Ken Binmore, Ariel Rubinstein, and Asher Wolinsky 1986). Although the idealized construct given above may appear arbitrary at first, its behavioral implications may well stand up to variant institutional assumption.

6. The use of a lower wage is only one aspect of subcontracting among many others.

7. See Note 2 for some details concerning this trend.

REFERENCES

Abegglen, James C. and Stalk, George, Jr. *Kaisha, the Japanese corporation.* NY: Basic Books, 1985.

Aoki, Masahiko. *The Co-operative game theory of the firm.* Oxford: Oxford U. Press, 1984a.

———. "Shareholders' Non-Unanimity on Investment Financing: Banks vs. Individual Investors," in *The economic analysis of the Japanese firm.* Ed.: M. Aoki. Amsterdam: North-Holland, 1984b, pp. 193–224.

———. "Horizontal vs. Vertical Information Structure of the Firm," *Amer. Econ. Rev.,* Dec. 1986, 76(5), pp. 971–83.

———. *Information, incentives, and bargaining in the Japanese economy.* NY and Cambridge: Cambridge U. Press, 1988a.

———. "Decentralization-Centralization in Japanese Organization: A Duality Principle," Mimeo., U. of Kyoto, 1988b. (To appear in *The political economy of Japan,* Vol. 3. Eds.: Shumpei Kumon and Henry Rosovsky. Stanford: Stanford U. Press.)

———. "The Participatory Generation of Information Rents and the Theory of the Firm," in *The firm as a nexus of treaties.* Eds.: Masahiko Aoki, Bo Gustafsson, and Oliver E. Williamson. London: Sage Publications, 1989, pp. 26–51.

Aoki, Masahiko; Koike, Kazuo and Nakatani, Iwao. *Nihon Kigyo Gurobaruka no Kenkyu: Jyoho-Sisutemu, R6-D, Jinzai Ikusei (The globalization of the Japanese firm).* Tokyo: PHP, 1989.

Aoki, Masahiko and Rosenberg, Nathan. "The Japanese Firm as an Innovating Institution," in *Economic institutions in a dynamic society.* Eds. Takashi Shiraishi and Shiceto Tsuru. London: Macmillan Press, 1989, pp. 137–54.

Archibald, G. C. "The Theory of the Firm," in *The new Palgrave*: *A dictionary of economics,* Vol. 2. London: Macmillan, 1987, pp. 357–63.

Atkinson, Anthony. "Worker Management and the Modern Industrial Enterprise," *Quart. J. Econ.,* Aug. 1973, 87(3), pp. 375–92.

Binmore, Ken; Rubinstein, Ariel and Wolinsky, Asher. "The Nash Bargaining Solution in Economic Modelling," *Rand J. Econ.,* Summer 1986, 17(2), pp. 176–88.

Cremer, Jacques. "Common Knowledge and the Coordination of Economic Activities," in *The firm as a nexus of treaties.* Eds: Masahiko Aoki, Bo Gustafsson, and Oliver E. Williamson. London: Sage Publications, 1989, pp. 53–76.

Dore, Ronald. *British factory, Japanese factory: The origins of national diversity in industrial relations.* Berkeley: U. of California Press, 1973.

Foulkes, Fred. *Personnel policies in large nonunion companies.* Englewood Cliffs, NJ: Prentice-Hall, 1980.

Hashimoto, Masanori and Raisian, John. "Employment Tenure and Earnings Profiles in Japan and the United States," *Amer. Econ. Rev.,* Sept. 1985, 75(4), pp. 721–35.

Itoh, Hideshi. "Information Processing Capacities of the Firm," *J of the Japanese and International Economies,* Sept. 1987, 1(3), pp. 299–326.

Jensen, Michael and Meckling, William. "Theory of the Firm: Managerial Behavior, Agency Costs and Capital Structure," *J. Finan. Econ.,* Oct. 1976, (4), pp. 305–60.

Koike, Kazuo. "Skill Formation Systems in the U.S. and Japan: A Comparative Study," in *The economic analysis of the Japanese firm.* Ed.: M. Aoki. Amsterdam: North-Holland, 1984, pp. 47–75.

———. *Understanding industrial relations in modern Japan.* London: Macmillan Press, 1988.

———. "Intellectual Skill and the Role of Employees as Constituent Members of Large Firms in Contemporary Japan," in *The firm as a nexus of treaties.* Eds.: Masahiko Aoki, Bo Gustafsson, and

Oliver E. Williamson. London: Sage Publications, 1989, pp. 185–208.

Komiya, Ryutaro. "Japanese Firms, Chinese Firms: Problems for Economic Reform in China. Part II," *J. of the Japanese and International Economies,* June 1987, 1(2), pp. 229–47.

MacLeod, Bentley W. and Malcomson, James M. "Reputation and Hierarchy in Dynamic Models of Employment." Mimeo., U. of Southampton, 1986.

Mailath, George J. and Postlewaite, Andrew. "Asymmetric Information and Bargaining Problems with Many Agents." Mimeo., U. of Pennsylvania, 1988.

Mansfield, Edwin. "Industrial R&D in Japan and the United States: A Comparative Study," *Amer. Econ. Rev.,* May 1988, 78(2), pp. 223–28.

Mincer, Jacob and Higuchi, Yoshio. "Wage Structures and Labor Turnover in the United States and Japan," *J. of the Japanese and International Economies,* June 1988, 2(2), pp. 97–133.

Miyazaki, Hajime. "Internal Bargaining, Labor Contracts, and a Marshallian Theory of the Firm," *Amer. Econ. Rev.,* June 1984, 74(3), pp. 381–93.

Mowery, David C. and Rosenberg, Nathan. "Commercial Aircraft: Cooperation and Competition Between the U.S. and Japan," *Calif. Manage. Rev.,* Summer 1985, 27(4), pp. 70–92.

Nakane, Chie. *Japanese society.* Berkeley and Los Angeles: U. of California Press, 1970.

Nash, John. "The Bargaining Problem," *Econometrica,* Apr. 1950, 18(2), pp. 155–62.

Piore, Michael and Sabel, Charles E. *The second industrial divide.* NY: Basic Books, 1984.

Shirai, Taishiro. "A Theory of Enterprise Union," in *Contemporary industrial relations in Japan.* Ed.: Taishiro Shirai. Madison: U. of Wisconsin Press, 1984, pp. 117–43.

Weitzman, Martin. *The share economy.* Cambridge: Harvard U. Press, 1984.

SOURCE: Aoki, Masahiko. 1990. Excerpt from "Toward an Economic Model of the Japanese Firm." *Journal of Economic Literature,* 28:3, 7–14, 18–24.

26

WORK ORGANIZATION, TECHNOLOGY, AND PERFORMANCE IN CUSTOMER SERVICE AND SALES

ROSEMARY BATT

There is considerable support for the idea that "high involvement" or "high performance" work systems lead to better organizational performance in manufacturing.[1] The argument is that work organized under the logic of mass production to minimize costs alone is no longer compatible with current markets, which demand competitiveness on the basis of quality, cost, innovation, and customization (Piore and Sabel 1984; Appelbaum and Batt 1994). High involvement systems, by contrast, produce better quality and efficiency because work is designed to use a higher-skilled work force with broader discretion in operational decision-making; human resource (HR) practices such as training, performance-based pay, and employment security provide complementary incentives for workers to continuously learn and innovate (Lawler 1986; Bailey 1992; Kochan and Osterman 1994; Pfeffer 1998).

At a time when high involvement work systems have gained considerable acceptance in manufacturing, however (for example, Lawler et al. 1995), many service operations are embracing mass production. For example, telemarketers, operators, and customer service and sales representatives in banking, insurance, airlines, telecommunications, and the service centers of manufacturing operations typically work in large call centers. Their work is individualized, repetitive, scripted, and machine-paced by expert systems rather than assembly lines.

In this paper I consider whether the concepts of participation and team work found in high involvement manufacturing systems also produce better performance among production-level workers in call centers—increasingly viewed as the factories of the information economy. Call center work is best conceptualized as "interactive service work" (Leidner 1993). The defining feature is the interaction of a worker with a customer to deliver a service or sell a product. In call centers, however, the interaction is mediated by telephones and computers. In this study, the subjects answer incoming calls for service inquiries (for example, billing, collections) and sales (for example, new orders, transfers, and enhanced features). As in most interactive service work, a tension exists between serving and selling: employees must take enough time with customers to answer their questions fully while simultaneously selling as much as possible and minimizing "call-handling" time. Service and sales appear to involve contradictory demands, and whether they can be "jointly optimized" is a central question in this paper.

Research on interactive service work is important because roughly 42% of the work force is employed in low-productivity service, sales, and clerical occupations (CPS 1996). Call centers have grown dramatically as a result of process reengineering. Heightened global competition in services (McKinsey 1992) and deregulation of national industries (for example, telecommunications, finance, airlines, trucking, and utilities) have led firms to search for higher productivity and quality strategies; and customer service and sales workers increasingly are viewed as critical to competitiveness because they are the face of the company to the customer.

This paper focuses on two questions. First, what is the most effective way to organize work in service and sales operations? Can work be organized to maximize both service quality and sales, or is there an inevitable trade-off? Second, where better performance occurs, what explains it? In addition, I explore what other human resource and industrial relations practices influence individual service and sales performance.

The paper answers these questions through a study of 223 unionized employees in 68 work groups in customer service centers in a large regional Bell operating company organized by the Communications Workers of America (CWA). The telecommunications services industry is an appropriate context for this research because this historically high-skill, high-wage industry achieved annual productivity growth of 6.9% in the three decades prior to 1980, but only 3.4% in the 1980s (Keefe and Boroff 1994). Since 1984, deregulation has led companies to pursue new strategies to cut costs and improve service delivery, and call centers are central to those strategies.

Previous Research

Management theorists have identified two basic strategies for competing in sales and service delivery. The first focuses on maximizing sales and minimizing costs, and adopts a mass production approach as inspired by Scientific Taylorism (Levitt 1972, 1976). The second seeks to maximize sales by providing good service, and is often referred to as "relationship management" (Gutek 1995; Keltner 1995). Under a relationship management strategy, companies build long-term relationships with customers by providing quality service. Good service is "a bridge to sales" because satisfied, loyal customers buy more and have more inelastic demand curves (Reichheld 1996; Jones and Sasser 1995). Keltner (1995) found that a strategy of relationship banking coupled with highly skilled and trained employees contributed significantly to German banks' outperforming U.S. banks in the 1980s.

For relationship management to succeed, firms need to design work so that employees have the skills and discretion to meet customer demands. Firms typically have accomplished this in one of two ways. The first draws on total quality management (TQM): individual discretion (or what TQM calls "empowerment") is coupled with employee involvement in "off-line" problem-solving groups or quality circles. The second applies the ideas of Socio-Technical Systems (STS) theory: workers organized into self-managed teams decide how to conduct their work and interact with customers. In sum, there are three common forms of work organization in service operations: a mass production approach that maximizes individual efficiency; a total quality approach that seeks to jointly maximize sales and quality by raising individual discretion and worker participation in quality circles, but leaves the supervisory structure in place; and a team approach that maximizes sales and quality through group self-regulation.

Work Organization and Customer Interaction

The mass production approach to service delivery includes a detailed functional division of labor, limited discretion for workers, and the management of customer behavior by limiting service options (Levitt 1972, 1976; Chase 1978; Lovelock 1990). Service quality is likely to suffer because customers have limited options, because employees have limited discretion to meet customer needs, and because the division of labor leads to multiple hand-offs. Individual efficiency is high because workers learn simple tasks through repetition ("practice makes perfect") and because there are few transactions costs associated with switching from one task to another or participating in training or problem-solving meetings (as in total quality or team systems). Customer dissatisfaction and employee boredom, however, lead to high turnover for both parties. High customer turnover creates a vicious cycle in which the firm focuses primarily on new sales to replenish lost customers (Schlesinger and Heskett 1991; Heskett et al. 1997). In sum, under Scientific Taylorism, sales productivity and service quality are inversely related, suggesting the following:

H1a: Workers who have limited discretion in how they conduct their work activities will have higher productivity, but offer lower service quality (compared to workers with greater discretion). Time spent in training or problem-solving meetings will decrease productivity.

In contrast to the engineering efficiency of mass production, work organization in TQM theory is driven by the characteristics and demands of customers. TQM is the source of lean production models in manufacturing, and management theorists have developed a functional equivalent for service operations (for example, Schlesinger and Heskett 1991; Bowen and Schneider 1988). Under TQM, service managers design jobs with greater discretion so that workers can meet a wide range of customer demands at any one time, referred to as "universal service" or "one-stop-shopping." Quality service leads to customer retention, and more interesting jobs reduce employee turnover. Customer service workers are viewed as strategically important because they are able to learn from customers and to build an information data base about them. As a result, workers are able both to serve the customer better and to know what sales opportunities exist, maximizing service and sales together. While "learning" under Taylorism is repetitive, "learning" under TQM is a continuous process of using new ideas and information as sources of innovation (Deming 1984).[2]

In addition to increased employee discretion, TQM usually includes the systematic use of "off-line" problem-solving or quality improvement teams (QITs): groups of workers who regularly meet with their supervisors (for example, one hour per week away from their work station) to discuss methods to improve work. Off-line teams are "consultative" in nature (Levine and Tyson 1990): that is, workers may influence management decisions, but do not have "substantive" decision-making rights to make operational changes without consulting management. Research has shown that employee involvement in offline teams has some positive effect on worker attitudes, but does not consistently affect performance (Griffin 1988; Steel et al. 1990; Adam 1991; Cotton 1993). While the use of QITs alone is unlikely to affect performance, the TQM model of greater employee discretion plus participation in QITs should produce better outcomes because workers can apply lessons from off-line teams to their daily work.

H1b: Workers who have more discretion in their work and who participate in off-line quality improvement teams will achieve higher service quality and sales than those who have less discretion and do not participate in QIT.

Team-based systems that draw on Socio-Technical Systems theory differ from the TQM model primarily because they allocate substantive decision-making rights to production-level employees and because the self-managed team (SMT) rather than the "empowered" individual is the unit of operation (Klein 1989; Adler and Cole 1993; Appelbaum and Batt 1994). Self-managed teams are defined as groups of workers who are self-managing, who have significant interdependent relations, who perceive themselves and are perceived by others as a group, and who have significant interdependent relations with other groups in a larger social system (Alderfer 1977). They are not "autonomous" or "self-designing," given that they are embedded in a large organization with hierarchical management structures fully intact (Hackman 1987).

STS theory predicts better quality and productivity because team members as a group "jointly optimize" the social and technical systems (for example, Trist and Bamforth 1951; Emery 1959; Cummings 1978; Pearce and Ravlin 1987). First, individual autonomy or discretion improves performance by shifting operational decision-making from supervisors to workers with tacit knowledge of the work process (Cummings 1978). Second, apart from individual autonomy or discretion, internal group self-regulation leads to better performance because group members learn from each other and solve problems across an entire process, rather than individually working on a small piece of it (Pearce and Ravlin 1987; Cohen 1994). Group self-regulation under STS is "substantive" rather than consultative (Levine and Tyson 1990). Finally, by reducing or eliminating supervision, teams assume more responsibility for external coordination and direct communication with employees and managers from other departments, and in the process they gain more knowledge and understanding of the broader work process. Most of the research on external coordination or "boundary maintenance" has focused on product development teams (Ancona 1990; Ancona and Caldwell 1992), but the lessons are applicable to production workers. By assuming coordination responsibilities of supervisors, employees learn more and reduce transactions costs associated with third-party (supervisory) intervention.

The empirical evidence on the performance of employees in self-managed teams is mixed, but stronger than that for individual job autonomy or participation in offline teams or quality circles.[3] Cohen and Bailey's (1997) review of research between 1990 and 1996 found 24 rigorous studies of work teams in organizations, and concluded that organizing work into self-managed teams or autonomous work groups generally produces positive performance outcomes. Most of the research on self-managed teams, however, has occurred among blue-collar workers in manufacturing. If team effectiveness is contingent on the nature of the task and technology, as STS and group effectiveness theories predict (Cummings 1978; Goodman et al. 1986; Hackman 1987), then findings from manufacturing may not generalize to services. A small number of studies of teams in production-level services have been conducted, and also have shown positive but still mixed results (Gladstein 1984; Yammarino and Dubinsky 1990; Cohen and Ledford 1994; Cohen, Ledford, and Spreitzer 1996);[4] but only one has found positive effects using objective data (Campion, Medsker, and Higgs 1993). In sum, despite some mixed results, theory and evidence support a positive hypothesized relationship between self-managed teams and performance.

H1c: Employees who work in self-managed teams will provide better-quality service and have higher sales than those who work under traditional supervision.

Work Organization and Information Technology

While the customer-worker interface is one dimension of service work, the use of information technology is a second factor affecting performance. Under mass production in services, the primary role of information technology (IT) is to electronically monitor workers and control operations (for example, Schlesinger and Heskett 1991). Under TQM, by contrast, IT becomes a resource for workers to manipulate (for example, Zuboff 1988). Skilled employees who have discretion in how they use IT systems are likely to come up with process innovations that improve service delivery and sales. One recent study, for example, found that individual autonomy and IT had a positive interactive effect on wages (Hunter and Lafkas 1998). This argument suggests the following:

H2a: The combined use of the TQM model and advanced information technology will have a positive interactive effect on individual service and sales performance.

The argument for a positive interaction between self-managed teams and technology in call centers is less straightforward. STS theory argues that if there is "fit" between the social and technical systems, the whole is greater than the sum of its parts. This fit argument, however, hinges largely on the type of technology-induced interdependence found in mining and manufacturing. Teams are appropriate in assembly-line operations because "group designs that account for necessary task interdependencies seem more appropriate than individual job designs" (Cummings 1978:627). Service and sales workers who interact individually with customers via telephones and computers do not have such interdependence.

In addition, the empirical evidence of a relationship between teams and technology in the STS literature is weak, although this is primarily because researchers have focused on social organization and have ignored technology (see Emery

1959; Cummings 1978; Goodman et al. 1986; Pasmore 1988; Cohen and Bailey 1997). In Pasmore's 1988 review of 134 studies of STS interventions, for example, only 16% included any consideration of technological change. The strongest evidence of the interactive effects of computer-aided technology and employee involvement in operational decisions comes from auto assembly (for example, MacDuffie 1995), but even in this context there is debate about what form of participation works best—a more decentralized STS-inspired team approach (Berggren 1992; Rubenstein 2000), or lean production that draws on TQM principles (for example, Adler 1993; Adler and Cole 1993).

Even where interdependence among workers is technically low, however, the three dimensions of team organization discussed above are likely to lead to positive interactive effects of teams and computer technology. As discussed above, compared to "empowered" workers under TQM, workers in self-managed teams have more opportunities to influence how work is done. Second, the group effectiveness literature argues that group work provides an opportunity structure for group goal-setting, learning, and problem-solving (for example, Hackman 1987). On-the-job learning from experienced peers is an important source of tacit knowledge, particularly in an environment where product information and service offerings are rapidly changing. That is, the nature of service and sales work itself does not change under group designs—workers sit at their individual computers and interact with customers—but each member has access to the collective knowledge of the group. Third, the external coordination and communication function is likely to provide team members with additional sources of knowledge for solving technical problems associated with computer-use. These arguments suggest the following:

H2b: The combined use of self-managed teams and advanced information technology will have a positive interactive effect on individual service and sales performance.

Dimensions of Teams and Performance

A final issue to consider is what explains the performance outcomes of teams. If teams have a positive effect on performance, are some dimensions of teams more important than others? Do some dimensions have differential effects on service versus sales performance? For example, group interaction may be a source of learning but may also reduce the amount of time spent with customers, thereby reducing opportunities to sell. Similarly, the external coordination function may be more important for providing good service—for example, consulting with other departments about the status of an order—but may not improve sales. The STS and teams literatures discussed above, however, theorize that all three dimensions contribute to performance outcomes, suggesting the following hypothesized relationship:

H3: Employee participation in self-managed teams leads to better service and sales in three ways: by creating a structure that encourages greater individual discretion at work; by creating a structure of group self-regulation that leads to better learning and problem-solving; and by creating responsibility for external coordination and information gathering across groups and individuals in other departments.

Work, Technology, and Organizational Context

The site for the study is a large, multi-state regional Bell operating company (RBOC), and the subjects are customer service representatives (CSRs) handling service inquiries and sales requests from residential customers through incoming telephone calls.[5] The organization of work has changed dramatically since the early 1980s, both because of industry deregulation beginning in 1984 and because of new technologies. Like the other former Bell companies, this company adopted a mass production approach to service delivery in response to deregulation, and shifted emphasis from customer service to sales productivity. Prior to deregulation, CSRs (called business office staff) were viewed as providing a public service because telephones were considered a basic necessity. Business office staff provided "universal service" to all customers in small local business offices. Since deregulation, CSRs have been viewed primarily as a sales force. Companies have consolidated operations into large "mega-centers" of several hundred workers, with different centers for functional specialties (for example, service and sales, collections, repair, tele-marketing). Process reengineering has routinized and standardized customer interactions.

The CSRs in this study handle service (for example, billing and product information) and sales (basic service, transfers, internet service, upgrades, voice mail, call waiting, and so on). CSRs simultaneously interact with the customer on the telephone and input information directly into computer data bases while the customer is on the line. For complex orders, CSRs do follow-up work on the computer or manually. CSRs receive thirteen weeks of initial training, and reach proficiency in six months to a year, according to manager interviews. The skill requirements for the job include customer interaction skills; keyboard skills; knowledge of procedures, products, services, and legal regulations (which vary by local and state regulation); and technical proficiency in programming language (the traditional AT&T UNIX or Legacy system) plus, on average, eight database programs.

All employees are organized into work groups, with one supervisor for every ten employees. Supervisors have three functions: to handle non-routine calls, customer complaints, and inquiries to managers or subject-matter experts in other departments; to teach or coach employees to improve their performance; and to monitor and discipline. Work is organized to emphasize the vertical relationship between the supervisor and each worker and to minimize co-worker interaction.

Management has sought to achieve high productivity through the use of advanced information systems that automate routine functions and electronically monitor performance. The information system records the content of customer-employee interactions and the time employees spend in each type of work activity: on-line open to receive a customer, on-line with a customer, on-hold with a customer (for example, checking information or completing an order), closed (completing paper work, going to the restroom or lunch, and so on). Company-developed algorithms provide targets for the time allowed for each type of activity; managers at a central control panel watch for flashing lights of various colors that indicate if an employee has gone beyond the allotted time in any one area. Supervisors then use their discretion to counsel or

discipline employees who are at variance from the targeted time allotments (known as "out of adherence"). Average call-handling time (cycle time for the job) is targeted at 300 seconds, and service representatives are expected to complete 90 calls per day. They complete transactions with customers individually and are discouraged from interacting with fellow employees.

At the time of the study, the company was in the process of upgrading the computer information system, and roughly half of the sample was using the new system. The new system automatically paced work by sending calls directly to "open" employees, rather than having them pick up the phone. Employees had less "closed time" away from the computer to finish up orders or handle non-routine problems. In order to cope with the system, employees had to develop "workarounds," or ways of working with the new technology to make sure that orders were written up or problems taken care of before another customer came on the line. They experienced the new technology as a "speed up" or intensification of the pace of work.

In this context, employees also were evaluated on "quality service." They experienced the twin demands of maximizing sales and service as contradictory because the latter took time away from the former. Employees had to use their own discretion to decide how much time to spend on each. Experienced CSRs often used their expertise to investigate a billing issue or a customer's record when they suspected fraud, to arrange for alternative pay schedules, or to provide what they considered to be good service—even though they risked receiving disciplinary action if they stayed on the line too long. Managers and union representatives alike agree that CSR jobs are the most stressful ones in the industry—higher-stress than telephone operator jobs because of intense pressure to simultaneously sell, provide "quality" service, and turn over calls, all in the context of pervasive electronic monitoring.

Joint Union-Management Work Innovations

In this context, the regional union and corporate management negotiated parameters for joint participation in a TQM program and a self-managed team program in order to improve service quality and reduce high stress levels among employees. Management also sought to cut staff; and the union viewed the programs as a way to save union jobs by eliminating supervisory positions. Participation in both programs was strictly voluntary, and implementation tended to occur where local union-management relations were cooperative. Pairs of union and management trainers worked with local officials to promote consistent implementation across the company. A joint union-management structure at the corporate, state, and local levels oversaw the programs.

The TQM program consisted of three dimensions: increased discretion or "empowerment" to meet customer demands or make adjustments in customers' bills up to $200 without prior approval; TQM training; and participation in off-line quality improvement teams (QITs). For the self-managed team program, local managers and union leaders developed written agreements specifying what supervisory tasks teams would assume; these included setting daily assignments, writing up reports, covering breaks and schedules, handling non-routine problems, and calling directly on subject matter experts as needed. With the supervisor absent, these teams were responsible for learning and problem-solving. They received additional training, but no additional pay, and remained under the same contractual provisions as other workers. They worked in the same offices and under the same managers as traditionally supervised groups (TSGs). Joining teams was voluntary; volunteers were selected jointly by local managers and union leaders, who said in interviews that they chose a mix of "good and bad" performers to participate in self-managed teams in order to reduce conflicts between them and traditional groups. . . .

Discussion

In summary, this research compares the effectiveness of three approaches to organizing work in call centers: mass production, total quality management, and self-managed teams. I found that compared to mass production, TQM had no statistically significant positive effects on performance; and there were no interactive effects associated with TQM and technology. By contrast, participation in self-managed teams raised objective sales by 9.3%. Time spent in SMT meetings, often a concern of management, had a statistically significant negative effect on sales of .1 %, so that the net effect of teams was 9.2%. The interactive effect of team participation and use of new technology raised sales by an additional 17.4%. Participation in teams also significantly raised self-reported service quality. In addition, the effects associated with teams did not erode over time.

Perceptions of job insecurity were associated with decreased service quality and higher sales. A reasonable interpretation is that job insecurity led workers to reduce the time and attention (quality of interactions) they gave to each customer in order to increase the number of calls they handled and, hence, sales volume. They probably did this because their performance evaluations were weighted more heavily toward maximizing sales and minimizing call handling time than toward providing high-quality service.

It is important to interpret these findings in context. The level of decentralized decision-making was minimal compared to the classic model of self-managed teams in the literature. The team model, for example, did not challenge the extensive process standardization in the call centers. The large and statistically significant performance advantages of teams are surprising given the context of this study. Four organizational factors would argue against the successful implementation of teams in this context: the nature of work and technology did not require interdependence; process standardization and organizational structure limited opportunities for self-regulation; setting boundaries around a small team's work in the context of a large office setting (considered critical for group effectiveness) (for example, Cummings and Huse 1989) was not possible; and human resource practices such as group-based pay and job security were not in place.

This raises the question of what dimensions of teams are really important as drivers of better service and sales, and the structural equation analysis points to the importance of group self-regulation, rather than individual discretion or external coordination. What does group "self-regulation" mean, however, in this highly routinized environment?

The results from qualitative field research suggest that the real value of teams centered around group goal-setting, problem-solving, and learning. Workers in teams emphasized that the program "got the supervisor off our backs and allowed us to work together." They said that they established group sales goals, rather than individual ones, and then helped each other with developing sales strategies, handling problem customers, and keeping up with rapid changes in product information, work procedures, and legal regulations. They explicitly noted the contradiction of "going self-managed" in the context of increasingly automated technology, but said that the benefits of teams were even more important in that context. Both the automated technology and management efforts to maximize call volume created a work environment in which social interactions in traditionally supervised groups were minimized. Employees were not supposed to talk to one another because that meant time away from call-handling and sales opportunities. The rapidity of change in both product and legal information and software technology, however, meant that both selling and good service required on-going learning and problem-solving that was more effectively accomplished in groups.

CONCLUSION

One reason the institutional context of this case is important is that the historic HR practices of the Bell System had created a highly skilled work force with tremendous tacit knowledge of the customers, the telecommunications infrastructure, and the use of information systems. In addition, a long history of mature collective bargaining created a climate of trust, and union support for the program provided employees with confidence to fully participate in ways that might otherwise not have occurred. Thus, arguably, the industrial relations system provided the kind of support viewed as necessary for successful implementation of high involvement work systems. The missing incentives were group-based pay and job security, and as indicated earlier, employees viewed self-managed teams as a vehicle to enhance security. Not long after the experimental implementation of total quality and team management, the company let both programs dissolve, and union-management relations deteriorated in the face of on-going

downsizing and reengineering. Management reasoning was that small teams are not consistent with reengineering, where the gains from automation and process standardization are significant; and participatory meetings are a waste of time. The company, like others, has moved in the direction of a mass production model of individualized work, faster cycle times, and stricter adherence to schedules. It has created training modules on-line to reduce initial training, and has shifted much of subsequent training to on-line, self-paced modules. Virtually all training and work-related information (work procedures, system capabilities, product information, legal regulations) are on-line; employees receive eight to ten e-mail messages per day advising them of any updates in any of their systems. Employees are discouraged from asking questions or talking with one another because doing so reduces productive work time. The company has also introduced individual sales commissions as an incentive plan. The evidence in this case, however, argues against this type of mass production model, even on the basis of sales efficiency, because effective sales as well as service quality depend on continuous learning, processing of information, and tacit knowledge that group collaboration appears to foster.

NOTES

1. See, for example, Levine and Tyson (1990); Cutcher-Gershenfeld (1991); Arthur (1992); Snell and Dean (1992); Adler (1993); MacDuffie (1995); Becker and Gerhart (1996); Berg et al. (1996); Kelley (1996); Ichniowski et al. (1995, 1996); Rubenstein (2000) Appelbaum et al. (2000); Pfeffer (1998).

2. The application of TQM to services differs from that of manufacturing because of differences in the nature of the work and technology (Zimmerman and Enell 1988). In manufacturing, workers interact with machines and use TQM tools such as statistical process control (SPC) to improve quality by reducing process variances (unprogrammed deviation from standards or procedures). In services, by contrast, the interaction with customers is the critical point of production. Whereas manufacturing workers "add value" through their knowledge of the production process to reduce variances, service workers "add value" through their direct knowledge of customers, and the use of that knowledge to increase customization.

3. Much of the early research lacked independent or objective outcome measures, suffering from single-source or common method bias where correlations between independent and dependent variables are likely to be inflated (Roberts and Glick 1981; Wagner and Gooding 1987). Early studies found strong positive results of SMTs for outcomes for workers (for example, satisfaction, safety), but inconsistent or negative results for firms (absenteeism, turnover, commitment, and various definitions of performance) (Pasmore, Francis, and Haldeman 1982; Wall, Jackson, and Clegg 1986; Pearce and Ravlin 1987; Cordery, Mueller, and Smith 1991). Guzzo, Jette, and Katzell (1985) found modest productivity improvements for 11 STS interventions, but no effect on absenteeism. Beekun's 1989 meta-analysis found some productivity improvements; Cotton (1993), Macy and Izumi (1993), and Cohen and Bailey (1997) reported the most consistent positive results.

4. Gladstein (1984), in a study of 100 sales teams in telecommunications, found that team processes had a statistically significant positive relationship with self-reported effectiveness, but not with objective sales. Yammarino and Dubinsky (1990) found that group autonomy was positively related to managerial ratings of sales workers in retail sales, but not insurance. Campion, Medsker, and Higgs (1993) found that group autonomy contributed to better performance among 80 groups of clerical workers in financial services. A study of 100 matched pairs of self-managed and traditionally supervised work groups in telecommunications (Cohen and Ledford 1994; Cohen, Ledford, and Spreitzer 1996) reported that team and manager evaluations (but not supervisor evaluations) of craft and administrative support teams were higher; but those for customer service and sales workers were not.

5. This section describes changes in one company, but my field research in several other Bell companies confirmed that the RBOCs have followed similar patterns in their management strategies, use of technology, and HR practices. The RBOCs still employ the overwhelming majority of the work force in telecommunications. For a fuller account of changes in markets, technology, and work organization in the industry, see Batt and Keefe (1999).

REFERENCES

Adam, Everett E. 1991. "Quality Circle Performance." *Journal of Management,* Vol. 17, No. 1 (March), pp. 25–39.

Adler, Paul. 1993. "The 'Learning Bureaucracy': New United Motor Manufacturing, Inc." In Barry Staw and Larry Cummings, eds., *Research in Organizational Behavior,* Vol. 15. Greenwich, Conn.: JAI Press, pp. 111–94.

Adler, Paul, and Robert Cole. 1993. "Designed for Learning: A Tale of Two Auto Plants." *Sloan Management Review,* Vol. 34, No. 3 (Fall), pp. 85–94.

Alderfer, Clayton P. 1977. "An Intergroup Perspective on Group Dynamics." In J. W. Lorsch, ed., *Handbook of Organizational Behavior.* Englewood Cliffs, N.J.: Prentice-Hall, pp. 190–222.

Ancona, Deborah G. 1990. "Outward Bound: Strategies for Team Survival in an Organization." *Academy of Management Journal,* Vol. 33, No. 2, pp. 334–65.

Ancona, Deborah G., and David F. Caldwell. 1992. "Demography and Design: Predictors of New Product Team Performance." *Organization Science,* Vol. 3, No. 3 (August), pp. 321–41.

Appelbaum, Eileen, Thomas Bailey, Peter Berg, and Arne Kalleberg. 2000. *Manufacturing Competitive Advantage: The Effects of High Performance Work Systems on Plant Performance and Worker Outcomes.* Ithaca, N.Y.: Cornell University Press, forthcoming.

Appelbaum, Eileen, and Rosemary Batt. 1994. *The New American Workplace: Transforming Work Systems in the United States.* Ithaca, N.Y.: ILR Press (an imprint of Cornell University Press).

Arthur, Jeffrey. 1992. "The Link between Business Strategy and Industrial Relations Systems in American Steel Minimills." *Industrial and Labor Relations Review,* Vol. 45, No. 3 (April), pp. 488–506.

Bailey, Thomas. 1992. "Discretionary Effort and the Organization of Work: Employee Participation and Work Reform since Hawthorne." Manuscript prepared for the Alfred P. Sloan Foundation, August.

Batt, Rosemary, and Jeffrey Keefe. 1999. "Human Resource and Employment Practices in Telecommunications Services." In Peter Cappelli, ed., *Employment Strategies: Why Similar Employers Manage Differently.* Oxford: Oxford University Press, forthcoming.

Becker, Brian, and Barry Gerhart. 1996. "Special Research Forum: Human Resource Management and Organizational Performance." *Academy of Management Journal,* Vol. 39, No. 4, pp. 777–985.

Beekun, Rafik I. 1989. "Assessing the Effectiveness of Sociotechnical Interventions: Antidote or Fad?" *Human Relations,* Vol. 42, No. 10, pp. 877–97.

Berg, Peter, Eileen Appelbaum, Thomas Bailey, and Arne Kalleberg. 1996. "The Performance Effects of Modular Production in the Apparel Industry." *Industrial Relations,* Vol. 35, No. 3, pp. 356–73.

Berggren, Christian. 1992. *Alternatives to Lean Production: Work Organization in the Swedish Auto Industry.* Ithaca, N.Y.: ILR Press (an imprint of Cornell University Press).

Bollen, Kenneth. 1989. *Structural Equations with Latent Variables.* New York: John Wiley & Sons.

Bowen, David E., and Benjamin Schneider. 1988. "Services Marketing and Management: Implications for Organizational Behavior." In B. M. Staw and L. L. Cummings, eds., *Research in Organizational Behavior,* Vol. 10. Greenwich, Conn.: JAI Press, pp. 43–80.

Campion, Michael A., Gina J. Medsker, and A. Catherine Higgs. 1993. "Relations between Work Group Characteristics and Effectiveness: Implications for Designing Effective Work Groups." *Personnel Psychology,* Vol. 46, No. 3, pp. 823–50.

Chase, Richard B. 1978. "Where Does the Customer Fit in a Service Operation?" *Harvard Business Review,* Vol. 56, No. 6, pp. 137–42.

Cohen, Jacob, and Patricia Cohen. 1983. *Applied Multiple Regression/Correlation Analysis in Behavioral Sciences,* 2nd ed. Hillsdale, N. J.: Lawrence Erlbaum.

Cohen, Susan G. 1994. "Designing Effective Self-Managing Work Teams." In M. Beyerlein and D. Johnson, eds., *Advances in Interdisciplinary Studies of Work Teams,* Vol. 1. Greenwich, Conn.: JAI Press, pp. 67–102.

Cohen, Susan, and Diane Bailey. 1997. "What Makes Teams Work: Group Effectiveness Research from the Shop Floor to the Executive Suite." *Journal of Management,* Vol. 23, No. 3 (June), pp. 239–90.

Cohen, Susan, and Gerald Ledford. 1994. "The Effectiveness of Self-Managing Teams: A Quasi-Experiment." *Human Relations,* Vol. 47, No. 1, pp. 13–43.

Cohen, Susan, Gerald Ledford, and Gretchen Spreitzer. 1996. "A Predictive Model of Self-Managing Work Team Effectiveness." *Human Relations,* Vol. 49, No. 5 (May), pp. 643–76.

Cordery, John L., Walter S. Mueller, and Leigh M. Smith. 1991. "Attitudinal and Behavioral Effects of Autonomous Group Working: A Longitudinal Field Study." *Academy of Management Journal,* Vol. 34, No. 2, pp. 464–76.

Cotton, John L. 1993. *Employee Involvement: Methods for Improving Performance and Work Attitudes.* Newbury Park, Calif.: Sage.

Cummings, Thomas G. 1978. "Self-Regulating Work Groups: A Socio-Technical Synthesis." *Academy of Management Review,* Vol. 3, No. 4 (July), pp. 625–34.

Cummings, Thomas G., and E. F. Huse. 1989. *Organizational Development and Change.* St. Paul, Minn.: West.

Current Population Survey (CPS). 1996. Merged Annual Earnings Files. Washington, D.C.

Cutcher-Gershenfeld, Joel. 1991. "The Impact on Economic Performance of a Transformation in Workplace Relations." *Industrial and Labor Relations Review,* Vol. 44, No. 2 (January), pp. 241–60.

Deming, Edward. 1984. *Out of the Crisis.* Cambridge, Mass.: MIT Press.

Emery, F. 1959. *Characteristics of Socio-Technical Systems.* Document No. 527. London: Tavistock Institute.

Erez, Amir, Diane Johnson, and Timothy Judge. 1995. "Self-Deception as a Mediator of the Relationship between Dispositions and Subjective Well-Being." *Person. Individual Differences,* Vol. 19, No. 5, pp. 597–612.

Gladstein, Deborah L. 1984. "Groups in Context: A Model of Task Group Effectiveness." *Administrative Science Quarterly,* Vol. 29, No. 4 (December), pp. 499–517.

Griffin, Ricky W. 1988. "Consequences of Quality Circles in an Industrial Setting: A Longitudinal Assessment." *Academy of Management Journal,* Vol. 31, No. 2, pp. 338–58.

Goodman, Paul S., Elizabeth C. Ravlin, and Linda Argote. 1986. "Current Thinking about Groups: Setting the Stage." In P. S. Goodman, ed., *Designing Effective Work Groups.* San Francisco: Jossey-Bass, pp. 1–33.

Gutek, Barbara. 1995. *The Dynamics of Service: Reflections on the Changing Nature of Customer/ Provider Interactions.* San Francisco: Jossey-Bass.

Guzzo, Richard A., Richard D. Jette, and Raymond A. Katzell. 1985. "The Effects of Psychologically Based Intervention Programs on Worker Productivity: A Meta-Analysis." *Personnel Psychology,* Vol. 38, No. 3, pp. 275–91.

Hackman. J. Richard. 1987. "The Design of Work Teams." In J. W. Lorsch, ed., *Handbook of Organizational Behavior.* Englewood Cliffs, N.J.: Prentice-Hall, pp. 315–42.

Heskett, James, W. Earl Sasser, Jr., and Christopher Hart. 1990. *Service Breakthroughs: Changing the Rules of the Game.* New York: Free Press.

Heskett, James, W. Earl Sasser, Jr., and Leonard A. Schlesinger. 1997. *The Service Profit Chain: How Leading Companies Link Profit and Growth to Loyalty, Satisfaction, and Value.* New York: Free Press.

Huber, P. J. 1967. "The Behavior of Maximum Likelihood Estimates under Non-Standard Conditions." *Proceedings of the Fifth Berkeley Symposium on Mathematical Statistics and Probability,* Vol. 1, pp. 221–33.

Hunter, Larry W., and John J. Lafkas. 1998. "Information Technology, Work Practices, and Wages." *Proceedings of the 50th Annual Meeting of the Industrial Relations Research Association.* Madison, Wisc: IRRA.

Ichniowski, Casey, Thomas Kochan, David Levine, Craig Olson, and George Strauss. 1996. "What Works at Work: Overview and Assessment." *Industrial Relations,* Vol. 35, No. 3, pp. 299–334.

Ichniowski, Casey, Kathryn Shaw, and Giovanna Prennushi. 1995. "The Effects of Human Resource Management Practices on Productivity." Working Paper No. 5333, National Bureau of Economic Research.

Jones, Thomas O., and W. Earl Sasser, Jr. 1995. "Why Satisfied Customers Defect." *Harvard Business Review* (Nov.–Dec.), pp. 88–99.

Joreskog, Karl G., and Dag Sorbom. 1993. *Lisrel 8 User's Reference Guide.* Chicago: Scientific Software International.

Keefe, Jeffrey, and Karen Boroff. 1994. "Telecommunications Labor Management Relations after Divestiture." In Paula Voos, ed., *Contemporary Collective Bargaining in the Private Sector.* Madison, Wis.: Industrial Relations Research Association.

Kelley, Maryellen R. 1996. "Participative Bureaucracy and Productivity in Machined Products." *Industrial Relations,* Vol. 35, No. 3, pp. 374–99.

Keltner, Brent. 1995. "Relationship Banking and Competitive Advantage: Evidence from the U.S. and Germany." *California Management Review,* Vol. 37, No. 4 (Summer), pp. 45–73.

Klein, Janice. 1989. "A Reexamination of Autonomy in Light of New Manufacturing Practices." *Human Relations,* Vol. 44, No. 1. pp. 21–38.

Kochan, Thomas, and Paul Osterman. 1994. *The Mutual Gains Enterprise.* Boston: Harvard Business School Press.

Lawler, Edward E. III. 1986. *High-Involvement Management: Participative Strategies for Improving Organizational Performance.* San Francisco: Jossey-Bass.

Lawler, Edward E. III, and Susan A. Mohrman. 1987. "Quality Circles: After the Honeymoon." *Organizational Dynamics,* Vol. 15 (Spring), pp. 42–54.

Lawler, Edward E. III, Susan Mohrman, and Gerald Ledford. 1995. *Creating High Performance Organizations: Practices and Results of Employee Involvement and Total Quality Management in Fortune 1000 Companies.* San Francisco: Jossey-Bass.

Leidner, Robin. 1993. *Fast Food, Fast Talk: Service Work and the Routinization of Everyday Life.* Berkeley: University of California Press.

Levine, David I. and Laura D'Andrea Tyson. 1990. "Participation, Productivity, and the Firm's Environment." In Alan S. Blinder, ed., *Paying for Productivity: A Look at the Evidence.* Washington, DC: The Brookings Institution, 183–241.

Levitt, Theodore. 1972. "Production Line Approach to Services." *Harvard Business Review,* Vol. 50 (September–October), pp. 41–52.

———. 1976. "The Industrialization of Service." *Harvard Business Review,* Vol. 54 (September–October), pp. 63–74.

Lovelock, Christopher. 1990. "Managing Interactions between Operations and Marketing and Their Impact on Customers." In David Bowen, Richard B. Chase, and Thomas Cummings, eds., *Service Management Effectiveness: Balancing Strategy, Organization and Human Resources, Operations, and Marketing.* Oxford: Jossey-Bass, pp. 343–68.

MacDuffie, John Paul. 1995. "Human Resource Bundles and Manufacturing Performance: Organizational Logic and Flexible Production Systems in the World Auto Industry." *Industrial and Labor Relations Review,* Vol. 48, No. 2 (January), pp. 197–221.

Macy, Barry A., and Hiroaki Izumi. 1993. "Organizational Change, Design, and Work Innovation: A Meta-Analysis of 131 North American Field Studies, 1961–1991." *Research in Organizational Change and Development,* Vol. 7, pp. 235–313.

McKinsey, G. I. 1992. *Service Sector Productivity.* Washington. D.C.: McKinsey.

Pasmore, William A. 1988. *Designing Effective Organizations: The Sociotechnical Systems Perspective.* New York: Wiley.

Pasmore, William A., C. Francis, and J. Haldeman. 1982. "Sociotechnical Systems: A North American Reflection on Empirical Studies of the Seventies." *Human Relations,* Vol. 35, No. 12, pp. 1179–1204.

Pearce, John A., and Elizabeth C. Ravlin. 1987. "The Design and Activation of Self-Regulating Work Groups." *Human Relations,* Vol. 40, No. 11, pp. 751–81.

Pfeffer, Jeffrey. 1998. *The Human Equation: Building Profits through People.* Cambridge, Mass.: Harvard Business School Press.

Piore, Michael, and Charles Sabel. 1984. *The Second Industrial Divide.* New York: Basic Books.

Reichheld, Frederick F. 1996. *The Loyalty Effect.* Boston: Harvard Business School Press.

Roberts, Karlene H., and William Glick. 1981. "The Job Characteristics Approach to Task Design: A Critical Review." *Journal of Applied Psychology,* Vol. 66, No. 2, pp. 193–217.

Rubenstein, Saul. 2000. "The Impact of Co-Management on Quality Performance: The Case of the Saturn Corporation." Forthcoming, *Industrial and Labor Relations Review.*

Schlesinger, Leonard, and James Heskett. 1991. "Breaking the Cycle of Failure in Services." *Sloan Management Review,* Vol. 32 (Spring), pp. 17–28.

Snell, Scott, and James Dean. 1992. "Integrated Manufacturing and Human Resource Management: A Human Capital Perspective." *Academy of Management Journal,* Vol. 35, No. 3, pp. 467–503.

Steel, Robert P., Kenneth R. Jennings, and James T. Lindsey. 1990. "Quality Circle Problem Solving and Common Cents: Evaluation Study Findings from a United States Mint." *Journal of Applied Behavioral Science,* Vol. 26, No. 3, pp. 365–82.

Trist, Eric L., and K. W. Bamforth. 1951. "Some Social and Psychological Consequences of the Long Wall Method of Coal-Getting." *Human Relations,* Vol. 4, pp. 3–38.

Wagner, John A., and Richard Z. Gooding. 1987. "Shared Influence and Organizational Behavior: A Meta-Analysis of Situational Variables Expected to Moderate Participation Outcome Relationships." *Academy of Management Journal,* Vol. 30, No. 3, pp. 524–41.

Wall, Toby, Nigel Kemp, Paul Jackson, and Chris Clegg. 1986. "Outcomes of Autonomous Work Groups: A Long-Term Field Experiment." *Academy of Management Journal,* Vol. 29, No. 2, pp. 280–304.

Yammarino, Francis J., and Alan J. Dubinsky. 1990. "Salesperson Performance and Managerially Controllable Factors: An Investigation of Individual and Work Group Effects." *Journal of Management,* Vol. 16, No. 1 (Spring), pp. 87–106.

Zimmerman, Charles, and John Enell. 1988. "Service Industries." In J. M. Duran and Frank Gryna, eds., *Juran's Quality Control Handbook,* 4th ed. New York: McGraw-Hill, pp. 33.1–72.

Zuboff, Shoshana. 1988. *In the Age of the Smart Machine.* New York: Basic Books.

SOURCE: Batt, Rosemary. 1999. "Work Organization, Technology and Performance in Customer Service and Sales." *Industrial and Labor Relations Review*, 52:539–64.

27

CONNECTIVE LEADERSHIP

Female Leadership Styles in the 21st-Century Workplace

JEAN LIPMAN-BLUMEN

American cultural traditions define personality, achievement, and the purpose of human life in ways that leave the individual suspended in glorious, but terrifying, isolation.

—Bellah, Madsen, Sullivan, Swidler, and Tipton 1985:6

CONNECTIVE LEADERSHIP: AN INTEGRATIVE MODEL FOR THE 21ST CENTURY

Contrary to traditional beliefs, female leadership is no longer an oxymoron. Viewed from the perspective of global interdependence, it contains the seeds of connective leadership, a new, integrative model of leadership more suited to the dramatically changing workplace of the twenty-first century. Inevitably, the workplace will reflect the increasingly interdependent, external environment, shaped by new realities and demands emanating from global political and economic trends (Starr 1988; Drucker 1989). Internally, the backgrounds, talents, and interests of a highly diverse work force will foster additional, yet consonant, transformations in the workplace (Pfeffer 1983; Gutek, Larwood, and

Stromberg 1986). To address the complex demands of the twenty-first-century workplace, organizational and political leadership will need to reflect certain behaviors to which females traditionally have been socialized, but which many women are being urged to abandon to ensure their occupational success.

"Connective leadership" derives its label from its character of connecting individuals not only to their own tasks and ego drives, but also to those of the group and community that depend upon the accomplishment of mutual goals. It is leadership that connects individuals to others and *others'* goals, using a broad spectrum of behavioral strategies. It is leadership that "proceed(s) from a premise of connection" (Gilligan 1982:38) and a recognition of networks of relationships that bind society in a web of mutual responsibilities. It shares responsibility, takes unthreatened pride in the accomplishments of colleagues and protégés, and experiences success without the compulsion to outdo others.

Connective leadership reaches out beyond its own traditional constituencies to presumed adversaries, using mutual goals, rather than mutual enemies, to create group cohesion and community membership (Gardner 1990). It is leadership able to resolve the tension between agency and communion (Bakan 1966), comfortable in integrating others' diverse needs, able to take pride in others' success that may even surpass one's own. This new, integrative form of leadership not only encompasses both transactional and transformational behaviors (Burns 1978; Tichy and Devanna 1986; Doig and Hargrove 1987; Bass 1990; Gardner 1990), but also stretches its practitioners beyond individualism and charisma (Gerth and Mills 1946; Kouzes and Posner 1987; Conger 1989), even beyond competition and collaboration (Gray 1989; Badaracco 1991).

THE PSYCHOLOGICAL ROOTS: GENDER DIFFERENCES

The components of connective leadership are familiar to women, but more worrisome to men. Gilligan (1982), Miller (1976), and Chodorow (1974) concur that the psychosocial trajectories of women and men are differentially characterized by their respective needs for connection and separation. For males, separation from the maternal figure is the path to individuation and maturity. Competitively moving out beyond others, in ways delineated by rule-bound, hierarchical structures, becomes the mark of mature male success. According to post-Freudian interpretations, only under highly structured conditions can adult males feel comfortable acknowledging their connections to others. According to Gilligan (1982:44), "Rule-bound competitive achievement situations, which for women threaten the web of connection, for men provide a mode of connection that establishes clear boundaries and limits aggression, and thus appears comparatively safe."

For many females, connecting to, caring for, and taking responsibility for mediating the conflicting needs of others indicate adult success and provide a sense of safety. Females commonly interpret the various stages in structural hierarchies as problematical way stations of separation, positions dangerously poised at the far reaches of the social web (Chodorow 1974; Miller 1976; Gilligan 1982). Females' definition of self involves altruistically helping and caring for others (Fowlkes 1983), a self-definition historically reflected in traditional female occupations.[1]

The traditional American concept of leadership is a pastiche based upon a masculine ego-ideal glorifying the competitive, combative, controlling, creative, aggressive, self-reliant individualist. It describes a leadership form better suited to a frontier society than to the interdependent global and organizational environments that will characterize the twenty-first century. This standard leadership image is dominated by behaviors focussed on task mastery, competition, and power, and encapsulated in a limited set of achieving styles, labeled "direct achieving styles."

THE AMERICAN EGO-IDEAL AND ACHIEVING STYLES

"Achieving styles,"[2] central to this discussion, are simply the characteristic ways in which individuals go about getting things done—the learned behaviors people use for achieving goals regardless of their substantive nature. One might conceptualize achieving styles as personal technologies or methods of attacking problems, or even implementation strategies. Achieving styles are divided into three sets, "direct," "instrumental," and "relational," each with three associated styles, which are described in detail below. Each individual uses a unique combination of these learned behaviors, ordinarily relying on styles associated with previous success, perhaps shifting emphases, to accomplish his or her current goals (Lipman-Blumen 1991). Occasionally, under crisis conditions, individuals may move to a somewhat different configuration; however, if the crisis is easily circumscribed and resolved, individuals subsequently revert to their former achieving styles.

The central argument of this paper presents five main points, in which achieving styles play a key role.

- First, American leadership images represent a masculine ego-ideal, that is, an ideal image of what we all would be, if only we could.
- Second, that ego-ideal draws on a very limited set of achieving styles, which we shall call "direct" styles, that emphasize individualism, self-reliance, and belief in one's own abilities, as well as power, competition, and creativity.
- Third, we reject two other sets of learned behaviors—"instrumental" and "relational" achieving styles—ordinarily associated with more traditional female behavior.

The set we dismiss as weak are the "relational" achieving styles, which focus on collaborating with, contributing to, and deriving a vicarious sense of accomplishment from others' success. They are the helpful, nurturant, vicarious role behaviors associated with the traditional female role. An ongoing study of achieving styles (Lipman-Blumen, Handley-Isaksen, and Leavitt 1983; Lipman-Blumen 1991) confirms that women engaged in full-time homemaker roles favor these achieving styles above all others. So do many women in the workplace,

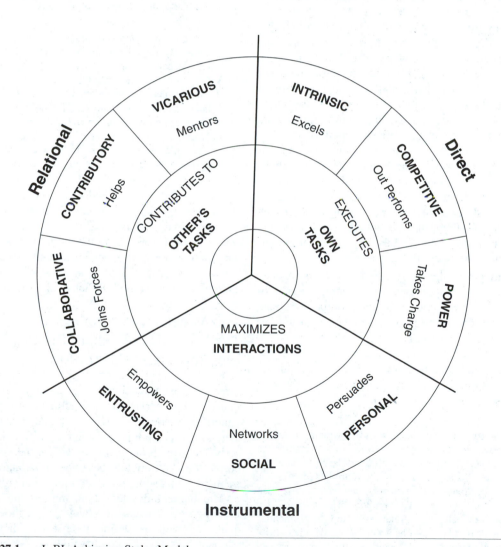

Figure 27.1 L-BL Achieving Styles Model

although they experience difficulty maintaining these styles in the absence of a critical mass of like-minded, usually female, coworkers.

Americans also reject a second set of learned achievement behaviors, the "instrumental" achieving styles, which, until recently, they perceived as manipulative and slightly unsavory behaviors. The instrumental styles take their name from the propensity to use the self and others as instruments for accomplishment.

Instrumental styles involve complex, subtle strategies. Individuals who prefer the instrumental styles use many aspects of the self, including intelligence, skill, wit, charm, family background, and previous accomplishments, to engage others in their tasks. They enjoy attracting followers by projecting and dramatizing themselves and their goals, through symbols and dramatic behavior, as well as counterintuitive, and therefore unexpected and unforgettable, gestures. For example, Indian independence leader Mohandas Gandhi was much enamored of instrumental styles, which also emphasize human interaction, group process, and informal systems (more recently understood as "networks"). Instrumental achieving styles involve accomplishing tasks through networks of relationships, believing in and entrusting one's vision to others, and thereby empowering others through one's confidence in them.

From pre-Biblical days, these styles have been attributed to women; however, the denigration associated with these styles generally prompts American women, not to mention men, to deny them. Earlier research (Lipman-Blumen et al. 1983) suggests that American women tend to rank two styles in the instrumental set much lower than the remaining seven achieving styles that complete the achieving styles spectrum.

- Fourth, the networked world in which all nations now live calls for new forms of leadership that connect people to each other, to their own and others' tasks and dreams, to their families, colleagues, institutions, and networks, as well as to their nations and global neighbors. The two rejected sets of behavior—"relational" and "instrumental" achieving styles—one accepted by, the other attributed to women—provide these important aspects of connective leadership.

To meet the leadership challenge of the 1990s and beyond, it will be necessary to integrate these two underutilized sets of achieving styles with our currently faltering masculine ego-ideal. In fact, to meet this need, female achieving styles—both actual and attributed—probably must predominate. Connective leadership, which connects individuals creatively to their tasks and visions, to one another, to the immediate group and the larger network, empowering others and instilling confidence, represents a crucial set of strategies for success, not only in the workplace, but in our interdependent world community.

- Fifth, connective leadership also integrates and creatively revitalizes individualism with a crucial female perspective, that is, seeing the world as a total system of interconnected, uniquely important parts, rather than as independent, competitive, isolated, and unequal entities. This perspective leads to an emphasis on external goals that all human groups can unite to accomplish, rather than on more internal objectives that set individuals, groups, and nations apart and often against one another.

Connective leadership repudiates the traditional use of external enemies to unite constituents behind their own parochial leaders. It also deconstructs hierarchies in which workers are urged to compete for the pinnacle positions, where many ostensibly successful individuals find themselves "suspended in glorious, but terrifying, isolation" (Bellah et al. 1985:6).

THE AMERICAN EGO-IDEAL: THE DIRECT ACHIEVER IN RUGGED INDIVIDUALIST'S CLOTHING

From our earliest national origins, the rugged individualist has served as the ultimate emblem of American leadership. This essentially masculine symbol melds the images, sounds, and smells of the early Western frontier (Taylor 1972): the cowboy's corral, the battlefield, the mine, the factory, the political back room, and the corporate boardroom.

The fierce individualist personifies the manner in which Americans are taught to achieve their goals, as well as define themselves, their most cherished dreams, and their values. These individualistic qualities also characterize the most admired

American leaders. Because they confront tasks directly through their own efforts, we shall call these leaders "direct achievers." As direct achievers, they tend to use three "direct" styles, all of which focus on realizing their own visions, whether through individualistic ("intrinsic direct"), competitive ("competitive direct"), or controlling ("power direct") behaviors.

Individuals who prefer the first "direct" style—the "intrinsic direct"—determinedly seek challenges and measure their visionary goals against personal, internalized standards of excellence that demand an exacting performance—perhaps a performance one can only count on oneself to deliver. Their stubborn pursuit of a dream is often associated with self-reliant creativity. Intrinsic direct achievers' passionate devotion to the vision or goal *they* have identified seeks only one reward: the intrinsic satisfaction derived from doing something well (much like McClelland's [1961] high-need achiever). Earlier research (Lipman-Blumen et al. 1983; Lipman-Blumen 1991) indicates that women, as well as men, endorse this behavior.

The second "direct" achieving style—the "competitive direct"—characterizes the rugged individualist who competes unrelentingly, determined to overcome all contenders, monumental odds, and immeasurable hardships. Perhaps, the most robust gender-linked finding in the achieving styles literature is the consistently lower valuation that women assign to competitive behavior (Axline, Billings, and VanderHorst 1991). Across virtually all age, occupational, and cultural groups, women consistently are less likely than men of their own group to report that they use competitive strategies to accomplish their goals.

The third "direct" style—the "power direct" achieving style—describes the "take charge" behavior of traditional American heroes. These independent heroes strive to be in total control of all resources, from people and situations to institutions and global events. Although leaders who prefer the "power direct" achieving style may delegate tasks to others, they retain strict control over both the targeted goals and the means to their accomplishment.

The second, but less pronounced, gender difference our research (Lipman-Blumen 1991) reveals is the predilection for power. According to these

data, men also tend to prefer power more intensely than women. With respect to power, however, many female executives are beginning to imitate their male colleagues, a strategy that threatens to undermine their connective leadership advantage.

These three "direct" achieving styles are the hallmarks of the self-reliant American hero. Americans perceive the "direct" achieving styles as the wellsprings of their unique admixture of pragmatism, innovation, creativity, and vision. Americans also associate these styles with determination and masculinity. That John Wayne's image is alive and well, not only in TV reruns and commercials, but also in the American psyche, is evidence from popular culture of "direct" achievers' enduring appeal.

"Direct" achieving leaders do not attract and unite their followers simply by the creativity and worthiness of their own dreams and goals. They also commonly draw constituents or followers to their cause by defining an external enemy, sometimes exaggerating that enemy's potential threat, and even creating enemies when none exist. This strategy brings internal cohesion to the leader's group, inflating both the leader's strength and the group's need for the leader's protection and guidance. Identifying an external enemy is an important strategy for the power-oriented, competitive leader.

Although many Western societies share this individualistic ideal, the American scene has provided the quintessential historical stage for the exploits of the rugged solo hero, the "direct achiever." For example, George Washington, Henry David Thoreau, Andrew Carnegie, Theodore and Franklin D. Roosevelt, John Wayne, Steve Jobs, Lee Iacocca, and Ronald Reagan all share to some degree this characteristic stance. Their examples encourage us to believe that we, as individuals, can make an important difference, should "go for it," can compete fiercely and win. These heroes embody the American ego-ideal: rugged individuals, with creative, visionary dreams, taking control, pitting themselves against impossible odds and winning.

American history texts depict archetypal American characters as individualistic, "direct" achievers, doing it all by themselves. Still, a healthy skepticism is warranted lest these allegedly "individual" exploits are taken as the whole, rather than the tip, of the human collaboration iceberg.

Despite historical accounts, the scope of their accomplishments suggests that these industrial and military leaders did not accomplish their feats single-handedly. Nevertheless, American mythology bathes them in an isolating spotlight, obscuring the many others whose contributions helped create their astounding successes—their aides-de-camp, their coaches or mentors, their assistants, their teammates, their parents, their wives and children. This misperception only encourages us to believe leaders succeed single-handedly, powerfully, and competitively.

If the heroes who exemplify the American ego-ideal appear larger than life or accomplish tasks that seem beyond the capabilities of a single individual, that is probably exactly the case. These are the makings of mythical figures, embodying cultural myths and images. Mythologized heroes serve as ego-ideals precisely because they inspire—and even goad—believers to reach beyond themselves to almost superhuman goals.

The cultural heroes Americans understand best speak to them of individual dreams, individual efforts, individual rights, individual property, individual problems. American culture encourages a profound, if irrational, faith that a nation of rugged individuals, working *separately*, often competing against one another, can produce a totality that miraculously will result in a successful *collective* effort.

The recent resurgence of the American entrepreneur (Gevirtz 1984; Drucker 1985) is consistent with this ego-ideal. The daring entrepreneur who starts a new business in his garage and takes on the industrial megagiants is the late-20th-century American hero. Still, that hero inevitably falters when success enlarges the task beyond the capabilities of one even larger-than-life individual. At that point, these self-reliant individuals have trouble sharing the challenge with peers, entrusting others with their dream, believing others can do it as well as they, collaborating, getting others to feel the task belongs to them, negotiating, helping others to fulfill their own dreams, making the group work synergistically, avoiding the pitfalls of team activities, and taking pride in others' success.

Individualistic leaders rarely embody these important aspects of connective leadership. More often than not, they fail to unite people and nations through their mutual needs. In fact, they commonly tend to set people in opposition to one another. They lack the skills of connective leaders who draw people to one another's goals, reach out to bring others into the process, and experience a sense of accomplishment when colleagues and protégés succeed. Connective leadership replaces egocentrism with mutuality.

When the task grows patently beyond the capabilities of one larger-than-life leader, the hero leaves, or is driven out, and starts again, as the lone hero. The "Lone Ranger rides again," or maybe now it is the *lonely* ranger—American images, all.

A Schizoid Love Affair With Teamwork

American culture partially tempers its devotion to individualism with a schizoid love affair with teamwork. Americans experience a deep-seated tension between the pursuit of individualism and a reflexive response to teamwork. Teamwork is a national shibboleth, deeply embedded in the core of democracy. In theory, at least, the team has an apparent leveling or democratizing effect. Everyone can try out for the team. All team members are equal. Still, Americans confront an abiding ambivalence that hobbles their unequivocal commitment to team effort. Even within teams, individualism remains their true love.

It is no accident that Americans anoint baseball the "all-American" sport. Baseball also serves as national metaphor. As the late Baseball Commissioner A. Bartlett Giamatti (1985) suggested,

> Baseball fits America so well because it embodies the interplay of individual and group that we so love, and because it expresses our longing for the rule of law while licensing our resentment of law givers . . . What each individual must do (is) obvious to all, and each player's initiative, poise, and skill are highlighted.

Baseball permits us the illusion of promoting teamwork, while simultaneously keeping a detailed scorecard on each player's hits, runs, and errors. The player's scorecard is tallied without acknowledging his teammates' contributions to that performance.

Periodically, of course, the "communal choreography" of the team takes over, fusing the individual players into a cohesive group, muting the loneliness, terror, and ecstasy of stardom (Giamatti

1985). Moreover, baseball enables team members to cooperate with one another while simultaneously competing with another team.

MISMATCH BETWEEN EGO-IDEAL AND INSTITUTIONAL NEEDS

To complicate matters, there is a growing lack of fit among (1) the American ego-ideal, (2) the needs of our increasingly large and complex institutions, and (3) the demands of an interdependent world. As previously noted, the American ego-ideal reifies individualistic, competitive, controlling behavior. Yet, as organizations grow in size and complexity, the tasks involved outstrip the capabilities of single-handed action. They require cooperation and coordination. Paradoxically, as the world shrinks through interdependence, that need increases. Still, the formal structure of large-scale institutions, from corporations to governments, makes it difficult to ensure quick and easy cooperation. Bureaucratic rules, reflecting an individualistic ego-ideal, present serious barriers.

According to Weber (Gerth and Mills 1946), formal hierarchies are designed to facilitate the coordination of complex tasks. In reality, however, the formal structure frequently inhibits goal attainment. As Weber (Gerth and Mills 1946) indicated, the informal system arises in the service of the formal structure. It offsets the barriers to cooperation within formal organizations and bureaucracies. One example of the informal system, the traditional "old boy network," stretched within and across institutions. It functioned as an uncharted, largely invisible, homosocial system (Lipman-Blumen 1976), excluding from membership less-powerful males and women. Non-isometric with the formal system, the "old boy network," nonetheless, ironically grafted the competition, power, and internal status differentials learned in the formal structure onto friendship patterns and alliances within the informal system. Within "the old boy network," resources moved to valued members in an efficient distribution system, reinforcing a system of obligations and reciprocations.

More recently, to offset their isolation, professional women have developed their own "old girl networks." It is my impression, based on observation, that these female networks commonly feature open, visible membership, even dues, with explicit criteria revolving around professional background and interests. As such, they are less like the traditional, covert, male informal networks and more reminiscent of the open, formal, but casual, associations described by de Toqueville ([1835] 1959) that included members from a broad range of backgrounds. Here, too, resources are distributed, but with seemingly less attention to power, competition, and internal status differentials. With some notable exceptions, these female professional networks thrive on inclusion and connection, potential models for the twenty-first-century workplace.

At its best, the informal system is a world of relationships and emotionality; familiar territory to women, but rather uncomfortable terrain for many male leaders. Through human interaction composed of friendships, understandings, and mutual help, members distribute various resources, particularly those essential to goal attainment. To partake of these resources, one must demonstrate political, social, and organizational "savvy." At its best, the system operates through inclusiveness and connection, rather than by exclusiveness and separation.

In the coming decades, the navigational skills required by the informal system will be increasingly distinguishable from the individualism, competitiveness, and power that currently permeate the byways of male networks. The new informal systems will call for a revised understanding of "connections"—connections between the self and others, as well as between the self and task, be it one's own or another's. They will require expertise in dealing with connections among people within and between groups, from small teams to far-flung networks, sometimes even networks of nations. The informal system will necessitate knowledge of relationships, human interaction, emotionality, and group processes.

NEW ACHIEVING STYLES FOR AN INTERDEPENDENT GLOBAL ORDER

Global interdependence increases the urgency of America's leadership problem. Fostering connective leadership demanded by the global environment requires integrating two other, more appropriate sets of achieving styles—more feminine behaviors—with the traditional American "direct" styles.

Instrumental Styles: Personal, Social, and Entrusting

The first additional set of achieving styles required for success in an interdependent order is the "instrumental" set, whose label reflects the characteristic use of (1) the self, (2) the system, and (3) others as instruments for goal attainment. Like the other achieving styles sets, this one also includes three styles: "personal," "social," and "entrusting."

Personal Instrumental

The "personal instrumental" style is evident in the action of leaders skilled in projecting and utilizing all aspects of their persona. Leaders who prefer the "personal instrumental" style utilize their intelligence, wit, compassion, humor, family background, previous accomplishments and defeats, courage, physical appearance, and sexual appeal to connect themselves to those whose commitment and help they seek to engage. The admiration and affection of followers may serve as both motive and sustenance for "personal instrumental" achievers. They unabashedly pursue an emotional connection with their followers, relationships based on compassion and inspiration, rather than competition and power. In 1987, a group of children attending an international women's peace conference in Moscow presented flowers to General Secretary Gorbachev. Touched by this gesture, Gorbachev turned his back to the audience to wipe his tears. Two thousand women in that audience wept openly in empathy.

Demonstrating and evoking compassion, even to the point of self-sacrifice (Miller 1976; Gilligan 1982), are traditional female behaviors. Connective leadership also draws on these instrumental strategies. Some examples include the following: (1) Mohandas Gandhi fasting to near-death to persuade Muslims and Hindus to work and live together in peace; (2) Corazon Aquino leading a national revolution without guns and bloodshed; (3) Gorbachev transforming traditional concepts of weakness into strength, by daring to unilaterally dismantle powerful weapons of war; (4) Martin Luther King linking arms

with other activists marching for civil rights. Each of these leaders, however, raised doubts and fears among both followers and adversaries still attuned to traditional power-driven, competitive images of leadership. Moreover, Aquino and Gorbachev have been pushed back repeatedly to more traditional "direct" leadership forms by both constituents and other contenders for power.

Leaders who dare step beyond the limits of their own followers to reach out to a broader, even a global constituency, risk the ire of their traditional constituents while simultaneously stirring fear and confusion in the hearts of outsiders. They draw upon their own "personal instrumental" skills as negotiators and persuaders to bridge interpersonal schisms. They use their gifts of persuasion and negotiation, rather than aggression, power, and competition, to accomplish their goals. They display a keen sense of symbolism and dramatic gestures, often creating counterintuitive gestures and symbols whose surprise and simplicity engrave their message upon the constituents' consciousness. For example, on his initial visit to Washington, Gorbachev unexpectedly stepped from his guarded limousine to shake the hands and touch the hearts of ordinary American citizens.

Leaders skilled in "personal instrumental" behavior understand the meaning, as well as the denial, of ritual and costume. Assuming the presidency in the wake of a dictatorship, Corazon Aquino symbolized her quest for a modest, democratic government by wearing a plain yellow dress and refusing the trappings of palaces and limousines. Her deliberately simple gestures and costume symbolized reconciliation and equality. Gandhi's rejection of Western, custom-tailored suits for a homespun *dhoti* symbolized his rejection of English rule, as well as his dedication to effecting Indian independence (Collins and Lapierre 1975).

With real genius, Gandhi could use a broad range of achieving styles in his nascent form of connective leadership (Gandhi 1957). Here, however, let us focus on Gandhi's use of the "personal instrumental" style. The Indian independence leader used dramatic, counterintuitive symbolism to draw people to his cause. He chose the spinning wheel, reflecting female and rural images, as a counterintuitive symbol of India's political independence through industrial self-reliance. This unforgettable symbol ignited an emotional connection between Gandhi and his followers. Commonplace now because his example has been followed by so many, Gandhi's "personal instrumental" fasts electrified the world, compelling both supporters and opponents to join hands, if only temporarily.

Charismatic leaders rely heavily on "personal instrumental" action. The drama of their behavior, from counterintuitive, symbolic gestures to their use of ritual, costume, and timing, telegraphs a magnetic message to potential followers. This "personal instrumental" style is part of the leadership repertoire exercised by many effective leaders, from Gandhi to Winnie Mandela at the height of her power.

Social Instrumental

Leadership behaviors that characterize the second "instrumental" style—the "social instrumental"—involve a heightened appreciation for process, for how human relationships offset the rigidity of structure and task. Leaders who use the "social instrumental" style demonstrate system or political "savvy." They are comfortable with informal processes. They appreciate institutions based on relationships. More specifically, leaders who use "social instrumental" strategies understand relationships and networks as vital and legitimate conduits for accomplishing their ends within and between institutions. They do things through other people, selecting specific individuals for specific tasks. "Social instrumental" actors first draw upon certain segments of their network for one task, then reshuffle the group, replacing some members with other, more relevant parties from the larger network for the next task.

"Social instrumental" actors build and draw upon networks of parties who, themselves, may not be congenial to one another. Since the alliances they string together are not necessarily intended as permanent structures, "social instrumental" achievers rely on their own "social" and "personal instrumental" skills to maintain the alliance for the endurance of the task. During the Gulf War, George Bush's masterful construction of an alliance of Gulf states, many of whom nursed long-standing enmities toward one another, was an exercise in "social instrumental" action.

Entrusting Instrumental

Connective leaders who use the third "instrumental" style—the "entrusting instrumental"—comfortably rely on everyone, not just specifically chosen individuals, to accomplish their tasks. "Entrusting instrumental" actors are adept at attracting others over whom they have no formal authority to help them realize their goals. By contrast to the "power direct" style, which involves command, delegation, and control over implementation, the "entrusting instrumental" style is used by leaders who believe in and rely on others, and simply expect others to help perform their tasks. Relinquishing their control over execution, "social instrumental" leaders entrust others with their vision, expecting others to implement their goals as well as, maybe better than, they could themselves. This expressed confidence empowers those in whom it is placed to meet the "entrusting instrumental" leader's expectations. In the Gulf War, George Bush's use of the "entrusting instrumental" style with parties over whom he had no formal control offered a new model for international action.

THE REPOSITORIES OF INSTRUMENTAL KNOWLEDGE AND SKILLS

Where are the repositories of instrumental knowledge and skill? Who, by training and circumstance, already understands instrumental action? Who knows how to make things happen without formal authority?

From necessity, those denied access to the penthouses of institutional power—those who cannot simply command others to comply—become expert in the byways of the informal interpersonal system (Janeway 1980). Those without formal power learn to interpret nuance, to negotiate and persuade. The informal system demands understanding the processes that occur in all social systems, particularly the subtle processes of human interaction. The less powerful become adept at micromanipulation (Lipman-Blumen 1984), the art of influence at the interpersonal level. From necessity, the powerless use micromanipulation, while the powerful engage in macromanipulation (Lipman-Blumen 1984), the process of influence at the societal or social-policy level.

Those without direct access to resources learn to rely on, rather than command, others to carry out tasks. Women's socialization to the complexities of human interaction, their social and emotional roles within all groups, as well as their resource-poor historical position, have taught them a special expertise, well-suited to this difficult arena. From early on, females are trained in "instrumental" achieving styles.

Still, these three "instrumental" styles that allow us to accomplish our tasks through relationships or by projecting our persona remain suspect in American culture. They offend our traditional, self-reliant ego-ideal. Traditionally, we have maligned such leadership strategies as "manipulative social climbing" or "weak dependence." We have deeply mistrusted the motives of leaders, such as President Lyndon Johnson, who demonstrated such skills (Caro 1983), regardless of the results they achieved.

In traditional American culture, those who overwhelm followers with their persona find their intentions questioned. We suspect dishonesty, incompetence, and possibly malevolence in those who use personal relationships, invoking family or group membership. We criticize as weak those who depend upon others to accomplish their ends.

In many other traditional societies, however, "social instrumental" behavior, particularly, is stitched into the cultural fabric. In countries as diverse as Japan, China, and Italy, the relationships that form one's social network represent an important part of a person's identity. Rather than stirring suspicion and distrust, these behaviors assure others that the individual can be held to his/her group's norms. Relationships offer the keys to success in all aspects of life. Instrumental achieving styles strengthen not only individuals, but the groups and institutions to which they belong.

Discomfort with "instrumental" styles forces individuals to deny these abilities within themselves and to disguise them from others. In fact, despite women's early training and reputation for instrumentality, research on achieving styles (Lipman-Blumen et al. 1983; Lipman-Blumen 1991) indicates that females, just like males, tend to reject these instrumental styles as self-descriptors. Driven under cover, these sensitivities and skills inevitably become one-sided, fail to evoke reciprocity, and, consequently, meet a dead end. Without the nutrients of openness and legitimacy, these processes cannot blossom into productive reciprocity, which, as Axelrod's (1984) research suggests, is a basic ingredient in stable cooperative systems.

Perhaps, in an earlier era, when survival depended upon an aggressive ability to wrest one's sustenance from a strange and hostile environment, self-reliance shielded individuals against those who would use, parasitize, or otherwise abuse relationships to accomplish their goals. The stark frontier society is gone. In its place, we have a different, complex environment, transformed by technology and the threat of mutual annihilation into a global community, where all actions affect and are visible to all.

Intricate institutional arrangements link groups separated by continents into interdependent economic, industrial, and political networks. These new conditions demand a greater sensitivity to organizational and human processes. Without the instrumental component of connective leadership, which incorporates such understanding, we shall have a difficult time adjusting to this new world community.

There is some indication that cultural attitudes are gradually changing. A new vocabulary is emerging to polish the image of these previously maligned styles. The positive connotations of "networking," "negotiating," and "consulting" provide preliminary lexical evidence of a budding awareness of "instrumental" behaviors' importance for the work environment of the 1990s and beyond.

Relational Achieving Styles: Contributory, Collaborative, and Vicarious

The final connective leadership component required by an interdependent environment involves an orientation toward others and their special goals. The third, or "relational," set of achieving styles contains three styles—"contributory," "collaborative," and "vicarious"—that encompass such inclinations. Complex alliances and institutions within a global community necessitate authentic teamwork toward common goals. They also call for helping others to accomplish their goals, for "mentoring" successors, and altruistically taking pride in others' achievements. We immediately recognize the relational styles as part of the traditional female milieu.

Individuals who prefer the three styles of the "relational" achieving styles set approach their goals by (1) collaborating on group goals, (2) contributing to others' objectives, and/or (3) deriving a vicarious sense of achievement from the success of others with whom they identify. Societies trapped in the thrall of individualism historically disdained and undervalued these "relational styles," while simultaneously offering them lip service, perhaps because of their association with women and children. "Relational" achievers receive public accolades for their altruistic contributions and collaboration, along with private suspicion that they do so more out of weakness than of will.

Cultural definitions portray women and children as weak partly because they achieve respectively through helping others and seeking help to accomplish their ends, rather than acting independently. We do not hail them as our heroes and leaders, even if they kindle a sentimental glow in our hearts. These conflicts between disdaining and commending "relational" styles present serious obstacles for leaders in an interdependent environment. What remedies, if any, exist for resolving these draining conflicts?

COOPERATION/COLLABORATION "WRONGLY UNDERSTOOD"

Organizational experts recommend cooperation and teamwork, but still have considerable difficulty explaining how to encourage these behaviors. The results from a recent study (Lefton and Buzzotta 1987) of 26 American executive teams, composed of 275 CEOs, company presidents and vice presidents, many from the *Fortune* 500 companies, are instructive.

The researchers report that "while these teams came much closer to the ideal than most, the members of the teams themselves acknowledged that less than 40 percent of their interaction could be called teamwork" (Lefton and Buzzotta 1987:8). The rest of the time, these top executives reported, their interaction was marked by internal conflict and competition at worst, and non-listening and hypocritical agreement at best.

Although cooperation in organizations has become a semantic touchstone, all our norms,

as well as our child-rearing practices, even our adult socialization methods, still shape people into self-reliant, independent (rather than strong *inter*dependent) individuals. Collaboration remains suspect. Even when people do successfully collaborate, society tends to single out a "leader," sometimes merely the most visible member of the group, and anoint that person the hero.

Most American leaders, like others worldwide, achieved their success with the help of others. Nonetheless, our cultural achieving styles spectacles only permit a vision of the leader, not the collaborators, nor the ones who relinquished their own dreams to help the leader succeed. The contributors are eclipsed in the shadow of the leader. For example, Chrysler CEO Lee Iacocca is crowned the "Corporate Messiah," while the workers whose labor and sacrifice were midwife to the Chrysler miracle are ignored, or even worse, blamed as the root of the problem.

Despite repeated calls for teamwork, the reward structure of American institutions favors primarily individual achievers, that is, stars, not their helpers. Professional baseball provides a useful example. Star players receive multimillion-dollar salaries, while their teammates must be satisfied with far less. In industry and government, reward systems offer assistants and collaborators less recognition, including lower salaries, smaller offices, and shorter vacations. Individuals, more often than groups, still receive the bonuses and awards, organizational slogans and academic treatises on teamwork notwithstanding. American organizations are caught in a circular dilemma. Because they prize individual achievement above all, American organizations barely reward cooperation and teamwork. Because rewards are lacking for cooperation and collaboration, it becomes virtually impossible to stimulate them in the workplace. This creates the classic case of "the Folly of Rewarding A, While Hoping for B" (Kerr 1989).

CREATING AND SUSTAINING COOPERATIVE SYSTEMS

Some relevant work from game theory casts new light on cooperation. Axelrod (1984) examined the conditions under which individuals or nations should cooperate, as well as the optimal strategies for eliciting cooperation rather than hostile acts and retaliation from others.

Axelrod invited various game theorists to write programs for a Computerized Prisoner's Dilemma Tournament. The Prisoner's Dilemma, a well-known laboratory game, allows players to seek their own self-interest or that of the group. Pursuing one's self-interest involves the risk of winning or losing "big" versus achieving slightly lower, but more dependable, mutual gains through cooperation. The game, rather than forcing cooperation, permits players to exploit or mutually resist cooperating with one another. The game also recognizes that, as in real life, players do not have totally opposing interests.

Game theorists in economics, psychology, sociology, political science, and mathematics submitted fourteen entries, which were run against each other in a round-robin tournament. Unexpectedly, the simplest program of all, Tit for Tat, was the clear winner. Tit for Tat offers a simple strategy in which a player starts by cooperating and subsequently merely mimics the other player's behavior on the last move. A second round-robin, this one with 62 entries representing as many different strategies, yielded the same result: Tit for Tat won again.

This led Axelrod to ask three questions. Limitations of space permit only the following over-simplified summary:

> First, how can a potentially cooperative strategy get an initial foothold in an environment which is predominantly noncooperative? [Translation: how can a female leadership perspective emerge in an essentially masculine environment?] Second, what type of strategy can thrive in a complex environment composed of other individuals using a wide diversity of more or less sophisticated strategies? Third, under what conditions can such a strategy, once fully established among a group of people, resist invasion by a less cooperative strategy? (1984:viii–ix).

First, "when there actually is a sufficiently high probability of continuing interaction between two individuals" (as in real life, long-term relationships within families, work groups and communities), cooperation is likely to emerge. The first tendrils of cooperative behavior are nourished by reciprocal cooperation on the second player's part. The expectation that cooperation will continue is important; however, so is the recognition that noncooperation breeds more noncooperation, to the detriment of all. (So, women, too, must also learn to use "direct" styles under certain conditions.)

Through a variety of computer simulations using all the submitted strategies, Axelrod (1984) demonstrated that, once established, cooperative efforts of a group can withstand the attack of a hostile, noncooperative group. A single individual trying to cooperate with a noncooperative party, however, has very little chance. Thus, for cooperation to take root, it is crucial to assemble a critical mass of individuals with cooperative, collaborative, and contributory skills.

Axelrod's (1984) work sheds light on why female leaders isolated in a male leadership environment may find that their "relational" styles are ineffective, commonly meeting serious resistance. Faced with serious opposition, solo female leaders are forced to forego "relational" action and resort to more typically masculine leadership strategies. Corazon Aquino is just one example. Separated from other collaborative, contributory, and vicarious colleagues, aspiring female leaders make a disheartening discovery. Only "direct" achieving, masculine leadership strategies, marked by controlling, authoritarian, competitive, and strictly independent behavior, win their male colleagues' grudging respect. Female leaders, forced back into the classical male leadership model, find themselves in a Catch-22 situation: they now risk being seen as "aggressive" and unfeminine.

The second condition for fostering ongoing cooperation occurs when each party has a reputation for toughness, that is, noncooperation will be responded to in kind. "Direct" achieving styles are useful here. In fact, the combination of tough and tender, "direct" and "relational" achieving styles is important.

The third condition critical to sustaining cooperative systems involves an understanding of group processes, a willingness to rely on others, and a predilection to allow relationships to develop into a stable system of reciprocity. Here "instrumental" achieving styles play an important role, emphasizing group process, human interaction, system savvy, reliance on others, and action through relationships that blossom into enduring networks.

A FINAL NOTE ABOUT WOMEN AND CONNECTIVE LEADERSHIP

The psychological literature (Miller 1976; Gilligan 1982) suggests that women take responsibility for keeping the group together, whether the group is the family or the work team. Females' need for connection, expressed in finely-tuned interpersonal skills, are legendary, although recent manuals on executive leadership warn women with serious leadership aspirations to steer clear of roles demanding such "instrumental," as well as "relational," styles.

Despite abundant mythology about women's competitiveness vis-à-vis one another, there is convincing evidence that women excel in collaborative, contributory, and mentoring behavior, all important aspects of connective leadership. Collaborating, contributing to others' tasks, taking vicarious pride in others' accomplishments, of course, are central to traditional female role behavior. Women have been ridiculed for taking pride in their children's and spouse's achievements, even though most societies socialize females to sacrifice themselves, first for their brothers, next for their husbands, and then for their children. The association between female behavior and powerlessness undoubtedly stirs fears, making these "female" styles suspect in societies dedicated to take-charge, competitive individualism.

Research data confirm women's greater propensity for putting the needs of others above their own. Laboratory studies of men and women playing the Prisoner's Dilemma (Axelrod 1984) and the Pollution Game (Dana and Rubenstein 1970) have demonstrated that, on average, women are significantly more likely than men to set aside their narrow self-interests for the sake of others. They exhibit vicarious or altruistic behavior. Women's socialization has taught them the importance of contributing to the goals of others, of collaborating in a group. They nurture others, basking vicariously and altruistically in the success of those they value and love (Gilligan 1982). Gilligan's (1982) work suggests that women often experience guilt and depression when their behavior violates these norms.

In other research (Lipman-Blumen et al. 1983; Lipman-Blumen 1991), full-time homemakers rank collaborative, contributory, and mentoring behavior (i.e., "relational" achieving styles) higher than men do. As indicated above, women across the entire occupational spectrum consistently rank competitiveness lower than do males matched in age, education, and occupation. Women's reluctance to act competitively holds up across cultures with differing levels of competitiveness. More specifically, Taiwanese subjects of both sexes had substantially higher competitive scores than American subjects, from high school students to senior executives. For example, Taiwanese housewives had competitive scores commensurate with those of American male senior executives. Still, compared to Taiwanese men of their own age and educational level, Taiwanese women produced significantly lower competitive achieving scores (Lipman-Blumen 1988).

One male group that consistently approximates this female pattern of moderated competition and elevated contributory, collaborative, or mentoring behavior is senior executives. They are significantly less competitive and more "relational" than mid-level male managers, still vying for promotion. This leads to a special paradox commonly observed in many American firms: "less competitive" females are bypassed for promotion to senior managerial positions, to which their "more aggressive" male colleagues are appointed. Once promoted to senior positions, male senior executives confront an ironic reality of top management: the need to moderate their competitiveness and increase their relational skills. A second paradox is also noticeable in American corporations: many women are succumbing to advice that urges them to eliminate their "instrumental" and "relational" styles, instead of integrating them with "direct" leadership skills. In doing so, these women may be depriving themselves of their advantage as connective leaders.

Earlier researchers (Hennig and Jardim 1977) suggested women experienced difficulty achieving in organizations because, as children, they had not played on teams. A clearer understanding of women's psychosocial development (Chodorow 1974; Miller 1976; and Gilligan 1982), not to mention baseball, prompts us to reconsider that assessment. Perhaps, a clarification of institutional processes and the conditions of cooperation and altruism will further legitimate both "instrumental" and "relational" achieving styles to which women traditionally were socialized. In turn, a revised interpretation of "relational" and "instrumental" styles will foster their dynamic integration with "direct" achieving styles that, together, provide the basis for connective leadership. Further research is needed to resolve a central paradox of the twenty-first-century American workplace: to regain their competitive edge in world markets, American organizations confront the necessity of de-emphasizing competition and developing connective leaders who can give them the connective edge.

NOTES

1. Fowlkes (1983) reminds us that the professionalization of these caretaking behaviors, however, commonly reduces and transforms them into impersonal, "interpersonal support" (Fowlkes 1983). We might speculate that this transformation from personal to impersonal is designed to demonstrate that these traditional female occupations genuinely meet the "affective neutrality" and "functional specificity" standards (Parsons 1951, 1968) embedded in the traditional/masculine definition of "professions."

2. Achieving styles described in this paper are based on the L-BL Achieving Styles Model (1983, 1991). Individual achieving styles are measured by the L-BL Achieving Styles Inventory (ASI), a 45-item Likert-style instrument. Organizational achieving styles, the achieving styles that a particular organization rewards, as perceived by knowledgeable observers or participants, are measured by the L-BL Organizational Achieving Styles Inventory (OASI).

REFERENCES

Axelrod, Robert. 1984. *The Evolution of Cooperation.* New York: Basic Books.

Axline, Sheryl, Jeanne Billings, and Nicole VanderHorst. 1991. "A Review of Gender-Linked Findings in the Achieving Styles Literature." Claremont, CA: Claremont Graduate School. Photocopy.

Badaracco, Joseph L., Jr. 1991. *The Knowledge Link: How Firms Compete through Strategic Alliances.* Cambridge: Harvard Business School.

Bakan, David. 1966. *The Duality of Human Existence.* Boston: Beacon Press.

Bass, Bernard M. 1990. *Bass and Stogdill's Handbook of Leadership: Theory, Research, and Managerial Applications,* 3d. ed. New York: Free Press.

Bellah, Robert N., Richard Madsen, William M. Sullivan, Ann Swidler, and Steven M. Tipton. 1985. *Habits of the Heart.* Berkeley: University of California Press.

Burns, James MacGregor. 1978. *Leadership.* New York: Harper and Row.

Caro, Robert A. 1983. *The Path to Power: The Years of Lyndon Johnson.* New York: Vintage.

Chodorow, Nancy. 1974. "Family Structure and Feminine Personality." Pp. 43–66 in *Women, Culture, and Society,* edited by Michelle Zimbalist Rosaldo and Louise Lamphere. Stanford, CA: Stanford University Press.

Collins, Larry, and Dominique Lapierre. 1975. *Freedom at Midnight.* New York: Simon and Schuster.

Conger, Jay A. 1989. *The Charismatic Leader: Behind the Mystique of Exceptional Leadership.* San Francisco: Jossey-Bass.

Dana, Jonathan, and Franklin D. Rubenstein. 1970. "The Psychology of Pollution and Other Externalities." Stanford, CA: Stanford Graduate School of Business. Photocopy.

de Toqueville, Alexis. [1835] 1959. *Democracy in America.* Translated by Henry Reeve, revised by Francis Bowen, and edited by Phillips Bradley. New York: Vintage Books.

Doig, Jameson W. and Erwin C. Hargrove, eds. 1987. *Leadership and Innovation: A Biographical Perspective on Entrepreneurs in Government.* Baltimore, MD: Johns Hopkins University Press.

Drucker, Peter F. 1985. *Innovation and Entrepreneurship: Practice and Principles.* New York: Harper and Row.

———. 1989. *The New Realities.* New York: Harper and Row.

Fowlkes, Martha R. 1983. "Katie's Place: Women's Work, Professional Work, and Social Reform." Pp. 143–159 in *Research in the Interweave of Social Roles: Families and Jobs,* Vol. 3, edited by Helena Z. Lopata and Joseph H. Pleck. Greenwich, CT: JAI.

Gandhi, Mohandas K. 1957. *Gandhi: An Autobiography.* Boston: Beacon Press.

Gardner, John W. 1990. *On Leadership.* New York: Free Press.

Gerth, H. H. and C. Wright Mills, eds. 1946. *From Max Weber: Essays in Sociology.* New York: Oxford University Press.

Gevirtz, Don. 1984. *The New Entrepreneurs: Innovation in American Business.* New York: Penguin.

Giamatti, A. Bartlett. 1985. Speech before the Massachusetts Historical Society.

Gilligan, Carol. 1982. *In a Different Voice: Psychological Theory and Women's Development.* Cambridge: Harvard University Press.

Gray, Barbara. 1989. *Collaborating: Finding Common Ground for Multiparty Problems.* San Francisco: Jossey-Bass.

Gutek, Barbara, Laurie Larwood, and Ann Stromberg. 1986. "Women at Work." Pp. 217–234 in *International Review of Industrial and Organizational Psychology,* edited by C. L. Cooper and I. Robertson. New York: Wiley.

Hennig, Margaret and Anne Jardim. 1977. *The Managerial Woman.* Garden City, NY: Anchor Press/Doubleday.

Janeway, Elizabeth. 1980. *Powers of the Weak.* New York: Knopf.

Kerr, Steven. 1989. "On the Folly of Rewarding A, While Hoping for B." Pp. 72–87 in *Readings in Managerial Psychology,* fourth edition, edited by Harold J. Leavitt, Louis R. Pondy, and David M. Boje. Chicago: University of Chicago Press.

Kouzes, James M. and Barry Z. Posner. 1987. *The Leadership Challenge: How to Get Extraordinary Things Done in Organizations.* San Francisco: Jossey-Bass.

Lefton, Robert E. and V. R. Buzzotta. 1987–1988. "Teams and Teamwork: A Study of Executive Level Teams." *National Productivity Review* 7:7–19.

Lipman-Blumen, Jean. 1976. "Toward a Homosocial Theory of Sex Roles: An Explanation of the Sex Segregation of Social Institutions." Pp. 15–31 in *Women and the Workplace: The Implications of Occupational Segregation,* edited by Martha Blaxall and Barbara Reagan. Chicago: University of Chicago Press.

———. 1984. *Gender Roles and Power.* Englewood Cliffs, NJ: Prentice-Hall.

———. 1988. *Individual and Organizational Achieving Styles: A Technical Manual for Researchers and Human Resource Professionals.* Claremont, CA: The Achieving Styles Institute.

———. 1991. *Individual and Organizational Achieving Styles: A Conceptual Handbook for Researchers and Human Resource Professionals,* 4th. ed. Claremont, CA: The Achieving Styles Institute.

Lipman-Blumen, Jean, Alice Handley-Isaksen, and Harold J. Leavitt. 1983. "Achieving Styles in Men and Women: A Model, An Instrument, and Some Findings." Pp. 147–204 in *Achievement and Achievement Motives: Psychological and Sociological Approaches,* edited by Janet T. Spence. San Francisco: W.H. Freeman.

McClelland, D. 1961. *The Achieving Society.* New York: Van Nostrand Reinhold.

Miller, Jean Baker. 1976. *Toward a New Psychology of Women.* Boston: Beacon Press.

Parsons, Talcott. 1951. *The Social System.* New York: Free Press.

———. 1968. "Professions." Pp. 536–547 in *International Encyclopedia of the Social Sciences,* Vol 12, edited by David L. Sills. New York: Macmillan.

Pfeffer, Jeffrey. 1983. "Organizational Demography." *Research in Organizational Behavior* 5:299–357. Greenwich, CT: JAI.

Starr, Martin K., ed. 1988. *Global Competitiveness: Getting the U.S. Back on Track.* New York: W.W. Norton.

Taylor, George Rogers. 1972. *The Turner Thesis: Concerning the Role of the Frontier in American History.* Lexington, MA: D.C. Heath.

Tichy, Noel and Mary Anne Devanna. 1986. *The Transformational Leader.* New York: Wiley.

SOURCE: Lipman-Blumen, Jean. 1992. "Connective Leadership: Female Leadership Styles in the 21st Century Workplace." *Sociological Perspectives*, 35(1):183–203.

28

TRUST AND INFLUENCE IN COMBAT

An Interdependence Model

PATRICK J. SWEENEY, VAIDA THOMPSON, AND HART BLANTON

Although leadership processes may be common across diverse situations, perhaps the most crucial setting in which to explore these processes is the combat zone. Beyond taking coercive measures, what is it that enables leaders, be they superiors or peers, to influence subordinates to risk injury or death to achieve the organization's objectives in combat? We propose that the mechanism is trust; not just trust in the leader, but mutual trust between leaders and subordinates.

Trust is no doubt a critical mechanism in all relationships: interpersonal, educational, and organizational. However, it seems critical in the military, particularly in a combat situation. Former senior military leaders and researchers have proposed that there will be neither leader nor unit effectiveness in combat in the absence of mutual trust between leaders and subordinates, and between the soldiers themselves. Without such trust, orders may not be fully obeyed, nor will the interests of the unit be placed above individual interests (Collins & Jacobs, 2002; Ulmer, 1989).

A major goal of the present research is to test our assumptions about trust by developing and testing a model of trust within the military, exploring the relationship of trust to influence and the factors that contribute to this relationship. The model guiding the research is that of interdependence theory (Kelley & Thibaut, 1978; Thibaut & Kelley, 1959). Never fully tested in relation to trust and influence, this theory sets forth a model pertaining to the development of trust, with the assumption that trust will result in influence. In testing and further developing the model, our basic questions are as follows: (a) How do military leaders develop trust with subordinates? and (b) How does subordinate trust in a leader relate to his or her ability to exercise influence?

The organizational behavior and social psychology literatures offer several models that outline the process necessary for the development of trust. However, for the most part, these models have not been tested empirically, generally are not grounded in a unifying theoretical framework, and do not link the development of trust explicitly to influence or leadership processes. Additionally, few of the many trust models deal specifically with trust in the leader from the perspective of the subordinate.

The interdependence model predicts how leaders can earn subordinates' trust by fostering cooperative interdependence, being competent, demonstrating good character traits, and showing intentions to trust subordinates. The current research extends this model by proposing that the level of trust subordinates have in their leaders determines the amount of influence subordinates will accept willingly beyond mere compliance. This extended model has not been tested or even proposed in earlier research. Results supporting the extended model should have important implications not only for the military, but also for leadership in other realms, including business and public safety.

We conducted two studies that tested a modified version of the interdependence trust development model and the link between trust and the acceptance of influence. The first study was conducted in a combat zone and used an instrument designed to test a modified version of the model of trust development set forth in interdependence theory. The second study extended the findings from the first study by using a refined instrument and a more experienced, non-combat sample.

For these studies, *trust* in an organizational setting is defined as one's willingness to be vulnerable to another group member's (i.e., leader, subordinate, or peer) actions. It is assumed that this form of trust is based on a sense of confidence in the group member's character and competence (Deutsch, 1958; Golembiewski & McConkie, 1975; Kelley & Thibaut, 1978; Mayer, Davis, & Schoorman, 1998; Zand, 1972). This definition suggests three precursors to trust: (a) certainty or confidence that a fellow group member will behave cooperatively; (b) belief that this group member has the competence to meet role expectations; and (c) willingness to place oneself in a position of vulnerability by placing one's fate in the group member's hands. All three components are considered in the model of trust tested in these studies.

Early research investigating trust development in interpersonal conflict situations found that the following led to the development of trust: concern for others' outcomes (cooperative orientation), open communication, shared power to retaliate (shared interdependence), intentions to trust others, and perceptions that one possesses the ability (e.g., skills, capability, power, resources) to produce benevolent acts (Deutsch, 1958, 1973). Deutsch (1958, 1962) proposed that individuals assess another person's intentions by considering the motivation behind the intentions and the commitment to the intentions. Essentially, they are assessing personal character traits to determine the reason and the extent of commitment or motivation to fulfill intentions to trust. Similarly, individuals assess another's ability to produce the intended benevolent act. Deutsch's (1958, 1962) work laid the foundation to the study of trust; however, he did not propose a model explaining how the factors interrelate to develop trust.

Later, researchers expanded on Deutsch's (1958, 1962) work by proposing that trust develops and deepens through cycles of interactions, similar to a spiral, in which parties in a relationship engage in behaviors that place them in positions of ever-increasing vulnerability or risk (Golembiewski & McConkie, 1975; Zand, 1972). Introducing these elements (i.e., reciprocating cycle and willingness to become increasingly vulnerable) furthered understanding of the nature of trust. However, neither Zand nor Golembiewski and McConkie proposed a comprehensive model to identify the factors and relationships between these factors that are presumed to influence development of trust.

Interdependence Model for Building Trust

Kelley and Thibaut's (1978) interdependence model of trust development, outlined in Figure 28.1, incorporates some of the concepts set forth by others, but stresses mutual trust, with trust developing through a reciprocating cycle in which each partner in a relationship acts to reduce the other's fear of exploitation and to show that the relationship will be rewarding. According to this theory, a partner can reduce the other's uncertainty about the relationship by taking action to show that one is dependable and has the ability to make the relationship rewarding. One earns an attribution of dependability by (a) demonstrating dependence on the relationship (interdependence); (b) highlighting the overlapping of interests (sharing of common interests); and (c) demonstrating willingness to act out of concern for all involved (cooperative motivational orientation; Kelley & Thibaut, 1978).

Simultaneously, while taking actions to demonstrate dependability, one must also show intention to

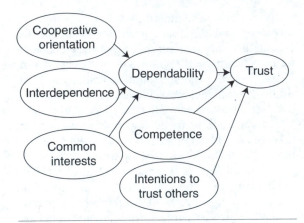

Figure 28.1 Kelley and Thibaut's (1978) original model for development of trust in close relationships (conceptual model).

trust and the ability to meet role expectations. One demonstrates intention to trust by engaging willingly in behavior that places oneself in a position of vulnerability or risk. Perceptions that one's partner has sacrificed his or her own interests in signaling intention to trust are thought to result in a reciprocation of risk.

According to Kelley and Thibaut (1978), the driving mechanism in the development of trust is this gradual reciprocation of risk taking between partners. Demonstrating the ability to meet role demands helps to assure the partner that the relationship will be rewarding. With perceptions that the partner is demonstrating good character, has the ability to meet role demands, has intention to trust, and demonstrates vulnerability, one is likely to make a stable, internal attribution regarding both the partner's dependability and his or her ability to deliver positive outcomes in the future (Kelley & Thibaut, 1978). Each cycle in which the partner behaves in a dependable and capable manner reduces fear of exploitation, thus fostering the development of a deeper level of trust in the relationship.

Links to Leadership

Influencing subordinates to achieve the organization's objectives is a major aspect of leadership (Gardner, 1990; Hollander, 1961; Jacobs, 1970; Yukl, 1998). Several researchers have found that the level of trust in leader-subordinate relationships

determines the amount of influence that subordinates and leaders would willingly accept from each other (Gabarro, 1978; Gibb, 1964; Golembiewski & McConkie, 1975; Roberts & O'Reilly, 1974; Zand, 1972). In an experiment investigating the impact of trust on group problem solving, Zand found that leaders in a high-trust condition had greater influence on group members and were more willing to accept influence attempts by group members than were leaders in a low-trust condition. This study also found that high trust led to greater acceptance of dependence, more cooperation, and enhanced information flow among all group members. Similarly, Gabarro, in a field study investigating how new company presidents establish working relationships with key subordinates, found that the level of influence both leaders and subordinates could exercise was a function of the amount of trust that existed between leaders and subordinates. Therefore, mutual trust seems to be a necessary condition for the exercise of influence in leader-subordinate relationships. This influence is mutual in that subordinates will accept—beyond mere compliance—influence attempts from a leader they trust, and leaders will allow trusted subordinates to influence them.

The leadership literature, in general, views trust as an outcome of various positive leader behaviors, with trust being important but not critical to the exercise of influence. For example, Bass (1985) proposed, in his transformational leadership theory, that trust is an outcome of leader behavior that provides followers with intellectual stimulation, individualized consideration, and charismatic influence. Bass developed the Multifactor Leadership Questionnaire (MLQ) to assess the extent to which leaders engage in these types of transformational behaviors.

Leader-member exchange (LMX) theory (Dansereau, Graen, & Haga, 1975; Graen & Cashman, 1975) proposes that leaders form a special relationship with a small group of subordinates based on followers' competence and reliability, as well as the leader's personal liking for them. These in-group members exchange greater commitment to the organization's objectives and loyalty to the leader for greater access to information, participation in decisions, flexibility to do their jobs, and leader attention. As these special relationships evolve, trust develops between the leader and the in-group members, which provides both the leader and followers with a greater ability to influence each other (Dansereau et al., 1975; Graen & Cashman, 1975). Further, Gardner (1990), in his book *On Leadership,* proposed that a leader earns followers' trust by respecting followers and behaving in a reliable and fair manner, thus enhancing leader ability to facilitate collaboration among group members. Bennis and Nanus (1985) proposed that trust bonds leaders and subordinates together and that it is the measure of a leader's legitimacy. In summary, the leadership literature views trust as an important outcome of leader behaviors, but not critical to the exercise of influence.

Proposed Modification to the Kelley and Thibaut Model

Although Kelley and Thibaut's (1978) model of trust would appear to be the most suitable to explore contributors to trust and the relationship of trust to noncoercive leadership, several modifications to the basic model are required, based on theory on the development of trust in leader-subordinate relationships. First, it is necessary to add influence specifically as an outcome of trust, because the literature suggests clearly that the level of mutual trust in a leader-subordinate relationship determines the amount of influence each party will willingly

accept from the other (Gabarro, 1978; Gibb, 1964; Golembiewski & McConkie, 1975; Roberts & O'Reilly, 1974; Zand, 1972). This proposed linking of the trust development process directly to the influence process results in a functional model of leadership. The central proposition of this modified model is that trust is necessary and essential to the exercise of influence beyond compliance.

Second, the concept of cooperative interdependence must be specified explicitly. Kelley and Thibaut (1978) focused on concepts of interdependence, sharing common interests, and being dependent on one another for outcomes. These are, in fact, the elements of cooperative interdependence. Their presence results in partner willingness to increase dependence on the relationship and to behave in a cooperative manner (Deutsch, 1962, 1973; Thibaut & Kelley, 1959).

Third, the modified model should include a factor that accounts for organizational structures (e.g., regulations, cultural norms, standard operating procedures) that encourage leaders to behave in a trustworthy manner (McKnight, Cummings, & Chervany, 1998). The addition of this factor broadens the scope of the model by investigating the role these structures play in controlling or influencing leaders to behave in a trustworthy manner. The proposed modified version of Kelley and Thibaut's (1978) model for trust building is presented in Figure 28.2.

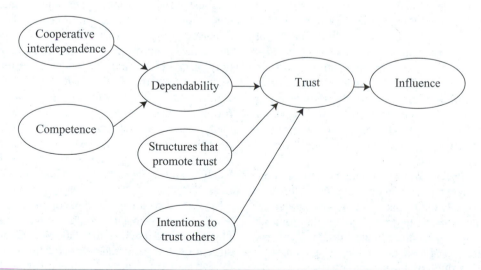

Figure 28.2   Proposed modified version of Kelley and Thibaut's model for development of trust in organizational relationships (conceptual model).

Hypotheses

Based on the previous literature review and the modified interdependence model for trust development, we propose the following hypotheses:

Hypothesis 1. Group members will perceive a leader as having dependable character if the leader is seen as promoting the establishment of cooperative interdependence, as competent to meet the role requirements of the leadership position, and as having enduring character qualities and skills that result in cooperative behavior and observed abilities.

Hypothesis 2. Group members will trust the leader if they perceive that the leader has a dependable character and intends to trust group members by engaging willingly in behaviors that make him or her vulnerable to the actions of the group. Additionally, they must perceive that organizational structure promotes cooperative and trusting behaviors by the leader.

Hypothesis 3. The level of trust that group members have in the leader will determine the amount of leader influence group members will accept willingly, beyond mere compliance. . . .

GENERAL DISCUSSION

Taken together, the findings from the two studies provide evidence suggesting that a modified interdependence model can account for both the development of trust between military leaders and their soldiers, and the link between soldiers' trust in leaders and perceptions of credibility and subordinates' willingness to accept leader influence. This model seems particularly useful because it explains trust development in the extreme environment of combat (Study 1), as well in non-combat situations (Study 2).

Study 1 provides the first known test of a model for trust development with data collected in a combat zone, which makes the results unique and compelling. Most importantly, the results from both studies suggest that subordinates' trust in their leaders/perceptions of leaders' credibility seem to determine the amount of leader influence subordinates will accept willingly, beyond compliance. This suggests that followers' trust in the leader/perceptions

of leader's credibility seem to determine the actual extent of influence a leader can exercise, which is the core premise of the modified interdependence model for trust development.

Further, the results suggest that the development of trust is influenced by relationship factors, person factors, and organizational factors. The relational factor consists of the establishment of cooperative interdependence in the leader-subordinate relationship, and establishing this type of relationship is a leader responsibility (Kelley & Thibaut, 1978; Likert, 1967). Trust thus develops in part from interactions in a relationship, creating an atmosphere of cooperation and shared interdependence in the relationship and setting the conditions for the growth of trust. The finding that a cooperative and interdependent relationship facilitates the development of trust is consistent with the literature (Deutsch, 1958, 1973; Gabarro, 1978; Golembiewski & McConkie, 1975; Holmes & Rempel, 1989; Zand, 1972).

Credibility is the person factor in the model. Leaders earn a perception of credibility by demonstrating competence and character. Competent leaders with good character are more likely to be successful in accomplishing the organization's objectives, while concomitantly assuring that they are taking care of organizational and subordinate needs. Credibility is also enhanced through the establishment of cooperative interdependence in the leader-subordinate relationship. The model thus suggests that trust arises in the context of the leader-subordinate relationship, but that it is only placed in a person or leader deserving of this trust (see Gabarro, 1978; Kelley & Thibaut, 1978; Kouzes & Posner, 1992). Furthermore, since a follower's decision to trust a leader rests on the leader's perceived competence and character, over time the follower might start to see trust and credibility as interchangeable concepts, as found in Study 2 and in the literature (Gabarro, 1978; Hall et al., 2001).

The third factor in the development and maintenance of trust—that is, organizational structures—played a small, albeit significant role. Organizational structures that require leaders to behave in a cooperative and trustworthy manner provide followers with a sense of control and predictability in that the structures set boundaries on leaders' behavior

(McKnight et al., 1998). Thus, subordinates can feel some assurance concerning how a leader, especially a new leader, will behave toward them. Organizational structures seem to provide subordinates with an insurance policy that their leaders will more than likely behave in a trustworthy manner, which probably plays a significant role in the beginning of a leader-subordinate relationship (McKnight et al., 1998).

Implications for Military Organizations

Although this model has implications for any organizational setting, the implications are most relevant to military organizations. The findings presented here provide the Army with an empirically plausible model that explains how leaders, at the platoon level, can go about earning their subordinates' trust and how this trust is linked to subordinates' willingness to accept leader influence, especially in combat.[1] The Army can use this model to teach leaders about the factors that influence trust, the theoretical relationships between these factors, and how trust is linked to their ability to influence subordinates. With this understanding, leaders should be better able to develop trust with their subordinates in order to exercise the necessary influence to lead in combat, which should enhance their own and the organization's effectiveness.

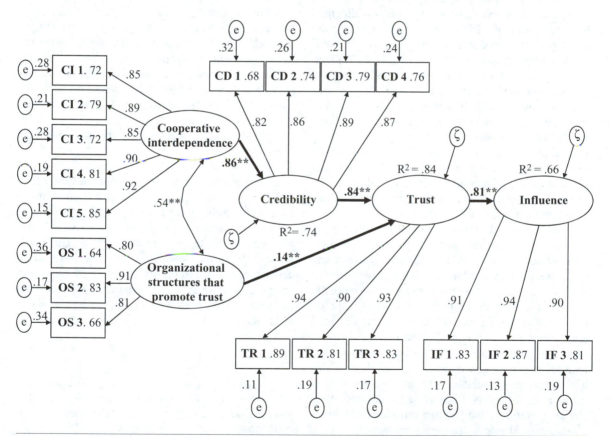

Figure 28.3 Structural equation model results from the test of the 5-LV (latent variable) interdependence model in Study 1. CI = cooperative interdependence measure; OS = organizational structure that promotes trust measure; CD = credibility measure; TR = trust measure; IF = influence measure; e = error; ζ = disturbance term; R^2 = squared multiple correlations. x^2(130. N = 315) = 318.74; goodness-of-lit index = .90; Tucker-Lewis Index = .96; comparative fit index = .97; root mean square error of approximation = .068.

Trust enhances leader and organizational performance because it provides both group members and leaders a sense of safety, which satisfies their basic need for security in the organization. When people feel secure—because they trust that leaders and the organization will protect their welfare—they can focus their energies on meeting higher order needs, such as forming strong and cohesive relationships (i.e., belongingness), mastering duties and achieving organizational objectives to gain recognition from others and a greater sense of self-efficacy (i.e., esteem), learning new knowledge and skills to prepare for future assignments (i.e., cognitive), and pursuing activities that promote growth and develop innate potential (i.e., self-actualization; Maslow, 1970).

Therefore, besides increasing one's willingness to accept influence from others, trust enhances the development of cooperative and cohesive relationships among group members (Kelley & Thibaut, 1978), promotes open communications throughout the organization (Roberts & O'Reilly, 1974), stimulates employee creativity and initiative (Gibb, 1964), increases problem-solving effectiveness (Zand, 1972), and facilitates learning and growth both in the people and the organization (Golembiewski & McConkie, 1975). All of these stem from trust, and result in enhanced individual and group performance. Figure 28.3 contains an updated conceptual model based on the results of these studies.

Furthermore, the relative stability of the model provides evidence suggesting that the model accounts for trust development and the links between trust and influence in both combat and non-combat settings. This should extend the applicability of the model to account for trust development in critical response organizations, such as law enforcement, fire, and emergency services; as well as business and education. The model also provides leaders with greater insights concerning why certain leader skills, traits, and behaviors are related to greater effectiveness in influencing followers. Finally, the results from these studies underscore the fact that trust should be given a more central role in leadership theories.

Limitations and Boundaries

The two studies reported here were conducted in a progressive sequence, with the second study designed to account for limitations in the first study. However, there are still several limitations that apply to both studies. First, since participants in Study 2 viewed trust and credibility as the same construct, thus prompting a modification to the interdependence model, it is best to use the 4-LV interdependence model with trust and credibility combined to guide future research. This would reduce the possibility of capitalizing on chance (MacCallum et al., 1992). Second, the use of correlation designs in both studies precludes drawing causal inferences from the results. Third, the studies tested the modified interdependence model for mutual trust development only from the subordinates' perspective. Fourth, the analytical method of SEM [structural equation modeling] tests only linear relationships between latent factors and measured variables; thus, the possibility exists that factors in the model could have nonlinear relationships. Fifth, both studies used cross-sectional designs, such that the results provide only a snapshot of the factors that affected subordinate trust in a current or former leader and subordinate willingness to accept the leader's influence based on recollections at the time the data were collected.

These studies provide important insights into trust development in a combat zone and the social psychological processes that affect a leader's influence in a military organization. It appears that leaders do earn their subordinates' trust in ways proposed by Kelley and Thibaut (1978; Thibaut & Kelley, 1959), by establishing a cooperative, interdependent relationship with followers; being competent; and possessing good character. Furthermore, subordinate trust is an essential ingredient in leader influence.

NOTE

1. A standard multiple regression analysis reveals no effects between MOS [military occupation specialty] groups. Thus, the results should generalize to all platoons in the Army.

REFERENCES

Bass, B. M. (1985). *Leadership and performance beyond expectations*. New York: Free Press.

Bennis, W., & Nanus, B. (1985). *Leaders: The strategy for taking charge.* New York: Harper & Row.

Collins, J., & Jacobs, T. (2002). Trust in the profession of arms. In D. Snider, G. Watkins, & L. Matthews (Eds.), *The future of the Army profession* (pp. 39–58). Boston: McGraw-Hill.

Dansereau, F., Graen, G., & Haga, W. (1975). A vertical dyad linkage approach to leadership within formal organizations: A longitudinal investigation of the role making process. *Organizational Behavior and Human Performance, 13,* 46–78.

Deutsch, M. (1958). Trust and suspicion. *Journal of Conflict Resolution, 2,* 265–279.

Deutsch, M. (1962). Cooperation and trust: Some theoretical notes. In M. R. Jones (Ed.), *Nebraska symposium on motivation* (pp. 275–319). Lincoln, NE: University of Nebraska Press.

Deutsch, M. (1973). *The resolution of conflict: Constructive and destructive processes.* New Haven, CT: Yale University Press.

Gabarro, J. J. (1978). The development of trust, influence, and expectations. In A. Athos & J. Gabarro (Eds.), *Interpersonal behavior: Communication and understanding in relationships* (pp. 290–303). Englewood Cliffs, NJ: Prentice Hall.

Gardner, J. W. (1990). *On leadership.* New York: Free Press.

Gibb, J. R. (1964). Climate for trust formation. In L. P. Bradford, J. R. Gibbs, & K. D. Benne (Eds.), *T-group theory and laboratory method: Innovations in re-education* (pp. 279–309). New York: John Wiley & Sons.

Golembiewski, R., & McConkie, M. (1975). The centrality of interpersonal trust in group processes. In C. Cooper (Ed.), *Theories of group processes* (pp. 131–185). London: John Wiley & Sons.

Graen, G., & Cashman, J. (1975). A role-making model of leadership in formal organizations: A developmental approach. In J. G. Hum & L. L. Larson (Eds.), *Leadership frontiers* (pp. 143–166). Kent, OH: Kent State University Press.

Hall, M. A., Dugan, E., Zheng, B., & Mishra, A. K. (2001). Trust in physicians and medical institutions: What is it, can it be measured, and does it matter? *The Milbank Quarterly, 79,* 613–639.

Hollander, E. P. (1961). Emergent leadership and social influence. In L. Petrullo & B. Bass (Eds.), *Leadership and interpersonal behavior* (pp. 30–47). New York: Holt, Rinehart, & Winston.

Holmes, J., & Rempel, J. (1989). Trust in close relationships. In C. Hendrick (Ed.), *Close relationships* (pp. 187–220). Newbury Park, CA: Sage.

Jacobs, T. O. (1970). *Leadership and exchange in formal organizations.* Alexandria, VA: Human Resources Research Organization.

Kelley, H. H., & Thibaut, J. W. (1978). *Interpersonal relations: A theory of interdependence.* New York: John Wiley & Sons.

Kouzes, J. M., & Posner, B. Z. (1992). The credibility factor: What people expect of leaders. In R. L. Taylor & W. E. Rosenbach (Eds.), *Military leadership: In pursuit of excellence* (pp. 133–138). Boulder, CO: Westview.

Likert, R. (1967). *The human organization.* New York: McGraw-Hill.

MacCallum, R. C., Roznowski, M., & Necowitz, L. B. (1992). Model modification in covariance structure analysis: The problem of capitalization on chance. *Psychological Bulletin, 111,* 490–504.

Maslow, A. H. (1970). *Motivation and personality* (2nd ed.). New York: Harper & Row.

Mayer, R. C., Davis, J. H., & Schoorman, F. D. (1998). An integrative model of organizational trust. *Academy of Management Review, 20,* 709–734.

McKnight, D. H., Cummings, L. L., & Chervany, N. L. (1998). Initial trust formation in new organizational relationships. *Academy of Management Review, 23,* 473–490.

Roberts, K. H., & O'Reilly, C. A. (1974). Failures in upward communication in organizations: Three possible culprits. *Academy of Management Journal, 17,* 205–215.

Thibaut, J. W., & Kelley, H. H. (1959). *The social psychology of groups.* New Brunswick, NJ: Transaction Books.

Ulmer, W. F. (1989). Introduction. In L. J. Matthews & D. E. Brown (Eds.), *The challenge of military leadership* (pp. xi–xviii). Washington, DC: Pergamon-Brassey.

Yukl, G. (1998). *Leadership in organizations* (4th ed.). Upper Saddle River, NJ: Prentice Hall.

Zand, D. (1972). Trust and managerial problem solving. *Administrative Science Quarterly, 17,* 230–239.

SOURCE: Sweeney, Patrick J., Vaida Thompson, and Hart Blanton. 2009. Excerpt from "Trust and Influence in Combat: An Interdependence Model." *Journal of Applied Social Psychology,* 39(1):235–41, 258–64.

PART V

ORGANIZATIONAL CULTURE

AN INTRODUCTION TO ORGANIZATIONAL CULTURE

Culture is one of those words so commonly used in ordinary language that wide agreement and understanding about its meaning are routinely assumed. Yet, *culture* is a broad and at times unwieldy umbrella term; depending on the context, various conceptual aspects are emphasized over others. For this reason it makes sense to explore how the term *culture* is generally used in the discipline of sociology as well as discuss and examine the trajectory of research on organizational culture.

Though Talcott Parsons was not the first to define culture, his description of its essential elements is both simple and comprehensive; he identifies three aspects that characterize culture: (1) knowledge (both empirical and existential), (2) values, and (3) forms of symbolic expression (Parsons, Shils, Neagele, and Pitts 1961). Cultures differ from one another in their understanding of the world (knowledge); their mores, ethics, and norms (values); and their rituals, music, art, language, and meaningful objects (symbolic expression). Yet, all cultures have some basic characteristics in common: Culture is learned and taught, shared to some significant degree by adherents, adaptive to changing conditions, and "focused on meanings and ideas rather than on . . . material production" (Levin 1994:128).

In "What Is Culture?" excerpted in this section, Edgar Schein's (1985) definition of organizational culture similarly emphasizes "conceptual sharing" (p. 245): He defines culture as a pattern of shared assumptions (knowledge and values) that have served the organization well in the past, that must be taught to new members of the group, and that can be adapted to external circumstances. Though objects and images can be emblematic of certain cultures, such as the association of the crescent moon and star with Islam, or a white wedding dress with purity, it is not the objects themselves that constitute culture, but the values, belief systems, authority, and underlying sentiment that symbols represent. Therefore, from the sociological perspective, culture is directed toward creating meaning, relationships, and identity rather than toward material production.

Within variegated, stratified, and complex contemporary societies, smaller subcultures arise that are differentiated from and resonate with the larger, dominant culture—this is true even of subcultures that are deliberately constituted in opposition to the dominant culture. The same elements of culture hold for subcultures: Distinct knowledge, values, and symbolic expression are shared by and taught to members. Subcultures are organized around myriad human qualities and experiences. Organizations, whether formal and bureaucratic or spontaneous and voluntary, often develop their own distinctive subcultures with which members come to identify. Subcultures are commonly formed around expertise, such as occupational and professional organizations; demographic characteristics, such as class, race, or gender; and interests and passions, such as religion, politics, or sports.

Organizational culture is a distinct subfield within the sociology of organizations, and as such it has its own history, body of scholarship, and set of assumptions. According to Michael Handel (2003), the recent interest in organizational culture was a response to the high level of productivity and economic success of Japanese businesses in the 1970s–1980s. "Intensely loyal and dedicated employees" were considered a key distinguishing feature of Japanese companies (Handel 2003:347). The hope was that the salient aspects of Japanese corporate culture could be identified and reconstituted in U.S. corporations, thereby improving morale and increasing worker commitment and loyalty to the company (Handel 2003). Gideon Kunda (2003) comments on this progression:

> In sum, the recent popularity of the idea of strong corporate culture may be seen as the culmination of a pronounced historical trend in managerial ideology and practice towards forms of normative control. In the most general terms, shaping the employees' selves in the corporate image is thought to be necessary in order to facilitate the management and increase the efficiency of large-scale bureaucratic enterprises faced with what the managerial literature refers to as "turbulent environments": rapid technological change, intense competition, and a demanding and unpredictable labor force. (P. 356)

Given this history, set of assumptions, and objectives, the scholarship in organizational culture is heavily skewed toward studying business cultures, especially cultures in traditional corporate hierarchies. Studies are often undertaken with the goal of how to find "the relationship between corporate culture and the 'bottom line'" (Kunda 2003:355). In this context, "culture" typically becomes synonymous with control techniques, and "organization" often refers to corporate organizations. Particular types of organizational culture are therefore strategically adopted as a means to enhance organizational effectiveness. In other words, culture is instrumentally developed so that employees internalize and accomplish specific company objectives. The investment in employee dedication is deemed valuable insofar as it ultimately advances profitability. Handel (2003) notes that the economic climate in the 1990s brought a reduction of the threat from Japan and provided a disincentive for developing communitarian workplace cultures. In response, corporations valued employee loyalty less and instead began encouraging employees "to act more like free agents" (p. 350). He writes, "When promises of security in return for commitment become too costly, they must be discontinued" (Handel 2003:350).

Exploring the Relationship Between Power and Culture

Randall Collins (1992) reflects on the fact that there are three common ways to exercise power: force, money, and solidarity. Each strategy has its drawbacks. The first strategy, force, is the most straightforward and is routinely used to elicit work from prisoners and slaves. However, force is not nearly as efficient as are noncoercive methods of exercising power for the simple reason that when people are coerced, they resist. Resistance can take many forms: People get anxious, angry, and frightened, and therefore are unable to apply much thought or energy to work. Additionally, they escape, and they rebel. A coercive workplace is inherently inefficient because some significant number of the labor force must be entrusted with forcing others to work and making sure workers do not escape. This circumstance is unlikely to create a workforce inclined to apply much initiative, judgment, or innovation to tasks.

The second strategy, money, also has significant flaws. When people work for money, they are concerned primarily with getting paid, rather than with their work product. Employers who want to maximize profit try to achieve the highest productivity with the lowest pay, while workers are attempting to earn the highest pay for the least effort. Paying by the hour incentivizes slower workers, while piecework or paying by the job encourages workers to hurry and sacrifice quality. Similar to the strategy of coercion, using money to elicit compliance engenders a basic conflict between worker and employer. Consequently, both workers and employers are removed, or alienated, from the work product or service provided. In fact, Kunda (2003) writes, "The concern with culture . . . reflect[s] the widespread and growing managerial interest in finding innovative solutions to the foremost problem of management: the conflict of interest that lies at the heart of the relations between organizations and their members" (p. 355).

However, the final strategy, solidarity, dissolves this conflict—it creates an alliance between managers and workers, organizations, and members. Collins (1992) writes, "If you want to get something done reasonably well, you have to find a way to make people *want* to do it . . . You need to make them feel that the work is part of their own identity, that they are contributing to something they believe in or some group that they belong to" (p. 69, emphasis added). The idea of creating a workplace culture where norms are internalized can hold the promise of high worker morale, give workers a sense of satisfaction, and increase their dedication and commitment to work. Further, the internalization of workplace norms means there is a reduced need for external controls such as monetary incentives or punishments. However, creating culture, solidarity, and loyalty within organizations can be time-consuming and requires a high investment in each employee. Moreover, feelings of loyalty and solidarity can be manipulated and exploited:

> Any individual can dominate other people mainly by taking advantage of their feelings of solidarity. Whoever can convince others that he or she is really one of them has a better chance of taking advantage of them. The most successful exploiter is the one who makes others feel that he or she has their best interests at heart. This means making an appeal precisely on that level and through those mechanisms by which nonrational sentiments of solidarity operate. This is a fundamental weapon of dictators, con-artists, politicians, and perhaps everyone who wishes to pursue their own self-interest aggressively in society. Feelings of solidarity are often called out in people, deep beneath their own rational calculations of self-interest. (Collins 1992:26)

Mary Parker Follett advances a plan to ensure that culture is not developed merely to manipulate and dominate others. As noted in our discussion on autonomy and control, Follett (1949) is a proponent of noncoercive control, which she refers to as "auto-control" (p. 83) or "self-generated control" (p. 88). She argues,

> If control is the process of the inter-functioning of the parts, if the most perfect control is where we have the inter-functioning of all the parts, then I think the workers should have a share, not from any vague idea of democracy, not because of their "rights," but simply because if you leave out one element in a situation you will have that much less control. (Follett 1949:85)

Follett ([1926] 2003) writes further,

> [Employee representation] should not be thought of as something added on to any scheme of organization in order to facilitate relations with labour . . . [or] primarily as a method of getting the consent of employees to certain decisions with the expectation that the workers will then be more likely to co-operate heartily in carrying them out . . . The most progressive view of employee representation to-day, as of democracy, is not *consent* of the governed, but *participation.* (Pp. 170–171, emphasis added)

If workers should share in the process of control, as Follett ([1926] 2003; 1949) argues, then it follows that they should be active participants in shaping their organization's culture: its knowledge, values, and forms of symbolic expression.

Loyalty and commitment hold organizations together and are based on *nonrational* sentiments: those emotional attachments that cause individuals to eschew calculations of self-interest and focus instead on the good of the community. To the degree that corporations develop organizational culture without employee participation and manipulate employee loyalty to serve the material ends of the organization, the solidarity and loyalty of workers are being exploited.

The Rational Paradigm in Organizational Culture

William Ouchi's scholarship is illustrative of how the rational paradigm can be used as a lens to consider organizational culture. His article "Markets, Bureaucracies, and Clans" (1980) appears in this volume in our section on the relational organizational form. Within rationalism, Ouchi's scholarship draws from the social exchange and rational choice theories. The fundamental assumption in these theories is that human relationships are based on a set of exchanges made by rational actors after they have completed a cost-benefit analysis. Ouchi focuses primarily on for-profit corporate organizations where the assumed goal is to increase productivity and profit. In this context, Ouchi emphasizes the "transactions cost approach" as best capturing organizational efficiency; that is, he links culture to the bottom line. Ouchi (1980) writes, "This transactions cost approach explicitly regards efficiency as the fundamental element in determining the nature of organizations" (pp. 129–30).

However, Ouchi mentions that there are limits to applying rational theories. Because they do not have price mechanisms or clear performance goals, organizations such as school systems and religious institutions "evade any form of rational control" (Ouchi 1980:140). Ouchi finds that clans, which he defines as organizations that achieve control through a common culture, are most efficient when goal incongruence is low (i.e., people agree on goals) and performance ambiguity is high (i.e., it is not clear how to evaluate performance). Hence, in some circumstances, Ouchi concedes that organizations must rely on the nonrational social elements of shared cultural values. Ouchi does not, however, discuss the possibility that organizations will exploit solidarity and shared values for the benefit of some and to the detriment of others.

Beyond Rationalism

In their article, "The Organizational Culture War Games: A Struggle for Intellectual Dominance" (1995), which is excerpted in the current section, Joanne Martin and Peter

Frost review four different approaches that emphasize the *qualities* of culture such as values, meanings, emotions, and ideas. These four approaches are integration, differentiation, fragmentation, and postmodernism (Martin and Frost 1995). Martin and Frost recognize that all four perspectives contribute to the understanding of organizational culture. The integrative approach defines cultures around "an internally consistent package of cultural manifestations that generates organization-wide consensus, usually around some set of shared values [and] . . . very little deep, collective conflict is acknowledged" (Martin and Frost 1995:603). This consensus-driven, unified, and optimistic portrait of cultures resonates with the functionalist paradigm associated with sociologists such as Emile Durkheim and Robert Merton.

In contrast to integration, the differentiation perspective does not view organizations as unitary, but instead studies subcultures within organizations with the hope that "opinions and interests of lower-level employees would be more fully represented" (Martin and Frost 1995:603). Among other things, the differentiation perspective emphasizes pluralism and challenges the status quo. The focus is on qualitative research and interpretive meaning. This perspective has aspects of a hermeneutic orientation and includes elements of critical theory such as the idea of an "emancipatory point of view" (Martin and Frost 1995:605). Differentiation theory therefore has elements in common with both conflict theory and interactionism.

Similar to Blumer's (1969) symbolic interaction, the fragmentation perspective stresses the complexity of organizations and emerging, negotiated reality. Martin and Frost (1995) write,

> According to the advocates of the fragmentation view, the relationships among the manifestations of a culture are neither clearly consistent nor clearly inconsistent; instead relationships are complex, containing elements of contradiction and confusion. Similarly, consensus is not organization-wide nor is it specific to a given subculture. Instead consensus is transient and issue-specific, producing short-lived affinities among individuals that are quickly replaced by a different pattern of affinities. (P. 609)

Finally, postmodernism takes fragmentation one step further as it discredits the modern habit of presenting an objective, coherent, and unified truth. In contrast to fragmentation, which focuses on confusions and ambiguities, postmodernism draws attention to the chaotic aspects of organizations that cannot be predicted or contained within rules and regulations:

> From a postmodern point of view, reality is a series of fictions and illusions. A text is not a closed system; it reflects the subjective view of its author, those who read it, and those whose views are quoted, included, suppressed or excluded. [Postmodernism] undermines any claim that a text can represent the objective truth about a reality that is "out there"—separate from the text. (Martin and Frost 1995:611)

Martin and Frost (1995) recognize that different approaches will appeal to different people. For instance, they note that integration literature is emphasized in publications written for executives and MBAs, and they predict that managers would be attracted to this view as it represents unified cultures that change in a controlled and predictable manner. On the other hand, employees might be more interested in the differentiation perspective on organizational culture because it investigates power dynamics and explores strategies of resistance.

Representations of Organizational Culture

Handel (2003) comments that "most people want a satisfying job, and self-fulfillment at work has often appeared to be the ideal antidote to the alienating qualities of bureaucracy. But a workplace that tries to serve both economic goals and human needs blurs the boundaries of self and work and threatens to absorb one's personal identity into a work role" (p. 350). This position assumes human needs do not include economic goals, and that one can (and should) have a personal self separate from a work identity. But are "economic goals" and "human needs" really separable? Is self-development separate from the work one does? In contrast to Handel (2003), Paul Willis (1990) represents another view often explored in organizational culture—that personal identity is developed in part through work: "Most people spend their prime waking hours at work, base their identity on work activities, and are defined by others essentially through their relations to work . . . people look for meaning . . . they repossess aspects of their experiences . . . This is a positive transformation of experience and a celebration of shared values . . . It allows people to recognize and even develop themselves" (pp. 184–85).

In this section on organizational culture, we include several articles that examine the development of self-identity at work, the interplay between ethics and instrumental behavior, and the relationship between culture and economics. In "Moral Economy and Cultural Work," Mark Banks (2006) challenges the notion that the expansion of free-market ideas has undermined the social and ethical foundations of human interaction. Like Willis (1990), Banks (2006) sees empirical evidence that people do imbue work environments with values and meaning and blur the lines between the material and the symbolic. He argues that this can have a positive rather than a detrimental effect:

> The collapsing of distinctions between public and private realms may well lead to the engulfment of the self by work, but can, potentially, have the converse effect of increasing the range and heterogeneity of (previously externalized) moral actions and judgments that can be brought to bear in the labor process . . . *perhaps we should consider equally how non-instrumental, political and social values may be feeding back into the work process.* (Banks 2006:462–63, emphasis added)

As Banks points out, rational-bureaucratic organizations do not always fulfill the promise of being impersonal, unbiased, and neutral with uniform and equal treatment for all. In fact, the very legitimacy of these organizations might come from how they reflect or undermine larger social and cultural values.

The remaining articles in this section focus on specific organizational cultures. "Hospitals as Cultures of Entrapment: Re-Analysis of the Bristol Royal Infirmary" by Karl E. Weick and Kathleen M. Sutcliffe (2003) provides evidence of how a bureaucratic and hierarchical structure can shield the incompetence of those at the top. By sheltering people who are unwilling to admit fallibility, even when confronted by empirical evidence of dire consequences, rigid hierarchies can protect those in power and impede change within organizational cultures. Two additional articles included in this section, "Representing Blue: Representative Bureaucracy and Racial Profiling in the Latino Community" by Vicky M. Wilkins and Brian N. Williams (2009) and "Representative Bureaucracy and Policy Tools: Ethnicity, Student Discipline, and Representation in Public Schools" by Christine H. Roch, David W. Pitts, and Ignacio Navarro, explore how and to what extent bureaucrats internalize and enact the prevailing institutional prejudices, even to the detriment of those they serve and sometimes at the expense of the demographic populations with which they identify.

On the other hand, there are organizations that deliberately build cultures in opposition to prevailing prejudice and discrimination. Women's Business Centers (WBCs) are such organizations. In "'This Place Makes Me Proud to Be a Woman': Theoretical Explanation for Success in Entrepreneurship Education for Low-Income Women," Mary Godwyn (2009) examines a women-centered organization where women are represented and perceived as normative entrepreneurs. She finds that the organizational culture in WBCs successfully creates solidarity around gender and neutralizes the prevailing negative stereotype that women are not business leaders. Despite being a socially and economically disadvantaged population, the female clients at WBCs start businesses at almost four times the rate of the national average for women.

Recognizing the interaction and mutability between workplace organizations and the larger culture, Follett ([1924] 1995) contends, "In commerce we may find culture . . . The divorce of our so-called spiritual life from our daily activities is a fatal dualism. We are not to ignore our industry, commerce, etc., and see spiritual development elsewhere; on the other hand we shall never find it in these, but only by an eternal influence and refluence" (p. 60). The articles included in this section explore the interface and permeability between commerce and culture, economics and ethics, and individualistic and communitarian forces.

DISCUSSION QUESTIONS

1. Are there common elements that define organizational culture? If so, what are they? Which are most important and under what circumstance?

2. How does organizational culture relate to power and control? Is it legitimate to use culture to achieve control? Why or why not?

3. In Mary Parker Follett's view, what is the difference between employee consent and employee participation? How do these concepts relate to organizational culture?

4. Would you expect the cultures of predominantly bureaucratic organizations to be different from the cultures in organizations that emphasize relationships and networks? Explain.

SUGGESTIONS FOR FURTHER READING

Alvesson, Matts. 1982. "The Limits and Shortcomings of Humanistic Organization Theory." *Acta Sociologica,* 25(2):117–31.

Bailyn, Lotte. 2002. "Time in Organizations: Constraints on and Possibilities for Gender Equity in the Workplace." Pp. 262–72 in *Advancing Women's Careers,* edited by Ronald J. Burke and Debra L. Nelson. Oxford: Blackwell Publishing.

Fourcade, Marion and Kieran Healy. 2007. "Moral Views of Market Society" *Annual Review of Sociology,* 33:285–311.

Hancock, Phillip. 2008. "Embodied Generosity and an Ethics of Organization." *Organizational Studies,* 29(10):1357–373.

O'Reilly, Charles and Jennifer Chatman. 1996. "Culture as Social Control: Corporations, Cults and Commitment." Pp. 157–200 in *Research in Organizational Behavior.* Greenwich, CT: JAI Press.

Sørensen, Jesper B. 2002. "The Strength of Corporate Culture and the Reliability of Firm Performance." *Administrative Science Quarterly,* 47(1):70–91.

Van Maanen, John. 1990. "The Smile Factory: Work at Disneyland." Pp. 58–76 in *Reframing Organizational Culture,* edited by Peter Frost et al. Thousand Oaks, CA: Sage.

REFERENCES

Banks, Mark. 2006. "Moral Economy and Cultural Work." *Sociology,* 40(3):455–72.

Blumer, Herbert. 1969. *Symbolic Interactionism: Perspective and Method.* Berkeley: University of California Press.

Collins, Randall. 1992. *Sociological Insight: An Introduction to Non-Obvious Sociology.* 2nd ed. New York: Oxford University Press.

Follett, Mary Parker. [1924] 1995. "Relating: The Circular Response." Pp. 35–65 in *Mary Parker Follett—Prophet of Management: A Celebration of Writings from the 1920s,* edited by Pauline Graham. Boston: Harvard Business School Press.

———. [1926] 1942. "The Influence of Employee Representation in a Remolding of the Accepted Type of Business Manager." Pp. 167–82 in *Dynamic Administration: The Collected Papers of Mary Parker Follett,* edited by Henry C. Metcalf and L. Urwick. New York: Harper and Brothers Publishers.

———. 1949. "The Process of Control." Pp. 77–89 in *Freedom and Co-ordination: Lectures in Business Organization by Mary Parker Follett,* edited by L. Urwick. London: Management Publications Trust, Ltd.

Godwyn, Mary. 2009. "'This Place Makes Me Proud to Be a Woman': Theoretical Explanation for Success in Entrepreneurship Education for Low-Income Women." *Research in Social Stratification and Mobility,* 27(1):50–64.

Handel, Michael. 2003. "Organizational Culture." Pp. 347–50 in *The Sociology of Organizations: Classic, Contemporary and Critical Readings,* edited by Michael J. Handel. Thousand Oaks, CA: Sage.

Kunda, Gideon. 2003. "Engineering Culture: Control and Commitment in a High-Tech Corporation." Pp. 351–69 in *The Sociology of Organizations: Classic, Contemporary and Critical Readings,* edited by Michael J. Handel. Thousand Oaks, CA: Sage.

Levin, William C. 1994. *Sociological Ideas: Concepts and Applications.* 4th ed. Belmont, CA: Wadsworth Publishing Company.

Martin, Joanne and Peter Frost. 1995. "The Organizational Culture War Games: A Struggle for Intellectual Dominance." Pp. 598–621 in *Handbook of Organizational Studies,* edited by S. Clegg, C. Hardy, and W. Nord. Newbury Park, CA: Sage.

Ouchi, William G. 1980. "Markets, Bureaucracies and Clans." *Administrative Science Quarterly,* 25(1):129–41.

Parsons, Talcott, Edward Shils, Kasper D. Neagele, and Jesse R. Pitts, eds. 1961. *Theories of Society.* New York: Free Press.

Roch, Christine H., David W. Pitts, and Ignacio Navarro. 2010. "Representative Democracy and Policy Tools: Ethnicity, Student Discipline, and Representation in Public Schools." *Administration & Society,* 42(38):38–65.

Schein, Edgar H. 1991. "What Is Culture?" Pp. 243–53 in *Reframing Organizational Culture,* edited by P. Frost, L. Moore, M. Louis, C. Lundberg, and J. Martin. Newbury Park, CA: Sage.

Weick, Karl E. and Kathleen M. Sutcliffe. 2003. "Hospitals as Cultures of Entrapment: Re-Analysis of the Bristol Royal Infirmary." *California Management Review,* 45(2):73–84.

Wilkins, Vicky M. and Brian N. Williams. 2009. "Representing Blue: Representative Bureaucracy and Racial Profiling in the Latino Community." *Administration & Society,* 40(8):775–98.

Willis, Paul. 1990. "Masculinity and Factory Labor." Pp. 183–98 in *Culture and Society: Contemporary Debates,* edited by Jeffrey Alexander and Steven Seidman. Cambridge, MA: Cambridge University Press.

29

WHAT IS CULTURE?

EDGAR H. SCHEIN

Organizational culture as a concept has taken hold, but it is not yet clear whether it will survive as a useful and viable addition to the conceptual armamentarium of organization studies. And the issue, as I see it, revolves around the core definition, both from a formal conceptual point of view and from a practical applied point of view. We cannot build a useful concept if we cannot agree on how to define it, "measure" it, study it, and apply it in the real world of organizations.

Right now I see several competing approaches to the definition and study of organizational culture:

1. *The Survey Research Approach.* In this approach the passion to measure and quantify leads to the de facto definition of culture as something that is measurable through individual questionnaires (e.g., Hofstede, 1980; Hofstede & Bond, 1988; Kilmann, 1984). Interestingly, the proponents of this method start with "deep" conceptual definitions of culture as "mental models" or "underlying assumptions," but their subsequent attempts to measure it by questionnaires and the forcing of the data into dimensions derived a priori or by factor analysis implies that culture is definable at the surface attitude level. In this approach culture and "climate" become virtually synonymous concepts and it is not clear why one should retain the culture concept at all. What does it add?

Furthermore, if one starts with a definition of culture as an aspect of the "deep structure" of an organization or some of its parts, it is highly unlikely that the pre-determined dimensions that lead to questionnaire construction adequately cover the conceptual terrain that culture deals with in human systems. This approach also presupposes that organizational cultures have common dimensions and that these dimensions are the most important aspect to study. Another possibility is that cultures, like personalities, are in part unique and that the power of the culture concept will ultimately lie in its ability to force us to look at the uniqueness of organizations rather than their common properties.

2. *The Analytical Descriptive Approach.* In this approach, as in the survey research approach, the dominant definitional force comes from the need to describe and measure culture. But in this approach one breaks culture down analytically into components that are empirically more tractable and settles for studies of those components (e.g., Harris & Sutton, 1986; Martin & Siehl, 1983; Schall, 1983; Trice & Beyer, 1984; Wilkins, 1983). Thus the core concept remains implicit and often undefined, while its manifestations such as rites, rituals, and organizational stories, symbolic manifestations of the "deeper" phenomena, occupy center stage and become the de facto definition of culture.

As a research strategy this approach is very practical, but as a conceptual strategy it imposes a possibly undesirable bias and makes assumptions that may not be valid from other points of view. Specifically, this approach fractionates a concept whose primary theoretical utility may be to draw attention to the holistic and systemic aspects of organizational phenomena. And in this analytical decomposition one may lose validity in that the true meaning of the symbolic or behavioral manifestations may not be decipherable without understanding a deeper set of phenomena that tie those manifestations together.

3. *The Ethnographic Approach.* The ethnographic approach taken from anthropology and sociology starts with the assumption that there are deeper structures and that those structures cannot be unraveled or understood without intensive and extensive observation supplemented by interview data from cultural insiders (informants). Such research leads to what have been called "thick descriptions" (Geertz, 1973) that bring out the uniqueness and complexity of cultural phenomena very well, but paradoxically leave unexamined the conceptual and definitional problems of the concept of culture as applied to organizations and subunits of organizations. Instead such research has focused more on occupational communities and broader issues such as the "management of emotions" in all kinds of organizational contexts (e.g., Barley, 1983a, 1983b; Van Maanen, 1988; Van Maanen & Barley, 1984; Van Maanen & Kunda, 1989).

One core assumption in this approach is that culture can ultimately only be deciphered as it is "enacted." In other words, the implication is that culture does not exist conceptually except in the observable behavioral manifestations enacted by the members of that culture. But when one examines the definitions that lie behind this observational strategy, one finds conceptually vague things like "the way we do things around here" or "common systems of meaning" that belie the "depth" of the observational methods.

Similarly, though conceptually the implication is that culture is a holistic systemic phenomenon, the ethnographic method often forces one to limit one's observations to some limited aspect of the group's behavior and explain that aspect in great detail without necessarily tying that entire behavioral set into other phenomena that may exist in that group.

Toward a Conceptual Resolution: Clinical/Analytic/Descriptive

Why do we need the concept of culture anyway? What does it add that concepts like norms, behavior patterns, and climate do not adequately convey? Why not just settle for the study of symbols and observed behavior patterns in their own right? Why do we need a conceptually "deeper" level? To answer these questions we should pause and ask ourselves a bit about the origin of the culture concept. Why was it taken out of the context of representing some of the more refined aspects of social phenomena into anthropology as a core concept for studying societies?

Culture implies stability. Without doing the necessary historical analysis, I will speculate that the concept was needed first of all to explain the fact that in most societies certain phenomena persisted over time and displayed remarkable stability even in the face of pressures toward change. This stability would be especially noticeable in some of the preliterate societies that had survived in a basically unchanged way for centuries. Culture, then, has something to do with long-range stability.

Culture emphasizes conceptual sharing. Secondly, I would speculate that what struck early ethnographers was the remarkable degree of similarity not only of manifest behavior but also the perceptions, cognitions, and feelings of the members of a given society, suggesting that there was something under the surface that new members learned that led to a high degree of similarity of outlook. Culture, then, has something to do with sharing or consensus among the members of a group. The most obvious aspect of such sharing is the common language and conceptual categories that are discovered whenever one studies a social group that has had any kind of history and shared experience. The study of socialization processes, especially their content, then became one of the primary ways of deciphering what the common underlying shared things were.

Culture implies patterning. Thirdly, I would speculate that what struck at least some anthropologists was the degree to which there were patterns evident in societies. The observed regularities reflected higher order phenomena that created patterns and paradigms, sometimes leading to premature formulations of cultural types. The fact that early typologies proved to be more stereotypic and ignored important variations among and within societies only reinforced the idea that patterns had to be studied carefully and were somehow at the crux of deciphering cultural phenomena.

Culture implies dynamics. How is one to explain the perpetuation of observed regularities and the ability of a group to perpetuate patterns over long periods of time and across many generations of membership? The analysis of culture pushes us to the analysis of how culture is created and perpetuated, thus leading to studies of the socialization process and a renewed emphasis on origins. Anthropologists had difficulty with cultural origins because one could not obtain historical data on the kinds of societies that were studied. Current attempts to apply culture to organizations do not suffer from this limitation because one can reconstruct historically the origin of organizations. In fact, some of the best cultural analyses in organization studies have been conducted by historians because they have been able to capture the dynamic, holistic patterning that is characteristic of cultures (e.g., Chandler, 1977; Dyer, 1986; Pettigrew, 1979; Westney, 1987).

Culture implies all aspects of group life. If one looks at early ethnographies, one is struck by the fact that cultural phenomena penetrate all of the aspects of daily life. There is virtually nothing that we do that is not colored by shared ways of looking at things. In analyzing culture, then, it becomes important not to develop simplistic models that rely only on a few key dimensions, but to find models that reflect the vastness that culture represents.

What we need is a model of culture that does justice to (a) what the concept connotes and (b) what has been its source of utility in other fields. Such a model comes out of an eclectic approach that draws on anthropology, sociology, and social psychology, and that reflects research methods broader than the traditional ones. Specifically, we need to add to other

methods what I have called the "clinical perspective" (Schein, 1987) by which I mean what one learns when one is in a helper/consultant role (as contrasted with a researcher role). Sometimes one learns most about what culture is, how it operates, and what its implications are when one is helping an organization to solve real problems. At such times the insiders are more open, more willing to reveal what they really think and feel, and, thereby, make it more obvious what things are shared and how things are patterned. At such times one also begins to understand what it means to go to "deeper" levels.

A Formal Definition of Culture

Culture is:

1. A pattern of shared basic assumptions,

2. invented, discovered, or developed by a given group,

3. as it learns to cope with its problems of external adaptation and internal integration,

4. that has worked well enough to be considered valid, and, therefore,

5. is to be taught to new members of the group as the

6. correct way to perceive, think, and feel in relation to those problems.

The Definition Examined and Explained

Culture, in any of its meanings, is a property of a human group. If one cannot define the group, then one cannot define the culture of that group. It will not help us in the conceptual domain to do what is sometimes done, namely, to define the group as "all those people who share some common behavior or attitude." In other words, to define a group as a set of people who share a culture is to be circular and to remain unenlightened on what precisely it is that they share. So we must start with group definitions that are more objective—sets of people who have a history with each other, who have shared experiences together, where membership is sufficiently stable to have allowed some common learning to occur.

At the simplest conceptual level, then, we can say that culture is the shared common learning output. But this does not yet tell us what sorts of things groups learn, retain, and pass on, or why they do this. What this "model" does say, however, is that only what is *shared* is, by definition, cultural. It does not make sense, therefore, to think about high or low consensus cultures or cultures of ambiguity or conflict. If there is no consensus or if there is conflict or if things are ambiguous, then, by definition, that group does not have a culture in regard to those things. It may have subcultures, smaller groups that have a shared something, a consensus about something, but the concept of sharing or consensus is core to the definition, not something about which we have an empirical choice.

The next part of the definition draws more on social, cognitive, and dynamic psychology. When one observes new groups or studies the histories of new organizations, one observes that all such organizations have to deal with two fundamental sets of issues—external adaptation and internal integration—and that they deal with such issues at the behavioral, cognitive, and emotional level.

The problems of external adaptation and internal integration specify what the learning focus is. Analyzing these problems, the primary issues faced by all groups, gives us an important insight into the likely "content" of any given culture. In other words, a given group's culture will reflect what that group has learned in solving its particular problems in its own history. A different group that has had different problems and experiences will, by definition, have a culture with different content.

NOTE

1. The material in this chapter is an expansion and elaboration of ideas originally presented in my 1985 book *Organizational Culture and Leadership*. Additional elaboration can be found in my recent article in the *American Psychologist* (Schein, 1990).

REFERENCES

Barley, S. R. (1983a). Codes of the dead: The semiotics of funeral work. *Urban Life, 10,* 459–461.

Barley, S. R. (1983b). Semiotics and the study of occupational and organizational cultures. *Administrative Science Quarterly, 28,* 393–413.

Chandler, A. P. (1977). *The visible hand.* Cambridge, MA: Harvard University Press.

Dyer, W. G. (1986). *Culture change in family firms.* San Francisco, CA: Jossey-Bass.

Geertz, C. (1973). *The interpretation of cultures.* New York: Basic Books.

Harris, S. G., & Sutton, R. I. (1986). Functions of parting ceremonies in dying organizations. *Academy of Management Journal, 19,* 5–30.

Hofstede, G. (1980). *Culture's consequences.* Beverly Hills, CA: Sage.

Hofstede, G., & Bond, M. H. (1988). The Confucius connection: From cultural roots to economic growth. *Organization Dynamics, 16*(4), 4–21.

Kilmann, R. H. (1984). *Beyond the quick fix.* San Francisco, CA: Jossey-Bass.

Martin, J., & Siehl, C. (1983). Organizational culture and counter-culture: An uneasy symbiosis. *Organizational Dynamics, 12,* 52–64.

Pettigrew, A. M. (1979). On studying organizational cultures. *Administrative Science Quarterly, 24,* 570–581.

Schall, M. (1983). A communication rules approach to organizational culture. *Administrative Science Quarterly, 28,* 557–581.

Schein, E. H. (1990). Organizational culture. *American Psychologist, 45,* 109–119.

Schein, E. H. (1985). *Organizational culture and leadership.* San Francisco, CA: Jossey-Bass.

Trice, H., & Beyer, J. (1984). Studying organizational cultures through rites and ceremonials. *Academy of Management Review, 9,* 653–669.

Van Maanen, J. (1988). *Tales of the field: On writing ethnography.* Chicago: University of Chicago Press.

Van Maanen, J., and Barley, S. R. (1984). Occupational communities: Culture and control in organizations. In B. M. Staw & L. L. Cummings (Eds.), *Research in organizational behavior* (Vol. 6, pp. 287–366). Greenwich, CT: JAI Press.

Van Maanen, J., & Kunda, G. (1989). Real feelings: Emotional expressions and organization culture. In B. Staw & L. L. Cummings (Eds.), *Research in organizational behavior* (Vol. 11, pp. 43–103). Greenwich, CT: JAI Press.

Westney, D. E. (1987). *Imitation and innovation.* Cambridge, MA: Harvard University Press.

Wilkins, A. L. (1983). Organizational stories as symbols which control the organization. In L. Pondy, P. Frost, G. Morgan, & T. Dandridge (Eds.), *Organizational symbolism* (pp. 81–92). Greenwich, CT: JAI Press.

SOURCE: Schein, Edgar H. 1991. Excerpt from "What Is Culture?" Pp. 243–48 in *Reframing Organizational Culture,* edited by P. Frost, L. Moore, M. Louis, C. Lundberg, and J. Martin. Newbury Park, CA: Sage.

30

THE ORGANIZATIONAL CULTURE WAR GAMES

A Struggle for Intellectual Dominance

JOANNE MARTIN AND PETER FROST

THE REVOLUTIONARY VANGUARD

There are many ways to tell the history of the renaissance of interest in culture in the late 1970s, but most organizational accounts cite the successes of Japanese management and the perceived failures of traditional organizational analysis as catalysts for awakening managerial interest in corporate culture (e.g. Turner 1990: 85–6). For example:

> The dearth of practical additions to old ways of thought was painfully apparent. It was never so clear as in 1980, when US managers, beset by obvious problems of stagnation, leaped to adopt Japanese management practices, ignoring the cultural difference, so much wider than even the vast expanse of the Pacific would suggest . . . The theorists from academe, we found, were wrestling with the same concerns. Our timing was good. The state of theory is in refreshing disarray. (Peters and Waterman 1982: 4–5)

Many members of the revolutionary vanguard of cultural researchers were highly critical of mainstream organizational research, which, at that time, emphasized quantitative, normal science in both the US (where it has long been the tradition) and the UK (where the Aston Studies were gaining momentum). They declared this approach to be arid and fruitless because it was overly reliant on a rational model of human behavior, a structural approach to questions of corporate strategy, and a love of numerical analysis. Business education based on such research, they argued, created a generation of managers who knew more about managing spreadsheets than people:

> A buried weakness in the analytic approach to business decision making is that people analyze what can be most readily analyzed, spend more time on it, and more or less ignore the rest. As Harvard's John Steinbruner [1974] observes, 'If quantitative precision is demanded, it is gained, in the current state of *things,* only by so reducing the scope of what is analyzed that most of the important problems remain *external* to the analysis.' (1982: 44)

Members of the revolutionary vanguard, whether or not they advocated the use of qualitative methods, shared a conviction that a cultural framework would

315

permit them to broaden the kinds of organizational phenomena they studied. For example:

> My interest in culture stemmed from a feeling of excitement: that through the cultural lens we could bring to the top of the agenda, in a constructive way, the emotional side of organizational life. I felt that our approaches to organizations were quite antiseptic and lifeless in many ways. Also I saw that we could begin to look at the texture of organizational life, again in ways that had been brushed aside/dismissed/discounted in the mainstream of research. It was now potentially ok to do qualitative research, to be playful and experimental, to collect, study, and learn from the stories, events, dramas, and tedium in organizations. It was a liberation from seemingly purely technical, *engineered* approaches to studying organizations. I experienced a sense of the fun and the theoretical potential of looking at organizations that way . . . We took risks and invented things that we would not likely have thought about in the previous era. (Frost 1995)

At these first stages of the cultural revolution, hope was in the air, new insights seemed likely, and the possibility of an organizational theory that was at once more broad and more useful was a heady tonic for many.

VALUE ENGINEERING AND THE INTEGRATION PERSPECTIVE

At this point, the game of king of the mountain had not yet begun. It was as if children drifted to the beach and began to play in the sand, at first without much interaction or coordination. Although publication dates can be misleading, and (as will be the case throughout this chapter) it is difficult to choose which of many exemplars to cite, many of the first widely influential culture publications were managerially oriented and written for a popular audience. Critics later labeled this cultural approach 'value engineering,' [1] because these authors had the temerity to argue that effective cultural leaders could create 'strong' cultures, built around their own values. Perhaps the most popular was Peters and Waterman's (1982) *In Search of Excellence: Lessons from America's Best-Run Companies*. This anecdote-filled, lively book began with many of the same premises outlined and quoted above. The key

to corporate financial success, according to Peters and Waterman, was a strongly unified culture. Top managers could build such a culture by articulating a set of values and then reinforcing those values, again and again, with formal policies, informal norms, stories, rituals, and jargon. In time, and with consistency, those values would become shared—with enthusiasm—by all employees. This would set up a domino effect: higher commitment, greater productivity, and ultimately, more profits. These seductive promises, complete with advice about how to create a 'strong' (meaning unitary) culture, were popularized in other books written primarily for executive and MBA audiences (e.g. Deal and Kennedy 1982; Ouchi 1981; Pascale and Athos 1981; see Fitzgerald 1988 for a rebuttal to some of these claims). Not surprisingly, culture quickly became the hottest product on the consulting market.

The value engineers touched a responsive chord in many managerially oriented academic researchers who shared the perception that organizational research had become dead-ended, boring, and/or too distant from the practical concerns of business. A flurry of culture research appeared (e.g. Enz 1988; Ott 1989; Ouchi and Jaeger 1978; Pennings and Gresov 1986; Pfeffer 1981; Pondy et al. 1983; Sathe 1985; Sergiovanni and Corbally 1984). These studies define culture as an internally consistent package of cultural manifestations that generates organization-wide consensus, usually around some set of shared values. In these cultural portraits all is clear; culture is 'an area of meaning carved out of a vast mass of meaninglessness, a small clearing of lucidity in a formless, dark, always ominous jungle' (Berger 1967: 23; quoted in Wuthnow et al. 1984: 26). Within the domain that is considered the culture, there is virtually no ambiguity (e.g. Schein 1991). Subcultures are noted only as a secondary consideration (if at all). Very little deep, collective conflict is acknowledged. Studies which share these characteristics (consistency, organization-wide consensus, and clarity) have been termed 'integration' research (Martin 1992). Many, *but not all*, integration studies have value engineering overtones, claiming that culture can be managed or that 'strong' cultures can lead to improved financial performance. Reviews which include a description of some of the historical roots of the integration literature are Ott (1989),

Ouchi and Wilkins (1985), Schultz (1994), and Trice and Beyer (1993).

The integration perspective conceptualizes cultural change as an organization-wide cultural transformation, whereby an old unity is replaced—hopefully—by a new one; in the interim, conflict and ambiguity may occur, but these are interpreted as evidence of the deterioration of culture before a new unity is established (e.g. Clark 1972; Greenwood and Hinings 1988; Jonsson and Lundin 1977; Selznick 1957). For example, Schein (1985) describes several organizational leaders who articulate their personal values and apparently generate harmonious and universal commitment to those values, reaping benefits of high morale and smoothly coordinated task performance. When dissent appears or ambiguities emerge, these anomalies are explained as evidence of individual deviance, insufficiently homogeneous employee selection procedures, poor socialization of new employees, a weak culture, a temporary period of confusion during a time of cultural realignment, or—in the case of ambiguity—as a domain of organizational life that is not part of its culture (Schein 1991). The bottom line is that homogeneity, harmony, and a unified culture are achievable.

Other good examples of integration studies include Barley's (1983) study of how funeral directors manipulated a variety of physical artifacts (e.g. changing the sheets on a death bed, washing and putting make-up on a corpse, closing the corpse's eyes) to create the illusion that death is life-like. Pettigrew (1979) described how headmasters used rituals, stories, and jargon to generate commitment to their schools.

McDonald (1991) described how uniforms, slogans, posters, a charismatic leader, well-defined rituals, and a strong work ethic combined to create a sense of excitement and a commitment to excellence among volunteers and employees of a temporary organization, the Los Angeles Olympic Organizing Committee.[2] These are generalist cultural studies, that is, in addition to formal practices, rules and structures they describe and interpret informal practices (such as norms about appropriate behavior or proper decision-making procedures), as well as organizational stories, rituals, specialized jargon, and physical artifacts, such as decor, dress norms, machinery, architecture. In contrast to 'generalist'

cultural studies, 'specialist' cultural studies focus on only a single cultural manifestation. Examples of specialist integration studies include Dandridge (1986) on ceremonies, Martin et al. (1983) on organizational stories, and Trice and Beyer (1984) on rituals. Specialist research done within the integration perspective assumes that the manifestations of a culture are consistent with each other, and thus sometimes, without adequate evidence, asserts that a single manifestation represents the culture as a whole (e.g. Martin et al. 1983).

ASSEMBLING THE TROOPS: THE DIFFERENTIATION PERSPECTIVE

Roughly at the same time as the flood of integration research began to appear, another group of scholars, mostly working independently, were drawn to some but not all the ideas expressed by the revolutionary vanguard. They too thought that mainstream organizational theory and research needed revitalization. They too thought that a renaissance of interest in organizational culture would bring an interdisciplinary creativity into the field, expanding the types of issues being studied and the kinds of methods considered valid.

Some of the members of this second group of cultural scholars had done work considered by many to be marginal to the managerial, quantitative emphases common to much mainstream organizational theory and research. Like many of the advocates of the integration viewpoint, some of this second group of scholars were qualitative researchers, who were excited because now ('at last' in the US) ethnographic research would have a home in organizational studies and qualitative case studies would be appreciated for their richly detailed, context-specific insights, rather than being dismissed as 'a nice story about an *N* of one.' Some scholars in this second group were also hopeful that cultural work would generate alternatives to the managerial orientation that had been dominant for so long; now the opinions and interests of lower-level employees would be more fully represented. These and other deviants, dissidents, and disenchanted organizational scholars seeking a fresh perspective were attracted to cultural studies. Because culture itself was so vaguely defined, because it lacked a clear and commonly accepted theoretical framework, and because so many of these scholars prided themselves individually on their iconoclastic openness to new ideas, this 'rag-tag' collection of marginals soon generated an impressive body of work that shared some common characteristics, labeled here and elsewhere (e.g. Martin and Meyerson 1988) as the differentiation perspective.

Differentiation studies developed commonalities without much intentional coordination (although meetings, such as the 1984 Vancouver Conference on Organizational Culture and the annual gatherings of the Standing Conference on Organizational Symbolism, did provide some opportunities for contact and interchange among a wide range of cultural researchers). These commonalities emerged from a disparate set of intellectual traditions and, as outlined in the next section of this chapter, this *de facto* alliance was shaky, soon to be threatened by dissension. In the terms of the king of the mountain game, it was as if children playing independently on the beach began to notice each other, eventually moving together to play in a parallel fashion: an unstable coalition at best.

Differentiation studies, like integration studies, stress the ideational aspects of culture, such as values, cognitions (meanings), symbolism (including aesthetics), and/or emotions—topics which were being *neglected* in mainstream organizational research. Rather than *defining* culture in purely ideational *terms,* however, differentiation studies preferred a less ethereal, more material approach that included within the definition of culture practical/structural *considerations* such as pay, task responsibilities, hierarchical reporting relationships, formal *policies* and procedures—in short, any organizational practice formal enough to be *written* down. Most differentiation studies seem to assume that a good *study* of a culture should be generalist rather than specialist, that is, it should include a wide range of *cultural* manifestations.

Such generalist breadth was not enough; a good cultural study also had to have depth, to 'penetrate the front' presented to strangers (e.g. Gregory 1983), and to observe conflicts, the unresolved, the shameful, what causes ambivalence—the chinks in the armor through which deeper, more complex considerations become visible. This emphasis on depth of understanding produced cultural accounts that were sensitive to inconsistencies between stated attitudes and actual behavior, between formal practices and informal norms, between one story and another, and—most important—between the interpretations of one person and another (e.g. Van Maanen and Barley 1984; Van Maanen and Kunda 1989). *Differences* in perception and opinion were associated with status, tasks, jobs, seniority, sex, occupation, race, and ethnicity—often coalescing into overlapping, nested subcultures (e.g. Louis 1985). Although Rosen (1991) rightly observes that true ethnographies of organizational cultures are rare, the best differentiation ethnographies are highly complex, full of nuance, open to conflict, pervaded by inconsistencies and ambivalences: a complex richness that indeed fulfilled many of the hopes of the cultural vanguard (e.g. Jaques 1951; Kunda 1991; Rosen 1985; Van Maanen 1991; Young 1989). These studies are bold, empirically well-supported challenges to the integration assumption that organizational culture can be a unitary monolith composed of clear values and interpretations perceived, enacted, and shared by all employees, in an organization-wide consensus.

In addition, differentiation research showed that the subcultures within an organization can reflect, and be partially determined by, cultural groupings in the larger society. For example, functional subcultures within a firm can reflect occupational subcultures that *cross* firm boundaries, as when accountants appear to be the 'same everywhere' (e.g. Gregory 1983). From this perspective, cultural change is localized within one or more subcultures, alterations tend to be incremental, and innovations are triggered primarily by pressures from an organization's environment (e.g. Meyerson and Martin 1987). That environment is *likely* to be segmented, so different subcultures within the same organization experience different kinds and rates of *change.* Thus, from a differentiation viewpoint, an organizational culture is not unitary; it is a *nexus* where environmental influences intersect, creating a nested, overlapping set of subcultures within a permeable organizational boundary (Martin 1992: 111–14).

Examples show the texture of this kind of cultural work. Christensen and Kreiner (1984) drew on several case studies to distinguish different aspects of cultures in organizations: the firm's external 'aura' (what economists refer to as its reputation in the market); its 'corporate culture' (the values and goals espoused by its top management—not necessarily accepted or even noticed by lower-level employees); and 'cultures in work' (reflecting the everyday working lives of groups of employees who share tasks). Rosen (1985) focused on the discordance between the espoused values of an advertising agency's top management and the reactions of various subcultures of employees, as they attended an annual company breakfast ritual. Van Maanen (1991) studied subcultures at Disneyland, as operators of various rides and concessions stands arranged themselves in a status hierarchy, harassed obnoxious customers, and ignored their supervisors. Bartunek and Moch (1991) described the non-too-enthusiastic reactions of various subcultures (in-house consulting staff, management of local plants, line employees, and machinists) to a management-initiated 'quality of working life' intervention. Young (1989) observed women working on an assembly line, describing their fission into two subcultures reflecting differences in age, marital status, and task assignments. A few researchers have delineated the difficulties women and minorities have in 'fitting into' corporate cultures dominated by white men (e.g. Bell 1990; Cox 1993; Kanter 1977; Mills 1992). Other studies consistent with a differentiation approach, broadly defined, include Brunsson (1985), Riley (1983), and Van Maanen (1986).

These studies have in common a willingness to acknowledge inconsistencies (i.e. attitudes versus behavior, formal policies versus actual practices, etc.). They see consensus as occurring only within subcultural boundaries. They acknowledge conflicts of interest, for example, between top management and other employees or within a top management group. These studies describe whatever inconsistencies and subcultural differences they find in clear terms: there is little ambiguity here, except in the interstices between subcultures. Thus, inconsistency, subcultural consensus, and subcultural clarity are the hallmark characteristics of differentiation research (Martin 1992).

DISSENSION IN THE RANKS OF THE DIFFERENTIATION PERSPECTIVE

Although differentiation studies share the common characteristics described above, these commonalities mask important distinctions (for an extended discussion of this issue, see Alvesson 1993; Alvesson and Berg 1992). For example, there is an important distinction between pluralism (the delineation of differences within a whole) and the awareness of power and conflicts of interest that come with a more critical perspective (i.e. Knights and Willmott 1987; Lucas 1987; Mumby 1988; Reed 1985; Riley 1983). There is a fundamental difference between the 'describe reality' tone of a historical-hermeneutic orientation (e.g. Agar 1986; Garfinkel 1967; Goffman 1967; Spradley 1979) and the challenge to the status quo represented by critical theories, for example what Habermas (1975) terms an emancipatory point of view. In Burrell and Morgan's (1979) terminology, some of these issues stem from differences between the interpretative and the radical humanist paradigms. Putnam et al.'s (1993) debate between ethnography and critical theory outlines some of these differences in orientation, and Stablein and Nord's (1985) review classifies organizational culture research according to the extent to which it represents an emancipatory point of view.

Clues to where differentiation studies stand on these issues can most easily be found in their theoretical introductions, rather than in the content of their descriptions of particular subcultures. Studies that stem from a more critical, rather than interpretative or pluralistic, tradition tend to cite some common intellectual predecessors to legitimate their theoretical orientation and anti-management tone. These include organizational scholars open to the insights of Marxist/critical theory (e.g. Burawoy 1979; Burrell and Morgan 1979; Deetz 1992; Perrow 1979; Reed 1985), occupational research in the tradition of the Chicago School of sociology (e.g. Becker et al. 1961; Hughes 1958; Manning 1977), and some early qualitative studies of organizations that included a focus on lower-level employees (e.g. Crozier 1964; Jaques 1951).

These intellectual predecessors share a concern with the everyday working lives of people of relatively low status, a focus which is congruent with a relatively leftist political ideology that challenges the top management's views and delineates the negative consequences of the status quo on those who are relatively disadvantaged. In this context, it is surprising to note that few differentiation studies, even those written from a critical theory viewpoint, go beyond the delineation of subcultural differences to examine processes of organizational change that might, for example in a grass roots collective action, benefit those who are at the bottom of an organizational hierarchy. Although several literatures are relevant to these questions of change (for example, research on social movements, unions, and sabotage), these issues have received relatively little attention to date from cultural researchers.

Thus, the differentiation perspective includes at least two subdivisions that have developed in distinctive ways from differing intellectual traditions. One documents pluralism within a culture, usually utilizing ethnographic methods and a hermeneutic epistemology, offering a single, presumably 'accurate' interpretation of what was observed without fundamentally challenging a managerial perspective (i.e. Barley et al. 1988; Louis 1985; Martin and Siehl 1983). The other adds a critical, anti-management reading of the data (empirical examples include Rosen 1985; Van Maanen 1991; Young 1989). In some critical studies, sometimes even the pluralist sensitivity to difference that is the foundation of all differentiation research is underemphasized, while critique of the hegemony of management takes precedence. Thus, these differences in intellectual orientation within the differentiation classification can sometimes blur the boundaries of the category. Some differentiation scholars, particularly those working from a critical theory perspective, have been concerned about delineating these differences within their ranks (see Alvesson and Berg 1992 and Alvesson 1993, for example), while others have directed their attention to criticizing integration research. Now the battle lines had been drawn and the attack was about to begin.

LET THE GAME BEGIN: THE ATTACK OF THE DIFFERENTIATION ADVOCATES

Literally hundreds of integration studies were published in the 1980s. In the vast majority of these publications, consultants and academics had adopted the language of cultural studies and transformed it into a barely recognizable variant (some would say, travesty). Suddenly 'strong' unitary cultures had become the latest 'new' answer to managers' desires for greater control over their employees and greater profitability for their firms (Barley et al. 1988). Differentiation scholarship, of both pluralistic and critical varieties, had been outflanked by a value engineering perspective; the integration view had become king of the mountain. Advocates of the differentiation viewpoint were, needless to say, not pleased by these developments and they regrouped and then counter-attacked on several different fronts.

Some noted that in spite of efforts to distinguish practitioner-oriented integrationist writings from academic integrationist studies, the boundaries between these two categories were permeable (for example, many academics consulted and many consultants had fine academic credentials); more importantly, they shared a managerial emphasis (Barley et al. 1988; Jeffcutt forthcoming) and came to similar conclusions: organizational cultures were supposedly characterized by consistency, organization-wide consensus, and clarity. Some noted such commonalities with contempt, as evidence that these integration studies had 'sold out' to the managerial perspective that dominated mainstream organizational research (see also Van Maanen and Kunda 1989: 92):

> The companies studied are the cream of America's corporate crop, and range from IBM to McDonald's hamburgers. The dedication and quasi-religious commitment which the new manager seeks to instill into his employees sometimes sits a little oddly with the nature of the company goal: it may be inspiring to hear of sales staff risking their life in a snow storm to ensure that the company goal of regular delivery of supplies is maintained, but when the reader learns that the product is a high-salt, high-calorie junk food, doubts about whether some of this shining dedication is perhaps misplaced begin to arise. (Turner 1986: 108)

Calás and Smircich (1987), noting the overwhelming numbers of integration studies being published, declared that the cultural revolution was in danger of becoming 'dominant, but dead.' As Calás and Smircich had hoped, this fear was premature. Many of those who were not willing to give up the fight to dethrone the integration view utilized a methodological critique, a move that ultimately had the effect of partially crosscutting the integration/differentiation battle lines and bringing different issues to the front.

THE METHODOLOGY BATTLE

The methodology battle was particularly fierce because underlying these method preferences were firmly held epistemological beliefs (e.g. Burrell and Morgan 1979). Although some skirmishes in this battle took place out in the open, most were more like guerrilla warfare, taking place in a series of out-of-sight maneuvers; the methods battle affected an editor's choice of journal reviewers for a culture article, a 'blind' reviewer's verdict about the merits of a particular manuscript, and even the content of letters from external reviewers in tenure cases. Of course, such out-of-sight maneuvers left few published traces that can be quoted here, without breaking norms of confidentiality and blind review. Nevertheless, we personally can testify that these non-public fights were, and are, fiercely contested. The stakes were high, at least in academic terms. Viewing culture from the differentiation perspective and studying it using qualitative methods can be a risky career strategy, particularly in the US where the field is dominated by managerial interests, integrationist theoretical preconceptions, and quantitative methods.

Some qualitative researchers were disappointed by this reaction. They responded by citing texts justifying their methods choices and outlining the fundamentals of good qualitative research methodology (some helpful texts include Agar 1986; Blau 1965; Glaser and Strauss 1967; Schein 1987; Van Maanen et al. 1982). Even among advocates of qualitative methods for studying culture there were strident disagreements, most of which surfaced in less public places, like journal reviews. The

purist ethnographers criticized short-term and/or interview-based qualitative studies as being 'smash and grab' ethnographies.[3] If a researcher was to truly 'penetrate the front' of cultural members, he or she had to, they argued, adopt 'true' ethnographic methods. This meant spending months or even years as a participant-observer in order to see things from an insider's 'emic' perspective (e.g. Gregory 1983). Anything less was worthy of being classified, at best, as exploratory pilot testing, anecdotal examples to illustrate ideas based on more solid evidence—in short, probably not worth mentioning, in print (see Sutton 1994 for a frank discussion of these issues).

Other cultural researchers, perhaps in response to criticisms of qualitative methods, developed quantitative measures of cultural phenomena, drawing primarily on techniques used in organizational climate research (Schneider 1990). Quantitative culture studies are generally 'specialist' in that they focus on only one kind of cultural manifestation—usually a measure of agreement with a series of espoused (rather than enacted) values or a self-report of behavioral norms (e.g. 'People in my work group are generally more cooperative than competitive'), measured using seven-point scales or more innovative techniques, such as adjective sorting tasks (e.g. O'Reilly et al. 1991).

There are several problems with these quantitative approaches. Specialist studies should not (although integration studies often do) assume or assert that the one kind of manifestation is consistent with or representative of the culture as a whole (see Martin et al. 1983 as an illustration of this problem). Additionally, respondents may not be aware that their espoused values are not being consistently enacted (e.g. Argyris and Schon 1978). They may fear that researchers' promises of anonymity will not be kept, endangering their jobs, and so may give misleading answers that are reflective of top management's expressed preferences, rather than actual behavior, thus creating an illusion of organizational consensus. To manage the impression given to researchers, respondents may give answers that seem socially desirable or that reflect their current levels of job satisfaction (high or low).

Furthermore, this kind of quantitative measure may give a misleading representation of a culture because the researcher has generated the alternatives that the respondents are evaluating. Most importantly, such quantitative studies are likely to provide empirical support for integrationist assumptions, if responses that do not reflect organization-wide consensus are excluded from discussion and analysis—as not part of the 'culture.' Significantly, other questionnaire-based specialist studies have used broader, random samples of respondents, across status levels, and have found evidence of subcultural differentiation (pockets of ignorance of and resistance to managerial values), rather than organization-wide consensus (Kilmann 1985; Rousseau 1990).

Some integration studies, which use specialist quantitative (questionnaire) measures of culture, have claimed to have found evidence of a link to financial performance (Denison 1990; Gordon 1985; Ouchi and Johnson 1978). Other specialist quantitative studies (for example, a content analysis of espoused managerial values in annual reports has been used as a measure of 'culture') conclude that valid empirical confirmation of a link to financial performance has not yet been found and is unlikely to be found, given the many non-cultural determinants of financial performance and the difficulty of developing adequately generalist measures of the cultures of large numbers of firms (see Siehl and Martin 1990 for a review of the research on this issue).

Advocates of ethnographic methods, from both the integration and differentiation perspectives, have been particularly critical of specialist studies which by definition lack the richly detailed, context-specific understandings that emerge from generalist ethnographic cultural portraits (e.g. Schein 1987; Smircich 1983; Smircich and Morgan 1982; Van Maanen et al. 1982), especially those with a longitudinal focus (e.g. Pettigrew 1985a; 1985b). Ethnographers also have disapproved of an exclusive focus on espoused values or self-reported behavioral norms. Because such a superficial focus cannot 'penetrate the front' of people's desires to present themselves in a favourable light, it is far inferior to the depth made accessible by long-term participant-observation. In organizational contexts, behavior is often constrained by managerial preferences or career ambitions and cannot be assumed to reflect an employee's true attitudes.

Many ethnographers had thought that the cultural movement would provide respect, particularly in the US where qualitative methods had been so disparaged. Many of these qualitative researchers were disappointed that this domain of organizational research, like all the others, was in danger of being taken over by the number crunchers, a reaction that was expressed, in public forums, by the usual strategies of silence and marginalization; in more private arenas, such as 'blind reviews,' the negative reaction was more pronounced and many researchers felt it was difficult to get their work recognized due to methods preferences of reviewers and editors (see, for example, Rousseau 1994).

The result was a strident debate over the merits of qualitative and quantitative methods for studying culture (for a particularly clear discussion of the underlying issues, although not within the context of this particular body of literature, see Blau 1965; Daft 1980; Light 1979), with some researchers advocating matching particular conventional methods with particular conceptual problems (e.g. McGrath 1982; Rousseau 1990), while others preferred an uneasy, but possibly innovative hybrid mix of the two approaches (e.g. Martin 1990a). For example, one such hybrid qualitative-quantitative approach to studying culture involved a two-step procedure (Martin et al. 1985). An open-ended, structured interview protocol was used to collect qualitative, context-specific event histories, generated by employees themselves, using such questions as: 'Describe the ten incidents that made your company what it is today. Give details. For each event, tell us what meanings this event holds for you personally and for the company as a whole.' These open-ended responses were then quantitatively content-analyzed, to measure subcultural or organization-wide agreement about what happened, to delineate which employees' actions were considered important, and which interpretations of the meanings of these events were shared. Such hybrid methods represent an uneasy compromise between quite different epistemologies. The qualitative/quantitative debates among cultural researchers continue (see the edited volumes by Schneider 1990, and Hassard and Pym 1990, for some recent salvos in this battle). Given the deep differences that underlie these disputes, agreement is unlikely.

Taken as a whole, qualitative cultural studies do not provide consistent, convincing support for the premises of either the integration or the differentiation perspectives. For those who thought quantitative research could resolve the conflict between these two viewpoints, the contradictory empirical record caused confusion: how could conscientious culture researchers come to such different conclusions? Was it the case simply that integration research generally focused on organizations where organization-wide consensus existed, while differentiation research picked organizations where subcultures prevailed? This was unlikely, given that integration studies dismissed evidence of non-unitary cultures as examples of weak or failed integration (e.g. Schein 1991), while differentiation research often failed to look for or report organization-wide agreement.

At this point, the conflict escalated, as advocates of each viewpoint accused each other of theoretical and methodological tautology, whether or not they used quantitative methods. Integration studies were accused (for examples from the literature, see Martin 1992: 65–7) of engaging in a kind of tautology because they defined culture as consistent and clear, then included in their cultural portraits only those manifestations which seemed to have consistent and clear interpretations. They defined culture (or a 'strong' culture) as organization-wide agreement with values espoused by top management, but their sampling procedures were seldom either random or stratified to include all levels of the hierarchy. Instead, integration studies tended to study those cultural members who were particularly articulate informants, or those who were most likely to have views similar to top managers (i.e. high-ranking and upwardly mobile managers, professionals such as accountants or engineers, or loyal lower-ranking members selected by management). Unfortunately, integration studies seldom hesitated to generalize from such limited subject samples to the culture of the whole organization.

Even studies which refrained from these nonstandard sampling procedures found organization-wide consensus by excluding from their cultural portraits (as 'not part of the culture' or 'evidence of a weak culture') all aspects of the culture that generated conflicting or ambiguous interpretations (see Schein 1991 for a cogent defense of this position). Not surprisingly, the portraits of culture that emerged from these research designs were entirely consistent with integrationist theoretical preconceptions: each 'strong' culture was a monolith where every manifestation reinforced the values of top management, employees complied with managerial directives, and preferences were assumed to share these values, and there was, apparently, only one interpretation of the meaning of events shared by all. These studies were designed so integration research would find what it was looking for.

Advocates of the integration point of view did not take all this criticism without fighting back. They accused differentiation research of also being tautological (for examples, see Martin 1992: 106–8). Differentiation studies, these critics argued, defined cultural manifestations as inconsistent, and then included in their cultural portraits those manifestations that fit these definitions. Differentiation studies were accused of seeking subcultural differentiation, by using focused, non-random samples of lower-level employees and ignoring (or not searching for) evidence of values shared on an organization-wide basis. Integration critics claimed that, if differentiation studies had only had sufficiently astute clinical and ethnographic skills, they would have understood that, at a deep enough level, fundamental assumptions (for example, about the nature of time) are shared by all or most members of an organization (e.g. Schein 1985, 1994). Of course, when such widely shared, deep assumptions are found, they may in fact be part of a society's culture, and not appropriately studied at the organizational level of analysis (Martin 1992: 53–6). And so it goes on: the openly combative exchanges in public, as well as the more private and less visible forms of battle, continue.

This academic battle about methodology and theory shows some considerable indifference to the fates of actual people in real organizations (see Donaldson 1989: 250 for an articulate version of this criticism); even differentiation research, ostensibly so concerned about the fate of the disadvantaged and oppressed, contributes little so far to understanding how to make people's organizational lives better. Outside academia, in corporations the stakes are high. Managers do not generally care about the hair splitting disputes of academics, but they do care, deeply, about the considerable expense and unwanted consequences of ill-thought-out cultural change interventions. Many executives, consultants, and lower-level employees dismiss culture as 'yesterday's fad,' and predictably have turned elsewhere to find another 'quick fix' for corporate ills.

The theoretical and methodological disputes described above have caused chaos in the field of cultural studies. In the struggle to be king of the mountain, skirmishes are constant among proponents of various epistemologies, methodologies, intellectual heritages, publication norms, and even different career paths (e.g. US versus European). Everyone is out to prove what they already believe in. It is not clear what has been learned, who is more correct, or even what methods could convincingly resolve these differences of opinion. In fact, for reasons explained in the next two sections of this review, such disputes may not be resolvable. In the short term, however, the confusion caused by the methods battle created an opening for other parties to enter the battlefield.

A New Contender: The Fragmentation Perspective

These new parties to the conflict each tried to redraw the battle lines so that their point of view would emerge triumphant—the king of the mountain. The first of these new contenders has been termed the fragmentation perspective (Martin 1992), as it is positioned as the third logical possibility on the dimensions that are the focus of the integration versus differentiation struggle. According to the advocates of the fragmentation view, the relationships among the manifestations of a culture are neither clearly consistent nor clearly inconsistent; instead, the relationships are complex, containing elements of contradiction and confusion. Similarly, consensus is not organization-wide nor is it specific to a given subculture. Instead, consensus is transient and issue-specific, producing short-lived affinities among individuals that are quickly replaced by a different pattern of affinities, as a different issue draws the attention of cultural members

(e.g. Kreiner and Schultz 1993). In such an ephemeral environment, culture is no longer a clearing in a jungle of meaninglessness. Now, culture is the jungle itself. According to the fragmentation point of view, the essence of any culture is ambiguity, which pervades all (e.g. Feldman 1991; Meyerson 1991). Clarity, then, is a dogma of meaningfulness and order propagated by management to create an illusion of clarity where there is none (e.g. Levitt and Nass 1989).

Lack of consistency, lack of consensus, and ambiguity are the hallmarks of a fragmentation view of culture. In a fragmentation account, power is diffused broadly at all levels of the hierarchy and throughout the organization's environment. Change is a constant flux, rather than an intermittent interruption in an otherwise stable state. Because change is largely triggered by the environment or other forces beyond an individual's control, fragmentation studies of change offer few guidelines for those who would normatively control the change process.

For example, Feldman (1989) studied policy analysts in a large government bureaucracy. They spent their days writing policy reports that might never be read and, in any case, were unlikely to influence the formation of a policy. In such a context, ambiguities became a protective cloud that prevented a clear analysis of the meaning(lessness) of the analysts' work. In Meyerson's (1991) studies of social workers, ambiguity pervaded an occupation whose practitioners had to operate in a world where the objectives of social work were unclear, the means to those goals were not specified, and sometimes it wasn't even clear when an intervention had been successful or even what success in this context might have meant.

Meyerson concluded that to study the culture of this occupation—while excluding ambiguity from the realm of what is defined as cultural—would have been dramatically incomplete, even misleading. Weick (1991) offered a fragmentation view of a foggy airport in Tenerife, as pilots, controllers, and cockpit crews struggled to make themselves understood across barriers of status, language, and task assignment. In this context, pervasive ambiguity was not benign: hundreds of lives were lost as two jumbo jets collided in the fog.

An Attempt to Redraw the Battle Lines: A Meta-Theoretical Move

What had been a war among two perspectives was now a war among many: among the integration, differentiation, and fragmentation views; between the qualitative and quantitative advocates; and between the critical theorists and their more interpretive colleagues. The game of king of the mountain was now being played in earnest; all of these contenders were competing for supremacy, although each was arguing for the use of different playing rules. Rather than going for a minor victory (a fourth perspective), the next obvious move in the king of the mountain game was to create a meta-theory that would encompass all three perspectives.

Martin (1992) outlined the problems of methodological tautology discussed above and argued that such tautologies were also evident in fragmentation research. Fragmentation studies focused on contexts (airports literally in the fog) and occupations (policy analyst, social worker) that were particularly ambiguous and then wrote cultural portraits emphasizing those ambiguities. Both fragmentation and differentiation studies tended to focus on a wide range of cultural manifestations, making it less likely that all manifestations would have consistent interpretations. Thus, integration, differentiation, and fragmentation researchers defined culture in a particular way and then designed studies which made it more likely they would find what they were looking for. This problem of tautology explained, to a large extent, why three traditions of research on ostensibly the same topic could produce such conflicting empirical records. (Indeed, some have argued that similar tautological problems characterize all of organizational research; see Morgan 1983.)

However, the fact remains that evidence congruent with each perspective had been found. Martin (1992) argues that it is not only that advocates of the various perspectives have sought and found cultural contexts that fit their preconceptions; in addition, *any* organizational culture contains elements congruent with all three perspectives. If any organization is studied in enough depth, some issues, values, and objectives will be seen to generate organization-wide consensus, consistency,

and clarity (an integration view). At the same time, other aspects of an organization's culture will coalesce into subcultures that hold conflicting opinions about what is important, what should happen, and why (a differentiation view). Finally, some problems and issues will be ambiguous, in a state of constant flux, generating multiple, plausible interpretations (a fragmentation view). A wide range of organizational contexts have been examined using the three-perspective framework, including studies of a temporary educational organization for unemployed women in England, a newly privatized bank in Turkey, truants from an urban high school in the US, and Peace Corps/ Africa volunteers (Baburoglu and Gocer 1991; Enomoto 1993; Jeffcutt forthcoming; Meyerson and Martin 1987). Implicit in the three-perspective framework is the assumption that these social scientific viewpoints are subjectively imposed on the process of collecting and interpreting cultural data. Often one perspective, labeled the 'home' viewpoint, is easy for cultural members and researchers to acknowledge, while the other two perspectives can be more difficult to access. It is therefore a misunderstanding to conclude that a particular organization has a culture that is best characterized by one of the three perspectives. Rather, any culture at any point in time will have some aspects congruent with all three perspectives (e.g. Frost et al. 1991; Martin 1992; Meyerson and Martin 1987).

The three-perspective framework is a meta-theory, which claims to encompass and thereby surpass prior, more narrow theories by moving to a higher level of abstraction, claiming that, when a cultural context is viewed from all three perspectives, a deeper understanding will emerge. Presumably, because the three-perspective theory is more inclusive and thereby possibly more insightful, it supposedly deserves to dominate other approaches to understanding cultures in organizations. This is a classic attempt to redraw the lines of battle and so become 'king of the mountain,' and as such, it arouses considerable antagonism.

Obviously, this approach does have limitations. To paraphrase and quote arguments made elsewhere (Martin 1992: 192), this tripartite classification scheme is based on a series of undeconstructed dichotomies that position the perspectives in opposition to one another. It ignores aspects of theories and studies that straddle boundaries among the perspectives (see, especially, rich ethnographies such as Kunda 1991 and Pettigrew 1985b), omits unclassifiable research or relegates it to marginalized places in the text, and reserves treatment of issues that transcend these categories for separate parts of the text (for example, see the discussion above of the differences between the critical theory and interpretative traditions or the qualitative versus quantitative methods debates). Most importantly, by using these tripartite categories to classify studies, the perspectives are reified and individual studies are pigeonholed, thereby diminishing the uniqueness of their contributions. Such a use of categories is common social scientific practice, and not unique to this particular attempt to build a meta-theory, but it does have harmful effects on the ways knowledge gets created and scholarly work is and is not evaluated (e.g. Gagliardi 1990; Turner 1989). And these criticisms are mild compared to the postmodern critiques of meta-theories outlined in the next section of this review.

To summarize the results of the last few battles described above: in spite of (or perhaps because of) the confusion caused by these disputes, the last decade of cultural research has produced a variety of insightful, innovative studies that might not have been completed within the narrower orthodoxies of theory and method that have constrained other kinds of organizational inquiry. Cultural studies have brought epistemological and methodological variety to the field, introduced ideas from other disciplines, and (speaking now of qualitative generalist work) offered richly detailed, context-specific descriptions of organizational life. Now, however, cultural research faces a new and formidable challenge: postmodernists have entered the culture wars. The postmodernists' bid to be king of the mountain has a very different tone than the modernist traditions of cultural research described so far. If the postmodernists are successful, cultural researchers will admit that it is impossible, ever, to know, or represent, the truth about a culture.

THE END OF THEORY: A POSTMODERN ROUT OF ALL ARMIES FROM THE FIELD OF BATTLE?

It is beyond the mandate of this chapter to discuss postmodernism at length but, nonetheless, we are able to discuss its implications for and contributions to the work on organizational culture. Postmodernism is the most profound, potentially disruptive, and possibly insightful development in cultural studies to date (e.g. Calás and Smircich 1987; Czarniawska-Joerges 1992; Jeffcutt forthcoming; Linstead and Grafton-Small 1991). There is not just one postmodernism: it is a discourse, rather than a unified theory, in part because it has attracted such a diverse group of advocates, including architects, philosophers, and literary critics. Some postmodernists have been accused of fascism, while others are leftist refugees from the political activism of the 1960s. In all these varieties, postmodernism challenges ideas which are the foundation of modern science: rationality, order, clarity, realism, truth, and intellectual progress (e.g. Baudrillard 1983; Derrida 1976; Foucault 1976; Grafton-Small and Linstead 1987; Lyotard 1984). When contrasted to postmodern ideas, modernist cultural scholarship is seen to share some preconceptions. For example, modern cultural studies (even those written from differentiation and fragmentation perspectives) attempt to provide coherent accounts—to order the disorder that is organizational life. Carrying this emphasis on order one step further, integration studies offer a portrait of unity, harmony, and in many instances, the promise of cultural control.

In contrast, postmodern accounts draw attention to disorder and offer a multiplicity of contradictory interpretations, making integration studies particularly suspect from a postmodern viewpoint. The relationship between the signifier and the signified, between an image and the original experience it was once produced to represent, is from a postmodern viewpoint attenuated, complex, and in part arbitrary (Alvesson and Berg 1992: 220). This arbitrariness should not be confused with the more tepid, manageable ambiguities, irrationalities, and randomness that are the focus of fragmentation research.

The key difference is that while ambiguity implies a surplus of meaning attached to a particular object, i.e., a somewhat unclear, fuzzy, vague, obscure or enigmatic relation, arbitrariness implies a capricious or willful relationship that cannot be determined by any rule or principle. While an ambiguous relationship means that there is a way of understanding and capturing this relationship and of understanding the inherent way in which the signifier represents the signified, an arbitrary relationship makes no such assumptions. (Alvesson and Berg 1992: 220)

Modern cultural scholarship, particularly that which uses ethnographic methods, attempts to cut through superficial cultural manifestations and interpretations to uncover a deeper reality, revealing knowledge that is closer to the truth. Modern scholarship is careful to draw distinctions among the objective truth about reality, the subjectivity of a researcher-author, and a text. These distinctions, however, are not inviolable. For example, modernist studies sometimes explore the flaws of an imperfect relationship between reality and data (which presumably can be improved by more rigorous ethnographic or quantitative methods). Modern scholars also sometimes acknowledge a flawed relationship between presumably objective data and their imperfect representation in a text (which presumably can be improved by clearer, more 'transparent' writing). More rarely, a modernist author may engage in self-reflexivity concerning the effects of his or her individualized subjectivity on a text (e.g. Kunda 1991; Van Maanen 1988). Such introspection is usually confined to the margins of a text (an introduction, an anecdote, or an appendix). Such marginalization enables the modern author, in the main body of the text, to maintain the impersonal, supposedly objective style and language that sustain scientific credibility by making the individualized subjectivity of the author invisible (e.g. Clifford and Marcus 1986; Geertz 1988).

In contrast, from a postmodern point of view, reality is a series of fictions and illusions (Alvesson and Berg 1992; Arac 1986; Clifford and Marcus 1986; Geertz 1988). A text is not a closed system; it reflects the subjective views of its author, those who read it, and those whose views are quoted, included, suppressed, or excluded (e.g. Hassard and Parker 1993; Linstead and Grafton-Small 1992). This focus on representational issues, such as the ways impersonal language reinforces the authority of an author, undermines any claim that a text can represent the objective truth about a reality that is 'out there'— separable from the text (e.g. Cooper and Burrell 1988; Jeffcutt 1995; Smircich 1995). Truth therefore becomes 'a matter of credibility rather than an objective condition' (Alvesson and Berg 1992: 223; Van Maanen 1988). This focus on textual *analysis* (rather than collective change efforts or data collection) is justified from a postmodern point of view because there is *nothing outside* or beyond the text (e.g. Moi 1985; Weedon 1987).

Whereas modern scholars argue about what the truth is or what methods or *modes* of engagement would bring research closer to truth, postmodernists use analytic techniques such as deconstruction to reveal strategies used to represent truth claims in a text, for example, how: an author establishes his or her credibility; particular data are selected and interpreted (to the exclusion of other, equally valid data and interpretations); uncertainties are hidden; opposing meanings are suppressed or omitted; and unintended and suppressed viewpoints emerge in the margins of a text (such as footnotes, asides, metaphors, etc.). (For introductions to and examples of deconstruction, see Calás and Smircich 1991; Czarniawska-Joerges 1992; Ferguson 1993; Flax 1990; Martin 1990b; Weedon 1987.) Reading in these ways, between the lines of a text, silences become eloquent and the false certainties inherent in language (such as the clarities of a dichotomy) are exposed.

Postmodernist cultural scholars use textual analysis to interrogate, disrupt, and overturn claims to truth or theoretical superiority (e.g. Gagliardi 1991; Jeffcutt 1995). Their goal is not to establish a better theory of culture (this would perpetuate the struggle for intellectual dominance of the field, as described for example by Kuhn 1970), but rather to challenge the foundations of modern cultural scholarship (Alvesson and Berg 1992; Smircich and Calás 1987). For example:

Not surprisingly, postmodern theorizing is adamantly disdainful of meta-theories, labeling them 'narratives of transcendence' because each claims to be better than its predecessors—more abstract and yet also closer to 'the' empirical 'truth.' Lyotard, for example, views meta-theories as totalitarian attempts, by those who are or wish to become dominant, to provide all-encompassing world views that silence diversity of opinion. Postmodern scholars argue that attempts to create meta-theories are misguided and futile; fragmentation and multiplicity will flourish, in spite of attempts to make particular meta-theories dominant. (Martin 1992: 193)

For this reason, postmodern analyses often take the form of critiques or parodies (e.g. Calás and Smircich 1988; Willmott 1993)—carnivalesque writing that steadfastly maintains a marginalized position. Such writing attempts to 'overturn a disciplinary and prejudicial order through the articulation of ambiguity and contradiction from the margin' but does not seek 'to co-ordinate this difference into a fresh hierarchy through the articulation of a superior vision of progress' (Jeffcutt forthcoming: 18–19).

Given the postmodern disdain for attempts to legitimize claims of theoretical supremacy, a postmodern history of cultural research would not be a linear tale of progress, with new insights learned and old errors abandoned. Postmodernism, if taken seriously, makes the structure and form of a traditional handbook or review chapter an impossibility. Instead, postmodernism, in accord with Kuhn's (1970) views of paradigm revolutions, views the history of research on a topic as a struggle for intellectual dominance. Each new development, whether theoretical or methodological, is seen as an attempt to declare superiority over prior efforts.

This handbook chapter has been structured around some of these ideas, using the metaphor of culture wars and a war game (king of the mountain) to describe developments in this field as struggles for intellectual dominance, rather than linear advancements in the progression toward greater knowledge. The various moves in the culture wars, outlined in the first sections of this chapter, are described as if these modernist culture scholars were saying 'My approach is deeper, more complex, or more inclusive than yours' (ethnography, a longitudinal approach, or the three-perspective framework); or 'My approach is more responsive to the needs of business than yours' (the integration framework);

or 'Look what you have been ignoring' (the fragmentation perspective). Such claims of superiority have in common the implication that each view is, somehow, closer to the truth about a culture. All are attempts to impose order and meaning.

A postmodern critique would deconstruct these attempts to establish dominance in a hierarchical order. For example, such a critique would show how all these modern studies refrain from fully exploring the inherent and inescapable limitations of textual representation. Rather than perpetuating the king of the mountain game, where each new theory or meta-theory attempts to dominate other current contenders, postmodernism apparently abandons claims of linear progress and superior insight. Postmodernism is an attempt to rout all contenders from the field of battle and change the terms of engagement in the culture wars: no longer are we discussing ways to 'penetrate the front' of cultural members and get closer to some truth; now truth is impossible to represent.

A Victory for Postmodernism or More of the Same?

Many academics have dismissed postmodernism on grounds that it is esoteric, reactionary, apolitical, too relativistic, or nihilistic (e.g. Okin 1994; Reed 1990). This reaction has been particularly strong among some empirical, relatively positivistic culture researchers, perhaps because postmodernism represents a deep challenge to basic tenets of the scientific method: rationality, order, truth, and progress. Modernist cultural scholars, rather than seeing only the threat that the burgeoning postmodern literature represents, could try to learn from and use some aspects of postmodern thinking (see, for example, Clegg 1990; Hassard and Parker 1993). For example, postmodernism offers a way of escaping the cycles of disillusionment that trouble relationships between cultural scholars and practitioners, whereby each attempt at theoretical innovation is oversimplified and transformed into yet another managerial panacea—an easy answer to managers' endless desire to use 'quick fix' remedies to attain greater productivity or profitability. Such easy answers are doomed, ultimately, to fall short of their advance press and be labeled a failure, only to start the cycle again (e.g. Calás and Smircich 1990). Indeed, some have said that organizational culture represents just such a failed managerial fad. Could deconstruction make this cycle visible and be a tool to prevent its recurrence?

In addition, cultural researchers have invested a considerable amount of time and effort trying to combat the unitary assumptions of the integration perspective (i.e. Gregory 1983; Lucas 1987; Martin and Siehl 1983; Turner 1986; Van Maanen and Kunda 1989; Young 1989). Every careful ethnography or quantitative study that tries to challenge integrationist assumptions is countered quickly by yet another assertion that any culture can be a haven of homogeneity and harmony—a place where management's values are shared by all, and an employee's major task is simply to find a culture where he or she will 'fit in.' Could this cycle be short-circuited by postmodernism, so that researchers could devote their time and energy to deeper and more important cultural questions?

A postmodern approach could most certainly offer insight into the representational strategies that make cultural accounts more like fiction than, supposedly, like science (e.g. Calás 1987; Jermier 1992; Van Maanen 1988). Our cultural texts could become more self-reflexive and we could seek, as anthropologists are now doing, new, polyphonic ways of writing about culture that allow multiple voices to be heard and deconstructed, without transforming the researcher into a transcriber who has given informants total control of and responsibility for the text (Clifford and Marcus 1986).

As Alvesson and Berg (1992) observe, such 'benefits' would not represent a major change in modern cultural research strategies and they would not fully acknowledge the depth of the challenge to the scientific method that would follow from a full acceptance of postmodern ideas. Common criticisms of postmodernism (e.g. nihilistic, relativist, apolitical, esoteric, etc.) could be redefined as problems in postmodernism that cultural scholars might be able to help solve. Not only might this reorientation represent a contribution to problems that many postmodernists have been struggling with; it might also open the minds of modern cultural—and more broadly organizational—scholars to the value of postmodern insights.

For example, some scholars are seeking clear ways of explaining postmodern ideas to a broader range of organizational researchers (at the risk of being accused of oversimplification and other intellectual crimes and misdemeanors) (e.g. Boje and Dennehy 1993; Clegg 1990; Cooper and Burrell 1988; Hassard and Parker 1993). Some are trying to align postmodern insights with activist social change agendas, focusing on small wins and the likelihood of ambiguous and random outcomes as more attainable, less romanticized views of what kinds of organizational change are possible in contemporary circumstances (e.g. Arac 1986; Bergquist 1993; Letiche 1991; Simons and Billig 1994). Still others (e.g. Ferguson 1993; Flax 1990; Okin 1994) are struggling with ways to reconcile the indeterminism of postmodernism with ideological certainties (for example, from moral philosophy and feminism) in order to avoid problems of ethical relativism. The insights from all these lines of inquiry could enrich cultural studies in helpful ways.

SOME LESSONS OF WAR

One striking aspect of the culture literature, at this point in its development, is that none of the cultural approaches outlined in this chapter have gone very far in *helping improve* the lives of people who work in organizations. Integration studies have perhaps gone the farthest, although this research seems aimed primarily at aiding managers without acknowledging conflicts of interest with other constituencies, such as lower-level employees. Some differentiation research, several ethnographies, and studies in the critical theory tradition have effectively chronicled the views and material conditions of work of non-management employees, but these *studies* say less about how to fix the problems they describe so eloquently. The fragmentation perspective and symbolic approaches also offer description and analysis, but *relatively* few tools for action. Postmodern organizational scholars have not, so far, taken as their mission helping employees take action, although such work is starting to emerge (e.g. Letiche 1991). Of course, not all cultural researchers have, as part of their agendas, the goal of *helping* others to improve their working lives. For those that do, we can draw on this analysis of the culture wars to see what might be learned and applied.

If managers, employee representatives, and other stakeholders in and around organizations paid attention to the culture literature and studied the debates as we have represented them here, they might at first blush throw up their hands and dismiss culture as a fad or as unimportant. Alternatively, they might fixate on one or the other theoretical viewpoint, borrowing only a subset of the available ideas about culture. We would predict, in the latter case, that most managers would want to create and control a unified and strong culture that would maximize productivity and performance, trying to manage cultural change in a controlled and predictable manner. If unreflective, they would draw primarily from the integration perspective, given its prevalence in publications written for executives and MBAs. Rather than relying on the integration literature, some employees might find differentiation research, with its emphasis on intergroup conflict, to be more attuned to their goals (for example, achieving job security, fair wages, equity, resistance to change). They might also be interested in differentiation ideas about cultural control, particularly when there is a perceived need for a unified resistance (e.g. to a management initiative) or a need to understand what management is thinking as it pushes its agenda. Other stakeholders, such as customers, legislators, shareholders, and environmentalists, may view an organizational arena as being fragmented and conflict-ridden, rather than highly integrated. Alternatively, those 'outsiders' with a skeptical eye may view cultures as purely symbolic representations used by managers and employees to influence outcomes in self-serving ways. This last view may be closer to a postmodern perspective on culture than any of the others.

The aspirations of these various stakeholders differ, as group members struggle to accomplish outcomes they believe serve their interests. This is neither good nor bad. If we take the position that understanding culture is important, and that having such understandings available to all stakeholders is a basis for more informed and just efforts to make organizations more profitable and humane, then sharing the intellectual 'spoils' of the culture wars with everyone may be a useful undertaking. We

think that trying to make sense of the ideas, insights, prescriptions, and the like that are currently reported in the various literatures might improve the chances of reflective, informed, and creative approaches to working and living with culture. Some examples are as follows:

First, practitioners tend to oversimplify the meaning of organizational culture as they borrow, adapt, or are fed the latest theory of organizational culture. This produces a high probability of a failed adaptation of culture to organizational issues, especially those related to improving productivity and performance. This, in turn, leads to disillusionment and dismissal of the cultural approach as a fad. Analysis of common oversimplifications of cultural theories and representative failed attempts at cultural change (e.g. Bartunek and Moch 1991) can be particularly useful in this regard.

Second, no one theory or collection of theories about culture can conclusively claim superiority over others. One is better off adopting a multi-perspective framework that assumes that, in any organizational setting, there will be some values, interpretations, and practices that generate organization-wide consensus, some that cause conflict, and some that are not clear. At any point in time, a subset of these will be easily visible (a 'home' perspective of a researcher or an employee), while other perspectives will be harder to see. To the extent that it is possible to work with culture to attain collectively desired ends, actions and processes will have to take into account these different, co-existing cultural possibilities. Accepting this proposition means that culture 'users' will have to understand and accept that there is no 'happy acculturated forever after' ending to change attempts. In all likelihood, there is no 'forever after' in the script. At best, there may be some combination of agreement, dispute, and confusion that can be stitched together by human agency, as managers and others move the action along, accomplish some objective, and then regroup around subsequent problems, issues, and opportunities.

Third, in attempting to manage change, it may be useful to try to accomplish collective objectives in a way that incorporates the postmodernist treatment of 'reality' as a series of fictions and illusions. In particular, if one understands that the culture theorist (or consultant) who promotes a perspective on organizational culture is providing a fictional account of the phenomenon (and plays a part in the story as well), then one is empowered to treat the 'story' with caution—preferably to rewrite, or better yet co-write, the script for the setting he or she is in. The application of theories of culture to organizational issues then becomes a joint venture between the theorist and those who work with the story or stories. This approach is likely to incorporate more improvisation and reflexivity than is usually the case when cultural theories are applied to managing organizational issues.

Fourth, at the same time, some stories about culture are more compelling than others and some are more influential than others (particularly if they are rooted in the values of those with power). Consequently, a useful additional source of value to a cultural theory—as story/representation—can be its deconstruction. While the tools of deconstruction may be outside the grasp of the typical organizational practitioner, they need not necessarily remain so. This may be a challenge that postmodernists can take on in the interests of helping improve the human condition in the work place (see Boje and Dennehy 1993; Clegg 1990). Application of deconstructive techniques might be used to help reconstruct a theory, strategy, action plan, or story in ways that would be more useful to a wider array of interested stakeholders.

Fifth, if truth is a matter of credibility rather than an objective condition (e.g. Alvesson and Berg 1992: 223), then management of change by practitioners (not necessarily only managers) becomes a matter of developing credible scripts and framing issues to bridge different understandings, rather than imposing or inserting a new set of values in a situation. There is likely to be much more emphasis on dialogue, process, co-creation, and finding ways to build credibility for such activities and outcomes than is typically prescribed by most cultural theories.

Sixth, wars don't typically end: they are settled for a time and then they flare up in new forms, perhaps with new armies, new 'would-be kings.' Other wars start up in different situations. We expect this to continue in the culture arena. What this might mean for change agents is a willingness to remain alert to the existence and nature of the wars, to learn from the 'dispatches' from the front lines, and to factor these messages into their plans and strategies for change. One cannot assume a 'settled once and for all' script, any more than a 'forever after' one.

Finally, the intentions and actions of members of groups sometimes identified as having strong cultures (e.g. 'the managers,' 'the workers') might be better understood, and their cultural roles in organizations more effectively identified, if we treated them as less homogeneous, more multidimensional in their intentions, and more tentative and experimental in their actions. If, as we suspect, the organizations that people negotiate have, simultaneously, elements of integration, conflict, power, uncertainty, and 'truth construction,' then there is exciting and challenging work to be done. Cultural researchers need to figure out what this means for their definitions, theories, investigations, and practices.

NOTES

1. We do not know the origins of this term, but it was first drawn to our attention as the title of the annual meeting theme of the Standing Conference on Organizational Symbolism, held in Montreal, Canada, in 1986.

2. Although the scope of this review does not include studies of national cultures performed by organizational scholars, it is worth noting that these studies tend to use an integration framework to describe national cultures in unitary terms. For example, Lincoln and Kallberg (1985) implicitly adopt an integration perspective for the study of international cultures, describing US and Japanese cultures as internally homogeneous, characterized by consistency, consensus, and clarity.

3. This felicitous phrase was, we believe, coined by Robert Sutton.

REFERENCES

Agar, M. (1986) *Speaking of Ethnography*. Beverly Hills, CA: Sage.

Alvesson, M. (1993) *Cultural Perspectives on Organizations*. Cambridge: Cambridge University Press.

Alvesson, M. and Berg, P. (1992) *Corporate Culture and Organizational Symbolism*. Berlin: Walter de Gruyter.

Arac, J. (ed.) (1986) *Postmodernism and Politics*. Minneapolis: University of Minnesota Press.

Argyris, C. and Schon, D. (1978) *Organizational Learning: A Theory of Action Perspective*. Reading, MA: Addison-Wesley.

Baburoglu, O. and Gocer, A. (1991) 'The impact of privatization on the organizational culture: the Sumerbank's case.' Paper presented at the International Conference on Organizational Symbolism and Corporate Culture, Copenhagen.

Barley, S. (1983) 'Semiotics and the study of occupational and organizational cultures,' *Administrative Science Quarterly,* 28: 393–414.

Barley, S., Meyer, G. and Gash, D. (1988) 'Cultures of culture: academics, practitioners, and the pragmatics of normative control,' *Administrative Science Quarterly,* 33: 24–61.

Bartunek, J. and Moch, M. (1991) 'Multiple constituencies and the quality of working life intervention at FoodCom,' in P. Frost, L. Moore, M. Louis, C. Lundberg and J. Martin (eds), *Reframing Organizational Culture.* Newbury Park, CA: Sage. pp. 104–14.

Baudrillard, J. (1983) *Simulations.* New York: Semiotext(e).

Becker, H., Geer, B., Hughes, E. and Strauss, A. (1961) *Boys in White; Student Cultures in Medical School* Chicago: University of Chicago Press.

Bell, E. (1990) 'The bicultural life experience of career-oriented black women.' *Journal of Organizational Behavior,* 11: 459–78.

Berger, P. (1967) *The Sacred Canopy.* Garden City, NY: Doubleday.

Bergquist, W. (1993) *The Postmodern Organization: Mastering the Art of Irreversible Change.* San Francisco: Jossey-Bass.

Blau, P. (1965) 'The comparative study of organizations,' *Industrial and Labour Relations Review,* 28: 323–38.

Boje, D. and Dennehy, R. (1993) *Managing in the Postmodern World: America's Revolution against Exploitation.* Dubuque, IA: Kendall-Hunt.

Brunsson, N. (1985) *The National Organization.* New York: Wiley.

Burawoy, M. (1979) *Manufacturing Consent: Changes in the Labor Process under Monopoly Capitalism.* Chicago: University of Chicago Press.

Burrell, G. and Morgan, G. (1979) *Sociological Paradigms and Organizational Analysis.* London: Heinemann.

Calás, M. (1987) 'Organizational science/fiction: the postmodern in the management disciplines.' Unpublished doctoral dissertation, Amherst, MA: University of Massachusetts.

Calás, M. and Smircich, L. (1987) 'Post-culture: is the organizational culture literature dominant but dead?' Paper presented at the International Conference on Organizational Symbolism and Corporate Culture, Milan.

Calás, M. and Smircich, L. (1988) 'Reading leadership as a form of cultural analysis,' in J. Hunt, B. Haliga, H. Dachler and A. Schriesheim (eds), *Emerging Leadership Vistas.* Lexington, MA: Lexington Books. pp. 201–26.

Calás, M. and Smircich, L. (1990) 'Thrusting towards more of the same,' *Academy of Management Review,* 15: 698–705.

Calás, M. and Smircich, L. (1991) 'Voicing seduction to silence leadership,' *Organizational Studies,* 12: 567–601.

Christensen, S. and Kreiner, K. (1984) 'On the origin of organizational cultures.' Paper presented at the International Conference on Organizational Symbolism and Corporate Culture, Lund, Sweden.

Clark, B. (1972) 'The organizational saga in higher education,' *Administrative Science Quarterly,* 17: 178–84.

Clegg, S. (1990) *Modern Organizations: Organization Studies in a Postmodern World.* London: Sage.

Clifford, J. and Marcus, O. (eds) (1986) *Writing Culture: the Poetics and Politics of Ethnography.* Berkeley, CA: University of California Press.

Cooper, R. and Burrell, G. (1988) 'Modernism, postmodernism, and organizational analysis,' *Organization Studies,* 9: 91–112.

Cox, T. (1993) *Cultural Diversity in Organizations: Theory, Research, and Practice.* San Francisco: Berrett-Koehler.

Crozier, M. (1964) *The Bureaucratic Phenomenon.* Chicago: University of Chicago Press.

Czarniawska-Joerges, B. (1992) *Exploring Complex Organizations: a Cultural Perspective.* Newbury Park, CA: Sage.

Daft, R. (1980) 'The evolution of organization analysis in *ASQ,* 1959–1979,' *Administrative Science Quarterly,* 25: 623–36.

Dandridge, T. (1986) 'Ceremony as an integration of work and play,' *Organization Studies,* 7: 159–70.

Deal, T. and Kennedy, A. (1982) *Corporate Cultures: the Rites and Rituals of Corporate Life.* Reading, MA: Addison-Wesley.

Deetz, S. (1992) *Democracy in an Age of Corporate Colonization: Developments in Communication and the Politics of Everyday Life.* New York: State University of New York Press.

Denison, D. (1990) *Corporate Culture and Organizational Effectiveness.* New York: Wiley.

Derrida, L (1976) *Speech and Phenomenon.* Evanston, IL: Northwestern University Press.

Donaldson, L. (1989) 'Redirections in organizational analysis,' *Australian Journal of Management,* 14: 243–54.

Enomoto, E. (1993) 'In-school truancy in a multiethnic urban high school examined through organizational culture lenses.' PhD dissertation, University of Michigan.

Enz, C. (1988) 'The role of value congruity in intraorganizational power.' *Administrative Science Quarterly,* 33: 284–304.

Feldman, M. (1989) *Order without Design: Information Processing and Policy Making.* Stanford, CA: Stanford University Press.

Feldman, M. (1991) 'The meanings of ambiguity: learning from stories and metaphors,' in P. Frost, L. Moore, M. Louis, C. Lundberg and J. Martin (eds), *Reframing Organizational Culture.* Newbury Park, CA: Sage. pp. 145–56.

Ferguson, K. (1993) *The Man Question: Visions of Subjectivity in Feminist Theory.* Berkeley, CA: University of California Press.

Fitzgerald, T. (1988) 'Can changes in organizational culture really be managed?' *Organizational Dynamics,* 17: 5–15.

Flax, J. (1990) *Thinking Fragments: Psychoanalysis, Feminism, and Postmodernism in the Contemporary West.* Berkeley, CA: University of California Press.

Foucault, M. (1976) *The Archeology of Knowledge,* translated by B. Smith. New York: Harper and Row.

Frost, P. (1995) Personal communication.

Frost, P., Moore, L., Louis, M., Lundberg, C. and Martin, J. (1991) *Reframing Organizational Culture.* Newbury Park, CA: Sage.

Gagliardi, P. (ed.) (1990) *Symbols and Artifacts: Views of the Corporate Landscape.* Hawthorne, NY: Walter de Gruyter.

Gagliardi, P. (1991) 'Reflections on reframing organizational culture.' Paper presented at the International Conference on Organizational Symbolism and Corporate Culture, Copenhagen.

Garfinkel, H. (1967) *Studies in Ethnomethodology.* Englewood Cliffs, NJ: Prentice-Hall.

Geertz, C. (1988) *Works and Lives: the Anthropologist as Author.* Stanford, CA:' Stanford University Press.

Glaser, B. and Strauss, A. (1967) *The Discovery of Grounded Theory.* Chicago, IL: Aldine.

Goffman, I. (1967) *Interaction Ritual.* New York: Anchor Books.

Gordon, G. (1985) 'The relationship of corporate culture to industry sector and corporate performance,' in R. Kilmann, M. Saxton, R. Serpa and Associates (eds), *Gaining Control of the Corporate Culture.* San Francisco: Jossey-Bass. pp. 103–25.

Grafton-Small, R. and Linstead, S. (1987) 'Theory as artifact.' Paper presented at the International Conference on Organizational Symbolism and Corporate Culture, Milan.

Greenwood, R. and Hinings, C. (1988) 'Organizational design types, tracks and the dynamics of strategic change,' *Organization Studies,* 9: 293–316.

Gregory, K. (1983) 'Native-view paradigms: multiple cultures and culture conflicts in organizations,' *Administrative Science Quarterly,* 28: 359–76.

Habermas, J. (1975) *Legitimation Crisis,* translated by T. McCarthy. Boston: Beacon Press.

Hassard, J. and Parker, M. (eds) (1993) *Postmodernism and Organizations.* London: Sage.

Hassard, J. and Pym, D. (eds) (1990) *The Theory and Philosophy of Organizations: Critical Issues and New Perspectives.* London: Routledge.

Hughes, E. (1958) *Men and Their Work.* New York: Free Press.

Jaques, E. (1951) *The Changing Culture of a Factory: a Study of Authority and Participation in an Industrial Setting.* London: Tavistock. New York: Dryden Press, 1952.

Jeffcutt, P. (1995) 'The interpretation of organization: a contemporary analysis and critique.' *Journal of Management Studies,* 31: 225–50.

Jeffcutt, P. (forthcoming) *Culture and Symbolism in Organizational Analysis.* Newbury Park, CA: Sage.

Jermier, J. (1992) 'Literary methods and organizational science: reflections on "When the sleeper wakes,"' in P. Frost and R. Stablein (eds), *Doing Exemplary Research.* Newbury Park, CA: Sage.

Jonsson, S. and Lundin, R. (1977) 'Myths and wishful thinking as management tools,' in P. Nystrom and W. Starbuck (eds), *Studies in Management Sciences. Vol. 5: Prescriptive Models of Organizations.* Amsterdam: North Holland, pp. 157–70.

Kanter, R. (1977) *Men and Women of the Corporation.* New York: Anchor Press.

Kilmann, R. (1985) *Beyond the Quick Fix: Managing Five Tracks to Organizational Success.* San Francisco: Jossey-Bass.

Knights, D. and Willmott, H. (1987) 'Organizational culture as management strategy: a critique and illustration,' *International Studies of Management and Organization,* 13: 40–63.

Kreiner, K. and Schultz, M. (1993) 'Informal collaboration in R&D: the formation of networks across organizations,' *Organization Studies,* 14: 189–209.

Kuhn, T. (1970) *The Structure of Scientific Revolutions,* 2nd edn (1st edn 1962). Chicago: University of Chicago Press.

Kunda, G. (1991) *Engineering Culture: Control and Commitment in a High-Tech Corporation.* Philadelphia: Temple University Press.

Letiche, H. (1991) 'Postmodernism goes practical.' Paper presented at the International Conference on Organizational Symbolism and Corporate Culture, Copenhagen.

Levitt, B. and Nass, C. (1989) 'The lid on the garbage can: institutional constraints on decision making in the technical core of college-text publishers,' *Administrative Science Quarterly,* 34: 190–207.

Light, D. Jr (1979) 'Surface data and deep structure: observing the organization of professional training,' *Administrative Science Quarterly,* 24: 551–60.

Lincoln, J. and Kallberg, A. (1985) 'Work organization and workforce commitment: a study of plants and employees in the U.S. and Japan,' *American Sociological Review,* 50: 738–60.

Linstead, S. and Grafton-Small, R. (1991) 'No visible means of support: ethnography and the end of deconstruction.' Paper presented at the International Conference on Organizational Symbolism and Corporate Culture, Copenhagen.

Linstead, S. and Grafton-Small, R. (1992) 'On reading organizational culture,' *Organization Studies,* 13: 331–55.

Louis, M. (1985) 'An investigator's guide to workplace culture,' in P. Frost, L. Moore, M. Louis, C. Lundberg and J. Martin (eds), *Organizational Culture.* Beverly Hills, CA: Sage. pp. 73–94.

Lucas, R. (1987) 'Political-cultural analysis of organizations,' *Academy of Management Review,* 12; 144–56.

Lyotard, J. (1984) *The Postmodern Condition.* Minneapolis: University of Minnesota Press.

Manning, P. (1977) *Police Work: the Social Organization of Policing.* Cambridge, MA: MIT Press.

Martin, J. (1990a) 'Breaking up the mono-method monopolies in organizational analysis,' in J. Hassard and D. Pym (eds), *The Theory and Philosophy of Organizations.* New York: Routledge. pp. 30–43.

Martin, J. (1990b) 'Deconstructing organizational taboos: the suppression of gender conflict in organizations,' *Organizational Science,* 1: 339–59.

Martin, J. (1992) *Cultures in Organizations: Three Perspectives.* New York: Oxford University Press.

Martin, J. and Meyerson, D. (1988) 'Organizational cultures and the denial, channeling, and acknowledgement of ambiguity,' in L. Pondy, R. Roland, and H. Thomas (eds), *Managing Ambiguity and Change.* New York: Wiley. pp. 93–125.

Martin, J. and Siehl, C. (1983) 'Organizational culture and counter culture: an uneasy symbiosis,' *Organizational Dynamics,* 12: 52–64.

Martin, J., Feldman, M., Hatch, M. and Sitkin, S. (1983) 'The uniqueness paradox in organizational stories,' *Administrative Science Quarterly,* 28: 438–53.

Martin, J., Sitkin, S. and Boehm, M. (1985) 'Founders and the elusiveness of a cultural legacy,' in P. Frost, L. Moore, M. Louis, C. Lundberg and J. Martin (eds), *Organizational Culture.* Beverly Hills, CA: Sage. pp. 99–124.

McDonald, P. (1991) 'The Los Angeles Olympic Organizing Committee: developing organizational culture in the short run,' in P. Frost, L. Moore, M. Louis, C. Lundberg and J. Martin (eds), *Reframing Organizational Culture.* Newbury Park, CA: Sage. pp. 26–38.

McGrath, J. (1982) 'Dilemmatics: the study of research choices and dilemmas,' in J. McGrath, J. Martin and R. Kulka, *Judgment Calls in Research.* Newbury Park, CA: Sage. pp. 69–102.

Meyerson, D. (1991) '"Normal" ambiguity? A glimpse of an occupational culture,' in P. Frost, L. Moore, M. Louis, C. Lundberg and J. Martin (eds), *Reframing Organizational Culture.* Newbury Park, CA; Sage. pp. 131–44.

Meyerson, D. and Martin, J. (1987) 'Cultural change: an integration of three different views.' *Journal of Management Studies,* 24: 623–47.

Mills, A. (1992) 'Organization, gender, and culture,' in A. Mills and P. Tancred (eds), *Gendering Organizational Analysis.* Newbury Park, CA: Sage. pp. 93–111.

Moi, T. (1985) *Sexual/Textual Politics: Feminist Literary Theory.* New York: Methuen.

Morgan, G. (ed.) (1983) *Beyond Method: Strategies for Social Research.* Beverly Hills, CA: Sage.

Mumby, D. (1988) *Communication and Power in Organizations: Discourse, Ideology and Domination.* Norwood, NJ: Ablex.

Okin, S. (1994) 'Gender and relativism.' Unpublished manuscript, Stanford University.

O'Reilly, C., Chatman, J. and Caldwell, D. (1991) 'People and organizational culture: a Q-sort approach to assessing person-organization fit,' *Academy of Management Journal,* 34: 487–516.

Ott, J. (1989) *The Organizational Culture Perspective.* Pacific Grove, CA: Brooks & Cole.

Ouchi, W. (1981) *Theory Z: How American Business Can Meet the Japanese Challenge.* Reading, MA: Addison-Wesley.

Ouchi, W. and Jaeger, A. (1978) 'Type Z organization: stability in the midst of mobility.' *Academy of Management Review,* 3: 305–14.

Ouchi, W. and Johnson, J. (1978) 'Types of organizational control and their relationship to emotional well-being,' *Administrative Science Quarterly,* 23: 293–317.

Ouchi, W. and Wilkins, A. (1985) 'Organizational culture,' *Annual Review of Sociology,* 11: 457–83.

Pascale, R. and Athos, A. (1981) *The Art of Japanese Management: Applications for American Executives.* New York: Simon and Schuster.

Pennings, J. and Gresov, C. (1986) 'Technoeconomic and structural correlates of organizational culture: an integrative framework,' *Organization Studies,* 7: 317–34.

Perrow, C. (1979) *Complex Organizations: A Critical Essay.* Glenview, IL: Scott, Foresman & Co.

Peters, T. and Waterman, R. (1982) *In Search of Excellence: Lessons from America's Best-Run Companies.* New York: Harper & Row.

Pettigrew, A. (1979) 'On studying organizational cultures,' *Administrative Science Quarterly,* 24: 570–8.

Pettigrew, A. (1985a) 'Examining change in the long-term context of culture and politics,' in J. Pennings and Associates (eds), *Organizational Strategy and Change.* San Francisco: Jossey-Bass. pp. 269–318.

Pettigrew, A. (1985b) *The Awakening Giant: Continuity and Change in ICI.* Oxford: Blackwell.

Pfeffer, J. (1981) 'Management as symbolic action: the creation and maintenance of organizational paradigms,' in B. Staw and L. Cummings (eds), *Research in Organizational Behavior.* Greenwich, CT: JAI Press. pp. 1–52.

Pondy, L., Frost, P., Morgan, G. and Dandridge, T. (eds) (1983) *Organizational Symbolism.* Greenwich, CT: JAI Press.

Putnam, L., Bantz, C., Deetz, S., Mumby, D. and Van Maanen, J. (1993) 'Ethnography versus critical theory: debating organizational research,' *Journal of Management Inquiry,* 2: 221–35.

Reed, M. (1985) *Redirections in Organizational Analysis.* London: Tavistock.

Reed, M. (1990) 'From paradigms to images: the paradigm warrior turns postmodernist guru,' *Personnel Review,* 19: 35–40.

Riley, P. (1983) 'A structurationist account of political cultures,' *Administrative Science Quarterly,* 28: 414–37.

Rosen, M. (1985) 'Breakfast at Spiro's: dramaturgy and dominance,' *Journal of Management,* 11: 31–48.

Rosen, M. (1991) 'Coming to terms with the field: understanding and doing organizational ethnography,' *Journal of Management Studies,* 28: 1–24.

Rousseau, D. (1990) 'Assessing organizational culture: the case for multiple methods,' in B. Schneider (ed.), *Organizational Climate and Culture.* San Francisco: Jossey-Bass. pp. 153–92.

Rousseau, D. (1994) 'A fresh start for organizational culture research,' *Contemporary Psychology,* 39: 194–5.

Sathe, V. (1985) *Culture and Related Corporate Realities: Text, Cases, and Readings on Organizational Entry, Establishment, and Chance.* Homewood, IL: Irwin.

Schein, E. (1985) *Organizational Culture and Leadership.* San Francisco: Jossey-Bass.

Schein, E. (1987) *The Clinical Perspective in Field Work.* Newbury Park, CA: Sage.

Schein, E. (1991) 'What is culture?' in P. Frost, L. Moore, M. Louis, C. Lundberg and J. Martin (eds), *Reframing Organizational Culture.* Newbury Park, CA: Sage. pp. 243–53.

Schein, E. (1994) 'Book review: Martin: Cultures in Organizations: *Three Perspectives,*' *Administrative Science Quarterly,* 39: 339–42.

Schneider, B. (ed.) (1990) *Organizational Climate and Culture.* San Francisco: Jossey-Bass.

Schultz, M. (1994) *On Studying Organizational Cultures: Diagnosis and Understanding.* Berlin: De Gruyter.

Selznick, P. (1957) *Leadership and Administration.* Evanston, IL: Row & Peterson.

Sergiovanni, T. and Corbally, J. (eds) (1984) *Leadership and Organizational Culture.* Urbana, IL: University of Illinois Press.

Siehl, C. and Martin, J. (1990) 'Organizational culture: a key to financial performance?' in B. Schneider (ed.), *Organizational Climate and Culture.* San Francisco: Jossey-Bass. pp. 241–81.

Simons, H. and Billig, M. (eds) (1994) *After Postmodernism: Ideology Critique.* Thousand Oaks, CA: Sage.

Smircich, L. (1983) 'Concepts of culture and organizational analysis,' *Administrative Science Quarterly,* 28: 339–58.

Smircich, L. (1995) 'Writing organizational tales: reflections on three books on organizational culture,' *Organizational Science,* 6: 232–7.

Smircich, L. and Calás, M. (1987) 'Organizational culture: a critical assessment,' in F. Jablin, L. Putnam, K. Roberts and L. Porter (eds), *Handbook of Organizational Communication.* Beverly Hills, CA: Sage. pp. 228–63.

Smircich, L. and Morgan, G. (1982) 'Leadership: the management of meaning,' *Journal of Applied Behavioral Science,* 18: 257–73.

Spradley, J. (1979) *The Ethnographic Interview.* New York: Holt, Rinehart & Winston.

Stablein, R. and Nord, W. (1985) 'Practical and emancipatory interests in organizational symbolism: a review and evaluation,' *Journal of Management,* 11: 13–28.

Steinbruner, J.D. (1974) *The Cybernetic Theory of Decision: New Dimensions of Political Analyses.* Princeton, NJ: Princeton University Press.

Sutton, R. (1994) 'The virtues of closet qualitative research.' Unpublished manuscript, Stanford University.

Trice, H. and Beyer, J. (1984) 'Studying organizational cultures through rites and ceremonials,' *Academy of Management Review,* 9: 653–69.

Trice, H. and Beyer, J. (1993) *The Cultures of Work Organizations*. Englewood Cliffs, NJ: Prentice-Hall.

Turner, B. (1986) 'Sociological aspects of organizational symbolism,' *Organizational Studies*, 7: 101–15.

Turner, B. (ed.) (1989) *Organizational Symbolism*. Hawthorne, NY: Walter de Gruyter.

Turner, B. (1990) 'The rise of organizational symbolism,' in J. Hassard and D. Pym (eds), *The Theory and Philosophy of Organizations: Critical Issues and New Perspectives*. London: Routledge. pp. 83–96.

Van Maanen, J. (1986) 'Power in the bottle: drinking patterns and social relations in a British police agency,' in S. Srivastava (ed.), *Executive Power*. San Francisco: Jossey-Bass. pp. 204–39.

Van Maanen, J. (1988) *Tales of the Field*. Chicago: University of Chicago Press.

Van Maanen, J. (1991) 'The smile factory: work at Disneyland,' in P. Frost, L. Moore, M. Louis, C. Lundberg and J. Martin (eds), *Reframing Organizational Culture*. Newbury Park, CA: Sage. pp. 58–76.

Van Maanen, J. and Barley, S. (1984) 'Occupational communities: culture and control in organizations,' in B. Staw and L. Cummings (eds), *Research in Organizational Behavior*, vol. 6. Greenwich, CT: JAI Press. pp. 287–366.

Van Maanen, J. and Kunda, G. (1989) '"Real feelings": emotional expression and organizational culture,' in L. Cummings and B. Staw (eds), *Research In Organizational Behavior*, vol. 11. Greenwich, CT: JAI Press. pp. 43–103.

Van Maanen, J., Dabbs, J. and Faulkner, R. (1982) *Varieties of Qualitative Research*. Newbury Park, CA: Sage.

Weedon, C. (1987) *Feminist Practice and Poststructuralist Theory*. New York: Basil Blackwell.

Weick, K. (1991) '"The vulnerable system: an analysis of the Tenerife air disaster,' in P. Frost, L. Moore, M. Louis, C. Lundberg and J. Martin (eds), *Reframing Organizational Culture*. Newbury Park, CA: Sage. pp. 117–30.

Willmott, H. (1993) 'Strength is ignorance; slavery is freedom: managing culture in modem organizations,' *Journal of Management Studies*, 30: 515–52.

Wuthnow, R., Hunter, J., Bergesen, A. and Kurzweil, E. (1984) *Cultural Analysis*. Boston: Routledge & Kegan Paul.

Young, E. (1989) 'On the naming of the rose: interests and multiple meanings as elements of organizational culture,' *Organization Studies*, 10: 187–206.

SOURCE: Martin, Joanne and Peter Frost. 1995. Excerpt from "The Organizational Culture Wars: A Struggle for Intellectual Dominance." pp. 601–14 in *Handbook of Organizational Studies*, edited by S. Clegg, C. Hardy, and W. Nord. Newbury Park, CA: Sage.

31

MORAL ECONOMY AND CULTURAL WORK

MARK BANKS

INTRODUCTION

Critics of neo-liberalism argue that the expansion of free market values has led to the concretization of individualistic tendencies and the undermining of the social and ethical foundations of societies (Bauman, 2000; Sennett, 1998; Smart, 2003). Much anguish has been expressed at the negative impacts on individuals of innovations such as more 'flexible' pay, terms and contractual conditions, the 'freedom' to work for oneself and the retreat of workplace collectivities leading to self-reliance and a sense of personal culpability in the advent of (structural) labour market shifts. This is compounded by the likelihood of further denudation of the social realm as insecurities endemic to our fragmented work lives bleed into the whole gamut of social and personal relationships (Beck, 2000; McRobbie, 2002a, 2002b; Sennett, 1998; Smart, 2003). A widespread belief is that rampant individualization, a culture of self-interest, and the primacy of market rationality have rendered the economy more unethical and immoral. While the mooted 'culturalization'[1] of the economy has led some critics to welcome the 'turn to life' (Heelas, 2002) and anticipate the remoralization of economic activity, others argue that the 'cultural turn' is conducive only to the continued demoralization of economic relations. At the core of this critique, the 'cultural industries' are identified as a high-profile sector promoting a culturalized work process that promises emancipation from the herd but provides only a new kind of individuated tyranny.

In this article I critically examine assumptions about the demoralization of cultural work and, more specifically, of cultural industries. In doing so I draw on Sayer's attempts to restore the concept of 'moral economy' to debates concerning the relative status and intersections of the 'economic' and the 'cultural' (1999, 2001, 2003, 2004). A rekindling of interest in moral values may, as Sayer suggests, fly in the face of much post-modern thinking and what he calls the fashionable 'refusal of normativity,' but is clearly stimulated by a concern to move beyond the stale confines of a debate that tends to see all values as either instrumental or purely aesthetic. Despite the primacy of an instrumental rationality, I suggest that contemporary capitalism is a sufficiently imperfect operation to accommodate a broad range of moral values that will potentially effect a diversity of outcomes at the level of practice (Willis, 1990). The intention here is to provide some empirical evidence of cultural entrepreneurs undertaking ethical work; that is, to show how they are self-consciously engaged in forms of practice that contain ideas about what is 'good' (and therefore 'bad'), exhibit moral ways of acting towards others and negotiate the balance between holding instrumental or non-instrumental values.

The broader aims of the article are twofold: firstly, to develop some closer understanding of workplace identities within cultural industries—the empirical data in this regard is curiously thin; and secondly, to enliven a debate that threatens to calcify between those who would uncritically celebrate the aesthetic, expressive individuality and potential for individual emancipation offered by cultural work, and those who would disregard its apparent 'freedoms' as merely complicit in the consolidation of a hegemonic, recursively 'flexible,' neo-liberal regime. The approach I take is empirically grounded, drawing closely on an ongoing programme of work being undertaken with cultural industry entrepreneurs in Manchester in the north-west of England. Initially, however, I want to more thoroughly map out the terrain of the debate regarding the (im)morality of the new economy and in particular its cultural industry components.

THE NEGLECT OF MORALITY IN CULTURAL INDUSTRIES RESEARCH

Cultural industries are conventionally described as those activities involved in the production of symbolic goods and services, whose principal value is derived from their function as carriers of meaning—through images, symbols, signs and sounds (see Du Gay and Pryke, 2002; Hesmondhalgh, 2002; Lash and Urry, 1994; Nixon, 2003; Scott, 2000). While cultural entrepreneurs are often judged to be motivated by the desire for money, creativity or generating cultural value, how moral or ethical considerations may inform their work remains unclear. As McRobbie (2002a) notes, at the populist end of the literature, questions of ethics and morality are not only deemed 'uncool' but regarded as 'old' economy hang-ups that serve only to undermine the heroic status of those go-getting entrepreneurs who have (apparently) triumphed simply through their own hard work, individual talent and force of personality (see for example Bentley, 1999; Florida, 2002; Leadbeater, 1999). In the social sciences a

more critical, but no less morally blind approach has been apparent. This is understandable given that contemporary social and cultural theory is generally antagonistic towards questions of morality and normative value. In ideal type, the post-modern cultural entrepreneur operates unfettered by tradition; a creative free spirit driven by the desire to make money but also broker creative alliances, combine previously disparate aspects of production and consumption, and to contribute to, and be drawn by, the cosmopolitan, diverse city and its sense of place (Florida, 2002; O'Connor and Wynne, 1996; Wittstock, 2000). Current policy discourse also tends to give positive affirmation to this image of the singular, independent 'creative' (DCMS, 2001; Smith, 1998). So while there has been some inferred suggestion that cultural entrepreneurs are in part motivated by a desire to contribute to the aesthetic 'vibrancy' of the city (Wynne and O'Connor, 1998) or helping to inspire 'creative' urban renaissance (Florida, 2002), demonstrating the political or social motivations of cultural workers has generated limited interest.

The neglect of moral concerns may also be explained by the tendency for sociological accounts of cultural entrepreneurship to overdraw on Bourdieu's (1984) notion of the 'cultural intermediary'—the creative producer, manager or fixer of the service and culture-based economy. Bourdieu argues that, as a subgroup of the 'new petit bourgeoisie,' the cultural intermediary is most commonly found in the plethora of media, communication and arts-based occupations that have emerged since the 1960s (Bourdieu, 1984; see also Featherstone, 1992; Nixon, 2003). Cultural intermediaries initially appear socially progressive, for while they may conventionally pursue materialist ambitions and have instrumental motives, they are more widely engaged in a quest for new forms of sociality and a reconfiguration of cultural hierarchies, understood by Bourdieu as a structurally embedded and comprehensive 'ethic of liberation' (1984: 371). For Bourdieu, cultural intermediaries are engaged in the search for an 'emancipatory life' (p. 370), free from bourgeois constraint, and attempt to achieve this through adopting a 'learning mode,' becoming culturally omnivorous and insinuating new patterns of taste into the social field—the consummation of their 'practical utopianism' (p. 370) being a state 'untrammelled by the constraints and brakes imposed by collective memories and interpretations' (p. 371). It is fair to suggest that Bourdieu's figure (though not unequivocally) has provided a clear template for more recent attempts to characterize the contemporary cultural entrepreneur as a creative, dynamic figure seeking out new 'practical Utopias' through experimental combinations of economic and cultural practice (Featherstone, 1992; Nixon, 2003; O'Connor and Wynne, 1996). Yet, for Bourdieu, this emancipatory promise will remain unfulfilled as long as cultural intermediaries tend to substitute one form of conformity ('bourgeois') for another ('alternative,' 'bohemian') and in doing so incline towards the same position-taking and status-seeking behaviour strategies of other social groups. Put another way, because Bourdieu portrays a social world driven by individualistic instrumentality, albeit within the shared confines of class and habitus, his analysis does tend to overlook the ways in which actors may possess values or follow courses of action that are not automatically geared to enhancing status or reinforcing social position. The emphasis on self-interest in the individualistic pursuit of status, prestige and new kinds of lifestyle tends to underplay the influence of non-instrumental or ethical motives in social and economic reproduction (see Sayer, 1999, for a fuller critique). It is arguable that the shadow of influence cast by Bourdieu's work has meant more recent observers have neglected to address non-instrumental aspects of cultural work.

THE DEMORALIZATION OF CULTURAL WORK

What possibility is there then for morally progressive or socially useful cultural work? At first glance, not much. Conventional accounts tend to emphasize the growing power and influence of global cultural industries of the kind described by Hesmondhalgh (2002), such as Hollywood studios, media conglomerates and so on, who are (by and large) involved in the production of mass appeal, deterritorialized, internationally marketable products or who seek to take advantage of 'local differences' by producing niche output for (usually) national markets. The moral purpose here is driven by the instrumental imperative to make money in a competitive market—and generating social outcomes or benefits is not usually prioritized. Even at the local or city level, social relations in cultural industries appear to be determined by an instrumental and functional 'network sociality' (Wittel, 2001) that appears to lack any explicit ethical foundation. Indeed, a critical orthodoxy has emerged carried by the conviction that something is being 'lost'—in moral-political or social terms—by the increased capitalization and commercialization of the cultural industries. Such a view echoes Sennett's (1998) wider, pessimistic view of the ethically 'corrosive' impact of the new, deregulated and disembedded global economy and Bauman's lament for the ethically significant and socially beneficial 'secure axis' (2000: 139) provided by work in industrial society.

The demoralization critique has tended to emphasize the improbability of cultural industries as a location for the enhancement of socially responsible or ethical values. This is exemplified by McRobbie (2002a), who identifies the decline of the 'first wave' independent cultural production sector and its replacement by a more aggressive, commercially driven 'second wave' in hock to the free market and global multinationals. As she herself acknowledges, this work departs from her earlier, more optimistic analyses of the capacity for cultural entrepreneurs to forge both creatively rewarding and commercially successful independent careers in the new economy (McRobbie, 1999). In her updated analysis, McRobbie argues that the acceleration and expansion of neo-liberal values in the cultural sector has disabled the capacity of entrepreneurs to remain independent of larger corporations and has, crucially, undermined the moral and reflexive aspects of cultural production, diminishing its socially useful character and disembedding it from its original utopian formulation in the context of local communities of interest—including those related to (for example) youth culture, feminism, ethnic minority cultures and other forms of heterodox social collectivity.

In McRobbie's view, drawing on Ulrich Beck, 'speed and risk negate ethics, community and politics' (2002a: 523) and the logical outcome of commercialization of the cultural industries is the destabilization of moral-political values other than those conducive to neo-liberalism. Depicting a system premised on asymmetrical power relations between powerful corporations and fragile independents, McRobbie suggests there is a lack of space and time for cultural entrepreneurs to consider the moral consequences of actions or to pursue an ethical path separate from that permitted under the terms and conditions directly or indirectly imposed by the market. With an emphasis on fluidity, speed and image, the cultural sector tends to deny notions of workplace rights, entitlements or responsibilities, as well as undercutting notions of participation and equality, historically embedded and negotiated for in a regulated, Fordist work regime. Additionally, rather than providing 'flexibility benefits,' the blurring of work and non-work now simply means that work begins to negatively invade and inhibit one's personal and social existence. The increased pressure to become a flexible and productive 'creative' worker overshadows other social roles, meaning that—in the wider context of a new punitive workfare meritocracy and diminished social contract (McDowell, 2004)—the 'problem of work' is now not that it has no meaningful link to the self as once argued,[2] but that it has now wholly captured the self and weakened the identity-forming powers of non-work elements (Grugulis et al., 2000). 'At this point,' McRobbie concludes, 'the possibility of a revived, perhaps reinvented, radical democratic politics that might usefully de-individuate and resocialize the world of creative work is difficult to envisage' (2002a: 528).

Others contend that the moral vacuum at the heart of cultural industries might stem from a form of false consciousness endemic amongst cultural workers themselves, who—beguiled by the charisma and prestige of working in a creative sector—may fail to recognize the conditions of their own exploitation or take steps to seek (say) appropriate pay, terms and conditions. As Gibson (2003) notes in a study of Australian music scenes, musicians often accept low pay, poor conditions and an uncertain future as an unfortunate but necessary side effect for the chance to 'make it.' In effect, the emphasis on individual creativity and the personal qualities required to become a success tends to undermine unionization

and other collective efforts to improve working conditions. Organizations that cohere to provide a material and moral framework for the appropriate treatment of employed musicians—such as the Musicians Union—tend to have limited impact on the ground, hampered not least by resistances from powerful groups within the industry itself.

Finally, Miller (2004) suggests that the illusory glamour of cultural industries has rendered Western societies insensible to the fundamentally exploitative relations upon which the 'new international division of cultural labor' now depends. Here the developing world is allocated the role of 'anthropological avant-garde laboratory for music, medication and minerals' (p. 59), providing Western consumers with opportunities to incarnate and indulge their new creative selves. In a withering critique, Miller contends that a 'new labour paradigm' must be formulated in order to expose the complicity of those 'culturalist mavens' (p. 59) who now appear indistinguishable from the 'prevailing neoliberal Washington Consensus' (p. 57) in their collective efforts to celebrate the sovereignty and creativity of the consumer in a culturalized and deregulated global market. By drawing attention to individuation and exploitation, this critique provides a necessary corrective to the more upbeat claims of advocates of the cultural economy. There are, however, two initial drawbacks with it. The first is its underdeveloped notion of agency; indeed the critique is virtually complete in its disregard for the capacity of cultural workers to think and act in ways that contradict market rationality. Secondly, the argument tends towards a universalist position; and I would argue that to merely assume that moral values are absent or that a blanket consensus exists whereby atomized individuals, either through choice or compulsion, automatically endorse neo-liberal values is to decontextualize and desocialize the varied conditions under which cultural industries operate.

A MORAL ECONOMY: AN UNINTENDED OUTCOME OF INDIVIDUALIZATION?

The remainder of the article is concerned with evaluating these generalized assumptions about the (im)moral nature of cultural work; not necessarily to diminish the critique, but to provide a point of contrast that draws attention to the varied and diverse motives and actions of cultural entrepreneurs, and reveals the possibilities for progressive social and political action contained within cultural work. I argue that the blurring of boundaries between work and non-work (often seen as a detrimental impact of the new economy) can also provide conditions for the increased integration and overlap of hitherto separate realms of obligation (moral-political and contractual) that can interact to effect forms of workplace identity that exhibit morally complex characteristics, some of which are translatable into socially useful actions.

To do this, we must begin by acknowledging the central role that moral values play in the economy at large. How we should behave ethically towards others and how we should show adequate regard for moral conventions is part of a broader conception of 'moral economy,'[3] defined thus:

> . . . the study of how economic activities of all kinds are influenced and structured by moral dispositions and norms, and how in turn these norms may be compromised, overridden or reinforced by economic pressures. (Sayer, 2004: 2)

Booth (1994) and Sayer (2004) remind us that in classical political economy (as in the work of Adam Smith), economies were judged to be morally constituted: that is, economic activity was embedded and entwined in non-economic social relations and shaped by moral values other than those effecting instrumental rationalization. However, the rise of a Modern 'formal' economy of institutions, and the emergent idea of the economy as an autonomous sphere operating under its own internal logic, appeared to 'lift' the economic from local or quotidian realms and induce a break between economic rationality and (non-economic) moral purpose. Conventional accounts of the development of Modern societies often refer to the downgrading of moral issues in economic life. As economic systems have become more abstract and distanced from the framework of personal experience provided by traditional societies, so local capacities for the moral regulation of economic life appear to diminish, and indeed be of less concern than establishing one's own position in the economic system—leaving

issues of moral judgment and action to be exercised in non-economic contexts (Sayer, 1999, 2004).

Yet, despite this apparent demoralization of Modern economics, it is clear that economic activity can only function with recourse to some value system that comprises a set of moral presumptions regarding how economic activity should be conducted and regulated. For example, as Smart admits, for markets to be able to function there has to be 'a degree of trust between participants . . . confidence that promises made will be kept, that people can be taken at their word' (2003: 109), and other deep-rooted moral sensibilities (for example honesty, obligation, fairness, restraint) are central to the development of efficient economic relations (Wilber, 1996). Indeed, while morality is always somewhere where 'there,' structuring market relations and shaping workplace interactions, more recent transformations in capitalism illustrate that morality may be reestablishing a firmer rooting in economic discourse and practice. The rise of 'social entrepreneurs,' Local Exchange Trading Schemes, various forms of ethical business and the growth of more aesthetically and spiritually directed 'slow' or 'soft' capitalism (Heelas, 2002) suggest that morally diverse business models with complex orientations to market rationality are now in evidence. Indeed, just at the point where neo-liberalism appears to have achieved a 'natural' supremacy (Smart, 2003) writers such as Crossley (2003), Klein (2000) and Williams (2004) point to the increasing emergence of a wide array of social relations and movements opposed to the dogma of free market fundamentalism, impelled to make new social and economic relations based on sustainability, mutuality and a sense of moral obligation.

The rise of such alternatives lends weight to Giddens' (1991) argument that the capacity for self-reflexivity and progressive social action may actually increase, rather than diminish, as modernization effects a radical rolling back of collective, institutional forms. Indeed, both Giddens and Beck have argued strongly that under conditions of reflexive modernization individuals are decreasingly presented with fixed and objective social roles and now have to actively construct their own identities in a situation of fluidity, anxiety and risk (Beck, 1992, 2000). Giddens, in particular, emphasizes the positive aspects of this transformation, highlighting the expanded opportunities for self-determination as detraditionalization opens up new avenues of choice and brokers opportunities for meaningful self-actualization. Such an argument premises a more proactive notion of agency than that prescribed by Marxism or 'neo-liberal fatalism' (Sayer, 2001: 700) which see modernization leading only to the destruction, rather than the adaptation, of the self. Giddens' view is summarized thus:

> A sense of self, with a degree of agency and reflexive control over work and life, is not therefore overwhelmed by new economic forms. Different groups in the workforce are differentiated in their responses to employers' demands for continuing adaptability and organizational commitment, with evidence of resistance to such pressures, whether because of socio-economic status, family commitments, life stage or *values* [my emphasis]. (Webb, 2004: 733)

Giddens is explicit about the possibility of new values, and the 'moral thread' (1991: 78) that underpins self-reflexivity may lead to the construction of new 'authentic' (in the sense of being 'true to oneself') identities, ones 'free from dependencies' and more geared to 'achieving fulfilment' as a 'good' or 'worthy' person (p. 79). The loosening of institutional bonds, be it at work, home or from the state, underwrites the absolute necessity to make choices about one's life project; with individual self-reflexivity now being creatively applied not just to the instrumental calculation of (say) employment risk and opportunity but also to the non-instrumental, moral and emotional aspects of selfhood—which, as we have seen, are already vital components of economic relations. Of course, at work (as in other arenas) the distributions of 'choice' and 'freedom' will be uneven and unequal (Mythen, 2005). However, this does not discount the possibility that, for some, the opportunity to reinvest work with a moral or ethical dimension has emerged as an ironic consequence of neo-liberal efficiency in dismantling clear distinctions between realms of work and non-work, and the transferring of moral authority and duties of care away from institutions to individual domains. The collapsing distinctions between public and private realms may well lead to the engulfment of the self by work (Grugulis et al., 2000; Ross, 2003), but can, potentially, have the converse effect of increasing the range and heterogeneity of (previously externalized) moral actions and judgments that can be brought to bear in the labour process. Thus, rather than assume that work unproblematically supplants the social (as McRobbie and others suggest), perhaps we should consider equally how non-instrumental, political and social values may be feeding back into the work process. The central research question here is: how, under conditions of reflexive modernization, are individuals (re)introducing moral sentiments into the context of their working lives?

MORAL ECONOMY AND CULTURAL ENTREPRENEURSHIP IN MANCHESTER

Leadbeater and Oakley (1999) argue that cultural entrepreneurs are not simply ideologically committed to the market economy, but may attempt to negotiate a space to develop additional non-economic interests. While these interests are assumed to be predominantly aesthetic or creative, they can extend into areas of politics and social practice not commonly associated with the cultural entrepreneur. For example, amongst our sample,[4] a number of entrepreneurs revealed their involvement in the Northern Quarter Association,[5] a voluntary group lobbying for environmental, social and cultural renewal in the bohemian fringe of Manchester city centre:

> It [the NQA] developed from an early meeting where really it was very very basic, talking about cleaning the streets and that kind of stuff (. . .) I'm voluntary I don't get paid for any of it, (. . .) currently I'm involved in negotiations over the Smithfield site which is the old market site, (. . .) I'm representing the community, I'm on the evaluation panel, so there's me, two senior councillors, a senior officer (. . .) it's not always a happy relationship . . .

While, for entrepreneurs, 'helping the community' or 'improving the neighbourhood' was motivated by a sense of social responsibility, the economic success of a cultural business was seen to be closely related to the ability to cultivate and access a 'unique' local environment that could provide a stimulating and diverse admixture of social and cultural groups and perspectives—showing how non-instrumental and instrumental values can mutually reinforce. Additionally, entrepreneurs' motivations for joining the NQA seemed to be less concerned with negotiating a position as a regeneration 'mover and shaker' or indulging in 'city imaging' and post-modern spectacle (Harvey, 1989), and more about attempting to preserve some kind of cultural pluralism and re-establish an ethical commitment to place in a city increasingly subject to gentrification and the commodification of public space. In this respect, cultural entrepreneurs, rather than being 'despatialized' and 'desocialized' (McRobbie, 2002b), appeared to be highly attuned to the social milieu into which they were embedded.

Our research revealed explicit historical and contemporary links between cultural entrepreneurs and higher education institutions (around 70% of entrepreneurs interviewed had been through humanities/liberal arts and/or design-based courses or were working in university 'spin-off' companies), the free and alternative press, as well as (usually leftist) political parties and organizations (see Banks and O'Connor, 2000). Many entrepreneurs were born in Manchester or hailed from nearby towns and cities, while others had attended college/university in the city and decided to 'stay on.' In contrast to Wittel's nomadic and desocialized new media entrepreneurs, devoid of 'common and shared history' (2001: 67), these entrepreneurs revealed an abundance of collective memories and shared experiences, cultivated through historical immersion in Manchester's various social, political and cultural 'scenes.' The reminiscences of these two designers were typical:

All the bands like the Happy Mondays and the Stone Roses would all pop in and see people because Affleck's [a retail and work space for small cultural firms] was the place where Things happened and it was great and then Hacienda was at its peak at that time as well . . . It was a great time and Affleck's was a great place to be, when the whole Madchester thing was on . . . it was MTV and all the world in there everyday, it was crazy.

As I said I came to college and stayed here. I'm emotionally attached to the city, I like the city, it accounted for most of my evolving from some spud who was at school to a human being (. . .) The city contains all the elements I require personally and professionally and it has evolved with me, or I have evolved with it (. . .). There's a natural magnetism for people to come into Manchester . . .

Throughout, a sense of community, strong social and cultural ties and a regard for the 'can-do' and creative 'atmosphere' of Manchester were cited as incentives to action. Manchester's diverse configurations of social and spatial relations, underwritten by a rich history of images, myths and narratives, were often alluded to as a source of inspiration and value:

. . . so there's a quite good feel about Manchester and that goes back a long long time. There is a sort of history of radical politics, there is a history of innovation, adventure I don't why . . . you go back to your geography it'll be all about the rivers, it'll be all about the availability of capital, be about the bridges, be about accumulation—once you have one innovation like the canal to the sea or a railway or whatever they start to build on one another. (Promoter/new media entrepreneur)

With many entrepreneurs expressing a strong, progressive sense of place it was not surprising that the desire to 'give something back' to the city was often expressed. To give some examples, entrepreneurs involved themselves in voluntary teaching and mentoring at local colleges, devoting services free to local arts and entertainment events, combining work with the provision of public art in the local community, driving a women's night-bus and, in the case of one local recording studio, working through colleges to offer local youth free use of their facilities. More directly, the links between cultural production and political and social action were ably demonstrated by one promoter/new media entrepreneur, recalling his own career development working in music promotion in the city:

I was putting on shows. They were mainly for global things, like anti-apartheid, anti-racism generally, the biggest one we did was in Albert Square [in

Manchester] called 'Jammin' for Jobs,' it was about the city being forced to shed workers. There were quite radical political movements meshing with the cultural stuff.

While, for our entrepreneurs, progressive social and political values may happily co-exist with economic instrumentality, non-instrumental moral values can also have more direct purchase on cultural work by shaping market relations and influencing economic choices and decisions. One fashion design and retail company described itself as a place where people were encouraged to pursue interests and express themselves in ways other than those defined by formal business. As the store manager had duly developed an interest in art, so the company had diversified into providing a small, accessible gallery space for local artists—the opportunity cost here being the growth of the retail arm of the business. Eschewing market rationality, the manager had wanted to see how far he could take the 'idea of the shop in the community,' as he further elaborated:

> We're about retail, we view retail and our business in a broader context and we involve ourselves in the wider community as well and we immerse ourselves in all aspects of popular street culture . . . and we express ourselves through that as we can.

Finally, entrepreneurs revealed the ability to reflect in depth on ethical aspects of management/employment, particularly regarding the treatment and development of staff. While much cultural work comprises vulnerable 'low-end' and casual employment, typically un-unionized and under-regulated, this entrepreneur set great store by staff training and development and consciously undertook constant reflexive evaluation of the aims and practices of the business, articulated thus:

> When we look at staffing issues are the means as important as the ends? Is customer service the most important thing that we do? Are we treating everybody with the same respect throughout? The more I go on the more I think reflection is actually a very important element rather than rote learning if you like.

To summarize, a number of our entrepreneurs revealed themselves to be self-reflexive and sensitive actors, acutely aware of the embeddedness of their firm within a particular geographical and social milieu, and concerned to achieve a balance between the pursuit of instrumental goals and the articulation of moral-political values of socially useful character. Overall—without wishing to fetishize localities and remaining cognisant of the fact that places and networks can both constrain as well as enable—our evidence of collective sentiments and an embedded moral economy (a shared culture, the emergence of agencies such as the Northern Quarter Association, strong interlinking with voluntary work and charitable enterprises and the recent development of a cluster of informal networks through the city council's Cultural Industries Development Service) would suggest that localities may not only provide cultural entrepreneurs with economic advantages and/or aesthetic inspiration (as is conventionally argued), but might potentially act as a framework for the articulation of moral-political and social values in the course of cultural work.

While I can make no generalizations about the wider applicability of this preliminary analysis, it does at least illustrate the existence of moral diversity in cultural work, the possibility of 'mixed opportunity' (Giddens, 1991: 176) in detraditionalized workplace politics and the enduring influence of place and local identity on cultural production (Banks et al., 2000; Drake, 2003; O'Connor and Wynne, 1996; Scott, 2000). Beyond the caricature of the individualized, desocialized creative, some entrepreneurs may be recast as progressive, politically motivated actors that pursue varied ends in the context of place-embedded cultural work. As McRobbie once argued, the cultural turn and aestheticization of work can open up 'desires for social transformation . . . too easily dismissed as marginal, merely cultural and politically insignificant' (1999: 30), and here I have provided one example of how these desires may persist and materialize as socially useful actions.

CONCLUSIONS—UNCOVERING PROGRESSIVE WORKPLACE IDENTITIES?

I have argued that non-instrumental motives can shape practices of cultural entrepreneurship, and that the binding effects of sense of place and community obligation can act as focus for social imperatives that mediate and impose limits around the pursuit of instrumental, profit-seeking goals—an issue hitherto unacknowledged by both supporters and critics of neo-liberalism and the 'cultural turn.' The accounts of these cultural entrepreneurs contrast with the pessimistic assessments of neo-liberal fatalists, as they reveal moral commitments that contradict the popular model of the self-interested and depoliticized creative. In this respect, empirical analysis of the micro-contexts of production have helped obtain a finer purchase on the complexities of cultural work, broadening our understanding of the range of biographical possibilities able to be realized in the context of this (still) relatively unexplored field (Slater, 2002).

A number of caveats are, of course, required. Firstly, the sample is small and unrepresentative, comprised of self-employed entrepreneurs in one city—working as sole traders or in micro-enterprises, rather than in larger, more global-corporate organizations, more significant in employment terms, such as those studied by Hesmondhalgh (2002). We should remember, however, that small and micro-enterprises are significant employment contributors and sources of innovation in the overall cultural sector (DCMS, 2001; Scott, 2000). Secondly, it is not my intention to recast cultural work as inherently progressive—clearly much of it is not. No one denies the fact that, even in local cultural sectors, commercial self-interest and instrumental rationality will tend to have primacy in underwriting economic actions—and the problems of gender and ethnic discrimination, lack of diversity (Richards and Milestone, 2000) and moral abjection identified by McRobbie (2002a, 2002b) are real and widely dispersed. A final caveat is that even if we acknowledge, like Giddens, that the compulsion to choose can be progressive and effect personal and social growth, there remains the danger that by over-emphasizing the positive potential of self-reflexive agency and fetishizing freedom of choice, we obscure the historical resilience of those socio-economic barriers that retard choice, and in doing so play into the hands of neo-liberal ideologues who would wish to promulgate a 'fantasy of individual omnipotence' (Webb, 2004: 724) at the heart of free market economies.

Despite these drawbacks I would maintain that the debate on cultural industries has hitherto been marked by a somewhat truncated understanding of the complexity of cultural work and a rather generalized view of the social relations experienced by its practitioners. As Webb (2004) avers, the relationships between work organization and identity are complex and multi-faceted. While there is a wealth of evidence to suggest that cultural work is increasingly subject to the disaggregating and corrosive forces of the global economy, it is also the case that the possibilities for reaffirming individual choices are opened up as workers are forced to shoulder the burden of responsibility for the 'career path,' as well as other non-economic aspects of the personal biography. These cultural entrepreneurs are pursuing careers underpinned by a diverse assemblage of motives and moral principles, and, as such, contrast markedly with the desocialized drones distinctive to the fatalist critique.

Where does this lead us? Like Williams' (2004) study of the hidden 'moral economy of favours' that underpins 'cash-in-hand' work, this article identifies the existence of morally progressive, non-instrumental rationales in what was previously thought to be a morally abject and apolitical sector. This recognition is important since it not only raises the prospect of uncovering alternative rationales in other robustly commercial sectors, but also helps to 'illuminate the possibility of alternative futures beyond the hegemony of profit-motivated monetised exchange' (Williams, 2004: 2). It provides hope that more 'sustainable,' embedded and morally diverse approaches to capitalism may be found or made possible elsewhere. Perhaps for the future, critical social science needs to more fully acknowledge the moral complexity inherent to (not just cultural) work and thus begin to formulate a critique that can divest neo-liberal models of their seductive (but dehumanized and decontextualized) notions of human agency as rational self-interest, avoid fatalist conceptions of abject, desocialized work, and provide the resources to develop counter-arguments that can both illustrate and advocate the progressive potential of the remoralization of economic relations.[6] We ought to reject the view that the culturalized economy can only be either 'emancipatory or enslaving' (Löfgren, 2003: 251), and suggest that further unpacking of the heterogeneity of motives and actions that underpin economic activity may now be essential in helping to develop more progressive workplace futures.

NOTES

1. This term is used to refer to a number of distinct and overlapping processes—most notably the expansion of cultural, creative and leisure-based occupations, increased demand for cultural (symbolic, aesthetic, meaning-laden) goods and services; greater identification and exploitation of culturally specific niche markets; the growth of workplace 'culture change' programmes designed to improve economic performance through manipulation of human resources; and increased recognition of the aesthetic, interpersonal, discursive and value-laden (hence broadly 'cultural') character of economic relations (see Du Gay and Pryke, 2002, for a useful overview).

2. As Heelas (2002) notes, any attempt to understand workplace identity as a complex of motivations means breaking with a theory most commonly invoked as the 'problem of work' (see Berger, 1964; Bell, 1976). By the 1960s, the tendency towards rationalization, bureaucratization and the apparent dehumanizing drift of work meant that many observers were arguing that work had lost its meaningful link to 'real' or 'authentic' selfhood, providing only material underpinnings for the more rewarding essences of life to be found in the private world of family, interpersonal relations and creative self-expression. Because it was argued that people did not value work in itself—it being nothing more than a means to an end, a source of money for pleasure (what Heelas identifies as the 'instrumental work ethic')—they could neither invest in nor derive any other kinds of benefits or values from it.

3. The idea of 'moral economy' has only recently re-emerged in critical social science, but has, of course, a long history. The central concern of a moral economy approach is to examine the relationship between embedded, socially constructed and mediated norms and values and the apparently disembedded and autonomous operations of the market (Booth, 1994). However, the extent to which these two spheres might be construed as theoretically and empirically distinct has always been open to question. Sayer's (2004) attempt to reassess (and perhaps reclaim) the legacy of Adam Smith reveals that as well as *The Wealth of Nations* (1776), Smith also (contemporaneously) wrote *The Theory of Moral Sentiments* (1759), an empirically grounded evaluation of the socially embedded (rather than economically determined) contexts of moral conduct; indeed *The Theory of Moral Sentiments* was considered by Smith to be his main work. In doing

this, Sayer seeks to remind us that Smith considered the relationships between morality and economic practices in a more nuanced and sophisticated way than is conventionally presented by his neo-liberal acolytes—moral values and the impacts, and indeed benefits, of social embeddedness were important considerations in Smith's political economy. While, later, Marx, Durkheim, Weber and Simmel were all in some way concerned with the demoralizing effects of industrial societies and the possibilities for remoralization, it is only more recently that the idea of embeddedness has resurfaced, reinvigorated by Polanyi's (1944) work examining the 'great transformation' and the deleterious effects of the disembedding of economic relations. While much classical theory has taken the view that economic morality has simply removed or replaced non-economic forms—for example, Schumpeter's observation that economic rationality removes the 'conscientious inhibitions' of the 'old moral tradition' (1976: 158)—more recent work by Booth and Sayer has insisted again that historically embedded and durable non-economic norms and values continue to shape the formation and reproduction of economic practices.

4. The sample is primarily drawn from the ESRC-sponsored 'Cultural Industries and the City' project: L130251048 and the 'Skills for the Missing Industry's Leaders and Enterprises' project, part sponsored by the European Social Fund. The primary data were generated through in-depth qualitative interviews with cultural entrepreneurs, managers and intermediaries. These were either self-employed freelancers or owner/managers of small and micro-enterprises. Thus, notwithstanding conventional contractual obligations with clients and customers and the need to generate a liveable income, these entrepreneurs had a high degree of control over their working conditions and considerable latitude regarding their choice of projects, contracts and the means and measures of delivery. While levels of self-employment in the cultural industries are high, the experiences of this sample are not necessarily generalizable and would likely contrast with workers in larger, more corporate enterprises, as well as those workers who conduct both skilled and non-skilled non-cultural activities in cultural firms and sectors. Though the projects had different target groups, the entrepreneurs tended to be white, British, aged 25–40, beneficiaries of a social science or arts-based higher education (in one project it was assessed that 70% had a degree). We interviewed roughly equal numbers of men and women, while noticing that men tended to work in new media, music, advertising and graphic design and women were more likely to be based in art, craft and fashion design-based enterprises. Common biographical themes emerged: notably that—attracted by the cultural

'buzz'—entrepreneurs had migrated to Manchester from other Northern and Midland towns and cities in order to undertake vocational and higher education, had developed strong linkages and decided to stay on and make their careers. Entrepreneurs tended to socialize in the city centre (in the emergent café bar and 'loft' districts) and conventionally resided in the traditional 'bohemian,' but economically marginal, districts adjacent to the city centre: e.g. Hulme, Whalley Range, Moss Side and the fringes of Chorlton-cum-Hardy. Interviews usually lasted between one and two hours. In total, interviews with 55 entrepreneurs and cultural intermediaries were undertaken on the 'Cultural Industries and the City' project and a further 20 on the 'Skills for the Missing Industry's Leaders and Enterprises' project. The interviews examined the role of 'the city' as an attractor for cultural entrepreneurs, the importance of social networks and the relevance of social, political and 'lifestyle' issues to the construction of entrepreneurial identities. The interview extracts used here were selected to illustrate the general point about the existence of moral diversity in cultural work and the possibility of 'mixed opportunity' (Giddens, 1991: 176) in detraditionalized workplace politics. Clearly, not all entrepreneurs profess social and political motivations in work: amongst our larger project sample of 55, approximately 23 entrepreneurs articulated some kind of non-economic rationale for being in business—roughly 40%.

5. The Northern Quarter is a transitional zone at the fringe of Manchester city centre. Its marginal status has proved attractive to cultural entrepreneurs for its cheap rents, 'alternative' atmosphere and opportunity for trading and networking.

6. It is important not to exaggerate the extent to which the remoralization of cultural work might be rooted in a desire to usurp capitalism. Despite the identification here of some radical interests, ethical imperatives and collectivist tendencies, it appears entrepreneurs were mostly concerned with negotiating a space to work *within* the capitalist system rather than rejecting it outright. There was however a widespread disavowal of the neo-liberal fantasy of the self-interested, profit-maximizer driven only by instrumental gain in a disembedded market situation.

REFERENCES

Banks, M. and J. O'Connor (2000) *Cultural Industries and the City: Final Report. Economic and Social Research Council: Cities, Competitiveness and Cohesion Programme.* Swindon: ESRC.

Banks, M., A. Lovart, J. O'Connor and C. Raffo (2000) 'Risk and Trust in the Cultural Industries,' *Geoforum* 3(4): 453–64.

Bauman, Z. (2000) *Liquid Modernity.* Cambridge: Polity Press.

Beck, U. (1992) *Risk Society.* London: Sage.

Beck, U. (2000) *The Brave New World of Work.* Cambridge: Polity Press.

Bell, D. (1976) *The Cultural Contradictions of Capitalism.* London: Heinemann.

Bentley, T. (1999) *The Creative Age.* London: Demos.

Berger, P. (1964) *The Human Shape of Work.* New York: Macmillan.

Booth, W. (1994) 'On the Idea of Moral Economy,' *The American Political Science Review* 88(3): 653–67.

Bourdieu, P. (1984) *Distinction: A Social Critique of the Judgement of Taste.* London: Routledge and Kegan Paul.

Crossley, N. (2003) 'Even Newer Social Movements? Anti-corporate Protests, Capitalists Crises and the Remoralization of Society,' *Organization* 10(2): 287–305.

DCMS (2001) *Creative Industries Mapping Document.* London: Department of Culture, Media and Sport.

Drake, G. (2003) '"This Place Gives me Space": Place and Creativity in the Creative Industries,' *Geoforum* 34(4): 511–24.

Du Gay, P. and M. Pryke (eds) (2002) *Cultural Economy.* London: Sage.

Featherstone, M. (1992) *Consumer Culture and Postmodernism.* London: Sage.

Florida, R. (2002) *The Rise of the Creative Class.* New York: Basic.

Gibson, C. (2003) 'Cultures at Work: Why "Culture" Matters in Research on the "Cultural" Industries,' *Social & Cultural Geography* 4(2): 201–15.

Giddens, A. (1991) *Modernity and Self-Identity.* Cambridge: Polity Press.

Grugulis, I., T. Dundon and A. Wilkinson (2000) 'Cultural Control and the "Culture Manager": Employment Practices in a Consultancy,' *Work, Employment and Society* 14(1): 97–116.

Harvey, D. (1989) *The Condition of Postmodernity.* Oxford: Blackwell.

Heelas, P. (2002) 'Work Ethics, Soft Capitalism and the "Turn to Life,"' in P. du Gay and M. Pryke (eds) *Cultural Economy,* pp. 78–96. London: Sage.

Hesmondhalgh, D. (2002) *The Cultural Industries.* London: Sage.

Klein, N. (2000) *No Logo.* London: Flamingo.

Lash, S and J. Urry (1994) *Economies of Signs and Space.* London: Sage.

Leadbeater, C. (1999) *Living on Thin Air: The New Economy*. Harmondsworth: Viking.

Leadbeater, C. and K. Oakley (1999) *The Independents*. London: Demos.

Löfgren, O. (2003) 'The New Economy: A Cultural History,' *Global Networks* 3(3): 239–54.

McDowell, L. (2004) 'Work, Workfare, Work/Life Balance and an Ethic of Care,' *Progress in Human Geography* 28(2): 145–63.

McRobbie, A. (1999) *In the Culture Society*. London: Routledge.

McRobbie, A. (2002a) 'Clubs to Companies: Notes on the Decline of Political Culture in Speeded Up Creative Worlds,' *Cultural Studies* 16(4): 516–31.

McRobbie, A. (2002b) 'From Holloway to Hollywood: Happiness at Work in the New Cultural Economy,' in P. du Gay and M. Pryke (eds) *Cultural Economy*, pp. 97–114. London: Sage.

Miller, T. (2004) 'A View from a Fossil: The New Economy, Creativity and Consumption—Two or Three Things I Don't Believe In,' *International Journal of Cultural Studies* 7(1): 55–65.

Mythen, G. (2005) 'Employment, Individualisation and Insecurity: Rethinking the Risk Society Perspective,' *The Sociological Review* 53(1): 129–49.

Nixon, S. (2003) *Advertising Cultures*. London: Sage.

O'Connor, J. and D. Wynne (eds) (1996) *From the Margins to the Centre: Cultural Production and Consumption in the Post-Industrial City*. Aldershot: Ashgate.

Polanyi, K. (1944) *The Great Transformation*. Boston, MA: Beacon Press.

Richards, N. and K. Milestone (2000) 'What Difference does it Make? Women's Pop Cultural Production and Consumption in Manchester,' *Sociological Research Online* 5(1), URL (consulted Jan. 2006): http://www.socresonline.org.uk/5/1/richards.html

Ross, A. (2003) *No Collar. The Humane Workplace and its Hidden Costs*. New York: Basic Books.

Sayer, A. (1999) 'Valuing Culture and Economy,' in L. Ray and A. Sayer (eds) *Culture and Economy after the Cultural Turn*, pp. 53–75. London: Sage.

Sayer, A. (2001) 'For a Critical Cultural Political Economy,' *Antipode* 33(4): 687–708.

Sayer, A. (2003) 'Decommodification, Consumer Culture and Moral Economy,' *Environment and Planning D: Society and Space* 21: 341–57.

Sayer, A. (2004) *Moral Economy*, URL (consulted Oct. 2004): http://www.lancs.ac.uk/fss/sociology/papers/sayer-moral-economy.pdf

Schumpeter, J. (1976) *Capitalism, Socialism and Democracy*. Loudon: Allen and Unwin.

Scott, A.J. (2000) *The Cultural Economy of Cities*. London: Sage.

Sennett, R. (1998) *The Corrosion of Character: The Personal Consequences of Work in the New Capitalism*. New York: W.W. Norton.

Slater, D. (2002) 'Capturing Markets from the Economists,' in P. du Gay and M. Pryke (eds) *Cultural Economy*, pp. 59–77. London: Sage.

Smart, B. (2003) *Economy, Culture and Society*. Buckingham: Open University Press.

Smith, C. (1998) *Creative Britain*. London: Faber and Faber.

Webb, J. (2004) 'Organizations, Self-identities and the New Economy,' *Sociology* 38(4): 719–38.

Wilber, C. (1996) 'Ethics and Economies,' in C.J. Whalen (ed.) *Political Economy for the 21st Century*, pp. 45–65. New York: M.E. Sharpe.

Williams, C. (2004) 'Cash-In Hand Work: Unravelling Informal Employment from the Moral Economy of Favours,' *Sociological Research Online* 9(1), URL (consulted Jan. 2006): http://www.socresonline.org.uk/cgi-bin/absrtact.pl?9/1/williams.html

Willis, P. (1990) *Common Culture*. Buckingham: Open University Press.

Wittel, A. (2001) 'Towards a Network Sociality,' *Theory, Culture & Society* 18(6): 51–76.

Wittstock, M. (2000) 'Are You a Bourgeois Bohemian?' *The Observer* (28 June).

Wynne, D. and J. O'Connor (1998) 'Consumption and the Post-modern City,' *Urban Studies* 35(5–6): 841–64.

SOURCE: Banks, Mark. 2006. "Moral Economy and Cultural Work." *Sociology*, 40(3):455–72.

32

REPRESENTING BLUE

Representative Bureaucracy and Racial Profiling in the Latino Community

VICKY M. WILKINS AND BRIAN N. WILLIAMS

The research on the theory of representative bureaucracy is concerned with understanding the conditions under which we can expect passive representation to lead to active representation. Numerous studies have highlighted the role that institutional and contextual factors play in the link between passive and active representation (Keiser, Wilkins, Meier, & Holland, 2002; Wilkins, 2007; Wilkins & Keiser, 2006). However, these studies of active representation have examined organizations with low to moderate levels of socializations (i.e., public schools, Child Support Enforcement, and Farmer's Home Administration) and found that minority bureaucrats use their discretion to reduce negative outcomes or increase positive outcomes for minority clientele. We offer a much harder test for the theory of representative bureaucracy by testing the link between passive and active representation for ethnicity in an organization that relies heavily on socialization—police departments. Police departments are known for their use of socialization to modify the behavior and attitudes of their employees.

We make this extension to the research on representative bureaucracy by examining the case of racial profiling in the Latino community. There is a longstanding research tradition examining the intersection of policing and race; however, most of this extant research focuses on the experience of African Americans. Little has been done to incorporate Latinos into policing research. Martinez's (2007) search of articles published between 1990 and 2006 with the keywords "Hispanic" or "Latino" and "police" in the *Criminal Justice Abstracts* netted 68 items when compared with 485 articles with the keywords "African-American" or "black" and "police." Even less research has examined racial profiling and the experience of the Latino[1] community. There is clear evidence that like African Americans, Latinos experience excessive vehicle stops and searches (Fagan & Davies, 2000; Spitzer, 1999). In addition, Latinos hold less favorable attitudes toward police than Whites (Weitzer, 2002) and the vast majority of Latinos believe that law enforcement should discontinue the use of racial profiling techniques (Newport, 1999). Given these findings, researchers should examine racial profiling from the perspective and context of the Latino community.

In this article, we turn to the literature on representative bureaucracy to examine one aspect of racial profiling in the Latino community. We focus on how the representation of Latino police officers influences vehicle stop behavior in their divisions. In other words, will the presence of Latino officers reduce the racial disparity in traffic stops in the division they work in? Using the lens of representative bureaucracy, we address the following question: Are there conditions under which minority bureaucrats will be less likely to provide active representation? We contend that organizational socialization may hinder the link between passive and active representation.[2] At first glance we should expect to find that the proportion of Latino officers working in a police department is correlated with a decrease in the racial disparity in vehicle stops, by that police department, all else being equal. But, does organizational socialization strip the racial identity of police officers, somehow changing them from "brown" to "blue" and limiting their provision of active representation?

PREVIOUS RESEARCH ON REPRESENTATIVE BUREAUCRACY AND ORGANIZATIONAL SOCIALIZATION

The bureaucrats working in public agencies are often the first, and sometimes the only, contact that the public has with the bureaucracy. Because this contact is most often with street-level bureaucrats who may exercise discretion, his or her attitudes, values, and predispositions are important in understanding policy implementation (Lipsky, 1980). The theory of representative bureaucracy concerns how the demographic characteristics of bureaucrats affect the distribution of outputs to clients who share these demographic characteristics.[3] The literature distinguishes between two forms of representation—passive and active. Passive representation is concerned with the bureaucracy having the same demographic origins (sex, race, income, class, religion) as the population it serves (Mosher, 1982). Studies of passive representation examine whether the composition of the bureaucracy mirrors the demographic composition of the general population or whether women and minorities are underrepresented in the bureaucracy (Dolan, 2000, 2002; Kellough, 1990: Naff & Crum, 2000; Riccucci & Saidel, 1997). These studies seldom examine the effects of representation or the lack of representation on the agency's policy outputs. Active representation, in contrast, is concerned with how representation influences policy making and implementation. Active representation assumes that bureaucrats will act purposely on behalf of their counterparts in the general population (Pitkin, 1967).

Early scholars assumed that passive representation would naturally translate into active representation, but recent work has identified a couple of necessary conditions for the link to occur (Keiser et al., 2002; Meier, 1993). First, the policy area must be salient to the demographic group in question (Keiser et al., 2002; Meier, 1993; Selden, 1997). As discussed earlier, the issue of racial profiling is highly salient in the Latino community. The second necessary condition is that the policy area must be one in which bureaucrats exercise discretion. Discretion is a necessary condition because it provides bureaucrats with the opportunity to shape outputs to reward a particular group (Meier, 1993). In bureaucracies where most decisions are dictated by rules, bureaucrats have few opportunities to shape outputs to reward a particular group within their clientele (Meier, 1993). Street-level bureaucrats normally make decisions, major and minor, that can influence the outcome of cases and the benefits received by agency clients. It is these decisions that can produce what we term as active representation—bureaucrats advocating the interest of their clients and eliminating discrimination that has an impact on one group or another among the agency's clientele (Mosher, 1982). Police officers, described by Muir (1977) as street corner politicians who can monopolize the exercise of power, are the quintessential street-level bureaucrats and clearly exercise a necessary amount of discretion (Davis, 1975; Lipsky, 1980; Vinzant & Crothers, 1998). There are numerous ways that minority police officers could influence outcomes for minority drivers, either through their own actions or by influencing the organization.

Race and ethnicity are the most common demographic characteristics examined by the existing research on both passive and active representation (Cayer & Sigelman, 1980; Hindera, 1993; Meier, 1975, 1993; Rehfuss, 1986; Riccucci & Saidel, 1997; Saltzstein, 1989; Selden, 1997; Thompson, 1976,

1978). In the case of race and ethnicity, numerous studies (Hindera, 1993; Meier & Stewart, 1992; Meier, Stewart, & England, 1989; Selden, 1997) have concluded that minority bureaucrats implement policies or use their discretion to reduce the disparate treatment minority clients have historically received from various public bureaucracies. At first glance we should expect, therefore, that passive representation will lead to active representation in police departments. However, previous research and our understanding of organizational socialization present in police departments require that we modify this expectation.

Recent research on representative bureaucracy focuses on the role that institutional and contextual factors play in the link between passive and active representation (Keiser et al., 2002). One of the institutional variables considered is organizational socialization. Scholars argue that administrators are socialized by the organizations they work in and they adopt behaviors and preferences that are consistent with organizational goals, thereby minimizing the influence of their own personal values on bureaucratic behavior (Downs, 1967; Gawthrop, 1969; Meier & Nigro, 1976; Simon, 1957; Thompson, 1976; Weber, 1946). Employees may be willing to adopt the organization's values to increase the chance of promotion and career success chances either because they feel peer pressure to do so, or simply because they come to agree with and internalize the dominant organizational view (Romzek, 1990; Simon, 1957: Thompson, 1976).

In previous research (Wilkins & Williams, 2008), we tested the hypothesis that the link between passive and active representation can be hindered by organizational socialization by examining how the presence of black police officers affect vehicle stops. Analyzing traffic stop data from the San Diego Police Department, we find that the presence of Black police officers in a division is related to an increase in racial disparity in traffic stops in the division. These findings, in conjunction with insights from individual interviews and focus group discussions with police officers and police executives, suggest that the behavior of Black police officers is influenced by the strong need to fit into the culture of the organization. It appeals that the structure and processes of an organization can affect the representation provided by the bureaucrats working there. In this article, we will test if the effect is similar for Latino police officers.

In related research, Smith and Holmes (2003) examine how the representation of minority police officers (both Black and Latino) affects the number of police brutality complaints filed each year in 114 U.S. cities. They argue that the demographic composition of the police departments will influence the likelihood that the citizens of the city will experience police brutality. Specifically, they hypothesize that when Blacks or Latinos are better represented among the police officers there will be fewer complaints of police brutality. Their findings offer mixed support for their hypotheses. The presence of Black police officers in the police department does not appear to be related to the number of complaints filed. On the other hand, they find a sizable positive effect for the variable measuring the representation of Latino police officers. Specifically, the findings indicate that the more closely the proportion of Latino officers in a police department matches the proportion of Latinos in the general population, there will be fewer complaints of police brutality. They speculate that the different findings for Black and Latino police officers stem from differences in the social organization of the Black and Latino communities. They suggest that "Latino police officers may be more integrated into their community producing empathy for Latino citizens and counteract socialization pressures from the occupational subculture" (Smith & Holmes, 2003, p. 1054).

Although Smith and Holmes (2003) do not test their proposition that Latino police officers may be more integrated into their community, there is some evidence of this from other lines of research. Studies of the social and economic structures of the African American and Latino communities describe rather different circumstances. African American communities are deeply impoverished and highly segregated (Massey & Denton, 1993; Wilson, 1987). Working- and middle-class African Americans have moved out of inner-city neighborhoods that were once heterogeneous with respect to social class, leaving behind the most disadvantaged segments of the population (Wilson, 1987). This has created a social and economic divide between relatively affluent African Americans and poor African Americans (Massey & Denton, 1993; Wilson, 1987). For a number of reasons, African Americans from these highly disadvantaged areas generally would be less-qualified police candidates than those from the working- and middle-class neighborhoods (Williams & Murphy, 1990). Given the significant separation within the African American community, African American police officers may perceive citizens in impoverished African American neighborhoods as threats to their physical well-being and authority (Alex, 1969).

Although the residents of Latino barrios have also experienced social and economic disadvantages, there are several factors present that may promote higher levels of social organization when compared with poor African American neighborhoods (Martinez, 2002). First, Latinos have higher rates of formal and informal labor force participation, albeit in lower paying jobs (Martinez, 2002). Furthermore, the close social networks of Latinos are often credited with assisting Latinos, especially new immigrants, in finding work (Mouw, 2003). Second, the Latino immigration has been a constant pattern since the 1800s. As a result, each successive wave of immigrants has served to reinforce various aspects of the Latino culture and encourage the use of the Spanish language within the United States (Martinez, 2002). Next, the size and distribution of the Latino population also serves to keep the community integrated. The majority of Latinos continue to live in neighborhoods with very high concentrations of Latino inhabitants. Thus, the potential for interaction with other Latinos is extremely high. Many, on a daily basis, will work, go to school, go to church, and attend various community events with other Latinos. Although Latinos confront difficult conditions, they may also experience high levels of social integration. These higher levels of integration may make Latino police officers less susceptible to organizational socialization and ultimately increase the likelihood that they work to eliminate racial disparities experienced by Latino citizens.

The theory of representative bureaucracy would predict that minority representation should create a police department that is more sensitive to the experiences of minority citizens and should reduce negative outcomes—such as excessive vehicle stops. The findings on this point are mixed. We have evidence that the number of Black police officers is related to an increase in racial disparity in traffic stops (Wilkins & Williams, 2008). Contrary to our findings. Smith and Holmes (2003) find that the representation of Black officers is not related to police brutality. However, they do find that the representation of Latino officers is associated with a lower incidence of police brutality complaints. In addition, there is evidence that the social organization of African American communities differs in important ways from the Latino communities and these differences could effect the provision of active representation by Latino police officers. These inconsistent findings motivate this research. We question whether organizational socialization can strip away the racial identity of Latino police officers and replace it with an organizational identity. In essence, can this process transform those officers so they no longer represent their ethnic identity and instead represent blue?

POLICE SOCIALIZATION

Police socialization is part and parcel of organizational socialization—the process by which members of an organization learn the required behaviors and attitudes to be recognized as a member of the organization (Caplow, 1964; Manning, 1970). The objective of police socialization, like occupational socialization, is the long-term internalization and subsequent action congruence with organizational values (Bennett, 1984). Similar to Milgram's (1974) concept of "agentic shift," police socialization seeks to control and limit individual behavior in order to facilitate a transition away from autonomous behavior by individual officers, toward organizational functioning of officers. This process may co-opt minority police officers to engage in conduct contrary to the interests of minority citizens, including racial profiling.

Police departments are characterized by a uniquely robust subculture that insulates its members and fosters in-group cohesiveness (Skolnick, 1975). The cohesion and degree of solidarity for police officers has long been noted as one of the most noticeable, yet unusual aspects of the police profession (Hahn, 1971). As such, this profession reflects and projects a sense of fraternal support and fidelity, which in turn encourages and reinforces an overarching police culture. This culture has been found to be a result of three factors: the continuous presence of danger, the use of coercive authority, and police professionalism (Harrison, 1998; Paoline, 2003; Paoline, Myers, & Worden, 2000; Waddington, 1999). Almost immediately new officers are cognizant that the brotherhood that they are members of transcends their jurisdictional, operational, or hierarchical boundaries. In theory, this esprit de corps or common spirit of comradeship and devotion to the cause of law enforcement is of value to the public. However, when carried too far this solidarity can produce negative outcomes, including racial profiling.

For several reasons we think that the solidarity promoted among police officers may actually facilitate profiling behavior, especially among minority officers. First, officers quickly learn that their allegiance is to each other and that they are to never "rat" on another officer. So, even in departments where racial profiling is not sanctioned and/or promoted, officers may look the other way if they observe their peers profiling. Second, the focus on group cohesion serves to give birth to the "us versus them" line of thinking and isolates the officers from the citizenry. This isolation can desensitize minority officers to the concerns of minority communities and citizens. Finally, in a culture where solidarity is so highly valued the behavior of minority officers is influenced by the strong need to fit into the organization. The following quote highlights this possibility.

> This one (white) sergeant here that loves to refer to black people as 'those people.' If you're black and you refer to black people as 'those people' you're treated okay by him. Otherwise, you may not be. You get a few black cops who do that sort of thing, guys who have no backbone. They're treated by this one sergeant as one of the guys. (Leinen, 1984, p. 38)

Furthermore, in a recent interview with the chief of a local police agency regarding the cultural and organizational dynamics affecting the working relationship between his agency and the local Latino community, the chief highlighted the pressure that one Latino officer faced to conform and better align himself with his occupational identity.[4]

> One of our greatest challenges is building and sustaining a strong relationship with our local Hispanic community. We've had some success. Right now we have approximately 8 officers who are Hispanic or bilingual. We are trying to recruit more, but it is a challenge. With our success, we also have had some frustrations. We had one Hispanic officer who was working in special operations—you know floating around town, spending time in the various Hispanic communities, meeting the people, building the needed rapport, gaining trust . . . A couple of months back he put in a request to switch back to shift work [working in a set geographic area, during a set time]. I asked him why did he want to make that move considering how effective he was in special operations—you know. Hispanic residents were responsive to him, they knew him, they trusted him, they liked and respected him . . . He said he felt as if he needed to prove himself to the other officers . . . I guess to let them know that he could do more than work with the Hispanic community . . . to let them know he was a police officer and not just a Hispanic police officer. (Interview with Police Chief of local department, June 2007)

Although we concede that all police officers face pressure to fit in, we argue that the pressure weighs more heavily on minority and female police officers, who have historically been outsiders in the field of law enforcement.

The desire to fit in and be treated as "one of the guys" likely influences their behavior, attenuates the provision of active representation, and can ultimately lead them to profile minority drivers.

Police socialization is not a one time phenomenon. To the contrary, it occurs at all stages of an officer's career and incorporates both a formal and informal dimension. The formal socialization process is hierarchical in nature and begins with a police cadet's initial contact with her instructor in a sterile, preoccupational environment—the classroom of the local police academy. This setting helps to instill the central values of the policing profession as outlined in the International Association of Chiefs of Police (IACP) Law Enforcement Code of Ethics: service mindedness, integrity, public trust, team work, courage, and respect.

This initial process of socialization is followed by subsequent post academy "street" experiences that further acclimate officers to the norms and mores of what it means to be blue. One very common process is the field training officer program that assigns more experienced officers to train and supervise recent academy graduates. The final phase of the formal socialization process persists along the career path of officers as they continue to come into contact and interact with more senior supervisors and managers. Conversely, the informal socialization process transcends the police officer seniority continuum and affects both novice police cadets and more seasoned police officers alike. The informal method counters the hierarchical characteristic of the formal socialization process and is characterized by peer to peer or officer to officer interactions. These interactions have been found to contradict the values articulated in the more formal socialization process. In particular, loyalty to the standards of the profession is often challenged by a standard of loyalty to one's peers or primary peer group.

In this research, we analyzed the data from a traffic stop study in San Diego, California, a large urban municipality located in the western United States. This local law enforcement agency employs in excess of 2,000 sworn police officers and its procedures and practices reflect those of most big-city police departments. The department embraces the community and problem-oriented philosophies that dominate the landscape of American police agencies. The police department utilizes a decentralized approach to policing with community collaboration in problem identification and problem solving playing a vital role in the coproduction of public safety and public order.

The police officer selection process in this city is typical to the process in other large, urban police departments in the United States. This process begins with an initial screening of potential applicants. Each applicant is required to meet or exceed the following requirements: be at least 20.5 years of age on the day of the written exam and 21 years of age at the time of academy graduation; be a U.S. citizen or permanent resident alien who is eligible and has applied for U.S. citizenship prior to application for employment; possess a valid Class C driver's license; and possess certification of graduation from

a high school in the United States or its equivalent (i.e., GED, successful completion of state proficiency examination). This initial screening phase is followed by eight other steps in the officer selection process: written examination, background investigation, physical ability test, polygraph exam, departmental interview, psychological evaluation, medical examination, and academy training.

Academy training consists of 32 weeks of college-level training. During this time period, recruits take courses that cover the principles of law enforcement, criminal law, rules and evidence, search and seizure, laws of arrest and control methods, traffic laws, juvenile laws, first aid, care and use of firearms, patrol theory and methods, the criminal justice system, and physical conditioning and self-defense. This preservice training concludes with 6 weeks of field training. On the successful completion of this curriculum, recruits graduate with the rank of Police Officer I and begin a 12-week field training program under the tutelage of an experienced field training officer. Based on this high level of occupational socialization within the San Diego Police Department, we expect a conditioning effect where the confluence of the formal and informal dimensions of police socialization will shape the values and behavior of police officers, regardless of race, and limit or negate the provision of active representation.

RACIAL/ETHNIC PROFILING: THE LATINO EXPERIENCE

The tension between the police and racial/ethnic minority communities remains a pressing issue facing American police organizations (Barak, Flavin, & Leighton, 2001; Culver, 2004; Websdale, 2001; Williams, 1998). American policing, with its history and heritage of legally sanctioned, disparate service delivery, and the enforcement of racially motivated laws and statutes, has affected, and in many instances, continues to marginalize segments of racial, ethnic, and socioeconomic communities (Cashmore & McLaughlin, 1991; Chambliss, 1994; Ellison & London, 1992; Fogelson, 1968; Hahn, 1971; Murty, Roebuck, & Smith, 1990; Radelet, 1986; Rossi, Beck, & Edison, 1974; Russell, 1998; Websdale, 2001; Williams, 1998). Consequently, much merit is found in the argument that the public perception of racial/ethnic profiling on the parts of racial and ethnic minorities is a contemporary by-product of the legacy of the disparate nature of American policing (Russell, 1998; Williams, 2000).

Racial profiling [emphasis added] is the term used to identify law enforcement practices that use the race or ethnicity of an individual to make discretionary judgments. Ramirez, McDevitt, and Farrell (2000) define racial profiling as

> Any police-initiated action that relies on the race, ethnicity, or national origin rather than the behavior of an individual or information that leads the police to a particular individual who has been identified as being, or having been, engaged in criminal activity. (p. 3)

Conceptualized as a perversion of criminal profiling,[5] Harriott (2004) has noted that criminal profiling becomes racial profiling when race is elevated to the primary principle for predicting criminality. Consequently, profiling no longer serves as an investigative tool for solving cases, "but instead as a tool for race differential surveillance and investigative arrests" (Harriott, 2004, p. 26). Moreover, this failure to focus and differentiate at the individual offender level suggests a shift in the strategy of policing: from utilizing profiling as an investigative tool to an institutional mechanism for control and repression of certain populations based exclusively on race (Verna, 1997).

Beginning in the early 1900s, "anti-drug warriors" invoked the image of Chinese, African Americans, and Latinos as drug users and criminals to pass the nation's earliest drug laws. By 1915, more than 500,000 Latinos had immigrated, bringing marijuana with them (Gray, 1998). In response to increasing anti-Latino sentiment, 16 western states passed laws that criminalized marijuana use (Gray, 1998). These laws targeted the growing Latino community and were promoted as a way to decrease violent crime (Gray, 1998). By the 1980s, the link between minorities, drugs, and crime was cemented in American rhetoric and motivated the effort of the U.S. government to tackle drug trafficking. The U.S. Drug Enforcement Administration (DEA) had, for some years, used lists of common characteristics of drug courier arrestees to construct what they called "drug courier profiles" (Harris, 2002). DEA agents would use these profiles to identify passengers of commercial airliners who might be transporting large quantities of narcotics. The DEA claimed that using these profiles succeeded and that agents using them made regular arrests of passengers carrying illegal drugs. Convinced of the effectiveness of using profiles and facing rising concerns about drug traffickers using the interstate highways to move large quantities of narcotics, the DEA sought to incorporate profiling into the enforcement of traffic laws (Harris, 2002). Traffic laws in the United States have always regulated both driving and the condition of vehicles in incredible detail (Harris, 1997). As a result, any American police officer can easily observe a traffic offense by almost any driver after following the vehicle for just a few blocks (Harris, 1997). This means that police officers have enormous discretion in making vehicle stops and could use traffic regulations as a mere pretext for drug enforcement investigations. Consequently, traffic stops were initiated by officers using these race/ethnicity-based profiles.

Beyond the DEA's actions, the U.S. government's intelligence bulletins for state and local police also encouraged officers involved in drug interdiction to be increasingly suspicious of particular racial and ethnic groups. At the same time that the DEA trained police officers in drug interdiction and profiling tactics, the U.S. government consistently disseminated intelligence reports to police agencies on drug trafficking that often included information pointing to particular ethnic groups (Harris, 2002). For example, the intelligence might indicate that Hispanic gangs were moving cocaine by vehicle across a particular state. This information encourages police officers to use visible physical characteristics of particular minority groups as indicators when making vehicle stops.

In addition to drug interdiction, law enforcement also relies on profiling to enforce immigration laws. Ethnicity remains central to the enforcement of the U.S. immigration laws, particularly in the southwestern part of the country. In fact, the Supreme Court stated in 1975 that "Mexican appearance" constitutes a legitimate consideration under the Fourth Amendment for making an immigration stop (*United States v. Brignoni-Ponce,* 1975). At first glance, the reliance on "Mexican appearance" in immigration enforcement might not appear problematic given the perception that a large percentage of undocumented persons are of Mexican origin. However, only about one-half of the undocumented persons in the United States are Mexican nationals (Johnson, 2001). More important, the vast majority of Latinos in the United States are U.S. citizens or lawful permanent residents. These persons suffer the brunt of race-based immigration enforcement. In addition to the impact that racial profiling has on the minority community, the allegation of racial profiling, and the perception of the police that it creates for minorities could lessen the likelihood of meaningful collaboration with minority citizens and communities in the coproduction of public safety and order (Williams, 1999; Williams, 2000).

Although the vast majority of research on racial profiling has focused on the experience of African Americans, there is a growing body of work that examines Latino/non-Latino differences in police stops and arrests practices. Spitzer (1999) and Fagan and Davies (2000) showed that Latinos (and African Americans) were overrepresented in vehicle stops and in some cases searches. A 1999 analysis by Spitzer and a follow-up study by Fagan and Davies (2000) of the New York City Police Department's stop and frisk practices found that Latinos (and African Americans) were stopped and/or frisked substantially more than their representation in the population would predict. When Fagan and Davies categorized the data by police division, they found that Latinos were two times more likely to be stopped for alleged weapons violations, especially in police divisions where the population was predominately Latino.

We build on this research and the research on representative bureaucracy and organizational socialization to examine how the representation of Latino police officers influences the vehicle stop behavior in their division. This is an important endeavor when you consider the recent demographic shift in terms of Latinos, who now make up the largest percentage of minorities within the United States population (as well as the projected continued growth of this population). Consequently, this investigation goes beyond the more traditional "driving while Black" approach of examining traffic stops and searches of Black drivers to examine how "being brown in blue" affects the behavior of Latino officers regarding traffic stops.

DATA AND METHOD

The data for this project come from the vehicle stop forms collected by the San Diego Police Department for 2000.[6] Starting on January 1, 2000, police officers in San Diego were required to complete a vehicle stop form each time they stopped a vehicle. Use of the vehicle stop form was discontinued in 2001. Vehicle stop forms recorded the context of traffic stop encounters (date and time), the reason for the stop, driver demographics (gender, race/ethnicity, age), actions taken during the stop (search, search authority, search outcome), and the disposition of the stop (citation, arrest). Officers turned these forms in at the end of their shifts. The data on the forms were entered into a database by personnel at police headquarters. For this project, we analyzed the 168,901 stop forms compiled in the 12 months of 2000.[7]

The only piece of individual-level information the police officer is required to provide is the division they are assigned to. Given this, our level of analysis for this project is aggregated to the division. The San Diego Police Department consists of eight divisions. These divisions (North, Northeast, East, Southeast, Central, West, South, and Mid-City) are geographically arranged throughout the area and serve as the first-line of command for the police officers.

Our dependent variable is the percentage of vehicle stops involving a Latino driver in each division for each month in 2000. This yields a sample size of 96 for our analysis. For example, in the month of May 11.59% of the stops made in the North division involved Latino drivers. For the same time period, the number of stops involving a Latino driver in the South division was 75.85%. The mean of this variable is 30%. Table 32.1 presents the vehicle stops by race/ethnicity of the driver by division compared to the driving age population for 2000.

Table 32.1   Vehicle Stops by Race/Ethnicity of Driver by Division for 2000

	Hispanic			White		
Division	*Stops (%)*	*Population (%)*	*Difference (%)*	*Stops (%)*	*Population (%)*	*Difference (%)*
Northern	12	10	2	76	80	−4
Northeastern	12	9	3	61	67	−6
Eastern	16	9	7	64	78	−14
Southeastern	40	33	7	12	15	−3
Central	39	52	−13	40	31	9
Western	18	17	1	64	69	−5
Southern	75	58	17	15	20	−5
Mid-City	33	24	9	29	47	−18

To test the link between passive and active representation, our variable of interest is the percentage of Latino sworn police officers in each division in 2000.[8] Latino officers are well represented in the San Diego Police Department. The mean of this variable is 17%. The division with the greatest representation of Latino police officers is the South division where 41.7% of the officers are Latino.[9] The theory of representative bureaucracy and past research on active representation for ethnicity would suggest that as the percentage of Latino police officers in a division increases, the percentage of Latino drivers involved in vehicle stops in that division will decrease. Prior findings (Wilkins & Williams, 2008) and our understanding of organizational socialization leads us to modify our expectations. Instead, we expect to find that intense organizational socialization will negate the possibility for active representation. In addition, the overwhelming pressure to fit into the culture of the organization may produce a "blue" mentality on the part of Latino officers and may result in the increase of ethnic disparity in the division.

Our model also includes a number of control variables that allow us to rule out alternative explanations for the increase in vehicle stops involving Latino drivers. The most important control variable included in our model is the percentage of the driving population in the division that is Latino. We use a measure of the Latino driving eligible population, as measured by the population that is 15 years or older, in the division. We expect that the percentage of stops that involve Latino drivers will be significantly related to the Latino driving eligible population in the division. In fact, scholars and politicians studying racial profiling often use the difference between the percentage of stops where the driver is Latino and some measure of the Latino population in the area as their primary measure of racial profiling (Harris, 1999: Lundman and Kaufman, 2003; Novak, 2004; Smith & Petrocelli, 2001).

Community-level factors are likely to influence vehicle stops and we can control for some of them in our model. First, we include the median income of the division area according to the 2000 census data.[10] Previous research has found that racial disparity in enforcement increases in high-poverty areas (Cox, Pease, Miller, & Tyson, 2001; Fagan & Davies, 2000; Smith & Petrocelli, 2001; Spitzer, 1999; Wilkins & Williams, 2008). It is possible that all police officers, regardless of race and ethnicity, target certain types of drivers. Findings from in-depth individual interviews and focus group discussions of police officers, as well as police executives, suggest the notion of "low hanging fruit" can impact police practice based on the race and socioeconomic status of the community. Given this, we expect to find that Latino drivers are more likely to be stopped in divisions with lower median incomes. An additional way to get at the effects of poverty on police behavior is to control for the monthly city unemployment rate. We hypothesize that unemployment will be positively related to traffic stops involving Latino drivers.

The final community variable that we control for is the monthly overall crime rate of the city.[11] The measure of crime rates includes seven crimes: homicide, forcible rape, robbery, aggravated assault, burglary, motor vehicle theft, and larceny. Research suggests that area crime rates are positively related to the incidences of racial profiling (Cox et al.,

Table 32.2   Description of Variables

Variable	Mean	Standard Deviation	Minimum and Maximum
Percentage Latino police officers in division	17	9.7	7–42
Median income for division (x1000$)	42.9	12.3	24.4–63.5
Unemployment rate	3.9	0.37	3.2–4.6
Crime rate	1,917	127	1,715–2,115
Percentage of the division driving eligible population that is Latino	26.5	18.3	9–58
Percentage of vehicle stops involving a Latino driver by division	31	20	10–77

2001; Fagan & Davies, 2000; Smith & Petrocelli, 2001; Spitzer, 1999). We hypothesize that divisions will react to rising crime rates at the city level by intensifying enforcement, which in turn could increase the percentage of vehicle stops involving Latino drivers. Table 32.2 presents the summary statistics for all our variables.

To test the relationship between the percentage of stops involving Latino drivers and the presence of minority officers in the eight divisions for the months of 2000, we use ordinary least squares regression. Because pooled cross-sectional time series data sets often exhibit heteroskedasticity (i.e., correlated error terms across units at each time point), we use panel-corrected standard errors (Beck & Katz, 1995, 1996). A second problem for our data set is correlation among error terms within the same unit (division) over time (i.e., autocorrelation). To control for bias in the standard errors, we specify an AR1 process.[12]

RESULTS

The results of the model predicting the relationship between the presence of Latino officers and vehicle stops involving Latino drivers are presented in Table 32.3.[13] The model performs well; the independent variables in the model predict 86% of the variance in the dependent variable.[14] However, it is the parameter estimates that are most interesting.

We expected to find that due to high levels of organizational socialization the percentage of Latino police officers in the division would not reduce the ethnic disparity in vehicle stops for that division. This hypothesis was well supported by the analysis.

The coefficient was both positive and statistically significant ($p < .01$). In other words, as the presence of Latino police officers increases, so does the percentage of vehicle stops in that division involving Latino drivers. Substantively speaking, the impact is large; a 1% increase in Latino police officers in a division leads to an almost 1% (0.98%) increase in the percentage of Latino drivers involved in vehicle stops for a division in a month.

Three of the control variables are also statistically significant ($p < .01$). However, they offer mixed support for our hypotheses. First, as expected, our regression results show that the percentage of the driving eligible population that is Latino had a

Table 32.3   Regression Estimates for Vehicle Stops Involving Latino Drivers in the San Diego Police Divisions in the Months of 2000

Varible	Unstandardized Coefficient (Panel Corrected SE)
Percentage Latino police officers	0.98 (0.144)***
Latino driving eligible population	0.59 (0.08)***
Unemployment rate	−0.92 (0.40)**
Median income	−0.02 (0.11)
Crime rate	−001 (0.0005)**
Constant	4.59 (6.76)
Rho	0.82
N	96
R^2	.86
F	1607.9***

**p < .05 (significance at better than .05, two-tailed test).
***p <. 01 (significance at better than .01; two-tailed test).

positive and statistically significant effect on the percentage of vehicle stops that involved Latino drivers. A 1% increase in the Latino driving eligible population resulted in an increase in stops by 0.59%. Next, the unemployment rate in the city is negatively related to the dependent variable. We hypothesized that higher unemployment rates would increase the percentage of vehicle stops involving Latino drivers, but this hypothesis is not supported. Instead, it appears that Latino drivers are more likely to be stopped during periods of lower unemployment. Although we have no evidence to support this, we might speculate that this finding is because of an increase in car usage by Latinos during periods of higher employment. Finally, our hypothesis that higher crime rates would lead to more Latino drivers being pulled over was also not supported. Lower crime rates are associated with more stops of Latino drivers. We might speculate that this finding has something to do with police officers having additional time to focus on traffic enforcement; however, we would need to conduct further research to support this proposition. Interestingly, the hypotheses for unemployment rate and the crime rate are derived from research on African Americans and racial profiling; our contrary findings suggest that additional research is necessary to understand the influence of these variables in the Latino context.

Caveats and Conclusions

In this article, we tested the hypothesis that the link between passive and active representation can be hindered by organizational socialization. We posed the following question: Are there conditions under which minority bureaucrats will not provide active representation? We addressed this question in an agency with high levels of formal and informal socialization and the answer appears to be yes. Consistent with our findings examining the presence of Black officers (Wilkins & Williams, 2008), the presence of Latino police officers is related to an increase in racial disparity in the division. Taken together, these findings suggest that the structure and processes of an organization affect the representation provided by the bureaucrats working there. If the socialization is intense enough the bureaucrats

may end up representing the occupational identity above all other identities. Regardless of the race and ethnicity, police officers may end up only representing the blue they wear. This finding raises several important questions, most of which require individual-level data to address.

Considering our finding, it is evident that more systematic individual-level research is necessary to explore the causal relationship behind these findings. With aggregate-level data, it is impossible to know whether Latino police officers, because of high levels of organizational socialization, actually profile Latino drivers, or if the presence of large numbers of Latino officers in a division changes the behavior of the other officers in the organization, resulting in an increase in Latino drivers being stopped. We could also examine how rank and/or tenure in the police department influences traffic stop behavior. By examining the number of years that a police officer has served on the force, we would have a better test of the effect of organizational socialization on officer behavior. Also, what about the impact or effect of partnering? In particular, how does the partnering of two Latino officers, two White officers, or a mixed tandem influence traffic stop behavior? Similarly, what about the effect of stratification? For example, does traffic stop behavior vary when there are Latino officers in senior positions in the department?

The data we use for our analysis have some advantages and disadvantages. First, the high levels of representation of Latino officers in the San Diego Police Department are important to the analysis. At the same time, we admit that the use of data from a border city may raise some concerns. In particular, it is likely that proximity to the border would influence the behavior of Latino officers in the San Diego Police Department and that their behavior would be different from that of Latino police officers in a Midwest city. It would be important to replicate this analysis with data from a nonborder town.

In sum, our findings make several contributions to the theory of representative bureaucracy. Most notably, our findings support our contention that institutional context affects whether passive representation will lead to active representation. Specifically, our results empirically support the hypothesis that organizational socialization can hinder the translation of passive representation into active representation. Further research into the effect of organizational socialization in additional policy areas is needed. Researchers should seek to identify cases where organizational socialization can be treated as an independent variable in the analysis so its direct influence can be ascertained. In addition, we see no reason why organizational socialization would not also affect the translation of passive into active representation for gender as well, although future research is needed to explore this in more detail.

NOTES

1. We realize that the term *Latino* is gendered and is associated with men. We choose to use the term for simplicity. However, it is not our contention that only males from the Latino community experience discriminatory treatment by police officers.

2. It is important to note that our data do not allow us to directly test the effect of organizational socialization. Instead, we are able to test the relationship between key factors and the presence of racial profiling in an organization where socialization is known to be intense. To test the influence of organization socialization directly we would need additional data.

3. Of particular note here is how the theory of representative bureaucracy connects with the underlying assumption for one of the recommendations of the Kerner Commission—the hiring of officers that better reflected and were more representative of the communities they served (i.e., the hiring of more minority officers). It was assumed that same-race police officers would be able to better understand the cultural norms associated with their racial/ethnic communities, act based on this understanding, and in turn, generate an increased community acceptance to improve police-community relations and decrease the likelihood of the recurrence of civil unrest.

4. This project is being conducted by Brian N. Williams at the University of Georgia, with the assistance of Regan Byrd from the University of Denver. Williams and Byrd have been conducting interviews with police executives, beat or patrol officers, members of the Latino community, and members of the social service network that serves the Latino community to explore and uncover the cultural and organizational dynamics that impede the coproduction of public safety and public order in the context of Latino communities.

5. Criminal profiling is defined as a technique that uses the major personality, behavioral and demographic characteristics of offenders for the purposes of analyzing the crimes those offenders have committed.

6. It is interesting to note that at the time of the data collection the Chief of Police of the San Diego Police Department was Chief David Bejarano. Chief Bejarano was the first Latino to serve as police chief since Antonio Gonzales who served as San Diego's top lawman from 1838 to 1845. Chief Bejarano led the department from 1999 to 2003. As chief, he led the efforts to investigate police brutality and racial profiling by the department.

7. Although it is possible that police officers were not completing a form for every stop they made qualitative research collected during focus groups suggest that the vehicle stop forms collected should be representative of all vehicle stops (Cordner, Williams, & Velasco, 2002). The focus group participants did not believe that officers were falsifying information on the stop forms or biasing the data by systematically completing forms for some stops and not others. Rather participants felt that a few officers were never filling out the forms, whereas most officers were completing forms when they had time, but not when they were busy (Cordner et al., 2002).

8. It would be preferable to have a time varying measure for this variable; unfortunately only the annual numbers are available. We took two steps to assess the stability of these numbers over time. First, we compared the percentage of Latino police officers in each division in 2000 with the same numbers for 2005 (the next year that this report was available). We found that these measures were still highly correlated at .87. In addition, we interviewed a data analyst with the San Diego Police Department to discuss transfer policies in the department (C. Haley, San Diego Police Department phone interview with authors, May 17, 2006). The data analyst reported that most transfers occur between service areas of the divisions and not between divisions. Transfers between divisions are considered only on an as-needed basis as the department's and individual division's needs are reevaluated. Both these pieces of information suggest that the percentage of Latino police officers in each division is relatively stable within a given year.

9. Unfortunately, the data are not available to separate the officers by rank so it is not possible to know if the officers are on patrol or in a supervisory position. This would be important to test because researchers (Meier et al., 1989) have found that when minorities gain access to upper levels of an organization, they create an internal environment more conducive to active representation. In addition, Wilkins and Keiser (2006) found that it was female supervisors in child support enforcement agencies, not female caseworkers, who provided active representation.

10. We divide median income by 1,000 to make it easier to interpret the coefficient.

11. Ideally, we would have a measure of the crime rate within each division; unfortunately these data are not available. However, we argue that the crime rate in the city is likely to influence the behavior across divisions. Increased levels of crime anywhere in the city are likely to heighten enforcement.

12. The model was estimated numerous ways with and without panel-corrected standard error, with a random effects model with and without the lagged dependent variable, and with and without the AR1 error process, and the substantive findings remained unchanged. In addition, alternative specifications of the model were tested. We ran the model using the measure for racial profiling commonly used in the criminal justice literature. For this analysis, the dependent variable was the difference between the percentage of stops in the division involving a Latino driver and the percentage of the driving age population in the division that is Latino for each month in 2000 the same set of independent variables were included, except for the driving population variable. This model produces identical substantive findings to the reported model.

13. We also ran an additional model to check the relationship between the representation of Black police officers and Latino traffic stops. In the model, we included the percentage of Black police officers in the division along with the percentage of Latino officers and the control variables. The results for the variables included in the original model do not change. The variable for the percentage of Black police officers in the division is also positive and statistically significant. This means that increasing the representation of Black police officers is also related to an increase in traffic stops of Latino drivers. There are several possible explanations for this finding. Although this finding could suggest that Black officers are more likely to stop Latino drivers; an alternative explanation is that as the presence of minority police officers, both Black and Latino, increases, White officers in the division begin to target Latino drivers. Future research and individual-level data are needed to fully understand this relationship.

14. To check for multicollinearity in the model, we examined the bivariate correlations and the variance inflation factors and no problems were detected.

REFERENCES

Alex, N. (1969). *Black in Black: A study of the Negro policeman.* New York: Appleton-Century-Crofts.

Barak, G., Flavin, J. M. & Leighton, P. S. (2001). *Class, race, gender, and crime: Social realities of justice in America.* Los Angeles: Roxbury.

Beck, N., & Katz, J. N. (1995). What to do (and not to do) with time-series cross-section data. *American Political Science Review, 89,* 634–647.

Beck, N., & Katz, J. N. (1996). Nuisance vs. substance: Specifying and estimating time-series cross-section models. *Political Analysis, 6,* 1–36.

Bennett, R. R. (1984). Becoming blue: A longitudinal study of police recruit occupational socialization. *Journal of Police Science and Administration, 12,* 47–58.

Caplow, T. (1964). *Principles of organization.* New York: Harcourt, Brace & World.

Cashmore, E., & McLaughlin, E. (1991). *Out of order: Policing Black people.* New York: Routledge.

Cayer, N. J., & Sigelman, L. (1980). Minorities and women in state and local government: 1973–1975. *Public Administration Review, 40,* 443–450.

Chambliss, W. (1994). Policing the ghetto underclass: The politics of law and law enforcement. *Social Problems, 41,* 177–195.

Cordner, G., Williams, B., & Velasco, A. (2002). *Vehicle stops in San Diego: 2001.* San Diego, CA: San Diego Police Department.

Cox, S. M., Pease, S. E., Miller D. S., & Tyson, C. B. (2001). *Interim report of traffic stop statistics for the state of Connecticut.* Rocky Hill, CT: Division of Criminal Justice.

Culver, L. (2004). *Adapting police services to new immigration.* New York: LFB Scholarly.

Davis, K. C. (1975). *Police discretion.* St Paul, MN: West.

Dolan, J. (2000). The senior executive service: Gender, attitudes, and representative bureaucracy. *Journal of Public Administration Research and Theory, 10,* 513–530.

Dolan, J. (2002). Representative bureaucracy in the federal executive: Gender and spending priorities. *Journal of Public Administration Research and Theory, 12,* 353–375.

Downs, A. (1967). *Inside bureaucracy.* Prospect Heights, IL: Waveland Press.

Ellison, C., & London, B. (1992). The social and political participation of Black Americans: Compensatory and ethnic community perspectives revisited. *Social Forces, 70,* 681–701.

Fagan, J., & Davies, C. (2000). Street stops and broken windows: Terry, race, and disorder in New York City. *Fordham Urban Law Journal, 28,* 457–504.

Fogelson, R. (1968). From resentment to confrontation: The police, the Negroes, and the outbreak of the nineteen-sixties riots. *Political Science Quarterly, 83,* 217–247.

Gawthrop, L. C. (1969). *Bureaucratic behavior in the executive branch.* New York: Free Press.

Gray, M. (1998). *Drug crazy.* New York: Random House.

Hahn, H. (1971). A profile of urban police. *Law and Contemporary Problems, 36,* 449–466.

Harriott, A. (2004). Presumed criminality, racial profiling, and policing in America—with special reference to the Diallo case. In D. Jones-Brown & K. Terry (Eds.), *Policing and minority communities: Bridging the gap* (pp. 22–35). Upper Saddle River, NJ: Pearson Prentice Hall.

Harris, D. A. (1997). Driving while Black and all other traffic offenses: The Supreme Court and pretextual traffic stops. *Journal of Criminal Law and Criminology, 87,* 544–581.

Harris, D. A. (1999). The stories, the statistics, and the law: Why "driving while Black" matters. *Minnesota Law Review, 84,* 265–326.

Harris, D. A. (2002). *Profiles in injustice: Why racial profiling cannot work.* New York: New Press.

Harrison, S. (1998). Police organizational culture: Using ingrained values to build positive organizational improvement. *Public Administration and Management: An Interactive Journal, 3*(2). http://www.pamij.con/harrison.html

Hindera, J. J. (1993). Representative bureaucracy: Imprimis evidence of active representation in the EEOC District Office. *Social Science Quarterly, 74,* 95–109.

Johnson, K. R. (2001). The case against race profiling in immigration enforcement. *Washington University Law Quarterly, 78,* 675–736.

Keiser, L, Wilkins, V. M., Meier, K. J., & Holland, C. (2002). Lipstick and logarithms: Gender, identity, and representative bureaucracy. *American Political Science Review, 96,* 553–565.

Kellough, J. E. (1990). Integration in the public workplace: Determinants of minority and female employment in federal agencies. *Public Administration Review, 50,* 557–566.

Leinen, S. (1984). *Black police, while society.* New York: New York University Press.

Lipsky, M. (1980). *Street-level bureaucracy: Dilemmas of individual in public services.* New York: Russell Sage Foundation.

Lundman, R. J., & Kaufman, R. L. (2003). Driving while Black: Effects of race, ethnicity, and gender on citizen self-reports of traffic stops and police actions. *Criminology, 41,* 195–220.

Manning, P. K. (1970). Talking and becoming: A view of organizational socialization. In J. D. Douglas (Ed.), *Understanding everyday life* (pp. 239–258). Chicago: Aldine.

Martinez, R. (2002). *Latino homicide: Immigration, violence and community.* New York: Routledge.

Martinez, R. (2007). Incorporating Latinos and immigrants in policing research. *Criminology and Public Policy, 6,* 57–64.

Massey, D. S., & Denton, N. A. (1993). *American apartheid: Segregation and the making of the underclass.* Cambridge, MA: Harvard University Press.

Meier, K. J. (1975). Representative bureaucracy: An empirical analysis. *American Political Science Review, 69,* 526–542.

Meier, K. J. (1993). Latinos and representative bureaucracy: Testing the Thompson and Henderson hypothesis. *Journal of Public Administration Research and Theory, 3,* 393–414.

Meier, K. J., & Nigro, L. G. (1976). Representative bureaucracy and policy preferences: A study in the attitudes of federal executives. *Public Administration Review, 36,* 458–469.

Meier, K. J., & Stewart, J. (1992). Active representations in educational bureaucracies: Policy impacts. *American Review of Public Administration, 22,* 157–171.

Meier, K. J., Stewart, J., Jr., & England, R. (1989). *Race, class and education.* Madison, Wisconsin: University of Wisconsin Press.

Milgram, S. (1974). *Obedience to authority: An experimental view.* New York: HarperCollins.

Mosher, F. (1982). *Democracy and the public service.* New York: Oxford University Press.

Mouw, T. (2003). Social capital and finding a job: Do contacts matter? *American Sociological Review, 68,* 868–897.

Muir, W. K. (1977). *Police: Streetcorner politicians.* Chicago: University of Chicago Press.

Murty, K., Roebuck, J., & Smith, J. (1990). The image of the police in Black Atlanta communities. *Journal of Police Science and Administration, 17,* 250–257.

Naff, C. C., & Crum, J. (2000). The president and representative bureaucracy: Rhetoric and reality. *Public Administration Review, 60,* 98–110.

Newport, F. (1999). *Racial profiling is seen as widespread, particularly among young Black men.* Gallup Poll, December 9, 1999. Northeastern University Racial Profiling Data Collection Resource Center.

Novak, K. (2004). Disparity and racial profiling in traffic enforcement. *Police Quarterly, 7,* 65–96.

Paoline, E. (2003). Taking stock: Toward a richer understanding of police culture. *Journal of Criminal Justice, 31,* 199–214.

Paoline, E., Myers, T., & Worden, R. (2000). Police culture, individualism and community policing: Evidence from two police departments. *Justice Quarterly, 17,* 575–605.

Pitkin, H. (1967). *The concept of representation*. Berkeley: University of California Press.

Radelet, L. (1986). *The police and the community* (4th ed.). New York: Macmillan.

Ramirez, D., McDevitt, J., & Farrell, A. (2000). *A resource guide on racial profiling data collection systems: Promising practices and lessons learned*. Washington, DC: Department of Justice.

Rehfuss, J. (1986). A representative bureaucracy: Women and minority executives in California career service. *Public Administration Review, 45,* 454–460.

Riccucci, N. M., & Saidel, J. R. (1997). The representativeness of state-level bureaucratic leaders: A missing piece of representative bureaucracy puzzle. *Public Administration Review, 57,* 423–430.

Romzek, B. (1990). Employee investment and commitment: The ties that bind. *Public Administration Review, 50,* 374–382.

Rossi, P., Beck, R., & Edison, B.(1974). *The roots of urban discontent*. New York: Wiley

Russell, K. (1998). *The color of crime: Racial hoaxes, While fear, Black protectionism, police harassment and other macroaggressions*. New York: New York University Press.

Saltzstein, G. H. (1989). Black mayors and public policies. *Journal of Politics, 51,* 525–547.

Selden, S. C. (1997). *The promise of the representative bureaucracy: Diversity and responsiveness in a government agency*. Armonk, NY: M. E. Sharpe.

Simon, H. A. (1957). *Administrative behavior* (2nd ed.). New York: Macmillan.

Skolnick, J. (1975). *Justice without trial*. New York: Wiley.

Smith, B. W., & Holmes, M. D. (2003). Community accountability, minority threat and police brutality: An examination of civil rights criminal complaints. *Criminology, 41,* 1035–1058.

Smith, M., & Petrocelli, M. (2001). Racial profiling? A multivariate analysis of police traffic stop data. *Police Quarterly, 4,* 4–27.

Spitzer, E. (1999). *The New York City Police Department's "stop and frisk" practices: A report to the people of the State of New York from the Office of the Attorney General*. Albany: New York Attorney General's Office.

Thompson, F. J. (1976). Minority groups in public bureaucracies: Are passive and active representation linked? *Administration & Society, 8,* 201–226.

Thompson, F. J. (1978). Civil servants and the deprived: Socio-political and occupational explanations of attitudes toward minority hiring. *American Journal of Political Science, 22,* 325–347.

United States v. Brignoni-Ponce, 422 U.S. 873 (1975).

Verna, A. (1997). Construction of offender profile using fuzzy logic. *Policing: An International Journal of Police Strategy and Management, 20,* 408–418.

Vinzant, J. C., & Crothers, L. (1998). *Street-level leadership: Discretion and legitimacy in front-line public service*. Washington, DC: Georgetown Press.

Waddington, P. (1999). Police (canteen) sub-culture: An appreciation. *British Journal of Criminology, 39,* 287–309.

Weber, M. (1946). *From Max Weber: Essays in sociology* (H. H. Gerth & C. Wright Mills, Eds. and Trans.). London: Oxford University Press.

Websdale, N. (2001). *Policing the poor: From slave plantation to public housing*. Boston: Northeastern University Press.

Weitzer, R. (2002). Incidents of police misconduct and public opinion. *Journal of Criminal Justice, 30,* 397–408.

Wilkins, V. M. (2007). Exploring the causal story: Gender, active representation, and bureaucratic priorities. *Journal of Public Administration Research and Theory, 17,* 77–94.

Wilkins, V. M., & Keiser, L. R. (2006). Linking passive and active representation for gender: The case of child support agencies. *Journal of Public Administration Research and Theory, 16,* 87–102.

Wilkins, V. M., & Williams, B. N. (2008). Black or blue: Racial profiling and representative bureaucracy. *Public Administration Review, 68,* 652–662.

Williams, B. N. (1998). *Citizen perspectives on community policing: A case study in Athens*, GA. Albany: State University of New York Press.

Williams, B. N. (1999). Perceptions of children and teenagers on community policing: A case study in Athens, GA: Implications for law enforcement leadership, training, and citizen evaluations. *Police Quarterly, 2,* 150–173.

Williams, B. N. (2000). Racial profiling: The personal costs and societal consequences of driving while Black: Implications for the minority academic community. In L. Jones (ed.), *Brothers of the Academy: Earning Our Way* (pp. 263–274). Herndon. VA: Stylus Publishers.

Williams, H., & Murphy, P. V. (1990). The evolving strategy of policing: A minority view. *Perspectives on Policing, 13,* 1–15.

Wilson, W. J. (1987). *The truly disadvantaged: The inner city, the underclass and public policy*. Chicago: University of Chicago Press.

SOURCE: Wilkins, Vicky M. and Brian N. Williams. 2009. "Representing Blue: Representative Bureaucracy and Racial Profiling in the Latino Community." *Administration & Society, 40*(8): 775 – 98.

33

"THIS PLACE MAKES ME PROUD TO BE A WOMAN"

Theoretical Explanations for Success in Entrepreneurship Education for Low-Income Women

MARY GODWYN

INTRODUCTION

Despite serving women who are socially and economically disadvantaged, and despite being chronically under-funded and short-staffed, Women's Business Centers (WBCs) have been extraordinarily successful in helping women to start businesses (Langowitz, Sharpe, & Godwyn, 2006). The purpose of this research is to determine the social mechanisms manifest in the success of WBCs. Two theories are applied: the macro-theory of middleman minorities (Bonacich, 1980; Butler, 2005a,b) and the microconcept of stereotype threat (Steele, 1997). Using the methodology of grounded theory (Strauss & Corbin, 1998), the two sociological theories being tested were not arbitrarily selected, but were suggested by data gathered in a previous study of WBCs (Langowitz et al., 2006). Applying survey, focus group and interview data, the goal of this research is to discover whether techniques used by WBCs provide the intra-group solidarity emblematic of middleman minorities and whether WBCs successfully neutralize the stereotype threat experienced by many female entrepreneurs.

Male entrepreneurs still outnumber their female counterparts (Minniti & Bygrave, 2004). However, women-owned businesses provide $1.19 trillion in revenues, represent 30% of all businesses in the United States and employ more than 9.8 million workers—women-owned businesses are central to the U.S. economy (http://www.nwbc.gov). In an attempt to boost the number of women entrepreneurs, the Women's Business Center movement, and federal funding of many Women's Business Centers through the Small Business Administration (SBA), emerged in the 1990s. These centers provide training in the form of business classes and one-on-one counseling to women, especially those who are socially and economically disadvantaged. Between 1997 and 2002, women-owned businesses increased at more than 150% the national rate, with about 13% of those businesses owned by women of color (Coughlin, 2002). Women's Business Centers have been part of this growth.

Though the WBC movement has persisted for over a decade, until recently few studies have been conducted to ascertain how many centers exist, client demographics, how successful WBCs are in assisting women in business formation, what pedagogical techniques are used and what challenges these centers face. In 2005, approximately 105 WBCs were identified across the country (Godwyn, Langowitz, & Sharpe, 2005). These centers work with a relatively disadvantaged population of women: 67% have a household income under $50,000, 43% identify as minority women, 49% have no college education, and 6% have less than a high school education. Women's Business Centers also operate on lean budgets as well as with lean organizations. Annual budgets range from a low of $25,000 to a maximum of $3.1 million, with an average budget of approximately $745,000 per year. The centers average five full-time and two part-time employees and service, on average, 1,000 clients annually.

In many ways, WBCs are similar to institutions such as the Grameen Bank. Some of these centers are able to offer their clients micro-credit loans, and like the Grameen Bank, WBCs strongly encourage solidarity among their clients by using a "relationship" orientation. For instance, each center provides their clients networking and support group opportunities that include regular breakfast and lunch meetings as well as large annual expos where members can display goods and services. Some centers even have "slumber parties" for rural clients who live far away. Long-term relationships between clients and staff members are also strongly encouraged; this priority is manifest in staff training, staff accessibility and the policy of numerous follow-up contacts between centers and their clients. Twenty staff members were interviewed for this study and almost half had once been WBC clients themselves. Muhammad Yunus, the founder of the Grameen Bank, recognizes the importance of group membership and solidarity for those who start new ventures:

> We discovered that support groups were crucial to the success of our operations: we required that each applicant join a group of like-minded people living in similar economic and social conditions. Convinced that solidarity would be stronger if the groups came into being by themselves, we refrained from managing them, but we did create incentives that encouraged the borrowers to help one another succeed in their businesses (Yunus, 2003: 62).

Though Women's Business Centers serve a disadvantaged population and are under-funded and short-staffed, they are astonishingly successful in their mission: Women's Business Center clients are almost four times more likely to start a business than women in the general population. Compared to the overall rate of entrepreneurship among U.S. women of 8.2%, the average center reported that more than 60% of their clients were managing a start-up business, and 34% of those entrepreneurs were managing a start-up that was more than 3 years old (Langowitz et al., 2006). Theories from the sociology of entrepreneurship and from social psychology can help explain why WBCs are so successful. With the goal of identifying the social mechanisms that WBCs use to turn a relatively disadvantaged population of women into entrepreneurs, two theoretical frameworks, the macro-level theory of middleman minorities (Bonacich, 1980; Butler, 2005a,b) and the micro-level framework of stereotype threat (Steele, 1997) will be explored to determine if the success of Women's Business Centers can be attributed to the creation of gender solidarity and identity safety for women clients.

Middleman Minorities and Strangers

The sociology of entrepreneurship examines the relationship between group characteristics and the initiation of business activity. By creating economic stability for a given population and establishing a place in the social and economic power structure, entrepreneurial enterprises directly contribute to group assimilation (Butler, 2005a,b). This field of sociology is an outgrowth of the sociology of race and ethnicity as these two factors were once perceived to be the salient group characteristics around which processes such as assimilation, colonialism, discrimination, racism and prejudice could be measured (Butler, 2005a,b).

Race and ethnicity, however, are not the only characteristics that have been used historically by sociologists to define groups. Classical sociological texts such as Emile Durkheim's *Elemental Forms of Religious Life* and Max Weber's *Protestant Ethic and the Spirit of Capitalism* use religion as one of the salient group characteristics around which to organize analyses—Weber specifically analyzed entrepreneurial activity and economic development based on religious affiliation. In addition to race, ethnicity and religion, gender has increasingly come to be perceived as an important aspect of identity. Until the 1970s, gender was largely ignored in social science research (Kimmel, 2004: 5), and perhaps because "money savvy is connected with masculinity in our culture" (Kimmel, 2004: 12), theoretical constructions in the sociology of entrepreneurship had routinely assumed a male business owner.

There have been recent efforts to extend sociological research to include gender as a salient group characteristic in its relationship to entrepreneurial activity (Brush, Carter, Gatewood, Greene, & Hart, 2004; Butler, 2005a,b: Coughlin, 2002; Langowitz & Morgan, 2003). John Butler writes, "The inquiry remains the same while the groups change" (2005a: 4). Edna Bonacich's theory of "middleman" minorities (1980) and John Sibley Butler's related concept of "Strangers" (2005b) might help explain the success of WBCs. Butler uses George Simmel's term "Strangers" to describe those groups that have restricted access to the social, political and economic opportunity structure (2005b). As a strategy to counteract discrimination, Strangers have initiated entrepreneurial enterprises (Bonacich, 1980; Butler, 2005a,b; Greene & Johnson, 1995: 65). These businesses tend to be family-owned and concentrate on trade, commerce and the circulation of goods and services (Butler, 2005a: 14). Because feminine characteristics are not as likely to be associated with the workplace as are masculine qualities (Valian, 1998: 125) and because women often move between domestic and workplace obligations, they are also Strangers. In addition, until recently, women have largely been subsumed into the same class category as their husbands or families of origin, while also having less ability than their male counterparts to generate independent capital (Baxter, 1994; Davis & Robinson, 1988).

In Bonacich's theory, those minority entrepreneurs, hereafter referred to as middle-group rather than middleman minorities, exhibit three characteristics: they are victims of discrimination; they are concentrated in service industry business; and they have strong intra-group solidarity (Bonacich, 1980; Greene & Johnson, 1995). This population tends to cluster in niche areas of commerce between the elites and the subordinates such as in small businesses that focus on petty finance, craftwork and marginalized service industries (Bonacich, 1980). Women are minorities not only because they have had to endure societal discrimination, but also, when compared to their male counterparts across all races, women make up a minority of business owners (Butler, 2005a,b). Further, like middle-group ethnic minorities, women tend to own small, service-oriented businesses (Sykes, 2008). WBC clients are most interested in training and education focused on the service industry, especially retail sales, food service and childcare (Langowitz et al., 2006).

Members of middle-group minorities are also characterized by their tendency to "take care of their own" and maintain a high level of group solidarity (Bonacich, 1980; Butler, 2005a,b: 16; Greene & Johnson, 1995). This intra-group solidarity is most often kept in place by mechanisms of private language, religious affiliation and attendant rituals, urban concentration, social organizations and other specific memberships and practices that serve to reinforce "relative solidarity within the group and [social separation] from the surrounding society" (Butler, 2005a,b). However, women are neither minorities nor Strangers insofar as they sometimes have majority status in race, ethnicity and class. Therefore, unlike the case of ethnic middle-group minority entrepreneurs, intra-group solidarity for women business owners has not been easily established, nor have the mechanisms of solidarity been clarified.

Greene and Johnson theorize that women entrepreneurs, unlike other minority groups, draw support from their family and friends, in other words, "people who are not [necessarily] exclusively members of the minority group defined as females" (1995: 67). However, many WBC directors cited instances where women's families actively discouraged them from starting businesses because the role of entrepreneur conflicted with women's caretaking role (Langowitz et al., 2006). Women in more traditional cultures were especially affected; center directors specifically mentioned Iranian, Hispanic, rural Caucasian Americans and Taiwanese women. WBC directors noted that disproportionate domestic and family obligations were both motivations for and obstacles to women starting businesses. As will be described later, this finding was replicated in interviews with clients. The mechanisms that create intra-group solidarity among women entrepreneurs therefore remain unclear. One hypothesis explored in this research is whether intra-group solidarity can be gender-based rather than familial.

Stereotype Threat

Claude Steele's micro-level social psychological theory suggests organizations that have successfully addressed "stereotype threat" can negate the self-doubt resulting from "situational pressure" that often plagues individuals who have been subject to discrimination (Steele, 1997: 620). Stereotype threat is the threat of being viewed as incompetent in some area, such as standardized test-taking, because of race, gender or other group characteristic, and then the fear of acting in a way that confirms that incompetence. "It is the social-psychological threat that arises when one is in a situation or doing something for which a negative stereotype about one's group applies" (Steele, 1997: 614). Moreover, Steele found that only those who identify with the domain enough to experience this threat will have their performance undermined by the pressure and anxiety caused by the stereotype.

Steele was able to demonstrate that the long-standing discrepancy in SAT scores between African-American students and white students could be mitigated by introducing the test to African-American students as academically insignificant. Similarly, women performed worse than men on standardized math tests when they were told that the test reproduced gender differences, but equal to men when the test was introduced as being without gender bias (Steele, 1997: 619–620). Steele chose subjects who identified with the domain in question; for instance, women were selected because they were very good at math (entering test scores in the top 15% of the Michigan student population) and reported being confident about their math aptitude (Steele, 2003: 117). Additionally, Steele found that the performances of students who do not identify with the domain are not affected by stereotype threat, "[We] had selected Black students who identified with verbal skills and women who identified with math. But when we tested participants who identified less with these domains . . . none of them showed any effect of stereotype threat whatsoever" (Steele, 2003: 120).

The concept of stereotype threat is so powerful because it demonstrates that enduring, socially embedded problems of racism and sexism do not have to be solved in order to create environments where the negative effect of stereotypes is dramatically diminished. Nor must individuals engage in extensive therapy in order to exorcise self-loathing and the internalization of social stigma. Steele has demonstrated that performance can be manipulated by techniques that are readily available and easily replicated. He shows that though societal stereotypes change slowly, niches that neutralize stereotype threat can be created almost instantly (Steele, 2003: 130). Stereotype threat is situational and social rather than individual and internal; therefore, it can be immediately changed by changing the environment. Steele writes:

> Thus, the gender-difference conditions (the normal condition under which people take these tests) could not have impaired their performance by triggering some greater internalized anxiety acquired, for example, through prior socialization. Rather, this condition had its effect through situational pressure. It set up an interpretive frame such that any performance frustration signaled the possible gender-based ability limitation alleged in the stereotype. For these women, this signal challenged their belongingness in a domain they cared about and, as a possibly newly met limit to their ability, could not be disproven by their prior achievements, thus its interfering threat (1997: 620).

What Steele does not explain in detail is what happens when he introduces standardized tests in a way that does not elicit the stereotype. What is the mechanism that neutralizes the stereotype threat—that creates alternative "interpretive frames," and allows participants to perform to their actual capacity? One explanation tested here is that the stereotype defines the participant as deviant in the domain—in the case of Steele's experiments; the stereotype defines African Americans as deviant, and thus inferior, test takers when compared to their Caucasian counterparts. Similarly, women are considered substandard, or deviant, in the domain of standardized math tests when compared to males. The negative association between women and math extends to women's perceived incompetence with numbers generally, is often used to deny women's skills in a host of business disciplines such as accounting and finance, as well as to claim that women are not skilled money managers.

Stereotypes such as "women are poor at math" subvert what Steele refers to as women's "belongingness in a domain" (1997: 620). Merely introducing the math test as one without gender bias has the effect of neutralizing the stereotype because it changes the interpretive framework, the social context, in which women perceive themselves and other women. The change can be described as women shifting identification from belonging to a group of people who are deviant and incompetent with regard to the task at hand or the role in question, to identifying as a member of a group that is recognized as nonnative and competent within a given social context. This phenomenon of identifying with the normative, dominant group is what Steele calls "identity safety" (2003), and is the opposite of stereotype threat. For those invested in a domain, Steele can successfully create an environment of identity safety and override stereotype threat simply by reframing the skill as one neutrally or positively associated with the gender and race identities of the participants. The skill itself is less important than whether the participant identifies with the domain and accepts the authority of the social context. This is also evident in Ruth Milkman's research on the shift in gender demographics of factory workers in the United States during World War II. Milkman writes, "Idioms of sex-typing can be flexibly applied to whatever jobs women and men happen to be doing" (1987: 50).

Identity safety is also illustrated in William Whyte's account of his context-specific bowling performance. In his famous ethnography, *Street Corner Society*, Whyte recounts that his bowling performance varied directly to his relationship with the high-status members of the Norton group. To Whyte's surprise, when he was associated with the leadership of the Norton group, his bowling ability was commensurate with his place in the social hierarchy. Identity safety is experienced subjectively and individually within a social context; it is a product of what Whyte refers to as "the relationship between individual performance and group structure" ([1943] 1981: 319):

> " . . . as a close friend of Doc, Danny, and Mike, I held a position close to the top of the gang and therefore should be expected to excel on this great occasion. I simply felt myself buoyed up by the situation. I felt my friends were for me, had confidence in me . . . I felt supremely confident that I was going to hit the pins that I was aiming at. I have never felt quite that way before—or since. Here at the bowling alley I was experiencing subjectively the impact of the group structure upon the individual. It was a strange feeling, as if something larger than myself was controlling the ball as I went through my swing and released it toward the pins" ([1943] 1981: 319).

If identity safety is the feeling of supreme confidence that comes from being associated with those of high social status, then stereotype threat is the fear and anxiety of acting in such a way that confirms that low social status is justified. In either case, performance can be profoundly affected. Like the female test takers in Steele's experiments, women entrepreneurs experience stereotype threat, and it affects their success. Porter and Geis (1981) found that sex-role stereotypes trump situational cues when determining leadership. Specifically, they found that when undergraduate students were shown slides of business people seated around a table in same-sex groups, groups of only men or only women, the person seated at the head of the table was consistently chosen as the leader. However, in mixed-sex groups, groups of women and men, even when women were seated at the head of the table, they were not consistently seen as the leader. Women are less likely to be granted the deference that situational indicators such as clothing and positioning provide for men.

Eagly and Johannesen-Schmidt found that women have a more negative self-assessment of their leadership skills than do men because women are faced with greater role incongruity in leadership positions (2001). Women are consistently rated lower than men on many of the characteristics seen as typical for successful managers; even women who are described as *successful* managers are seen as having less leadership ability than successful managers who are male (Heilman, Block, Martell, & Simon, 1989). The negative effect of stereotype threat on women's entrepreneurial performance, though not as quantifiable as standardized test scores, is evident. According to the Global Entrepreneurship Monitor, a "strong positive and significant correlation exists between a women's belief of having the knowledge, skills and experience required to start a new business and her likelihood of starting one . . . and a strong, negative and significant correlation exists between fear of failure and a women's likelihood of starting a new business" (Minniti, Arenius, & Langowitz, 2005). However, in the female-oriented environment of WBCs, women's perceptions of themselves, and therefore their response to stereotype threat is very different from the larger cultural environment.

Michael Kimmel asserts that even in institutions labeled gender-neutral, male characteristics and male needs are prioritized in ways that reflect the male-dominated cultural bias of our society: this bias often remains unrecognized (2004: 101). Interviews with WBC clients and directors indicate that a significant population of women served by WBCs have not been able to complete training or to successfully network at various gender-neutral organizations such as Service Corps of Retired Executives (SCORE), the Small Business Development Centers (SBDCs) and local Chambers of Commerce.[1] Perhaps WBCs have changed the social frame of reference and thus created the heretofore-elusive intra-group solidarity for women entrepreneurs. This sense of solidarity cultivated in an environment where women entrepreneurs are perceived as normative and competent might explain the high rate of entrepreneurship in WBC clients.

METHODS AND DATA

In order to understand the social mechanisms involved in the success of Women's Business Centers, I visited four centers: Montpelier, Vermont;

Springfield, Virginia, Ft. Worth, Texas and Medford, Oregon. I also conducted phone interviews with staff members from the Albuquerque, New Mexico Women's Business Center, and collected surveys from clients there. The centers were selected to provide geographic and ethnic diversity, as well as a combination of established and new centers, and centers that serve rural and urban populations of women. During visits to WBCs, I attended networking groups, business classes, staff meetings and observed a one-on-one counseling session between a staff member and a client. Focus groups were conducted with 26 WBC clients from the Springfield, Virginia and Dallas/Ft. Worth, Texas centers. (See Appendix A for interview questions.) Clients from the focus groups were gathered from volunteers who were attending classes and networking events at the centers. The hypothesis associated with middle-group minority theory is that WBCs provide an interactive space wherein women from various races, ethnicities, class and religious backgrounds identify with each *other primarily on the basis of gender.* Because gender is such a liability for women in business, Women's Business Centers might create a space where women are seen and see themselves as normative and typical entrepreneurs rather than as deviant and unusual.

To establish inter-judge agreement, 38 independent coders were given illustrative exemplar statements from unrelated interviews (see Appendix B). I selected five separate illustrative statements to demonstrate gender, race, religious, class and ethnic identification/solidarity. These illustrative exemplars were evaluated by a panel of independent scholars. These scholars agreed that the illustrative exemplars adequately represented the solidarities being examined. Using a five point scale where 0 = no solidarity and 4 = very strong solidarity, coders were asked for their impression of the solidarities demonstrated in the narratives of the WBC focus groups. Coders were not aware of the theories being tested.

Additionally, 44 WBC clients and 44 undergraduate business students responded to an imaged-based survey. Stereotype threat toward women entrepreneurs is not as easy to quantify as scores on standardized tests; however, the survey provides evidence about whether clients at WBCs are more likely to view women as being in positions of authority and leadership in the workplace than are undergraduate business students. Both WBC clients and undergraduate business students are invested in the domain of business; therefore, according to Steele's theory, both groups should be aware of and vulnerable to stereotype threat. Using Porter and Geis's model, WBC clients and undergraduate business students were shown eight images of men and women of various races and ages, dressed in typical business attire and working in an office setting (see Appendix C for examples of the images). To test perceptions of leadership, respondents were asked to look at the images and answer two questions: 1. "Who is in charge?" and 2. "How do you know?" All respondents were also invited to write comments or reactions they had to the survey images.

The stereotype and common perception is that men are business leaders and women are not (Eagly & Johannesen-Schmidt, 2001; Heilman et al., 1989; Kimmel, 2004; Porter & Geis, 1981; Valian, 1998). In other words, businessmen are perceived as normative and typical and businesswomen are perceived as deviants, minorities, and Strangers—especially in leadership positions. The hypothesis being tested in regard to the theory of stereotype threat was that undergraduate business students and WBC clients would respond differently to the images in the survey. The expectation was that business students would respond as they had in Porter and Geis's experiment and identify men as being leaders in business situations more often than women. If the environment at Women's Business Centers creates the perception that women are normative in business leadership positions, then WBC clients would perceive women as being leaders as often or more often than men.

RESULTS

Interview and Focus Group Data

In focus groups and interviews, clients consistently referenced solidarity created around gender identification. Class was also referenced or alluded to insofar as many of the women had low incomes and lack of money was commonly a topic of conversation. Race, religion and sexual orientation were rarely mentioned. When race was mentioned, it was most often used as a category to describe outsiders, specifically "white men." One representative statement came from a client in Ft. Worth:

> I went to SCORE one time and that guy is so old! But, unfortunately they are old white guys from corporate America who don't think women can do anything but have kids. One told me I should just keep cleaning houses.

Though there are many white women staff members as well as many white women clients, throughout the interviews, their race was rarely mentioned either by women of color or by other white women. In the culture of WBCs, regardless of race or class, gender status seemed to define all women as minorities—people who are subject to prejudice and discrimination in business settings in the larger society. This is consistent with Hacker's claim that women are minorities (1951) and with Butler (2005a,b) and Greene and Johnson (1995) that women are Strangers. When race was mentioned, it was often used to demonstrate that all women were embraced regardless of race:

> It is hard to have trust when you are in the Spanish community. But, now I tell people to come [to WBCs]. If they come, they don't leave.

> Counseling support for us minorities is amazing. They just keep going and going. Once you come here they keep you excited. It is like a good family—they never kick you out.

Many of the clients spoke of an emotional connection to their Women's Business Center as a place they have turned to for help in times of crisis. One client volunteered this interpretation:

> We genuinely care about each other. It is a whole continuum of care—not just business. When Daisy's[3] husband got diagnosed with cancer, everyone was so supportive.

Others said:

> I feel like a member of this family. After going to the Community Service Center, I really felt lost. Here they were like, 'What can we do for you? How can we help?'

I was like what? Is this for real? I felt really happy and lucky.

There is unconditional loving support here.

It is easy for everyone to get in because the open arms are so huge.

Clients also described how they met and forged bonds with other clients and with staff. They describe a sense of safety and acceptance as they contrast WBCs with other organizations and "women's" style of interaction with "men's" style:

[My friend] calls me and says, 'You missed a [WBC networking] breakfast! Why weren't you there!' No one calls me if I miss a Chamber [of Commerce] event.

They tell you right away this is a cooperative place not a competitive place. Men compete; women share. We network differently; men ask you for money and women ask you what they can do to help you.

One man came [to a networking lunch] two months in a row. It puts it on a different level. We put on a mask like 'I'm a professional.' The whole table stopped being emotional and personal. Women on the corporate side have had to take on a man's role. I don't think you have to play a particular role when you come to this.

Everyone is just themselves. You can feel comfortable here. Not embarrassed about anything. Free to learn.

When I talk to good ol' boys I'm different than when I talk here. I am not trying to put on a face, but my cadence changes as I'm interacting with them. They'll never be a level playing field, but at least we're getting into the game.

This place makes me proud to be a woman.

Unlike data from Greene and Johnson (1995: 67), few WBC clients mentioned their families as being either supportive or non-supportive of their business ventures—the exception was when women were in business with a family member—most often a husband or sister. The few times family members (outside of business partners) were mentioned, they were most often viewed as undermining and unsupportive. Here are some representative comments:

My family didn't believe in me. They had no entrepreneurial experience. I didn't get the feeling of support until I came here.

Nobody 1 knew on a personal level was supportive. Everybody laughed at me. The only support I got was from here.

Many friends and family have no concept of what you do.

For months I tried to sell the idea to friends and family, and myself. But they were silent. When the WBC people heard and said, 'You're fine,' then I had confidence. When my family saw my work, they said, 'We had no idea you were that good.'

The results of the solidarity analysis based on scoring of the focus group interviews were striking. Gender solidarity dwarfed all other solidarities combined.

Table 33.1 presents descriptive statistics on the ratings of solidarity across the five focus group participant characteristics. The ratings ranged from a mean of 0.16 for solidarity based on religion (representing very slight solidarity) to a mean of 3.84 for solidarity based on gender (representing very strong solidarity). The ratings for solidarity based on the other three participant characteristics fell in between these extremes: race (0.49 = very slight solidarity), ethnicity (0.98 = slight solidarity), and class (1.91 = moderate solidarity). This pattern was similar for both the Virginia and Texas focus groups.

Table 33.2 presents the results of a multivariate ANOVA across the five solidarity ratings, which explored (1) differences among raters' judgments of solidarity across the five focus group participant characteristics and (2) differences between the solidarity ratings for the Virginia and Texas focus groups.

The between-subject analyses showed no main effect for focus group. The univariate results, however, showed that the Texas focus group was rated significantly higher in solidarity based on religion (F = 7.61, p = .0073) and gender (F = 7.28, p = .0086), whereas the Virginia focus group was rated higher in solidarity based on ethnicity (F = 3.34, p = .0717)

Table 33.1   Means and standard deviations for ratings of solidarity based on five focus group participant characteristics.

Focus group participant characteristics	M	s.d.	Virginia focus group		Texas focus group	
			M	s.d.	M	s.d.
Race	0.49	0.68	0.50	0.69	0.47	0.68
Class	1.91	1.07	2.11	0.89	1.71	1.21
Ethnicity	0.98	0.99	1.18	1.01	0.78	0.94
Religion	0.16	0.43	0.03	0.16	0.29	0.57
Gender	3.84	0.46	3.70	0.61	3.97	0.16

Table 33.2   Multivariate analysis of variance on ratings of solidarity in two focus groups across five focus group participant characteristics, with contrasts between participant characteristics.

Focus group participant characteristics	Focus Groups		Contrasts
	F	F	F
Univariate results			
Race	0.03		
Class	2.63[+]		
Ethnicity	3.34[-]		
Religion	7.61**		
Gender	7.28**		
Between-subjects effects	0.43		
Within-subjects effects			
Solidarity ratings		893.36*	
Contrasts			
Gender vs. race			1546.88***
Gender vs. class			257.05***
Gender vs. ethnicity			595.35***
Gender vs. religion			2886.84***
Solidarity x sample		3.83**	

$^{+}p < .15.$ $^{-}p < .10.$ $^{**}p < .01.$ $^{***}p < .001.$

and class ($F = 2.63$, $p = .1093$), with the latter differences approaching statistical significance. This pattern of focus group differences in solidarity ratings was reflected in the within-subject effects by the statistically significant solidarity by focus group interaction ($F = 3.83$, $p = .0071$). The within-subjects effects also included a very large main effect for solidarity ratings ($F = 893.36$, $p < .0001$), indicating that there are large differences in solidarity ratings across the five focus group participant characteristics. Contrasts between the participant characteristic ratings show that solidarity was rated significantly higher for gender than for each of the other four participant characteristics, as detailed in Table 33.2.

Many WBC clients have forged ties around their gender identification; it appears that WBC networking events, mentorship, classes and counseling create a forum for intra-group solidarity for women entrepreneurs. The interview and focus group data presented here are consistent with the survey data gathered from WBC directors (Godwyn et al., 2005) and suggest that WBCs have, in Steele's words, affirmed women's "belongingness" to the business domain with which they identify as entrepreneurs.

Survey Data

The survey distributed to 44 WBC clients asked the respondents to state their gender, the racial background with which they identify [Steele notes that asking respondents to provide race and gender information can sensitize them to stereotype threat (1997)] and the number of years they have been associated with the Women's Business Center. Next, respondents viewed eight images of groups of men and women of various races (Caucasian, Hispanic, Asian and African American) in workplace settings. Respondents were asked to identify who was in charge and how they knew. The surveys tested the respondents' ideas and assumptions about how people are valued in society and in the workplace, and how authority is distributed along the lines of gender. This survey continues a tradition of research scholarship testing perceptions linking gender and leadership qualities, employability and competence (Eagly & Johannesen-Schmidt, 2001; Heilman et al., 1989; Miller, Taylor, & Buck, 1991; Minniti ct al., 2005; Porter & Geis, 1981; Valian, 1998: 110–114, 125–134). The surveys were also distributed to 44 undergraduate business students.

Of the 44 undergraduate business students to complete the survey, 23 were women and 21 were men. Like WBC clients, undergraduate business students are invested in being successful in the business domain. Eleven female students identified as Caucasian/White, one as Turkish, five as Latina/Hispanic, three as Indian, one as Asian, one as Pakistani and one had no racial identification. Ten of the male students identified as Caucasian/White, five as Latino/Hispanic, four as Indian, one as Asian, and one had no racial identification.

In the eight images asking who was in charge, undergraduate business students interpreted men as being leaders more often than women (see Figure 33.1). Of 352 student responses, 158 perceived men as in charge, 132 perceived women in charge, and 62 times neither men nor women were identified as being in charge. Of 168 male responses, men perceived other men in charge 75 times, women in charge 61 times and were unsure who was in charge 32 times (see Figure 33.2). Female students also guessed that men were in charge more often than women were. Of 184 female student responses, women perceived men in charge 81 times, women in charge 71 times and they were unsure who was in charge 32 times (see Figure 33.3).

Of the 44 WBC respondents (41 women and 3 men), 29% identified as minorities, 16 were

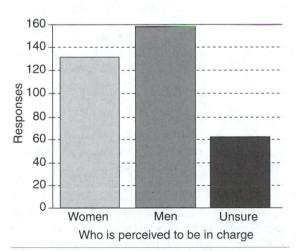

Figure 33.1   Undergraduate Business Students' Perception of Gender Authority in a Business Setting

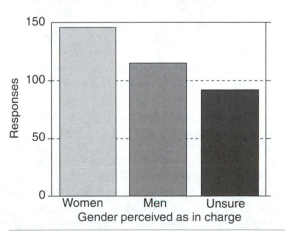

Figure 33.2   Women's Business Center Clients' Perception of Gender Authority in a Business Setting

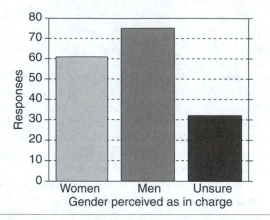

Figure 33.3 Male Undergraduate Business Students' Perception of Gender Authority in a Business Setting

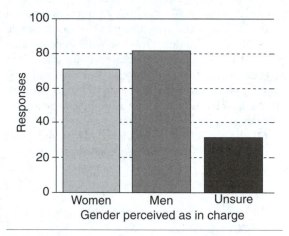

Figure 33.4 Female Undergraduate Business Students' Perception of Gender Authority in a Business Setting

staff members and 9 had been clients for more than 1 year. However, only 34% of WBC respondents answered the question about how long they had been associated with the WBC. Additionally, as mentioned earlier, a high percentage of staff members have also been WBC clients. Unlike the business students, when asked to interpret who held authority in a group of business people, WBC respondents interpreted women as being in charge more often than men. Out of 352 responses, WBC clients perceived women in charge 146 times, men

Table 33.3 Chi-square Women's Business Center clients' versus business students' perception of women or men in charge (excluding ambiguous responses).

	Men in charge	Women in charge	Total
WBC clients	115	146	261
Students	158	132	290
Total	273	278	551

Degrees of freedom: 1. Fisher's exact test, the two-tailed p-value = 0.0l69. Chi-square with Yates correction = 5.559; the two-tailed $p = 0.0184$. The distribution is statistically significant.

in charge 115 times and were unsure 92 times (see Figure 34.4). This interpretation is remarkable not only because it is in sharp contrast to that of the more educated undergraduate business students tested here, but because it is a singular finding. In all other survey data testing perceptions about the relationship between gender and workplace authority, employability and competence conducted over the last 30 years, no other population has perceived women as being in charge more than men (see Valian 125–131 for literature review).

Duplicating results from all previous studies of leadership in business situations, undergraduate business students were more likely to identify men as being in charge, and they were more certain about who was in charge (not sure 18% of the time). By contrast, WBC clients and staff were more likely to see women as holding authority in business situations, and they were also more likely to interpret the image as ambiguous (not sure 27% of the time) (see Table 33.3).

DISCUSSION

Among the limitations of this study is the small sample size of the participants. Further study on stereotype threat and gender-based intra-group solidarity using a larger sample size as well as testing for the impact of both race and gender in workplace authority would be very useful in determining the wider applicability of the findings in this study. The interdependence of race and gender could be determined with images that systematically present various race/gender combinations to determine the significance of such combinations on who is perceived to be in charge.

Another limitation of the study is that there is no precise way to measure the impact of intra-group solidarity and stereotype threat on entrepreneurial success. However, WBC clients are nearly four times as likely to open businesses than the general population of women in the U.S., and this study demonstrates that Women's Business Center clients are also more likely to interpret women as being authorities in workplace images than are undergraduate business students. This is especially surprising because undergraduate business students are younger and are, on average, more educated than WBC clients. Undergraduates also have less actual work experience. As students rather than workers, they might get much of their understanding of the value, status and authority that women possess from media representations rather than from real-life business experience. Media representations often depict sexism and racism as remnants of the past (Coontz, 1992; Dow, 1996). Moreover, young college-educated women who study business are presumably optimistic that their chances of establishing and maintaining leadership positions are similar to their male counterparts' chances.

But does the experience at Women's Business Centers *cause* women to view other women as having authority—or were WBC clients inclined to see women as business leaders before coming to the centers? Based on the data from this study, the latter seems unlikely: WBC directors consistently report that many clients are initially not at all confident of their ability to succeed. In fact, they are often too intimidated to pursue business training in mixed-sex classes and therefore seek out Women's Business Centers. Before becoming WBC clients, many women had also experienced rejection from lending institutions and had been discouraged by family and friends. Directors describe a situation where women are drawn to WBCs not because they are confident of their own and other women's leadership ability and business acumen, but because they feel unprepared and unsupported sitting in business classes next to men. In the interviews I conducted, WBC clients talked openly about their lack of confidence, and they were acutely aware of negative social stereotypes that give rise to common beliefs such as "women

don't have a head for business" and "women can't handle money." When WBC clients described their experiences in mixed-sex classes, their presumption was that men, by virtue of their gender, though often race and class were conflated with gender—"white-college-men"—had advantages over them. Here are some representative quotes:

> I didn't like sitting next to some white man whose Daddy had given him a wad of money to start something. I felt like a nobody who knew nothing.

> They just didn't take me seriously and half the time I didn't even know what they were talking about.

> The class wasn't set up for people like me.

CONCLUSION

One male director of an SBDC said this about Women's Business Centers:

> WBCs were started because of blatant discrimination against women. But, I don't think that's true in 2005. You see as many women loan officers as men. So, over the last ten years things have changed a lot. I just think the landscape has changed so that we don't need Women's Business Centers anymore.

Though his is a conventional response to gender discrimination, the data here strongly counter that conclusion. Race and/or gender-specific programs that attempt to help populations disadvantaged by stereotype threat have always been controversial (Clayton & Crosby, 1992). The prevailing view is that discrimination no longer exists so programs tailored to minority groups are anachronistic. However, by undermining women's confidence that they can be successful business leaders, stereotype threat continues to have direct economic consequences (Langowitz & Minniti, 2005).

Women's Business Centers fit Claude Steele's model: committing to a female-centered culture. WBCs allow women to have identity safety (Steele, 2003) through optimistic teacher-student relationships, affirmation of domain belongingness, valuation of multiple perspectives and the provision of role models and self-efficacy (1997). However, as previous research has demonstrated, WBCs, like many federally supported gender and/or race specific organizations, are in jeopardy because of cuts in funding (Langowitz et al., 2006). Despite the tremendous contribution women's businesses make to the overall economy and the high success rate of Women Business Center clients, WBCs remain largely under-funded, under-staffed and, as evidenced by the above comment of the SBDC director, under-appreciated. One WBC client commented:

> There is a huge disconnect. WBCs are so under-funded. These women [staff members] are wearing two or three hats. Think of how much better it could be if there were more [staff members] or if [staff members] could work full-time. Because it is a women's thing, they are being held to the standard of super-women. They are supposed to be able to do everything on few resources.

A WBC director commented:

> What's not fair is SBDC gets some amount of money that they can count on and they have fewer numbers [of clients], less counseling and we have better numbers [of clients] and have to do fundraising. SBDC doesn't put on expos; they don't have networking. They run classes on a budget. I could do that with my eyes shut.

WBCs are a very valuable tool for launching women-owned businesses among populations of socially and economically disadvantaged women. This research suggests that Women's Business Centers neutralize the stereotypes that women entrepreneurs face and provide an environment that fosters intra-group solidarity and defines women as normative business leaders. The women at WBCs display gender solidarity in much greater proportion than solidarity around race, class, ethnicity or religion. WBC clients are therefore more likely to perceive other women as business leaders than are college students trained in the nominally gender-neutral setting of undergraduate business classes.

Continued federal support of current programming in SBDCs and SCORE, ostensibly gender-neutral organizations, may inadvertently undermine women's ability to start businesses. Similarly, the typical business school curriculum that includes teaching cases focused primarily on white, male business owners reinforces stereotypical assumptions regarding the race and gender of entrepreneurs. John Ogbor writes that the "concept of entrepreneurship is discriminatory, gender-biased, ethnocentrically determined and ideologically controlled, sustaining not only prevailing societal biases, but serving as a tapestry for unexamined and contradictory assumptions and knowledge about the reality of entrepreneurs" (2000: 605). Bonacich and Butler's work frames entrepreneurship as a path to economic solvency for marginalized populations, but clearly entrepreneurship education can either advance or thwart the emancipatory or "self-help" (Butler, 2005a,b) potential of entrepreneurship. The strategies used in WBCs are consistent with Steele's model for creating identity safety and belongingness in a domain. Further research is needed to determine whether strategies that cultivate intra-group gender solidarity at WBCs can be applied to women in a range of domains and can therefore affect outcomes in areas where women are both invested and suffer from stereotype threat.

APPENDIX A

Focus Group/Interview Questions for WBC Clients

What has your experience been like at WBCs?

What do you need from the centers?

What are your concerns?

What is your favorite story?

APPENDIX B

Illustrative Examples of Identification and Solidarity: Race, Class, Ethnicity, Religion and Gender

Race

"The Southern Whites dislike more and more the educated colored man. They hate the intelligent colored man who is accumulating something. The respectable, intelligent colored people are 'carefully un-known'; their good traits and virtues are never mentioned. On the other hand, the ignorant and vicious are carefully known and all of their traits cried aloud" (Holt [1906] 2000: 223–4).

"To the white man these old people may not seem important, but to us young Indians they are very important. The family tie is strong among Indians. White people are aggravated because so many young Indians, after their schooling, go back to their reservations and are soon seen dressed and living just like others. But they must do that if they desire to keep touch with the others" (Holt [1906] 2000: 137).

Class Identification and Solidarity

"By the most frugal living and strict economy we saved enough to buy for a home a house of four rooms, which has since been increased to eight. Since our marriage we have bought and paid for two other places, which we rent . . . I would be contented and happy if I, an American citizen, could say, 'There are no aristocrats to push us down and that we are not worthy because our fathers were poor'" (Holt [1906] 2000: 220).

"There were officers there, too, but they never noticed me. They belong to the high families, and go about the streets with their noses up in the air and their moustaches waxed up, trying to look like the Emperor" (Holt [1906] 2000: 81).

Ethnicity/Culture/Nationality Identification and Solidarity

"There is no country like France and no city like Paris" (Holt [1906] 2000: 67).

"All the world knows that we French have the true artistic taste and we show it most in our dress. The Germans or the English cannot make dresses or hats, and even when we make it for them they cannot wear the clothes properly. There is something wrong somewhere, probably with the color scheme. Those other people do not understand, they cannot comprehend, it is impossible to convey to them the conception of true harmony. It is like trying to teach the blind about light. They lack the soul of the artist, and so their

dresses are shocking, hideous discords of form and color. When I see them I simply want to scream" (Holt [1906] 2000: 71).

"Like all Greeks, we were naturally inclined to temperance. There was no gluttony and no drunkenness, although we had plenty of good strong wine. All loved our king and the royal family. Next to God we revered the king and his whole family shared our love for him. Greeks are very democratic, but the members of this royal family are fit to be the first citizens in a pure democracy—they have done so much for the country and for all the people" (Holt [1906] 2000: 41).

Religious Identification and Solidarity

"There are two Sabbaths here—our own Sabbath, that comes on a Saturday, and the Christian Sabbath that comes on Sunday. It is against our law to work on our own Sabbath, so we work on their Sabbath" (Holt [1906] 2000: 23).

"The school was for Catholics, and I was glad I was a Catholic it was so good to be there; and I heard that at the school to which the Lutheran children went the teachers were very severe" (Holt [1906] 2000: 78).

Gender Identification and Solidarity

"After I had been working as a cap maker for three years it began to dawn on me that we girls needed an organization. The men had organized already, and had gained some advantages, but the bosses had lost nothing, as they took it out on us. The girls and women by their meetings and discussions came to understand and sympathize with each other and more and more easily they act together" (Schneiderman in Lerner [1905] 1979: 300)

"Specific to VMI [Virginia Military Institute], he said, that their style of education has benefits for a certain type of young man who can't do quite as well in a coed environment and thrives on this kind of boot camp thing, builds self-confidence. You know you can do anything if you can survive this, that sort of thing, and that, if you admit women, even a few women, he claims, the benefit, the uniqueness of the place would largely be destroyed" ("Exclusionary Politics," http://www.pbs.org/news-hour/bb/law/vmi_1–17b.html).

APPENDIX C

Sample Images from Survey

NOTES

1. Women's Business Center clients often cross-enroll in several programs, some of which are housed in the same building, but data gathered on WBC members does not reflect cross-enrollment, so it is not possible to directly compare the entrepreneurial success of women who enroll only in WBC programs versus women who enroll only in other non-gender specific programs. Therefore, qualitative data from cross-enrollees describing their experiences, and from WBC directors is examined here.

2. Patricia Greene, a sociologist who has applied Bonacich and Butler's theories in her own research on female entrepreneurs, Candida Brush, who holds a doctorate in business administration and in the 1980's conducted the first and largest study on women entrepreneurs, and Wynn Schwartz, a psychologist who specializes in social psychology and experimental methods.

3. Names of individuals and organizations are fictitious.

REFERENCES

Baxter, J. (1994). Is Husband's class enough? Class location and class identity in the United States, Sweden,

Norway and Australia. *American Sociological Review, 59,* 220–225.

Bonacich, E. (1980). *The economic basis of ethnic solidarity: Small businesses in the Japanese American community.* Berkeley: University of California Press.

Brush, C., Carter, N., Gatewood, E., Greene, P., & Hart, M. (2004). *Clearing the hurdles: Women building high-growth businesses.* Upper Saddle River, NJ: Financial Times Prentice Hall.

Butler, J. S. (2005a). *Entrepreneurship and self-help among Black Americans: A reconsideration of race and economics.* NY: State University of New York Press.

Butler, J. S. (2005b). *Regional wealth creation and the 21st century: Women and "Minorities" in the tradition of economic strangers.* Unpublished manuscript. IC@ Institute/Herb Kelleher Center. The University of Texas at Austin.

Clayton, S. D., & Crosby, F. J. (1992). *Justice, gender and affirmative action.* Ann Arbor, MI: The University of Michigan Press.

Coontz, S. (1992). *The way we never were: American families and the nostalgia trap.* New York: Basic Books.

Coughlin, J. H. (2002). *The rise of women entrepreneurs.* Westport, Conn: Quorum Books.

Davis, N., & Robinson, R. (1988). Class identification of men and women in the 1970's and 1980's. *American Sociological Review, 53,* 103–112.

Dow, B. J. (1996). *Prime-time feminism: Television, media culture and the women's movement since 1970.* Philadelphia: University of Pennsylvania Press.

Eagly, A. H., & Johannesen-Schmidt, M. J. (2001). The leadership styles of women and men. *Journal of Social Issues, 57*(4), 781–797.

Exclusionary Politics. (2005). PBS Online Newshour. Transcript. January 1996. http://www.pbs.org/newshour/bb/law/vmi_1–17b.html.

Godwyn, M., Langowitz, N., & Sharpe, N. 2005. *The impact and influence of Women's Business Centers in the United States.* Godwyn, M., Langowitz, N., & Shorpe, N., in association with the Association of Women's Business Centers, sub-award funding by the Kauffmann Foundation, The Center for Women's Leadership at Babson College, Research Monograph.

Greene, P. G., & Johnson, M. A. (1995). Social learning middleman minority theory: Explanations for self-employed women. *National Journal of Sociology, 9*(1), 60–83.

Hacker, H. M. (1951). Women as a minority group. *Social Forces,* 60–69.

Heilman, M. E., Block, C. J., Martell, R., & Simon, M. (1989). Has anything changed? Current characterizations of men, women, and managers. *Journal of Applied Psychology, 74*(6), 935–942.

Holt, H. ([1906] 2000). *The life stories of undistinguished Americans as told by themselves.* NY: Routledge.

Kimmel, M. (2004). *The gendered society.* New York: Oxford University Press.

Langowitz, N., & Morgan, C. (2003). The myths and realities of women entrepreneurs. In John E. Butler (Ed.), *New perspectives on women entrepreneurs.* Greenwich, Conn: Information Age Publishing.

Langowitz, N., & Minniti, M. (2005). Gender differences and early stage entrepreneurship. *Working Paper.* Babson Park, MA: Center for Women's Leadership at Babson College.

Langowitz, N., Sharpe, N., & Godwyn, M. (2006). Women's Business Centers in the United States: Effective entrepreneurship training and policy implementation. *Journal of Small Business and Entrepreneurship, 19*(2), 167–181.

Miller, D. T., Taylor, B., & Buck, M. L. (1991). Gender gaps: Who needs to be explained? *Journal of Personality and Social Psychology, 67*(1), 5–12.

Milkman, R. (1987). *Gender at work: The dynamics of job segregation during World War II.* Urbana: University of Illinois Press.

Minniti, M., & Bygrave, W. (2004). *Global entrepreneurship monitor: National entrepreneurship assessment, United States of America, 2003 executive report.* Babson Park, MA: Babson College.

Minniti, M., Arenius, P., & Langowitz, N. (2005). *Global entrepreneurship monitor 2004 report on women and entrepreneurship.* Babson Park, MA: The Center for Women's Leadership at Babson College.

Ogbor, J. (2000). Mythisizing and reification in entrepreneurial discourse: Ideology-critique of entrepreneurial studies. *Journal of Management Studies, 37*(5), 605–635.

Porter, N., & Geis, F. (1981). Women and nonverbal leadership cues: When seeing is not believing. In C. Mayo & N. M. Henley (Eds.), *Gender and nonverbal behavior.* New York: Springer-Verlag.

Schneiderman, R. ([1905] 1979). The cap maker's story. In G. Lerner (Ed.), *The female experience.* 1st ed. Fourth Printing. Indianapolis: Bobbs-Merrill Educational Publishing.

Steele, C. (1997). A threat in the air: How stereotypes shape the intellectual identities and performance of women and African-Americans. *American Psychologist, 52,* 613–629.

Steele, C. (2003). Stereotype threat and African-American student achievement. In T. Perry, C. Steele, & A. G.

Hilliard III (Eds.), *Young, gifted and black*. Boston: Beacon Press.

Strauss, A., & Corbin, J. (1998). *Basics of qualitative research*. Thousand Oaks, CA: Sage.

Sykes, T. A. (2008). *Grrrrl power: Top 10 women-run businesses*. Retrieved March 19, 2011, from http://www.inc.com/inc5000/2008/articles/women-owned.html

Valian, V. (1998). *Why so slow? The advancement of women*. Boston: MIT Press.

Whyte, W. F. ([1943] 1981). *Street corner society: The social structure of an Italian slum*. 3rd ed. Chicago: The University of Chicago Press.

Yunus, M. (2003). *Banker to the poor: Micro-lending and the battle against world poverty*. New York: Public Affairs.

SOURCE: Godwyn, Mary. 2009. "'This Place Makes Me Proud to Be a Woman': Theoretical Explanations for Success in Entrepreneurship Education for Low-Income Women." *Research in Social Stratification and Mobility*, 27(1):50–64.

34

HOSPITALS AS CULTURES OF ENTRAPMENT

A Re-Analysis of the Bristol Royal Infirmary

KARL E. WEICK AND KATHLEEN M. SUTCLIFFE

Organizational culture is often used to explain extraordinary organizational performance. In fact, the term "safety culture" has recently emerged in the healthcare literature to describe the set of assumptions and practices necessary for healthcare organizations to provide optimal care.[1] Culture enables sustained collective action by providing people with a similarity of approach, outlook, and priorities.[2] Yet these same shared values, norms, and assumptions can also be a source of danger if they blind the collective to vital issues or factors important to performance that lie outside the bounds of organizational perception.[3] Cultural blind spots can lead an organization down the wrong path, sometimes with dire performance consequences. This was the case at the Bristol Royal Infirmary (BRI).

The example of BRI represents a sustained period of blindness associated with organizational culture. Culture can entrap hospitals into actions from which they cannot disengage and which subsequently lead to repeated cycles of poor performance. The working definition of culture used in the BRI inquiry was "those attitudes, assumptions, and values which condition the way in which individuals and the organization work."[4] While Schein provides a more detailed definition,[5] a more compact definition is used here to treat culture as "what we expect around here."[6] Cultural entrapment means the process by which people get locked into lines of action, subsequently justify those lines of action, and search for confirmation that they are doing what they should be doing. When people are caught up in this sequence, they overlook important cues that things are not as they think they are.

The Bristol Royal Infirmary pediatric cardiac surgery program had significantly higher mortality rates than other centers in England and failed to follow the overall downward trend in mortality rates seen in the other cardiac surgery programs.[7] The case shows how small actions can enact a social structure that keeps the organization entrapped in cycles of behavior that preclude improvement. The question is why did Bristol Royal Infirmary continue to perform pediatric cardiac surgeries for almost fourteen years (1981–1995) in the face of poor performance? This persistence was the result of a cultural mindset about risk, danger, and safety that was anchored by a process of behavioral commitment that shaped interpretation, action, and communication.

Description of Events at Bristol Royal Infirmary Pediatric Cardiac Surgery[8]

The Bristol Royal Infirmary (BRI) and the Bristol Royal Hospital for Sick Children, also known as Bristol Children's Hospital (BCH), are teaching hospitals associated with Bristol University's Medical School located in southwest England.[9] In 1984, the BRI and BCH were designated by the National Health Service as one of nine Supra Regional Service (SRS) centers to provide pediatric cardiac surgical care for infants and neonates under 1 year old. (To put things into perspective, this involves surgery to correct anomalies on hearts no bigger than a peach pit.) BRI was designated to provide open-heart surgery, while the BCH was designated to provide closed-heart surgery.

The decision to centrally fund specialized services and establish the SRS center system was made by the National Health Service to control and concentrate resources and to assure that clinicians would encounter a sufficient number of rare cases to acquire necessary experience and expertise. As noted in the BRI Inquiry final report, the assumption was that "[a] unit should undertake a certain volume of cases to ensure good results in this very exacting field."[10] The idea was that the more practice, the better a center would become, and the more likely it would be to experience over time a complete range of rare conditions and complications.

Very few open-heart surgeries on children under 1 had been performed at BRI when it was initially designated. In contrast to other units in the UK that had developed special expertise in pediatric cardiac surgery, Bristol did not stand out in this area. In fact, government officials admitted that the case for making Bristol an SRS was weak because it was unlikely to have sufficient volume to maintain the proficiency of its participants.[11] Still a decision to designate it as an SRS was made primarily on geographic grounds—there were no other locations in southwest England nearly as capable as Bristol, and to have no program in southwest England at all would

have led to quite long transfer distances. As noted in the report, "the Advisory Group was concerned to see that part [southwest England] covered . . . if you are designating a service for the first time and you are endeavoring to cover the country, you may well have to identify a unit which at that moment in time is not performing as well as some of the other centers which may have been established for many years, the intention is to develop that service, nurture that service."[12]

The physical setting at Bristol is worth noting since it figures prominently in the inquiry report. BRI is located two-blocks away from the BCH. Open-heart surgery is done at Bristol Infirmary and closed heart is done at Children's Hospital. Cardiologists are located at Children's Hospital, there are none at the BRI, and surgeons are based at BRI. Most of the children are kept in wards at BRI after they are operated on with an open-heart procedure. At BRI, open-heart surgery is done on the fourth floor, while the ICU unit is on the sixth floor. The ICU unit can only be reached by a non-dedicated elevator, so it is necessary to have somebody moving out of surgery waiting for an elevator, with the possibility of getting on an elevator that has several other people on it. Once children are moved up to the sixth floor, they are taken care of for a short period of time until they are stabilized. Then they are taken back down in the elevator, transferred to an ambulance that moves them to the BCH where they are cared for on a ward. These transfers and hand-offs all have the potential to magnify small problems that linger after surgery. The problems with the split site and split service were noted in the early 1980s by hospital officials and the regional health authority and the aim was to unify the care of children on one site and to recruit a surgeon who specialized in pediatric cardiac surgery.

Several other features need mentioning. First, the regional health authority and hospital board relied on the CEO, Dr. John Roylance, for direction. Dr. Roylance in turn relied on Dr. James Wisheart, one of the two pediatric surgeons who did the work. Wisheart was a man of many trades, holding other positions in BRI such as associate director of cardiac surgery and the chairman of the hospital's medical committee. Wisheart is described in the report in rather negative terms; he arrives late to surgery, his patients typically are on bypass before he shows up (not highly recommended), and when he gets into complicated problems he is faulted for not being able to step back and see what is developing. Moreover, he's intimidating and autocratic enough that the rest of the team is reluctant to tell him what they see unfolding in front of them. The other surgeon is Dr. Janardan Dhasmana, who is described as being more deferential. He is seen to have adequate skills with the exception of the neonatal switch procedure. He is also described as self critical, disengaged from his surgical team, and unaware of their importance as a "whole team."[13]

Dr. Wisheart and Dr. Dhasmana operated both on children and adults. However, pediatric cardiac surgery was only a small part of the overall cardiac surgery activity. Experts agreed that the minimum caseload necessary for a center to maintain sufficient expertise was approximately 80–100 open-heart operations annually for two surgeons (40–50 per surgeon).[14] As noted, the Bristol open-heart pediatric caseload for children under 1 year of age was low, averaging about 46 between the two surgeons per year.

When the pediatric cardiac surgical program began, its performance was roughly commensurate with the other programs. However, over the next seven years, while all other centers improved their performance, Bristol did not. Between 1988 and 1994, the mortality rate at Bristol for open-heart surgery in children under one was roughly double the rate of any other center in England in five of the seven years. The mortality rate (defined as deaths within 30 days of surgery) between 1984 and 1989 for open-heart surgery under 1 at Bristol was 32.2% and the average rate for the other centers for the same period was 21.2%.[15] For the year 1989–1990, the mortality rate for Bristol was 37.5% and the comparable figure for other UK centers was 18.8%.[16] For the period 1991 to 1995, data analyses showed that Bristol had between 30 and 35 excess deaths over what would have been expected if the unit had been "typical" based on the performance of the other eleven centers around the UK. The mortality rate for closed-heart procedures in children under 1 year at BCH did not differ significantly from those of the other centers around the UK.[17] Although some clinicians explained the differences in mortality

rates on the ground that Bristol was seeing a more complex mix of cases, clear evidence indicated "divergent performance in Bristol."[18] Bristol simply had failed "to progress."[19]

Clues that things were not going as well as they seemed were abundant. In fact, concerns about pediatric performance began to surface as early as October 1986 when a professor at the University of Wales wrote to the Regional Health Authority to report: "It is no secret that their [BRI pediatric cardiac] surgical service is regarded as being at the bottom of the UK league for quality."[20] Government officials investigated the issue, but in the absence of supporting evidence, they concluded that the problem was related to the volume of cases, not the quality of care.[21] As events unfolded there were at least 100 formal concerns raised about the quality of care being delivered, including those raised by Dr. Stephen Bolsin, a consultant anesthetist who joined BRI in 1988.[22] Bolsin immediately noted differences between his previous experience at Brompton hospital and his experience at BRI. In contrast to Brompton, operations at BRI were longer, which meant that the babies were being kept on the by-pass machines much longer with consequent adverse outcomes.

In addition to Bolsin's explicit and repeated complaints to colleagues, he complained to the hospital's CEO John Roylance, who dismissed him by saying the issue was a clinical matter, one that was the domain of the pediatric cardiac surgeons. While Bolsin wasn't shy about expressing his concerns to the CEO and colleagues within his specialty, he never directly confronted either of the surgeons with his concerns. Concerns surfaced in other places as well. An article written by the Pediatric Pathologist at Bristol reporting on postmortem examinations of seventy-six Bristol children who had undergone surgery for congenital heart disease was published in the *Journal of Clinical Pathology* in 1989. Among the findings reported in that article are 29 cases of cardiac anomalies and surgical flaws that contributed to death.[23] In January 1991, the Royal College of Physicians refused to accredit the BRHSC as an institution to train pediatric cardiology because of the split site and split services.[24] A series of six exposé articles criticizing pediatric care at BRI, written by Dr. Phillip Hammond, were published in

Private Eye (Bolsin was the source of the information for these articles).[25] Events reached a climax in early 1995 after the death during surgery of a child, Joshua Loveday, whose operation had been resisted by everyone except the two surgeons. An external review by two people selected by Dr. Wisheart described "confusion" at Bristol and pediatric cardiac surgeries were essentially halted. Parents called for an inquiry in 1996. The inquiry itself started June 18, 1998 and ended with the publication of the report in July 2001.

What Happened?

There is no disagreement that the pediatric cardiac service provided at Bristol was less than adequate and continued as such for many years in the face of growing evidence of the poor quality of care. Although there are many plausible interpretations of what went wrong, one of the most striking findings of the Bristol inquiry is the conclusion by investigators that "while the pediatric cardiac service *was* less than adequate, it would have taken a different mindset from the one that prevailed on the part of the clinicians at the center of the service, and senior management, to come to this view. It would have required abandoning the principles which then prevailed: of optimism, of 'learning curves,' and of gradual improvements over time. It would have required them to adopt a more cautious approach rather than 'muddling through.' That this did not occur to them is one of the tragedies of Bristol."[26]

How did the mindset originate and why was it impervious to change? A single organizational process of behavioral commitment explains the origins of the BRI mindset and its persistence. While this mindset may look like "muddling through" from the outside, it has a different standing inside. The mindset at BRI was sufficiently workable and reasonable that it explained away both poor performance and the need to learn.

The basic ideas of behavioral commitment are summarized by Salancik and Pfeffer.[27] "Commitment binds an individual to his or her behavior. The behavior becomes an undeniable and unchangeable aspect of the person's world, and when he makes sense of the environment, behavior is the point on which constructions or interpretations are based.

This process can be described as a rationalizing process, in which behavior is rationalized by referring to features of the environment which support it. Such sensemaking also occurs in a social context in which norms and expectations affect the rationalizations developed for behavior, and this can be described as a process of legitimating behavior. People develop acceptable justifications for their behavior as a way of making such behavior meaningful and explainable."[28]

That description is noteworthy for its connections between micro and macro levels of analysis. At the macro level of hospitals and their environments, the description links micro rationalizing processes such as justification to the larger setting when it refers to: features of the environment that offer support to the justification; the social context whose norms and expectations supply the content of justification; legitimacy of actions and justification in the eyes of key stakeholders; and justifications that are explainable and meaningful to people outside the circle of action at the sharp end of the error chain.

At the micro level, the description links justification to specific details in day-to-day medical work. When people take important actions that are visible and hard to undo, it is hard for them to deny that the actions actually occurred. If those clear actions are also seen as volitional, then those actions are also harder to disown and the actor is held responsible for them. Public, irrevocable, chosen actions put reputations on the line and compel some kind of explanation and justification. The content of those justifications is not chosen casually because so much is at stake. Only a limited number of justifications are socially acceptable, and people have to live with the justifications they adopt. Thus, whatever justifications people voice tend to have considerable tenacity, they tend to influence subsequent perceptions and action, and they focus disproportionately on information that confirms their validity rather than disconfirms it. Behavioral commitment, therefore, has three components: an elapsed action, socially acceptable justification for that action, and potential for subsequent activities to validate or threaten the justification.

It is important to understand that the idea of justification as used here is not synonymous with mere individual self-justification or defensiveness. Justification is "rationalizing done within socially acceptable bounds."[29] Rationalization will not work unless it is culturally appropriate.

These ideas help us make sense of what happened at BRI. Bristol is described as a collection of fragmented, loosely coupled, self-contained subcultures (the inquiry board calls them "tribes"),[30] managed by a CEO whose idea of leadership and oversight was to say, "You fix it." The BRI culture is one in which people share the practice "of explaining or justifying . . . mediocre or poor results on the basis of case severity rather than directing attention to producing better results."[31] The prevailing explanation for bad results at BRI is not "we are doing something wrong and need to improve," but rather that these are "bad patients . . . and we are doing our best."[32]

If this pattern at BRI is translated into the language of behavioral commitment, then there is high autonomy and choice within each sub-culture of professionals. There is high irrevocability since surgical interventions on tiny patients are hard to reverse. In addition, there is high visibility for the actions and outcomes among people within the same specialty, surgical teams and ICU personnel, and among referring cardiologists, the families of patients, and regional and National Health Service monitors. BRI, as is true of many hospitals, enacted a context of choice, irrevocability, publicity, and rationales within which adversity was an outcome that was easier to justify than to remedy. The initial justifications that focused on *unusual case complexity* had a surprising tenacity that is explained by the fact that they served to reduce uncertainty, they were supported when "tested" against records maintained by the affected personnel, and they were plausible in the sense that a case can be complex either because of the patient's presenting condition or because of the physician's inadequate treatment of that condition. Moreover, right when the justification seemed most endangered, there was an anomalous year in 1990 where mortality rates at BRI came back into line with those of the other centers.[33] Rather than question why there was this change, people treated it as evidence that the justifications were correct (i.e., we're learning and gradually improving).

The BRI board of inquiry summarized the essentials of what we call a culture of entrapment, this way: "The surgeons were working in a relatively new and developing field of highly complex surgery.

They were dealing with small numbers of disparate congenital cardiac anomalies. Perhaps unsurprisingly, they tended to turn to their own logs of operations as the most detailed, relevant and reliable sources of data. In these logs they saw a pattern of complex cases. In this hard-pressed service, which was attempting to offer the full range of specialist care to these children, as well as meeting all the other needs of a cardiac surgical unit, the poor results achieved were believed then, and are still believed, by Mr. Wisheart to be the result of this pattern of complex cases, the result of caring for an unusually high proportion of unusually difficult cases."[34] Tenacious justifications make it harder to learn, harder to discontinue the justified action, and easier to spot information that confirms their validity. Carried to the extreme, this is one mechanism by which people developed "professional hubris."[35]

This basic social process for constructing reality is common to organizations of all kinds, both those experiencing adversity and those experiencing success.[36] Even though this social process is fundamental, it gets ignored because people tend to blame adversity on operators at the sharp end of the accident chain and fail to look at earlier moments when commitments are hardening. The analytic error is compounded when people are then removed from their organizational contexts (which favor some justifications and discourage others) and are then judged one at a time, in isolation, as if they alone intended to err.

Static renderings of organizational structure can mask ongoing interpretations, expectations, and learning that enable action to continue. Medical work turns either toward adversity or away from it because of the content of culture. However, content alone is not sufficient to produce adversity or to protect against it. Content needs to matter. When it is selectively mobilized to justify actions that might otherwise raise doubts about legitimacy, then content matters a lot. Content that matters can either open current practices to closer inspection and improvement, or it can seal them off—as was the case at BRI.

DISCUSSION

"Medicine used to be simple and ineffective and relatively safe, but now it is complex, effective, and potentially dangerous."[37] Surgeons at BRI did not expect that their learning would be so gradual, or that other centers would outperform them, or that their own management would inadvertently undermine possibilities for improvement. When the unexpected occurs, sensemaking intensifies. As Diane Vaughan made clear in her analysis of the *Challenger* disaster: "When an unexpected event occurs, we need to explain it not only to others, but to ourselves. So we imbue it with meaning in order to make sense of it. We correct history, reconstructing the past so that it will be consistent with the present, reaffirming our sense of self and place in the world. We reconstruct history every day, not to fool others but to fool ourselves, because it is integral to the process of going on. . . . People attempt to rescue order from disorder."[38]

BRI reconstructed a history of excess deaths and transformed it into a history of excess complexity. That reconstruction rescued order from disorder and imbued the past with meaning, all of which is perfectly understandable. What is harder to accept is the persistence of a rationale that precludes learning, reduces openness to information, and minimizes cross-specialty communication. The reconstructed rationale persists because layers of bureaucrats above the surgical unit, people who had some say in the original choice to designate BRI as a center of excellence, find their own judgments in jeopardy. The unintended consequence is that the whole chain of decision makers comes to support an explanation that makes it difficult for an underperforming unit to improve or to stop altogether.

To analyze BRI as a setting that entraps people in behavioral commitments does provide a compact synopsis of a sprawling, complex lapse in patient safety. However, there is always the danger that such an analysis seems like little more than an exercise in re-labeling. That is not the case here. There are some unusual implications that follow from the analysis, three in particular.

One unexpected twist is that those who are in a better position to learn from adversity are those who have *low* choice to become involved in adverse events. If high choice sets justification in motion, then low choice reduces the pressure to justify and reduces the necessity to engage in a biased search for the sources of adversity. Choice is higher at the top of hierarchies than at the bottom (e.g., surgeons are higher than anesthetists who are higher than nurses). People at the bottom of hierarchies also tend to be closer to the patient's bedside, for longer periods, with richer data. They see adversity as it unfolds; and their reduced sense of volition reduces pressure on them to justify and construct acceptable reasons for errant actions.

However, there is a catch. Their actions are visible to everyone above them in the hierarchy and they are also at the sharp end of the chain of events leading to adversity where the last irrevocable act occurs. This increases pressure on them to justify adverse outcomes. People at the bottom are torn between justification and candor. Their public irrevocable acts tempt them to justify, but their forced compliance with directives from above tempts them toward candor. The tensions created by these opposing temptations may mean that frontline medical workers are people at a tipping point. That possibility is important because it means that they may welcome surprisingly small interventions of support, security, and psychological safety[39] that could tip the balance toward candor and learning and away from concealment and justification. The point here is that fear of punishment may not be the only dynamic that leads people to cover up error. Errors may look like they are being covered up when in fact they are being explained away in order to justify public, irrevocable, volitional actions that have turned into mistakes.[40]

If attempts to improve patient safety focus on justification rather than on fear of punishment, then the targets for change are quite different. Interventions would tend to focus on perceived choice with the intent to show that earlier choices were less voluntary than first thought (e.g., you really had no choice but to go in), and/or focus on perceived irrevocability with the intent to show that treatment can be started over (e.g., let's stop all medications and see where we are), and/or focus on perceived visibility with the intent to demonstrate that observers forgot what they saw, were unimportant to begin with, or understood how the system conspired to make things worse (e.g., they have rotated onto a different service and are seeing a different set of problems). The central and simple idea is that people with less of a stake in what they can afford to see and what they must ignore, will see more, spot the development of adversity at earlier stages, and contain adversity more effectively.

A second unexpected twist is that the much-discussed "autonomy" of professionals such as surgeons and hospital CEOs takes on a different meaning. Hospitals are contexts in which autonomy works against learning. When physicians contract with hospitals, call their own shots, and, as in the case of BRI, "report to" a CEO who says "you work it out, the quality of clinical care is your exclusive preserve,"[41] then they experience relatively high levels of choice. If you add in the fact that when physicians are concerned about accountability and liability, these are proxies for visibility and irrevocability, then it is clear that hospitals are sites where professional action is exceedingly binding and where justifications are consequential. The net result is that change is next to impossible, even when no one is satisfied with current performance levels. Through repeated cycles of justification, people enact a sensible world that matches their beliefs, a world that is not clearly in need of change. Increasingly shrill insistence that change is mandatory changes nothing, since neither the rationales nor the binding to action change. Inadequate performance persists.

Finally, the idea of a "safety culture" is applicable in medical settings, but not for the reasons people usually think. Discussions of culture typically focus on content and refer to shared beliefs, shared norms, and shared assumptions. The BRI board of inquiry variously referred to BRI as a provider-oriented culture,[42] a culture of blame,[43] a club culture where your career depends on whether you fit into the inner circle[44] and not on your performance,[45] a culture of fear,[46] an oral culture,[47] a culture of justification,[48] a culture of paternalism (professionals know best so don't ask questions),[49] and a culture of uncertainty.[50] As investigators combed through the BRI data with the benefit of hindsight, they sought some kind of "invisible hand" that preserved the same interpretation of the same inadequate performance for several years. People at BRI persistently believed that things were anomalous rather than unacceptably poor.[51] It was the combination of choice, irrevocability, and publicity that preceded this interpretation and not the content

of the interpretation per se that precluded learning. Accelerated learning, in this view, is more likely when the committing context itself is weakened and not when the content of justifications dwells more on maxims of safety.

If there is a maxim implied in this analysis, it reads "challenge easy explanations." An "easy" explanation is one that that has shallow plausibility, meaning that it can explain away any outcome, is not readily refuted, and the best that can be done to disarm it is to doubt it. Easy explanations for the poor outcomes at BRI included: "our poor outcomes will improve over time with experience," "outcomes will improve once we get a hoped-for new surgeon"[52] and "our poor outcomes are an artifact of small numbers that look worse when convened into percentages, and they are inevitable because we are treating sicker children."[53] As the board of inquiry said, "All of these arguments hail sufficient plausibility at the time that they could be believed, and they could not be readily refuted, though they might be doubted."[54]

Justification turns a conspicuous action into a meaningful action. The resulting meaning can promote or impede improvement. Culture plays at least two roles in this transformation. First, culture supplies the meaning. Second, culture supplies the conspicuousness that influences the intensity with which the meaning is defended.

The lesson for hospitals is also twofold. First, be certain that the socially acceptable reasons that are available as content for justifications center on a learning orientation that values communication, openness, mutual aid, and mindful attention to patient care. As Marc de Laval put it, "physicians must become more open and comfortable with their fallibility and the patients must accept their own vulnerability."[55] Second, hospitals should try to weaken the committing context that surrounds adverse events so that people are not forced to justify inadequate performance. This is the tougher assignment of the two. The BRI inquiry board said that the better professional mindset at BRI would have been "to abandon the principles which then prevailed of optimism, of learning curves, and of gradual improvement over time, and adopting what may be called the precautionary principle."[56] However, that is as far as the board went. One way to give substance to their precautionary principle is to translate it into the image of tempered commitment. To temper a committing context is to create moderate levels of choice, publicity, and revocability. One means to do this is to make the interdependencies that are involved in medical work more explicit. The unwillingness and inability to see and improve interdependence at BRI was the feature most often criticized.[57] This feature is the one that makes the biggest difference in performance improvement.

When people understand interdependence, behavioral commitment can be moderated. Thus, choice is refrained as a collective responsibility such that the buck stops everywhere. Publicity is reframed as a collective commitment to provide constructive feedback to one another in order to improve performance. Irrevocability is reframed as a collective responsibility to identify escape routes, contingency plans, and to mentally simulate potential interventions in order to spot potential traps. When choice, publicity, and irrevocability are treated as collective responsibilities necessitated by task interdependence, this spreads responsibility but it does *not* diffuse it.

The dangerous person in a scenario of behavioral commitment is an exposed individual, in search of perfection, who is reluctant to admit fallibility, but who also feels momentarily vulnerable in the face of adverse behavioral commitments. Vulnerability continues until he or she finds a plausible justification that explains the adversity away. What began as merely a plausible justification is likely to harden into dogma because it performs such an important function. Dogma precludes learning, and it precludes improvement. This is what happened at BRI and it need not happen again.

NOTES

1. L.T. Kohn, J.M. Corrigan, and M.S. Donaldson, *To Err Is Human: Building a Safer Health System* (Washington, D.C.: National Academy Press, 2000).

2. B.A. Turner and N.F. Pidgeon, *Man-Made Disasters,* 2nd edition (Oxford: Butterworth-Heinemann, 1997: 47).

3. Ibid.

4. *Learning from Bristol* (Crown Copyright 2002), p. 266.

5. See Chapter 1 in E.H. Schein, *Organizational Culture and Leadership* (San Francisco, CA: Jossey-Bass, 1985).

6. K.E. Weick and K.M. Sutcliffe, *Managing the Unexpected: Assuring High Performance in an Age of Complexity* (San Francisco, CA: Jossey-Bass, 2001), pp. 121–122.

7. *Leaning from Bristol* [see note 8], p. 4.

8. All details concerning the Bristol Royal Infirmary are taken from the Bristol Royal Infirmary Inquiry Final Report. The Report of the Public Inquiry into children's heart surgery at the Bristol Royal Infirmary 1984–1995, *Learning from Bristol,* Presented to Parliament by the Secretary of State for Health by Command of Her Majesty, July 2001, Crown Copyright 2001. The inquiry was conducted between October 1998 through July 2001. The magnitude of the inquiry is daunting. The final printed version of the report is 530 pages and includes two CDs of raw data. The investigators received written evidence from five hundred and seventy-seven witnesses (two hundred and thirty-eight of those witnesses were parents). They also received and reviewed over nine hundred thousand pages of documents, eighteen hundred medical records, and took oral evidence for ninety-six days. They commissioned a hundred and eighty papers that were presented at seven different seminars. There are no restrictions on quoting or using the report. See www .bristol-inquiry.org.uk.

9. *Learning from Bristol*, op. cit., p. 23.

10. Ibid., p. 25.

11. Ibid., p. 105.

12. Ibid., p. 105.

13. Ibid., p. 175.

14. Ibid., p. 104.

15. Ibid., p. 139.

16. Ibid., p. 136.

17. Ibid., pp. 4–5.

18. Ibid., p. 4.

19. Ibid., p. 4.

20. Ibid., p. 134.

21. Ibid., p. 134.

22. Ibid., pp. 134–151.

23. Ibid., p. 136.

24. Ibid., pp. 138, 210.

25. Ibid., p. 141.

26. Ibid., p. 4.

27. G.R. Salancik and J. Pfeffer, "A Social Information Processing Approach to Job Attitude and Task Design," *Administrative Science Quarterly,* 23/2 (June 1978): 224–253.

28. Ibid., p. 231.

29. Ibid., p. 235, footnote 3.

30. *Learning from Bristol*, op. cit., p. 266.

31. Ibid., p. 161.

32. Ibid., p. 161.

33. Ibid., p. 4.

34. Ibid., pp. 239–240.

35. Ibid., p. 164.

36. For examples, see M.L. Tushman and C.A. O'Reilly III, *Winning through Innovation: A Practical Guide to Leading Organizational Change and Renewal* (Boston, MA: Harvard Business School Press, 1997), pp. 132–141; J. Ross and B.M. Slaw, "Expo 86: An Escalation Prototype," *Administrative Science Quarterly,* 31/2 (June 1986): 274–298.

37. Sir Cyril Chantler, former Dean, Guy's, King's and St. Thomas's Medical and Dental School, cited in *Learning from Bristol,* op. cit., p. 355.

38. D. Vaughan, *The* Challenger *Launch Decision: Risky Technology, Culture and Deviance at NASA* (Chicago, IL: University of Chicago Press, 1996), p. 281.

39. A.C. Edmondson, "Psychological Safety and Learning Behavior in Work Teams." *Administrative Science Quarterly,* 44/2 (June 1999): 350–383.

40. M. Paget, *The Unity of Mistakes: A Phenomenological Interpretation of Medical Work* (Philadelphia, PA: Temple University Press, 1988).

41. *Learning from Bristol*, op. cit., p. 74.

42. Ibid., p. 257.

43. Ibid., p. 16.

44. Ibid., p. 302.

45. Ibid., pp. 68, 201.

46. Ibid., p. 201

47. Ibid., p. 202.

48. Ibid., p. 161.

49. Ibid., p. 268.

50. Ibid., p. 273.

51. Ibid., p. 163.

52. Ibid., p. 148.

53. Ibid., p. 247.

54. Ibid., p. 247.

55. Ibid., p. 272.

56. Ibid., p. 248.

57. Ibid., p. 4.

35

REPRESENTATIVE BUREAUCRACY AND POLICY TOOLS

Ethnicity, Student Discipline, and Representation in Public Schools

CHRISTINE H. ROCH, DAVID W. PITTS, AND IGNACIO NAVARRO

Although the idea that public policy influences politics was first explored in the writings of Schattschneider (1935) and then Lowi (1964), the link between policy and political behavior has received renewed attention in recent research. Scholars have considered how policy influences the development of norms and rules that shape citizens' views and expectations of government as well as their involvement in political and civic life (Campbell, 2002; Mettler, 2002; Soss, 1999). As discussed by Schneider and Ingram (1993), "Policy teaches lessons about the type of groups people belong to, what they deserve from government, and what is expected from them" (p. 340). Researchers also have examined these linkages empirically, linking experiences with specific programs and corresponding sets of policy tools, such as those evident in the G.I. Bill or Social Security Disability Insurance, to general political and civic orientations and engagement.

Less research, however, has examined the design of programs and choice of policy tools, treating these as exogenous constraints rather than areas for empirical investigation. In recent research, the architects of these policy tools are largely public officials who shape particular bills and programs. The link between officials and the selection of policy tools has not received much attention empirically, perhaps in part because of the difficulty of obtaining data that can be used to explore and document the dynamics underlying this process. Conceptually, scholars have argued that the motivations of public officials when considering policy design are grounded in their social constructions of target populations, which are based on their own values as well as on their perceptions about the constructions held by groups that they view as politically important (see Schneider & Ingram, 1993, pp. 335–336).

In this research, we examine the processes underlying the selection of policy tools by public officials, specifically focusing on representational effects. Representative bureaucracy research demonstrates that representation, via socialization processes and shared norms, supports practices that lead to more effective outcomes. This would suggest that representation is one means of explaining the process by which policy tools are selected. We expect that public officials will alter the policy tools they choose depending on whether they "match" the service recipients by race and ethnicity. For example, we suspect that public officials will be more likely to choose learning-oriented, rehabilitative tools when they reflect the racial and ethnic makeup of the target population of the agency. On the other hand, we believe that public officials will be more likely to choose sanction-oriented tools when they are not representative. The root of the connection between representation and policy tools is in the process of social construction. As argued by Schneider and Ingram (1993), "The theory advanced here contends that some elements of design (especially the policy tools and the policy rationales) will differ depending on the social construction and political power of the target population" (p. 338). In this research, we examine the link between bureaucratic representation and variation in the use of policy tools. As representation increases, we expect that it will become more likely that bureaucrats formulate positive social constructions of the target population, because they will share underlying norms and values. As representation decreases, bureaucrats will be likely to formulate more negative social constructions, because the shared norms and values will begin to decrease. We outline the basis for our expectations in the sections below.

This is an important area of inquiry because bureaucrats often have discretion to wield significant influence on policy. The representative bureaucracy stream of research has demonstrated empirically that such influence exists. For example, representation in public schools has been shown to relate to higher test scores for students of color (Meier et al., 2001; Meier, Wrinkle, & Polinard, 1999), higher academic achievement for female students (Keiser, Wilkins, Meier, & Holland, 2002), and fewer students dropping out of school (Pitts, 2005). In other policy settings, research has shown that representation can lead to more Equal Employment Opportunity complaint filings (Hindera, 1993, 2004), more favorable farm loan application outcomes for people of color (Selden, 1997), more balanced spending priorities in executive agencies (Dolan, 2002), and higher

citizen satisfaction for people of color (Bradbury & Kellough, in press).

We consider how bureaucrats influence policy in public education by examining the particular policy tools that they choose to implement. To distinguish between the types of policy tools available, we rely on Schneider and Ingram's (1990, 1993, 1997) framework. Their research identifies several different types of tools; we consider the use of sanctions and force, which are used to stigmatize behavior, and learning tools, which focus on methods that support problem solving. This is an important distinction with potentially long-lasting implications: Stigmatizing tools may support the disenfranchisement of target groups, whereas learning tools are more likely to support problem solving and capacity building, which in turn leads to political participation. We argue that higher levels of racial and ethnic representation will lead to the selection of learning tools, whereas lower levels of racial and ethnic representation will lead to the selection of sanctions and force. Because bureaucrats that match service recipients by race and ethnicity are more likely to create positive social constructions of them, we expect that they will be more likely to choose policy tools that serve the target population's long-term interest.

To explore how representation might increase the use of learning-oriented tools, we use data from the public education policy setting, specifically information concerning the use of disciplinary actions. Because policy tools are defined by Schneider and Ingram as "aspects of policy intended to motivate the target populations to comply with policy or utilize policy opportunities" (1993, p. 338), we believe student discipline is a valid and interesting application of the framework. A school's discipline policy is aimed toward incentivizing students against disrupting the learning environment and those policy tools (whether carrots or sticks) all focus on such motivation to comply. For example, the use of some disciplinary practices, such as expulsions, can have a negative effect on student achievement (Brown, 2007; Skiba & Noam, 2002), and evidence suggests that these types of actions may be used disproportionately in cases of racial and ethnic minorities (Skiba & Peterson, 1999; Verdugo, 2000; Verdugo & Glenn, 2002). Given that one of the key roles of public education is to provide an understanding of the responsibilities of democratic citizenship and the requisite skills for effective political participation, the success of these endeavors may depend in part on the types of policy tools favored by teachers and administrators.

We see our contributions as twofold. First, we contribute to the growing policy tools literature by providing an empirical test of the argument that social views toward target populations influence the choice of policy tools. Second, we contribute to the literature on representative bureaucracy by providing a framework that extends the influence of bureaucratic representation beyond the immediate goals and practices of the organization to citizens' views and expectations of government, as well as their involvement in political and civic life. This builds on the traditional representative bureaucracy framework, which has shown extensively that passive and active representation are linked for race and ethnicity in public schools (see, e.g., Meier, 1993b; Meier et al., 1999; Meier et al., 2001; Pitts, 2007).

We begin by considering the use of policy tools within the larger system of policy feedbacks. We then consider research that has explored the relationship between representative bureaucracy, organizational performance, and target population outcomes. Next, we consider how disciplinary practices can be viewed as policy tools. We then examine the relationship between representative bureaucracy and disciplinary practices empirically, relying on data from Georgia public schools. We consider our findings in the article's conclusion.

Policy Feedbacks

Central to the policy feedback argument is the notion that varying sets of policy tools will "coproduce" citizen outcomes that have implications beyond more narrow organizational goals. These broader effects have been demonstrated empirically in recent research. For instance, Soss (1999) demonstrates that when comparing the program structures of SSDI and AFDC, close casework relationships and the significant personal discretion associated with them caused AFDC clients to see agency decision making as arbitrary and unresponsive. He found that these attitudes also influenced clients'

more general orientations toward government and levels of external political efficacy. Policy feedbacks are also demonstrated in recent research by Campbell (2002), who indicates that Social Security influences participation levels among recipients from low- to moderate-income backgrounds, and by Mettler (2002), who demonstrates the positive influence of the G.I. Bill on civic involvement.

The larger system of linkages that encompasses the causal effect of policy on participation also links participation to future demand making and to the further formulation of policy (see Schneider & Ingram, 1997). Thus, the resulting patterns of participation, along with the actions of public officials, help determine the changing structure of policy. Policy making may be carried out through many stages, suggesting that policy design that invites such feedback can be thought of as occurring during multiple processes, ranging from its initial formulation to the day-to-day policy decision making by bureaucrats. When considering the role of public officials, the balance between their attention to the behavior and psychological constructions held by groups perceived as politically powerful and their own beliefs is likely to vary across these processes and according in part to the sets of constraints imposed on officials—for example, whether the official is subject to election—as well as to their personal norms and predispositions.

It is within this larger system that we focus on how bureaucrats' constructions of target groups influence policy making. When considering the policy-related behavior of these unelected officials, individual norms and beliefs are likely to have a greater influence on behavior than those constructions held by politically powerful groups. We discuss in the following section how the literature on representative bureaucracy provides compelling evidence that these constructions affect the actions of bureaucrats and how these beliefs may exert greater influences in some circumstances than others.

Representative Bureaucracy

Representative bureaucracy considers whether a public organization employs a bureaucracy that matches the general population on salient indicators of diversity, such as race, ethnicity, or gender (for a review, see Dolan & Rosenbloom, 2003; Meier, 1975; Mosher, 1982; Pitkin, 1967; Saltzstein, 1979; Selden, 1997). The theory holds that passive representation—the bureaucracy matching the general population on these indicators—will lead to active representation, which is the formulation of policies that will benefit the interests of diverse groups (Meier, 1993a; Mosher, 1982). The link between passive and active representation is premised on research showing that people with similar characteristics–such as race, for example—will have similar values and beliefs (Meier, 1975; Mosher, 1982; Pitkin, 1967; Selden, 1997). For example, representative bureaucracy at its simplest suggests that based on shared values and beliefs, an African American bureaucrat will be more likely than a White bureaucrat to represent the policy preferences of African American citizens. The motivation for representation varies widely, with arguments on legal, normative, and strategic grounds (Naff, 2001, 2004; Naylor & Rosenbloom, 2004; Riccucci, 2002). Representational effects formed an early basis for affirmative action in the public sector (Selden, 1997), and they also support the argument that bureaucrats who match service recipients by race are more likely to form positive social constructions of them than those who do not match by race. This process is particularly likely to occur when race is a salient factor in the delivery of policy. In the context of policy tools, we would expect that racial and ethnic representation would yield specific patterns of social construction, which in turn determine the policy tools that bureaucrats choose for different subsets of an organization's target population.

If passive representation leads bureaucrats to choose policy tools that benefit service recipients of the same race or ethnicity, then this would constitute a transition from passive to active representation. Generally, research shows that this is more likely to occur when bureaucrats are afforded discretion in their jobs vis-à-vis policy making or implementation and when the policy issue is salient to the specific group being represented (Meier, 1993a; Selden, 1997). Even if these criteria are met, active representation may not occur, and ongoing research has attempted to identify

additional factors that affect this transition (Meier, 1993b; Selden, 1997; Sowa & Selden, 2003). This growing body of research suggests that social constructions are more likely to influence the choice of policy tools in some instances rather than others. For instance, Meier and Stewart (1992) and Meier (1993b) found that active representation may be more likely among street-level bureaucrats than managerial-level administrators. In their studies of Florida schools, they found that socialization to professional norms may inhibit the transition from passive to active representation among administrators. Other research has demonstrated that the transition from passive to active representation is more likely when officials see themselves as advocates of minority rights or needs (Selden, 1997).

This research suggests that the translation of passive representation into active representation is particularly likely in the case of public education. For example, public education bureaucrats enjoy immense discretion in their jobs. Teachers operate under standard curricula, but the implementation of those curricula through teaching methods and interpersonal interactions varies substantially by instructor. In addition, race and ethnicity are consistently among the most salient dimensions of diversity when it comes to education outcomes. By satisfying these two criteria, we can formulate a firm hypothesis that educators who represent their students by race and ethnicity will choose policy tools that are particularly beneficial for those students. As the match becomes weaker, policy tools will be less likely to reflect the needs of students. As noted above, we expect that social constructions of students are more likely to be positive when bureaucrats match students by race and ethnicity. As social constructions become more positive, we expect that bureaucrats will be more likely to choose learning tools for student discipline.

One of the key goals of this research is to demonstrate the important connection between research on policy feedbacks and representative bureaucracy. Empirical research in representative bureaucracy has been unable to establish a link between bureaucratic representation and broad social outcomes like political participation. Instead, it has focused on more narrow organizational goals that are often specific to a particular policy setting.

For instance, research has linked representation to higher test score performance, increased filings in response to minority complaints at EEOC offices, and increased number of awards of grant loans to minority clients (Hindera, 1993; Meier & Stewart, 1992; Selden, 1997). In limited cases, research has considered the broader effects of representation on outcomes by focusing on whether representational gains made for one racial group appear to occur at the expense of others. At this point, these findings are inconsistent, with some researchers finding no evidence of redistribution (Meier et al., 1999) and others finding that an increase in organizational effectiveness for some groups is associated with a corresponding decline for others (Andrews et al., 2005; Pitts, 2005, 2007). We argue that broad, long-term outcomes are important potential consequences of representation that are underexplored by research in representative bureaucracy. The policy feedbacks literature demonstrates that policy design can strongly influence citizen development and political participation. If representation is one process through which policy design is altered, then it seems likely that representation's impacts extend far beyond immediate organizational goals. Although we do not have the data necessary to test such a complex question, we argue that marrying these two literatures conceptually provides a good first start at thinking about the true impact of representation.

In sum, we rely on this literature while arguing that the influence of representation, and underlying beliefs held by individuals with similar racial identities, extends beyond the choice and use of tools that affect organizational outcomes. Following the larger literature on policy tools and feedbacks, we view the underlying beliefs held by bureaucrats as influencing the choice and use of tools in ways that also help construct and sustain constructions of racially defined target groups. These constructions then potentially influence the future civic and political behavior of those groups. As argued by Schneider and Ingram (1997), for majority groups, those in power, or those deemed "deserving" by policy makers and implementers, the policy tools used tend to support citizen development, empowerment, and capacity building. For minority groups, or those deemed less "deserving," tools involving sanctions

or force are more likely to be used (Schneider & Ingram, 1997, p. 517).

Disciplinary Measures as Policy Tools

In the public education context, policy tools designed to respond to student behavioral problems can be easily defined as either more likely to support learning and capacity building or as more closely associated with potentially stigmatizing sanctions. For example, schools might execute simple "punishments" that provide little in the way of rehabilitation—these tools might include expulsion or out-of-school suspension. The use of such tools in recent years has been heightened, as a number of schools have initiated "zero-tolerance" policies toward some student behaviors, leading to automatic suspension or expulsion. Research indicates that feelings of exclusion and denigration are prevalent among those who are subject to these types of disciplinary actions (DeRidder, 1991; Gershoff, 2002; Owen, 2005; Strauss, 2001). On the other hand, schools also have the option of using more complex and costly disciplinary techniques that are rehabilitative in nature, such as in-school suspension or alternative school arrangements. In these cases, students are kept in the school environment and usually receive some sort of counseling or behavioral therapy aimed to address the issues behind the student's misbehavior (Green & Barnes, 1993; Lawrence & Olvey, 1994; Short, Short, & Blanton, 1994). These types of actions, particularly when compared to simple punitive actions, are more likely to promote self-discipline and personal responsibility for conduct (Kadel & Follman, 1993; Short et al., 1994; Siskind et al., 1993).

Research overwhelmingly indicates that disciplinary tools involving punitive measures like out-of-school suspension and expulsion are disproportionately used when students are minorities (U.S. Department of Education, 1999). Research has also shown that Black students are most often suspended because they were disrespectful, appeared threatening, or presented ambiguous behavioral concerns (Skiba, 2000; Skiba, Michael, & Peterson, 2002). Whites, on the other hand, may be disproportionately suspended when the infraction is clear—involving guns, weapons, or drug violations.

Given the role of discretion in facilitating the transition from passive to active representation, this is an important point to raise in the context of this article: It appears that minority students are more likely to be disciplined when teacher or administrator discretion must be used to impose order on an ambiguous behavioral problem.

The choice of disciplinary tools can have far-reaching consequences. First, the selection of tools may influence the degree to which a school is successful in educating its students. Research has shown that students who are expelled or suspended out of school are more likely to drop out (DeRidder, 1991). Furthermore, as Schneider and Ingram argue, policy tools may coproduce outputs that have implications that extend beyond more narrow organizational goals. For instance, a significant volume of research in political science demonstrates that education is a critical precursor to civic and political involvement; as discussed by Verba, Schlozman, and Brady (1995, p. 433), "Education is the prime factor in most analyses of political activity" (see also Nie et al., 1996). Thus, students who fail to complete a high school education are left with fewer skills and resources to support engagement, linking increased use of expulsions and suspensions with lowered participatory rates and also a feedback process in which individuals continue throughout adulthood to exert little influence on politics, such as those surrounding the local school board. The stigmatizing effects of sanctions are also likely to encourage withdrawal, as well as to reinforce negative assessments of government and a lack of interest in conventional forms of participation (Schneider & Ingram, 1993, p. 342). Thus, policy tools such as sanctions may not only interfere with the attainment of educational goals but also coproduce behaviors that are likely to lower the overall quality of democratic governance and reinforce persistent negative constructions of some target populations. The concentration of such effects may have particularly pernicious, long-term impacts on some communities (see Croninger & Lee, 2001; Owen, 2005; Smith, Beaulieu, & Israel, 1992).

We argue that the degree of representation, and thus the underlying sets of beliefs held by officials, influences how target groups are perceived and the selection of policy tools. We hypothesize that in representative schools, a larger proportion of offenses will be addressed by tools like in-school suspensions and alternative school settings, and a smaller proportion of offenses will be addressed by out-of-school suspensions and expulsions, for two reasons. First, in schools where teachers and administrators "look like" the students they serve, we expect that constructions of the target populations will largely be more positive. In these environments, we expect that it is more likely that students will be perceived as deserving and capable and that we should see a greater use of disciplinary tools like in-school suspension and use of alternative schools. Second, we expect that these officials will also use their discretion to ensure that students of color are not disproportionately expelled or suspended out of school; thus, we expect to see more limited use of these types of simple punitive tools.

Data and Variables

To consider the relationship between ethnic representation and the selection of policy tools, we use data from all public schools in the state of Georgia for the school years 2002–2003, 2003–2004, and 2004–2005. These data provide an excellent opportunity for examining the influence of representation in the public sector for several reasons. Representation variables are easily constructed at the organizational level for both teachers and administrators, student data are readily available, and data are available for a host of control variables that help to account for environmental influences that might confuse the relationship between ethnicity and the selection of policy tools. Most useful perhaps for this current research is that Georgia schools are required to report student infractions that resulted in a disciplinary action, and the Georgia Department of Education (GDOE) classifies and archives these disciplinary incidents. Table 35.1 shows the average number of disciplinary incidents of each type for the schools in our sample.

Dependent Variables

In Table 35.2, we list the types of disciplinary actions used in response to the various infractions summarized in Table 35.1. Table 35.2 summarizes the average number of each type of disciplinary

Table 35.1   Summary of Disciplinary Incidents (per school)

Incident Type (GADOE classification)	School Year 2002–2003 (n = 1,959)		School Year 2003–2004 (n = 1,990)		School Year 2004–2005 (n = 2,037)		Pooled Data 2002–2005 (N = 5,986)	
	M	SD	M	SD	M	SD	M	SD
Alcohol	0.560	2.374	0.579	1.873	0.579	1.876	0.573	2.051
Arson	0.076	0.531	0.070	0.506	0.054	0.330	0.066	0.463
Battery	4.493	24.020	4.274	25.218	4.207	24.412	4323	24.553
Burglary	0.289	1.304	0.183	0.971	0.136	0.737	0.202	1.029
Computer trespass	0.682	2.690	0.787	9.415	0.591	2.659	0.686	5.851
Disorderly conduct	96.245	271.253	78.543	267.771	81.414	281.381	85.313	273.667
Drugs—except alcohol	2.462	7.542	2.758	7.642	2.701	6.920	2.641	7.371
Fighting	34.423	52.492	35.835	54.459	34.708	52.564	34.990	53.173
Homicide	0	0	0	0	0.000	0.000	0.000	0.000
Kidnapping	0.001	0.023	0	0	0.000	0.022	0.000	0.018
Larceny and theft	3.351	5.861	2.763	5.255	2.396	4.740	2.830	5.312
Motor vehicle theft	0.021	0.180	0.020	0.191	0.019	0.225	0.020	0.200
Robbery	0.151	1.712	0.065	0.524	0.038	0.372	0.084	1.048
Sexual battery	0.029	0.230	0.069	0.547	0.025	0.225	0.041	0.366
Sexual harassment	2.580	7.817	2.032	4.385	1.730	3.793	2.108	5.603
Sex offenses	1.793	5.028	1.509	4.203	1.392	3.800	1.562	4.368
Threat or intimidation	12.062	27.251	12.459	31582	10.635	27.235	11.709	28.764
Tobacco	5.350	13.654	5.784	15.144	5.855	15.392	5.666	14.760
Trespassing	0.478	2.594	0.465	2.072	0.416	1.793	0.453	2.173
Vandalism	3.111	6.291	2.645	5.290	2.474	5.057	2.739	5.570
Other discipline incident	330.464	503.748	372.666	561.578	368.535	557.905	357.449	542.280
Weapons								
Knife	1.076	1.707	1.318	2.003	1.381	2.048	1.260	1.932
Other	0.962	2.621	1.035	3.735	1.118	4.511	1.039	3.716
Handgun	0	0	0.278	7.519	0.075	0.405	0.118	4.343
Rifle	0	0	0.010	0.182	0.012	0.167	0.008	0.143

SOURCE: Georgia Department of Education (GADOE).

Table 35.2   Summary of Disciplinary Actions (per school)

Discipline Actions (GADOE Classification)	School Year 2002–2003 (n = 1,959)		School Year 2003–2004 (n = 1,989)		School Year 2004–2005 (n = 2,037)		Pooled Data 2003–2005 (N = 5,986)	
	M	*SD*	*M*	*SD*	*M*	*SD*	*M*	*SD*
Corporal punishment	10.27	33.02	10.33	34.40	19.70	76.48	13.50	52.53
In-school suspension	103.62	144.55	109.52	153.62	247.44	381.76	154.53	262.15
Out-of-school suspension	74.11	102.27	80.41	111.48	154.64	253.31	103.61	175.31
Expulsion	1.21	4.15	1.63	5.56	1.99	7.36	1.62	5.87
Suspension from riding the bus	24.07	33.05	25.61	35.29	36.23	54.29	28.72	42.47
Juvenile court referral	0.94	4.67	1.06	5.31	1.23	5.77	1.08	5.28
Other discipline action	22.50	47.02	17.98	41.46	30.88	115.49	23.85	76.56
Removed from classroom at teacher's request	0.32	3.49	0.54	6.76	1.38	26.38	0.75	16.01
Referral to an alternative school	3.09	11.41	3.65	11.05	4.22	14.23	3.66	12.34

SOURCE: Georgia Department of Education (GADOE).

Table 35.3   Dependent Variables

Action[a]	School Year 2002–2003 (n = 1,959)		School Year 2003–2004 (n = 1,989)		School Year 2004–2005 (n = 2,035)		Pooled Data 2002–2005 (N = 5,983)	
	M	*SD*	*M*	*SD*	*M*	*SD*	*M*	*SD*
Expulsions	0.48	3.83	0.51	3.48	0.44	3.79	0.48	3.70
In-school suspensions	29.58	26.65	29.72	27.1	32.1	30.14	30.48	28.05
Out-of-school suspensions	36.85	27.22	37.05	25.48	37.61	27.3	37.18	26.68
Alternative school referrals	0.87	4.4	0.76	2.03	0.55	2.65	0.72	3.18

[a] Expressed in percentage of total number of actions.

action for the schools in our sample. In-school and out-of-school suspensions appear to be the most common responses by teachers and administrators to those infractions presented in Table 35.1. We use four disciplinary action variables as dependent variables for this research. Two of these—being sent to an alternative school setting and in-school suspension—represent rehabilitative measures that schools might use in an effort to assist the disciplined student in reforming his or her behavior. These are policy tools that one might characterize as "learning tools." The other two—out-of-school suspensions and expulsions—represent more punitive measures that schools might use to rid themselves of a "problem" student. These are policy tools that might be categorized more as punishments or sanctions.[1] In our models, we use as dependent variables the proportion of all disciplinary actions that fall into each of these categories—that is, the percentage of all disciplined students who received a given sanction or punishment as a result of problematic behavior (see Table 35.3).[2] As we have discussed, we expect that ethnic representation will be positively related to the proportion of students who are sent to an alternative school or in-house suspension and negatively related to the proportion of students who are expelled or suspended out of school.

Representation Variables

Our key independent variables are those reflecting the extent to which the school's staff is representative of the target population by ethnicity. To measure the degree of ethnic representation, we created two separate representation indices: one for teachers (R_t) and one for administrators (R_a). The teacher representation index was created using the following formula:

$$R_t = (1 - \sqrt{((H_s - H_t)^2 + (W_s - W_t)^2 + (B_s - B_t)_2} + (A_s - A_t)_2 + (O_s - O_t)_2)) * 100$$

Where H_s = Proportion of Hispanic students in the school,

H_t = Proportion of Hispanic teachers,
W_s = Proportion of White students,
W_t = Proportion of White teachers,
B_s = Proportion of African American students,
B_t = Proportion of African American teachers,
A_s = Proportion of Asian students,
A_t = Proportion of Asian teachers,
O_s = Proportion of other students, and
O_t = Proportion of other teachers.

The result is a basic measure of distance, but we inverted the measure so that lower numbers indicate less representation and higher numbers indicate more representation. Thus, in those cases where teachers largely do not represent the school's students, the index may fall under zero. When constructing the index for administrative representation, we relied on the same formula, replacing the proportion of teachers with proportion of administrators. Representative bureaucracy researchers have formulated a variety of methods for measuring representation, but this approach permits us to test the extent to which an organization is representative across all ethnic groups (Nachmias & Rosenbloom, 1973; Riccucci & Saidel, 1997).

The teacher representation variable ranged from the least ethnically represented school in Georgia with a score of 28 to perfectly represented schools with a score of 100. The median score was 66 whereas the mean score was 63, showing a slight skew toward higher representation values. The top 5% of the teacher representation index distribution was composed of 92 schools, of which about 11% had a majority of Black students and 89% a majority of White students. On the other hand, the schools in the 5th percentile of the teacher representation index distribution were schools with high proportions of Hispanic population.

For the administrators' representation index, the values ranged from –40 to 100, with about 60 schools having a score of less than 0 and four perfectly represented schools. The mean score for the administrators' representation index was 64.

Environmental Control Variables

A vast literature links resources and constraints in the environment to student outcomes (Burtless, 1996; Fuller, Eggers-Pierola, Holloway, Liang, & Rambaud, 1996; Necochea & Cune, 1996). Following the lead of this research, we included three series of control variables to tap various factors that might have an impact on disciplinary actions. First, we controlled for factors specific to the teachers and administrators for whom the representation indices were constructed. We include average salary and experience variables for both administrators and teachers, as well as the percentage of each group that holds graduate degrees.

Second, we controlled for factors that might influence the larger school environment as well as those that might influence the likelihood of the use of disciplinary actions. For example, we include a Blau index of variability for student ethnicity to take into account the overall level of student ethnic diversity, allowing us to control for possibility that the extent to which the school staff is representative of the target population is influenced by the degree of homogeneity across the student body. We also include the percentage of students who qualified for federally funded reduced-price lunch, the percentage of students with disabilities, the percentage of students who were language impaired, and the percentage of students with 15 or more absences.

To control for the severity of student misbehavior, we included variables for the percentage of disciplinary incidents in a series of state-created categories, including those of a personal nature, those involving property, those involving weapons, misdemeanors, and other minor incidents. We also included a series of control variables to account further for particularities about each school: the student-teacher ratio; the student-administrator ratio; whether it was a high school, middle school, or elementary school (dichotomous); and the total number of students.

Model and Method

We used a linear pooled model, which under strict exogeneity[3] offers consistent estimates, to test our hypothesis. The model was specified as follows:

$$\text{Action}_{jit} = \alpha + \beta_1 \text{ (teacher rep.)}_{it} + \beta_2 \text{ (manager rep.)}_{it}$$
$$+ \theta_1 X1_{it} + \theta_2 X2_{it} + \theta_3 X3_{it} + u_{it}$$

Action_{jit} stands for the number of times action j is used, expressed as a proportion of the total number of actions for school i at time t.[4] Representation indices for teachers and managers are drawn respectively for school i at time t. $X1_{it}$ is a vector of discipline infraction counts classified into five groups[5] (see above) for school i at time t. $X2_{it}$ is a vector of school characteristics including students', teachers', and administrators' characteristics. $X3_{it}$ is a vector of time dummies to allow for a change in intercept over time. In the appendix, we present descriptive statistics for our independent variables pooled over time.

Findings and Discussion

We present our results in Table 35.4. We test our model on four different dependent variables, with two "learning tool" models and two "sanction" models. The first two columns show results from regressing our sanction dependent variables on the model. In both cases, we find that teacher representation results in a lower proportion of disciplinary actions that are sanctions. The coefficient for teacher representation is negative and statistically significant at the .05 level for expulsions and the .001 level for out-of-school suspensions. The analysis yields interesting substantive results as well. Increasing teacher representation by 20 points leads to, on average, a decrease of 0.2 points in the percentage of actions that are expulsions. Although this effect may seem somewhat small, it is important to consider that the schools in our sample average about 1 such action per year. In the case of out-of-school suspensions, a similar increase in teacher representation means, on average, a decrease of approximately 4 points in the percentage of disciplinary infractions that result in out-of-school suspensions—equivalent to 12 fewer out-of-school suspensions in a given year.

In schools where teachers match students by ethnicity, the discipline profile for the school seems to be oriented less toward sanctions than in schools with less ethnic representation. Although we are unable to test the causal path directly, we believe this is likely to occur through a complex process of social construction and advocacy. Teachers create more positive social constructions of students they match by ethnicity, and they are also more likely to serve as advocates for students of the same ethnicity. In the aggregate, those processes result in broad organizational behaviors that translate passive representation into learning-oriented policy tools.

Note that our findings replicate those of previous research suggesting that the transition from active to passive representation is more likely among street-level bureaucrats than managerial-level administrators; that is, although administrator representation is associated with fewer expulsions and fewer students sent to out-of-school suspension, it is not significant in either model. In addition, although administrators are typically responsible for disciplinary actions, we

Table 35.4 Linear Pooled Model of Disciplinary Actions

	% Out-of-School Suspensions	% Expulsions	% In-School Suspensions	% Alternative School Referrals
Representation indexes				
Teacher representation index	−0.194*** (0.033)	−0.01*(0.006)	0.078**(0.030)	0.005**(0.002)
Administrator representation index	−0.003(0.023)	−0.002(0.003)	0.012(0.02)	−0.001(0.002)
Teacher characteristics				
Teacher average salary ($1,000)	2.206***(0.274)	−0.018(0.078)	−0.323(0.26)	0.026(0.017)
Teacher average experience	−2.033***(0.261)	−0.048(0.073)	0.605**(0.237)	−0.032(0.025)
% Teachers with graduate degrees	−0.198***(0.059)	−0.003(0.012)	−0.069(0.051)	0.003(0.004)
Administrator characteristics				
Administrator average experience	0.021(0.086)	0.026(0.017)	0.25***(0.088)	−0.014*(0.008)
Administrator average salary ($ 1,000)	0.099(0.107)	−0.024(0.017)	−0.308***(0.093)	0.021**(0.009)
% Administrator with graduate degrees	0.099**(0.040)	0.018*(0.01)	0.076*(0.041)	0.01***(0.002)
Student characteristics				
Student diversity index	−21.226***(3.391)	−0.671(0.419)	2.231(3.218)	0.412(0.373)
% Free lunch–qualifying studs	7.619***(2.932)	−1.59**(0.749)	−3.726(2.986)	0.459(0.384)
% Students with disabilities	−15.369(11.197)	0.126(1.163)	−2.562(5.504)	0.114(0.46)
% Language–impaired students	−1.971(7.751)	−0.467(0.875)	5.075(6.514)	0.201(0.514)
% Students with ≥ 15 absences	38.151***(7.061)	−1.694(2.087)	−23.353***(6.460)	−2.808***(1.323)
School characteristics				
Total number of students	−0.003*(0.002)	−0.001**(0.001)	0.003*(0.002)	0.0002(0.0002)
Student–teacher ratio	−0.046(0.057)	0.068(0.084)	−0.071(0.044)	0.001(0.003)
Student–administrator ratio	0.006(0.005)	−0.002*(0.001)	−0.01*(0.005)	0.00004(0.0004)
High school	−3.372*(1.996)	2.3***(0.671)	25.59***(1.929)	1.85***(0.381)
Middle school	−7.998***(1.142)	0.884***(0.252)	28.104***(1.277)	1.178***(0.214)
Incident controls				
Personal incidents	0.059***(0.011)	0.001(0.001)	−0.046***(0.013)	0.003***(0.001)
Property incidents	−0.427***(0.064)	−0.016***(0.005)	0.406***(0.074)	−0.034***(0.005)
Weapon incidents	0.024(0.049)	0.003(0.004)	0.016(0.042)	0.009(0.007)
Misdemeanor incidents	0.024***(0.006)	0.001**(0.001)	−0.033***(0.006)	0.002***(0.001)
Other minor incidents	−0.006***(0.001)	0.0003**(0.0001)	0.008***(0.001)	−0.0002(0.0001)
Intercept	−19.826(11.208)	1.058(2.8)	8.287(10.456)	−1.465***(0.636)
Observations and schools	5966/2173	5966/2173	5966/2173	5966/2173
Adjusted R^2	0.16	0.08	0.33	0.05

NOTE: Standard errors are in parentheses. Not shown: Year dummy variables.
***p < .001. **p <.05.

believe these findings indicate that teachers influence the process more than administrators. As gatekeepers to disciplinary action, teachers are typically the school officials who first witness a disciplinary infraction. They choose which infractions to report and how severely to describe them. Moreover, we believe that administrators may be socialized to use their discretion in very specific ways, such that infractions result in very specific consequences that are not influenced by the administrator's subjective judgment. A similar logic might suggest that administrators choose to use the full range of disciplinary options available to them, in part to demonstrate that they are "'tough on crime" and move up the organizational hierarchy. Because the same incentive structure would not necessarily exist for teachers, who are unlikely to see promotion to assistant principal on this basis, the finding for administrators would be clouded.

It could also be that our data and measurement approach do not lend themselves to a significant finding on this variable. Because there are relatively few administrators in each school, a composite measure of representation like ours is a very blunt tool by which to measure the ethnic match. Other approaches to this variable were equally unsuccessful, and given the theoretical justification for this specific measure of representation, we chose to use it in the model. Future research should consider the issue of managerial representation in greater detail as a number of questions remain as to whether administrators can shape outcomes through this particular causal path.

Results from the two models linking representation and more rehabilitative outcomes were similar. In the second two columns of Table 35.4, we present the results from our models for in-school suspension and alternative school referral. We find that teacher representation is associated with a larger proportion of students being sent to in-school suspension and alternative schools. The coefficients for teacher representation are statistically significant at the .01 level for both models. As in the models for punitive tools, the substantive findings are also interesting. For in-school suspension, a 20-point increase in our index of teacher representation leads, on average, to an increase of 1.5 percentage points in the proportion of all disciplinary actions that involve

in-school suspensions—equivalent to an additional five in-school suspensions in a given year. For alternative school assignment—a similar increase leads on average to a 0.1-point increase in the percentage of all disciplinary actions that involve alternative school assignments. Again, although this increase may seem small, it is important to consider that the schools in our sample average between three and four such assignments per year. As with the other models, administrative representation is not significant in either case.

It is important to keep in mind that representation is not out of the hands of school officials—it can be manipulated in ways that ultimately benefit student outcomes. Although schools cannot choose their students, they can certainly choose the teachers that they hire, and keeping the two sets of ethnic profiles similar can encourage a particular orientation to student discipline. For many school districts, immigration and growing demographic diversity make the labor market more diverse than it has ever been, giving school systems an opportunity to hire teachers from diverse backgrounds. Even in areas where diverse applicants may be difficult to find, aggressive recruitment strategies can result in an applicant pool that is more heterogeneous than the labor market might predict (Riccucci, 2002; Selden, 2006; Selden & Selden, 2001). Ethnic representation is not simply an area for empirical inquiry but is also a managerial lever that can be used by school officials to effect a particular outcome. In this case, representation can be used to encourage learning-oriented discipline.

Some have argued that representation as a management lever is inappropriate because it tilts the policy direction of the organization in favor of a particular minority interest group (see, e.g., Lim, 2006; Nielsen & Wolf, 2001). If organizations hire more racial- and ethnic-minority employees, and those employees actively represented their group's interests, then other groups would theoretically suffer. We argue that this is not necessarily the case. Our research demonstrates that shifts in representation can potentially change the *culture* of the organization by modifying overall policy direction. Overall racial and ethnic representation can lead to a more rehabilitative policy direction for student discipline, perhaps making it more likely that all students would avoid punitive discipline. Although we are unable to test how representation affects the discipline outcomes for individual racial and ethnic groups, we do control for the racial and ethnic makeup of the students in the models, meaning that the results hold regardless of the makeup of the student body. Disentangling these relationships further would be a fruitful avenue for future research.

Interesting policy implications also arise from these findings. Rehabilitative discipline is more expensive to administer than punitive discipline. It costs more to staff in-school suspension than to send students home, and it is more expensive to operate an alternative school than it is to expel students (see, e.g., Irvin, Tobin, Sprague, Sugai, & Vincent, 2004). Public schools do not typically operate in an environment with slack resources, which creates a zero-sum game where money put toward one focus is necessarily taken from another. If funds are dedicated to student discipline that might otherwise be put toward other special programs, such as English as a Second Language initiatives, enrichment programs for gifted students, and supplies for science courses, then schools must evaluate whether the benefit of learning oriented discipline outweighs the drawback of being unable to offer other programs. Moreover, in an era of emphasis on student test scores and objective benchmarks, schools are actually incentivized to remove problem students from the school in whatever ways possible (Bohte & Meier, 2000). By removing students who are unlikely to perform well on standardized tests from the pool of students, schools increase the likelihood that they meet test score targets. This creates a dilemma for discipline policy, where school officials must choose between a learning-oriented policy tool and the ability to meet objective benchmarks and provide other programs. It also potentially creates a problem of goal congruence, where street-level bureaucrats would focus on discipline but political overseers require a focus on test scores or college preparedness (Meyers, Riccucci, & Lurie, 2001). We are unable to test the extent to which educators choose between competing demands, but the policy implications of these choices are nonetheless vital to understanding the full spectrum of these decisions.

Whether schools choose to devote resources to discipline or another area of education, the policy feedback literature suggests that students will see long-term impacts from educators' choices. Rehabilitative discipline can encourage students to engage in effective political participation, creating a cycle through which they will form more positive opinions of government and bureaucrats. As a result, school officials may be motivated to focus on rehabilitative discipline because it results in broad social benefit, but they may also be motivated by self-interest to promote more positive views toward public officials. It is not possible to test the extent to which officials weigh these political considerations against conclusions drawn from the social constructions they create of students, but they both seem to contribute to the choice of policy design.

CONCLUSION

This research has explored the relationship between bureaucratic representation and the choice of disciplinary tools in the schools. The results demonstrate that for schools in which teachers are more representative of their target populations, there is less frequent use of punitive disciplinary practices such as expulsions and out-of-school suspensions. Instead, in schools with greater representation, we are more likely to observe disciplinary practices that involve a greater rehabilitative component—such as in-school suspensions and the use of alternative school settings.

This provides empirical support for the argument that social perspectives of target populations held by public officials influence the choice of policy tools. Although scholars such as Schneider and Ingram have argued persuasively that constructions of target populations are likely to influence the selection of policy tools, little work has examined this link empirically. The role of socialization processes and norms in determining policy actions of public officials is well documented in the literature on representative bureaucracy and allows for a valuable test of this argument that is critical to the larger literature on policy tools and feedbacks.

It is also important to consider that we have approached our study somewhat differently than that of much previous research that has explored the relationship between bureaucratic representation and organizational performance. Our approach supports a framework that extends the influence of representation beyond the immediate goals and practices of the organization to citizens' views and expectation of government as well as their political and civic involvement. It also results in management and policy implications that reflect the complexity of the goal environment in public schools. As managers aim to choose the most effective set of policy tools, they must confront a complex set of consequences that may affect other policy areas in ways that are difficult to discern.

Of course, these results must be considered within the context of the limitations of this research. These variables, models, and findings are context specific, and it is not clear whether the results could be generalized to other policy settings. Disciplinary actions represent one type of policy tool and they operate within a policy setting where street-level bureaucrats enjoy immense discretion. For other policy areas, where perhaps the target population is less clearly defined, street-level bureaucrats enjoy less discretion, or choice of tools is more limited, it could be that representation does not have these impacts. A second limitation is that of the data—we used data from public schools in only one state. Although it is a fairly large and diverse state, and data are at the school level, not the district level, it would still be ideal to have data from all states to provide the most generalizable set of findings. Finally, we can offer only quantitative evidence for the role of representation in promoting rehabilitative policy design. The complex set of causal mechanisms at play in this study could be further disentangled by well-crafted qualitative research. Future research should also consider administrative representation in greater detail, testing whether alternative measures would better illuminate the relationship between ethnic representation and outcomes. It is also possible that administrators are shaping target population outcomes through teacher representation as a mediator. Administrators hire teachers, manage them, and provide them with feedback and direction. It could be that administrators are actually shaping the policy tools chosen by teachers indirectly.

These results provide an interesting first glimpse into representation's impact on policy design in the context of student discipline and public education. Several other priorities might be considered by other representative bureaucracy researchers. First, it is increasingly important to understand the consequences of representation for the outcomes of different target population groups. Do majority clients and citizens suffer as minority clients and citizens benefit from representation? Can the organization as a whole derive benefit from representation through a synergy of sorts? Second, the causal path that explains the shift from passive to active representation should be explored further in the context of Schneider and Ingram's framework. If social construction is a key aspect of representation, then it should be understood in more detail than our quantitative analysis can provide. Qualitative research or well-designed mixed-method case studies could push theory forward on social construction and representation questions. Finally, the field would benefit from exploring the policy feedback-representation relationship in greater detail. What citizen outcomes are affected by representation? What is the time horizon for such effects—short-term, middle-term, or long-term? Are the impacts direct, indirect, or both? The knowledge base on representation will build significantly as it finds answers to these more complicated questions, pushing beyond focus on the passive-active link.

NOTES

1. There is some variation in the implementation of in-school suspension and alternative school programs, such that some will create more of a sanctionative atmosphere than a rehabilitative one. We are unable to control for this potential error in the measure, but given that this error would bias our results against findings, not toward them, we believe that the consequences would be only in underestimating the findings we present below.

2. We use the proportion of incidents because we believe that this provides us with the best gauge of the use of one type of disciplinary tool relative to the use of others. A simple count of disciplinary actions would reflect the size of the student population.

3. In this case, strict exogeneity means no correlation between the regressors and the error term for each observation at each point in time: $E(X_{it}'U_{it}) = 0$, where X stands for all the regressors in the model.

APPENDIX

Descriptive Statistics for Independent Variables

Variable	Pooled N	M	SD
Teacher representation index	5,969	63.58	23.08
Administrator representation index	5,969	64.81	26.65
Teacher average salary	5,969	45605	3077
Teacher average experience	5,979	12.70	2.74
% Teachers with graduate degrees	5,979	51.75	11.63
Administrator average salary	5,979	72987	7608
Administrator average experience	5,979	20.65	5.43
% Administrators with graduate degrees	5,969	96.49	11.03
Student diversity index[6]	5,986	0.38	0.19
% Free lunch-qualifying students	5,986	52	25
% Students with disabilities	5,986	10.42	8.94
% Language-impaired students	5,986	3.98	8.22
% Students with $\geq$15 absences	5,986	11.57	7.68
Student-teacher ratio	5,979	13.94	7.30
Student-administrator ratio	5,969	254	111
High school	5,969	0.17	0.38
Middle school	5,986	0.20	0.40
Total number of students	5,986	740	436
Incidents			
Personal	5,986	4.51	24.62
Property	5,986	3.05	5.64
Weapon	5,986	2.43	6.37
Misdemeanor	5,986	61.56	86.90
Other minor	5,986	442.76	636.60

4. Even though the dependent variables are similar to one another, the errors do not appear to be correlated to the extent that estimates would be inefficient.

5. Discipline actions are a direct consequence of discipline infractions so we include counts of discipline infractions classified into four groups: serious incidents against property, serious incidents against persons, weapons incidents, misdemeanors, and other minor incidents.

6. For the student diversity measure we use the Blau index calculated with the formula $1 - \Sigma p^2 i$, where p is the proportion of group members in a given category and i is the number of different categories.

REFERENCES

Andrews, R., Boyne, G., Meier, K. J., O'Toole, L. J., & Walker, R. (2005). Representative bureaucracy, organizational strategy, and public service performance: An empirical analysis of English local government. *Journal of Public Administration Research and Theory, 15,* 489–504.

Bohte, J., & Meier, K. J. (2000). Goal displacement: Assessing the motivation for organizational cheating. *Public Administration Review, 60,* 173–182.

Bradbury, M. D., & Kellough, J. E. (in press). Representative bureaucracy: Exploring the potential for active representation in local government. *Journal of Public Administration Research and Theory.*

Brown, T. M. (2007). Lost and turned out: Academic, social, and emotional experiences of students excluded from school. *Urban Education, 42,* 432–455.

Burtless, G. (1996). *Does money matter? The effect of school resources on student achievement and adult success.* Washington, DC: Brookings Institution.

Campbell, A. (2002). Self-interest, social security, and the distinctive participation patterns of senior citizens. *American Political Science Review, 96,* 565–574.

Croninger, R. G., & Lee, V. E. (2001). Social capital and dropping out of high school: Benefits to at-risk students of teachers' support and guidance. *Teachers College Record, 103,* 548–581.

DeRidder, L. M. (1991). How suspension and expulsion contribute to dropping out. *Education Digest, 56*(6), 44–47.

Dolan, J. (2002). Representative bureaucracy in the federal executive: Gender and spending priorities. *Journal of Public Administration Research & Theory, 12,* 353–376.

Dolan, J., & Rosenbloom, D. H. (2003). *Representative bureaucracy: Classic readings and continuing controversies.* Armonk, NY: M. E. Sharpe.

Fuller, B., Eggers-Pierola, C., Holloway, S. D., Liang, X., & Rambaud, M. F. (1996). Rich culture, poor markets: Why do Latino parents forego preschooling? *Teachers College Record, 97,* 400–418.

Gershoff, E. T. (2002). Corporal punishment by parents and associated child behaviors and experiences: A meta-analytic and theoretical review. *Psychological Bulletin, 128,* 539–579.

Green, J., & Barnes, D. (1993). *Discipline in secondary schools: How administrators deal with student misconduct* (ERIC Document Reproduction Service No. 357–507). Indiana: Ball State University.

Hindera, J. J. (1993). Representative bureaucracy: Imprimis evidence of active representation in the EEOC district offices. *Social Science Quarterly, 74,* 95–108.

Hindera, J. J. (2004). Representative bureaucracy: Further evidence of active representation in the EEOC district offices. *Journal of Public Administration Research and Theory, 3,* 415–429.

Irvin, L. K., Tobin, T. J., Sprague, J. R., Sugai, G., & Vincent, C. G. (2004). Validity of office discipline referral measures as indices of school-wide behavioral status and effects of school-wide behavioral interventions. *Journal of Positive Behavior Interventions, 6,* 131–147.

Kadel, S., & Follman, J. (1993). *Reducing school violence in Florida: Hot topics, usable research.* (ERIC Document Reproduction Series No. 355–614). Florida: Southeastern Regional Vision for Education.

Keiser, L. R., Wilkins, V. M., Meier, K. J., & Holland, C. A. (2002). Lipstick and logarithms: Gender, institutional context, and representative bureaucracy. *American Political Science Review, 96,* 553–564.

Lawrence, P. A., & Olvey, S. K. (1994). Discipline: A skill not a punishment. *American School Board Journal, 181*(7), 31–32.

Lim, H. (2006). Representative bureaucracy: Rethinking substantive effects and active representation. *Public Administration Review, 66,* 193–204.

Lowi, T. (1964). American business, public policy studies, and political theory. *World Politics, 16,* 677–715.

Meier, K. J. (1975). Representative bureaucracy: An empirical assessment. *American Political Science Review, 69,* 526–542.

Meier, K. J. (1993a). Representative bureaucracy: A theoretical and empirical exposition. In J. L. Perry (Ed.), *Research in public administration* (pp. 1–35). Greenwich, CT: JAI.

Meier, K. J. (1993b). Latinos and representative bureaucracy: Testing the Thompson and Henderson hypotheses. *Journal of Public Administration Research and Theory, 3,* 393–414.

Meier, K. J., Eller, W., Wrinkle, R., & Polinard, J. L. (2001). Zen and the art of policy analysis: A reply to Nielsen and Wolf. *Journal of Politics, 63,* 616–629.

Meier, K. J., & Stewart, J. S. (1992). The impact of representative bureaucracies: Educational systems and public policies. *American Review of Public Administration, 22,* 157–171.

Meier, K. J., Wrinkle, R. D., & Polinard, J. L. (1999). Representative bureaucracy and distributional equity: Addressing the hard question. *Journal of Politics, 61,* 1025–1039.

Mettler, S. (2002). Bringing the state back in to civic engagement: Policy feedback effects of the G.I. Bill for World War II veterans. *American Political Science Review, 96,* 351–365.

Meyers, M. K., Riccucci, N. M., & Lurie, I. (2001). Achieving goal congruence in complex environments: The case of welfare reform. *Journal of Public Administration Research and Theory, 11,* 165–202.

Mosher, F. (1982). *Democracy and the public service* (2nd ed.). New York: Oxford University Press.

Nachmias, D., & Rosenbloom, D. H. (1973). Measuring bureaucratic representation and integration. *Public Administration Review, 33,* 590–597.

Naff, K. C. (2001). *To look like America*. Boulder, CO: Westview.

Naff, K. C. (2004). From Bakke to Grutter and Gratz: The Supreme Court as a policymaking institution. *Review of Policy Research, 21,* 405–427.

Naylor, L. A., & Rosenbloom, D. H. (2004). Does Affirmative Action in federal employment matter? *Review of Public Personnel Administration, 24,* 150–174.

Necochea, J., & Cune, Z. (1996). A case study of within district school funding inequities. *Equity and Excellence in Education,* 29(3), 69–77.

Nie, H. N., Junn, J., & Stehlik-Barry, K. (1996). *Education and democratic citizenship in America*. Chicago: University of Chicago Press.

Nielsen, L. B., & Wolf, P. J. (2001). Representative bureaucracy and harder questions: A response to Meier, Wrinkle, and Polinard. *Journal of Politics, 63,* 598–615.

Owen, S. S. (2005). The relationship between social capital and corporal punishment in schools: A theoretical inquiry. *Youth & Society, 37,* 85–112.

Pitkin, H. (1967). *The concept of representation*. Berkeley: University of California Press.

Pitts, D. W. (2005). Diversity, representation, and performance: Evidence about ethnicity in public organizations. *Journal of Public Administration Research and Theory, 15,* 323–339.

Pitts, D. W. (2007). Representative bureaucracy, ethnicity, and public schools: Examining the link between representation and performance. *Administration & Society, 39,* 497–526.

Riccucci, N. (2002). *Managing diversity in public sector workforces*. Boulder, CO: Westview.

Riccucci, N. M., & Saidel, J. M. (1997). The representativeness of state-level bureaucratic leaders: A missing piece of the representative bureaucracy puzzle. *Public Administration Review, 57,* 423–430.

Saltzstein, G. H. (1979). Representative bureaucracy and bureaucratic responsibility. *Administration and Society, 10,* 465–475.

Schattschneider, E. E. (1935). *Politics, pressure and the tariff*. New York: Prentice Hall.

Schneider, A., & Ingram, H. (1990). The behavioral assumptions of policy tools. *Journal of Politics, 52,* 511–529.

Schneider, A., & Ingram, H. (1993). Social construction of target populations: Implications for politics and policy. *American Political Science Review, 87,* 334–347.

Schneider, A., & Ingram, H. (1997). *Policy design for democracy*. Lawrence: University Press of Kansas.

Selden, S. C. (1997). *The promise of representative bureaucracy: Diversity and responsiveness in a government agency*. Armonk, NY: M. E. Sharpe.

Selden, S. C. (2006). A solution in search of a problem? Discrimination, affirmative action, and the new public service. *Public Administration Review, 66,* 911–923.

Selden, S. C., & Selden, F. (2001). Rethinking diversity in public organizations for the 21st century: Moving toward a multicultural model. *Administration & Society, 33,* 303–329.

Short, P. M., Short, R. J., & Blanton, C. (1994). *Rethinking student discipline: Alternatives that work*. Thousand Oaks, CA: Corwin Press.

Siskind, T. G., Leonard, G., Carnucci, M., Gibson, M., Jeng, J., Nevarre, A., et al. (1993). *An evaluation of in-school suspension programs*. Paper presented at the Annual Meeting of the Eastern Educational Research Association. Clearwater, Florida, February 1–3.

Skiba, R. J. (2000). *Zero tolerance, zero evidence: A critical analysis of school disciplinary practice*. Bloomington: Indiana University Press.

Skiba, R. J., Michael, R. S., & Peterson, R. L. (2002). The color of discipline: Sources of racial and gender disproportionality in school punishment. *The Urban Review, 34,* 317–342.

Skiba, R. J., & Noam, G. G. (Eds.). (2002). *Zero tolerance: Can suspension and expulsion keep schools safe?* San Francisco: Jossey-Bass.

Skiba, R. J., & Peterson, R. (1999). The dark side of zero-tolerance: Can punishment lead to safe schools? *Phi Delta Kappan, 80,* 372–382.

Smith, M. H., Beaulieu, L. J., & Israel, G. D. (1992). Effects of human capital and social capital on dropping out of high school in the south. *Journal of Research on Rural Education, 8,* 75–87.

Soss, J. (1999). Lessons of welfare: Policy design, political learning, and political action. *American Political Science Review, 93,* 363–380.

Sowa, J. E., & Selden, S. C. (2003). Administrative discretion and active representation: An expansion of the theory of representative bureaucracy. *Public Administration Review, 63,* 700–710.

Strauss, M. A. (2001). *Beating the devil out of them: Corporal punishment in American Families* (2nd ed.). New Brunswick, NJ: Transaction Publishing.

U.S. Department of Education. (1999). *Elementary and secondary school civil rights compliance report: National and state projections*. Washington, DC: Office for Civil Rights.

Verba, S., Schlozman, K. L., & Brady, H. E. (1995). *Voice and equality: Civic voluntarism in American politics.* Cambridge, MA: Harvard University Press.

Verdugo, R. R. (2000). *Zero tolerance policies: A critical review.* Washington, DC: National Education Association.

Verdugo, R. R., & Glenn, B. C. (2002, April). *Race-ethnicity class, and zero tolerance policies: A policy discussion.* Paper presented at the Annual Meeting of the American Educational Research Association, New Orleans, LA.

SOURCE: Roch, Christine H., David W. Pitts, and Ignacio Navarro. 2010. "Representative Bureaucracy and Policy Tools: Ethnicity, Student Discipline and Representation in Public Schools." *Administration & Society*, 42(38):38–65.

PART VI

ORGANIZATIONAL CONFLICT

AN INTRODUCTION TO ORGANIZATIONAL CONFLICT

Conflict in organizations is usually discussed as a zero-sum game: One side's win depends on the other side's loss. Competition, dominance, and subordination are inherent to this model of conflict. Most scholars consider Karl Marx to be the progenitor of conflict theory. Marx observed that the Industrial Revolution not only changed the manufacturing and distribution of goods, but also changed the relationship between people and their work. He further proposed that factories ushered in a new class system. In this system, two classes, the owners and the workers (Marx calls them capitalists and proletariats), have different and opposing interests in the workplace. Factory work is economically disadvantageous to workers because they do not have access to capital and do not own what Marx refers to as the "means of production"—this includes material such as factory equipment, buildings, and land. Unlike capitalists who benefit from the ability to purchase the labor power of others, workers have only their own labor to sell, and are therefore severely restricted in the capital they can accumulate. In addition to economic disadvantages, Marx argues that workers on assembly lines are disadvantaged in another way as well: Workers are organized into a highly managed and very restricted division of labor. Because factory work is routinized to such a degree, it quickly becomes boring and stultifying. As the product, pace, and profits of labor are controlled by capitalists, workers lose the autonomous, creative dimension of their own labor. This process changes what Marx refers to as "relations of production"—that is, the relationship between people and their work. He theorizes that the relations of production are also replicated in relations among people. Consequently, in capitalist systems, all human interaction is subject to the structure of domination and subordination.

Though Marx emphasizes the underlying *economic* motivations in social behavior, he also contends that there is a connection between work and self-development. For him, work is mainly the reconfiguration of material through human activity. Both individual self-development and social progress are mediated through the relations of production—that is, through the interaction between people and their work. Before the automated process of mass production, highly skilled artisans used their imagination and knowledge to change raw material into one-of-a-kind goods—wool into dresses, leather into shoes, and silver into teaspoons. But the assembly line reduces a worker to the repetition of a single task in the production process. Rather than creating an entire dress or constructing a pair of shoes, an assembly line worker might only insert zippers or punch the holes for shoelaces.

One hundred years after Marx wrote *Capital,* Ben Hamper's father worked on the trim line at the GM plant. His job was installing windshields. Watching his father work for the first time, Hamper (1986) writes,

> Car, windshield. Car, windshield. Car, windshield . . . And here all of this time, I had assumed that Dad just built the vehicles all by his lonesome. I had imagined that building adult cars was identical to building cars in model kits. You were given a large box with illustrated directions, a clutter of fenders, wheels and trunk lids, and some hip-high vat of airplane glue . . . We stood there for forty minutes or so, a miniature lifetime, and the pattern never changed. Car, windshield. Car, windshield. (P. 2)

For Marx, labor on the assembly line is a dehumanizing process in which workers are just another tool, no different from the machines over which they toil. In *Capital,* excerpted in this section, Marx writes, "The habit of doing only one thing converts him into a never failing instrument, while his connexion with the whole mechanism compels him to work with the regularity of the parts of a machine" (Marx [1867] 1967: 348). Labor is bought and sold, and so is no longer meaningful in itself. Workers become alienated from, rather than invested in, the outcome of their labor. They are thereby reduced to, in Marx's words, "crippled monstrosit[ies] . . . a mere fragment" of their own bodies (1886: 360). Instead of work being a source of self-expression and fulfillment, an end in itself, work becomes an economic necessity, only a means to money. Workers are estranged from their work process and product, and, since work is also an avenue for self-development, workers can experience self-estrangement as well. In this scenario, workers seek to maximize their earnings and minimize their efforts. Capitalists, on the other hand, try to get the highest production for the lowest wages, thereby increasing the profit they make on goods. The conflict between workers and capitalists is a power struggle over control of the labor process wherein more autonomy for the workers indicates lower profits for capitalists.

Marx also proposes that ideas and belief systems play an important part in reproducing relations of dominance and subordination. In his concept of ideology, he argues that power relations are replicated not only in the relations of production, but throughout society in both material and symbolic ways. John Lye (1997) explains:

> Ideology is a term developed in the Marxist tradition to talk about how cultures are structured in ways that enable the group holding power to have the maximum control with the minimum of conflict. This is not a matter of groups deliberately planning to oppress people or alter their consciousness (although this can happen), but rather a matter of how the dominant institutions in society work through values, conceptions of the world, and symbol systems . . . this legitimization is managed through the widespread teaching (the social adoption) of ideas about the way things are, how the world "really" works and should work. These ideas (often embedded in symbols and cultural practices) orient people's thinking in such a way that they accept the current way of doing things, the current sense of what is "natural," and the current understanding of their roles in society.

Marx contends that once dominant and subordinate roles have been solidified, it is common for those in dominant positions to believe the order is natural, justified, and fair. This belief system, or ideology, maintains and perpetuates established power relations. It is also common for those in subordinated positions to accept and even unwittingly contribute to their own subordination. When exploited populations embrace the dominant ideology, Marx calls it "false consciousness." He contends that workers remain in subordinated positions because they accept various false beliefs: perhaps a religious belief that encourages pacifism and promises poor people freedom in the afterlife, or the belief that through hard work and perseverance, factory workers will one day become rich. Marx predicts that when workers recognize their subordination under capitalism, they will revolt. Under this circumstance, workers would replace false consciousness with workers' consciousness, unite in collective action, and eliminate private property. The result would represent the next stage of social and economic development: collective ownership and management of the government and the economy. It is worth noting that, though Marx focuses on factories, his analysis has been also been applied to low-wage service work, and even to the work of professionals.

Given this history, conflict theory tends to take a critical, or change-oriented, perspective—that is, a perspective that disagrees with the view that the current relations of production are benign and in the best interests of all members. Conflict theory focuses on improvement through the emancipation of oppressed populations and calls for more equal distribution of economic and symbolic power. However, conflict theory does not always assume the dualistic division of domination and subordination: Mary Parker Follett has another model of conflict theory where the emphasis is on the inclusion and reconciliation of a multiplicity of views.

Follett understands conflict as potentially emancipatory and enlightening for all involved. In "Constructive Conflict" included in this section, Follett recognizes three ways to solve conflict: domination, compromise, and integration. While domination might be the most common, Follett ([1926] 1942) opines it is the "easiest for the moment but not usually successful in the long run" (p. 31). Compromise, too, is less than ideal, because it implies "giving up something" (Follett ([1926] 1942:32). Follett advocates a third possibility: integration. The concept of noncoercive integration assumes that the self is constructed and developed through social interaction, or what Follett refers to as the "circular response." In this emergent process of self-development and interaction, we mutually rely on one another such that the stagnant division of domination and subordination is replaced by a dynamic, continuous feedback system; "we are creating each other all the time" (Follett [1924] 1995:41). Follett gives an example of integration when her friend, a potential juror, is nearly rejected by a judge because he does not believe in capital punishment. In the end, neither perspective dominates the other, nor is either view compromised. Instead, the views are integrated:

> My friend summed up the incident to me in these words: "After the judge had subjected me to a kind of cross-examination, I was put into the jury box, but neither the judge nor myself was left as victor; the experience had changed us both. We found the solution instead of vindicating the pre-judgment of either of us; the solution being that it is possible to render a verdict in accordance with evidence so that you need not evade your duties as a citizen whatever your opinion of capital punishment." (Follett [1926] 1942:33)

Integration disrupts the simple dualistic notion of domination and subordination and instead imagines a complex interplay wherein people are continuously and mutually changing and influencing one another. In this model, power is diffused throughout human interactions.

In addition to Marx and Follett, the articles in this section focus on several different aspects of conflict. In "Organizational Conflict: Concept and Models," Louis Pondy (1967) explains that conflict is not constant or uniform; instead, Pondy asserts that conflict is a process, experienced at different levels, in various ways, and through a series of stages. Like Follett, Pondy does not see conflict as necessarily destructive; he thinks conflict can create progressive, functional change. However, Pondy reminds us that conflict will be perceived positively or negatively within a context of values and belief systems. He writes,

> It has become fashionable to say that conflict may be functional or dysfunctional and is not necessarily either. What this palliative leaves implicit is that the effects of conflict must be evaluated relative to some set of values. The argument with those who seek uniformly to abolish conflict is not so much with their *a priori* assertion that conflict is undesirable, as it is with their failure to make explicit the value system on which their assertion rests. (Pondy 1967:307)

Continuing to contextualize and expand on conflict theory in "Marx, Globalization and Alienation: Received and Underappreciated Wisdoms," W. Peter Archibald (2009) applies the Marxist concept of alienation to contemporary capitalism and to workers in the global economy. Archibald uses alienation to examine employees in both factories and offices, and in developed and developing countries. He concludes that alienation from work continues to be a salient concept for all workers, but that even in capitalistic economies alienation can be ameliorated, depending on the degree of worker ownership and autonomy. Archibald (2009) writes,

> We found strong effects for ownership, absolutely and relative to one's position in occupational hierarchies and complexity in and control over work itself. On the other hand . . . capitalism and class are not the only sources of alienation . . . the effects of ownership do operate mainly through complexity in and control over work itself . . . it is indeed possible for alienation to decrease within the life of capitalism. (P. 162)

According to Archibald (2009), Marx attributes alienation in part to owners and managers forcing workers to be "ever more productive" and to the common assumption that owners and managers must "overcome the 'unavoidable' resistance of workers" (p. 163). However, as Archibald reminds us, Marx also recognizes that easing the demand for surplus value and increasing worker autonomy leads to less alienation even within capitalist economies. Here we recommend putting Archibald in conversation with Follett as she discusses the potential positive and noncoercive consequences of conflict, as long as the integration of perspectives, rather than domination or compromise, governs the outcome.

In her article, "Racial Inequality in the Workplace: How Critical Management Studies Can Inform Current Approaches," Brenda Johnson (2009) explores the contributions of critical management studies (CMS) to our understanding of conflict. In addition to Marxism, CMS includes a wide range of alternative paradigms, such as postmodernism, postcolonialism, and feminism, all of which question and seek to reform current practice and research. As Johnson (2009) examines the enduring racial inequality in the workplace, she writes that "the emancipatory intent of CMS, the historical, sociological approach, the challenge to the myth of objectivity, and the assertion that managers are pursuing agendas that can reinforce stereotypes and inequities are all elements that have been missing from the discourse of diversity in American organizations and from diversity education" (p. 277).

The critical management studies approach locates the causes of and solutions to inequality in social forces that govern the historical and cultural contexts of opportunities. These social forces overwhelm individual differences in talent and effort. Johnson (2009) writes,

If managers learned about the current and historical patterns of employment for demographic groups they would at minimum have an opportunity to see how their decisions can reproduce or potentially change the patterns of racial segregation in the workplace. Managers are not aware of these patterns because it is not part of management education, which has divorced itself form a sociological and historical approach. (P. 275)

Johnson (2009) outlines a series of recommendations to redress the deficiencies in management education and diversity training. She suggests that organizations are not "neutral and disinterested" but instead primarily represent the political and economic interests of owners and managers (p. 277).

Finally, in "Mythicizing and Reification in Entrepreneurial Discourse: Ideology-Critique of Entrepreneurial Studies," John O. Ogbor (2000) recognizes the potential for entrepreneurship to reunite individuals with their work as they experience autonomy, control, and economic security though business ownership. However, using the traditions of postmodernism, deconstructionism, and critical theory, Ogbor (2000) challenges the discourse of entrepreneurship as "discriminatory, gender-biased, ethnocentrically determined and ideologically controlled, sustaining not only prevailing societal biases, but serving as a tapestry for unexamined and contradictory assumptions and knowledge about the reality of entrepreneurs" (p. 605). Ogbor argues that conventional entrepreneurial discourse replicates Western ideology, promotes the "archetype of the white male hero," and, rather than live up to its emancipatory potential, instead sustains and reinforces the current power structure of privilege and oppression (p. 607). Similar to Johnson's entreaty to management and diversity educators, Ogbor encourages researchers and theorists in entrepreneurship to critically examine the ideological, historical, and cultural contexts in which entrepreneurial conventions and assumptions are generated.

QUESTIONS FOR DISCUSSION

1. What are the two main models of conflict theory? Which do you find most compelling, and why?
2. Why is conflict theory a "critical" perspective? How is this perspective developed in critical management studies?
3. What is the connection between conflict and control?
4. What are some of the potential negative and positive outcomes of organizational conflict? What are some of the factors that determine whether conflict results in primarily negative or positive outcomes?

SUGGESTIONS FOR FURTHER READING

Hochschild, Arlie. 2003. *The Managed Heart: Commercialization of Human Feeling.* 2nd ed. Berkeley: University of California Press.

Stoudt, Margaret. 2010. "Back to the Future: Toward a Political Economy of Love and Abundance" *Administration & Society,* 42:3.

Walton, Richard and Robert McKersie. 1965. *A Behavioral Theory of Labor Negotiations: An Analysis of a Social Interaction System.* New York: McGraw-Hill (reprinted in 1991 by Cornell University Press).

REFERENCES

Archibald, W. Peter. 2009. "Marx, Globalization and Alienation: Received and Underappreciated Wisdoms." *Critical Sociology,* 35(2):151–74.

Follett, Mary Parker. [1924] 1995. "Relating: The Circular Response." Pp. 35–66 in *Mary Parker Follett—Prophet of Management: A Celebration of Writings from the 1920s,* edited by Pauline Graham. Boston: Harvard Business School Press.

Follett, Mary Parker. [1926] 1942. "Constructive Conflict." Pp. 30–49 in *Dynamic Administration: The Collected Papers of Mary Parker Follett.* New York: Harper and Brothers.

Hamper, Ben. 1986. *Rivethead: Tales from the Assembly Line.* New York: Warner Books.

Johnson, Brenda. 2009. "Racial Inequality in the Workplace: How Critical Management Studies Can Inform Current Approaches." Pp. 271–28 in *Critical Management Studies at Work: Negotiating Tensions Between Theory and Practice,* edited by Julie Wolfram Cox, Tony G. LeTrent-Jones, Maxim Voronov, and David Weir. Northampton, MA: Edward Elgar.

Lye, John. 1997. *Ideology: A Brief Guide.* Retrieved August 25, 2010, from http://www.scribd.com/doc/103252/Ideology-a-Brief-Guide

Marx, Karl. [1867] 1967. *Capital: A Critique of Political Economy.* Volume 1. Translated by Samuel Moore and Edward Aveling. Edited by Frederick Engels. New York: International Publishers.

Ogbor, John. 2000. "Mythicizing and Reification in Entrepreneurial Discourse: Ideology-Critique of Entrepreneurial Studies." *Journal of Management Studies,* 35(5):606–35.

Pondy, Louis. 1967. "Organizational Conflict; Concepts and Models." *Administrative Science Quarterly,* 12(2):296–320.

36

CAPITAL

A Critique of Political Economy

KARL MARX

The collective labourer, formed by the combination of a number of detail labourers, is the machinery specially characteristic of the manufacturing period. The various operations that are performed in turn by the producer of a commodity, and coalesce one with another during the process of production, lay claim to him in various ways. In one operation he must exert more strength, in another more skill, in another more attention; and the same individual does not possess all these qualities in an equal degree. After manufacture has once separated, made independent, and isolated the various operations, the labourers are divided, classified and grouped according to their predominating qualities. If their natural endowments are, on the one hand, the foundation on which the division of labour is built up, on the other hand, manufacture, once introduced, develops in them new powers that are by nature fitted only for limited and special functions. The collective labourer now possesses, in an equal degree of excellence, all the qualities requisite for production, and expends them in the most economical manner, by exclusively employing all his organs, consisting of particular labourers, or groups of labourers, in performing their special functions. The one-sidedness and the deficiencies of the detail labourer become perfections when he is part of the

collection labourer. The habit of doing only one thing converts him into a never failing instrument, while his connexion with the whole mechanism compels him to work with the regularity of the parts of a machine.

Since the collective labourer has functions, both simple and complex, both high and low, his members, the individual labour-powers, require different degrees of training, and must therefore have different values. Manufacture, therefore, develops a hierarchy of labour-powers, to which there corresponds a scale of wages. If, on the one hand, the individual labourers are appropriated and annexed for life by a limited function; on the other hand, the various operations of the hierarchy are parceled out among the labourers according to both their natural and their acquired capabilities. Every process of production, however, requires certain simple manipulations, which every man is capable of doing. They too are now severed from their connexion with the more pregnant moments of activity, and ossified into exclusive functions of specially appointed labourers. Hence, Manufacture begets, in every handicraft that it seizes upon, a class of so-called unskilled labourers, a class which handicraft industry strictly excluded. If it develops a one-sided speciality into a perfection, at the expense of the whole of a man's working capacity, it also begins to make a speciality of the absence of all development. Alongside of the hierarchic gradation there steps the simple separation of the labourers into skilled and unskilled. For the latter, the most of apprenticeship vanishes; for the former, it diminishes, compared with that of artificers, in consequence of the functions being simplified. In both cases the value of labour-power falls. An exception to this law holds good whenever the decomposition of the labour-process begets new and comprehensive functions, that either had no place at all, or only a very modest one, in handicrafts. The fall in the value of labour-power, caused by the disappearance or domination of the expenses of apprenticeship, implies a direct increase of surplus value for the benefit of capital; for everything that shortens the necessary labour-time required for the reproduction of labour-power, extends the domain of surplus-labour. . . .

In manufacture . . . , the collective working organism is a form of existence of capital. The mechanism that is made up of numerous individual detail labourers belongs to the capitalist. Hence, the productive power resulting from a combination of labourers appears to be the productive power of capital. Manufacture proper not only subjects the previously independent workman to the discipline and command of capital, but, in addition, creates a hierarchic gradation of the workmen themselves. While simple co-operation leaves the mode of working by the individual for the most part unchanged, manufacture thoroughly revolutionizes it, and seizes labour-power by its very roots. It converts the labourer into a crippled monstrosity, by forcing his detail dexterity at the expense of a world of productive capabilities and instincts, just as in the Sates of La Plata they butcher a whole beast for the sake of his hide or his tallow. Not only is the detail work distributed to the different individuals, but the individual himself is made the automatic motor of a fractional operation, and the absurd fable of Menenius Agrippa, which makes man a mere fragment of his own body, becomes realized. If at first, the workman sells his labour-power to capital, because the material means of producing a commodity fail him, now his very labour-power refuses its services unless it has been sold to capital. Its functions can be exercised only in an environment that exists in the workshop of the capitalist after the sale. By nature unfitted to make anything independently, the manufacturing labourer develops productive activity as a mere appendage of the capitalist's workshop. As the chosen people bore in their features the sign manual of Jehovah, so division of labour brands the manufacturing workman as the property of capital.

SOURCE: Marx, Karl. [1867] 1967. Excerpt (pp. 348–350, 360) from *Capital: A Critique of Political Economy*. Volume 1. Translated by Samuel Moore and Edward Aveling. Edited by Frederick Engels. New York: International Publishers.

37

CONSTRUCTIVE CONFLICT

MARY PARKER FOLLETT

The subject I have been given for these lectures is *The Psychological Foundations of Business Administration,*[1] but as it is obvious that we cannot in four papers consider all the contributions which contemporary psychology is making to business administration—to the methods of hiring, promoting and discharging, to the consideration of incentives, the relation of output to motive, to group organization, etc.—I have chosen certain subjects which seem to me to go to the heart of personnel relations in industry. I wish to consider in this paper the most fruitful way of dealing with conflict. At the outset I should like to ask you to agree for the moment to think of conflict as neither good nor bad; to consider it without ethical pre-judgment; to think of it not as warfare, but as the appearance of difference, difference of opinions, of interests. For that is what conflict means—difference. We shall not consider merely the differences between employer and employee, but those between managers, between directors at the Board meetings, or wherever difference appears.

As conflict—difference—is here in the world, as we cannot avoid it, we should, I think, use it. Instead of condemning it, we should set it to work for us. Why not? What does the mechanical engineer do with friction? Of course his chief job is to eliminate friction, but it is true that he also capitalizes friction. The transmission of power by belts depends on friction between the belt and the pulley. The friction between the driving wheel of the locomotive and the track is necessary to haul the train. All polishing is done by friction. The music of the violin we get by friction. We left the savage state when we discovered fire by friction. We talk of the friction of mind on mind as a good thing. So in business, too, we have to know when to try to eliminate friction and when to try to capitalize it, when to see what work we can make it do. That is what I wish to consider here, whether we can set conflict to work and make it *do* something for us.[2]

METHODS OF DEALING WITH CONFLICT

There are three main ways of dealing with conflict: domination, compromise and integration. Domination, obviously, is a victory of one side over the other. This is the easiest way of dealing with conflict, the easiest for the moment but not usually successful in the long run, as we can see from what has happened since the War.

The second way of dealing with conflict, that of compromise, we understand well, for it is the way we settle most of our controversies; each side gives up a little in order to have peace, or, to speak more accurately, in order that the activity which has been interrupted by the conflict may go on. Compromise is the basis of trade union tactics.[3] In collective bargaining, the trade unionist asks for more than he expects to get, allows for what is going to be lopped off in the conference. Thus we often do not know what he really thinks he should have, and this ignorance is a great barrier to dealing with conflict fruitfully. At the time of a certain wage controversy in Massachusetts, the lowest paid girls in the industry were getting about $8.00 or $9.00 a week. The demand made by two of the representatives of the girls was for $22.40 (for a minimum wage, note), obviously too great an increase for anyone seriously to think of getting at one time. Thus the employers were as far as ever from knowing what the girls really thought they ought to have.

But I certainly ought not to imply that compromise is peculiarly a trade union method. It is the accepted, the approved, way of ending controversy. Yet no one really wants to compromise, because that means a giving up of something. Is there then any other method of ending conflict? There is a way beginning now to be recognized at least, and even occasionally followed: when two desires are *integrated,* that means that a solution has been found in which both desires have found a place, that neither side has had to sacrifice anything. Let us take some very simple illustration. In the Harvard Library one day, in one of the smaller rooms, someone wanted the window open, I wanted it shut. We opened the window in the next room, where no one was sitting. This was not a compromise because there was no curtailing of desire; we both got what we really wanted. For I did not want a closed room, I simply did not want the north wind to blow directly on me; likewise the other occupant did not want that particular window open, he merely wanted more air in the room.

I have already given this illustration in print. I repeat it here because this instance, from its lack of any complications, shows my point at once I think. Let us take another illustration. A Dairymen's Co-operative League almost went to pieces last year on the question of precedence in unloading cans at a creamery platform. The men who came down the hill (the creamery was on a down grade) thought they should have precedence; the men who came up the hill thought they should unload first. The thinking of both sides in the controversy was thus confined within the walls of these two possibilities, and this prevented their even trying to find a way of settling the dispute which would avoid these alternatives. The solution was obviously to change the position of the platform so that both up-hillers and down-hillers could unload at the same time. But this solution was not found until they had asked the advice of a more or less professional integrator. When, however, it was pointed out to them, they were quite ready to accept it. Integration involves invention, and the clever thing is to recognize this, and not to let one's thinking stay within the boundaries of two alternatives which are mutually exclusive.[4]

Take another case. There is sometimes a question whether the meetings of works committees should be held in the plant or outside: the argument for meeting inside is the obvious advantage of being near one's work; the argument against, the fear of company influence. I know one factory that made what I consider an integration by having the meetings of the works committee held in the separate club building of the employees situated within the factory grounds. Here the men felt much freer than in any other part of the plant.

A friend gave me this example. He was called on jury service in a murder trial. The District Attorney asked him whether he had any objection to capital punishment. He replied, "Yes, definitely so." The "conflict" was then on, for the judge thought this opinion incapacitated him for service in a murder trial. My friend summed up the incident to me in these words: "After the judge had subjected me to a kind of cross-examination, I was put into the jury box, but neither the judge nor myself was left as victor; the experience had changed us both. We found the solution instead of vindicating the pre-judgment of either of us; the solution being that it is possible to render a verdict in accordance with evidence so that you need not evade your duties as a citizen whatever your opinion of capital punishment." By far the most interesting examples of integration which have come to my attention recently were four sent to the London *Times* by Gilbert Murray, four integrations which he had found in the Report of the Dawes Committee.[5] It is often difficult to decide whether a decision is a true integration or something of a compromise, and there is a flaw I think in one of the four cited by Gilbert Murray. But signs of even partial integration, signs even that people want integration rather than domination or compromise, are encouraging.

Some people tell me that they like what I have written on integration, but say that I am talking of what ought to be instead of what is. But indeed I am not; I am talking neither of what is, to any great extent, nor of what ought to be merely, but of what perhaps may be. This we can discover only by experiment. That is all I am urging, that we try experiments in methods of resolving differences; differences on the Board of Directors, with fellow managers or heads of departments, with employees, or in other relations. If we do this, we may take a different attitude toward conflict.

The key-word of psychology to-day is desire. If we wish to speak of conflict in the language of contemporary psychology, we might call it a moment in the interacting of desires. Thus we take from it any connotation of good or bad. Thus we shall not be afraid of conflict, but shall recognize that there is a destructive way of dealing with such moments and a constructive way. Conflict as the moment of the appearing and focusing of difference may be a sign of health, a prophecy of progress. If the Dairymen's League had not fought over the question of precedence, the improved method of unloading would not have been thought of. The conflict in this case was constructive. And this was because, instead of compromising, they sought a way of integrating.

Compromise does not create, it deals with what already exists; integration creates something new, in this case a different way of unloading. And because this not only settled the controversy but was actually better technique, saved time for both the farmers and the creamery, I call this: setting friction to work, making it *do* something.

Thus we see that while conflict as continued unintegrated difference is pathological, difference itself is not pathological. The fights in the Democratic convention were a hopeful sign for the Democratic party. What I think we should do in business organization is to try to find the machinery best suited for the normal appearing and uniting of diversity so that the difference does not stay too long crystallized, so that the pathological stage shall not be reached.

One advantage of integration over compromise I have not yet mentioned. If we get only compromise, the conflict will come up again and again in some other form, for in compromise we give up part of our desire, and because we shall not be content to rest there, sometime we shall try to get the whole of our desire. Watch industrial controversy, watch international controversy, and see how often this occurs. Only integration really stabilizes. But by stabilization I do not mean anything stationary. Nothing ever stays put. I mean only that that particular conflict is settled and the next occurs on a higher level.

Psychology has given us the phrase "progressive integratings"; we need also the phrase progressive differings. We can often measure our progress by watching the nature of our conflicts. Social progress is in this respect like individual progress; we become spiritually more and more developed as our conflicts rise to higher levels. If a man should tell you that his chief daily conflict within himself is—Shall I steal or not steal?—you would know what to think of his stage of development. As someone has said, "A man is known by the dilemmas he keeps." In the same way, one test of your business organization is not how many conflicts you have, for conflicts are the essence of life, but *what* are your conflicts? And how do you deal with them? It is to be hoped that we shall not always have strikes, but it is equally to be hoped that we shall always have conflict, the kind which leads to invention, to the emergence of new values.

Having suggested integration as perhaps the way by which we can deal most fruitfully with conflict, with difference, we should now consider the method by which integration can be obtained. But before we do that I want to say definitely that I do not think integration is possible in all cases. When two men want to marry the same woman, there can be no integration; when two sons both want the old family home, there can usually be no integration. And there are many such cases, some of little, some of great seriousness, I do not say that there is no tragedy in life. All that I say is that if we were alive to its advantages, we could often integrate instead of compromising. I have a friend who annoys me in this way. She makes a statement. I say, "I don't agree with that because . . ." and I intend to give my reasons, but before I have a chance she says, "Well, let's not fight about it." But I had no intention of fighting.

BASES OF INTEGRATION

If, then, we do not think that differing necessarily means fighting, even when two desires both claim right of way, if we think that integration is more profitable than conquering or compromising, the first step toward this consummation is *to bring the differences into the open*. We cannot hope to integrate our differences unless we know what they are. I will give some illustrations of the opposite method—evading or suppressing the issue.

I know a factory where, after the War, the employees asked for a 5 per cent increase in wages, but it was not clear to either side whether this meant a 5 per cent raise over present wages or over pre-War wages. Moreover, it was seen that neither side wished to know! The employees naturally preferred to think the former, the managers the latter. It was some time before both sides were willing to face the exact issue; each, unconsciously, hoped to win by keeping the whole problem hazy.

One of the longest discussions I ever heard on a minimum wage board was in regard to the question of fares to and from work: first, whether this item should be included at all with board, lodging, etc., in a cost-of-living budget, that is, whether transportation to and from the plant should be a cost on production. When finally it was decided to leave the item in and allow 60 cents a week for it, instead of the $1.20 which the 10-cent Boston car fare would necessitate if this item were to be allowed for in full, it seemed to me a clear case of evasion or suppression. That is, the employers were not willing to face at that moment the question whether wages should include transportation. I sat on that board as a representative of the public, and I suggested more than once during the discussion that we should find out whether most of the girls in that particular industry did live near the plant or at a distance too great for walking. Also I suggested that we should find out whether, if they lived near the plant, the cost of board and lodging in that neighbourhood was so high that it would more than offset car fares. But the employers in this instance were not ready to face the

issue, and therefore the clearly evasive decision of 60 cents was made.

Another interesting case of suppression occurred in a committee of which I was a member. The question was a disagreement concerning the pay of two stenographers who were working for us. Those who urged the higher amount persisted in speaking of the stenographers' day as an eight-hour day because the hours are from nine to five, although with the hour out for lunch that obviously makes a seven-hour day.

Wherever you have the fight-set, you are in danger of obscurities, conscious or unconscious. As long as trade unionism is a defensive movement, as long as employers' associations are defensive movements, we shall have obscurities. As long as internationalism is what it is, evasion will go on. Of course not to *appear* to evade is part of good diplomacy, for you don't want the other side to think you are trying to "get by" on anything. But we shall continue to evade or suppress as long as our real aim is not agreement, but domination. Lord Shaw, chairman of the Coal Commission, put it as one of the essentials in arbitration that both sides should genuinely desire agreement. Here we get a very direct lesson from psychology.

The psychiatrist tells his patient that he cannot help him unless he is honest in wanting his conflict to end. The "uncovering" which every book on psychology has rubbed into us for some years now as a process of the utmost importance for solving the conflicts which the individual has within himself is equally important for the relations between individuals, or between groups, classes, races, nations. In business, the employer, in dealing either with his associates or his employees, has to get underneath all the camouflage, has to find the real demand as against the demand put forward, distinguish declared motive from real motive, alleged cause from real cause, and to remember that sometimes the underlying motive is deliberately concealed and that sometimes it exists unconsciously.

The first rule, then, for obtaining integration is to put your cards on the table, face the real issue, uncover the conflict, bring the whole thing into the open.

One of the most important reasons for bringing the desires of each side to a place where they can be clearly examined and valued is that evaluation often leads to *revaluation*. We progress by a revaluation of desire, but usually we do not stop to examine a desire until another is disputing right of way with it. Watch the evolution of your desires from childhood, through youth, etc. The baby has many infantile desires which are not compatible with his wish for approbation; therefore he revalues his desires. We see this all through our life. We want to do so-and-so, but we do not estimate how much this really means to us until it comes into conflict with another desire. Revaluation is the flower of comparison.

This conception of the revaluation of desire it is necessary to keep in the foreground of our thinking in dealing with conflict, for neither side ever "gives in" really, it is hopeless to expect it, but there often comes a moment when there is a simultaneous revaluation of interests on both sides and unity precipitates itself. This, I think, happened in Europe at the London Conference last summer, or rather it happened before that and led to the Conference. Integration is often more a spontaneous flowing together of desire than one might think from what I have said; the revaluing of interests on both sides may lead the interests to fit into each other, so that all find some place in the final solution.

The bearing of all this on business administration is, I hope, obvious. A business should be so organized (this is one of the tests for us to apply to our organization) that full opportunity is given in any conflict, in any coming together of different desires, for the whole field of desire to be viewed. Our employees should be able to see, as we should be able ourselves to see, the whole field of desire. The *field of desire* is an important psychological and sociological conception; many conflicts could, I believe, be prevented from ending disastrously by getting the desires of each side into one field of vision where they could be viewed together and compared. We all believe to a certain extent in Freud's "sublimation," but I believe still more that various desires get orientated toward one another and take on different values in the process of orientation.

It will be understood, of course, that all this applies to ourselves as well as to the other side; we have to uncover our sub-articulate egoisms, and then, when we see them in relation to other facts and desires, we may estimate them differently. We often think it is a question of eliminating motives when it

is only a question of subordinating them. We often, for instance, treat personal motives as more ignoble than we need. There is nothing necessarily discreditable in the politician "standing by" his friends. The only ethical question is how much that motive is weighing against others. The unethical thing is to persuade yourself that it is not weighing at all.

I have time barely to mention a very important point: the connection between the *realignment of groups* and a revaluation of interests. I have found this important in watching the realignments of political parties. We must in any conflict between groups watch every realignment to see how far it changes the confronting desires, for this means how far it changes the conflict.

I began this section by saying that the first step in integration is to bring the differences into the open. If the first step is to put clearly before ourselves what there is to integrate, there is something very important for us to note—namely, that the highest lights in a situation are not always those which are most indicative of the real issues involved. Many situations are decidedly complex, involve numerous and varied activities, overlapping activities. There is too great a tendency (perhaps encouraged by popular journalism) to deal with the dramatic moments, forgetting that these are not always the most significant moments. We should not follow literary analogies here. You may have a good curtain with, to quote Kipling, the lovers loving and the parents signing cheques. Yet, after all, this may not be the controlling moment in the lives of these people. To *find the significant rather than the dramatic features* of industrial controversy, of a disagreement in regard to policy on board of directors or between managers, is essential to integrative business policies.

Such search is part of what seems to me the second step in integration. If the first step is to uncover the real conflict, the next is to take the demands of both sides and break them up into their constituent parts.[6] Contemporary psychology shows how fatal it is to try to deal with conglomerates. I know a boy who wanted a college education. His father died and he had to go to work at once to support his mother. Had he then to give up his desire? No, for on analysis he found that what he wanted was not a college education, but an education, and there were still ways of his getting that. You remember the southern girl who said, "Why, I always thought damned Yankee was one word until I came north." This method of *breaking up wholes* is the way you deal with business problems; it is the method which precedes business decisions. Take the case of inaugurating a system of approval shipment. A. W. Shaw, in his *Approach to Business Problems,* shows the sub-problems involved here:

1. What will be the effect on collections and on the cost of shipment?
2. What is to be the credit policy?
3. Will the stock in transit or in the hands of customers reduce the number of turnovers per year?
4. Will the risk of damage to returned goods be great enough to jeopardize the regular profit?
5. Will the increase in sales more than offset any added cost in the administrative department?
6. Also psychological factors, as customers' curiosity and caution.

I have given this illustration at length because it seems to me that this is the method which should be applied to controversy. I wish indeed that every controversy might be considered a problem.

You will notice that to break up a problem into its various parts involves the *examination of symbols,* involves, that is, the careful scrutiny of the language used to see what it really means. A friend of mine wanted to go to Europe, but also she did not want to spend the money it would cost. Was there any integration? Yes, she found one. In order to understand it, let us use the method I am advocating; let us ask, what did "going to Europe" symbolize to her? In order to do that, we have to break up this whole, "going to Europe." What does "going to Europe" stand for to different people? A sea voyage, seeing beautiful places, meeting new people, a rest or change from daily duties, and a dozen other things. Now, this woman had taught for a few years after leaving college and then had gone away and led a somewhat secluded life for a good many years. "Going to Europe" was to her a symbol, not of snow mountains, or cathedrals, or pictures, but of meeting people—that was what she wanted. When she was asked to teach in a summer school of young men and women where she would meet a rather interesting staff of teachers and a

rather interesting group of students, she immediately accepted. This was her integration. This was not a substitution for her wish, it was her *real* wish fulfilled.

I have given other illustration of symbols in Chapter IX of my book, *Creative Experience.* There was an interesting one in the Loeb-Leopold case. I think there should have been taken into consideration in that case what life imprisonment symbolized. As there was no question of freeing the boys, the decision was to be made between death and life imprisonment. Therefore, when the latter sentence was given, that was a symbol, it seemed to me, of victory for the boys, especially since everyone thought that their detention would last only a few years. In many cases, on the other hand, life imprisonment is a symbol of defeat. I do not think that this was taken into account sufficiently in considering the effect of the sentence on the country.

It is, of course, unavoidable to use symbols; all language is symbolic; but we should be always on our guard as to what is symbolized. For instance, the marketing cooperatives say that they want their members to keep their pledges. That statement is a symbol for what they *really* want, which is to get enough of the commodity to control the market. Every day we use many more not-understood symbols, many more whole-words, unanalysed words, than we ought to. Much of what is written of the "consumer" is inaccurate because consumer is used as a whole-word, whereas it is quite obvious that the consumer of large wealth has different desires and motives from the consumer of small means.

We have been considering the breaking up of the whole-demand. On the other hand, one often has to do just the opposite; find the whole-demand, the real demand, which is being obscured by miscellaneous minor claims or by ineffective presentation. The man with a genius for leadership is the one who can make articulate the whole-demand, unless it is a matter of tactics deliberately to conceal it. I shall not stop to give instances of this, as I wish to have time for some consideration of a point which seems to me very important for business, both in dealings with employees and with competing firms, and that is the anticipation of demands, of difference, of conflict.

Mr. Earl Howard, labour manager for Hart, Schaffner and Marx, said to me once, "It isn't enough merely to study the actual reactions of your employees; you must anticipate their reactions, beat them to it." That—to beat them to it—is exactly what each firm does try to do with its competing firms, but I do not think many managers study and anticipate the reactions of their employees as carefully as they do those of competing firms. It would be just as useful.

You could probably give me many illustrations of the *anticipation of response*. We could find innumerable examples in our households. A man liked motoring, his wife walking; he anticipated what her response might be to a suggestion that they motor on Sunday afternoon by tiring her out playing tennis in the morning.

The middlemen are deliberately anticipating response on the part of the farmers. In their struggle with the marketing co-operatives, they are basing their calculations of the future on the assumption that the particularistic tendency of the farmer is such that he cannot be held in line permanently, that he has been carried off his feet by victory and promises; moreover, that the use of legal power in enforcing contracts will in the end defeat the movement, that the farmer will surely rebel against this sort of coercion.

The anticipation of conflict, it should be noted, does not mean necessarily the avoidance of conflict, but playing the game differently. That is, you integrate the different interests without making all the moves. A friend of mine says that my theory of integration is like a game of chess. I think it is something like that. The tyro has to find his solution by making his actual moves, by the crude method of changing the places of his chessmen. A good chess player does not need to do this, he sees the possibilities without playing them out. The business man in dealing with competitive firms is like the good chess player. As the real conflict between two good chess players is a conflict of possibilities that would be realized if they played them out, so in business you do not have to make all the moves to make your integrations; you deal with antecedents, premonitory symptoms, etc. You do not avoid doing certain things, you have done them without doing them.

But assuming that in our business we do watch response and anticipate response, that still is not going far enough. It is not enough to ask to what

our employee or our business confrère or business competitor is responding, nor even to what he is likely to respond. We have to prepare the way for response, we have to try to build up in him a certain attitude. Of course every good salesman does this, but its necessity is not so fully recognized in other departments, and we shall therefore consider this question further in a later paper.

Yet even *preparation for response* is only a small part of the matter; we shall have to go deeper than that. There is *circular* as well as *linear* response, and the exposition of that is I think the most interesting contribution of contemporary psychology to the social sciences.[7] A good example of circular response is a game of tennis. A serves. The way B returns the ball depends partly on the way it was served to him. A's next play will depend on his own original serve plus the return of B, and so on and so on. We see this in discussion. We see this in most activity between one and another. Mischievous or idle boys say, "Let's start something"; we must remember that whenever we act we have always "started something," behaviour precipitates behaviour in others. Every employer should remember this. One of the managers in a factory expressed it to me thus: "I am in command of a situation until I behave; when I act I have lost control of the situation." This does not mean that we should not act! It is, however, something to which it is very important that we give full consideration.

Circular response seems a simple matter, quite obvious, something we must all accept. Yet every day we try to evade it, every day we act and hope to avoid the inescapable response. As someone has said in another connection, "We feed Cerberus raw meat and hope that when we lie between his paws, he will turn out to be a vegetarian."

The conception of circular behaviour throws much light on conflict, for I now realize that I can never fight you, I am always fighting you plus me. I have put it this way: that response is always to a relation. I respond, not only to you, but to the relation between you and me. Employees do not respond only to their employers, but to the relation between themselves and their employer. Trade unionism is responding, not only to capitalism, but to the relation between itself and capitalism. The Dawes plan, the London Conference, were obviously moments in circular behaviour. Circular behaviour as the basis of integration gives us the key to constructive conflict.

OBSTACLES TO INTEGRATION

Finally, let us consider the chief *obstacles to integration*. It requires a high order of intelligence, keen perception and discrimination, more than all, a brilliant inventiveness; it is easier for the trade union to fight than to suggest a better way of running the factory. You remember that the Socialist Party in Italy had a majority before Mussolini came in. But they would not take responsibility; they preferred to stay fighting, to attack what others were doing rather than to do themselves. They do not, I think, compare favourably with the English Labour Party.

Another obstacle to integration is that our way of life has habituated many of us to enjoy domination. Integration seems to many a tamer affair; it leaves no "thrills" of conquest. I knew a dispute within a trade union where, by the skilful action of the chairman, a true integration was discovered and accepted, but instead of the satisfaction one might have expected from such a happy result, the evening seemed to end rather dully, flatly; there was no climax, there was no side left swelling its chest, no one had conquered, no one had "won out." It is even true that to some people defeat, as well as conquest, is more interesting than integration. That is, the person with decided fight habits feels more at home, happier, in the fight movement. Moreover, it leaves the door open for further fighting, with the possibility of conquest the next time.

Another obstacle to integration is that the matter in dispute is often theorized over instead of being taken up as a proposed activity. I think this important in business administration. Intellectual agreement does not alone bring full integration. I know one factory which deliberately provides for this by the many activities of its many sub-committees, some of which seem rather trivial unless one sees just how these activities are a contribution to that functional unity which we shall consider in a later paper.

I have been interested to watch how often disagreement disappears when theorizing ends and the question is of some definite activity to be undertaken. At a trade union conference, someone brought up the question of waste: how could the workmen help to eliminate waste? But it was found that most of the union men did not think it the job of the workmen to eliminate waste; that belonged to the management. Moreover, they did not think it to their interest to eliminate waste; wages were fixed by the union, by collective bargaining; everything saved went to swell profits; no more went into their pockets. It was seen, however, that there was another side, and the argument went on, but without coming to any agreement. Finally, however, by some manœuvring on the part of the chairman, it was acknowledged that there were certain forms of waste which the unions could be got to take cognizance of. A machinist, a plumber and a carpenter undertook to take up with their unions the question of how far they could agree to take some responsibility for these particular types of waste. I hope the fact then emerged, when it was considered as a practical issue, that for some forms of waste the management is responsible, for some forms the employees, and for some forms the union.

A serious obstacle to integration which every business man should consider is the language used. We have noted the necessity of making preparation in the other man, and in ourselves too, for the attitude most favourable to reconciliation. A trade unionist said to me, "Our representatives didn't manage it right. If instead of a 15 per cent increase they had asked for an adjustment of wages, the management would have been more willing to listen to us; it would have put them in a different frame of mind." I don't quite see why we are not more careful about our language in business, for in most delicate situations we quite consciously choose that which will not arouse antagonism. You say to your wife at breakfast, "Let's reconsider that decision we came to last night." You do not say, "I wish to give you my criticism of the decision you made last night."

I cannot refrain from mentioning a personal experience. I went into the Edison Electric Light Company and said to a young woman at a counter, "Where shall I go to speak about my bill?" "Room D for complaints," she replied. "But I don't wish to make a complaint," I said. "I thought there was a mistake in your bill." "I think there is," I said, "but I don't wish to complain about it; it was a very natural mistake." The girl looked nonplussed, and as she was obviously speechless a man came out from behind a desk and said: "You would prefer to ask for an adjustment, wouldn't you?" and we had a chat about it.

I think that the "grievance committees" which exist in most factories are a mistake. I do not like the "trouble specialists" of the Ford plant. I wish it were not so often stated that shop or department committees were formed to "settle disputes." If you will get lists of these so-called "disputes," you will find that often they have not so much of the fight element in them as this word implies. But much of the language expressing the relation between capital and labour is that of a fight: "traditional enemies," the "weapon of the union," etc.

I have left untouched one of the chief obstacles to integration—namely, the undue influence of leaders—the manipulation of the unscrupulous on the one hand and the suggestibility of the crowd on the other. Moreover, even when the power of suggestion is not used deliberately, it exists in all meetings between people; the whole emotional field of human intercourse has to be taken fully into account in dealing with methods of reconciliation. I am deliberately omitting the consideration of this, not because I do not feel its importance as keenly as anyone, but because in these few papers we cannot cover everything.

Finally, perhaps the greatest of all obstacles to integration is our lack of training for it. In our college debates we try always to beat the other side. In the circular announcing the courses to be given at the Bryn Mawr Summer School for Workers, I find: "English Composition and Public Speaking; to develop the art of oral and written expression." I think that in addition to this there should be classes in discussion which should aim to teach the "art" of cooperative thinking, and I was disappointed that there was no such course in the programme of a school for workers. Managers need it just as much. I have found, in the case of the wage boards which I have been on, that many employers (I ought in fairness to say not the majority) came to these joint conferences of employers and employees with little notion of conferring, but to push through, to force through, plans *previously* arrived at, based on *preconceived* ideas of what employees are like. It seems as if the methods of genuine conference have yet to be learned. Even if

there were not the barriers of an unenlightened self-interest, of prejudice, rigidity, dogmatism, routine, there would still be required training and practice for us to master the technique of integration. A friend of mine said to me, "Open-mindedness is the whole thing, isn't it?" No, it isn't; it needs just as great a respect for your own view as for that of others, and a firm upholding of it until you are convinced. Mushy people are no more good at this than stubborn people.

As an indirect summing up of this discussion, I should like to emphasize our responsibility for integration. We saw in our consideration of circular response that my behaviour helps create the situation to which I am responding. That implies (what we have daily to take into account) that my behaviour is helping to *develop* the situation to which I am responding. The standard of living goes up not only while, but partly because, it is being studied. This conception of the developing situation is of the utmost importance for business administration. It makes it impossible to construct a map of the future, yet all our maxims of foresight hold good; every business should reconcile these two statements. We should work always with the evolving situation, and note what part our own activities have in that evolving situation.

This is the most important word, not only for business relations, but for all human relations: not to adapt ourselves to a situation—we are all more necessary to the world than that; neither to mould a situation to *our* liking—we are all, or rather each, of too little importance to the world for that; but to take account of that reciprocal adjustment, that interactive behaviour between the situation and ourselves which means a change in both the situation and ourselves. One test of business administration should be: is the organization such that both employers and employees, or co-managers, co-directors, are stimulated to a reciprocal activity which will give more than mere adjustment, more than an equilibrium? Our outlook is narrowed, our activity is restricted, our chances of business success largely diminished when our thinking is constrained within the limits of what has been called an either-or situation. We should never allow ourselves to be bullied by an "either-or." There is often the possibility of something better than either of two given alternatives. Every one of us interested in any form of constructive work is looking for the plus values of our activity. In a later paper, on *Business as an Integrative Unity,* we shall consider how we can find in business administration those plus values which alone mean progress, progress for the individual and for whatever business or service we have undertaken for ourselves and for our community.

NOTES

1. This and the three succeeding papers reprinted from *Scientific Foundations of Business Administration,* Henry C. Metcalf, *Editor,* The Williams and Wilkins Company, Baltimore, 1926. Miss Follett's main theme in these four contributions to this series of conferences was "The *Psychological* Foundations." This paper was first presented before a Bureau of Personnel Administration conference group in January, 1925.

2. *Cf. Creative Experience,* p. 300: "What people often mean by getting rid of conflict is getting rid of diversity, and it is of the utmost importance that these should not be considered the same. We may wish to abolish conflict, but we cannot get rid of diversity. We must face life as it is and understand that diversity is its most essential feature . . . Fear of difference is dread of life itself. It is possible to conceive conflict as not necessarily a wasteful outbreak of incompatibilities, but a *normal* process by which socially valuable differences register themselves for the enrichment of all concerned."

3. *Cf. The New State,* Chapter XIV, for a discussion of the relations of capital and labour. "The weakness of arbitration and conciliation boards, with their 'impartial' member, is that they tend to mere compromise even when they are not openly negotiations between two warring parties" (p. 115).

4. For a fuller exposition of the principle of integration as the foundation of Mary Follett's thought on the subject of group psychology, see *Creative Experience,* Chapter IX, "Experience as Creating." *Cf.* p. 156: "Integration, the most suggestive word of contemporary psychology, is, I believe, the active principle of human intercourse scientifically lived."

5. In a Letter to the Editor in *The Times,* June 6th, 1924, Professor Gilbert Murray writes to draw attention to the influence of previous decisions and methods of the League of Nations on the members of the Dawes Committee. He quotes four matters on which French and British opinion was widely divergent, but where agreement was reached by the mutual adoption of League solutions in previous comparable problems. These instances are illustrations of the method of "integration" that Mary Follett was so keen to expound. (The matters in dispute were: the currency of German reparations payments; the fixation of total German liability; the necessity of external control, or wisdom of trusting completely to German good faith; the relation of German capacity to pay to the problem of fixing the final total liability.)

6. *Cf. Creative Experience,* pp. 167–8: "Again, labour and capital can never be reconciled as long as labour persists in thinking that there is a capitalist point of view and capitalists that there is a labour point of view. There is not. These are imaginary wholes which must be broken up before capital and labour can co-operate."

7. *Cf. Creative Experience,* Chapter III, "Experience in the Light of Recent Psychology: Circular Response."

SOURCE: Follett, Mary Parker. [1926] 1942. "Constructive Conflict." Pp. 30–49 in *Dynamic Administration: The Collected Papers of Mary Parker Follett.* New York: Harper and Brothers.

38

ORGANIZATIONAL CONFLICT

Concepts and Models

LOUIS R. PONDY

There is a large and growing body of literature on the subject of organizational conflict. The concept of conflict has been treated as a general social phenomenon, with implications for the understanding of conflict within and between organizations.[1] It has also assumed various roles of some importance in attempts at general theories of management and organizational behavior.[2] Finally, conflict has recently been the focus of numerous empirical studies of organization.[3]

Slowly crystallizing out of this research are three conceptual models designed to deal with the major classes of conflict phenomena in organizations.[4]

1. *Bargaining model.* This is designed to deal with conflict among interest groups in competition for scarce resources. This model is particularly appropriate for the analysis of labor-management relations, budgeting processes, and staff-line conflicts.

2. *Bureaucratic model.* This is applicable to the analysis of superior-subordinate conflicts or, in general, conflicts along the vertical dimension of a hierarchy. This model is primarily concerned with the problems caused by institutional attempts to control behavior and the organization's reaction to such control.

3. *Systems model.* This is directed at lateral conflict, or conflict among the parties to a functional relationship. Analysis of the problems of coordination is the special province of this model.

Running as common threads through each of these models are several implicit orientations. The most important of these orientations follow:

1. Each conflict relationship is made up of a sequence of interlocking conflict episodes; each episode exhibits a sequence or pattern of development, and the conflict relationship can be characterized by stable patterns that appear across the sequence of episodes. This orientation forms the basis for a working definition of conflict.

2. Conflict may be functional as well as dysfunctional for the individual and the organization; it may have its roots either within the individual or in the organizational context; therefore, the desirability of conflict resolution needs to be approached with caution.

3. Conflict is intimately tied up with the stability of the organization, not merely in the usual sense that conflict is a threat to stability, but in a much more complex fashion; that is, conflict is a key variable in the feedback loops

that characterize organizational behavior. These orientations are discussed before the conceptual models are elaborated.

A WORKING DEFINITION OF CONFLICT

The term "conflict" has been used at one time or another in the literature to describe: (1) *antecedent conditions* (for example, scarcity of resources, policy differences) of conflictful behavior, (2) *affective states* (e.g., stress, tension, hostility, anxiety, etc.) of the individuals involved, (3) *cognitive states* of individuals, i.e., their perception or awareness of conflictful situations, and (4) *conflictful behavior,* ranging from passive resistance to overt aggression. Attempts to decide which of these classes—conditions, attitude, cognition, or behavior—is really conflict is likely to result in an empty controversy. The problem is not to choose among these alternative conceptual definitions, since each may be a relevant stage in the development of a conflict episode, but to try to clarify their relationships.

Conflict can be more readily understood if it is considered a dynamic process. A conflict relationship between two or more individuals in an organization can be analyzed as a sequence of conflict episodes. Each conflict episode begins with conditions characterized by certain conflict potentials. The parties to the relationship may not become aware of any basis of conflict, and they may not develop hostile affections for one another. Depending on a number of factors, their behavior may show a variety of conflictful traits. Each episode or encounter leaves an aftermath that affects the course of succeeding episodes. The entire relationship can then be characterized by certain stable aspects of conditions, affect, perception, and behavior. It can also be characterized by trends in any of these characteristics.

This is roughly analogous to defining a "decision" to include activities preliminary to and following choice, as well as the choice itself. In the same sense that a decision can be thought of as a process of gradual commitment to a course of action, a conflict episode can be thought of as a gradual escalation to a state of disorder. If choice is the climax of a decision, then by analogy, open war or aggression is the climax of a conflict episode.

This does not mean that every conflict episode necessarily passes through every stage to open aggression. A potential conflict may never be perceived by the parties to the conflict, or if perceived, the conflict may be resolved before hostilities break out. Several other alternative courses of development are possible. Both Coleman and Aubert make these points clearly in their treatments of the dynamics of conflict.[5]

Just as some decisions become programmed or routinized, conflict management in an organization also becomes programmed or institutionalized sometimes. In fact, the institutionalization of means for dealing with recurrent conflict is one of the important aspects in any treatment of the topic. An organization's success hinges to a great extent on its ability to set up and operate appropriate mechanisms for dealing with a variety of conflict phenomena.

Five stages of a conflict episode are identified: (1) latent conflict (conditions), (2) perceived conflict (cognition), (3) felt conflict (affect), (4) manifest conflict (behavior), and (5) conflict aftermath (conditions). The elaboration of each of these stages of a conflict episode will provide the substance for a working definition. Which specific reactions take place at each stage of a conflict episode, and why, are the central questions to be answered in a theory of conflict. Only the framework within which those questions can be systematically investigated is developed here.

Latent Conflict

A search of the literature has produced a long list of underlying sources of organizational conflict. These are condensed into three basic types of latent conflict: (1) competition for scarce resources, (2) drives for autonomy, and (3) divergence of subunit goals. Later in the paper each of these fundamental types of latent conflict is paired with one of the three conceptual models. Briefly, competition forms the basis for conflict when the aggregated demands of participants for resources exceed the resources available to the organization; autonomy needs form the basis of conflict when one party either seeks to exercise control over some activity that another party regards as his own province or seeks to insulate itself from such control;

goal divergence is the source of conflict when two parties who must cooperate on some joint activity are unable to reach a consensus on concerted action. Two or more types of latent conflict may, of course, be present simultaneously.

An important form of latent conflict, which appears to be omitted from this list, is role conflict. The role conflict model treats the organization as a collection of role sets, each composed of the focal person and his role senders. Conflict is said to occur when the focal person receives incompatible role demands or expectations from the persons in his role set.[6] This model has the drawback that it treats the focal person as merely a passive receiver rather than as an active participant in the relationship.

It is argued, here, that the role conflict model does not postulate a distinct type of latent conflict. Instead, it defines a conceptual relationship, the role set, which may be useful for the analysis of all three forms of latent conflict described.

Perceived Conflict

Conflict may sometimes be perceived when no conditions of latent conflict exist, and latent conflict conditions may be present in a relationship without any of the participants perceiving the conflict.

The case in which conflict is perceived when no latent conflict exists can be handled by the so-called "semantic model" of conflict.[7] According to this explanation, conflict is said to result from the parties' misunderstanding of each others' true position. It is argued that such conflict can be resolved by improving communications between the parties. This model has been the basis of a wide variety of management techniques aimed at improving interpersonal relations. Of course, if the parties' true positions *are* in opposition, then more open communication may only exacerbate the conflict.

The more important case, that some latent conflicts fail to reach the level of awareness, also requires explanation. Two important mechanisms that limit perception of conflict are the suppression mechanism and the attention-focus mechanism.[8] Individuals tend to block conflicts that are only mildly threatening out of awareness.[9] Conflicts become strong threats, and therefore must be acknowledged, when the conflicts relate to values central to the individual's personality. The suppression mechanism is applicable more to conflicts related to personal than to organizational values. The attention-focus mechanism, however, is related more to organizational behavior than to personal values. Organizations are characteristically faced with more conflicts than can be dealt with, given available time and capacities. The normal reaction is to focus attention on only a few of these, and these tend to be the conflicts for which short-run, routine solutions are available. For organizations successfully to confront the less programmed conflicts, it is frequently necessary to set up separate subunits specifically to deal with such conflicts.

Felt Conflict

There is an important distinction between perceiving conflict and feeling conflict. *A* may be aware that *B* and *A* are in serious disagreement over some policy, but it may not make *A* tense or anxious, and it may have no effect whatsoever on *A*'s affection towards *B*. The personalization of conflict is the mechanism which causes most students of organization to be concerned with the dysfunctions of conflict. There are two common explanations for the personalization of conflict.

One explanation is that the inconsistent demands of efficient organization and individual growth create anxieties within the individual.[10] Anxieties may also result from identity crises or from extra-organizational pressures. Individuals need to vent these anxieties in order to maintain internal equilibrium. Organizational conflicts of the three latent types described earlier provide defensible excuses for displacing these anxieties against suitable targets. This is essentially the so-called "tension-model."[11]

A second explanation is that conflict becomes personalized when the whole personality of the individual is involved in the relationship. Hostile feelings are most common in the intimate relations that characterize total institutions, such as monasteries, residential colleges, and families.[12] In order to dissipate accumulated hostilities, total institutions require certain safety-valve institutions such as athletic activities or norms that legitimize solitude and withdrawal, such as the noncommunication norms prevalent in religious orders.

Thus, felt conflict may arise from sources independent of the three types of latent conflict, but latent conflicts may provide appropriate targets (perhaps symbolic ones) for undirected tensions.

Manifest Conflict

By manifest conflict is meant any of several varieties of conflictful behavior. The most obvious of these is open aggression, but such physical and verbal violence is usually strongly proscribed by organizational norms. Except for prison riots, political revolutions, and extreme labor unrest, violence as a form of manifest conflict in organizations is rare. The motivations toward violence may remain, but they tend to be expressed in less violent form. Dalton has documented the covert attempts to sabotage or block an opponent's plans through aggressive and defensive coalitions.[13] Mechanic has described the tactics of conflict used by lower-level participants, such as apathy or rigid adherence to the rules, to resist mistreatment by the upper levels of the hierarchy.[14]

How can one decide when a certain behavior or pattern of behavior is conflictful? One important factor is that the behavior must be interpreted in the context in which it takes place. If A does not interact with B, it may be either because A and B are not related in any organizational sense, or because A has withdrawn from a too stressful relationship, or because A is deliberately frustrating B by withdrawing support, or simply because A is drawn away from the relationship by other competing demands upon his time. In other words, knowledge of the organizational requirements and of the expectations and motives of the participants appears to be necessary to characterize the behavior as conflictful. This suggests that behavior should be defined to be conflictful if, and only if, some or all of the participants perceive it to be conflictful.

Should the term *manifest conflict* [emphasis added] be reserved for behavior which, in the eyes of the actor, is deliberately and consciously designed to frustrate another in the pursuit of his (the other's) overt or covert goals? But what of behavior which is not *intended* to frustrate, but does? Should not that behavior also be called conflictful? The most useful definition of manifest conflict seems to be that behavior which, in the mind of the actor, frustrates the goals of at least some of the other participants. In other words, a member of the organization is said to engage in conflictful behavior if he consciously, but not necessarily deliberately, blocks another member's goal achievement. He may engage in such behavior *deliberately* to frustrate another, or he may do so in spite of the fact that he frustrates another. To define manifest conflict in this way is to say that the following question is important: "Under what conditions will a party to a relationship *knowingly* frustrate another party to the relationship?" Suppose A unknowingly blocks B's goals. This is not conflictful behavior. But suppose B informs A that he perceives A's behavior to be conflictful; if then A acknowledges the message and *persists* in the behavior, it is an instance of manifest conflict.

The interface between perceived conflict and manifest conflict and the interface between felt conflict and manifest conflict are the pressure points where most conflict resolution programs are applied. The object of such programs is to prevent conflicts which have reached the level of awareness or the level of affect from erupting into noncooperative behavior. The availability of appropriate and effective administrative devices is a major factor in determining whether conflict becomes manifest. The collective bargaining apparatus of labor-management disputes and budgeting systems for internal resource allocation are administrative devices for the resolution of interest-group conflicts. Evan and Scott have described due process or appeal systems for resolving superior-subordinate conflicts.[15] Mechanisms for resolving lateral conflicts among the parties to a functional relationship are relatively undeveloped. Transfer-pricing systems constitute one of the few exceptions. Much more common are organizational arrangements designed to *prevent* lateral conflicts, e.g., plans, schedules, and job descriptions, which define and delimit subunit responsibilities. Another alternative is to reduce the interdependence between conflicting subunits by introducing buffers, such as inventories, which reduce the need for sales and production departments in a business firm to act in perfect accord.

The mere availability of such administrative devices is not sufficient to prevent conflict from becoming manifest. If the parties to a relationship do not value the relationship, or if conflict is strategic in the pursuit of subunit goals, then conflictful behavior is likely. Furthermore, once conflict breaks out on some specific issue, then the conflict frequently widens and the initial specific conflict precipitates more general and more personal conflicts which had been suppressed in the interest of preserving the stability of the relationship.[16]

Conflict Aftermath

Each conflict episode is but one of a sequence of such episodes that constitute the relationships among organization participants.[17] If the conflict is genuinely resolved to the satisfaction of all participants, the basis for a more cooperative relationship may be laid; or the participants, in their drive for a more ordered relationship, may focus on latent conflicts not previously perceived and dealt with. On the other hand, if the conflict is merely suppressed but not resolved, the latent conditions of conflict may be aggravated and explode in more serious form until they are rectified or until the relationship dissolves. This legacy of a conflict episode is here called "conflict aftermath."[18]

However, the organization is not a closed system. The environment in which it is imbedded may become more benevolent and alleviate the conditions of latent conflict, for example, by making more resources available to the organization. But a more malevolent environment may precipitate new crises. The development of each conflict episode is determined by a complex combination of the effects of preceding episodes and the environmental milieu. The main ideas of this view of the dynamics of conflict are summarized in Figure 38.1.

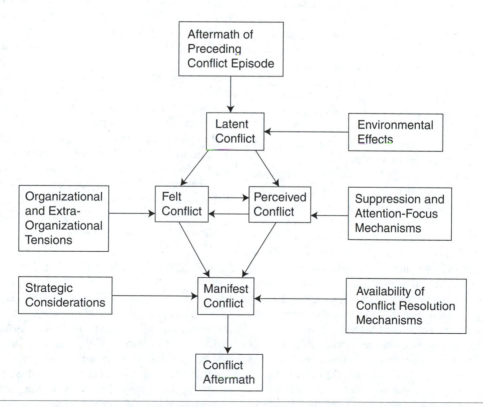

Figure 38.1   The Dynamics of a Conflict Episode

FUNCTIONS AND DYSFUNCTIONS OF CONFLICT

Few students of social and organizational behavior have treated conflict as a neutral phenomenon to be studied primarily because of scientific curiosity about its nature and form, its causes, and its effects. Most frequently the study of conflict has been motivated by a desire to resolve it and to minimize its deleterious effects on the psychological health of organizational participants and the efficiency of organization performance. Although Kahn and others pay lip service to the opinion that "one might well make a case for interpreting some conflict as essential for the continued development of mature and competent human beings," the overriding bias of their report is with the "personal costs of excessive emotional strain," and, they state, "the fact that common reactions to conflict and its associated tensions are often dysfunctional for the organization as an on-going social system and self-defeating for the person in the long run."[19] Boulding recognizes that some optimum level of conflict and associated personal stress and tension are necessary for progress and productivity, but he portrays conflict primarily as a personal and social cost.[20] Baritz argues that Elton Mayo has treated conflict as "an evil, a symptom of the lack of social skills," and its alleged opposite, cooperation, as "symptomatic of health."[21] Even as dispassionate a theory of organization as that of March and Simon defines conflict conceptually as a "*breakdown* in the standard mechanisms of decision making"; i.e., as a malfunction of the system.[22]

It has become fashionable to say that conflict may be either functional or dysfunctional and is not necessarily either one. What this palliative leaves implicit is that the effects of conflict must be evaluated relative to some set of values. The argument with those who seek uniformly to abolish conflict is not so much with their *a priori* assertion that conflict is undesirable, as it is with their failure to make explicit the value system on which their assertion rests.

For the purposes of this research, the effects of organizational conflict on individual welfare are not of concern. Conflict may threaten the emotional well-being of individual persons; it may also be a positive factor in personal character development; but this research is not addressed to these questions.

Intra-individual conflict is of concern only in so far as it has implications for organizational performance. With respect to organizational values, *productivity*, measured in both quantitative and qualitative terms, is valued; other things being equal, an organization is "better" if it produces more, if it is more innovative, and if its output meets higher standards of quality than other organizations. *Stability* is also valued. An organization improves if it can increase its cohesiveness and solvency, other things being equal. Finally *adaptability* is valued. Other things being equal, organizations that can learn and improve performance and that can adapt to changing internal and environmental pressures are preferred to those that cannot. In this view, therefore, to say that conflict is functional or dysfunctional is to say that it facilitates or inhibits the organization's productivity, stability, or adaptability.

Clearly, these values are not entirely compatible. An organization may have to sacrifice quality of output for quantity of output; if it pursues policies and actions that guarantee stability, it may inhibit its adaptive abilities. It is argued here that a given conflict episode or relationship may have beneficial or deleterious effects on productivity, stability, and adaptability. Since these values are incompatible, conflict may be simultaneously functional and dysfunctional for the organization.

A detailed examination of the functional and dysfunctional effects of conflict is more effectively made in the context of the three conceptual models. Underlying that analysis is the notion that conflict disturbs the "equilibrium" of the organization, and that the reaction of the organization to disequilibrium is the mechanism by which conflict affects productivity, stability, and adaptability.

CONFLICT AND EQUILIBRIUM

One way of viewing an organization is to think of each participant as making contributions, such as work, capital, and raw materials, in return for certain inducements, such as salary, interest, and finished goods. The organization is said to be in "equilibrium," if inducements exceed contributions (subjectively valued) for every participant, and in "disequilibrium" if contributions exceed inducements for some or all of the participants. Participants will be motivated to restore equilibrium either by leaving the organization for greener pastures, when the disequilibrium is said to be "unstable," or by attempting to achieve a favorable balance between inducements and contributions within the organization, when it is considered "stable." Since changing organizational affiliation frequently involves sizable costs, disequilibria tend to be stable.

If we assume conflict to be a cost of participation, this inducements-contributions balance theory may help in understanding organizational reactions to conflict. It suggests that the perception of conflict by the participants will motivate them to reduce conflict either by withdrawing from the relationship, or by resolving the conflict within the context of the relationship, or by securing increased inducements to compensate for the conflict.

The assumption that conflict creates a disequilibrium is implicit in nearly all studies of organizational conflict. For example, March and Simon assume that "where conflict is perceived, motivation to reduce conflict is generated," and conscious efforts to resolve conflict are made.[23] Not all treatments of the subject make this assumption, however. Harrison White attacks the March-Simon assumption of the disequilibrium of conflict as "naive."[24] He bases his assertion on his observation of chronic, continuous, high-level conflict in administrative settings. This, of course, raises the question, "Under what conditions *does* conflict represent a disequilibrium?"

To say that (perceived) conflict represents a state of disequilibrium and generates pressures for conflict resolution is to say three things: (1) that perceived conflict is a *cost* of participation; (2) that the conflict disturbs the inducements-contributions balance; and (3) that organization members react to perceptions of conflict by attempting to resolve the conflict, in *preference to* (although this is not made explicit in the March-Simon treatment) other reactions such as withdrawing from the relationship or attempting to gain added inducements to compensate for the conflict.

1. *Conflict as a cost.* Conflict is not necessarily a cost for the individual. Some participants may actually enjoy the "heat of battle." As Hans Hoffman argues, "The unique function of man is to live in close creative touch with chaos and thereby experience the birth of order."[25]

Conflict may also be instrumental in the achievement of other goals. One of the tactics of successful executives in the modern business enterprise is to create confusion as a cover for the expansion of their particular empire,[26] or, as Sorensen observes, deliberately to create dissent and competition among one's subordinates in order to ensure that he will be brought into the relationship as an arbiter at critical times, as Franklin D. Roosevelt did.[27] Or, conflict with an out-group may be desirable to maintain stability within the in-group.

In general, however, conflict can be expected to be negatively valued; particularly if conflict becomes manifest, and subunit goals and actions are blocked and frustrated. Latency or perception of conflict should be treated as a cost, only if harmony and uniformity are highly valued. Tolerance of divergence is not generally a value widely shared in contemporary organizations, and under these conditions latent and perceived conflict are also likely to be treated as costly.

2. *Conflict as a source of disequilibrium.* White's observation of *chronic* conflict creates doubt as to whether conflict represents a disequilibrium.[28] He argues that if conflict *were* an unstable state for the system, then only transient conflict or conflict over shifting foci would be observable. Even if organizational participants treat conflict as a cost, they may still endure intense, chronic conflict, if there are compensating inducements from the organization in the form of high salary, opportunities for advancement, and others. To say that a participant will endure chronic conflict is not to deny that he will be motivated to reduce it; it is merely to say that if the organization member is unsuccessful in reducing conflict, he may still continue to participate if the inducements offered to him exceed the contributions he makes in return. Although conflict may be one of several sources of disequilibrium, it is neither a necessary nor a sufficient condition of disequilibrium. But, as will be shown, equilibrium nevertheless plays an important role in organizational reactions to conflict.[29]

3. *Resolution pressures a necessary consequence of conflict.* If conflicts are relatively small, and the inducements and contributions remain in equilibrium, then the participants are likely to try

to resolve the conflict within the context of the existing relationship.[30] On the other hand, when contributions exceed inducements, or when conflict is intense enough to destroy the inducements-contributions balance and there is no prospect for the re-establishment of equilibrium, then conflict is likely to be reduced by dissolving the relationship. Temporary imbalances, of course, may be tolerated; i.e., the relationship will not dissolve if the participants perceive the conflicts to be resolvable in the near future.

What is the effect of conflict on the interaction rate among participants? It depends on the stability of the relationship. If the participants receive inducements in sufficient amounts to balance contributions, then perception of conflict is likely to generate pressures for *increased* interaction, and the content of the interaction is likely to deal with resolution procedures. On the other hand, if conflict represents a cost to the participant and this cost is not compensated by added inducements, then conflict is likely to lead to *decreased* interaction or withdrawal from the relationship.

To summarize, conflict is frequently, but not always, negatively valued by organization members. To the extent that conflict *is* valued negatively, minor conflicts generate pressures towards resolution without altering the relationship; and major conflicts generate pressures to alter the form of the relationship or to dissolve it altogether. If inducements for participation are sufficiently high, there is the possibility of chronic conflict in the context of a stable relationship.

THREE CONCEPTUAL MODELS OF ORGANIZATIONAL CONFLICT

As Ephron points out, only a very abstract model is likely to be applicable to the study of all organizational conflict phenomena.[31] To be useful in the analysis of real situations, a general theoretical framework must at least fit several broad classes of conflict, some or all of which may occur within the same organization. This suggests that different ways of abstracting or conceptualizing a given organization are required, depending on what phenomena are to be studied. The three models of organization

described at the beginning of this paper are the basis of the general theory of conflict presented here.

Bargaining Model

A reasonable measure of the potential conflict among a set of interest groups is the discrepancy between aggregated demands of the competing parties and the available resources. Attempts at conflict resolution usually center around attempting either to increase the pool of available resources or to decrease the demands of the parties to the conflict. Because market mechanisms or elaborate administrative mechanisms have usually evolved to guarantee orderly allocation of scarce resources, bargaining conflicts rarely escalate to the manifest level, except as strategic maneuvers.[32] Walton and McKersie describe such conflicts as complex relationships which involve both integrative (cooperative) and distributive (competitive) subprocesses.[33] Each party to the conflict has an interest in making the total resources as large as possible, but also in securing as large a share of them as possible for itself. The integrative subprocess is largely concerned with joint problem solving, and the distributive subprocess with strategic bargaining. A major element of strategy in strategic bargaining is that of attitudinal structuring, whereby each party attempts to secure the moral backing of relevant third parties (for example, the public or the government).

An important characteristic of interest-group conflicts is that negotiation is frequently done by representatives who face the dual problems of (1) securing consensus for the negotiated solution among respective group members, and (2) compromising between the demands for flexibility by his opposite number and the demands for rigidity by his own group.[34] The level of perceived conflict will increase as the deadline for a solution approaches; and interest-group conflicts are invariably characterized by deadline pressures.

Most of Walton and McKersie's framework has been developed and applied within the context of labor-management relations. But the interest-group model is not limited to this sphere of activity. Pondy has described the process of capital budgeting as a process of conflict resolution among departments competing for investment funds.[35] Wildavsky has described government budgeting as a political process involving the paraphernalia of bargaining among legislative and executive interest groups.[36] Just as past labor agreements set precedents for current labor agreements, budgeting is an incremental process that builds on the residues of previous budgetary conflicts. But, whereas the visible procedures of bargaining are an accepted part of labor-management relations, there are strong pressures in budgeting (particularly *business* budgeting) to conceal the bargaining that goes on and to attempt to cloak all decisions in the guise of rationality.[37]

Bureaucratic Model

The bureaucratic model (roughly equivalent to Ephron's "political" model) is appropriate for the analysis of conflicts along the *vertical* dimension of a hierarchy, that is, conflicts among the parties to an authority relation. Vertical conflicts in an organization usually arise because superiors attempt to control the behavior of subordinates, and subordinates resist such control. The authority relation is defined by the set of subordinate activities over which the subordinate has surrendered to a superior the legitimacy to exercise discretion.[38] The potential for conflict is thus present when the superior and subordinate have different expectations about the zone of indifference. The subordinate is likely to perceive conflict when the superior attempts to exercise control over activities outside the zone of indifference; and the superior perceives conflict when his attempts at control are thwarted. Superiors are likely to interpret subordinate resistance as due to resentment of the exercise of *personal* power. A typical bureaucratic reaction to subordinate resistance is therefore the substitution of impersonal rules for personal control. As numerous students of bureaucracy are quick to point out, however, the unanticipated reaction to rules is more conflict, not less. The usual reasoning goes as follows: The imposition of rules defines the authority relation more clearly and robs the subordinate of the autonomy provided by ambiguity. Replacing supervision with control by rules invariably narrows the subordinate's freedom of action, makes his behavior more predictable to others, and thus weakens his power position in the organization. Control

over the conditions of one's own existence, if not over others', is highly valued in organizations, particularly in large organizations. The subordinate therefore perceives himself to be threatened by and in conflict with his superiors, who are attempting to decrease his autonomy.

But why should autonomy be so important? What is the drawback to being subject to a benevolent autocrat? The answer, of course, is that autocrats seldom are or seldom remain benevolent. There is no assurance that the superior's (the organization's) goals, interests, or needs will be compatible with those of the subordinate, especially when: (1) organizations are so large that the leaders cannot identify personally with the rank and file; (2) responsibilities are delegated to organizational subunits, and subunit goals, values, etc. become differentiated from those of the hierarchy; and (3) procedures are formalized, and the organization leaders tend to treat rank and file members as mere instrumentalities or executors of the procedures.

In short, numerous factors influence goals and values along the vertical dimension of an organization; therefore, because subordinates to an authority relation can not rely on superiors to identify with their goals, autonomy becomes important. This leads to resistance by subordinates to attempts by superiors to control them, which in turn generates pressures toward routinization of activities and the institution of impersonal rules. This may lead to relatively predictable, conflict-free behavior, but behavior which is rigid and largely immune to personal persuasion. It is ironic that these very factors provide the potential for conflict when the organization must adapt to a changing environment. Rigidity of behavior, which minimizes conflict in a stable environment, is a major source of conflict when adaptability is required.

Research on leadership and on role conflict also provides important insights into vertical conflict. Whereas bureaucratic developments have sought to minimize conflict by altering the *fact* of supervision (for example, the use of impersonal rules and emphasis on procedure), leadership developments have sought to alter the *style* of supervision (for example, Likert's "linking pin" proposal and the various techniques of participative management).[39] Instead of minimizing dependence and increasing autonomy, leadership theorists have proposed minimizing conflict by using personal persuasion and group pressures to bring subordinate goals more closely into line with the legitimate goals of the organization. They have prescribed solutions which decrease autonomy and increase dependence. By heightening the individual's involvement in the organization's activities, they have actually provided the basis for the intense personal conflict that characterizes intimate relations.[40]

Both the bureaucratic and the leadership approaches to vertical conflict, as discussed here, take the superior-subordinate dyad as the unit of analysis. The role-conflict approach opens up the possibility of examining the conflicts faced by a man-in-the-middle between the demands of his subordinates and the demands of his superiors. Blau and Scott have suggested that effective leadership can occur only on alternate levels of a hierarchy.[41] The "man-in-the-middle" must align himself with the interests of either his superior or his subordinate, and in so doing he alienates the other. Of the three conceptual models of conflict, the bureaucratic model has probably received the most attention from researchers from a wide variety of disciplines. Partly because of this diversity, and partly because of the case with which researchers identify with values of efficiency or democracy, this model is the least straightforward of the three.

Systems Model

The systems model, like Ephron's "administrative" model, derives largely from the March-Simon treatment of organizational conflict.[42] It is appropriate for the analysis of conflicts among the parties to a functional relationship. Or to use Walton's terminology, the systems model is concerned with "lateral" conflicts or conflicts among persons at the same hierarchial level.[43] Whereas the authority-structure model is about problems of control, and the interest-group model is about problems of competition, the systems model is about problems of coordination.

The dyad is taken as the basic building block of the conceptual system. Consider two individuals, each occupying some formal position in an organization and playing some formal role with respect to the other. For example, A is the production manager and B the marketing manager of the XYZ company. The production manager's position is defined by the responsibility to use resources at his disposal (for example, raw materials, workers, machines) to manufacture specified products within certain constraints of quantity, quality, cost, time, and perhaps procedure. The marketing manager's position is defined by the responsibility to use resources at his disposal (for example, promotional media, salesmen, salable goods) to market and sell the company's products within certain constraints of product mix, cost, profitability, customer satisfaction, and so on. The constraints under which each manager operates and the resources at his disposal may be set for him by himself, by the other manager, or by someone else either in or outside of the company. The role of each with respect to the other is specified by the set of directions, requests, information, and goods which he minimally must or maximally may give to or receive from the other manager. The roles may also specify instances of and procedures for joint selection of product mix, schedules, and so on. These *formal* specifications of position and role are frequently described in written job descriptions, but may also form part of a set of unwritten, stable, widely shared expectations legitimized by the appropriate hierarchial authorities. If certain responsibilities and activities are exercised without legitimization, that is, without the conscious, deliberate recognition and approval of the appropriate authorities, then they constitute *informal* positions and roles. Such expectations may still be widely shared, and are not necessarily illegitimate, i.e., specifically proscribed by the hierarchial authorities.

The fundamental source of conflict in such a system arises out of the pressures toward suboptimization. Assume first that the organization is goal-oriented rather than procedure-oriented. The subunits in a goal-oriented system will, for various reasons, have different sets of active goals,[44] or different preference orderings for the same set of goals. If in turn, two subunits having differentiated goals are functionally interdependent, then conditions exist for conflict. Important types of interdependence matter are: (1) common usage of some service or facility, (2) sequences of work or information flow prescribed by task or hierarchy, and (3) rules of unanimity or consensus about joint activity.

Two ways of reducing conflict in lateral relationships, if it be desirable to do so, therefore, are to reduce goal differentiation by modified incentive systems, or by proper selection, training, or assignment procedures; and to reduce functional interdependence. Functional interdependence is reduced by (1) reducing dependence on common resources; (2) loosening up schedules or introducing buffers, such as inventories or contingency funds; and (3) reducing pressures for consensus. These techniques of preventing conflict may be costly in both direct and indirect costs. Interpersonal friction is one of the costs of "running a tight ship."

If the parties to the conflict are flexible in their demands and desires,[45] the conflict is likely to be perceived only as a transient disturbance. Furthermore, the conflict may not be perceived, if alternative relationships for satisfying needs are available. This is one of the persuasive arguments for building in redundant channels of work and information flow.

Some relationships may be traditionally conflictful (e.g., administration-faculty, sales-production, and others). The parties to such a relationship have a set to expect conflict, and therefore may perceive conflict when none exists.

As to the forms of manifested conflict, it is extremely unlikely that any violent or aggressive actions will occur. First, strongly held norms proscribe such behavior. Secondly, the reaction of other parties to the relationship is likely to be that of withdrawing all cooperation. A much more common reaction to perceived conflict is the adoption of a joint decision process characterized by bargaining rather than problem solving. Walton, Dutton, and Fitch have described some of the characteristics of a bargaining style: careful rationing of information and its deliberate distortion; rigid, formal, and circumscribed relations; suspicion, hostility, and disassociation among the subunits.[46] These rigidities and negative attitudes, of course, provide the potential for conflict over other issues in future episodes of the relationship.

Summary

It has been argued that conflict within an organization can be best understood as a dynamic process underlying a wide variety of organizational behaviors. The term *conflict* [emphasis added] refers neither to its antecedent conditions, nor individual awareness of it, nor certain affective states, nor its overt manifestations, nor its residues of feeling, precedent, or structure, but to all of these taken together as the history of a conflict episode.

Conflict is not necessarily bad or good, but must be evaluated in terms of its individual and organizational functions and dysfunctions. In general, conflict generates pressures to reduce conflict, but chronic conflict persists and is endured under certain conditions, and consciously created and managed by the politically astute administrator.

Conflict resolution techniques may be applied at any of several pressure points. Their effectiveness and appropriateness depends on the nature of the conflict and on the administrator's philosophy of management. The tension model leads to creation of safety-valve institutions and the semantic model to the promotion of open communication. Although these may be perfectly appropriate for certain forms of imagined conflict, their application to real conflict may only exacerbate the conflict.

A general theory of conflict has been elaborated in the context of each of three conceptual models: (1) a bargaining model, which deals with interest groups in competition for resources; (2) a bureaucratic model, which deals with authority relations and the need to control; and (3) a systems model, which deals with functional relations and the need to coordinate.

Notes

1. Jessie Bernard, T. H. Pear, Raymond Aron, and Robert C. Angell, *The Nature of Conflict* (Paris: UNESCO, 1957); Kenneth Boulding, *Conflict and Defense* (New York: Harper, 1962); Lewis Coser, *The Functions of Social Conflict* (Glencoe, Ill.: Free Press, 1956); Kurt Lewin, *Resolving Social Conflict* (New York: Harper, 1948); Anatol Rapaport, *Fights, Games, and Debates* (Ann Arbor: University of Michigan, 1960); Thomas C. Schelling, *The Strategy of Conflict* (Cambridge, Mass.: Harvard Univ., 1961); Muzafer Sherif and Carolyn Sherif, *Groups in Harmony and Tension* (Norman, Okla.: University of Oklahoma, 1953); Georg Simmel, *Conflict*, trans. Kurt H. Wolff (Glencoe, Ill.: Free Press, 1955).

2. Bernard M. Bass, *Organizational Psychology* (Boston, Mass.: Allyn and Bacon, 1965); Theodore Caplow, *Principles of Organization* (New York: Harcourt, Brace, and World, 1964); Eliot D. Chapple and Leonard F. Sayles, *The Measure of Management* (New York: Macmillan, 1961); Michel Crozier, *The Bureaucratic Phenomenon* (Glencoe, Ill.: Free Press, 1964); Richard M. Cyert and James G. March, *A Behavioral Theory of the Firm* (Englewood Cliffs, N. J.: Prentice-Hall, 1963); Alvin W. Gouldner, *Patterns of Industrial Bureaucracy* (Glencoe, Ill.: Free Press, 1954); Harold J. Leavitt, *Managerial Psychology* (Chicago: University of Chicago, 1964); James G. March and Herbert A. Simon, *Organizations* (New York: Wiley, 1958); Philip Selznick, *TVA and the Grass Roots* (Berkeley: University of California, 1949): Victor Thompson, *Modern Organization* (New York: Knopf, 1961).

3. Joseph L. Bower, The Role of Conflict in Economic Decision-making Groups, *Quarterly Journal of Economics,* 79 (May 1965), 253–257; Melville Dalton, *Men Who Manage* (New York: Wiley, 1959); J. M. Dutton and R. E. Walton, "Interdepartmental Conflict and Cooperation: A Study of Two Contrasting Cases," dittoed, Purdue University, October 1964; William Evan, Superior-Subordinate Conflict in Research Organizations, *Administrative Science Quarterly,* 10 (June 1965), 52–64; Robert L. Kahn, *et al., Studies in Organizational Stress* (New York: Wiley, 1964); L. R. Pondy, Budgeting and Inter-Group Conflict in Organizations, *Pittsburgh Business Review,* 34 (April 1964), 1–3; R. E. Walton, J. M. Dutton, and H. G. Fitch, *A Study of Conflict in the Process, Structure, and Attitudes of Lateral Relationships* (Institute Paper No. 93; Lafayette, Ind.: Purdue University, November 1964); Harrison White, Management Conflict and Sociometric Structure, *American Journal of Sociology,* 67 (September 1961), 185–199; Mayer N. Zald, Power Balance and Staff Conflict in Correctional Institutions, *Administrative Science Quarterly,* 7 (June 1962), 22–49.

4. The following conceptualization draws heavily on a paper by Lawrence R. Ephron, Group Conflict in Organizations: A Critical Appraisal of Recent Theories, *Berkeley Journal of Sociology,* 6 (Spring 1961), 53–72.

5. James S. Coleman, *Community Conflict* (Glencoe, Ill.: Free Press, 1957); Vilhelm Aubert, Competition and Dissensus: Two Types of Conflict and Conflict Resolution, *Journal of Conflict Resolution,* 7 (March 1963), 26–42.

6. Kahn, *et al., op. cit.,* pp. 11–35.

7. Bernard, Pear, Aron, and Angell, *op. cit.*

8. These two mechanisms are instances of what Cyert and March, *op. cit.,* pp. 117–118, call the "quasi-resolution" of conflict.

9. Leavitt, *op. cit.,* pp. 53–72.

10. Chris Argyris, *Personality and Organization: The Conflict Between the System and the Individual* (New York: Harper, 1957).

11. Bernard, Pear, Aron, and Angell, *op. cit.*

12. It should be emphasized that members of total institutions characteristically experience both strong positive and negative feelings for one another and toward the institution. It may be argued that this ambivalence of feeling is a primary cause of anxiety. See Coser, *op. cit.,* pp. 61–65; and Amitai Etzioni and W. R. Taber, Scope, Pervasiveness, and Tension Management in Complex Organizations, *Social Research,* 30 (Summer 1963), 220–238.

13. Dalton, *op. cit.*

14. David Mechanic, "Sources of Power of Lower Participants in Complex Organizations," in W. W. Cooper, H. J. Leavitt, and M. W. Shelly (eds.), *New Perspectives in Organization Research* (New York: Wiley, 1964), pp. 136–149.

15. Evan, *op. cit.*; William G. Scott, *The Management of Conflict: Appeals Systems in Organizations* (Homewood, Ill.; Irwin, 1965). It is useful to interpret recent developments in leadership and supervision (e.g., participative management, Theory Y, linking-pin functions) as devices for preventing superior-subordinate conflicts from arising, thus, hopefully, avoiding the problem of developing appeals systems in the first place.

16. See Coleman, *op. cit.,* pp. 9–11, for an excellent analysis of this mechanism. A chemical analogue of this situation is the supersaturated solution, from which a large amount of chemical salts can be precipitated by the introduction of a single crystal.

17. The sequential dependence of conflict episodes also plays a major role in the analysis of role conflicts by Kahn, *et al., op. cit.,* pp. 11–35. Pondy, *op. cit.,* has used the concept of "budget residues" to explain how precedents set in budgetary bargains guide and constrain succeeding budget proceedings.

18. Aubert, *op. cit.*

19. Kahn, *et al., op. cit.,* p. 65.

20. Boulding, *op. cit.,* pp. 305–307.

21. Loren Baritz, *The Servants of Power* (Middletown, Conn.: Wesleyan University, 1960), p. 203.

22. March and Simon, *op. cit.,* p. 112, italics mine. At least one author, however, argues that a "harmony bias" permeates the entire March-Simon volume. It is argued that what March and Simon call conflicts are mere "frictions" and "differences that are not within a community of interests are ignored." See Sherman Krupp, *Pattern in Organization Analysis* (New York: Holt, Rinehart and Winston, 1961), pp. 140–167.

23. March and Simon, *op. cit.,* pp. 115, 129.

24. Harrison While, *op. cit.*

25. Quoted in H. J. Leavitt and L. R. Pondy, *Readings in Managerial Psychology* (Chicago: University of Chicago, 1964), p. 58.

26. Dalton, *op. cit.*

27. Theodore Sorensen, *Decision Making in the White House* (New York: Columbia University, 1963), p. 15. This latter tactic, of course, is predicated and the fact that, *for the subordinates,* conflict is indeed a cost!

28. Harrison White, *op. cit.*

29. Conflict may actually be a source of equilibrium and stability, as Coser, *op. cit.*, p. 159, points out. A multiplicity of conflicts internal to a group, Coser argues, may breed solidarity, provided that the conflicts do not divide the group along the same axis, because the multiplicity of coalitions and associations provide a web of affiliation for the exchange of dissenting viewpoints. The essence of his argument is that some conflict is inevitable, and that it is better to foster frequent minor conflicts of interest, and thereby gradually adjust the system, and so forestall the accumulation of latent antagonisms which might eventually disrupt the organization. Frequent minor conflicts also serve to keep the antagonists accurately informed of each other's relative strength, thereby preventing a serious miscalculation of the chances of a successful major conflagration and promoting the continual and gradual readjustment of structure to coincide with true relative power.

30. For example, labor unions, while they wish to win the economic conflict with management, have no interest in seeing the relationship destroyed altogether. They may, however, choose to threaten such disruptive conflict as a matter of strategy.

31. Ephron, *op. cit.*, p. 55.

32. However, the Negro demonstrations of the 1960's and the labor riots of the early twentieth century testify to the futility of managing interest-group conflicts when mechanisms for resolution are not available or when the parties in power refuse to create such mechanisms.

33. R. E. Walton and R. B. McKersie, *A Behavorial Theory of Labor Negotiations* (New York: McGraw-Hill, 1965).

34. These two negotiator problems are termed "factional conflict" and "boundary conflict" by Walton and McKersie, *op. cit.*, p. 283 ff.

35. Pondy, *op. cit.*

36. Aaron Wildavsky, *The Politics of the Budgetary Process* (Boston: Little, Brown, 1964).

37. March and Simon, *op. cit.*, p. 131.

38. This set of activities is usually called the "zone of indifference" or "zone of acceptance." See Chester Barnard, *The Functions of the Executive* (Cambridge, Mass.: Harvard University, 1960), pp. 168–170, and Herbert A. Simon, *Administrative Behavior* (New York: Macmillan, 1960), pp. 11–13.

39. Rensis Likert, *New Patterns of Management* (New York: McGraw-Hill, 1961); see, for example, Chris Argyris, *Interpersonal Competence and Organizational Effectiveness* (Homewood, Ill.: Dorsey, 1962), or Douglas McGregor, *The Human Side of Enterprise* (New York: McGraw-Hill, 1960).

40. Coser, *op. cit.*, pp. 67–72.

41. Peter Blau and Richard Scott, *Formal Organizations* (San Francisco: Chandler, 1962), pp. 162–163.

42. March and Simon, *op. cit.*, pp. 112–185.

43. R. E. Walton, "Theory of Conflict in Lateral Organizational Relationships" (Institute Paper No. 85; Lafayette, Ind.: Purdue University, November 1964).

44. Following Simon, we treat a goal as any criterion of decision. Thus, both purposes and constraints are taken to be goals. See Herbert A. Simon, On the Concept of Organizational Goal, *Administrative Science Quarterly,* 9 (June 1964), 1–22.

45. Such flexibility is one of the characteristics of a problem-solving relationship. Conversely, a bargaining relationship is characterized by rigidity of demands and desires.

46. Walton, Dutton, and Fitch, *op. cit.*

SOURCE: Pondy, Louis R. 1967. "Organizational Conflict: Concepts and Models." *Administrative Science Quarterly*, 12(2):296–320.

39

MARX, GLOBALIZATION, AND ALIENATION

Received and Underappreciated Wisdoms

W. PETER ARCHIBALD

ABSTRACT

At the World Congress of Sociology in 2006, the official rationale for re-examining 'alienation' within a global context was that alienating factory work has now been eradicated, humanized and/or simply compensated for by high levels of consumption in post-industrialized societies, with alienation from work having been 'exported' to offices there and sweatshops in newly industrializing countries. However, alienation from work in industrially developed countries does not appear to have decreased, nor have longstanding inequalities in alienation favoring high status employees been reversed. Instead, any credible account must recognize cyclical and long-term economic crises and continued downsizing that have produced levels of un- and under-employment and job insecurity in industrially developed countries that have sometimes rivaled those in the Great Depression of the 1930s. Specifically how these trends have affected alienation is taken up in a subsequent article. . . .

WHY AND HOW WE SHOULD USE MARX'S 'ALIENATION' EMPIRICALLY

One would think that when others suggest that Marx's theory of alienation no longer has much relevance, Marxists would man (person) the barricades to defend it by doing their own, systematic empirical research. However, as noted above, this has seldom happened. In fact, it did not occur much in the 1960s and 1970s either, even when Blauner (1964), Kohn (1976) and others claimed that their own research indicated that capitalism and classes based on ownership of the means of production are not important sources of alienation, and certainly much less important than one's place in bureaucratic hierarchies and the nature of the technologies with which one works. Instead, many Marxists have acted like ruling classes by exercising 'repressive tolerance' (let your opponents speak but then do not listen or respond to them), or taking various maneuvers to dismiss or drastically restrict the use of empirical methods to study alienation in the first place. Indeed, two reviewers of an earlier draft of this article attempted to discourage this Marxist from defending Marx with empirical research on psychic alienation.

One argument of Hegelian Marxists is that the latter research is not appropriate because Marx's own assignments and explanations for alienation are based upon a view of individuals' human nature, their 'species-being,' as only an ontology; an abstract, conceptual, philosophical and prescriptively normative 'shell' that is only metaphysical. Since our human nature exists only as an abstract potential that has no current empirical referents, neither it nor our estrangement from it can be measured and explained by other, empirically verifiable circumstances (Mezaros, 1972; Ollman, 1971). A less extreme claim is that alienation can be studied empirically in *principle,* but since our nature as humans is open-ended and continuously evolving, alienation from it is also difficult to study empirically, in *practice.*

However, the latter stance is then sometimes fortified with another consideration. Since everything is related to everything else empirically as well as conceptually, for Marx both human nature and alienation refer to collectivities and social systems rather than distinct and autonomous individuals. Furthermore, all members of societies with industrial capitalist modes of production will be alienated, and equally. Moreover, since alienation comes only from capitalism or other class systems, Marx correctly believed that alienation cannot be substantially reduced by reforms to capitalism, even when the latter are achieved by workers' own struggles. Simply arguing otherwise, let alone claiming to have demonstrated it, is to be non-Marxist.

Althusser (1969) and his structuralist followers (e.g. Molina, 1978) agreed that Marx did not take individuals as his unit of analysis, but otherwise they have been distinct from Hegelians. Whereas the latter had used the philosophical, normative models in Marx's earliest writings to criticize authoritarian socialist regimes like the Soviet Union (e.g. Fromm, 1967), Althusser defended the latter by maintaining that the mature Marx himself had rejected not only the baseline of distinct and autonomous individuals, but any notions of a common human nature whatsoever, and therefore also 'alienation.' They are not only 'unscientific,' because they are only

philosophical and normative, but simply aspects of bourgeois ideology. Nevertheless, here too there are more moderate positions. Specifically, it is alright to retain the concept of alienation, providing one

a) leaves behind philosophical, and perhaps also methodologically individualistic and psychological, views of human nature and alienation, or, at least,
b) restricts alienation to the objective powerlessness of individuals.

Mills (1951) came close to the latter position, but Braverman (1974) is a more recent and purer case.

These various positions have been critiqued earlier (Archibald, 1978a, 1989/1993; Israel, 1970, 1979) and cannot be fully repeated here. However, here is a brief summary.

First, while Marx used 'alienation' at various levels of analysis at all stages of his career—that is, the philosophical/normative, objective powerlessness and subjective, psychic processes and states—he did rely less and less on the first. After all, this was the major point of both *The German Ideology* and *The Poverty of Philosophy.* Furthermore, when he became aware that he was regressing to his early Hegelianism, Marx (1973[1857]: 151) then seemed embarrassed and apologetic, and vowed to convert the merely conceptual into more causal and empirical terms.

Secondly, the historical materialism of his middle writings did represent a major shift in other aspects of his thinking. Nevertheless, contrary to Althusser, this shift was much more methodological than substantive. One should ground one's theorizing in systematic, comparative, historical and cross-sectional empirical research, rather than 'armchair,' abstract, *a priori* speculation about anything. In addition, one cannot simply take allegedly distinct and autonomous individuals as one's initial units of analysis. Yet, these need not mean that one should not take *relatively* distinct and autonomous 'individuals' as units of analysis, or that one cannot infer commonalities to human nature.

The whole point of Marx's theories of individuation and agency (1973[1857]: 471–514; see Archibald, 1989/1993) is that the distinctiveness and autonomy of individuals vary greatly, not only across modes of production, classes and periods of history, but within capitalism itself. Indeed, for most of its 'life,' capitalism severely 'atomizes' workers. For example, their employment contracts with their employers are between 'individuals' rather than occupational groups and classes (Marx, 1973[1857]: 157, 589; no date[1867]: 96). Also, even though workers often succeed in organizing themselves into unions and broader organizations, those organizations are just as often then broken up by cyclical economic crises and political repression (1976b: 493; no date[1867]: 595–8).

Similarly, Marx's criticisms of Feuerbach, Smith and Bentham were not that they had *any* theories of 'human nature in general' at all, but that they had formulated them by observing only 'individuals' in capitalist societies, and generalized them to all individuals on this narrow and often ideological basis. Thus Feuerbach used the allegedly ubiquitous powerlessness of all individuals in the face of nature as his explanation for Christianity, yet used bourgeois individuals and their families for evidence. Smith explained *workers'* repulsion from their labor as an indication of their *natural* laziness, and Bentham presumed that all of us are narrowly calculative and utilitarian because he had only been observing English shopkeepers (Marx, 1973[1857]: 612; 1976a: 7–8; no date[1867]: 571n). But Marx continued to use many of his own, substantive assumptions about human nature and alienation from his earliest works.

Thus, just as human creativity is possible because of our capacity to distance ourselves from our animal instincts, plan our projects ahead of time and view the results through the eyes of others, so we are the only animal species that can cognitively and emotionally withdraw from instinctual relationships and activities that are personally depriving and frustrating (Marx, 1975a: 227–8; no date[1867]: 174). We have common needs for affiliation and activity, and variety in and influence over our relationships and activities (see Archibald, 1989/1993: chapter 4), but how much of what types of these we expect and aspire to will depend upon a host of social and personal circumstances (Marx, 1973[1857]: 92; no date[1867]: 168). As a consequence, how much we experience objective as subjective powerlessness is also likely to vary greatly (Marx, no date[1867]: 91, 474, 689), as are our responses to deprivation and frustration.

We may actually seek out moderate barriers to gratification, as we do with puzzles and games, because they provide variety and challenges which are then gratifying to overcome (Karasek and Theorell, 1990; Marx, 1973[1857]: 611) and subjective alienation is not likely to be the immediate response even to moderately high objective powerlessness. Rather, our first response is likely to be leaving our employer or job physically, but when that is difficult we are likely to organize with others and voice our grievances in an attempt to redress them. Psychic alienation ('leaving the field' emotionally and cognitively) is mainly our last resort.

Marx (1977a[1864]: 535) put it this way with regard to political alienation: 'All the efforts made at keeping up, or remodelling, the Chartist Movement failed signally; the press organs of the working class died one by one by the *apathy* of the masses, and, in point of fact, never before seemed the English working class so thoroughly *reconciled* to a state of political nullity.' (Emphases added.) This model appears to explain Seeman's (1972) findings about Parisian workers and the protests in 1968. Those who did not feel very powerless did not participate much, but those who felt extremely so did not participate either. Presumably the former were not provoked enough to, while the latter had no confidence that it would make a difference. Meanwhile, the moderately powerless were provoked by threats to their control but still felt confident enough to protect it.

For Marx, the key aspects of psychic alienation are emotional and cognitive withdrawal from relationships and activities (and products and oneself), especially those one cannot leave physically (Marx, 1975b: 274–5), and these often entail lowering one's aspirations for gratification (Marx, 1975b: 308–9). This is so subsequent deprivation and frustration will be less frequent and painful (Marx, 1975b: 313). A common result of this lowering is regarding others and one's work mainly in 'extrinsic,' 'instrumental' or utilitarian terms. 'No Admittance Except on Business' characterizes the relationship between capitalists and workers: one side wants only labor power to exploit; the other wants only a job, and works only in order to live. Similarly, workers often treat fellow workers merely as competitors (Marx, no date[1867]: 172, 595–8).

Marx often phrased these claims in empirically observable and verifiable ways. Thus, we 'shun' others as well as our labor 'like the plague'; 'as soon as there is no physical or other compulsion' (Marx, 1975b: 274–5). That this is a prediction Marx meant to be testable seems clear in a later work (1973[1857]: 282): 'If capital were willing to pay [labour] without making it labour it would enter the bargain with pleasure.' As it happens, the vast majority of large lottery winners leave their jobs forever; the more money they win, the more likely they are to quit; and most of those who stay anyway have particularly fulfilling work (Kaplan, 1978). Marx (1976a: 512) also defended Fourier's experiments with making work more attractive. Were one to restrict oneself to the German ideologist Grun's conceptual rants, 'all psychological experiment would be impossible.'

A more difficult issue is consciousness. Some Marxists maintain that even if one moves beyond objective powerlessness, whether individuals are consciously aware of their lack of intrinsic involvement in their work is irrelevant. Others go further: to not be aware that one is objectively powerless, that one has an interest in eradicating capitalism, is to be '*falsely* conscious.' This is actually the highest stage of alienation. Here one might recall Mills' (1951: 228–9) references to workers as 'happy robots.'

Since Marx used the proto-Freudian notions of 'regression' and 'scapegoating' others who are not sources of one's deprivation and frustration, it is not a huge psychological leap to see him having also thought of 'repression,' and there are hints of this (Marx, 1975b: 313). On the other hand, Marx (1975b: 274–5) often referred to subjective feelings like a lack of enjoyment in work, and he does not appear to have regarded workers as the judgmental dopes that Althusser clearly did (see Archibald, 1989/1993: 25–31, 34–6).

Mills was undoubtedly correct about job satisfaction: it can result from many things besides intrinsic involvement in work itself (see e.g. Archibald, 1978b: 125). Furthermore, high dissatisfaction may mean that one still cares about one's work, has yet to lower one's aspirations for it, and therefore is not in fact alienated from it. Still, large differences in degrees of dissatisfaction between individuals and occupations probably do indicate differences in alienation (Archibald, 1978b: 129; Archibald et al., 1981).

When my colleagues and I began to study alienation empirically we experimented with quit rates and other objective indicators of repulsion from work, but often found little variation to explain. However, this is not surprising when one remembers Marx's important qualification: work is only physically shunned 'when there is no physical or other compulsion.' With this in mind, we then looked at actions and intentions over which interview and survey respondents had more control, and their answers to questions about whether they came in to do extra work on their own, even when they were not required to; whether they would choose the same job if they had the same choice now; and whether their choices would be made on the basis of income or intrinsic interest. Such measures indicated both higher levels of alienation and larger differences among occupational strata than job satisfaction typically does, yet simply asking workers how involved in or committed to their work they were often yielded results similar to those from asking them to describe their overt actions and hypothetical choices (Archibald, 1978a, 1978b; Archibald et al., 1981).

Surely, Marxists should pursue such lines of inquiry. Otherwise, claims that Marx's theories are wrong or outmoded will remain unanswered. Thus, Blauner (1964) argued that since there were such large differences in alienation within manual workers themselves, capitalism and class are not important sources. Similarly, after comparing the alienation of those who did and did not own stocks, and those who did and did not own the means of production at their own workplaces, Kohn (1976) concluded that ownership has only very weak and indirect effects upon alienation, and that position in the supervisory hierarchy explains almost all the variation in alienation. However, Blauner and Kohn used Seeman's conceptualization and theorizing of alienation, which relies more upon Durkheim's and Merton's 'anomie' than Marx's alienation (Archibald, 1978a), and therefore confounds research purporting to test Marx.

Thus, Blauner and Kohn relied heavily upon subjective powerlessness, but as we have seen, the latter is not in a one-to-one relationship, even with subjective alienation. Furthermore, one can still have important differences *between* classes, even with large variation *within* classes, and small amounts of stock ownership or owning a small business do not assure one of much control over either markets or one's own work. When we corrected these problems we found strong effects for ownership, absolutely and relative to one's position in occupational hierarchies and complexity in and control over work itself (Archibald, 1978b; Archibald et al., 1981).

On the other hand, research like Blauner's and Kohn's should force us to recognize that capitalism and class are not the only sources of alienation, that the effects of ownership do operate mainly through complexity in and control over work itself, and that it is indeed possible for alienation to decrease within the life of capitalism. Although these claims are heretical for most Marxists, they were definitely not so for Marx himself. '*All* combined labour on a large scale,' Marx (no date[1867]: 313, 320) wrote, 'requires a directing authority, in order to secure the harmonious working of the individual activities . . . [However, once] a function of capital, it acquires *special* characteristics.' (Emphases added.)

Marx then proceeded to specify that the latter features center around capitalists' 'need' to extract surplus value, and therefore

a) make labor ever more productive, and
b) overcome the 'unavoidable' resistance of workers.

Nevertheless, '[T]his division of labour is [only] a particular sort of co-operation, and many of its disadvantages spring from the general character of co-operation, and not from this particular form of it.' (All emphases added.)

One consequence of this will be a minimum, unavoidable amount of objective powerlessness and psychic alienation from their work, even if workers were to socialize the means of production. Marx's position here parallels Marcuse's (1962) distinction between 'basic' and 'surplus' repression. However, those higher in hierarchies of knowledge, skill and supervisory responsibility should still have more control and less psychic alienation. This may well be true whether or not individuals own their means of production, yet owning means of production and employing large numbers of others does seem to give one more control over more intrinsically interesting work.

But Marx believed that some types of workers would also experience less objective and subjective alienation, long before the advent of full-fledged socialism. For example, after struggling together and presumably achieving some degree of security about their subsistence, skilled artisans in Paris had moved up to intrinsic relationships with each other (Marx, 1975b: 313), and the same was true for unionized, skilled English workers: 'once the worker's material situation has become better . . . he himself can cultivate his mind more . . . and he becomes socialist without noticing it' (Marx, 1977b[1869]: 538). Finally, Marx (1973[1857]: 705) himself envisioned a stage of capitalism where increasingly larger proportions of workers would be educated and trained to tend more automated machinery, which would allow them respite from hard manual labor and more control over its new forms, as watchmen and regulators in teams as well as individuals. In turn, this would both raise their aspirations for ownership as well as more control, and for decreased working time for self-development beyond it. As we shall see, here Marx may have been as naive as Blauner, but this does not take away from my main point: Marx recognized that alienation can decrease within capitalism.

With these caveats in mind, let us return to the rest of our agenda.

HAVE NEW TECHNOLOGIES AND WORK ORGANIZATIONS DECREASED ALIENATION FOR FACTORY WORKERS AND INCREASED IT FOR SERVICE EMPLOYEES?

If these claims are true, there is little 'hard' empirical evidence for them, and lots suggesting that they should at least be highly qualified.

Thus, there are still many more assembly lines than continuous processes in factories, and while the latter may lessen the physical burden of work, they do not necessarily make work more stimulating and challenging, and some substantial amount of work time is spent worrying about system failures and rectifying them (Karasek and Theorell, 1990; Liker et al., 1999). Whereas professionals like ourselves who make much use of computers in our work usually feel that they have given us more freedom, manual production workers and low-status service workers report no more freedom than their low-use counterparts (Hughes and Lowe, 2000). They also report *less* job security and 'too many job demands and long hours.' As well, computerization has given management more opportunities to pressure, monitor and discipline workers, often while they are at home as well as in the workplace (Burris, 1998).

Similarly, the shortening of assembly lines; rotation, expansion or more fundamental redesign of jobs; and increased participation by workers can and sometimes have increased commitment to employers, involvement in work and productivity, and decreased absenteeism and turnover (Hogue, 1999; Karasek and Theorell, 1990; McKay, 2003; Schouteten and Benders, 2004). Nevertheless, 'cut-throat' competition and the changes in the social organization of work it has led to have often threatened managers as well as workers, to the point where such programs have not been fully and genuinely implemented (Betcherman et al., 1994; MacDuffie, 2003), and workers have had neither job security nor much effective influence over their work. Instead, managers' claims for them have often raised workers' expectations but the latter have seldom been realized (Milkman, 1997; Rinehart et al., 1997). Furthermore, production deadlines tend to be very short, absent team members are seldom replaced, and there is 'management by stress' rather than substantial increases in workers' control (Godard and Delaney, 2000; Liker et al., 1999; V. Smith, 1997).

Surely, the 'acid test' for such HPWs [high-performance workplaces] has been Sweden. There, workers have had almost complete unionization and considerable sympathy from managers as well as a comprehensive and interventionist welfare state, and have often themselves initiated redesigned work, but assembly lines in HPWs have remained alienating (Berggren, 1992). Yet, unionization and sympathetic states have been less frequent in Anglo-Saxon countries and other countries in the first place, and both have been more seriously eroded there (Jeffreys, 2001; Korpi, 2003).

Claims about post-industrialism's effects upon alienation are also dubious. There has been an overall upgrading of the knowledge and skill of the labor forces of FICs [fully industrialized countries], and if this is true, one would expect an overall lowering of alienation from work, as the Durban rationale claims. However, recall that the rationale also predicts an opposite trend for high status service workers, allegedly because of an increase in the division of labor and de-skilling. Yet, available research suggests no uniform trend toward either massive upgrading or de-skilling, and to the extent that Braverman was correct at all, he was so for manual industrial more than professional service workers, and for the USA more than other FICs (Clement and Myles, 1994: 73–80).

Instead, in many FICs there has been a 'hollowing out' of occupational hierarchies, with an increase in *both* 'good' (hi-tech, high control) *and* 'bad' (unskilled, low control) jobs, and within non-manual, 'white collar' as well as manual, 'blue collar' occupations (Livingstone, 1998: 145, 159–61; Myles, 1988: 337, 351). The latter applies to service industries as well as those producing and distributing goods. In addition, there are large differences within industries and occupations themselves.

Thus there are low-skilled, low-waged 'servant' industries populated mainly by women versus high-skilled, high-waged private financial and public service industries whose upper echelons are made up almost wholly of men. Whereas a majority of men in both of these types of service industries reported being able to slow the pace of their work and introduce new tasks for themselves, the reverse was true for women. Moreover, men in the production and distribution of goods were much less likely to claim control over their work than those in services did (Boyd et al., 1991).

Note that neither these results for the skill and control of high status service versus manual production employees nor the earlier ones about the effects of working closely with computers support the Durban claim for a reversal of past inequalities by occupational status. Since these results rely on the independent ratings of experts as well as workers' own descriptions of how much skill and control they usually exercise while working, it is still possible that there are differences in relative deprivation between occupations which confirm the Durban claim. Yet, there is not much support here either.

On one hand, the actual amounts of training necessary for most service work, use of knowledge and skill obtained in one's formal education, and actual autonomy at work, are all far less than those predicted and claimed by experts using formal models; substantial minorities of service workers of all types do feel under-employed; and in Ontario the proportions feeling this at least doubled from 1984 to 1996. On the other hand, these proportions tripled for skilled industrial workers, and their 66% for 1996 is much higher than those for skilled service workers (42%), supervisors (42%), semi-professionals (45%), professionals (46%), managers (37%) and corporate executives (20%). Age and education were also important here: it was the youngest and most highly educated who felt the most under-employed, but this applied to manual as well as service workers (Livingstone, 1998: 214–22).

REFERENCES

Althusser, L. (1969) *For Marx.* Penguin: Harmondsworth.

Archibald, W.P. (1978a) Using Marx's Theory of Alienation Empirically. *Theory and Society* 6(Summer): 119–32.

Archibald, W.P. (1978b) *Social Psychology as Political Economy.* McGraw-Hill Ryerson: Toronto.

Archibald, W.P. (1989/1993) *Marx and the Missing Link: 'Human Nature.'* Macmillan/Humanities Press: London/New Jersey.

Archibald, W.P., Adams, O. and Gartrell, J. (1981) Propertylessness and Alienation: Reopening a 'Shut' Case. F. Geyer and D. Schweitzer (eds) *Alienation: Problems of Meaning, Theory and Method,* pp. 149–74. Routledge: London.

Berggren, C. (1992) *Alternatives to Lean Production: Work Organization in the Swedish Auto Industry.* ILR Press: Ithaca.

Betcherman, G., McMullen, K., Leckie, N. and Caron, C. (1994) *The Canadian Workplace in Transition.* IRC Press: Kingston.

Blauner, R. (1964) *Alienation and Freedom.* University of Chicago Press: Chicago.

Boyd, M., Mulvihill, M.A. and Myles, J. (1991) Gender, Power and Postindustrialism. *Canadian Review of Sociology and Anthropology* 28(4): 407–36.

Braverman, H. (1974) *Labor and Monopoly Capital.* Monthly Review Press: New York.

Burris, B. (1998) Computerization of the Workplace. *Annual Review of Sociology* 24: 141–57.

Clement, W. and Myles, J. (1994) *Relations of Ruling: Class and Gender in Postindustrial Societies.* McGill/Queen's University Press: Montreal/Kingston.

Fromm, E. (ed.) (1967) *Socialist Humanism.* Doubleday (Anchor): Garden City.

Godard, J. and Delaney, J.T. (2000) Reflections on the 'High Performance' Paradigm's Implications for Industrial Relations as a Field. *Industrial and Labor Relations Review* 53(3): 482–502.

Hogue, K. (1999) Human Resource Management and Performance in the UK Hotel Industry. *British Journal of Industrial Relations* 37(3): 419–43.

Hughes, K. and Lowe, G. (2000) Surveying the 'Post-Industrial' Landscape: Information Technologies and Labour Market Polarization in Canada. *Canadian Review of Sociology and Anthropology* 37(1): 29–53.

Israel, J. (1970) The Principle of Methodological Individualism and Marxist Epistemology. *ACTA Sociologica* 14: 145–50.

Israel, J. (1979) *Alienation: From Marx to Modern Sociology.* Humanities Press: New Jersey.

Jeffreys, S. (2001) Western European Trade Unionism at 2000. L. Panitch and C. Leys (eds), *Socialist Register 2001,* pp. 143–69. Merlin Press: London.

Kaplan, R. (1978) *Lottery Winners.* Harper and Row: New York.

Karasek, R. and Theorell, T. (1990) *Healthy Work: Stress, Productivity and the Reconstruction of Working Life.* Basic Books: New York.

Kohn, M. (1976) Occupational Structure and Alienation. *American Journal of Sociology* 82(1): 111–30.

Korpi, W. (2003) Welfare State Regress in Western Europe. *Annual Review of Sociology* 29: 589–609.

Liker, J., Haddad, C. and Karlin, J. (1999) Perspectives on Technology and Work Organization. *Annual Review of Sociology* 25: 575–96.

Livingstone, D.W. (1998) *The Education-Jobs Gap: Underemployment or Economic Democracy.* Westview Press: Boulder.

MacDuffie, J.P. (2003) Leaning toward Teams: Divergent and Convergent Trends in Diffusion of Lean Production Work Practices. T. Kockan and D. Lipsky (eds) *Negotiations and Change: From the Workplace to Society,* pp. 94–116. ILR Press: Ithaca.

McKay, S.C. (2003) Securing Commitment in an Insecure World: Workers in Multinational High-Tech Subsidiaries. *Economic and Industrial Democracy* 25(3): 375–410.

Marcuse, H. (1962) *Eros and Civilization.* Random House (Vintage): New York.

Marx, K. (1973[1857]) *Grundrisse: Introduction to the Critique of Political Economy.* Translated and edited by M. Nicolaus. Penguin Books: Harmondsworth.

Marx, K. (1975a) Comments on James Mill, *Eléments d'économie politique.* Volume 3, *Collective Works.* International Publishers: New York.

Marx, K. (1975b) *Economic and Philosophic Manuscripts.* Volume 3, *Collective Works.* International Publishers: New York.

Marx, K. (1976a) *The German Ideology.* Volume 5, *Collective Works.* International Publishers: New York.

Marx, K. (1976b) *Manifesto of the Communist Party.* Volume 6, *Collective Works.* International Publishers: New York.

Marx, K. (1977a[1864]) *Inaugural Address to the First International.* D. McLellan (ed.) *Karl Marx: Selected Writings,* pp. 531–7. Oxford University Press: Oxford.

Marx, K. (1977b[1869]) On Trade Unions. D. McLellan (ed.) *Karl Marx: Selected Writings,* p. 538. Oxford University Press: Oxford.

Marx, K. (no date[1867]) *Capital.* Volume 1. Progress Publishers: Moscow.

Mezaros, I. (1972) *Marx's Theory of Alienation.* Harper: New York.

Milkman, R. (1997) *Farewell to the Factory: Autoworkers in the Late Twentieth Century.* University of California Press: Berkeley.

Mills, C.W. (1951) *White Collar: The American Middle Classes.* Oxford University Press: New York.

Molina, V. (1978) Notes on Marx and the Problem of Individuality. Centre for Contemporary Cultural Studies *On Ideology,* pp. 230–58. Hutchinson: London.

Myles, J. (1988) The Expanding Middle: Some Canadian Evidence on the De-Skilling Debate. *Canadian Review of Sociology and Anthropology* 25(3): 335–64.

Ollman, B. (1971) *Alienation: Marx's Conception of Man in Capitalist Society.* Cambridge University Press: Cambridge.

Rinehart, J., Huxley, C. and Robertson, D. (1997) *Just Another Car Factory? Lean Production and Its Discontents.* ILR Press: Ithaca.

Schouteten, R. and Benders, J. (2004) Lean production Assessed by Karasek's Job Demand–Job Control Model. *Economic and Industrial Democracy,* 25(3): 347–73.

Seeman, M. (1972) Alienation in Pre-Crisis France. *American Sociological Review* 37(August): 385–402.

Smith, V. (1997) New Forms of Work Organization. *Annual Review of Sociology* 23: 315–39.

SOURCE: Archibald, W. Peter. 2009. Excerpt from "Marx, Globalization and Alienation: Received and Underappreciated Wisdoms." *Critical Sociology*, 35(2):151, 158–65.

40

RACIAL INEQUALITY IN THE WORKPLACE

How Critical Management Studies Can Inform Current Approaches

BRENDA JOHNSON

Many researchers before me (see for example Nkomo 1992) have suggested that a dramatically different perspective on race in organizations must be taken to increase the relevance of organizational research and practice. Nkomo pointed out that 'Organizations are not race-neutral entities' (p. 501), and called on organizational scholars to consider alternative paradigms and research questions. More than fifteen years later, many of these questions still need to be addressed. This chapter revisits how racial inequality is addressed in American organizations and suggests some changes to the ways managers and others are educated about racial inequality, and how the issue is managed in organizations. I chose the lens of the critical management studies (CMS) literature because it encompasses alternative paradigms that question current practice and research. This CMS-informed approach to racial inequality will examine the current state of affairs in US organizations and offer some alternative perspectives and possible options beyond diversity training based on my reading of some of the relevant

CMS literature. As such, this is not an exhaustive study of all that CMS can add to this topic. Rather it is an exploration by an organizational researcher who is troubled by racial inequality and interested in alternative approaches that may be useful to practitioners who address these issues.

First, I present an overview of racial inequality in the US, and the changes in the workplace since legislation required equal opportunities for more US workers. Following this is a discussion of the backlash against the initiatives intended to create equal opportunities, namely, affirmative action and the ensuing rise of the diversity industry. In the next section a critical approach is outlined and used as the basis of suggested changes in current approaches to workplace racial segregation and inequality.

RACIAL INEQUALITY IN THE USA

Race continues to be a factor in the allocation of power and resources in organizations and in US society at large, with Whites controlling a disproportionate share (Danziger and Gottschalk 2005; Huffman and Cohen 2004). The civil rights legislation of 1964 attempted to address the issues of access to education and employment opportunities for White women and under-represented racial minorities, but disparities in employment across racial groups are still significant, particularly between Blacks and Whites (Brief, Butz and Dietch 2005; Huffman and Cohen 2004). According to the United States Equal Employment Opportunity Commission's most recent data (2007a), Whites are over-represented proportionally in professional and managerial occupations and under-represented in service jobs, while Blacks and Hispanics are under-represented in professional and managerial occupations and over-represented in service occupations. For example. White men make up 36 per cent of the private industry workforce, yet they comprise 55 per cent of all officials and managers, in comparison with racial minority men, who comprise 16 per cent of the workforce but only 9 per cent of officials and managers. The differences in occupation are subsequently reflected in the wages of racial groups, with Blacks and Whites disproportionately represented in the low and high ends of the income spectrum respectively (Grodsky and Pager 2001; Huffman and Cohen 2004).

BACKLASH AGAINST AFFIRMATIVE ACTION—RISE OF THE DIVERSITY INDUSTRY

Racial minorities and White women gained substantial ground between 1966 and 1990, as organizations complied with the 1964 legislation that made racial discrimination illegal, but the rate of change slowed in the 1990s when they ran into the so-called glass ceiling, while their White male counterparts with no more experience or education were promoted on what David Maume (1999) dubbed the 'glass escalator.' Asian-Americans on the other hand are faring better than any other non-White group, in terms of wages, but their movement into, and within, the managerial ranks is still restricted; they tend to be funneled into professional rather than managerial roles (Cheng 1997; Woo 1994). Notwithstanding the slowing pace of change, and their continued domination of organizations, Whites began reacting negatively to

the changes and a backlash against affirmative action began (Crosby, Iyer and Sincharoen 2006).

During the 1970s and early 1980s, affirmative action legislation was strongly enforced, and organizations hired compliance specialists; when political pressure reduced the strength of enforcement in the 1980s, these experts shifted their focus to diversity training (Kelly and Dobbin 1998; Konrad 2003). By 2003, 75 per cent of Fortune 500 companies in the USA had diversity training programs, and 36 per cent of all American firms had them, while only 22 per cent of the workforce was in an organization required to comply with the affirmative action laws (United Stales Department of Labor 2003). The diversity training industry has grown steadily since then and currently generates US $8–10 billion per year, as more organizations attempt to both avoid lawsuits and realize the benefits that the proponents of the business case for diversity have proffered (Hansen 2003). The size of the diversity training industry and the amount of money spent creates the appearance that organizations are improving the work environment, but attitudes and behaviors have not been significantly impacted and individual and class action discrimination lawsuits continue to be filed against US organizations, according to the data gathered by the US Equal Opportunity Employment Commission (2007b). While this may be coincidental, conclusions about the business case for diversity or the effect of training programs are hard to make in the absence of data, as organizations are not collecting data on the effects of diversity programs (Kelly and Dobbin 1998).

Thus far we have discussed inequality of access by various racial groups in the American workplace, the changes catalysed by affirmative action, the backlash against those policies, and the rising popularity of diversity training as an alternative. Now we turn to consider how CMS might help understand this situation from a different perspective, and develop some alternatives.

A CRITICAL APPROACH

A key similarity among CMS scholars is the 'questioning of taken-for-granteds, both about practice and its social and institutional context . . .

identifying and questioning both purposes, and conflicts of power and interest' (Reynolds 1998, p. 192). This questioning is the central strength of the CMS approach, and I will draw on the work of those who are asking questions about the supposed success stories of diversity training in organizations (for example, Prasad and Mills 1997). At this point I now turn to the questions that arise for me as an organizational psychologist, and to the CMS-inspired approach that has changed my perspective on these questions. The major touchstones are the following: the social construction of organizational problems; the questioning of basic assumptions through critical reflection; the historical and sociological perspective on organizational issues; and the post-colonial perspective on racial inequality. These are not the only aspects of the critical management literature that pertain to this issue, but they are important starting points and will now be considered.

Problem Definition—Who Frames It and What Is Not Included?

One of the basic assumptions of CMS is that problems in organizations are social constructions reflecting the agendas and interests of the most powerful constituents (Alvesson 1984; Fournier and Grey 2000; Reynolds 1998). As it is currently framed, the increase in numbers of White women and racial minorities has been constructed as the problem to be addressed rather than the resistance from White men. In the diversity training literature I see an unquestioned assumption that the problem is the 'diversity' for which workers and managers need to be 'trained,' not the resistance of the Whites who do not want to work in racially integrated workplaces. Steffy and Grimes's critical examination of personnel/organizational psychology (1992) helps contextualize the use of diversity training as a reflection of how managers address problems. They contend that the function of human resource management is to respond to organizational issues as they arise in such a way as to maximize productivity with the appropriate policies and procedures. When civil rights legislation required organizations to address discrimination, the issue was framed as a problem brought in

from the outside, and not a problem of resistance from within. The power to define organizational problems, to name who or what is the source of those problems, is central to how racial inequality is constructed and reproduced. As a few women and racial minorities have made their way into the managerial ranks, White men have constructed a new problem—reverse discrimination in spite of the lack of evidence to support their claims (Pincus 2000). When an organizational constituency has the power to define a problem, the solutions will suit their purposes, and the trope of reverse discrimination has become a powerful tool in shaping organizational policy choices.

The focus on White men as beleaguered victims of reverse discrimination exemplifies how organizational issues are determined by the most powerful organizational and societal constituents. Many White Americans are unaware of how history has shaped current organizational demographics and how that history affords them access to and mobility within the workplace (Pincus 2000). However, group-based power differences are not currently an important element in the discussion of diversity, which essentially serves the status quo (Hernandez and Field 2003). The perspective offered by Steffy and Grimes (1992) suggests that we turn our attention to who defines the problem and how that perspective may be limiting current initiatives.

Managers might be less biased decision makers if they were aware of how racial attitudes and organizational policies are shaped by economic, political and ideological patterns (Wetherell and Potter 1992). For example, White managers have different attitudes towards Blacks and Asians, who fare differently in organizational mobility (Cheng 1997), and this can be traced back to the history of intergroup contact, which evolved based on economics, political and historical events and ideological trends (Sidanius and Pratto 1999). If managers learned about the current and historical patterns of employment for demographic groups they would at minimum have an opportunity to see how their decisions can reproduce or potentially change the patterns of racial segregation in the workplace. Managers are not aware of these patterns because it is not part of management education, which has divorced itself from a sociological and historical approach (Reynolds 1998).

Has the Problem Definition Supported Collusion?

While it is tempting to suggest that there is money being wasted by organizations because diversity consultants are colluding with White male managers to maintain the status quo, a broader view of the situation suggests that the issue of racial inequality has simply been left unaddressed by American society. Indeed, human resource managers and the diversity-training consultants they hire have merely responded to the problem as defined by organizational leaders. Does this imply that diversity consultants are colluding consciously or unconsciously with organizational leaders not to advocate for substantial change? Diversity professionals are making a living by training individuals to become aware of and respect differences, but this has not altered the status quo (Hernandez and Field 2003). However, they appear to have been left to address the issue of racial discrimination without much support from organizational leaders (Brief and Hayes 1997). A recent study comparing the relative effectiveness of diversity policies found that the most effective policy is the establishment of a centralized cross-functional organizational body that is responsible and accountable for addressing diversity and inequality (Kalev, Dobbin and Kelly 2006). Rather than relying on diversity training alone, such an approach would involve organizational resources from all functions, and establish accountability throughout the organization.

Since the problem of racial inequality remains substantially unaddressed in the nation at large, the methods that many diversity consultants have employed appear to reflect the ideology of the country as a whole. It is widely believed that America is a meritocracy and that those who do not succeed simply don't deserve it because they did not work hard enough (Sidanius and Pratto 1999). This ideology is communicated throughout American society in many ways and diversity training that focuses only on individual awareness of differences is one example. Centralized organizational responsibility

and accountability for diversity and equality is a very different approach and the fact that it increases the effectiveness of all diversity programs suggests that accountability at multiple levels is needed (Kalev, Dobbin and Kelly 2006).

Rethinking the Ahistorical Individual

The individual focus employed by diversity trainers also reflects the approach taken by mainstream race researchers in the USA. As Wetherell and Potter (1992) point out in their analysis of racism in New Zealand, the social psychological focus on the individual has dominated the study of racial attitudes, particularly in the USA, and this has influenced diversity-related initiatives. As Prasad (1997) has elaborated organizations are themselves products of culture and history, and American organizations have been influenced by the myths of the American frontier and the protestant work ethic. This link from the individual to the intergroup and the historical societal levels reframes our understanding of how individual racial attitudes are formed and how much more is required than brief training programs about individual differences. This is not to suggest that just learning a bit of history is going to change the nature of an intergroup conflict. It will however increase the awareness of how power dynamics in organizations reflect the history and intergroup tensions of the society in which they are embedded (Prasad and Mills 1997). One recommendation is that managers learn how they have been shaped by the history of intergroup relations and cultural tensions, and what that means for the advancement opportunities of different groups within organizations. My own experience as a White Canadian doing research in the USA on racial inequality has deepened my awareness of how my attitudes have been shaped and how my own blind spots have developed. Our attitudes are not individual inventions. We are socialized into particular cultures, hence a broader understanding of this is helpful to anyone trying to comprehend how that socialization impacts our current work.

As many CMS scholars assert, social and cultural arrangements are constructions that can be reconfigured (Alvesson 1984; Fournier and Grey 2000). When this is taken as a starting point in examining a problem, the consistent patterns of who dominates the hierarchy in organizations become an object for examination rather than a natural outcome.

The emancipatory intent of CMS, the historical, sociological approach, the challenge to the myth of objectivity, and the assertion that managers are pursuing an agenda that can reinforce stereotypes and inequities are all elements that have been missing from the discourse of diversity in American organizations and from diversity education (Acosta 2004; Alvesson and Willmott 1992; Deetz 2003; Konrad 2003; Linnehan and Konrad 1999; Litvin 2006; Marsden and Townley 1996; Nord and Jermier 1992; Proudford and Nkomo 2006). The insights of CMS scholars are a natural addition to the analysis of and response to the complex issue of racial inequality, and how diversity initiatives might evolve. In this conceptualization, all organizational constituents need to participate in the conceptualization of organizational change, members of the dominant group as well as those who feel marginalized. For example, Clayton Alderfer's work on systemic organizational change (1987) involves all stakeholders. His race relations analysis and change process is grounded in the belief that race and gender affect one's perceptions of organizational inequality, and therefore all perspectives are taken into consideration in the design of organizational analysis and change.

CRITICAL REFLECTION

One of the key concepts that the CMS literature offers to this discussion is the necessity of critical reflection. It is missing from the education of managers (Reynolds 1998; Reynolds and Vince 2004), and from the diversity training offered by human resource professionals and diversity consultants. Reynolds (1998) makes the case for critical reflection in management education, and his list points to many of the missing pieces in the treatment of race in American organizations: the questioning of assumptions; the social rather than the individual focus; the attention to power dynamics; and the concern with emancipation. Because management is 'not a neutral or disinterested activity' (Reynolds 1998, p. 190) this kind of interrogation is essential to locating and naming the interests, the power imbalances and the manner in which they are reinforced and reconstructed in daily practice in organizations.

There is a need for critical reflection and questioning the taken-for-granted assumptions about how racial dynamics affect how people work in organizations (Acosta 2004; Litvin, 2006). If management is not a neutral practice, and it reflects the political and economic interests of White male owners and managers (Nkomo 1992; Proudford and Nkomo 2006), then racial dynamics and inequality can be fruitfully examined in this light. This simple observation changes the focus of any question in an organization, moving our gaze from the individual to the societal level and to the analysis of the broader power relations that undergird those found in the organization. The issue of race in American organizations needs the kind of critical reflection that brings about change in thinking, in management education and in management practice. If managers learn how to reflect critically on how their racial attitudes and behaviours have been molded, they may be less likely to discriminate unconsciously. Furthermore, if accountability for equality becomes an organization-wide issue, as Kalev and colleagues' research suggests it should, managers may find more support for different behaviour through shared accountability (Kalev, Dobbin and Kelly 2006).

Ignoring History and Sociology

The severing of the connection between behaviours within organizations and the social structuring of interactions in society (Marsden and Townley 1996) has left the issue of race relations in organizations in somewhat of a vacuum. An historical perspective on the demographic patterns in US organizations might shed some light on how workplace differences are managed, particularly a perspective that would address the legacy of slavery. The historical relationships of slavery, with the concomitant beliefs in White superiority and legal discrimination against African Americans are not so distant; racial discrimination was made illegal in the USA just over 40 years ago. In order to address what goes on inside American organizations, one needs to acknowledge the social relations of the society at large. Not to acknowledge this serves the purpose of the owners, because within the 'boundary of private property' they are free to serve their own purposes (Marsden and Townley 1996, p. 663) rather than the interests of the workers who are part of that 'property.' When we think of racial issues and private property, what comes to mind is the historical development of American corporations, which is interwoven with the development of slavery (Cooke 1999).The postcolonial literature provides an important foundation for examining the effect of history on current organizational practices. While it is a diverse literature that cannot be simply defined, an important characteristic of much of it is the inclusion of colonization and slavery as a central element in the history of US corporations and the development of management theory (Cooke 1999; Mir, Mir and Upadhyaya 2003). This is omitted from the history that organizational psychologists are taught, and even Loren Baritz's history of industrial psychology, aptly named *Servants of Power* (1960), does not include the role of slavery. This remains a painful part of US history, and the backlash against affirmative action policies may well be embedded in the wish to avoid having to address that past. The theories of modern or aversive racism suggest that many Whites believe they are not racist, that they accept Blacks as equals. What the researchers find however is that even those who want to believe they are not racist feel ambivalent about Blacks (Dovidio and Gaertner 2000; Gaertner and Dovidio 1986).

The postcolonial theorists, who look at the issue of racial attitudes more broadly than social psychologists, also suggest that this is the case. As Prasad (2003) describes in an overview of postcolonial theory, the colonial discourse contains ambivalent messages about the nature of Blacks, simultaneously describing them as animals and as obedient servants. Such ambivalence creates instability in the colonial discourse and, and in order to shore up the superiority of Whites, the negative stereotypes and 'old stories' must be repeated (Prasad 2003). This brings to mind the successful racial discrimination lawsuit brought against the oil company Texaco. Taped conversations among White executives of Texaco included a host of offensive terms to describe their Black co-workers (Hansen 2003). Considering such behaviour, it is difficult to believe that the problems associated with diversity are solely the 'diverse' workers entering the workforce and not the racist attitudes of the White managers. Postcolonial theory makes clear that there are historical cultural issues that impact intergroup dynamics in organizations (Prasad 2006), and so it is important to examine the social environment that allowed White executives to behave in this way rather than simply suggest that they are just a few of the 'bad apples' out there (Prasad and Mills 1997).

In the next and final section I am going to introduce briefly some suggestions for rethinking current approaches to addressing racial inequality in the workplace.

SUGGESTIONS FOR A CMS-INSPIRED APPROACH

So what would a CMS-inspired approach to creating more truly egalitarian workplaces for all include? The major touchstones discussed from the CMS literature include reconsidering race relations in the light of the structural historical dynamics of US society, rather than continuing to pursue changing individual attitudes through diversity training. This approach dovetails well with the recent research of Kalev and her colleagues (2006), who found that structures of responsibility within the organization were effective in increasing racial diversity among managers, while diversity training was the least effective. The structures included dedicated staff roles, interdepartmental committees and coordination plans. Their research found that across the more than 700 US firms they surveyed, there was a significant drop in the number of Black female managers after diversity training programs. While the reasons for this are not known in detail, the fact that the number of Black female managers decreased after a program intended to raise awareness of racial inequality in the workplace may reflect some sort of backlash among Whites. It also highlights the lack of effectiveness of programs aimed at simply changing the attitudes of individuals, a point which others have made as well (for example, see Wetherell and Potter 1992). The stall roles, committees and plans dedicated to diversity were found to be much more effective by Kalev *et al.* (2006); this may be so because the structures provide clear norms for decision making and behaviour, and create structures of accountability.

So how can one infuse such structures with the spirit of the CMS approach, one that creates a space for critical reflection, and potentially involve more organizational voices, both of the dominant groups and the marginalized, in creating structures of accountability? I now consider one approach that is solidly founded on an understanding of power and the effect of historical intergroup relations on racial segregation and organizational dynamics.

Education and Interventions Based on Embedded Group Relations Theory

One type of intervention that has potential as part of the process of creating effective structures of accountability is a group relations framework that focuses on authority and leadership in organizations. Clayton Alderfer (1987) developed a model and multi-stage intervention for improving race relations in organizations. His model examines the embedded social groups within organizations (for example, based on gender and race) and the meaning that emerges from the patterns of segregation or integration throughout the organization. This approach would be an effective aspect of an integrated organizational program to decrease racial segregation while also addressing status concerns of the dominant group. The finding of a recent study of willingness to support policies to increase racial equality in the workplace suggests that both status concerns and hidden hostility of Whites towards Blacks may be factors in negative reactions to racial integration in the workplace (Johnson 2007). Johnson's results suggest that both affective responses and status concerns impede the willingness of Whites to support racial equality. Alderfer's model includes a steering committee comprised of representative members of all the races and gender groups in an organization, so the process would involve White men and White women, thus potentially allaying fears of rapid loss of status for them individually or as a group. Concerns about loss of status were salient for both White men and women in the workshop component of Alderfer's intervention model (Alderfer *et al.* 1992). While no definitive conclusions can be made regarding how specifically to mitigate status

concerns, Alderfer and colleagues found that the workshop and the intervention did have an important effect on the White participants, for whom the fear that increased racial equality would hurt Whites was decreased.

Alderfer's workshop and intervention are concerned with questioning the taken-for-granted assumptions about racial and gender segregation in the workplace and how this reflects the broader social and historical context of the organization. The focus is social rather than individual, and pays particular attention to the analysis of the socially and historically based power relations that are imported into the organization. This is just the sort of focus that CMS scholars have applied to other organizational issues.

CONCLUSION

The CMS literature adds valuable dimensions to the analysis of race relations in American organizations. I have briefly outlined the problem of racial inequality in these organizations, with domination by White men, and limited freedom of choice and movement for White women and racial minorities. I have suggested a few of the insights of CMS scholars that appear immediately useful to this analysis, though by no means is this discussion complete. Finally I have briefly outlined how linking some of the principles of CMS with a group relations approach and recent research findings might be useful in conceptualizing a different approach to addressing racial inequality in the workplace. I hope that this has served to introduce the reader to the richness that CMS scholars can bring to this important issue.

If diversity practitioners have created a niche for themselves working on racial diversity in the American workplace, but have not succeeded in improving the status of women and racial minorities, what then is the role of the academic who wants to help practitioners address the problem more effectively? This is similar to the question that others have asked regarding the role of CMS researchers in influencing management practices generally (Reynolds and Vince 2004). My answer is similar to theirs. By using the CMS literature as a guide to examine the assumptions that undergird the design of diversity initiatives, and engaging in a critically reflective dialogue with managers and consultants, we may begin to design interventions that alleviate racial inequality within organizations.

REFERENCES

Acosta, A.S. (2004), 'A diversity perspective on organizational learning and a learning perspective on organizational diversity,' *Academy of Management Best Conference Paper Proceedings,* D1–D6.

Alderfer, C.P. (1987), 'An intergroup perspective on group dynamics,' in J.W. Lorsch (ed.), *Handbook of Organizational Behavior,* Englewood Cliffs, NJ: Prentice-Hall, pp. 190–222.

Alderfer, C.P., C.J. Alderfer, E.L. Bell and J. Jones (1992), 'The race relations competence workshop: Theory and results,' *Human Relations,* 45(12), 1259–1291.

Alvesson, M. (1984), 'Questioning rationality and ideology: On critical organization theory,' *International Studies of Management and Organization,* XIV(1), 61–79.

Alvesson, M. and H. Willmott (1992), 'On the idea of emancipation in management and organization studies,' *Academy of Management Review,* 17(3), 432–464.

Baritz, L. (1960), *Servants of Power,* Middletown, CT: Wesleyan University Press.

Brief, A.P., R.M. Butz and E.A. Dietch (2005), 'Organizations as reflections of their environments: The case of race composition,' in R.L. Dipboye and A. Colella (eds), *Discrimination at Work: The Psychological and Organizational Bases,* Mahwah, NJ: Lawrence Erlbaum Associates, pp. 119–148.

Brief, A.P. and E. Hayes (1997), 'The continuing "American Dilemma": Studying racism in organizations,' in C.L. Cooper and D.M. Rousseau (eds), *Trends in Organizational Behavior,* Volume 4, New York: John Wiley and Sons, pp. 89–104.

Cheng, C. (1997), 'Are Asian American employees a model minority or just a minority?' *The Journal of Applied Behavioral Science,* 33(3), 277–290.

Cooke, B. (1999), 'The flag on the cover, part one: Once a slave driver,' paper presented in the post colonialism stream of the *International Critical Management Studies Conference,* Manchester School of Management, UMIST, Manchester UK, 14–16 July.

Crosby, F., A. Iyer and S. Sincharoen (2006), 'Understanding affirmative action,' *Annual Review of Psychology,* 57, 586–611.

Danziger, S. and P. Gottschalk (2005), Diverging fortunes: Trends in poverty and inequality,' in F. Reynolds and J. Haaga (eds), *The American People: Census 2000,* New York: Russell Sage Foundation, pp. 49–75.

Deetz, S. (2003), 'Disciplinary power, conflict suppression and human resources management,' in M. Alvesson and H. Wilimott (eds), *Studying Management Critically,* London: Sage, pp. 23–45.

Dovidio, J.F. and S.L. Gaertner (2000), 'Aversive racism and selection decisions: 1989–1999,' *Psychological Science,* 11, 315–319.

Fournier, V. and C. Grey (2000), 'At the critical moment: Conditions and prospects for critical management studies,' *Human Relations,* 53(1), 7–32.

Gaertner, S.L. and J.F. Dovidio (1986), 'The aversive form of racism," in J.F. Dovidio and S.L. Gaertner (eds), *Prejudice, Discrimination and Racism,* Orlando: Academic Press, pp. 61–89.

Grodsky, E. and D. Pager (2001), 'The structure of disadvantage: Individual and occupational determinants of the black-white wage gap,' *American Sociological Review,* 66(4), 542–568.

Hansen, F. (2003), 'Diversity's business case doesn't add up,' *Workforce Management,* April, 28–32.

Hernandez, D. and K. Field (2003), 'The diversity industry,' *Colorlines Magazine: Race, Action, Culture,* 6(4), 23–25.

Huffman, M.L. and P.N. Cohen (2004), 'Racial wage inequality: Job segregation and devaluation across U.S. labor markets,' *The American Journal of Sociology,* 109(4), 902–936.

Johnson, B.K. (2007), *Understanding Racial Inequality in the American Workplace: The Persistence of the Principle-Implementation Gap and its Relationship to Social Dominance Orientation and Modern Racism,* unpublished doctoral dissertation, Columbia University.

Kalev, A., F. Dobbin and E. Kelly (2006), 'Best practices or best guesses? Assessing the efficacy of corporate affirmative action and diversity policies,' *American Sociological Review,* 71(4), 589–617.

Kelly, E. and F. Dobbin (1998), 'How affirmative action became diversity management,' *The American Behavioral Scientist,* 41(7), 960–984.

Konrad, A.M. (2003), 'Defining the domain of workplace diversity scholarship,' *Group and Organization Management,* 28(1), 4–17.

Linnehan, F. and A. Konrad (1999), 'Diluting diversity: Implications for intergroup inequality in organizations,' *Journal of Management Inquiry,* 8(4), 399–414.

Litvin, D.R. (2006), 'Making space for a better case,' in A.M. Konrad, P. Prasad and J.K. Pringle (eds), *Handbook of Workplace Diversity,* London: Sage Publications, pp. 76–94.

Marsden, R. and B. Townley (1996), The owl of Minerva: Reflections on theory and practice,' in S.R. Clegg, C. Hardy and W. Nord (eds), *Managing Organizations: Current Issues,* London: Sage, pp. 660–675.

Maume, D.J. (1999), 'Glass ceilings and glass elevators: Occupational segregation and race and sex differences in management promotions,' *Work and Occupation,* 26(4), 483–509.

Mir, R.A., A. Mir and P. Upadhyaya (2003), 'Toward a postcolonial reading of organizational control,' in A. Prasad (ed.), *Postcolonial Theory and Organizational Analysis: A Critical Engagement,* New York: Palgrave, pp. 47–73.

Nkomo, S. (1992), 'The emperor has no clothes: Rewriting "race in organizations,"' *Academy of Management Review,* 17(3), 487–513.

Nord, W. and J.M. Jermier (1992), 'Critical social science for managers? Promising and perverse possibilities,' in M. Alvesson and H. Willmott (eds), *Critical Management Studies,* London: Sage, pp. 202–222.

Pincus, F.L. (2000), "Reverse discrimination vs. White privilege: An empirical study of alleged victims of affirmative action,' *Race and Society,* 3, 1–22.

Prasad, A. (2003), 'The gaze of the Other: Postcolonial theory and organizational analysis,' in A. Prasad (ed.), *Postcolonial Theory and Organizational Analysis: A Critical Engagement,* New York: Palgrave, pp. 21–45.

Prasad, A. (2006), 'The jewel in the crown: Postcolonial theory and workplace diversity,' in A.M. Konrad, P. Prasad and J.K. Pringle (eds), *Handbook of Workplace Diversity,* London: Sage Publications, pp. 121–144.

Prasad, P. (1997), "The protestant ethic and the myths of the frontier: Cultural imprints, organizational structuring and workplace diversity,' in P. Prasad and A.J. Mills (eds), *Managing the Organizational Melting Pot: Dilemmas of Workplace Diversity,* London: Sage Publications, pp. 129–147.

Prasad, P. and A.J. Mills (1997), 'From showcase to shadow: Understanding the dilemmas of managing workplace diversity,' in P. Prasad and A.J. Mills (eds), *Managing the Organizational Melting Pot: Dilemmas of Workplace Diversity,* London: Sage Publications, pp. 3–25.

Proudford, K.L. and S. Nkomo (2006). 'Race and ethnicity in organizations,' in A.M. Konrad, P. Prasad and J.K. Pringle (eds), *Handbook of Workplace Diversity,* London: Sage Publications, pp. 323–344.

Reynolds, M. (1998), 'Reflection and critical reflection in management learning,' *Management Learning,* 29, 183–200.

Reynolds, M. and R. Vince (2004), 'Critical management education and action-based learning: Synergies and contradictions,' *Academy of Management Learning and Education,* 3(4), 442–456.

Sidanius, J. and F. Pratto (1999), *Social Dominance: An Intergroup Theory of Social Hierarchy and Oppression,* Cambridge: Cambridge University Press.

Steffy, B.D. and A.J. Grimes (1992), 'Personnel/organizational psychology: A critique of the discipline,' in M. Alvesson and H. Willmott (eds), *Critical Management Studies,* London: Sage, pp. 181–201.

United States Department of Labor, Bureau of Labor Statistics (2003), *Equal Employment Opportunity,* http://www.dol.gov/dol/topic/discrimination/index.htm, accessed 8 May 2007.

United States Equal Employment Opportunity Commission (2007a), *Occupational Employment in Private Industry by Race/Ethnic Group/Sex and by Industry,* http://www.eeoc.gov/stats/jobpat/2005/national.html, accessed 8 May 2007.

United States Equal Opportunity Employment Commission (2007b), *Race/Color Discrimination,* http://www.eeoc.gov/types/race.html, accessed 8 May 2007.

Wetherell, M. and J. Potter (1992), *Mapping the Language of Racism: Discourse and the Legitimation of Exploitation,* New York: Columbia University Press.

Woo, D. (1994). The glass ceiling and Asian-Americans, Washington, DC: U.S. Department of Labor, Glass Ceiling Commission.

SOURCE: Johnson, Brenda. 2009. "Racial Inequality in the Workplace: How Critical Management Studies Can Inform Current Approaches." Pp. 271–84 in *Critical Management Studies at Work: Negotiating Tensions Between Theory and Practice.* Northampton, MA: Edward Elgar.

41

MYTHICIZING AND REIFICATION IN ENTREPRENEURIAL DISCOURSE

Ideology-Critique of Entrepreneurial Studies

JOHN O. OGBOR

ABSTRACT

This article discusses the effects of ideological control in conventional entrepreneurial discourses and praxis. Following postmodernist, deconstructionist and critical theory traditions, the ideas expressed about the phenomenon of entrepreneurship, and its contiguous notions and concepts, are deconstructed to reveal the dysfunctional effects of ideological control both in research and in praxis. It is shown that the concept of entrepreneurship is discriminatory, gender-biased, ethnocentrically determined and ideologically controlled, sustaining not only prevailing societal biases, but serving as a tapestry for unexamined and contradictory assumptions and knowledge about the reality of entrepreneurs. . . .

IDEOLOGY-CRITIQUE OF ENTREPRENEURSHIP DISCOURSES AND PRAXIS

From an ideology-critique perspective, we are encouraged to understand how societal and organizational life reflect a process of 'power-based reality construction' (Morgan, 1986) and trace how people become trapped by ideas that serve specific sets of interests. Critical inquiry inspires people to explore the relationship between illusion and reality as it stimulates self-reflection in order to free individuals from the restrictions and repression of the established social order and its ideologies (Alvesson, 1991). In other words, ideological critique involves a process of resistance to hegemonic discursive practices, leading to an opening up of the discourses articulated in a particular social domain (Deetz and Mumby, 1990).

In concert with a postmodernist tradition, feminist efforts have been made to critique and challenge male-dominated ideologies and assumptions in Western society, and the effects these have had on some aspects of life. Similarly, the 'genderness' of traditional organization theory has been subjected to critical inquiry (Balsamo, 1985; Calas and Smircich, 1992; Calvert and Ramsey, 1992; Ferguson, 1984; Ramsey and Calvert, 1994; Smircich, 1985) in order to unveil and de-mystify a form of patriarchical knowledge. The impetus for a feminist perspective on organizational analyses can be traced to gender critique-studies such as the seminal work of Gilligan (1982) and others who have questioned why the pursuit of knowledge has always taken place within a given masculine paradigm. In the discourse on entrepreneurship, a process of gender criticism is in the process of gestation as in the work of Baker et al. (1997) and Chio and Calas (1991).

Although research in entrepreneurship has been critiqued for silencing a feminist perspective (Bowen and Hisrich, 1986; Chio and Calas, 1991), the ideological basis upon which the dominant perspective is perpetuated, produced and reproduced has not been given enough attention. And although there is growing recognition that the conventional discourse on entrepreneurship is rooted in the heroic myth which defines the dominant, rational, European/North American male model (Bull and Willard, 1993; Bygrave, 1993; Fondas, 1997; Van de Ven, 1993), very few attempts have been made to provide an understanding of the mechanisms through which this dominant ideology is perpetuated or its effect on entrepreneurship in discourse and in praxis.

In a similar manner and following a postmodernist/critical theory tradition, issues of race and ethnicity in management and organization discourse have also been brought to the fore (Aldrich and Waldinger, 1990; Nkomo, 1992). Although this area is diverse and growing, very few attempts have been made to examine the underlying ideological assumptions through which race relations are silenced in the management literature. In entrepreneurship studies, generally, Butler (1991) argues that nested within the realities of racism, prejudice and discrimination is a history of business enterprise, which has been overlooked by contemporary scholars of race relations in general. Consequently, 'when the Afro-American tradition has been recognized, it has been misinterpreted and scandalized' (Butler, 1991, p. 34).

It could be said that the ideology-critique of the discourse on entrepreneurship has remained one of the last taboos in management and organization discourses, waiting to be de-mystified.

The purpose of this article, apart from enhancing our understanding of *whose* image the conventional discourse on entrepreneurship promotes, is to show *how* and *why* the representation of the dominant power structure in contemporary Western society is perpetuated in the discourse, including its effects on entrepreneurial praxis. The discussion is organized in the following manner.

The concept of ideology and its role in social science research are discussed. This is done in an attempt to understand the processes through which research objectives are legitimized via ideological control, while recognizing the fact that ideological control in science is, to some extent, inevitable. This is followed by a critical examination of the conventional discourse on entrepreneurship within the framework of ideological reproduction of societal myths and ideologies. Here, the major themes informing our present knowledge about entrepreneurship are examined against the background of how these theories reflect the dominant societal myth. A discussion of how ideological control has affected theory, research and practice of minority and female-owned businesses is then offered. The discussion is brought to a conclusion by suggesting a re-examination of the concept of entrepreneurship, and the various notions within which it is associated, in order to free ourselves from a form of false consciousness.

Following a deconstructionist approach, Schumpeter's discourse on entrepreneurship is used to mirror existing biases and knowledge claims about the phenomenon of entrepreneurship. The choice of Schumpeter's theses is premised on his indelible imprint on entrepreneurial discourses; Schumpeter has remained the most quoted (and sometimes misquoted) source in the discourse on entrepreneurship generally.

THE CONCEPT OF IDEOLOGY AND ITS ROLE IN SOCIAL SCIENCE RESEARCH

Central to the concept of ideology are the concepts of values, ideals, beliefs, cultural systems through which it is defined and conceptualized. I see ideology as that part of culture, which is actively concerned with the establishment, and defense, of patterns of belief and values. Hence, it is seen as an instrument for legitimization and 'justificatory' (Berger and Luckmann, 1967). According to Geertz (1973, pp. 231–2) ideology not only 'objectifies moral sentiments,' but 'makes empirical claims about the condition and direction of society.' As a system for legitimating actions, an important instrument for explaining or justifying social order is the ideology (Berger and Luckmann, 1967). Hence 'ideology is both a mask and a weapon, a symptom and a remedy' Geertz (1973, p. 201). Schumpeter (1954, p. 43) suggests that, 'The first thing a man will do for his ideals is to lie.' Thus, ideology has also been seen as 'a relatively coherent set of assumptions, beliefs, and values about a demarcated part of social reality, being illuminated in a selective and legitimizing way, restricting autonomous and critical reflection and sometimes favoring sectional interests' (Alvesson, 1991, p. 209). Schumpeter (1954) believes that people have a tendency to rationalize events or otherwise engage in ideological behavior:

> Comforting ourselves and impressing others by drawing a picture of ourselves, our motives, our friends, our enemies, our vocation, our church, our country, which may have more to do with what we like them to be than with what they are. (Schumpeter, 1954, pp. 34–5)

The connection between ideology and social theory is that most social science researchers rely on ideology to justify their claim to knowledge. In other words, a social theory strives after validity claims by functioning as an instrument for legitimizing a group's pretext to dominance (Rosen, 1984). This validity claim is tied to societal ideological claims and legitimation. Feyerabend (1975, p. 55) argues that facts are constituted by the ideologies they seek to explain, and are maintained by the community's adherence to a body of theory tied to a particular social reality. Hence, scientists, according to Schumpeter, do not work in ideological neutral problems or issues, because 'we start from the work of our predecessors or contemporaries or else from the ideas that float around us in the public mind' (Schumpeter, 1949, p. 350). For Schumpeter (1954), 'scientific ideas belong to the social circumstances given to scientists: Analytic work begins with material provided by our vision of things, and this is ideological almost by definition' (p. 42).

In as much as the image of society (vision) starts from the preconceptions of scientists (ideology) it is necessary to ask questions about *the* processes through which research activities are legitimated via ideological control. This is especially important when the subject matter is entrepreneurship and its role in society. Hence, Schumpeter cautioned against the role of ideology in his theses:

> . . . but we do not know enough in order to form valid generalizations or even enough to be sure whether there are generalizations to form. As it is, most of us economists have some opinions on these matters. But these opinions have more to do with our preconceived ideas or ideals than with solid fact, and our habit of illustrating them by stray instances that have come to our notice is obviously a poor substitute for serious research. (Schumpeter, 1947, p. 150)

It can be said that there exist a number of reasons why social science in general, and entrepreneurship research in particular, should be placed under ideological scrutiny. The nature of science itself and its knowledge as severely determined by socioeconomic, cultural, psychological, religious forces makes it desirable for the evaluation of scientific work against the paradigmatic nature of the scientist. Topic selection and assessment criteria, for instance, are affected by individual and collective values so that what is seen as constituting social scientific knowledge is dependent on either personal or collective preferences and interests. This limited 'social autonomy of researchers' (Alvesson, 1991) is thus of crucial importance for the way values and ideologies affect social science research. In a practically oriented field such as management, which in most cases seeks to improve managerial/organizational practices, the identification of what constitutes managerial problems, and the preferred solutions are based on what a particular sector identifies as the relevant problems. As Whitley (1984, p. 375) has pointed out, 'practitioners' goals, perceptions and beliefs enter into the formulation of research goals and evaluation criteria.' To work on 'relevant' research is equivalent to attending to problems of current interests to powerful managers, funding institutions and other reputable organizations, formulated in their terms. Thus, Rosen (1984, p. 319) points out that: 'relevance as a criticism is evoked not infrequently when a body of theory rather than mirroring and reinforcing the dominant *Weltanschauung* implicitly or explicitly challenges it.'

Thus, when the explanatory product of a group of theorists significantly diverges from the interests of the practitioners or that of the dominant ideology, particularly when this product no longer functions to legitimate and mystify the societal bases of power and relations of domination, such a theory is not surprisingly unacknowledged or backgrounded (Rosen, 1984).

The socio-political relevance of research issues is another source of ideological control in social science research. Socio-political relevance indicates the extent to which research is considered particularly important in terms of political exigencies and interests. As Alvesson (1991) has pointed out, there are instances in which research issues, topics and projects come closer to overtly or potentially political topics. The interest in research on minority-owned business, for example, can be traced to the Civil Rights Movement of the early 1960s to late 1970s. The surge of interest was precipitated by the political climate and movement, which focused, among other things, on a poor resource base that inhibited the development of an entrepreneurial class among African-Americans. The civil-rights movement prompted the development of legislation and a number of government agencies to ensure that the social, political and economic rights of African-Americans are attended to. The key reports issued during this period maintained that African-American business lacked the developmental, educational and training opportunities of their major counterparts. The African-American 'entrepreneurial experience,' such as it was, was poorly organized, under-resourced and lacked political, institutional and economic support from significant segments of American society. The interest in research in this area was also fueled by 'political' objectives, which, arguably, set out to remedy the evils of the past through such programs as Affirmative Action. Research objectives and problem formulations were designed, ideally, to lend support to the political culture and movement prevailing at the time.

Schumpeter (1941) refers to this aspect of political influence both in economics generally, and in entrepreneurship in particular, as he says that:

I have first to say that I am not running a drugstore. I have no pills to hand out; no clear-cut solutions for any practical problems that may arise. For these problems are largely political and it is up to you to say what you want to do and fight for it, to say what you will extol and what you will destroy. The economist has no particular qualification to speak about that aspect of any subject. What he can do and what I wanted to do, to the best of my ability, is to present the problem . . . as I see it. (Schumpeter, in a speech in Detroit, April, 1941, in Richard Swedborg, 1991)

The crucial problem in instances of this nature is not necessarily when it can be recognized that there is a presence of ideological control in the formulation of research problems, 'but when it exists as part of what is taken for granted and is unreflectively reproduced, thereby legitimating the status quo' (Alvesson, 1991, p. 212). Related to this aspect of ideological control in the social sciences is the attractiveness of theory and research issues at a particular time (Alvesson, 1991). As has been indicated by a number of researchers, management's core knowledge has developed less as the accumulative discovery of truth about managerial reality than as the product of a political interplay between theorists engaged in sophistry (Astley, 1984). This political interplay could be said to be quintessentially related to what particular groups considered as 'academic vogue' at a particular period.

In the same manner, Schumpeter's *Theorie der wirtschaftlichen Entwicklung* did not get the reception it deserved when it was published in 1911. According to Schumpeter, himself, the overriding reason for the non-receptivity of his theory in that book was its unconventional treatment of the economic doctrine prevailing in Germany at that time, which was contrary to the dominant prevailing Austro-Germanic economic ideology. Thus Schumpeter was later to write that:

When this book first appeared in 1911, both the general view of the economic process embodied in it and about half a dozen of the results it tried to establish, seemed to many people so strikingly uncongenial and so far removed from traditional teaching that it met almost universal hostility. (Schumpeter in Richard Swedborg, 1991, p. 39)

Again, when Schumpeter came to Harvard from Vienna, Austria, the same hostility arising from the unconventionality of his theory was met. Aitken

(1965), one of Schumpeter's colleagues at Harvard, notes that:

> There was . . . much in the Schumpeterian system that we found hard to digest. Our positivistic stomachs rebelled at the taint of mysticism in Schumpeter's concept of creativity; our ideological palates, conditioned during the late 1930s, found the . . . aristocratic element in his thinking distasteful. None of this was reasonable, of course; but it is perhaps understandable. (Aitken, 1965, p. 10)

Thus ideology (or ideological palates) plays an important part in the degree to which a theory is accepted or rejected. The attractiveness of each theory and/or methodology is related also to a particular frame of reference or paradigm. As Kuhn has shown, science typically proceeded by seeking confirmations of the prevailing paradigm. Far from subjecting the existing paradigm itself to constant testing, normal science avoids contradicting it by routinely reinterpreting conflicting data in ways that would support the paradigm, or by neglecting such awkward data altogether. Kuhn argues that allegiance to a particular paradigm depends as much on the established customs of the scientific community, on aesthetics, prevailing belief systems, psychological and religious dispositions which are all shaped by the researcher's ideological and value consciousness. Hence 'the competition between paradigms is not the sort of battle that can be resolved by proofs' (Kuhn, 1970, p. 143) as 'the proponents of each paradigm are engaged in political efforts to gain dominance within the discipline as a means of imposing their own conceptions of reality on the practical events of social life' (Astley and Van de Ven, 1983, p. 270). In other words, for a theory to gain acceptability, it is far less related to objective truth than to ideological and value consensus, namely, the incorporation of research agenda and scientific knowledge into institutionalized ideologies, myths and value preferences prevalent in society.

A theory may be 'useful' in terms of its ability to justify and legitimize underlying societal ideologies, myths and assumptions. Berger (1963) points out that legitimation involves the task of explaining or justifying the social order in such a way as to make institutional arrangements plausible. An important instrument for explaining, advocating or justifying social order is the ideology. Conventional entrepreneurship theory is justified in terms of its appeal to a free market system, the capitalist state and a kind of Utopian goal of economic freedom for everyone. An academic product, thus, might be beneficial for a certain group externally, through its impact on the general public. Hence a theory which fits into the prevalent institutionalized ideologies, myths and values enables a particular interest group to affect other groups in a tactical way. Ideology, like social theory, 'is a set of ideas which is used to legitimate vested interests of sectors of society, communities, professional bodies, etc.' (Berger, 1963, p. 111). Researchers, like ideologues (those who invoke ideology), state social problems or any other problems for the larger society, take sides on the issues involved and present them in the court of the ideological market place. Hence, Geertz (1973, p. 232) makes the point that 'the social function of science vis-à-vis ideologies is first to understand them—what they are, how they work, what gives rise to them—and second, to criticize them, to force them to come to terms with reality.'

What is important about these points for our purpose of examining ideological control and the discourse on entrepreneurship is that they enable us not only to examine the extent to which ideology has penetrated the discourse but also enable us to be skeptical about what is considered self-evident truth. If we are able to achieve this, perhaps it could be possible to free ourselves from the repression of our discourses.

THE DISCOURSE ON ENTREPRENEURSHIP AS A REPRODUCTION OF SOCIETAL MYTHS

Although entrepreneurship has long been regarded as one of the most promising fields in management and organization studies, a search for a theory and a conceptual definition has been problematic (Cooper and Dunkelberg, 1986; Low and MacMillan, 1988; Worthman, 1987). The problem arising from a lack of working definition and theory has been seen as the greatest impediment to knowledge development in this field (Bull and Willard, 1993; Bygrave, 1993; Gartner, 1985, 1993). Other commentators with a more pessimistic view (Low and MacMillan, 1988) have suggested that it seems likely that the desire for common definitions and a clearly defined area of inquiry will remain unfulfilled in the foreseeable future. The problematic nature of the concept of entrepreneurship is reflected in a history of efforts by entrepreneurial researchers to explain 'who' is an entrepreneur and 'what' constitutes entrepreneurship. The who and what in entrepreneurial discourses constitute an ongoing debate, beginning from the time the concept first appeared in Cantillon's (1755) *Essai sur la nature du commerce en general,* through Knight's (1921) theory of risk, uncertainty and profit; Schumpeter's (1934) *Theory of Economic Development,* Cole's (1959) discussion of 'Business Enterprise'; Collins and Moore's (1964) thesis on *The Enterprising Man* and to present-day discourse on entrepreneurship and small business creation.

The term *entrepreneur* [emphasis added] is traditionally recognized to be rooted in Cantillon's (1755) *Essai sur la nature du commerce en general.* Cantillon's vision of an entrepreneur is likened to anyone who is either a farmer or who conducts business (undertaking) in the face of uncertainty. 'The farmer,' according to Cantillon, 'is an undertaker [*entrepreneur*] who promises to pay to the landowner for his farm or land, a fixed sum of money without assurance of the profit he will derive from his enterprise.' What was important for Cantillon is the entrepreneur who invests in the face of risk and uncertainty because 'he employs part of the land to feed flocks, produce corn, wine, hay, etc. according to his judgement without being able to foresee which of these will pay best . . . The price of the farmer's product depends naturally upon these unforeseen circumstances, and consequently he conducts the enterprise of his farm at an uncertainty' (Cantillon, 1755, p. 49).

If ever there was a consensus in the analysis of entrepreneurship, it must be that Schumpeter's contribution to it has been widely recognized as the most influential in the discourse. Schumpeter's discussion of *entrepreneur* and *entrepreneurship* [emphases added] is related to how the economy changes by basically putting together already existing elements into new combinations. Indeed, Schumpeter defines the entrepreneur with this very process in mind: 'The carrying out of new combinations we call "enterprise" (or entrepreneurship); the

individuals whose function it is to carry them out we call "entrepreneurs"' (Schumpeter, 1934, p. 74). The emphasis on Schumpeter's theory of entrepreneurship is consequently not on creating something new from scratch, but on combining what already exists in new ways. Schumpeter therefore draws a sharp conceptual distinction between 'innovation' and 'invention.' For Schumpeter, the 'entrepreneur innovates, but he never invents: Economic leadership in particular must hence be distinguished from "invention." As long as they are not carried into practice, inventions are economically irrelevant' (Schumpeter, 1934, p. 88).

Economic change, which is the Schumpetarian essence of entrepreneurship, can come in many different forms. One can, he says, distinguish between five major categories of 'new combinations':

> (1) The introduction of a new good . . . or a new quality of a good. (2) The introduction of a new method of production . . . (3) The opening of a new market . . . (4) The conquest of a new source of supply of raw materials or half-manufactured good . . . (5) The carrying out of the new organization of any industry, like the creation of a monopoly position . . . or the breaking up of a monopoly position. (Schumpeter, 1934, p. 66)

Arguably, the classics in economics and management recognize the entrepreneur to be someone special as '*he*' (the emphasis in the discourse has always been on 'he') has to be able to break through the resistance to change that exists in any society (Cole, 1959; Collins and Moore, 1964; Knight, 1921; Schumpeter, 1934). The discourse says that most people are unable to do this since they can only handle what is familiar to them. The entrepreneur, on the other hand, has the strength and the courage to challenge the accepted ways of doing things and to sweep aside the forces of tradition. Such people, according to Schumpeter (1934, p. 82), have 'super-normal qualities of intellect and will' and, hence 'essentially more masculine than feminine' whose 'values and activities have become part of the character of America and intimately related to our ideas of personal freedom, success, and above all, individualism' (Collins and Moore, 1964, p. 6).

Following these classical contributions to the understanding of entrepreneurs as agents of the capitalist system, researchers have focused their attention on the individual entrepreneur and sought to understand not only *his* roles in the economic system, but also the masculine personality attributes that are supposedly congruent with these roles, namely, 'his' psychological or personality traits. Such an attempt has also led to a search for the 'heroic' entrepreneur—those 'special breed . . . the truly indigenous epic types' (Collins and Moore, 1964, p. 5). Consequently, the discourse has insisted that the concept of *entrepreneur* and *entrepreneurship* be limited to the study of personality/psychological characteristics (see, for instance, Baumol, 1993; McClelland, 1961; Schere, 1982; Smith and Miner, 1985; among others).

David McClelland's (1961) work on the psychological characteristics of entrepreneurs provides some of the impetus for studies that examined the relationship between entrepreneurial performance and psychological variables. Since McClelland argues that 'high need for achievement' is a key characteristic of entrepreneurs a host of other researchers have sought to establish a relationship between individual characteristics (such as a strong internal locus of control, high need for autonomy, dominance, aggressiveness, low need for support and conformity, independence, task orientation, high risk-taking propensity) and entrepreneurial actions (Cooper and Dunkelberg, 1986; Sexton and Bowman, 1985). With insights drawn from this conceptualization, there emerged a proliferation of studies concerned with the formulation of research problems and questions, including the validation of hypotheses, ostensibly designed to explain and reproduce the dominant ideology of the heroic rational man who 'went through the recurrent process of imposing man's will and man-conceived structures on a wilderness of primeval forests' (Collins and Moore, 1964, p. 5). The idea of entrepreneurship as a masculine notion derives from the conceptualization of entrepreneurial undertaking in terms of 'the wilderness' and this 'wilderness is essentially feminine. It is the *mother* out of which man has built and created things' (Collins and Moore, 1964, p. 5).

Others have insisted on Knightian concepts of risk and uncertainty (Amit et al., 1993). Here, entrepreneurship is defined or conceptualized as the ability to predict the future correctly (Bull and Willard, 1993; Bygrave, 1993; Kirzner, 1985;

Knight, 1921). The central role of uncertainty in the Cantillonian concept is replaced in an interesting way with notions of alertness, predictability, sound judgement, etc. Kirzner (1985), for instance, recognizes the role played by alertness of the entrepreneur and the speculative ability to see into the future because 'man acts in the light of the future as he envisages it, to enhance his position in that future' (1985, p. 55). Thus the term *entrepreneur* [emphasis added] evokes the images of the hero—the historical literature of America about the 'first' white-male European who 'discovered' and 'conquered' the land of opportunity, symbolizing the heroic representation of the positive American male model of aggressiveness, assertiveness and the conqueror of Mother Nature. The impact of this representation on present-day discourses on entrepreneurship is undeniably potent, as evidenced in the type of definitions provided by authors who claim to seek an understanding of the phenomenon of entrepreneurship. Collins and Moore (1964, p. 5) point out apropos this heroic myth that was later to colonize entrepreneurial discourses:

> The symbolism expressed in the American image of the entrepreneur is a profound reflection of our national history and character. We are a people who for nearly twelve generations went through the recurrent process of imposing man's will and man-conceived structures on a wilderness of primeval forests . . . Thus, in American symbolic life, the natural order—the wilderness—is essentially feminine. It is the mother out of which man has built and created things.

Following these heroic, and sometimes Darwinian, notions, Collins and Moore's (1964) conceptualization of an entrepreneur is nearly poetical:

> What we have learned is that the way of the entrepreneur is a long, lonely and difficult road. The men who follow it are by necessity a special breed . . . The road they can follow is one that is lined with difficulties, which most of us could not even begin to overcome. As a group they do not have the qualities of patience, understanding, and charity many of us may admire and wish for in our fellows. This is understandable. In the long and trying way of the entrepreneur such qualities may come to be so much excess baggage. What is necessary to the man who travels this way is great imagination, fortitude, and hardness of purpose . . .

The men who travel the entrepreneurial way are, taken in balance, not remarkably likeable people . . . As any one of them might say in the vernacular of the world of the entrepreneur, 'Nice guys don't win.' (p. 244)

Apart from the fact that entrepreneurship has long been theorized within a gendered framework corresponding to the dominant American folklore, more recent studies have conceptualized it ethnocentrically, explaining the phenomenon of entrepreneurship with racio-ethnic variables (Charboneau, 1981; Chotigeat et al., 1991; De Carlos and Lyons, 1979; Hisrich and Brush, 1984). Many of these researchers seek to understand the ethnic and racial variables that inhibit entrepreneurship among people who are non-European in origin. Others have seen it as a cultural variable (McClelland, 1961; Takyi-Asiedu, 1993) or as the product of the environment (Woo et al., 1994). Here, a Darwinian notion of the environment has been used to conceptualize the ideal entrepreneur through theories of population ecology. This view contends that new business creation is an evolutionary process of 'variation, selection, retention, and diffusion and the struggle for existence' (Aldrich and Zimmer, 1986, p. 9).

These notions of entrepreneurship correspond to a conceptualization of the phenomenon in terms of a configuration of attributes such as abilities, traits and idiosyncrasies necessary for the 'hero' to 'organize the universe around him' (Collins and Moore, 1964). Hence, it is suggested that:

In some respects, the entrepreneur is a heroic figure in American folklore akin perhaps, to Davy Crockett and other truly indigenous epic types—stalwart independents who hewed forests, climbed over the mountains, built new communities, rose from nothing to something, and did all the things American heroes must have done to build a great nation. (Collins and Moore, 1964, pp. 4–5)

Entrepreneurship is thus equated with the way we strive to conquer and master nature; to see into the future, to predict it and to act upon our predictions. As researchers, we are thus seduced into representing entrepreneurs in terms of our ideological constructs regarding heroes with in-born attributes. Entrepreneurship is conceptualized by this ideological orientation as if it were a concrete means by which the rational European/North American male model exhibits the propensity to take risks, to conquer the environment and to survive in a Darwinian world. Commenting on this dominant idea on entrepreneurship, Bull and Willard (1993) suggest that 'Americans have long been interested in a Horatio Alger fiction, where the hero achieves success through self-reliance and hard work. It is not surprising, therefore, that the focus of much of the early work was directed towards identifying the traits or characteristics that distinguish entrepreneurs from mere mortals' (p. 186).

Parallel to this conceptualization is the equally ideologically controlled belief that the traits associated with entrepreneurship and, by implication, capitalism, are not only psychologically given, but are culturally and ethno-racially determined. In this context, Weber's (1930) discussion of 'The Protestant Ethic and the Spirit of Capitalism' has been used to explain why entrepreneurs can only emerge in societies or among people whose culture derives from the Judeo-Christian world-view.

THE LEGITIMATION OF THE DOMINANT IDEOLOGY VIA ETHNOCENTRISM IN THE CONVENTIONAL DISCOURSE ON ENTREPRENEURSHIP

The subject of class, race and ethnicity was prominent in the writings of the classics in entrepreneurial discourses. According to Schumpeter (1951), the concept of class (and race) was extremely important and promised to solve a number of difficult problems not only in entrepreneurial analysis but also in the social sciences in general. It was in the context of discussing the omnipresence of race and class in entrepreneurship that Schumpeter suggests that:

The subject [of class and race]—and this is what constitutes its fascination—poses a wealth of new questions, offers outlooks on untitled fields, foreshadows sciences of the future. Roaming it, one often has a strange feeling, as though the social sciences of today, almost on purpose were dealing with relative side-issues; as though some day—and perhaps soon—the things we now believe will be discounted. (Schumpeter, 1951, p. 103)

In the discourse on entrepreneurship, there seems to be a double rejection and a double acceptance of ethnic and/or racial issues. Although issues about race and/or ethnicity have been very prominent in the discourse, most of the existing research has treated the participation of minorities in entrepreneurial praxis as dysfunctional to theory development (Baker et al., 1997; Butler, 1991; Jackson and Konz, 1998; Nkomo, 1992). What has been repressed or neglected in the discourse is how societal racial and ethnic biases have created the particular conditions in which minority business owners have found themselves. Perhaps, the reason for this neglect may be found in Blauner (1972, p. 2) who suggests that research on racial minorities (i.e., African-Americans, Latinos, Asian-Americans and Native-Americans) was premised on several assumptions such as: (a) racial groups were not viewed as central or persistent elements of society and (b) racism and racial oppression were ultimately reducible to other causal determinants—usually economic or psychological.

In this sense, research has centered on the mechanisms through which the experiences of the non-dominant group (both in entrepreneurship and other aspects of organizational life) can become amenable to suit the dominant paradigm of entrepreneurship or assimilated into what is considered appropriate entrepreneurial behavior. Assimilation is thus seen as a one-way process that requires non-European, non-English-speaking groups (the 'others') to change to fit the dominant culture (Feagin, 1987). A manifestation of this assimilation mentality in the wider society is the tendency of researchers to focus on questions of 'why aren't they like us, or how can they become like us?' (Nkomo, 1992, p. 496). Not surprisingly, over two-thirds of research on minority-owned businesses from 1962 to 1995 are prescriptive, describing programs to assist minority-owned businesses to act in ways prescribed by the dominant culture (Williams and Ramsey, 1996).

The reason why issues of race, ethnicity and class are repressed or neglected in the discourse could be related to the fact that theorists concerned are intimately driven by an identification with the particular class or race to which they not only belong, but which is most admirable in the order of things. Hence Schumpeter (1951) maintains that:

Class members behave towards one another in a fashion characteristically different from their conduct toward members of other classes. They are in closer association with one another; they understand one another better; they work more readily in concert; they close ranks and erect barriers against the outside; they look out into the same segment of the world, with the same eyes, from the same viewpoint, in the same direction. (Schumpeter, 1951, p. 107)

The most important consequence of this tendency to use constructed frameworks which reflect ideological orientations of a 'hierarchically superior race' is that most theorists (and researchers) delineate an analytical space which constitutes an arena of knowledge and which provides the basis for the operation of power. Not surprisingly, outsiders are encouraged to adopt ways that fit into those of the dominant culture.

The influence of ideological control on minority business research in terms of theoretical assumptions has been critiqued as a result of its ahistorical and decontextualized nature (Butler, 1991; Nkomo, 1992). Secondly, the conventional discourse has been criticized for its undue focus on attitudinal problems as explanations for the performance of minority business firms (for such explanations, see Chotigeat et al., 1991; De Carlos and Lyons, 1979; Feldman et al., 1991; Hisrich and Brush, 1984). At the heart of this criticism is that issues related to minority businesses are treated as antitheses and dysfunctional, inhibiting entrepreneurial development.

What has been obscured and/or neglected in the discourse related to the participation of minorities in entrepreneurial activities are the processes through which knowledge is constructed. The discourse, in its dismissal of sociological, historical and other political factors, ultimately left the entrepreneur to psychological determinism. Perhaps this 'dismissal' is understandable since conventional discourse embraced much of the theorizing of psychologists where socio-cultural and other non-psychological factors are de-emphasized. The point I wish to make here is that the current emphasis on the search for psychological variables as a way of explaining the conditions of minority-owned businesses is theoretically inadequate in building an entrepreneurial theory. I wish to point out also that this way of 'understanding' the nature of minority-owned business has contributed to and reinforced the prevailing myth that non-dominant groups have psychological and racial characteristics which inhibit entrepreneurial development. This tendency has been all too pervasive in the conventional literature. For instance, it has been suggested that non-minority entrepreneurs place a higher value on achievement, recognition and independence while minority entrepreneurs place greater value on conformity and benevolence: the antithesis of entrepreneurial performance (see, for example, De Carlos and Lyons, 1979). In a similar manner, Sonfield (1978, pp. 98–9), in an 'attitudinal comparison of black and white small businesses,' described the failure of a 'black capitalism' as a result of attitudinal differences.

Through ethnocentrism, the very concepts of 'entrepreneur' and 'entrepreneurship' as used in the conventional discourse have served as social artifacts reflecting the social relations, or power order, in contemporary society, based on what Rosen (1984) calls 'hierarchical segmentation and value appropriation.' As researchers, we have treated entrepreneurship as we treat other forms of social relations of domination.

LEGITIMATION OF THE DOMINANT IDEOLOGY THROUGH THE GENDERING OF ENTREPRENEURIAL IDEAS

The discourse on entrepreneurship, following a pattern within a general 'Eurocentric' character of Western thought, has sustained traditional dichotomies, oppositions and dualities—between male and female—where the male-oriented definition of reality is upheld as the legitimate world-view celebrating masculine concepts of control, competition, rationality, dominance, etc. Not surprisingly, Collins and Moore (1964) posit that:

> However we may personally feel about the entrepreneur, he emerges as essentially *more masculine than feminine, more heroic than cowardly* . . . His values and activities have become part of the character of America and intimately related to our ideas of personal freedom, success, and, above all, individualism . . . the myth of the entrepreneur is a drama in which the

protagonists challenge the established order . . . (pp. 5–6, italics added)

In this world-view, males are seen as the archetype of entrepreneurs whereas females, at best, are restricted to what Bowen and Hisrich (1986) termed as 'entrepreneurial ghettos.' Female participation in entrepreneurship is reasoned to be the antithesis of entrepreneurial norms as a result of gender qualities: male achievement versus female subjugation; male dominance versus female submissiveness; male control versus female appreciation; male autonomy versus female support; male aggression versus female co-operation; male independence versus female dependence; male idiosyncrasy versus female conformity.

Thus, not only are entrepreneurial ideas ethnocentrically presumed, its discourse has also been influenced and controlled by gender-biased strategies and metaphors supporting a patriarchical conception of nature. Chio and Calas (1991, p. 7) point out that 'in analyzing the potential "effectiveness" of women-owned businesses, prescriptive academic literature often calls for an increase in activities which are task oriented' reflecting a male definition of reality. In this context, the term 'invisible entrepreneurs' has been used to describe the limited or lack of attention provided female business owners in the literature and research on entrepreneurship (Baker et al., 1997).

The reason for this 'invisibility' could be seen as quintessentially the result of the fact that entrepreneurial research has been undertaken with assumptions derived from male-oriented dominant cultural ideologies that have pervaded theoretical constructions. Following a feminist/postmodernist tradition, Chio and Calas (1991) draw attention to how the existing discourse on businesses owned by dominant groups legitimates a certain world of actions over another and point out the necessity of researchers to start asking not only in whose image conventional organizations have been formulated, but also whose experiences traditional organization theory represents.

In a feminist-critique of organization studies generally, Calvert and Ramsey (1992) also draw attention to the tendency, for researchers who study women, to use men as standards of comparison.

This approach, according to Calvert and Ramsey, serves to maintain the status quo because 'we are still asking the same questions, repeating the same answers, and operating on the same set of assumptions' (pp. 80–1). To the extent that entrepreneurial ideas are gendered, they reflect and maintain the system of social relations that privileges one-half of the masculine/feminine dichotomy; namely, the masculine half. And, as gendered ideas, they themselves have become instruments of control over resources, over people, and especially over the drawing of boundaries between people of different sexes. Some scholars such as Chio and Calas (1991) have taken this point seriously and suggest that regardless of what has been written about minority-owned businesses and their owners, 'the scholarly literature has been incapable of questioning the epistemological lenses that provide the assessments. The knowledge-makers coalesce in separating "those who think" and "those who do," and in legitimizing with their theoretical activities a certain world and not another, the legitimate world has already been made' (p. 8).

As has been noted by a number of radical organization theorists, contemporary organizations and management practices are both White-male dominated and White-male defined because white males have created organizations and adopted management practices that have met male needs, reinforced male values and best fit male experiences of the world around them (Calvert and Ramsey, 1992). I am suggesting that the traditional discourse on entrepreneurship has not only taken the experience of the male species as a self-evident unit with which to produce knowledge about entrepreneurship, but also the discourse itself has served to maintain the existing dichotomy between maleness and femaleness, and thus the existing societal bias on inequality.

REFERENCES

Aitken, H. G. J. (1965). 'Entrepreneurial history: the history of an intellectual innovation.' In Aitken, H. G. J. (Ed.), *Explorations in Enterprise*. Cambridge, MA: Harvard University Press, 3–19.

Aldrich, H. and Zimmer, C. (1986). 'Entrepreneurship through social networks.' In Sexton, D. L. and Smilor, R. W. (Eds), *The Art and Science of Entrepreneurship*. Cambridge, MA: Ballinger Publishing, 2–23.

Aldrich, H. and Waldinger, R. (1990). 'Ethnicity and entrepreneurship.' *Annual Review of Sociology*, **18**, 111–35.

Alvesson, M. (1991). 'Organizational symbolism and ideology.' *Journal of Management Studies*, **28**, 3, 207–25.

Amit, R., Glosten, L. and Muller, E. (1993). 'Challenges to theory development in entrepreneurship *research.*' *Journal of Management Studies*, **30**, 5, 815–34.

Astley, W. G. (1984). 'Subjectivity, sophistry and symbolism in management science.' *Journal of Management Studies*, **21**, 3, 259–273.

Astley, W. Graham and Andrew H. Van de Ven. (1983). "Central Perspectives and Debates in Organization Theory." *Administrative Science Quarterly*, **28**(2):245–73.

Baker, T., Aldrich, H. E. and Liou, N. (1997). 'The invisible entrepreneurs: the neglect of women business owners by mass media and scholarly journals in the USA.' *Entrepreneurship and Regional Development*, **9**, 221–38.

Balsamo, A. (1985). 'Beyond female as a variable: constructing a feminist perspective on organizational analysis.' *Paper presented at the conference on 'Critical Perspective on Organizational Analysis.'* Baruch College.

Baumol, W. J. (1993). 'Formal entrepreneurship theory in economics: the existence and bounds.' *Journal of Business Venturing*, **8**, 197–210.

Berger, P. L. (1963). *Invitation to Sociology*. Garden City, NY: Doubleday.

Berger, P. L. and Luckmann, T. (1967). *The Social Construction of Reality*. New York: Doubleday.

Blauner, R. (1972). *Racial Oppression in America*. New York: Harper & Row.

Bowen, D. D. and Hisrich, R. D. (1986). 'The female entrepreneur: a career development perspective.' *Academy of Management Review*, **11**, 2, 393–407.

Bull, I. and Willard, G. E. (1993). 'Towards a theory of entrepreneurship.' *Journal of Business Venturing*, **8**, 183–95.

Butler, J. S. (1991). *Entrepreneurship and Self-help among Black Americans*. New York: State University of New York Press.

Bygrave, W. D. (1993). 'Theory building in the entrepreneurship paradigm.' *Journal of Business Venturing*, **8**, 255–80.

Calas, M. B. and Smircich, L. (1992). 'Re-writing gender into organizational theorizing: directions from feminist perspectives.' In Reed, M. I. and Hughes, M. D. (Eds), *Rethinking Organizations: New Directions on Organizational Research and Analysis.* London: Sage.

Calvert, L. M. and Ramsey, V. J. (1992). 'Bringing women's voice to research on women management: a feminist perspective.' *Journal of Management Inquiry,* **Vol. 1**, 79–88.

Cantillon, R. (1755). *Essai sur la nature du commerce en general.* Translated by Higgs, H. (1931). Oxford: Oxford University Press.

Charboneau, F. J. (1981). 'The woman entrepreneur.' *American Demographics,* **June**, 21–3.

Chio, V. C. and Calas, M. B. (1991). 'Understanding small business owners' organizational approaches: possible influences of gender roles.' *Paper presented at the Proceedings of the Eastern Academy of Management.*

Chotigeat, T., Balsmeier, W. and Stanley, T. (1991). 'Fueling Asian immigrants' entrepreneurship: a source of capital.' *Journal of Small Business Management,* **7**, 50–68.

Cole, A. H. (1959). *Business Enterprise in its Social Setting.* Cambridge, MA: Harvard University Press.

Collins, O. F. and Moore, D. G. (1964). *The Enterprising Man.* East Lansing, MI: Michigan State University Press.

Cooper, A. C. and Dunkelberg, W. (1986). 'Entrepreneurship and paths to ownership.' *Strategic Management Journal,* **7**, 53–68.

de Carlos, J. F. and Lyons, P. R. (1979). 'A comparison of selected personal characteristics of minority and non-minority female entrepreneurs.' *Proceedings of the 39th Annual Meeting of the Academy of Management.*

Deetz, S. and Mumby, D. (1990). 'Power, discourse, and the workplace: reclaiming the critical tradition in communication studies in organizations.' In Anderson, J. (Ed.), *Communication Yearbook. Vol. 13.* Newbury Park, CA: Sage.

Feagin, F. (1987). 'Changing black Americans to fit a racist system?' *Journal of Social Issues,* **43**, 1, 85–9.

Feldman, H. D., Koberg, C. S. and Dean, T. J. (1991). 'Minority small business owners and their paths to ownership.' *Journal of Small Business Management,* **Oct.**, 13–27.

Ferguson, K. (1984). *The Feminist Case against Bureaucracy.* Philadelphia: Temple University Press.

Feyerabend, P. (1975). *Against Method.* London: Redwood Burn Limited.

Fondas, N. (1997). 'Feminization unveiled: management qualities in contemporary writings.' *Academy of Management Review,* **22**, 1, 257–84.

Gartner, W. B. (1985). 'A framework for describing and classifying the phenomenon of new venture creation.' *Academy of Management Review,* **10**, 4, 696–708.

Gartner, W. B. (1993). 'Words lead to deeds: towards an organizational emergence vocabulary.' *Journal of Business Venturing,* **8**, 231–9.

Geertz, C. (1973). *The Interpretation of Cultures.* New York: Basic Books.

Gilligan, C. (1982). *In a Different Voice.* Cambridge, MA: Harvard University Press.

Hisrich, R. D. and Brush, C. (1984). 'The woman entrepreneur: management skills and business problems.' *Journal of Small Business Management,* **22**, 30–7.

Jackson, J. and Konz, G. (1998). 'Black women entrepreneurs.' In Biberman, J. and Alkhafaji, A. (Eds), *Business Research Yearbook,* **5**, 536–9.

Kirzner, I. (1985). *Discovery and the Capitalist System.* Chicago: University of Chicago Press.

Knight, F. (1921). *Risk, Uncertainty, and Profit.* Boston, MA: Houghton-Mifflin.

Kuhn, T. S. (1970). *The Structure of Scientific Revolution* (3rd edition). Chicago: University of Chicago Press.

Low, M. B. and MacMillan, I. C. (1988). 'Entrepreneurship: past research and future challenges.' *Journal of Management,* **14**, 20, 139–61.

McClelland, D. (1961). *The Achieving Society.* Princeton, NJ: Van Nostrand.

Morgan, G. (1986). *Images of Organization.* London: Sage.

Nkomo, S. M. (1992). 'The emperor has no clothes: rewriting "race in organizations."' *Academy of Management Review,* **17**, 3, 489–513.

Ramsey, V. J. and Calvert, L. M. (1994). 'A feminist critique of organizational humanism.' *Journal of Applied Behavioral Science,* **30**, 83–97.

Rosen, M. (1984). 'Myth and reproduction: the contextualization of management theory, method and practice.' *Journal of Management Studies,* **21**, 3, 303–22.

Schere, J. L. (1982). 'Tolerance and ambiguity as a discriminatory variable between entrepreneurs and managers.' *Proceedings, Academy of Management,* 404–8.

Schumpeter, J. (1934). *The Theory of Economic Development: An Inquiry into Profits, Capital, Credit, Interest, and the Business Cycle* (trans. by Redvers Opie). Cambridge, MA: Harvard University Press.

Schumpeter, J. (1947). 'The creative response in economic history.' *Journal of Economic History,* **7**, 149–59.

Schumpeter, J. (1949). 'Science and ideology.' *American Economic Review,* **39**, 345–59.

Schumpeter, J. (1951). *Imperialism and Social Classes.* Oxford: Blackwell.

Schumpeter, J. (1954). *History of Economic Analysis.* London: Allen & Unwin.

Sexton, D. L. and Bowman, N. (1985). 'The entrepreneur: a capable executive and more.' *Journal of Business Venturing,* **1**, 129–40.

Smircich, L. (1985). 'Toward a woman-centered organization theory.' *Paper presented at the Academy of Management National Meeting.* San Diego, CA.

Smith, N. R. and Miner, J. B. (1985). 'Motivational considerations in the success of technologically innovative entrepreneurs.' In Hornaday, J. et al. (Eds), *Frontiers of Entrepreneurship Research.* Wellesley, MA: Babson College.

Sonfield, M. C. (1978). 'An attitudinal Comparison of Black and White Small Businessmen.' *American Journal of Small Business,* **2**, 94–111.

Swedborg, R. (1991). *Schumpeter: A Biography.* Princeton, NJ: Princeton University Press.

Takyi-Asiedu, S. (1993). 'Some socio-cultural factors retarding entrepreneurial activity in sub-Saharan Africa.' *Journal of Business Venturing,* **8**, 91–8.

Van de Ven, A. H. (1993). 'The development of an infrastructure for entrepreneurship.' *Journal of Business Venturing,* **8**, 211–30.

Weber, M. (1930). *The Protestant Ethic and the Spirit of Capitalism.* London: Allen & Unwin.

Whitley, R. (1984). 'The scientific status of management research as a practically-oriented science.' *Journal of Management Studies,* **21**, 4, 369–90.

Williams, J. and Ramsey, J. V. (1996). 'What do we know about minority-owned businesses? A review and critique.' *Business and Economic Review,* **3**, 39–56.

Woo, C. Y., Daellenbach, U. and Nicholls-Nixon, C. (1994). 'Theory building in the presence of "randomness": the case of venture creation and performance.' *Journal of Management Studies,* **31**, 4, 507–23.

Worthman, M. S. (1987). 'Entrepreneurship: an integrated typology and evaluation of the empirical research in the field.' *Journal of Management,* **13**, 2, 259–79.

SOURCE: Ogbor, John O. 2000. Excerpt from "Mythicizing and Reification in Entrepreneurial Discourse: Ideology-Critique of Entrepreneurial Studies." *Journal of Management Studies,* 35(5):606, 609–22, 629–35.

PART VII

DIVERSITY WITHIN ORGANIZATIONS

AN INTRODUCTION TO DIVERSITY WITHIN ORGANIZATIONS

Why be concerned with diverse populations within workplace organizations? The power of social ties and mutual identification allows group members to work cooperatively toward common goals. However, this same solidarity can create hostility directed at "outsiders" who are not included in the group. Those excluded others often feel resentment and hostility. They can also suffer socially, politically, and economically. Though there are virtually limitless reasons to be interested in different points of view and in diverse populations, in this section we focus on practical and ethical considerations.

On a practical level, when workplace organizations welcome diverse members, they benefit from a larger pool of applicants and have greater opportunity to hire the most qualified and talented employees. Additionally, diversity in workplace populations, whether demographic, educational, or experiential, provides a variety of perspectives on any problem. Charlan Nemeth argues that majority and minority views contribute differently to processes. The views of majorities "foster convergence of attention, thought, and the number of alternatives considered" (Nemeth 1986:23). On the other hand, minority views "are important . . . because they stimulate divergent attention and thought. As a result, even when [minority views] are wrong, they contribute to the detection of novel solutions and decisions that, on balance, are qualitatively better . . . for creativity, problem-solving and decision-making, both at the individual and group levels" (Nemeth 1986:23). Further, when employee diversity mirrors diversity in the larger society, the organization can be most responsive to the needs of those it serves since a range of demographic groups is already represented within company ranks.

On the other hand, because of the lack of uniformity that different perspectives ensure, diverse populations can be more challenging to manage. Consensus and stability can be elusive as people from various cultures and backgrounds struggle to reconcile conflicting values and understandings. Additionally, in uncertain environments, trust and reliability become even more important, which further strengthens the tendency for people to affiliate with those they consider to be like themselves. Homosocial reproduction is the tendency to hire, mentor, and form professional relationships with those who are socially similar. Rosabeth Moss Kanter (1977) writes,

> It is the uncertainty quotient in managerial work, as it has come to be defined in the large modern corporation, that causes management to become so socially restricting: to develop tight inner circles excluding social strangers; to keep control in the hands of socially homogeneous peers; to stress conformity and insist upon a diffuse, unbounded loyalty; and to prefer ease of communication and thus social certainty over the strains of dealing with people who are "different." (P. 49)

The ideal, which is easier said than done, is to maintain creativity and innovation and also provide predictability and efficiency by uniting diverse perspectives under a set of agreed-upon goals.

In addition to the impact on the interests of the organization, there are other practical and measurable consequences of the historical underrepresentation of certain demographic groups. For instance, there is evidence that exclusion and underrepresentation of women and minorities in entrepreneurial narratives and workplace images anchors low social and psychological expectations for these groups that undermine their confidence and, as a result, their likelihood to successfully engage in entrepreneurial activity (Godwyn 2009; Minniti, Arenius, and Langowitz 2005). Therefore, underrepresentation in scholarly research, teaching tools, and media coverage effectively impedes access to the economy through entrepreneurship. Additionally, studies over the years have established that women are less likely than men to be identified as business leaders (Eagly and Johannesen-Schmidt 2001; Heilman et al. 1989) and that feminine characteristics are not as likely to be associated with the workplace as are masculine qualities (see literature review in Valian 1998). Researchers have also demonstrated that racial stereotypes can negatively affect self-esteem (Clark and Clark 1939) and diminish performance (Steele 1997). This not only affects members of these groups, but also has negative economic consequences for the broader society.

On a brighter note, there is also evidence that frames of reference can be changed by including women and minorities in normative representations (Godwyn 2009; Steele 1997). When marginalized groups are represented and included in social networks, performance can be positively affected. Claude Steele (1997) demonstrated that the standardized test scores of African American students were higher if tests were introduced as academically insignificant, thereby removing the expectation that black students would perform less well than their white counterparts, while Casper et al. (2007) found that social inclusion at work increased organizational commitment for single employees.

On an ethical level, organizations can either reinforce or challenge the conventions that result in unequal opportunities, discrimination, and prejudice. The valuation of diversity resonates with the democratic emphasis on the inclusion and representation of a multiplicity of views and interests. People increasingly recognize that the workplace is not an autonomous sphere governed solely by instrumental logic and operating independently of social rules and concerns. All interactions are rife with social implications, moral and ethical considerations; material exchanges involve relationships among sensitive, reflexive actors as they recursively define their identity in their relation to work (Godwyn 2006).

In an effort to include demographic minorities and in recognition that the unequal distribution of wealth, status, and power does not necessarily reflect differences in individual talent or efforts, some public and private organizations have instituted practices, such as equal opportunity policies and diversity training programs, that actively invite and support heretofore underrepresented populations. During the twentieth century, class, race, religion, ethnicity, age, and gender became the central social referents identified in discrimination. In the twenty-first century, the range of qualities covered by the rubric of diversity is expanding. In addition to the referents already mentioned, organizations are also concerned about rights, representation, and inclusion with regard to sexual orientation, gender identity, physical and mental challenges, and marital and parental status. The valuation of diversity can be understood not only as providing access to the economy to more people, but also as promoting the representation of a variety of values and perspectives as they are communicated in workplace interactions, and practices.

The vastness of diversity eludes comprehensive representation; however, the articles in this section include a wide range of populations and workplaces. In "Women's Careers in Static and Dynamic Organizations," Elin Kvande and Bente Rasmussen (1995) investigate the experiences of women engineers as they attempt to join the workforce in six large male-dominated Norwegian companies. Kvande and Rasmussen challenge the idea that individual differences, or differences between men and women, are salient in workplace success. Instead, they find organizational structures to be the leading driver of the unequal, gendered distribution of career opportunities. Most significantly they challenge the notion that bureaucratic hierarchies are *the* structures of modern organizations (Kvande and Rasmussen 1995). Kvande and Rasmussen (1995) write,

> The companies where we find that men have systematically better opportunities than women are characterized by a hierarchical structure of work organization. The "opportunity"-firms where opportunities do not vary systematically according to gender are characterized by a less hierarchical and more flexible network-type of work organization. According to their market position and organization of work we labeled them *static hierarchies* and *dynamic networks* respectively in order to treat them as ideal types. (P. 124)

The effects of gender vary in organizational settings, and Kvande and Rasmussen (1995) report that bureaucratic hierarchies are associated with inflexibility and intolerance such that they impede diversity, inclusion, and innovation. Similarly, in his article "We Have to Make a MANagement Decision: Challenger and the Dysfunctions of Corporate Masculinity," Mark Maier (1997) finds that gender remains a social category of "master status" (p. 226). Maier provides a feminist critique of conventional management practices and points out that bureaucratic hierarchies are "infused with a 'masculine ethic'" (p. 229), arguing that this masculinist management mind-set created a context of risk that led to the *Challenger* tragedy. He writes, "From a diversity perspective, one need look no further than *Challenger* for the compelling case to embrace a multicultural approach to organizational development" (Maier 1997:253).

In her article, "Just One of the Guys: How Transmen Make Gender Visible at Work," Kristen Schilt (2006) interviews female-to-male transsexuals. As men, these individuals receive "more authority, reward and respect" (Schilt 2006:465) in the workplace than they did as women. Though gender is a "master status," other social referents are important as well. In Schilt's study, body type, ethnicity, height, and race are also relevant to whether or not these employees experienced prejudice and discrimination on the job.

Stella Nkomo's "The Emperor Has No Clothes: Rewriting 'Race in Organizations,'" (1992) has become foundational to the discourse on workplace diversity. By critiquing various theories of race, Nkomo persuasively argues that the notion of "race," as it is generally situated and studied in organizations, assumes a Eurocentric ideological construction that often escapes detection and challenge. She argues that organizations are not "race neutral" (Nkomo 1992:489). In fact, "the concepts and approaches used in Western academics help to maintain the political and intellectual superiority of Western cultures and people" (Nkomo 1992:490). Therefore, under the current scholarly and scientific inquiry, racial inequality is perpetuated and reinforced rather than examined and dismantled.

Using postcolonial theory, Anshuman Prasad's "The Colonizing Consciousness and Representations of the Other: A Postcolonial Critique of the Discourse of Oil," (1997) contextualizes the oil industry within a historical and cultural narrative. Prasad (1997) demonstrates that the construction of an "ontological Other" (p. 303) and the attendant system of colonialist binaries (1997)—wherein all things associated with the West are positive, civilized, and modern and all things associated with non-Western cultures are negative, savage, and backward—provide a medium of dehumanization and economic exploitation. Echoing Nkomo (1992), Prasad (1997) explains the implications for this critique on workplace diversity:

> One of the basic purposes of such critique would be to understand how, at the fundamental level, the diversity industry may primarily be occupied in echoing and enacting the central propositions of colonialist discourse, and consequently, in being complicit with the continual production, reproduction, and perpetuation of a hegemonic system that is the source of immense material and symbolic violence directed against those cultural and demographic groups that mostly inhabit the margins of contemporary Western organizations. (P. 305)

The last two articles in this section focus on very different populations. In "The Disclosure Dilemma for Gay Men and Lesbians: 'Coming Out' at Work," Kirstin H. Griffin and Michelle R. Hebl (2002) discuss sexual orientation as visible diversity. And in "Identification of Work Environments and Employers Open to Hiring and Accommodating People with Disabilities," Dennis Gilbride et al. (2003) examine the workplace experiences of individuals with disabilities. Despite their differences, both articles explore the attributes of tolerant organizations: job sites that make it safe for gay men and lesbians to disclose their identities, and workplaces that are open to hiring employees with disabilities.

Gilbride et al. (2003) found that there is a "culture of inclusiveness" (p. 131) in companies that routinely hire people with disabilities. In these cultures, employees with disabilities comment frequently about the importance of feeling integrated into the organization. Emphasis on performance rather than disability creates a sense that people with disabilities are like everyone else. One employee commented, "I don't think they see the disabilities. They treat us like we're—like you want to be treated, like a regular human being, and that's the way they treat us here" (Gilbride et al. 2003:133).

Similarly Griffin and Hebl (2002) underscore that "one of the most fundamental motivations that people possess is a need to belong and have social support, and this same motivation has profound implications in the workplace. Those who acknowledge and receive favorable and supportive reactions from others feel happier and less stressed in the workplace" (p. 1196). To this end, gay men and lesbians "do take into account the extent to which companies are gay-supportive employers" (Griffin and Hebl 2002). Griffin and Hebl also found that "organizations that promote diversity *do not* do so at the risk of decreasing majority members' positivity toward the organization" (p. 1197, emphasis added).

This notion of openness, toleration, and appreciation of differences, *without sacrificing one group for another* or one's individuality for the group, resonates with Mary Parker Follett's position in 1918: "Give *your* difference, welcome *my* difference, unify *all* difference in the larger whole—such is the law of growth. The unifying of difference is the eternal process of life—the creative synthesis, the highest act of creation, the atonement. The implications of this conception when we come to define democracy are profound" (p. 40, emphasis in the original).

QUESTIONS FOR DISCUSSION

1. What are some ways that diverse populations and perspectives affect organizations?
2. How might diversity within organizations, or the lack thereof, affect the broader society?
3. How is inclusion related to democracy? How do these concepts differ?
4. How can diverse populations achieve consensus and efficiency? Give specific examples.

SUGGESTIONS FOR FURTHER READING

Heath, Melanie. 2003. "Soft-Boiled Masculinity: Renegotiating Gender and Racial Identities in the Promise Keepers Movement." *Gender & Society,* 17(3):423–44.

Kanter, Rosabeth Moss. 1993. *Men and Women of the Corporation.* New York: Basic Books.

Ortleib, Renate and Barbara Sieben. 2010. "Migrant Employees in Germany: Personnel Structures and Practices." *Equality, Diversity and Inclusion,* 29(4):364–79.

Park, Jaihan, Eva Malachi, Orit Sternin and Roni Tevet. 2009. "Subtle Bias against Muslim Job Applicants in Personnel Decisions." *Journal of Applied Psychology,* 39(9):2174–90.

REFERENCES

Casper, Wendy J., David Weltman, and Eileen Kwesiga. 2007. "Beyond Family Friendly: The Construct and Measurement of Singles-Friendly Work Culture." *Journal of Vocational Behavior,* 70(3):478–501.

Clark, Kenneth B., and Mamie K. Clark. 1939. "The Development of Consciousness of Self and the Emergence of Racial Identification in Negro Pre-School Children." *The Journal of Social Psychology*, 10: 591–99.

Eagly, Alice H. and Mary J. Johannesen-Schmidt. 2001. "The Leadership Styles of Women and Men." *Journal of Social Issues,* 57(4):781–97.

Follett, Mary Parker. 1918. *The New State: Group Organization, the Solution of Popular Government.* London: Longmans, Green and Co.

Gilbride, Dennis, Robert Stensrud, David Vandergoot, and Kristie Golden. 2003. "Identification of Work Environments and Employers Open to Hiring and Accommodating People with Disabilities." *Rehabilitation Counseling Bulletin,* 46(3):130–37.

Godwyn, Mary. 2006. "Using Emotional Labor to Create and Maintain Relationships in Service and Sales Interactions." *Symbolic Interaction,* 29:487–505.

———. 2009. "'This Place Makes Me Proud to be a Woman': Theoretical Explanations for Success in Entrepreneurship Education for Low-Income Women." *Research in Social Stratification and Mobility,* 27(1):50–64.

Griffin, Kirstin H. and Michelle R. Hebl. 2002. "The Disclosure Dilemma for Gay Men and Lesbians: 'Coming Out' at Work." *Journal of Applied Psychology,* 87(6):1191–99.

Heilman, M. E., C. J. Block, R. Martell, & M. Simon. (1989). "Has anything changed? Current characterizations of men, women, and managers." *Journal of Applied Psychology,* 74(6):935–42.

Kanter, Rosabeth Moss. 1977. *Men and Women of the Corporation.* New York: Basic Books.

Kvande, Elin and Bente Rasmussen. 1995. "Women's Careers in Static and Dynamic Organizations." *Acta Sociologica,* 38:115–30.

Maier, Mark. 1997. "We Have to Make a MANagement Decision: Challenger and the Dysfunctions of Corporate Masculinity." Pp. 226–54 in *Managing the Organizational Melting Pot: Dilemmas of Workplace Diversity*. Thousand Oaks, CA: Sage.

Minniti, M., P. Arenius, and N. Langowitz. 2005. *Global Entrepreneurship Monitor 2004 Report on Women and Entrepreneurship*. Babson Park, MA: The Center for Women's Leadership at Babson College.

Nemeth, Charlan Jeanne. 1986. "Differential Contributions of Majority and Minority Influence." *Psychological Review,* 93(1):23–32.

Nkomo, Stella. 1992. "The Emperor Has No Clothes: Rewriting 'Race in Organizations.'" *Academy of Management Review,* 17(3):487–513.

Prasad, Anshuman. 1997. "The Colonizing Consciousness and Representations of the Other: A Postcolonial Critique of the Discourse of Oil." Pp. 285–311 in *Managing the Organizational Melting Pot: Dilemmas of Workplace Diversity*. Thousand Oaks, CA: Sage.

Schilt, Kristen. 2006. "Just One of the Guys: How Transmen Make Gender Visible at Work." *Gender & Society,* 20(4):465–49.

Steele, Claude. 1997. "A Threat in the Air: How Stereotypes Shape the Intellectual Identities and Performance of Women and African-Americans." *American Psychologist,* 52:613–29.

Valian, Virginia. 1998. *Why So Slow? The Advancement of Women*. Boston: MIT Press.

42

WOMEN'S CAREERS IN STATIC AND DYNAMIC ORGANIZATIONS

ELIN KVANDE AND BENTE RASMUSSEN

The focus in this article is on how structural conditions in organizations either limit or give women opportunities for mobility. Most organizational researchers see the bureaucratic and hierarchical structure of organizations as *the* structure of modern organizations. We apply a structural perspective but unlike former studies we look at *variations* in structural conditions between organizations. We ask whether the effects of gender vary in different types of organizations.

The changes in women's situation in the Norwegian society over the last 20 years have been labelled 'The Norwegian Women's Revolution' (Skrede & Tornes 1986). This 'revolution' has been brought about by the dramatic increase in women in the labour-force and in the political arena. Norway is now among the countries with the highest rate of women in the workforce (Esping-Andersen 1993). First, this movement of women was into part-time work, but the development in the 1980s has been towards full-time employment, noticeably by the growing rate of mothers of small children working full time (Kjeldstad 1993).

Although women's participation in the labour-market became more like men's, the labour-market was still segregated according to gender. To de-segregate the labour market, the official policy was to promote campaigns to encourage non-traditional choices in education among boys and girls. These efforts had a positive effect. In the 1980s Norway saw a marked increase in women in male-dominated educations and professions. Before 1979 the rate of women graduating from the Norwegian Institute of Technology (NTH) never exceeded 5 per cent (Kvande 1982). In 1985 the rate reached 25 per cent, which was at that time considered sensational on a world scale (Kvande & Rasmussen 1990).

These changes in education, however, did not directly manifest themselves in changes in work organizations. While Norwegian women have entered the top positions in politics, the number of women in middle- and top-management positions is still very low. Even though more women are in the labour force in Norway and the facilities for working mothers are much better than those in the US, the rate of women with top-management positions is 5 per cent in the US, which is twice as high as in Norway (Powell 1993; Kjeldstad 1993).

In Norway the engineering profession has been an important recruiting ground for business managers (Kvande & Rasmussen 1990). The women graduating as engineers are not only moving into one of the world's most male-dominated professions, they also compete with men for managerial careers. Using this professional group we wanted to investigate the processes of career development for women who were in the right starting place as far as education was concerned. What are the processes that result in a low representation of women in top positions in work organizations in Norway? What organizational conditions contribute to this situation?

In this article we will address these questions with data from a research project on Norwegian male and female graduate engineers and their career development in different work organizations. The study was carried out in 1984–86 and full results have been published elsewhere (Kvande & Rasmussen 1990).

From Women in Management to Gender and Organization

Organization studies as a field have been criticized for neglecting gender in their analyses, or, when gender is introduced, for inadequately analysing it (Hearn & Parkin 1987). Gender in organization has until recently been treated only indirectly, either as part of Women in Management research (WIM) (Henning & Jardim 1978; Donnell & Hall 1980; Marshall 1984) or as part of women and work research (Kaul & Lie 1982; Cockburn 1983; 1985; Knights & Wilmott 1986). At the same time organization theory and organization research have not, until recently, been a focus of feminist scholarship. Thus organization studies need to confront the gender issue and gender studies need to put organizations on their research agenda (Kvande & Rasmussen 1992). Organizations are, after all, the area where the sex-segregation of the labour-market, the unequal distribution of rewards as well as gendered cultural images and identities are created (Acker 1990). We can now observe a move from studies focusing on women in management to studies exploring gender in organizations (Acker 1992; Mills & Tancred 1992).

The WIM tradition, developed from the mid-1970s mainly in the USA, focuses on individual characteristics of women, sex role socialization and gender roles. This research on women in management, such as female graduate engineers, uses a sex role model that attaches importance to socialization. It emphasizes women's lack of self-confidence and ambition in order to answer the 'why so few' question, which is the typical research question in this research tradition. We have structured the studies in this research tradition in the following four categories:

(1) The 'trait' approach, where the main emphasis is whether women are 'suited' to management (Bartol 1978; Donnell & Hall 1980; Terborg 1977). This approach is part of an Anglo-American tradition of research where certain characteristics of managers are seen as important elements of management theory (Yukl 1981). A 'modern' variant of a 'trait' approach is the research on women's values in management and leadership (Marshall 1984; Loden 1986; Rosener 1990). According to this research male and female managers use different management styles.

(2) The 'motivation' approach, with the focus on women's 'lack of' self-confidence or motivation. This approach is based on the idea that women hold traditional women's jobs because they lack motivation and self-confidence; they score lower than men on these variables (Terborg 1977; Hackett & Betz 1981).

(3) The 'strategy' approach, where the emphasis is on whether or not women are good enough strategists, making use of the right informal channels (Henning & Jardim 1978).

(4) The 'choice' approach, showing that women choose to give priority to their home and family rather than a career. This is the most predominant approach of the four. It is supported by studies showing that relatively few of the women who make a career in public or private business are married compared to the corresponding group of men (Hernes 1982; Henning & Jardim 1978; Business Week 1987).

A common denominator of the four categories is that they refer to characteristics of the individual woman rather than factors related to the work conditions offered to men and women by the organizations where they work. They can be located within the American tradition of organizational research which has been preoccupied with management and the problems of managing organizations. The selection processes of managers have been an important focus in this tradition. The European sociology of work, in contrast, has focused upon the behaviour of workers in the structural setting of the capitalist firm. The socio-technical tradition where workers' behaviour and motivation are explained by the content and conditions of work has been very strong in Scandinavian work research (Emery & Thorsrud 1976; Gustavsen & Hunnius 1981). Feminist scholars inspired by this tradition have used a work role model rather than a sex role model in their analysis of women workers (Acker & Van Houten 1974; Kanter 1977; Feldberg & Glenn 1979; Kaul & Lie 1982; Kaul 1982). Thus they attach more importance to structural conditions in the organizations where women work than to individual characteristics of women.

The classic example of such an approach in the study of organizations can be found in Rosabeth Moss Kanter's book *Men and Women of the Corporation* (1977). She shows how the structural conditions in a large corporation limit women's opportunities. Kanter's approach must be read as a criticism of individual-oriented explanations. Women's positions in the labour-market are on the lower levels of the corporate hierarchy with limited opportunities for mobility. According to Kanter (1977) it is therefore unreasonable to conclude that women limit their career aspirations because of their sex roles or family responsibilities. Her alternative model involves three factors. First, the structure of opportunity, meaning the challenges available, the chances of learning new skills and the earning of organizational rewards. Secondly, the power or ability to get things done. Thirdly, the social composition of groups, meaning the relative number of women in work groups and departments.

Kanter, however, studied only one company, with a traditional hierarchical structure. Therefore she does not take into account that different types of organizations may involve different structures of opportunity for the employees. Although we find her structural approach interesting, it needs to be applied to different organizations which vary in organizational structure.

According to the contingency tradition in organization theory there will be variations in organization structure depending on the organizations' environments (Mintzberg 1979). The structure of an organization is seen as dependent upon its *market* and *technology* (Pfeffer & Salancik 1978; Mintzberg 1979). The organizational environment differs according to stability and predictability and a formalized bureaucratic structure is considered to be better able to handle stable and predictable market conditions and technology. An organic structure with more complex and flexible communication structures is better suited to a market and technology in rapid change (Lawrence & Lorsch 1967). The size of a firm is also of importance where there is a need for formal structuring of the organization (Pugh & Hickson 1976). According to contingency theory, there will be variations in organization structure in relation to the organizations' environments (Mintzberg 1979).

The structure of opportunity of the organization will vary according to the differences in structural factors of the organization. According to the tradition of the dual labour-market theory, the career opportunities are dependent upon the existence of internal labour-markets. We can expect to find internal labour-markets in large firms that have control over their environments whereas one would not expect to find these in smaller firms that are more dependent upon the market (Averitt 1968). Therefore one would expect to find better internal career opportunities in large firms and in firms that control their environments than in smaller firms and in firms that operate in unpredictable and changing markets.

A study of women engineers in the USA reveals that men have better opportunities than women in organizations where the engineers have a powerful position, where growth and technical innovation are high and where authority relations are less bureaucratic (i.e. electrical engineers in high-tech firms). Women achieve equality with men where engineering work is more routine, where the engineers have lower status and where the work-place is most bureaucratic in structure (i.e. in mechanical engineering and aerospace) (Robinson & McIlwee 1989). One would thus expect to find better opportunities for women in traditional engineering firms that are large and have a stable environment and a bureaucratic structure. We would also expect to find better opportunities where there are affirmative action programmes that counter the preference for men in management (Robinson & McIlwee 1989; Cockburn 1991).

It has been the general understanding that bureaucratic structures with fixed rules for advancement often found in public organizations would give women better opportunities. In private organizations with informal criteria and procedures men would be chosen instead of women (Robinson & McIlwee 1989). This is also in accordance with the dual labour-market theories. We could therefore expect to find better opportunities for women in *public* or publically owned organizations than in *private* ones.

Finally, according to Kanter's theory on *relative numbers* we would expect to find less discrimination and better opportunities for women in organizations where there are many women employed and where the organization is used to employ women than in organizations that only employ a few women (Kanter 1977).

In the Women in Management tradition, as also in Robinson & McIlwee's (1989) study of women engineers, *gender* is understood as differences between women and men. The structure of the organization is understood as gender neutral. When feminist scholars have studied organizations in a gender perspective, they also tend to deal with organization structures as gender neutral (Ferguson 1984; Ressner 1986). Ressner is a good example of this when she analyses bureaucracy as two parallel structures hierarchy and patriarchy working together. Thus the hierarchy of bureaucracy is still gender neutral while the gendering occurs in the parallel structure, the patriarchy.

Recent feminist theory on gender and organization understands organizations as basically gendered; shaped by gendered processes (Acker 1990; 1992). They must therefore be understood in gendered terms (Martin 1990; Calas & Smircich 1991). Acker (1992) describes gendered organizations in terms of four sets of processes. The first is the production of gendered divisions of jobs, hierarchies, power, etc. The second is the creation of symbols, images and forms of consciousness that explain, justify or oppose the gendered divisions. The third

is the interactions between women and men, among women, and among men that enact dominance and subordination and create alliances and exclusions. The last of the processes is the internal mental work of individuals as they consciously construct their understanding of the organization's gendered structure of work and opportunity and the demands for gender-appropriate behaviour and attitudes (Acker 1992). This includes creating the appropriate gendered personae or gendered professional identity.

According to Acker, gendered processes: 'means that advantages and disadvantages, exploitation and control, actions and emotions, meaning and identity are patterned through and in terms of distinctions between male and female, masculine and feminine' (Acker 1990:146). Gendering is thus the processes which constitute the organization as a gender-political system. We apply the term *gender-political system* to organizations in order to stress a perspective of change and that women are agents in the processes. Women challenge the reigning gender arrangement by intruding into male-dominated organizations and by seeking challenges and careers. They compete with men for restricted goods such as challenges and they have an influence on important decisions (Harlan & Weiss 1980; Kvande & Rasmussen 1994).

The obvious issues in such a competition are contrasting interests and power within the organization. This perspective of organizations as an arena for power, conflicts and interests is a central element in the theories of organization as political systems (Pfeffer 1981; Morgan 1986). Modern organizations promote forms of political behaviour because at one and the same time they are systems for both cooperation and competition. The employees must cooperate in order to carry out the organization's assignments, while they are also in competition with one another for the limited resources, status and career opportunities. These conflicting dimensions are clearly symbolized in the hierarchical organization chart which is a system of cooperation, a rational division of tasks, and a career ladder which will motivate one to perform well and want to climb it. As there are fewer places the higher one climbs in the hierarchy, the competition increases upwards. Therefore the hierarchy ensures the competitiveness that is the basis for running organizational politics (Burns 1961).

We can summarize our theory on structural factors creating variations in organizational effects on women's opportunities in the following model:

METHOD

We sought to investigate whether the career development opportunities for women engineers varied within different work organizations. In order to answer this question we needed information about the structural conditions of the organization and the processes of gender differentiation within the organizations. The main data set comprised case studies carried out in six large Norwegian companies that employed a substantial number of graduate engineers. We needed organizations that had more than a few engineers in order to be able to analyse the effects of structural factors and we chose organizations that employed at least ten female graduate engineers. We therefore ended up with six large companies according to Norwegian standards.

The companies represented different branches of industry in order to cover changing and stable market conditions and technology. We chose chemical industry and oil as well as research and development in technical chemistry to represent stable market conditions and stable technology. To represent unstable markets and changing technologies we chose construction for the oil business and electronics and both research and development in computer science and automation. Among these companies we included both public and private ownership within the stable and the changing environments. By varying the branches of industry we also covered different types of engineers so that we would have chemical engineers where women have been a substantial group of students for many years as well as construction and electronics where women were always a minority. We also chose organizations with and without affirmative action programmes for women engineers.

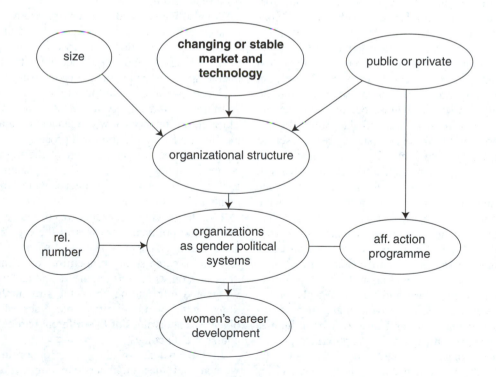

Figure 42.1   Factors affecting women's opportunities

	Changing environment	Stable environments
Public	Techno, Computer science Techno, automation Eltron (A)	Spoil (A)
Private	Construct Elcorp	Chemo

Figure 42.2 Companies according to market positions, ownership and affirmative action programmes. The companies with affirmative action programmes are labeled (A).

We selected the following six enterprises (the names are fictitious):

- two electronic enterprises, one in the public sector (Eltron) and another (Elcorp) in the private sector.
- one oil company (Spoil)
- one engineering firm working for an oil company (Construct)
- one industrial chemical enterprise (Chemo)
- one research company in the computer, chemical and mechanical industries (Techno)

Within the companies our main source of information was in-depth interviews with matched *pairs* of graduate engineers. We matched the women/men pairs on the basis of the criteria that they came from the same department in the company and had graduated the same year from NTH (Norwegian Institute of Technology) or a corresponding foreign university. We chose pairs from different sectors of the organization so that all the main types of engineering work in the company were represented (research and development, design and construction, technical management). We interviewed 24 pairs or 48 graduate engineers. Each pair faced the *same* structural conditions and were interviewed about the same conditions. We asked about their backgrounds, their experience and career development, their work and the management and organization of their tasks, their career plans, their family situation and division of work at home and about their interests and activities outside work and family. We also asked them about their views on women and men as colleagues and managers and on career opportunities for women and affirmative action programmes.

We had long interviews, which were generally longer with the women than with the men as they often developed into reflections on their experiences that they had not consciously revealed before. After

interviewing in one company we decided to concentrate upon engineers who had worked for three years or more as they were the ones who had some experience with the work organization and could be expected to have started both their career development and to think about their future plans. Thus we compared the experiences, interpretations, reactions and objectives of the women and men engineers. We could compare career objectives with *actual* career development for women and men in the same organizational setting.

We also interviewed the pairs' respective department heads about the work of the department, the work organization, career opportunities and their attitudes to and experience with female and male employees. Since the managers were graduate engineers, we interviewed them about their careers and families as well (Kvande & Rasmussen 1994). Through the interviews with managers we attained insight into the gender-political processes.

Data on the market position of the companies, company strategy and policies and personnel management were obtained by interviewing key informants in the companies.

By interviewing representatives of the three 'parties' in the political processes in the organizations about the tasks, the organization of work, the opportunities for careers, the competition for rewards and the views on women as engineers and as managers, we gained information about the structural conditions for the gender-political processes, about the objectives and values of the different parties, and of course the outcomes.

In the analysis of the career opportunities of women and men engineers we employ different types of comparisons. In all the case studies we look at the *career opportunity objectives* and *actual* career development. The analysis was carried out in several steps:

- First we compared all the women.
- Then we compared all the women with all the men.
- Then we compared the matched pairs.
- In the end we compared the different companies.

In the comparison of the pairs we looked at the level of management position for those with management responsibilities. For the others we assessed them according to the challenges they had been given and their evaluation of their situation. We also included the evaluation their managers did of them.

In addition, we used a postal survey of all female members of the Norwegian Engineering Society, asking questions about their work and work experience, career, management, family and housework. The response rate was 57 per cent and the survey included 479 persons. Through this survey we could check out and confirm that a large majority of women engineers below 35 years of age worked in private industry and that almost all women engineers above 25 years of age were married and had more than one child, just like our sample. The selection of pairs was determined by our decision to focus on a comparison between organizations. In spite of this, however, we found a group of women engineers which was representative of women engineers in general.

WOMEN AND MEN IN MANAGEMENT

The first step in our analysis was to compare all the women with all the men regarding their career objectives and career development. To do this we divided the engineers into two groups: 'the older' engineers (with five or more years' experience) and 'the younger' engineers. The former being those who at the time of interview were possible candidates for management responsibility, and the latter being those who were not yet ready for management positions. Here we will concentrate on the possible candidates with five years' or more experience, who comprised 14 out of the total 24 pairs.

In our data there are just as many women as men who have management responsibilities. Among the older female engineers two-thirds—or nine—of the 14 were managers. Thus a relatively large proportion of women as well as men have jobs with management responsibilities. However, when we examine the type of positions, we find differences between the women and the men:

The men have higher management positions than the women. We find no women above the department-head level, while their male pair counterparts are at the division level. The women appear to stagnate at the level of supervisor or in more favourable cases at the department-head level. We find the same development in the gender distribution of the growing numbers of management positions in the 1980s in general in Norway. Women came into middle-management positions while men increased their numbers in higher level positions as well (Kjeldstad 1993).

Turning to the 5 out of 14 of the 'older' male engineers who were not managers, all had been asked to take on such responsibilities. They were either considering the offer or had turned it down because they were interested in a technical career. Three of the five 'older' female engineers who were not managers would like to have had management responsibilities, but only one of them had received an offer.

The motivation for management positions among the ten pairs of younger engineers was also high, and slightly higher among the men than the women.

DIFFERENT ORGANIZATIONS—DIFFERENT OPPORTUNITIES

Following Kanter, we expected to find differences in career development between the men and the women varying in relation to their positions in the companies and the opportunity structures of these positions. We also expected to find that opportunity structures varied with structural differences between the organizations. Therefore we had chosen organizations that varied along structural dimensions.

Table 42.1 Women and men in management positions

Type of position	Women	Men
Supervisor	7	5
Middle-manager	2	2
Higher management position	–	2

In order to determine whether there were systematic differences between the organizations, we analysed them according to two criteria: First, the relative position in the organizational hierarchy of women and men in the pairs; whether the man was at a higher level, whether they were at the same level or whether the woman was at a higher level than the man, and, secondly, how many of the 'older' women engineers who wanted management responsibilities did in fact have such responsibilities.

Analysing the relative positions of the women and men in the pairs that were possible candidates for management, we found the following picture:

From the table we can see that there are two companies that differ markedly from the rest by having just as many women above men as men above women in the pairs. In all the other companies we see that there is a distribution in favour of men. In half the pairs the men have a position above the women. In the companies Construct and Elcorp, however, we found no systematic differences in career development between the men and the women in the pairs. We therefore labelled these companies the 'opportunity'-firms.

In all the other four companies we found variations in the 'normal' pattern of men having systematically better opportunities than women. The companies differed in their 'normal' pattern from Techno where the men in the pairs *always* were above the women, to Chemo where we found one pair where the woman was above the man. One could say that in these four companies there were variations in the degree to which women had fewer opportunities than men.

Turning to the second criterion, whether women with five years' or more experience had a position with management responsibilities if they wanted it, we found a similar picture. *All* the men with five years' or more experience either had management responsibilities or had been offered such possibilities.

In the 'opportunity'-firms (Construct and Elcorp) *all* women with experience who wanted management responsibility had achieved it. In the 'opportunity'-firms the motivation for management responsibilities was also the highest; all the women with five years' or more experience were motivated for management responsibilities.

In the other four firms, only some of the women who wanted management responsibilities were given them. Their experience varied from Techno, where none of the women had management responsibilities, to Chemo where two-thirds of the women who wanted management responsibilities had them. Thus, in these companies a substantial number of women who wanted management responsibilities did not have them, nor had they been offered them.

What are the differences between the 'opportunity'-firms and the other companies where men have systematically better career opportunities than women? In our selection of companies we had chosen companies that varied according to whether or not they had affirmative action programmes. One

Table 42.2 The relative positions of the 24 pairs in the companies, ratio

	Construct	Elcorp	Chemo	Spoil	Eltron	Techno
Man above woman	1/3	1/3	1/2	1/2	1/2	1
Equal	1/3	1/3	2/6	1/2	1/2	–
Woman above man	1/3	1/3	1/6	–	–	–

Table 42.3 Women in management among the motivated women

Women motivated for management	Construct	Elcorp	Chemo	Spoil	Eltron	Techno
In management position	1	1	2/3	1/2	1/2	–
Not in management position	–	–	1/3	1/2	1/2	1

could assume that the 'opportunity'-firms would be the ones that had an equal opportunity policy and affirmative action programmes. This was not so; neither of the 'opportunity'-firms had such programmes.

Both of the 'opportunity'-firms had private ownership. The two publicly owned companies Eltron and Spoil were the ones that had affirmative action programmes. These public companies and a non-profit research foundation were among the companies where men had systematically better opportunities than women. This was not what one would have expected according to the general assumption that public and non-profit organizations are friendlier toward women workers. The third private company, Chemo, had better opportunities for women than the other three companies where men systematically had better opportunities than women.

Differences between old and new firms failed to show a clear pattern in opportunities for women. Both of the 'opportunity'-firms were relatively new. Elcorp was a new electronics company within an older corporation, whereas Construct was a new engineering enterprise of an old ship-building corporation. On the other hand, the oil company Spoil was a new industry as well as Techno computer science.

The 'opportunity'-firms differed from the rest of the companies in their market situation. They operated within markets that were turbulent and in constant change and they had no control over their markets. In the construction business for oil-drilling, Construct faced a fierce national and international competition for large contracts with very short time limits. There is also great emphasis on security and quality control and numerous changes are underway. For Elcorp the electronic products as well as the technology were changing and they faced a growing international competition due to the internationalization of the market.

The other firms where we found that men had systematically better opportunities than women operated either within markets that they could control or that were stable and gave them the possibility to plan for a longer period of time. The publicly owned Eltron held a monopoly position on distribution and networks and could concentrate on technical development. The oil company, Spoil, also saw a steady and unchanging demand albeit with varying prices for crude oil on the international market. The R&D foundation faced fluctuations in demand but little competition because of its strong national position and its influence over the public funding of research. In the computer department the organization had a large university and research market to cater to that gave them a secure basis.

We found some striking differences in organizational structure between the 'opportunity'-firms and the others. The companies where we find that men have systematically better opportunities than women are characterized by a hierarchical structure of work organization. The 'opportunity'-firms where opportunities do not vary systematically according to gender are characterized by a less hierarchical and more flexible network-type of work organization. According to their market position and organization of work we labelled them *static hierarchies* and *dynamic networks* respectively in order to treat them as ideal types.

The work organization in the dynamic network was characterized by a flexible and changing organization of tasks. The tasks were organized in teams where everybody could have their say. The communication channels within the groups and between groups in different departments were horizontal and used according to need. The decision-making was decentralized. The influence was dependent upon relevant information and qualifications in the matters to be decided upon. This does not mean that the dynamic network-type of companies did not have a formal hierarchy. They did, but the *organization of work* within the projects, the working-groups and departments, was organized as team-work where planning, decision-making and coordination were discussed by the team. In the static hierarchy-type of companies, the organization of work was hierarchical with a head of department and a project leader designing tasks that were then delegated to individual employees who carried them out and then returned them to the project manager for integration into the end product.

The work organization in the static hierarchy was characterized by a strict and specialized division of work between and within departments. The communication channels were vertical and all contact went through formal channels. The decision-making was centralized and the influence of the people in the organization was exercised according to their formal position in the hierarchy.

There were variations within the group that we have labelled static hierarchies. We had chosen firms with and without programmes for affirmative action for women. We have seen that the dynamic networks Construct and Elcorp were not the ones with affirmative action programmes. When we compared the static hierarchies that had affirmative action programmes, Spoil and Eltron, with the ones that did not have such programmes, we found that they were neither among the best nor the worst in opportunities for women. They are the companies where women in half of the pairs were at the same level as the men and in the other half of the pairs were below the men.

The company among the static hierarchies with the best opportunities for women, Chemo, differs from the other six companies. They have hired women for a long time due to their comparatively low wages and the relatively large number of female chemical engineers on the labour-market. The relative number of women in the organization is therefore high, and has been so for many years. Women are thus more 'normal' and visible as professionals in this organization than in the other companies. The firm with the lowest rate of women employed is Techno where women have no opportunities and where there is no policy on hiring or promoting women.

We can sum up our findings in Figure 42.3 where the companies are shown with the 'opportunity'-firms at the top and the one with no opportunities at the bottom.

	Dynamic network	Static hierarchy	
	Changing market	Relative number	Affirmative action
Construct	X		
Elcorp	X		
Chemo		X	
Spoil			X
Eltron			X
Techno			

Figure 42.3 The organizational factors of the different organizations

The most important factor in determining women's career opportunities was the market situation with changes and turbulence and the network-type of organization that could respond to this situation. Among the static hierarchies the relative number of women seems to be most important for women's career opportunities followed by affirmative action which also seems to have some impact.

ORGANIZATIONS AS GENDER POLITICAL SYSTEMS

We will now proceed to the question of how the two types of organization constitute different gender political systems with different outcomes for women engineers. The dynamic network and the static hierarchy can be analysed as gender-political systems. We will show how different organization structures are gendered differently. They are different gender-political systems.

To explain the differences in opportunities for men and women in the two types of organizations we will use some of the structural characteristics of the organizations. They are stability and change, division of work and recruitment of managers. These characteristics are discussed below.

DYNAMIC NETWORKS

The organizations with no systematic differences in opportunities between male and female graduate engineers were the ones where the market was turbulent and unpredictable. Therefore the companies had developed an organization structure which was flexible and open to changes and new approaches. These companies had to be dynamic; they have profited from trying out new ideas and non-traditional approaches. This in turn created a corporate culture which welcomes change and new ways of doing things, including trying out women in non-traditional positions. Hard competition forces them to use all their resources. One of the women in a dynamic network organization said: 'I'm surprised at the opportunities we have here. There is room for new ways of thinking in the organization. It doesn't have a fixed structure but has to keep alert and be innovative all the time. It has to follow the signs of the times. I think this is what makes it more open to taking on women and giving us opportunities.'

The power structure in network organizations strengthens the dynamic aspect. The decentralized structure is based on the idea that everyone who has relevant knowledge of the problem in question is involved in decision-making. Different ways of thinking, values and opinions represent a resource for interpreting signals from the market and the environment and in working out solutions to new challenges. Women and their points of view are seen as a resource for the organization.

In dynamic networks the work is organized in teams where all members are equally important and all contribute knowledge and effort on an equal basis. As they work, the graduate engineers get to know one another's academic and personal qualifications. The women become visible as professionals for their colleagues and superiors instead of invisible as professionals and overly visible as women (Kanter 1977).

The organization of tasks is flexible in the dynamic networks. The employees here do *not* have clearly defined tasks and areas of responsibility, but their tasks and responsibilities alter progressively as the situation changes. The employees are given responsibility and challenges whether they want them or not. One of the women said: 'What I don't like is never having time enough to follow up all the challenges in the job, at least not in a normal working day.'

A woman manager told us how she solved the pressure between having a family and a demanding job: 'I am known as one who uses flexitime in the extreme. I have done it the way *I* want, and it has been accepted. Maximum flexitime is an important condition in my life. The kids decide the tempo in the morning. When I get to my job, I work hard. I like it that way.'

In dynamic networks the engineers get a gradual training for leadership through their work, and this seems to suit women well. It also makes it easier for women to volunteer for new tasks. Managerial careers in dynamic networks tend to follow 'natural' routes where the position is a direct result of the tasks and responsibility one has had beforehand (see also Kanter 1984b). One of the women told us how she had suggested that she take a course

in a technology that was new at that time. After the course she went to her boss and said that she thought that it was important to Elcorp to follow this technological development. She was given the task of following it up, and was at the time of the interview the head of a small group that worked with the application of the technology.

Their career is therefore not dependent upon competing with male colleagues for challenges and management positions. They can take initiatives in their work and be judged by what they do, not in competition with men. In that way there is less chance that they will encounter the mechanisms of homosocial reproduction for management positions (Kanter 1977).

When we find that the dynamic organizations give women good opportunities for career and development, and equal opportunities with their male colleagues, that does not mean that they are de-gendered or gender neutral. Dynamic networks will make use of women to further *their* ends, and they will use the women to the point of exploitation if they are allowed. They are based on the masculine principle of work orientation that the job should be the foremost in your life, and that family should accommodate to job demands. They may be flexible and you may do the job wherever or whenever you want, *as long as it is ready on time.* The women engineers use this flexibility to juggle their job and family responsibilities in cooperation with their spouses. Only as long as women are willing to conform to this traditional masculine work ethic are they given opportunities. The fact that these organizations give women a good opportunity does not therefore mean that they are tailored for women's needs.

STATIC HIERARCHIES

The other group of companies that we have labelled static as opposed to the dynamic organizations operate in very stable markets with few requirements to change. The centralized pyramid structure of the static hierarchy ensures a continual reproduction of the culture, which makes such organizations very *stable.* The organization will try to maintain the status quo in order to avoid disturbances. Therefore it is not open to change or ready to accept anything new or different even if the engineers felt that change was needed in order to meet the needs in the market. One frustrated man said: 'The responsibility for change lies with the managers, and they do not always welcome initiatives from below. We send proposals for new methods or new products the formal right way, but get no response. We, who receive the signals, are not allowed to follow them up, and the ones who are responsible for the follow-up are not in the position to understand the signals.'

In the static hierarchies we find all the well-known mechanisms described by Kanter (1977). Women become invisible as professionals and get stuck in blind alleys. A young woman in a static hierarchy told us: 'I never get any feed-back on my performance. When I prepare a paper, my boss never tells me that it is OK, or suggests any changes. The only thing he ever said, when I *asked* him once, was that my handwriting was very nice. I only manage in this job because I can discuss my work with my husband at home.'

A career in a hierarchy involves promotion to a higher position. To be given new challenges, new tasks and increased responsibility in a hierarchical organization, one must apply for another job, either in a different department or upwards in one's own department. A woman's chances of getting a better job are poor because they depend on whether she has been *visible* as a capable and important member of the organization. One woman told us how her group manager would always step in and take over her presentation of the project she was responsible for. Even though he meant well, this prevented her from doing it herself and gaining the necessary experience.

In order to become visible women must have challenges, meet them successfully and show their superiors that they are professionally outstanding. In hierarchical organizations a woman is professionally *invisible* and this puts her in the back row for more important jobs. This strengthens the processes of homosocial reproduction in the management of the organization (Mills 1963, Kanter 1977). A newly appointed female manager of a department told us: 'I did not get this position without a struggle. There were some old men in the department, and they had their crown-princes. Because I knew that, I contacted the union representative when the job was announced. I applied, and I went to the Board of Equal Opportunity when I was passed by. The old

men were very angry when they had to give me the job after all.'

In organizations dominated by men, women represent something new and different and will therefore tend to meet with rejection or scepticism (Kanter 1977). Women are, or are assumed to be, different from men and therefore they have problems being considered relevant and central to the organization. Women are allowed to do traditional women's work in women's jobs, such as office or secretarial work where they are subordinated to men in a 'natural' way in these organizations. If, on the other hand, women impinge on areas dominated by men, such as technical work and managerial positions, they challenge the *existing gender order* and hence the *stability* of the organization.

If we once again return to the influence of affirmative action on women's opportunities, when comparing Spoil and Eltron with Techno we saw that such measures may be effective within the static hierarchies precisely because they make women visible as potential managers. If the company has a policy to promote women, their managers are forced to look at women as candidates in the same way that they normally look at men. Affirmative action in hiring may also be a means to increase the number of women in the organization. In the case of Chemo we saw that the relative number of women was important for women's opportunities for careers.

The affirmative action we found was typically not directed at structural conditions at work but at the motivation of individual women. According to our findings the organization of work and responsibilities within the organization is the most important factor influencing women's career opportunities. We find that dynamic networks do not need affirmative action to make place for women. They are open to differences and new approaches and are willing to give women responsibilities in their work organization. The static hierarchies discriminate against women as being potentially different. Affirmative action programmes as a means to counter the processes that cause the discrimination against women are focused on individual women. By doing so the problem is defined as a problem of gender and not a structural one. The organization structure is treated as gender neutral and the responsibility for changes is moved to the women. Instead of looking at the organization and structural changes they make women responsible for changing in order to fit in with the existing gender-political system.

WOMEN'S OPPORTUNITIES IN CHANGING ORGANIZATIONS

We found that women's career opportunities were better and equal to those of men in organizations that were dynamic and changing in the competition-ridden private sector. These organizations had informal and less hierarchical structures, and they did not have any policy on hiring or promoting women. Our findings did not confirm what one might have expected from studies of career structures in different organizations or the findings of former research on the careers of women engineers (Robinson & McIlwee 1989). From these studies one would expect to find that women's career opportunities were better in organizations that were large, stable and bureaucratic, especially in public organizations, and in organizations that had affirmative action programmes. The reason for the difference in results in Robinson and McIlwee's study and ours, might be the character of the affirmative action programmes. These programmes in the companies we studied were 'motivation' programmes directed towards the individual woman in order to help her to become more self-assertive, etc. In the US the affirmative action programmes are more structural and directed towards the organization level. To attain government contracts the companies have to show that they have hired women and minorities. In Norway it is up to the different companies whether they want to do anything with equal opportunities. The social democratic state with its tradition for state intervention thus displays a more liberalistic attitude towards equal opportunities at company level.

Our findings indicate that dehierarchization is an important measure in increasing women's opportunities. Studies of industrial development and changes in the structure of organizations (Piore & Sabel 1984; Handy 1984; Kern & Schumann 1984; Kanter 1989; Clegg 1990) have recently focused upon trends towards dehierarchization and broadening of functions along the same lines as we have found in the dynamic networks.

Rosabeth Moss Kanter's more recent work on large corporations in North America and Europe (Kanter 1989) suggests that these companies are moving away from diversification towards maximizing their core business competence. Companies develop by delayering the hierarchy and making the company leaner. They try to strengthen their relations to the customers and to their business partners through alliances. Kanter calls these firms post-bureaucratic or post-entrepreneurial because they try to combine the strength and stability of a big corporation with the agility and innovative capacity of the entrepreneur. The reasons for these changes are the changes in market conditions and increased competition.

Stewart R. Clegg (1990) uses studies of new organizational forms especially in Asian industrialized countries, but also in French, Italian and Swedish industry, to advocate the decline of modernist organizational principles based on a differentiation of tasks, familiar in Tayloristic and bureaucratic organizations. Clegg sees many examples of organizations that are highly competitive but that do not conform to these principles. He sees tendencies to de-differentiation and dehierarchization which he labels as the emerging postmodern organizations (Clegg 1990).

If these tendencies are dominant, we could expect that women's opportunities at work are changing for the better. Better career opportunities, however, also mean that the demands at work increase. The opportunities are given to women because the organization needs the resources of all employees regardless of their gender. The companies are willing to give women opportunities as long as they conform to the male work ethic.

Recent research shows the same tendencies. They find increasing demands for qualifications and increasing responsibilities in jobs of almost all categories for women as well as for men. At the same time that the quality of the jobs get better, the demands on the worker increase, the work is intensified and the symptoms of stress increase (Gallie 1994). This development may thus mean that women get better jobs and career opportunities, but it may also mean a normalization of the work situation of the '60-hour man,' the man who works overtime in a job that gives him a lot but that also means that he must sacrifice time with his family and social life (Kvande 1994). This development may not further women's participation in management, and the career opportunities offered to women may after all not lead to an increase in women in management. Whether this will happen depends upon which norms and values will dominate the work organizations in the future. The pressure upon deregulation of the normal working day and on flexibilization of working hours may not encourage women's participation on an equal footing with men. Our conclusion when looking at recent trends in the labour-market is that although dehierarchization is an appropriate measure in order to increase women's opportunities, we might also be facing lesser representation of women in management because of the intensification of work which is an important effect of the same development.

REFERENCES

Acker, J. 1990. Hierarchies, Jobs, Bodies: A Theory of Gendered Organizations. *Gender & Society,* 4, 139–158.

Acker, J. 1992. Gendering Organization Theory. *In* J. Mills & P. Tancred, *Gendering Organizational Analysis.* London: Sage.

Acker, J. & Van Houten, D. 1974. Differential Recruitment and Control: The Sex Structuring of Organizations. *Administrative Science Quarterly,* 19, 52–63.

Averitt, R. T. 1968. *The Dual Economy: The Dynamics of American Industry Structure.* New York: Norton.

Bartol, K. M. 1978. Sex Structuring of Organizations: A Search for Possible Causes. *Academy of Management Review,* 3, 805–815.

Burns, T. 1961. Mechanisms of Institutional Change. *Administrative Science Quarterly,* 68, 257–282.

Business Week, 1987. June 22.

Calas, M. & Smircich, L. 1991. Voicing Seduction to Silence Leadership. *Organizations Studies,* 12, 567–601.

Clegg, S. R. 1990. *Modern Organizations. Organization Studies in the Postmodern World.* London: Sage.

Cockburn, C. 1983. *Brothers.* London: Pluto.

Cockburn, C. 1985. *Machinery of Dominance.* London: Pluto.

Cockburn, C. 1991. *In the Way of Women.* Basingstoke: Macmillan.

Donnell, S. & Hall, J. 1980. Men and Women as Managers: A Significant Case of No Significant Difference. *Organizational Dynamics,* 8, 60–76.

Emery, F. & Thorsrud, E. 1976. *Democracy at Work.* The Hague: Nijhoff.

Esping-Andersen, G. et al. 1993. Trends in Contemporary Class Structuration: A Six-nation Comparison. *In* G. Esping-Andersen (ed.), *Changing Classes. Stratification and Mobility in Post-Industrial Societies.* London: Sage.

Feldberg, R. & Glenn, E. N. 1979. Male and female: Job Versus Gender Models in the Sociology of Work. *Social Problems,* 26, 524–538.

Ferguson, K. 1984. *The Feminist Case Against Bureaucracy.* Philadelphia: Temple University Press.

Gallie, D. 1994. *Skill, Gender and Technological Change.* Paper presented at a seminar at Warwich Business School, 12 October.

Gustavsen, B. & Hunnius, G. 1981. *New Patterns of Work Reform—The Case of Norway.* Oslo: Universitetsforlaget.

Hackett, G. & Betz, N. E. A. 1981. A Self-Efficacy Approach to the Career Development of Women. *Journal of Vocational Behaviour,* 18, 326–339.

Handy, C. 1984. *The Future of Work.* Oxford: Basil Blackwell.

Harlan, A. & Weiss, C. 1980. *Women in Managerial Careers; Third Progress Report.* Wesley, Mass: Wesley Centre for Research on Women.

Hearn, J. & Parkin, W. 1987. *Sex at Work. The Power and the Paradox of Organization Sexuality.* Brighton: Wheatsheaf.

Henning, M. & Jardim, A. 1978. *The Managerial Woman.* London: Marion Boyars.

Hernes, H. M. 1982. *Staten—kvinner ingen adgang?* Oslo: Universitetsforlaget.

Kanter, R. M. 1977. *Men and Women of the Corporation.* New York: Basic Books.

Kanter, R. M. 1984a. *The Change Masters.* London: Allen & Unwin.

Kanter, R. M. 1984b. Variations in Managerial Career Structures in High-Technology Finns: The Impact of Organizational Characteristics on Internal Labour Market Patterns. *In* P. Osterman (ed.), *Internal Labour Markets.* Boston: MIT Press.

Kanter, R. M. 1989. *When Giants Learn to Dance.* London: Simon & Schuster.

Kaul, H. 1982. *Når Fravær er Nærvær.* Trondheira: IFIM.

Kaul, H. & Lie, M. 1982. When Paths are Vicious Circles— How Women's Working Conditions Limit Influence. *Economic and Industrial Democracy,* 3, 466–481.

Kern, H. & Schumann, M. 1984. *Das Ende der Arbeitsteilung. Rationalisierung in der industriellen Produktion.* Munchen: C. H. Beck.

Kjeldstad, R. 1993. Kvinner og menn på arbeidsmarkedet. *In* R. Kjeldstad & J. Lyngstad, *Arbeid, Lonn og Likestilling.* Oslo: Universitetsforlaget.

Knights, D. & Wilmott, H. 1986. *Gender and the Labour Process.* Aldershot: Gower.

Kvande, E. 1982. Anpassning och protest. *Kvinnovetenskaplig tidsskrift,* 3, 42–51.

Kvande, E. 1994. 6-timers kvinnen og 60-timersmannen. *In* B. Fougner & M. Larsen-Asp (eds.), *Norden— Kvinners Paradis?* København: Nordisk Ministerrad.

Kvande, E. & Rasmussen, B. 1990. *Nye kvinneliv. Kvinner i menns organisasjoner.* Oslo: Ad Notam.

Kvande, E. & Rasmussen, B. 1992. *Fra kvinner og ledelse til kjønn og organisasjoner.* Oslo: NORAS/LOS, LOS-notat 1992:3.

Kvande, E. & Rasmussen, B. 1994. Men in Male-Dominated Organizations and their Encounter with Women Intruders. *Scandinavian Journal of Management,* 10, 163–175.

Lawrence, P. & Lorsch, J. 1967. *Organization and Environment.* Boston: Harvard Business School.

Loden, M. 1986. *Feminine Leadership or How to Succeed in Business without Being One of the Boys.* New York: Times Books.

Marshall, J. 1984. *Women Managers—Travellers in a Male World.* Chichester: Wiley.

Martin, J. 1990. Deconstructing Organizational Taboos; The Suppression of Gender Conflict in Organizations. *Organization Science,* 4, 339–359.

Mills, J. & Tancred, P. 1992. *Gendering Organizational Analysis.* London: Sage.

Mills, C. W. 1963. The American Business Elite: A Collective Portrait. *In* I. L. Horowitz (ed.), *Power, Politics and People.* New York: Ballantine.

Mintzberg, H. 1979. *The Structuring of Organizations.* Englewood Cliffs: Prentice-Hall.

Morgan, G. 1986. *Images of Organization.* Newbury Park, CA: Sage.

Pfeffer, J. 1981. *Power in Organizations.* Boston: Pitman.

Pfeffer, J. & Salancik, G. R. 1978. *The External Control of Organizations. A Resource Dependence Perspective.* New York: Harper & Row.

Piore, M. J. & Sabel, C. F. 1984. *The Second Industrial Divide: Prospects for Prosperity.* New York: Basic Books.

Powell, G. N. 1993. *Women and Men in Management.* Newbury Park, CA: Sage.

Pugh, D. S. & Hickson, D. J. 1976. *Organization Structure in its Context: the Aston Programme I.* London: Saxon House.

Ressner, U. 1986. *The Hidden Hierarchy.* London: Gower.

Robinson, J. G. & McIlwee, J. S. 1989. Women in Engineering: A Promise Unfulfilled? *Social Problems,* 36, 455–473.

Rosener, J. B. 1990. Ways Women Lead. *Harvard Business Review,* 68, 119–125.

Skrede, K., & Tornes, K. 1986. *Den Norske Kvinnerevolusjonen.* Oslo: Universitetsforlaget.

Terborg, J. R. 1977. Organizational and Personal Correlates of Attitudes Toward Women as Managers. *Academy of Management Journal,* 20, 85–100.

Yukl, G. 1981. *Leadership in Organizations.* Englewood-Cliffs: Prentice-Hall.

SOURCE: Kvande, Elin and Bente Rasmussen. 1995. "Women's Careers in Static and Dynamic Organizations." *Acta Sociologica,* 38:115–30.

43

"WE HAVE TO MAKE A MANAGEMENT DECISION"

Challenger and the Dysfunctions of Corporate Masculinity

MARK MAIER

Prologue. On January 28, 1986, the space shuttle Challenger lifted off on the 25th mission of NASA's shuttle program. Its voyage was tragically cut short by an explosion just 73 seconds into flight. Its seven crew members, including New Hampshire school teacher Christa McAuliffe, perished on impact as their crew cabin slammed into the Atlantic Ocean. The shock of the tragedy humbled a once-proud agency and was followed by months of investigations as a presidential commission searched for the cause. In its final report, the commission (Rogers, 1986) noted that the immediate, technical reason for the disaster was the inability of a pair of slim (one quarter inch) rubber O-rings in one of the shuttle's reusable solid rocket boosters (SRBs) to seal properly. Hopelessly hardened by frigid temperatures preceding liftoff, the twin O-rings between two of the interlocking rocker segments on Challenger's righthand SRB lacked the resiliency necessary to maintain an impermeable seal. Searing combustion gases penetrated the joint, causing the fuel tank to rupture and snap the orbiter into pieces. But the commission also singled out flaws in the decision-making process, noting that explicit warnings—some dating back years and others voiced just hours before the fateful launch—were repeatedly ignored.

"Is it a boy or a girl?"

This seemingly innocuous question carries within it the roots of the space shuttle Challenger disaster. For the question lays bare our society's preoccupation with gender as a master status, a preoccupation that indelibly shapes our lives from the moment of our birth. From that day forward, society goes to great lengths to ensure that males and females become gendered in significantly different ways. Gender, it is generally accepted, is socially constructed, and even though societal conceptions of masculinity (as well as femininity) are neither monolithic nor static, at any given point in time and place, there is clearly a dominant form of masculinity that may be described as *hegemonic* (Connell, 1989), and to which all other forms of masculinity will be subordinate. Of equal import is the oft-noted point that masculinity is generally "elevated" as the human standard, serving implicitly as the norm against which *both* genders are measured (Hare-Mustin, 1988). Hegemonic masculinity, then, assures that "man" becomes the generic, but hidden, referent in our culture (Gilligan, 1982). As Spender (1984) noted, "Women can only aspire to be as good as a man; there is no point in trying to be 'as good as a woman'" (p. 201).

As organizational scholars have similarly discovered, the values that under-gird bureaucratic functioning and managerial styles in the United States are similarly "masculine" (Ferguson, 1984; Kanter, 1977; Maier, 1993b). Powell and Butterfield (1989) discovered in a review of the literature that "managerial identity remains as masculine as it ever was" (p. 230). Schaef (1981) describes the cultural ethos of organization as following the norms of a "white male system." Because corporate masculinity has been unconsciously assumed and largely uncritically accepted as the organizational behavior standard, little attention has been devoted to exploring its implications for managerial dysfunction in the workplace.

The 1986 space shuttle Challenger disaster serves as a prominent focal point for this exploration. Not only is the selection of Challenger appropriate to this endeavor, as an occurrence that most readers have at least some familiarity (and perhaps even identification) with, but also—it turns out—because it resulted from practices and dynamics that are fairly common in hierarchical organizations (Maier, 1992, 1994). We assume here that because the Challenger debacle was not only widely experienced but had painful impact, if people recognize the connection between the causes of Challenger and the masculinist dynamics that undergird conventional organizational assumptions and managerial styles, they will be motivated to question those assumptions and challenge those styles. In essence, we will demonstrate that a primary factor in *not* "launching a Challenger" in one's own career or organization is a willingness to abandon the attachment to the standard (hierarchical) way of organizing and the conventional masculinist managerial approaches it promotes, in favor of alternatives. We aim—using the legacy of Challenger—to enhance awareness of and "unfreeze" attachment to that taken-for-granted system, with its underlying gender bias, thus providing further support to diversity initiatives aimed at transforming existing

organizational cultures rather than blindly assimilating others into its dysfunctional ways.

Specifically, then, this chapter identifies the largely taken-for-granted features of conventional managerial practices and how they are inherently "gendered" (e.g., coincide with a *masculine ethos*) and demonstrates how these features were at work in the organizational dynamics and decision processes that led to the tragic space shuttle Challenger launch decision 10 years ago. Selected events from the year immediately preceding the disaster will be reviewed, along with an assessment of the final decision-making process itself, to demonstrate how the men who made the decisions that culminated in the ill-fated launch may have internalized (all too well) our culture's prescriptions for "manhood." The data from which the Challenger story has been reconstructed here come from a number of sources, assembled over a 6-year period (1988–1994). Principal among these are: original interviews with several of the key participants in the launch decision (including NASA and Morton Thiokol insiders); a review of the videotaped testimony by NASA and Morton Thiokol officials and employees before the presidential commission (obtained under the Freedom of Information Act); dozens of hours of historical video footage from the NASA archives; and the presidential commission report itself (Rogers, 1986).

A FEMINIST CRITIQUE OF MANAGEMENT: ON THE GENDERED FOUNDATIONS OF ORGANIZATION

Our review of the gendered foundations of organization begins with the Industrial Revolution, Frederick Taylor's ideal of *scientific management,* and the writings of the 19th-century sociologist, Max Weber. Taylor was captivated by the ascendancy of science, fascinated in particular with the potential organizational applications of the empirical method of knowledge and control. Like Taylor, Weber saw the rationalization of life under bureaucratic structures as essential to social progress, embracing rationality as the central ideal of organizational life; the culmination of organizational development was an institution devoid of emotion and passion. Paraphrasing Weber's classic title, Kanter (1977) has pointed out that "the evolving 'spirit of managerialism' was infused with a 'masculine ethic'" (p. 20)—a legacy that persists to this day. This ethic, according to Kanter,

> elevates the traits assumed to belong to some men to necessities for effective management: a tough-minded approach to problems; analytic abilities to abstract and plan; a capacity to set aside personal, emotional considerations in the interests of task accomplishment; and a cognitive superiority in problem solving and decision making. (p. 22)

One lasting consequence of the industrialization of society (and the related sex segregation of human activity) was to create a bureaucratic social order grounded in norms conventionally—and increasingly—ascribed to men. Feminist responses to that order offer a valuable political and epistemological lens through which to view the events surrounding the launch of the Challenger.[1]

One central idea in much feminist theory addresses the relationship between gender and the shape of human experience in daily life. In other words, whether we proceed through the world in a male or female body makes all the difference in the world. These different life worlds, generally speaking, shape each sex in profoundly different ways and produce significant outcomes not only for individual behavior, but for how others interpret and react to that behavior. In a society that differentiates sharply between males and females from birth, and that accords greater status and worth to males, the dominant understandings of selfhood and society that are available to men and women (and the prevailing assumptions about social relations, measures of success, organizational structure, leadership, ways of communicating, reasoning, and decision making, practices of power, politics, and morality) tend to differ along gendered lines. Although such categories are not ironclad (men and women do partake of the life worlds of the other), they nonetheless form distinct arenas in which the experiences and perspectives of women as a group are distinguished from, and usually subordinated to, the experiences and perspectives of men as a group. These differences may be conceptualized along the *masculinist and feminist* dimensions delineated in Table 43.1.

Thus, we use the designations masculinist and feminist largely as potent metaphors for contrasting modes of apprehending and acting upon the world. To call upon such differentiation to understand organizations and to imagine alternatives is not to claim that such differences are biologically determined, or that they reflect some essence of male and/or female. Men can sometimes be put into situations in which they are perceived, and come to act, "like women," just as women can come to act "like men." The point is not that all individual women and men always act in predictably feminine or masculine ways, but that organizational structures and processes generally reinforce and legitimize a particular form of masculinity while dismissing that which appears feminine. The pyramidal structure ensures that management and masculinity will be virtually synonymous. Indeed, gender emerges as perhaps the dominant factor driving the Challenger launch decision, even though no women were present in decision-making roles.

Women's perspectives on self and society are, like everyone else's, shaped and sometimes distorted by their interactions with the dominant points of view. But because women's subjectivity and worldviews emerge within a context of subordination to men, feminine experiences and interpretations are not by themselves sufficient to generate an alternative perspective. But, interpreted in a way that is attentive to the consequences of the differences in power between women and men, female experience can offer a substantially different approach to the understandings of self, relations with other, strategies of power, and practices of organizations (as suggested in Table 43.1). From this perspective, gender becomes central to understanding organizational phenomena . . . even when women are absent. Thus, when we suggest that organizational practices are gendered, we do so here not to focus attention on male privilege (although that, too, does result), but to provide graphic evidence of how men's organizational experience is profoundly influenced by *men's* conformity to bureaucratic, that is, masculinist, prescriptions. In the case of Challenger, as shall be demonstrated, that influence should no

Table 43.1   Contrasting male system and female system archetypes

	Male System	*Female System*

Selected core values	Hierarchy-status
	Competitive/winning
	   Maximizing-quantity ("More/bigger
	   is better")
	Action/agency
	Success (advancement)
	   Dependence-responsibility/
	   "Leadership" at top
		Equality-intimacy
		   Collaborative/sharing
		   Optimizing-quality
		("Small is beautiful")
		   Reflection/communion
		Balance (life/work)
		   Interdependence-shared
		   responsibility/leadership

Image of strength and power	Rigid uncompromising "command &
	   control"
	Authoritarian father
	Standing at the top; being at
	   the head
	Fighting; power over (win-lose)
	Leader as commander
		Adaptive, flexible; "inspire
		   and entrust"
		   Nurturing mother
		   Standing in the center;
		   being in the circle
		Engaging; power with (win-win)
		   Leader as servant

View of social relations	Exclusionary politics/ranking
	   (rivals/subordinates)
	   Task-focused ("get the job done!")
	   Telling-demanding
	Dissent = Disloyalty
		Inclusionary politics/linking
		   (colleagues)
		   Process-focused
		   ("how are we doing?")
		   Hearing-responding
		   Dissent – Loyal opposition

View of self	Autonomous, separate, independent	Relational, connected, interdependent
Basis of reasoning	Sensing, thinking (mind) Distanced, objective, logical/rational	Intuitive, feeling (heart) Connected subjective, emotional
Key influence strategies	Intimidating, "forcing," complying	Supporting, "submitting," enabling
Decisional guide	Authority or majority rule	Participation and consensus

Principal ethic	Rights (consistency-
	   impartiality-universality)
		Caring (exceptions-empathic-
		   situational)

Organizational metaphors	Pyramids, channels, chains of command	Webs, networks, teams

longer be uncritically taken for granted but should be examined for the ways in which it can become dysfunctional.

Women's worlds typically require of their participants a particular kind of labor: maintaining relationships, attending to the needs of others, caring for bodies as well as minds and spirits. Women (generally) learn to see themselves and others as embedded in relations, as interdependent with others and responsible for their collective well-being (see Gilligan, 1982). In contrast, men's worlds (typically) entail a very different set of language and labors, one that conceives of individuals as separate, autonomous beings, that values independent achievement, and that eschews commitments that might hinder success in competitive endeavors. Success in the masculine worldview becomes defined as distancing oneself from those lower in the hierarchy, competing successfully with those positioned similarly, and emulating (and eventually joining) those placed "above." In a feminine framework, however, actions that allow the maintenance of relations (e.g., mentoring, vicarious achievement) are more highly valued than those that advance the individual but leave others behind.

Consequently, communication in the female life world—where individuals struggle to minimize differences and reach consensus—is used primarily to establish intimacy; in the male life world, as Tannen (1990) explains in her influential work, communication is a primary means for establishing and maintaining one's position; hence,

> independence is key because a primary means of establishing status is to tell others what to do, and taking orders is a marker of low status. Though all humans need both intimacy and independence, women tend to focus on the first and men on the second. (p. 26)

As a result, men (generally) find hierarchical relations comfortable and look to such arrangements to legitimate the process of ranking and exclusion, as well as to mediate the conflicting rights of autonomous selves. Conflicts are resolved by relying on an *ethic of rights* (Gilligan, 1982), which emphasizes consistency and impartial and objective evaluations of competing claims, as well as due process and equal treatment for all individuals, regardless of their place in the social order. Women, on the other hand, tend to find greater comfort in inclusive relations, to value their links to others more than their ranking over them (Eisler, 1987). The feminine worldview is thus more likely to be grounded in an *ethic of care* (Gilligan, 1982), in which rules are regarded as inherently context dependent (and exceptions legitimized by attention to circumstance).

Power, in a feminine framework, is used to give "voice" to the conventionally disenfranchised; it is a basis for empowering others. Feminine notions of justice call for the avoidance of harm to others, for an active response to others' needs, and for an appreciation of the particularities of time and place.

Where masculine politics is grim and instrumental, suppressing dissent frequently to the point of violence (even physical), feminine politics aims for cooperation, compromise, and allowance for—even encouragement of—difference (Chodorow, 1978; Di Stefano, 1991; Gilligan, 1982; Hartsock, 1983; Ruddick, 1989). Where masculine leadership often relies on force (expressed or implied) to get the job done, feminine leadership is responsive and focused on the process by which common objectives are defined and pursued.

In symbolic terms, the masculine manager stands at the top of an exclusionary pyramid, the feminine manager in the center of a web of inclusion. Where organizational subordinates in a masculine system are expected to know their place, focusing narrowly on compartmentalized duties in the horizontal division of labor and ingratiating themselves to "higher-ups" in the vertical chain of command, in a feminine system, they are expected and encouraged to share responsibility for reaching the common vision—even if it means that superiors' authority (and colleagues'—or one's own—"turf") will be challenged.

As one can surmise, the worldviews that men typically bring to organizational life in many ways mesh neatly with the requirements of bureaucracies, whereas those that women bring tend to clash with that social order. The managerial viewpoint stresses instrumental rationality, orderliness, conformity to the requirements of authority, and respect for the chain of command. Objectivity is defined as lifting oneself above the particulars of one's situation and applying universal standards in an impartial and consistent fashion, to embrace a "separate" way of knowing, in which one distances oneself from the object of inquiry and truth emerges from impersonal procedures (Belenky, Clinchy, Goldberger, & Tarule, 1986; Harding, 1986; Kanter, 1977). Reason and logic are construed rather narrowly, referring mainly to quantifiable factors that count as evidence in a linear process of sensing, thinking, and deduction. "Disinterested reason," unblinded by passion (i.e., objectivity), is the ultimate value in a discourse built on challenge, argument, suspicion, and critical judgment. The resulting "doubting game" constitutes "a rational form of masculine ceremonial combat" (Ong, quoted in Belenky et al., 1986, p. 110), in which the listener is perceived as a potentially hostile judge, not as a potential ally in conversation. As Belenky et al. note, the objectivity demanded by this perspective expects participants to

> exclude your own concerns and to adopt a perspective that your adversaries may respect, as in their own self-interest. It means to exclude all feelings, including those of the adversary, examining the issue from a strictly pragmatic, strategic point of view. (p. 109)

In contrast, women's worldviews tend to a more *situated* objectivity, to value those kinds of insights that are difficult to quantify but that come from the heart, from feeling and from intuition. From a feminine perspective, truth is discovered not through separation but through connection and direct personal experience, through an essential subjectivity (Belenky et al., 1986). Where doubting and judgment occupy center stage in masculinist discourse, trust and understanding predominate in its feminist counterpart; where masculinist discourse derives its moral legitimacy from impersonal procedures, feminist discourse stakes its moral claim in caring; where masculinist discourse aims for generalities, feminist discourse focuses on particularities; and where masculinist discourse stresses agency and action (separation and control), feminist discourse strives for community (acceptance and fusion) (Belenky et al., 1986).

Which discourse one employs, and with what consequences, is not only a function of one's prior socialization but of one's current context; one's organizational structure, in particular. Although it exceeds the scope of this chapter to elaborate, readers should assume the sociological maxim that individual behaviors are structure-bound (if not determined): Masculine managerial styles flow inexorably from hierarchical, pyramidal organizational structures.

Men and women recruited into positions of dominance within organizations tend to internalize the requirements of their position, becoming "like men"—valuing competition over cooperation, focusing more on rights than on needs, internalizing the requirements of a narrow technical rationality, and so on. Women and men recruited into subordinate positions or relations tend, correspondingly, to become the kind of people their organization requires them to be; they become "like women" in their attention to the requirements of others, need to please their superiors, reluctance to assert themselves, and so on. In complex ways, therefore, masculine dominance and feminine subordination are reproduced and reinforced, and gender becomes a potent metaphor for power (Ferguson, 1984).

Schaef's (1981) classic elaboration contrasting the *White Male System* with the *Female System* offers similar distinctions. In Schaef's view, the White Male System (or WMS) is characterized by the following:

1. "One-up; one-down" relations (vs. egalitarian/peer relations typical of the Female System)
2. Self and work ("doing") as one's center of focus (as opposed to self-awareness or relations with others)
3. A "zero-sum/scarcity" model of power (in contrast to a synergistic orientation, which assumes that power, life, love, or knowledge is not diminished by sharing it, but in fact is enhanced)
4. A vision of "leading" anchored in commanding or directing others (vs. facilitating or enabling)
5. Differences seen as competitive threats that must be reduced, assimilated, or eliminated, instead of (in what Schaef describes as the Female System) being seen as collaborative opportunities to learn, grow, and change.

Using a feminist lens to focus on the consequences of the White Male System allows us to shift our attention away from the traits of the individual men making decisions about Challenger (were they intelligent or foolish? Cautious or rash?) and toward the characteristics of the structures and processes within which men and women are required to operate. These structures and processes tend to be gendered in predictable ways; ways that elevate typically male experiences to the level of unquestioned norm, while dismissing that which appears "feminine" as irrational, illogical, unsubstantiated, or irrelevant. When managers—male and female alike—are acting "normally" as bureaucracy defines it, they are acting masculine. We shall argue that decision-making processes such as those producing the ill-fated launch of the Challenger are not aberrations or "flaws" in the standard operating procedure of organizations—they are its logical and inexorable consequences. As my colleague Kathy Ferguson (personal communication, August 4, 1992) put it to me, "Masculinity run amok is not bad bureaucracy; it is bureaucracy as usual." Drawing on previous work (Maier, 1993a), we shall demonstrate how these gendered power factors literally managed, as Messerschmidt (1995) has asserted, to kill the crew of Challenger.

We turn now to the Challenger chronology, keeping these gendered foundations of MANagement and the White Male System in mind.

CHALLENGER: A MANAGEMENT CHRONICLE

The Historical Context of Challenger

Although most of us were stunned by the news of Challenger, the presidential commission observed that, in fact, this had been a disaster waiting to happen, an "Accident Rooted in History." Concerns with the rocket boosters dated back to 1977, when engineers at NASA's Marshall Space Flight Center (MSFC, the unit responsible for monitoring the development and performance of the shuttle's components) first warned of deficiencies in the contractor's (Morton Thiokol's) design of the reusable rockets. Those early fears were confirmed when the shuttle actually began flying in 1981. Although President Reagan declared the system to be "fully operational" after just four test flights, recovery and inspection of the boosters revealed that, in fact, hot gases from inside the rockets were somehow impinging on the fragile quarter-inch thick, 12-foot diameter twin rubber O-rings intended to seal the rocket segments, causing them to be partially eaten away. In the years that followed, flights continued unabated, despite increasing incidents of erosion. Because the missions were "successful" (i.e., the integrity of the joints had never been *fully* compromised to the point of a total burn-through), NASA officials concluded the damage constituted "an acceptable flight risk." Each incidence of erosion reinforced a "can't-fail" decision-making philosophy that Commissioner Richard Feynman described as "a kind of Russian Roulette. . . . We can lower our

standards a little bit because we got away with it last time" (Rogers, 1986, p. 2469).

Two near disasters in early 1985 put that complacency to the test. During a particularly cold (53 degrees Fahrenheit) launch in January 1985, hot gases for the first time actually *burned through* the primary O-ring in one of the SRB joints, charring (but not eroding) the critical secondary seal, the booster's thin last line of defense. Alarmingly, two missions later, a primary seal in a nozzle joint failed completely, allowing its secondary O-ring to be partially eaten away. The seal failures sent shock waves through Morton Thiokol, Inc. (MTI) and NASA. At MTI, Roger Boisjoly, the rocket engineer who had inspected the disassembled rockets from both missions, sent a blistering memo to Vice President of Engineering Robert Lund, warning that "the mistakenly accepted position on the joint problem was to fly without fear of failure." Boisjoly stressed that failure to address the problem head-on could result in "a catastrophe of the highest order: Loss of human life." A task force was established at MTI to rectify the problem.

At NASA, meanwhile, Richard Cook, a newly hired budget analyst, had just interviewed headquarters engineers at the Office of Space Flight about the potential budgetary implications of the O-ring dilemma. Told by the engineers that they "held their breath" at each liftoff because "this thing could blow up" (Maier, 1994), Cook sent a detailed memo to his superior, warning that "there is little question that flight safety has been and is still being compromised by potential failure of the seals, and it is acknowledged that failure during launch would certainly be catastrophic." The worst case scenario, he noted, would require halting shuttle flights while the boosters were redesigned and existing rockets were scrapped. The potential budgetary impact was "immense."

In August 1985, NASA's top shuttle official, Associate Administrator for Space Flight Jesse Moore, convened a meeting with senior MTI and MSFC personnel for a comprehensive review of the O-ring problems. Although MTI stressed that "the lack of a good secondary seal in the joint is most critical" and urged that "efforts need to continue at an accelerated pace to eliminate SRM [Solid Rocket Motor] erosion," NASA decided against a flight ban, electing instead to continue flying the shuttle "as is," searching for the solution as they went along. The commission would later conclude that the briefing was sufficiently detailed to require corrective action before the next flight. No action was taken because meeting flight schedules and cutting costs were given a higher priority than flight safety (Maier, 1994).

By the fall of 1985, complacency had sunk in again at NASA and MTI. The Seal Task Force at MTI, which had been established in response to Boisjoly's memo, was turning out to be a paper tiger, stymied in its efforts by bureaucratic inertia. Bob Ebeling, the task force leader, wrote an unusually blunt appeal to MTI's SRM Project Director, Allan McDonald, which began simply: "HELP! The seal task force is constantly being delayed by every possible means." It ended, "We wish we could action by verbal request, but such is not the case. This is a red flag." The Vice President of the Space Boosters Program at MTI, Joseph Kilminster, met with the task force to appease them. He insisted they continue to follow established policies and routines, working through existing channels to do "whatever was necessary" to "nurse each task" through to completion.

On January 21, 1986—just one week prior to the eventual Challenger launch date—NASA, responding to pressure from Congress, announced that it was seeking bids from four competitors to supply additional rocket boosters for the shuttle. MTI's exclusive contract with the agency—a contract worth over $1 billion—was up for grabs.

Challenger's Final Hours: "We Have to Make a Management Decision"

On January 27, 1986, following its third postponement in 6 days (and right on the heels of the most delayed flight in shuttle history), Challenger appeared destined for yet another delay: A cold front was approaching and the temperature forecast for launch time the next morning was 29 degrees F—well below the record coldest launch of January 1985 (53 degrees). An afternoon telephone conference call (telecon) took place between MTI in Utah and MSFC personnel in Alabama and Florida.

MTI was resolute: Based on their engineering judgment, they would oppose the launch as long as the temperature fell below their previous experience base (53 degrees). NASA asked the contractor to fax its data to MSFC and the Kennedy Space Center for a fuller deliberation and final determination during a subsequent telecon beginning at 8:45 p.m.

Unwilling to vouch for the safety of the seals in the rocket motor joints at such a low temperature, MTI, as anticipated, entered the final telecon recommending against the launch. But their stance was challenged with unprecedented vigor. Larry Mulloy, the SRB Program Manager for NASA, aggressively attacked the MTI position, pressing the engineers for quantitative proof that the joint would fail. Exasperated by MTI's intransigence, and stressing that no official launch criterion for joint temperature existed, Mulloy bristled, "My God, Thiokol. When do you want us to launch? Next April? The eve of a launch is a hell of a time to be generating new Launch Commit Criteria!" Because NASA had "successfully flown with the existing LCC 24 previous times," Mulloy questioned whether it was "logical—*truly logical*—that we really have to have a system that has to be 53 in order to fly?" (Rogers, 1986, p. 1541). George Hardy, the Deputy Director of Science and Engineering for NASA's Marshall Center, was asked for his reaction to the MTI recommendation. Hardy responded that he was "appalled" by their no-go decision but added that he "would not recommend launching over the contractor's objection" (Maier, 1992).

Accustomed to defending the wisdom of recommendations *to* launch, the company now found itself on the defensive for a conservative stance. It was the first time in the entire history of space flight that a contractor's recommendation not to launch had been challenged. When Mulloy summed up the deliberations with the statement that the MTI data were inconclusive (i.e., they had not established with certainty that the joint *would* fail . . . not work), Stanley Reinartz asked MTI's Joe Kilminster for a final recommendation. Pressed to establish with absolute certainty that the joint would not work, MTI management instead called for a short "time-out" from the telecon in order to caucus and, ostensibly, "re-evaluate their data." As soon as the mute button was pushed, Jerry Mason, the Senior

Vice President at MTI, turned to the vice presidents clustered around him and softly announced, "We have to make a management decision."

Correctly anticipating that Mason's comment was a signal the managers would reverse the no-launch recommendation, the company's two top engineering experts on the O-ring seals—Arnie Thompson and Roger Boisjoly—vigorously urged their superiors to stand by their original decision. Thompson rose from his position at the end of the table and sketched the problems with the joint on a note pad in front of the managers. He abandoned his effort and returned to his seat after Mason disciplined him with an unfriendly look, as if to say, as Boisjoly described it, "Go away and don't bother us with the facts."

Infuriated by the brushoff given his colleague, Boisjoly (1991) stood up from his seat across from the managers, slammed his photographic evidence from previous postflight inspections down in front of them, and, "literally screaming at them, admonished them to look at what the data are telling us: Namely that cold temperature indeed increases the risk of hot gas blowing by the joint." But he, too, backed down when Mason glared at him icily with "the kind of look you get just prior to being fired." Although Thompson and Boisjoly both knew the launch would be unsafe, they were unable to get their managers to listen to them. Instead, as Boisjoly observed, "The managers were having their own little meeting right in front of us, to the total exclusion of myself and my engineering colleagues." About midway through the caucus, Mason threw down the gauntlet before his executive subordinates, asking pointedly, "Am I the only one who wants to launch?" (Maier, 1992).

"What followed made me both sad and angry," Boisjoly explained. "They were taking our data, which supported a position *not* to launch, and trying to turn it around to support a launch decision. It was really disgusting" (Boisjoly, 1991). The lone holdout among the senior managers, Bob Lund, the Vice President of Engineering, finally capitulated 25 minutes into the caucus when Mason turned to him and instructed, "Take off your engineering hat and put on your management hat." A poll was taken of only the four senior managers, who voted unanimously to launch. As the General Manager explained to the Rogers commission, "We only polled the management people, because we had already established that we were *not* going to be unanimous" (Rogers, 1986, p. 1362).

At 11 p.m., MTI went "back on the line," and Joe Kilminster announced their reversal to Reinartz, who promptly accepted the new recommendation. MTI had provided NASA with the perfunctory "green light" to proceed with the fatal countdown. Challenger would be launched just a few hours later, at 11:38 a.m. (EST).

On the basis of the available evidence, it is clear that the ensuing disaster could—and should—have been prevented. The string of warnings unheeded, of recommendations ignored—from the early developmental stages all the way through to the "flawed decision-making process" (Rogers, 1986) of Challenger's final hours—culminated in the disaster that has become part of our collective consciousness.

As has been noted elsewhere, those horrific twisted-Y plumes etched into our memories represent an inevitable outcome of fairly typical organizational processes (Maier, 1992; Starbuck & Milliken, 1988; Vaughan, 1996). Less obvious, however, is how these processes reflect the tragic triumph of a decidedly masculinist managerial system. This connection is made explicit below, in an analysis of how the events in the Challenger chronology mesh neatly with several key dimensions of our culture's prevailing blueprint for masculinity; it raises serious questions about the extent to which any organizational participant—female or male—should be expected to conform to such a standard.

THE CHALLENGER LAUNCH DECISION: "BOYS WILL BE BOYS?"

Perhaps the most well-known framework that articulates the core dimensions of masculinity is the one developed by David and Brannon (1976). According to David and Brannon, the central dimensions of masculinity include

1. "No Sissy Stuff": The Stigma of Anything Vaguely Feminine
2. "The Big Wheel": Success, Status, and the Need to Be Looked Up To

3. "The Sturdy Oak": A Manly Air of Toughness, Confidence, and Self-Reliance
4. "Give 'Em Hell": The Aura of Aggression, Violence, and Daring

Played out in organizational roles, this gives rise to the White Male System summarized above (Schaef, 1981). Although this enumeration is not all-encompassing, it provides a useful and appropriate starting point for analysis.[2]

Theme No. 1: "No Sissy Stuff": The Stigma of Anything Vaguely Feminine

One of the earliest messages males in this culture receive is to distance themselves from girls and anything vaguely feminine. Leaving aside for a moment the obvious fact that NASA and its contractor were virtually (white) male-only clubs, the men whose actions ultimately cost the seven Challenger astronauts their lives show ample evidence of such conditioning. This correspondence is most vividly reflected in the events surrounding the evening telephone conference call between NASA officials and MTI on January 27, 1986.

Shortly before the final telecon took place, the NASA officials who would lead it (Stanley Reinartz and Larry Mulloy) caucused with their institutional superior, MSFC Director William Lucas to apprise him of the impending "no-launch" recommendation from MTI. Lucas had an autocratic reputation among MSFC employees, creating, according to one source, "an atmosphere of rigid, often fearful, conformity among Marshall managers. . . . Like many demanding task-masters, he demanded absolute personal loyalty" (McConnell, 1987, p. 108). According to Mulloy (personal communication, May 15, 1991), the Solid Rocket Booster Program Manager for NASA, when Lucas was told of MTI's position, he responded, "This sure is interesting: We get a little cold nip, and they want us to shut the Shuttle System down? I sure would like to see their reasons for that." Lucas's reaction harkens back to the old mental tape, "What-a-bunch-of-wussies!" It also not incidentally encapsulates the masculine world-view that presupposes scientific dominion over nature (as in "man's conquest of space").

Reflecting on his meeting with Lucas, Mulloy explained,

> If they [MTI] were going to come in and say, "We can't launch tomorrow 'cause we can't operate an SRM [Solid Rocket Motor] at 30," we were going to demand to know *why* and *not accept it on the basis of some hand-wringing emotion.* [italics added] (personal communication, May 15, 1991)

Although he couched it in more articulate language, Mulloy was essentially admonishing the MTI engineers for being "cry-babies."

During the teleconference itself, Mulloy rejected Boisjoly's data as qualitative, insisting the rocket engineer "quantify" his concerns. His invocation of logic, rationality, and data (i.e., masculine-gendered values) to claim legitimacy for himself while simultaneously framing (and thus disqualifying) the engineers' data as based on "hand-wringing emotion" and "gut feelings" (i.e., feminine qualities) is summed up in his assertion that the 53-degree lower limit advocated by MTI was not "truly logical." As he elaborated in his testimony,

> If somebody is giving me a recommendation and a conclusion, I *probe* the data to assure that it is sound and it is logical. I think that has been interpreted [that] when one challenges someone [i.e., Boisjoly] who says, "I don't have anything too quantitative, but I'm worried," that that is pressure, and I don't see it that way. (Rogers, 1986, p. 1532)

Even 4 years after Challenger, Mulloy (1990) clung stubbornly to this masculinist-anchored defense:

> You could not reach that conclusion [not to launch] on a quantitative basis alone. I kept examining what we had done, and I concluded then—and I'm confident now—that we made, based on the information available to us, a logical decision that had a disastrous result. (pp. 23–24)

After MTI called for the time out on the telecon and the managers began caucusing on how to deal with the rebuke from their major customer, Boisjoly and Thompson vigorously attempted to persuade their managers to stand firm. Shaken by NASA's unprecedented refusal to accept a conservative "don't-fly" recommendation, however, Jerry Mason, the Senior MTI official, dismissed Iris engineers' vociferous warnings on the basis that, "Although they were outspoken . . . we listened to their *reasons* more than their *intensity*, and the reasons boiled down to the fact that we found ourselves in a position of uncertainty that we were unable to quantify" (Rogers, 1986, p. 1365). Coding Boisjoly's confrontational outburst as intensity, he in essence feminized the rocket engineer and therefore discounted him. Note also the specious reasoning that the launch could proceed on the basis of uncertain and inconclusive data, suggestive of the "Go for it; No-guts, No-glory" theme of masculinity we will take up below ("The aura of daring"). The irony, of course, is that although the managers requested the caucus ostensibly to "Reevaluate their data" and determine a quantifiable justification for their position, they ended up, by Mason's own admission, relying "on a judgment, rather than a precise engineering calculation, in order to conclude what we needed to conclude" (Maier, 1992).

Theme No. 2: "The Big Wheel": Success, Status, and the Need to Be Looked Up To

This theme actually subsumes several powerful subdimensions of hegemonic masculinity: (a) a near-compulsive orientation to task accomplishment and competitive advancement (sometimes euphemistically referred to as ambition or dedication); (b) a corresponding ingrained respect for hierarchy, exclusionary politics, and established procedure (wanting to be "on top," which r equires the presence of others who can be "looked down upon"); and (c) a willingness to subordinate all other life obligations to one's employment/economic role and a focus on self as the metaphorical "center of the universe."

"Just Do It": The Masculine Premium on Action and Being "Number One"

The masculinist focus on *activity, action,* and *achievement,* on "giving 150%" and the obsession with "being Number One," played themselves out on Challenger in a number of ways, reflected in the following examples.

Although NASA had normalized the anomalous O-ring erosion as acceptable, two near disasters in 1985 called that judgment into question. Yet, fearful of bursting NASA's "Can-Do" bubble, no one was willing to do what it took to correct the problem. The Seal Task Force at MTI is an excellent illustration of this. When engineers informed management that standard operating procedures were obstructing the task force in its efforts to find a solution, management was unwilling to authorize exceptions to those procedures. Joe Kilminster, the Vice President of Space Boosters, met with the rocket engineers, but gladly told them that they would just have to make do with the resources at their disposal. As Boisjoly made clear in an Activity Report dated October 4, 1985, "He plain doesn't understand that there are not enough people to do that kind of nursing of each task, but he doesn't seem to mind directing that the task nevertheless gets done." Clearly, the task force efforts were *not,* as Boisjoly correctly surmised, a top priority to management. ("The basic problem boils down to the fact that *all* MTI problems have No. 1 priority and that upper management apparently feels that the SRM project is ours for sure and the customer be damned!") Rather than acknowledge the flaws in its design, MTI management elected to project a "strong front" by continuing to support NASA's flight program.

The excessive devotion to task (meeting flight projections) is similarly reflected in the fact that despite warnings raised at the NASA headquarters briefing in August 1985, top shuttle officials decided not to ground the fleet, believing the problem posed "an acceptable flight risk." Although the Rogers commission noted that the briefing was "sufficiently detailed to require corrective action prior to the next flight" (Rogers, 1986, p. 148), no corrective action was taken, according to a congressional investigation of the tragedy, because meeting flight schedules and cutting costs were given a higher priority than flight safety ("Investigation," 1986).

William Lucas, the autocratic Director of the MSFC, had consistently made it known to his subordinates that "under no circumstances is the Marshall Center to be the cause for delaying a launch" (cited in McConnell, 1987, p. 109).

Pyramidal Politics: Team Players and Kings of the Mountain

To grow up masculinized is to learn to value hierarchies. We are taught that it is a positive thing to "move up" (this overlaps with the achievement theme discussed previously). Emulate, imitate, *join,* if possible, those "above" you (the "higher ups"); distance and disassociate yourself from the people on your level or "below." In this manner, the values of stratification, exclusion, and an ethic of rights (Gilligan, 1982) occupy center stage in the lives of boys, at the expense of the more feminine values of egalitarianism, inclusion, and an ethic of care enumerated previously. These tendencies to emphasize ranking (one-up/one-down relations) over linking (peer relations), dominance over empowerment, winning over sharing, authority over participation, are central themes not only in masculinity (see Belenky et al., 1986; Eisler, 1987; Tannen, 1990) but in bureaucratic life (Ferguson, 1984). Here is how they were painfully well-represented in the events of the evening telecon proceeding the Challenger launch.

"Going by the Book": The Primacy of Procedure. The lives that were at stake were rarely, if ever, mentioned during the entire 2-hour telecon; that fact is a telling reflection on the masculine preoccupation with bureaucratic/procedural matters; a blind devotion to task that can render all other factors invisible and/or irrelevant. Mulloy was distressed not only by the *content* of MTI's message (i.e., "don't launch") but also by its *timing.* His bellicose reaction ("My God, Thiokol! When do you want me to launch? Next April? The *eve of a launch is a hell of a time* [italics added] to be generating new Launch Commit Criteria!") is nonsensical from a feminine perspective attuned to safety and caution, regardless of what "proper protocol" dictated. As MTI's Director of the SRM Project, Al McDonald (who was seated next to Mulloy at the Kennedy Space Center for the telecon) opined in an interview (July 1, 1992), "He was believing more in the system than in the people inputting into that system." As such, Mulloy's approach *does* mesh with the respect for organizationally

sanctioned rules (and for one's institutional superiors) typical of masculinist systems anchored in rank and hierarchy.

MTI, by advocating a 53-degree threshold for *this* particular launch, was—in Mulloy's view—essentially proposing the establishment of a new Launch Commit Criteria "after we have successfully flown with the existing LCC 24 previous times." Mulloy was incensed partly because his (masculine) reasoning did not allow him to accept that MTI's recommendation was restricted to this particular launch. He saw a conflict between the MTI position and *existing* policy ("no LCCs existed for joint temperature"; higher-ups had committed to accepting erosion anyway). Whereas MTI was following a (feminine) logic of being attuned to this specific context, Mulloy was also concerned about the *future* policy implications of accepting the MTI recommendation ("How are we going to live with this in the future?"). According to Mulloy, "The logic for [MTI's] recommendation did *not* specifically address, 'Don't launch 51-L [Challenger].' What it said was, 'Within our experience base, we should not operate *any* Solid Rocket Motor at any temperature colder than 53'" (Rogers, 1986, p. 1529).

Defending one's actions with reference to the masculinist ethic of procedure occurred with predictable regularity during presidential commission testimony. When middle-level NASA managers Larry Mulloy (the fourth-ranking launch official) and Stanley Reinartz (the third-ranking shuttle official) were asked why they reportedly did not pass the MTI concerns (including their original "no" vote on launch) up their chain of command, they retreated into a classic I-was-going-by-the-book stance, insisting that "no launch commit criteria were violated" (Rogers, 1986, p. 1680) and that "it was clearly a Level III issue that had been resolved" (p. 1557).

In a similar vein, MSFC director William Lucas, who *was* informed by Reinartz and Mulloy of the Thiokol concerns but did not mention those reservations to higher level launch officials even though he sat side-by-side with them throughout the morning of the launch, explained, "That would not be my reporting channel" (Rogers, 1986, p. 1877).

Exclusionary Politics: The Significance of Rank. In masculinist interactions, confrontation and intimidation are implicit. In feminine-gendered interactions, intimacy and connection predominate. As Tannen (1990) notes, both styles can be effective influence strategies, but men tend to use communication primarily as a means of establishing status and telling others what to do, whereas taking orders (or compromising) is perceived as a marker of low status. An approach more attuned to a feminine worldview (which is possible for both men and women, but more common of the latter), instead of focusing on jockeying for position, focuses on making connections, deliberately minimizing status differences while striving for consensus and mutual understanding. How was masculinist discourse in evidence during the Challenger launch decision process?

When Jerry Mason, the Senior Vice President of MTI, softly announced at the onset of the MTI caucus, "We have to make a management decision," it was for the benefit of the other senior officials seated close to him in the Management Information Center; a signal about who would be included and who would be excluded from the discussion. As Boisjoly (1991) explained, "He wasn't talking to me. He was talking to his three vice presidential colleagues." By emphasizing that a management decision was necessary, Mason was effectively defining both the *type* of decision that would be made and *who* would be entitled to make it: It would be based on *managerial* criteria (a point punctuated by Mason's eventual command to Bob Lund, the Vice President of Engineering, to "take off your engineering hat and put on your management hat!"). And it would also be a decision made by the *managers* (and only the managers). To *belong* to this team, you had to prove your loyalty by voting to launch; to continue to resist (as Lund at first did) resulted in ostracism and conformity pressure. Only "real men" (i.e., men willing to launch!) could belong to this team; "No Girls Allowed" (i.e., anyone who was fearful or subordinate).

The masculinist attachment to rank is also reflected in the engineers' acquiescence to management. As Boisjoly emphasized, "I had my say, and I never take away any management right to take the input of an engineer and then make a decision based on that input. . . . There was no point in

me doing anything any further." The stratification between managers and engineers was also alluded to by Brian Russell, another telecon participant, who noted, "We were not asked as the *engineering people* [italics added]. It was a management decision at the vice presidents' level" (Rogers, 1986, p. 1486). Engineering people were a disempowered class in the Management Information Center. Of the 14 men in the room, evidently the only ones entitled to speak were the four vice presidents.

The masculinist tendency to deny voice to the less powerful, and to respect the voices of the powerful, is further captured in Mason's incredulous explanation for why he did not even ask the engineers to participate in the final vote; "We only polled the management people because we had already established that we were not going to be unanimous" (Rogers, 1986, p. 1362). This non sequitur is meaningful only in a context in which dissent, especially from below, is unwelcome. In this case, the managers had every reason not to listen to the (hysterical) warnings of the engineers, because, after all, they were subordinate (inferior). Note that because Mulloy's emotionally charged challenge ("My God . . . When do you want me to launch? Next April?") originates from a "one-up" position (MSFC vis-à-vis MTI), it is not labeled (or denigrated) as emotional but is simply evidence of his entitlement to demand what he regards as a logical argument. This contradiction was lost on the participants that night.

Lurking in the background through all of the deliberations about "getting Challenger up" by January 28 was the pressure (however direct or indirect, however real or implied) to please the ultimate authority: President Reagan himself. He was the one who prematurely had declared the system "operational" in 1982; that declaration had provided the basis for his "Civilian-in-Space" program (announced during a 1984 election campaign stop); and he had personally insisted that the first such civilian would be a schoolteacher, picking out New Hampshire's Christa McAuliffe for the mission from among 142 applicants. Everyone at NASA knew how important this particular mission was to Reagan. Having Challenger aloft in time for the State of the Union Address on January 28 was clearly a priority for the White House, as evidenced by a flurry of telephone calls between the President's scheduling office and the Kennedy Space Center in the days leading up to the launch. The wishes of the "King of the Mountain" were known to all.

Work and Male Identity

One of the central themes of the male system in organizations is the expectation that one should subordinate all other life interests to one's work. If the earlier theme on "action" defines men by what they do, then this theme reminds us that a cornerstone of masculinity is one's paid employment status. There were numerous examples where this primacy of economics and the "male model of work" ultimately factored in to doom the Challenger and its crew.

Boisjoly's description of Mason's disciplinary gazes (during the MTI caucus) as "the kind of looks you get just prior to being fired" reminds us that one of the most powerful means of controlling men in organizations is to threaten this cultural centerpiece of adult manhood, gainful employment. Not incidentally, both Boisjoly and Richard Cook noted elsewhere that this may have been a crucial factor in why no one with sufficient authority stepped forward sooner to insist on a flight moratorium. As Cook pointed out, "You aren't going to find an engineer with 20 years experience *and a livelihood to protect* stand up and say, 'Excuse me, but we might have an explosion on the next flight because the O-rings might break!'" (Maier, 1992). Or, as Boisjoly (1991) explained, "It would have been tantamount to terminating one's career in the Space Program."

Economic considerations almost certainly affected MTI's submission to NASA's pressure ("Say Uncle!"). When it was clear that their major customer was displeased with their no-launch recommendation (as evidenced by their outright refusal to accept it), MTI asked for a time-out from the telecon to "re-evaluate the data." In hierarchical terms, MTI was being "bullied" into submission. As the less powerful of the two units (MTI depended more on NASA's good graces than vice versa, especially in the midst of ongoing contract negotiations), MTI (inferior = feminized) understood it had to be responsive to NASA (superior = masculinized) or suffer potentially drastic consequences. With a substantial continuing contract at risk, it is no wonder the Rogers commission concluded that,

"Thiokol Management reversed its position and recommended the launch . . . in order to accommodate a major customer" (Rogers, 1986, p. 104).

When the Seal Task Force at MTI ran up against the bureaucratic brick wall, Kilminster's lack of responsiveness to members' plight meant overtime working hours for them. Roger Boisjoly noted in his October 4 Activity Report that "I for one resent working at full capacity all week long, and then being required to support activity on the weekend that could have been accomplished during the week." Employers can make such demands only on employees they assume are unfettered by domestic concerns (i.e., men) . . . or whom they assume to be married to people (i.e., "wives") who will accommodate to the spillover effects of work on family life.

Excessive work involvement was directly implicated as a contributor to the Challenger disaster by the Rogers commission:

> One factor which may have contributed significantly to the atmosphere of the teleconference at Marshall is the effect on managers of several days of irregular working hours and insufficient sleep. . . . The willingness of NASA employees to work excessive hours, while admirable, raises serious questions when it jeopardizes job performance, particularly when critical management decisions are at stake. (Rogers, 1986, p. G-5)

As long as work and success are presumed to reign supreme in men's lives (and therefore be more highly valued than familial obligations which are—still—presumed to be "women's work"), then organizations can and will make demands on *men qua men* to "be there." This same rationale applied to why the MTI and MSFC representatives who flew to Florida for the launch, leaving their families behind, "happened" to be male.

Theme No. 3: "The Sturdy Oak": A Manly Air of Toughness, Confidence, and Self-Reliance

Appearing tough and in control, whatever the reality, is another hallmark of American hegemonic masculinity that plays out in organizations. This theme also implies that "real men stand tall"; they do not allow themselves to be put down, nor do they back down. Here is a sampling of how this theme permeates the events around Challenger.

From its inception, space flight was an arena where our self-image as a nation was placed on the line, the gauntlet having been thrown down by the Soviet launch of Sputnik. It was Cold War posturing that led John F. Kennedy to commit the United States, "to achieving the goal, before this decade is out, of landing a man on the moon and returning him safely to the earth." The unstated subtext, of course, was that we would get there *before* the Soviets; that we would "beat" them in this "space race."

Our successful moon landings, which rank undeniably among the top technological achievements of our time, sowed the seeds, however, of an arrogant hubris within the space agency. As Richard Cook pointed out, when the early evidence of O-ring damage began to emerge, NASA management failed to interpret the developments with alarm. According to Cook (1991), "NASA, with its history of spectacular successes, tended to view itself as a uniquely all-knowing and perfected entity." The agency boldly promised to accelerate the flight schedule from 9 missions in 1985, to 15 in 1986, up to 24 a year by 1990 (unrealistically ambitious, yet still well below the original 60 missions a year projected by the agency when it sold the program to Congress in the 1970s).

Hardy, the Deputy Director of Science and Engineering at MSFC, who during the telecon indicated he was "appalled" by MTI's data, offered a sublimely circular rationale for why his challenge was justified, one that encapsulates the masculinist fascination with toughness: "I have found in most cases [that] engineers, managers, or whatever else who have a true conviction in the data that they are presenting to you will 'hang tough' and not resent someone probing and penetrating that data" (Rogers, 1986, p. 1632). In other words, he was correct to challenge them because, after all, they backed down in the end. Obviously, MTI's initial tenacious defense of the 53-degree threshold for launch did not constitute "hanging tough" (a masculine virtue), but was pure "resentment" at being "probed and penetrated" (i.e., analogous to feminine irrationality).

Theme No. 4: "Give 'Em Hell": The Aura of Aggression, Violence, and Daring

The dominant themes of masculinity overlap and intersect to reinforce one another. As alluded to above, the toughness and confidence evidenced by NASA in its race to the moon and its willingness to press ahead with an accelerated flight schedule despite increasing incidents of erosion can also be construed as evidence of a near reckless bravado. The clearest example of this is the virtual absence, in thousands of pages of testimony, of any hint that the decision makers on Challenger considered the *possibility* of being wrong. In all of the debate about whether procedures were followed or not, about who communicated what to whom and when, about who was responsible, with rare exception did the lives of the astronauts themselves emerge as an issue. There are many other instances where the masculine aura of aggression shone through to ultimately take the lives of the Challenger crew.

Richard Cook revealed that safety concerns got submerged at the space agency because "the whole culture of the place calls for a can-do attitude that NASA can do whatever it tries to do, can solve any problem that comes up as it roars ahead toward 24 shuttle flights a year" (Boffey, 1986, p. B4).

The media, for all of their grandstanding *after* the disaster, chimed in to compound NASA's problems prior to it. When the launch was delayed, rather than welcoming the news as evidence of respect for the safety of the astronauts, the TV networks ridiculed the agency, referring to the postponement as "another red-faces-all-around space shuttle launch delay" (CBS), or quipping, "a flawless lift-off proved too much of a challenge for Challenger" (ABC). From a masculine-gendered perspective, such ridicule constitutes an implicit dare for the target to "deliver" (translated, "Nyah-nyah-nyah-nyah-nyah! NASA can't get it up! Betcha-can't-launch-on-time!").

The dare would be made more explicit during the pivotal telecon, with Mulloy setting the tone by lambasting MTI with "When do you want us to launch? Next April?" In other words, "What's wrong with you? *We're* ready!" The aura was embellished with profanity (*"My God,* Thiokol . . ." and "[This] is a *hell of a time* to be generating new Launch Commit Criteria!"). Mulloy's institutional superior, William Lucas, had signaled his view to the SRB Manager before the telecon had begun: "We get a little cold nip, and they want to shut the Shuttle System down? I sure would like to see their reasons for that!"

During the MTI caucus, while the managers were midway through their private discussion, the General Manager, Jerry Mason, rhetorically asked his vice presidential subordinates, "Am I the only one who wants to launch?" (translated, "What'samatter? You *chicken?*").

Mason's outright rejection of Boisjoly's and Thompson's input to the discussion (in effect, "Sit down and shut up. We didn't ask you!") and his willingness to exclude the engineers from the final vote ("because we had already established that we were not going to be unanimous") is a form of aggression and psychological violence common in (and to) hierarchical systems. To silence the voices of those who dissent, on the grounds of their disagreement and/or on the basis of their "inferior status," is a deliberate act of intimidation in order to get one's own way. The same can be said for his virtual dictation to Bob Lund, "Take off your engineering hat and put on your management hat."

CONCLUSIONS

As the foregoing elaboration attests, the pressures and dynamics, the organizational processes that allowed Challenger to happen reflect the tragic triumph of a decidedly masculinist (and *unfortunately* pervasive) managerial mind-set. We have seen how the processes and actions that contributed to what the presidential commission referred to as "the flawed decision" are strikingly linked to the four cornerstones of masculinity identified by David and Brannon (1976): No Sissy Stuff, The Big Wheel, The Sturdy Oak, and Give 'Em Hell, which parallel the elements of the White Male System presented by Schaef (1981). As such, it raises a question that strikes at a central dilemma in the diversity debate: By focusing on white males' relative ease of *success* in the White Male System, attention has been diverted away from the more fundamental issue of whether we should be encouraging anyone—including white males—to assimilate to (and hence replicate, maintain, and perpetuate) that system. Indeed, the foregoing analysis suggests that our organizations, and white males in particular, stand to benefit tremendously from questioning the normative foundations upon which organizational and individual success has been predicated. In diversity

terms, this means grappling with the central issue of changing the culture of corporate masculinity; or moving beyond MANagement.

As hierarchical systems, NASA and MTI empowered superiors and denied voice to subordinates. Views that challenged managerial prerogatives or that violated NASA's "can-do operational shuttle" ideology were suppressed or submerged. In effect, the managers in this chain of events were men, the engineers women (metaphorically speaking). NASA management's invocation of logic to invalidate the "qualitative, gut feelings" and "hand-wringing emotion" of the MTI engineers allowed NASA to insist that "no data showed conclusively that cold temperature increased the risk" (Mulloy, personal communication, May 15, 1991). Following the rule of reason, NASA managers felt insulated from blame for having made a "logical decision that had a disastrous result." Those who were opposed to the launch essentially were branded as "sissies" and pressured to change their stance ("Real men take risks. Real men are always ready to fly.")

In acting out adult equivalents of "King of the Mountain" and "Chicken," NASA and MTI were, by the time the telecon took place on the evening of January 27, already at the edge of the precipice. The "Russian Roulette" that allowed top NASA officials to keep the shuttles flying (at an ever-accelerating pace, no less) all but guaranteed the tragic outcome that resulted on January 28, 1986. The willingness to take ever greater (institutional) risks while denying one's weaknesses and neglecting to even consider the consequences of being wrong (Give 'Em Hell), the blind devotion to and projection of the image of an operational shuttle that never was (The Sturdy Oak) were fueled in part by these men's fears that ferreting out and speaking the truth might have threatened their personal livelihood or the viability of their organizations (The Big Wheel).

I find it impossible to reflect back to Challenger without experiencing deep regret and pain, feelings that are probably shared by many readers recalling the event, exacerbated by the knowledge that it was entirely preventable. My research into the disaster, as explored herein, has convinced me that we would not have experienced that loss or pain if the key decision makers and the organizations themselves had been guided by a different set of managerial principles and organizational priorities than the masculine ones that so indelibly shaped their actions. This analysis does not assume that men are inherently "bad," but that the norms by which they are expected to pattern their lives can be dysfunctional to the point of disaster. Gender is central to our understanding of organizational phenomena, even when (as illustrated here) all of the participants are male. Masculinity, as currently conceived, is both inherent to organizations and problematic. By making corporate masculinity (the implicit and unquestioned norm of organizational life) both visible and problematic, it is hoped that organizations and the people (i.e., men) who run them will commit to adopting alternatives (e.g., empowerment over dominance; participation and linking over authority and ranking; connection over confrontation; intimacy over intimidation; egalitarianism and inclusion over stratification and exclusion), alternatives I explore in greater depth elsewhere (Maier, 1996). Absent such a commitment, countless Challengers, metaphorically speaking, will be launched every day. Exposing this factor as one of the root causes, if not the ultimate source, of the tragedy can serve as a catalyst to inspire managers and organizations to reexamine their basic assumptions not only about masculinity (i.e., about what it means to "be a man" in this society), but also about *management* and the masculine underpinnings of organization.

Thus, we are left with a final dilemma: To adopt such alternative managerial approaches requires more than just the "will," as the saying goes. It also requires a "way," an altogether different form of organizational culture . . . and structure, than those which predominate today.

From a diversity perspective, one need look no further than Challenger for the compelling case to embrace a multicultural approach to organizational development, rather than blindly assimilating more numbers of diverse people *and* white males themselves into the existing (and dysfunctional) white male system.

NOTES

1. Kathy Ferguson collaborated extensively on the analysis in this section.

2. The analysis in this section draws from my previous research in masculinities (1993a).

REFERENCES

Belenky, J., Clinchy, B., Goldberger, N., & Tarule, T. (1986). *Women's ways of knowing.* New York: Basic.

Boffey, P. (1986, February 14). Analyst who gave shuttle warning faults "gung-ho, can-do" attitude. *New York Times,* p. B-4.

Boisjoly, R. M. (1991, April 18). *Ethical decision-making in organizations: Morton Thiokol and the space shuttle Challenger disaster.* Paper presented at the GTE Lectureship on Technology and Ethics, Binghamton, NY.

Chodorow, N. (1978). *The reproduction of mothering,* Berkeley: University of California Press.

Connell, B. (1989). Masculinity, violence, and war. In M. Kimmel & M. Messner (Eds.), *Men's lives* (pp. 176–183). New York: Macmillan.

Cook, R. C. (1991, April 18). *The NASA space shuttle Challenger disaster: The view from within.* Paper presented at the GTE Lectureship on Technology and Ethics, Binghamton, NY.

David, D. S., & Brannon, R. (1976). *The forty-nine percent majority: The male sex role.* Reading, MA: Addison-Wesley.

Di Stefano, C. (1991). *Configurations of masculinity: A feminist perspective on modern political theory.* Ithaca, NY: Cornell University Press.

Eisler, R. (1987). *The chalice and the blade.* New York: Harper-Collins.

Ferguson, K. (1984). *The feminist case against bureaucracy.* Philadelphia: Temple University Press.

Gilligan, C. (1982). *In a different voice.* Cambridge, MA: Harvard University Press.

Harding, S. (1986). *The science question in feminism.* Ithaca, NY: Cornell University Press.

Hare-Mustin, R. T. (1988). Family change and gender differences: Implications for theory and practice. *Family Relations, 37,* 36–41.

Hartsock, N. (1983). *Money, sex, and power; Toward a feminist historical materialism.* New York: Longman.

Investigation of the Challenger accident (House Report #99–1016). (1986, October 29.) Washington, DC: Government Printing Office.

Kanter, R. M. (1977). *Men and women of the corporation.* New York: Basic.

Kimmel, M., & Messner, M. (1992). *Men's lives* (2nd ed.). New York: Macmillan.

Maier, M. (Writer/Director). (1992). *"A major malfunc-tion . . ." The story behind the space shuttle Challenger disaster. A pedagogical documentary about orga-nizational politics, ethics, and decision making* (Videotape and Instructional Materials). Albany: The Research Foundation of the State University of New York.

Maier, M. (1993a). "Am I the only one who wants to launch?" Corporate masculinity and the space shuttle Challenger disaster. *Masculinities, 1*(1-2), pp. 34–45.

Maier, M. (1993b). Revisiting (and resolving?) the androg-yny/masculinity debate in management. *Journal of Men's Studies,* 2(2), 157–171.

Maier, M. (1994). Challenger: The path to disaster. *Case Research Journal, 14*(1), 1–49; 150–155.

Maier, M. (1996, August). *Confronting the (f)laws of the pyramid: The enduring legacy of the space shuttle Challenger disaster?* Paper presented at the Academy of Management Annual Meetings, Cincinnati, OH.

McConnell, M. (1987). *Challenger: A major malfunction.* New York: Doubleday.

Messerschmidt, J. (1995). Managing to kill: Masculinities and the space shuttle Challenger explosion. *Masculinities,* 3(4): 1–22.

Mulloy, L. (1990). Interview transcript, Cosgrove-Meurer Productions *(The story behind the story).* Courtesy of Larry Mulloy.

Powell, G. N., & Butterfield, D. A. (1989). The "good manager": Did androgyny fare better in the 1980s? *Group and Organization Studies, 14,* 216–233.

Rogers, W. (1986). *Report on the space shuttle Challenger accident.* Washington, DC: Government Printing Office.

Ruddick, S. (1989). *Maternal thinking.* New York: Doubleday.

Schaef, A. W. (1981). *Women's reality.* New York: Harper-Collophon.

Spender, D. (1984). Defining reality: A powerful tool. In C. Kramarae, M. Schulz, & W. O'Barr (Eds.), *Language and power* (pp. 194–205). Beverly Hills, CA: Sage.

Starbuck, W., & Milliken, F. (1988). Challenger: Fine-tuning the odds until something breaks. *Journal of Management Studies, 25*(4), 319–340.

Tannen, D. (1990). *You just don't understand.* New York: Ballantine.

Vaughan, D. (1990). Autonomy, interdependence, and social control: NASA and the space shuttle Challenger. *Administrative Science Quarterly, 35*(2), 225–257.

Vaughan, D. (1996). *The Challenger launch decision.* Chicago: University of Chicago Press.

SOURCE: Maier, Mark. 1997. "'We Have to Make a MANagement Decision': Challenger and the Dysfunctions of Corporate Masculinity." Pp. 226–54 in *Managing the Organizational Melting Pot: Dilemmas of Workplace Diversity.* Thousand Oaks, CA: Sage.

44

JUST ONE OF THE GUYS?

How Transmen Make Gender Visible at Work

KRISTEN SCHILT

Theories of gendered organizations argue that cultural beliefs about gender difference embedded in workplace structures and interactions create and reproduce workplace disparities that disadvantage women and advantage men (Acker 1990; Martin 2003; Williams 1995). As Martin (2003) argues, however, the practices that reproduce gender difference and gender inequality at work are hard to observe. As these gendered practices are citations of established gender norms, men and women in the workplace repeatedly and unreflectively engage in "doing gender" and therefore "doing inequality" (Martin 2003; West and Zimmerman 1987). This repetition of well-worn gender ideologies naturalizes workplace gender inequality, making gendered disparities in achievements appear to be offshoots of "natural" differences between men and women, rather than the products of dynamic gendering and gendered practices (Martin 2003). As the active reproduction of gendered workplace disparities is rendered invisible, gender inequality at work becomes difficult to document empirically and therefore remains resistant to change (Acker 1990; Martin 2003; Williams 1995).

The workplace experiences of female-to-male transsexuals (FTMs), or transmen, offer an opportunity to examine these disparities between men and women at work from a new perspective. Many FTMs enter the workforce as women and, after transition, begin working as men.[1] As men, they have the same skills, education, and abilities they had as women; however, how this "human capital" is perceived often varies drastically once they become men at work. This shift in gender attribution gives them the potential to develop an "outsider-within" perspective (Collins 1986) on men's advantages in the workplace. FTMs can find themselves benefiting from the "patriarchal dividend" (Connell 1995, 79)—the advantages men in general gain from the subordination of women—after they transition. However, not being "born into it" gives them the potential to be cognizant of being awarded respect, authority, and prestige they did not have working as women. In addition, the experiences of transmen who fall outside of the hegemonic construction of masculinity, such as FTMs of color, short FTMs, and young FTMs, illuminate how the interplay of gender, race, age, and bodily characteristics can constrain access to gendered workplace advantages for some men (Connell 1995).

In this article, I document the workplace experiences of two groups of FTMs, those who openly transition and remain in the same jobs (open FTMs) and those who find new jobs posttransition as "just men" (stealth FTMs).[2] I argue that the positive and negative changes they experience when they become men can illuminate how gender discrimination and gender advantage are created and maintained through workplace interactions. These experiences also illustrate that masculinity is not a fixed character type that automatically commands privilege but rather that the relationships between competing hegemonic and marginalized masculinities give men differing abilities to access gendered workplace advantages (Connell 1995).

THEORIES OF WORKPLACE GENDER DISCRIMINATION

Sociological research on the workplace reveals a complex relationship between the gender of an employee and that employee's opportunities for advancement in both authority and pay. While white-collar men and women with equal qualifications can begin their careers in similar positions in the workplace, men tend to advance faster, creating a gendered promotion gap (Padavic and Reskin 2002; Valian 1999). When women are able to advance, they often find themselves barred from attaining access to the highest echelons of the company by the invisible barrier of the "glass ceiling" (Valian 1999). Even in the so-called women's professions, such as nursing and teaching, men outpace women in advancement to positions of authority (Williams 1995). Similar patterns exist among blue-collar professions, as women often are denied sufficient training for advancement in manual trades, passed over for promotion, or subjected to extreme forms of sexual, racial, and gender harassment that result in women's attrition (Byrd 1999; Miller 1997; Yoder and Aniakudo 1997). These studies are part of the large body of scholarly research on gender and work finding that white- and blue-collar workplaces are characterized by gender segregation, with women concentrated in lower-paying jobs with little room for advancement.

Among the theories proposed to account for these workplace disparities between men and women are human capital theory and gender role socialization. Human capital theory posits that labor markets are neutral environments that reward workers for their

skills, experience, and productivity. As women workers are more likely to take time off from work for child rearing and family obligations, they end up with less education and work experience than men. Following this logic, gender segregation in the workplace stems from these discrepancies in skills and experience between men and women, not from gender discrimination. However, while these differences can explain some of the disparities in salaries and rank between women and men, they fail to explain why women and men with comparable prestigious degrees and work experience still end up in different places, with women trailing behind men in advancement (Valian 1999; Williams 1995).

A second theory, gender socialization theory, looks at the process by which individuals come to learn, through the family, peers, schools, and the media, what behavior is appropriate and inappropriate for their gender. From this standpoint, women seek out jobs that reinforce "feminine" traits such as caring and nurturing. This would explain the predominance of women in helping professions such as nursing and teaching. As women are socialized to put family obligations first, women workers would also be expected to be concentrated in part-time jobs that allow more flexibility for family schedules but bring in less money. Men, on the other hand, would be expected to seek higher-paying jobs with more authority to reinforce their sense of masculinity. While gender socialization theory may explain some aspects of gender segregation at work, however, it leaves out important structural aspects of the workplace that support segregation, such as the lack of workplace child care services, as well as employers' own gendered stereotypes about which workers are best suited for which types of jobs (Padavic and Reskin 2002; Valian 1999; Williams 1995).

A third theory, gendered organization theory, argues that what is missing from both human capital theory and gender socialization theory is the way in which men's advantages in the workplace are maintained and reproduced in gender expectations that are embedded in organizations and in interactions between employers, employees, and coworkers (Acker 1990; Martin 2003; Williams 1995). However, it is difficult to study this process of reproduction empirically for several reasons. First, while men and women with similar education and workplace backgrounds can be compared to demonstrate the disparities in where they end up in their careers, it could be argued that differences in achievement between them can be attributed to personal characteristics of the workers rather than to systematic gender discrimination. Second, gendered expectations about which types of jobs women and men are suited for are strengthened by existing occupational segregation; the fact that there are more women nurses and more men doctors comes to be seen as proof that women are better suited for helping professions and men for rational professions. The normalization of these disparities as natural differences obscures the actual operation of men's advantages and therefore makes it hard to document them empirically. Finally, men's advantages in the workplace are not a function of simply one process but rather a complex interplay between many factors, such as gender differences in workplace performance evaluation, gendered beliefs about men's and women's skills and abilities, and differences between family and child care obligations of men and women workers.

The cultural reproduction of these interactional practices that create and maintain gendered workplace disparities often can be rendered more visible, and therefore more able to be challenged, when examined through the perspective of marginalized others (Collins 1986; Martin [S.] 1994, [P.] 2003; Yoder and Aniakudo 1997). As Yoder and Aniakudo note, "marginalized others offer a unique perspective on the events occurring within a setting because they perceive activities from the vantages of both nearness (being within) and detachment (being outsiders)" (1997, 325–26). This importance of drawing on the experiences of marginalized others derives from Patricia Hill Collins's theoretical development of the "outsider-within" (1986, 1990). Looking historically at the experience of Black women, Collins (1986) argues that they often have become insiders to white society by virtue of being forced, first by slavery and later by racially bounded labor markets, into domestic work for white families. The insider status that results from being immersed in the daily lives of white families carries the ability to demystify power relations by making evident how white society relies on racism and sexism, rather than superior ability or intellect,

to gain advantage; however, Black women are not able to become total insiders due to being visibly marked as different. Being a marginalized insider creates a unique perspective, what Collins calls "the outsider-within," that allows them to see "the contradictions between the dominant group's actions and ideologies" (Collins 1990, 12), thus giving a new angle on how the processes of oppression operate. Applying this perspective to the workplace, scholars have documented the production and reproduction of gendered and racialized workplace disparities through the "outsider-within" perspective of Black women police officers (Martin 1994) and Black women firefighters (Yoder and Aniakudo 1997).

In this article, I posit that FTMs' change in gender attribution, from women to men, can provide them with an outsider-within perspective on gendered workplace disparities. Unlike the Black women discussed by Collins, FTMs usually are not visibly marked by their outsider status, as continued use of testosterone typically allows for the development of a masculine social identity indistinguishable from "bio men."[3] However, while both stealth and open FTMs can become social insiders at work, their experience working as women prior to transition means they maintain an internalized sense of being outsiders to the gender schemas that advantage men. This internalized insider/outsider position allows some transmen to see clearly the advantages associated with being men at work while still maintaining a critical view to how this advantage operates and is reproduced and how it disadvantages women. I demonstrate that many of the respondents find themselves receiving more authority, respect, and reward when they gain social identities as men, even though their human capital does not change. This shift in treatment suggests that gender inequality in the workplace is not continually reproduced only because women make different education and workplace choices than men but rather because coworkers and employers often rely on gender stereotypes to evaluate men's and women's achievements and skills.

METHOD

I conducted in-depth interviews with 29 FTMs in the Southern California area from 2003 to 2005.

My criteria for selection were that respondents were assigned female at birth and were currently living and working as men or open transmen. These selection criteria did exclude female-bodied individuals who identified as men but had not publicly come out as men at work and FTMs who had not held any jobs as men since their transition, as they would not be able to comment about changes in their social interactions that were specific to the workplace. My sample is made up of 18 open FTMs and 11 stealth FTMs.

At the onset of my research, I was unaware of how I would be received as a non-transgender person doing research on transgender workplace experiences, as well as a woman interviewing men. I went into the study being extremely open about my research agenda and my political affiliations with feminist and transgender gender politics. I carried my openness about my intentions into my interviews, making clear at the beginning that I was happy to answer questions about my research intentions, the ultimate goal of my research, and personal questions about myself. Through this openness, and the acknowledgment that I was there to learn rather than to be an academic "expert," I feel that I gained a rapport with my respondents that bridged the "outsider/insider" divide (Merton 1972).

Generating a random sample of FTMs is not possible as there is not an even dispersal of FTMs throughout Southern California, nor are there transgender-specific neighborhoods from which to sample. I recruited interviewees from transgender activist groups, transgender listservers, and FTM support groups. In addition, I participated for two years in Southern California transgender community events, such as conferences and support group meetings. Attending these community events gave me an opportunity not only to demonstrate long-term political commitment to the transgender community but also to recruit respondents who might not be affiliated with FTM activist groups. All the interviews were conducted in the respondents' offices, in their homes, or at a local café or restaurant. The interviews ranged from one and a half to four hours. All interviews were audio recorded, transcribed, and coded.

Drawing on sociological research that reports long-standing gender differences between men and women in the workplace (Reskin and Hartmann 1986; Reskin and Roos 1990; Valian 1999; Williams 1995), I constructed my interview schedule to focus on possible differences between working as women and working as men. I first gathered a general employment history and then explored the decision to openly transition or to go stealth. At the end of the interviews, I posed the question, "Do you see any differences between working as a woman and working as a man?" All but a few of the respondents immediately answered yes and began to provide examples of both positive and negative differences. About half of the respondents also, at this time, introduced the idea of male privilege, addressing whether they felt they received a gender advantage from transitioning. If the concept of gender advantage was not brought up by respondents, I later introduced the concept of male privilege and then posed the question, saying, "Do you feel that you have received any male privilege at work?" The resulting answers from these two questions are the framework for this article.

In reporting the demographics of my respondents, I have opted to use pseudonyms and general categories of industry to avoid identifying my respondents. Respondents ranged in age from 20 to 48. Rather than attempting to identify when they began their gender transition, a start date often hard to pinpoint as many FTMs feel they have been personally transitioning since childhood or adolescence, I recorded how many years they had been working as men (meaning they were either hired as men or had openly transitioned from female to male and remained in the same job). The average time of working as a man was seven years. Regarding race and ethnicity, the sample was predominantly white (17), with 3 Asians, 1 African American, 3 Latinos, 3 mixed-race individuals, 1 Armenian American, and 1 Italian American. Responses about sexual identity fell into four main categories, heterosexual (9), bisexual (8), queer (6), and gay (3). The remaining 3 respondents identified their sexual identity as celibate/asexual, "dating women," and pansexual. Finally, in terms of region, the sample included a mixture of FTMs living in urban and suburban areas. (See Table 44.1 for sample characteristics.)

The experience of my respondents represents a part of the Southern California FTM community

Table 44.1   Sample Characteristics

Pseudonym	Age	Race/Ethnicity	Sexual Identity	Approximate Number of Years Working as Male	Industry	Status at Work
Aaron	28	Black/White	Queer	5	Semi-Professional	Open
Brian	42	White	Bisexual	14	Semi -Professional	Stealth
Carl	34	White	Heterosexual	16	Higher Professional	Stealth
Christopher	25	Asian	Pansexual	3	Semi-Professional	Open
Colin	31	White	Queer	1	Lower Professional	Open
Crispin	42	White	Heterosexual	2	Blue-Collar	Stealth
David	30	White	Bisexual	2	Higher Professional	Open
Douglas	38	White	Gay	5	Semi-Professional	Open
Elliott	20	White	Bisexual	1	Retail/Customer Service	Open
Henry	32	White	Gay	5	Lower Professional	Open
Jack	30	Latino	Queer	1	Semi-Professional	Open
Jake	45	White	Queer	9	Higher Professional	Open
Jason	48	White/Italian	Celibate	20	Retail/Customer Service	Stealth
Keith	42	Black	Heterosexual	1	Blue-Collar	Open
Kelly	24	White	Bisexual	2	Semi-Professional	Open
Ken	26	Asian/White	Queer	6 months	Semi-Professional	Open
Paul	44	White	Heterosexual	2	Semi-Professional	Open
Peter	24	White/Armenian	Heterosexual	4	Lower Professional	Stealth
Preston	39	White	Bisexual	2	Blue-Collar	Open
Riley	37	White	Dates women	1	Lower Professional	Open
Robert	23	Asian	Heterosexual	2	Retail/Customer Service	stealth
Roger	45	White	Bisexual	22	Lower Professional	Stealth
Sam	33	Latino	Heterosexual	15	Blue-Collar	Stealth
Simon	42	White	Bisexual	2	Semi-Professional	Open
Stephen	35	White	Heterosexual	1	Retail/Customer Service	Stealth
Thomas	42	Latino	Queer	13	Higher Professional	Open
Trevor	35	White	Gay/Queer	6	Semi-Professional	Open
Wayne	44	White/Latino	Bisexual	22	Higher Professional	Stealth
Winston	40	White	Heterosexual	14	Higher Professional	Stealth

from 2003 to 2005. As Rubin (2003) has demonstrated, however, FTM communities vary greatly from city to city, meaning these findings may not be representative of the experiences of transmen in Austin, San Francisco, or Atlanta. In addition, California passed statewide gender identity protection for employees in 2003, meaning that the men in my study live in an environment in which they cannot legally be fired for being transgender (although most of my respondents said they would not wish to be a test case for this new law). This legal protection means that California transmen might have very different workplace experiences than men in states without gender identity protection. Finally, anecdotal evidence suggests that there are a large number of transgender individuals who transition and then sever all ties with the transgender community, something known as being "deep stealth." This lack of connection to the transgender community means they are excluded from research on transmen but that their experiences with the workplace may be very different than those of men who are still connected, even slightly, to the FTM community.

TRANSMEN AS OUTSIDERS WITHIN AT WORK

In undergoing a physical gender transition, transmen move from being socially gendered as women to being socially gendered as men (Dozier 2005). This shift in gender attribution gives them the potential to develop an "outsider-within" perspective (Collins 1986) on the sources of men's advantages in the workplace. In other words, while they may find themselves, as men, benefiting from the "patriarchal dividend" (Connell 1995, 79), not being "born into it" can make visible how gendered workplace disparities are created and maintained through interactions. Many of the respondents note that they can see clearly, once they become "just one of the guys," that men succeed in the workplace at higher rates than women because of gender stereotypes that privilege masculinity, not because they have greater skill or ability. For transmen who do see how these cultural beliefs about gender create gendered workplace disparities, there is an accompanying sense that these experiences are visible to them only because of the unique perspective they gain from undergoing a change in gender attribution. Exemplifying this, Preston reports about his views on gender differences at work posttransition: "I swear they let the guys get away with so much stuff! Lazy ass bastards get away with so much stuff and the women who are working hard, they just get ignored. . . . I am really aware of it. And that is one of the reasons that I feel like I have become much more of a feminist since transition. I am just so aware of the difference that my experience has shown me." Carl makes a similar point, discussing his awareness of blatant gender discrimination at a hardware/home construction store where he worked immediately after his transition: "Girls couldn't get their forklift license or it would take them forever. They wouldn't make as much money. It was so pathetic. I would have never seen it if I was a regular guy. I would have just not seen it. . . . I can see things differently because of my perspective. So in

some ways I am a lot like a guy because I transitioned younger but still, you can't take away how I was raised for 18 years." These comments illustrate how the outsider-within perspective of many FTMs can translate into a critical perspective on men's advantages at work. The idea that a "regular guy," here meaning a bio man, would not be able to see how women were passed over in favor of men makes clear that for some FTMs, there is an ability to see how gender stereotypes can advantage men at work.

However, just as being a Black woman does not guarantee the development of a Black feminist perspective (Collins 1986), having this critical perspective on gender discrimination in the workplace is not inherent to the FTM experience. Respondents who had held no jobs prior to transition, who were highly gender ambiguous prior to transition, or who worked in short-term, high-turnover retail jobs, such as food service, found it harder to identify gender differences at work. FTMs who transitioned in their late teens often felt that they did not have enough experience working as women to comment on any possible differences between men and women at work. For example, Sam and Robert felt they could not comment on gender differences in the workplace because they had begun living as men at the age of 15 and, therefore, never had been employed as women. In addition, FTMs who reported being very "in-between" in their gender appearance, such as Wayne and Peter, found it hard to comment on gender differences at work, as even when they were hired as women, they were not always sure how customers and coworkers perceived them. They felt unable to speak about the experience of working as a woman because they were perceived either as androgynous or as men.

The kinds of occupations FTMs held prior to transition also play a role in whether they develop this outsider-within perspective at work. Transmen working in blue-collar jobs—jobs that are predominantly staffed by men—felt their experiences working in these jobs as females varied greatly from their experiences working as men. This held true even for those transmen who worked as females in blue-collar jobs in their early teens, showing that age of transition does not always determine the ability to see gender discrimination at work. FTMs working in the "women's professions" also saw a great shift in their treatment once they began working as men. FTMs who transitioned in their late teens and worked in marginal "teenage" jobs, such as fast food, however, often reported little sense of change posttransition, as they felt that most employees were doing the same jobs regardless of gender. As a gendered division of labor often does exist in fast food jobs (Leidner 1993), it may be that these respondents worked in atypical settings, or that they were assigned "men's jobs" because of their masculine appearance.

Transmen in higher professional jobs, too, reported less change in their experiences posttransition, as many of them felt that their workplaces guarded against gender-biased treatment as part of an ethic of professionalism. The experience of these professional respondents obviously runs counter to the large body of scholarly research that documents gender inequality in fields such as academia (Valian 1999), law firms (Pierce 1995), and corporations (Martin 1992). Not having an outsider-within perspective, then, may be unique to these particular transmen, not the result of working in a professional occupation.

Thus, transitioning from female to male can provide individuals with an outsider-within perspective on gender discrimination in the workplace. However, this perspective can be limited by the age of transition, appearance, and type of occupation. In addition, as I will discuss at the end of this article, even when the advantages of the patriarchal dividend are seen clearly, many transmen do not benefit from them. In the next section, I will explore in what ways FTMs who expressed having this outsider-within perspective saw their skills and abilities perceived more positively as men. Then, I will explore why not all of my respondents received a gender advantage from transitioning.

TRANSITION AND WORKPLACE GENDER ADVANTAGES[4]

A large body of evidence shows that the performance of workers is evaluated differently depending on gender. Men, particularly white men, are viewed as more competent than women workers (Olian, Schwab, and Haberfeld 1988; Valian 1999). When men succeed, their success is seen as stemming from their abilities while women's success often is attributed to luck (Valian 1999). Men are rewarded more than women for offering ideas and opinions and for taking on leadership roles in group settings (Butler and Geis 1990; Valian 1999). Based on these findings, it would be expected that stealth transmen would see a positive difference in their workplace experience once they have made the transition from female to male, as they enter new jobs as just one of the guys. Open FTMs, on the other hand, might find themselves denied access to these privileges, as they remain in the same jobs in which they were hired as women. Challenging these expectations, two-thirds of my respondents, both open and stealth, report receiving some type of posttransition advantage at work. These advantages fell into four main categories: gaining competency and authority, gaining respect and recognition for hard work, gaining "body privilege," and gaining economic opportunities and status.

Authority and Competency

Illustrating the authority gap that exists between men and women workers (Elliott and Smith 2004; Padavic and Reskin 2002), several of my interviewees reported receiving more respect for their thoughts and opinions posttransition. For example, Henry, who is stealth in a professional workplace, says of his experiences, "I'm right a lot more now. . . . Even with folks I am out to [as a transsexual], there is a sense that I know what I am talking about." Roger, who openly transitioned in a retail environment in the 1980s, discussed customers' assumptions that as a man, he knew more than his boss, who was a woman: "People would come in and they would go straight to me. They would pass her and go straight to me because obviously, as a male, I knew [sarcasm]. And so we would play mind games with them. . . . They would come up and ask me a question, and then I would go over to her and ask her the same question, she would tell me the answer, and I would go back to the customer and tell the customer the answer." Revealing how entrenched these stereotypes about masculinity and authority are, Roger added that none of the customers ever recognized the sarcasm behind his actions. Demonstrating how white men's opinions are seen to carry more authority, Trevor discusses how, post-transition, his ideas are now taken more seriously in group situations—often to the detriment of his women coworkers: "In a professional workshop or a conference kind of setting, a woman would make a comment or an observation and be overlooked and be dissed essentially. I would raise my hand and make the same point in a way that I am trying to reinforce her and it would be like [directed at me], 'That's an excellent point!' I saw this shit in undergrad. So it is not like this was a surprise to me. But it was disconcerting to have happen to me." These last two quotes exemplify the outsider-within experience: Both men are aware of having more authority simply because of being men, an authority that happens at the expense of women coworkers.

Looking at the issue of authority in the women's professions, Paul, who openly transitioned in the field of secondary education, reports a sense of having increased authority as one of the few men in his work environment:

I did notice [at] some of the meetings I'm required to attend, like school district or parent involvement [meetings], you have lots of women there. And now I feel like there are [many times], mysteriously enough, when I'm picked [to speak]. . . . I think, well, why me, when nobody else has to go to the microphone and talk about their stuff? That I did notice and that [had] never happened before. I mean there was this meeting . . . a little while ago about domestic violence where I appeared to be the only male person between these 30, 40 women and, of course, then everybody wants to hear from me.

Rather than being alienated by his gender tokenism, as women often are in predominantly male workplaces (Byrd 1999), he is asked to express his opinions and is valued for being the "male" voice at the meetings, a common situation for men in "women's professions" (Williams 1995). The lack of interest paid to him as a woman in the same job demonstrates how women in predominantly female workspaces can encourage their coworkers who are men to take more authority and space in these careers, a situation that can lead to the promotion of men in women's professions (Williams 1995).

Transmen also report a positive change in the evaluation of their abilities and competencies after transition. Thomas, an attorney, relates an episode in which an attorney who worked for an associated law firm commended his boss for firing Susan, here a pseudonym for his female name, because she was incompetent—adding that the "new guy" [i.e., Thomas] was "just delightful." The attorney did not realize that Susan and "the new guy" were the same person with the same abilities, education, and experience. This anecdote is a glaring example of how men are evaluated as more competent than women even when they do the same job in careers that are stereotyped requiring "masculine" skills such as rationality (Pierce 1995; Valian 1999). Stephen, who is stealth in a predominantly male customer-service job, reports, "For some reason just because [the men I work with] assume I have a dick, [they assume] I am going to get the job done right, where, you know, they have to second guess that when you're a woman. They look at [women] like well, you can't handle this because you know, you don't have the same mentality that we [men] do, so there's this sense of panic . . . and if you are a guy, it's just like, oh, you can handle it." Keith, who openly transitioned in a male-dominated blue-collar job, reports no longer having to "cuddle after sex," meaning that he has been able to drop the emotional labor of niceness women often have to employ to when giving orders at work. Showing how perceptions of behavior can change with transition, Trevor reports, "I think my ideas are taken more seriously [as a man]. I had good leadership skills leaving college and um . . . I think that those work well for me now. . . . Because I'm male, they work better for me. I was 'assertive' before. Now I'm 'take charge.'" Again, while his behavior has not changed, his shift in gender attribution translates into a different kind of evaluation. As a man, being assertive is consistent with gendered expectations for men, meaning his same leadership skills have more worth in the workplace because of his transition. His experience underscores how women who take on leadership roles are evaluated negatively, particularly if their leadership style is perceived as assertive, while men are rewarded for being aggressive leaders (Butler and Geis 1990; Valian 1999).[5]

This change in authority is noticeable only because FTMs often have experienced the reverse: being thought, on the basis of gender alone, to be less competent workers who receive less author-ity from employers and coworkers. This sense of a shift in authority and perceived competence was particularly marked for FTMs who had worked in blue-collar occupations as women. These transmen report that the stereotype of women's incompetence often translated into difficulty in finding and main-taining employment. For example, Crispin, who had worked as a female construction worker, reports being written up by supervisors for every small infraction, a practice Yoder and Aniakudo (1997, 330) refer to as "pencil whipping." Crispin recounts, "One time I had a field supervisor confront me about simple things, like not dotting i's and using the wrong color ink. . . . Anything he could do, he was just constantly on me. . . . I ended up just leaving." Paul, who was a female truck driver, recounts, "Like they would tell [me], 'Well we never had a female driver. I don't know if this works out.' Blatantly tell-ing you this. And then [had] to go, 'Well let's see. Let's give it a chance, give it a try. I'll do this three days for free and you see and if it's not working out, well then that's fine and if it works out, maybe you want to reconsider [not hiring me].'" To prove her competency, she ended up working for free, hoping that she would eventually be hired.

Stephen, who was a female forklift operator, described the resistance women operators faced from men when it came to safety precautions for loading pallets:

[The men] would spot each other, which meant that they would have two guys that would close down the aisle . . . so that no one could go on that aisle while you know you were up there [with your fork lift and load] . . . and they wouldn't spot you if you were a female. If you were a guy . . . they got the red vests and the safety cones out and it's like you know—the only thing they didn't have were those little flashlights for the jets. It would be like God or somebody responding. I would actually have to go around and gather all the dykes from receiving to come out and help and spot me. And I can't tell you how many times I nearly ran over a kid. It was maddening and it was always because [of] gender.

Thus, respondents described situations of being ignored, passed over, purposefully put in harm's

way, and assumed to be incompetent when they were working as women. However, these same indi-viduals, as men, find themselves with more author-ity and with their ideas, abilities, and attributes evaluated more positively in the workforce.

Respect and Recognition

Related to authority and competency is the issue of how much reward workers get for their work-place contributions. According to the transmen I interviewed, an increase in recognition for hard work was one of the positive changes associated with working as a man. Looking at these stories of gaining reward and respect, Preston, who transi-tioned openly and remained at his blue-collar job, reports that as a female crew supervisor, she was frequently short staffed and unable to access neces-sary resources yet expected to still carry out the job competently. However, after his transition, he sud-denly found himself receiving all the support and materials he required:

I was not asked to do anything different [after transi-tion]. But the work I did do was made easier for me. [Before transition] there [were] periods of time when I would be told, "Well, I don't have anyone to send over there with you." We were one or two people short of a crew or the trucks weren't available. Or they would send me people who weren't trained. And it got to the point where it was like, why do I have to fight about this? If you don't want your freight, you don't get your freight. And, I swear it was like from one day to the next of me transitioning [to male]. I need this, this is what I want and [snaps his fingers]. I have not had to fight about anything.

He adds about his experience, "The last three [per-formance] reviews that I have had have been the absolute highest that I have ever had. New manage-ment team. Me not doing anything different than I ever had. I even went part-time." This comment shows that even though he openly transitioned and remained in the same job, he ultimately finds him-self rewarded for doing less work and having to fight less for getting what he needs to effectively do his job. In addition, as a man, he received more positive reviews for his work, demonstrating how men and women can be evaluated differently when doing the same work.

As with authority and competence, this sense of gaining recognition for hard work was particularly noticeable for transmen who had worked as women in blue-collar occupations in which they were the gender minority. This finding is not unexpected, as women are also more likely to be judged negatively when they are in the minority in the workplace, as their statistical minority status seems to suggest that women are unsuited for the job (Valian 1999). For example, Preston, who had spent time in the ROTC as a female cadet, reported feeling that no matter how hard she worked, her achievements were passed over by her men superiors: "On everything that I did, I was the highest. I was the highest-ranking female during the time I was there. . . . I was the most decorated person in ROTC. I had more ribbons. I had more medals, in ROTC and in school. I didn't get anything for that. There was an award every year called Superior Cadet, and guys got it during the time I was there who didn't do nearly what I did. It was those kinds of things [that got to me]." She entered a blue-collar occupation after ROTC and also felt that her workplace contributions, like designing training programs for the staff, were invisible and went unrewarded.

Talking about gender discrimination he faced as a female construction worker, Crispin reports,

I worked really hard. . . . I had to find myself not sitting ever and taking breaks or lunches because I felt like I had to work more to show my worth. And though I did do that and I produced typically more than three males put together—and that is really a statistic—what it would come down to a lot of times was, "You're single. You don't have a family." That is what they told me. "I've got guys here who have families." . . . And even though my production quality [was high], and the customer was extremely happy with my work . . . I was passed over lots of times. They said it was because I was single and I didn't have a family and they felt bad because they didn't want Joe Blow to lose his job because he had three kids at home. And because I was intelligent and my qualities were very vast, they said, "You can just go get a job anywhere." Which wasn't always the case. A lot of people were—it was still a boy's world and some people were just like, uh-uh,

there aren't going to be any women on my job site. And it would be months . . . before I would find gainful employment again.

While she reports eventually winning over many men who did not want women on the worksite, being female excluded her from workplace social interactions, such as camping trips, designed to strengthen male bonding.

These quotes illustrate the hardships that women working in blue-collar jobs often face at work: being passed over for hiring and promotions in favor of less productive male coworkers, having their hard work go unrecognized, and not being completely accepted.[6] Having this experience of being women in an occupation or industry composed mostly of men can create, then, a heightened appreciation of gaining reward and recognition for job performance as men.

Another form of reward that some transmen report receiving posttransition is a type of bodily respect in the form of being freed from unwanted sexual advances or inquiries about sexuality. As Brian recounts about his experience of working as a waitress, that customer service involved "having my boobs grabbed, being called 'honey' and 'babe.'" He noted that as a man, he no longer has to worry about these types of experiences. Jason reported being constantly harassed by men bosses for sexual favors in the past. He added, "When I transitioned . . . it was like a relief! [laughs] . . . I swear to God! I am not saying I was beautiful or sexy but I was always attracting something." He felt that becoming a man meant more personal space and less sexual harassment. Finally, Stephen and Henry reported being "obvious dykes," here meaning visibly masculine women, and added that in blue-collar jobs, they encountered sexualized comments, as well as invasive personal questions about sexuality, from men uncomfortable with their gender presentation, experiences they no longer face posttransition. Transitioning for stealth FTMs can bring with it physical autonomy and respect, as men workers, in general, encounter less touching, groping, and sexualized comments at work than women. Open FTMs, however, are not as able to access this type of privilege, as coworkers often ask invasive questions about their genitals and sexual practices.

Economic Gains

As the last two sections have shown, FTMs can find themselves gaining in authority, respect, and reward in the workplace posttransition. Several FTMs who are stealth also reported a sense that transition had brought with it economic opportunities that would not have been available to them as women, particularly as masculine women.

Carl, who owns his own company, asserts that he could not have followed the same career trajectory if he had not transitioned:

I have this company that I built, and I have people following me; they trust me, they believe in me, they respect me. There is no way I could have done that as a woman. And I will tell you that as just a fact. That when it comes to business and work, higher levels of management, it is different being a man. I have been on both sides [as a man and a woman], younger obviously, but I will tell you, man, I could have never done what I did [as a female]. You can take the same personality and it wouldn't have happened. I would have never made it.

While he acknowledges that women can be and are business entrepreneurs, he has a sense that his business partners would not have taken his business venture idea seriously if he were a woman or that he might not have had access to the type of social networks that made his business venture possible. Henry feels that he would not have reached the same level in his professional job if he were a woman because he had a nonnormative gender appearance:

If I was a gender normative woman, probably. But no, as an obvious dyke, I don't think so . . . which is weird to say but I think it's true. It is interesting because I am really aware of having this job that I would not have had if I hadn't transitioned. And [gender expression] was always an issue for me. I wanted to go to law school but I couldn't do it. I couldn't wear the skirts and things females have to wear to practice law. I wouldn't dress in that drag. And so it was very clear that there was a limit to where I was going to go professionally because I was not willing to dress that part. Now I can dress the part and it's not an issue. It's not putting on drag; it's not an issue. I don't love putting on a tie, but I can do it. So this world is open to me that would not have been before just because of clothes. But very little has changed in some ways. I look very

different but I still have all the same skills and all the same general thought processes. That is intense for me to consider.

As this response shows, Henry is aware that as an "obvious dyke," meaning here a masculine-appearing woman, he would have the same skills and education level he currently has, but those skills would be devalued due to his nonnormative appearance. Thus, he avoided professional careers that would require a traditionally feminine appearance. As a man, however, he is able to wear clothes similar to those he wore as an "obvious dyke," but they are now considered gender appropriate. Thus, through transitioning, he gains the right to wear men's clothes, which helps him in accessing a professional job.

Wayne also recounts negative workplace experiences in the years prior to his transition due to being extremely ambiguous or "gender blending" (Devor 1987) in his appearance. Working at a restaurant in his early teens, he had the following experience:

The woman who hired me said, "I will hire you only on the condition that you don't ever come in the front because you make the people uncomfortable." 'Cause we had to wear like these uniforms or something and when I would put the uniform on, she would say, "That makes you look like a guy." But she knew I was not a guy because of my name that she had on the application. She said, "You make the customers uncomfortable." And a couple of times it got really busy, and I would have to come in the front or whatever, and I remember one time she found out about it and she said, "I don't care how busy it gets, you don't get to come up front." She said I'd make people lose their appetite.

Once he began hormones and gained a social identity as a man, he found that his work and school experiences became much more positive. He went on to earn a doctoral degree and become a successful professional, an economic opportunity he did not think would be available had he remained highly gender ambiguous.

In my sample, the transmen who openly transitioned faced a different situation in terms of economic gains. While there is an "urban legend" that FTMs immediately are awarded some kind of "male privilege" posttransition (Dozier 2005), I did not find that in my interviews. Reflecting this common belief, however, Trevor and Jake both recount that women colleagues told them, when learning of their transition plans, that they would probably be promoted because they were becoming white men. While both men discounted these comments, both were promoted relatively soon after their transitions. Rather than seeing this as evidence of male privilege, both respondents felt that their promotions were related to their job performance, which, to make clear, is not a point I am questioning. Yet these promotions show that while these two men are not benefiting undeservedly from transition, they also are not disadvantaged. Thus, among the men I interviewed, it is common for both stealth and open FTMs to find their abilities and skills more valued posttransition, showing that human capital can be valued differently depending on the gender of the employee.

Is It Privilege or Something Else?

While these reported increases in competency and authority make visible the "gender schemas" (Valian 1999) that often underlie the evaluation of workers, it is possible that the increases in authority might have a spurious connection to gender transitions. Some transmen enter a different work field after transition, so the observed change might be in the type of occupation they enter rather than a gender-based change. In addition, many transmen seek graduate or postgraduate degrees posttransition, and higher education degrees afford more authority in the workplace. As Table 44.2 shows, of the transmen I interviewed, many had higher degrees working as men than they did when they worked as women. For some, this is due to transitioning while in college and thus attaining their bachelor's degrees as men. For others, gender transitions seem to be accompanied by a desire to return to school for a higher degree, as evidenced by the increase in master's degrees in the table.

A change in educational attainment does contribute to getting better jobs with increased authority, as men benefit more from increased human capital in the form of educational attainment (Valian 1999). But again, this is an additive effect, as higher education results in greater advantages for men than for women. In addition, gender advantage alone also is apparent in these experiences of increased authority, as transmen report seeing an increase in others' perceptions of their competency outside of the workplace where their education level is unknown. For example, Henry, who found he was "right a lot more" at work, also notes that in daily, nonworkplace interactions, he is assumed, as a man, to know what he is talking about and does not have to provide evidence to support his opinions. Demonstrating a similar experience, Crispin, who had many years of experience working in construction as a woman, relates the following story:

Table 44.2   Highest Level of Education Attained

	Stealth FTMs		Open FTMs	
Highest Degree Level	*As Female*	*As Male*	*As Female*	*As Male*
High school/GED	7	2	3	2
Associate's degree	2	3	3	3
Bachelor's degree	2	4	7	5
Master's degree	0	1	2	4
Ph.D.	0	1	1	2
J.D.	0	0	1	2
Other	0	0	1	1
Total	11	11	18	18

NOTE: FTMs = female-to-male transsexuals.

I used to jump into [situations as a woman]. Like at Home Depot, I would hear . . . [men] be so confused, and I would just step over there and say, "Sir, I work in construction and if you don't mind me helping you." And they would be like, "Yeah, yeah, yeah" [i.e., dismissive]. But now I go [as a man] and I've got men and women asking me things and saying, "Thank you so much," like now I have a brain in my head! And I like that a lot because it was just kind of like, "Yeah, whatever." It's really nice.

His experience at Home Depot shows that as a man, he is rewarded for displaying the same knowledge about construction—knowledge gendered as masculine—that he was sanctioned for offering when he was perceived as a woman. As a further example of this increased authority outside of the workplace, several FTMs report a difference in their treatment at the auto shop, as they are not assumed to be easy targets for unnecessary services (though this comes with an added expectation that they will know a great deal about cars). While some transmen report that their "feminine knowledge," such as how to size baby clothes in stores, is discounted when they gain social identities as men, this new recognition of "masculine knowledge" seems to command more social authority than prior feminine knowledge in many cases. These stories show that some transmen gain authority both in and out of the workplace. These findings lend credence to the argument that men can gain a gender advantage, in the form of authority, reward, and respect.

BARRIERS TO WORKPLACE GENDER ADVANTAGES

Having examined the accounts of transmen who feel that they received increased authority, reward, and recognition from becoming men at work, I will now discuss some of the limitations to accessing workplace gender advantages. About one-third of my sample felt that they did not receive any gender advantage from transition. FTMs who had only recently begun transition or who had transitioned without using hormones ("no ho") all reported seeing little change in their workplace treatment. This group of respondents felt that they were still seen as women by most of their coworkers, evidenced

by continual slippage into feminine pronouns, and thus were not treated in accordance with other men in the workplace. Other transmen in this group felt they lacked authority because they were young or looked extremely young after transition. This youthful appearance often is an effect of the beginning stages of transition. FTMs usually begin to pass as men before they start taking testosterone. Successful passing is done via appearance cues, such as hairstyles, clothes, and mannerisms. However, without facial hair or visible stubble, FTMs often are taken to be young boys, a mistake that intensifies with the onset of hormone therapy and the development of peach fuzz that marks the beginning of facial hair growth. Reflecting on how this youthful appearance, which can last several years depending on the effects of hormone therapy, affected his work experience immediately after transition, Thomas reports, "I went from looking 30 to looking 13. People thought I was a new lawyer so I would get treated like I didn't know what was going on." Other FTMs recount being asked if they were interns, or if they were visiting a parent at their workplace, all comments that underscore a lack of authority. This lack of authority associated with looking youthful, however, is a time-bounded effect, as most FTMs on homones eventually "age into" their male appearance, suggesting that many of these transmen may have the ability to access some gender advantages at some point in their careers.

Body structure was another characteristic some FTMs felt limited their access to increased authority and prestige at work. While testosterone creates an appearance indistinguishable from bio men for many transmen, it does not increase height. Being more than 6 feet tall is part of the cultural construction for successful, hegemonic masculinity. However, several men I interviewed were between 5' 1" and 5' 5," something they felt put them at a disadvantage in relation to other men in their workplaces. Winston, who managed a professional work staff who knew him only as a man, felt that his authority was harder to establish at work because he was short. Being smaller than all of his male employees meant that he was always being looked down on, even when giving orders. Kelly, who worked in special education, felt his height affected the jobs he was assigned:

"Some of the boys, especially if they are really aggressive, they do much better with males that are bigger than they are. So I work with the little kids because I am short. I don't get as good of results if I work with [older kids]; a lot of times they are taller than I am." Being a short man, he felt it was harder to establish authority with older boys. These experiences demonstrate the importance of bringing the body back into discussions of masculinity and gender advantage, as being short can constrain men's benefits from the "patriarchal dividend" (Connell 1995).

In addition to height, race/ethnicity can negatively affect FTMs' workplace experiences posttransition. My data suggest that the experience of FTMs of color is markedly different than that of their white counterparts, as they are becoming not just men but Black men, Latino men, or Asian men, categories that carry their own stereotypes. Christopher felt that he was denied any gender advantage at work not only because he was shorter than all of his men colleagues but also because he was viewed as passive, a stereotype of Asian men (Espiritu 1997). "To the wide world of America, I look like a passive Asian guy. That is what they think when they see me. Oh Asian? Oh passive. . . . People have this impression that Asian guys aren't macho and therefore they aren't really male. Or they are not as male as [a white guy]." Keith articulated how his social interactions changed with his change in gender attribution in this way: "I went from being an obnoxious Black woman to a scary Black man." He felt that he has to be careful expressing anger and frustration at work (and outside of work) because now that he is a Black man, his anger is viewed as more threatening by whites. Reflecting stereotypes that conflate African Americans with criminals, he also notes that in his law enforcement classes, he was continually asked to play the suspect in training exercises. Aaron, one of the only racial minorities at his workplace, also felt that looking like a Black man negatively affected his workplace interactions. He told stories about supervisors repeatedly telling him he was threatening. When he expressed frustration during a staff meeting about a new policy, he was written up for rolling his eyes in an "aggressive" manner. The choice of words such as "threatening" and "aggressive," words often used to describe Black

men (Ferguson 2000), suggests that racial identity and stereotypes about Black men were playing a role in his workplace treatment. Examining how race/ethnicity and appearance intersect with gender, then, illustrates that masculinity is not a fixed construct that automatically generated privilege (Connell 1995), but that white, tall men often see greater returns from the patriarchal dividend than short men, young men and men of color.

CONCLUSION

Sociological studies have documented that the workplace is not a gender-neutral site that equitably rewards workers based on their individual merits (Acker 1990; Marlin 2003; Valian 1999; Williams 1995); rather "it is a central site for the creation and reproduction of gender differences and gender inequality" (Williams 1995, 15). Men receive greater workplace advantages than women because of cultural beliefs that associate masculinity with authority, prestige, and instrumentality (Martin 2003; Padavic and Reskin 2002; Rhode 1997; Williams 1995)—characteristics often used to describe ideal "leaders" and "managers" (Valian 1999). Stereotypes about femininity as expressive and emotional, on the other hand, disadvantage women, as they are assumed to be less capable and less likely to succeed than men with equal (or often lesser) qualifications (Valian 1999). These cultural beliefs about gender difference are embedded in workplace structures and interactions, as workers and employers bring gender stereotypes with them to the workplace and, in turn, use these stereotypes to make decisions about hiring, promotions, and rewards (Acker 1990; Martin 2003; Williams 1995). This cultural reproduction of gendered workplace disparities is difficult to disrupt, however, as it operates on the level of ideology and thus is rendered invisible (Martin 2003; Valian 1999; Williams 1995).

In this article, I have suggested that the "outsider-within" (Collins 1986) perspective of many FTMs can offer a more complex understanding of these invisible interactional processes that help maintain gendered workplace disparities. Transmen are in the unique position of having been socially gendered as both women and men (Dozier 2005). Their workplace experiences, then, can make the underpinnings of gender discrimination visible, as well as illuminate the sources of men's workplace advantages. When FTMs undergo a change in gender attribution, their workplace treatment often varies greatly—even when they continue to interact with coworkers who knew them previously as women. Some posttransition FTMs, both stealth and open, find that their coworkers, employers, and customers attribute more authority, respect, and prestige to them. Their experiences make glaringly visible the process through which gender inequality is actively created in informal workplace interactions. These informal workplace interactions, in turn, produce and reproduce structural disadvantages for women, such as the glass ceiling (Valian 1999), and structural advantages for men, such as the glass escalator (Williams 1995).

However, as I have suggested, not all of my respondents gain authority and prestige with transition. FTMs who are white and tall received far more benefits posttransition than short FTMs or FTMs of color. This demonstrates that while hegemonic masculinity is defined against femininity, it is also measured against subordinated forms of masculinity (Connell 1995; Messner 1997). These findings demonstrate the need for using an intersectional approach that takes into consideration the ways in which there are crosscutting relations of power (Calasanti and Slevin 2001; Collins 1990; Crenshaw 1989), as advantage in the workplace is not equally accessible for all men. Further research on FTMs of color can help develop a clearer understanding of the role race plays in the distribution of gendered workplace rewards and advantages.[8]

The experiences of this small group of transmen offer a challenge to rationalizations of workplace inequality. The study provides counterevidence for human capital theories: FTMs who find themselves receiving the benefits associated with being men at work have the same skills and abilities they had as women workers. These skills and abilities, however, are suddenly viewed more positively due to this change in gender attribution. FTMs who may have been labeled "bossy" as women become "go-getting" men who seem more qualified for managerial positions. While FTMs may not benefit at equal levels to bio men, many of them do find themselves receiving an advantage to women in the workplace they did not have prior

to transition. This study also challenges gender socialization theories that account for inequality in the workplace. Although all of my respondents were subjected to gender socialization as girls, this background did not impede their success as men. Instead, by undergoing a change in gender attribution, transmen can find that the same behavior, attitudes, or abilities they had as females bring them more reward as men. This shift in treatment suggests that gender inequality in the workplace is not continually reproduced only because women make different education and workplace choices than men but rather because coworkers and employers often rely on gender stereotypes to evaluate men and women's achievements and skills.

It could be argued that because FTMs must overcome so many barriers and obstacles to finally gain a male social identity, they might be likely to overreport positive experiences as a way to shore up their right to be a man. However, I have reasons to doubt that my respondents exaggerated the benefits of being men. Transmen who did find themselves receiving a workplace advantage posttransition were aware that this new conceptualization of their skills and abilities was an arbitrary result of a shift in their gender attribution. This knowledge often undermined their sense of themselves as good workers, making them continually second-guess the motivations behind any rewards they receive. In addition, many transmen I interviewed expressed anger and resentment that their increases in authority, respect, and recognition came at the expense of women colleagues. It is important to keep in mind, then, that while many FTMs can identify privileges associated with being men, they often retain a critical eye to how changes in their treatment as men can disadvantage women.

This critical eye, or "outsider-within" (Collins 1986) perspective, has implications for social change in the workplace. For gender equity at work to be achieved, men must take an active role in challenging the subordination of women (Acker 1990; Martin 2003; Rhode 1997; Valian 1999; Williams 1995). However, bio men often cannot see how women are disadvantaged due to their structural privilege (Rhode 1997; Valian 1999). Even when they are aware that men as a group benefit from assumptions about masculinity, men typically still "credit their successes to their competence" (Valian

1999, 284) rather than to gender stereotypes. For many transmen, seeing how they stand to benefit at work to the detriment of women workers creates a sense of increased responsibility to challenge the gender discrimination they can see so clearly. This challenge can take many different forms. For some, it is speaking out when men make derogatory comments about women. For others, it means speaking out about gender discrimination at work or challenging supervisors to promote women who are equally qualified as men. These challenges demonstrate that some transmen are able, at times, to translate their position as social insiders into an educational role, thus working to give women more reward and recognition at these specific work sites. The success of these strategies illustrates that men have the power to challenge workplace gender discrimination and suggests that bio men can learn gender equity strategies from the outsider-within at work.

Notes

1. Throughout this article, I endeavor to use the terms "women" and "men" rather than "male" and "female" to avoid reifying biological categories. It is important to note, though, that while my respondents were all born with female bodies, many of them never identified as women but rather thought of themselves as always men, or as "not women." During their time as female workers, however, they did have social identities as women, as coworkers and employers often were unaware of their personal gender identities. It is this social identity that I am referencing when I refer to them as "working as women" as I am discussing their social interactions in the workplace. In referring to their specific work experiences, however, I use "female" to demonstrate their understanding of their work history. I also do continue to use "female to male" when describing the physical transition process, as this is the most common term employed in the transgender community.

2. I use "stealth," a transgender community term, if the respondent's previous life as female was not known at work. It is important to note that this term is not analogous with "being in the closet," because stealth female-to-male transsexuals (FTMs) do not have "secret" lives as women outside of working as men. It is used to describe two different workplace choices, not offer a value judgment about these choices.

3. "Bio" man is a term used by my respondents to mean individuals who are biologically male and live

socially as men throughout their lives. It is juxtaposed with "transman" or "FTM."

4. A note on pronoun usage: This article draws from my respondents' experiences working as both women and men. While they now live as men, I use feminine pronouns to refer to their female work histories.

5. This change in how behavior is evaluated can also be negative. Some transmen felt that assertive communication styles they actively fostered to empower themselves as lesbians and feminists had to be unlearned after transition. Because they were suddenly given more space to speak as men, they felt they had to censor themselves or they would be seen as "bossy white men" who talked over women and people of color. These findings are similar to those reported by Dozier (2005).

6. It is important to note that not all FTMs who worked blue-collar jobs as women had this type of experience. One respondent felt that he was able to fit in, as a butch, as "just one of the guys." However, he also did not feel he had an outsider-within perspective because of this experience.

7. Open transitions are not without problems, however. Crispin, a construction worker, found his contract mysteriously not renewed after his announcement. However, he acknowledged that he had many problems with his employers prior to his announcement and had also recently filed a discrimination suit. Aaron, who announced his transition at a small, medical site, left after a few months as he felt that his employer was trying to force him out. He found another job in which he was out as a transman. Crispin unsuccessfully attempted to find work in construction as an out transman. He was later hired, stealth, at a construction job.

8. Sexual identity also is an important aspect of an intersectional analysis. In my study, however, queer and gay transmen worked either in lesbian, gay, bisexual, transgender work sites, or were not out at work. Therefore, it was not possible to examine how being gay or queer affected their workplace experiences.

References

Acker, Joan. 1990. Hierarchies, jobs, bodies: A theory of gendered organizations. *Gender & Society* 4:139–58.

Butler, D., and F. L. Geis. 1990. Nonverbal affect responses to male and female leaders: Implications for leadership evaluation. *Journal of Personality and Social Psychology* 58:48–59.

Byrd, Barbara. 1999. Women in carpentry apprenticeship: A case study. *Labor Studies Journal* 24(3):3–22.

Calasanti, Toni M., and Kathleen F. Slevin. 2001. *Gender, social inequalities, and aging.* Walnut Creek, CA: Alta Mira Press.

Collins, Patricia Hill. 1986. Learning from the outsider within: The sociological significance of Black feminist thought. *Social Problems* 33(6): S14–S31.

———. 1990. *Black feminist thought.* New York: Routledge.

Connell, Robert. 1995. *Masculinities.* Berkeley: University of California Press.

Crenshaw, Kimberle. 1989. Demarginalizing the intersection of race and sex: A Black feminist critique of antidiscrimination doctrine, feminist theory, and antiracist politics. *University of Chicago Legal Forum* 1989:139–67.

Devor, Holly. 1987. Gender blending females: Women and sometimes men. *American Behavioral Scientist* 31(1):12–40.

Dozier, Raine. 2005. Beards, breasts, and bodies: Doing sex in a gendered world. *Gender & Society* 19:297–316.

Elliott, James R., and Ryan A. Smith. 2004. Race, gender, and workplace power. *American Sociological Review* 69:365–86.

Espiritu, Yen. 1997. *Asian American women and men.* Thousand Oaks, CA: Sage.

Ferguson, Ann Arnett. 2000. *Bad boys: Public schools in the making of Black masculinity.* Ann Arbor: University of Michigan Press.

Leidner, Robin. 1993. Fast food, fast talk: Service work and the routinization of everyday life. Berkeley: University of California Press.

Martin, Patricia Yancy. 1992. Gender, interaction, and inequality in organizations. In *Gender, interaction, and inequality,* edited by Cecelia L. Ridgeway. New York: Springer-Verlag.

———. 2003. "Said and done" versus "saying and doing": Gendering practices, practicing gender at work. *Gender & Society* 17:342–66.

Martin, Susan. 1994. "Outsiders-within" the station house: The impact of race and gender on Black women police officers. *Social Problems* 41:383–400.

Merton, Robert. 1972. Insiders and outsiders: A chapter in the sociology of knowledge. *American Journal of Sociology* 78(1):9–47.

Messner, Michael. 1997. *The politics of masculinities: Men in movements.* Thousand Oaks, CA: Sage.

Miller, Laura. 1997. Not just weapons of the weak: Gender harassment as a form of protest for army men. *Social Psychology Quarterly* 60(1):32–51.

Olian, J. D., D. P. Schwab, and Y. Haberfeld. 1988. The impact of applicant gender compared to qualifications on hiring recommendations: A meta-analysis of experimental studies. *Organizational Behavior and Human Decision Processes* 41:180–95.

Padavic, Irene, and Barbara Reskin. 2002. *Women and men at work.* 2d ed. Thousand Oaks, CA: Pine Forge Press.

Pierce, Jennifer. 1995. *Gender trials: Emotional lives in contemporary law firms.* Berkeley: University of California Press.

Reskin, Barbara, and Heidi Hartmann. 1986. *Women's work, men's work: Sex segregation on the job.* Washington, DC: National Academic Press.

Reskin, Barbara, and Patricia Roos. 1990. *Job queues, gender queues.* Philadelphia: Temple University Press.

Rhode, Deborah L. 1997. *Speaking of sex: The denial of gender inequality.* Cambridge, MA: Harvard University Press.

Rubin, Henry. 2003. *Self-made men: Identity and embodiment among transsexual men.* Nashville, TN: Vanderbilt University Press.

Valian, Virginia. 1999. *Why so slow? The advancement of women.* Cambridge, MA: MIT Press.

West, Candace, and Don Zimmerman. 1987. Doing gender. *Gender & Society* 1:13–37.

Williams, Christine. 1995. *Still a man's world: Men who do "women's" work.* Berkeley: University of California Press.

Yoder, Janice, and Patricia Aniakudo. 1997. Outsider within the firehouse: Subordination and difference in the social interactions of African American women firefighters. *Gender & Society* 11:324–41.

SOURCE: Schilt, Kristen. 2006. "Just One of the Guys: How Transmen Make Gender Visible at Work." *Gender & Society,* 20(4):465–90.

THE EMPEROR HAS NO CLOTHES

Rewriting "Race in Organizations"

STELLA M. NKOMO

"Now, is not that magnificent?" said both the worthy officials. "Will your Majesty deign to note the beauty of the patterns and the colors?" And they pointed to the bare loom for they supposed that all the rest could certainly see the stuff. "What's the meaning of this?" thought the Emperor. "I can't see a thing! This is terrible! Am I stupid? Am I not fit to be Emperor? That would be the most frightful thing that could befall me." "Oh, it's very pretty, it has my all highest-approval!" said he, nodding complacently and gazing on the empty loom: of course, he wouldn't say he could see nothing. The whole of the suite he had with him looked and looked, but got no more out of that than the rest. However, they said, as the Emperor said: "Oh, it's very pretty!" And they advised him to put on this splendid new stuff for the first time, on the occasion of a great procession which was to take place shortly . . .

So the Emperor walked in the procession under the beautiful canopy, and everybody in the streets and at the windows said: "Lord! How splendid the Emperor's new clothes are. What a lovely train he has to his coat! What a beautiful fit it is!" Nobody wanted to be detected seeing nothing: that would mean that he was no good at his job, or that he was very stupid.

"But he hasn't got anything on!" said a little child. . . . "Why he hasn't got anything on!" The whole crowd was shouting at last; and the Emperor's flesh crept, for it seemed to him they were right. "But all the same,"

he thought to himself, "I must go through with the procession." So he held himself more proudly than before, and the lords in waiting walked on bearing the train—the train that wasn't there at all. (Excerpt from "The Emperor's New Clothes," by Hans Christian Andersen, 1968: 104–107)

The children's fairy tale, "The Emperor's New Clothes," is an excellent allegory for the primary way in which organization scholars have chosen to address race in organizations. For the most part, research has tended to study organization populations as homogeneous entities in which distinctions of race and ethnicity are either "unstated" or considered irrelevant. A perusal of much of our research would lead one to believe that organizations are race neutral (Cox & Nkomo, 1990).

Although the emperor, his court suitors, and his tailors recognize that he is naked, no one will explicitly acknowledge that nakedness. Even as the innocent child proclaims his nakedness, the emperor and his suitors resolutely continue with the procession. Similarly, the silencing of the importance of race in organizations is mostly subterfuge because of the overwhelming role of race and ethnicity in every aspect of society.

Race in the United States has been a profound determinant of one's political rights, one's location in the labor market, one's access to medical care, and even one's sense of identity (Omi & Winant, 1986). Its immediacy is manifested in everyday life experiences and social interactions (Blauner, 1989; Essed, 1991; van Dijk, 1987). Most important, race is one of the major bases of domination in our society and a major means through which the division of labor occurs in organizations (Reich, 1981). As I will argue later, race has been present all along in organizations, even if silenced or suppressed.

One might ask, why use a European fairy tale to call attention to the exclusion of race in the study of organizations? I have purposefully used a Eurocentric parable to signify this problem through parody, in the African-American tradition of what Gates (1988: 82) has called "black signifyin(g)"— the figurative difference between the literal and the metaphorical, between surface and latent meaning. In this article, the emperor is not simply an emperor but the embodiment of the concept of Western knowledge as both universal and superior and white males as the defining group for studying organizations. The court suitors are the organizational scholars who continue the traditions of ignoring race and ethnicity in their research and excluding other voices. All have a vested interest in continuing the procession and not calling attention to the omissions.

Who then is most likely to call attention to these omissions? As has been the case in other disciplines, it is most likely to be the *other,* the excluded, who is assumed to be childlike and inferior. Even as these *other* voices point to the omissions and errors and the need for inclusiveness, the dominant group refuses to hear the message and continues with the procession. The real issue for the *others* is getting truly heard, rather than simply "added on." As noted by Minnich (1990), it is difficult to add new knowledge to anything that has been defined as the whole. The challenge must strike directly at the center of the kingdom and its attendant theoretical foundations.

The purpose of this article then is to analyze how race has been written into the study of organizations in incomplete and inadequate ways. It demonstrates how our approaches to the study of race reflect particular historical and social meanings of race, specifically a racial ideology embedded in a Eurocentric view of the world. This view is evident first in the general exclusion of race when organizational theories are developed and, second, in the theoretical and methodological orientation of the limited body of research on race. Finally, suggestions are made for ways of making race a necessary and productive analytical category for theorizing about organizations. Perspectives are drawn from several disciplines including African-American studies and race and ethnic relations. The intent is not to provide a specific theory of race but to suggest ways of "re-visioning" the study of race in organizations.

ON THE EXCLUSION OF RACE IN THE STUDY OF ORGANIZATIONS

Why do we as organizational scholars continue to conceptualize organizations as race neutral? Why has race been silenced in the study of organizations? One way of explaining this exclusion is to examine what Minnich (1990) has called intellectual errors in the production of knowledge. The root error might be labeled faulty generalization or noninclusive universalization. This error occurs when we take a dominant few (white males) as the inclusive group, the norm, and the ideal of humankind (Minnich, 1990). The defining group for specifying the science of organizations has been white males. Only recently have we begun to study the experiences of women in management, and even this body of literature focuses mainly on white women (Nkomo, 1988). We have amassed a great deal of knowledge about the experience of only one group, yet we generalize our theories and concepts to all groups. We do not acknowledge that these universal theories emanate from an inadequate sample and, therefore, there is the possibility that the range of a theory or construct is limited (Cox & Nkomo, 1990).

According to Minnich (1990), faulty generalization leads to a kind of hierarchically invidious monism. Not only are dominant group members the defining group, but they are taken to be the highest category—the best—and all other groups must be defined and judged solely with reference to that hegemonic category (Keto, 1989). Other racial and ethnic groups are relegated to subcategories; their experiences are seen as outside of the mainstream of developing knowledge of organizations.

This point can be illustrated by examining the use of prefixes in the description of research samples in our work. The prefix "white" is usually suppressed, and it is only other racial groups to which we attach prefixes (Minnich, 1990). "Race" becomes synonymous with *other* groups, and whites do not have "race." A study based on a sample of white male managers is unlikely to state that the results may be valid only for that group. More likely than not the term *manager* will be used. The problem is the usurpation of the category *manager* by the dominant group and the lack of awareness that white managers also have race.

Concomitantly, a study that has a minority group sample will rarely be accepted for developing and generalizing organization theory. The results of the study would be viewed as valid only for that group with minimal or little relevance for organization knowledge. Thus, instead of race being an analytical category critical to the fundamental understanding of organizations, it is marginalized. Unless the study is explicitly about race (e.g., affirmative action or bias in performance ratings) or has a minority-group sample, it is not included as an important variable, even when contextual factors may indicate otherwise.

The faulty generalization error stems mainly from bias in science. The practices of science reflect the values and concerns of dominant societal groups (Harding, 1986). The concepts and approaches used in Western academia help to maintain the political and intellectual superiority of Western cultures and people (Joseph, Reddy, & Searle-Chatterjee, 1990). Kuhn (1962) argued that problem selection and the search for explanations by scholars are influenced by the social and political conditions of the times. To the extent that white males have dominated the production of knowledge, their values and concerns are predominant. The study of race is an especially sensitive issue because scholars must not only be aware of how prevailing societal race relations influence their approach to the study of race but they must also understand the effects of their own racial identity and experiences on their work (Alderfer, 1982).

The tendency toward faulty generalization is further explained by the adherence to the assumption, embedded in Western philosophy from Socrates to the Enlightenment, that there is one ultimate objective truth and the scholar's mission is to search for that truth. This truth cannot come from *other* non-Western views of knowledge (Keto, 1989). Hence, there is a relationship between the desire for universal theories and the suppression of the experience of *others*. Researchers who ignore the influence of race in understanding organizations may reflect a veiled hope that, indeed, management theories and constructs are universal. Once there is acceptance of the idea that the major theories and concepts of the field of management do not address all groups, the holding of and search for universal theories is undermined.

It is illusory to think that other views are socially located while one's own are not. We cannot avoid the implicit influence of the scholar's perspective and values in the theories we develop (Morgan, 1983). The research questions that are asked and not asked and the chosen methodology of research on race in organizations parallel the dominant theoretical, political, and social meanings of race.

THEORETICAL AND IDEOLOGICAL FOUNDATIONS OF RESEARCH ON RACE

Before race can be re-visioned as an analytical category in the formulation of organization theory, a first step is to understand the historical and theoretical foundations of research on race and its influence on the ways in which we have studied race in organizations.

According to Omi and Winant (1986), the meaning, transformation, and significance of racial theories are shaped by actual existing race relations in any given historical period. Blanton (1987) added that within any given historical period, a particular racial theory is dominant, despite the existence of competing paradigms. The dominant racial theory provides society with a framework for understanding race relations and serves as a guide for research with implications for the kinds of questions scholars address. The dominant racial paradigm in the field of race and ethnic studies for the last half century has been that of ethnicity (Blanton, 1987; Omi & Winant, 1986; Thompson, 1989).

The Ethnicity Paradigm

The basic premises and assumptions of this paradigm are reflected in much of the research and writing in the management literature. Ethnicity-based theory emerged in the 1920s as a challenge to biological and social Darwinian conceptions of race (Blanton, 1987). Sociological concepts primarily replaced biological ones, and racial and ethnic forms of identification and social organizations were viewed as "unnatural" (Thompson, 1989). Becoming predominant by World War II, the ethnic paradigm has shaped academic research about race and guided policy formation (Omi & Winant, 1986). Despite serious challenges from alternative paradigms during the 1970s and 1980s, the rise of neoconservatism in the United States has led to a resurgence of ethnicity theory in a new guise, which has been labeled the *new ethnicity* (Omi & Winant, 1986; Steinberg, 1981; Thompson, 1989).

Ethnicity theorists' main empirical reference point was the study of immigration and the social patterns and experiences of European immigrants (Omi & Winant, 1986). Dominated by two recurrent oppositional themes, assimilation versus cultural pluralism, ethnicity theory was focused on the incorporation and separation of ethnic minorities, the nature of ethnic identity, and the impact of ethnicity on life experiences (Omi & Winant, 1986). One of the earliest explications of assimilationalism appeared in Park's 1939 essay, "The Nature of Race Relations" (Park, 1950/1939). Park focused on the problem of European migration and what he called *culture contact*. Park's famous race *relations cycle* became the basis for further development of assimilation theory (e.g., Gordon, 1964). Park argued that this cycle "which takes the form of contacts, competition, accommodation and eventual assimilation, is apparently progressive and irreversible" (Park, 1950/1939: 150). Despite Park's (1950/1939) acknowledgment that it was possible that a particular stage might be prolonged, assimilation was viewed as the most logical and natural antidote for racism and ethnocentricism. The widespread view of assimilation as a process

of interpenetration and fusion in which persons and groups acquire the mentality, sentiments, and attitudes of dominant groups led to the well-known *melting pot* concept (Omi & Winant, 1986). For example, much of the early research on management was developed during a period of widespread European immigration to the United States. The new immigrants, urban white workers, particularly the Irish and people from Eastern Europe, were often degraded as "children" and "savage" and as being more interested in seeking lower rather than higher pleasures (Takai, 1979: 127). These early factory workers were scolded for their idleness and their lack of punctuality and industry (Gutman, 1977: 20). The theme of assimilation pervaded efforts by industrial capitalists to teach these workers the requisite attitudinal and work ethic skills needed to perform industrial jobs.

Other early proponents of assimilation theory included Myrdal (1944) and Gordon (1964). Gunnar Myrdal's classic work, *The American Dilemma,* called into question the contradiction between continued discrimination against African-Americans and the democratic ideals of equality and justice espoused in U.S. society. Both Myrdal's and Gordon's works attempted to extend ethnicity theory, which has been largely derived from the experience of European immigrants, to the situation of African-Americans (Thompson, 1989). It was assumed that the experience of racial minorities could be theorized in much the same way as the experience of ethnic immigrants. Thus, race in the United States was largely reduced to a question of integration and assimilation of racial minorities into the mainstream of a consensus-based society (van den Berghe, 1967). Within the assimilation framework, legal remedies like the Civil Rights Act of 1964 were viewed as necessary for removing barriers so that racial minorities would encounter the same conditions as white ethnics (Omi & Winant, 1986; Thompson, 1989). However, preferential treatment remedies like affirmative action were not supported (Glazer, 1987; Gordon, 1964). Blauner (1972: 2) pointed out that research on racial minorities (i.e., African-Americans, Latinos, Asian Americans, and Native Americans) from the ethnicity perspective was premised on several assumptions: (a) racial groups were not viewed as central or persistent elements of society; (b) racism and racial oppression were ultimately reducible to other causal determinants—usually economic or psychological; and (c) there were no essential long-term differences between the experience of racial minorities and the European ethnic groups that immigrated to the United States.

Research on race emanating from the ethnic-based paradigm centered on questions of why racial minorities were not becoming incorporated or assimilated into mainstream society. Or directly stated, "What obstructs assimilation?" Much of this research was devoted to problems of prejudice and discrimination and grew out of social psychological approaches to the study of intergroup relations (Oudenhoven & Willemsen, 1989). It was based on the belief that relations between dominant group members and racial minorities resulted from prejudiced attitudes of individuals. For example, Merton (1949) argued that discrimination might be practiced by unprejudiced people who were afraid not to conform to the prejudices of others. Adorno, Frenkel-Brunswick, Levinson, and Sanford (1950: 8) studied the relationship between prejudice and personality. He argued that prejudiced persons differed from tolerant persons in central personality traits—specifically, that they exhibited authoritarian *personalities*. Allport (1954) suggested that there was a direct link between prejudiced people and discriminatory acts. Unlike Adorno et al. (1950), Allport (1954) did not view prejudice as an aberrant cognitive distortion. Allport argued that prejudice was a natural extension of normal cognitive processes (Pettigrew, 1979). Thus, prejudice and discrimination were mainly reduced to either an individual aberration or faulty generalization (Henriques, 1984). Adorno's and Allport's emphasis on prejudice as an attitude also found widespread acceptance because of its amenability to quantification and statistical measurement (Henriques, 1984).

This traditional stress on the expressive function of prejudice by individuals is still manifested in much of contemporary social psychology research on race (Oudenhoven & Willemsen, 1989). For example, dominant contemporary social psychology theories for explaining prejudice include social identity or social categorization theory, social attribution theory, and the contact hypothesis (Dovidio & Gaertner, 1986).

The phenomenological approach of social identity or social categorization theory postulates that an individual's identity depends to a large extent on social group memberships where individuals seek positive social identity (Tajfel, 1969, 1970; Tajfel & Turner, 1979, 1986). The evaluation of one's own group is determined with reference to specific other groups through social comparisons in terms of value-laden attributes and characteristics. This mechanism is basic to the evaluation of one's social identity. These comparisons involve perceptual accentuation of similarities of people belonging to the same group and differences between people belonging to a different social group or category (Tajfel, 1981). Accordingly, if categorization is in terms of a racial or an ethnic criterion, then it is likely that this process is responsible in part for the prejudices found in the judgment of people belonging to different groups. Tajfel (1981) stressed the influence of the social factors of status, power, and material interdependence in the categorization process.

Social attribution theory or intergroup attribution theory refers to "how members of different social groups explain the behavior and social condition of members of their own group (ingroup) and other social groups (outgroups)" (Hewstone, 1989: 25). In this case, research emphasis is placed on explaining the behavior of individuals who act as members or representatives of social groups. An important explanatory concept in this theory is the fundamental attribution error—the phenomenon that one tends to explain the behavior of others by internal factors rather than situational factors (Oudenhoven & Willemsen, 1989). The extreme manifestation of social attribution is what Pettigrew has called the ultimate attribution error—"a systematic patterning of intergroup misattributions shaped in part by prejudice" (Pettigrew, 1979: 464). On the one hand, when blacks or other minority group members behave in a manner perceived to be negative, majority group members, especially those who are prejudiced, are likely to attribute this behavior to the personal character of the group (Pettigrew, 1979). On the other hand, prejudiced majority group members can explain away behavior that is seen as positive by attributing it to (a) the exceptional, special-case individual who is contrasted with his or her group; (b) luck or special advantage, which is viewed as unfair; (c) high motivation and effort, which is ultimately unsustainable; or (d) a manipulated situational context (Pettigrew, 1979: 469). Therefore, the ingroup (majority group) can still hold negative assessments of the outgroup (minority group), despite contrary evidence.

Finally, a third social psychology theory used to explain prejudice is the contact hypothesis. This is best understood as a solution to intergroup conflict which posits that positive contacts between ingroups and outgroups will reduce prejudice (Wilder, 1986). The success of contact is contingent upon the favorability of the interaction, especially the ingroup's perception of the interaction. Proponents of this theory underscore the important role of structuring the situation to promote cooperation rather than competition (Pettigrew & Martin, 1987). A major assumption underlying the contact hypothesis is that frequent positive contact between groups will minimize the information-processing errors (e.g., stereotyping) by ingroup members.

Although social psychologists like Tajfel argued that the major contribution of their work was its focus on the group rather than on individuals, making it more social and progressive, a close reading reveals it also ultimately relies on individual cognitive processing to explain prejudice and discrimination (Henriques, 1984). The results of Tajfel's minimal intergroup laboratory experiments led him to conclude that the mere perception of belonging to two distinct groups (i.e., social categorization per se) is sufficient to trigger intergroup discrimination favoring the ingroup. In other words, ingroup bias is a natural feature of intergroup relations. Therefore, if groups have no real bases for conflict, then discrimination lies in failures in the mechanism of individual cognition (Henriques, 1984).

Additionally, the primary solution offered by these social psychological approaches—the contact hypothesis—falls within the assimilation approach through the assumption that the reduction of the salience of group boundaries will improve intergroup interaction (Oudenhoven & Willemsen, 1989).

The New Ethnicity

During the mid-1970s, the ethnic-based paradigm was reformulated (Thompson, 1989). The upheavals during the Civil Rights movement of the 1960s and the urban riots of the 1970s underscored the fact that for African-Americans assimilation into dominant society was less than forthcoming. The major failure of assimilationists to explain the lack of African-American assimilation spawned a new paradigm, which has been called the *new ethnicity* (Steinberg, 1981; Thompson, 1989; Yinger, 1986). The *new* in *new ethnicity* is not so much a significant shift in theory as an attempt by assimilationists to explain the enduring nature of racial stratification (Thompson, 1989). According to Thompson (1989: 91), this paradigm is based on two interrelated positions: (a) that ethnic and racial criteria have become major forms of group-based sociopolitical behavior because of the changing nature of industrial society and (b) that ethnic and racial groups ought to maintain their separate boundaries and seek their separate interests provided such interests recognize and respect the multitude of other, different ethnic interests (i.e., the cultural pluralism creed). The popular origins of the new ethnicity lie in the revival of the ethnic consciousness of white ethnics in response to the perceived preferential treatment of racial minority groups (Steinberg, 1981).

The theoretical dilemma that existed within the new ethnicity paradigm was how to explain the persistence of racial and ethnic stratification. Two different explanations have been offered. One explanation is that the persistence of racial and ethnic stratification reflects biological tendencies and that people, by nature, have a basic, primordial need for group identification. This explanation is grounded in sociobiology and primordialism. In his more recent work, entitled *Human Nature, Class and Ethnicity,* Gordon (1978), one of the major early proponents of assimilation theory, emphasized the importance of understanding human nature (i.e., biological predisposition) and its interaction with the social and cultural environment. Gordon (1978: 74) wrote, "Some observers, including myself, . . . have begun to wonder whether there are not biological constants or propensities in human behavior which fall short of the instinct category but which predispose the actor to certain kinds of behavior." In a similar vein, van den Berghe (1981: 80) theorized that ethnic and racial sentiments are extensions of kinship sentiments and, as such, express the sociobiological principle of inclusive fitness. In his analysis, van den Berghe (1981) argued that genetic predisposition for kin selection causes people to behave in racist and ethnocentric ways. Accordingly, racism and discrimination in society and culture were viewed as the sum of individually motivated behaviors that were rooted in genetic predisposition. **According to this essentialist explanation, racial and ethnic stratification are viewed as an almost permanent and inevitable part of human society.**

The alternate explanation rejects biological criteria and relies upon social psychological theories that attribute the failure of minority group assimilation to improper attitudes of majority group members or the lack of self-reliance on the part of minorities (Thompson, 1989). The common denominator for all of these explanations is that they stress some essential property of individuals.

Problems With the Ethnic Paradigm

There are several problems with the ethnic-based paradigm and its so-called new form for producing knowledge for understanding race in organizations. In this paradigm, the dualistic oppositional categories of assimilation versus pluralism are emphasized as the solution to questions of discrimination and racism (Glazer & Moynihan, 1970; Omi & Winant, 1986; Thompson, 1989).

Assimilationalism is basically individualistic in its ontology, and in this case, race is largely conceptualized as a problem of prejudiced attitudes or personal and cultural inadequacies of racial and ethnic groups (Thompson, 1989). The fact that certain groups have not been successfully assimilated is not due to the structure of U.S. society and institutions but to psychological or personality characteristics of both whites and minorities (Henriques, 1984; Thompson, 1989). Assimilation is conceptualized as a one-way process that requires non-European, non-English-speaking groups to change to fit the dominant culture (Feagin, 1987). Consequently, researchers have tended to focus on other groups as having race, and questions of "why aren't they like us, or how can they become like us?" dominate. Herein lies one of the major deficiencies in the very premise of the assimilation approach. Inequality is accepted as a natural feature of U.S. society or any other complex social structure and, therefore, inequality itself is a "nonissue" and not part of the analysis (Thompson, 1989: 85).

Assimilation represents an inadequate model for understanding racial hierarchy in organizations. Its best answer to why racial and ethnic minorities are underrepresented in higher level positions in organizations would lie in social psychological explanations, which emphasize cognitive causes of prejudice and discrimination. Sole emphasis on microlevel or individualistic remedies are unlikely to affect existing social and power relations in organizations. Billig (1985) noted that the emphasis placed upon explaining cognitive biases by social categorization theory and other cognitive theories winds up confirming the status quo in the sense that changing the cognitions of individuals is often viewed as less amenable to intervention. Users of the individual-focused social psychology approaches are silent on the sociohistorical dynamics of the capitalist system in creating and maintaining inequality in organizations. Such explanations detract from issues of power and domination in racial dynamics and reflect a failure to analyze both the historically specific experience of racial minorities in U.S. society and the influence that this history has had on their status in organizations (Foner & Lewis, 1982; Takai, 1979).

Furthermore, assimilation within the ethnic paradigm often leads to a "blame-the-victim" explanation of why certain groups have not been assimilated as successfully as other groups (Omi & Winant, 1986). According to Thompson (1989), one of the less explicit assumptions of the ethnic paradigm is the acceptance of the neoclassical view of the very nature of a capitalist economy. In this view, individual opportunity is widely available, and the kind of job one has is a function of choice and skill level. People who fail are seen as making bad choices or not exhibiting the appropriate character traits (Sowell, 1975). Minority group members who do not succeed have abnormal cultural patterns or other deficiencies.

The essentialist element of this argument often results in tautological explanations of success whereby a minority group that has not been subjected to the social and historical conditions of another group is seen as a "good group," which has been successfully assimilated. For example, the contemporary view of Asian Americans as the model minority reinforces the notion that only "good groups," whose members do the right thing, become assimilated. Successful achievement and mobility reflect a group's willingness and ability to accept the norms and values of the majority group.

The theoretical alternative to assimilation, cultural pluralism, supposedly allows for the possibility that groups do not assimilate but remain distinct in terms of cultural identity. However, similar to users of assimilation theory, proponents of cultural pluralism still maintain the existence of an allegedly "normal" (understood to mean superior) majority culture, to which other groups are juxtaposed (Omi & Winant, 1986). Further, they suggest that separation of racial and ethnic groups is natural and immutable. Steinberg (1981) pointed out that cultural pluralism is not a viable option in a society where inequality exists because true cultural pluralism would be based on equality among different groups. In the words of Henriques (1984: 63), "It is a case of putting the ideal cart before the real horse."

Unfortunately, cultural pluralism has often been superficially interpreted as an opportunity to celebrate difference (Yinger, 1986). For example, the influence of this school of thought is reflected in the nascent "managing diversity" discourse appearing in management literature (Thomas, 1990). Yet underlying some work in this area are assumptions like, "Minority workers are less likely to have had satisfactory schooling and training. They may have language, attitude, and cultural problems that prevent them from taking advantage of the jobs that will exist" (Johnston & Packer, 1987: xxvi).

THE WRITING OF RACE IN THE ORGANIZATION LITERATURE

The influence of the ethnic paradigm and its assumptions are reflected in much of the extant research on race found in the organization literature. Thus, not surprisingly, when management researchers have studied race, much of the research is narrowly focused, ahistorical, and decontextualized; in this research, race is mainly treated as a demographic variable. In their review of 20 journals during the period 1965–1989, Cox and Nkomo (1990) identified 201 articles focusing on race. They reported a notable decline in this type of research during the

1980s. For the most part, the topics and approaches in these articles reproduced the standard organization literature with emphasis on five content areas: affirmative action/equal employment opportunity; staffing, including test validation; job satisfaction; job attitudes and motivation; and performance evaluation.

Research designs were dominated by comparative studies of black and white workers to the neglect of other racial and ethnic groups (Cox & Nkomo, 1990). Within these studies, race was treated mainly as a demographic variable whereby blacks and whites were compared on a standard organizational theory or concept. Studies in the area of job satisfaction typically compared job satisfaction levels of black and white workers (e.g., Jones, James, Bruni, & Sell, 1977; Konar, 1981; Milutinovich & Tsaklanganos, 1978; Moch, 1980; Slocum & Strawser, 1972; Veechio, 1980; Weaver, 1978). Results in this area were largely inconsistent—some studies reported that white employees were more satisfied than black employees, and other studies reported the opposite effect. Although a few of these studies attempted to identify the factors that contributed to differences in levels of satisfaction (e.g., Konar, 1981), in general, the research provides little insight into the complexity of the psychological, organizational, and societal variables that may account for such findings. Often, the results appear to be tautological. For example, to explain their finding that whites were more satisfied with their jobs and that whites associated overall satisfaction more closely with promotion than nonwhites, O'Reilly and Roberts (1973) concluded that whites and nonwhites approach their jobs with different frames of reference.

One of the pervasive questions found within all topics was: "Does discrimination exist?" In this research, emphasis was placed on searching for objective and quantifiable evidence of racial discrimination. For example, a majority of the early articles in the area of affirmative action/equal employment opportunity were focused on whether or not discrimination existed in the occupational distribution of jobs (e.g., Franklin, 1968; Kovarshy, 1964; Northrop, 1969; Taylor, 1968). Representative questions included: To what extent are blacks overrepresented in lower socioeconomic jobs? (Franklin,

1968); Where are blacks employed within the aerospace industry? (Northrop, 1969); and is there discrimination within the governmental apprentice training program? (Kovarshy, 1964). In the area of staffing, research was focused on discrimination and bias in recruitment and selection outcomes for blacks and whites in organizations (e.g., Brown & Ford, 1977; Newman, 1978; Newman & Krzytofiak, 1979; Stone & Stone, 1987; Terpstra & Larsen, 1980). Typically, explanations were centered on the stereotyping of minority groups.

Over the years, a number of studies have been used to examine bias in performance ratings and evaluation. The level of activity in this area is evidenced by the existence of three comprehensive literature reviews on the subject (Dipboye, 1985; Kraiger & Ford, 1985; Landy & Farr, 1980). According to some studies, ratees received significantly higher ratings from evaluators of their own race (e.g., Schmitt & Lappin, 1980), whereas other studies failed to support the existence of significant race effects on performance evaluation (Mobley, 1982). Still other studies reported results that indicated a complex interaction between the race of the ratee and his or her performance (Hamner, Kim, Baird, & Biogness, 1974). In their 1985 meta-analysis, Kraiger and Ford concluded that ratees tend to receive higher ratings from raters of the same race and that these effects were more pronounced in field studies than in laboratory ratings. Only a handful of researchers explored the processes underlying differences (Cox & Nkomo, 1986; Dipboye, 1985; Pettigrew & Martin, 1987). Most often the explanations were based on a social psychology perspective with an emphasis on rater bias, including stereotyping and perceptual error in information processing.

The other prototypical question underlying much of this literature was: Do racial and ethnic minorities have what it takes to succeed in organizations? or more concisely, Why aren't they like us? Illustrative of this theme are studies that were conducted regarding job attitudes, motivation, and affirmative action. A common question in the research on job attitudes was: Do blacks have different attitudes toward their jobs and work environment than whites? (Alper, 1975; Gavin & Ewen, 1974). Several studies were focused on race differences in motivation (e.g., Bhagat, 1979; Bankart, 1972; Brenner &

Tomkiewicz, 1982; Greenhaus & Gavin, 1972; Miner, 1977; Watson & Barone, 1976). An unstated assumption in much of this research might be labeled the deficit hypothesis—whether or not minorities possessed the necessary motivational profile and values needed by organizations. Bhagat (1979) created a model to explain how black ethnic values coupled with negative job experiences have prevented a large majority of the black population from identifying strongly with the work ethic. The approach used in these studies included using a well-known theory of motivation and comparing scores of black employees to white employees. In the few studies that addressed the behavioral dimensions of affirmative action, authors emphasized the assimilation of minorities into organizations. Typical questions included: What changes are needed to assimilate the hard-core black into organizations? (Domm & Stafford, 1972) and Can the Afro-American be an effective executive? (Goode, 1970).

The final theme permeating much of this research was an emphasis on the legal, technical, and mechanical aspects of how organizations could comply with affirmative action and Title VII guidelines. Indeed, the highest concentration of research on race was conducted on the topic of affirmative action (e.g., Hitt & Keats, 1984; Marimont, Maize, Kennedy, & Harley, 1976; Marino, 1980). Some of the authors prescribed mathematical and computer simulation models for effectively implementing affirmative action programs (e.g., Hopkins, 1980; Ledvinka & Hildreth, 1984; Solomon & Messmer, 1980). Effectiveness in this area was most often defined by specifying the technical requirements of affirmative action and equal employment opportunity and fitting those requirements to existing organizational systems. Only a few studies were used to examine the behavioral and social ramifications of affirmative action and equal employment (e.g., Goodman, 1969; Lakin, 1966; Rubin, 1967). A similar emphasis on techniques and mechanics is found in the test validation literature where the issue of differential validity dominated personnel/ human resource management research for a number of years (e.g., Bartlett & O'Leary, 1969; Bayroff, 1966; Boehm, 1977; Hunter, Schmidt, & Hunter, 1979; Schmidt, Pearlman, & Hunter, 1980). In this area there was very little discussion of theory about why researchers expected differential validity to occur among different racial and ethnic groups or why test score differentials persisted (Arvey & Faley, 1988). Little attention was given regarding the roles that educational opportunities and other societal factors play in explaining differences or that "universal knowledge" may not be value free.

Several observations can be drawn from the way race was considered in management studies. Much of the research lies along the prejudice-discrimination axis, with an emphasis on discovering objective evidence of racial discrimination and racial differences in behavior, primarily between blacks and whites. This is consistent with the premises underlying the ethnicity paradigm that race can largely be understood as a problem of prejudiced attitudes or personal and cultural inadequacies of racial minorities. A notable exception was the work of Alderfer, Alderfer, Tucker, and Tucker (1980). Using an intergroup framework that emphasized the interaction of power differences at the group, organizational, and societal levels, they examined the broad issue of race relations within an organizational setting.

What is most striking about the management literature is researchers' fixation on searching for differences. Although this fixation may reflect the positivist approach to research adopted by many management scholars, it raises important issues for how race has been conceptualized. When no significant differences were found, authors were likely to conclude that race had no effect. This might be interpreted as an affirmation of the universality of management concepts. Another interpretation, consistent with the theoretical premises of the ethnicity paradigm, is that there really are no differences between racial minority groups and the European immigrants who successfully achieved assimilation. In contrast, when significant behavioral differences were reported, explanations were often focused on inadequate socialization of racial minorities to the norms and requirements for successful accomplishment or prejudice or stereotyping by majority group members. Conspicuously absent from these articles is any suggestion or recognition of the different sociohistorical experience of African-Americans or other racial minorities in the United States. There was little awareness that racial minorities may have something to contribute to organizations or

that perhaps race can inform our understanding of organizations in other ways. For the most part, in this literature, race has been considered an issue or a problem. Or race enters the discussion of organizations only when "minority" employees are studied. Aside from Alderfer and his colleagues (1980), there were no researchers in the studies reviewed who examined the meaning of race for majority group members. This omission reflects an unconscious assumption by organizational researchers that majority group members do not have a racial identity and, consequently, it is a "nontopic" for research.

In summary, the questions that addressed race in the organizational literature echo the assumptions and themes of the ethnicity paradigm. Further, lest we think that the *managing diversity* discourse represents a new approach, we should be reminded that it may be only as *new* as the *new ethnicity*. Our conceptualization of race in organizations has been constrained by these theoretical orientations, and, consequently, a necessary step toward rewriting race is recognizing these influences.

REWRITING RACE INTO THE STUDY OF ORGANIZATIONS

To rewrite race, we must not continue the emperor's procession by remaining silent about race or studying it within the narrowly defined ethnicity-based paradigm that has dominated much of our research. First, we must acknowledge that the emperor is indeed naked. Organizations are not race-neutral entities. Race is and has been present in organizations, even if this idea has not been explicitly recognized. Second, rewriting race is not a matter of simply clothing the emperor, but the emperor must be dethroned as the universal, the only reality. We need to revise our understanding of the very concept of race and its historical and political meaning. Only then can race be used as a productive analytical concept for understanding the nature of organizations.

Alternative Frameworks

A useful starting point is to examine alternative theoretical frameworks for understanding the complexity and nature of race. For example, power-conflict theories of race and ethnic relations offer ways to move beyond sole reliance on assimilation models.

Power-conflict approaches to race and ethnicity emphasize issues of economic power, inequalities in access to material resources and labor markets, and the historical development of racism (Bonacich, 1980; Cox, 1948; Reich, 1981). One of the earliest proponents of these approaches (Cox, 1948) argued that racial exploitation and race prejudice developed with the rise of capitalism and nationalism. In Cox's analysis, American colonies imported African slaves to fill a particular labor need and simultaneously incorporated the ideology of racism as a justification of slavery. He contended that the idea of racial inferiority didn't precede the use of minority groups as servile labor but that an ideology of racial inferiority developed to maintain Africans and other racial minorities in a servile status. According to Cox, the racial division of labor into white and black workers hindered any positive contact between the white and black masses. Thus, the persistence of racial stratification in society was not a function of atomistic individuals or cultural deficiencies of minorities but was rooted in the class positions of workers.

Reich's (1981) class-conflict theory of racial inequality attempts to explain the meaning of race within the context of an advanced capitalist system. Like Edwards (1979), Reich (1981) conceptualized the workplace as contested terrain wherein workers and capitalists engage in power struggles over income distribution and material resources. White workers do not benefit from racial inequality but capitalists do, and the very organization of jobs in the workplace is structured to exploit the existence of racial and other divisions among workers. Racial antagonism among workers inhibits the collective strength of workers and sustains the power of capitalists.

These and other power-conflict theories attempt to analyze race within the relations of capitalists' production without reducing it to an epiphenomenon (Thompson, 1989; Wilhelm, 1983).

Thus, if applied to organizational analysis, power-conflict theories would focus our attention on understanding how organizations have become racially constructed, the power relations that sustain racial divisions and racial domination, and the important role of capitalist modes of production in maintaining these divisions.

Omi and Winant's (1986) racial-formation theory represents another alternative formulation of race. They argued that race is preeminently a sociohistorical concept whose meanings and categories are given concrete expression by the specific social relations and historical context in which they are embedded. They noted, for example, that in the United States with the consolidation of racial slavery, a racially based understanding of society was set in motion, which resulted in the shaping of a specific racial identity for both slaves and European settlers. Africans with specific ethnic identities became simply "black," and European settlers previously identified as Christian or English and free became "white" (Omi & Winant, 1986: 64).

Race occupies a central position in our understanding of social relations, and in their theory, Omi and Winant (1986: 66) distinguish between two levels of social relations: micro and macro. At the microlevel, race is a matter of individuality, of the formation of identity. The ways we understand ourselves, our experiences, our interactions with others, and our day-to-day activities are all shaped by racial meanings and racial awareness. At the macrolevel, race is a matter of collectivity, of the formation of social structures. These authors conceived of social structures as a series of economic, political, and cultural/ideological sites, which represented a region of social life with a coherent set of constitutive social relations. For example, at the economic level, the very definition of labor and the allocation of jobs among workers have been dependent on race as an organizing principle. Consequently, in this case, the racial order is organized and enforced by the continuity and interaction between the microlevel and macrolevel of social relations. Racial discrimination within the economic structure has consequences for individual identity at the microlevel.

The term *racial formation* in Omi and Winant's (1986: 61) model refers to the process by which social, economic, and political forces determine the content and importance of racial categories and the subsequent process through which these categories are, in turn, shaped by racial meanings. Accordingly, the meaning of race is defined and contested throughout society, in both collective action and personal practice. In the process, racial categories themselves are formed, transformed, destroyed, and reformed. These authors caution not only against the tendency to view race as an essence (i.e., as something fixed or objective) but also against the tendency to view race as a mere illusion that will disappear with the correct social order.

Similarly, Essed (1991) argued that because race is an organizing principle of many social relations, the fundamental social relations of society are *racialized* relations. She conceptualized race as both an ideological and a social construction with structural expressions. Using cross-cultural empirical data, Essed (1991) developed a theory of everyday racism, which attempts to build upon both the micro and macro perspectives of race and ethnicity. Essed defined *everyday racism* as "a process in which (a) socialized racist notions are integrated into meanings that make practices immediately definable and manageable, (b) practices with racist implications become in themselves familiar and repetitive, and (c) underlying racial and ethnic relations are actualized and reinforced through these routine or familiar practices in everyday situations" (1991: 52). The three main practices are marginalization (a form of oppression), containment (a form of repression), and problematization (ideological constructions legitimizing exclusion through hierarchical organization of difference). The integration of racism into everyday situations through these practices activates and reproduces underlying power relations.

Omi and Winant's (1986) theory of racial formation and Essed's (1991) theory of everyday racism emphasize the instability of race as a natural category and the impossibility of maintaining the essentialist position about race that sustains the ethnicity paradigm. At the same time, these theories help in understanding the reproduction of race from its historical to contemporary site in particular forms that occupy every part of society. They suggest that we have left out an important analytical concept for understanding organizations and that if race forms the core of individual, social, and institutional life in the United States, then we need explicit theories of race and ethnicity to overcome this omission.

Other theoretical approaches that have race at the center can be found in the literature and research in African-American and African studies, Asian studies, and Chicano/Latino studies. This literature can also provide a focus for developing theoretical content specifically about race and can help us to ask different questions than those that stem solely from the ethnicity paradigm.

For example, African-American and African studies, or Black studies, are ideologically and philosophically distinct from European social scientific theory because in them Africa is viewed as the genesis and foundation of knowledge and study of black people (Anderson, 1990). *Black studies* has been defined as "an analysis of the factors and conditions which have affected the economic, political, psychological, and legal status of African-Americans as well as the African in the Diaspora from the social reality of their own experience" (Gordon, 1978: 231). The early work of Black studies scholars called attention to the exclusion of the culture and experience of blacks from textbooks and curricula of educational institutions (Karenga, 1984). Despite this exclusion from mainstream academia, a great deal of scholarly work had been previously produced and generated about the experience of black people (e.g., Bennett, 1966; Diop, 1955; Du Bois, 1961; Fanon, 1963). Initial goals of Black studies were to add to the body of knowledge about blacks within the various disciplines. Taylor (1990) noted that most early attempts failed to move theory substantially beyond the extant paradigms of mainstream social science and research centered around relabeling familiar concepts and adapting existing research strategies.

A second strand of Black studies emerged that has been devoted to a critical assessment of traditional social science paradigms and the systematic articulation of a "black perspective," from which the development of new theories and alternative interpretation of the black community and its relation to the larger society could be advanced (e.g., Cheek, 1987; Gates, 1985; Kershaw, 1990). An effort was made to move away from the "pathological behavior" model of the black community. These strands have appeared as black psychology and black sociology, and they can be found in many other social science disciplines.

For example, within black psychology the attempt has been to build conceptual models to organize, explain, and understand the psychosocial behavior of

African-Americans. These models are based on the primary dimensions of an African-American world view instead of the traditional psychology concerned mainly with categorization, mental measurement, and the establishment of norms (Azibo, 1990; Guthrie, 1976; White, 1984). Cross (1978) and others (e.g., Parham, 1989) have developed a model of racial identity for African-Americans. The model describes a process of psychological Nigrescence that hypothesizes the kinds of changes that occur in the racial identity of African-Americans at various points in the life cycle. Research addressing specific applications of Nigrescence theories can be found in the areas of value orientations (Carter & Helms, 1987) and self-actualization (Parham & Helms, 1985). More recently, research has been focused on models of white racial identity (Helms, 1990). Another useful concept for understanding the experiences of racial and ethnic minorities that has been widely used is *biculturalism* (Bell, 1990), or what Du Bois (1961) called *double consciousness*. Users of this concept recognize that African-Americans have both Afrocentric and Eurocentric elements of culture and racial identity.

Within the discipline of history, scholars researching African-American experiences have sought to correct the theoretical and methodological errors that questioned the historical actuality of African societies (Davidson, 1991; Rodney, 1974) and the nature and effect of slavery upon African-Americans. By examining slave narratives, songs, and other historical documents, scholars in the field have offered re-visions that characterize slaves as more than empty vessels who were acted upon, shaped, and dominated by their European American enslavers (Blassingame, 1979; White, 1984). Slaves had cultural, psychological, and technical resources from their African heritage that not only contributed to the development of the United States but also helped them to resist the devastation of slavery. Revisiting the early history of African-American and other minority workers and their exclusion from skilled industrial jobs in organizations also can inform our understanding of their present status (Foner & Lewis, 1982; Takai, 1979).

A third strand of research has developed, which calls attention to the need for theoretical development and construction of ideas toward building a new social science (Taylor, 1990). The aim of such research is to move beyond explanations of black institutional life and behavior toward theoretical formulations that build upon a more expansive lens. That is, how would social science concepts differ if we used race as a core analytical concept? What concepts and constructs have been omitted? Other areas of development include analyses that examine the intersection of race with gender and class (e.g., Hill-Collins, 1990; King, 1988; Wilson, 1984).

Implications of Alternative Frameworks

Although I have expanded upon African-American studies as a body of knowledge from which management studies can draw, analogous work can be found for other racial groups. My purpose is not to suggest the replacement of Eurocentric theories with Afrocentric or Asian-centered ones. Yes, these approaches do imply efforts toward accounting for the absence of or any reference to perspectives from other groups in understanding organizations; they also imply that we not view racial minorities solely as deviants or problems in the study of organizations. Yet, such changes do not simply mean *adding* on studies of these groups. The major point is that we re-vision the very way we "see" organizations. Clearly, the specific historical context of race should be considered in the development and use of concepts. A ready example can be found in Thomas's (1989) study of mentoring in organizations. He explicitly draws on the historical impact of social taboos from our legacy of slavery in order to understand the dynamics of present-day cross-race mentoring relationships. Finally, new approaches would suggest different questions about race in organizations. Table 45.1 contains a comparison of the questions that have emanated from the ethnicity paradigm and the kinds of questions supported from the alternative theoretical frameworks and bodies of literature discussed in this section.

Rewriting race also suggests recognizing the limitations of positivist research methods. Research strategies determine the kinds of knowledge produced, and a realistic view of the research process encourages us to use these strategies in different ways (Morgan, 1983). A majority of the organizational studies mentioned in this article relied upon comparative designs

Table 45.1   Asked and Unasked Questions About Race

Research Questions From Ethnicity Paradigm

Does discrimination exist in recruitment, selection, etc.?

Can the Afro-American be an effective executive?

Do blacks identify with the traditional American work ethic?

Do blacks' and whites' problem-solving styles differ?

How can blacks/minorities be assimilated into organizations?

How can organizations manage diversity?

How can organizations comply with equal employment opportunity/affirmative action requirements?

Do blacks and whites have the same job expectations?

Are there different levels of motivation between black and white employees?

Is there racial bias in performance ratings?

What is the role of stereotyping in job bias? Does differential test validity exist?

Does discrimination exist in recruitment, selection, etc.?

Silenced Research Questions From Alternative Paradigms

How are societal race relations reproduced in the workplace?

How did white males come to dominant management positions?

To what extent is race built into the definition of a "manager"?

What are the implications of racial identity for organization theories based on individual identity?

How does racial identity affect organizational experiences?

How does the racial identity of white employees influence their status and interaction with other groups?

Why, despite national policies like affirmative action, does inequality still exist in the workplace?

Are assimilation and managing diversity the only two means of removing racial inequality in the workplace?

How do organizational processes contribute to the maintenance of racial domination and stratification?

Are white male-dominated organizations also built on underlying assumptions about gender and class?

What are the patterns of relationships among different racial minorities in organizations?

---

in which race was categorized as a two-level variable (i.e., black and white). There are two basic problems with this approach. First, comparative designs too often adopt a position of cultural monism that assumes equivalence of groups across race (Azibo, 1990). In such a case, meaningful and valid interpretations of any observed differences are hindered. An awareness of the appropriate use of emic (within culture) and etic (cross-culture) approaches is critical (Triandis, 1972). Azibo (1990) noted that researchers must seek a balance between the assumption that cultures can best be understood in their own terms and the desire to establish universal theories of human behavior. Research efforts in this direction can be found in the works of Marin and Triandis, 1985; Triandis, Marin, Lisansky, and Betancourt, 1984; and Cox, Lobel, and McLeod, 1991.

Second, categorization of subjects is an essentialist view of race as a discrete, demographic variable that can be objectively observed and measured.

Reconceptualizing race not as a simple property of individuals but as an integral dynamic of organizations implies a move toward phenomenological and historical research methods that would contribute toward building theories and knowledge about both how race is produced and how it is a core feature of organizations.

CONCLUSION

I have argued that we should not continue our silence about race, and when we do study it, that we expand our approaches beyond the ethnicity-based paradigm that has implicitly dominated much of our research. This expansion would allow race to become a productive analytical category used in understanding organizations. What does it mean to use race as an analytical category? This use suggests a view of organizations as made up of race relations played out in power struggles, which includes the realization that "race" is not a stable category. Then, not only would we not conduct research on "race in organizations" the way we have done it in the past, but we would also need to rethink the very nature of organizations.

Finally, it is important to point out that race is just one part of a more complicated web of socially constructed elements of identity formation such as gender and class. Race, gender, and class can form interlocking bases of domination in social relations (Hill-Collins, 1990; Spelman, 1988). Although each part may be manifested in its own peculiar and distinct way, the common factor is domination based on notions of inferiority and superiority. To the extent that each system reinforces and reproduces the other, an analysis of organizations cannot exclude the importance of these significant elements of identity. Indeed, the challenge before us becomes much more complex than simply clothing the emperor!

REFERENCES

Adorno, T. W., Frenkel-Brunswick, E., Levinson, D. J., II, & Sanford, R. N. 1950. *The authoritarian personality.* New York: Harper & Row.

Alderfer, C. P. 1982. Problems of changing white males' behavior and beliefs concerning race relations. In P. S. Goodman & Associates (Eds.), *Change in organizations:* 122–165. San Francisco: Jossey-Bass.

Alderfer, C. P., Alderfer, C. J., Tucker, L., & Tucker, R. 1980. Diagnosing race relations in management. *Journal of Applied Behavioral Science,* 16: 135–166.

Allport, G. 1954. *The nature of prejudice.* New York: Doubleday.

Alper, S. W. 1975. Racial differences in job and work environment priorities among newly hired college graduates. *Journal of Applied Psychology,* 60: 120–134.

Andersen, H. C. 1968. *Forty-two stories* (M. R. James, Trans.). London: Faber & Faber.

Anderson, T. (Ed.). 1990. *Black studies: Theory, method, and cultural perspectives.* Pullman: Washington State University Press.

Arvey, R. D., & Faley, R. H. 1988. *Fairness in selecting employees.* Reading, MA: Addison-Wesley.

Azibo, D. A. Y. 1990. Personality, clinical, and social psychological research on blacks: Appropriate & inappropriate research frameworks. In T. Anderson (Ed.), *Black studies: Theory, method and cultural perspectives:* 25–41. Pullman: Washington State University Press.

Bankart, P. C. 1972. Attribution of motivation in same-race and different race stimulus persons. *Human Relations,* 215: 35–45.

Bartlett, C. J., & O'Leary, B. S. 1969. A differential prediction model to moderate the effects of heterogeneous groups in personnel selection and classification. *Personnel Psychology,* 22: 1–18.

Bayroff, A. 1966. Test technology and equal employment opportunity. *Personnel Psychology,* 19: 35–39.

Bell, E. L. 1990. The bicultural life experiences of career-oriented black women. *Journal of Organizational Behavior,* 11: 459–477.

Bennett, L. 1966. *Before the Mayflower: A history of the negro in America, 1619–1964.* Baltimore: Penguin Books.

Bhagat, R. 1979. Black-white ethnic differences in identification with the work ethic: Some implications for organizational integration. *Academy of Management Review,* 4: 381–391.

Billig, M. 1985. Prejudice, categorization and particularization: From a perceptual to a rhetorical approach. *European Journal of Social Psychology,* 15: 79–103.

Blanton, M. 1987. *Racial theories.* Cambridge: Cambridge University Press.

Blassingame, J. 1979. *The slave community: Plantation life in the antebellum south.* New York: Oxford University Press.

Blauner, R. 1972. *Racial oppression in America.* New York: Harper & Row.

Blauner, B. 1989. *Black lives, white lives: Three decades of race relations in America.* Berkeley: University of California Press.

Boehm, V. R. 1977. Differential prediction—A methodological artifact. *Journal of Applied Psychology,* 62: 146–154.

Bonacich, E. 1980. Class approaches to ethnicity and race. *Insurgent Sociologist,* 10: 9–23.

Brenner, O. C., & Tomkiewicz, J. 1982. Job orientation of black and white college graduates in business. *Personnel Psychology,* 35: 89–103.

Brown, H. A., & Ford, D. L., Jr. 1977. An exploratory analysis of discrimination in the employment of black MBA graduates. *Journal of Applied Psychology,* 62: 50–56.

Carter, R. T., & Helms, J. E. 1987. Relationship of black value orientation to racial identity attitudes. *Measurement and Evaluation in Counseling and Development,* 19: 185–195.

Cheek, D. K. 1987. Social science: A vehicle for white supremacy? *International Journal for the Advancement of Counseling,* 10: 59–69.

Cox, O. C. 1948. *Caste, class, and race: A study in social dynamics.* New York: Doubleday.

Cox, T., Jr., & Nkomo, S. M. 1986. Differential appraisal criteria based on race of the ratee. *Group and Organization Studies,* 11: 101–119.

Cox, T., Jr., & Nkomo, S. M. 1990. Invisible men and women: A status report on race as a variable in organization behavior research. *Journal of Organizational Behavior,* 11: 419–431.

Cox, T., Jr., Lobel, S., & McLeod, P. 1991. Effects of ethnic group cultural differences on cooperative versus competitive behavior in a group task. *Academy of Management Journal,* 34: 827–847.

Cross, W. E. 1978. The Cross and Thomas models of psychological nigrescence. *Journal of Black Psychology,* 5: 13–19.

Davidson, B. 1991. *African civilization revisited.* Trenton, NJ: Africa World Press.

Diop, C. A. 1955. *The African origin of civilization: Myth or reality.* Paris: Presence Africaine.

Dipboye, R. L. 1985. Some neglected variables in research on discrimination in appraisals. *Academy of Management Review,* 10: 116–127.

Domm, D., & Stafford, J. 1972. Assimilating blacks into the organization. *California Management Review,* 15(1): 46–51.

Dovidio, J. F., & Gaertner, S. L. (Eds.). 1986. *Prejudice, discrimination, and racism.* Orlando, FL: Academic Press.

Du Bois, W. E. B. 1961. *The souls of black folk.* Greenwich, CT: Fawcett.

Edwards. R. 1979. *Contested terrain.* New York: Basic Books.

Essed, P. 1991. *Everyday racism.* Newbury Park. CA: Sage.

Fanon, F. 1963. *The wretched of the earth.* New York: Grove Press.

Feagin, J. 1987. Changing black Americans to fit a racist system? *Journal of Social Issues,* 43(1): 85–89.

Foner, P. S., & Lewis, R. L. (Eds.). 1982. *The black worker: A documentary history from colonial times to the present.* Philadelphia: Temple University Press.

Franklin, R. 1968. A framework for the analysis of interurban negro-white economic differentials. *Industrial and Labor Relations Review,* 2: 209–223.

Gavin, J., & Ewen, R. 1974. Racial differences in job attitudes and performance—Some theoretical considerations and empirical findings. *Personnel Psychology,* 27: 455–464.

Gates, H. L., Jr. 1985. Editor's introduction: Writing "race" and the difference it makes. In H. L. Gates, Jr. (Ed.), *"Race," writing, and difference:* 1–20. Chicago: University of Chicago Press.

Gates. H. L., Jr. 1988. *The signifying monkey: A theory of Afro-American literary criticism.* New York: Oxford University Press.

Glazer, N. 1987. *Affirmative discrimination: Ethnic inequality and public policy.* Cambridge, MA: Harvard University Press.

Glazer, N., & Moynihan, D. P. 1970. *Beyond the melting pot: The Negroes, Puerto Ricans, Jews, Italians, and Irish of New York City.* Cambridge, MA: MIT Press.

Goode, K. 1970. Can the Afro-American be an effective executive? *California Management Review,* 13(1): 27–30.

Goodman, R. 1969. A hidden issue in minority employment. *California Management Review,* 11(1): 22–26.

Gordon, M. M. 1964. *Assimilation in American life: The role of race, religion, and national origin.* New York: Oxford University Press.

Gordon, M. M. 1978. *Human nature, class, and ethnicity.* New York: Oxford University Press.

Guthrie, R. V. 1976. *Even the rat was white: A historical view of psychology.* New York: Harper & Row.

Gutman, H. G. 1977. *Work, culture, and society in industrializing America.* New York: Knopf.

Greenhaus, J., & Gavin, J. 1972. The relationship between expectancies and job behavior for white and black employees. *Personnel Psychology,* 25: 449–455.

Hamner, W. C., Kim, J. S., Baird, L., & Biogness, W. J. 1974. Race and sex as determinants of ratings by potential employers in a simulated work-sampling task. *Journal of Applied Psychology,* 59: 705–711.

Harding, S. 1986. *The science question in feminism.* Ithaca, NY: Cornell University Press.

Helms, J. G. 1990. *Black and white racial identity: Theory, research, and practice.* Westport, CT: Greenwood Press.

Henriques, J. 1984. Social psychology and the politics of racism. In J. Henriques, W. Hollway, C. Urwin, C. Venn, & V. Walkerdine (Eds.), *Changing the subject: Psychology, social regulations and subjectivity:* 60–89. London: Methuen.

Hewstone, M. 1989. Intergroup attribution: Some implications for the study of ethnic prejudice. In J. P. Van Oudenhoven & T. M. Willemsen (Eds.), *Ethnic minorities: Social psychological perspectives:* 25–42. Amsterdam: Sivets & Zeitlinger.

Hill-Collins, P. 1990. *Black feminist thought: Knowledge consciousness, and the politics of empowerment.* Boston: Unwin Hyman.

Hitt, M., & Keats, B. 1984. Empirical identification of the criteria for effective affirmative action programs. *Journal of Applied Behavioral Science,* 20: 203–222.

Hopkins, D. 1980. Models for affirmative action planning and evaluation. *Management* Science, 26: 994–1006.

Hunter, J. E., Schmidt, F. L., & Hunter, R. 1979. Differential validity of employment tests by race: A comprehensive review and analysis. *Psychological Bulletin,* 85: 721–735.

Johnston, W., & Packer, A. 1987. *Workforce 2000: Work and workers for the 21st century.* Indianapolis, IN: Hudson Institute.

Jones, A. P., James, L. R., Bruni, J. R., & Sell, S. B. 1977. Black white differences in work environment perceptions and job satisfaction and its correlates. *Personnel Psychology,* 30: 5–16.

Joseph, G. G., Reddy, V., & Searle-Chatterjee, M. 1990. Eurocentrism in the social sciences. *Race & Class,* 31(4): 1–26.

Karenga, R. 1984. *Introduction to black studies.* Los Angeles: Kawaida Publications.

Kershaw, T. 1990. The emerging paradigm in black studies. In T. Anderson (Ed.), *Black studies: Theory, method, and cultural perspectives:* 17–24. Pullman: Washington State University Press.

King, D. K. 1988. Multiple jeopardy, multiple consciousness: The context of black feminist ideology. *Signs,* 14: 42–72.

Keto, C. T. 1989. *The Africa centered perspective of history.* Blackwood, NJ: KA Publications.

Konar, E. 1981. Explaining racial differences in job satisfaction: A reexamination of the data. *Journal of Applied Psychology,* 66: 522–524.

Kovarshy, I. 1964. Management, racial discrimination, and apprentice training programs. *Academy of Management Journal,* 7: 196–203.

Kraiger, K., & Ford, J. 1985. A meta-analysis of ratee race effects in performance ratings. *Journal of Applied Psychology,* 70: 56–65.

Kuhn, T. 1962. *The structure of scientific revolutions.* Chicago: University of Chicago Press.

Lakin, M. 1966. Human relations training and interracial social action: Problems in self and client definition. *Journal of Applied Behavioral Science,* 2(2): 139–149.

Landy, F. J., & Farr, S. L. 1980. Performance rating. *Psychological Bulletin,* 87: 72–107.

Ledvinka, J., & Hildreth, W. B. 1984. Integrating planned change intervention and computer simulation technology: The case of affirmative action. *Journal of Applied Behavioral Science,* 20(2): 125–140.

Lefkowitz, J. 1972. Differential validity: Ethnic groups as a moderator in predicting tenure. *Personnel Psychology,* 25: 223–240.

Marimont, R. B., Maize, B., Kennedy, P., & Harley, E. 1976. Using FAIR to set numerical EEO goals. *Public Personnel Management,* 5(3): 191–198.

Marin, G., & Triandis, H. C. 1985. Allocentrism as an important characteristic of the behavior of Latin Americans and Hispanics. In R. Diaz-Guerrero (Ed.), *Cross-cultural and national studies in social psychology:* 85–104. Amsterdam: Elsevier Science.

Marino, K. E. 1980. A preliminary investigation into the behavioral dimensions of affirmative action compliance. *Journal of Applied Psychology,* 65: 346–350.

Merton, R. K. 1949. Discrimination and the American creed. In R. MacIver (Ed.), *Discrimination and national welfare:* 99–126. New York: Harper & Row.

Milutinovich, J. S., & Tsaklanganos, A. 1976. The impact of perceived community prosperity on job satisfaction of black and white workers. *Academy of Management Journal,* 19: 49–65.

Miner, J. 1977. Motivational potential for upgrading among minority and female managers. *Journal of Applied Psychology,* 62: 691–697.

Minnich, E. K. 1990. *Transforming knowledge.* Philadelphia: Temple University Press.

Mobley, W. 1982. Supervisor and employee race and sex effects on performance appraisals: A field study of adverse impact and generalizability. *Academy of Management Journal,* 25: 598–606.

Moch, M. 1980. Racial differences in job satisfaction: Testing four common explanations. *Journal of Applied Psychology,* 65: 299–306.

Morgan, G. 1983. Toward a more reflective social science. In G. Morgan (Ed.), *Beyond method: Strategies for social research:* 368–376. Beverly Hills, CA: Sage.

Myrdal, G. 1944. *An American dilemma.* New York: Harper & Row.

Newman, J. M. 1978. Discrimination in recruitment: An empirical analysis. *Industrial and Labor Relations Review,* 32: 15–23.

Newman, J. M., & Krzytofiak, F. 1979. Self-reports versus unobtrusive measures: Balancing method variance and ethical concerns in employment discrimination research. *Journal of Applied Psychology,* 64: 2–85.

Nkomo, S. M. 1988. Race and sex: The forgotten case of the black female manager. In S. Rose & L. Larwood (Eds.), *Women's careers: Pathways and pitfalls:* 133–150. New York: Praeger.

Northrop, H. 1969. The negro in aerospace work. *California Management Review,* 11(4): 11–26.

Omi, M., & Winant, H. 1986. *Racial formation in the United States: From the 1960s to the 1980s.* New York: Routledge & Kegan Paul.

O'Reilly, C. A., & Roberts, K. M. 1973. Job satisfaction among whites and nonwhites: A cross-cultural approach. *Journal of Applied Psychology,* 57: 295–299.

Oudenhoven, I. P. V., & Willemsen, T. M. (Eds.). 1989. *Ethnic minorities: Social psychological perspectives.* Amsterdam: Sivets & Zeitlinger.

Parham, T. A. 1989. Cycles of psychological nigrescence. *Counseling Psychologist,* 17(2): 187–225.

Parham, T. A., & Helms, J. E. 1985. Relation of racial identity attitudes to self-actualization and affective statements of black students. *Journal of Counseling Psychology,* 32: 431–440.

Park, R. E. 1950. *Race and culture.* Glencoe, IL: Free Press. (Original work published in 1939)

Pettigrew, T. F. 1979. The ultimate attribution error. Extending Allport's cognitive analysis of prejudice. *Personality and Social Psychology Bulletin,* 5: 461–476.

Pettigrew, T. F., & Martin, I. 1987. Shaping the organizational context for black American inclusion. *Journal of Social Forces,* 43(1): 41–78.

Reich, M. 1981. *Racial inequality.* Princeton, NJ: Princeton University Press.

Rodney, W. 1974. *How Europe underdeveloped Africa.* Washington, DC: Howard University Press.

Rubin, I. 1967. The reduction of prejudice through laboratory training. *Journal of Applied Behavioral Science,* 3(1): 29–51.

Schmidt, F. L., Pearlman, K., & Hunter, J. 1980. The validity and fairness of employment and educational tests for Hispanic Americans: A review and analysis. *Personnel Psychology,* 33: 705–724.

Schmitt, N., & Lappin, M. 1980. Race and sex as determinants of the mean and variance of performance ratings. *Journal of Applied Psychology,* 65: 428–435.

Slocum, J., Jr., & Strawser, R. 1972. Racial differences in job attitudes. *Journal of Applied Psychology,* 56: 28–32.

Solomon, R. J., & Messmer, D. J. 1980. Implications of the Bakke decision in implementing affirmative action programs: A decision model. *Decision Sciences,* 11: 312–324.

Sowell, T. 1975. *Race and economics.* New York: David McKay.

Spelman, E. V. 1988. *Inessential woman: Problems of exclusion in feminist thought.* Boston: Beacon Press.

Steinberg, S. 1981. *The ethnic myth.* New York: Atheneum.

Stone, D. L., & Stone, E. F. 1987. Effects of missing application-blank information on personnel selection decisions: Do privacy protection strategies bias the outcome? *Journal of Applied Psychology,* 72: 452–456.

Tajfel, H. 1969. Cognitive aspects of prejudice. *Journal of Social Issues,* 25(4): 79–97.

Tajfel, H. 1970. Experiments in intergroup discrimination. *Scientific American,* 223(5): 96–102.

Tajfel, H., & Turner, J. C. 1979. *An integrative theory of intergroup conflict: The social psychology of intergroup relations.* Monterey, CA: Brooks/Cole.

Tajfel, H. 1981. *Human groups and social categories.* Cambridge: Cambridge University Press.

Tajfel, H., & Turner, J. C. 1986. The social identity of theory of intergroup behavior. In S. Worchel & W. G. Austin (Eds.), *Psychology of intergroup relations:* 7–24. Chicago: Nelson-Hall.

Takai, R. 1979. *Iron cages: Race and culture in nineteenth-century America.* New York: Knopf.

Taylor, D. 1968. Discrimination and occupational wage differences in the market for unskilled labor. *Industrial and Labor Relations Review,* 21: 373–390.

Taylor, Ronald L. 1990. The study of black people: A survey of empirical and theoretical models. In T. Anderson (Ed.), *Black studies: Theory, method and cultural perspectives:* 11–15. Pullman: Washington State University Press.

Terpstra, D., & Larsen, M. 1980 A note on job type and applicant race as determinants of hiring decisions. *Journal of Occupational Psychology,* 53(3): 117–119.

Thomas, D. A. 1989. Mentoring and irrationality: The role of racial taboos. *Human Resource Management,* 28: 279–290.

Thomas, R. R. 1990. From affirmative action to affirming diversity. *Harvard Business Review,* 68(2): 107–117.

Thompson, R. H. 1989. *Theories of ethnicity: A critical appraisal.* New York: Greenwood Press.

Triandis, H. C. 1972. *The analysis of subjective culture.* New York: Wiley.

Triandis, H. C., Marin, G., Lisansky, J., & Betancourt, H. 1984. Simpatia as a cultural script of hispanics. *Journal of Personality and Social Psychology,* 47: 1363–1375.

van den Berghe, P. 1967. *Race and racism.* New York: Wiley.

van den Berghe, P. 1981. *The ethnic phenomenon.* New York: Elsevier.

van Dijk, T. A. 1987. *Communicating racism: Ethnic prejudice in thought and talk.* Newbury Park, CA: Sage.

Veechio, R. 1980. Worker alienation as a moderator of the job quality-job satisfaction relationship: The case of racial differences. *Academy of Management Journal,* 23: 479–486.

Watson, J. G., & Barone, S. 1976. The self-concept, personal values, and motivational orientations of black and white managers. *Academy of Management Journal,* 19: 36–48.

Weaver, C. N. 1978. Black-white correlates of job satisfaction. *Journal of Applied Psychology,* 63: 255–258.

White, J. L. 1984. *The psychology of blacks: An African-American perspective.* Englewood Cliffs, NJ: Prentice-Hall.

Wilder, D. A. 1986. Cognitive factors affecting the success of intergroup contact. In S. Worchel & W. G. Austin (Eds.), *Psychology of intergroup relations:* 49–66. Chicago: Nelson Hall.

Wilhelm, S. 1983. *Black in white America.* Cambridge, MA: Schenkman.

Wilson, W. J. 1984. *The declining significance of race.* Chicago: Chicago University Press.

Yinger, J. M. 1986. Intersecting strands in the theorization of race and ethnic relations. In J. Rex & D. Mason (Eds.), *Theories of race and ethnic relations:* 20–41. Cambridge: Cambridge University Press.

SOURCE: Nkomo, Stella M. 1992. "The Emperor Has No Clothes: Rewriting 'Race in Organizations.'" *The Academy of Management Review,* 17(3):487–513.

46

THE COLONIZING CONSCIOUSNESS AND REPRESENTATIONS OF THE OTHER

A Postcolonial Critique of the Discourse of Oil

ANSHUMAN PRASAD

The conquest of the earth, which mostly means the taking it away from those who have a different complexion or slightly flatter noses than ourselves, is not a pretty thing when you look into it too much. What redeems it is the idea only. An idea at the back of it; not a sentimental pretence but an idea; and an unselfish belief in the idea—something you can set up, and bow down before, and offer a sacrifice to. . . .

Joseph Conrad, Heart of Darkness

Language is the perfect instrument of empire.
Bishop of Avila to Queen Isabella of Castille, 1492, quoted in Peter Hulme, Colonial Encounters

The present chapter represents an attempt to strengthen the theoretical bases of diversity research and practice—and, in the process, to enhance our own understanding of the dilemmas of workplace diversity—by means of drawing upon some of the insights emerging from postcolonial theory (or postcolonialism),[1] a new and increasingly important scholarly approach for analyzing the cultural dynamics of control and resistance in the period of colonialism and its aftermath (Ashcroft, Griffiths, & Tiffin, 1995; Barker, Hulme, Iversen, & Loxley, 1985; Bhabha, 1994; Guha & Spivak, 1988;

Nandy, 1983, 1987; Prakash, 1995; Said, 1979, 1993; Spivak, 1990; Williams & Chrisman, 1994b).

As this chapter's reliance upon postcolonialism may suggest, the chapter seeks to theorize workplace diversity within the wider context of the (continuing?) history and experience of Euro-American imperialism and colonialism.[2] The use of colonialism/imperialism as a broad conceptual matrix for understanding workplace diversity is somewhat new and unusual in management research and practice. Even a brief look at the diversity literature is sufficient to suggest that, for the most part, diversity scholars and practitioners have tended to ignore colonialism as a sense-making framework. This chapter, however, submits that the colonial experience can provide a useful window for analyzing diversity and for developing a more complete understanding of the multiplicity of issues that seem to surround this complex phenomenon.

There are at least three reasons that render postcolonial theory a worthwhile perspective for developing a deeper understanding of workplace diversity. First, immigrants and people of color happen to provide one of the principal dimensions of the diversity phenomenon. In historical terms, however, it is important to remember that the ancestors and forebears of the same groups (who have now come to be identified in North America and parts of Europe as "immigrants" or as "people of color") also served as the objects or targets of Euro-American conquest, expansion, and colonization. The colonial encounter of the past several centuries, hence, was one of the most decisive and meaningful historical processes that influenced and shaped the West's perceptions of the non-West, that is, of the West's Others (Said, 1979, 1993). Moreover, as Edward Said's meticulous scholarship suggests, even today, the West[3] continues to view immigrants, people of color, and similar other members of the non-West through an imperial lens that was originally crafted during the colonial era. Postcolonial theory, therefore, can be a valuable perspective for understanding some of the complexities attending cultural and racial dynamics in contemporary Western organizations.

Second, for the West, the colonial experience holds some significant implications for gender relations and sexuality. As postcolonial scholars such as Nandy (1983) have noted, one of the most unfortunate by-products of colonialism was the production, reification, and privileging of a culture of aggressive hypermasculinity in the West—a culture that; among other things, devalued the role and importance of women and denigrated femininity. Postcolonial theory, therefore, can be helpful in shedding some extra light on the contentious diversity-related issues that surround sexuality and gender relations at the workplace. Finally, the postcolonial perspective is valuable also for its important insights into the dynamics of social and cultural marginality. As postcolonial theorists have frequently noted, at the

paradigmatic level the discourse[4] of colonization is structured around the exchanges taking place between the metropolitan "center" and the provincial "periphery." Postcolonial inquiry, accordingly, has devoted considerable scholarly effort toward understanding the center-periphery discourse. As a result, postcolonial theory can be a valuable aid for analyzing dominant group-marginal group dynamics. The next section of the chapter provides a brief overview of postcolonial theory.

POSTCOLONIAL THEORY: A BRIEF OVERVIEW

The twin processes of colonial conquest and decolonization represent a massive upheaval of truly global proportions, which touched and profoundly affected most of the world. To provide just one index of the scope of colonialism, by the early decades of the present century—when the infamous "Age of Empires" was at its zenith—Europe's colonies covered almost 85% of the Earth's surface (Headrick, 1981; Said, 1979). Given this magnitude of the colonial encounter, it is not surprising that colonialism has long served as a major object of scholarly research and inquiry. Such being the case, it may be useful and worthwhile to point out that postcolonial theory differs from earlier theorizations of imperialism and colonialism in some important respects.

Briefly stated, whereas early research on colonialism mostly concentrated upon "brute" aspects and sought to analyze the political, economic, and military impact of Western colonization, the primary focus of postcolonial theory is upon the more subtle dimensions of imperialism spanning culture, ideology, and discourse (Dirks, 1992; Nandy, 1983; Niranjana, 1992; Prakash, 1995; Said, 1979, 1993; Tiffin & Larson, 1994). One of the major objectives of such focus upon the subtle aspects of colonialism is to understand the complex web of processes by means of which the colonial encounter worked to produce the subjectivities[5] of the colonizers and the colonized. In this process of focusing upon the subtle dimensions of colonialism, it is not as if postcolonial theory completely disregards or overlooks the political, the economic, and the military. Rather, instead of totally neglecting to consider the brute features of colonialism, postcolonial theory textualizes those features and aims to understand the role and effect of such features in the constitution of colonizer/colonized subjectivities. Postcolonialism, hence, may be seen as providing a more sophisticated, nuanced, and complex reading of imperialism, and as attempting to analyze those cultural and ideological aspects of colonialism that are sometimes said to have survived the formal end of the colonial era itself (Nandy, 1983; Tiffin & Lawson, 1994).[6]

Postcolonial theory came into prominence with Said's (1979) authoritative study, *Orientalism*. In this highly influential work, Said (1979) proffers an analysis[7] of the structures of the Western discourse (both scholarly as well as popular) on the Middle East and Islam, a discourse that he labels *Orientalism*. In brief, according to Said (1979), the discourse of Orientalism posited that the Occident and the Orient represented ontologically distinct and opposite entities and that the "essence" of the Orient consisted of such elements as "despotism, . . . splendor, cruelty, sensuality" (p. 4), untruthfulness, lack of logic, absence of energy and initiative, intrigue, cunning, unkindness, lethargy, and suspicion (pp. 38–39), as well as eccentricity, backwardness, indifference, feminine penetrability, supine malleability, and so on (p. 206). Thus, with the assistance of these and similar other tropes, the discourse of Orientalism constructed an image of the Orient around the themes of "decline, degradation, and decadence" (Dirks, 1992, p. 9), portraying the Orient as being fit (*in an ontological sense*) only for conquest, subjugation, and colonization.

Following the lead given by Said (1979), postcolonialism has gone through a period of intense and explosive growth, and any comprehensive overview of postcolonial research and inquiry is clearly beyond the scope of the present chapter. Nevertheless, it may still be useful to provide a brief catalog of some of the major tendencies exhibited by postcolonial theoretic scholarship. One important direction taken by postcolonial inquiry, for instance, broadly emulates Said's (1979) approach, seeking to provide in-depth analyses of the language and rhetoric of imperialism (e.g., Brantlinger, 1988; Spurr, 1993; Suleri, 1992). Another subfield of postcolonial scholarship (represented by Subaltern Group, the influential collective of South Asian historians) regards the old, colonialist

accounts of history as instruments of domination and seeks to reinterpret the past with a view to recovering an insurrectionary history of the dominated groups (e.g., Guha, 1983; Guha & Spivak, 1988). On the other hand, the proponents of the *hybridization* thesis (e.g., Bhabha, 1985, 1994) work toward unveiling the record of the hybrid construction of *both* the West and the non-West, and another important group of scholars (e.g., Cesaire, 1972; Nandy, 1983, 1987) seeks to analyze the negative, psychological and cultural consequences of colonialism *not only* for the non-West, but for the West as well. Simultaneously, other groups of postcolonial theorists can be seen to be occupied in such overlapping scholarly programs as (a) investigating the complicity of past and present Western scholarship with imperialism and the imperial mindset (e.g., Asad, 1973; Bishop, 1990; Chakrabarty, 1992), (b) critiquing and problematizing the idea of the nation-state (Chatterjee, 1986, 1993; Nandy, 1992), and (c) deconstructing the mythic notion of (economic) development (Sachs, 1992).

Taken as a whole, the combined analytics of the various streams of postcolonial theory provide some important insights into the overall nature of the discourse of colonization. To begin with, according to postcolonial scholars, the discourse of colonization may be said to be fundamentally premised upon the constructed availability of an ontological Other, an Other that serves as the focal point for distilling and concentrating the *opposites* of all those privileged moral, ethical, and aesthetic attributes that have gradually accreted to constitute the very core of the colonizer's own self-image. Such being the case, the discourse of colonization needs to be seen as having worked simultaneously to produce (and naturalize) the subjectivities of both the colonizer and the colonized. Hence, for instance, Said's (1979) important observation that the discourse of "the Orient has helped to *define* [italics added] Europe (or the West) as . . . [the Orient's] contrasting image, idea, personality, experience" (pp. 1–2).

The discourse of colonialism conceived of the West's non-Western Other as the epistemological and ontological opposite of the West and saw the West as "superior" and the non-West as "inferior." The construction of the West/non-West dichotomy was fleshed out and completed by means of the production and institutionalization of an elaborate series of hierarchical binary polarities (Dirks, 1992; Nandy, 1983; Prakash, 1995). Table 46.1 provides a brief list of such binaries.

Along with the above, however, colonial discourse also evinced a great deal of ambivalence toward the "inferior" non-West, which gradually came to serve as the object of Western colonization. For instance, even though it was clearly the goal of this discourse to define the non-West as inferior and undesirable, the non-West was also regarded by this discourse as a highly desirable object for Western possession. Similarly, although the non-West was seen as "weak and effeminate," it was also viewed as a grave threat that represented "the unpleasant likelihood of a sudden eruption that would destroy . . . [the Western] world" (Said, 1979, p. 251). Thus, the discourse of colonization saw the non-West as simultaneously being undesirable and desirable, weak and potentially lethally explosive, something to be possessed and something to be feared, something needing to be controlled and something that never would (or could) be completely controlled (Said, 1979, 1993; Spurr, 1993). Against this backdrop of colonialism and postcolonial theory, the next section of the chapter will venture into the world of the American and Western European petroleum industry with a view to exploring, unraveling, unveiling, documenting, and theorizing the persistent imprint of the colonizing consciousness in the petroleum sector's representations of the Other.

The Colonizing Consciousness and the Discourse of Oil

This chapter's interest in the oil industry (and in the discourse of oil)[8] springs from the privileged position occupied by oil in contemporary Western civilization. Oil, as the title of Tugendhat and Hamilton's (1975) remarkable book declares, is "the world's biggest business" (see also Yergin, 1991, p. 13). Quite apart from sheer size, moreover, oil (as the preeminent source of energy and as an important raw material for such diverse products as adhesives, animal feeds, dyestuffs, explosives, fertilizers, paints, pesticides, plastics, synthetic fibers, etc.) so thoroughly saturates people's everyday lives in the West that, following Yergin (1991, p. 14), contemporary

Western society may well be best understood as a Hydrocarbon Society. According to Yergin (p. 15) and several others, for the West, the 20th century is truly "the century of oil." Furthermore, for the United States in particular, oil is part and parcel of the myths and dreams that make up "the life of the mind in America," being inextricably linked with the legends and the sagas of the frontier, the wildcatter, and the pioneer and with rags to riches tales. Symbolically and materially, therefore, petroleum occupies a position of great eminence in the Western life world, with the result that the discourse of oil is rightfully deserving of serious scholarly attention. Before turning toward the discourse of oil, however, some basic familiarity with the broad contours of the history of the Western oil industry may be useful.

The history of the present-day Western oil industry begins roughly around the middle of the last century (Ai-Chalabi, 1980; Blair, 1976; Hamilton, 1986; Karlsson, 1986; Prasad, 1994; Roncaglia, 1985; Sampson, 1975; Terzian, 1985; Tugwell, 1988; Turner, 1978; Vallenilla, 1975; Yergin, 1991).

Table 46.1   The Hierarchical System of Colonialist Binaries

West	Non-west
Active	Passive
Center	Margin/periphery
Civilized	Primitive/savage
Colonizer	Colonized
Developed	Backward/undeveloped/ underdeveloped/developing
Fullness/plenitude/ completeness	Lack/inadequacy/ incompleteness
Historical (people with history)	Ahistorical (people without history)
The liberated	The savable
Masculine	Feminine/effeminate
Modern	Archaic
Nation	Tribe
Occidental	Oriental
Scientific	Superstitious
Secular	Nonsecular
Subject	Object
Superior	Inferior
The vanguard	The led
White	Black/brown/yellow

In the United States, the fledgling industry soon came under the control of John D. Rockefeller's Standard Oil Company, which controlled as much as 90% of the industry by the 1880s (Prasad, 1994). During the early years of the present century, however, Standard Oil witnessed the rise of some important domestic competition in the shape of Gulf Oil Company[9] and the Texas Company (today's Texaco). At the global level, after an initial period characterized by both competition and collusion, control over the petroleum sector came to be wielded first by the "Big Three" (namely, Standard Oil of New Jersey,[10] Royal Dutch/Shell, and British Petroleum), and later by the Seven Sisters, the well-organized international cartel of seven Euro-American oil companies.[11] To give just a brief hint of the extent of the Seven Sisters' domination of the international petroleum system, in 1950, these seven companies controlled virtually the entire crude oil production of the Middle East, Venezuela, and Indonesia (the three major oil producing regions outside the United States and the then-U.S.S.R.) and accounted for about 85% of the total crude oil production outside North America and the Socialist countries. Similar levels of global control were wielded by the Sisters in other oil industry segments (e.g., refining, transportation etc.) as well.

Even a brief look at the history of oil is sufficient to reveal that the international dominance of the Seven Sisters was simply one of the plum fruits of colonialism. That is to say, the work involved in creating a Euro-American hegemony in the international petroleum system had gone hand in hand with the projection, establishment, and consolidation of European and American political and military power over the rest of the world during the colonial era. It was inevitable, therefore, that the political end of Western colonialism would be followed by an intense struggle (waged by those who had been colonized) aimed at changing the asymmetries of power that had so far characterized the political economy of international oil. In a nutshell, this is exactly what took place by means of the OPEC offensive of the 1960s and the 1970s.[12]

With the preceding introduction to the historical context, we now turn our attention toward examining the representation of Otherness in the discourse of oil. For this purpose, the present chapter isolates two key discursive events from the recent history of the Western petroleum sector and attempts to analyze and understand the two events from the perspective of postcolonial theory. In view of the fact that the Middle East has been at the very heart of Western oil imperialism for close to a century, we begin, appropriately enough, with the labeling (by the Seven Sisters) of the Saudi Arabian sheikh, Abdullah Tariki, as the *Red* Sheikh.

The Red Sheikh

Sheikh Abdullah Tariki of Saudi Arabia, who left an indelible imprint on the international political economy of oil and who is commonly regarded as one of the two cofounders of the Organization of the Petroleum Exporting Countries (OPEC),[13] was a pan-Arab nationalist and an ardent admirer of Egypt's charismatic leader, Gamal Abdel Nasser (Terzian, 1985; Yergin, 1991). Tariki's importance in the history of oil stems from the decisive role that he played in opposing oil imperialism.

A trained geologist, Tariki first rose to prominence in 1948, when he became the Director of the Oil Affairs Supervisory Bureau in the Ministry of Finance in Saudi Arabia. He came to head the Saudi Directorate of Oil and Mining Affairs in 1955 and was appointed the Oil Minister of Saudi Arabia in 1960, the same year in which OPEC was founded. An outspoken critic of (oil) imperialism, Tariki strongly denounced the activities and policies of the Seven Sisters on more than one occasion. He also insisted on invoking the Saudi rights to two directorships (which had never been used by Saudi Arabia in the past) on Aramco[14] and was himself appointed an Aramco director in 1959. As a result of his activism, he was promptly dubbed by the Seven Sisters as the Red Sheikh. From the perspective of postcolonial theory, this representation of Sheikh Tariki needs to be viewed as an important discursive event in the history and the "text" of imperial oil. The remainder of this section of the chapter will aim to briefly understand what such an act of naming or labeling may reveal about the colonizing consciousness itself.

To begin with, in a post-World War II hermeneutic context overwhelmingly defined by frenzied anti-communism in America and (parts of) Western Europe, the Seven Sisters' use of the Red (i.e., communist/socialist) label for pigeonholing and categorizing Sheikh Tariki offers a revealing glimpse into Western colonialism's frequently commented-upon tendency to quickly and hastily define the Other as embodying a grave danger that supposedly imperils the very existence of Western civilization (see, e.g., Said, 1979, 1993; Spurr, 1993). In addition, however, the use of the specific descriptor Red seems to tell us something more about the colonizing consciousness as it manifested itself through the Seven Sisters.

It can be rightfully argued, for instance, that the use of this particular label (Red) may be viewed as an index of the Seven Sisters' need to see Sheikh Tariki as an element (or a component) of a larger, anti-Western conspiracy—that is, as something much more sinister and diabolical than an isolated, stand-alone danger, howsoever menacing or threatening. In other words, by using the Red label, the Seven Sisters may have been attempting to impute far greater potential danger to Sheikh Tariki (because now he was represented as being a part of a large, powerful, and well-organized, communist conspiracy) than would have been the case if he were to be considered just another (non-Red) threat, enemy, or opposition. This, however, may not be all. Given the highly negative understanding that people generally have of words such as conspiracy, conspirators, and so forth (which carry not-so-subtle hints of intrigue, deviousness, betrayal, back stabbing, and double crossing), in calling the sheikh Red, the Seven Sisters may also be seen as suggesting that the sheikh was dishonorable and treacherous enough to be a part of something as evil and immoral as a conspiracy. Hence, in labeling the sheikh Red, colonizing oil may be said to be claiming not only that the sheikh was an enemy of the West, but also that the sheikh was an evil and ethically debased enemy, undeserving of the courtesies and considerations that one normally extended to those enemies or opponents who were honorable and morally upright.[15] However, the use of the Red label for the Saudi sheikh also points to a crucial paradox, tension, or ambivalence that invests colonialism's engagement with its Others. For, if on the one hand, the Red label is suggestive of colonialism's tendency to represent the colonized as ominous and threatening, and/or to demonize and vilify the Other, on the other hand,

the same label is also indicative of colonialism's intense desire to seek to reduce the menace of the *difference* of Otherness by means of constituting the colonized (i.e., the Other) in the form of images that are already familiar to the colonizing consciousness. By the middle of this century, we need to recall, the discourse of revolutionary communism (the Red menace) had been a prominent part of Western history and imagination for more than 100 years,[16] with the result that communism, while undoubtedly being regarded as a grave generalized threat, nevertheless represented (for the West) something familiar and manageable, something which the West was capable of successfully containing and dealing with. Somewhat paradoxically, therefore, even as the label of the Red Sheikh underscored the material and moral graveness of the threat embodied in the Other, simultaneously, by means of gesturing toward the familiar and the already known, the selfsame label also made an attempt to redefine the different as not-so-different, and the new as not-so-new, and thus, to contain and reduce the Otherness of the colonized to more manageable proportions.

Thus, in part, the act of labeling Sheikh Abdullah Tariki as the Red Sheikh may be seen as a somewhat desperate effort on colonialism's part to seek to preserve and maintain an earlier, simpler, and more familiar (Western) sociocultural schema for sense making, which was being subjected to increasing pressure and distortion as it confronted other, rival, cultural schemata that were unavoidably brought to the colonizers' consciousness during the course of colonialism's extended encounter with its Others. However, in labeling the sheikh Red, the colonizing consciousness can also be said to be attempting to achieve more than a simple containment of differences embodied in, and exhibited by, the colonized.

Specifically, one may argue that, buried in the act of naming Sheikh Tariki the Red Sheikh, was an implicit claim that it was *only* the "red devil" that opposed the West's imperial project, and that, actively or passively, the rest of the world supported, valued, and cherished the colonialist enterprise of "bringing light and civilization" to the dark corners of the Earth.[17] In other words, we could say that in declaring the Saudi sheikh to be Red, (oil) imperialism may also be said to have been making the claim that the whole world, *except* the evil communists, was deeply appreciative (or welcomingly accepting) of the West's colonial rule and domination as a beacon of Hope, Prosperity, and Progress.

Carefully analyzed, the claim (which is implicitly embedded in the Red Sheikh label) that only reds oppose the West offers us an important insight into the colonizing consciousness. We need to begin by noting that, in the West, communism has long been regarded as the devil's own handmaiden and as a symbol of all that is evil and immoral in this world. In such a context (where communism is synonymous with evil), the claim that it is *only* the Red devil that opposes the imperial West has the effect of reflexively creating an image of colonialism in the form of a contrasting figure to the evil that is communism. That is to say, the claim that only evil communism opposes Western imperialism works to produce a self-representation of Western colonialism as the repository of universal good. As noted by countless postcolonial scholars, such a self-representation of colonialism is crucial for the success of the colonialist enterprise.

Finally, in labeling Sheikh Tariki the Red Sheikh, colonialism also allows us a glimpse into its own conceptualization of global history. As postcolonial scholarship has frequently noted (see, e.g., Chakrabarty, 1992), the Hegelian notion of teleological history (e.g., Hegel, 1900)—which came to be reified and naturalized in the Western consciousness during the period of modernity—conceives of the West as the vanguard of human history and imagines the rest of the world to be by fate ordained to follow into the West's footsteps.[18] Concomitantly, this view of human history believes also in the universal applicability and validity of Western historiographical categories such as capital, feudal, bourgeois, liberal, and so on. Indeed, it may even be declared with due merit that the modernistic view of history considers these and other Western categories to be of universal *ontological* significance. Hence, the act of labeling Sheikh Abdullah Tariki a Red communist—which has the effect of interpretively situating the (Saudi) Arabian resistance to oil imperialism within a Eurocentric story of the conflict between bourgeois liberalism and communism—may be seen as an elisionary discursive maneuver that denies the uniqueness and the particularities of Arab history and that seeks to absorb Arab history in a

globalizing and totalizing Western narrative with a view to reiterating/reinforcing the West's claim to its own universality.

Admittedly, the preceding is a fairly condensed reading of what may be called the Red Sheikh episode in the discourse of imperial oil. Even such a brief reading, however, does not fail to offer a number of important and interesting insights into the colonizers' consciousness. We will now turn our attention toward yet another discursive event in the history of the Western oil industry with a view to illuminating some other facets and aspects of the colonizing consciousness.

Oil, Camels, Sheikhs, and Bananas

In his immensely readable and highly impressive analysis of the politics, economics, and deadly intrigue surrounding international oil and oil imperialism, Terzian (1985) documents an incredible colonialist moment (in which extreme imperial hauteur seems to have freely and lavishly commingled with pique, exasperation, bitterness, contempt, derision, dismissal, rage, dread, and several other conflicting and not-so-conflicting passions) when he narrates how an American newspaper, the *Washington Post*—a newspaper that incidentally is frequently seen in the United States as one of the leading symbols of liberal America—once snappishly referred to OPEC as "a quarrelling collection of camel sheikhdoms and banana republics" (p. 163). For the postcolonial reader, such a representation of OPEC seems simply to overflow with rich meaning. The purpose of this section of the chapter, accordingly, is to provide a reading of this angry and tense *Washington Post* outburst with a view to affording some further insights into the colonizer's consciousness.

Founded in 1960, OPEC came into existence as a united front of a group of large oil-exporting countries[19] deeply desirous of overthrowing oil imperialism, with its legacy of exploitative petroleum concessions, colonial spheres of influence, and untrammelled Western control and domination of the political and economic lives of the oil-producing countries. That the founders of OPEC clearly envisioned this body as a coalition for opposing Western imperialism seems obvious when we consider the secrecy that shrouded the negotiations leading to the creation of OPEC (Terzian, 1985; Yergin, 1991).[20] Nor was such secrecy unwarranted. The founding of OPEC took place against the backdrop of the 1953 coup in Iran (following Iran's nationalization of its oil industry), which had been orchestrated by the secret intelligence agencies of Britain and the United States,[21] and the invasion of Egypt in 1956 by Britain, France, and Israel, after the Egyptian government of Gamal Abdel Nasser had nationalized the Suez Canal.

In the colonialist discourse of oil, OPEC appears as something of an enigma. Looking at the Western discourse of oil and imperialism, it would seem that, although this discourse recognizes the clear nature of the challenge posed by OPEC to the enterprise of colonization and empire, it never quite succeeds in making up its mind about whether to treat OPEC seriously or not. Here an example or two may be useful in clarifying what is being suggested above. For instance, right from the moment of its inception, OPEC forced the Western oil cartel to give up the latter's unilateral control of the pricing of oil (Ghanem, 1986), and, as a result of such radical dilution of colonialist control, the activities and practices of international oil were fundamentally transformed. Notwithstanding such transformation effected by OPEC in the "text" of oil, however, somewhat surprisingly, the Western discourse of oil continued also to represent OPEC as incapable of posing a serious challenge to Western imperialism, and as something that could simply be brushed aside in a brief, dismissive gesture. As evidence, one may consider the in-depth report on Middle East oil prepared by the U.S. Central Intelligence Agency (CIA) in November 1960—that is, 2 full months after OPEC came into existence—which dismissed OPEC in "a mere four lines" (Yergin, 1991, p. 523).[22]

Similarly, a report in the *New York Times* on the occasion of OPEC's founding stated that the "'cartel' [i.e., OPEC] . . . would only last a year or two . . . following which everything would go back to normal" (Terzian, 1985, p. vii). This report is interesting on account of the deep ambivalence that it exhibits toward OPEC. On the one hand, the report's nostalgia for the pre-OPEC "good, old days" (as suggested by the report's prophecy that things would "go back to normal" after OPEC's

hoped-for demise) indicates a clear acknowledgment of OPEC's *power* to affect the course of history and to make the state of oil affairs not-so-normal (from the Western perspective). Thereby, the report undoubtedly recognizes OPEC as a serious threat to oil imperialism. On the other hand, however, by stating that OPEC "would only last a year or two," the report also seems to suggest that OPEC may not be powerful enough to survive for long and, therefore, may not really be a serious threat to the imperial project. Hence, as a result of the highly uncertain position accorded to OPEC in the discourse of oil, this discourse would appear to be deeply ruptured and fissured. And it is from within such an ambivalent and fractured discourse that the *Washington Post* quip about camels, sheikhs, and bananas may be seen as emerging.

Recall that the *Washington Post*'s representation of OPEC reads: "a quarrelling collection of camel sheikhdoms and banana republics." The important question that we face here is how does one read this representation of OPEC. In short, are there meanings, allusions, and nuances buried deep in this representation that are in need of being excavated? In what follows, it will be argued that, from a postcolonial perspective, it is possible to read the preceding representation of OPEC as a complex and ambivalent outcome of the conflict and commingling among a number of discordant Western discourses including those of the Orient, the Savage, and the Nation-State.

To begin with, note that OPEC is not being referred to as, say, a collection of quarrelling nations (or, states, countries, peoples, etc.). Why not, for example, call OPEC a collection (quarrelling or otherwise) of republics and monarchies spread over Asia, Africa, and South America? Why, in sum, the hesitation and reluctance on part of the *Washington Post* (in its references to OPEC) to employ signifiers that are commonly understood to suggest the nation and/or the nation-state? In part, the answer to this question may be found in the hierarchy of colonialist binaries referred to above (see Table 46.1). In brief, as Table 46.1 indicates, the ideas of the nation and the nation-state are such an intimate component of the "civilized, superior" West's own self-representation (and self-constitution) that any suggestion of the possible existence of nation-states in the non-West would seem to have the effect of denying the very Otherness of that non-West and, consequently, of radically disturbing the ontology of colonialism.[23] In other words, the reluctance to refer to the OPEC countries as modern nations may well be a reflection of the danger that such a mode of referring to OPEC poses for the West's own (sense of) reality.

However, if the discourse of oil must evince a reluctance toward addressing the OPEC countries as full-fledged, civilized nations, are there any valid reasons that may offer some likely explanation as to why this discourse must be equally shy of referring to OPEC as a group of barbarians? Why not, for instance, designate OPEC as a quarrelling collection of primitives? What are the constraints, in other words, that inhibit the discourse of oil from calling OPEC, say, a horde of wild savages? In order to understand such constraints, we need to take a brief look at the historical trajectory followed by the Western discourse of the Savage (see, e.g., Hulme, 1986).

According to Hulme (1986), schematically, the discourse of the Savage is traceable to Herodotus of Classical Greece.[24] Constructed around notions of purely Other creatures, such as Amazons, Anthropophagi and Cynocephali,[25] the discourse of the Savage exhibited an amazing degree of continuity and changelessness in the European imagination as this discourse wound its way down through the millennia. During the centuries following the European voyages of discovery, however, the discourse of the Savage became exclusively tied to specific parts and sections of certain unique geographical locales, such as Africa, the Caribbean[26] and the Americas, the Andaman Islands, and the Malay Archipelago. As a result, by the 20th century, the discourse of the Savage was no longer available to be employed freely for representing Europe's Others. Even more specifically, that discourse was not unrestrictedly available for purposes of representing Iranians, Iraqis, Saudi Arabians, and so on, who formed a significant majority of OPEC's membership. Hence, working inevitably within the boundaries decreed by the preexisting Western discourses of Savagery and the Nation-State, the discourse of oil was placed in the unenviable position of being able to call OPEC neither savage nor civilized, neither modern nor primeval, neither the same nor a pure Other.

The discourses of the Savage and the Nation-State were, of course, not the only preexisting discourses operating to prescribe enunciatory limits to what could be articulated by the discourse of oil. A third such earlier discourse was that of the Orient. Similar to the discourse of the Savage, the origins of the discourse of the Orient may also be found in European antiquity (Said, 1979, p. 68). By all accounts, however, it would appear that the discourse of the Orient achieved a new intensity and salience following Marco Polo, the 13th-century Venetian traveler to the East, who is said to have visited the opulent and radiantly magnificent court of the Great Mongol Khan himself (Hulme, 1986). Briefly staled, this discourse saw the Orient as a land of gold, of immense riches, of mighty empires,[27] and of hoary, splendorous civilizations, as well as of mystery, novelty, danger, and terror. Through various twists and turns, the discourse of the Orient eventually came to take the form of what Said (1979) calls Orientalism, with its distinctly pejorative construction of the Orient.[28]

One may well suppose that in Said's Orientalism the discourse of oil would have found precisely what it could be said to have been looking for, namely, the vocabulary, imagery, idioms, and styles of representation for addressing those of the non-West who could not have been rendered (in light of the already discussed enunciatory limits imposed by the discourses of the Savage and the Nation-State) as either pure savages or as fully civilized. However, for at least two reasons the discourse of oil seems to have been denied such an easy resolution of the dilemma that it faced. First of all, there was the issue of (what the discourse of oil understood as) the banana republics. As is generally known, OPEC began as an alliance between two of the richest oil-producing areas of the world, namely the Middle East and South America. And to a large extent, the perception of OPEC as being a group of Middle Eastern and South American countries (a perception that was formed at the moment of OPEC's origin) continues to persist. Orientalist vocabulary, however, as the discourse of oil could not fail to realize, was capable of being appropriately employed only in the case of the Middle East (or by extension, that of the East as such), but not for purposes of representing Latin America. Hence, as far as the discourse of oil was concerned, Orientalism could only offer a partial solution to its problems.

Second, there was the all-too-important matter of oil—the black gold. As suggested by our previous discussions, the transformation and evolution of the discourse of the Orient into its latest incarnation (namely, Orientalism) can be seen as involving the substantive displacement of an earlier chain of key tropes (in outline form, "gold," "immense wealth," "mighty empire," "the Great Khan," "powerful armies," "grand civilization," and so on) by another chain (to wit, "moribund society," "backward populace," "decadent sheikhs," "puny principalities," "weak armies," "degraded civilization," and so forth). One of the most significant shifts involved in this transformation seems to have been the gradual eclipse and disappearance of gold as a leading metaphor employed in conjunction with the Orient. Indeed, one may well argue that the successful discursive transformation of the Orient from the domicile of "the magnificently civilized" to that of "the not-fully civilized" was most crucially dependent upon this very effacement of gold from the sequence of key metaphors used in connection with the Orient. With the arrival of the *black* gold on the Middle Eastern scene, however, Orientalism's masterful elimination of gold (from the series of major Oriental metaphors) becomes questionable, with the result that (as far as the discourse of oil was concerned) Orientalist tropes alone may not have been considered sufficient for successfully representing the essence of the not-savage-yet-not-fully-civilized Others of the Western world.

Said (1979) has pointed out that, during the last couple of centuries or so, the pejorative discourse of Orientalism took such a powerful hold of the Western imagination that the very designation of someone or something as Oriental was sufficient to create a strongly negative impression of the object or the person so characterized. That is to say, as a result of the sedimentation and naturalization of the discourse of Orientalism, *Orient* (and the panoply of terms used for describing the Orient) had become a shorthand term for quickly and accurately telegraphing a dense constellation of overwhelmingly negative images to the Western mind. Thus, for instance,

referring to a country as a *sheikhdom* was usually enough to clearly indicate to the average Western person that the country in question was backward, apathetic, squalid, nonmodern, despotic, and so on.

As suggested earlier, however, with oil becoming a symbol of richness and wealth, and the consequent reemergence of the trope of gold in the chain of key metaphors used for referring to the Orient, the (so far unambiguous) pejorative connotations of Orientalist vocabulary seem to have come under new pressures and strains. One possible result of this could be a degree of uncertainty (exhibited within the discourse of oil) regarding the stability and unambiguity of the senses, meanings, and images connoted by the old Orientalist terminology. Could it have been the case that it was this very uncertainty that found expression in the *Washington Post*'s compelling need to refer not simply to sheikhdoms, but to *camel* sheikhdoms, in its own representation of OPEC?

In a nutshell, what is being suggested above is that, with the arrival of oil (and the reemergence of the trope of Oriental riches), the term sheikhdom alone may no longer have appeared sufficient for communicating what was one of the long-established dogmas of Orientalism, namely, the pejorative essence of the Orient. Hence the need, apparently, to further calibrate and finetune the precise connotation of the term sheikhdom by means of adding the adjectival qualifier, camel. The sheikhs may be as wealthy as the richest in the capitalist West, this adjective seems to aver, but the sheikhs' wealth is not the dynamic, sleek, jet-setting, modern wealth that "we" have; the sheikhs' wealth is the discredited and compromised wealth of those who are organically linked to something as slow, bizarre, awkward, and premodern as the camel. And lest there be any doubts about the precise connotation of the phrase, camel sheikhdoms, the *Washington Post* thoughtfully provides its readers with a symmetrical phrase, *banana republics*. OPEC, as this newspaper's quote under scrutiny is careful to point out, is "a quarrelling collection of camel sheikhdoms *and* banana republics."

The *Washington Post*'s juxtaposition of camel sheikhdoms and banana republics would seem to be significant. The term banana republics has long been used in the West for derisively referring to a group of small Caribbean and Latin American countries that traditionally derived an overwhelming proportion of their foreign exchange earnings through the export of tropical fruits such as bananas (see, e.g., Enloe, 1989). The fruit plantations in these countries tend to be controlled by large foreign conglomerates such as the United Brands Corporation (formerly, United Fruit Company) of the United States, and the banana republics themselves are seen as being ruled by corrupt tinhorn dictators said to be in the pay of overseas governments and corporations. In sum, the expression, banana republics, conveys contempt rather than respect. And it is this contempt that is seemingly sought to be evoked by means of mentioning, in the same breath, the two expressions, camel sheikhdoms and banana republics. In addition, however, the reference to banana republics may be seen as also serving to make explicit OPEC's contiguity and imbrication with "that [wild and] primordial part of America, the Caribbean" (Hulme, 1986, p. xiii), and thus attempting to reintroduce (through the back door, as it were) the Savage into the discourse of oil.

Finally, of course, one cannot ignore the use of the epithet, *quarrelling.* After all, according to the *Washington Post,* OPEC is not any simple collection of camel sheikhdoms and banana republics, OPEC is a *quarrelling* collection of camel sheikhdoms and banana republics. Nations, according to one of the inviolable dogmas of the Western liberal doctrine of international relations, have no permanent friends, they only have permanent interests. Hence, nations (even Western ones) frequently quarrel among themselves. Indeed, nations (or, at least, their presidents, kings, and ruling elites) have fought and warred with one another since time immemorial. Such being the case, one may rightfully ask, what is so new or different about the OPEC member nations quarrelling among themselves? In other words, why this insistence by the *Washington Post* on this particular label (quarrelling) over the plethora of other labels that might have been available for characterizing OPEC? It is possible, at least to some extent, that the use of this label expresses a desire and a hope for OPEC's disintegration: If OPEC as a group is not cohesive— if its members are always at loggerheads with one another—the West may justifiably hope that OPEC will soon collapse, and, for the West, things may quickly go back to "normal." But there may be more

to the use of the word quarrelling than a simple expression of the hope for OPEC's decline and fall.

In his impressive book, *The Rhetoric of Empire,* Spurr (1993) draws the reader's attention to an article in the *Harper's Magazine* that quotes a senior representative of the Iranian Revolution of 1978–1979 as saying: "You westerners . . . why do you always talk about us as having power struggles while you yourselves merely have politics?" (p. 190). In his analysis following this quotation, Spurr perspicaciously points to the important rhetorical distinction between the "barbarism of 'power struggles'" and "the relative civility of 'politics'" (p. 191). In a similar vein, we need to note that the use of the word quarrelling may have the crucial rhetorical function of denigrating the politics and the internal differences that inevitably attend the coming together of a number of sovereign states. Indeed, the word quarrelling almost has the effect of conjuring the image of a pack of ill-bred children who are in need of firm, adult supervision. And given that the ideology of colonialism often pictures the colonizer in the role of a mature adult who is duty-bound to be a trustee, guardian, and protector of the immature child that is the colonized (see, e.g., Nandy, 1983, 1987), could we not claim with sufficient reason that the *Washington Post*'s use of the word quarrelling may be seen as working to represent the OPEC as an underdeveloped child needing firm Western control, guidance, and discipline?

In sum, the preceding postcolonial analysis of two significant discursive events from the recent history of oil and imperialism offers some important insights into the colonizer's consciousness. It will be our endeavor in the rest of this chapter to use this understanding of the colonizing consciousness for purposes of developing a deeper appreciation of the dilemmas of workplace diversity in the West.

THE COLONIZING CONSCIOUSNESS AND THE DILEMMAS OF WORKPLACE DIVERSITY

As we have already noted, the discourse of colonization is fundamentally dependent upon the construction of an ontological other. Our foregoing analysis of the discourse of oil was intended to (a) develop a more sophisticated understanding of the topography of the discursive terrain that seems to condition and regulate the nature of the material and symbolic exchanges taking place between the colonizing Self and the colonized Other, and, in the process, (b) to adumbrate the persistent imprint of colonial discourse on the mundane and quotidian activities of one of the foremost spheres of Western political economy, namely, the petroleum sector.

To recapitulate briefly, our analysis suggests that the colonizing consciousness mostly tends to conceptualize the Other in a highly pejorative vein—to wit, as morally debased, as immature and not fully developed, as something that menaces the safety and well-being of the Western society, and so on. Moreover, employing simple contrast, the colonizing consciousness seems to view the colonial West itself as the storehouse of universal good, as developed and mature, and as morally obliged to serve in the capacity of a guardian and trustee for the non-West. At the same time, the colonial discourse is also the site where a number of somewhat discrepant discourses may be said to intersect and collide, with the result that the colonizing consciousness exhibits some deep ambivalence in its reception of the colonized Other. All in all, therefore, the colonizing consciousness sees the colonized as being, at the same time, a grave threat and as something too weak to pose a credible threat, as something needing to be contained that never can be fully contained, and as beings representing pure difference who can, nonetheless, be assimilated in the totalizing narratives of Western history. Not surprisingly, therefore, the colonizer's approach toward the colonized seems to be characterized by a sense of deep schizophrenia. It is this very schizophrenic attitude, this chapter submits, which the contemporary West brings in its encounters with workplace diversity, and it is only by grasping the implications of such schizophrenia that we may hope to develop a better understanding of the dilemmas of diversity faced by contemporary Western organizations.

The introductory parts of this chapter have already drawn our attention to the importance of postcolonial theory for understanding the dilemmas of workplace diversity. Nevertheless, at this point, the skeptical reader may be somewhat justified in posing the question: Is this chapter's analysis of colonial discourse of any continued relevance

today? After all, isn't colonialism supposed to be dead now? In order to address this question, we do not necessarily need to enter into the contentious debate as to whether we inhabit a *neo*-colonial or a *post*-colonial world. What may be more important to point out is that discourses saturate us; they provide us with the everyday language, the idioms, and the vocabulary for speaking and thinking about "things" of interest to us. As a result, in the West, it may be virtually impossible to think and speak about the non-West without employing a colonialist vocabulary, the political demise of colonialism notwithstanding. Such vocabulary, furthermore, does not become impartial and nonpartisan simply because colonialism may have come to a political end. "Beneath the idioms," as Said (1979) observes in the context of Orientalism, there is always "a layer of [partisan] doctrine" (p. 203).[29] For instance, the imprint of such partisan, colonialist doctrine is visible whenever the various apparatuses of the Western world (and that includes Western individuals, governments, academics, scholarly journals, media, cultural agencies, corporations, and all the rest) assert their right (or obligation) to "guide" the rest of the world, be it for intellectual, economic, social, or political "development." Discourses, therefore, have enormous staying power. It is this chapter's claim, accordingly, that in order to develop a deeper appreciation of the dilemmas of diversity in Western organizations, we need to unveil the imprint of colonial discourse upon the handling of workplace diversity in the West.

As far as workplace diversity is concerned, given the continued persistence of colonial discourse, the white male power structure is likely to approach differences of race, culture, ethnicity, gender, sexuality, and so on within contemporary Western organizations with an incongruous combination of contempt and schizophrenia that may closely resemble the manner of the erstwhile colonizers in their engagement with the colonized Others. To varying degrees, the power structure is likely to see such differences as representing inferiority, irrationality, backwardness, immaturity, immorality, corruption, "a menace to society," a grave threat to meritocracy, an evil conspiracy designed to destroy the Christian West, and so forth. In addition, although they experience a sense of being threatened by such differences, the dominant groups are also likely to believe, at the same time, that different races, cultures, genders, and so on are too weak, contemptible, and so on to pose a strong threat to their own power, privilege, and hegemony. In other words, the dominant are likely to sense deep ambivalence as they are simultaneously buffeted by a host of often-conflicting feelings, ideas, and beliefs.

This brief list of ideas and emotions that seemingly constitute the worldview of the dominant gives us some indication of the problems faced by organizations seeking to "manage" workplace diversity. But this is not all. Although the preceding catalog is a good enough pointer to the formidable nature of the problems surrounding diversity, the real dilemma of managing diversity would seem to be that, with varying degrees of intensity, these same ideas, beliefs, passions, and emotions are likely to have a hold of the life worlds of even those who want to value diversity and to promote the interests of the marginal. Indeed, given that the discourse of colonialism saturates us (so that our very vocabulary for addressing difference is highly colonialist in nature), it could not be otherwise. In sum, what is being suggested here is that the discourse of workplace diversity is inextricably (and fatally) linked with the discourse of colonialism. In which case, are we caught in a labyrinth, and there is simply no way out? The question that we are ultimately brought to confront, therefore, is how do we deconstruct that discourse of colonialism that (by means of crucially configuring and conditioning the discourse of workplace diversity) permeates the very fabric of the practices that constitute management of diversity in Western organizations?

"The first step toward an alternative to colonial discourse, for Western readers at least," says Spurr (1993), "has to be a critical understanding of its structures" (p. 185). Analogously, a search for alternatives to the contemporary discourse of workplace diversity must begin with a critique of all those practices (engaged in by managers, researchers, consultants, workshop facilitators, etc.) that constitute the corpus of the diversity management industry. One of the basic purposes of such critique would be to understand how, at the fundamental level, the diversity industry may primarily be occupied in echoing and enacting the central propositions of colonialist discourse, and consequently, in being complicit with the continual production, reproduction, and perpetuation of a hegemonic system that is the source of immense material and symbolic violence directed against those cultural and demographic groups that mostly inhabit the margins of contemporary Western organizations.

Along with the above, the practical project of deconstructing the discourse of workplace diversity needs to proceed along a "double-gesture" or a "double movement" (Derrida, 1981). The first movement (although not necessarily in a strictly chronological sense) is what may be referred to as inversion, or the "phase of overturning" (Derrida, 1981, p. 40). In this phase, the system of hierarchical binaries (see Table 46.1) that, as colonialism's legacy, continues to cast its shadow upon the diversity industry needs to be overturned and inverted. As Derrida (1981) put it, this is the phase "which brings low what was high" (p. 42). The enormous practical difficulties of this phase alone cannot be overemphasized. For this deconstruction to succeed, however, merely inverting the system of hierarchical binaries is not enough, because the phase of overturning continues "to operate on the terrain of and from within the deconstructed system" (Derrida, 1981, p. 42). Hence, the necessity of the second phase of deconstruction, which results in "the irruptive emergence of a new 'concept,' a concept that can no longer be, and never could be, included in the previous regime" (Derrida, 1981, p. 42). Only when we have engaged in both these phases of deconstruction would it be possible for us to contemplate organizations "in which the play of difference could range free of the structures of inequality" (Spurr, 1993, p. 201).

NOTES

1. Despite sharing a somewhat similar label, postcolonialism, it is important to note, differs from other "posts," such as postmodernism, post-structuralism, and so on in many important respects. Any discussion of those differences, however, will clearly take us far afield from the principal concerns of this chapter. The reader interested in exploring the tensions among the various posts is referred to such sources as Adam and Tiffin (1990), Bhabha (1994), and Prasad (1997).

2. Although in a strictly technical sense, colonialism, that is, the direct control and administration of other people's territories, is only one form of imperialism (see, e.g., Lichtheim, 1974; Williams & Chrisman, 1994a), the distinction is not particularly important for our purposes. This chapter, accordingly, uses the two terms, colonialism and imperialism, somewhat interchangeably.

3. Sooner or later, all (postcolonial) theorists must wrestle with the wider implications of employing such sweeping terms as America, Europe, the West, non-West and so forth. Needless to mention, postcolonial theory is fully aware of the epistemological sins of essentialism, homogenization, and so on associated with the use of these and similar other terms. In his seminal article, "Postcoloniality and the Artifice of History: Who Speaks for 'Indian' Pasts?" Chakrabarty (1992, p. 1), for instance, emphasizes that such expressions need to be viewed as hyperreal terms, or "as figures of the imaginary." Along with such awareness, however, numerous postcolonial scholars (including Chakrabarty, 1992) continue to insist on the *value* of employing such terminology in their writings. In brief, this insistence may be said to be rooted in a concrete reality in which expressions such as Europe, the West, and so on, although undoubtedly fictive, are fictions of enormous material consequence. See, for example, Chakrabarty (1992), Nandy (1983, especially pp. xiii–xiv), Prasad (1997).

4. The recent discursive turn in the social sciences (including organization studies) has led to a far-reaching reconceptualization of such terms as *discourse, text, reading, writing, representation,* and so on. In brief, texts now refer not only to linguistic artifacts, but to extra-linguistic artifacts (e.g., culture, rituals, music, painting, architecture, social practices and institutions, history, etc.) as well, with the result that "textuality has become a metaphor for reality in general" (Dirks, Eley, & Ortner, 1994, p. 25). This chapter, accordingly, often uses words such as text and discourse in their expanded sense.

5. Following the turn to discourse in social theory, human subjectivities are no longer conceptualized as occurring "naturally" but are seen as effects or products of specific texts or discourses. For a brief and lucid analysis of the implications of the discursive turn, see Dirks et al. (1994). For a discussion (in organization studies) of the discursive constitution of human subjectivities, see, for example, Jermier, Knights, and Nord (1994).

6. Nandy (1983) refers to such continuation of colonialism by ideological means as the "second colonization" (p. xi). For a subtle critique of the second colonization thesis, see Prakash (1992).

7. Said (1979) bases his analysis upon the works of some of the leading 19th- and 20th-century Orientalist scholars in Britain, France, and America—"the three great empires" (p. 15).

8. In the interest of clarity, it may be important to note here that the phrase, *discourse of oil,* employs the expression discourse in this term's expanded sense mentioned earlier.

9. Gulf Oil was acquired by Chevron Corp. (one of the descendants of Standard Oil) in 1984 for a sum of $13.2 billion, at that time the largest corporate takeover in U.S. history.

10. Incorporated in 1882 for purposes of skirting some legal problems. Standard Oil of New Jersey (often called Jersey Standard) eventually became the holding company that owned the shares of the various Standard Oil subsidiaries. The subsidiaries were given independent legal existence in 1911 following the U.S. Supreme Court-directed dissolution of Standard. Despite the so-called dissolution, the various Standard offshoots continued to act as a unified company for many years (Roncaglia, 1985; Sampson, 1975; Tugwell, 1988). In 1972, Jersey Standard was renamed Exxon Corporation.

11. The cartel of the Seven Sisters consisted of: Exxon Corp., Mobil Corp., Chevron Corp., Gulf Oil Corp., Texaco Inc., Royal Dutch/Shell, and British Petroleum. Exxon, Mobil, and Chevron are direct descendants of the original Standard Oil Company. Except for Gulf (which was taken over by Chevron in 1984), all the other Sisters continue to be very large and successful petroleum companies. However, as a result of (a) the OPEC revolution of the early 1970s and (b) the rise of large and powerful National Oil Companies (NOCs) all over the world, the global role and importance of the Sisters has considerably diminished. Nevertheless, the Sisters continue to be politically and economically influential organizations, especially in their home countries.

12. OPEC is the well-known acronym for the Organization of the Petroleum Exporting Countries.

13. The honor of being the other cofounder of OPEC belongs to Juan Pablo Perez Alfonzo of Venezuela.

14. Aramco, the Arabian American Oil Company, was the joint-production consortium of Exxon, Mobil, Texaco, and Chevron, which controlled crude oil production in Saudi Arabia.

15. The theme of being opposed by evil conspiracies has long been an integral part of the self-representation of the colonialist project. For example, traces of this theme may be discerned even in the myth of "a City upon a Hill," one of the important enabling myths of colonialism attending a significant moment in the history of Western imperialism, namely the colonization of North America. The origins of this myth are traceable to an oration given by John Winthrop to a group of Puritan colonizers he

was leading from England to America in what became known as the Great Migration of 1630 (Miller, 1956). Emphasizing the momentous nature of this "errand into wilderness," Winthrop said to his fellow travelers: "wee must Consider that wee shall be as a City upon a Hill, the eies of all people are uppon us" (Miller, 1956, p. 11). If the colonizing pilgrims failed in this enterprise, warned Winthrop, God would make them "a story and a by-word through the world, wee shall open the mouthes of enemies to speak evill of the wayes of god and all professours for God's sake" (Miller, 1956, p. 11). In the pilgrims' consciousness, thus, while on the one hand, the project of America was endowed with sacredness and divine grace, on the other hand, the project was also threatened by a conspiracy of its numerous, powerful enemies. In that event, one may offer that just as John Winthrop saw the Puritans' project of American colonization as imperiled by the existence of a conspiracy of that project's enemies, the Seven Sisters also saw the existence of a major conspiracy as threatening the global enterprise of oil and imperialism. For Winthrop, the conspiracy was of people who spoke "evill of the wayes of god" (Miller, 1956, p. 11); for the Seven Sisters, the conspiracy was that of international communism (of which, according to the Western oil cartel, Sheikh Tariki happened to be an important part).

16. Karl Marx and Frederick Engels' famous *Communist Manifesto,* for instance, first appeared in 1848 (see, e.g., Marx & Engels, 1948).

17. In order to clarify the point being made here, we need only to look at an illustrative argument of the following form: (a) only Reds oppose the West, (b) Sheikh Tariki opposes the West, (c) hence, the sheikh is Red. On the basis of the structure of the preceding syllogism, one can rightfully contend that the act of labeling the sheikh a Red may be said to contain an implicit claim that only Reds oppose the West.

18. It should come as no surprise that "the emergence of [this view of] history in European thought is coterminous with the rise of modern colonialism" (Ashcroft et al., 1995, p. 355).

19. In 1960, OPEC began with five founding members, namely, Iran, Iraq, Kuwait, Saudi Arabia, and Venezuela. During subsequent years, OPEC was joined by the following countries: Algeria, Ecuador, Gabon, Indonesia, Libya, Nigeria, Qatar, and the United Arab Emirates. Recently, Ecuador ceased to be a member.

20. Yergin (1991) quotes the Iranian participant in these negotiations as saying: "We met in a James Bond atmosphere" (p. 518).

21. Sampson (1975, p. 135) notes that for several years after the Iranian coup, Western oil companies would frequently warn Third World nationalist leaders by, in effect,

saying, look what happened to Mossadeq. Dr. Mossadeq was the Iranian prime minister overthrown in the Anglo-American coup.

22. Yergin (1991) also points to the Seven Sisters' dismissive view of OPEC when he quotes Howard Page, one of the top Jersey Standard executives, as saying: "We attached little importance to . . . [OPEC], because we believed it would not work" (p. 523).

23. According to the linear "conveyer belt" view of history, only the countries of the West have so far succeeded in "reaching" nationhood; an overwhelming majority of the non-Western countries are still "on their way" to full nationhood. Achieving nationhood, in this view, also implies "arriving" in the modem era of universal history.

24. Right from the days of European antiquity, the discourse of the Savage displayed a basic dualism that eventually came to express itself along two dimensions, that of "fierce cannibal" on the one hand, and of the "noble savage" on the other. The following brief discussion, however, confines itself to the first dimension alone. See, in this connection, Hulme (1986, especially p. 45 ff).

25. In standard European teratology, Cynocephali refer to men who have the head (or face) of a dog.

26. By way of understanding the special association (between the Caribbean and the discourse of the Savage) that developed in the European imagination following the voyages of discovery, it may be interesting to note that the word *cannibal* comes from *Canibalis,* the name used by Christopher Columbus for referring to the Carib people of the Antilles. Columbus ultimately came to claim that these people were man-eaters. For an erudite and fascinating analysis of how the discourse of the Savage uncertainly emerges to a position of dominance in Columbus's *Journal* (with the result that the Carib people eventually come to be labeled as anthropophagi), see Hulme (1986). On the basis of an in-depth analysis of extensive historical sources, Hulme (1986) arrives at the conclusion that "the entry of the word 'cannibal' into European discourse with the meaning 'man-eating savage' was, despite appearances, unsupported by what would legally be accepted as 'evidence'" (p. 47).

27. For several centuries right up to the 17th and the 18th, Europe's trade with the East (including with China and India) ran huge deficits and involved the eastward flow of large quantities of gold and silver (Abu-Lughod, 1989a, 1989b; Hulme, 1986). This fact may partly account for the prominent place accorded to Oriental wealth and power in the discourse of the Orient preceding Orientalism.

28. Because this part of the present chapter draws upon the scholarship of Said (1979) and Hulme (1986) in order to sketch the outlines of the discourse of the Orient, it is important to point out that whereas Said's primary

analytical focus is the Western discourse with respect to the Middle East and Islam, that of Hulme focuses upon the civilization of China (see Hulme, 1986, p. 270, n.8). In addition, Hulme's historical period of reference precedes that of Said. Both of these variants of the discourse of the Orient, however, share common origins in European antiquity, and despite considerable differences, do contain important parallels and overlaps. In many respects, the discourse of the Orient (including its latest version, Said's Orientalism) can be said to represent Europe's portrayal of the entire East.

29. Derrida (1981) makes a similar point when he notes that "'everyday language' is not innocent or neutral" (p. 19). As a result, however, what Said (1979) observes in the context of analyzing Orientalism assumes crucial significance. Says Said (1979): "Orientalism was . . . a [partisan] system of truths. . . . It is therefore correct that *every* . . . [Westerner], in what he could say about the Orient, was consequently a *racist,* an imperialist, and almost totally ethnocentric" (p. 204; italics added). The stamp of such Orientalist racism and imperialism is visible, for instance, even in the writings of Karl Marx, the leading Western prophet of revolutionary emancipation (see, e.g., Said, 1979, pp. 153 ff; Spurr, 1993, pp. 99–100). And this despite the fact that Marx (and several other Westerners like him) may not have consciously desired to be racists, imperialists, and so on.

REFERENCES

Abu-Lughod, J. (1989a). *Before Europe's hegemony.* New York: Oxford University Press.

Ahu-Lughod, J. (1989b). On the remaking of history. In B. Kruger & P. Mariani (Eds.), *Remaking history* (pp. 111–129). Seattle: Bay Press.

Adam, I., & Tiffin, H. (Eds.). (1990). *Past the last post: Theorizing post-colonialism and post-modernism.* Calgary: University of Calgary Press.

Al-Chalabi, F. J. (1980). *OPEC and the international oil industry.* Oxford: Oxford University Press.

Asad, T. (Ed.). (1973). *Anthropology and the colonial encounter.* New York: Humanities Press.

Ashcroft, B., Griffiths, G., & Tiffin, H. (Eds.). (1995). *The post-colonial studies reader.* London: Routledge.

Barker, R., Hulme, P., Iversen, M., & Loxley, D. (Eds.). 1985. *Europe and its others* (2 vols.). Colchester, UK: University of Essex.

Bhabha, H. K. (1985). Signs taken for wonders: Questions of ambivalence and authority under a tree outside Delhi, May 1817. In F. Barker, P. Hulme, M. Iversen, & D. Loxley (Eds.), *Europe and its others*

(Vol. 1, pp. 89–106). Colchester, UK: University of Essex.

Bhabha, H. K. (1994). *The location of culture.* London: Routledge.

Bishop, A. (1990). Western mathematics: The secret weapon of cultural imperialism. *Race and Class, 52*(2), 51–65.

Blair, J. M. (1976). *The control of oil.* New York: Pantheon.

Brantlinger, P. (1988). *Rule of darkness: British literature and imperialism, 1830–1914.* Ithaca, NY: Cornell University Press.

Cesaire, A. (1972). *Discourse on colonialism.* New York: Monthly Review Press.

Chakrabarty, D. (1992). Postcoloniality and the artifice of history: Who speaks for "Indian" pasts? *Representations, 37*(Winter), 1–26.

Chatterjee, P. (1986). *Nationalist thought and the colonial world.* Minneapolis: University of Minnesota Press.

Chatterjee, P. (1993). *The nation and its fragments: Colonial and postcolonial histories.* Princeton, NJ: Princeton University Press.

Conrad, J. (1983). *Heart of darkness* (P. O'Prey, ed.). Harmondsworth, UK: Penguin.

Derrida, J. (1981). *Positions* (A. Bass, trans.). Chicago: University of Chicago Press.

Dirks, N. (1992). Introduction: Colonialism and culture. In N. Dirks (Ed.), *Colonialism and culture* (pp. 1–25). Ann Arbor: University of Michigan Press.

Dirks, N., Eley, G., & Ortner, S. (1994). Introduction. In N. Dirks, G. Eley, & S. Ortner (Eds.), *Culture/power/history* (pp. 3–45). Princeton, NJ: Princeton University Press.

Enloe, C. (1989). *Bananas, beaches, and bases.* Berkeley: University of California Press.

Ghanem, S. (1986). *OPEC: Rise and fall of an exclusive club.* London: KPI.

Guha, R. (1983). *Elementary aspects of peasant insurgency in colonial India.* Delhi: Oxford University Press.

Guha, R., & Spivak, G. C. (Eds.). (1988). *Selected subaltern studies.* New York: Oxford University Press.

Hamilton, A. (1986). *Oil: The price of power.* London: Michael Joseph/Rainbird.

Headrick, D. (1981). *The tools of the empire.* New York: Oxford University Press.

Hegel, G. W. F. (1900). *Philosophy of history* (J. Sibree, trans.). New York: P. F. Collier.

Hulme, P. (1986). *Colonial encounters.* London: Routledge.

Jermier, J., Knights, D., & Nord, W. (Eds.). (1994). *Resistance and power in organizations.* London: Routledge.

Karlsson, S. (1986). *Oil and the world order.* Leamington Spa, UK: Berg.

Lichtheim, G. (1974). *Imperialism.* Harmondsworth, UK: Penguin.

Marx, K., & Engels, F. (1948). *The communist manifesto.* New York: International Publishers.

Miller, P. (1956). *Errands into wilderness.* Cambridge, MA: Harvard University Press.

Nandy, A. (1983). *The intimate enemy: Loss and recovery of self under colonialism.* Delhi: Oxford University Press.

Nandy, A. (1987). *Traditions, tyranny, and Utopias.* Delhi: Oxford University Press.

Nandy, A. (1992). State. In W. Sachs (Ed.), *The development dictionary* (pp. 264–274). London: Zed Books.

Niranjana, T. (1992). *Siting translation: History, post-structuralism, and the colonial context.* Berkeley: University of California Press.

Prakash, G. (1992). Science "gone native" in colonial India. *Representations, 40*(Fall), 153–178.

Prakash, G. (1995). *After colonialism: Imperial histories and postcolonial displacements.* Princeton, NJ: Princeton University Press.

Prasad, A. (1994). *Institutional ideology and industry-level action: A macro analysis of corporate legitimation in the United States petroleum industry.* Unpublished doctoral dissertation, University of Massachusetts at Amherst.

Prasad, A. (1997). Provincializing Europe: Towards a post-colonial reconstruction. *Studies in Cultures, Organizations, and Societies,* Vol. 3.

Roncaglia, A. (1985). *The international oil market.* Armonk, NY: M. E. Sharpe.

Sachs, W. (Ed.). (1992). *The development dictionary: A guide to knowledge as power.* London: Zed Books.

Said, E. W. (1979). *Orientalism.* New York: Vintage.

Said, E. W. (1993). *Culture and imperialism.* New York: Knopf.

Sampson, A. (1975). *The seven sisters.* New York: Viking.

Spivak, G. C. (1990). *The post-colonial critic.* New York: Routledge.

Spurr, D. (1993). *The rhetoric of empire.* Durham, NC: Duke University Press.

Suleri, S. (1992). *The rhetoric of English India.* Chicago: University of Chicago Press.

Terzian, P. (1985). *OPEC: The inside story.* London: Zed Books.

Tiffin, C., & Lawson, A. (Eds.). (1994). *Describing empire: Post-colonialism and textuality.* London: Routledge.

Tugendhat, C., & Hamilton, A. (1975). *Oil: The biggest business.* London: Eyre Methuen.

Tugwell, F. (1988). *The energy crisis and the American political economy.* Stanford: Stanford University Press.

Turner, L. (1978). *Oil companies in the international system.* London: George Allen & Unwin.

Vallenilla, L. (1975). *Oil: The making of a new economic order: Venezuelan oil and OPEC.* New York: McGraw-Hill.

Williams, P., & Chrisman, L. (1994a). Colonial discourse and post-colonial theory: An introduction. In P. Williams & L. Chrisman (Eds.), *Colonial discourse and post-colonial theory: A reader* (pp. 1–26). New York: Columbia University Press.

Williams, P., & Chrisman, L. (Eds.). (1994b). *Colonial discourse and post-colonial theory: A reader.* New York: Columbia University Press.

Yergin, D. (1991). *The prize.* New York: Simon & Schuster.

SOURCE: Prasad, Anshuman. 1997. "The Colonizing Consciousness and Representations of the Other: A Postcolonial Critique of the Discourse of Oil." Pp. 285–311 in *Managing the Organizational Melting Pot: Dilemmas of Workplace Diversity.* Thousand Oaks, CA: Sage.

47

THE DISCLOSURE DILEMMA FOR GAY MEN AND LESBIANS

"Coming Out" at Work

KRISTIN H. GRIFFITH AND MICHELLE R. HEBL

Building a support system of trusted coworkers who respect you and your sexual identity is an important first step toward fully coming out.

The Lesbian Almanac (1996, p. 152)

Self-disclosure was defined by Collins and Miller (1994) as the "act of revealing personal information about oneself to another" (p. 457), and disclosures often involve surprising, if not stigmatizing, information such as criminal activity, marital infidelity, or sexual orientation (see Derlega, Metts, Petronio, & Margulis, 1993; Ludwig, Franco, & Malloy, 1986). Although largely unexamined by previous research, the current study attempts to examine one set of self-disclosures in the workplace, those in which individuals reveal to coworkers (superordinates, subordinates, and colleagues) that they are gay or lesbian.

The present investigation is particularly important for several reasons. First, estimates reveal that 10–14% of the U.S. workforce is composed of nonheterosexual workers (Powers, 1996), and there is a recognized need to better understand minorities working in a majority context (e.g., see Waldo, 1999). Second, disclosing one's sexual orientation is one of the toughest issues that gay men and lesbians face because it involves considerable emotional turmoil and a fear of retaliation and rejection (Bohan, 1996; Cain, 1991; Ellis & Riggle, 1996; Franke & Leary, 1991; Goffman, 1963; Kronenberger, 1991; Wells & Kline, 1987). At the same time, those who remain closeted report lower levels of psychological well-being and life satisfaction (Garnets & Kimmel, 1993; Lane & Wegner, 1995; Savin-Williams & Rodriquez, 1993), increased health risks (Cole, Kemeny, Taylor, & Visscher, 1996; Kalichman & Nachimson, 1999), and extensive and energy-draining activities focused on covering up their stigmatized identity (e.g., see Ellis & Riggle, 1996).

Third, it is unclear how attitudes toward lesbians and gay men translate into workplace behaviors. Most Americans continue to have negative attitudes toward those who are gay/lesbian, although these attitudes may be changing (e.g., Herek, Gillis, & Cogan, 1999; Kite & Whitley, 1996). Although a recent study found that 66% of Americans support laws that protect gay and lesbian workers against job discrimination (Yang, 1997), 62% of gay men and 59% of lesbians continue to report that they experience employment discrimination (National Gay and Lesbian Task Force Survey, 1991; Waldo, 1999). Further evidence from a laboratory-based résumé study suggests that discrimination in the hiring of gay and lesbian job applicants is still prevalent (Griffith & Quiñones, 2001).

A recent comprehensive analysis, however, suggests that overt, formal displays of discrimination are becoming less frequent (Dovidio & Gaertner, 2000). A field study by Hebl, Foster, Mannix, and Dovidio (2002), for instance, found no differences in hiring rates but found that employers spoke fewer words, terminated interactions, and engaged in more nonverbal discrimination with gay/lesbian than heterosexual applicants. Thus, discrimination in the workplace may still exist, but may manifest itself in more subtle ways. Such results, coupled with the fact that many organizations (e.g., over half of Fortune 1000 companies) are beginning to include sexual orientation as a protected class and offer diversity training (e.g., see also Baker, Strub, & Henning, 1995; Neely Martinez, 1993; Powers, 1996), establish the need to better understand the changing workplace that gay and lesbian workers are experiencing. At present, it seems that gay/lesbian workers face a double-edged sword when managing their stigmatized sexual identity at work—they face problems if they don't disclose, and they face problems if they do.

The current study empirically examined self-disclosure of sexual orientation in the workplace; there is almost no previous research addressing this. One exception involves a study by Day and Schoenrade (1997) in which they examined how communication about sexual orientation is related to critical work attitudes. They found that "out" workers had higher job satisfaction, were more committed to their organization, perceived top management to be more supportive of their rights, experienced less conflict between work and home, and had lower role conflict and lower role ambiguity. Day and Schoenrade's (1997) research demonstrated benefits to disclosure in the workplace; however, their research focused primarily on the relationship between disclosure and work attitudes. The current research replicated the examination of the relationship between disclosure and both organizational support and work attitudes but expanded this work by examining the relationship between self-disclosure and individual differences as well as the potential importance of formal organizational policies and coworkers' reactions.

IMPORTANCE OF ORGANIZATIONAL SUPPORTIVENESS

The extent to which an organization supports demographically relevant characteristics is extremely important to minority employees (see Rynes, 1990). Similarly, Button (2001) revealed that organizational efforts to affirm sexual diversity result in increased views of fair and equitable treatment by employees. The present research extends this to examine how the workplace atmosphere impacts the disclosure behaviors of gay/lesbian workers. Driscoll, Kelley, and Fassinger (1996) commented that " . . . it is likely that perceived and actual tolerance in the workplace climate regarding lesbians and gay men will be related to disclosure of homosexual identify in the workplace" (p. 229). As Driscoll et al. noted, organizational support for diversity in sexual orientation may manifest itself in the perceptions of support among coworkers (e.g., subjective estimates) or of actual organizational structures (e.g., nondiscriminatory policies, special interest groups). Thus, we believe that organizational support will lead to increased disclosures because organizational supportiveness may signal to the gay/lesbian worker that the organization is a safe place in which to disclose their sexual orientation. Thus, we predicted the following:

Hypothesis 1: The more that an organization is perceived to be supportive towards gay/lesbian employees (H1a) and has supportive structures (H1b), the more gay/lesbian workers will have disclosed their sexual orientation at work.

Job Attitudes

Consistent with Day and Schoenrade's (1997) study, we examined how disclosure relates to job satisfaction and job anxiety. Research conducted outside the workplace has shown that those individuals who disclose their identity to others tend to have higher psychological adjustment and life satisfaction (e.g., see Savin-Williams & Rodriquez, 1993; D'Augelli & Hershberger, 1993; Ellis & Riggle, 1996; Garnets & Kimmel, 1993). We anticipated similar outcomes in the workplace, particularly given that employees who hide their sexual orientation report strategies (e.g., making up lies, switching the gender of their partners in conversation) for dealing with the related psychological distress (e.g., shame, fear) that can consume their time and energy. Likewise, employees who disclose may be able to establish closer and more honest relationships with coworkers and feel accepted for who they are. We anticipated that these outcomes related to workplace disclosure will influence job attitudes, such that:

Hypothesis 2: Gay and lesbian workers who have disclosed their sexual orientation to more coworkers will report increased job satisfaction (H2a) and decreased job anxiety (H2b).

These predictions are partially based on Day and Schoenrade's (1997) findings. Although they found evidence for differential job satisfaction, they found no differences in reported job anxiety. Our research will reexamine both findings.

ORGANIZATIONAL SUPPORTIVENESS AND JOB ATTITUDES

In addition to the influence of disclosure, we anticipated that the supportiveness of an organization will also influence job-related attitudes. Specifically, an organization that is gay supportive and recognizes the needs of workers will likely have a positive effect on workers' attitudes and their general well-being (Croteau & Lark, 1995; Hallowell, Schlesinger, & Zornitsky, 1996; Rynes, 1990). Button's (2001) work showed initial evidence for this in that policies affirming and recognizing

sexual diversity in the workplace resulted in less workplace discrimination. By extension, we anticipated that more support and less discrimination will also result in more positive job attitudes. Thus, we predicted the following:

Hypothesis 3: The more that an organization is perceived to be supportive towards gay/lesbian employees, the higher the gay/lesbian workers' job satisfaction (H3a) and the lower their job anxiety (H3b).

Not only did we anticipate that perceived gay supportiveness may influence gay/lesbian workers' job attitudes, but we also anticipated the following:

Hypothesis 4: The more gay-supportive structures present in the organization, the higher the gay/lesbian workers' job satisfaction (H4a) and the lower their job anxiety (H4b).

INDIVIDUAL DIFFERENCES

Few studies have previously addressed how individual differences relate to self-disclosure of sexual orientation in the workplace, and we proposed that such differences must be considered to fully understand disclosure behavior at work (see Bohan, 1996). For instance, Button (2001) revealed that attitudes about a stigmatized sexual identity influence work-related behaviors. In this initial investigation, we were particularly interested in three individual differences: the centrality of sexual orientation to one's self-concept, the degree of self-acceptance that one has, and the extent to which one has disclosed to others. Each of these variables provide some measure of the individual's attitude toward their identity as a gay man or lesbian woman, and in general, we predicted the following:

Hypothesis 5: Individual differences will influence the extent to which gay and lesbian workers disclose their sexual identity to others in the workplace.

We will discuss each of these three individual difference variables in more detail.

Centrality of Sexual Orientation to One's Self-Concept

The centrality of sexual orientation concerns the extent to which an individual defines themselves in terms of a gay man or a lesbian woman. In some cases, a gay/lesbian identity may be so central to individuals that they may not feel accepted or at ease with others until they have disclosed (see Bohan, 1996; Laurenceau, Barrett, & Pietromonaco, 1998). Similarly, Crocker and Major (1989) suggested that the centrality of identity was one of the most influential predictors of coping success and well-being (see also Branscombe, Schmitt, & Harvey, 1999). Thus, we predicted the following:

Hypothesis 5a: Individuals with a central gay/lesbian identity will be more likely to disclose their sexual identity to others in the workplace (H5a).

Degree of Self-Acceptance

Another individual difference is the extent to which gay men or lesbians accept their identity. Although some people may feel comfortable with and embrace their sexual orientation, other people may reject their sexual orientation and view themselves as inferior to heterosexuals or flawed. Self-acceptance is one of the major dimensions of psychological well-being (Ryff & Keyes, 1995) and may be particularly important for gay/lesbian individuals because it is associated with better mental health and coping skills in dealing with prejudice (Bohan, 1996; Garnets, Herek, & Levy, 1990; Hershberger & D'Augelli, 1995). It is also positively correlated with the length of time one is "out" (Savin-Williams & Rodriquez, 1993), and many believe coming to terms with and accepting their sexual orientation is a precursor to disclosing it to others (e.g., Bohan, 1996; Coleman, 1982). Thus, we predicted the following:

Hypothesis 5b: Gay men or lesbians who are more accepting of their sexual orientation are more likely to disclose their identity to coworkers (H5b).

Extent to Which One Has Disclosed to Others

Finally, this individual difference assesses the extent to which individuals are "out" to others. Although some individuals are "out" to all of their friends and families, other individuals remain fully "closeted." The extent to which individuals are "out" to their families and friends may buffer individuals' fears and anxieties in the workplace and may lead to a heightened integration of one's personal and professional life (e.g., see Lewis, 1984; Savin-Williams, 1989). In addition, prior disclosures may increase social support, decrease fears of rejection, and increase practice and experience with the coming "out" process. Therefore, we predicted the following:

Hypothesis 5c: Disclosure to more family members and friends will predict increased self-disclosures at work (H5c).

REACTIONS OF COWORKERS

Feedback from others plays a critical role in determining whether individuals are better off revealing or maintaining their secrets (see Ellis & Riggle, 1996), and we believe this is the case in the reactions that coworkers have toward workers who disclose their sexual orientation. Gay and lesbian workers often report hesitancy in disclosing information about their significant others, their families, or even their weekend plans because they fear retaliation or rejection from coworkers (Vargo, 1998). Supporting this, Franke and Leary (1991) found that lesbians' concerns regarding coworkers' reactions to their disclosures predicted their actual willingness to disclose. In hiding their identities, closeted workers report the need to use extensive and energy-draining strategies to conceal their stigmatized identity (Ellis & Riggle, 1996). These anxiety ridden strategies include: self-editing, divulging fictitious personal details that do not add up, relying on the use of neutral pronouns ("they" rather than "she" or "he") when discussing significant others or more drastic measures such as altogether avoiding certain coworkers (see Rogers & Hebl, 2001).

Given that much of the concealment of disclosure focuses on preventing negative reactions, the benefits of disclosures are predicted to occur only when positive reactions from coworkers occur. Likewise, if coworkers have negative reactions to an "out" gay/lesbian worker (e.g., by showing hostility, treating them unfairly, avoiding them), we predicted that disclosing will not be associated with more positive job attitudes. So, we believe that positive job-related attitudes will only emerge when people disclose to coworkers who have favorable reactions. As a result, we predict that coworkers' reactions fully mediate the relationship between self-disclosure and job-related attitudes.

Hypothesis 6: The relationship between disclosing and job satisfaction (H6a) and between disclosing and job anxiety (H6b) will be mediated by coworkers' reactions to the disclosure.

METHOD

Participants

To meet inclusionary criteria for the study, participants had to self-identify as gay or lesbian on the questionnaire, were required to be at least 21 years of age, and had to have been currently employed at the time of the study. A total of 220 gay men and 159 lesbians from Houston, Texas, served as participants. There were 309 Caucasians, 34 Hispanics, 9 African Americans, 7 Native Americans, 3 Asian Americans, and 15 self-reported "other ethnicity." The mean age of respondents was 39 years of age ($SD = 10$), and 69% of participants had a college degree or an advanced degree. The average salary for respondents was $49,430 ($SD = $37,755$), and the average number of years that participants worked in their current job was 7.5 years ($SD = 8$ years). The demographics of the gay/lesbian participants matched those of previous studies in that they tended to be more White, more educated, and make higher salaries than generally observed with heterosexual participants (see Rothblum, 1995).

Data Collection

We collected data by using three different strategies. First, we relied on a 350-page publication listing nonprofit clubs, businesses, and establishments that self-identified as gay/lesbian-related or friendly. If the groups and places that we randomly selected from this list agreed to participate, we sent them surveys and instructed them to give the surveys to their gay or lesbian members and patrons, who also

were invited to further distribute questionnaires. We included postage-paid, self-addressed envelopes inside each package of questionnaires and paid $5 for each completed survey that was returned. We imposed a cap of $100 to each club, business, or establishment to ensure that we could minimize bias caused by collecting too many surveys from a single source. Second, we solicited participants through a citywide gay/lesbian monthly publication and a similar e-mail listserver within the metropolitan area. Using these two methods, we received a total of 173 completed surveys from at least 19 different clubs, businesses, and establishments.

Third, we rented a booth at a gay/lesbian business exposition that lasted 2 days and had thousands of area attendees. Research assistants successfully recruited 206 (of a total of approximately 250 approached) gay/lesbian attendees to complete surveys at the booth and afterward enter a raffle to win a $20 gift certificate to a local bookstore.

Survey Instrument

A cover letter attached to a six-page survey informed participants that the study investigated the experiences of both "out" and "closeted" gay and lesbian workers. Participants were told that all responses would be anonymous and confidential and that if they knew others who might want to participate (particularly those not "out"), they should take additional questionnaires. The first page of the survey contained demographic questions and the next five pages contained the study measures.

Measures

The survey was composed of a number of measures, and we briefly describe these and refer readers to Table 47.1 for details concerning the scales and subscales used, example items, anchors, and reliability coefficients.

Disclosure behavior at work. Disclosure behavior at work was measured by adapting the identity management behaviors scale developed by Croteau (1996). This 12-item measure assesses the extent to which individuals engage in avoidant behaviors (e.g., avoid discussing, lie) and overt behaviors

Table 47.1   Descriptions and Characteristics of Measures

Scale or subscale	Example item and scale anchors	No. of items	α
Disclosure behaviors	At work, I pretend that I have a partner of the opposite sex[a]	12	.91
Job attitudes			
Job satisfaction	In general, I am satisfied with my job.[a]	3	.95
Job anxiety	I experience considerable anxiety at work.[a]	1	
Organizational supportiveness			
Policies	My company offers diversity training programs. (1= *true*, 0 = *false*)	7	.86
Perceived gay supportiveness	My company is committed to the fair treatment of lesbian and gay workers.[a]	3	
Individual differences			
"Out" to family	How many immediate family members are you out to? (1 = *not out to anyone*, 7 = *"out" to all of them*.)	1	
"Out" to heterosexual friends	How many heterosexual friends are you to? (1 = *not out to anyone*, 7 = *"out" to all of them*.)	1	
Centrality of sexual orientation	My identity as a gay man or lesbian is extremely central to my self-concept.[a]	4	.67
Self-acceptance	I really wish I could change my sexual orientation (become heterosexual).[a]	5	.68
Coworker reactions	My coworkers are hostile toward me.[a]	10	.89

[a] Unless otherwise indicated, participants responded to all items on 7-point Likert scales: 1 = *strongly disagree*, 4 = *neither agree nor disagree*, and 7 = *strongly agree*.

(disclose, directly address) concerning their sexual orientation. Consonant with Croteau, higher scores reflect increased disclosure behaviors.

Job attitudes. Job satisfaction was measured with three items adapted from Ironson, Smith, Brannick, Gibson, and Paul's (1989) Job in General Scale. Job anxiety was measured with the item, "I experience considerable anxiety at work."

Organizational support. Consistent with Driscoll et al. (1996), participants reported the policies in their organizations that specifically support gay and lesbian employees as well as their perceptions of the organization's gay supportiveness. Gay and lesbian workers were asked if any of seven different gay-supportive policies (e.g., a written non-discrimination policy, same-sex partner benefits)

were present at their place of employment (a more complete list appears later in Table 47.5). A composite of gay-supportive policies was calculated by summing all of the "yes" responses to the individual policy items. Perceived supportiveness towards gay and lesbian employees was adapted from Waldo's (1999) WHEQ questionnaire.

Individual differences. The centrality of one's sexual orientation was measured by adapting four items from Phinney's (1990) Multigroup Ethnic Identity Measure and from Luhtanen and Crocker's (1992) "importance to identity" subscale. The degree of self-acceptance was measured by adapting five items from Waldo's (1999) study. To assess the extent to which one was "out," individuals reported the extent to which they were out to their family members and heterosexual friends (see Cole et al., 1996).

Coworkers' reactions. Because coworkers' reactions is a novel contribution to the existing body of research, there were no preexisting scales so we developed our own (see Table 47.1). The 10 items that we developed assessed the extent to which coworkers (superordinates, peers, subordinates) treated gay and lesbian workers fairly and were inclusive, felt comfortable with, and were accepting of gay and lesbian workers. These items allowed employees to evaluate their coworkers' reactions even if no disclosure was made.

RESULTS

Correlations

Table 47.2 provides descriptive statistics and zero-order correlation coefficients for all study variables.

Tests of Hypotheses

Organizational supportiveness, individual differences, and disclosure behaviors. Table 47.3 presents the results of the regression analyses testing Hypotheses 1 and 5. Working in an organization that is perceived to be more gay supportive was strongly related to being more "out" at work, fully supporting H1a. However, the presence of more gay-supportive policies was not significantly related to disclosure behaviors at work; thus, H1b was not supported. Centrality of a gay/lesbian identity was not related

to a gay/lesbian's disclosure behaviors at work. Therefore, H5a was not supported. Increased self-acceptance was significantly related to increased disclosure behaviors, fully in support of H5b. Being more "out" to heterosexual friends was significantly related to exhibiting more disclosure behaviors at work. In addition, a nonsignificant trend in the data showed that being more "out" to family members was also related to being more "out" at work. Thus, H5c was partially supported.

Disclosure and job attitudes. The results revealed that disclosing more at work was related to higher job satisfaction ($r = .36$, $p < .01$) and lower job anxiety ($r = -.28$, $p < .01$), supporting H2a and H2b.

Organizational supportiveness and job attitudes. We conducted two regressions (see Table 47.4) examining whether job satisfaction and job anxiety were predicted by the two measures of organizational support (Hypotheses 3 and 4). Indeed, gay-supportive policies and perceived gay supportiveness accounted for a significant proportion of variance in job satisfaction and job anxiety. Perceived gay supportiveness was positively related to job satisfaction, in support of H3a, but negatively related to job anxiety, in support of H3b. The presence of gay-supportive policies was not related to job satisfaction or job anxiety after accounting for the effects of perceived gay supportiveness. Thus, H4a and H4b were not supported.

Table 47.2   Means, Standard Deviations, and Intercorrelations Among Study Variable

Variable	M	SD	1	2	3	4	5	6	7	8	9	10
1 "Out" to family	5.73	1.99	–									
2 "Out" to heterosexual friends	5.55	1.83	.38**	–								
3 Centrality	5.25	1.16	.25**	.43**	(.67)							
4 Acceptance	5.75	1.08	.24**	.40**	.42**	(.68)						
5 Policies	1.68	1.93	.11*	.18**	.20**	.08	–					
6 Gay supportiveness	5.37	1.48	.12*	.28**	.18**	.23**	.26**	(.86)				
7 Disclosure behaviors	5.68	1.39	.28**	.58**	.32**	.52**	.21**	.54**	(.91)			
8 Coworkers' reactions	6.18	1.05	.04	.21**	.00	.28**	.12*	.60**	.45**	(.89)		
9 Job satisfaction	6.37	1.11	−.04	.16**	−.01	.21**	.07	.53**	.36**	.85**	(.95)	
10 Job anxiety	2.83	2.11	.02	−.13*	.10	−.17**	−.05	−.28**	−.28**	−.45**	−.42**	

NOTE: Internal consistency reliability coefficients (alphas) appear in parentheses along the diagonal *$p < .05$; **$p < .01$.

Table 47.3   Means, Standard Deviations, and Intercorrelations Among Study Variable

$\propto$ for:

Dependent variable	"Out" to family	"Out" to heterosexual friends	Centrality	Acceptance	Policies	Perceived gay supportiveness	R^2	F
Disclosure behaviors	08†	.32**	.00	.28**	.02	.36**	.54	58.09**

†$p < .10$; *$p < .05$; ** $p < .01$.

Table 47.4   Means, Standard Deviations, and Intercorrelations Among Study Variable

$\propto$ for:

Dependent variable	Policies	Perceived gay supportiveness	R^2	F
Job satisfaction	−.07	.54**	.27	62.21**
Job anxiety	.02	−.26**	.07	9.82**

*$p < .05$; **$p < .01$.

Reactions of coworkers. We used the criteria outlined by Baron and Kenny (1986) to test for mediation effects (Hypothesis 6): (a) disclosure behaviors must be significantly correlated with coworkers' reactions; (b) there should be a significant increase in R² when coworkers' reactions are added hierarchically after controlling for disclosure behaviors to the regression equation that predicts job attitudes; and (c) there should not be an increase in R² when disclosure behaviors are added hierarchically after controlling for coworkers' reactions when predicting job attitudes.

The first analysis (H6a) revealed that coworkers' reactions fully mediated the relationship between disclosure behaviors and job satisfaction. Specifically, disclosure behaviors were significantly correlated with coworkers' reactions ($r = .45$, $p < .01$), the change in R^2 when coworkers' reactions were added after controlling for disclosure behaviors was .56 ($p < .01$), and the change in R^2 when disclosure behaviors were added after controlling for coworkers' reactions was .00 (*ns*). Similarly, the second analysis (H6b) also revealed that coworkers' reactions fully mediated the relationship between disclosure behaviors and job anxiety. That is,

disclosure behaviors were significantly correlated with coworkers' reactions ($r = .45$, $p < .01$), the change in R^2 when coworkers' reactions were added after controlling for disclosure behaviors was .14 ($p < .001$), and the change in R^2 when disclosure behaviors were added after controlling for coworkers' reactions was .00 (*ns*). Thus, Hypothesis 6 was supported.

Additional Exploratory Analyses

To examine in more detail how specific, supportive organizational structures potentially benefit gay/lesbian workers, we conducted t-tests on six specific company policies (see Table 47.5 for the policies and statistical results). Of the six policies, the presence of diversity training (that did not include gay/lesbian issues) was the only variable not related to increased disclosure behaviors. In addition, having a written nondiscrimination policy, diversity training that specifically includes gay/lesbian issues, and showing support for gay/lesbian activities was related to more disclosure behaviors, more positive coworker reactions, less perceived job discrimination, and less unfair treatment from a boss or supervisor.

Table 47.5   The Impact of Specific Company Policies

Experiences of gay/lebisan employess	Written nondiscrimination policy			Diversity training only			Diversity training with gay/lesbian issues		
	No	Yes		No	Yes		No	Yes	
		M	t		M	t		M	t
Disclosure behaviors	5.50	5.99	3.05**	5.62	5.76	.85	5.58	6.06	2.74**
Coworker reactions	6.05	6.32	2.15	6.19	6.22	.24	6.14	6.45	2.20**
Job satisfaction	6.32	6.46	1.09	6.47	6.33	1.01	6.40	6.52	.85
Job anxiety	3.08	2.56	1.96	2.85	2.87	.05	2.92	2.59	1.03
Coworkers ridicule me	1.65	1.56	.65	1.49	1.68	1.31	1.52	1.55	.18
Experienced job discrimination	2.33	1.85	2.32*	2.20	1.88	1.55	2.24	1.53	3.36**
Boss/supervisor treats me unfairly	1.67	1.34	2.38*	1.58	1.43	1.11	1.62	1.21	3.03**

Experiences of gay/lesbian employees	Support for gay/lesbian activities			Same-sex partner benefits			Recognized gay/lesbian employee organization		
	No	Yes		No	Yes		No	Yes	
		M	t		M	t		M	t
Disclosure behaviors	5.35	6.24	6.03**	5.62	6.02	2.25*	5.55	6.21	4.22**
Coworker reactions	6.00	6.53	4.23**	6.20	6.17	.20	6.18	6.26	.55
Job satisfaction	6.20	6.65	3.68**	6.38	6.39	.06	6.36	6.41	.31
Job anxiety	3.06	2.65	1.48	2.85	2.78	.23	2.81	2.82	.04
Coworkers ridicule me	1.75	1.52	1.42	1.61	1.71	.58	1.64	1.66	.09
Experienced job discrimination	2.36	1.54	4.33**	2.05	2.08	.11	2.13	1.86	1.04
Boss/supervisor treats me unfairly	1.69	1.32	2.59*	1.57	1.39	1.03	1.60	1.40	1.06

$*p < .05$; $**p < .01$.

DISCUSSION

The current results add to an almost nonexistent body of research examining gay men and lesbians' experiences in the workforce, and particularly clarifies the work of Day and Schoenrade (1997). Our findings are consistent with Day and Schoenrade to the extent that we also found that disclosure was related to job satisfaction, but our findings are not consistent to the extent that in our study, disclosure was also related to job anxiety. Our results are congruent with other research (e.g., Baumeister & Leary, 1995; Leary, Springer, Negel, Ansell, & Evans, 1998), which has shown that one of the most fundamental motivations that people possess is a need to belong and have social support, and this same motivation has profound implications in the workplace. Those who acknowledge and receive favorable and supportive reactions from others feel happier and less stressed in the workplace.

Individual differences (e.g., acceptance, degree of being "out") and perceived organizational supportiveness also relate significantly to disclosure behaviors. In terms of supportive organizational policies, gay/lesbian workers are more likely to be "out," report less job discrimination, more favorable coworker reactions, and more fair treatment from their boss or supervisor when their organizations have written nondiscrimination policies, actively show support for gay/lesbian activities, and offer diversity training that specifically includes gay/lesbian issues. It is unclear why our predictions involving some measures of organizational policies (Hypotheses 1b, 4a, and 4b) did not emerge. Perhaps the construct of perceived gay-supportiveness is an overarching measure of climate that is composed of many different cues (e.g., policies, how supportive coworkers and bosses are, and the number of other diverse workers) and policies alone are less predictive than the whole. Or perhaps, gay/lesbian workers are not entirely accurate about the extent to which their companies have policies. However, the fact that organizational policies were significantly correlated with disclosure behaviors ($r = .21, p < .01$), and some individual policies were significantly correlated with disclosure behaviors (e.g., five of the six tested), did provide some indication that organizational policies are related to increased disclosures behaviors.

Gender Differences

Although past research has revealed some gender differences between gay and lesbian workers (e.g., see Kimmel & Sang, 1995; Sang, 1993), the only difference the current study found was that lesbians were more accepting of their sexual identity than gay men. Rather, the process of coming out seemed to affect men and women similarly in this study.

Limitations

One of the study's limitations is that participants may have been more "out" than the general population of gay and lesbian workers because "closeted" gay and lesbian workers are more difficult to identify and may be more reluctant to participate, a problem that research using gay and lesbian participants generally faces. However, the extent to which our participants were "out" closely corresponds to those reported "out" in national samples (see Badgett, 1996). In addition, Rothblum (1995) defends the generalizability of such results on the basis of a potentially constrained sample by citing that although "participants of such studies are sometimes considered to be nonrepresentative or nonrandom . . . they are representative of lesbians and gay men who are active in the communities" (p. 2). Rothblum further states that those who are "out" may be most important because they are the group that is most visible to the public and most affect how heterosexual women and men view gay men and lesbians (see also Day & Schoenrade, 1997). Furthermore, it is important to consider that we did attempt to achieve some representation by recruiting participants from multiple sources (see Rothblum, 1995) and by stressing in the recruitment stage that we were seeking less "out" participants as well. Indeed, 11% of participants reported not being "out" to anyone at work, and there was substantial variation in the percentage of coworkers to whom they were "out" ($M = 59\%$; $SD = 39.20$; range = 0–100%) and disclosure behaviors they displayed ($M = 5.68$; $SD = 1.39$; range = 1.17–7.00).

Another limitation involves some of the measures. Because of time and length limitations, all study variables could not be measured with multiple-item or full-length scales. In addition, well-established and previously validated scales for some measures simply do not exist (see Day & Schoenrade, 1997). However, we did rely heavily on measures and constructs used in past research on issues related to gay men and lesbians, albeit some of this research was not necessarily focused on workplace implications (e.g., see Bailey, Kim, Hills, & Linsenmeier, 1997). As a result, the reliabilities of some of the scales (e.g., centrality) may have attenuated the results, and we hope that future research will improve in this area. Future research might also improve on the potential single source bias present in the current research. For instance, it is possible that individual difference variables (e.g., degree of self-acceptance) might influence perceptions of constructs (e.g., perceptions of coworkers' reactions). Disentangling such biases is important to fully understanding the experiences of gay/lesbian employees.

A final limitation involves interpreting the direction of causality. For instance, self-acceptance may lead to disclosure behaviors, and disclosing more often may lead to greater self-acceptance. Likely this is a bidirectional process. The current results also suggest that employees who are "out" are more likely to be satisfied, have supportive coworkers, and have supportive organizational policies. Although it is possible that employees self-select into organizations that are tolerant and gay friendly, it is also possible that employees who "come out" may pave the way for organizational changes. Past research reveals that few corporations adopted domestic partnership benefits, antigay discrimination policies, and other supportive organizational structures without first receiving pressure from some informal social group (Baker et al., 1995). That is, active and vocal gay/lesbian employees were often a key factor in affecting change within an organization. However, such forces within an organization often result in shifts in the type of people who are attracted, selected, and retained (see Schneider, 1983). Future research might clarify the process of change and the direction of causality.

Implications

The present results have implications for the recruitment of qualified gay and lesbian candidates. Recruitment efforts might apply Schneider's (1987) attraction-selection-attrition theory, which suggests that organizations who want to attract, select, and retain gay and lesbian workers should have formal, visible cues and structures reflecting that they already have such representation in their workforce or that there is organizational support and policies in place (see also Schneider, Goldstein, & Smith, 1995). Such organizations should consider what the candidates value and reinforce such values by creating and maintaining a culture that reflects this. Furthermore, recent research suggests that organizations that promote diversity do not do so at the risk of decreasing majority members' positivity toward the organization (see Avery, Hernandez, & Hebl, in press; Perkins, Thomas, & Taylor, 2000; Thomas & Wise, 1999).

Certainly our results showing that corporate supportiveness of diversity has a very favorable impact on gay/lesbian employees provide substantiation that such initiatives are worthwhile. In addition, gay/lesbian workers actually do take into account the extent to which companies are gay supportive when seeking employment (see Badgett, 1996). In fact, books and other listings even publish the most gay-supportive employers (e.g., Baker et al., 1995; Mickens, 1994). As a result, the institution of organizational policies and a supportive atmosphere may provide employers with a competitive advantage in the recruitment process.

Finally, Powers (1996) suggested that "people in organizations lack the skills, knowledge, tools, and resources to effectively address gay, lesbian, bisexual, and transgender workplace issues" (p. 79). To compensate for this, diversity training may need to specifically address issues of sexual orientation. For instance, management might consider greater attempts to educate workers specifically about gay/lesbian issues, foster a climate of acceptance, and articulate policies that clearly indicate that discrimination will not be tolerated, particularly because coworker reactions are so important to gay/lesbian employees' job satisfaction and job anxiety.

Issues concerning disclosures of sexual orientation in the workplace are complex but can be understood with an increased focus on the workplace experiences of gay and lesbian employees. Given that attitudes about gay and lesbian individuals, laws, and organizational policies are continually changing, it is important to empirically examine critical issues that gay/lesbian workers face. We can't rely on outdated research—or the entire absence of it—to understand organizational implications in an evolving workplace.

References

Avery, D. R., Hernandez, M., & Hebl, M. (in press). Recruiting diversity: The race is on. *Journal of Applied Social Psychology*.

Badgett, M. V. L. (1996). Employment and sexual orientation: Disclosure and discrimination in the workplace. In Alan L. Ellis & E. D. B. Riggle (Eds.), *Sexual identity on the job: Issues and services*. New York: Haworth Press.

Bailey, J. M., Kim, P. Y., Hills, A., & Linsenmeier, J. A. W. (1997). Butch, femme, or straight acting? Partner preferences of gay men and lesbians. *Journal of Personality and Social Psychology, 73*, 960–973.

Baker, D. B., Strub, S. O., & Henning, B. (1995). *Cracking the corporate closet: The 200 best (and worst) companies to work for, buy from, and invest in if you're gay or lesbian—and even if you aren't.* New York: HarperCollins.

Baron, R. M., & Kenny, D. A. (1986). The moderator-mediator variable distinction in social psychological research: Conceptual, strategic, and statistical considerations. *Journal of Personality and Social Psychology, 51*, 1173–1132.

Baumeister, R. F., & Leary, M. R. (1995). The need to belong: Desire for interpersonal attachment as a fundamental human motivation. *Psychological Bulletin, 117*, 497–529.

Bohan, J. S. (1996). *Psychology and sexual orientation: Coming to terms.* New York: Routledge.

Branscombe, N. R., Schmitt, M. T., & Harvey, R. D. (1999). Perceiving pervasive discrimination among African-Americans: Implications for group identification and well-being. *Journal of Personality and Social Psychology, 77*, 135–149.

Button, S. B. (2001). Organizational effectors to affirm sexual diversity: A cross-level examination. *Journal of Applied Psychology, 86*, 17–28.

Cain, R. (1991). Stigma management and gay identity development. *Social Work, 36*, 67–73.

Cole, S. W., Kemeny, M. E., Taylor, S. E., & Visscher, B. R. (1996). Elevated physical health risk among gay men who conceal their homosexual identity. *Health Psychology, 15*, 243–251.

Coleman, E. (1982). Developmental stages of the coming out process. *Journal of Homosexuality, 7*, 31–43.

Collins, N. L., & Miller, L. C. (1994). Self-disclosure and liking: A meta-analytic review. *Psychological Bulletin, 116*, 457–475.

Crocker, J., & Major, B. (1989). Social stigma and self-esteem: The self-protective properties of stigma. *Psychological Review, 96*, 608—630.

Croteau, J. M. (1996). Research on the work experience of lesbian, gay, and bisexual people: An integrative review of methodology and findings. *Journal of Vocational Behavior, 48*, 195–209.

Croteau, J. M., & Lark, J. S. (1995). On being lesbian, gay, or bisexual in student affairs: A national survey of experiences on the job. *NASPA Journal, 32*, 189–187.

D'Augelli, A. R., & Hershberger, S. L. (1993). Lesbian, gays, and bisexual youth in community settings: Personal challenges and mental health problems. *American Journal of Community Psychology, 21*, 421–448.

Day, N. E., & Schoenrade, P. (1997). Staying in the closet versus coming out: Relationships between communication about sexual orientation and work attitudes. *Personnel Psychology, 50*, 147–163.

Derlega, V. J., Metts, S., Petronio, S., & Margulis, S T. (1993). *Self-disclosure.* Newbury Park, CA: Sage.

Dovidio, J. F., & Gaertner, S. L. (2000). Aversive racism and selection decisions: 1989 and 1999. *Psychological Science, 11*, 315–319.

Driscoll, J. M., Kelley, F. A., & Fassinger, R. E. (1996). Lesbian identity and disclosure in the workplace: Relation to occupational stress and satisfaction. *Journal of Vocational Behavior, 48*, 229–242.

Ellis, A. L., & Riggle, E. D. B. (1996). *Sexual identity on the job: Issues and services.* New York: Haworth Press.

Franke, R., & Leary, M. R. (1991). Disclosure of sexual orientation by lesbians and gay men: A comparison of private and public processes *Journal of Social and Clinical Psychology, 10*, 262–269.

Garnets, L., Herek, G., & Levy, B. (1990). Violence and victimization of lesbians and gay men: Mental health consequences. *Journal of Interpersonal Violence, 5*, 366–383.

Garnets, L., & Kimmel, D. (1993). *Psychological perspectives on lesbian and gay male experiences.* New York: Columbia University Press.

Goffman, E. (1963). *Stigma: Notes on the management of spoiled identity.* Englewood Cliffs, NJ: Prentice Hall.

Griffith, K. H., & Quiñones. M. A. (2001). *Lesbian construction workers and gay flight attendants: The effects of sexual orientation, gender, and job type on job applicant ratings.* Unpublished manuscript, Rice University.

Hallowell, R., Schlesinger, L. A., & Zornitsky, J. (1996). Internal service quality, customer and job satisfaction: Linkages and implications for management. *Human Resource Planning, 19*, 20–31.

Hebl, M., Foster, J. M., Mannix, L. M., & Dovidio, J. F. (2002). Formal and interpersonal discrimination: A field study bias toward homosexual applicants. *Personality and Social Psychology Bulletin, 28*, 815–825.

Herek, G. M., Gillis, J. R., & Cogan, J. C. (1999). Psychological sequalae of hate-crime victimization among lesbian, gay, and bisexual adults. *Journal of Consulting and Clinical Psychology, 67*, 945–951.

Hershberger, S. L., & D'Augelli, A. R. (1995). The impact of victimization on the mental health and suicidality of lesbian, gay, and bisexual youths. *Developmental Psychology, 31,* 65–74.

Ironson, G. H., Smith, P. C., Brannick, M. T., Gibson, W. M., & Paul, K. B. (1989). Construction of a job in general scale: A comparison of global, composite, and specific measures. *Journal of Applied Psychology, 74,* 193–200.

Kalichman, S. C., & Nachimson, D. (1999). Self-efficacy and disclosure of HIV-positive serostatus to sex partners. *Health Psychology, 18,* 281–287.

Kimmel, D. C., & Sang, B. E. (1995). Lesbians and gay men in midlife. In A. R. D'Augelli & C. J. Patterson (Eds.), *Lesbian, gay, and bisexual identities over the lifespan* (pp. 190–214). New York: Oxford University Press.

Kite, M. E., & Whitley, B. E. (1996). Sex differences in attitudes toward homosexual persons, behaviors, and civil rights: A meta-analysis. *Personality and Social Psychology Bulletin, 22,* 336–353.

Kronenberger, G. K. (1991). Out of the closet. *Personnel Journal, 70,* 40–44.

Lane, J. D., & Wegner, D. M. (1995). The cognitive consequences of secrecy. *Journal of Personality and Social Psychology, 69,* 237–253.

Laurenceau, J., Barrett, L. F., & Pietromonaco, P. R. (1998). Intimacy as an interpersonal process: The importance of self-disclosure, partner disclosure, and perceived partner responsiveness in interpersonal exchanges. *Journal of Personality and Social Psychology, 74,* 1238–1251.

Leary, M. R., Springer, C., Negel, L., Ansell, E., & Evans, K. (1998). The causes, phenomenology, and consequences of hurt feelings. *Journal of Personality and Social Psychology, 74,* 1225–1237.

The Lesbian Almanac. (1996). Compiled by the National Museum & Archive of Lesbian and Gay History. New York: Berkley Books.

Lewis, L. A. (1984). The coming-out process for lesbians: Integrating a stable identity. *Social Work, 29,* 464–469.

Ludwig, D., Franco, J. N., & Malloy, T. E. (1986). Effects of reciprocity and self-monitoring on self-disclosure with a new acquaintance. *Journal of Personality and Social Psychology, 50,* 1077–1032.

Luhtanen, R., & Crocker, J. (1992). A collective self-esteem scale: Self-evaluation of one's social identity. *Personality and Social Psychology Bulletin, 18,* 302–318.

Mickens, E. (1994). *The 100 best companies for gay men and lesbians.* New York: Pocket Books.

National Gay and Lesbian Task Force. (1991). National Gay and Lesbian Task Force Survey (National Gay and Lesbian Task Force records, 1973–2000). Division of Rare and Manuscript Collections, Cornell University.

Neely Martinez, M. (1993, June). Recognizing sexual orientation is fair and not costly. *HR Magazine, 38,* 66–72.

Perkins, L. A., Thomas, K. M., & Taylor, G. A. (2000). Advertising and recruitment: Marketing to minorities. *Psychology & Marketing, 17,* 235–255.

Phinney, J. S. (1990). Ethnic identity in adolescents and adults: Review of research. *Psychological Bulletin, 10,* 499–514.

Powers, B. (1996). The impact of gay, lesbian, and bisexual workplace issues on productivity. In Ellis, A. L., & Riggle, E D. B. (Eds.), *Sexual identity on the job: Issues and services.* New York: Haworth Press.

Rogers, A., & Hebl, M. R. (2001, June). *To disclose or not to disclose: A micronarrative account.* Poster session presented at the annual meeting of the American Psychological Society, Toronto, Ontario, Canada.

Rothblum, E. (1995). "I only read about myself on bathroom walls": The need for research on the mental health of lesbians and gay men. *Journal of Consulting and Clinical Psychology, 62,* 213–220.

Ryff, C. D., & Keyes, C. L. M. (1995). The structure of psychological well-being revisited. *Journal of Personality and Social Psychology, 69,* 719–727.

Rynes, S. L. (1990). Recruitment, job choice and post-hire consequences: A call for new research directions. In M. D. Dunnette & L. M. Hough (Eds.), *Handbook of industrial and organizational psychology* (2nd ed., Vol. 2, pp. 399–444). Palo Alto, CA: Consulting Psychologists Press.

Sang, B. (1993). Some existential issues of midlife lesbians. In L. Garnets & D. Kimmel (Eds.), *Psychological perspectives on lesbian and gay-male experiences* (pp. 500–516). New York: Columbia University Press.

Savin-Williams, R. (1989). Coming out to parents and self-esteem among gay and lesbian youths *Journal of Homosexuality, 18,* 1–35.

Savin-Williams, R., & Rodriquez, R. G. (1993). A developmental, clinical perspective on lesbian, gay male, and bisexual youths. In T. P. Gullotta, G. R. Adams, & R. Montemayer (Eds.), *Advances in adolescent development* (Vol. 5, pp. 77–101). Newbury Park, CA: Sage.

Schneider, B. (1983). An interactionist perspective on organizational effectiveness. In K. S. Cameron & D. A. Whetten (Eds.), *Organizational effectiveness: A comparison of multiple models* (pp. 27–54). Orlando, FL: Academic Press.

Schneider, B. (1987). The people make the place. *Personnel Psychology, 40,* 437–453.

Schneider, B., Goldstein, H. W., & Smith, B. D. (1995). The ASA framework: An update. *Personnel Psychology, 48,* 747–773.

Thomas, K. M., & Wise, P. G. (1999). Organizational attractiveness and individual differences: Are diverse applicants attracted by different factors? *Journal of Business and Psychology, 13,* 375–390.

Vargo, M. E. (1998). *Acts of disclosure: The coming-out process of contemporary gay men.* Binghamton, NY: Haworth Press.

Waldo, C. R. (1999). Working in a majority context: A structural model of heterosexism as minority stress in the workplace. *Journal of Counseling Psychology, 46,* 218–232.

Wells, J. W., & Kline, W. B. (1987). Self-disclosure of homosexual orientation. *Journal of Social Psychology, 127,* 191–197.

Yang, A. S. (1997). The polls-trends: Attitudes toward homosexuality. *Public Opinion Quarterly, 61,* 477–507.

SOURCE: Griffin, Kristin H. and Michelle R. Hebl. 2002. "The Disclosure Dilemma for Gay Men and Lesbians: 'Coming Out' at Work." *Journal of Applied Psychology*, 87(6):1191–99.

48

Identification of the Characteristics of Work Environments and Employers Open to Hiring and Accommodating People with Disabilities

Dennis Gilbride, Robert Stensrud, David Vandergoot,
and Kristie Golden

It has been more than a decade since the Americans with Disabilities Act of 1990 (ADA) was signed into law, yet the unemployment rate for people with significant disabilities has remained virtually unchanged. Public policy makers recognized the persistent problem of unemployment among people with significant disabilities and responded by strengthening the employment outcome focus of the Rehabilitation Act of 1973 and initiating new programs such as the Ticket to Work and Work Incentives Improvement Act (TWWIIA, Pub. L. 106–170).

Although these initiatives are important, it is clear that by themselves they cannot solve the employment challenges of many people with disabilities.

To effectively meet the employment goals desired by many consumers, rehabilitation providers also need to increase the effectiveness of placement services. One way to accomplish this is to increase our understanding of employers. Many employers do hire and effectively accommodate and include people with disabilities. Identification of the specific characteristics of those employers who are open to and successful in hiring and accommodating people with disabilities can help us focus our placement services and improve the targeting of our consulting, education, and advocacy activities.

Prior researchers have recognized the importance of understanding employers and how they perceive disability issues (Millington, Asner, Linkowski, &

Der-Stepanian, 1996). Research has been conducted on employer attitudes toward people with various disabilities (Gilbride, Stensrud, Ehlers, Evans, & Peterson, 2000), employer's perceptions of the ADA (Hernanadez, Keys, & Balcazar, 2000), how to develop relationships with employers (Fry, 1997), and the types of consulting services that rehabilitation professionals might provide to employers (Gilbride & Stensrud, 1992, 1999; Jenkins & Strauser, 1999).

Stone and Colella (1996) developed a comprehensive model of factors that they believed affected the treatment of people with disabilities in organizations. They identified three clusters of variables: attributes of the people with disabilities, environmental factors (public policy issues), and organizational characteristics. The organizational variables that they hypothesized to have the most effect on people with disabilities included organizational norms and values, human resource policies, and the nature of the reward systems.

A number of other researchers have concurred with Stone and Colella, and they have attempted to identify the specific characteristics of the workplace that improve an organization's capacity to effectively hire and include people with disabilities (Akabas, 1994; Butterworth, Hagner, Helm, & Whelley, 2000; Kirsh, 2000a). Akabas asserted that placement professionals need to identify and reach out to employers who celebrate diversity and provide an individualized and supportive workplace.

Butterworth, Whitney-Thomas, and Shaw (1997) found that supported employment consumers had higher success rates in organizations that had a "culture of inclusiveness." In a qualitative study of eight young adults with developmental disabilities, Butterworth et al. (2000) identified four organizational characteristics that were related to successful integration of the consumers they studied. They found that successful employers allowed opportunities for multiple context relationships among employees, provided specific opportunities for social interactions, used a personal and team-building management style, and had an interdependent job design. Similarly, Kirsh (2000b) found that consumers with psychiatric disabilities were more successful in workplaces whose norms included acceptance of diversity and an atmosphere of respect and caring.

This initial research on workplace culture suggests that employers do vary in their openness to hiring and including people with disabilities and that there are specific organizational characteristics that enhance this inclusiveness. The present study was designed to extend this research. In this study, focus groups and interviews were conducted with successfully employed people with disabilities, employers who have successfully hired and included employees with disabilities, and successful placement providers. This facilitated the identification of specific workplace factors that characterize employers open to inclusion of people with disabilities.

METHOD

A grounded theory qualitative design (Straus & Corbin, 1998) was chosen for this study. Although some research has been conducted on employer openness, it is in a formative stage and lacks specificity and broad empirical validation. Grounded theory is an effective method for developing a theory from the bottom up; that is, rather than beginning with a theory about employer openness and testing it, this strategy allows the theory to emerge from the data. In grounded theory, qualitative data are carefully obtained, and through a systematic procedure of data analysis and coding, categories and concepts are developed and then integrated into larger components. These larger components become the conceptual building blocks of hypotheses and theory, which can then be tested explicitly. A major advantage of qualitative research is the emphasis on data that identify the meaning people give to events in context (Hagner & Helm, 1994). A central component of employer openness to hiring persons with disabilities is the perception of consumers about the inclusiveness of the worksite. The importance of consumers' experiences of acceptance and inclusion make grounded theory appropriate for use in addressing this research area at its current stage of development.

Procedures

Focus groups and interviews were conducted with three groups: successfully employed people with disabilities, employers who have successfully hired and integrated people with disabilities into their workforces, and placement providers who have worked closely with employers and have successfully placed many people with disabilities. Only successful participants were included in this study because our purpose was identification of employer characteristics that enhanced hiring and inclusion of persons with disabilities.

Two groups of successfully employed consumers were recruited for this study ($n = 6$ and $n = 10$). One group was conducted in a large city, the other in a midsize regional city. These two locations were chosen because they represented very different labor markets and consumer populations. Local rehabilitation providers and the state vocational rehabilitation (VR) agency in each area nominated consumers. The consumer groups consisted of people with a wide range of disabilities, including mobility limitations, cognitive disabilities, psychiatric disabilities, substance abuse, and AIDS. The consumer groups contained 11 women and 6 men, of which 9 individuals were African American and 1 person was Hispanic. The average age was 47.4 years. Four participants were married, 3 were divorced, 5 had never been married, and 4 provided no information on their marital status. Consumers were paid $100 plus expenses and lunch for their participation. The focus groups lasted approximately 4 hours, with a lunch break in the middle, and were tape-recorded and transcribed. The first consumer group met a second time toward the end of the study to review findings and serve as a member check of the emerging theory. Consumers were asked to describe their employment experiences and discuss employer behaviors, policies, and procedures and other characteristics of the workplace that increased or decreased their feelings of acceptance and their ability to be a successful employee.

Five focus groups and nine individual interviews were conducted with employers. Employers included human resource directors from hospitals, manufacturing, and service industries; owners of small businesses; and mid-level supervisors of retail stores. The number of participants in each group varied from 6 to 10. Employers were identified by local rehabilitation providers as organizations that had hired consumers, and they were viewed

in the community as open to hiring people with disabilities. Initial employer groups were asked to discuss their experiences with employees with disabilities. As potential issues for the consumers and placement providers were identified, employers were asked more specific questions that arose out of certain emerging topics. This process of feeding initial results back into the data collection process is viewed as essential to theory building from the grounded theory perspective (Straus & Corbin, 1998).

A focus group was also conducted with providers of placement services ($n = 5$), and individual interviews with placement providers ($n = 3$) were conducted. The focus group consisted of agencies that provided services to members of the second consumer group. Consumers indicated which service providers they believed had the strongest relationships with employers and which agencies were the most helpful to them in transitioning to work. The placement providers identified by the consumers were invited to participate in the focus group and agreed to participate. Placement providers were asked (a) how they identified which employers to contact for potential employment opportunities and (b) their perceptions of the characteristics of employers open to hiring people with disabilities.

Coding and Data Analysis

Independent open coding (Straus & Corbin, 1998) of the initial transcripts was conducted by each of the three primary investigators. After each focus group, investigators identified statements that they viewed as related to employer openness. Statements were collected and patterns and themes identified. Those themes were then compared to the literature and refined into categories. As indicated in the grounded theory methodology, further questions were developed that related to those categories, and the next focus group was asked to answer these questions. The employer focus groups were conducted both before and after the second consumer group and the service provider group.

Differences among the three primary researchers in the coding of statements were discussed and negotiated as a group. During the final coding, a fourth, independent researcher was asked to review the categories, and items were discussed until consensus was reached. Categories were continually refined and reexamined after each focus group. The resulting model consisted of three major categories and 13 specific characteristics of employers open to hiring individuals with disabilities.

Credibility of Findings

In qualitative research, issues of reliability and validity are often discussed in terms of the credibility of the findings (Bogdan & Bicklen, 1993; Hagner & Helm, 1994; Straus & Corbin, 1998). The credibility of findings in a qualitative study is based upon the quality of the data obtained (often called *thick description*) and other specific techniques designed to limit potential bias and enhance the usefulness and generalizability of results. To enhance the credibility of this study, a number of techniques were utilized. First, as indicated previously, careful attention was paid to transcript coding and analysis, with an extensive audit trail and field notes from the three primary researchers. Thick description was ensured by examination and coding of more than 600 transcript pages. Second, triangulation of data was accomplished by obtaining information from multiple sources with different perspectives (consumers, employers, and service providers). Third, all the transcripts were reexamined after categories were developed to identify' potential discrepant data and adjust the model to address those inconsistencies. Fourth, a participant check was conducted toward the conclusion of the data collection phase of the study. The participant check was conducted by reconvening the initial consumer group and presenting the emerging categories and model to the group members. They reviewed the categories and model and provided feedback that resulted in a number of the categories being extended and refined. At the conclusion of the participant check, the consumer focus group members confirmed that the revised model reflected their experiences in workplaces that were open to them as people with significant disabilities.

Results

As indicated previously, the extensive data collection and analysis process resulted in identification of 13 specific employer characteristics organized into three major categories: Work Cultural Issues, Job Match, and Employer Experience and Support. Each of these categories will be discussed, along with the specific employer characteristics within each category. Direct quotations from all three data sources (people with disabilities, employers, and providers) will be provided to illustrate the employer characteristics. A complete list of categories and employer characteristics can be found in Table 48.1.

Work Cultural Issues

Work Cultural Issues was the largest category and included values and norms concerning diversity, work performance, organizational practices, and policies. The central issue for consumers was feeling included and respected. Consumers indicated that a good employer was one who included them with all employees and listened to their concerns and needs. The importance of feeling integrated into the organization was best expressed by one consumer, who used some version of the word "include" five times in one statement:

> They include us in everything that they do. I mean we are included. We were having a Christmas party a couple of weeks ago, and they are including us in it. Everything they do we are included. We have staff meetings for, like, company meetings every month because how our production was the past month, how much scrap was there for the whole place, what new contracts were in, what old contracts were going out. They include us in everything.

Employers also indicated that diversity and inclusion of people who are different have become increasingly important to their organization's success. Reflecting on this, one employer stated, "Diversity is important to us as a company. Our customer base is getting more diverse. Our employees are getting more diverse. If we can't handle

Table 48.1.   Key Characteristics of Employers Who Are Open to People With Disabilities

Work cultural issues	Job match	Employer experience and support issues
1. Employers include people with disabilities with all workers and treat them equally	1. The employer focuses on the consumer's capabilities and effectively matches the worker with the job requirements	1. The employer has the ability to supervise a diverse workforce.
2. Employers welcome diversity; they are egalitarian and inclusive	2. The employer obtains input from people with disabilities on their ability to perform job duties, and he or she includes people with disabilities in all accommodation discussions.	2. The employer views the community rehabilitation program (or other rehabilitation agency) as a partner and as an on-going employment support resource.
3. Employers' management style is more personal and flexible	3. The employer focuses on essential, rather than marginal, functions.	
4. Employers focus on a worker's performance, not his or her disability.	4. The employer offers interships, and they often lead to jobs.	
5. Senior management expects and rewards diversity.		
6. Employers are comfortable providing accommodations to all their employees.		
7. The organization provides "cafeteria style" benefits		

differences and handle them really well, it will cost us money."

A second cultural value expressed by both consumers and employers was a focus on job performance rather than disability. One consumer said,

> I don't think they see the disabilities. They treat us like we're—like you want to be treated, like a regular human being, and that's the way they treat us there. You know they don't see disabilities. They see our performance. As long as we perform to the best of our abilities, that's all they ask.

Employers also indicated that they focus exclusively on job performance. One employer noted, "I hire for attitude and train for skills. After that,

the cost of accommodations is nothing. I want employees who will stay and do good work."

Participants identified a number of other cultural issues that were related to the manner in which employers managed, supervised, and accommodated employees with disabilities. A key consideration was the employer's ability to be flexible regarding and sensitive to the employee's specific situation. These employers frequently did not single out people with disabilities for special treatment, but rather understood, as one employer stated, that "everybody needs some kind of accommodation sometime." Another employer indicated, "We have the approach that, hey, if we can do anything to make your life easier at home or work, we try to work with the employee to do it."

Employers also recognized that values and norms concerning inclusion and flexibility should come from senior management. One employer said, "But I think it starts at the top; you have to hold people accountable and our managers have objectives that their bonuses depend upon in terms of working with diversity."

Consumers also indicated how important it was for employers to be flexible and accommodating. One consumer stated,

> My disability is obvious; you can see it, but I get somewhat treated different, not in a bad way. They accommodate. Like we just moved from one area to another, so they make sure everything was accessible for me like the bathroom, the area.

Medical benefits were also frequently discussed by both consumers and employers. Participants recognized that people with disabilities may have unique medical needs that aren't effectively covered by traditional plans. One consumer stated, "The employer is hiring people with disabilities, so they need to look at that [benefits options], and it was looked at and it was changed." An employer said, "We've got five health plans and three vision plans and so on, but to go beyond this to accommodate a disability, we would look at that on a case-by-case basis."

A great deal of agreement existed among consumers, employers, and providers regarding the type of work culture that is welcoming of and supportive to people with disabilities. Seven specific employer characteristics that were identified in this category can be found listed in Table 48.1.

Job Match

The second major category was Job Match. All three groups discussed the importance of a specific match between the consumer and the job. The actual ability of the applicant to perform the essential functions of the job was emphasized, whereas disability issues were de-emphasized.

One consumer stated, "I was having trouble because I had to fit it [a particular part] a certain way into the gauge, and I couldn't do it. They said, 'Okay, we'll put somebody else on this,' and they put me on a job I knew how to do." Another consumer said, "They're focusing on what it is you can do and trying to encourage you to look at yourself as an employee and not as a person with a special situation."

Employers were also concerned about focusing on the ability of the person to be a good employee. One employer said, "I can pick out the people that are nervous versus an attitude—you ask them why they want the job, and if they can explain that to you, that means a lot to me, that means the person is going to show up."

A placement provider emphasized focusing on job skills when working with employers. The provider stated, "You must make sure the person with a disability can do the job. I tell them I am here to help with your employment needs, I won't send you someone who can't do the job." Another provider indicated that focusing on just the essential functions of the job was key: "A closed employer stands by the job description to the letter; an open employer is more flexible and will try and make it work."

Many of the providers had consumers who developed their job skills by participating in internships. Although the use of internships is not a widely employed rehabilitation technique, it was very successful for many of these consumers and placement providers. Said one provider,

> I mean, an internship, it's a no cost collaboration between [the agency] and the employer, so they basically get to see without any risk what this person is like, so it just—it's really a very casual way of working with employers . . . I would say a very small percentage of students [providers call consumers *students*] don't get placed right from internships.

All of the participants consistently emphasized the importance of a good match between the consumer and the specific job. Consumers wanted employers to recognize and allow them to use their skills and talents, whereas employers wanted good, reliable employees. The four specific employer characteristics from this category are listed in Table 48.1.

Employer Experience and Support

The key components of the third category were the extent to which an employer was skilled at managing differences and the level of support the employer believed he or she had to include and accommodate workers with disabilities. Employers who were comfortable and had experience with an ethnically diverse workforce found it easier to accommodate a person with a disability. For these employers, disability was just another form of diversity. As one employer said, "So you are so used to that [accommodating existing employees] that then hiring a person with a disability is not really an issue, and it gives you insight into how you can be creative, to make the choice work." Another employer said, "I think we can kind of stretch ourselves when we're making an accommodation, and we have done that, we haven't had anybody ask for anything unreasonable yet."

A consumer also recognized that at his organization, disability was just another type of diversity. He said,

It is the same thing with the ethnic part of it, and in the plant that I'm in there are a lot of people who are from different countries . . . you know everybody helps each other out. Being disabled out there where I am, it doesn't really make any difference.

The second factor was the availability of human resources support. Having the necessary support, either from the disability community or an in-house human resource department, was viewed as essential. One employer said,

I think what I could use the most is a point of contact, someone that I know I can pick up the phone and call and ask questions . . . about reasonable accommodations . . . the ADA, especially that, what it is we're expected to do, what's reasonable.

When responding to this type of expressed employer need, a vocational rehabilitation provider indicated that she had placed seven consumers with one employer. She said, "I became their HR staff, I did the paperwork and the interviewing, I did the hiring for them sight unseen."

Developing strong, effective relationships between community rehabilitation programs (CRPs) and employers was identified by both groups as a key support strategy. The need for support, and the willingness to rely on a CRP for that support, was underscored by an employer who said, "So perhaps that could go back to the education of us and supervision about disability in general, and you know, going beyond the obvious [disability issue] and you know, help us to understand and not, say, be afraid." A provider indicated that the profession's commitment to assisting employers and maintaining a strong relationship increased employer openness to hiring people with disabilities: "There are mutual benefits [between the agency and employers], and we try to make sure they see, [we want to] help them with their general employee who might have problems . . . we get a lot of positive feedback on that." The two specific employer characteristics from this category are listed in Table 48.1.

DISCUSSION

The results of this study support and extend prior research concerning the characteristics of employers who are open to hiring and supporting workers with disabilities. The three categories identified in this study—Work Cultural Issues, Job Match, and Employer Experience and Support—are consistent with the factors discussed in the theoretical literature. Furthermore, during the member check, all of the consumers agreed that the employer characteristics identified in this study were on target. As one consumer concluded, "These are good things!"

The importance of Work Cultural Issues concerning diversity, egalitarianism, and flexibility found in the work of Stone and Colella (1996), Akabas (1994), and Butterworth et al. (1997) was strongly supported by the results of this study, which indicate that organizations that authentically embrace those values and have strong senior management support create a culture in which people with disabilities can work and succeed. Employer values and culture vary. In this study, seven specific characteristics were identified that can be used to differentiate employers who may be more open to hiring and accommodating people with disabilities.

The second category, Job Match, has always been a key component of quality vocational rehabilitation (Gilbride, Stensrud, & Johnson, 1994; Spirito-Dalgin & Gilbride, in press). The current study underscores the importance of this match for both the consumer and employer. These results are consistent with the findings of Colella, DeNisi, and Varma (1997), who found more negative bias directed at a worker with a disability in a poor fit situation. Successful placement professionals understand the importance of job match and work closely with consumers and employers to ensure that the position is appropriate before a placement is made.

The results of this study concerning the category of Employer Experience and Support also confirm and extend the current literature. Employers with successful diversity experience find inclusion and accommodation of people with disabilities much easier. These results indicate that employment outcomes for people with disabilities can be enhanced if the rehabilitation community plays an active role in providing support for employers with less experience and limited internal personnel resources. Employers are likely to utilize members of the disability community to help them with personnel issues if those services are provided consistently and are focused on job performance.

From the perspective of consumers, three issues seemed to emerge: inclusion and respect, an employer who listens to them, and a good job match that utilizes their capabilities. Although the importance of these factors is not surprising, it does suggest that along with a thoughtful analysis of the match between the consumer and the job, rehabilitation professionals need to attend much more to the culture of the specific employer. The employment success of the consumers in this study was significantly affected by these environmental factors, indicating that employment outcomes can be improved if consideration is given to the extent of these factors in the employer's environment prior to placement.

The results of this study suggest that even employers who are open to hiring and accommodating workers with disabilities are very concerned about maintaining explicit and rigorous hiring guidelines. Their first objective is to hire the person who most effectively demonstrates that he or she can perform the essential functions of the job, with or without accommodations. Their second objective is to hire people with the soft skills (i.e. positive attitude) to be reliable workers. In order to hire a person with a disability, employers consistently emphasized that applicants had to meet these criteria before they would be considered for a position. If the applicant was referred by an agency, employers wanted assurance that the worker could do the job. If the applicant posed a challenge to the existing system by needing accommodations with which the employer was unfamiliar or needing occasional rehabilitation counseling interventions, employers wanted ongoing support in understanding these needs. Employers without strong human resource departments would look toward the disability community for personnel support; however, they wanted that support to be job related, effective, and timely.

Limitations

The limitations of this study are those common to most qualitative research—the small sample size and the limited representativeness of the sample, both of which reduce generalizability. As indicated in the Method section, a number of procedures were employed to mitigate the inherent limitations of a qualitative design. Nonetheless, these results must be understood as preliminary, and they need further validation through other qualitative and quantitative research.

Implications for Rehabilitation Counselors

These results have a number of implications for rehabilitation counselors and other placement providers. First, placement should always be done in a thoughtful manner that matches employee ability with the essential functions of the job. The results of this study underscore the importance of rehabilitation and placement professionals having a comprehensive understanding of the essential functions of positions in their local labor markets and using that knowledge to find appropriate fits for their consumers. Labor market knowledge and accurate consumer assessment have long been considered essential functions within rehabilitation counseling. The results of this study emphasize the importance of these skills in assisting consumers in finding meaningful and successful employment.

Second, rehabilitation professionals should go beyond traditional labor market research that emphasizes job openings and salary by also evaluating the organizational culture of the target employer. Rehabilitation professionals can use the characteristics of open employers found in this study to help direct their analysis to identify employers most willing and capable of hiring people with disabilities. For example, rehabilitation providers can ask (or determine) some of the following key questions:

- How much diversity does the employer have in the workforce?
- Is the organization's management style personal and flexible?
- Does the organization provide ongoing training for frontline supervisors and see it as a critical factor in managing employees?
- Does the employer have experience working with people with disabilities?
- Does the employer have a source of support? If not, can my agency provide that support?

Rehabilitation professionals can use the answer from these types of questions to focus placement efforts on those employers most likely to provide quality employment opportunities.

Third, the rehabilitation community can use the characteristics outlined in this study to provide a direction and focus for employer education and consulting. In large part, the characteristics that make an employer open to a person with a disability are factors that would benefit all employees, particularly in the increasingly diverse society. Not all employers (even very progressive ones) will embody all of these characteristics. Rehabilitation counselors can use these factors to help employers conduct a self-assessment from which they can identify areas in need of improvement. Rehabilitation professionals can also be involved in advocacy and educational initiatives that challenge other employers to authentically evaluate and change their organizational culture to enhance their openness.

Finally, the results of this study suggest that many employers require, and would welcome, thoughtful support in meeting their personnel needs. These results support prior suggestions in the literature that rehabilitation counselors should "horizontally expand" their role to include services to support employers (Gilbride & Stensrud, 1999; Jenkins & Strauser, 1999). Most of the employers in this study had received ongoing support and assistance from rehabilitation professionals. They were consistent in their appreciation for that support and the role that it played in their ability to successfully hire and accommodate people with disabilities. These results suggest that more opportunities for people with disabilities could be generated if rehabilitation professionals expanded their support to more employers. Although many rehabilitation agencies support the concept of providing services directly to an employer (Gilbride, 2000) few have committed the necessary organizational resources. Providing services directly to employers requires significant conceptual and systemic change. These results challenge rehabilitation professionals to consider those changes and find ways to reach out and support employers.

Conclusions

These results suggest that employment outcomes for people with disabilities can be enhanced if rehabilitation providers pay more attention to the specific characteristics of the organization in which they want to place their consumer. Specifically, this study provides preliminary empirical data on some of the characteristics of work environments that are related to increased employer openness to hiring and accommodating employees with disabilities. A number of issues suggested by this study require additional research. First, future research needs to confirm, revise, and expand these employer characteristics in order to deepen our understanding of the types of work environments that are conducive to success for workers with disabilities. Second, we need to develop a simple but valid method to measure these factors. In order to be helpful to rehabilitation counselors, placement professionals, consumers, and others interested in employment of people with disabilities, we need to find an easy, reliable method for accessing the type of employer information suggested by this study. Third, we need to determine if providing services and support directly to employers does increase the number and quality of placements. If rehabilitation agencies redirect resources toward employer support, we need to be sure that those resources result in increased numbers of quality placements.

Successful employment of people with disabilities is complex and challenging, but it is vitally significant. We must continue to build our understanding of employers and work environments so that we can reduce the barriers to employment that many people with disabilities confront.

REFERENCES

Akabas,. S. (1994). Workplace responsiveness: Key employer characteristics in support of job maintenance for people with mental illness. *Psychosocial Rehabilitation Journal, 17*(3), 91–101.

Americans with Disabilities Act of 1990. 42 U.S.C. § 12101 *et seq.*

Bogdan, R., & Biklen, S. (1998). *Qualitative research for education: An introduction to theory and methods* (3rd ed.). Boston: Allyn & Bacon.

Butterworth, J., Hagner, D., Helm, D., & Whelley, T. (2000). Workplace culture, social interactions, and supports for transition-age young adults. *Mental Retardation, 38*, 342–353.

Butterworth, J., Whitney-Thomas, J., & Shaw, D. (1997). The changing role of community based instruction: Strategies for facilitating supports. *Journal of Vocational Rehabilitation, 8*, 9–20.

Colella, A., DeNisi, A., & Varma, A. (199S). The impact ratee's disability on performance judgments and choice as partner: The role of disability-job fit stereotypes and interdependence of rewards. *Journal of Applied Psychology, 83*, 102–111.

Fry, R. (Ed.). (1997). *Developing effective partnerships with employers as a service delivery mechanism.* Menomonie, WI: Stout Vocational Rehabilitation Institute.

Gilbride, D. (2000). Going to work: Placement trends in public rehabilitation. *Journal of Vocational Rehabilitation, 14*, 89–94.

Gilbride, D., & Stensrud, R. (1992). Demand-side job development: A model for the 1990s. *Journal of Rehabilitation, 58*(4), 34–39.

Gilbride, D., & Stensrud, R. (1999). Demand-side job development and system change. *Rehabilitation Counseling Bulletin, 42*, 329–342.

Gilbride, D., Stensrud, R., Ehlers, C., Evans, E., & Peterson, C. (2000). Employers' attitudes toward hiring persons with disabilities and vocational rehabilitation services. *Journal of Rehabilitation, 66*(4), 17–23.

Gilbride, D., Stensrud, R., & Johnson, M. (1994). Current models of job placement and employer development: Research, competencies and educational considerations. *Rehabilitation Education, 7*, 215–239.

Hagner, D., & Helm, D. (1994). Qualitative methods in rehabilitation research. *Rehabilitation Counseling Bulletin, 37*, 290–303.

Hernanadez, B., Keys, L., & Balcazar, F. (2000). Employer attitudes toward workers with disabilities and their ADA employment rights: A literature review. *Journal of Rehabilitation, 66*(4), 4–16.

Jenkins, W., & Strauser, D. (1999). Horizontal expansion of the role of the rehabilitation counselor. *Journal of Rehabilitation, 65*(1), 4–9.

Kirsh, B. (2000a). Organizational culture, climate and person-environment fit: Relationships with employment outcomes for mental health consumers. *Work, 14*, 109–121

Kirsh, B. (2000b). Work, workers, and workplaces: A qualitative analysis of narratives of mental health consumers. *Journal of Rehabilitation, 66*(4), 24–30.

Millington, M., Asner, K., Linkowski, D., & Der-Stepanian, J. (1996). Employers and job development: The business perspective. In R. Parker & E. Siymanski (Eds), *Rehabilitation counseling: Basics and beyond* (pp. 277–308). Austin. TX: PRO-ED.

Rehabilitation Act of 1973. 29 U.S.C. § 701 *et seq.*

Spirito-Dalgin, R., & Gilbride, D. (in press). Perspective of people with psychiatric disabilities on employment disclosure. *Journal of Psychosocial Rehabilitation.*

Stone, D., & Colella, A. (1996). A model of factors affecting the treatment of disabled individuals in organizations. *Academy of Management Review, 21*, 352–401.

Strauss, A., & Corbin, J. (1998). *Basics of qualitative research: Techniques and procedures for developing grounded theory* (2nd ed.). Thousand Oaks, CA: Sage.

SOURCE: Gilbride, Dennis, Robert Stensrud, David Vandergoot, and Kristie Golden. 2003. "Identification of Work Environments and Employers Open to Hiring and Accommodating People With Disabilities." *Rehabilitation Counseling Bulletin, 46*(3):130–37.

PART VIII

ORGANIZATIONAL LEARNING AND CHANGE

AN INTRODUCTION TO ORGANIZATIONAL LEARNING AND CHANGE

Although the previous sections on conflict and diversity strongly suggest the need for organizational learning and change, change can be hard to achieve. Scholars have documented the likelihood that organizational change efforts will fail and the likelihood, when they do succeed, that changes will not be sustained over time. Theories of organizational learning and change therefore tend to focus attention on the obstacles that impede learning and change.

One potential explanation for the difficulty of change can be found in our earlier discussion of organizational culture. If organizational culture is composed of taken-for-granted assumptions, many of which may remain invisible to organizational members (Parsons et al. 1961; Schein 1991), it is likely that an organization's culture will inhibit any change efforts that violate its assumptions. Indeed, Edgar Schein makes the functionalist argument that organizational culture is based on assumptions that have been retained over time because they have "worked" in the past—that is, they have enabled the organization to survive. If these assumptions are perceived to have worked in the past, organizational members will likely be attached to them, especially the organizational members whose interests they have served most effectively.

Jesper Sørensen (2002) argues that strong cultures create a clear framework for action but that they also inhibit fundamental change. Therefore, strong cultures are conducive to organizational performance in stable environments that require only incremental change, but they undermine organizational performance in more volatile environments that require fundamental change. Despite this negative impact on performance, however, it is difficult to question the assumptions embedded in the organization's culture because these assumptions have served the organization well in the past and have therefore become normatively sanctioned.

Organization design scholars Paul Lawrence and Jay Lorsch (1967) suggest a rationalist model of organizational change. Organizations succeed to the extent that their structures match the requirements of their environments, including both competitive conditions and the technological requirements of their tasks. Lawrence and Lorsch suggest that one of the key roles of leaders is to understand the multiple environments in which their organization operates, to differentiate their organization into departments that correspond to these different environments, and then to achieve integration across these departments "to achieve unity of effort . . . as required . . . by the demands of the environment" (p. 11). Organizational change is therefore a process of differentiating and reintegrating the organization in response to diverse environmental demands. Jeffrey Pfeffer and Gerald Salancik (1978) suggest an alternative rationalist model of organizational change based on the concept of *resource dependence,* arguing that organizations succeed to the extent that they adjust their activities and external relationships to access the resources they need to survive. However, neither of these theories explicitly addresses *how* these changes occur.

Alternatively, Michael Hannan and John Freeman's (1977) population ecology approach is predicated on the idea that organizations do *not* change, and that change occurs instead through an evolutionary process that is akin to "survival of the fittest." Organizations that happen to be well adapted to their environments will survive, while those with less adaptive characteristics will fail, resulting in change over time at the population level. Organizations are not completely helpless, however; they can identify an environmental niche to which they are well adapted, and seek to compete in it. For example, when the airline industry shifted toward a demand for low fares, some airlines with high costs tried to reduce their costs while maintaining quality, with mixed success, while others sought to compete in a higher cost niche offering luxury amenities for high-end travelers. The niche strategy is based not on an organization's ability to change its characteristics, but rather on its ability to identify a niche environment that fits the characteristics it already has. This population ecology approach to change is consistent with Durkheimian functionalism in the sense that both make use of natural science concepts, such as survival of the fittest, to explain social realities. Functional arguments like population ecology assume that group characteristics and behavior reflect the best strategies for group coherence and survival.

Paul DiMaggio and Walter Powell (1983) argue that organizations can and do change, but while one or two early adopters change in order to adapt to the requirements of their environment, later adopters simply imitate the organizations whose practices have become perceived as legitimate. Instead of a rational search for best practices, therefore, organizations more typically seek to imitate legitimized practices whether or not those practices are conducive to their own performance. According to this institutional theory of change, the problem is not organizations' inability to change, but their desire to optimize legitimacy rather than performance as they engage in the process of change.

So far, these theories do not consider learning to be part of the change process. Of course change can occur *without* learning, just as learning can occur *without* change, but the most useful theories of change might be those that address how organizations can change in a way that is informed by learning. Chris Argyris's classic (1976) theory of single- and double-loop learning explores how taken-for-granted assumptions inhibit the ability to learn, and how organizations can overcome that disability. He defines learning as "the detection and correction of errors, and error as any feature of knowledge or of knowing that makes action ineffective" (Argyris 1976:365). The primary inhibitors to learning are (1) factors that impede the production of valid information that would enable decision makers to monitor the effectiveness of their decisions, such as "interdepartmental and interpersonal conflicts, ineffective and incomplete search, avoidance of uncertainty, political exchanges, annexation of other units, . . . competitive games, bargaining, parochial priorities, personal goals, interest, stakes, and stands, misperception and miscommunication" (p. 366) and (2) the receptivity of decision makers to corrective feedback. The problem of generating valid information and openness to hearing it becomes more severe the more important the decision, because the stakes become higher. Argyris concludes,

> One might say that participants in organizations are encouraged to learn to perform as long as the learning does not question the fundamental design, goals and activities of their organizations. This learning may be called single-loop learning. In double-loop learning, a participant would be able to ask questions about changing fundamental aspects of the organization. (P. 367)

The fact that fundamental questions cannot easily be asked might be attributed to a strong organizational culture, one whose taken-for-granted assumptions are shared widely by members of the organization. But in Argyris's (1976) view, the problem is different. Single-loop learning and the failure to ask fundamental questions is reinforced by a desire to unilaterally control other people by controlling their assumptions. The leader of an organization can overcome this problem by creating an environment that is conducive to open inquiry. In double-loop learning,

> Articulateness and advocacy are coupled with an invitation to confront one another's views and to alter them, in order to produce the position that is based on the most complete and valid information possible and to which participants can become internally committed. This means that the *leader must be skilled in eliciting* double-loop learning. (Argyris 1976:369, emphasis added)

The obstacles are significant, however. The change to double-loop learning is often misconstrued as requiring the withdrawal of power and structure. Organizational structures are needed, according to Argyris (1976), though they should be structures that support rather than suppress open inquiry. But even then, changing structures is not sufficient:

> Change based on the double-loop model would require a shift in the behavior of individuals and in group, intergroup and organizational processes . . . Changes in organizational structure, management information systems and organizational norms will not lead directly to changes in behavior of the people within the new system. (Argyris 1976:371)

Organizational change therefore requires behavioral change as well as structural change; neither is sufficient in itself. Argyris's (1976) theory of learning is clearly informed by a relational perspective on power and conformity and the associated dysfunctions of organizations. At the same time, he draws upon the rationalist paradigm in his insistence that good decisions, informed by valid information, can be made if organizational actors are encouraged by their leaders and supported by their organizational structures to challenge assumptions and engage in an open exchange of ideas.

Returning to Sørensen's (2002) argument that strong organizational cultures create an obstacle for change, we would argue instead that it depends. A strong culture that values the open exchange of ideas would tend to support organizational learning and change, whereas a strong culture that values the protection of assumptions and the unilateral control of others through control over their assumptions would tend to inhibit organizational learning and change. The important variable, we would suggest, is not the *strength or weakness* of the culture but rather the extent to which the culture *supports or inhibits* the open exchange of ideas and the ability to question taken-for-granted assumptions.

Barbara Levitt and James March (1988) suggest that organizational learning is shaped by the limits of human cognition, or the so-called "bounded rationality" of human actors.

To capture learning, organizations use routines or established patterns of behavior that are interpreted to have worked in the past. Organizational behavior is oriented toward using those routines to close the gap between actual and desired outcomes. The ability to automate routines enables greater standardization, reducing conflicting interpretations of what has worked in the past, as well as reducing the need to "reinvent the wheel." But automation and standardization can also reduce mindfulness, thus keeping an organization and its members trapped in single-loop learning, unable to break through to more fundamental change. Culture is the accumulation of routines that have been successful in the past, and it also tends to promote single-loop learning. Although organizations can in principle develop routines that are conducive to double-loop learning, this tends not to happen. They conclude rather pessimistically,

> Problems in learning from experience stem partly from inadequacies of human cognitive habits, partly from features of organizations, partly from characteristics of the structure of experience. They are strategies for ameliorating some of these problems, but ordinary organizational practices do not always generate behavior that conforms to such strategies. (Levitt and March 1988:335)

While Levitt and March (1988) suggest the potential for organizational structures to facilitate double-loop learning, they provide little or no insight into what these organizational structures might look like.

More recent theorists have moved beyond this pessimism to identify ways that organizations and actors within them can promote organizational learning and change. Amy Edmondson (2002) presents learning as an interpersonal, relational process and argues that psychological safety—the perception that it is safe to express disagreement—is a necessary condition for radical learning, as opposed to incremental learning, to occur. Psychological safety varies widely even within organizations, depending upon group and leader behaviors at a local level. Her argument is reminiscent of Argyris's (1976) view of the impediments to double-loop learning and his claim that leaders must be skilled in order to overcome those impediments and elicit double-loop learning. Edmondson's theory of learning, like Argyris's, draws upon both rationalist and relational paradigms of sociological theory: Their theories are rationalist in the sense that good decisions can be made through the process of open inquiry, and relational in the sense that relational dynamics determine whether or not open inquiry can be achieved.

Poststructuralist approaches to organizational change have gained prominence in recent years, building on the idea that change occurs when opportunities are created to have conversations that identify and question organizational assumptions. These theorists argue that organizational change does not occur simply by changing formal organizational structures—those structures will not be embraced or sustained unless the assumptions that underlie them are openly identified and questioned. In effect these theorists are saying that learning needs to occur in order for real change to occur. They challenge the rationalist view of change that is implicit in organization design theories, in which organizations develop structures that conform to the needs of their environments, and that participant behaviors somehow change in response to the new structures. Poststructuralist theorists argue that, to achieve real change, one must create the "discursive space" in which organizational participants can identify and question current organizational assumptions and, from there, advocate for the adoption of new ways of working. These new ways of working can include new structures, but structures that are informed and supported by new assumptions and that therefore do not function merely as "window dressing." Joyce Fletcher, Stacy Beard, and Lotte Bailyn (2009) describe this approach to change:

> The goal . . . is to create "discursive space" where new ways of thinking can surface and dominant meanings can be resisted. Creating discursive space means offering an alternative interpretation of reality that relaxes taken-for-granted assumptions, thereby creating a place where new things can be said and new social structures envisioned.

Katherine Kellogg (2009) adopts a similar lens for understanding organizational change, demonstrating the importance of relational space for challenging taken-for-granted assumptions about how work is done, and the role that power plays in either enabling these assumptions to be challenged or preventing them from being challenged. For example, given the macho pride associated with long working hours despite their documented impact on patient errors, the "iron man" culture found in surgical departments does not readily give way to new regulatory restrictions on resident work hours. Kellogg finds that cross-level coalitions enable organizational assumptions to be openly identified and challenged, thus leading to changes in how work gets done. In the absence of these coalitions, organizational actors merely present the appearance or "window dressing" of change while continuing to adhere to the old assumptions. Kellogg's finding that coalitions create relational efficacy to challenge the dominant culture, and to create the discursive space for new assumptions to be formed and new organizational structures to be adopted, leaves the field of organizational learning and change in a more optimistic place than where we started.

We conclude by asking whether the relational or the bureaucratic organizational form is more conducive to learning and change. The bureaucratic organizational form is more notable for its stability than for its ability to change (Weber 1920). In Part II, "The Bureaucratic Organizational Form," we argued that the absence of horizontal ties at multiple levels of the organization not only slows the speed of response, but also hampers the cognitive process through which workers understand the whole process and how their work relates to the whole. This lack of holistic vision not only impedes the day-to-day coordination of work, but very likely hampers the ability to innovate. Comparing the organic and mechanistic organizational forms, Burns and Stalker ([1961] 1995) argue that these "two management systems represent for us the two polar extremities of the forms which such systems can take when they are *adapted to a specific rate of technical and commercial change*" (p. 119, emphasis added), where the organic form is well adapted to conditions of rapid change and the mechanistic form is well adapted to conditions of high stability. In the organic form, ideas can readily be combined and shared across areas of specialization via dense relational networks, and initiative can more easily be taken at multiple levels of the organization. As noted in Part I, "The Relational Organizational Form," Burns and Stalker's conception of organic and mechanistic organizational forms is reminiscent of the Durkheimian distinction between organic and mechanistic solidarity, where organic solidarity is made possible by the extensive differentiation of functions found in more modern societies.

Mary Parker Follett's relational conception of the organization emphasizes this latter point. Just as she envisions workers as sharing in the control of their work (see Part IV, "Autonomy and Control"), she also envisions workers throughout the organization taking initiative for organizational learning and change. "Some people want to give the workmen a share in carrying out the purpose of the plant and do not see that this involves a share in creating the purpose of the plant" (Follett [1924] 1995:56). So the relational organizational form would appear to be conducive to change due to its widespread distribution of leadership throughout the organization, enabled by a widespread understanding of organizational purpose, which evolves through the cognitive process of interrelating across functional boundaries. As Follett emphasizes, purpose does not just drive activity; it emerges from activity. In this sense, "activity always does more than embody purpose, it evolves purpose" (Follett [1924] 1995:57). Purpose itself emerges from the activity of interrelating. This broader and more dynamic understanding of organizational purpose may also reduce attachment to one's own parochial goals, thereby reducing the barriers to challenging assumptions that Argyris (1976), Edmondson (2002), Fletcher et al. (2009), and Kellogg (2009) argue is essential for real change to occur.

The advantage of bureaucracy, on the other hand, is the ability to codify and sustain new routines once they have been learned. As noted by Levitt and March (1988), routines can lock an organization into a pattern of single-loop learning by fostering mindlessness. But Adler and Borys (1996) argue that routines are one of several bureaucratic attributes that can be transformed to play an enabling rather than a coercive role. As we did in our introduction to the bureaucratic organizational form, we once again encourage creative theorizing about hybrid organizational forms that embody the best attributes of the relational and bureaucratic organizational forms. For the purpose of organizational learning and change, this would include the development of routines that capture past learning while at the same time institutionalizing the ability of all participants to continually rethink "how we do things here."

QUESTIONS FOR DISCUSSION

1. How are organizational learning and change different? How are they related?
2. Describe a situation where organizational change occurred, but not organizational learning. Describe another situation where organizational learning occurred, but not organizational change. How would you explain these phenomena theoretically?
3. For organizational change to be successful, is it more important to change formal structures, or patterns of belief and behaviors? If you were to engage in a change effort, which would you focus on? Why? If both, how would you sequence your efforts? Why?
4. What are the advantages of the relational organizational form for learning and change? Advantages of the bureaucratic organizational form?

RECOMMENDATIONS FOR FURTHER READING

Briscoe, Forrest and Sean Safford. 2008. "The Nixon-in-China Effect: Activism, Imitation and the Institutionalism of Contentious Practices." *Administrative Science Quarterly,* 53(3):460–91.

Durant, Robert. 2007. "Toxic Politics, Organizational Change and the 'Greening' of the U.S. Military: Toward a Polity-Centered Perspective." *Administration & Society,* 39:409–46.

Fiol, C. Marlene and Marjorie Lyles. 1985. "Organizational Learning." *Academy of Management Review,* 10(4):803–13.

Holmes, Janet, Stephanie Schnurr, and Meredith Marra. 2007. "Leadership and Communication: Discursive Evidence of a Workplace Culture Change." *Discourse & Communication,* 1(4):433–51.

Huber, George P. 1991. "Organizational Learning: The Contributing Processes and the Literatures." *Organization Science,* 2(1):88–115.

REFERENCES

Adler, Paul and Brian Borys. 1996. "Two Types of Bureaucracy: Enabling and Coercive." *Administrative Science Quarterly,* 41:61–89.

Argyris, Chris. 1976. "Single-Loop and Double-Loop Models in Research on Organizational Decision-Making." *Administrative Science Quarterly,* 21:363–75.

Burns, Tom and G. M. Stalker. [1961] 1995. "Mechanistic and Organic Systems of Management." Pp. 96–125 in *The Management of Innovation.* Oxford: Oxford University Press.

DiMaggio, Paul and Walter Powell. 1983. "The Iron Cage Revisited: Institutional Isomorphism and Collective Rationality in Organization Fields." *American Journal of Sociology,* 48:147–60.

Edmondson, Amy. 2002. "The Local and Variegated Nature of Learning in Organizations: A Group-Level Perspective." *Organization Science,* 13:128–46.

Fletcher, Joyce K., Lotte Bailyn, and Stacy Blake Beard. 2009. "Practical Pushing: Creating Discursive Space in Organizational Narratives." Pp. 82–93 in *Critical Management Studies at Work: Negotiating Tensions between Theory and Practice*, edited by Julie Wolfram Cox, Tony G. LeTrent-Jones, Maxim Voronov, and David Weir. Northampton, MA: Edward Elgar.

Follett, Mary Parker. [1924] 1995. "Relating: The Circular Response." Pp. 25–65 in *Mary Parker Follett—Prophet of Management: A Celebration of Writings from the 1920s*, edited by Pauline Graham. Boston: Harvard Business School Press.

Hannan, Michael T. and John H. Freeman. 1977. "The Population Ecology of Organizations." *American Journal of Sociology,* 82:929–64.

Kellogg, Katherine. 2009. "Operating Room: Relational Spaces and Micro-institutional Changes in Surgery." *American Journal of Sociology,* 115(3):657–711.

Lawrence, Paul and Jay Lorsch. 1967. *Organization and Environment: Managing Differentiation and Integration.* Boston: Graduate School of Business Administration, Harvard University.

Levitt, Barbara and James March. 1988. "Organizational Learning." *Annual Review of Sociology,* 14:319–38.

Parsons, Talcott, Edward Shils, Kasper D. Neagele, and Jesse R. Pitts, eds. 1961. *Theories of Society.* New York: Free Press.

Pfeffer, Jeffrey and Gerald Salancik. 1978. *The External Control of Organizations: A Resource Dependence Perspective.* New York: Harper and Row.

Schein, Edgar H. 1991. "What Is Culture?" Pp. 243–53 in *Reframing Organizational Culture,* edited by P. Frost, L. Moore, M. Louis, C. Lundberg, and J. Martin. Newbury Park, CA: Sage.

Sørensen, Jesper B. 2002. "The Strength of Corporate Culture and the Reliability of Firm Performance." *Administrative Science Quarterly,* 47(1):70–91.

Weber, Max. 1920. "Bureaucracy." Pp. 956–1005 in *Economy and Society: An Outline of Interpretive Sociology.* Volume 2. Berkeley: University of California Press.

49

SINGLE-LOOP AND DOUBLE-LOOP MODELS IN RESEARCH ON DECISION MAKING

CHRIS ARGYRIS

RESEARCH AND THE STATUS QUO

Cohen and March (1974: 205) state explicitly: "First, we do not believe that any major new cleverness that would conspicuously alter the prevailing limits in our ability to change the course of history (in organizational theory and practice) will be discovered." However, a few pages later (Cohen and March, 1974: 215), in the fascinating section on "Technology of Foolishness," they raise questions about certain "robust faiths" that have become segments of contemporary Western civilization, such as the concept of choice, which assumes pre-existence of purpose, the necessity of consistency, and the primacy of rationality. Their questions seem to imply that the course of history may be alterable, and it is not surprising that this inconsistency appears in a section in which Cohen and March attempt to apply their framework to develop practical advice to administration.

The problem has two aspects. The first is that Cohen and March recommend a leadership strategy that has been called (by March) mini-Machiavellian and derivable from the major properties of decision making in organized anarchies that Cohen and March found as a result of their research. They recommended that the leader should (1) be involved in the organization in order to provide the energy needed to influence major decisions, (2) become informed so that in an information poor system (characteristic of organized anarchies) he will then become valued, (3) persist in promoting his views, since a decision defeated today may be accepted tomorrow, (4) exchange status for substance, (5) facilitate opposing factors to participate, and (6) overload the system thereby making themselves more necessary.

This advice appears to be a framework for maintaining organizations as Cohen and March found them: mini-Machiavellian and organized anarchies. The advice could also perpetuate the expectations of subordinates, especially the ineffective and/or less involved ones, that organizations and their leadership will never change, and can lead to physical and psychological exhaustion in leaders. Imagine being advised to work hard, to be present at most meetings, to provide energy in a system whose participants refuse to energize (and through their bickering are capable of using up any energy input), and to facilitate opposition because it is the best way to correct excesses or polarizations of positions.

Finally, the advice appears to sanction deceit. The effectiveness of a mini-Machiavellian leadership is based on the assumption that the reasons for behavior or strategy are kept secret. For example, Cohen and March (1974: 211) recommend that if the president of a university wants to untangle a curriculum reform from an issue of social justice, he should create a garbage can attractive enough to seduce the social justice proponents away from the immediate action.

To those familiar with organizational activity, Cohen and March have elevated leadership strategy to what some would consider dysfunctions in organizations.

Cohen and March might object to calling the strategy dysfunctional, since they described organizations as they were and since they provided a section on the technology of foolishness which raised some basic questions about orthodoxy in decision making. The term, foolishness, indicates that Cohen and March were aware how radical their questions would appear to many theorists on decision making. What Cohen and March reported was a rational theory of leadership, consistent with their model, which, in turn, was consistent with the organizations they studied.

In examining other literature, to learn what can be done about this problem, one finds mostly conjectures and almost no empirical research. The primary objective stated in almost all of the studies is to attempt a rigorous description of the problem. This position is predictable because the underlying assumption of much research in social science is to conduct rigorous research about conditions, systems, relationships, and so forth as they are (Argyris, 1968, 1971, 1973, 1974, 1975; Hackman and Morris, 1975). Such an assumption is considered in that useful insights for correcting problems can be derived from the accurate description of a problem.

A paradoxical assumption is that change is possible even though the factors causing the problems are taken as given. For example, Cohen and March (1974) view intergroup coalition rivalries, avoidance of uncertainty, interpersonal threat, and mistrust as factors inhibiting decision-making effectiveness; but they were viewed as factors to be understood, not altered. This does not mean that suggestions are not made in the literature to increase decision-making effectiveness. For example, a collegial style of decision making might be recommended, but no insight provided on this could be attained without first reducing conflict, mistrust, and so on.

ALTERNATIVE VIEWS

An earlier model called "synoptic" described a decision maker going through a set of processes where he or she (1) identified and systematically ordered objectives and values, (2) comprehensively surveyed all possible means of achieving those values, (3) exhaustively examined the sequences, and (4) made a choice that maximized or reached some acceptable level of achievement. Lindblom (1959, 1965: 137–138, 1968) described this model, but with other researchers argued that this view was not adapted to man's limited intellectual capacities, to the inadequacy of information, to the high cost of analysis, to learning from failures, or to the close relationship between fact and value in policy making. Consequently they proposed a third model described as an incremental approach to decision making (Pressman and Wildavsky, 1973; Moynihan, 1972). Researchers proposing this model consider analysis to be drastically limited and the definition of a good policy arbitrary, and it is probably not possible to select rigorous criteria for effectiveness. The closest one could come to understanding effectiveness would be to define key questions, which, if answered, would make it possible to evaluate effectiveness. Effective action is more a succession of comparisons between actions and feedback from the environment, which provide information for the next action or decision. Since decisions are made on necessarily incomplete information, once executed, feedback is required to evaluate their effectiveness.

It is not the purpose here to argue for any of these approaches, but rather to explore the importance that learning processes play in problem solving and decision making. The effectiveness of this approach depends upon being able to subdivide problems and upon the actions being repeatable enough so that decision makers can learn from their actions and adapt their decision making and behavior accordingly; also upon the availability of valid information from the environment within realistic time constraints to make corrections possible.

Underlying Role of Learning in Decision Making

Learning is here defined as the detection and correction of errors, and error as any feature of knowledge or of knowing that makes action ineffective. Error is a mismatch: a condition of learning, and matching a second condition of learning. The detection and correction of error produces learning and the lack of either or both inhibits learning.

It is difficult to conceive of how decision-making processes that include such activities as search, design, and choice could operate effectively without valid information. It is here assumed that the more complex and ill-structured a problem, the higher the probability of ambiguity and so the higher the probability of errors; that is, the lower the probability that actions will match plans effectively. Furthermore, problems become increasingly complex and ill-structured, the need for learning increases, but so does the difficulty in carrying out effective learning.

An assumption in the three models of decision-making processes just described is that complex decisions can be subdivided and the subordinate problems solved in some sort of functional sequence. Such an approach would be especially appropriate for decisions that once made are not intended to be altered. This makes crucial the learning processes before the decision. For example, Allison (1971), George (1972), and Neustadt (1970) provide illustrations of decisions where the learning could have occurred before the decisions were made, though in many cases, it did not.

Factors That Inhibit Learning

At least two important sets of variables can be altered to increase the effectiveness of learning, no matter at what point the learning is to occur. One is the degree to which interpersonal, group, intergroup, and bureaucratic factors produce valid information for the decision makers to use to monitor the effectiveness of their decisions. The other is the receptivity to corrective feedback of the decision-making unit—that is, individual, group, or organization.

Allison (1971) presented evidence that organizational and bureaucratic political factors significantly influenced the amount and quality of the learning during decision making. Examples of organizational factors are partial resolutions of interdepartmental and interpersonal conflicts, ineffective and incomplete search, avoidance of uncertainty, political exchanges, and annexation of other units. Examples of bureaucratic and political factors among individuals are competitive games; bargaining, parochial priorities, personal goals, interests, stakes, and stands; use of power; misperception; and miscommunication.

Halperin (1974: 235–279) suggested that there were "maneuvers" to affect the information given and received; for example, (1) reporting only those factors that support one's view, (2) biasing reports to senior participants to promote one's own view, (3) not reporting facts that indicate danger, and (4) avoiding senior officers who might report facts that one wished to suppress.

Hoopes (1969) described the distortion and manipulation of information by subordinates and the lack of open debate. Wildavsky (1964) and Pressman and Wildavsky (1973) focused especially on the competitiveness and bureaucratic win-lose politics among bureaus and departments. Thomson (1968) and Halberstam (1972) provided vivid examples of how personal ideologies, cognitive rigidities, and concepts of loyalty inhibited the generation and communication of valid information to upper levels. Geyelin (1966) and Halberstam (1972) provided evidence that key officials repeatedly and privately attributed motives to others, which then influenced the information that the officials gave or expected to receive. Schlesinger (1973) and Sorensen (1963) stated that secrecy had been a governing principle of presidential decision making nationally, and that conflict was the "one quality which characterizes most issues likely to be brought to the President." Moynihan (1972) suggested that bureaucratic political strife and competitiveness led to "competitive depreciation." Wildavsky (1964) provided informative descriptions of the political warfare, one-upmanship, and power maneuverings that occurred during budgetary processes. Donovan (1970: 32, 33) described how the decision related to the Bay of Pigs moved to execution without President Kennedy being able either to control or to reverse it, and how President Johnson was misled into signing community-action legislation that provided for citizen participation, a concept which he did not like. Gawthrop (1971) described administrative politics as games in which the basic rules were to maximize winning and self-interest. Schlesinger (1973) described the compelling need, especially of the President, for "passports to reality" since the world that immediately surrounds superiors is so often unreal. Neustadt's (1960, 1970) work presaged many of the observations above and suggested that key top figures seem to forget the constraints others have placed upon them by their national governance processes as well as by deeply held norms developed over years of national political activity.

Moreover, the literature suggests that the factors that inhibit valid feedback tend to become increasingly more operative as the decisions become more important and as they become more threatening to participants in the decision-making processes; that is, valid information appears to be more easily generated for less important and less threatening decisions. This is a basic organizational problem for it is found not only in governmental organizations, but also in business organizations, schools, religious groups, trade unions, hospitals, and so on (Argyris, 1970, 1972).

One might say that participants in organizations are encouraged to learn to perform as long as the learning does not question the fundamental design, goals, and activities of their organizations. This learning may be called single-loop learning. In double-loop learning, a participant would be able to ask questions about changing fundamental aspects of the organization (Allison, Neustadt, Halperin, and others).

Furthermore, most groups and organizations studied in their usual settings permit only single-loop learning. Recent research on individual adult learning suggests that human beings are also acculturated to be primarily single-loop learners in dealing with other human beings and with substantive,

controversial issues (Argyris and Schon, 1974). This high degree of consonance between learning acculturation and the kind of limitations placed on learning within groups and organizations results in processes that limit exploration and information and so help provide stability but also inhibit learning in fundamental organizational issues.

To intervene in these circular processes, one needs a model that helps to explain what aspects of current behavior of decision makers and policy makers inhibit double-loop learning, a model that would increase the effectiveness of decision making and policy making, and finally one that would make it possible to use the explanatory model to achieve effectiveness.

THEORIES OF ACTION

Argyris and Schon (1974) stated that all human action was based on theories of action. One can differentiate between espoused theories of action and theories-in-use. Espoused theories of action are those that people report as a basis for actions. Theories-in-use are the theories of action inferred from how people actually behave (taken from video or audio tapes, or other instruments that focus on collecting relatively directly observable behavior). Most individuals studied seem to be able to detect the discrepancies between their espoused theories and theories-in-use of others, but were not able to detect similar discrepancies in themselves. People observe the discrepancies manifested by others but they are programmed with theories-in-use that say, "If you observe others behaving incongruently with what they espouse, in the name of effectiveness, concern, diplomacy, do not tell them."

Single-Loop Model

A model of the theory-in-use was found to account for much of the behavior relevant to this study (Argyris and Schon, 1974). It was hypothesized that human behavior, in any situation, represents the most satisfactory solution people can find consistent with their governing values or variables, such as achieving a purpose as others define it, winning, suppressing negative feelings, and emphasizing rationality.

It was also hypothesized that human beings learned to associate behavioral strategies with their governing values or variables. The primary strategies are to control the relevant environment and tasks unilaterally and to protect themselves and their group unilaterally. The underlying behavioral strategy is control over others, although people vary widely in how they control others. Giving the meaning of a concept to others and defining its validity for them is one of the most powerful ways to control others.

Control as a behavioral strategy influences the leader, others, and the environment in that it tends to produce defensiveness and closedness, because unilateral control does not tend to produce valid feedback. Moreover, controlling behavior unilaterally may be seen by others as defensiveness. Groups composed of individuals using such strategies will tend to create defensive group dynamics, reduce the production of valid information, and reduce free choice. Consequently it was hypothesized that a particular kind and quality of learning would take place. There would be relatively little public testing of ideas, especially important or threatening ones. As a result, leaders would tend to receive little genuine feedback and others would tend not to violate their governing values and so disturb the accepted fundamental framework. Many of the hypotheses or hunches that the leaders generate would then tend to become limited and accepted with little opposition. Moreover, whatever a leader learned would tend to be within the confines of what was acceptable.

Under these conditions, problem solving about technical or interpersonal issues would be rather ineffective. Effective problem solving occurs to the extent individuals are aware of the major variables relevant to their problem and solve the problem in such a way that it remains solved (at least until the external variables change); and, moreover, that they accomplish these without reducing the current level of problem-solving effectiveness (Argyris, 1970). Under these conditions, top administrators tend to become frustrated with the ineffectiveness of the decision-making process and react by striving to increase control, by increasing secrecy about their own strategies, and by demanding loyalty of subordinates that borders on complete agreement with their views.

Besides the acculturation of individuals to these interpersonal group and intergroup dynamics, the consequences just described would be compounded by pyramidal structures, management information systems, including budgets (Argyris, 1965). In other words, the activities documented in the literature cited above exist at the individual, interpersonal, group, intergroup, organizational, and intraorganizational level in such a way that they mutually reinforce each other to create a stable, indeed, an ultra stable slate (Schon, 1971).

Double-Loop Model

A model incorporating double-loop learning can avoid the consequences of a model based on single-loop learning (Argyris and Schon, 1974). The governing variables or values of Model II are not the opposite of Model I. The governing variables are valid information, free and informed choice, and internal commitment. The behavior required to satisfice these values also is not the opposite of Model I. For example, Model I emphasizes that the individuals are expected to be articulate about their purposes, goals, and so forth, and simultaneously control the others and the environment in order to ensure achievement of their goals. However, in the double-loop model, the unilateral control that usually accompanies advocacy is rejected because the typical purpose of advocacy is to win; and so, articulateness and advocacy are coupled with an invitation to confront one another's views and to alter them, in order to produce the position that is based on the most complete valid information possible and to which participants can become internally committed. This means that the leader must be skilled in eliciting double-loop learning. Every significant action in the double-loop model is evaluated in terms of the degree it helps the participants generate valid and useful information, including relevant feelings, and solve the problem so that it remains solved without reducing the level of problem-solving effectiveness.

The behavioral strategies of this model involve sharing power with anyone who has competence, and with anyone who is relevant in deciding or implementing the action, in the definition of the task, or the control over the environment, Face saving is resisted because it is seen as a defensive nonlearning activity, and any face-saving action that must be taken is planned jointly with the people involved, with the exception of individuals vulnerable to such candid and joint solutions.

Under these conditions individuals would not tend to compete to make decisions for others or to outdo others for self-gratification. They would try to find the most competent people for the decision to be made, and would try to build viable decision-making networks in which the major function of the group would be to maximize the contributions of each member so that when a synthesis was developed, the widest possible exploration of views would have taken place.

Finally, if new concepts were formulated, the meaning given to them by the formulator and the inference processes used to develop them would be open to scrutiny by those who were expected to use them. Evaluations and attributions would be the result of directly observable data after the concepts were used. Also, the formulator would feel responsible to present the evaluations and attributions so as to encourage open and constructive confrontations.

If the governing values and behavioral strategies just outlined are used, then the degree of defensiveness in individuals, within, between, and among groups, would tend to decrease and free choice would tend to increase, as would feelings of commitment. The end result should be increased effectiveness in decision making or policy making in the monitoring of the decisions and policies and in the probabilities that errors and failures would be communicated openly and that actors would learn from the feedback.

Transitional Model

It is not easy to conceptualize models of transition from a single-loop to a double-loop model that do not violate the requirements of the latter. Moreover, if one is able to design such processes, the probability of being able to test them empirically is low. Few subjects are interested in genuinely new options, especially if learning them may be difficult and if having learned them there is little support from subordinates' peers, and superiors, as well as from organizational policies and practices to use the new skills.

Learning to become aware of one's present theory-in-use and then altering it is a very difficult process, because it requires that individuals question the theories of action that have formed the framework for their actions. Learning about double-loop learning through lectures, reading, and case discussions will lead to learning at the espoused level rather than at the level of theory-in-use.

For example, the single-loop model teaches individuals to be high on articulate advocacy and simultaneously high on unilateral control over others in order to win. Governmental and private executives can be taught to be articulate advocates in such a way that control is shared in order to increase time for study, and the executives might even come to value the new behavior highly, yet they are unable to behave according to the new requirements, or to experience the appropriate feelings. In the single-loop model inquiry may be seen as weakness; in the double-loop model, it is seen as strength.

Another difficulty is that in organizations, human beings are acculturated to accept a role in a pervasive atmosphere of deception. For example, A would not tell B that he or she was about to act destructively toward B; C would not tell D that he or she was distorting information to D; and E would not tell F that he or she was flattering F. Yet all six know that they and others act in such ways, and that the accepted behavior is to act as if no one knows that such activities go on.

Second, if theories-in-use are the basis of behavior, then they represent a source of confidence that one has in functioning effectively in one's world. To change one's theory-in-use would be risky. There are few group, organizational, or societal supports for significantly different behaviors. New behavior, for example, a focus on real-time inquiry and shared power and trust, could actually cause difficulties for a person because it would be considered deviant behavior. New behavior could also harm the individual because others might use the new power and the trust against him or her.

Third, changing to a double-loop model involves exploration of certain basic values and feelings. For example, if an individual decides to explore reducing his unilateral control over others, he will soon confront himself with the question, why does he control others? Typically, he may respond by saying that if he did not control others, he could not get things done. "People respect what I inspect." All this is confirmable in a Model I world.

In exploring new behaviors some top officials have checked their hypotheses about their lack of confidence with their subordinates. To their dismay they have learned that their subordinates felt the officials' mistrust, and that they kept this knowledge hidden just as the officials were keeping their attributions of mistrust of the subordinates hidden. Also the subordinates could give officials valid reasons for behaving in ways that required the officials' control. In short, the officials learned that much of their sense of a need for unilateral control was a self-fulfilling prophecy (Argyris, 1976a).

Such experiences help one to understand why people accustomed to single-loop learning find it difficult to change. For example, many "alternative schools" were started because certain teachers and students were against the Model I schools. A major strategy of alternative schools included going from a highly structured to a very loose school; from unilateral control by teachers to complete equality with students; from teachers evaluating students to students evaluating teachers. These strategies did not work for two reasons. One cannot have effective school organizations without structure with complete equality, and without evaluations of performance of students. Moreover, when one examines carefully the actual behavior of the teachers and the students, it went from the opposite of Model I to an oscillating Model I (Argyris, 1974). The same analysis appears to be relevant to the experiments for community participation projects. Many floundered between the competitive win-lose tactics of militant minorities to the opposite role of withdrawal of power and structure related to such learning experiences as T-groups or sensitivity training. A large portion of T-group practice (not theory) is based on a model that is the opposite to the single-loop model; that is, one characterized by withdrawal and passivity. Such a model is not apt to produce more effective decision making; it may actually produce an increase in participant narcissism and, therefore, increased problems when the participant strives to behave with others who have not been in his or her T-groups (Argyris, 1972).

Such data raise questions about two commonly held assumptions by researchers in this field. The first assumption is that changes can be produced directly from descriptive research. Bauer (1974), for example, suggested that there is a continuous relationship from understanding a given situation, to designing a new one and then realizing it. Research tends to suggest that change based on the double-loop model would require a shift in the behavior of individuals and in group, intergroup, and organizational processes.

The second assumption is that changes to make the environment approximate the requirements of the double-loop model would lead to behavior and values appropriate to the model. This assumption is not predicted by the theory, which states that no changes will occur toward a double-loop model unless the individuals change their current theories-in-use. This also means that changes in organizational structure, management information systems, and organizational norms will not lead directly to changes in behavior of the people within the new system.

MULTIPLE ADVOCACY MODEL

George (1972) showed that it is possible for researchers to develop normative prescriptive models that are systematic and empirically testable. He (1972: 758) hypothesized that a system of multiple advocacy worked best and was likely to produce better decisions when three conditions were satisfied:

(1) no major maldistribution of power, weight, influence, competence, information, or analytical resources; (2) bargaining and persuasive skills among members, participation of chief executives to monitor and regulate the workings of multiple advocacy; and (3) time for adequate debate and exchange of ideas.

On the basis of espoused theories and theories-in-use, however, if for example, power, weight, and influence are functions of a role, then maldistribution of such variables would be alterable by order of the chief executive. However, the theories-in-use of individual members also influence their power, weight, and influence in groups. In studies (Argyris, 1969) of nearly 300 policy-making and decision-making sessions in the government and private sectors, such theory-in-use variables made significant differences in the effectiveness of individual members and in the quality of the decisions. However, the variables were rarely, if ever, discussed openly because such discussions violated the governing values of suppressing threatening issues and the negative feelings against the norms against interpersonal risk taking. Questions can also be raised about bargaining and persuasive skills. In a single-loop model, such skills are closely correlated with unilateral control and manipulation of information, secrecy, and so on, which inhibit the kind of discussion required in multiple advocacy if it is to be effective.

Analysis of tapes (Argyris, 1969) of policy-making and decision-making meetings suggests that groups rarely have enough time for adequate debate partially because the win-lose dynamics coupled with single-loop learning and the emphasis on control of others make discussions competitive. Consequently, if the theories-in-use of groups inhibit effective discussion, how effective can the chief executive be in monitoring such factors? George (1972: 761) stated that the multiple advocacy required that the chief executive define his or her own role as that of a magistrate who evaluates, judges, and chooses among the various policies proposed by advocates. Some research (Argyris, 1956, 1968, 1974; Blake and Mouton, 1968) would indicate that this would tend to magnify the win-lose dynamics and/or create a greater sense of hidden conformity.

George suggested that with the introduction of the magistrate role, the advocates will no longer compete against each other but they will compete for the magistrate's attention. Our research would raise some doubts because some of the key variables that influence the magistrate's attention are related to the effectiveness with which the members compete with each other. George may wish that the individuals carrying out the custodian role focus on reducing the competitiveness that is destructive. But there is nothing in George's model to suggest that presently such behavior would be seen, by the participants, as deviant and odd. Also, if our research to date is valid, there are few top administrators who hold such skills.

George also suggests that collegial decision making coupled with the three conditions mentioned would increase the effectiveness of decision making. The path to increased effectiveness may be more difficult. Several decades ago executives in government and private industry associated with the production of complex electronic equipment developed what they called product planning groups, task forces, and matrix organizations. The idea was congruent with the one espoused by George. If one could bring together competent people, with adequate resources and time, and with relatively equal weight of power and influence, more effective decisions should be made. A study of nine such teams in matrix organizations showed that as time progressed the participants, through their behavior (theory-in-use), altered these groups to look more like little pyramidal organizations with little genuine collegial style (Argyris, 1967).

Finally, George identified nine possible malfunctions of policy making that could not be ignored, no matter what model of decision making was used. These included: (1) the chief executive and his other advisors agree too readily on the kind of problem and on a response to it; (2) disagreements do not cover the full range of relevant hypotheses and options; (3) there is no advocate for an unpopular policy action, and so on. These malfunctions were confirmed by other research (Janis, 1972).

George's case for multiple advocacy, with which this writer agrees, points up some important gaps that can begin to be reduced by examining literature and by pursuing further empirical research. The gaps become evident when the distinction is made between espoused theory and theory-in-use. The latter type of data is necessary for the empirical test of any model as well as for knowledge that will be helpful in practice, but these data are still lacking.

DISCUSSION AND SUMMARY

It is acknowledged that the research on the two models is only beginning, although from the data available so far, one can conclude that many espouse the double-loop model or some combination of both models. The data on theory-in-use indicate that most behavior may be categorized as approximately the single-loop model.

One difficulty with these results is that they may be based on research in which the categories are poorly defined. A more differentiated conceptual scheme might produce different results. The results of studies so far range from high interobserver reliability to studies where the subjects scored their own behavior and judged it to approximate the single-loop model, even though they had originally claimed it to be double-looped (Argyris, 1976c). Finally, predictions on the basis of the present conceptual scheme were confirmed (Argyris and Schon, 1974).

Double-loop learning can occur under the conditions of the single-loop model under extreme crisis or revolution. Unfortunately, there are no directly observable data, such as tape recordings, that could lead to inferences if the changes in behavior were those of the double-loop model. Under such extreme conditions, members can be brutally candid, discount the negative impact upon them from such behavior on the grounds that the stakes are very high and the members' motives are sincere; that is, they are not capable of more effective behavior, yet the need for honesty is greater than the need to avoid hurt feelings (Janis). An excellent example of this state in the deliberations of the Marshall Plan is where Kennan felt so punished that he left the meeting to cry and regain his composure (Janis, 1972).

This mode of behavior depends upon having members who can tolerate competitiveness in the group, but this may exclude individuals who may have substantive contributions to make, but cannot tolerate severe competition. Groups composed of highly competitive people also tend to create norms that make other groups "outsiders" and "competitors" if not enemies (Janis, 1972). Moreover, participants from other groups coming into these groups, in order to give reports, tend to feel intimidated and then presentations tend to be less effective, which may be viewed by the competitive group as evidence of their superiority. In short, the presentation may be pessimistic and there may be more individuals, groups, and organizations falling into the double-loop model, implied by our admittedly incomplete research; but further empirical research is needed to make the case convincing. Such research would have to obtain directly observable data (for instance, transcripts) and not remain at the espoused level (questionnaires and reports). Another way of interpreting the findings is that they illustrate the scope and depth of the problem and help to explain why much research in social science tends to support the status quo.

REFERENCES

Alderfer, Clayton P., and L. Dave Brown Learning from Changing. Beverly Hills, Calif.: Sage, in press.

Allison, Graham T. 1971 Essence of Decision: Explaining the Cuban Missile Crisis. Boston, Mass.: Little Brown.

Argyris, Chris 1956 Diagnosing Human Relations in Organizations: A Case Study of a Hospital. New Haven, Conn.: Labor and Management Center, Yale University.

———. 1965 Organization and Innovation. Homewood, Ill.: Irwin-Dorsey.

———. 1966 Some Causes of Organizational Ineffectiveness within the Dept. of State, Center for International Systems Research, Occasional Paper, No. 2.

———. 1967 "Today's problems with tomorrow's organizations." Journal of Management Studies, 4: 31–55.

———. 1968 "Some unintended consequences of rigorous research." Psychological Bulletin, 70(3): 185–197.

———. 1969 "The incompleteness of social psychology theory." American Psychologist, 24: 893–908.

———. 1970 Intervention Theory and Method. Reading, Mass.: Addison-Wesley.

———. 1971 Management and Organizational Development. New York: McGraw Hill.

———. 1972 "Do personal growth laboratories represent an alternative culture?" Journal of Applied Behavioral Science, 8: 7–28.

———. 1973 On Organizations of the Future. Albert Schweitzer Lecture given at Syracuse University on May 11, 1972. Published as Sage Professional Paper in Administration and Policy Studies #03–006.

———. 1973 The CEO's Behavior: Key to Organizational Development, Harvard Business Review, March-April, Vol. 51, No. 2: 55–64.

———. 1973 "Some limits of rational man organizational theory." Public Administration Review, 33: 253–267.

———. 1974 "Alternative schools: a behavioral analysis." Teachers College Record, 75: 429–452.

———. 1975 "Some dangers in applying results from experimental social psychology." American Psychologist, 30: 469–485.

———. 1976a Increasing Leadership Effectiveness. New York: Inter-Science, John Wiley.

———. 1976b "Problems and new directions for industrial psychology." In Marvin Dunnette, ed., Handbook of Industrial and Organizational Psychology. Chicago: Rand-McNally.

———. 1976c "Theories of action that inhibit individual learning." American Psychologist, in press.

Argyris, Chris and Donald Schon 1974 Theory in Practice: Increasing Professional Effectiveness. San Francisco: Jossey-Bass Publishers.

Bauer, Raymond A. 1974 The Convergence of What Is and What Should Be. Division of Research, Harvard Business School HBS-7.

Blake, Robert R., and Jane Mouton 1968 Corporate Excellence through Good Organizational Development. Houston, Texas: Gulf Publishing Co.

Cohen, Michael D., and James G. March 1974 Leadership and Ambiguity, The American College President. New York: McGraw Hill Book Co.

Cyert, Richard M., and James G. March 1963 A Behavioral Theory of the Firm. Englewood Cliffs, N.J.: Prentice-Hall.

Donovan, John C. 1970 The Policy Makers. Indianapolis, In.: Pegasus-Western Publishers.

Gawthrop, Louis 1971 Administrative Politics and Social Change. New York: St. Martin's Press.

George, Alexander 1972 "The case for multiple advocacy in making foreign policy." American Political Science Review, LXVI: 751–785.

Geyelin, Philip 1966 Lyndon B. Johnson and the World. New York: Frederick A. Praeger.

Golembiewski, R. T. 1972 Renewing Organizations. Itasca, Ill.: F. E. Peacock.

Hackman, J. Richard, and C. G. Morris 1975 "Group tasks, group interaction process, and group performance effectiveness—a review and proposed integration." In L. Berkowitz (ed.), Advances in Experimental Social Psychology, Vol. 8. New York: Academic Press.

Halberstam, David 1972 The Best and the Brightest. New York: Random House.

Halperin, Morton H. 1974 Bureaucratic Politics and Foreign Policy. Washington, D.C.: The Brookings Institution.

Hoopes, Clement R. 1969 A Frolic of His Own. New York: The Devin-Adair Company.

Janis, Irving L. 1972 Victims of Groupthink. Boston: Houghton Mifflin.

Katz, Daniel, and Robert L. Kahn 1966 The Social Psychology of Organizations. New York: John Wiley.

Lawrence, Paul R., and Jay W. Lorsch 1967 Organization and Environment Managing Differentiation and Integration. Boston: Division of Research, Harvard University, Graduate School of Business Administration.

Likert, Rensis 1961 The Human Organization. New York: McGraw Hill.

Lindblom, Charles E. 1959 "The science of 'muddling through.'" Public Administration Review, XIX: 79–88.

———. 1965 The Intelligence of Democracy: Decision Making through Mutual Adjustment. New York: The Free Press.

———. 1968 The Policy Making Process. Englewood Cliffs, N.J.: Prentice-Hall.

Marrow, A. J., D. G. Bowers, and S. E. Seashore 1967 Management by Participation. New York: Harper and Row.

Moynihan, Daniel P. 1972 Coping. New York: Random House.

Neustadt, Richard E. 1960 Presidential Power: The Politics of Leadership. New York: Wiley.

———. 1970 Alliance Politics. New York: Columbia University Press.

Porter, Lyman W., E. E. Lawter, and J. R. Hackman 1975 Behavior in Organizations. New York: McGraw Hill.

Pressman, Jeffrey L., and Aaron Wildavsky 1973 Implementation. Berkeley, Calif.: University of California Press.

Schein, Edgar 1965 Organizational Psychology. Englewood Cliffs, N.J.: Prentice-Hall.

Schlesinger, Arthur M. Jr. 1973 The Imperial Presidency. Boston: Houghton Mifflin.

Schon, Donald 1971 Beyond the Stable State. New York: Random House.

Simon, Herbert A. 1970 The Sciences of the Artificial. Cambridge, Mass.: M.I.T.

Sofer, Cyril 1961 The Organization from Within. London: Tavistock Publications.

Sorensen, Theodore 1963 Decision-making in the White House: The Olive Branch or the Arrows. New York: Columbia University Press.

Steinbruner, John D. 1974 The Cybernetic Theory of Decision. Princeton, N.J.: Princeton University Press.

Thomson, James C. Jr. 1968 "How could Vietnam happen?" The Atlantic, pp. 47–53.

Wildavsky, Aaron 1964 The Politics of the Budgetary Process. Boston: Little Brown.

SOURCE: Argyris, Chris. 1976. "Single-Loop and Double-Loop Models in Research on Organizational Decision-Making." Administrative Science Quarterly, 21:363–75.

50

THE IRON CAGE REVISITED

Institutional Isomorphism and Collective Rationality in Organizational Fields

PAUL J. DIMAGGIO AND WALTER W. POWELL

In *The Protestant Ethic and the Spirit of Capitalism,* Max Weber warned that the rationalist spirit ushered in by asceticism had achieved a momentum of its own and that, under capitalism, the rationalist order had become an iron cage in which humanity was, save for the possibility of prophetic revival, imprisoned "perhaps until the last ton of fossilized coal is burnt" (Weber, 1952:181–82). In his essay on bureaucracy, Weber returned to this theme, contending that bureaucracy, the rational spirit's organizational manifestation, was so efficient and powerful a means of controlling men and women that, once established, the momentum of bureaucratization was irreversible (Weber, 1968).

The imagery of the iron cage has haunted students of society as the tempo of bureaucratization has quickened. But while bureaucracy has spread continuously in the eighty years since Weber wrote, we suggest that the engine of organizational rationalization has shifted. For Weber, bureaucratization resulted from three related causes: competition among capitalist firms in the marketplace; competition among states, increasing rulers' need to control their staff and citizenry; and bourgeois demands for equal protection under the law. Of these three, the most important was the competitive marketplace. "Today," Weber (1968:974) wrote:

> it is primarily the capitalist market economy which demands that the official business of administration be discharged precisely, unambiguously, continuously, and with as much speed as possible. Normally, the very large, modern capitalist enterprises are themselves unequalled models of strict bureaucratic organization.

We argue that the causes of bureaucratization and rationalization have changed. The bureaucratization of the corporation and the state have been achieved. Organizations are still becoming more homogeneous, and bureaucracy remains the common organizational form. Today, however, structural change in organizations seems less and less driven by competition or by the need for efficiency. Instead, we will contend, bureaucratization and other forms of organizational change occur as the result of processes that make organizations more similar without necessarily making them more efficient. Bureaucratization and other forms of homogenization emerge, we argue, out of the structuration (Giddens, 1979) of organizational fields.

This process, in turn, is effected largely by the state and the professions, which have become the great rationalizers of the second half of the twentieth century. For reasons that we will explain, highly structured organizational fields provide a context in which individual efforts to deal rationally with uncertainty and constraint often lead, in the aggregate, to homogeneity in structure, culture, and output.

ORGANIZATIONAL THEORY AND ORGANIZATIONAL DIVERSITY

Much of modern organizational theory posits a diverse and differentiated world of organizations and seeks to explain variation among organizations in structure and behavior (e.g., Woodward, 1965; Child and Kieser, 1981). Hannan and Freeman begin a major theoretical paper (1977) with the question, "Why are there so many kinds of organizations?" Even our investigatory technologies (for example, those based on least-squares techniques) are geared towards explaining variation rather than its absence.

We ask, instead, why there is such startling homogeneity of organizational forms and practices; and we seek to explain homogeneity, not variation. In the initial stages of their life cycle, organizational fields display considerable diversity in approach and form. Once a field becomes well established, however, there is an inexorable push towards homogenization.

Coser, Kadushin, and Powell (1982) describe the evolution of American college textbook publishing from a period of initial diversity to the current hegemony of only two models, the large bureaucratic generalist and the small specialist. Rothman (1980) describes the winnowing of several competing models of legal education into two dominant approaches. Starr (1980) provides evidence of mimicry in the development of the hospital field; Tyack (1974) and Katz (1975) show a similar process in public schools; Barnouw (1966–68) describes the development of dominant forms in the radio industry; and DiMaggio (1981) depicts the emergence of dominant organizational models for the provision of high culture in the late nineteenth century.

What we see in each of these cases is the emergence and structuration of an organizational field as a result of the activities of a diverse set of organizations; and, second, the homogenization of these organizations, and of new entrants as well, once the field is established.

By organizational field, we mean those organizations that, in the aggregate, constitute a recognized area of institutional life: key suppliers, resource and product consumers, regulatory agencies, and other organizations that produce similar services or products. The virtue of this unit of analysis is that it directs our attention not simply to competing firms, as does the population approach of Hannan and Freeman (1977), or to networks of organizations that actually interact, as does the inter-organizational network approach of Laumann et al. (1978), but to the totality of relevant actors. In doing this, the field idea comprehends the importance of both *connectedness* (see Laumann et al., 1978) and *structural equivalence* (White et al., 1976).[1]

The structure of an organizational field cannot be determined a priori but must be defined on the basis of empirical investigation. Fields only exist to the extent that they are institutionally defined. The process of institutional definition, or "structuration," consists of four parts: an increase in the extent of interaction among organizations in the field; the emergence of sharply defined interorganizational structures of domination and patterns of coalition; an increase in the information load with which organizations in a field must contend; and the development of a mutual awareness among participants in a set of organizations that they are involved in a common enterprise (DiMaggio, 1982).

Once disparate organizations in the same line of business are structured into an actual field (as we shall argue, by competition, the state, or the professions), powerful forces emerge that lead them to become more similar to one another. Organizations may change their goals or develop new practices, and new organizations enter the field. But, in the long run, organizational actors making rational decisions construct around themselves an environment that constrains their ability to change further in later years. Early adopters of organizational innovations are commonly driven by a desire to improve performance. But new practices can become, in Selznick's words (1957:17), "infused with value beyond the technical requirements of the task at hand." As an innovation spreads, a threshold is reached beyond which adoption provides legitimacy rather than improves performance (Meyer and Rowan, 1977). Strategies that are rational for individual organizations may not be rational if adopted by large numbers. Yet the very fact that they are normatively sanctioned increases the likelihood of their adoption. Thus organizations may try to change constantly; but, after a certain point in the structuration of an organizational field, the aggregate effect of individual change is to lessen the extent of diversity within the field.[2] Organizations in a structured field, to paraphrase Schelling (1978:14), respond to an environment that consists of other organizations responding to their environment, which consists of organizations responding to an environment of organizations' responses.

Zucker and Tolbert's (1981) work on the adoption of civil-service reform in the United States illustrates this process. Early adoption of civil-service reforms was related to internal governmental needs, and strongly predicted by such city characteristics as the size of immigrant population, political reform movements, socioeconomic composition, and city size. Later adoption, however, is not predicted by city characteristics, but is related to institutional definitions of the legitimate structural form for municipal administration.[3] Marshall Meyer's (1981) study of the bureaucratization of urban fiscal agencies has yielded similar findings: strong relationships between city characteristics and organizational attributes at the turn of the century, null relationships in recent years. Carroll and Delacroix's (1982) findings on the birth and death rates of newspapers support the view that selection acts with great force only in the early years of an industry's existence.[4] Freeman (1982:14) suggests that older, larger organizations reach a point where they can dominate their environments rather than adjust to them.

The concept that best captures the process of homogenization is *isomorphism*. In Hawley's (1968) description, isomorphism is a constraining process that forces one unit in a population to resemble other units that face the same set of environmental conditions. At the population level, such an approach suggests that organizational characteristics are modified in the direction of increasing compatibility with environmental characteristics; the number of organizations in a population is a function of environmental carrying capacity; and the diversity of organizational forms is isomorphic to environmental diversity. Hannan and Freeman (1977) have significantly extended Hawley's ideas. They argue that isomorphism can result because nonoptimal forms are selected out of a population of organizations *or* because organizational decision makers learn appropriate responses and adjust their behavior accordingly. Hannan and Freeman's focus is almost solely on the first process: selection.[5]

Following Meyer (1979) and Fennell (1980), we maintain that there are two types of isomorphism: competitive and institutional. Hannan and Freeman's classic paper (1977), and much of their recent work, deals with competitive isomorphism, assuming a system rationality that emphasizes market competition, niche change, and fitness measures. Such a view, we suggest, is most relevant for those fields in which free and open competition exists. It explains parts of the process of bureaucratization that Weber observed, and may apply to early adoption of innovation, but it does not present a fully adequate picture of the modern world of organizations. For this purpose it must be supplemented by an institutional view of isomorphism of the sort introduced by Kanter (1972:152–54) in her discussion of the forces pressing communes toward accommodation with the outside world. As Aldrich (1979:265) has argued, "the major factors that organizations must take into account are other organizations." Organizations compete not just for resources and customers, but for political power and institutional legitimacy, for social as well as economic fitness.[6] The concept of institutional isomorphism is a useful tool for understanding the politics and ceremony that pervade much modern organizational life.

Three Mechanisms of Institutional Isomorphic Change

We identify three mechanisms through which institutional isomorphic change occurs, each with its own antecedents: 1) *coercive* isomorphism that stems from political influence and the problem of legitimacy; 2) *mimetic* isomorphism resulting from standard responses to uncertainty; and 3) *normative* isomorphism, associated with professionalization. This typology is an analytic one: the types are not always empirically distinct. For example, external actors may induce an organization to conform to its peers by requiring it to perform a particular task and specifying the profession responsible for its performance. Or mimetic change may reflect environmentally constructed uncertainties.[7] Yet, while the three types intermingle in empirical setting, they tend to derive from different conditions and may lead to different outcomes.

Coercive isomorphism. Coercive isomorphism results from both formal and informal pressures exerted on organizations by other organizations upon which they are dependent and by cultural expectations in the society within which organizations function. Such pressures may be felt as force, as persuasion, or as invitations to join in collusion. In some circumstances, organizational change is a direct response to government mandate: manufacturers adopt new pollution control technologies to conform to environmental regulations; nonprofits maintain accounts, and hire accountants, in order to meet tax law requirements; and organizations employ affirmative-action officers to fend off allegations of discrimination. Schools mainstream special students and hire special education teachers, cultivate PTAs and administrators who get along with them, and promulgate curricula that conform with state standards (Meyer et al., 1981). The fact that these changes may be largely ceremonial does not mean that they are inconsequential. As Ritti and Goldner (1979) have argued, staff become involved in advocacy for their functions that can alter power relations within organizations over the long run.

The existence of a common legal environment affects many aspects of an organization's behavior and structure. Weber pointed out the profound impact of a complex, rationalized system of contract law that requires the necessary organizational controls to honor legal commitments. Other legal and technical requirements of the state—the vicissitudes of the budget cycle, the ubiquity of certain fiscal years, annual reports, and financial reporting requirements that ensure eligibility for the receipt of federal contracts or funds—also shape organizations in similar ways. Pfeffer and Salancik (1978:188–224) have discussed how organizations faced with unmanageable interdependence seek to use the greater power of the larger social system and its government to eliminate difficulties or provide for needs. They observe that politically constructed environments have two characteristic features: political decision makers often do not experience directly the consequences of their actions; and political decisions are applied across the board to entire classes of organizations, thus making such decisions less adaptive and less flexible.

Meyer and Rowan (1977) have argued persuasively that as rationalized states and other large rational organizations expand their dominance over more arenas of social life, organizational structures increasingly come to reflect rules institutionalized and legitimated by and within the state (also see Meyer and Hannan, 1979). As a result, organizations are increasingly homogeneous within given domains and increasingly organized around rituals of conformity to wider institutions. At the same time, organizations are decreasingly structurally determined by the constraints posed by technical activities, and decreasingly held together by output controls. Under such circumstances, organizations employ ritualized controls of credentials and group solidarity.

Direct imposition of standard operating procedures and legitimated rules and structures also occurs outside the governmental arena. Michael Sedlak (1981) has documented the ways that United Charities in the 1930s altered and homogenized the structures, methods, and philosophies of the social service agencies that depended upon them for support. As conglomerate corporations increase in size and scope, standard performance criteria are not necessarily imposed on subsidiaries, but it is common for subsidiaries to be subject to standardized reporting mechanisms (Coser et al., 1982). Subsidiaries must adopt accounting practices, performance evaluations, and budgetary plans that are compatible with the policies of the parent corporation. A variety of service infrastructures, often provided by monopolistic firms—for example, telecommunications and transportation—exert common pressures over the organizations that use them. Thus, the expansion of the central state, the centralization of capital, and the coordination of philanthropy all support the homogenization of organizational models through direct authority relationships.

We have so far referred only to the direct and explicit imposition of organizational models on dependent organizations. Coercive isomorphism, however, may be more subtle and less explicit than these examples suggest. Milofsky (1981) has described the ways in which neighborhood organizations in urban communities, many of which are committed to participatory democracy, are driven to developing organizational hierarchies in order to gain support from more hierarchically organized donor organizations. Similarly, Swidler (1979) describes the tensions created in the free schools she studied by the need to have a "principal" to negotiate with the district superintendent and to represent the school to outside agencies. In general, the need to lodge responsibility and managerial authority at least ceremonially in a formally defined role in order to interact with hierarchical organizations is a constant obstacle to the maintenance of egalitarian or collectivist organizational forms (Kanter, 1972; Rothschild-Whitt, 1979).

Mimetic processes. Not all institutional isomorphism, however, derives from coercive authority. Uncertainty is also a powerful force that encourages imitation. When organizational technologics are poorly understood (March and Olsen, 1976), when goals are ambiguous, or when the environment creates symbolic uncertainty, organizations may model themselves on other organizations. The advantages of mimetic behavior in the economy of human action are considerable; when an organization faces a problem with ambiguous causes or unclear solutions, problemistic search may yield a viable solution with little expense (Cyert and March, 1963).

Modeling, as we use the term, is a response to uncertainty. The modeled organization may be unaware of the modeling or may have no desire to be copied; it merely serves as a convenient source of practices that the borrowing organization may use. Models may be diffused unintentionally, indirectly through employee transfer or turnover, or explicitly by organizations such as consulting firms or industry trade associations. Even innovation can be accounted for by organizational modeling. As Alchian (1950) has observed:

> While there certainly are those who consciously innovate, there are those who, in their imperfect attempts to imitate others, unconsciously innovate by unwittingly acquiring some unexpected or unsought unique attributes which under the prevailing circumstances prove partly responsible for the success. Others, in turn, will attempt to copy the uniqueness, and the innovation-imitation process continues.

One of the most dramatic instances of modeling was the effort of Japan's modernizers in the late nineteenth century to model new governmental initiatives on apparently successful western prototypes. Thus, the imperial government sent its officers to study the courts, Army, and police in France, the Navy and postal system in Great Britain, and banking and art education in the United States (see Westney, forthcoming). American corporations are now returning the compliment by implementing (their perceptions of) Japanese models to cope with thorny productivity and personnel problems in their own firms. The rapid proliferation of quality circles and quality-of-work-life issues in American firms is, at least in part, an attempt to model Japanese and European successes. These developments also have a ritual aspect; companies adopt these "innovations" to enhance their legitimacy, to demonstrate they are at least trying to improve working conditions. More generally, the wider the population of personnel employed by, or customers served by, an organization, the stronger the pressure felt by the organization to provide the programs and services offered by other organizations. Thus, either a skilled labor force or a broad customer base may encourage mimetic isomorphism.

Much homogeneity in organizational structures stems from the fact that despite considerable search for diversity there is relatively little variation to be selected from. New organizations are modeled upon old ones throughout the economy, and managers actively seek models upon which to build (Kimberly, 1980). Thus, in the arts one can find textbooks on how to organize a community arts council or how to start a symphony women's guild. Large organizations choose from a relatively small set of major consulting firms, which, like Johnny Appleseeds, spread a few organizational models throughout the land. Such models are powerful because structural changes are observable, whereas changes in policy and strategy are less easily noticed. With the advice of a major consulting firm, a large metropolitan public television station switched from a functional design to a multidivisional structure. The stations' executives were skeptical that the new structure was more efficient; in fact, some services were now duplicated across divisions. But they were convinced that the new design would carry a powerful message to the for-profit firms with whom the station regularly dealt. These firms, whether in the role of corporate underwriters or as potential partners in joint ventures, would view the reorganization as a sign that "the sleepy nonprofit station was becoming more business-minded" (Powell, forthcoming). The history of management reform in American government agencies, which are noted for their goal ambiguity, is almost a textbook case of isomorphic modeling, from the PPPB of the McNamara era to the zero-based budgeting of the Carter administration.

Organizations tend to model themselves after similar organizations in their field that they perceive to be more legitimate or successful. The ubiquity of certain kinds of structural arrangements can more likely be credited to the universality of mimetic processes than to any concrete evidence that the adopted models enhance efficiency. John Meyer (1981) contends that it is easy to predict the organization of a newly emerging nation's administration without knowing anything about the nation itself, since "peripheral nations are far more isomorphic—in administrative form and economic pattern—than any theory of the world system of economic division of labor would lead one to expect."

Normative pressures. A third source of isomorphic organizational change is normative and stems primarily from professionalization. Following Larson (1977) and Collins (1979), we interpret professionalization as the collective struggle of members of an occupation to define the conditions and methods of their work, to control "the production of producers" (Larson, 1977:49–52), and to establish a cognitive base and legitimation for their occupational autonomy. As Larson points out, the professional project is rarely achieved with complete success. Professionals must compromise with nonprofessional clients, bosses, or regulators. The major recent growth in the professions has been among organizational professionals, particularly managers and specialized staff of large organizations. The increased professionalization of workers whose futures are inextricably bound up with the fortunes of the organizations that employ them has rendered obsolescent (if not obsolete) the dichotomy between organizational commitment and professional allegiance that characterized traditional professionals in earlier organizations (Hall, 1968). Professions are subject to the same coercive and mimetic pressures as are organizations. Moreover, while various kinds of professionals within an organization may differ from one another, they exhibit much similarity to their professional counterparts in other organizations. In addition, in many cases, professional power is as much assigned by the state as it is created by the activities of the professions.

Two aspects of professionalization are important sources of isomorphism. One is the resting of formal education and of legitimation in a cognitive base produced by university specialists; the second is the growth and elaboration of professional networks that span organizations and across which new models diffuse rapidly. Universities and professional training institutions are important centers for the development of organizational norms among professional managers and their staff. Professional and trace associations are another vehicle for the definition and promulgation of normative rules about organizational and professional behavior. Such mechanisms create a pool of almost interchangeable individuals who occupy similar positions across a range of organizations and possess a similarity of orientation and disposition that may override variations in tradition and control that might otherwise shape organizational behavior (Perrow, 1974).

One important mechanism for encouraging normative isomorphism is the filtering of personnel. Within many organizational fields filtering occurs through the hiring of individuals from firms within the same industry; through the recruitment of fast-track staff from a narrow range of training institutions; through common promotion practices, such as always hiring top executives from financial or legal departments; and from skill-level requirements for particular jobs. Many professional career tracks are so closely guarded, both at the entry level and throughout the career progression, that individuals who make it to the top are virtually indistinguishable. March and March (1977) found that individuals who attained the position of school superintendent in Wisconsin were so alike in background and orientation as to make further career advancement random and unpredictable. Hirsch and Whisler (1982) find a similar absence of variation among *Fortune* 500 board members. In addition, individuals in an organizational field undergo anticipatory socialization to common expectations about their personal behavior, appropriate style of dress, organizational vocabularies (Cicourel, 1970; Williamson, 1975) and standard methods of speaking, joking, or addressing others (Ouchi, 1980). Particularly in industries with a service or financial orientation (Collins, 1979, argues that the importance of credentials is strongest in these areas), the filtering of personnel approaches what Kanter (1977) refers to as the "homosexual reproduction of management." To the extent managers and key staff are drawn from the same universities and filtered on a common set of attributes, they will tend to view problems in a similar fashion, see the same policies, procedures and structures as normatively sanctioned and legitimated, and approach decisions in much the same way.

Entrants to professional career tracks who somehow escape the filtering process—for example, Jewish naval officers, woman stockbrokers, or Black insurance executives—are likely to be subjected to pervasive on-the-job socialization. To the extent that organizations in a field differ and primary socialization occurs on the job, socialization could reinforce, not erode, differences among organizations. But when organizations in a field are similar and occupational socialization is carried out in trade association workshops, in-service educational programs, consultant arrangements, employer-professional school networks, and in the pages of trade magazines, socialization acts as an isomorphic force.

The professionalization of management tends to proceed in tandem with the structuration of organizational fields. The exchange of information among professionals helps contribute to a commonly recognized hierarchy of status, of center and periphery, that becomes a matrix for information flows and personnel movement across organizations. This status ordering occurs through both formal and informal means. The designation of a few large firms in an industry as key bargaining agents in union-management negotiations may make these central firms pivotal in other respects as well. Government recognition of key firms or organizations through the grant or contract process may give these organizations legitimacy and visibility and lead competing firms to copy aspects of their structure or operating procedures in hope of obtaining similar rewards. Professional and trade associations provide other arenas in which center organizations are recognized and their personnel given positions of substantive or ceremonial influence. Managers in highly visible organizations may in turn have their stature reinforced by representation on the boards of other organizations, participation in industry-wide or inter-industry councils, and consultation by agencies of government (Useem, 1979). In the nonprofit sector, where legal barriers to collusion do not exist, structuration may proceed even more rapidly. Thus executive producers or artistic directors of leading theatres head trade or professional association committees, sit on government and foundation grant-award panels, or consult as government- or foundation-financed management advisors to smaller theatres, or sit on smaller organizations' boards, even as their stature is reinforced and enlarged by the grants their theatres receive from government, corporate, and foundation funding sources (DiMaggio, 1982).

Such central organizations serve as both active and passive models; their policies and structures will be copied throughout their fields. Their centrality is reinforced as upwardly mobile managers and staff seek to secure positions in these central organizations in order to further their own careers. Aspiring managers may undergo anticipatory socialization into the norms and mores of the organizations they hope to join. Career paths may also involve movement from entry positions in the center organizations to middle-management positions in peripheral organizations. Personnel flows within an organizational field are further encouraged by structural homogenization, for example the existence of common career titles and paths (such as assistant, associate, and full professor) with meanings that are commonly understood.

It is important to note that each of the institutional isomorphic processes can be expected to proceed in the absence of evidence that they increase internal organizational efficiency. To the extent that organizational effectiveness is enhanced, the reason will often be that organizations are rewarded for being similar to other organizations in their fields. This similarity can make it easier for organizations to transact with other organizations, to attract career-minded staff, to be acknowledged as legitimate and reputable, and to fit into administrative categories that define eligibility for public and private grants and contracts. None of this, however, insures that conformist organizations do what they do more efficiently than do their more deviant peers.

Pressures for competitive efficiency are also mitigated in many fields because the number of organizations is limited and there are strong fiscal and legal barriers to entry and exit. Lee (1971:51) maintains this is why hospital administrators are less concerned with the efficient use of resources and more concerned with status competition and parity in prestige. Fennell (1980) notes that hospitals are a poor market system because patients lack the needed knowledge of potential exchange partners and prices. She argues that physicians and hospital administrators are the actual consumers. Competition among hospitals is based on "attracting physicians, who, in turn, bring their patients to the hospital." Fennell (p. 505) concludes that:

> Hospitals operate according to a norm of social legitimation that frequently conflicts with market considerations of efficiency and system rationality. Apparently, hospitals can increase their range of services not because there is an actual need for a particular service or facility within the patient population, but because they will be defined as fit only if they can offer everything other hospitals in the area offer.

These results suggest a more general pattern. Organizational fields that include a large professionally trained labor force will be driven primarily by status competition. Organizational prestige and resources are key elements in attracting professionals. This process encourages homogenization as organizations seek to ensure that they can provide the same benefits and services as their competitors.

NOTES

1. By *connectedness* we mean the existence of transactions tying organizations to one another: such transactions might include formal contractual relationships, participation of personnel in common enterprises such as professional associations, labor unions, or boards of directors, or informal organizational-level ties like personnel flows. A set of organizations that are strongly connected to one another and only weakly connected to other organizations constitutes a *clique*. By *structural equivalence* we refer to similarity of position in a network structure: for example, two organizations are structurally equivalent if they have ties of the same kind to the same set of other organizations, even if they themselves are not connected: here the key structure is the *role* or *block*.

2. By organizational change, we refer to change in formal structure, organizational culture, and goals, program, or mission. Organizational change varies in its responsiveness to technical conditions. In this paper we are most interested in processes that affect organizations in a given field: in most cases these organizations employ similar technical bases; thus we do not attempt to partial out the relative importance of technically functional versus other forms of organizational change. While we shall cite many examples of organizational change as we go along, our purpose here is to identify a widespread class of organizational processes relevant to a broad range of substantive problems, rather than to identify deterministically the causes of specific organizational arrangements.

3. Knoke (1982), in a careful event-history analysis of the spread of municipal reform, refutes the conventional explanations of culture clash or hierarchal diffusion and finds but modest support for modernization theory. His major finding is that regional differences in municipal reform adoption arise not from social compositional differences, "but from some type of imitation or contagion effects as represented by the level of neighboring regional cities previously adopting reform government" (p. 1337).

4. A wide range of factors—interorganizational commitments, elite sponsorship, and government support in form of open-ended contracts, subsidy, tariff barriers and import quotas, or favorable tax laws—reduce selection pressures even in competitive organizational fields. An expanding or a stable, protected market can also mitigate the forces of selection.

5. In contrast to Hannan and Freeman, we emphasize adaptation, but we are not suggesting that managers' actions are necessarily strategic in a long-range sense. Indeed, two of the three forms of isomorphism described below—mimetic and normative—involve managerial behaviors at the level of taken-for-granted assumptions rather than consciously strategic choices. In general, we question the utility of arguments about the motivations of actors that suggest a polarity between the rational and the nonrational. Goal-oriented behavior may be reflexive or prerational in the sense that it reflects deeply embedded predispositions, scripts, schema, or classifications; and behavior oriented to a goal may be reinforced without contributing to the accomplishment of that goal. While isomorphic change may often be mediated by the desires of managers to increase the effectiveness of their organizations, we are more concerned with the menu of possible options that managers consider than with their motives for choosing particular alternatives. In other words, we freely concede that actors' understandings of their own behaviors are interpretable in rational terms. The theory of isomorphism addresses not the psychological states of actors but the structural determinants of the range of choices that actors perceive as rational or prudent.

6. Carroll and Delacroix (1982) clearly recognize this and include political and institutional legitimacy as a major resource. Aldrich (1979) has argued that the population perspective must attend to historical trends and changes in legal and political institutions.

7. This point was suggested by John Meyer.

REFERENCES

Alchian, Armen
    1950 "Uncertainty, evolution, and economic theory." Journal of Political Economy 58:211–21.

Aldrich, Howard
    1979 Organizations and Environments. Englewood Cliffs, NJ: Prentice-Hall.

Barnouw, Erik
    1966–68 A History of Broadcasting in the United States, 3 volumes. New York: Oxford University Press.

Carroll, Glenn R. and Jacques Delacroix
    1982 "Organizational mortality in the newspaper industries of Argentina and Ireland: an ecological approach." Administrative Science Quarterly 27:169–98.

Child, John and Alfred Kieser
    1981 "Development of organizations over time." Pp. 28–64 in Paul C. Nystrom and William H. Starbuck (eds.), Handbook of Organizational Design. New York: Oxford University Press.

Cicourel, Aaron
    1970 "The acquisition of social structure: toward a developmental sociology of language." Pp. 136–68 in Jack D. Douglas (ed.), Understanding Everyday Life. Chicago: Aldine.

Collins, Randall
    1979 The Credential Society. New York: Academic Press.

Coser, Lewis, Charles Kadushin and Walter W. Powell
    1982 Books: The Culture and Commerce of Book Publishing. New York: Basic Books.

Cyert, Richard M. and James G. March
    1963 A Behavioral Theory of the Firm. Englewood Cliffs, NJ: Prentice-Hall.

DiMaggio, Paul
    1981 "Cultural entrepreneurship in nineteenth-century Boston. Part 1: The creation of an organizational base for high culture in America." Media, Culture and Society 4:33–50.
    1982 "The structure of organizational fields: an analytical approach and policy implications." Paper prepared for SUNY-Albany Conference on Organizational Theory and Public Policy. April 1 and 2.

Fennell, Mary L.
    1980 "The effects of environmental characteristics on the structure of hospital clusters." Administrative Science Quarterly 25:484–510.

Freeman, John H.
    1982 "Organizational life cycles and natural selection processes." Pp. 1–32 in Barry Staw and Larry Cummings (eds.), Research in Organizational Behavior. Vol. 4. Greenwich, CT: JAI Press.

Giddens, Anthony
    1979 Central Problems in Social Theory: Action, Structure, and Contradiction in Social Analysis. Berkeley: University of California Press.

Hall, Richard
    1968 "Professionalization and bureaucratization." American Sociological Review 33:92–104.

Hannan, Michael T. and John H. Freeman
    1977 "The population ecology of organizations." American Journal of Sociology 82:929–64.

Hawley, Amos
    1968 "Human ecology." Pp. 328–37 in David L. Sills (ed.), International Encyclopedia of the Social Sciences. New York: Macmillan.

Hirsch, Paul and Thomas Whisler
    1982 "The view from the boardroom." Paper presented at Academy of Management Meetings, New York, NY.

Kanter, Rosabeth Moss
    1972 Commitment and Community. Cambridge, MA: Harvard University Press.

1977 Men and Women of the Corporation. New York: Basic Books.

Katz, Michael B.
1975 Class, Bureaucracy, and Schools: The Illusion of Educational Change in America. New York: Praeger.

Kimberly, John
1980 "Initiation, innovation and institutionalization in the creation process." Pp. 18–43 in John Kimberly and Robert B. Miles (eds.), The Organizational Life Cycle. San Francisco: Jossey-Bass.

Knoke, David
1982 "The spread of municipal reform: temporal, spatial, and social dynamics." American Journal of Sociology 87:1314–39.

Larson, Magali Sarfatti
1977 The Rise of Professionalism: A Sociological Analysis. Berkeley: University of California Press.

Laumann, Edward O., Joseph Galaskiewicz and Peter Marsden
1978 "Community structure as interorganizational linkage." Annual Review of Sociology 4:455–84.

Lee, M. L.
1971 "A conspicuous production theory of hospital behavior." Southern Economic Journal 38:48–58.

March, James C. and James G. March
1977 "Almost random careers: the Wisconsin school superintendency, 1940–72." Administrative Science Quarterly 22:378–409.

March, James G. and Johan P. Olsen
1976 Ambiguity and Choice in Organizations. Bergen, Norway: Universitetsforlaget.

Meyer, John W.
1979 "The impact of the centralization of educational funding and control on state and local organizational governance." Stanford, CA: Institute for Research on Educational Finance and Governance, Stanford University, Program Report No. 79-B20.
1981 Remarks at ASA session on "The Present Crisis and the Decline in World Hegemony." Toronto, Canada.

Meyer, John W. and Michael Hannan
1979 National Development and the World System: Educational, Economic, and Political Change. Chicago: University of Chicago Press.

Meyer, John W. and Brian Rowan
1977 "Institutionalized organizations: formal structure as myth and ceremony." American Journal of Sociology 83:340–63.

Meyer, John W., W. Richard Scott and Terence C. Deal
1981 "Institutional and technical sources of organizational structure explaining the structure of educational organizations." In Herman Stein (ed.), Organizations and the Human Services: Cross-Disciplinary Reflections. Philadelphia, PA: Temple University Press.

Meyer, Marshall
1981 "Persistence and change in bureaucratic structures." Paper presented at the annual meeting of the American Sociological Association, Toronto, Canada.

Milofsky, Carl
1981 "Structure and process in community self-help organizations." New Haven: Yale Program on Non-Profit Organizations, Working Paper No. 17.

Ouchi, William G.
1980 "Markets, bureaucracies, and clans." Administrative Science Quarterly 25:129–41.

Perrow, Charles
1974 "Is business really changing?" Organizational Dynamics Summer: 31–44.

Pfeffer, Jeffrey and Gerald Salancik
1978 The External Control of Organizations: A Resource Dependence Perspective. New York: Harper & Row.

Powell, Walter W.
Forthcoming "The Political Economy of Public Television." New Haven: Program on Non-Profit Organizations.

Ritti, R. R. and Fred H. Goldner
1979 "Professional pluralism in an industrial organization." Management Science 16:233–46.

Rothman, Mitchell
1980 "The evolution of forms of legal education." Unpublished manuscript. Department of Sociology, Yale University, New Haven, CT.

Rothschild-Whitt, Joyce
1979 "The collectivist organization: an alternative to rational bureaucratic models." American Sociological Review 44:509–27.

Schelling, Thomas
1978 Micromotives and Macrobehavior. New York: W. W. Norton.

Sedlak, Michael W.
1981 "Youth policy and young women. 1950–1972: the impact of private-sector programs for pregnant and wayward girls on public policy." Paper presented at National Institute for Education Youth Policy Research Conference, Washington, D.C.

Selznick, Philip
1957 Leadership in Administration. New York: Harper & Row.

Starr, Paul
1980 "Medical care and the boundaries of capitalist organization." Unpublished manuscript. Program on Non-Profit Organizations, Yale University, New Haven, CT.

Swidler, Ann
  1979 Organization Without Authority: Dilemmas of Social Control of Free Schools. Cambridge: Harvard University Press.
Tyack, David
  1974 The One Best System: A History of American Urban Education. Cambridge, MA: Harvard University Press.
Useem, Michael
  1979 "The social organization of the American business elite and participation of corporation directors in the governance of American institutions." American Sociological Review 44:553–72.
Weber, Max
  1952 The Protestant Ethic and the Spirit of Capitalism. New York: Scribner.
  1968 Economy and Society: An Outline of Interpretive Sociology. Three volumes. New York: Bedminster.
Westney, D. Eleanor
  Forthcoming Organizational Development and Social Change in Meiji, Japan.
White, Harrison C, Scott A. Boorman and Ronald L. Breiger
  1976 "Social structure from multiple networks. I. Blockmodels of roles and positions." American Journal of Sociology 81:730–80.
Williamson, Oliver E.
  1975 Markets and Hierarchies, Analysis and Antitrust Implications: A Study of the Economics of Internal Organization. New York: Free Press.
Woodward, John
  1965 Industrial Organization, Theory and Practice. London: Oxford University Press.
Zucker, Lynne G. and Pamela S. Tolbert
  1981 "Institutional sources of change in the formal structure of organizations: the diffusion of civil service reform, 1880–1935." Paper presented at American Sociological Association annual meeting, Toronto, Canada.

SOURCE: DiMaggio, Paul J. and Walter W. Powell. 1983. Excerpt from "The Iron Cage Revisited: Institutional Isomorphism and Collective Rationality in Organization Fields." *American Sociological Review*, 48:147–54, 158–60.

51

ORGANIZATIONAL LEARNING

BARBARA LEVITT AND JAMES G. MARCH

INTRODUCTION

Theories of organizational learning can be distinguished from theories of analysis and choice which emphasize anticipatory calculation and intention (Machina 1987), from theories of conflict and bargaining which emphasize strategic action, power, and exchange (Pfeffer 1981), and from theories of variation and selection which emphasize differential birth and survival rates of invariant forms (Hannan & Freeman 1977). Although the actual behavioral processes and mechanisms of learning are sufficiently intertwined with choice, bargaining, and selection to make such theoretical distinctions artificial at times, ideas about organizational learning are distinct from, and framed by, ideas about the other processes (Grandori 1987, Scott 1987).

Our interpretation of organizational learning builds on three classical observations drawn from behavioral studies of organizations. The first is that behavior in an organization is based on routines (Cyert & March 1963, Nelson & Winter 1982). Action stems from a logic of appropriateness or legitimacy more than from a logic of consequentiality or intention. It involves matching procedures to situations more than it does calculating choices. The second observation is that organizational actions are history-dependent (Lindblom 1959, Steinbruner 1974). Routines are based on interpretations of the past more than anticipations of the future. They

adapt to experience incrementally in response to feedback about outcomes. The third observation is that organizations are oriented to targets (Simon 1955, Siegel 1957). Their behavior depends on the relation between the outcomes they observe and the aspirations they have for those outcomes. Sharper distinctions are made between success and failure than among gradations of either.

Within such a framework, organizations are seen as learning by encoding inferences from history into routines that guide behavior. The generic term "routines" includes the forms, rules, procedures, conventions, strategies, and technologies around which organizations are constructed and through which they operate. It also includes the structure of beliefs, frameworks, paradigms, codes, cultures, and knowledge that buttress, elaborate, and contradict the formal routines. Routines are independent of the individual actors who execute them and are capable of surviving considerable turnover in individual actors.

The experiential lessons of history are captured by routines in a way that makes the lessons, but not the history, accessible to organizations and organizational members who have not themselves experienced the history. Routines are transmitted through socialization, education, imitation, professionalization, personnel movement, mergers, and acquisitions. They are recorded in a collective memory that is often coherent but is sometimes jumbled, that often endures but is sometimes lost. They change as a result of experience within a community of other learning organizations. These changes depend on interpretations of history, particularly on the evaluation of outcomes in terms of targets.

In the remainder of the present paper we examine such processes of organizational learning. The perspective is narrower than that used by some (Starbuck 1976, Hedberg 1981, Fiol & Lyles 1985) and differs conceptually from that used by others. In particular, both the emphasis on routines and the emphasis on ecologies of learning distinguish the present formulation from treatments that deal primarily with individual learning within single organizations (March & Olsen 1975, Argyris & Schön 1978) and place this paper closer to the traditions of behavioral theories of organizational decisionmaking (Winter 1986, House & Singh 1987), and to population level theories of organizational change (Carroll 1984, Astley 1985).

LEARNING FROM DIRECT EXPERIENCE

Routines and beliefs change in response to direct organizational experience through two major mechanisms. The first is trial-and-error experimentation. The likelihood that a routine will be used is increased when it is associated with success in meeting a target, decreased when it is associated with failure (Cyert & March 1963). The underlying process by which this occurs is left largely unspecified. The second mechanism is organizational search. An organization draws from a pool of alternative routines, adopting better ones when they are discovered. Since the rate of discovery is a function both of the richness of the pool and of the intensity and direction of search, it depends on the history of success and failure of the organization (Radner 1975).

Learning by Doing

The purest example of learning from direct experience is found in the effects of cumulated production and user experience on productivity in manufacturing (Dutton et al 1984). Research on aircraft production, first in the 1930s (Wright 1936) and subsequently during World War II (Asher 1956), indicated that direct labor costs in producing airframes declined with the cumulated number of airframes produced. If C_i is the direct labor cost of the ith airframe produced, and a is a constant, then the empirical results are approximated by: $C_n = C_1 n^{-a}$. This equation, similar in spirit and form to learning curves in individuals and animals, has been shown to fit production costs (in constant dollars) reasonably well in a relatively large number of products, firms, and nations (Yelle 1979). Much of the early research involved only simple graphical techniques, but more elaborate analyses have largely confirmed the original results (Rapping 1965). Estimates of the learning rate, however, vary substantially across industries, products, and time (Dutton & Thomas 1984).

Empirical plots of experience curves have been buttressed by three kinds of analytical elaborations. First, there have been attempts to decompose experience curves into several intercorrelated causes and to assess their separate contributions to the observed improvements in manufacturing costs. Although it has been argued that important elements of the improvements come through feedback from customers who use the products, particularly where those products are complex (Rosenberg 1982), most of the research on experience curves has emphasized the direct effects of cumulative experience on production skills. Most studies indicate that the effects due to cumulative production are greater than those due to changes in the current scale of production, transformation of the technology, increases in the experience of individual production workers, or the passage of time (Preston & Keachie 1964, Hollander 1965, Argote et al 1987); but there is evidence that the latter effects are also involved (Dutton & Thomas 1984, 1985). Second, there have been attempts to use experience curves as a basis for pricing strategies. These efforts have led to some well-publicized successes but also to some failures attributable to an inadequate specification of the basic model, particularly as it relates to the sharing of experience across organizations (Day & Montgomery 1983, Dutton & Freedman 1985). Third, there have been attempts to define models that not only predict the general log-linear result but also accommodate some of the small but theoretically interesting departures from that curve (Muth 1986). These efforts are, for the most part, variations on themes of trial-and-error learning or organizational search.

Competency Traps

In simple discussions of experiential learning based on trial-and-error learning or organizational search, organizations are described as gradually adopting those routines, procedures, or strategies that lead to favorable outcomes; but the routines themselves are treated as fixed. In fact, of course, routines are transformed at the same time as the organization learns which of them to pursue, and discrimination among alternative routines is affected by their transformations (March 1981, Burgelman 1988).

The dynamics are exemplified by cases in which each routine is itself a collection of routines, and learning takes place at several nested levels. In such multilevel learning, organizations learn simultaneously both to discriminate among routines and to refine the routines by learning within them. A familiar contemporary example is the way in which organizations learn to use some software systems rather than others and simultaneously learn to refine their skills on the systems that they use. As a result of such learning, efficiency with any particular procedure increases with use, and differences in success with different procedures reflect not only differences in the performance potentials of the procedures but also an organization's current competences with them.

Multilevel learning typically leads to specialization. By improving competencies within frequently used procedures, it increases the frequency with which those procedures result in successful outcomes and thereby increases their use. Provided this process leads the organization both to improve the efficiency and to increase the use of the procedure with the highest potential, specialization is advantageous. However, a competency trap can occur when favorable performance with an inferior procedure leads an organization to accumulate more experience with it, thus keeping experience with a superior procedure inadequate to make it rewarding to use. Such traps are well-known both in their new technology version (Cooper & Schendel 1976) and in their new procedures version (Zucker 1977).

Competency traps are particularly likely to lead to maladaptive specialization if newer routines are better than older ones. One case is the sequential exposure to new procedures in a developing technology (Barley 1988). Later procedures are improvements, but learning organizations have

problems in overcoming the competences they have developed with earlier ones (Whetten 1987). The likelihood of such persistence in inferior procedures is sensitive to the magnitude of the difference between the potentials of the alternatives. The status quo is unlikely to be stable if the differences in potential between existing routines and new ones are substantial (Stinchcombe 1986). The likelihood of falling into a competency trap is also sensitive to learning rates. Fast learning among alternative routines tends to increase the risks of maladaptive specialization, while fast learning within a new routine tends to decrease the risks (Herriott et al 1985).

The broader social and evolutionary implications of competency traps are considerable. In effect, learning produces increasing returns to experience (thus typically to scale) and leads an organization, industry, or society to persist in using a set of procedures or technologies that may be far from optimal (Arthur 1984). Familiar examples are the standard typewriter keyboard and the use of the internal combustion gasoline engine to power motor vehicles. Since they convert almost chance actions based on small differences into stable arrangements, competency traps result in organizational histories for which broad functional or efficiency explanations are often inadequate.

INTERPRETATION OF EXPERIENCE

The lessons of experience are drawn from a relatively small number of observations in a complex, changing ecology of learning organizations. What has happened is not always obvious, and the causality of events is difficult to untangle. What an organization should expect to achieve, and thus the difference between success and failure, is not always clear. Nevertheless, people in organizations form interpretations of events and come to classify outcomes as good or bad (Thompson 1967).

Certain properties of this interpretation of experience stem from features of individual inference and judgment. As has frequently been observed, individual human beings are not perfect statisticians (Kahneman et al 1982). They make systematic errors in recording the events of history and in making inferences from them. They overestimate the probability of events that actually occur and of events that are available to attention because of their recency or saliency. They are insensitive to sample size. They tend to overattribute events to the intentional actions of individuals. They use simple linear and functional rules, associate causality with spatial and temporal contiguity, and assume that big effects must have big causes. These attributes of individuals as historians are important to the present topic because they lead to systematic biases in interpretation, but they are reviewed in several previous publications (Slovic et al 1977, Einhorn & Hogarth 1986, Starbuck & Milliken 1988) and are not discussed here.

Stories, Paradigms, and Frames

Organizations devote considerable energy to developing collective understandings of history. These interpretations of experience depend on the frames within which events are comprehended (Daft & Weick 1984). They are translated into, and developed through, story lines that come to be broadly, but not universally, shared (Clark 1972, Martin et al 1985). This structure of meaning is normally suppressed as a conscious concern, but learning occurs within it. As a result, some of the more powerful phenomena in organizational change surround the transformation of givens, the redefinition of events, alternatives, and concepts through consciousness raising, culture building, double-loop learning, or paradigm shifts (Argyris & Schön 1978, Brown 1978, Beyer 1981).

It is imaginable that organizations will come to discard ineffective interpretive frames in the very long run, but the difficulties in using history to discriminate intelligently among alternative paradigms are profound. Where there are multiple, hierarchically arranged levels of simultaneous learning, the interactions among them are complex, and it is difficult to evaluate higher order alternatives on the basis of experience. Alternative frames are flexible enough to allow change in operational routines without affecting organizational mythology (Meyer & Rowan 1977, Krieger 1979), and organizational participants collude in support of interpretations that sustain the myths (Tirole 1986). As a result, stories, paradigms, and beliefs are conserved in the face of considerable potential disconfirmation (Sproull 1981); and what is learned appears to be influenced

less by history than by the frames applied to that history (Fischhoff 1975, Pettigrew 1985).

Although frameworks for interpreting experience within organizations are generally resistant to experience—indeed, may enact that experience (Weick 1979)—they are vulnerable to paradigm peddling and paradigm politics. Ambiguity sustains the efforts of theorists and therapists to promote their favorite frameworks, and the process by which interpretations are developed makes it relatively easy for conflicts of interest within an organization to spawn conflicting interpretations. For example, leaders of organizations are inclined to accept paradigms that attribute organizational successes to their own actions and organizational failures to the actions of others or to external forces, but opposition groups in an organization are likely to have the converse principle for attributing causality (Miller & Ross 1975). Similarly, advocates of a particular policy, but not their opponents, are likely to interpret failures less as a symptom that the policy is incorrect than as an indication that it has not been pursued vigorously enough (Ross & Staw 1986). As a result, disagreements over the meaning of history are possible, and different groups develop alternative stories that interpret the same experience quite differently.

The Ambiguity of Success

Both trial-and-error learning and incremental search depend on the evaluation of outcomes as successes or failures. There is a structural bias toward post-decision disappointment in ordinary decision-making (Harrison & March 1984), but individual decisionmakers often seem to be able to reinterpret their objectives or the outcomes in such a way as to make themselves successful even when the shortfall seems quite large (Staw & Ross 1978).

The process is similar in organizational learning, particularly where the leadership is stable and the organization is tightly integrated (Ross & Staw 1986). But where such conditions do not hold, there are often differences stemming from the political nature of an organization. Goals are ambiguous, and commitment to them is confounded by their relation to personal and subgroup objectives (Moore & Gates 1986). Conflict and decision advocacy within putatively rational decision processes lead to inflated expectations and problems of implementation and thus to disappointments (Olsen 1976, Sproull et al 1978). Different groups in an organization often have different targets and evaluate the same outcome differently. Simple euphoria is constrained by the presence of individuals and groups who opposed the direction being pursued, or who at least feel no need to accept responsibility for it (Brunsson 1985). New organizational leaders are inclined to define previous outcomes more negatively than are the leaders who preceded them (Hedberg 1981). As a result, evaluations of outcomes are likely to be more negative or more mixed in organizations than they are in individuals.

Organizational success is ordinarily defined in terms of the relation between performance outcomes and targets. Targets, however, change over time in two ways. First, the indicators of success are modified. Accounting definitions change (Burchell et al 1985); social and policy indicators are redefined (MacRae 1985). Second, levels of aspiration with respect to any particular indicator change. The most common assumption is that a target is a function of some kind of moving average of past achievement, the gap between past achievement and past targets, or the rate of change of either (Cyert & March 1963, Lant 1987).

Superstitious Learning

Superstitious learning occurs when the subjective experience of learning is compelling, but the connections between actions and outcomes are misspecified. Numerous opportunities exist for such misunderstandings in learning from experience in organizations. For example, it is easy for technicians to develop superstitious perceptions of a new technology from their experience with it (Barley 1988). Cases of superstition that are of particular interest to students of organizations are those that stem from special features of life in hierarchical organizations. For example, the promotion of managers on the basis of performance produces self-confidence among top executives that is partly superstitious, leading them to overestimate the extent to which they can control the risks their organizations face (March & Shapira 1987).

Superstitious learning often involves situations in which subjective evaluations of success are insensitive to the actions taken. During very good times, or when post-outcome euphoria reinterprets outcomes

positively, or when targets are low, only exceptionally inappropriate routines will lead an organization to experience failure. In like manner, during very bad times, or when post-outcome pessimism reinterprets outcomes negatively, or when targets are high, no routine will lead to success. Evaluations that are insensitive to actions can also result from adaptive aspirations. Targets that adapt very rapidly will be close to the current performance level. This makes being above or below the target an almost chance event. Very slow adaptation, on the other hand, is likely to keep an organization either successful for long periods of time or unsuccessful for long periods of time. A similar result is realized if targets adapt to the performance of other organizations. For example, if each firm in an industry sets its target equal to the average performance of firms in that industry, some firms are likely to be persistently above the target and others persistently below (Levinthal & March 1981, Herriott et al 1985).

Each of these situations produces superstitious learning. In an organization that is invariantly successful, routines that are followed are associated with success and are reinforced; other routines are inhibited. The organization becomes committed to a particular set of routines, but the routines to which it becomes committed are determined more by early (relatively arbitrary) actions than by information gained from the learning situation (Nystrom & Starbuck 1984). Alternatively, if failure is experienced regardless of the particular routine that is used, routines are changed frequently in a fruitless search for some that work. In both cases, the subjective feeling of learning is powerful, but it is misleading.

ORGANIZATIONAL MEMORY

Organizational learning depends on features of individual memories (Hastie et al 1984, Johnson & Hasher 1987), but our present concern is with organizational aspects of memory. Routine-based conceptions of learning presume that the lessons of experience are maintained and accumulated within routines despite the turnover of personnel and the passage of time. Rules, procedures, technologies, beliefs, and cultures are conserved through systems of socialization and control. They are retrieved through mechanisms of attention within a memory structure. Such organizational instruments not only record history but shape its future path, and the details of that path depend significantly on the processes by which the memory is maintained and consulted. An accounting system, whether viewed as the product of design or the residue of historical development, affects the recording and creation of history by an organization (Johnson & Kaplan 1987). The ways in which military routines are changed, maintained, and consulted contribute to the likelihood and orchestration of military engagement (Levy 1986).

Recording of Experience

Inferences drawn from experience are recorded in documents, accounts, files, standard operating procedures, and rule books; in the social and physical geography of organizational structures and relationships; in standards of good professional practice; in the culture of organizational stories; and in shared perceptions of "the way things are done around here." Relatively little is known about the details by which organizational experience is accumulated into a structure of routines, but it is clearly a process that yields different kinds of routines in different situations and is only partly successful in imposing internal consistency on organizational memories.

Not everything is recorded. The transformation of experience into routines and the recording of those routines involve costs. The costs are sensitive to information technology, and a common observation is that modern computer-based technology encourages the automation of routines by substantially reducing the costs of recording them. Even so, a good deal of experience is unrecorded simply because the costs are too great. Organizations also often make distinction between outcomes that will be considered relevant for future actions and outcomes that will not. The distinction may be implicit, as for example when comparisons between projected and realized returns from capital investment projects are ignored (Hagg 1979). It may be explicit, as for example when exceptions to the rules are declared not to be precedents for the future. By creating a set of actions that are not precedents, an organization gives routines both short-term flexibility and long-term stability (Powell 1986).

Organizations vary in the emphasis placed on formal routines. Craft-based organizations rely more

heavily on tacit knowledge than do bureaucracies (Becker 1982). Organizations facing complex uncertainties rely on informally shared understandings more than do organizations dealing with simpler, more stable environments (Ouchi 1980). There is also variation within organizations. Higher level managers rely more on ambiguous information (relative to formal rules) than do lower level managers (Daft & Lengel 1984).

Experiential knowledge, whether in tacit form or in formal rules, is recorded in an organizational memory. That memory is orderly, but it exhibits inconsistencies and ambiguities. Some of the contradictions are a consequence of inherent complications in maintaining consistency in inferences drawn sequentially from a changing experience. Some, however, reflect differences in experience, the confusions of history, and conflicting interpretations of that history. These latter inconsistencies are likely to be organized into deviant memories, maintained by subcultures, subgroups, and subunits (Martin et al 1985). With a change in the fortunes of the dominant coalition, the deviant memories become more salient to action (Martin & Siehl 1983).

Conservation of Experience

Unless the implications of experience can be transferred from those who experienced it to those who did not, the lessons of history are likely to be lost through turnover of personnel. Written rules, oral transitions, and systems of formal and informal apprenticeships implicitly instruct new individuals in the lessons of history. Under many circumstances, the transfer of tradition is relatively straightforward and organizational experience is substantially conserved. For example, most police officers are socialized successfully to actions and beliefs recognizable as acceptable police behavior, even in cases where those actions and beliefs are substantially different from those that were originally instrumental in leading an individual to seek the career (Van Maanen 1973).

Under other circumstances, however, organizational experience is not conserved. Knowledge disappears from an organization's active memory (Neustadt & May 1986). Routines are not conserved because of limits on the time or legitimacy of the socializing agents, as for example in deviant subgroups or when the number of new members is large (Sproull et al 1978); because of conflict with other normative orders, as for example with new organization members who are also members of well-organized professions (Hall 1968); or because of the weaknesses of organizational control, as for example in implementation across geographic or cultural distances (Brytting 1986).

Retrieval of Experience

Even within a consistent and accepted set of routines, only part of an organization's memory is likely to be evoked at a particular time, or in a particular part of the organization. Some parts of organizational memory are more available for retrieval than others. Availability is associated with the frequency of use of a routine, the recency of its use, and its organizational proximity. Recently used and frequently used routines are more easily evoked than those that have been used infrequently. Thus, organizations have difficulty retrieving relatively old, unused knowledge or skills (Argote et al 1987). In cases where routines are nested within more general routines, the repetitive use of lower level routines tends to make them more accessible than the more general routine to which they are related (Merton 1940). The effects of proximity stem from the ways the accumulation of history is linked to regularized responsibility. The routines that record lessons of experience are organized around organizational responsibilities and are retrieved more easily when actions are taken through regular channels than when they occur outside those channels (Olsen 1983). At the same time, organizational structures create advocates for routines. Policies are converted into responsibilities that encourage rule zealotry (Mazmanian & Nienaber 1979).

Availability is also partly a matter of the direct costs of finding and using what is stored in memory. Particularly where there are large numbers of routines bearing on relatively specific actions, modern information technology has reduced those costs and made the routinization of relatively complex organizational behavior economically feasible, for example in the preparation of reports or presentations, the scheduling of production or logistical support, the design of structures or engineering systems, or the analysis of financial statements (Smith & Green 1980). Such automation of the recovery of routines makes retrieval more reliable. Reliability is, however, a mixed blessing. It standardizes retrieval and thus typically underestimates the conflict of interest and ambiguity about preferences in an organization. Expert systems of the standard type have difficulty capturing the unpredictable richness, erratic redundancy, and casual validity checking of traditional retrieval procedures, and they reduce or eliminate the fortuitous experimentation of unreliable retrieval (Simon 1971, Wildavsky 1983). As a result, they are likely to make learning more difficult for the organization.

LEARNING FROM THE EXPERIENCE OF OTHERS

Organizations capture the experience of other organizations through the transfer of encoded experience in the form of technologies, codes, procedures, or similar routines (Dutton & Starbuck 1978). This diffusion of experience and routines from other organizations within a community of organizations complicates theories of routine-based learning. It suggests that understanding the relation between experiential teaming and routines, strategies, or technologies in organizations will require attention to organizational networks (Hakansson 1987) as well as to the experience of the individual organization. At the same time, it makes the derivation of competitive strategies (e.g. pricing strategies) more complex than it would otherwise be (Hilke & Nelson 1987).

Mechanisms for Diffusion

The standard literature on the epidemiology of disease or information distinguishes three broad processes of diffusion. The first is diffusion involving a single source broadcasting a disease to a population of potential, but not necessarily equally vulnerable, victims. Organizational examples include rules promulgated by governmental agencies, trade associations, professional associations, and unions (Scott 1985). The second process is diffusion involving the spread of a disease through contact between a member of the population who is infected and one who is not, sometimes mediated by a host carrier. Organizational examples include routines diffused by contacts among organizations, by consultants, and by the movement of personnel (Biggart 1977). The third process is two-stage diffusion involving the spread of a disease within a small group by contagion and then by broadcast from them to the remainder of a population. Organizational examples include routines communicated through formal and informal educational institutions, through experts, and through trade and popular publications (Heimer 1985a). In the organizational literature, these three processes have been labeled *coercive, mimetic,* and *normative* (DiMaggio & Powell 1983). All three are involved in a comprehensive system of information diffusion (Imai et al 1985).

Dynamics of Diffusion

The possibilities for learning from the experience of others, as well as some of the difficulties, can be illustrated by looking at the diffusion of innovations among organizations. We consider here only some issues that are particularly important for organizational learning. For more general reviews of the literature, see Rogers & Shoemaker (1971) and Kimberly (1981).

Although it is not easy to untangle the effects of imitation from other effects that lead to differences in the time of adoption, studies of the spread of new technologies among organizations seem to indicate that diffusion through imitation is less significant than is variation in the match between the technology and the organization (Mansfield 1968), especially as that match is discovered and molded through learning (Kay 1979). Imitation, on the other hand, has been credited with contributing substantially to diffusion of city manager plans among American cities (Knoke 1982) and multidivisional organizational structures among American firms (Fligstein 1985). Studies of the adoption of civil service reform by cities in the United States (Tolbert & Zucker 1983) and of high technology weaponry by air forces (Eyre et al 1987) both show patterns in which features of the match between the procedures and the adopting organizations are more significant

for explaining early adoptions than they are for explaining later ones, which seem better interpreted as due to imitation. The latter result is also supported by a study of the adoption of accounting conventions by firms (Mezias 1987).

The underlying ideas in the literature on the sociology of institutionalization are less epidemiological than they are functional, but the diffusion of practices and forms is one of the central mechanisms considered (Zucker 1987). Pressure on organizations to demonstrate that they are acting on collectively valued purposes in collectively valued ways leads them to copy ideas and practices from each other. The particular professions, policies, programs, laws, and public opinion that are created in the process of producing and marketing goods and services become powerful institutionalized myths that are adopted by organizations to legitimate themselves and ensure public support (Meyer & Rowan 1977, Zucker 1977). The process diffuses forms and procedures and thereby tends to diffuse organizational power structures as well (Fligstein 1987).

The dynamics of imitation depend not only on the advantages that come to an organization as it profits from the experience of others, but also on the gains or losses that accrue to those organizations from which the routines or beliefs are drawn (DiMaggio & Powell 1983). In many (but not all) situations involving considerations of technical efficiency, diffusion of experience has negative consequences for organizations that are copied. This situation is typified by the case of technical secrets, where sharing leads to loss of competitive position. In many (but not all) situations involving considerations of legitimacy, diffusion of experience has positive consequences for organizations that are copied. This situation is typified by the case of accounting practices, where sharing leads to greater legitimacy for all concerned.

The critical factor for the dynamics is less whether the functional impetus is a concern for efficiency or legitimacy than whether the feedback effects are positive or negative (Wiewel & Hunter 1985). Where concerns for technical efficiency are associated with positive effects of sharing, as for example in many symbiotic relations within an industry, the process will unfold in ways similar to the process of institutionalization. Where concerns for legitimacy are associated with negative effects of sharing, as for example in cases of diffusion where mimicking by other organizations of lower status reduces the lead organization's status, the process will unfold in ways similar to the spread of secrets.

ECOLOGIES OF LEARNING

Organizations are collections of subunits learning in an environment that consists largely of other collections of learning subunits (Cangelosi & Dill 1965). The ecological structure is a complication in two senses. First, it complicates learning. Because of the simultaneously adapting behavior of other organizations, a routine may produce different outcomes at different times, or different routines may produce the same outcome at different times. Second, an ecology of learners complicates the systematic comprehension and modeling of learning processes. Environments change endogenously, and even relatively simple conceptions of learning become complex.

Learning in a World of Learners

Ecologies of learning include various types of interactions among learners, but the classical type is a collection of competitors. Competitors are linked partly through the diffusion of experience, and understanding learning within competitive communities of organizations involves seeing how experience, particularly secrets, are shared (Sitkin 1986), and how organizational actors come to trust one another, or not (Zucker 1986). Competitors are also linked through the effects of their actions on each other. One organization's action is another organization's outcome. As a result, even if learning by an individual organization were entirely internal and direct, it could be comprehended only by specifying the competitive structure.

Suppose competitors learn how to allocate resources to alternative technologies (strategies, procedures) in a world in which the return received by each competitor from the several technologies is a joint consequence of the potentials of the technologies, the changing competences of the several competitors within the technologies, and the allocations of effort by the several competitors among the technologies (Khandwalla 1981). In a situation of this type, it has been shown that there are strong ecological effects (Herriott et al 1985). The learning outcomes depend on the number of competitors, the rates at which they learn from their own experience, the rates at which they adjust their targets, the extent to which they learn from the experience of others, and the differences in the potentials of the technologies. There is a tendency for organizations to specialize and for faster learners to specialize in inferior technologies.

Learning to Learn

Learning itself can be viewed as one of the technologies within which organizations develop competence through use and among which they choose on the basis of experience. The general (non-ecological) expectation is that learning procedures will become common when they lead to favorable outcomes and that organizations will become effective at learning when they use learning routines frequently. The ecological question is whether there are properties of the relations among interacting organizations that lead some of them to learn to learn and others not to do so.

In competitive situations, small differences in competence at learning will tend to accumulate through the competency multiplier, driving slower learners to other procedures. If some organizations are powerful enough to create their own environments, weaker organizations will learn to adapt to the dominant ones, that is they will learn to learn (Heimer 1985b). By the same token, powerful organizations, by virtue of their ability to ignore competition, will be less inclined to learn from experience and less competent at doing so (Engwall 1976). The circumstances under which these learning disabilities produce a disadvantage, rather than an advantage, are more complicated to specify than might appear, but there is some chance that a powerful organization will become incapable of coping with an environment that cannot be arbitrarily enacted (Hannan & Freeman 1984).

LEARNING AS A FORM OF INTELLIGENCE

Organizational learning from experience is not only a useful perspective from which to describe organizational change; it is also an important instrument of organizational intelligence. The speculation that learning can improve the performance, and thus the intelligence, of organizations is confirmed by numerous studies of learning by doing, by case observations, and by theoretical analyses. Since we have defined learning as a process rather than as an outcome, the observation that learning is beneficial to organizations is not empty. It has become commonplace to emphasize learning in the design of organizations, to argue that some important improvements in organizational intelligence can be achieved by giving organizations capabilities to learn quickly and precisely (Starbuck & Dutton 1973, Duncan & Weiss 1979). As we have seen, however, the complications in using organizational learning as a form of intelligence are not trivial.

Nor are those problems due exclusively to avoidable individual and organizational inadequacies. There are structural difficulties in learning from experience. The past is not a perfect predictor of the future, and the experimental designs generated by ordinary life are far from ideal for causal inference (Brehmer 1980). Making organizational learning effective as a tool for comprehending history involves confronting several problems in the structure of organizational experience: (*a*) The paucity of experience problem: Learning from experience in organizations is compromised by the fact that nature provides inadequate experience relative to the complexities and instabilities of history, particularly when the environment is changing rapidly or involves many dangers or opportunities each of which is very unlikely. (*b*) The redundancy of experience problem: Ordinary learning tends to lead to stability in routines, to extinguish the experimentation that is required to make a learning process effective. (*c*) The complexity of experience problem: Organizational environments involve complicated causal systems, as well as interactions among learning organizations. The various parts of the ecology fit together to produce learning outcomes that are hard to interpret.

Improving the Structure of Experience

The problems of paucity, redundancy, and complexity in experience cannot be eliminated, but they can be ameliorated. One response to the paucity of experience is the augmentation of direct experience through the diffusion of routines. Diffusion increases the amount of experience from which an organization draws and reduces vulnerability to local optima. However, the sharing of experience through diffusion can lead to remarkably incomplete or flawed understandings. For example, if the experiences that are combined are not independent, the advantages of sharing are attenuated, and organizations are prone to exaggerate the experience base of the encoded information. Indeed, part of what each organization learns from others is likely to be an echo of its own previous knowledge (Anderson 1848).

Patience is a virtue. There is considerable evidence that organizations often change through a sequence of small, frequent changes and inferences formed from experience with them (Zald 1970). Since frequent changes accentuate the sample size problem by modifying a situation before it can be comprehended, such behavior is likely to lead to random drift rather than improvement (Lounamaa & March 1987). Reducing the frequency or magnitude of change, therefore, is often an aid to comprehension, though the benefits of added information about one situation are purchased at a cost of reduction in information about others (Levinthal & Yao 1988).

The sample size problem is particularly acute in learning from low probability, high consequence events. Not only is the number of occurrences small, but the organizational, political, and legal significance of the events, if they occur, often muddies the making of inferences about them with conflict over formal responsibility, accountability, and liability. One strategy for moderating the effects of these problems is to supplement history by creating hypothetical histories of events that might have occurred (Tamuz 1987). Such histories draw on a richer, less politically polarized set of interpretations, but they introduce error inherent in their hypothetical nature.

Difficulties in overcoming the redundancy of experience and assuring adequate variety of experience is a familiar theme for students of organizational change (Tushman & Romanelli 1985). Organizational slack facilitates unintentional innovation (March 1981), and success provides self-confidence in managers that leads to risk-taking (March & Shapira 1987); but in most other ways success is the enemy of experimentation (Maidique & Zirger 1985). Thus, concern for increasing experimentation in organizations focuses attention on mechanisms that produce variations in the failure rate, preferably independent of the performance level. One mechanism is noise in the measurement of performance. Random error or confusion in performance measurement produces arbitrary experiences of failure without a change in (real) performance (Hedberg & Jonsson 1978). A second mechanism is aspiration level adjustment. An aspiration level that tracks past performance (but not too closely) produces a failure rate-thus a level of search and risk taking-that is relatively constant regardless of the absolute level of performance (March 1988).

A second source of experimentation in learning comes from imperfect routine-maintenance—failures of memory, socialization, or control. Incomplete socialization of new organizational members leads to experimentation, as do errors in execution of routines or failures of implementation (Pressman & Wildavsky 1973). Although it seems axiomatic that most new ideas are bad ones (Hall 1976), the ideology of management and managerial experience combine to make managers a source of experimentation. Leaders are exhorted to introduce change; they are supposed to make a difference (MacCrimmon & Wehrung 1986). At the same time, individuals who have been successful in the past are systematically more likely to reach top level positions in organizations than are individuals who have not. Their experience gives them an exaggerated confidence in the chances of success from experimentation and risk taking (March & Shapira 1987).

Overcoming the worst effects of complexity in experience involves improving the experimental design of natural experience. In particular, it involves making large changes rather than small ones and avoiding multiple simultaneous changes (Miller & Friesen 1982, Lounamaa & March 1987). From this point of view, the standard version of incrementalism with its emphasis on frequent, multiple, small changes cannot be, in general, a good learning strategy, particularly since it also violates the patience imperative discussed above (Starbuck 1983). Nor, as we have suggested earlier, is it obvious that fast, precise learning is guaranteed to produce superior performance. Learning that is somewhat slow and somewhat imprecise often provides an advantage (Levinthal & March 1981, Herriott et al 1985).

The Intelligence of Learning

The concept of intelligence is ambiguous when action and learning occur simultaneously at several nested levels of a system (March 1987). For example, since experimentation often benefits those who copy successes more than it does the experimenting organization, managerial illusions of control, risk taking, and playful experimentation may be more intelligent from the point of view of a community of organizations than from the point of view of organizations that experiment. Although legal arrangements, such as patent laws, attempt to reserve certain benefits of experimentation to those organizations that incur the costs, these complications seem, in general, not to be resolved by explicit contracts but through sets of evolved practices that implicitly balance the concerns of the several levels (March 1981). The issues involved are closely related to similar issues that arise in variation and selection models (Holland 1975, Gould 1982).

Even within a single organization, there are severe limitations to organizational learning as an instrument of intelligence. Learning does not always lead to intelligent behavior. The same processes that yield experiential wisdom produce superstitious learning, competency traps, and erroneous inferences. Problems in learning from experience stem partly from inadequacies of human cognitive habits, partly from features of organization, partly from characteristics of the structure of experience. There are strategies for ameliorating some of those problems, but ordinary organizational practices do not always generate behavior that conforms to such strategies.

The pessimism of such a description must, however, be qualified by two caveats. First, there is adequate evidence that the lessons of history as encoded in routines are an important basis for the intelligence of organizations. Despite the problems, organizations learn. Second, learning needs to be compared with other serious alternatives, not with an ideal of perfection. Processes of choice, bargaining, and selection also make mistakes. If we calibrate the imperfections of learning by the imperfections of its competitors, it is possible to see a role for routine-based, history-dependent, target-oriented organizational learning. To be effective, however, the design of learning organizations must recognize the difficulties of the process and in particular the extent to which intelligence in learning is often frustrated, and the extent to which the comprehension of history may involve slow rather than fast adaptation, imprecise rather than precise responses to experience, and abrupt rather than incremental changes.

REFERENCES

Anderson, H. C. 1848. Det er ganske vist. In *H. C. Andersens Eventyr*, ed. P. Høybe, pp. 72–75. Copenhagen: Forlaget Notabene

Argote, L., Beckman, S., Epple, D. 1987. The persistence and transfer of learning in industrial settings. Paper presented at the St. Louis meetings of the Institute of Management Sciences (TIMS) and the Operations Research Society of America (ORSA)

Argyris, C., & Schön, D. 1978. *Organizational Learning*. Reading, MA: Addison-Wesley

Arthur, W. B. 1984. Competing technologies and economic prediction. *IIASA Options* 2:10–13

Asher, H. 1956. *Cost-Quantity Relationships in the Airframe Industry*. Santa Monica, CA: Rand

Astley, W. G. 1985. The two ecologies: population and community perspectives on organizational evolution. *Admin. Sci. Q.* 30:224–41

Barley, S. R. 1988. The social construction of a machine: ritual, superstition, magical thinking and other pragmatic responses to running a CT Scanner. In *Knowledge and Practice in Medicine: Social Cultural and Historical Approaches,* ed. M. Lock, D. Gordon. Hingham, MA: Reidel. In press

Becker, H. S. 1982. *Art Worlds*. Berkeley, CA: Univ. Calif. Press

Beyer, J. M. 1981. Ideologies, values, and decision making in organizations. See Nystrom & Starbuck 1981, 2:166–202

Biggart, N. W. 1977. The creative-destructive process of organizational change: the case of the post office. *Admin. Sci. Q.* 22:410–26

Brehmer, B. 1980. In one word: not from experience. *Acta Psychol.* 45:223–41

Brown, R. H. 1978. Bureaucracy as praxis: toward a political phenomenology of formal organizations. *Admin. Sci. Q.* 23:365–82

Brunsson, N. 1985. *The Irrational Organization: Irrationality as a Basis for Organizational Action and Change*. Chichester, UK: Wiley

Brytting, T. 1986. The management of distance in antiguity. *Scand. J. Mgmt. Stud.* 3:139–55

Burchell, S., Colin, C., Hopwood, A. G. 1985. Accounting in its social context: towards a history of value added in the United Kingdom. *Account. Organ. Soc.,* 10:381–413

Burgelman, R. A. 1988. Strategy-making as a social learning process: the case of internal corporate venturing. *Interfaces* 18:In press

Cangelosi, V. E., Dill, W. R. 1965. Organizational learning: observations toward a theory. *Admin. Sci. Q.* 10:175–203

Carroll, G. R. 1984. Organizational ecology. *Ann. Rev. Sociol.* 10:71–93

Clark, B. R. 1972. The organizational saga in higher education. *Admin. Sci. Q.* 17:178–84

Cooper, A. C., Schendel, D. E. 1976. Strategic responses to technological threats. *Bus. Horizons* Feb: 19(1):61–63

Cyert, R. M., March, J. G. 1963. *A Behavioral Theory of the Firm*. Englewood Cliffs, NJ: Prentice-Hall

Daft, R. L., Lengel, R. H. 1984. Information richness: a new approach to managerial behavior and organization design. In *Research in Organizational Behavior,* ed. B. M. Staw, L. L. Cummings, 6:191–223. Greenwich, CT: JAI Press

Daft, R. L., Weick, K. E. 1984. Toward a model of organizations as interpretation systems. *Acad. Mgmt. Rev.* 9:284–95

Day, G. S., Montgomery, D. B. 1983. Diagnosing the experience curve. *J. Mark.* 47:44–58

DiMaggio, P. J., Powell, W. W. 1983. The iron cage revisited: institutional isomorphism and collective rationality in organizational fields. *Am. Sociol. Rev.* 48:147–60

Duncan, R., Weiss, A. 1979. Organizational learning: implications for organizational design. In *Research in Organizational Behavior,* ed. B. M. Staw, 1:75–123. Greenwich, CT: JAI Press

Dutton, J. M., Freedman, R. D. 1985. External environment and internal strategies: calculating, experimenting, and imitating in organizations. In *Advances in Strategic Management,* ed. R. B. Lamb 3:39–67. Greenwich, CT: JAI

Dutton, J. M., Starbuck, W. H. 1978. Diffusion of an intellectual technology. In *Communication and Control in Society,* ed. K. Krippendorff, pp. 489–511. New York: Gordon & Breach

Dutton, J. M., Thomas, A. 1984. Treating progress functions as a managerial opportunity. *Acad. Mgmt. Rev.* 9:235–47

Dutton, J. M., Thomas, A. 1985. Relating technological change and learning by doing. In *Research on Technological Innovation, Management and Policy,* ed. R. S. Rosenbloom, 2:187–224. Greenwich, CT: JAI

Dutton, J. M., Thomas, A., Butler, J. E. 1984. The history of progress functions as a managerial technology. *Bus. Hist. Rev.* 58:204–33

Einhorn, E. J., Hogarth, R. M. 1986. Judging probable cause. *Psychol. Bull.* 99:3–19

Engwall, L. 1976. Response time of organizations. *J. Mgmt. Stud.* 13:1–15

Eyre, D. P., Suchman, M. C., Alexander, V. D. 1987. The social construction of weapons procurement: proliferation as rational myth. Pap. pres. Ann. Meet. Am. Sociol. Assoc. Chicago

Fiol, C. M., Lyles, M. A. 1985. Organizational learning. *Acad. Mgmt. Rev.* 10:803–13

Fischhoff, B. 1975. Hindsight or foresight: The effect of outcome knowledge on judgment under uncertainty. *J. Exper. Psychol.* 1:288–99

Fligstein, N. 1985. The spread of the multi-divisional form among large firms, 1919–1979. *Am. Sociol. Rev.* 50:377–91

Fligstein, N. 1987. The intraorganizational power struggle: rise of finance personnel to top leadership in large corporations, 1919–1979. *Am. Sociol. Rev.* 52:44–58

Gould, S. J. 1982. Darwinism and the expansion of evolutionary theory. *Science* 216: 380–87

Grandori, A. 1987. *Perspectives on Organization Theory*. Cambridge, MA: Ballinger Publishing Company

Hagg, I. 1979. Reviews of capital investments: empirical studies. *Finn. J. Bus. Econ.* 28:211–25

Hakansson, H. 1987. *Industrial Technological Development: A Network Approach*. London: Croom Helm

Hall, R. H. 1968. Professionalization and bureaucratization. *Am. Sociol. Rev.* 33:92–104

Hall, R. L 1976. A system pathology of an organization: the rise and fall of the old Saturday Evening Post. *Admin. Sci. Q.* 21:185–211

Hannan, M. T., Freeman, J. 1977. The population ecology of organizations. *Am. J. Sociol.* 82:929–64

Hannan, M. T., Freeman, J. 1984. Structural inertia and organizational change. *Am. Sociol. Rev.* 49:149–64

Harrison, J. R., March, J. G. 1984. Decision making and post-decision surprises. *Admin. Sci. Q.* 29:26–42

Hastie, R., Park, B., Weber, R. 1984. Social memory. In *Handbook of Social Cognition,* ed. R. S. Wyer, T. K. Srull, 2:151–212. Hillsdale, NJ: Erlbaum

Hedberg, B. L. T. 1981. How organizations learn and unlearn. See Nystrom & Starbuck 1981, 1:3–27

Hedberg, B. L. T., Jonsson, S. 1978. Designing semi-confusing information systems for organizations in changing environments. *Account. Organ. Soc.* 3:47–64.

Heimer, C. A. 1985a. *Reactive Risk and Rational Action: Managing Moral Hazard in Insurance Contracts.* Berkeley, CA: Univ. Calif. Press

Heimer, C. A. 1985b. Allocating information costs in a negotiated information order: interorganizational constraints on decision making in Norwegian oil insurance. *Admin. Sci. Q.* 30:395–417

Herriott, S. R., Levinthal, D., March, J. G. 1985. Learning from experience in organizations. *Am. Econ. Rev.* 75:298–302

Hilke, J. C., Nelson, P. B. 1987. Caveat innovator: strategic and structural characteristics of new product innovations. *J. Econ. Behav. Organ.* 8:213–29

Holland, J. H. 1975. *Adaptation in Natural and Artificial Systems: An Introductory Analysis with Applications to Biology, Control and Artificial Intelligence.* Ann Arbor, MI: Univ. Mich. Press

Hollander, S. 1965. *The Sources of Increased Efficiency: A Study of DuPont Rayon Manufacturing Plants.* Cambridge, MA: MIT Press

House, R. J., Singh, J. V. 1987. Organizational behavior: some new directions for i/o psychology. *Ann. Rev. Psychol.* 38:669–718

Imai, K., Nonaka, I., Takeuchi, H. 1985. Managing the new product development process: how Japanese companies learn and unlearn. In *The Uneasy Alliance,* ed. K. Clark, R. Hayes, C. Lorentz, pp. 337–75. Boston: Harvard Grad. Sch. Bus.

Johnson, H. T., Kaplan, R. S. 1987. *Relevance Lost: The Rise and Fall of Management Accounting.* Boston, MA: Harvard Bus. Sch. Press

Johnson, M. K., Hasher, L. 1987. Human learning and memory. *Ann. Rev. Psychol.* 38:631–68

Kahneman, D., Slovic, P., Tversky, A., eds. 1982. *Judgment under Uncertainty: Heuristics and Biases.* Cambridge: Cambridge Univ. Press

Kay, N. M. 1979. *The Innovating Firm: A Behavioral Theory of Corporate R&D.* New York: St. Martin's Press

Khandwalla, P. N. 1981. Properties of competing organizations. See Nystrom & Star-buck 1981, 1:409–32

Kimberly, J. R. 1981. Managerial innovation. See Nystrom & Starbuck 1981, 1:84–104

Knoke, D. 1982. The spread of municipal reform: temporal, spatial, and social dynamics. *Am. J. Sociol.* 87:1314–39

Krieger, S. 1979. *Hip Capitalism.* Beverly Hills, CA: Sage

Lant, T. K. 1987. *Goals, search, and risk taking in strategic decision making.* PhD thesis. Stanford Univ.

Levinthal, D. A., March, J. G. 1981. A model of adaptive organizational search. *J. Econ. Behav. Organ.* 2:307–33

Levinthal, D. A., Yao, D. A. 1988. The search for excellence: organizational inertia and adaptation. *Unpubl. ms.* Carnegie-Mellon Univ. In press

Levy, J. S. 1986. Organizational routines and the causes of war. *Int. Stud. Q.* 30:193–222

Lindblom, C. E. 1959. The "science" of muddling through. *Public Admin. Rev.* 19:79–88

Lounamaa, P. H., March, J. G. 1987. Adaptive coordination of a learning team. *Mgmt. Sci.* 33:107–23

Machina, M. J. 1987. Choice under uncertainty: problems solved and unsolved. *J. Econ. Perspect.* 1:121–54

MacCrimmon, K. R., Wehrung, D. A. 1986. *Taking Risks: The Management of Uncertainty.* New York: Free Press

MacRae, D. 1985. *Policy Indicators.* Chapel Hill, NC: Univ. North Carolina Press

Maidique, M. A., Zirger, B. J. 1985. The new product learning cycle. *Res. Policy* 14:299–313

Mansfield, E. 1968. *The Economics of Technological Change.* New York: Norton

March, J. G. 1981. Footnotes to organizational change. *Admin. Sci. Q.* 26:563–77

March, J. G. 1987. Ambiguity and accounting: the elusive link between information and decision making. *Account. Organ. Soc.* 12:153–68

March, J. G. 1988. Variable risk preferences and adaptive aspirations. *J. Econ. Behav. Organ.* 9:5–24

March, J. G., Olsen, J. P. 1975. The uncertainty of the past: organizational learning under ambiguity. *Eur. J. Polit. Res.* 3:147–71

March, J. G., Shapira, Z. 1987. Managerial perspectives on risk and risk taking. *Mgmt. Sci.* 33:1404–18

Martin, J., Siehl, C. 1983. Organizational culture and counterculture: an uneasy symbiosis *Organ. Dynam.* Autumn:52–64

Martin, J., Sitkin, S. B., Boehm, M. 1985. Founders and the elusiveness of a culture legacy. In *Organi-zational Culture,* ed. P. J. Frost, L. F. Moore, M. R. Louis, C. C. Lundberg, J. Martin, pp. 99–124. Beverly Hills, CA: Sage.

Mazmanian, D. A., Nienaber, J. 1979. *Can Organizations Change? Environmental Protection, Citizen Participation, and the Corps of Engineers.* Washington, DC: The Brookings Inst.

Merton, R. K. 1940. Bureaucratic structure and personality. *Soc. Forces* 18:560–68

Meyer, J. W., Rowan, B. 1977. Institutionalized organizations: formal structure as myth and ceremony. *Am. J. Sociol.* 83:340–63

Mezias, S. J. 1987. *Technical and Institutional Sources of Organizational Practices: The Case of a Financial Reporting Method.* PhD thesis. Stanford Univ.

Miller, D. T., Ross, M. 1975. Self-serving biases in the attribution of causality. *Psychol. Bull.* 82:213–25

Miller, D., Friesen, P. 1982. Structural change and performance: quantum vs. piecemeal-incremental approaches. *Acad. Mgmt. J.* 25:867–92

Moore, M. H., Gates, M. J. 1986. *Inspector-General: Junkyard Dogs or Man's Best Friend?* New York: Russell Sage Found.

Muth, J. F. 1986. Search theory and the manufacturing progress function. *Mgmt. Sci.* 32:948–62

Nelson, R. R., Winter, S. G. 1982. *An Evolutionary Theory of Economic Change.* Cambridge, MA: Harvard Univ.

Neustadt, R. E., May, E. R. 1986. *Thinking in Time: The Uses of History for Decision Makers.* New York, NY: Free Press

Nystrom, N. C., Starbuck, W. H., eds. 1981. *Handbook of Organizational Design.* Oxford: Oxford Univ. Press

Nystrom, N. C., Starbuck, W. H. 1984. To avoid organizational crisis, unlearn. *Organ. Dynam.* Spring:53–65

Olsen, J. P. 1976. The process of interpreting organizational history. In *Ambiguity and Choice in Organizations,* ed. J. G. March, J. P. Olsen, pp. 338–50. Bergen, Norway: Universitetsforlaget

Olsen, J. P. 1983. *Organized Democracy.* Bergen, Norway: Universitetsforlaget

Ouchi, W. G. 1980. Markets, bureaucracies and clans. *Admin. Sci. Q.* 25:129–41

Pettigrew, A. M. 1985. *The Awakening Giant: Continuity and Change in Imperial Chemical Industries.* Oxford: Blackwell

Pfeffer, J. 1981. *Power in Organizations.* Marshfield, MA: Pitman

Powell, W. W. 1986. How the past informs the present: the uses and liabilities of organizational memory. Paper read at the Conference on Communication and Collective Memory, Annenberg School, University of Southern California.

Pressman, J. L., Wildavsky, A. B. 1973. *Implementation.* Berkeley: Univ. Calif. Press

Preston, L., Keachie, E. C. 1964. Cost functions and progress functions: an integration. *Am. Econ. Rev.* 54:100–7

Radner, R. 1975. A behavioral model of cost reduction. *Bell J. Econ.* 6:196–215

Rapping, L. 1965. Learning and World War II production functions. *Rev. Econ. Stat.* 47:81–86

Rogers, E. M., Shoemaker, F. F. 1971. *Communication of Innovations.* New York: Free Press

Rosenberg, N. 1982. *Inside the Black Box: Technology and Economics.* Cambridge: Cambridge Univ. Press

Ross, J., Staw, B. M. 1986. Expo 86: an escalation prototype. *Admin Sci. Q.* 31:274–97

Scott, W. R. 1985. Conflicting levels of rationality: regulators, managers, and professionals in the medical care sector. *J. Health Admin. Educ.* 3:113–31

Scott, W. R. 1987. *Organizations: Rational, Natural, and Open Systems.* Englewood Cliffs, NJ: Prentice-Hall. 2nd ed.

Siegel, S. 1957. Level of aspiration and decision making. *Psychol. Rev.* 64:253–62

Simon, H. A. 1955. A behavioral model of rational choice. *Q. J. Econ.* 69:99–118

Simon, H. A. 1971. Designing organizations for an information rich world. In *Computers, Communications and the Public Interest,* ed. M. Greenberger, pp. 37–52. Baltimore, MD: Johns Hopkins Univ. Press

Sitkin, S. B. 1986. *Secrecy in Organizations: Determinants of Secrecy Behavior among Engineers in Three Silicon Valley Semiconductor Firms.* PhD thesis. Stanford Univ.

Slovic, P., Fischhoff, B., Lichtenstein, S. 1977. Behavioral decision theory. *Ann. Rev. Psychol.* 28:1–39

Smith, H. T., Green, T. R. G., eds. 1980. *Human Interaction with Computers.* New York: Academic

Sproull, L. S. 1981. Beliefs in organizations. See Nystrom & Starbuck 1981, 2:203–24

Sproull, L. S., Weiner, S., Wolf, D. 1978. *Organizing an Anarchy: Belief, Bureaucracy, and Politics in the National Institute of Education.* Chicago, IL: Univ. Chicago Press

Starbuck, W. H. 1983. Organizations as action generators. *Am. Sociol. Rev.* 48:91–102

Starbuck, W. H. 1976. Organizations and their environments. In *Handbook of Industrial and Organizational Psychology,* ed. M. D. Dunnette, pp. 1067–1123. Chicago: Rand McNally

Starbuck, W. H., Dutton, J. M. 1973. Designing adaptive organizations. *J. Bus. Policy* 3:21–28

Starbuck, W. H., Milliken, F. J. 1988. Executives' perceptual filters; what they notice and how they make sense. In *Executive Effect: Concepts and Methods for Studying Top Managers,* ed. D. Hambrick. Greenwich, CT: JAI In press

Staw, B. M., Ross, J. 1978. Commitment to a policy decision: a multi-theoretical perspective. *Admin. Sci. Q.* 23:40–64

Steinbruner, J. D. 1974. *The Cybernetic Theory of Decision.* Princeton, NJ: Princeton Univ. Press

Stinchcombe, A. L. 1986. *Stratification and Organization.* Cambridge: Cambridge Univ. Press

Tamuz, M. 1987. The impact of computer surveillance on air safety reporting. *Columbia J. World Bus.* 22:69–77

Thompson, J. D. 1967. *Organizations in Action.* New York: McGraw-Hill

Tirole, J. 1986. Hierarchies and bureaucracies: on the role of collusion in organizations. *J. Law Econ. Organ.* 2:181–214

Tolbert, P. S., Zucker, L. G. 1983. Institutional sources of change in the format structure of organizations: the diffusion of civil service reform, 1880–1935. *Admin. Sci. Q.* 28:22–39

Tushman, M. L., Romanelli, E. 1985. Organizational evolution: a metamorphosis model of convergence and reorientation. In *Research in Organizational Behavior,* ed. L. L. Cummings, B. M. Staw, 7:171–222. Greenwich, CT: JAI Press

Van Maanen, J. 1973. Observations on the making of policemen. *Hum. Organ.* 32:407–18

Weick, K. E. 1979. *The Social Psychology of Organizing.* Reading, MA: Addison Wesley. 2nd ed.

Whetten, D. A. 1987. Organizational growth and decline processes. *Ann. Rev. Sociol.* 13:335–58

Wiewel, W., Hunter, A. 1985. The interorganizational network as a resource: a comparative case study on organizational genesis. *Admin. Sci. Q.* 30:482–96

Wildavsky, A. 1983. Information as an organizational problem. *J. Mgmt. Stud.* 20:29–40

Winter, S. G. 1986. The research program of the behavioral theory of the firm: orthodox critique and evolutionary perspective. In *Handbook of Behavioral Economics,* ed. B. Gilad, S. Kaish, 1:151–87. Greenwich, CT: JAI Press

Wright, T. P. 1936. Factors affecting the cost of airplanes. *J. Aeronautical Sci.* 3:122–28

Yelle, L. E. 1979. The learning curve: historical review and comprehensive survey. *Decision Sci.* 10:302–28

Zald, M. N. 1970. *Organizational Change: The Political Economy of the YMCA.* Chicago, IL: Univ. Chicago Press

Zucker, L. G. 1977. The role of institutionalization in cultural persistence. *Am. Sociol. Rev.* 42:726–43

Zucker, L. G. 1986. Production of trust: institutional sources of economic structure, 1840 to 1920. In *Research in Organizational Behavior,* ed. L. L. Cummings, B. M. Staw, 8:55–111. Greenwich, CT: JAI Press

Zucker, L. G. 1987. Institutional theories of organization. *Ann. Rev. Sociol.* 13:443–64

SOURCE: Levitt, Barbara and James G. March. 1988. "Organizational Learning." *Annual Review of Sociology,* 14:319–40.

52

THE LOCAL AND VARIEGATED NATURE OF LEARNING IN ORGANIZATIONS

A Group-Level Perspective

AMY C. EDMONDSON

INTRODUCTION

The notion of organizational learning has been explored in the management literature for several decades (e.g., March and Simon 1958, Argyris and Schön 1978, de Geus 1988, Hayes et al. 1988, Levitt and March 1988, Stata 1989, Senge 1990, Huber 1991, Schein 1993, Garvin 2000). This interest stems from the premise that success in changing environments requires learning—recognizing a need for change, evaluating new possibilities, and implementing new courses of action. Organizational learning is an encompassing rubric under which researchers have studied, in remarkably varied ways, this fundamental need to adapt and change. Understanding the processes by which organizations learn and how these processes might be better managed is of central importance to management scholars and practitioners alike. This paper takes a group-level perspective to shed light on interpersonal processes that influence organizational learning outcomes.

Organizational learning is defined here as a process of improving organizational actions through better knowledge and understanding (Fiol and Lyles 1985, Garvin 2000). Although the literature includes numerous definitions of organizational learning (e.g., see Edmondson and Moingeon 1998), not all of them encompass change in behavior or action.[1] Learning, more generally, is viewed as an iterative process of action and reflection, in which action is taken, assessed by the actor, and modified to produce desired outcomes (Kolb 1984, Schön 1983, Dewey 1938). Consistent with this general framework, I concur with Garvin (2000) that a useful conception of organizational learning must include change, such that an organization can be said to learn when its actions have been modified as a result of reflection on new knowledge or insight.[2] This definition leaves much about the adaptive learning process in an organization unspecified, such as how new insights are developed and applied, who carries out what learning objectives, and whether different parts of an organization must learn different things for effective learning by the whole organization.

In this paper, I start with the premise that an organization "learns" through actions and interactions that take place between people who are typically situated within smaller groups or teams. Through these subunits making appropriate changes in how they do their work—driven by both team-specific and organizational objectives—an organization maintains its effectiveness in a changing world. Although there is an emergent literature on team learning, we know little about how organizations change, or fail to change, through adaptive processes carried out by teams. To better understand this process, I conducted an intensive study of learning in five different types of teams—top management, middle management, product development, internal services, and production—in a medium-sized manufacturing company.

In the next section, I summarize previous individual- and organizational-level explanations of why organizations fail to adapt effectively, and propose a third, group-level explanation. I then elaborate on a theoretical argument that conceptualizes organizational learning as an aggregation of local action and reflection cycles in teams. This group-level perspective calls attention to the roles of group process and perceptions of interpersonal risk in hindering organizational learning.

LEVELS OF ANALYSIS IN THE ORGANIZATIONAL LEARNING LITERATURE

The organizational learning literature includes both organizational-level and individual-level theories to explain change and resistance to change in complex organizations (Miner and Mezias 1996, Edmondson and Moingeon 1998). These levels of analysis have emphasized different phenomena, giving rise to complementary but disconnected pictures of organizational learning. Organizational-level theories focus on the stabilizing effects of routines, a tendency to execute a limited search, and a preference for current competencies—all shortcomings of the unsystematic trial and error process through which organizations adapt over time (Levitt and March 1988). For example, theorists have argued that organizations favor learning that exploits current capabilities

("exploitation") rather than learning that develops necessary new capabilities through "exploration" (March 1991), and that organizations cling to outmoded identities that thwart adaptive action (Brown and Starkey 2000). Although human cognition is implicated in these adaptation failures, interpersonal mechanisms through which cognitive limitations lead to organizational outcomes are not directly investigated. In contrast, individual-level theories point to the behavior of individuals in organizational contexts as limiting effective organizational change. For example, Argyris and Schön (1978) showed that people hold tacit theories ("theories-in-use") that disable their own and others' learning and tend to favor "single-loop learning" (detecting and correcting error) over "double-loop learning" (analyzing and altering underlying causes of error, such as norms and policies). Individuals' learning gaps are assumed to hinder effective organizational adaptation, without specifying intervening processes through which this occurs. These two perspectives on organizational learning—macro and micro—provide a foundation for a third perspective that investigates learning phenomena at the group level of analysis. A group-level or "meso" approach is inherently integrative, incorporating factors from two or more levels simultaneously (Rousseau and House 1994).

Toward a "Meso" Approach to Organizational Learning

A decade ago, Senge (1990) suggested that teams are the fundamental learning unit in an organization. An increasing amount of work in organizations is carried out by teams (Osterman 1994) and the context for organizational learning—for evaluating the current state and making changes—is often a team. Teams, or work groups,[3] are also important in that individual cognition and behavior—through which organizational learning necessarily occurs—is shaped by social influences, that is, by the attitudes and behaviors of others with whom they closely work (Salancik and Pfeffer 1978, Hackman 1992). The localness of social influence gives rise to subcultures in organizations (Trice and Beyer 1993), and propensity to learn varies across organizational cultures (Schein 1985). Organizational learning is thus likely to be a variegated phenomenon, with potentially dramatic differences in learning approach or learning effectiveness across organizational subunits. For example, Edmondson (1996) found that group-level differences in norms for reporting medication errors in hospitals had the potential to limit organizational learning about how to prevent similar errors in the future. There is little empirical research in the organizational learning literature investigating this variation or exploring how an organization's teams affect its overall learning goals. Thus, the implications of Senge's (1990) proposition that teams are the unit of organizational learning have remained largely undeveloped, with limited empirical research on team learning in real organizations and a lack of theoretical work on how different kinds of teams and team processes affect organizational adaptation.

Existing Research on Team Learning. Team learning has been defined as a process in which a team takes action, obtains and reflects upon feedback, and makes changes to adapt or improve (Edmondson 1999, Argote et al. 2000). This is consistent with the dominant conception of individual learning as cited above.

Recent research in the laboratory and field has established a foundation for understanding organizational learning at this level of analysis, but has made limited connections to organizational outcomes. Laboratory studies of group learning found that stable membership promotes learning and tacit coordination (e.g., Moreland et al. 1998) and showed that teams of management students participating in a computer simulation and acting as top management teams respond to performance feedback by adjusting aspiration levels, much the way individuals do (Lant 1992). In field research, Brown and Duguid (1991) found that organizational work practices are modified in small networks called "communities of practice," by sharing stories and insights in the context of doing work. Although communities of practice are loosely tied networks of common interest rather than formal work groups, this research showed that learning occurs in small collectives within organizations. A small number of detailed case studies highlight the remarkable potential for tacit coordination and adaptive learning in teams (Hutchins 1991, Weick and Roberts 1993). Other field research finds that learning in teams is driven by interpersonal perceptions and concerns,

and that a lack of psychological safety can inhibit experimenting, admitting mistakes, or questioning current team practices (Edmondson 1999).

Even when teams learn effectively, team learning may not translate to organizational learning. Groups often fail to communicate with others in the organization (Ancona and Caldwell 1992), or else they communicate but are unable to convince others in the organization to adopt new ways of working (Roth and Kleiner 2000). Similarly, early research on organizational change found that instituting new work practices in one part of an organization gave rise to "star envy." This is a phenomenon in which other organizational groups' envy of the success and attention earned by those selected for the change effort leads to the others' rejection of the changes, stifling progress (Walton 1975). In this way, learning in organizations often remains local—driven by goals and concerns of individuals and groups rather than serving organizational goals.

LINKING TEAM LEARNING TO ORGANIZATIONAL LEARNING

In this paper, I propose that organizations can fail to carry out essential adaptation due to incomplete reflection and action in teams situated at multiple levels in the organization's hierarchy. As defined above, team learning breaks down when teams fail to reflect on their own actions, or when teams reflect but fail to make changes following reflection. In case of either failure, a team is unlikely to contribute new knowledge or new ways of working that could help its organization succeed in an ambiguous or changing environment.

Why might these failures occur? First, reflection at the group level is a discussion process, and if teams are busy or accustomed to routine (Gersick and Hackman 1990), such reflective discussion may simply not occur. Second, considerable research shows that group discussion that does occur is often ineffective—vulnerable to process failures such as ignoring relevant information not already shared by group members (Stasser 1999) or inappropriate deference to authorities (Janis 1982). These process failures are likely to be exacerbated by a lack of psychological safety, where group members believe that they are at risk if they speak openly (Edmondson 1999). Interpersonal concerns are particularly salient when members engage in evaluative discussion about their team's activities, including evaluation of individual or collective performance. Negative evaluation or criticism that is needed to trigger learning is inherently psychologically threatening (Argyris and Schön 1978), and so it may be difficult for teams to have high-quality reflective discussion about their shortcomings without considerable psychological safety. Third, teams may reflect (well or badly) but fail to implement changes in team activities due to such constraints as inability to break out of routines, or lack of necessary resources or motivation.

In conceptualizing the relationship between team and organizational learning, I also suggest that different teams may serve different learning goals for the organization. Specifically, researchers have long drawn a distinction between two types of learning—exploitation and exploration (March 1991), first- and second-order learning (Lant and Mezias 1992), single- and double-loop learning (Argyris 1982), and Learning I and Learning II (Bateson 1972). The former is characterized by improving existing routines or capabilities and the latter by reframing a situation, developing new capabilities, or solving ambiguous problems. Recent work maintains that no theory of organizational learning is complete without this distinction (Crossan et al. 1999). Following Miner and Mezias (1996), I use the terms *incremental* and *radical* learning to capture this distinction and to develop a model in which organizational learning consists of learning processes within multiple teams, some of which help an organization explore and develop new capabilities while others help to execute and improve existing capabilities. Serving these two goals simultaneously is another way in which organizational learning may be variegated. Finally, I speculate that teams pursuing either learning goal may face challenges to carrying out effective reflection and action.

In summary, the present study uses a group-level lens to explore variation in learning within an organization. I conceptualized team learning as an iterative action-reflection process that serves either an incremental or radical learning goal for the organization. As described above, this conceptualization implies that organizational learning is likely to be *local* (focused on specific organizational tasks),

interpersonal (influenced by individuals' perceptions of the social climate), and *variegated* (non-uniform in both learning and learning goals). The broad questions guiding my investigation were as follows: How does learning occur in organizational work teams? What factors are associated with different patterns of action and reflection in different teams? How is the distinction between radical and incremental learning manifested in a set of organizational teams? In the next section, I describe my research method, followed by a section that presents and discusses qualitative data from a subset of the teams. Finally, I integrate these empirical analyses with the theoretical argument presented above to refine my model of how organizational learning is enabled and hindered by team processes. . . .

IMPLICATIONS FOR ORGANIZATIONAL LEARNING

To summarize the lessons of this study, I draw from my analyses of 12 work teams to suggest new insights for organizational learning theory. By using a group-level lens, I developed a different, but complementary, understanding of the phenomenon of organizational learning than organizational- and individual-level perspectives have previously provided. In this section, I build on the arguments and data presented earlier to elaborate on organizational learning as a process that is local, interpersonal, and variegated.

A Group-Level Perspective on Organizational Learning

First, as predicted, this qualitative study provides suggestive evidence that organizational learning is a variegated phenomenon. Quality and use of collective reflection varied across teams in the same company and industry context, even when teams faced similar tasks. This provides preliminary empirical support for the theoretical argument presented at the outset of this paper. A core argument in this paper is that the collective learning process in an organization is inherently local. The learning process itself necessarily focuses on some bounded task or opportunity, and it occurs through conversations among a limited number of interdependent people. As such, it is subject to variance from group to group. Past

Table 52.1   How Organizational Teams Map to Radical and Incremental Learning Goals

	The Teams			*The Learning Process*	
Type of Team	*Role in Organizational Learning*	*Type of Learning*	*Developing Insight (Reflection)*	*Taking Action (Change/mprovement)*	
Top management team	Diagnosing context, creating strategy and vision, developing and communicating strategy and vision.		Acquire market and competitor information, analyze company product lines and customer perceptions of company, develop strategic options. Assess new projects and changes.	Make tough strategic choices, communicate new strategy, and authorize new development projects.	
		Radical *(Doing new things)*			
Product Development team	Developing new products (to implement strategy and vision).		Listen to customers, diagnose needs, design solutions and options. Integrate customer voice with manufacturing needs and strategic direction.	Experiment with solutions, make choices, deliver designs to manufacturing.	
Middle management team	Execute and continuously improve specific facets of the organization's existing operations.		Self-assess performance in specialized area: based on meeting customer and employee expectations. Assess changes.	Implement changes as needed.	
Internal services team	Deliver and continuously improve services that allow different parts of the organization to coordinate with each other, promoting the effectiveness of the organization as a whole.	Incremental *(Doing things better)*	Deliver services, self-assess current performance, ask others in the organization for feedback, design appropriate changes. Assess changes.	Implement changes as needed.	
Production team	Execute and continuously improve manufacturing and/or delivery of organization's products.		Make products, diagnose quality problems, self-assess current performance, ask others for feedback, propose changes. Assess changes.	Implement changes as needed.	

*The terminology of *radical* and *incremental learning* was used by Miner and Mezias (1996); similar conceptualizations of two types of learning include *second-order* vs. *first-order learning* (Lant and Mezias 1992), and *exploration* vs. *exploitation* (March 1991). *Incremental and radical* effectively communicate the intended distinction in this paper [italics added].

work on organizational learning has not examined the extent or nature of variance in learning within a given organization or considered how this localness may affect an organization's ability to adapt to critical changes in its environment. Thus, one contribution of a group-level perspective is to call attention to variation across work groups within the same organization. In contrast, conceptualizing organizational learning as a process in which an organization as an entity adapts (or fails to adapt) to its environment threatens to obscure the way some groups can learn while others adhere to routine.

Table 52.2   Organizational Effects of Team Learning Failures

Type of Team	Organizational Effects of Breakdown Between Insight and Action	Implications for Organizational Learning
TMT	The organization's ability to respond to changes in the market is severely limited: New strategies are not articulated; other organizational teams are left improving (or doing) activities that are not optimally suited to the new environment.	Inadequate or insufficient exploration of new capabilities to meet changing market needs
PDT	A potential new product is not introduced, or a suboptimal product is introduced. Over time, the performance of the organization suffers from a shortage of timely, high-quality products that serve market needs	
MMT	Business as usual persists. As context changes, organizational performance suffers from failure to adapt ongoing operations accordingly.	
PT	A product or set of products suffers from inadequate quality and cost improvement, potentially harming customer satisfaction or profitability.	Inadequate exploitation of current capabilities—lost opportunities to improve cost, efficiency, or quality.
IST	Efficiency of coordination across organizational subunits suffers, opportunities for individual performance improvement and training on the job are lost.	

A second theoretical contribution is the salience of power and fear in teams and its consequences for collective learning. Previous research has shown that individuals with less power in organizations are particularly concerned about appearing incompetent in front of those with more power and thereby losing access to valued resources and professional rewards (Lee 1997; Winter 1973, 1993). Here, the observation that beliefs about power and psychological safety can disable individuals' willingness to actively and honestly contribute their ideas, evaluations, or suggestions provides new insight into the interpersonal nature of organizational learning that goes beyond defensive theories in use (Argyris 1982). The implications of psychological safety, previously shown to vary significantly across organizational work groups, are that an organization's ability to adapt—to make sound decisions and implement timely changes in response to changes in the environment—can be thwarted by interpersonal processes that take place within the context of smaller groups. In sum, not only do teams differ in psychological safety, these differences can have far-reaching implications for the organization's ability to learn.

Third, not only is the learning process variegated at the group level of analysis, the nature of the learning goal also is nonuniform across teams within an organization. I found that both radical and incremental learning goals were simultaneously addressed in the same organization because of different learning tasks faced by different types of teams. Data analysis further implied that both radical and incremental organizational learning are inhibited by fears about speaking up in one's own team, when team leaders' power over other members is salient. This observation was as salient in the boardroom as on the front lines, and had consequences ranging from the strategic and far reaching to the operational and highly bounded. For example, when interpersonal concerns inhibit learning in a TMT [top management team], the organization may lose an opportunity to pursue radical learning goals that allow it to successfully meet changes in the market. This certainly appeared to be the case in this organization, where the strategy team met for six months without articulating a new strategy. When the same concerns inhibit learning in an IST [internal services team], the organization may suffer from inefficiency in a specific work process, such as computer support or order processing, both of which occurred in the teams studied here.

Organizational learning, from a group-level perspective, is both radical and incremental at the same time. Both are, in fact, essential for effective organizational adaptation. The ability to produce new ideas and capabilities is vital to ongoing competitiveness in a changing world, while the ability to assess changes, modify tasks accordingly, and continue to improve efficiency and quality throughout organizational departments is an important component of reducing costs in a competitive marketplace. Table 52.1 summarized this relationship between team type and learning goal. Specifically, the TMTs and PDTs [product development teams] in this study served radical learning goals for the organization, while MMTs [middle management teams], ISTs and PTs [production teams] focused on incremental learning goals. Table 52.2 showed that a breakdown in the team learning process has different implications depending on the type of team. The TMTs (and to a lesser extent, the PDTs) in this study had the potential to limit the scope of learning activities in which other teams could engage. In this way, incremental learning can be constrained by opportunities created by radical learning.

Limitations

This study was exploratory and its findings are limited in several ways. First, the study sought to develop rather than test theory, and patterns that emerged in the data do not constitute formal tests of the categories identified. Second, although the studied teams varied considerably, they all worked in the same organization and may not reflect variation in teams in other companies, limiting the study's generalizability.

A few observations from the study have strong face validity and suggest directions for future meso-level research on organizational learning. First, the distinction between reflection and action at the group level emerges as helpful to understanding collective learning processes in an organization,

because it allowed a distinction between teams that had the "look" of reflective learning without real change and those who engaged in more complete learning cycles.[4] Second, factors such as leader behavior and task interdependence that were associated with patterns of reflection and action are worth testing systematically in future research. Third, the question of how organizations can balance the need for radical and incremental learning by allocating different learning responsibilities to different teams emerges as an opportunity for future research.

CONCLUSIONS

Organizations are complex systems that carry out a variety of tasks. This paper contributes to long-standing interest in the management literature in how such systems learn—by digging into the details of how people work together to carry out and modify the tasks that together produce and deliver products and services to customers. By focusing on work groups, this study calls attention to certain factors and necessarily ignores others. Most notably, a group-level perspective on organizational learning emphasizes interpersonal perceptions and behaviors. Its lens is squarely focused on interactions among a small number of individuals and how these enhance or inhibit the process of building new knowledge and initiating new action. Team leaders whose behaviors encourage input and discussion, resulting perceptions of psychological safety, and tasks that require interaction all seemed conducive to a healthy cycle of reflection and action that enabled progress on organizational goals. These observations add to—rather than supplant—theories at other levels of analysis.

A group level of analysis in organizational learning, consistent with the meso approach as presented by Rousseau and House (1994), is important in linking individual-level factors such as cognition and behavior to organizational-level outcomes. Individual-level theory identified self-protective cognition as a constraint on learning (Argyris and Schön 1978), and organizational-level theory observed traps and biases that companies fall prey to as entities (Levitt and March 1988). A group-level perspective begins to connect these disparate observations. In the face-to-face setting of the team, individuals make sense of their organization—its interpersonal climate, norms, goals, and how it serves its market. They use this understanding to make implicit decisions about what the organization should do, but also about what can be said and what is better left unsaid in their local work group. These teams—through discussion and task execution—produce outcomes through which their organization designs, produces, and delivers products and services that meet (or fail to meet) customers' needs.

Further, although this study found that some teams learned more than others did, it also produced evidence that a collective learning process can occur naturally, without outside intervention. Half of the teams studied seemed eager and able to reflect, engage new possibilities, and implement improvements that served organizational goals. In this way, the study suggests that an organization can learn—team by team—through many simultaneous and partially overlapping team-learning journeys. It also suggests that much can go wrong in this process. When power differences created perceptions of interpersonal risk, interpretive learning processes gave rise to an enacted goal of self-protection. Ensuring that individual or collective insights or ideas were applied to initiate change or improvement, thus, could not be taken for granted.

This study points to a particular kind of organizational tragedy. It is possible for teams deep within an organization to be learning and taking action with energy and excitement—while at the same time, a TMT is unable to act upon what *its* members know, such that impressive pockets of team learning are limited in their impact on the organization by a lack of effective team learning at the top. Organizational learning can be seen as a process of cascading team learning opportunities, independently carried out, but interdependent in their impact on company performance. The independence of different teams means that teams within the same company can serve either as a safe laboratory in which to experiment or a dangerous proving ground in which interpersonal risks are avoided. Finally, past work noted the need for both radical and incremental learning for ongoing organizational effectiveness, not just the former (March 1991, Miner and Mezias 1996, Edmondson and Moingeon 1996). This study begins

to identify different teams responsible for carrying out these two organizational-learning objectives. Future research has much to gain by investigating the boundary processes between different teams, to better understand how team processes interrelate to produce an integrated organizational-learning response.

NOTES

1. For example, Huber (1991) defines organizational learning as diffusion of information in an organization.

2. Pfeffer and Sutton (2000) note, similarly, that organizational "knowing" does not always translate into organizational "doing," and that knowledge management should only be considered effective if new knowledge is used to produce new action.

3. The terms *work group* and *team* [italics added] are used interchangeably in this paper to refer to groups of individuals that exist within the context of a larger organization, have clearly defined membership, and are responsible for a shared product or service (Alderfer 1987, Hackman 1987).

4. I am indebted to Teresa Lant (1992) for this insight, and for showing me how these teams' reflection was qualitatively different from other teams studied.

REFERENCES

Alderfer, C. P. 1987. An intergroup perspective on organizational behavior. J. W. Lorsch, ed. *Handbook of Organizational Behavior*. Prentice-Hall, Englewood Cliffs, NJ.

Ancona, D. G., D. F. Caldwell. 1992. Bridging the boundary: External activity and performance in organizational teams. *Admin. Sci. Quart.* **37** (4) 634–655.

Argote, L., D. Gruenfeld, C. Naquin. 2000. Group learning in organizations. M. E. Turner, ed. *Groups at Work: Advances in Theory and Research*. Erlbaum, New York.

Argyris, C. 1982. *Reasoning, Learning and Action: Individual and Organizational*. Jossey-Bass, San Francisco, CA.

———, D. Schön, 1978. *Organizational Learning: A Theory of Action Perspective*. Addison-Wesley, Reading, MA.

Bateson, G. 1972. *Steps to an Ecology of Mind*. Chandler, San Francisco, CA.

Brown, A. D., K. Starkey. 2000. Organizational identity and learning: A psychodynamic perspective. *Acad. Management Rev.* **25** (1) 102–120.

Brown, J., P. Duguid. 1991. Organizational learning and communities-of-practice: Toward a unified view of working, learning, and innovation. *Organ. Sci.* **2** (1) 40–57.

Crossan, M. M., H. W. Lane, R. E. White. 1999. An organizational learning framework: From intuition to institution. *Acad. Management Rev.* **24** (3) 522–537.

de Geus, A. P. 1988. Planning as learning. *Harvard Bus. Rev.* **66** (March–April) 70–74.

Dewey, J. 1938. *Logic: The Theory of Inquiry*. Holt, New York.

Edmondson, A. 1996. Three faces of eden: The persistence of competing theories and multiple diagnoses in organizational intervention research. *Human Relations* **49** (5) 571–595.

———. 1999. Psychological safety and learning behavior in work teams. *Admin. Sci. Quart.* **44** 350–383.

———, B. Moingeon. 1996. When to learn how and when to learn why: Appropriate organizational learning processes as a source of competitive advantage. B. Moingeon and A. Edmondson, eds. *Organizational Learning and Competitive Advantage*. Sage Publications, London, U.K.

———, ———. 1998. From organizational learning to the learning organization. *Management Learn.* **29** (1) 5–20.

Fiol, C. M., M. A. Lyles. 1985. Organizational learning. *Acad. Management Rev.* **10** (4) 803–813.

Garvin, D. 2000. *Learning in Action*. Harvard Business School Press, Boston, MA.

Gersick, C. J. G., J. R. Hackman. 1990. Habitual routines in task-performing teams. *Organ. Behavior and Human Decision Processes* **47** (1) 65–97.

Hackman, J. R. 1987. The design of work teams. J. Lorsch, ed. *Handbook of Organizational Behavior*. Prentice-Hall, Englewood Cliffs, NJ.

———. 1992. Group influences on individuals in organizations. M. D. Dunnette and L. M. Hough, eds. *Handbook of Industrial and Organizational Psychology*. Consulting Psychologists Press, Inc., Palo Alto, CA.

Hayes, R. H., S. C. Wheelwright, K. B. Clark. 1988. *Dynamic Manufacturing: Creating the Learning Organization*. The Free Press, London, U.K.

Huber, G. 1991. Organizational learning: The contributing processes and a review of the literature. *Organ. Sci.* **2** (1) 88–115.

Hutchins, E. 1991. Organizing work by adaptation. *Organ. Sci.* **2** (1) 14–39.

Janis, I. L. 1982. *Victims of Groupthink,* 2nd ed. Houghton Mifflin, Boston, MA.

Kolb, D. A. 1984. *Experiential Learning*. Prentice-Hall, Englewood Cliffs, NJ.

Lant, T. K. 1992. Aspiration-level adaptation: An empirical exploration. *Management Sci.* **38** (5) 623–644.

———, S. J. Mezias. 1992. An organizational learning model of convergence and reorientation. *Organ. Sci.* **3** (1) 47–71.

Lee, D. Y. 1997. The impact of poor performance on risk-taking attitudes: A longitudinal study with a PLS causal modeling approach. *Decision Sci.* **28** (1) 59–80.

Levitt, B., J. March. 1988. Organizational learning. *Ann. Rev. Sociology* **14** 319–340.

March, J. G. 1991. Exploration and exploitation in organizational learning. *Organ. Sci.* **2** (2) 71–87.

———, H. A. Simon. 1958. *Organizations*. Wiley, New York.

Miner, A. S., S. J. Mezias. 1996. Ugly duckling no more: Pasts and futures of organizational learning research. *Organ. Sci.* **7** (1) 88–99.

Moreland, R. L., L. Argote, R. Krishnan. 1998. Training people to work in groups. R. S. Tindale and L. Heath, eds. *Theory and Research on Small Groups: Social Psychological Applications to Social Issues*. Plenum Press, New York, 37–60.

Osterman, P. 1994. How common is workplace transformation and who adopts it? *Indust. Labor Relations Rev.* **47** (2) 172–188.

Pfeffer, J., R. I. Sutton. 2000. The knowing-doing gap: How smart companies turn knowledge into action. Harvard Business School Press, Boston, MA.

Roth, G., A. Kleiner. 2000. *Car Launch: The Human Side of Managing Change*. Oxford University Press, New York.

Rousseau, D. M., R. J. House. 1994. Meso-organizational behavior: Avoiding three fundamental biases. *J. Organ. Behavior* **1** (1) 13–30.

Salancik, G., J. Pfeffer. 1978. A social information processing approach to job attitudes and task design. *Admin. Sci. Quart.* **23** 224–253.

Schein, E. 1985. Organizational culture and leadership. Jossey-Bass, San Francisco, CA.

———. 1993. How can organizations learn faster? The challenge of entering the green room. *Sloan Management Rev.* **34** (2) 85–90.

Schön, D. 1983. *The Reflective Practitioner*. Basic Books, New York.

Senge, P. M. 1990. *The Fifth Discipline: The Art and Practice of the Learning Organization*. Doubleday, New York.

Stasser, G. 1999. The uncertain role of unshared information in collective choice. L. Thompson,

J. Levine, and D. Messick, eds. *Shared Cognition in Organizations*. Lawrence Erlbaum Associates, Mahwah, NJ, 49–69.

Stata, R. 1989. Organizational learning: The key to management innovation. *Sloan Management Rev.* **12** (1) 63–74.

Trice, H. M., J. M. Beyer. 1993. *The Cultures of Work Organizations*. Prentice-Hall Inc., Englewood Cliffs, NJ.

Walton, R. E. 1975. The diffusion of new work structures: Explaining why success didn't take. *Organ. Dynamics* **3** (3) 2–22.

Weick, K. E., K. H. Roberts. 1993. Collective mind in organizations: Heedful interrelating on flight decks. *Admin. Sci. Quart.* **38** (3) 357–381.

Winter, D. G. 1973. *The Power Motive*. Free Press, New York.

———. 1993. Power, affiliation, and war: Three tests of a motivational model. *J. Personality and Soc. Psych.* **65** (3) 532–545.

SOURCE: Edmondson, Amy C. 2002. Excerpt from "The Local and Variegated Nature of Learning in Organizations: A Group-Level Perspective." *Organization Science*, 13:128–31, 141–46.

53

PRACTICAL PUSHING

Creating Discursive Space in Organizational Narratives

JOYCE K. FLETCHER, LOTTE BAILYN, AND STACY BLAKE BEARD

For the past ten years a group of action researchers in the Boston area has been using a feminist poststructural lens to do organizational change work (Bailyn 2005; Ely and Meyerson 2000; Fletcher 1999; Fletcher and Bailyn 2005; Fletcher and Rapoport 1996; Kolb and Merrill-Sands 1999; Merrill-Sands *et al.* 1999; Meyerson and Fletcher 2000; Perlow 1997; Rapoport *et al.* 1996; Rapoport *et al.* 2002). The goal of the action research has been to make visible—and discussable—the gendered power dynamic embedded in an organization's discourse so that we can help organizational members disrupt that dynamic, thereby creating discursive space in which new, more equitable possibilities might surface. Two of the co-authors of this chapter, Joyce K. Fletcher and Lotte Bailyn, were founding members of this group and the third, Stacy Blake Beard, has joined more recently. In this chapter, we give an overview of the approach we use, summarize some of our findings and share what we have learned about the practical application of a poststructural diagnosis and critique.

WHAT DO WE MEAN BY A FEMINIST POSTSTRUCTURAL LENS?

What underlies our method is an acknowledgement of the relationship between knowledge, power and discourse (Alvesson and Deetz 1996; Lukes 1974). It starts from the premise that some voices in the discourse are heard and counted as knowledge, while others are silenced, marginalized or excluded (Clegg 1989; Foucault 1980; Nicholson 1990). Our approach gives voice to (at least) one of these marginalized perspectives and brings it into the mainstream. The goal is to disrupt the status quo and call attention to the systems of power that account for a group's marginal status. We think of ourselves as feminist poststructuralists because we adopt poststructural principles but with a specific focus on the gendered nature of knowledge production and the way it maintains and reinforces the power relationships between the sexes (Calás and Smircich 1992; Diamond and Quinby 1988; Jacobsen and Jacques 1997; Weedon 1987). Thus, feminist poststructuralism adds a particular marginalized voice to organizational discourse (women's voice) and by so doing, seeks to disrupt a particular system of power (patriarchy).

While poststructuralist inquiry has many distinguishing characteristics, the most relevant to our approach are (1) its perspective on the relationship between power and knowledge, (2) its emphasis on the role of language and other forms of representation in constructing experience and (3) its concept of resistance.

Power and Knowledge

Unlike other perspectives that assume that facts speak for themselves, the poststructural perspectives cited above see the production of knowledge as an exercise of power where only some voices are heard and only some experience is counted as knowledge. Poststructuralists challenge the notion of transcendent or universalizing truth and assert that the set of rules used to determine if something is 'true' or 'false' is not value free but is instead ideologically determined. The goal of poststructuralist inquiry is to disrupt the relationship between power and knowledge by bringing 'subversive stories' into the discourse (Ewick and Silbey 1995). The strength of adding a marginalized voice to the discourse is that it forces recognition of the arbitrary nature of what is considered true. The goal is to offer the dominant group an opportunity to question these truths, or at least to consider that they are not universal.

Language and the Social Construction of Experience

Another key feature of poststructuralist inquiry is its emphasis on the role that language and other forms of representation play in mediating the relationship between power and knowledge (Fairclough 1989). This perspective considers social reality—and its pattern of dominancy—not as a given, but as something that is constructed through the process of representing experience. Thus, language not only reflects a certain reality, it also actively creates that reality and sustains the power relationships that are embedded in it. From a poststructuralist perspective, then, textual and material representations are never neutral but are instead powerful means of constructing an ideological worldview that furthers the interest of some dominant group.

Resistance

Resistance, the third key feature of poststructuralism, refers to the process of disrupting, or resisting, the unobtrusive exercise of power that occurs in the process of representing experience (Clegg 1989; Collinson 1994; Flax 1990). The goal of the action research is to create 'discursive space,' where new ways of thinking can surface and dominant meanings can be resisted. Creating discursive space means offering an alternative interpretation of reality that relaxes taken-for-granted assumptions, thereby creating a place where new things can be said and new social structures envisioned.

Putting our action research methodology in the language of this perspective, we can describe it as an effort to destabilize the definition of work in organizational discourse by telling a feminist subversive story. The goal is to call attention to the masculine nature of the truth rules and knowledge production processes that create seemingly commonsense definitions of concepts like work, competence and skill in organizations. In our work with organizations, we uncover and give voice to a feminist alternative that has been silenced or obscured. We add this voice to the discourse, thereby momentarily relaxing taken-for-granted assumptions about the nature of work, creating discursive space in which new, less masculine ways of thinking about work, competence and leadership skills might be considered.

WHAT DO WE DO?

The 'Dual Agenda'[1]

Our stated goal is to look at an organization's work culture to identify routine, everyday work practices as well as assumptions about competence and leadership that are both a barrier to women's advancement AND a barrier to work effectiveness. We use the term 'dual agenda' to describe the goal of the change effort, because we want to make clear how our approach differs from others. Indeed, organizations usually contact us because they have tried more traditional approaches (for example, work–family policies, hiring and recruiting guide-lines, sensitivity training) which have not yielded the hoped-for results. Linking equity and effective-ness is a way of operationalizing the goal of creating discursive space in which new ways of doing work might surface. Focusing on work practices that have effectiveness as well as equity implications relaxes the adversarial positioning of marginalized versus dominant perspectives, and also engages a broader constituency. This bringing together of equity and effectiveness is what makes our approach different, even though the steps in our process are similar to those of any change effort: formation of an internal advisory group, data collection, data analysis, feed-back and action planning.

Development of an Internal Advisory Group

Once an organization contracts with us to work with them, the first step is to create an internal advisory group. This group, which is typically small in size, becomes our internal partner in the interven-tion process. We work collaboratively with them to determine the direction of the work—including interview questions and suggestions for participants in the data collection phase. From a logistical per-spective, we need a group that is large enough to represent multiple perspectives in the organization, yet small enough to work together with a measure of flexibility and closeness. Finally, the internal advi-sory group provides a sounding board to interpret the information that we gather in the data collection phase. This group has the potential to become the agents of ongoing organizational change as well as carriers of an alternative narrative about barriers to women's advancement.

Data Collection

The second step in our process is data collection. In this phase, we interview a range of employees to understand the discourse of success, leadership and work used in this particular organization. We inter-view across levels and where appropriate, across functions. It is also important to have both men and women in different family structures. The purpose is not only to collect data about the work culture and the narrative used to describe it, but also to

begin the change process itself. Often, interviewees are surprised to hear the nature of our questions. Their understanding of why we have been brought in is often limited, and because 'gender equity' is in the title, they expect to be asked only about bias and barriers. Instead, we ask questions in three broad areas: work culture (for example, about how work gets done, what it takes to be—and to be seen as—successful, and about what types of behaviour get rewarded); women' advancement (for example, personal explanations about why women are not advancing as fast as expected, advice you would give women, advice you would give the organiza-tion), and third, the strategic challenges facing the organization or unit. Reflecting on these three areas in one interview begins to connect the three organi-zational narratives about these issues and is a critical part of the change initiative. More specifically, it is a way of advancing another of the goals of feminist poststructuralist critique, which is to surface the role of language in mediating the relationship between power and knowledge and to momentarily disrupt it.

Analysis

The third step is data analysis. We are looking for themes and patterns in the data about work culture that will allow us to name three or four underlying assumptions about success in that orga-nization that have an impact both on work effec-tiveness and on women's advancement. It is in this step of the process that our feminist poststructural-ist lens is most apparent. The heroic myths, the lan-guage used, the way women are positioned in the stories people tell, help us identify the particular assumptions about work that are likely to have the greatest impact. Our data analysis begins with each of us reflecting (individually and before meeting) on how to fill the blank in the following sentence: 'People at X work as if (blank) is true.' The goal is to build a narrative about what constitutes truth about success and effectiveness in this organiza-tion. When we meet we share our reflections and begin to think about what we call the 'unintended consequences' of these assumptions on women's advancement (equity) and on the business (effective-ness). We choose (at least) three assumptions that have the clearest power–knowledge connection and brainstorm phrases that use organization-specific language to describe them.

Feedback as Intervention

After preliminary analysis, we begin the feedback process. The presentation of the findings is an important step in the intervention process because it is the place in which a new narrative—and new language to represent the experience of a subset of the organization's members—can begin to emerge. We first present our findings in rough, draft form to the internal advisory group, using quotes from interviews to illustrate. The goal is an extensive, interactive session where it is clear that we are seeking their feedback and are interested in their experience of the aspects of the culture we have observed. Often the session feels less like feedback and more like a deeper discussion of the phenomenon. Indeed, the reaction of this group generates important new data about the culture.

Key to our methodology is our way of presenting these findings to organizational members so that they hear the poststructural critique as actionable and practical rather than theoretical and abstract. For each cultural assumption we offer five observations. First we name and describe the assumption using language, examples and quotes from the interviews. Second we name the intended effect of the assumption, that is, why it is there ant the useful function it serves or served. Third, we name the unintended consequences for women, that is, why this cultural assumption might make it more difficult for women to advance. Fourth, we name the potential unintended consequences of this assumption on the work itself. And finally, we offer a sample of suggestions for ways to interrupt the norm and relax its grip on work practices. Identifying leverage points for change is a way of articulating concrete, specific acts of resistance to the dominant discourse. We make it clear in this part of the feedback that the group will have much more input during the discussion on leverage points for change, and that our observations are meant only as examples.

After a general discussion of the feedback, we engage participants in what we think of as a process to identify opportunities to interrupt and resist power dynamics embedded in the status quo. To operationalize it in a work setting, however, we entitle the exercise 'identifying leverage points for change' and break people into small groups to discuss and brainstorm ideas. We find that organizing the groups by function, discipline or, if possible, in actual working teams is useful. We ask them to choose the cultural assumption they believe has the most serious consequences for their particular area and then discuss two questions:

- What are the dysfunctional work practices related to this assumption?
- If we wanted to relax its hold, what could we do? (Ideas must be specific, concrete, and actionable.)

Below is a sample of one cultural assumption with its five feedback components, drawn from an organizational diagnosis of a high-tech firm. Our organizational example is drawn from a firm that prides itself on its cutting-edge research and rigorously trained scientists and technicians. Although the firm has a reputation as a good place for women to work (high salaries, autonomy and flexible work), senior management was aware that they had difficulty moving women into the highest scientific ranks. They did not regard this as a serious problem because they accepted the conventional wisdom that the reason was not systemic but had to do with the individual choices women made. But when approached by members of a women's network within the firm requesting a cultural analysis to determine if there were systemic reasons in addition to individual ones, they agreed to fund our consultation.

The four 'dual agenda' cultural assumptions we identified were:

- Leadership will seek you.
- We know smart when we see it.
- Technical competence is key.
- You sink or swim on your own.

To illustrate the feedback process, we detail the observations about one of these cultural assumptions: Leadership will seek you.

Naming the Norm

Leadership will seek you means that there is a belief that truly gifted employees don't seek leadership. They just work hard and excel, and leadership seeks them. Perceptions of leadership potential are enhanced by not being overly concerned about leadership or career progression.

Purpose of the Norm

At its best, this norm encourages employees to focus on the work and what is best for the company, not on what is best for 'me.' This norm also exemplifies the best of what we hope to see in a meritocracy—it suggests that hard work is the best determiner of career advancement, not politics or other considerations.

Unintended Consequences for Women

First, being noticed and assessed as a high-potential contributor is a subjective process highly dependent on what excellence and hard work 'look like.' For those whose social identity does not fit the mould, it is less likely that leadership will seek them. In this case, because women do not fit the traditional image of a senior scientist, they are less likely to be recognized and tapped for leadership opportunities and development. Second, having one's competence recognized means being in the right place at the right time. In this organization, that means being invited to informal brainstorming meetings on new technology. Conveners or these groups note that they do not intentionally come to mind. Thus, if women want to be included they need to 'make the ask.' But the belief that accomplishment speaks for itself puts women in a double bind. If they ask, they are calling attention to themselves in a way that is inappropriate to the culture. If they do not ask, they 'do not come to mind.'

A third aspect of the norm has to do with reluctance. In a culture where a mark of leadership potential is indifference to hierarchy and position, it is common for those who are tapped to disavow interest. But this disavowal is perceived differently based on sex. Reluctance in women is often met with acceptance. Her reluctance fits with conventional wisdom that women opt out, are not comfortable with power or not willing to make the sacrifices needed to lead effectively. Reluctance in men is often met with persuasion, encouragement and expressions of confidence in their potential.

Unintended Consequences for Business

Consequences are not limited to women. Undoubtedly there are men who do not fit the senior scientist mould and therefore do not fit the image of leader in this organization. So the organization is missing opportunities to develop and fully tap into the human resource potential of women *and* men who are not visible because they do not fit preconceived notions of who will succeed and be effective leaders.

Allowing old images of leadership and competence to dictate who is chosen does not take into account new demands and the changing nature of work at the company. Leaders have historically come from the same functional area. This practice may have been appropriate in the past but given the strategic challenges mentioned in the interviews, is this the best way to identify leaders in the future?

Possible Leverage Points for Change: Small Wins

- Develop guidelines for selection of 'brainstorming meeting' participants.
- Set up an organization-wide workshop to discuss leadership qualities for the future.
- Create a succession planning process.
- Create processes to deal with 'reluctant leadership.'

In the exercise described above, the general discussion on small wins yielded two concrete suggestions. The first was that they make the issue of how people are selected for brainstorming groups an object of discussion at a senior scientist meeting. Part of this discussion would include a suggestion that someone in the group pulling together a brainstorming meeting take up what they called a 'conscience-role.' The task would be to help the group reflect on the list of invitees and raise the possibility that they have selected a group who looks just like them. The conscience person would say something like, 'As the informal "conscience person" I want to ask: Are there skill sets missing? Are there people who "don't come to mind" but who would if we thought about it a little more?' Although done half-jokingly, it was thought that this type of intervention would be enough to begin to change to norm and get people to be more reflective about their choices.

The second suggestion was to establish what the organization called a 'fourth frame' mentoring programme. Fourth frame refers to a framework for thinking about ways of addressing gender equity.[2] Fourth frame approaches deal with systemic, cultural issues rather than focusing on women and their individual characteristics of deficiencies. A fourth frame mentoring programme puts in place institutional supports to help mentors push back on system factors that might inhibit protégé career advancement.

We have found that brainstorming exercises such as this operationalize the notion of resistance by engaging in discussion of concrete actions that could interrupt the status quo. Many ideas surface in these discussions. Although only one or two gain support and proceed to an action planning stage at an organizational level, we have found that individuals themselves often incorporate many of the original ideas in their work patterns (Kolb and Merrill-Sands 1999).

WHAT WE HAVE LEARNED ABOUT THIS METHOD

We believe that this method is a powerful way of challenging organizational norms. There are limits and challenges in the approach, however, and we briefly mention them here and summarize them in Table 53.1.

First, we have learned that the particular change is less important than the process of getting there and that this process requires time. That is, the thing is not the thing. For example, in one organization where we introduced a reallocation of activities during the day, the intervention worked well in that unit, but when another unit tried it, it failed.[3] It is the process described above—not the particular intervention—that creates change.

We also found that naming assumptions begins to change the organizational narrative in important ways and is a key part of the intervention. Surfacing an alternative story about organizational norms and their consequences creates a tool to continue the change process. For example, we found that people used the shorthand phrases to interrupt organizational routines, asking questions such as 'are we acting like leadership will seek you?' This attention to language allows the change effort to stay connected to the diagnosis, and is a way people can carry the message with them during their day-to-day activities. Such 'seed carriers' can be powerful agents of change.[4]

Finally, we discovered that it is not always easy to keep both equity and effectiveness on the table at the same time. For example, on one surgical ward the change introduced was to allow nurses to self-schedule within the constraints of the needs of the ward. This recommendation required a collective commitment to meet all the staff requirements while having the flexibility of some choice. Unfortunately, nurses began instead to see this opportunity as an individual entitlement and the experiment had to be stopped, even though they felt that it had helped their lives and their ability to give good care to their patients.[5] Systemic change needs to be collective, but there is a powerful tendency to translate everything into individual terms and counteracting this tendency is a serious challenge.

Table 53.1 Learnings and challenges

Learning	Challenge
The thing is not the thing.	Sustainability: process requires time and long-term orientation to change.
Changing the narrative is key.	Naming the assumptions succinctly so they can be used to challenge the status quo.
'Seed carriers' can be a powerful force for change.	Empowering individuals to foster collective, systemic-level change.
Effectiveness and equity must remain linked and equally valued.	Establishing a way to re-link effectiveness and equity should one begin to dominate.

CONCLUSION

One of the common critiques of poststructural inquiry into organizational systems is that it is not actionable. We have experience that suggests otherwise. And while the organizations we have worked with might not recognize the language of power and resistance we use to describe our approach to the audience of this book, their members would, we believe, attest to the way in which a diagnosis such as we describe here has opened up new avenues for change in work practices and routines that have long gone unquestioned.

NOTES

1. See also Rapoport et al. (2002) and Bailyn and Fletcher (2007).
2. For a description of the four frames see Kolb et al. (1998).
3. See Perlow (1997) for a full description.
4. For an analysis of organizational catalysts see Sturm (2006).
5. For a full description of this example see Bailyn, Collins and Song (2007).

REFERENCES

Alvesson, M. and S. Deetz (1996), 'Critical theory and postmodernism approaches to organizational studies,' in S. Clegg, C. Hardy and W. Nord (eds), *Handbook of Organization Studies*, London: Sage, pp. 191–217.

Bailyn, L. (2005), 'Filling the gap by redesigning work,' in S.M. Bianchi, L.M. Caspar and R.B. King (eds), *Workforce/Workplace Mismatch: Work, Family, Health and Well-being*, Mahwah, NJ: Erlbaum.

Bailyn, L. and J.K. Fletcher (2007), 'Collaborative interaction research, sloan work and family research network,' Boston College, available at: http://wfnetwork.bc.edu/encyclopedia_entry.php?id=6386&area=academics.

Bailyn, L., R. Collins and Y. Song (2007), 'Self-scheduling for hospital nurses: An attempt and its difficulties,' *Journal of Nursing Management*, **15**(1), 72–77.

Calás, M. and L. Smircich (1992), 'Rewriting gender in organization theory,' in M. Read and M. Hughes (eds), *Rethinking Organizations*, London: Sage, pp. 227–253.

Clegg, S. (1989), *Frameworks of Power*, Newbury Park, CA: Sage.

Collinson, D. (1994), 'Strategies of resistance: Power, knowledge and subjectivity in the workplace,' in J. M. Jermier, D. Knights and W. Nord (eds), *Resistance and Power in Organizations*, London: Routledge, pp. 25–69.

Diamond, I. and L. Quinby (1988), *Feminism and Foucault*, Boston, MA: Northeastern University Press.

Ely, R.J. and D.E. Meyerson (2000), 'Advancing gender equity in organizations: The challenge and importance of maintaining a gender narrative,' *Organization*, **7**(4), 589–608.

Ewick, P. and S. Silbey (1995), 'Subversive stories and hegemonic talks: Toward a sociology of narrative,' *Law & Society Review*, **29**(2), 197–226.

Fairclough, N. (1989), *Language and Power*, New York: Longman.

Flax, J. (1990), *Thinking Fragments*, Berkeley: University of California Press.

Fletcher, J.K. (1999), *Disappearing Acts: Gender Power and Relational Practice at Work*, Cambridge, MA: MIT Press.

Fletcher, J.K. and L. Bailyn (2005), 'The equity imperative: redesigning work for Work-Family integration,' in E. Kossek and S. Lambert (eds), *Work and Life Integration: Cultural and Individual Perspectives*, Mahwah, NJ: Erlbaum.

Fletcher, J.K. and R. Rapoport (1996), 'Work-family issues as a catalyst for change,' in S. Lewis and J. Lewis (eds), *Rethinking Employment: The Work Family Challenge*, London: Sage.

Foucault, M. (1980), 'Truth and power,' in C. Gordon (ed.), *Power/Knowledge: Selected Interviews and Other Writings, 1972–1977, by Michel Foucault*, New York: Pantheon, pp. 109–133.

Jacobsen, S. and R. Jacques (1997), 'Destabilizing the field,' *Journal of Management Inquiry*, **6**(1), 42–59.

Kolb, D.M., J.K. Fletcher, D. Merrill-Sands and R. Ely (1998), *Making Change: A Framework for Promoting Gender Equity in Organizations*, Boston, MA: Center for Gender in Organizations, Simmons School of Management.

Kolb, D.M., and D. Merrill Sands (1999), 'Waiting for outcomes: Anchoring a dual agenda for change to cultural assumptions,' *Women in Management Review*, **14**, 194–202.

Lukes, S. (1974), *Power*, London: Macmillan.

Merrill-Sands, D., J.K. Fletcher, and A. Acosta (1999), 'Engendering organizational change: A case study of strengthening gender-equity and organizational effectiveness in an international agricultural research institute,' in A. Aruna Rao, R. Stuart, and D. Kelleher (eds), *Gender at Work: Organizational Change for Equality*, West Hartford, CT: Kumarian Press, pp. 77–128.

Meyerson, D.E. and J.K. Fletcher (2000), 'A modest manifesto for shattering the glass ceiling,' *Harvard Business Review*, **78**(1), 126–136.

Nicholson, L.J. (1990), *Feminism/Postmodernism,* New York: Routledge.

Perlow, L. (1997), *Finding Time: How Corporations, Individuals and Families can Benefit from New Work Practices*, Ithaca, NY: Cornell University Press.

Rapoport, R., L. Bailyn, J.K. Fletcher and B.H. Pruitt (2002), *Beyond Work-Family Balance: Advancing Gender Equity and Workplace Performance*, San Francisco, CA: Jossey-Bass.

Rapoport, R., L. Bailyn, with D. Kolb, J.K. Fletcher, D.E. Friedman, S. Eaton, M. Harvey and B. Miller. (1996), *Relinking Life and Work: Toward a Better Future*, Darby, PA: DIANE Publishing.

Sturm, S. (2006), 'The architecture of inclusion: Advancing workplace equity in higher education,' *Harvard Journal of Law and Gender*, **29**, 247–334.

Weedon, C. (1987), *Feminist Practice and Poststructuralist Theory*. Oxford: Basil Blackwell LTD.

SOURCE: Fletcher, Joyce K., Lotte Bailyn, and Stacy Blake Beard. 2009. "Practical Pushing: Creating Discursive Space in Organizational Narratives." Pp. 82–93 in *Critical Management Studies at Work: Negotiating Tensions between Theory and Practice*, edited by Julie Wolfram Cox, Tony G. LeTrent-Jones, Maxim Voronov, and David Weir. Northampton, MA: Edward Elgar.

54

OPERATING ROOM

Relational Spaces and Microinstitutional Change in Surgery

KATHERINE C. KELLOGG

One of the great paradoxes of institutional change is that even when top managers in organizations provide support for change in response to new regulation, the employees whom new programs are designed to benefit often do not use them. This 15-month ethnographic study of two hospitals responding to new regulation demonstrates that using these programs may require subordinate employees to challenge middle managers with opposing interests. The article argues that relational spaces—areas of isolation, interaction, and inclusion that allow middle-manager reformers and subordinate employees to develop a cross-position collective for change—are critical to the change process. These findings have implications for research on institutional change and social movements.

INTRODUCTION

How is change in institutionalized practice accomplished in response to regulation? Sociologists have long documented the complex ways that law influences organizational action (e.g., Dobbin et al. 1988; Fligstein 1990; Powell 1996; Edelman and Suchman 1997; Heimer and Staffen 1998; Scott 2007). On the one hand, top managers in organizations may adopt new formal programs to signal compliance to external audiences but decouple these formal programs from everyday work practice (Meyer and Rowan 1977; DiMaggio and Powell 1983; Silbey 1984; Oliver 1991; Edelman 1992). On the other hand, even when top managers provide support for a change in practice to benefit subordinate employees, the employees for whom the programs are designed frequently do not use them (e.g., Kalev, Dobbin, and Kelly 2006; Kelly and Kalev 2006). Often middle managers who administer the programs serve their own interests by actively discouraging the programs' intended beneficiaries from taking advantage of them (e.g., Edelman, Erlanger, and Lande 1993; Heimer 1999; Edelman, Fuller, and Mara-Drita 2001). Yet, despite such pressures to preserve the status quo, real change sometimes does occur in response to regulation. How?

In this article, I draw on empirical data from 15 months of ethnographic research at two U.S. teaching hospitals to demonstrate that change in an institutionalized work practice can be effected by developing a unified group of reformers from each of the different work positions involved in the practice targeted for change. The regulation I studied was designed to improve safety for patients and quality of work life for surgical residents.[1] Historically, surgical residents in U.S. hospitals have worked 100–120 hours per week; the new regulation required 80-hour workweeks for residents starting in July 2003. In response, top managers in hospitals across the country created new programs (described in further detail below). Despite these new resources, at many hospitals residents did not use the programs that were established for their benefit. A recent study documents that compliance by interns with the 80-hour-workweek regulation (i.e., averaging 80 work hours per week or less each month) during 2003–4 occurred in only 33% of general surgery residency programs (Landrigan et al. 2006). To put it differently, merely ceremonial compliance in surgery occurred in 67% of hospitals.

This study of two teaching hospitals (pseudonyms Advent and Bayshore) responding to this regulation can help us understand the process by which an institutionalized work practice can change in response to regulation. Advent and Bayshore were exposed to the same regulation at the same time. The hospitals were comparable in terms of industry sector, work organization, prior organizational performance, and other characteristics that have been shown to affect organizational response to regulation. Top managers at Advent and Bayshore created similar programs designed to help residents reduce their work hours. At both hospitals, middle managers had equal power vis-à-vis the subordinates who were the intended beneficiaries of these programs. In both sites, the crux of the problem was that the new programs required these subordinates to challenge their managers. I observed the hospitals from three months before the new formal programs were introduced to 12 months after they were introduced. Despite their similarities, by the end of my 15 months of observation, the daily practice targeted by the regulation was changed at Advent but not at Bayshore.

In this article, I combine an understanding of institutional change with the concept of "free spaces" from social movement theory and extend this concept in important ways to explain the process that

accounted for the difference in outcomes at Advent and Bayshore. Social movement theorists employ the term "free spaces" to describe small-scale settings—such as the women-only consciousness-raising groups of the feminist movement or the black churches of the Civil Rights movement—that are isolated from the direct observation of defenders of the status quo and allow for interaction among reformers apart from daily work (e.g., Fantasia and Hirsch 1995; Gamson 1996; Polletta 1999). These theorists argue that free spaces enable reformers to develop an oppositional sense of efficacy (e.g., Hirsch 1990b), an oppositional identity (e.g., Taylor and Whittier 1992), and oppositional frames (e.g., Snow et al. 1986) that enable them to challenge defenders (e.g., Ewick and Silbey 1995).

In the context I studied, the challenge being mounted required coordination among reformers in different work positions. I find that in order for free spaces to facilitate a cross-position challenge, they must allow not only for isolation and interaction but also for inclusion: they must include reformers from each of the work positions involved in the practice targeted for change so that these reformers can build a unified collective that enables them to sustain their challenge against defenders outside of these spaces. I call the subset of free spaces that allow not only for isolation and interaction but also for inclusion *relational spaces,* and I call the cross-position collective building that occurs in such spaces *relational mobilization.*

Below, I first review the existing literature on institutional change in response to regulation and on free spaces and describe the research setting and the details of the research design. I then recount how defenders of the status quo (e.g., many middle-manager surgeons) successfully resisted change initially at both hospitals and how the hospitals' change processes subsequently diverged. I contrast Advent's change process with that of Bayshore to highlight the way relational spaces at Advent enabled middle-manager reformers and subordinate beneficiaries to build a cross-position collective and ultimately to change the daily practice targeted by the regulation. I end by discussing the implications of relational spaces and relational mobilization for understanding microinstitutional change as well as social movement processes.

INSTITUTIONAL CHANGE IN RESPONSE TO REGULATION IN THE LITERATURE

Social movements often fight for new regulation intended to protect organizations' employees or customers (e.g., Soule and Olzak 2004; Soule and King 2006). But regulations won by social movements do not automatically lead organizations to change practices (e.g., McCann 1994; Katzenstein 1998; Binder 2002). Sometimes regulations run counter to the interests of powerful organization members (e.g., Edelman 1990), and often regulations provide only ambiguous criteria by which to identify compliance (Silbey 1981). In response, organizations may adopt new policies or programs to create believable displays of conformity for important external constituencies but decouple these policies or programs from actual daily practices (Meyer and Rowan 1977; DiMaggio and Powell 1983; Silbey 1984; Oliver 1991; Edelman 1992).

Organizational response to institutional pressure is shaped by environmental characteristics, organizational characteristics, and the actions of top managers. Organizations are more likely to adopt and use new formal policies in response to regulation when legal objectives are clear, sanctions for noncompliance are strong, and beliefs and norms support compliance as the right and proper thing to do (e.g., Edelman 1990, 1992). Organizations are also more likely to embrace new policies if they are nonprofit organizations or public agencies that are highly visible because of their large size or if they are more receptive to innovations in employment practices because they have separate personnel offices (Baron, Dobbin, and Jennings 1986; Dobbin et al. 1988; Edelman 1990, 1992). When institutional pressures run counter to the interests of top managers, they may engage in merely symbolic versus real change according to their power vis-à-vis external audiences (Westphal and Zajac 1994) and according to whether the change that is called for is consistent with their backgrounds (Fligstein 1985), their professional identities (Binder 2002;

Rao, Monin, and Durand 2003), or the behavior of high-status actors in their organizational field (Rao, Monin, and Durand 2005).

Middle managers also play an important role in organizational response to institutional pressure because change requires overcoming commitment to existing routines and practices (Dutton and Ashford 1993; Kalev and Dobbin 2006). Middle managers who are sympathetic to a reform, such as personnel officers, often become internal advocates for the implementation of new compliance programs (e.g., Kelly 2003; Bendersky 2007; Dobbin and Kelly 2007). These middle-manager reformers assist in the elaboration and enforcement of employee rights both because they are committed to these ideals and because they seek to increase their power within their organizations (Edelman 1990; Dobbin et al. 1993; Heimer and Stevens 1997). They may use new models proffered in their professional journals, conferences, and networks to persuade top managers to adopt particular programs (Edelman 1990, 1992; Sutton et al. 1994). Over time, they may even come to disassociate these new programs from regulation and justify them in economic terms (Dobbin and Sutton 1998; Kelly and Dobbin 1998; Edelman, Uggen, and Erlanger 1999; Edelman et al. 2001).

However, while adoption and strong support of new programs by middle-manager reformers is important, it is but one step in the process of changing institutionalized work practices. For real change to occur, subordinate employees must actually use these new programs to change their day-to-day work behaviors. Yet institutional theorists studying a wide range of programs—from those established in response to civil rights law to those established in response to OSHA regulation—have found that the employees who would benefit most from changing work practices often avoid using these new programs and instead continue to work in traditional ways (e.g., Edelman 1992). For example, when top managers responded to civil rights law by setting up internal dispute-resolution systems, many African-Americans who believed that they were passed over for promotion or were assigned undesirable tasks kept their complaints to themselves (Kaiser and Major 2006). When top managers responded to equal employment opportunity law by broadly defining sexual harassment and prescribing mechanisms for protecting employee rights, women who were targets of harassment rarely reported it (Marshall 2005). And when top managers responded to OSHA regulation by hiring safety engineers and committing funds to safety programs to prevent illness and injury, employees often did not bring safety problems to managers' attention (Rees 1988).

The failure of subordinate employees to use such programs can be attributed to multiple factors. Sometimes the programs serve the interests of outsiders rather than insiders (e.g., Gouldner 1954) or do not address the issues that need attention (Selznick 1949). In other cases, the programs offer ineffective mechanisms; for example, some purportedly flexible work programs require employees to choose starting and stopping times and to adhere to them for months rather than allowing them to shift hours daily as needed (Kelly and Moen 2007).

One major factor in the nonuse of new programs by intended beneficiaries is a constraining social context (Morrill 1995; Blair-Loy and Wharton 2002, 2004). In particular, unsupportive actions on the part of midlevel line managers who administer the programs often lead subordinates not to use them. Middle managers who administer these new programs may ignore the goals of the programs as they juggle multiple work demands (Kalev et al. 2006). They may even actively discourage the use of the programs to serve their own interests (Edelman 1990; Edelman et al. 1993; Harlan and Robert 1998; Heimer and Staffen 1998; Heimer 1999; Edelman et al. 2001; Kelly and Kalev 2006), interests that may differ considerably from those of the top managers who established the programs (Edelman and Petterson 1999; Morrill, Zald, and Rao 2003).

Individuals make decisions about compliance according to cognitive scripts, moral beliefs, and material self-interest (Silbey 1981; Suchman 1997), and interactions between subordinates and their midlevel line managers around the use of such new programs often lead subordinates not to do the "naming, blaming, and claiming" (Felstiner, Abel, and Sarat 1981) necessary to invoke their rights. Middle managers sometimes discourage subordinates from naming a traditional practice as unfair by portraying antidiscrimination law in a negative light and depoliticizing legal ideals (Edelman

et al. 2001). They may also encourage subordinates to blame themselves for the perpetuation of these practices by recasting complaints as due to personality conflicts or employee deficiencies rather than discrimination (Edelman et al. 1993; Harlan and Robert 1998). Finally, they may lead subordinates not to claim their rights by encouraging fear of retaliation or the belief that their efforts will not result in change (Edelman et al. 1993; Harlan and Robert 1998; Fuller, Edelman, and Matusik 2000; Albiston 2005; Marshall 2005).

Despite these pressures for maintenance of the status quo, past studies show that change in institutionalized daily work practices in response to regulation does sometimes occur (e.g., Edelman 1990). However, the process by which it occurs has not been elaborated before, perhaps because doing so requires intensive observation of day-to-day interaction over an extended period of time (Barley and Tolbert 1997; Barley 2008) and because it is difficult for researchers to gain access to study the implementation of regulation inside organizations (Gunningham, Kagan, and Thornton 2003; Suchman and Edelman 2007). In this study, I combine the concept of free spaces with insights gained from my longitudinal ethnographic study inside two organizations to demonstrate the relational mobilization process by which real change in an institutionalized daily work practice in response to regulation can occur.

FREE SPACES AND OPPOSITIONAL MOBILIZATION FOR CHANGE

Social movement theorists have developed the notion of free spaces to explain how subordinate groups generate the capacities needed to engage in political challenge (e.g., Polletta 1999). According to these theorists, free spaces include such spaces as work departments and union halls (Fantasia 1988; Hirsch 1990b), women's social meetings on the margins of big meetings of the Student Nonviolent Coordinating Committee (Evans and Boyte 1986), and traditional homes in the Algerian revolt against French colonialism (Fantasia and Hirsch 1995). These spaces can be virtual as well as physical, and their security, as well as the ease of limiting access to them, can vary over time (Gamson 1996). Within these spaces, reformers can engage in oppositional mobilization against defenders of the status quo; they can build a sense of *oppositional efficacy* (a feeling that their collective action against defenders can be successful; Fantasia 1988; Fantasia and Hirsch 1995; Gamson 1996), an *oppositional identity* that allows them to act together against newly defined adversaries (Taylor and Whittier 1992; Snow and McAdam 2000; Polletta and Jasper 2001), and *oppositional frames* that highlight problems with the traditional system and prescribe collective action solutions (Snow et al. 1986; Snow and Benford 1988).

Two characteristics of free spaces are important to the analysis presented here: where the spaces are located (namely, apart from defenders of the status quo) and what happens in them (interactions different from daily work). The isolation of free spaces from defenders is critical to mobilization because, for oppositional capacities to develop and become shared, reformers need some autonomous space where they are at least temporarily shielded from agents of social control (Fantasia and Hirsch 1995; Gamson 1996). The setting for interaction apart from daily work provided by free spaces is critical because oppositional efficacy, identity, and frames are created in encounters in intimate settings (Snow and Anderson 1987; Fantasia 1988; Hirsch 1990a). The examination of where these free spaces are and what happens in them is useful to understanding the oppositional mobilization processes by which reformers ready themselves to challenge defenders. However, to explain the intraorganizational change processes I saw, it is necessary to analyze an additional element—the inclusion of reformers from each of the work positions required for change.

In this study, I address two problems with the concept of free spaces to help explain the dynamics I observed. First, since social movement scholars have previously invoked free spaces as an explanation for successful mobilization efforts without also studying failed efforts (to determine if there were no free spaces available in those efforts), it is not clear that free spaces can really explain success. Second, because the free spaces that have previously been studied have been homogeneous, collecting people who are already similarly situated and like-minded,

they seem to be ill suited for building new role relationships across reformers in different work positions. In the context I studied, reformers needed to build not only an oppositional collective against defenders but also a cross-position collective with other reformers because the challenge required coordination among reformers in different work positions (e.g., middle managers and subordinates). I find that in order for free spaces to facilitate this kind of coordinated challenge across multiple positions, they must allow not only for isolation and interaction but also for inclusion of reformers from each of the work positions that need to be part of the new role relationships.

I suggest that relational spaces—a subset of free spaces that allow such inclusion—give reformers in different work positions a forum for building a sense of efficacy around accomplishing change with newly developed task allocations. These spaces allow reformers to develop an identity dictating how reformers in different work positions should behave with one another. Finally, the spaces facilitate the creation of frames justifying these new task and role expectations. Through the creation of new relational efficacy, identity, and frames, reformers can build a cross-position collective that enables them to sustain a challenge against defenders of the status quo and change a long-standing work practice. In what follows, I review the methods used in this study and then describe how relational spaces at Advent were necessary for reformers to engage in relational mobilization and subsequently challenge and change an institutionalized work practice. . . .

DISCUSSION

Relational Spaces and the Importance of Inclusion

These findings contribute to the literature on institutional change in response to regulation and to the literature on social movements in several ways. Institutional theorists have shown that organizational response to institutional pressure is associated with particular environmental characteristics such as dominant beliefs, norms, and resources (e.g., Edelman 1990; Ruef and Scott 1998; Scott et al. 2000), regulatory regimes (Tolbert and Zucker

1983; Baron et al. 1986; Katzenstein 1998) and community-specific requirements (Lounsbury 2007; Marquis, Glynn, and Davis 2007), particular organizational characteristics such as alignment with the public sector (Dobbin et al. 1988; Edelman 1992), existence of a personnel office (Baron et al. 1986; Edelman 1992), and organizational performance (Westphal and Zajac 1994), and particular top-manager characteristics such as work background (Fligstein 1990) and professional identity (Binder 2002; Rao et al. 2003). Since Advent and Bayshore were matched on each of these environmental, organizational, and top-manager characteristics, these characteristics alone may not be sufficient for explaining change in an institutionalized work practice. Such change may also depend on microlevel processes occurring inside organizations (Barley 1986, 2008; Zilber 2002; Reay, Golden-Biddle, and Germann 2006; Powell and Colyvas 2008). The present study adds to our understanding of micro-institutional change by demonstrating that, in the face of resistance by defenders of the status quo, the emergence of relational efficacy, identity, and frames are necessary for change to occur, and relational spaces are at least one route to getting there.

The isolation from defenders that relational spaces provide is critical to change because midlevel reformers and their subordinates are often not comfortable trying out new task allocations, expressing new identities, or discussing nontraditional ideas when defenders are present, for fear of retaliation. This discomfort may be especially pronounced for lower-status reformers who are in the numeric minority (Loyd 2008). Having a setting for interaction apart from work itself is crucial because it facilitates discussion of new tasks, identities, and frames. Finally, inclusion of reformers from all of the different work positions involved in the practice targeted for change is important because it enables collective coordination and negotiation of new relational tasks, roles, and frames. Since shared communication contexts have been shown to reduce conflict (Hinds and Mortensen 2005), one might think that to accomplish change in a work practice in response to regulation it is necessary to bring defenders and reformers together to plan and implement compliance programs with one another. However, the findings presented here suggest the opposite. For routine practices to change

when defenders of the status quo resist it, reformers from each of the work positions involved in the work practice must have spaces apart from defenders to coordinate their efforts with one another.

In addition to contributing to institutional theory, the concept of relational spaces contributes to social movement theory. Social movement theorists have highlighted the importance of free spaces in allowing reformers to ready themselves for a collective challenge of defenders of the status quo (e.g., Fantasia and Hirsch 1995; Gamson 1996; Polletta 1999).

Yet previous studies of free spaces have documented successful mobilization efforts without detailing failed efforts (to determine if there were no free spaces available in those efforts), so it is not clear from past research that free spaces can really explain success. In addition, social movement theorists have not explored what kinds of spaces are necessary when the challenge being mounted requires reformers to carry out different yet interdependent tasks. This is unfortunate because challenges interesting to social movement theorists often require such a division of labor. For example, during the bus boycotts of the Civil Rights movement, a division of labor was required for successful challenge: some reformers needed to avoid using buses, while others needed to provide transport for the boycotters (e.g., McAdam 1982). According to the argument presented here, reformers likely used relational spaces to coordinate their efforts in this case, but these spaces and the processes occurring within them have not been previously examined.

The role of relational spaces in social movement processes may be particularly important inside organizations. Theorists have used social movement concepts to describe how mobilization occurs in organizational fields and inside organizations (e.g., Rao, Morrill, and Zald 2000; Lounsbury, Ventresca, and Hirsch 2003; Davis et al. 2005; McAdam and Scott 2005; Briscoe and Safford 2008; Davis et al. 2008) and inside organizations (e.g., Zald and Berger 1978; Lounsbury 2001; Scully and Creed 2005; Kaplan 2008; O'Mahony and Bechky 2008). These scholars have argued that mobilization may look different inside organizations because of the important role played by top managers (Scully and Segal 2002; Raeburn 2004; Clemens 2005; Zald, Morrill, and Rao 2005; Weber, Thomas, and Rao

2009). The findings presented here suggest that even when top managers are committed to change, relational spaces may be necessary for mobilization inside organizations to occur. Reformers trying to create a unified group across different work positions may need such spaces to coordinate their completion of different yet interdependent tasks before they can effectively challenge defenders.

Relational Mobilization and the Building of a Cross-Position Collective

In addition to explaining the importance of relational spaces, these findings add to social movement theory and institutional theory by detailing the institutional change process of relational mobilization—the building of capacity for challenge among reformers in different positions. While social movement theorists have explained how oppositional mobilization (mobilization against defenders) occurs (e.g., Fantasia 1988; Gamson 1992; Taylor and Whittier 1992; Polletta and Jasper 2001), they have not explored how relational mobilization (mobilization in relation to other reformers) happens. As social movement theorists would predict, reformers at both Advent and Bayshore used free spaces to build oppositional capacities that allowed them to challenge defenders of the status quo. They built a sense of oppositional efficacy that made them willing to take risks and assured them that others would act with them to challenge defenders. They created an oppositional identity that made it easier for them to act "inappropriately" to challenge defenders and gave them a sense of obligation to act on behalf of their group. They developed oppositional frames that identified a problem and specified a collective solution.

Despite this, change occurred at Advent and not at Bayshore because at Advent, in addition to generating oppositional capacities for collective action against defenders, reformers generated relational capacities for collective action with one another. The building of relational efficacy—a sense of hope that change was possible through the use of a new division of labor among reformers—occurred as reformers collectively identified task problems and jointly negotiated task solutions. The development of relational identity was accomplished as

reformers demonstrated new language and demeanors and offered help across positions in front of one another. Relational frames were created as reformers justified new task allocations and reinforced new relational frames with one another. Relational mobilization facilitated the development of a cross-position collective that allowed reformers to be successful in their fight against defenders in a situation where the challenge being mounted required coordination and cooperation among reformers in different work positions.

An understanding of relational mobilization contributes to institutional theory as well as to social movement theory. Theorists have begun to build an institutional theory of the remediation of inequality, suggesting that the structure of workplace programs can counteract work practices that disadvantage particular groups of employees (Kalev et al. 2006; Castilla 2008), particularly since lack of structure makes opportunities for inequality more likely (Fernandez-Mateo 2009). For example, Kalev et al. (2006) have documented that workplace programs that assign accountability for change to line managers are effective in increasing the proportions of white women, black women, and black men in management positions while programs that attempt to train managers in the benefits of diversity or help women and minorities to combat social isolation through networking are not.

The findings presented here suggest that a workplace process—relational mobilization—can also help remediate inequality. At both Advent and Bayshore, directors created weak structures of accountability: they assigned responsibility for the change to the chief residents but did not track residents' weekly work hours to evaluate progress because they feared that this tracking might be seen by the regulatory agency before they had successfully accomplished change. Yet, despite a weak structure of accountability similar to the one at Bayshore, relational mobilization enabled change at Advent.

Future Research

This analysis raises several questions for future research. Since studies of compliance with this work-hours regulation show that only a third of hospitals that have introduced compliance programs have actually used these programs to make the required change (Landrigan et al. 2006), there must be a number of reasons for merely symbolic compliance. A claim that relational spaces are the only factor accounting for the difference in outcomes at these hospitals would not do justice to other possible conditioning factors that a comparative ethnographic study cannot detect.

First, there were several factors that were present at both Advent and Bayshore that were clearly important to the change process—supportive top managers, a cadre of committed reformers, and free spaces—and because these factors were present at both sites it is not possible to know how they each affected the process. Future research could explore what critical mass of reformers is required for successful change. It could also investigate what types of top-manager resources best enable change in daily work behaviors. Finally, it could elaborate whether some oppositional mobilization processes that occur in free spaces are more important than others.

Second, this kind of observational study cannot identify unobservable factors that may have influenced the change process. For example, defenders' or reformers' relationships with their superiors, colleagues, or professional association may have led to power differences playing out in the two different hospitals and beyond that were not detected. In addition, it is possible that unobserved personality differences or social skill differences (Fligstein 1997) between reformers at the two hospitals led Advent reformers to be more open to change or better at accomplishing it. Future research mapping structure in the patterns of ties between groups of actors (e.g., Wheat 2005) and testing for reformer characteristics could examine the effects of these additional factors.

In sum, this study elaborates how change in institutionalized practice inside an organization can be accomplished in response to regulation in the face of resistance from defenders of the status quo. Even when top managers support a new program to change an institutionalized practice, middle managers whose interests run counter to the new program are likely to resist it and to attempt to persuade their subordinates to refrain from using it. I demonstrate here that middle managers sympathetic to reform and their subordinates can successfully change

practice in such a situation by interacting with one another in spaces of isolation, interaction, and inclusion to build new task allocations, new role expectations, and justifications for these new tasks and roles. This relational mobilization can enable reformers to sustain a cross-position challenge in the face of defender resistance and to pressure defenders to change practice. In this way, relational spaces and relational mobilization enable the microinstitutional change that new regulation is designed to promote.

NOTE

1. Residents are doctors who are undergoing hands-on training in their specialties after medical school.

REFERENCES

Albiston, Catherine R. 2005. "Bargaining in the Shadow of Social Institutions: Competing Discourses and Social Change in Workplace Mobilization of Civil Rights." *Law and Society Review* 39:11–49.

Barley, Stephen R. 1986. "Technology as an Occasion for Structuring: Evidence from Observations of CT Scanners and the Social Order of Radiology Departments." *Administrative Science Quarterly* 31:78–108.

———. 2008. "Coalface Institutionalism." Pp. 491–518 in *The Sage Handbook of Organizational Institutionalism,* edited by Royston Greenwood, Christine Oliver, Roy Suddaby, and Kerstin Sahlin-Andersson. Thousand Oaks, Calif.: Sage.

Barley, Stephen R., and Pamela S. Tolbert. 1997. "Institutionalization and Structuration: Studying the Links between Action and Institution." *Organization Studies* 18: 93–117.

Baron, James N., Frank R. Dobbin, and P. Devereaux Jennings. 1986. "War and Peace: The Evolution of Modern Personnel Administration in U.S. Industry." *American Journal of Sociology* 92:350–83.

Bendersky, Corrine. 2007. "Complementarities in Organizational Dispute Resolution Systems: How System Characteristics Affect Individuals' Conflict Experiences." *Industrial and Labor Relations Review* 60:204–24.

Binder, A. 2002. *Contentious Curricula: Afrocentrism and Creationism in American Public Schools.* Princeton, N.J.: Princeton University Press.

Blair-Loy, M., and A. S. Wharton. 2002. "Employees' Use of Work-Family Policies and the Workplace Social Context." *Social Forces* 80:813–45.

———. 2004. "Organizational Commitment and Constraints on Work-Family Policy Use: Corporate Flexibility Policies in a Global Firm." *Sociological Perspectives* 47: 243–67.

Briscoe, F., and S. Safford. 2008. "The Nixon-in-China Effect: Activism, Imitation, and the Institutionalization of Contentious Practices." *Administrative Science Quarterly* 53:460–91.

Castilla, Emilio J. 2008. "Gender, Race, and Meritocracy in Organizational Careers." *American Journal of Sociology* 113:1479–1526.

Clemens, Elisabeth. 2005. "Two Kinds of Stuff: The Current Encounter of Social Movements and Organizations." Pp. 351–66 in *Social Movements and Organization Theory,* edited by G. Davis, D. McAdam, W. R. Scott, and Mayer N. Zald. New York: Cambridge University Press.

Davis, Gerald F., Doug McAdam, W. Richard Scott, and Mayer N. Zald, eds. 2005. *Social Movements and Organization Theory.* New York: Cambridge University Press.

Davis, G. F., C. Morrill, H. Rao, and S. A. Soule. 2008. "Introduction: Social Movements in Organizations and Markets." *Administrative Science Quarterly* 53:389–94.

DiMaggio, Paul J., and Walter W. Powell. 1983. "The Iron Cage Revisited: Institutional Isomorphism and Collective Rationality in Organizational Fields." *American Sociological Review* 48:147–60.

Dobbin, Frank, Lauren B. Edelman, John W. Meyer, W. Richard Scott, and A. Swidler. 1988. "The Expansion of Due Process in Organizations." Pp. 71–100 in *Institutional Patterns and Organizations: Culture and Environment,* edited by L. G. Zucker. Cambridge, Mass.: Ballinger.

Dobbin, Frank, and Erin L. Kelly. 2007. "How to Stop Harassment: Professional Construction of Legal Compliance in Organizations." *American Journal of Sociology* 112:1203–43.

Dobbin, Frank, and John R. Sutton. 1998. "The Strength of a Weak State: The Rights Revolution and the Rise of Human Resources Management Divisions." *American Journal of Sociology* 104:441–76.

Dobbin, Frank, John R. Sutton, John W. Meyer, and W. Richard Scott. 1993. "Equal Opportunity Law and the Construction of Internal Labor Markets." *American Journal of Sociology* 99:396–427.

Dutton, J. E., and S. J. Ashford. 1993. "Selling Issues to Top Management." *Academy of Management Review* 18:397–428.

Edelman, Lauren B. 1990. "Legal Environments and Organizational Governance: The Expansion of Due Process in the American Workplace." *American Journal of Sociology* 95:1401–40.

———. 1992. "Legal Ambiguity and Symbolic Structures: Organizational Mediation of Civil Rights Law." *American Journal of Sociology* 97:1531–76.

Edelman, Lauren B., Howard S. Erlanger, and J. Lande. 1993. "Internal Dispute Resolution: The Transformation of Civil Rights in the Workplace." *Law and Society Review* 27:497–534.

Edelman, Lauren B., Sally Riggs Fuller, and Iona Mara-Drita. 2001. "Diversity Rhetoric and the Managerialization of Law." *American Journal of Sociology* 106: 1589–1641.

Fuller, Sally R., Lauren B. Edelman, and Sharon F. Matusik. 2000. "Legal Readings: Employee Interpretation and Mobilization of Law." *Academy of Management Review* 25:200–216.

Edelman, Lauren B., and Stephen Petterson. 1999. "Symbols and Substance in Organizational Response to Civil Rights Law." In "The Future of Affirmative Action," special issue, *Research in Social Stratification and Mobility* 17:107–35.

Edelman, Lauren B., and Mark Suchman. 1997. "The Legal Environments of Organizations." *Annual Review of Sociology* 23:479–515.

Edelman, Lauren B., Christopher Uggen, and Howard S. Erlanger. 1999. "The Endogeneity of Legal Regulation: Grievance Procedures as Rational Myth." *American Journal of Sociology* 105:406–54.

Evans, S. M., and H. C. Boyte. 1986. *Free Spaces: The Sources of Democratic Change in America.* New York: Harper & Row.

Ewick, P., and S. S. Silbey. 1995. "Subversive Stories and Hegemonic Tales: Toward a Sociology of Narrative." *Law and Society Review* 29:197–226.

Fantasia, Rick. 1988. *Cultures of Solidarity: Consciousness, Action, and Contemporary American Workers.* Berkeley and Los Angeles: University of California Press.

Fantasia, Rick, and Eric L. Hirsch. 1995. "Culture in Rebellion: The Appropriation and Transformation of the Veil in the Algerian Revolution." Pp. 144–59 in *Social Movements and Culture,* edited by Hank Johnston and Bert Klandermans. Minneapolis: University of Minnesota Press.

Felstiner, W. L. F., R. L. Abel, and A. Sarat. 1981. "The Emergence and Transformation of Disputes: Naming, Blaming, Claiming." *Law and Society Review* 15:631–54.

Fernandez-Mateo, Isabel. 2009. "Cumulative Gender Disadvantage in Contract Employment." *American Journal of Sociology* 114:871–923.

Fligstein, Neil. 1985. "The Spread of the Multidivisional Form among Large Firms, 1919–1979." *American Sociological Review* 50:377–91.

———. 1990. *The Transformation of Corporate Control.* Cambridge, Mass.: Harvard University Press.

———. 1997. "Social Skill and Institutional Theory." *American Behavioral Scientist* 40:397–405.

Gamson, William A. 1992. *Talking Politics.* New York: Cambridge University Press.

———. 1996. "Safe Spaces and Social Movements." *Perspectives on Social Problems* 8:27–38.

Gouldner, Alvin Ward. 1954. *Patterns of Industrial Bureaucracy.* Glencoe, Ill.: Free Press.

Gunningham, N., R. A. Kagan, and D. Thornton. 2003. *Shades of Green: Business, Regulation, and Environment.* Stanford, Calif.: Stanford University Press.

Harlan, S. L., and P. M. Robert. 1998. "The Social Construction of Disability in Organizations: Why Employers Resist Reasonable Accommodation." *Work and Occupations* 25:397–135.

Heimer, Carol A. 1999. "Competing Institutions: Law, Medicine, and Family in Neonatal Intensive Care." *Law and Society Review* 33:17–66.

Heimer, Carol A., and Lisa R. Staffen. 1998. *For the Sake of the Children: The Social Organisation of Responsibility in the Hospital and the Home.* Chicago: University of Chicago Press.

Heimer, C. A., and M. L. Stevens. 1997. "Caring for the Organization: Social Workers as Frontline Risk Managers in Neonatal Intensive Care Units." *Work and Occupations* 24:133–63.

Hinds, P. J., and M. Mortensen. 2005. "Understanding Conflict in Geographically Distributed Teams: The Moderating Effects of Shared Identity, Shared Context, and Spontaneous Communication." *Organisation Science* 16:290–307.

Hirsch, Eric L. 1990a. "Sacrifice for the Cause: Group Processes, Recruitment, and Commitment in a Student Social-Movement." *American Sociological Review* 55:243–54.

———. 1990b. *Urban Revolt.* Berkeley and Los Angeles: University of California Press.

Kaiser, C. R., and B. Major. 2006. "A Social Psychological Perspective on Perceiving and Reporting Discrimination." *Law and Social Inquiry* 31:801–30.

Kalev, Alexandra, and Frank Dobbin. 2006. "Enforcement of Civil Rights Law in Private Workplaces: The Effects of Compliance Reviews and Lawsuits over Time." *Law and Social Inquiry* 31:855–903.

Kalev, Alexandra, Frank Dobbin, and Erin Kelly. 2006. "Best Practices or Best Guesses? Assessing the Efficacy of Corporate Affirmative Action and Diversity Policies." *American Sociological Review* 71:589–617.

Kaplan, S. 2008. "Framing Contests: Strategy Making under Uncertainty." *Organization Science* 19:729–52.

Katzenstein, Mary Fainsod. 1998. *Faithful and Fearless: Moving Feminist Protest inside the Church and Military.* Princeton, N.J.: Princeton University Press.

Kelly, Erin L. 2003. "The Strange History of Employer-Sponsored Child Care: Interested Actors, Uncertainty, and the Transformation of Law in Organizational Fields." *American Journal of Sociology* 109:606–49.

Kelly, E., and Frank Dobbin. 1998. "How Affirmative Action Became Diversity Management: Employer Response to Antidiscrimination Law, 1961 to 1996." *American Behavioral Scientist* 41:960–84.

Kelly, Erin L., and Alexandra Kalev. 2006. "Managing Flexible Work Arrangements in U.S. Organizations: Formalized Discretion or 'A Right to Ask.'" *Socio-economic Review* 4:379–416.

Kelly, E. L., and P. Moen. 2007. "Rethinking the Clockwork of Work: Why Schedule Control May Pay Off at Work and at Home." *Advances in Developing Human Resources* 9:487–506.

Landrigan, Christopher P., Laura K. Barger, Brian E. Cade, Najib T. Ayas, and Charles A. Czeisler. 2006. "Interns' Compliance with Accreditation Council for Graduate Medical Education Work-Hour Limits." *Journal of the American Medical Association* 296:1063–70.

Lounsbury, Michael. 2001. "Institutional Sources of Practice Variation: Staffing College and University Recycling Programs." *Administrative Science Quarterly* 46:29–56.

———. 2007. "A Tale of Two Cities: Competing Logics and Practice Variation in the Professionalizing of Mutual Funds." *Academy of Management Journal* 50:289–307.

Lounsbury, Michael, Marc J. Ventresca, and Paul M. Hirsch. 2003. "Social Movements, Field Frames and Industry Emergence: A Cultural-Political Perspective on U.S. Recycling." *Socio-economic Review* 1:71–104.

Loyd, Denise L. 2008. "Avoiding the Appearance of Favoritism in Evaluating Others: The Importance of Status and Distinctiveness." Manuscript. Massachusetts Institute of Technology, Organization Studies Department.

Marquis, C., M. A. Glynn, and G. F. Davis. 2007. "Community Isomorphism and Corporate Social Action." *Academy of Management Review* 32:925–45.

Marshall, A. M. 2005. "Idle Rights: Employees' Rights Consciousness and the Construction of Sexual Harassment Policies." *Law and Society Review* 39:83–123.

McAdam, Doug. 1982. *Political Process and the Development of Black Insurgency, 1930–1970.* Chicago: University of Chicago Press.

McAdam, Doug, and W. Richard Scott. 2005. "Organizations and Movements." Pp. 4–49 in *Social Movements and Organization Theory,* edited by Gerald F. Davis, Doug McAdam, W. Richard Scott, and Mayer N. Zald. Cambridge: Cambridge University Press.

McCann, Michael W. 1994. *Rights at Work: Pay Equity Reform and the Politics of Legal Mobilization.* Chicago: University of Chicago Press.

Meyer, John W., and Brian Rowan. 1977. "Institutionalized Organizations: Formal Structure as Myth and Ceremony." *American Journal of Sociology* 83:340–63.

Morrill, Calvin. 1995. *The Executive Way.* Chicago: University of Chicago Press.

Morrill, Calvin, Mayer N. Zald, and Hayagreeva Rao. 2003. "Covert Political Conflict in Organizations: Challenges from Below." *Annual Review of Sociology* 29:391–415.

Oliver, Christine. 1991. "Strategic Responses to Institutional Processes." *Academy of Management Review* 16:145–79.

O'Mahony, S., and B. A. Bechky. 2008. "Boundary Organizations: Enabling Collaboration among Unexpected Allies." *Administrative Science Quarterly* 53:422–59.

Polletta, Francesca. 1999. "'Free Spaces' in Collective Action." *Theory and Society* 28: 1–38.

Polletta, Francesca, and James M. Jasper. 2001. "Collective Identity and Social Movements." *Annual Review of Sociology* 27:283–305.

Powell, Walter W. 1996. "Fields of Practice: Connections between Law and Organizations." *Law and Social Inquiry* 21:959–66.

Powell, Walter, and Jeannette Colyvas. 2008. "Microfoundations of Institutional Theory." Pp. 276–98 in *The Sage Handbook of Organisational Institutionalism,* edited by Royston Greenwood, Christine Oliver, Roy Suddaby, and Kerstin Sahlin-Andersson. Thousand Oaks, Calif.: Sage Publications.

Raeburn, X. 2004. *Inside Out: The Struggle for Lesbian, Gay, and Bisexual Rights in the Workplace.* Minneapolis: University of Minnesota Press.

Rao, Hayagreeva, Philippe Monin, and Rodolphe Durand. 2003. "Institutional Change in Toque Ville: Nouvelle Cuisine as an Identity Movement in French Gastronomy." *American Journal of Sociology* 108:795–843.

———. 2005. "Border Crossing: Bricolage and the Erosion of Categorical Boundaries in French Gastronomy." *American Sociological Review* 70:968–91.

Rao, Hayagreeva, Calvin Morrill, and Mayer N. Zald. 2000. "Power Plays: How Social Movements and Collective Action Create New Organizational Forms." Pp. 237–81 in *Research in Organizational Behavior,* edited by B. M. Staw and R. I. Sutton. New York: JAI-Elsevier Science.

Reay, Trish, Karen Golden-Biddle, and Kathy Germann. 2006. "Legitimizing a New Role: Small Wins and Microprocesses of Change." *Academy of Management Journal* 49:977–98.

Rees, J. V. 1988. *Reforming the Workplace: A Study of Self-Regulation in Occupational Safety.* Philadelphia: University of Pennsylvania Press.

Ruef, Martin, and W. Richard Scott. 1998. "A Multidimensional Model of Organizational Legitimacy: Hospital Survival in Changing Institutional Environments." *Administrative Science Quarterly* 43:877–904.

Scott, W. 2007. *Institutions and organizations: Ideas and interests* (3rd ed.). Thousand Oaks, Calif.: Sage Publications.

Scott, W. Richard, Martin Ruef, Peter J. Mendel, and Carol A. Caronna. 2000. *Institutional Change and Healthcare Organizations: From Professional Dominance to Managed Care.* Chicago: University of Chicago Press.

Scully, Maureen A., and W. E. Douglas Creed. 2005. "Subverting Our Stories of Subversion." Pp. 310–32 in *Social Movements and Organization Theory,* edited by Gerald F. Davis, Douglas McAdam, W. Richard Scott, and Mayer X. Zald. Cambridge: Cambridge University Press.

Scully, Maureen A., and A. Segal. 2002. "Passion with an Umbrella: Grassroots Activists in the Workplace." Pp. 127–70 in *Research in the Sociology of Organizations,* edited by Michael Lounsbury and Marc J. Ventresca. Oxford: JAI.

Selznick, Philip. 1949. *TVA and the Grass Roots.* Berkeley: University of California Press.

Silbey, Susan S. 1981. "Case Processing: Consumer Protection in an Attorney General's Office." *Law and Society Review* 15:849–81.

———. 1984. "The Consequences of Responsive Regulation." Pp. 147–70 in *Enforcing Regulation,* edited by J. Thomas and K. Hawkins. Boston: Kluwer Nijhof.

Snow, David A., and Leon Anderson. 1987. "Identity Work among the Homeless: The Verbal Construction and

Avowal of Personal Identities." *American Journal of Sociology* 92:1336–71.

Snow, David A., and Robert D. Benford. 1988. "Ideology, Frame Resonance, and Participant Mobilization." *International Social Movement Research* 1:197–217.

Snow, David A., and Doug McAdam. 2000. "Identity Work Processes in the Context of Social Movements: Clarifying the Identity/Movement Nexus." Pp. 41–67 in *Self, Identity, and Social Movements,* edited by Sheldon Stryker, Timothy J. Owens, and Robert W. White. Minneapolis: University of Minnesota Press.

Snow, David A., E. B. Rochford, S. K. Worden, and R. D. Benford. 1986. "Frame Alignment Processes, Micromobilization, and Movement Participation." *American Sociological Review* 51:464–81.

Soule, Sarah A., and Brayden G. King. 2006. "The Stages of the Policy Process and the Equal Rights Amendment, 1972–1982." *American Journal of Sociology* 111:1871–1909.

Soule, Sarah A., and Susan Olzak. 2004. "When Do Movements Matter? The Politics of Contingency and the Equal Rights Amendment." *American Sociological Review* 69:473–97.

Suchman, Mark C. 1997. "On Beyond Interest: Rational, Normative and Cognitive Perspectives in the Social Scientific Study of Law." *Wisconsin Law Review,* pp. 475–501

Suchman, Mark C., and Lauren B. Edelman. 2007. "The Interplay of Law and Organizations." Pp. xi– in *The Legal Lives of Private Organisations,* edited by L. B. Edelman and M. C. Suchman. Aldershot: Ashgate.

Sutton, John R., Frank Dobbin, John W. Meyer, and W. Richard Scott. 1994. "The Legalization of the Workplace." *American Journal of Sociology* 99:944–71.

Taylor, V., and N. E. Whittier. 1992. "Collective Identity in Social Movement Communities: Lesbian Feminist Mobilization." Pp. 104–30 in *Frontiers in Social Movement Theory,* edited by Aldon D. Morris and Carol McClurg Mueller. New Haven, Conn.: Yale University Press.

Tolbert, Pamela S., and Lyrine G. Zucker. 1983. "Institutional Sources of Change in the Formal Structure of Organizations: The Diffusion of Civil Service Reform, 1880–1935." *Administrative Science Quarterly* 28:22–39.

Weber, K., L. G. Thomas, and H. Rao. 2009. "From Streets to Suites: How the Anti-biotech Movement Affected German Pharmaceutical Firms." *American Sociological Review* 74:106–27.

Westphal, James D., and Edward J. Zajac. 1994. "Substance and Symbolism in CEOs' Long-term Incentive Plans." *Administrative Science Quarterly* 39:367–90.

Wheat, Christopher O. 2005. "Organizational Positions and the Social Structure of Exchange." Ph.D. dissertation. Harvard University.

Zald, Mayer N., and M. A. Berger. 1978. "Social Movements in Organizations: Coup d'Etat, Insurgency, and Mass Movements." *American Journal of Sociology* 83:823–61.

Zald, Mayer N., Calvin Morrill, and Hayagreeva Rao. 2005. "The Impact of Social Movements on Organizations: Environment and Responses." Pp. 253–79 in *Social Movements and Organization Theory,* edited by Gerald F. Davis, Douglas McAdam, W. Richard Scott, and Mayer N. Zald. New York: Cambridge University Press.

Zilber, Tammar B. 2002. "Institutionalization as an Interplay between Actions, Meanings, and Actors: The Case of a Rape Crisis Center in Israel." *Academy of Management Journal* 45:234–54.

SOURCE: Kellogg, Katherine C. 2009. Excerpt from "Operating Room: Relational Spaces and Micro-institutional Changes in Surgery." *American Journal of Sociology*, 115(3):657–64, 701–11.

PART IX

New Technology, Social Media, and Emerging Communities

An Introduction to New Technology, Social Media, and Emerging Communities

New technology is transforming the ways in which we communicate, congregate, and form organizations. It is also challenging and expanding the narratives and viewpoints that influence social values and ways of understanding the world. Integrating a multiplicity of identities produces emergent selves within pluralistic communities. Multifaceted selfhood challenges antiquated notions of unification and solidarity built around rigid definitions of static personal characteristics. Anthony Giddens (1991) argues that the decrease in fixed identities and stagnant social roles can lead individuals to construct fluid identities within any context of dynamic negotiation and risk. Because individuals and communities are changing rapidly and in unprecedented ways, Zygmunt Bauman (2000) refers to the present time as "liquid modernity."

Our ability to reinvent ourselves has continued to increase dramatically through mounting expectations that individuals might have several different careers, a series of marriages and blended families; speak more than one language; and live in many places over time. In cyber reality, the options for experimenting with different identities and personas are almost limitless (Turkle 1994). In her article included in this section, "Constructions and Reconstructions of Self in Virtual Reality," Sherry Turkle (1994) examines the implications for self-development and interpersonal interaction through the medium of interactive computer games:

> [Multiuser games] provide worlds for social interaction in a virtual space, worlds in which you can present yourself as a "character," in which you can be anonymous, in which you can play a role or roles as close or as far away from your "real self" as you choose . . . Authorship is not only displaced from a solitary voice, it is exploded. The self is not only decentered but multiplied without limit. There is an unparalleled opportunity to play with one's identity and to "try out" new ones. (P. 158)

Turkle (1994) argues that the anonymity and intimacy of online interactions can provide the context for transformative self-development:

Engagement with computational technology facilitates a series of "second chances" for adults to work and rework unresolved personal issues and more generally, to think through questions about the nature of self, including questions about definitions of life, intentionality, and intelligence . . . Where the computer is used as communications medium, there is more room to use the control provided by the computer to develop a greater capacity for collaboration and even intimacy. The medium enables the self to explore a social context as well as to reflect on its own nature and powers. (P. 159)

Since Turkle's observations in 1994, the number of online communities has increased at an astonishing rate. The possibilities are seemingly endless and include not only gaming, but social media, dating services, political activism, social support networks, and special interest groups around almost anything: music, parenting, sports teams, gardening, and so on. The articles in this section discuss the impact of new technology on organizing and organizations within worlds that are increasingly virtual.

In their article, "Link, Search, Interact: The Co-Evolution of NGOs and Interactive Technology," Jonathan Bach and David Stark (2004) contend that one important ramification of online organizing is that heterarchical, collaborative organizations now coexist with bureaucratic, hierarchical organizations providing a greater range of organizational forms, some of which are coevolving with new media and technology. One such organizational form—nonprofit, nongovernment "civil society organizations" (NGOs)—has grown exponentially since the 1980s (Bach and Stark 2004:102). Describing the connection between the growth of NGOs and new technology, Bach and Stark write,

NGOs are embedded within the oft-described network paradigm that is displacing central-planning and strictly hierarchical thinking. Networks operate more fluidly and can improve on accounts of complex social interaction over the methodological individualism of positivist social science. They have the significant effect of enhancing flows and creating a shared acceleration that corresponds to the compressed space-time of our late modern era. This spatio-temporal compression is part and parcel of the function of interactive technologies, which combine real-time and many-to-many communication in ways that fundamentally rearrange the way firms produce, states fight wars, and people's lives are structured. (P. 103)

Bach and Stark (2004) argue that NGOs are effective as self-organizing communities because the interactivity among various social networks is directly linked to knowledge generation. In other words, NGOs succeed both because they transcend the traditional limits and borders of government agencies as they tend to be in "de-territorialized" virtual space and because they connect multiple populations and "older spatio-temporal order" to new knowledge of global transformation (Bach and Stark 2004:113). In this way, NGOs provide both a social, political, and knowledge space *within* which something can happen and a space *for* something to happen (Bach and Stark 2004).

In their article, "Tweeting the Night Away: Using Twitter to Enhance Social Presence," Joanna C. Dunlap and Patrick R. Lowenthal (2009) discuss how they found that using Twitter to augment their discussions with students in their online class extended their teaching presence with a "just-in-time" communications tool (p. 133). Similar to Bach and Stark (2004), Dunlap and Lowenthal (2009) found that the medium itself strongly influenced the users' relationship to one another and to the community at large:

Because [students] know they can count on us being available through Twitter, they continue to use Twitter as a just-in-time way to connect and interact with each other and us. This has been helpful for continued advising, coaching, and mentoring. Ultimately, following this guideline has helped us achieve the level of social presence we crave in support of on-going social learning and student engagement. (P. 133)

Though the impact of new technology cannot be denied, in "E-mail in Government: Not Post-Bureaucratic but Late Bureaucratic Organizations," Albert Jacob Meijer (2008) contends that new forms of communication may not always dramatically alter organizational structure. In his study of three bureaucratic organizations in the Netherlands, Meijer found that e-mail communication did not create radical transformations. Instead, the rigidity of the bureaucratic structure became the context within which the use and possibilities of e-mail as a medium of communication were interpreted. Therefore, changes in the organizations attributed to the use of e-mail were in degree rather than in type. The bureaucratic structure was modified in response to e-mail communications, but the structural changes were incremental rather than radical. Meijer (2008) writes,

The formalization of previously informal communications facilitates both vertical and horizontal control. The conclusion is that the use of email does not change government agencies into post-bureaucratic organizations. The resulting organizational form is a hybrid combination of bureaucratic and network forms. (P. 444)

In their article, "On-line Dating in Japan: A Test of Social Information Processing Theory," James Farrer and Jeff Gavin (2009) discuss how they found that organizations in cyberspace are not culturally neutral, nor is the organizational culture necessarily created through a consensus of members. Hearkening back to issues raised in the introduction to "organizational culture" (see Part V), online organizations can carry cultural markers from the population that initiated them. For instance, Match.com, a Western-based online dating service that now has an international presence, assumes aspects of social interactions that are common in North America but foreign to other regions. Farrer and Gavin found that despite unfamiliarity and initial discomfort with some of the social cues, the Japanese clientele on Match.com modified their behavior and expectations to conform to the established Western standards of the website:

Japanese online daters adapt their efforts to present and acquire social information using the cues that the online dating platform provides . . . The choice of a particular platform also is a form of social cueing. The choice of a "branded" site such as Match.com is described as a way of conveying a message about one's "seriousness" as well as a way of controlling for the seriousness and honesty of others. Sites can also be associated with particular types of people, such as foreigners, a special appeal of international sites such as Match.com. (P. 411)

In the final article in this section, "Online Organization of the LGBT Community in Singapore," Joe Phua (2008) demonstrates how online organizing is the only option for some communities. Though Singaporeans embrace many aspects of social and economic progress, there still remains a general intolerance of any nonheterosexual sexual orientation. For instance, homosexual relations among men are illegal, and most lesbian, gay, bisexual, and transsexual (LGBT) groups have been denied government approval to organize. Therefore, the majority of the LGBT organizations have moved online. In addition to providing a supportive community for their members, these LGBT groups often attempt to raise social and political awareness that would lead to more acceptance, both in Singapore and in other antihomosexual nations. Phua writes,

> The general consensus among the majority of interviewees is that political lobbying must take place using a "soft" approach, in which the government is "pressured" into changing their policies toward the LGBT community through local and, particularly, overseas coverage of LGBT issues and problems. Also, interviewees (N=5) expressed that their websites are able to indirectly influence policy development by creating dialogue and debate among intellectuals in the heterosexual community, including researchers, journalists and government officials. (Pp. 12–13)

Currently, the Singaporean government has decided not to close LGBT websites unless they display overtly pornographic material. Therefore, these online organizations provide a way for members to interact and keep in touch with one another as well as come together as a political force. In fact, Singaporeans might be becoming more tolerant of the LGBT community. Phua (2008) notes that many of his interviewees report an increase in positive media coverage of the LBGT community, a greater number of gay-owned and -operated businesses, and positive public reception to the "coming out" of local celebrities.

Organizing and organizations are coevolving with technologies that provide new ways to communicate and that connect populations that have heretofore remained isolated from one another. This has implications not only for self-development and emerging communities, but also for changes in organizational structure and knowledge generation that have the potential to dramatically redefine social, political, and economic power.

QUESTIONS FOR DISCUSSION

1. To what degree and in what ways does technology influence organizing and organizations?
2. What are some ways that organizations influence technology?
3. Some of the authors in this section claim that people can be more themselves online, while others claim that online interaction encourages participants to try on new identities. Explain various ways that new technologies can impact self-identity and self-development.
4. Describe some shifts in political, social, and/or economic power that can be attributed to new technology.

SUGGESTIONS FOR FURTHER READING

Matzat, Uwe. 2009. "A Theory of Relational Signals in Online Groups." *New Media & Society,* 11(3):375–94.

Shaw, Adrienne. (2009. "Putting the Gay in Games: Cultural Production and GLBT Content in Video Games." *Games and Culture,* 4(3):228–53.

Suarez, David. 2009. "Nonprofit Advocacy and Civic Engagement on the Internet." *Administration & Society,* 41:267–89.

REFERENCES

Bach, Jonathan and David Stark. 2004. "Link, Search, Interact: The Co-Evolution of NGOs and Interactive Technology." *Theory, Culture & Society,* 21:101–17.

Bauman, Zygmunt. 2000. *Liquid Modernity.* Cambridge, UK: Polity Press.

Dunlap, Joanna C. and Patrick R. Lowenthal. 2009. "Tweeting the Night Away: Using Twitter to Enhance Social Presence." *Journal of Information Systems Education,* 20(2):129–35.

Farrer, James and Jeff Gavin. 2009. "On-line Dating in Japan: A Test of Social Information Processing Theory." *CyberPsychology and Behavior,* 12(4):407–12.

Giddens, Anthony. 1991. *Modernity and Self-Identity.* Cambridge, UK: Polity Press.

Meijer, Albert Jacob. 2008. "E-mail in Government: Not Post-Bureaucratic but Late Bureaucratic Organizations." *Government Information Quarterly,* 25(3):429–47.

Phua, Joe. 2008. *Online Organization of the LGBT Community in Singapore.* Paper presented at the International Communication Association Conference, Montreal, Canada, May.

Turkle, Sherry. 1994. "Constructions and Reconstructions of Self in Virtual Reality: Playing in the MUDs." *Mind, Culture and Activity,* 1(3):158–63.

55

CONSTRUCTIONS AND RECONSTRUCTIONS OF SELF IN VIRTUAL REALITY

Playing in the MUDs

SHERRY TURKLE

PLAYING IN THE MUD

In an interactive computer game designed to represent a world inspired by the television series *Star Trek: The Next Generation,* over 1000 players spend up to 80 hours a week participating in intergalactic exploration and wars. They create characters who have casual and romantic sex, who fall in love and get married, who attend rituals and celebrations. "This is more real than my real life," says a character who turns out to be a man playing a woman who is pretending to be a man. In this game the rules of social interaction are built not received.

In another, more loosely structured game, each player creates a character or several characters, specifying their genders and other physical and psychological attributes. The characters need not be human and there are more than two genders. All interactions take place "in character." Beyond this, players are invited to help build the computer world itself. Using a relatively simple programming language, they can make a "room" in the game space where they can set the stage and define the rules. That is, they make objects in the computer world and specify how they work. Rachel, an 11-year-old, built a room she calls "the condo." It has jewelry boxes containing magical pieces that transport her to different places and moments in history. When Rachel visits the condo, she invites her friends, she chats, orders pizza, and flirts: Other players built TVs showing scenes taking place in the rooms of the game, a transportation system to navigate the space, and a magical theater that replays past game events. Some have built robots, for example a program named "Julia," that "pretends" to be a person as she offers directions and helps to locate your friends.

Both worlds exist on international computer networks, which of course means that in a certain sense, a physical sense, they don't exist at all. From all over the world, people use their individual machines to access a program which presents them with a game space—in the high tech world such spaces have come to be called "virtual"—in that they can navigate, converse, and build.

The first game, Trek Muse, and the second, LambdaMOO, are examples of a class of virtual worlds known as MUDs—an acronym for "Multi-User Dungeons."[1] In the early 1970s, a role playing game called "Dungeons and Dragons" swept the game cultures, a game in which a "dungeon master" created a world in which people created characters and played out complex adventures. Several years later, Dungeons and Dragons was interpreted for computational space in a program called "Adventure." There, players proceeded through a maze that was presented to them through text description on a computer screen. The term "dungeon" has persisted in both the games and hi-tech culture, and in the case of MUDs, refers to a virtual social space that exists on a machine.

There are over 300 multi-user games based on at least 13 different kinds of software on the international computer network known as the Internet. Here I use the term "MUD" to refer to all the various kinds. All provide worlds for social interaction in a virtual space, worlds in which you can present yourself as a "character," in which you can be anonymous, in which you can play a role as close or as far away from your "real self" as you choose. Where they differ is in how constrained that world is. It can be built around a medieval fantasy landscape in which there are dragons to slay and gold coins and magical amulets to collect, or it can be a relatively open space in which you can play at whatever captures your imagination, both by playing a role and by participating in building a world.

In the MUDs, the projections of self are engaged in a resolutely postmodern context. There are parallel narratives in the different rooms of the MUD; one can move forward or backward in time. The cultures of Tolkien, Gibson, and Madonna coexist and interact. Authorship is not only displaced from a solitary voice, it is exploded. The MUDs are authored by their players, thousands of people in all, often hundreds of people at a time, all logged on from different places. And the self is not only decentered but multiplied without limit. There is an unparalleled opportunity to play with one's identity and to "try out" new ones.

My past research into the experiences of individuals working with computers has led me to underscore the power of this technology not only as a medium for getting things done but for thinking through and working through personal concerns (Turkle, 1984). Engagement with computational technology facilitates a series of "second chances" for adults to work and rework unresolved personal issues and more generally, to think through questions about the nature of self, including questions about definitions of life, intentionality, and intelligence.

What is true of individuals working alone with a computer is raised to a higher power when people use computers to communicate with other people as they do on the MUDs. In the first case, the person alone with the computer, I have found that individuals use computers to work through identity issues that center around control and mastery; in the second, where the computer is used as a communications medium, there is more room to use the control provided by the computer to develop a greater capacity for collaboration and even intimacy. The medium enables the self to explore a social context as well as to reflect on its own nature and powers.

My method of investigation of MUDs has been ethnographic and clinical: play the games, "hang out" with game players in virtual as well as real space, interview game players in person both individually and in groups. Some of my richest data came from a series of weekly "pizza parties" for MUDders within the Boston area.[2] There the topic was open and conversation turned to what was on the players' minds: most often love, romance, and what can be counted on as real in virtual space.

I begin my report from this new social and psychological world by taking one step back to general considerations of how role playing games enable people to work through issues of identity and then move on to the form this takes in MUDs, which enhance the evocative potential of traditional games by further blurring the line between the game and what players refer to as RL, "real life," or TRW, "the real world."[3]

Traditional role playing prompts reflection on personal and interpersonal issues, but in games that take place in ongoing virtual societies such as MUDs, the focus is on larger social and cultural themes as well. The networked computer serves as an "evocative object" for thinking about community. Additionally, people playing in the MUDs struggle towards a new, still tentative discourse about the nature of a social world that is populated both by people and by programs. In this, life in the MUD may serve as a harbinger of what is to come in the social spaces that we still contrast with the virtual by calling the "real."

Role Playing Games

As identity workshops, MUDs have much in common with traditional role playing games, for example, the role playing games played by Julee, a 19-year-old who has dropped out of Yale after her freshman year. Part of the reason for her leaving college is that she is in an increasingly turbulent relationship with her mother, a devout Catholic, who turned away from her daughter when she discovered that she had had an abortion the summer before beginning college.

From Julee's point of view, her mother has chosen to deny her existence. When asked about her most important experience playing role playing games, Julee described a game in which she had been assigned the role of a mother facing a conflict with her daughter. Indeed, in the game, the script says that the daughter is going to betray, even kill, the mother.

In the role playing game, played over a weekend on the Boston University (BU) campus, Julee and her "daughter" talked for hours: Why might the daughter have joined her mother's opponents, how could they stay true to their relationship and the game as it had been written? Huddled in a corner of an empty BU classroom, Julee was having the conversation that her mother had not been willing to have with her. In the end, Julee's character chose to ignore her loyalty to her team in order to preserve her daughter's life.

Clearly, Julee projected feelings about her "real" mother's choice onto her experience of the game, but more was going on than a simple reenactment. Julee was able to reexperience a familiar situation in a setting where she could examine it, do something new with it, and revise her relationship towards it. In many ways, what happened was resonant with the psychoanalytic notion of "working through."

Julee's experience stands in contrast to images of role playing games that are prevalent in the popular culture. A first popular image portrays role playing games as depressing and dangerous environments. It is captured in the urban legend which describes an emotionally troubled student disappearing and committing suicide during a game of Dungeons and Dragons. Another popular image, and one that has been supported by some academic writing on role playing games, turns them into places of escape. Players are seen as leaving their "real" lives and problems behind to lose themselves in the game space. Julee's story belies both stereotypes. For her the game is psychologically constructive rather than destructive. And she uses it not for escape but as a vehicle for engaging in a significant dialogue with important events and relationships in her "real" life.

Role playing games are able to serve in this evocative capacity precisely because they are not simple escapes from the real to the unreal, but because they stand betwixt and between, both in and not in real life. But in the final analysis, what puts Julee's game most firmly in the category of game is that it had an end point. The weekend was over and so was the game.

MUDs present a far more complicated case. In a certain sense, they don't have to end. Their boundaries are more fuzzy; the routine of playing them becomes part of their players' real lives. The virtual reality becomes not so much an alternative as a parallel life. Indeed, dedicated players who work with computers all day describe how they temporarily put their characters to "sleep," remain logged on to the game, pursue other activities, and periodically return to the game space.

Such blurring of boundaries between role and self present new opportunities to use the role to work on the self. As one experienced player put it, "you are the character and you are not the character both at the same time." And "you are who you pretend to be." This ambiguity contributes to the games' ability to be a place in which to address issues of identity and intimacy. They take the possibilities that Julee found in role playing games and raise them to a higher power.

Virtual Realities: Role Playing to a Higher Power

The notion "you are who you pretend to be" has a mythic resonance. The Pygmalion story endures because it speaks to a powerful fantasy: that we are not limited by our histories, that we can be recreated or can recreate ourselves. In the real world, we are thrilled by stories of self transformation. Madonna is our modern Eliza Doolittle; Ivana Trump is the object of morbid fascination. But of course, for most people such recreations of self are difficult. Virtual worlds provide environments for experiences that may be hard to come by in the real.

Not the least of these experiences is the opportunity to play an "aspect of your self" that you embody as a separate self in the game space.[4]

Peter is a 23-year-old physics graduate student at the University of Massachusetts. His life revolves around his work in the laboratory and his plans for a life in science. He says that his only friend is his roommate, another student whom he describes as being even more reclusive than he. This circumscribed, almost monastic life does not represent a radical departure for Peter. He has had heart trouble since he was a child; his health is delicate, one small rebellion, a ski trip when he first came up to Boston, put him in the hospital for three weeks. His response has been to circumscribe his world. Peter has never traveled. He lives in a small compass.

In an interview with Peter he immediately made it clear why he plays on MUDs: "I do it so I can talk to people." He is logged on for at least 40 hours a week, but it is hard to call what he does "playing" a game. He spends his lime on the MUDs constructing a life that in only a seeming paradox is more expansive than his own. He tells me with delight that the MUD he frequents most often is physically located on a computer in Germany.

> And I started talking to them [the inhabitants of the MUD] and they're like, "This costs so many and so many Deutschmarks." And I'm like, "What are Deutschmarks? Where is this place located?" And they say: "Don't you know, this is Germany."

It is from MUDs that Peter has learned what he knows of politics, of economics, of the differences between capitalism and welfare state socialism. He revels in the differences between the styles of Americans and Europeans on the MUDs and in the thrill of speaking to a player in Norway who can see the Northern lights.

On the MUD, Peter shapes a character, Achilles, who is his ideal self. Life in a University of Massachusetts dorm has put him in modest and unaesthetic circumstances. Yet the room he inhabits on the MUD is elegant, romantic, out of a Ralph Lauren ad.

Peter's story illustrates several aspects of the relationship of MUDding and identity. First, the MUD serves as a kind of Rorschach inkblot, a projection of inner fantasies. Second, unlike a Rorschach, it does not stay on a page. It is part of Peter's everyday life. Beyond expanding his social reach, MUDs have brought Peter the only romance and intimacy he has ever known. At a social event held in virtual space, a "wedding" of two regular players on his favorite Germany-based MUD. Peter met Winterlight, one of the three female players. Peter, who has known little success with women, was able to charm this most desirable and sought after player. Their encounter led to a courtship in which he is tender and romantic, chivalrous and poetic. One is reminded of Cyrano who could only find his voice through another's persona. It is Achilles, Peter's character on the MUD, who can create the magic and win the girl.

While people work one-on-one with the computer, the machine becomes an evocative object for thinking through issues of identity which tend to be centered on control and mastery. But Peter's experience (where the computer is a mediator to a reality shared with other people) has put computation more directly in the service of the development of a greater capacity for friendship, the development of confidence for a greater capacity for intimacy.

But what of the contrast between Peter and Julee? What can we say about the difference between role playing games in the corridors of BU and on computer virtual worlds?

Julee and Peter both use games to remake the self. Their games, however, are evocative for different reasons. Julee's role playing has the powerful quality of real-time psychodrama, but on the other hand Peter's game is ongoing and provides him with anonymity, invisibility, and potential multiplicity. Ongoing: He can play it as much as he wants, all day if he wants, every day if he chooses as he often does. There are always people logged on to the game; there is always someone to talk to or something to do. Anonymous: Once Peter creates his character, that is his only identity on the game. His character need not have his gender or share any recognizable feature with him. He can be who he wants and play with no concern that "he," Peter, will be held accountable in "real life" for his characters' actions, quarrels, or relationships. The degree to which he brings the game into his real life is his choice. Invisible: The created character can have any physical description and will be responded to as a function of that description. The plain can experience the self presentation of great beauty; the nerdy can be elegant; the obese can be slender. Multiplicity: Peter can create several characters, playing out and playing with different aspects of his self. An ongoing game, an anonymous personae, physical invisibility, and the possibility to be not one but many, these are the qualities at the root of the holding power and evocative potential of MUDs as "identity workshops."[5] Faced with the notion that "you are what you pretend to be," Peter can only hope that it is true for he is playing his ideal self.

Peter plays what in the psychoanalytic tradition would be called an "ego ideal." Other players create a character or multiple characters that are closer to embodying aspects of themselves that they hate or fear or perhaps have not ever consciously confronted before. One male player describes his role playing as

> daring to be passive. I don't mean in having sex on the MUD. I mean in letting other people take the initiative in friendships, in not feeling when I am in character that I need to control everything. My mother controlled my whole family, well, certainly me. So I grew up thinking 'never again.' My 'real life' is exhausting that way. On MUDs I do something else. I didn't even realize this connection to my mother until something happened in the game and somebody tried to boss my pretty laid-back character around and I went crazy. And then I saw what I was doing.

The possibilities the medium offers for projecting both conscious and unconscious aspects of the self suggest an analogy between MUDs and psychotherapeutic milieus. The goal of psychotherapy is not of course to simply provide a place for "acting out" behavior that expresses one's conflicts, but to furnish a contained and confidential environment for "working through" unresolved issues. The distinction between acting out and working through

is crucial to thinking about MUDs as settings for personal growth. For it is in the context of this distinction that the much-discussed issue of "MUDs addiction" should be situated. The accusation of being "addicted" to psychotherapy is only made seriously when friends or family suspect that over a period of time, the therapy is supporting repetitions and reenactments rather than new resolutions. MUDding is no more "addictive" than therapy when it works as a pathway to psychological growth.

Robert is a college freshman who in the months before beginning college had to cope with his father's having lost his job and disgraced his family because of alcoholism. The job loss led to his parents' relocation to another part of the country, far away from all of Robert's friends. For a period of several months, Robert, now at college, MUDded over 80 hours a week. Around the time of a fire in his dormitory which destroyed all his possessions, Robert was playing over 120 hours a week, sleeping four hours a night, and only taking brief breaks to get food, which he would eat while playing.

At the end of the school year, however, Robert's MUD experience was essentially over. He had gotten his own apartment; he had a job as a salesman; he had formed a rock band with a few friends. Looking back on the experience he thought that MUDding had served its purpose: it kept him from what he called his "suicidal thoughts," in essence by keeping him too busy to have them; it kept him from drinking ("I have something more fun and safe to do"); it enabled him to function with responsibility and competency as a highly placed administrator; it afforded an emotional environment where he could be in complete control of how much he revealed about his life, about his parents, even about something as simple for other people as where he was from. In sum, MUDs had provided what Erik Erikson would have called a "psychosocial moratorium." It had been a place from which he could reassemble a sense of boundaries that enabled him to pursue less bounded relationships.[6] Through theories which stress the decentered subject and through the fragmented selves presented by patients,[7] contemporary psychology confronts what is problematic in traditional notions of a unitary self. MUDs have become a new context which provokes reflection on such questions. Virtual communities such as MUDs are the most dramatic example of the way the culture of simulation challenges traditional notions of human identity. Indeed, they make possible the construction of an identity that is so fluid and multiple that it strains the very limits of the notion. Identity, after all, literally means *one*. When we live through our electronic self-representations we have unlimited possibilities to be *many*. People become masters of self-presentation and self-creation. The very notion of an inner, "true self" is called into question.

These remarks have addressed MUDs as privileged spaces for thinking through and working through issues of personal identity. Additionally, when role playing moves from circumscribed "weekend encounters" such as those Julee participated in onto a sustained virtual stage, a new social world grows up too. The development of virtual social life is of signal importance: it makes MUDs very special kinds of evocative objects.

Evocative Objects: Gender, Community, and "Bots"

In *The Second Self* (1984) I called the personal computer an evocative object because it provoked self-reflection and stimulated thought. It led to reevaluations and reconsiderations of things taken for granted, for example, about the nature of intelligence, free will, and our notions of what is alive. And I found that the computer did this not just because it presented people with ideas as did traditional philosophy, but because it presented them with experiences, an ongoing culture of personal computing that provoked a new philosophy in everyday life.

The same kind of process, this provocation of new discourse and reflection, is taking place around computer-mediated communications in virtual realities such as MUDs. But the emphasis of the new discourse and reflection is on social and cultural issues as well as individual ones.

One dramatic example is the novel and compelling discourse that surrounds the experience of "gender swapping" in virtual reality, whereby men may play the roles of women and women the roles of men. As MUD players talked to me about their experiences with gender swapping, they certainly gave reason to believe that through this practice they were working through personal issues that had to do with accepting the feminine and/or the masculine in their own personalities. But they were doing something else as well which transcended the level of individual personality and its dynamics. People were using gender swapping as a first hand experience through which to form ideas about the role of gender in human interactions. In the ongoing culture of MUDs, these issues are discussed both within the space of the games and in a discussion group on USENET called "rec.games.mud."

Discussion on USENET about gender swapping has dealt with how female characters are besieged with attention, sexual advances, and unrequested offers of assistance which imply that women can't do things by themselves. It has dealt with the question of whether women who are consistently treated as incompetent may start to believe it. Men playing women on role playing games have remarked that other male players (read male characters) sometimes expect sexual favors in return for technical assistance. In this case, offering technical help, like picking up the check at dinner, is being used to purchase rather man win a woman's regard. While such expectations can be subtly expressed, indeed sometimes overlooked in real life, when such things happen in MUDs, they are more visible, often widely witnessed, and openly discussed. As this takes place, the MUD becomes an evocative object for a richer understanding not only of sexual harassment but of the social construction of gender. MUDding throws issues of the impact of gender on human relations into relief and brings the issue home; the seriousness and intensity of discussions of gender among MUDders speaks to the fact that the game allows its players to experience rather than merely observe what it feels like to be the opposite gender or to have no gender at all. MUDs are objects for thinking about gender, but there are similar stories to tell about discussions in MUD environments about violence, property, and privacy. Virtual communities compel conversations about the nature of community itself.

On an early MUD known as Habitat, which ran as an experiment in the United States and has become a successful commercial venture in Japan, players were originally allowed to have guns. However, when you are shot, you do not cease to exist but simply lose all the things you were carrying and are transported back to your virtual home. For some players, thievery and murder became the highlight of the "game." For others, these activities were experienced as a violent intrusion on their peaceful world. An intense debate ensued.[8]

Some players argued that guns should be eliminated; unlike in the real world, a perfect gun ban is possible with a few lines of code. Others argued that what was damaging was not the violence but the trivialization of violence, and maintained that guns should persist, but their consequences should be made more real: when you are killed, your character should cease to exist and not simply be sent home. Still others believed that since Habitat was "just a game," and playing assassin was part of the fun, there could be no harm in a little virtual violence.

As the debate raged, a player who was a priest in real life founded the "Order of the Holy Walnut" whose members pledged not to carry guns. In the end, the game designers divided the world into two parts: in town, violence was prohibited; in the wilds outside of town, it was allowed. Eventually a democratic voting process was installed and a sheriff elected. Debates then ensued about the nature of Habitat laws and the proper balance between individual freedom and law and order. What is remarkable is not just the solution, but the quality of the debate which led up to that solution. The denizens of Habitat were spending their leisure time debating pacifism, the nature of good government, and the relationships between representations and reality.

Virtual reality is not "real" but it has a relationship to the real. By being betwixt and between, it becomes a play space for thinking about the real world. It is an exemplary evocative object. When a technology serves as an evocative object, old questions are raised in new contexts and there is an opportunity for fresh resolutions. I conclude with a final example of how MUDs are able to recast some old questions about personhood and program.

When in the context of "traditional" computation, people meet a program that exhibits some behavior that would be considered intelligent if done by a person, they often grant the program a "sort of" intelligence, indeed a "sort of" life, but then insist that the essence of human intelligence or indeed of human uniqueness is what "the computer cannot

do." Computers cannot have intentions, feelings, the sense of an "I" (Turkle, 1984).[9]

In MUDs, however, intelligent computational entities are present in a context which gives new saliency to questions about their status. Some of the inhabitants of these virtual worlds are artificial intelligences, robots, affectionately referred to as "bots" that have been built by enterprising players. When you wander about in a MUD, you find yourself in conversations with them, you find yourself asking them for directions, thanking them for being helpful, ordering drinks from them at a virtual bar, telling them a joke. And you find yourself doing all of these things before you know that they are not people but "things." (Of course, you may be a person "playing" the role "an intelligent Batmobile" or "a swarm of bees.") The "thingness" of the bots is not part of your initial encounter or the establishment of your relationship with them. You have unintentionally played out a Turing test in which the program has won.

Reaction to such experiences is strong, much of it still centered on the question of human uniqueness and "whether a program can be an 'I.'" (For example, within the Narrative Intelligence electronic discussion group centered at MIT, there was heated debate about "bots" and the question of the "I." In this debate, sophisticated programmers of and players in virtual worlds admitted to being nonplussed when they first realized that they have unknowingly participated in casual social conversation with these virtually "ambulatory" artificial intelligences [AIs].) But another way of talking about the bots has grown up as well, a discourse marked by two new themes.

First, instead of dwelling on the essence of "bots," conversation among MUDders turns to the ethics of whether "they" (the bots) should or should not be required to announce their artificiality. This discussion of "full disclosure" is of course taking place in the context of a virtual world where changing gender, race, and species is the norm. With people playing robots, there is a new level of self-consciousness about the asymmetry of demanding that robots not play people.

In the film *Blade Runner* sophisticated androids almost indistinguishable from humans have been given the final defining human qualities: childhood memories and the knowledge of their mortality. This is a world obsessed with the Turing test; the film's hero, Decker, makes his profession diagnosing the real from the artificial. But by the end of the film, Decker, who has spent his life tracking down and destroying androids, is less concerned with whether he is dealing with an artificial being and more concerned with how to thank one of them for saving his life and how to escape with another of them with whom he has fallen in love. The film speaks to an increasing tension in our traditional notions of the real and the artificial. As we live in a world of cyborgs, the important distinctions may not follow from *a priori* essences but from ongoing relationships.

And indeed, the second new theme in MUD-based conversations about "bots" turns discussion away from questions of essence and towards the most practical matters. How exactly should the AIs function within the community? Are specific bots disruptive or facilitating? Are they rude or are they kind? In this sense, MUDs may be harbingers of the discourse about the artificial in a post Turing test world.

There is a lot of excitement about virtual reality. In both the popular and academic press there is enthusiasm and high expectation for a future in which we don gloves and masks and bodysuits and explore virtual space and sensuality. However, from the point of view of how we think about identity and community, there is reason to feel great excitement about where we are in the present. In the text-based virtual realities that exist today, people are exploring, constructing, and reconstructing their identities. They are doing this in an environment infused with a postmodern ethos of the value of multiple identities and of playing out aspects of the self and with a constructionist ethos of "Build something, be someone." And they are creating communities that have become privileged contexts for thinking about social, cultural, and ethical dilemmas of living in constructed lives that we share with extensions of ourselves we have embodied in program.

Watch for a nascent culture of virtual reality that underscores the ways in which we construct gender and the self, the ways in which we *become* what we play, argue about, and build. And watch for a culture that leaves new space for the idea that he or she who plays, argues, and builds might be doing so with a machine.

NOTES

1. For a general introduction to LambdaMOO and MUDding, see Pavel Curtis (1992), *MUDding: Social phenomena in text-based virtual realities,* and Amy Bruckman (1992), *Identity workshops: Emergent social and psychological phenomena in text-based virtual reality.* On virtual community in general, see Allucquere Rosanne Stone (1992), "Will the real body please stand up? Boundary stories about virtual cultures" in Michael Benedikt, Ed., *Cyberspace: First Steps* (Cambridge: MIT Press).

2. Amy Bruckman, a graduate student at MIT's Media Laboratory, was my research assistant and dialogue partner during a summer of intensive work on the MUD phenomena; my understanding of this activity and its importance owes much to our collaboration.

3. For more material on the contrast with traditional role playing see Gary Alan Fine, *Shared Fantasy: Role-Playing Games as Social Worlds* (Chicago: The University of Chicago Press, 1983). Henry Jenkins' study of fan culture, *Textual Poachers: Television Fans and Participatory Culture* (New York: Routledge, 1992), illuminates the general question of how individuals appropriate fantasy materials in the construction of identity.

4. "The Well" has a "topic" (discussion group) on "On Line Personae." In a March 24, 1992 posting to this group, F. Randall Farmer noted that in a group of about 50 Habitat users about a quarter experienced their online personae as a separate creature that acted in ways they do in real life, and a quarter experienced their online personae as a separate creature that acted in ways they do not in real life.

5. This felicitous phrase was coined by Amy Bruckman (1992).

6. Of course, taking the analogy between a therapeutic milieu and virtual reality seriously means that incidents when players lose their anonymity are potentially psychologically damaging. In therapy, the transference is to the person of the therapist or to the therapy group; in virtual space, the transference is to the "body" of the MUD often as represented by its "wizards" or system administrators.

7. Perhaps most dramatically demonstrated by the increasing numbers of patients who present with multiple personality disorder, literally "divided selves."

8. For more detail on this example, see Chip Morningstar and F. Randall Farmer (1992, pp. 289–91).

9. See Turkle (1984), Thinking of oneself as a machine, pp. 271–305.

REFERENCES

Bruckman, A. (1992). *Identity workshops: Emergent social and psychological phenomena in text-based virtual reality.* Unpublished manuscript.

Curtis, P. (1992). Mudding: Social phenomena in text-based virtual realities. *Proceedings of DIAC '92.* (Available via anonymous ftp from parcftp.xerox.com.pub/MOO)/papers/DIAC92. {ps,txt}).

Morningstar, C., & Farmer, F. R. (1992). The lessons of Lucasfilm's Habitat. In M. Benedikt (Ed.), *Cyberspace: First steps.* Cambridge, MA: MIT Press.

Stone, A. R. (1992). Will the real body please stand up? Boundary stories about virtual cultures. In M. Benedikt (Ed.), *Cyberspace: First steps.* Cambridge, MA: MIT Press.

Turkle, S. (1984). *The second self: Computers and the human spirit.* New York: Simon & Schuster.

SOURCE: Turkle, Sherry. 1994. "Constructions and Reconstructions of Self in Virtual Reality: Playing in the MUDs." *Mind, Culture and Activity*, 1(3):158–63.

56

LINK, SEARCH, INTERACT

The Co-Evolution of NGOs and Interactive Technology

JONATHAN BACH AND DAVID STARK

We are witnesses to an epochal transformation in the analytically distinct domains of production and communication. On one side, we see a shift from mass production to network modes of organizing, as hierarchical, bureaucratic forms coexist with hierarchical, collaborative forms. On the other, we see a shift from mass communication to interactive media, as the uni-directional channels of one-to-many coexist with the hypertextual world of increasing interactivity. The dual shifts are, in fact, a twinned transformation: from mass production/mass communication to network production/network communication. To understand the new organizational forms of our epoch we must study how their roles and practices co-evolve with the new interactive technologies.

These transformations are being exponentially accelerated by digital tools that make it possible to access text, audio, visual and database information in an encompassing, interactive environment. Actors now participate in complex digital ecologies consisting of the Internet, intranets, extranets, web sites, virtual collaborative workplaces and the like. Within this encompassing environment of extended connectivity and near-ubiquitous computing, the new

media do not simply allow organizations to communicate faster or to perform existing functions more effectively, they also present opportunities to communicate in entirely new ways and to perform radically new functions. Especially because these are interactive media, their adoption becomes an occasion for innovation that restructures interdependencies, reshapes interfaces and transforms relations.

The impact of such developments is as far-reaching for international order as for individual organizations. Among the many actors of this rapidly changing environment, non-governmental organizations (NGOs) have exploded in number and visibility as the 20th century neared its end. We use the term NGO to refer to the broad array of civil society organizations that together constitute what Anheier and Themudo (2002: 191) call the organizational infrastructure of global civil society. We are aware of the inherent limitations of any covering term, and use NGOs to refer to nonprofit organizations formally independent from government. These include community-based, national and international NGOs. The irreducibility of civil society-based organizations to a set organizational form is precisely of interest in understanding how, by any definition, the NGO has become a key actor in the global order by the beginning of the current century. The numbers vary according to method but all tell a similar story: NGOs of all types have increased from negligible numbers—a few dozen to just under 200—at the beginning of the 20th century, to a modest presence by the 1970s; then there was a period of exponential growth from the 1980s to the present day, with estimates ranging (depending on method) from 17,000 international NGOs (active in at least three countries) to 250,000 (Anheier and Themudo, 2002; Union of International Associations, 1999; World Resources Institute, 2003). The World Bank estimates that over 15 percent of total overseas development aid is channeled through NGOs (World Bank, 2001).

Today NGOs are engaged, directly or at the margins, in the transformation of national, international and transnational political space. In their engagement they appear in various, often conflicting, guises: as building blocks for a global civic culture, incubators for new international institutions, barefoot revolutionaries carrying out globalization from below, or new missionaries imposing Western ideals from above. While an ever-increasing literature on NGOs implicitly recognizes their growing power, NGOs are most often discussed, however, as if their form were given and only their effect remains to be worked out. Thus NGOs appear as an incipient global civil society, as functional equivalents of democracy, as tools of the ruling class or as the vanguard for globalization from below (Appadurai, 2000; Falk, 1999; Rosenau, 1998; Warkentin, 2001).

Interactive technology is generally regarded as instrumental support for one or the other of these guises. Technology is appended to a constellation of factors that are used to explain the recent growth and prominence of NGOs, most notably the retrenchment of the welfare state, the end of the Cold War (with its dual legacy of democratization and new civil wars) and a rise in private donations (Lindenberg and Bryant, 2001: 8–12). In nearly all of these scenarios, interactive technology appears in a diffusionist fashion as either speeding up the process, presenting obstacles, or both. Viewing technology as an external actant misses the way in which intelligence is distributed across actors and artifacts

(Hutchins, 1995). We would like to approach NGOs and interactive technology as co-evolving actants embedded in an era where knowledge is increasingly a resource for creating enduring associations (i.e. as a source of power). Our approach is part of a growing body of social science research that seeks to overcome the artificial divide between 'society' and 'technology' by viewing the social as consisting of humans and non-humans (objects, things, artifacts).[1] Viewing technology not as a tool but as part of a co-evolutionary process that shapes organizational forms and practices will help us understand why NGOs have been able to assume a more powerful and controversial role as co-constituents of global transformation.

This article proceeds in two parts: first it examines how NGOs are embedded within epochal shifts that are unbundling, as Saskia Sassen (1999) puts it, the centralized forms of authority that govern the nation-state. NGOs are among the new actors engaged in what is often loosely termed global governance. More precisely, at stake is a coming to terms with decentralized, distributed power, 'its reproduction, its diversification, its growth and multiplication' (Sassen, 1999). In this article we trace a shift among NGOs from pseudo-autarky to collaboration that enabled their structural role in globalization to become increasingly prominent. This expanded role itself has been enhanced through NGOs' use of interactive technology, often within the confines of an information broker model. The second part of the article moves beyond the diffusionist model of technology and the limits of information brokering to focus on the recombinatory logic of interactive technology. We highlight the multiplicative properties of the Internet as an example of how NGOs can facilitate knowledge to form incipient knowledge communities—communities that use a logic of what we call 'link, search, interact' to sustain themselves and grow.

FROM AUTARKY TO COLLABORATION

NGOs are embedded within the oft-described network paradigm that is displacing central-planning and strictly hierarchical thinking (Castells, 1999). Networks operate more fluidly and can improve on accounts of complex social interaction over the methodological individualism of positivist social science. They have the significant effect of enhancing flows and creating a shared acceleration that corresponds to the compressed space-time of our late modern era. This spatio-temporal compression is part and parcel of the function of interactive technologies, which combine real-time and many-to-many communication in ways that fundamentally rearrange the ways firms produce, states fight wars, and people's lives are structured. This rearranging is, significantly, a form of de-territorialization, both because the electronic space in which power and action are being reconstituted is literally not located in territorial space, and because the institutions that evolved to regulate life within territorial borders are ill-suited to the tasks of regulating transborder flows (Deleuze and Guattari, 1987; Sassen, 1998; Strange, 1996).

De-territorialization is the process at the core of the unbundling of the nation-state. It forces a transformation of the spatial organization of politics away from the single-point perspective that John Ruggie (1993: 159) pegs as the defining doctrinal characteristic of sovereignty. Most of us will have little difficulty agreeing minimally that an increase in flows of money, people and commodities has challenged the ability of the nation-state to exert its social ordering functions, that global issues exist beyond the control of any one state and that, consequently, the global political system is undergoing a significant transformation. But few will agree on what this is a transformation *to*.

We would be charlatans if we claimed to know what the new spatial organization of politics will be. We can, however, identify elements of the transformation, in particular three shifts (these are ongoing shifts, not completed processes):

• First, there is a shift among states and intergovernmental organizations from a concern about the sanctity of sovereignty to a concern about the enforcement of universal norms. This can be viewed cynically or hopefully, through the lens of empire or Enlightenment. Certainly not all governments embrace such a shift (ironically the United States is foremost among the obstructionists while also one of the greatest proselytizers of universal principles), but a global agenda that prioritizes humanitarian, environmental and even economic justice issues has established itself as a dominant discourse.

• Second, there is a shift from decentralized to distributed structures. Decentralized governing structures emerged to (over)compensate for the inability of centralized forms of government and market to efficiently provide the resources or results deemed necessary for the good life, resulting in privatization or political structures such as subsidiarity and devolution. Decentralized production enabled capital to increase its mobility. But decentralization is an effect. Distribution, on the other hand, is the capacity for a collective actor to act strategically based on an emergent effect of the patterns of association and not on the basis of a single person alone, or even a network of humans (Girard and Stark, 2002; Hutchins, 1995; Law and Hassard, 1999; Suchman, 1987).

• Third, in the analytical methodology that informs (social) scientific development we see a shift from a way of thinking that Latour called a diffusion model to a model of translation (Latour, 1986: 266–9). The diffusion model is a model of inertia and friction, where changes are explained by theorizing about what retards or accelerates an order or an object's trajectory—for example, the idea of the nation-state as a stable, given combination of traits and territory whose trajectory can be explained by a mixture of hard times that slow down its progress (perhaps covetous neighbors who invade their territory) or good times that speed it up (such as economic boom, or the nation-state's own military conquests).[2] The nation is merely transmitted from one generation to the next with a rich history of (and potential for future) friction. A translation model dispenses with inertia and sees an object or order as being continuously transformed by the actors themselves who engage in continuous reinterpretation.[3] In more fashionable terms a translation model could be seen as a process akin to social construction. But we have to remember that translation is *also always* a misunderstanding. Sites of translation therefore are thus also sites of interpretation, contention and renegotiation.

These shifts are harbingers of a new space-time construct. Again, we cannot know the outcome, but we can identify NGOs as an intriguing actor involved in the co-evolutionary process concomitant with the shifts presented above, since for many NGOs the concept of network is closely intertwined with their operational logic. Indeed, at first glance NGOs possess a superficial isomorphism with the perceived properties of interactive technology. When viewed mainly as a tool for processing information, interactive technology increases NGOs' communication and facilitates networking by enhancing the core tasks of getting information to constituents, channeling and interpreting information from varied sources, aggregating information and demands, transmitting them to diverse audiences, and mobilizing individuals and groups.[4] Interactive technology thus seemed ideal for lowering transaction costs, increasing participation and impact, and streamlining operations. The democratic rhetoric that accompanied the early years of the Internet was also a strong plus—social and organizational change could be seen as complementing each other.

It would be an error, however, to see NGOs as having an elective affinity with interactive technology, and then to use this a priori affinity to claim that NGOs plus IT equals new organizational forms capable of transforming global space if only the forces of friction are sufficiently overcome. This, however, is the sentiment that pervades much popular discussion about NGOs. It is a diffusionist model that presents NGOs as moving under their own inertia. This inertia is connected, often indirectly, to the quasi-mythical view of NGOs from the 1960s and 1970s as an anti-state and anti-market force. Let us take the example of development NGOs.

As Bishwapriya Sanyal explains, NGOs were privileged in the 1970s as 'the most appropriate catalytic agent for fostering development from below because their organizational priorities and procedures are diametrically opposed to those of the institutions at "the top"' (1994: 37). To fulfill this avant garde role Sanyal shows how NGOs valorized a form of pseudoautarky for two negative and one positive reasons: collaboration with the state was ruled out because it was seen as leading to control or co-option, while collaboration with the market would poison community solidarity bondings. In both cases legitimacy and effectiveness were thought to suffer. These were negative reasons for maintaining independence. A positive reason was

that the principles of self-sufficiency, self-reliance and social innovation would become the motor for self-reproduction. The basic analytic unit was the isolated NGO engaged in a form of autopoiesis. There was indeed a self-generating quality to this approach, but what it generated was isolation and contradictions. NGOs competed fiercely with each other for money and avoided forming institutional linkages with government, the commercial sector or even other NGOs. The lack of institutional support doomed all but the smallest projects and precluded replication or expansion. When they began to fall apart as a result of these incapacities it only intensified competitiveness and isolation and made a mockery of the attempt to create a broad base 'from below' (Sanyal, 1994).

The relative success and high growth of NGOs in the latter part of the 1980s, and especially the 1990s, can be attributed not only, or even primarily, to increased externalities, but to the NGOs' shift from self-imposed isolation to collaboration. NGOs moved to collaboration as they began to recognize that success, when it happened, was because they were already engaging in semi-conscious forms of collaboration that went unacknowledged. For example, NGOs' own leaders were drawn from an elite with informal linkages to all the types of institutions—banks, bureaucracies and parties—that form the 'top.' Sanyal (1994: 45) gives the example of the founders of the Grameen Bank, Doctors Yunus and Latifee, who are mythologized as visionaries whose sole efforts resulted in this paradigmatic development from below. They doubtless possessed great vision, but, as he points out, they also had an institutional association with the top university that provided both salary and legitimacy, and Yunus's efforts to convince the bank to make loans was not made on the strength of his grassroots organizing ability but because of his family's long-standing relationship as a major depositor. As the project expanded and became the famous Grameen Bank, it was on the firm basis of a tripartite alliance between NGOs, government and market institutions.[5]

The need to be self-sustaining caused conflicts within NGOs because of the siren call of alliances with the market as a source of generating independent income, especially as foundations began to require better accountability and plans for sustainability. Over the last 15 years, in the search for self-sustainability, some NGOs have indeed turned to income-generation alternatives that mimic commercial enterprises. For example the 'dot-corg' dual enterprise model combines social and business ventures, separating revenue generation from NGOs' social mission and evaluating it according to business metrics. There is also a minority of NGOs who, from early on, set their long-term goal as evolution into a socially oriented, for-profit venture, such as many Internet Service Providers in Eastern Europe who began as non-profits and grew into viable businesses (Peizer, 2000). When you consider the early resistance of NGOs to allying themselves too closely with the market it is striking (or even shocking) to watch partnerships emerge such as the CARE-Starbucks partnership (Lindenberg and Bryant, 2001: 164–5; see also Austin, 2000) or the 'Libraries Online Partnership' between Microsoft Corporation and the non-profit American Library Association (Sagawa and Segal, 2000).[6]

Alliances with the market certainly do open up new forms of sustainability and even synergy, and cannot be dismissed out of hand. If NGOs reject cooperation with state and market forces too completely they risk slipping into an exclusively oppositional role with diminished opportunities for agenda-setting (though some may relish precisely this oppositional role).

Yet the benefits of collaboration do not mean that old problems of co-option have disappeared—on the contrary, they may even be exacerbated by the new hybrid forms. The values of the market and of the non-profit world remain antagonistic. As NGOs spread their accountability unevenly among constituents, board members, donors and the public they find themselves faced with a proliferation of performance criteria that catches them between the value systems of business (efficiency, solvency) and social mission (adherence to principles, ideological agenda) (Edwards and Hulme, 1996b). In the best case they may exploit these contradictions, but the danger is real that actors who are accountable according to many principles become accountable to none (Stark, 2001).

Most importantly, success for NGOs came less from developing innovative ideas than from basing their efforts:

. . . on relatively old ideas which may have been tried, even by the government, in another context. . . . Successful NGOs did not pursue only a decentralized approach . . . their success was due to a skilful blending of centralization and decentralization of decisions, cooperation and competitiveness . . . (Sanyal, 1994: 43)

In other words, successful NGOs used logics that are distributed and recombinatory.

This shift from pseudo-autarky to collaboration, rather than the amassing of successes per se, made NGOs increasingly important players at a time when the dominant image of the Cold War gave way to globalization. We can see how NGOs were able to embody (and thereby help define) each of the major shifts we sketched above:

• NGOs were in the forefront in the shift from sovereign sanctity to universal norms, particularly in the realms of the environment and human rights. The stunning successes of Médecins sans Frontières (Doctors without Borders) and the Campaign to Ban Landmines, both of which won the Nobel Peace Prize, gave NGOs publicity and legitimacy that far surpassed previous efforts. From a different angle, the anti-World Trade Organization (WTO) protests in Seattle and similar 'anti-globalization' protests from Ottawa to Prague criticized the distributed modes of production and called attention to the new forms of connectedness under globalization. In an intriguingly isomorphic fashion the protesters, especially the more radical of them, also used a distributed logic to achieve their seeming chaotic but well-orchestrated effect: the weird coalitions of the anti-globalization movement, as Katharine Viner (2000) notes, are also wired coalitions.

• It is not only protesters, however, that use distributed logic. This can also be seen in the networks that formed in support of a variety of causes, such as humanitarian relief efforts for earthquake and war victims, preserving the Arctic wildlife reservation from oil drilling or pressing for minority rights. This does not mean that competition between, or hierarchy within, NGOs has disappeared. But the isolation of NGOs diminishes as networks become increasingly standard operating procedure, especially when linked through the Internet, as most of them are. This allows the leveraging of knowledge across multiple logics and ordering principles, creating new opportunities and conundrums, including the thorny problem of how to make *networks* accountable.[8]

• This leveraging of knowledge through distributed cognition allows NGOs to engage in translation as one of their major functions.[9] However, because translation is always also a misunderstanding, they are sites where negotiations of meaning take place. NGOs occupy a particularly strategic position in this regard: they work upwards with governments and corporations (e.g. through lobbying, media campaigns, protest and participation in policy processes) and downwards with local and marginalized populations (e.g. through in-country projects, training, re-granting and consciousness-raising). They thus are in a position to embody *the tension* between diffusion and translation that has become, in various academic and popular guises, the central debate of postmodernity.

From Knowledge — via Associations — to Power: The Logic of Link, Search, Interact

The shift from pseudo-autarky to collaboration enabled the structural role of NGOs in globalization to become increasingly prominent. This expanded role itself has been enhanced through NGOs' use of interactive technology within the confines of an information broker model. This model is a reasonable and conditioned reaction from the age of mass communication and mass production. Modern society is organized along lines of access to quantifiable information brokered between those who have information and those who want or need it. It has an hourglass structure, with information passing through the broker in the middle on the way from A to B, similar to Burt's (1992) bridges across structural holes or Latour's (1987) obligatory passage points. This can take the ruthless form of a monopolistic corporation or the benevolent form of an NGO seeking to spread formerly guarded information. Structurally, however, brokers work in the same way by exploiting gaps and, accordingly, gaining rents.

They have a vested interest in maintaining the gap between information producers and consumers. The affordances of interactive technology can be used to maximize this brokering role, along with the power (and perils) that come with it.

NGOs do not mimic those who 'hold' power in principle, such as states or rulers (whose claim to power can be tautological and often chimerical). But in their enhanced brokering role NGOs do gain power in Latour's sense, where power accrues to 'those who practically define or redefine what "holds" everyone together' (1986: 273). Engaging in this practical redefinition enhances NGOs' power. Transnational NGOs are particularly important in this respect. To the extent that NGOs become obligatory passage points, power can be exerted through the discursive production of the subjects they claim to represent, be they aid recipients, organizations to be included in a civil society database, or the creation of a regional identity.[10] As Paige West documents in her study of environmental NGOs in Papua New Guinea, NGOs use their structural and rhetorical power 'to discursively produce "local peoples," "indigenous peoples," "peasants" . . . and have their productions taken very seriously' (2001: 29).[11]

But since translation is always also misunderstanding, NGOs do not only produce identities but also renegotiate them. And since interactive technology affords the ability to shift from information as a discrete property to 'knowledge' that requires a knowing subject, there is more out there than the brokerage model. Here the emphasis is not on information per se but communication and distributed intelligence. Knowledge, unlike 'information,' cannot exist independently of a subject and cannot be conceived of independent of the communication network in which it is both produced and consumed (thus blurring the notion itself of producer and consumer). This does not displace or solve the practical and epistemological problems occasioned by 'information' (e.g. how to process large amounts of data, how to ensure data protection, how to ascribe meaning to data), but raises different questions of an ontological nature. These question the very a priori (diffusionist) assumptions of the institutional and organizational forms that order our world.

NGOs themselves transform when shifting their emphasis from brokering information to facilitating knowledge. This could make a difference for their potential to be genuinely transformative of social structure. Facilitating knowledge is powerful for forming associations that are not just linked communities, but what we can call knowledge communities—communities that use a recombinant and multiplicative logic of link, search, interact to sustain themselves and grow.

We refer to this as the logic of 'link, search, interact' to express concisely what it is about interactive technology—particularly its most widespread instantiation in the Internet—that makes it resonate deeply in the NGO community and in so many registers across the globe. This is certainly not the first technology to enable each of these functions: using a telephone you can search by dialing the operator to get 'information' and can then use the same phone to link you with a party with whom you interact. But consider the popular search engine Google: when it suggests sites to match your query it is also performing a search and establishing a link. To prioritize your answer it considers all the other sites that have linked to the potentially relevant sites that match your query and ranks them, based on patterns of links (i.e. the site with the highest number of links to it is considered more relevant). In other words it searches based on the pattern of links. For the telephone the process of link, search and interact is merely additive.[12] For Google they are multiplicative and recombinatory: each of these processes forms the basis for the other.

This recombinant technology allows search not only on the pattern of links, but also on the pattern of interactions. If you are even a casual user of Amazon. com the web site will suggest titles to you based on a book or CD you are looking at. This is done not by matching terms in the title or abstract of the book, which would entail a high degree of potentially humorous error, but by tracking patterns of purchase and preferences and then using an algorithm to determine that 'people who bought this book also bought . . .'[13] The output of Google or Amazon, of course, is web sites or books, while the output of the telephone is interaction with a person. What if you could harness the properties of the Web's recombinatory logic to suggest interaction with people?

This would be desirable even at a merely practical level; the glut of information available on the web is such that even if you know what you are looking for, you need a way to find the most relevant information expeditiously. Since the creators of all this content are *people,* not machines, it stands to reason that asking the right person might be the best way to find the information you are looking for. Researchers have developed such 'word of mouth' software (one is appropriately named 'gab,' as in talk, but also for Group Asynchronous Browsing) (Wittenburg et al., 1998). But there is an even more compelling reason to prefer a recombinatory over an additive approach—when you *don't* know what you are looking for but would recognize it when you find it (e.g. what happens every night at a singles bar). Unlike finding a phone number from "information," this way you find things you didn't know and come into contact with people whom you don't know. Most people would probably balk at interacting directly with other customers of Amazon, but there are communities where direct interaction would be quite an asset. For example, a doctor who wants to know who else is treating patients for similar rare diseases, or a member of an NGO community that wants to share best practices. Paul Mylea, the editor of an NGO website called Alternet.org that facilitates collaboration among humanitarian aid agencies, recounts how:

> During the Gujarat earthquake a member was based very close to the center—and they were experienced in drought relief rather than earthquake relief. A member from our advisory board contacted the member on the ground because he had experience of earthquake relief and was able to offer advice and guidance on how to deal with the crisis. They went off site and spoke on the phone. (Lewis, 2001)

Using the patterns of search or interact, one can link social structures (who knows who) and knowledge networks (who knows what). Amazon. com's collaborative filtering software is a commercial variant of similar programs such as the aptly named Yenta, Beehive or the browser Alexa.[14] For members of an NGO or non-profit community this could help develop and promote their respective knowledge networks. Working with a group of 285 such organizations in the Midwest, researchers at the University of Illinois at Urbana-Champaign developed a software program that could help the organizations identify those in the community who shared common or complementary interests and show how they may be directly or indirectly connected.[15] This software, based on a tool called IKNOW, is distinctive because the users can find out not only 'who knows who' and 'who knows what,' but also '*who* knows who knows who' and '*who* knows who knows what' (Contractor et al., 1998).[16] This works by capturing network data of both knowledge networks (based on links between actors' web sites, on common links from their web sites to third-party sites, on similarity in content between different web sites, and on an inventory of skills and expertise provided by the actors) and communication networks (based on an inventory of existing task and project links between them).

From social structures and knowledge networks we thus get at cognitive social structures and cognitive knowledge networks (*who* knows whom or what). The cognitive perceptions of the members of a knowledge community taken individually may be incomplete or inaccurate, but together they form a transactive memory system that shares domains of knowledge (Contractor, 2000; Contractor et al., 1998). This hints at a larger significance for what at first might seem like just a good way to sell books: communities of knowledge can not only be identified, but also created. IKNOW does not just enable dyadic relationships in the manner of personal ads, but also facilitates communities of knowledge.

In a similar vein, a group of researchers are working on Augmented Social Networks, or ASN. Unlike IKNOW, ASN is not software, and unlike Alternet.org, it is not a web site. Rather ASN seeks to establish a model for a 'persistent online identity' for individuals moving between different Internet communities. This identity can be the centerpiece for enhancing:

> . . . the power of social networks by using interactive digital media to exploit the transitive nature of trust through the principle of six degrees of connection. As a result, people will be able to inform themselves and self-organize more effectively—in non-hierarchical, rhizomatic social formations—leading to more opportunities for engaged citizenship. (Jordan et al., 2003: 2)

The idea for ASN builds on the work of Robert Metcalfe, whose Metcalfe's Law holds that: 'The total value of a network where each node can reach every other node grows with the square of the number of nodes,' and on research on Group Forming Networks by David Reed, who studied the exponential growth in new, and previously unknown, types of value created by the online interconnection of social networks. ASN seeks specifically to support civil society and citizen participation in governance structures through its model, and is developing software, protocols, open standards and principles of implementation (Jordan et al., 2003).

CONCLUSION: TRANSLATION AND TRANSFORMATION

Whether idealistic, as with ASN, or practical, as with Alternet, the rise of knowledge communities opens up a space—let us call it a 'knowledge space'—that is dissimilar to the established means of communication because it integrates discursive and non-discursive elements (see Levy, 1997). This is as much a space *within* which something happens as it is a space *for* something to happen (Johnson, 1997). As a space within which something happens we can trace empirically the creation and circulation of knowledge communities. As a space for something to happen we can speculate that new forms of social organization—including new social bonds (Levy, 1997: 10–13)—will develop on the basis of a relation to knowledge (for example, by the relocating of ties in social structures such as the family or the workplace, the valorization of programming skills and the mobility of electronic labor, and so forth). Such a transformation does not imply that knowledge is a function of interactive technology, any more than exchange is a function of capitalism. But just as exchange acquired specific characteristics under capitalism that became the basis for a complex system, so does knowledge acquire new characteristics in our (infelicitously but popularly titled) information age.

For NGOs in particular, knowledge communities engender deliberative associations that involve negotiations across ordering principles and multiple logics (Stark and Bruszt, 1998: 109–36). As Charles

Sabel (1992) points out in his study of economic developmental associations, no state can possibly have superior knowledge to the economic actors, or coordinate restructuring better than regional developmental associations—it is the associations, not the states, that do the developing. Likewise, as NGOs become deliberative associations they can play a greater role in both develop*ment* (in the traditional sense) and develop*ing* global, regional and national structures and institutions. This is because deliberative association leads to new associations, both in the literal sense of new networks and in the figurative sense of a mental connection between ideas.

An example is the now-famous moment during the 1999 anti-WTO protests in Seattle, when, as William Greider (2000) recounts it, 'a squad of activists dressed as sea turtles was marching alongside members of the Teamsters union. "Turtles love Teamsters," the turtles began to chant. "Teamsters love turtles," the truck drivers replied.' One associative outcome was the (partial) mental morphing of labor unions' and environmentalists' respective ideas on the environment and economics. Another was the creation of coalitions that turned the 'anti-globalization' movement that emerged from the protests in Seattle into a community of deliberative associations where the lines between environment, economic development and human rights increasingly blurred. A much smaller-scale example of an associative solution is a Roma rights organization in Hungary, which began solely by trying to link disparate organizations and individuals to each other. As a result of the subsequent interaction, the one-time clients moved from being serviced by the organization to claiming the organization as their own, eventually becoming involved in the governance of the organization. From its origins as an information broker, the organization transformed into a knowledge community (Bach and Stark, 2002).

When we employ analytical concepts that bridge the society/technology divide, NGOs appear as a molecular technology, a large, self-organizing community of deliberative associations (Latour, 1991; Levy, 1997: 41). They translate (i.e. misunderstand, interpret and renegotiate) between multiple logics, such as indigenous peoples and government bureaucrats. They also translate between an older

spatio-temporal order (the Cold War, the sovereign state system, Fordism, etc.) and what we have provisionally marked as a knowledge space.[17] It would be a mistake to assume this form predetermines any a priori normative outcome for NGOs—as we mentioned earlier the problems of accountability alone present substantial challenges to future development. NGOs could quite conceivably operate nefariously as the moral instruments of a new global society of control precisely *because* they are networked, molecular structures, functioning as 'the capillary ends of the contemporary networks of power' (Hardt and Negri, 2000: 313). This shift in form, however, makes NGOs axial organizations whose import extends beyond the negotiation of specific issues (e.g. carbon dioxide emissions or landmines) to the re-negotiation of justificatory regimes upon which the global temporal-spatial order is based. This, more than any particular event, accounts for NGOs' growing prominence. NGOs' use of recombinatory logics allows them to go beyond service provision and function as a global navigational resource for exploring a knowledge space full of uncertainties and unknowns. The best advice for observers of global transformation is to follow that of the old advertisements: watch this space.

NOTES

1. This approach draws on the work of French sociologists Michel Gallon (1998) and Bruno Latour (1991), and other social scientists in the United States who have been working with similar concepts. Hutchins (1995), for example, argues that cognition is distributed across a network of persons and instruments. Suchman's (1987) path-breaking work on human–machine interaction similarly resonates with the work of Gallon and Latour, and provides the basis for further studies on distributed design.

2. See here Appadurai's (2000) notion of process geographies and trait geographies, and Stephen Toulmin's (1990) notion of a Newtonian image of power exerted with a central force through sovereign agencies.

3. Latour (1986: 266–7) uses the example of rugby players and a rugby ball:

The initial force of the first in the chain is no more important than that of the second, or the fortieth, or of the four hundredth person. Consequently, it is clear that the energy cannot be hoarded or capitalized: if you want the token to move on you have to find fresh sources of energy all the time; you can never rest on what you did before, no more than rugby players can rest for the whole game after the *first* player has given the ball its *first kick*.

Latour's preference for a translation model is that it allows power to be seen as a consequence and not a cause of collective action, a point we will return to later.

4. Increased communication, however, is in itself not a good. Not everything works better with email (O'Mahony and Barley, 1999).

5. See also Sanyal's (1994) accounts of the Bangladeshi NGO Proshika, and the Indian NGO SEWA (the Self-employed Women's Association).

6. Of course Microsoft and Starbucks were themselves once upon a time anti-establishment upstarts. On the phenomenon of voluntary-commercial cooperation and its attendant challenges, see Edwards and Hulme (1996a) and Bendell (2000).

7. Because the state and market themselves are not static but are undergoing fundamental changes, an even bigger problem may be distinguishing cooperation from co-option in certain cases (Bach and Stark, 2002).

8. Because authority is distributed, accountability becomes highly problematic, especially when thought of in the juridical sense of locating responsibility in a figure or specific institution of authority (see Stark and Bruszt, 1998).

9. Compare the concept of translation with Fox and Brown's (1998) 'bridging individuals.'

10. This bears similarities to how non-profits in the US helped construct the categories and stigma of welfare recipients (Cruikshank, 1999).

11. See also our discussion of meta-NGOs in Bach and Stark (2002).

12. Which is not to downplay linking by itself—after all, we do have a very real use for the one-to-one technology of the telephone.

13. This form of search is known as collaborative filtering (Gladwell, 1999).

14. See, respectively, http://foner.www.media.mit.edu/people/foner/Yenta/; http:// info.alexa.com/; ftp://parcftp.xerox.com/pub/dynamics/heehive.html

15. PrairieNet communityware can be seen at http://www.tec.spcomm.uiuc.edu/ nosh/prairienet.

16. IKNOW stands for Inquiring Knowledge Networks On the Web. The IKNOW web site is: http://www.tec.spcomm.uiue.edu/nosh/IKNOW.

17. This space controls what came before, in the sense of paradigm, rather than eliminates it (see Levy, 1997).

REFERENCES

Anheier, H. and N. Themudo (2002) 'Organizational Forms of Global Civil Society,' pp. 191–216 in Marlies Glasius, Mary Kaldor and Helmut Anheier (eds) *Global Civil Society 2002*. Oxford: Oxford University Press.

Appadurai, A. (2000) 'Grassroots Globalization and the Research Imagination.' *Public Culture* 12(1): 1–19.

Austin, J. (2000) *The Collaboration Challenge*. San Francisco, CA: Jossey-Bass.

Bach, J. and D. Stark (2002) 'Innovative Ambiguities: NGOs' Use of Interactive Technology in Eastern Europe.' *Studies in International and Comparative Development* 37(2): 3–23.

Bendell, J. (2000) *Terms for Endearment: Business, NGOs and Sustainable Development*. Sheffield: Greenleaf.

Burt, R. (1992) *Structural Holes*. Cambridge, MA: Harvard University Press.

Gallon, M. (1998) *The Laws of the Markets*. Oxford: Blackwell.

Castells, M. (1999) *The Network Society*. London: Blackwell.

Contractor, N. (2000) *Social Network Formulations of Knowledge and Distributed Intelligence: Using Computational Models to Extend and Integrate Theories of Transactive Memory and Public Goods*. Heterarchies: Distributed Intelligence and the Organization of Diversity Project. Santa Fe, New Mexico: Santa Fe Institute.

Contractor, N., D. Zink et al. (1998) 'IKNOW: A Tool to Assist and Study the Creation. Maintenance, and Dissolution of Knowledge Networks,' pp. 210–17 in T. Ishida (ed.) *Community Computing and Support Systems: Lecture Notes in Computer Science 1519*. Berlin: Springer Verlag.

Cruikshank, B. (1999) *The Will to Empower*. Ithaca, NY: Cornell University Press.

Deleuze, G. and F. Guattari (1987) *A Thousand Plateaus*. Minneapolis: University of Minnesota Press.

Edwards, M. and D. Hulme (eds) (1996a) *Too Close for Comfort: NGOs, States and Donors*. London: Earthscan Press.

Edwards, M. and D. Hulme (1996b) *Beyond the Magic Bullet: NGO Performance and Accountability in the Post-Cold War World*. West Hartford, CT: Kumarian Press.

Falk, R. (1999) *Predatory Globalization*. Oxford: Polity Press.

Fox, J.A. and L.D. Brown (1998) *The Struggle for Accountability: The World Bank, NGOs and Grassroots Movements*. Cambridge, MA: MIT Press.

Girard, M. and D. Stark (2002) 'Distributing Intelligence and Organizing Diversity in New Media Projects.' *Environment and Planning A* 34(11): 1927–50.

Gladwell, M. (1999) 'The Science of the Sleeper.' *The New Yorker* 4 October: 48.

Greider, W (2000) 'Global Agenda: After the WTO Protest in Seattle, It's Time to Go on the Offensive. Here's How.' *The Nation* 270(4): 11.

Hardt, M. and A. Negri (2000) *Empire*. Cambridge, MA: Harvard University Press.

Hutchins, E. (1995) *Cognition in the Wild*. Cambridge, MA: MIT Press.

Johnson, S. (1997) *Interface Culture: How New Technology Transforms the Way We Create and Communicate*. San Francisco, CA: HarperCollins.

Jordan, K., J. Hauser et al. (2003) 'The Augmented Social Network: Building Identity and Trust into the Next-generation Internet,' The Link Tank, online www.asn.planetwork.netAvhitepaper.html.

Latour, B. (1986) 'Powers of Association,' pp. 264–80 in J. Law (ed.) *Power, Action, and Belief: A New Sociology of Knowledge*. New York: Routledge.

Latour, B. (1987) *Science in Action. How to Follow Scientists and Engineers Through Society*. Milton Keynes: Open University Press.

Latour, B. (1991) 'Society is Technology Made Durable,' pp. 103–31 in J. Law (ed.) *A Sociology of Monsters: Essays on Power, Technology, and Domination*. New York: Routledge.

Law, J. and J. Hassard (eds) (1999) *Actor Network Theory and After*. Oxford: Blackwell.

Levy, P. (1997) *Collective Intelligence*. New York: Plenum Trade.

Lewis, E. (2001) 'Red Alert.' *The Guardian* (London).

Lindenberg, M. and C. Bryant (2001) *Going Global*. Bloomfield, CT: Kumarian Press.

O'Mahony, S. and S.R. Barley (1999) 'Do Digital Telecommunications Affect Work and Organization?' *Research in Organizational Behavior* 21: 125–61.

Peizer, J. (2000) 'Sustainable Development in the Digital Age.' *Media Channel,* available online www.mediachannel.org/views/oped/peizer.shtml.

Rosenau, J. (1998) 'Governance and Diplomacy in a Globalizing World,' in D. Archibugi, D. Held and M. Kohler (eds) *Re-imagining Political Community*. Stanford, CA: Stanford University Press.

Ruggie, J. (1993) Territoriality and Beyond: Problematizing Modernity in International Relations.' *International Organization* 47(1): 139–74.

Sabel, C. (1992) 'Studied Trust: Building New Forms of Cooperation in a Volatile Economy,' in F. Pyke and W. Sengenberger (eds) *Industrial Districts and Local Economic Regeneration*. Geneva: International Labor Organization.

Sagawa, S. and E. Segal (2000) *Common Interest, Common Good: Creating Value Through Business and Social Sector Partnerships*. Cambridge, MA: Harvard Business School Press.

Sanyal, B. (1994) *Cooperative Autonomy: The Dialectic of State–NGO Relationships in Developing Countries*. Geneva: International Labor Organization.

Sassen, S. (1998) *Globalization and its Discontents: Essays on the New Mobility of People and Money*. New York: New Press.

Sassen, S. (1999) *Losing Control? Sovereignty in an Age of Globalization*. New York: Columbia University Press.

Stark, D. (2001) 'Ambiguous Assets for Uncertain Environments: Heterarchy in Postsocialist Firms,' pp. 69–104 in P. DiMaggio (ed.) *The Twenty-first-century Firm: Changing Economic Organization in International Perspective*. Princeton, NJ: Princeton University Press.

Stark, D. and L. Bruszt (1998) *Postsocialist Pathways: Transforming Politics and Property in East Central Europe*. Cambridge: Cambridge University Press.

Stewart, P.J. and A. Strathem (eds) (2001) *Anthropology and Consultancy*. Adelaide: University of Adelaide Press.

Strange, S. (1996) *The Retreat of the State: The Diffusion of Power in the World Economy*. Cambridge: Cambridge University Press.

Suchman, L. (1987) *Plans and Situated Actions: The Problem of Human-machine Communication*. New York: Cambridge University Press.

Toulmin, S. (1990) *Cosmopolis: The Hidden Agenda of Modernity*. Chicago, IL: University of Chicago Press.

Union of International Associations (1999) *Yearbook of International Organizations 1909/1999*. http://www.uia.org/statistics/organizations/ytb299.php.

Viner, K. (2000) '"Luddites" We Should Not Ignore: Instead of Vilifying the Prague Protester, We Could Learn from Them.' *The Guardian* (London) 29 September.

Warkentin, C. (2001) *Reshaping World Politics: NGOs, the Internet and Global Civil Society*. New York: Rowman and Littlefield.

West, P. (2001) 'Environmental NGOs and the Nature of Ethnographic Inquiry,' *Social Analysis* 45(2): 55–77.

Wittenburg, K., D. Das, W. Hill and L. Stead (1998) 'Group Asynchronous Browsing on the World Wide Web,' http://www.w3.org/Conferences/WWW4/Papers/98/.

World Bank (2001) 'Nongovernmental Organizations and Civil Society/Overview,' http://wbln0018.worldhank.org/essd/essd.nsf/NGOs/home, accessed 8 June 2001.

World Resources Institute (2003) 'Environmental Governance and Institutions,' http://earthtrends.wri.org/text/GOv7variahles/575notes.htm.

SOURCE: Bach, Jonathan and David Stark. 2004. "Link, Search, Interact: The Co-Evolution of NGOs and Interactive Technology." *Theory, Culture & Society*, 21:101–17.

57

TWEETING THE NIGHT AWAY

Using Twitter to Enhance Social Presence

JOANNA C. DUNLAP AND PATRICK R. LOWENTHAL

INTRODUCTIONS

Many online educators tend to design the scope, structure, and function of an online course based on the tools available within a learning management system (LMS); that is, an LMS (e.g., eCollege, Blackboard, WebCT, Moodle) can constrain how online educators design and develop their online courses (Lane, 2007; Morgan, 2003; Siemens, 2006). While adequate for some basic learning activities (e.g., information and document sharing, asynchronous and synchronous discussion, and assessment via quizzes), LMSs are modeled after classroom settings with drop boxes, grade books, announcements, and so on. What tends to be missing is the just-in-time, and sometimes playful, interactions that happen before and after class, during a break, and when students and faculty bump into each other between class meetings. Out-of-the-classroom interactions like these and many others have potential instructional value (Kuh, 1995) and can help strengthen interpersonal relationships between and among students and faculty that enhance the learning community inside the classroom.

In this teaching tip, we describe our use of Twitter (2009)—a Web 2.0, microblogging tool—to enhance social presence in an online course by

providing a mechanism for just-in-time social interactions. We also touch on some other instructional benefits of using Twitter in online courses and conclude with guidelines to consider when using Twitter with students.

THE IMPORTANCE OF SOCIAL PRESENCE

> Learning is a very human activity. The more people feel they are being treated as human beings—that their human needs are being taken into account—the more they are likely to learn and learn to learn. (Knowles, 1990, pp. 129)

When we design and teach online, we build in authentic and relevant opportunities for our students to interact and connect not only with the content but also with the instructor and each other (Dunlap, Dobrovolny, & Young, 2008; Dunlap, Furtak, & Tucker, 2009; Dunlap, Sobel. & Sands, 2007). In fact, students see social interaction and connection as a foundational attribute of our courses. We attend to the "socialness" of the courses we design and teach because we subscribe to the theory that learning, as a human activity, occurs within a social context, with higher cognitive processes originating from social interactions (Vygotsky, 1978). We also believe that social interaction and connection has significant influence over student engagement.

A commonly used framework for "best practices" in undergraduate and graduate education, Chickering and Gamson's (1987) Seven Principles of Good Practice in Education, describes seven principles that faculty can embrace to improve education. Developed from a review of fifty years of educational literature, Chickering and Gamson's first principle is, "Encourages contact between students and faculty." This first principle is influenced by instructor immediacy behaviors and participant interaction, with both having a positive influence on student learning and course satisfaction (Arbaugh, 2001, 2005; Baker, 2004; Hiltz and Wellman, 1997; Swan, 2002).

Contact between students and faculty in and outside of class is critical for student engagement because it influences student motivation and involvement. When faculty stay in touch with students through formal and informal communication and dialogue, students report that it helps them get through the rough times and keep on working. Knowing their instructors enhances students' intellectual commitment and encourages them to think about their own values and plans (Chickering and Ehrmann, 1996).

Social presence, along with cognitive and teaching presence, is well established in the online education literature as a way of thinking about social connection and interaction for student engagement in online courses. As a component of the Community of Inquiry framework (see Garrison, Anderson, & Archer, 2000), social presence refers to the "ability of participants in a Community of Inquiry to project their personal characteristics into the community, thereby presenting themselves to other participants as 'real people'" (Garrison, Anderson, & Archer, 2000, p. 89). Originally developed to explain the effect telecommunications media can have on communication, social presence was used to describe the degree of salience (i.e., quality or state of "being there") between two communicators using a communication medium (Short, Williams, & Christie, 1976).

Social presence theory took on new importance with the rise of computer-mediated communication (CMC) and later online learning (Lowenthal, in press, 2009). Now a central concept in online learning,

researchers have shown—to varying degrees—a relationship between social presence and student satisfaction (Gunawardena, 1995; Gunawardena and Zittle, 1997; Richardson and Swan, 2003), social presence and the development of a community of learners (Rourke, Anderson, Garrison, & Archer, 2001; Rovai, 2002), and social presence and perceived learning (Richardson and Swan, 2003). Because of results like these, researchers and practitioners alike continue to try out different ways to establish and maintain social presence in online courses. For instance, Aragon (2003) identified over a dozen different ways to create social presence in online courses (e.g., incorporating audio and video, posting introductions, frequent feedback). Others have looked at ways to create and maintain social presence by using tools outside of an LMS. For instance, DuVall, Powell, Hodge, and Ellis (2007) investigated using text messaging to improve social presence. Also, Keil and Johnson (2002) investigated using Internet based voice mail to increase social presence.

Social Presence and Twitter

Although the typical LMS provides tools that—when used appropriately—can establish and increase social presence (e.g., asynchronous discussions, synchronous chat tools), the tools reside within the online system. Because students and faculty have to login and navigate to several different locations in the course to engage in discussion, collaboration, and sharing, the communication is sometimes forced and out of the context of day-to-day, hour-to-hour, and minute-to-minute experience. In other words, communication between and among students and faculty is scheduled based on when they have a moment to login to the LMS. This means that there are many lost opportunities during the day to interact and connect.

Another challenge of encapsulating all social interaction and connection opportunities within a LMS is that we tend to lose the informal, free-flowing, just-in-time banter and chitchat that we have with students in our on-campus courses- the banter that helps us get to know each other, experience our personalities, and connect on a more emotional level. This sort of informal connection between and among students and faculty is one aspect of cultivating student engagement and social presence. Although we have tried to address this within the LMS by incorporating weekly fun activities (such as coming up with captions for goofy photos, or competing in online games), establishing discussion forums on non-academic topics, having students produce music playlists for the week, and the like, these strategies do not seem to do enough to enhance social presence. As a result, we have been looking for additional ways to enhance social presence.

Twitter immediately seemed like an additional way to enhance social presence. Twitter (2009) is a multiplatform Web 2.0, part social networking–part microblogging tool, freely accessible on the Web (Stevens, 2008). Other popular Web 2.0 microblogging tools include Jaiku, Tumblr, MySay, Hictu, and Edmodo. Twitter, however, is one of the most popular of these microblogging tools (Java, Song, Finin, & Tseng, 2007; McFedries, 2007) and, therefore, was our tool of choice because it is well-established, has a large and growing participant base, interfaces well with other Web 2.0 tools, and is easily accessible.

According to the Twitter website, *Twitter is a service for friends, family, and co-workers to communicate and stay connected through the exchange of quick, frequent answers to one simple question: What are you doing?* (Twitter, 2009). However, the people who participate in the Twitter community—people who are geographically distributed across all continents (with North America, Europe, and Asia having the highest adoption rate) (Java et al., 2007)—use it for more than providing updates on their current status.

In 140 characters or less, people share ideas and resources, ask and answer questions, and collaborate on problems of practice; in a recent study, researchers found that the main communication intentions of people participating in Twitter could be categorized as daily chatter, conversations, sharing resources/URLs, and reporting news (Java et al., 2007). Twitter community members post their contributions via the Twitter website, mobile phone, email, and instant messaging—making Twitter a powerful, convenient, community-controlled microsharing environment (Drapeau, 2009). Depending on whom you choose to follow (i.e., communicate with) and

who chooses to follow you, Twitter can be effectively used for professional and social networking (Drapeau, 2009; Thompson, 2007) because it can connect people with like interests (Lucky, 2009). And all of this communication happens in real-time, so the exchange of information is immediate (Parry, 2008a; Young, 2008).

TWITTER IN ACTION

Faculty have recently begun experimenting with how to use Twitter in the "classroom" (Parry, 2008a). Parry explains that despite his initial skepticism, he found that Twitter could be an effective tool in the classroom in part because of its ability to "blur the lines of the classroom" (Parry, 2008b). An example of how Parry uses Twitter in his classroom can be found online (see Parry, 2007).

Communication faculty are not the only ones using Twitter in the classroom. Twitter has also been used in public relations (Sweetser, 2008), project management (Keefer, 2008), medical education (van den Brock, 2009), language learning (Ullrich, Borau, Luo, Tan, L. Shen, & R. Shen, 2008), and information systems (Sendall, Ceocucci, & Peslak, 2008) courses, to name a few. During the fall of 2008, we incorporated Twitter into our online instructional design and technology courses. We did not require students to participate, but invited them to join us in our Twitter adventure as we tested its instructional potential. Although not everyone chose to participate, most did with positive results. The following describes our students' typical experiences using Twitter:

- A student is reading something in the textbook and has a question about the chapter on multimodal learning. She immediately tweets (i.e., posts) her question to the Twitter community, and gets three responses within ten minutes)—two responses from classmates, and one from Joni (her professor). This leads to several subsequent posts, including comments from two practicing professionals.

- A student is working on an assignment and is wondering about embedding music into a slideshow presentation. He tweets a question to the group and gets a response from Patrick (his professor) and a practicing professional. Both point the student to different online resources that explain how to embed music and provide examples to deconstruct. Within a half hour, the student has embedded music in his slideshow presentation.

• A student sends a private tweet (i.e., a private message that only the named recipient receives) to Joni regarding a difficult situation with a project team member. While in the middle of a departmental meeting, Joni immediately tweets back, arranging a time to talk with the student outside of Twitter.

• A student cannot believe what she has just heard on the news regarding federal funding of higher education and needs to share. She tweets her comment, and immediately connects with others who cannot believe it either.

• A student finds a great video about storyboarding on YouTube and posts the URL to Twitter. Her find is retweeted (i.e., reposted) three times because others also think the video is great and worth sharing.

• Joni and Patrick, who are both away at conferences, tweet various updates about what they are hearing and seeing at the conference.

• Several of the students are posting comments to Twitter while they watch a political debate. They provide commentary, along with several thousand others who are also in Twitter while watching the debate.

• A student tweets that he just posted a new entry to his blog on how vision trumps all other senses during instruction and provides the URL. His classmates, as well as other practicing professionals, read his blog post. He receives three tweets thanking him for sharing his ideas.

• As part of a research project on legacy systems, a student poses a question to the Twitter community regarding the prevalent need for COBOL programmers. She receives responses from several IT professionals, some with links to helpful resources and contacts that can help her with research.

• A student tweets that she is tired and going off to bed. She receives two tweets back from classmates wishing her a good night.

Throughout the course, we used Twitter in this way. By using a tool that enables just-in-time communication with the local (our course) and global (practicing professionals) community, we were able to engage in sharing, collaboration, brainstorming, problem solving, and creating within the context of our moment-to-moment experiences.

Because of Twitter's ability to enable persistent presence (Siemens, 2007), our social interactions occurred more naturally and immediately than when we have to login to the LMS, navigate to the appropriate discussion forum, post a message, and then wait for someone to respond (after we already moved on to other work, thoughts, and issues).

OTHER INSTRUCTIONAL BENEFITS OF TWITTER

Besides the benefit of enhancing the potential for positive social presence during online learning opportunities, Twitter has other instructional benefits.

Addressing Student Issues in a Timely Manner

Our students used Twitter for time-sensitive matters: to ask us for clarification on content or assignment requirements, notify us of personal emergencies, and alert us to issues that need our attention and action. Even though we log into the LMS several times a day, this immediate communication allowed us to attend to issues in a timely manner. On a few occasions, we were able to intervene before an issue spiraled out of control, as with a team that was having trouble meeting the requirements of a project. Twitter is a helpful tool for addressing student issues quickly.

Writing Concisely

Because a tweet is limited to 140 characters, this encourages students to write clearly and concisely. Although a very informal writing style, it is a professionally useful skill for students to develop, especially given the growing popularity of this category of communication tool.

Writing for an Audience

Although Twitter elicits open sharing and an informal writing style, it is nevertheless critical to know your audience and share accordingly. Participating in the Twitter community helped our students learn to be sensitive to their audience, and make professional decisions about what perspectives and ideas they should publically contribute and what perspectives and ideas should remain private.

Connecting With a Professional Community of Practice

A great benefit of participating in Twitter is that many practicing professionals also participate. In our courses, for example, a number of the textbook authors participate in Twitter. Besides the networking potential, students receive immediate feedback to their questions and ideas from practicing professionals, which serves to reinforce the relevance of Twitter participation and enhance their understanding of our course content and their enculturation into the professional community of practice.

Supporting Informal Learning

Informal learning involves "activities that take place in students' self-directed and independent learning time, where the learning is taking place to support a formal program of study, but outside the formally planned and tutor-directed activities" (Aspden and Thorpe, 2009). Twitter was one tool that students used to support their informal learning activities. Through their participation in the Twitter community, they discovered resources and tools that they effectively applied to their coursework.

Maintaining On-going Relationships

Student and faculty use of Twitter is not bound by the structure of an LMS or the timing of a semester. Twitter enables faculty and students to maintain on-going relationships after a course ends. Although the semester is over, we are still in daily communication with several students from the courses. This allows us to continue to advise students academically and professionally. It has also allowed for a much more natural and organic progression of our relationships; instead of severing our connections at the end of the semester, we are able to continue to be in community together, learning from each other and sharing our moment-to-moment experiences.

Possible Drawbacks of Twitter

Like most, if not all Web 2.0 tools, Twitter is not appropriate for all instructional situations. For instance, Grosseck and Holotescu (2008) identify a number of problems with using Twitter for educational purposes. For instance, Twitter can be time-consuming, addictive, and possibly even encourage bad grammar as a result of its 140-character limit (Grosseck and Holotescu, 2008). Further, while Twitter is free to use on a computer connected to the Web (whether accessed via a web browser or a Twitter client like Twirl), faculty and students might be charged texting or data fees if they access Twitter on their cell phone (depending on their cell phone plans). See Grosseck and Holotescu (2008) and Lavallee (2007) for a complete list of drawbacks of using Twitter for educational purposes.

Despite possible drawbacks like these, the instructional benefits encourage us to continue to incorporate Twitter in our online courses (as one more tool in our toolbox), and look at other Web 2.0 tools that may help us extend the instructional power of a LMS and further enhance the social-presence potential of the online learning opportunities we design and facilitate.

GUIDELINES FOR USING TWITTER WITH STUDENTS

Based on our experience using Twitter with our online students, we offer the following five guidelines:

Establish Relevance for Students

First and foremost, the use of Twitter in an online course needs to be relevant—have a clear purpose—for students to attend to it in personally, professionally, and academically meaningful ways. If students see using Twitter in a particular course as irrelevant then they will fail to participate in Twitter as hoped, and will fail to take anything of value away from the experience. Our strategy has been to show students examples of the ways we have benefited from using Twitter, such as the resources we have discovered that support our work, writing, and course learning activities; professionals we have met and are now in consistent contact with; and the audience we have attracted to our various projects and products. We also share with students the fun (e.g., tweeting with a celebrity) and informative (e.g., receiving product updates or news items) networking opportunities available via Twitter. When students see the possibilities and how those possibilities can help them meet specific learning goals and objectives, they are willing to give it a try.

Define Clear Expectations for Participation

Regardless of your expectations for student participation in Twitter, expectations for participation have to be clearly articulated. Our preference has been to invite and strongly encourage students to participate instead of requiring their participation. In support of our invitation, we define our expectations as setting up a Twitter account adding all class members and faculty as tweets, adding 2–3 professionals (usually our textbook authors) as tweets, and committing to logging into Twitter three times a day for two weeks. If after that point students determine it is not of value to them, then we do not expect them to continue participating. In fact, we post any important questions asked about the course on Twitter back in the LMS (in much the same way we do with questions asked via email) in an effort not to penalize students who do not continue to use Twitter. However, we have found that after those initial two weeks most students decide to continue to participate in Twitter for the duration of the course and beyond. Note: Related to expectations for participation, it is important to remind students that Twitter is a public forum requiring them to exhibit decorum in all of their Twitter interactions.

Model Effective Twitter Use

We make every effort to model effective Twitter use for our students by being active participants in the Twitter community. Through our modeling, students are exposed to effective strategies for connecting with other professionals, asking and answering questions, sharing resources, and friendly networking. Enhancing social presence using Twitter requires being socially present in Twitter.

Build Twitter-Derived Results Into Assessment

We encourage students to use information and resources derived through Twitter participation—triangulated with other more conventional references in research papers and presentations. We then assess students on the relevance and accuracy of their citations, including those derived from Twitter. In this way, we reinforce the value of Twitter as a professional resource, and give students credit—and points—for using Twitter to meet professional and academic goals.

Continue to Actively Participate in Twitter

We have made a commitment to continue to participate in the Twitter community after courses are completed. We believe that this community further encourages students to engage in Twitter, building their own valuable network of professional and academic contacts. Because they know they can count on us being available in Twitter, they continue to use Twitter as a just-in-time way to connect and interact with each other and us. This has been helpful for continued advising, coaching, and mentoring. Ultimately, following this guideline has helped us achieve the level of social presence we crave in support of on-going social learning and student engagement.

CONCLUSION

We set out to enhance the social-presence potential of our online courses using Twitter. That is, we believed that the synchronous just-in-time nature of Twitter could provide us and our students with opportunities to connect and be perceived as "real" in ways that traditional LMS contained tools could not. The feedback from our students suggests that Twitter accomplished just this for many of them:

> Twitter has been a great way for me to check in with everyone who is using it. I found out how others were feeling about school, how life was treating them, how

their jobs and families were doing. This is something much more intimate than mandatory weekly discussions, although they carry their own merit.

I really LOVE twittering with everyone. It really made me feel like we knew each other more and were actually in class together.

Twitter was a big part of my connected-ness, with course colleagues and with you. Even though I didn't post a lot of tweets, I watched the Twitter dialogue. It made the connections stronger and helped me learn more about folks in the course and you. And, Twitter led me to some great resources. Thanks, Joni, for being such a responsive Twitterer.

We also, and unexpectedly, concluded that involving students in the Twitter community also helps us attend to the other two components of the Community of Inquiry framework: cognitive and teaching presence.

Cognitive Presence

Cognitive presence is "the extent to which the participants in . . . a community of inquiry are able to construct meaning through sustained communication" (Garrison, Anderson, & Archer, 2000, p. 89). Interacting with us and other professional practitioners in Twitter, our students constructed meaning through sustained communication.

Teaching Presence

Teaching presence is the ability of a teacher or teachers to support and enhance social and cognitive presence through instructional management, building understanding, and direct instruction. Reflecting on the additional instructional benefits of Twitter, we clearly engaged in interactions with our students via Twitter that helped us attend to instructional management issues and students' knowledge building.

We encourage others to begin experimenting with Twitter in their classroom. However, formal and systematic research is needed to truly assess the value of using Twitter in the classroom as well as its relationship to social presence. All in all, though, we have found Twitter to be a powerful tool for establishing informal, free-flowing, just-in-time communication between and among students and faculty, and with the professional community at large.

REFERENCES

Aragon, S. (2003) "Creating Social Presence in Online Environments." New Directions for Adult and Continuing Education. San Francisco, pp. 57–68

Arbaugh, J. B. (2001) "How Instructor Immediacy Behaviors Affect Student Satisfaction and Learning in Web-Based Courses." Business Communication Quarterly, Vol. 64, No. 4, pp. 42–54

Arbaugh, J. B. (2005) "Is There an Optimal Design for On-Line MBA Courses?" Academy of Management Learning & Education, Vol. 4, pp. 135–149

Aspden, E. J., and Thorpe, L. P. (2009) "'Where Do You Learn?' Tweeting to Inform Learning Space Development." Educause Quarterly, Vol. 32, No. 1. Retrieved April 10, 2009, from http://www.educause.edu/EDUCAUSEH+Quarterly/EDUCAUSEQuarterlyMagazineVolum/WhereDoYouLearnTweetingtoInfor/163852

Baker, J. D. (2004) "An Investigation of Relationships Among Instructor Immediacy and Affective and Cognitive Learning in the Online Classroom." The Internet and Higher Education, Vol. 7, pp. 1–13

Chickering, A. W., and Ehrmann, S. C. (1996) "Implementing the Seven Principles: Technology as Lever." AAHE Bulletin, Vol. 49, No. 2, pp. 3–6

Chickering, A. W., and Gamson, Z. (1987) "Seven Principles for Good Practice in Undergraduate Education." AAHE Bulletin, Vol. 40, No. 7, pp. 3–7

Drapeau, M. D. (2009, February 2) "What is Twitter's Vision?" Retrieved February 2, 2008, from http://mashable.com/2009/02/02/what-is-twitters-vision/

Dunlap, J. C., Dobrovolny, J. L., and Young, D. L. (2008) "Preparing Learning Designers Using Kolb's Model of Experiential Learning." Innovate, Vol. 4, No. 4. [Online journal—http://innovateonline.info/?view=article&id=490]

Dunlap, J. C., Furtak, T. E., and Tucker, S. A. (2009) "Designing for Enhanced Conceptual Understanding in an Online Physics Course." TechTrends, Vol. 53, No. 1, pp, 67–73

Dunlap, J. C., Sobel, D. M., and Sands, D. (2007) "Supporting Students' Cognitive Processing in Online Courses: Designing for Deep and Meaningful Student-to-Content Interactions." TechTrends, Vol. 51, No. 4, pp. 20–31

DuVall, J. B., Powell, M. R., Hodge, E., and Ellis, M. (2007) "Text Messaging To Improve Social Presence in Online Learning." Educause Quarterly, Vol. 30, No. 3, pp. 24–28

Garrison, D. R., Anderson, T., and Archer, W. (2000) "Critical Inquiry in a Text-based Environment: Computer Conferencing in Higher Education." The Internet and Higher Education, Vol. 2, No. 2–3, pp. 87–105

Grosseck, G., and Holotescu, C. (2008, April) "Can we use Twitter for Educational Activities?" Paper presented at the 4th International Scientific Conference, eLearning and Software for Education. Bucharest, Romania.

Gunawardena, C. N. (1995) "Social Presence Theory and Implications for Interaction and Collaborative Learning in Computer Conferences." International Journal of Educational Telecommunications, Vol. 1, No. 2/3, pp. 147–166

Gunawardena, C. N., and Zittle, F. J. (1997) "Social Presence as a Predictor of Satisfaction Within a Computer-mediated Conferencing Environment." The American Journal of Distance Education, Vol. 11, No. 3, pp. 8–26

Hiltz, S. R., & Wellman, B. (1997) "Asynchronous Learning Networks as a Virtual Classroom." Communications of the ACM, Vol. 40, No. 9, pp. 44–49

Java, A., Song, X., Finin, T., and Tseng, B. (2007, August) "Why we Twitter: Understanding Microblogging Usage and Communities." Proceedings of the Joint 9th WEBKDD and 1st SNA-KDD Workshop 2007. Retrieved February 2, 2008, from http://ebiquity. umbc.edu/get/a/publication/369.pdf

Keefer, J. (2008, March) "How to use Twitter in Higher Education." Retrieved April 1, 2008, from http://silenceandvoice.com/archives/2008/03/31/how-to-use-twitter-in-higher-education/

Keil, M., and Johnson, R. D. (2002) "Feedback Channels: Using Social Presence Theory to Compare Voice Mail to E-mail." Journal of Information Systems Education, Vol. 13, No. 4, pp. 295–302

Knowles, M. S. (1990) The Adult Learners: A Neglected Species (4th ed.). Houston, TX: Gulf Publishing Co.

Kuh, G. D. (1995) "The Other Curriculum: Out-of-class Experiences Associated with Student Learning and Personal Development." The Journal of Higher Education, Vol. 66, No. 2, pp. 123–155

Lane, L. M. (2007) "Course Management Systems and Pedagogy." Retrieved October 1, 2007, from http://lisahistory.net/pages/CMSandPeoagogy.htm

Lavallee, A. (2007, March) "Friends Swap Twitters, and Frustration: New Real-time Messaging Services Overwhelm Some Users with Mundane Updates From Friends." Retrieved April 1, 2007, from http://online.wsj.com/public/article/SB117373145818634482-ZwdoPQ0PqPrcFMDHDZLz_P60snI_20080315.html

Lowenthal, P. R. (2009) "Social Presence," in Encyclopedia of Distance and Online Learning, 2nd Edition, P. Rogers, G. Berg, J. Boettcher, C. Reward, L. Justice, and K. Schenk (eds.). IGI Global, Hershey, PA, pp. 1900–1906.

Lowenthal, P. R. (in press) "The Evolution of Social Presence Theory and its Influence on Online Learning." To appear in T. T. Kidd (Ed.), Online Education and Adult Learning: New frontiers for teaching practices. IGI Global, Hershey, PA.

Lucky, R. W. (2009) "To Twitter or Not to Twitter?" IEEE Spectrum, Vol. 46, No. 1, pp. 22–22

Morgan, G. (2003, May) "Faculty Use of Course Management Systems." Research Study from the Educause Center for Applied Research, Vol. 2, pp. 1–6. Retrieved January 1, 2009, from http://net.educause.edu/ir/library/pdf/ERS0302/ekf0302.pdf

McFedries, P. (2007) "Technically Speaking: All A-Twitter." IEEE Spectrum, Vol. 44, No. 10, pp. 84.

Parry, D. (2007, November 1) Twitter away your weekend. Retrieved January 1, 2009, from http://outsidethetext.com/trace/38/

Parry, D. (2008a. January) "Twitter for Academia." Retrieved January 1, 2009, from http://academhack.outsidethetext.com/home/2008/twitter-for-acailemia/

Parry, D. (2008b, February) "Teaching With Twitter." The Chronicle of Higher Education. Retrieved March 1, 2008, from http://chronicle.com/media/video/v54/i25/twitter/

Richardson, J. C., and Swan, K. (2003) "Examining Social Presence in Online Courses in Relation to Students' Perceived Learning and Satisfaction." Journal of Asynchronous Learning Networks, Vol. 7, No. 1, pp. 68–88

Rourke, L., Anderson, T., Garrison, D. R., and Archer, W. (2001) "Assessing Social Presence in Asynchronous Text-based Computer Conferencing." Journal of Distance Education, Vol. 14. Retrieved January 1, 2008, from http://cade.athabascau.ca/v0114.2/rourke_et_al.html

Rovai, A. P. (2002) "Building a Sense of Community at a Distance." International Review of Research in Open and Distance Learning, Vol. 3, No. 1. Retrieved January 1, 2008, from http://www.irrodl.org/index.php/irrodl/article/view/79/15

Sendall, P., Ceocucci, W., and Peslak, A. (2008) "Web 2.0 Matters: An Analysis of Implementing Web 2.0 in the Classroom." Information Systems Education

Journal, Vol. 6, No. 64. Retrieved February 2, 2008, from http://isedj.org/6/64/

Short, J., Williams, E., and Christie, B. (1976) The Social Psychology of Telecommunications. John Wiley & Sons, London, p. 206.

Siemens, G. (2006) "Learning or Management System? A Review of Learning Management System Reviews." Retrieved January 1, 2009, from http://ltc.umanitoba.ca/wordpress/wpcontent/uploads/2006/10/learning-or-managememt-system-with-reference-list.doc

Siemens, G. (2007) "Connectivism: Creating a Learning Ecology in Distributed Environment," in Didactics of Microlearning: Concepts, discourses, and examples, in T. Hug. (ed.), Waxmann Verlag, New York, pp. 53–68

Stevens, V. (2008) "Trial by Twitter: The Rise and Slide of the Year's Most Viral Microblogging Platform." TESLEJ: Teaching English as a Second or Foreign Language, Vol. 12, No. 1. Retrieved October 1, 2008, from http://tesl-ej.org/ej45/int.html

Swan, K. (2002) "Building Learning Communities in Online Courses: The Importance of Interaction." Education Communication and Information, Vol. 2, No. 1, pp. 23–49

Sweetser, K. D. (2008, February) "Teaching Tweets." Retrieved March 1, 2008, from http://www.kaye-sweetser.com

Thompson, C. (2007, June) "Clive Thompson on How Twitter Creates a Social Sixth Sense." Wired Magazine, Vol. 15, No. 7. Retrieved January 1, 2009, from http://www.wired.com/techbiz/media/magazine/15–07/st_thompson

Twitter. (2009). Twitter [computer software]. Available at http://www.twitter.com/

Ullrich, C., Borau, K., Luo, H., Tan, X., Shen, L., and Shen, R. (2008, April) "Why Web 2.0 is Good for Learning and for Research: Principles and Prototypes." Proceeding of ACM's 17th international conference on World Wide Web, Beijing, China. Retrieved February 2, 2008, from http://portal.acm.org/citation.cfm?id=367497.1367593

van den Brock, W. (2009, January) "Twitter and Medical Education." Retrieved January 29, 2009, from http://www.shockmd.com/2009/01/14/twitter-and-medical-education/

Vygotsky, L. S. (1978). Mind In Society: The Development of Higher Psychological Processes. Cambridge, MA: Harvard University Press

Young, J. (2008, February) "Forget e-mail: New Messaging Service has Students and Professors atwitter." The Chronicle of Higher Education, Vol. 54, No. 25. Retrieved December 1, 2008, from http://chronicle.com/free/v54/i25/25a01501.htm

SOURCE: Dunlap, Joanna C., and Patrick R. Lowenthal. 2009. "Tweeting the Night Away: Using Twitter to Enhance Social Presence." *Journal of Information Systems Education*, 20(2): 129 - 135,

58

E-MAIL IN GOVERNMENT

Not Post-Bureaucratic but Late-Bureaucratic Organizations

ALBERT JACOB MEIJER

INTRODUCTION

The relation between e-mail and organization has been studied widely and intensively. Studies have highlighted that e-mail replaces other media, forms an addition to them, and leads to new patterns of communication in organizations (Fulk & DeSanctis, 1995; Hinds & Kiesler, 1995; Kock, Lynn, Dow & Akgun, 2006; Sproull & Kiesler, 1991). Most of this research makes no distinction between corporate and government organizations. However, the formalized and hierarchical character of government organizations seems to be at odds with the characteristics of a medium that enables informal and horizontal communication. One can ask whether government organizations lose these traits when civil servants transform organizations through the use of e-mail. Literature about corporate organizations suggests that electronic media transform these organizations in post-bureaucracies (Fulk & DeSanctis, 1995; Hinds & Kiesler, 1995). Key characteristics of post-bureaucracies are horizontal coordination and steering through influencing network interactions. We do not know whether electronic media have the same influence on government

organizations. One can pose the question whether electronic media have the same influence on government. Are government entities becoming post-bureaucratic organizations?

The effects of the use of e-mail on the structure of government organizations warrant special attention because representatives of the people need to be able to hold these accountable. Public oversight depends on the ability of political representatives to control the functioning of bureaucracies and steer bureaucratic outputs (Behn, 2001; Bovens, 1998). Bureaucracy is a key element in the chain of political and hierarchical control through which democratic oversight over government is ensured. Civil servants are controlled by public managers; these are controlled by political appointees which, in their turn, are held accountable by representatives. If the use of e-mail results in a lack of accountability in government bureaucracies, civil servants escape the chain of democratic control.

Systematic empirical research concerning the effects of e-mail on government organizations is needed to understand these transitions in government organizations. This paper presents a first exploration of this issue on the basis of interviews with a limited number of respondents. The paper deals with the following research question: Does the use of e-mail change government agencies into post-bureaucratic organizations? Structuration Theory and Bureaucracy Theory are used to analyze interactions between the use of e-mail and characteristics of government organizations. The use and the effects of e-mail were investigated in three government bureaucracies in the Netherlands: the Royal Navy, a local government (which was promised anonymity), and the National Bank. Theories from the domains of Public Administration and Information Systems are combined with this empirical research to understand transitions in bureaucratic organizations.

CONCEPTUAL FRAMEWORK

Structuration Theory and New Medium Studies

There has been a long debate about the effects of information and communication technologies (ICTs) on organizations (for an overview, see Taylor, Groleau, Heaton & Van Every, 2001; Williams & Edge, 1996). Traditional perspectives include a *techno-deterministic perspective* (i.e. organizational structures and cultures change because of the use of technologies) and a *voluntaristic perspective* (i.e. organizations choose how to use technologies to fit their specific situation). A sophisticated perspective on the interrelation between technology and organization has been developed on the basis of Giddens' (1984) Structuration Theory (Jones & Karsten, 2003; Orlikowski, 1992; Orlikowski, Yates, Okamura & Fujimoto, 1995). Structuration Theory poses that the introduction of ICTs in organizations has to be studied as a process of institutional change. ICTs have certain properties, but these properties are enacted by employees who use ICTs in a specific institutional context. A simplified version of this Structuration perspective is used for studying the relation between e-mail and bureaucratic organization (see Figure 58.1).

The bottom part of the figure highlights the interrelations between use of e-mail and communication patterns of civil servants. Arrow A indicates that civil servants will adapt the use of e-mail to their communication patterns. At the same time, however,

these communication patterns are influenced by the introduction of the new medium (arrow B). The availability of e-mail offers new opportunities for communication and hence leads to shifts in communication patterns.

The top part of the figure shows the interrelations between the communication patterns of civil servants and the characteristics of bureaucratic organization. Arrow C highlights the influence of bureaucratic organization on the communication patterns of civil servants. These patterns can be attributed to bureaucratic rules stipulating how to communicate in various situations. At the same time, bureaucratic only exists because civil servants communicate in a certain way (arrow D). Changes in their communication patterns will lead to changes in bureaucratic organization.

In this framework, e-mail is not an empty container. Technologies have certain characteristics, and the characteristics of communication media are a central tenet of the so-called "new medium studies" (Deibert, 1997; Hutchby, 2001, 2003). These studies highlight the way media structures communication by facilitating certain forms of interactions while hindering other forms. The concept of "affordance" plays a key role in these studies. Sellen and Harper (2002) wrote: "An affordance refers to the fact that the physical properties of an object make possible different functions for the person perceiving or using that object."

The following affordances of e-mail have been highlighted in various researches (Sproull & Kiesler, 1991; Trevino, Daft & Lengel, 1990):

1. text oriented (although increasingly images are used in messages);
2. asynchronous (no direct feedback required);
3. one-to-many (easy to send one message to a very large group);
4. inexpensive (compared to telephone or paper mail); and
5. instant memory (since all messages are, at least temporarily, stored).

New medium studies, however, highlight that these affordances do not determine outcomes. The outcome should be conceptualized as the results of affordance, the context of use and individual choices. This makes this theoretical approach

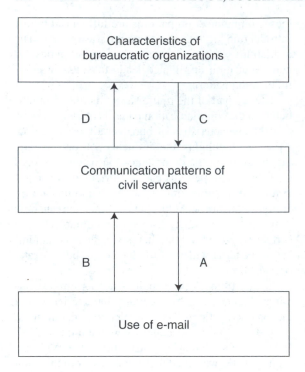

Figure 58.1   Interrelation between use of e-mail and characteristics of bureaucratic organizations.

compatible with Structuration Theory, although new medium studies do not emphasize that the context of use also changes in the use of technology.

Bureaucracy Theory

The (institutional) context of e-mail used in this study is formed by bureaucratic organizations and Bureaucracy Theory is the body of theory that has been developed about this institutional context. Colloquially, the term *bureaucracy* refers to an organization that is rigidly devoted to the details of administrative procedures. In this paper, however, bureaucracy is used in the Weberian sense. Weber developed his ideal type of a bureaucracy and indicated that a core assumption of bureaucracy is that it obeys its ruler. In democratic societies, the ruler of bureaucracies is a political appointee (a minister or a secretary or their local equivalents) who is held accountable by a parliament of representatives. Optimal bureaucracies should result in effective and

efficient organizations, and furthermore these organizations should be reliable (Weber, 1968). Bureaucratic structures are formed according to the following principles (Perrow, 1986; Zuurmond, 1994):

1. hierarchy (clear division of competencies in vertical positions);
2. centralization (bureaus are organized in a single line of command);
3. formalization (work processes are documented in an impersonal form);
4. specialization (specific job descriptions and good education); and
5. standardization (task execution according to fixed rules).

This paper focuses on the changes in two of the above mentioned principles: hierarchy and formalization. The reason for this limitation is pragmatic as an evaluation of the impact of e-mail on all these principles would require a book rather than a research paper. There is also a substantial rationale for this limitation—previous research (Frissen, 2003; Meijer, 2002; Stasz & Bikson, 1986; Van den Hooff, 1997) has indicated that the use of e-mail leads to less hierarchical and less formal organizations.

Formalization in the Weberian bureaucracy means that personal matters and execution of tasks need to be strictly separated (Perrow, 1986; Weber, 1968). Weber also emphasizes that the results of work processes need to be documented. *Schriftligkeit* is an important characteristic of bureaucracies, and written documents play a key role in control in and over these organizations (Zuurmond, 1994). Public officials can be called to account, and bureaucracies can demonstrate their functioning on the basis of written documents.

Formalization also plays an important role in literature on organizational analysis and design. In his influential work on Organizational Theory, Scott (2003) defines formal structures as the norms and communication patterns that are meant to function independent from individuals. Individuals are replaceable. In contrast, informal structures are based on personal characteristics and relations between individuals. On the basis of their well-known Hawthorne experiments, Roethlisberger and

Wilson (1939) equate formal structures to the "logic of costs and efficiency" and informal structures as the "logic of emotions." Selznick (1957) highlights the reduction of organizational dependency on personal characteristics by routinizing supervision and externalizing discipline and incentives.

Three key aspects can be identified in these discussions of formalization. First is the divide between work and private interests. Employees should not use their positions for improving their personal situations since the domains of work and private interest are to be separated. A second aspect refers to the style of communication. Formalized communication contains a style of writing that is non-personal and anticipates the use of documents in other contexts. Finally, a third aspect relates to the type of contact between employees in an organization. Formalization means a reduction in personal and relational elements of coordination and an emphasis on objectively documenting decisions, discussions, and work processes.

Hierarchy is another key principle and, as formulated by Max Weber (1968), is the system of vertical positioning of functions in organizational structures. Vertical lines play a crucial role in bureaucratic organizations since they ensure control and accountability. Hierarchy in government is crucial for the chain of command from citizens to representatives to political leaders to civil servants (Strøm, 2000). Through hierarchy, abuse of power and corruption in government can be prevented, and the activities of civil servants can be steered into the direction of political objectives.

In the organizational sciences hierarchy is generally acknowledged as a crucial aspect of organizations since it enables coordination, steering, and control (Mintzberg, 1983; Tannenbaum, Kavcic, Rosner, Vianello & Wieser, 1974). Vroom (1969) emphasizes that hierarchical channels for processing information enable organizations to solve problems quickly and communication between every individual in an organization would generate a communication overload. One could even say that hierarchy has become one of the dominant characteristics of bureaucratic organizations (Wilensky, 1967). The omnipresent organigrams (organizational charts) stress, above all, hierarchical relations in organizations.

Hierarchy can be conceptualized in three aspects. A first aspect of hierarchy concerns the limitation of the autonomy of employees. Autonomy can broadly be described as the degree of freedom in making decisions, but also in gathering information and executing organizational tasks (Harley, 1999). Second, hierarchy structures communication patterns in organizations (Schofield & Alt, 1983). Communication takes place within an organizational unit, and the head of this unit is the only one who communicates with other units. The hierarchy as means to structure communication is shown in Figure 58.2.

A third aspect of hierarchy is its function as a funnel for information from the bottom of the organization to its top (Van Thijn & Cardoso Ribiero, 2004). Employees inform their managers about their work and other relevant developments. These managers collect information from all their employees and inform political appointees. An adequate hierarchy should result in bringing relevant information to those in charge of the organization.

Formalization and hierarchy are well-established but in the last decade various researchers have been arguing that these characteristics of bureaucratic organizations are losing their central position in coordinating activities of members of these organizations. They stipulate that bureaucratic organizations are turning into post-bureaucratic organizations with lower degrees of formalization and hierarchy and coordination through informal, horizontal networks (Fulk & DeSanctis, 1995; Hekscher & Donnellon, 1994; Hinds & Kiesler, 1995). According to their argument, the use of information and communication technologies plays an important role in this transition.

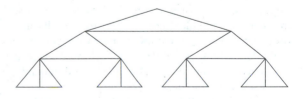

Figure 58.2 Communication follows hierarchical lines.

Hypotheses

The Structuration Theory framework brings together discussions about the use of information and communication technologies and characteristics of organizations. Although this framework stresses that outcomes of processes of change are unpredictable, the framework can be used to trace dominant—but not deterministic—outcomes of these processes. What is the outcome of the confrontation of e-mail and government bureaucracy?

Let us look at the expected effects of e-mail on the degree of formalization of government bureaucracies. Explorative research suggests that the distinction between work and private interest may become blurred with the use of e-mail compared with communication through paper documents since employees use e-mail not only for work-related communication, but also for private communication (Frissen, 2003; Meijer, 2002). Various researchers have also concluded that the style of e-mail communication is much more informal than the style of written documents since conventions that guide communication through paper documents do not apply as strictly to communication through e-mail (Ball, 1991; Burgess, Jackson & Edwards, 2005; Murray, 1988; Ngwenyama, 1998, p. 11; Taylor, Fieldman & Lahlou, 2005; Yunus, 2005). Finally, personal style becomes more important in e-mail communication at the cost of less systematically and objectively documenting work processes (Landry, 2000). On the basis of this overview, the following hypothesis is proposed:

> **H1.** The outcome of the changes triggered by the use of e-mail in government bureaucracies is a lower degree of formalization than before the introduction of this medium.

Now we will examine the anticipated effects of e-mail on the degree of hierarchy of government organizations. The use of e-mail is expected to raise the level of individual control, and this results in a drop of the degree of hierarchy since managers have fewer opportunities to steer the behavior of their employees (Hinds & Kiesler, 1995). Additionally, new e-mail communication patterns take the form of networks and result in a limitation of the role of hierarchy in structuring organizational communication (Sproull & Kiesler, 1991; Van den Hooff, 1997). The

third aspect of hierarchy was the information funnel. E-mail can be expected to form a barrier to this funnel of information because of the horizontal communication patterns (see also Thaens, 2001). On the basis of this overview, the following hypothesis is proposed:

> **H2.** The outcome of the changes triggered by the use of e-mail in government bureaucracies is a lower degree of hierarchy than before the introduction of this medium.

The lower degrees of formalization and hierarchy are key characteristics of post-bureaucratic organizations (Fulk & DeSanctis, 1995; Hekscher & Donnellon, 1994). This paper presents new empirical work to test the two propositions. The design of this research is presented in the next section.

RESEARCH DESIGN

The research was carried out in line with the interpretative research tradition in information systems research (Walsham, 2006). The combination of qualitative and quantitative research presented in this paper focused on creating an in-depth understanding of how e-mail is actually used by office workers in bureaucratic organizations. The research focused on e-mail communication from the perspective of civil servants to reconstruct the changes they experience in their work environment in bureaucratic organizations.

The research was explorative, and three cases were selected for the empirical research. The cases differed in the level of government, the level of autonomy from central departments, and the policy domain. The idea behind this unique case design was to get a broad understanding of the changes in government bureaucracies (George & Bennett, 2006). The following three cases were selected: the Headquarters of the Royal Navy, the Administrative Department of a local government (which requested anonymity), and the National Bank.

In line with the interpretative tradition, a combination of research methods was used to study e-mail practices in the three organizations. The conceptualizations of formalization and hierarchy presented in the conceptual framework guided the data collection and resulted in specific questions for the empirical research (see Table 58.1).

Table 58.1   Questions for Empirical Research

Bureaucratic characteristic	Specific questions
Formalization	Are work and private interests separated?
	Is the style of communication formal or informal?
	Are formal and informal communication separated?
Hierarchy	What is the degree of autonomy of employees?
	To what extent does communication follow hierarchical lines?
	Are superiors informed about the work of their subordinates?

The specific research method varied per case because access to the contents of the messages was problematic in the Royal Navy and the National Bank.

• The research consisted of extensive semistructured interviewing with civil servants with different hierarchical and functional positions in the organizations. Nine civil servants were interviewed at the Royal Navy, 13 respondents in the local government, and 8 respondents at the National Bank, which made a total of 14 managers and 16 employees. Respondents were selected on the basis of maximum variation since that fits this type of explorative study. Positions varied from secretaries to directors to Web masters to lawyers to IT auditors.

• To enhance the reliability of the research, the content of 1522 e-mail messages of a group of 13 civil servants in the local government were analyzed. This analysis focused on formal and informal use of language and e-mail patterns in terms of CCs, forwards, BCCs, etc.

• In the Royal Navy, seven civil servants registered their e-mail communication during a period of several days. They indicated whether this communication was task related or personal.

• In each organization, one or two interviews were held with IT experts to obtain information about the e-mail facilities at the organization.

• A total of 16 documents concerning e-mail facilities and policies were studied in all three organizations.

The original objective of the study was to track and explain differences between bureaucratic organizations. However, an analysis of the three cases showed very similar changes in communication patterns with the introduction of e-mail, and hence also similar effects on the degree of formalization and the hierarchy of organizations. Therefore, the research findings are presented collectively. The results are presented according to the two bureaucratic characteristics and the specific questions that were formulated for each of them.

EMPIRICAL RESULTS: FORMALIZATION

Are Work and Private Interests Blurring?

Does the use of e-mail result in blurring the distinction between task-related and private communication? Quantitative (though limited) evidence comes from the research at the Royal Navy. The respondents' registrations indicate that e-mail is used for personal communication in less than 10% of the messages. These findings were confirmed through qualitative research. Seventy percent of the respondents indicated that they make limited use of e-mail for private communication. Some respondents emphasized that limited private use is acceptable. One said: "I also call my wife from the office when I go home. Organizations should allow for limited private use of email." Thirty percent of the respondents make regular use of it. Another respondent reported that: "A great part of my personal life (. . .) is conducted through work email."

It is possible to question these answers since they are based on self-reporting. Use of e-mail for personal communication could be seen as undesirable behavior, and therefore respondents might be inclined to downplay this type of e-mail use. The content analysis at the local government, however, does not show a gap between self-reporting and actual messages and gave no reason to question the self-reports. Of 100 sample messages, five contained content which could be considered private.

Another possible blur of work and private interests is that employees use their private e-mail accounts for work-related communication. A large majority of the respondents at the three organizations have an e-mail account at home and a minority of them occasionally open this e-mail box at work. Private e-mail accounts are hardly used for work-related communications. Some respondents indicated that they e-mail documents to their private accounts so they can work on these documents at home.

Informal Style of Communication?

Does the use of e-mail result in a more informal style of communication? This part of the research is complicated to present since these changes in style are difficult to translate into English while they concern distinctions that are specific to the Dutch language. The distinction between a formal and an informal *you* provides an example. This distinction does not exist in English, whereas it plays an important role in Dutch interactions.

Eighty percent of the respondents confirmed that the style of communication in e-mail messages is more informal than in written documents. Nearly all respondents in the three organizations highlighted the informal heading. Written documents generally start with "To Whom it May Concern," whereas e-mail messages usually open with "Hi John." E-mail messages end with "Bye, Tim" instead of a formal "Best regards, Dr. T. Limber." This example also shows that first names are used instead of professional titles and formal abbreviations of positions in bureaucratic organizations.

E-mail messages in all three organizations are written is a sloppier manner. Rules of grammar are applied in a loose sense and the respondents do not make as much of an effort to formulate messages precisely. Some respondents highlighted that they do not use capitals and write e-mail messages as telegrams. Other respondents indicated that they tolerate spelling errors in e-mail that they would not tolerate in written documents. Many respondents,

however, emphasized that this does not mean that "anything goes." One respondent reported that, "I find quality important: no spelling errors and no yuppie language."

A few respondents emphasized that external e-mail messages are written in the same formal manner as written documents. A respondent indicated that the e-mail message he once wrote to the President of the National Bank was as formal as an internal memo. Two respondents indicated that, in the end, their messages are still relatively formal in style. They stressed that they have been trained to write in a certain way and they do not find it easy to suddenly change their style. One of these respondents recounted that, "My daughters always tell me that I write very formal email messages."

Some respondents emphasized that the style of communication in e-mail messages is closer to oral communication than to written communication. They emphasize that they write messages in the same way as they would speak to people. One respondent indicated that a rapid exchange of messages makes this type of communication feel like a conversation. He claimed that, "Email is similar to the telephone."

Mixing Formal and Informal Communication?

Do personal and task-related communications become intertwined in e-mail communication? Nearly 90% of the respondents indicated that personal and task-related communications are not mixed. To the contrary, e-mail is used almost exclusively for work-related matters. Some respondents indicated that e-mail contacts are more informal than communication through written documents. One respondent observed that, "In email you can easily write something such as, 'That was quite an emotional meeting!'" Another respondent stresses that relatively unimportant issues—still nice to know—are more easily communicated through e-mail.

Some respondents in all three organizations commented that the use of e-mail leads to more precise communication since agreements which were formerly not documented are now written down and kept in an electronic memory. One respondent said that, "Previously, we would not have made minutes of minor meetings. Now the outcomes of these meetings are recorded." Another respondent affirmed this saying, "The CC-option is used to inform others about agreements."

A few respondents highlighted that contacts are less personal and only related to the execution of tasks. One respondent claimed that, "Sending email messages is easier than walking to someone's office and, therefore, email leads to less face-to-face and telephone contact. In oral contacts personal matters are discussed. E-mail messages only contain work-related communication." Another respondent stressed that contacts through e-mail are more efficient but lose their personal touch. Some respondents reported that e-mail is not useful for communicating emotions. One reason why they do not include emotional statements in their e-mail messages is that these messages can be forwarded. Another reason is that emotional statements in e-mail can easily be misinterpreted. One observed that, "In sensitive matters I prefer using the telephone."

EMPIRICAL RESULTS: HIERARCHY

Decline in Autonomy?

Civil servants were asked whether e-mail enhanced their autonomy in the execution of tasks, in the management of information and communication, and in decision making. The results are shown in Table 58.2 (the scores reflect the number of positive answers minus the negative answers divided by the number of respondents: "1" means that all respondents see an increase in autonomy, "–1" means that all respondents see a decrease in autonomy).

The table shows that a substantial number of respondents see a positive effect of e-mail on their autonomy in information and communication management. The qualitative research confirms these findings. Several respondents highlighted that access to information is easier through e-mail. One respondent explained that, "I can request all sorts of information and they'll send it to me."

Other respondents indicated that their autonomy in communication is increased. They can decide at what time they want to communicate and, more importantly, with whom they want to communicate.

One respondent indicated that he also finds it important that he has a larger degree of autonomy in choosing the style of communication. Many respondents stressed that they have a large degree of autonomy in managing information. One respondent lauded his autonomy saying, "There are no rules that indicate how I should structure the storage of email."

The table also shows a positive effect of e-mail on employee autonomy in executing tasks. Three out of 10 respondents see a positive effect. In the qualitative research most respondents emphasized that e-mail does not change the contents of their tasks but their autonomy increases in terms of temporal and spatial autonomy. They can decide when and where to execute the task. One respondent said, "You do not get disturbed. You can decide when to do your job." Another respondent added, "You can work where you want. I sometimes work at home." Other respondents highlighted that additional opportunities to communicate with outside contacts increases their autonomy in executing tasks.

E-mail has a limited positive effect on employee autonomy in decision making. Most respondents stressed that decision making in bureaucratic organizations is bound by formal rules and formal responsibilities. A minority of the respondents saw a positive effect. They emphasized that decisions are made according to formal rules but indicated that e-mail increases their autonomy in preparing these decisions. One respondent indicated that employee autonomy has been increased for small budget purchases (up to a thousand euros).

There were no significant differences in the perceptions of the effect e-mail has on autonomy between employees and managers. Most managers evaluated the changes in autonomy as having positive effects. One manager commented that, "Managers must not control everything and must not even want to control their employees all the time. Trusting people is the way to motivate them." Another manager added, "Employee autonomy has been strengthened and this undermines hierarchy. (. . .) That is a good thing. (. . .) If they do not do their jobs correctly, we should hire better people." Only one manager disagreed, concluding that employee autonomy has attained unacceptable levels.

Table 58.2   Impact of E-Mail on Autonomy of Civil Servants

	Autonomy in information and communication management	Autonomy in tasks	Autonomy in decision making
Royal Navy ($n = 9$)	0.4	0.0	0.0
Local government ($n = 13$)	0.3	0.4	0.2
National Bank ($n = 8$)	0.4	0.4	0.1
Total ($N = 30$)	0.4	0.3	0.1

Is Hierarchy Less Important for Structuring Communication?

Does e-mail make employees skip hierarchical positions in their communication more frequently and/or does e-mail make them communicate more directly with employees in other departments? The results are shown in Table 58.3 (the scores reflect the number of positive answers minus the negative answers divided by the number of respondents: "1" means that all respondents indicate that they communicate more directly with employees in other departments, "–1" means that all respondents indicate that they communicate less directly with employees in other departments).

Most respondents in all three organizations indicated that it is easier to contact persons higher up in the hierarchy. One respondent reported, "Employees find it easier to send an email to the head of their department or to one of the directors." Employees indicated that they sometimes skip hierarchical positions in their e-mail communication, whereas they would not skip them in other written documents.

More significantly, respondents stressed that *horizontal communication* is facilitated. One affirmed that, "Before the introduction of e-mail, a memo would pass the head of my department and the head of another department before it would finally end up on the addressee's desk. Secretaries channeled the communication. Now I can send the message directly to the addressee." Another respondent emphasized that—in contrast with the situation in the past—e-mail communication is more related to the expertise of employees than to their formal positions.

Generally, heads of departments are informed through CCs. One respondent said that, "If I think there may be problems in the coordination I send a CC to the head of my department. If I think the issue

is harmless, I don't." The answers also reflected strategic considerations in sending a CC to the head of a department. One respondent stressed that, "If problems arise, I can say that he could have known because I did send him a CC."

Most managers valued the increase in horizontal communication as a positive development. One manager specifically highlighted that he is glad that his employees follow horizontal lines because it enables him to steer on key issues. Only one manager objected to the new communication patterns. He claimed that, "Email creates confusion in hierarchical organizations . . . It is an anarchistic medium which confounds formal procedures." Most managers value horizontal communication but emphasize that they should receive a CC to be able to monitor communication.

Limited Information to the Top of the Organization?

Respondents were asked whether they keep their managers better informed about their work because of e-mail communication. The results are shown in Table 58.4 (the scores reflect the number of positive answers minus the negative answers divided by the number of respondents: "1" means that all respondents indicated that they keep their managers better informed, "–1" means that all respondents indicated that they do not keep their managers as well informed).

Most respondents indicated that they keep their managers better informed because they send CCs. The respondents from the Royal Navy form an exception to the general perception that managers are better informed. The most probable explanation is that the Royal Navy, as a military organization,

Table 58.3   Impact of E-Mail on Communication Patterns

	Deviation from hierarchical lines
Royal Navy ($n = 9$)	0.6
Local government ($n = 13$)	0.5
National Bank ($n = 8$)	0.8
Total ($N = 30$)	0.6

Table 58.4   Impact of E-Mail on Informing Managers

	Do employees inform manager better?
Royal Navy ($n = 9$)	0.000
Local government ($n = 13$)	0.615
National Bank ($n = 8$)	0.600
Total ($N = 30$)	0.433

puts greater emphasis on directly informing superiors than the other organizations. The added value of sending CCs is then less notable. Testing this explanation requires more systematic research into the specific effects of e-mail on military organizations. The qualitative analysis yielded information about the variety of opposing positions taken by the respondents: why e-mail makes managers less informed, why it does not have any effect, and why it makes them better informed. The minority of respondents who answered that their managers are not as well informed stressed that managers lose their central position and cannot keep track of all the communication. One respondent pointed out that, "Our bosses don't know half of what goes on through email." Another respondent emphasized that communication is faster and does not pass the manager's desk. A third respondent indicated that his (older) boss does not feel comfortable with e-mail as a communication technology.

Quite a few respondents indicated that e-mail does not have any effect on the information managers receive. One respondent downplayed the role e-mail plays in his employment saying, "My boss is the assistant-director. E-mail does not make him better or worse informed about my work. He gets his information through meetings and not through email." One manager stressed that what he knows about the work his employees do depends on what they tell him and not on the communication technology they use.

A substantial group of respondents indicated that they are of the opinion that their managers are better informed, mainly because of CCs. One respondent observed that, "I send many CCs to my manager to keep him informed. This saves me from having to report my activities to him every week." Some respondents see CCs as an important precondition for coordination. One wrote, "Managers need to be informed through CCs to enable them to intervene." Most managers also indicated that they feel they are better informed about their employees' work. Information overload is not considered to be a problem. Said one, "You can get the main thrust of a message in 2 seconds. After that you can delete messages. I also put unread messages in my folders so they are available for later reading."

The analysis of e-mail communications within local government confirms that CCs are important (see Table 58.5). One fifth of the messages are received through CCs, and for the superiors, this is nearly one out of four messages. Subordinates sent slightly more messages than superiors.

ANALYSIS: TESTING THE HYPOTHESES

Testing the Informalization Hypothesis

We have seen that e-mail challenges existing conventions governing the division between work and private matters. E-mail is used for some private matters, and this type of use is generally accepted. This shows a shift in communication patterns. At the same time, however, civil servants emphasize that work-related and private communication should be separated and they strive for this separation. This can be seen as a reproduction of bureaucratic characteristics in the way e-mail is used.

Additionally, the style of communication is modified by the use of e-mail. The style of writing is sloppier and less formalized than in written documents. This shows how communication patterns and bureaucratic characteristics are challenged by the new medium. The actual use of the medium, however, is still fairly bureaucratic. And when it comes to important communication, the formal style of communication that is a hallmark of bureaucratic organizations is reproduced in e-mail messages.

Finally, e-mail is used for formalizing contacts in bureaucratic organizations. Agreements are recorded in e-mail messages to ensure that they are not misunderstood and so that they may be retrieved at a later stage. This shows how the use of e-mail is conditioned by the characteristics of bureaucratic organizations. At the same time, communication patterns are challenged by the medium and the degree of formalization rises.

These processes of structuration are similar in shape and outcome in the three bureaucratic organizations I investigated. This brings us to the research hypothesis. The following hypothesis was formulated:

H3. The outcome of the changes triggered by the use of e-mail in government bureaucracies is a lower degree of formalization than before the introduction of this medium.

There was mixed support for this proposition. E-mail is used for private communication but to a limited extent, e-mail enhances an informal style of communication, but also formalizes the content of communications. These findings seem to point at a paradoxical effect: the style of communication is becoming more informal whereas the content becomes formalized. One can label this outcome as *informal formalization:* the style of communication is more informal but the content focuses less on personal issues and emphasizes efficient recordings of agreements.

Testing the Horizontalization Hypothesis

E-mail challenges the notion of hierarchy by enhancing employee autonomy in information and communication management and in executing tasks. The new medium facilitates access to information, lets employees communicate with a wider network of contacts, gives them autonomy in managing information, and enables them to choose when and where they want to do their work. At the same time, employee autonomy is still limited by formal decision-making procedures. New forms of autonomy are limited by existing convention based on the hierarchical nature of bureaucratic organizations. Interesting processes of structuration are taking place in the preparation of decisions. Autonomy is strengthened and may challenge formal procedures.

Communication patterns deviate from hierarchical lines and thus challenge institutional structures. The *tree* as formal for intra-organizational communication is increasingly inadequate as horizontal communication becomes more important. This horizontal communication, however, takes place in the shadow of hierarchy, and managers are informed about important communications through a CC. Hierarchy does not become superfluous in conditioning communication but takes on a different role.

The new medium enables employees to continuously inform their managers about their work. Hierarchy conditions this type of e-mail usage and, at the same time, hierarchy takes a different form.

Table 58.5 CCs Within Local Government (percentage of total number of messages)

	CCs received	CCs sent
Superiors	23	13
Subordinates	17	15
Total	20	14

The cycle of control is shortened and managers are informed on a continuous basis.

These processes of structuration in the three aspects of hierarchy are similar in shape and outcome in the three bureaucratic organizations I investigated. This brings us to the research hypothesis.

H4. The outcome of changes triggered by the use of e-mail in government bureaucracies is a lower degree of hierarchy than before the introduction of this medium.

The empirical research provides mixed support for this proposition. The research indicated that in all three organizations e-mail enables communication which deviates from hierarchical lines. The respondents also indicated that their autonomy is enhanced. This indicates that the outcome of changes triggered by the use of e-mail in government bureaucracies is more individual control and less central steering. At the same time, these changes do not mean that managers lose control. Most respondents indicated that through e-mail managers are better informed about what they are doing. CCs are important. This means that there is less central steering but more central monitoring. This paradoxical effect can be labeled as *hierarchical horizontalization*. Horizontal contacts take a more central position in bureaucratic organizations, but these horizontal contacts are tightly linked to vertical structures.

CONCLUSIONS AND LESSONS LEARNED

On the basis of these findings, we can now answer the research question: Does the use of e-mail change government agencies into post-bureaucratic organizations? In the findings, the contours of a new type of organization can be recognized. This organization deviates from the formal bureaucratic organizations as described by Weber but also reflects its key traits. There is less ex ante control, but civil servants enable monitoring by their managers by keeping them informed with CCs. Managers survey e-mail messages and intervene when they feel their input is needed. The formalization of previously informal communications facilitates both vertical and horizontal control. The conclusion is that the use of e-mail does not change government agencies into post-bureaucratic organizations. The resulting organizational form is a hybrid combination of bureaucratic and network forms.

Orlikowski's (1992) perspective on the interplay between technology and organization was used to interpret the results and the emerging type of organization. One can conclude that the use of e-mail reflects the properties of government organizations. The emphasis on record making and informing managers results from the bureaucratic nature of government. The introduction of e-mail also challenges the properties of government organizations. Bureaucracy is not reproduced but shifts to a new form of coordination. This emerging form of organization results from the interplay between organizational and technological properties and the way these properties are combined in the context of use.

A first lesson from this research is that e-mail definitely has a different effect on the structure of government bureaucracies than the large scale information systems studied by Zouridis (2000), Zuurmond (1994), and Fountain (2001). E-mail does not enhance bureaucracy. Although the rise of the new form of coordination cannot be attributed only to the use of e-mail, affordances of e-mail facilitate the functioning of this new type of organization. Three affordances of e-mail were specifically relevant in this specific context: asynchronicity, instant memory, and one-to-many communication. These affordances trigger the change from a bureaucratic organization to a "network in the shadow of hierarchy" (cf. Scharpf, 1994). Asynchronicity is required for loose couplings. In a network organization, civil servants need to interact with many other people inside and outside the organization. Instant memory is needed for reliable contacts between civil servants in the absence of hierarchical relations. One-to-many communication is required to keep managers and other contacts informed and thus keep the network together.

A second lesson concerns the practical implications for the flexibility and accountability of government organizations. A key characteristic of the new form of coordination is the linkage between vertical and horizontal coordination. The *informal formalization* (recording agreements in an informal style) plays a crucial role in this linkage. This linkage is not new, per se, but now extends both vertically and horizontally with coordination

Table 58.6   Comparing Types of Bureaucracy

	Bureaucracy	*Late-bureaucracy*	*Post-bureaucracy*
Coordination	Predominantly vertical	Horizontal and vertical	Predominantly horizontal
Role of formalization	Vertical accountability	Vertical and horizontal accountability	No important role
Management control	Command and control	Monitoring	Network ineractions

documented in e-mail messages. Horizontal communication is directly linked to vertical structures through CCs. Public managers monitor their employees' messages and intervene when needed. E-mail facilitates these linkages and enables bureaucratic organizations to be both flexible and accountable.

The final and most important lesson of this research is that government agencies do not change into post-bureaucratic but into late-bureaucratic organizations. The autonomy of civil servant grows and coordination takes place in horizontal networks, typified by reciprocal patterns of communication and exchange (Powell, 1990). However, these post-bureaucratic organizations function in the shadow of hierarchy. Hierarchical and network forms of coordination are directly coupled through formalized electronic communications. This concept of the *late-bureaucratic organization* is based upon the idea of radicalized modernity as presented by Giddens (1990); Beck, Giddens & Lash, (1994). Bureaucracy is not surpassed but radicalized. Formalization has expanded and now encompasses communication that was previously considered to be informal, and hierarchy extends its control to day-to-day operations in organizations. Continuous monitoring replaces systems of ex ante command and ex post control. The differences between bureaucracies, late-bureaucracies, and post-bureaucracies are shown in Table 58.6.

Weber (1968) has called our attention to the central role of bureaucracy in public administration. This organizational form is being transformed under the influence of electronic communications. Studying these transformations is crucial for our scientific and pragmatic understanding of modern government. The concept of late-bureaucracy that was formulated on the basis of this empirical research sheds a new light on these transitions of modern government organizations, advances the scientific understanding of government organizations, and helps in designing and managing better governments.

REFERENCES

Ball, R. R. (1991). The effects of electronic mail on organisational structure. *Proceedings of the International Conference an Information Technology in the Workplace* (pp. 49–53).

Beck, U., Giddens, A., & Lash, S. (1994). *Reflexive modernization: Politics, tradition and aesthetics in the modern social order.* Oxford: Blackwell.

Behn, R. D. (2001). *Rethinking democratic accountability.* Washington DC: Brookings Institution Press.

Bovens, M. A. P. (1998). *The quest for responsibility: Accountability and citizenship in complex organizations.* Cambridge: Cambridge University Press.

Burgess, A., Jackson, T. W., & Edwards, J. (2005). Email training significantly reduces email defects. *International Journal of Information Management, 25,* 71–83.

Deibert, R. D. (1997). *Parchment, printing and hypermedia.* New York: Columbia University Press.

Frissen, V. (2003). De digitalisering van de werkvloer: De integratie van ICT in dagelijkse werkprocessen [Digitization at the Workfloor: The integration of ICT in routine business processes]. In P. Ester (Ed.), *ICT, arbeid en organisatie* (ICT, labour and organization) Den Haag: Reed Business Information.

Fountain, J. E. (2001). *Building the virtual state. Information technology and institutional change.* Washington DC: The Brookings Institute.

Fulk, J., & DeSanctis, G. (1995). Electronic communication and changing organizational forms. *Organization Science, 6,* 337–349.

George, A. L., & Bennett, A. (2006). *Case studies and theory development in the social sciences.* Cambridge MA: MIT Press.

Giddens, A. (1984). *The constitution of society: Outline of the theory of structure.* Berkeley CA: University of California Press.

Giddens, A. (1990). The *consequences of modernity.* Stanford CA: Stanford University Press.

Harley, B. (1999). The myth of empowerment: Work organization, hierarchy and employee autonomy in contemporary australian workplaces. *Work, Employment and Society, 13,* 41–66.

Hekscher, C., & Donnellon, A. (Eds.). (1994). *The post-bureaucratic organization. New perspectives on organizational change.* Thousand Oaks (CA): Sage Publications.

Hinds, P., & Kiesler, S. (1995). Communication across boundaries: Work, structure, and use of communication technologies in a large organization. *Organization Science, 6,* 373–393.

Hutchby, I. (2001). *Conversation and technology. From the telephone to the Internet.* Cambridge (UK): Polity.

Hutchby, I. (2003). Affordances and the analysis of technologically mediated interaction: A response to Brian Rappert. *Sociology, 37,* 581–589.

Jones, M., & Karsten, H. (2003). *A review of Structuration Theory in information systems research.* Research papers in management studies. Cambridge: University of Cambridge.

Kock, N., Lynn, G. S., Dow, K. E., & Akgun, A. E. (2006). Team adaptation to electronic communication media: Evidence of compensatory adaptation in new product development teams. *European Journal of Information Systems, 15,* 331–341.

Landry, E. M. (2000). Scrolling around the new organization: The potential for conflict in the on-line environment. *Negotiation Journal, 16,* 133–142.

Meijer, A. J. (2002). *De doorzichtige overheid. Parlementaire en juridische controle in het informatietijdperk* [Transparent government. Parliamentary and legal control in an Information Age]. Delft: Eburon.

Mintzberg, H. (1983). *Structures in fives. Designing effective organizations.* Englewood Cliffs: Prentice Hall.

Murray, D. (1988). Computer mediated communication: Implication for ESP. *English for Specific Purposes, 7,* 3–18.

Ngwenyama, O. K. (1998). Groupware, social action and organizational emergence: On the process dynamics of computer mediated distributed work. *Accounting Management and Information Technology, 8,* 127–146.

Orlikowski, W. J. (1992). The duality of technology: Rethinking the concept of technology in organizations. *Organization Science, 3,* 398–427.

Orlikowski, W. J., Yates, J., Okamura, K., & Fujimoto, M. (1995). Shaping electronic communication: The metastructuring of technology in the context of use. *Organization Science, 6,* 423–444.

Perrow, C. (1986). *Complex organizations: A critical essay.* New York: Random House.

Powell, W. W. (1990). Neither market nor hierarchy: Network forms of organization. *Research in Organizational Behavior, 12,* 295–336.

Roethlisberger, F. J., & Wilson, W. J. (1939). *Management and the worker.* Cambridge (MA): Harvard University Press.

Scharpf, F. W. (1994). Games real actors could play: Positive and negative coordination in embedded negotiations. *Journal of Theoretical Politics, 6,* 27–53.

Schofield, N., & Alt, J. (1983). The analysis of relations in an organization. *Quality and Quantity, 17,* 269–279.

Scott, W. R. (2003). *Organizations: Rational, natural and open systems,* 5th edition. Upper Saddle River: Prentice Hall.

Sellen, A. J., & Harper, R. H. R. (2002). *The myth of the paperless office.* Cambridge: MIT Press.

Selznick, O. (1957). *Leadership in administration. A sociological interpretation.* Berkeley: University of California Press.

Sproull, L., & Kiesler, S. (1991). *Connections. New ways of working in the networked organization.* Cambridge (MA): The MIT Press.

Stasz, C., & Bikson, T. K. (1986). Computer-supported cooperative work: Examples and issues in one federal agency. *Proceedings of the 1986 ACM Conference on Computer-Supported Cooperative Work* (pp. 318–324).

Strøm, K. (2000). Delegation and accountability in parliamentary democracies. *European Journal of Political Research, 37,* 261–289.

Tannenbaum, A. S., Kavcic, B., Rosner, M., Vianello, M., & Wieser, G. (1974). *Hierarchy in organizations.* Washington DC: Jossey-Bass.

Taylor, H., Fieldman, G., & Lahlou, S. (2005). The impact of a threatening e-mail reprimand on the recipient's blood pressure. *Journal of Managerial Psychology, 20,* 43–50.

Taylor, J. R., Groleau, C, Heaton, L., & Van Every, E. (2001). *The computerization of work. A communication perspective.* Thousand Oaks (CA): Sage Publications.

Thaens, M. (2001). *ICT en ministeriële verantwoordelijkheid: Verbinding en betekenis* [ICT and ministerial responsibility: Linkages and meanings].

Onderzoeksprogramma Internet en openbaar bestuur.

Trevino, L. K., Daft, R. L., & Lengel, R. H. (1990). Understanding manager's media choices: A symbolic interactionist perspective. In J. Fulk & C.W. Steinfield (Eds.), *Organizations and Communication Technology* (pp. 71–94). Newbury Park (CA): Sage.

Van den Hooff, B. J. (1997). *Incorporating electronic mail: Adoption, use and effects of electronic mail in organizations.* Amsterdam: Cramwinckel.

Van Thijn, E., & Cardoso Ribeiro, T. (2004). *De informatie-paradox: een blinde vlek in het openbaar bestuur [The information paradox: A blind spot in public administration].* Utrecht (NL): Lemma.

Vroom, V. H. (1969). Industrial social psychology. In G. Lindzey & E. Aronson (Eds.), *Handbook of social psychology* (pp. 196–268). Reading (MA): Addison-Wesley.

Walsham, G. (2006). Doing interpretive research. *European Journal of Information Systems, 15,* 320–330.

Weber, M. (1968). *Economy and society: An outline of interpretive sociology.* New York: Bedminister Press.

Wilensky, H. L. (1967). *Organizational intelligence. Knowledge and policy in government and industry.* New York: Basic Books.

Williams, R., & Edge, D. (1996). The social shaping of technology. *Research Policy, 25,* 865–899.

Yunus, H. (2005). E-mail communication in a distance learning programme and its implication to language teaching and learning. *Internet Journal of e-Language Learning & Teaching, 2,* 26–45.

Zouridis, S. (2000). *Digitale disciplinering. Over ICT, organisatie, wetgeving en het automatiseren van beschikkingen* [Digital discipline. ICT, organization, lawmaking and automating government decision]. Delft: Eburon.

Zuurmond, A. (1994). *De Infocratie, Een theoretische en empirische heroriëntatie op Weber's ideaaltype. In het informatietijdperk* [The infocracy. A theoretical and empirical re-orientation on Weber's idealtype in the Information Age]. Delft: Eburon.

SOURCE: Meijer, Albert Jacob. 2008. "E-Mail in Government: Not Post-Bureaucratic but Late Bureaucratic Organizations." *Government of Information Quarterly*, 25(3):429–47.

59

ONLINE DATING IN JAPAN

A Test of Social Information Processing Theory

JAMES FARRER AND JEFF GAVIN

INTRODUCTION

Japan is an early Internet adopter with its own online cultural norms, including a preference for mobile platforms such as cell phones.[1] Traditionally, Japanese preferred mediated forms of dating as a way of reducing the uncertainties and anxieties associated with meeting complete strangers.[2] With the traditional form of mediated introductions—*omiai*—now accounting for less than one tenth of marriages,[3] Japanese increasingly are turning to other forms of organized "marriage hunting" (*konkatsu*), including online dating.[4] The practice of peer-mediated blind group dates—*gokon*—has long been prevalent among college students in Japan but is less available for older Japanese adults, especially the increasingly large number of adults outside of regular corporate employment. Recently, online sites have become a popular form of mediated introduction, and they also offer some advantages over *gokon* and other face-to-face introductions. The Internet provides a way of getting to know a person "from the inside out" without having to risk first meeting that person face to face. However, there is also some distrust of Internet dating in Japan. The practice of *deai-kei*, arranging meetings online, became associated with prostitution and sexual assaults in Japan.[6] The bad reputation of *deai-kei* was described by Match.com Japan managers as a problem for mainstream online "matching" services in Japan (personal communication). On the other hand, Japanese men and women are marrying increasingly late or not at all, leading to increased anxieties about unmarriageable singles and declining birthrates.[7] All these trends have lowered social resistance to online dating.[4]

Although the same communicative acts can have different meanings in different cultures, online dating sites worldwide tend to follow the same, originally North American, model. Members of online dating sites post profiles describing themselves and their ideal partners, they send and receive e-mails on the basis of these initial descriptions, and in many cases continue to communicate using a variety of online and offline channels in order to get to know each other more fully. This process often culminates in the formation of offline romantic relationships, at which point membership of the dating site is canceled. Since most studies of online dating have looked at European or North American cases, this Japanese case study allows us to address questions about cultural differences in the use of online dating platforms and to explore the extent to which Western-based theories of computer mediated communication (CMC) and the development of online relationships are relevant to the Japanese experience.

Theories of CMC

Online communication has apparent disadvantages in terms of building personal relationships, as compared to face-to-face interactions, which make an abundance of verbal and nonverbal cues available.[8] Early "cues filtered out" models argue that important nonverbal and contextual cues are missing (or filtered out) in CMC[9-11] and that the fewer cue systems a channel offers, the greater the barrier to intimate relational development. This approach, however, does not take into account the intent of communicators. To this end, Walther's[12,13] social information processing theory (SIPT) argues that CMC users adapt their efforts to present and acquire social information using whatever cues a medium provides. To compensate for the lack of nonverbal cues, CMC users employ content and linguistic strategies as well as timing-related[14] and typographic cues[15] to glean information about a CMC partner. Furthermore, Walther[16] found that, proportionately, CMC partners ask more questions and disclose more about themselves than do their face-to-face counterparts. In these ways, impressions and relational communication improve over time in CMC to parallel face-to-face interactions.[17] A central premise of SIPT is that relational processes take time, and CMC interactions are relatively slower than face-to-face interactions.[12] Given enough time, however, CMC partners can adapt to the lack of cues inherent in text-based communication and eventually achieve interpersonal outcomes comparable to face-to-face relationships.

Recent extensions to this model highlight its relevance to online dating. For example, the anticipation of future interaction has been included as a variable in modifications to SIPT, as it is assumed to increase intimacy and self-disclosure.[18] Further, Walther's hyperpersonal model argues that not only can CMC partners overcome the limitations of CMC, they can use text-based communication to develop relationships more intimate than their face-to-face counterparts.[17] Interactants compensate for the limitations of CMC by hyperpersonalizing their interactions.

That is, CMC partners exploit the benefits of text-based communication to engage in, for example, selective self-presentation and partner idealization. This can lead to positively skewed perceptions leading to elevated feelings of intimacy. A recent study offers support for SIPT in the setting of online relationships by demonstrating the importance of small cues in online dating, in both the profiles and initial e-mails.[19] Online daters attend to subtle, almost minute cues in others' profiles and e-mail messages, including spelling ability, timing (e.g., time of day or night), message length, as well as broader cues such as whether the online partner is an active user of the dating site or the type of photograph included. All of these strategies are consistent with SIPT.

Cross-Cultural Differences in Communication Styles

The meanings and limitations of online communication are not necessarily uniform across cultures, with recent researchers calling into question early theorizing of the Internet as "deterritorialized" or "borderless."[20] The Internet is not culture neutral but is shaped by local cultures of politics, community, Internet use, the social shaping of technology, and language. Therefore, the lack of social context cues in text-based communication could be particularly problematic in Japanese culture, where social context plays a much greater role in the communication process.[21] Cross-cultural psychologists usually describe a Japanese preference for "high-context" communication in which information is conveyed not directly in the message itself but more indirectly through the larger context of communication.[22] Communication focuses on implicit communicative cues, such as body language and use of silence, implying a message through what is not said, including the situation, behavior, and paraverbal cues. These contextual cues are precisely the type of information that is often considered to be lacking in CMC. Other cultures (e.g., North America) communicate predominantly through explicit statements in text and speech and are thus categorized as "low-context" communicators.[21,23] Most information is contained in the message itself, so there is a need for information to be conveyed in a direct and unambiguous way.[24]

Research indicates that differences in communication styles between low-context and high-context cultures have carried over into various areas of online communication. Cross-cultural comparisons of Web-site content,[25,26] e-business negotiations, and international marketing[28] all indicate that cultural values are reflected in online communication styles and that the Internet should not automatically be assumed to be a culturally neutral medium. The presence of cross-cultural differences in online communication styles suggests that the techniques put forward by SIPT models, such as asking direct questions and increasing self-disclosure, may not be equally available in some online settings, particularly in Japan, a culture in which a reliance on high-context communication may preclude asking direct questions or providing explicit information, thus robbing the interaction of some of the elements said to aid relational development in CMC. For example, within Japanese culture, "being far more specific or elaborate than the situation demands is likely to be interpreted as a sign of incompetence, or *yabo* (insensitivity, or 'uncool')."[29(p171)] Similarly, as Mushakoji states, "In Japan it is considered virtuous to 'catch on' quickly . . . to adjust to someone's position before it is logically and clearly enunciated."[30(p43)] Japanese young people put a great value on the idea of "implied communication" in dating relationships, using conventional social cues to indicate a desire for increased commitment or intimacy.[3] Given the continuation of cross-cultural differences in communication styles in online settings, the Japanese preference for high-context communication, and the characterization of the Internet as a low-context medium,[2–5] this study examines whether Walther's SIPT is applicable to Japanese online dating interactions. Specifically, it explores how and to what extent Japanese daters overcome the limitations of CMC through the use of contextual and other cues.

Data and Method

The data were generated using an online survey consisting of a combination of 20 closed-ended and 35 open-ended questions, with 36 current and 27 former members of Match.com Japan, 40 female and 23 male. All women were looking for male partners, and all men were looking for female partners. Sixteen of the informants had married since beginning their use of Match.com. The others were never married (39) or divorced (8). Seventeen had never dated anyone on the site but were active users. Fifty-one lived in the Tokyo area, with rest spread out through Japan. Three were Japanese using the site from abroad. The median age of the informants was 32, with all but three between the ages of 25 and 45 (one below 25 and 2 over 45). Former members of Match.com were recruited via an e-mail sent to 89 participants of an earlier study on people who had married or formed a long-term relationship using the Match.com interface and provided an e-mail address indicating their willingness to participate in a future study. Current members were recruited via e-mails sent to 80 randomly selected members of Match.com who had been active on the site in the previous 2 weeks. The response rates were 40.4% and 33.3% respectively. After agreeing to participate in the study, respondents were directed to an online survey, which took about 15 minutes to complete. The survey was conducted using the online survey software Surveymonkey (http://www.surveymonkey.com). The survey instrument consisted of three sections: a set of closed-ended demographic questions; a section of open-ended questions on online dating behavior in general, including construction of a profile, searching behavior, and communication; and a section of questions about the formation of relationships online and any experiences of offline meetings.

Data analysis followed issue-based procedures for grounded theory.[31,32] This method generates generalizations based on interviewees' responses. Transcripts were read and files of excerpted quotes and coder comments were created. In what Weiss calls "local integration" of data, similar responses were grouped together to generate sets of common themes. Two native Japanese-speaking student assistants independently worked on categorizing the themes, with thematic categorizations confirmed by the principal investigator. As the data from the former and current members were comparable in terms of the relevant themes identified, they have been collapsed in the following analysis.

Findings

General Patterns

Contact is initiated between members via the sending of either an introductory e-mail or a virtual kiss. Most informants correspond with many people online rather than with just one, and send introductory e-mails and virtual kisses to many potential partners. There is a clear gender pattern in the sending and receiving of these initial messages. Most men (63.7%) have sent more than five introductory e-mails/virtual kisses to female members, with 27% of men sending 50 or more of these messages. On the other hand, only one woman has sent 50 or more messages, with most women (73.1%) sending five or fewer. Not surprisingly, this pattern is reversed with respect to receiving e-mails/virtual kisses, with women receiving many more than men. Fifty-six percent of women report having received 50 or more introductory e-mails/virtual kisses, with only one woman receiving five or fewer. On the other hand, only 9% of men report receiving 50 or more introductory e-mails/virtual kisses, with most (50%) receiving five or fewer.

These findings point to the great volume of direct and unsolicited communication established on this site, and on the whole, both men and women were responsive to the introductory messages they received. Although some men said they generally replied to every message they received, most informants, both male and female, generally checked photos and profiles before replying to introductory e-mails/virtual kisses. Our interest is on the cues that are drawn upon in deciding with whom to initiate contact, whether to respond to an introductory message, and whether to continue with the correspondence once an exchange of e-mail messages is underway.

The Choice of the Online Platform as a Filtering and Signaling Device

Before a profile is even created, the choice of an online platform is itself a social signal. Given the general suspicion of online dating in Japan, choosing a "reliable" and "trusted" site is an especially important strategy of conveying social information in online dating interactions, including a sense of purpose (such as seriousness or play). Our findings support Holden and Tsuruki's findings that the social stigma of *deai-kei* sites (online meeting sites) is itself a source of anxiety among Japanese users of online matching sites.[6] This may work to the advantage of mainstream online dating sites such as Match.com. Informants perceived it as trustworthy because it is a brand-name company and did not seem to have employees paid to pose as members (known as *sakura* in Japan and common on *deai-kei* sites). Informants stated that because the site charges a member fee, it excluded people who were not serious about finding a partner. A few mentioned its success in the United States and elsewhere as a reason for choosing it over other sites. There is still some stigma attached to online dating, however, even among our sample of online daters. Thirty-two percent of informants said that they had not told any of their friends or family about their participation in online dating. Some explained this was because it was "embarrassing" but also because of the negative image of online dating or *deai-kei* in Japan.

> Maybe I still have an image of it being dangerous myself. I am scared of acknowledging that "it might be safe" to meet people through this kind of medium. And it is embarrassing if someone you know sees you. (No. 2, 25–29, female)

Explicit and Implicit Social Cues in Profiles

The informants relied heavily on explicit information provided in self-descriptions provided via drop-down boxes in the online profile template. Using the Match.com search facility, this information then can be used to narrow down the potential "market" when browsing profiles. Ninety percent of the informants used the search function that allows them to specify parameters on profile elements such as age, language, and region to restrict their searches for appropriate partners and avoid certain types of members. Factors that were often used to limit searches included smoking (with a preference for nonsmokers), age, location, nationality, language, level of education, and marital history. Informants varied in their attitudes toward dating non-Japanese. Some said that they had no interest in foreigners or would be put off by different languages and values. Conversely, others used Match.com specifically to find a foreign partner or said they would prefer a foreign partner:

> If there is someone who I could speak Japanese with, I actually would prefer him to a Japanese guy. (No. 62, 35–39, female)

> As an Asian, I have looked for Asian ladies, especially Koreans and Chinese. It is the advantage of Match.com. Personally, I'm in favor of international marriage. (No. 41, 40–44, male)

While explicitly provided information such as nationality, age, occupation, geographical location, and hobbies was important, so too was the more implicit information conveyed by the way the profile was written. Some profiles included indirect forms of communication, such as self-deprecating humor or irony and sexual innuendo. Many profiles, especially those of younger users, use emoticons and other nonlinguistic symbols, such as musical notations or creative punctuation, to hint at emotional tone or personality traits. Photos were generally described as very important as a clue not only to attractiveness but also to personality.

> You can tell what kind of person they are by the way it is taken. (No. 35, 35–39, female)

> Seventy-nine percent of informants said they put up a photo with their profiles. These photos were chosen partly to convey physical appearance but also to convey more nebulous information; for example, "a smiling picture that shows who I am, and makes people think that I am having fun." (No. 63, 30–34, female).

Social Cueing Through Levels of Politeness

As outlined previously, online daters send out e-mails and virtual kisses to many partners. It is at this stage that nonverbal and other contextual cues take on their greatest importance as part of the communication process. When describing their first messages, most informants answered that they tried not to write long e-mails at the beginning, with two to three lines being the norm. Members introduced themselves and wrote about what interested them

when reading others' profiles. Members tried to write trivial things in first e-mails:

> I write something simple and short just to make sure the person is interested in me. (No. 28, 25–29, female)

Once communication was established and an exchange of e-mails was underway, Japanese online daters drew on indirect cues, such as writing style, humor, and the speed of replies, in getting to know their potential partners. This is consistent with the strategies used by online daters in western countries.[19]

> I was attracted by the polite tone in mails, humorous sentences, and wealth of subjects. I was able to perceive his serious character and reliability from the messages. (No. 19, 25–29, female)

> I observe whether the person shows an interest in me or not (I do not reply to people who just introduce themselves); people who can use proper keigo; in cases where I can sense kindness in what is written; when I look at the profile and the photo is nice, and I feel that we share the same values. (No. 63, 30–34, female)

Japanese daters also incorporate cues that are unique to the Japanese language and writing styles. In Japanese-language online interactions, degrees of formality and informality in language are an especially important form of social cueing. In writing and replying to e-mails from other Match.com members, most informants used polite Japanese, or *keigo*. However, they also found ways of indicating familiarity and friendliness while using the polite forms of writing.

> I use keigo while being careful not to appear too serious, so I use hiragana a lot [instead of Chinese characters]. I will try not to be rude. (No. 63, 30–34, female)

This use of polite language often continued until the first meeting. But it could also change in the course of online communication, in which case one partner might suggest that they drop formal language.

> I will stop using keigo if we get to know one other, but will keep using keigo unless the person says, "You don't have to speak in keigo." (No. 19, 30–34, female)

For many informants, there was thus a pattern of relatively distant and formal communication with a large number of members, then settling on a smaller number of members with whom an exchange of e-mails occurred and a level of intimacy developed that could be signaled by dropping formal/polite language in favor of a more informal and intimate style of writing.

Communication Channels as a Social Cue

An important means of signaling increased intimacy was broadening the means of communication used to include other media, including short text messaging, instant messaging, and telephone calls, and finally meeting in person. Although phone text messaging was also virtual, it was a way of signaling increased trust and intimacy in the relationship. Usually, the man asked to switch to talking on the cell phone and then to meet in person.

> First it was mail in Match.com, next mail by computer, third cell phone mail, fourth cell phone, and at last, the direct line. (No. 17, 30–34, male)

We can see a pattern in which CMC is perceived as the least intimate means of communication, telephone text messaging as a step more intimate, and talking on the telephone as more intimate still. Changing the technical means of communication is thus a way of both developing and signaling intimacy. This is consistent with the pattern of intimacy found in other cultural contexts, such as Australia.[33]

Controlling the Context of Communication

Flexibility and control are important perceived advantages of online dating. Informants said they could meet various types of people on this site and choose their ideal type of partner, controlling how much time they spend interacting with online partners and communicating when and where they choose. They could also meet people from different backgrounds and do not have to worry about dealing personally with mediators as one does in group dates (or *gokon*). Getting to know a person before meeting them face to face is an advantage of online dating, as is the fact that online daters can easily stop contacting their online partners.

The merit is that you can search for someone who fits your standards and start communicating. If you feel that he is not your type, you can stop communicating before you meet. You also can meet people who you cannot meet only in the Net. (No. 52, 25–29, female)

Online dating platforms, while perceived as unreliable by some informants, were perceived as allowing more control over the context of relationship development, especially in the early phases. In general, face-to-face meetings were perceived to have more social costs than online meetings.

> Meeting at office is troublesome after you break up. An introduction by friends or *omiai* is good if you are introduced by your friends who you trust. However, if you do not go well with your partner, it is troublesome that you need to care about your friends' feelings . . . A marriage introduction service is expensive and has an image that people use that place as a last resort. The people who use them seem to be the people who are not popular. Also it is troublesome that there are mediators. (No. 63, 30–34, female)

These findings point to a perceived flexibility that online sites offer Japanese users in managing the breadth of social contexts and the cues of communication. Rather than understanding online communication as simply low-context communication and Japanese culture as favoring high-context communication, these findings highlight the active ways in which Japanese users can manipulate the context to achieve control over self-presentations and relationship outcomes.

DISCUSSION AND CONCLUSIONS

These findings strongly support Walther's SIPT.[12,13] Japanese online daters adapt their efforts to present and acquire social information using the cues that the online dating platform provides. Research on Japanese communication strategies suggests that Japanese prefer indirect cues over direct messages and high-context to low-context communication strategies.[22,29] This tendency would seem to pose particular problems for Japanese people engaging in online dating interactions in which much of the typically available social context of dating interactions (such as membership in a common social circle) is missing and in which there are seemingly fewer opportunities to engage in nonverbal cueing (such as glances and body gestures). Our findings suggest the opposite. From this research, it seems that online dating provides tools of social cueing and contextual communication that differ from but are not inferior to the contextual tools used in face-to-face interactions. One feature of online dating that informants discussed was that it allowed very effective means of *managing social contexts* as a way of controlling the flow of information and the development of relationships.

Consistent with SIPT, our research also supports previous findings[19] in that the Japanese users are able to find many contextual cues in the ways that others communicate. Most informants described themselves as competent at managing their uncertainties over online interactions. They felt that they could discern true from false self-representations through interacting with people online. Informants reported that they tended to start with very brief and indirect ("trivial") messages as a way of signaling the appropriate level of social distance. In describing how they judged the sincerity of messages, many informants attached importance of indirect cues such as the speed of reply and length of responses, the style of writing, the use of humor, and the degree of politeness. In particular, the proper use of formal polite Japanese (*keigo*) without, however, seeming too formal or stiff, was taken as a sign of proper social distance, similar to what would be expected in the initial phases of face-to-face dating. Using styles of language as a cue to personality traits and intentions shows the importance of indirect communication and contextual cues even without face-to-face communication.

Another way in which indirect cues were used to signal intimacy was in supplementing the technical means of communication. The shifts from CMC to cell phone text messaging and then to calling on the cell phones were all ways in which a desire for increased intimacy was signaled without being explicitly articulated in a verbal message. The choice of a particular platform also is a form of social cueing. The choice of a "branded" site such as Match.com is described as a way of conveying a message about one's "seriousness" as well as a way of controlling for the seriousness and honesty of

others. Sites can also be associated with particular types of people, such as foreigners, a special appeal of international sites such as Match.com.

Many uses of online dating tools can be described as tactics of managing social risks. In general, Japanese people prefer mediated forms of dating as a way of reducing the uncertainties and anxieties that go with meeting complete strangers. Web sites provide a way of getting to a person "from the inside out" without having to risk first meeting that person face to face.[5] Not only do online sites reduce the anxieties of meeting people face to face, but our informants point out that they allow people to more easily *end* interactions without embarrassment and the other psychological costs of breaking off an interaction. Finally, unlike the personal go-betweens and organizers of face-to-face meetings, who are commonly involved in group dating (*gokon*), the mediator in online dating, the Web site, is impersonal and requires no special considerations or social interaction. Perhaps because Japanese users put an even greater importance on the context of communication and forms of indirect communication, online dating is perceived as an effective means of managing the social costs of interactions.

This research thus suggests a more complex understanding of the presumed Japanese preference for high-context communication. One attractive feature of online communication for Japanese users may in fact be that it allows more direct communication than in face-to-face contexts. The much discussed "disinhibition effect" of CMC allows people to do things online that they might not be able to in face-to-face contact.[34,35] This research provides some evidence that Japanese online dating users experience this disinhibition effect as well. The patterns of communication engaged in by our informants indicate that both men and women approach numerous strangers online. People who might be unlikely to approach a stranger on the street—a practice known derisively as *nanpa*—may send dozens of virtual kisses and messages to strangers on the dating site. So, while Japanese remain sensitive to contextual markers in online communication, they are also able to use online spaces to engage in more direct forms of communication without the social costs associated with many face-to-face contexts. This research shows that SIPT is very relevant for understanding online communication in Japan, while cautioning us about overly simple applications of the distinction between high-context and low-context communication styles.

REFERENCES

1. Gottlieb N, McLelland M. (2003) The Internet in Japan. In Gottlieb N, McLelland M, eds. *Japanese cybercultures*. London: Routledge, pp. 1–16.

2. Applbaum KD. Marriage with the proper stranger: arranged marriages in metropolitan Japan. Ethnology 1995; 34:37–51.

3. Farrer J, Tsuchiya H, Bagrowicz B. Emotional expression in tsukiau dating relationships in Japan. Journal of Social & Personal Relationships 2008; 25:169–88.

4. Shirakawa T, Yamada M. (2008) *Konkatsu jidai (Marriage-hunting era)*. Tokyo: Discover Press.

5. Baker A. Two by two in cyberspace: getting together and connecting online. CyberPsychology & Behavior 2000; 3:237–42.

6. Holden TJM, Tsuruki T. (2003) Deiai-kei: Japan's new culture of encounter. In Gottlieb N, McLelland M, eds. *Japanese cybercultures*. London: Routledge, pp. 34–49.

7. Retherford RD, Naohiro O, Rikiya M. Late marriage and less marriage in Japan. Population & Development Review 2001; 27:65–102.

8. Yum V, Hara K. Computer-mediated relationship development: a cross-cultural comparison. Journal of Computer-Mediated Communication 2005; 11:133–52.

9. Sproull L, Kiesler S. Reducing social context cues: electronic mail in organizational communication. Management Science 1986; 32:1492–512.

10. Culnan MJ, Markus ML. (1987) Information technologies. In Jablin FM, Putnam LL, Roberts KH, et al., eds. *Handbook of organizational communication: an interdisciplinary perspective*. Newbury Park, CA: Sage, pp. 420–43.

11. Dubrovsky VJ, Kiesler S, Sethna BN. The equalization phenomenon: status effects in computer-mediated and face-to-face decision-making groups. Human Computer Interaction 1991; 6:119–46.

12. Walther JB. Interpersonal effects in computer-mediated interaction. Communication Research 1992; 19:52–90.

13. Walther JB. Anticipated ongoing interaction versus channel effects on relational communication in computer-mediated interaction. Human Communication Research 1994; 20:473–501.

14. Walther JB, Tidwell LC. Nonverbal cues in computer-mediated communication and the effect of chronemics on relational communication. Journal of Organizational Computing 1995; 5:355–78.

15. Walther JB, D'Addario KP. The impacts of emoticons on message interpretation in computer-mediated communication. Social Science Computer Review 2001; 19:323–45.

16. Walther JB. Impression development in computer-mediated communication. Western Journal of Communication 1993; 57:381–98.

17. Tidwell LC, Walther JB. Computer-mediated communication effects on disclosure, impressions, and interpersonal evaluations: getting to know one another a bit at a time. Human Communication Research 2002; 28:317–48.

18. Walther JB, Slovacek CL, Tidwell LC. Is a picture worth a thousand words? Photographic images in long-term and short-term computer-mediated communication. Communication Research 2001; 28:105–34.

19. Ellison N, Heino R, Gibbs, J. Managing impressions online, self-presentation processes in the online dating environment. Journal of Computer-Mediated Communication 2006; 11:415–41.

20. Goggin C, McLelland M. (2008) Internationalizing Internet studies: beyond Anglophone paradigms. In Goggin G, McLelland M, eds. *Internationalizing Internet studies: beyond Anglophone paradigms*. London Routledge, pp. 1–17.

21. Hall ET. (1976) *Beyond culture*. London: Anchor.

22. Hofstede G. (2004) *Cultures and organizations: software of the mind*. New York: McGraw-Hill.

23. Hall E, Hall M. (1990) *Understanding cultural differences: Germans, French and Americans*. Yarmouth, MA: Intercultural Press.

24. Ting-Toomey S. Intimacy expressions in three cultures: France, Japan, and the United States. International Journal of Intercultural Relations 1991; 15:29–46.

25. Wurtz E. A cross-cultural analysis of Websites from high-context cultures and low-context cultures. Journal of Computer-Mediated Communication 2005; 11:13.

26. Singh N, Zhao H, Hu X. Analyzing the cultural content of Websites: a cross-national comparison of China, India, Japan, and US. International Marketing Review 2005; 22: 129–46.

27. Koeszegi S, Vetschera R, Kersten G. National cultural differences in the use and perception of Internet-based NSS: does high or low context matter? International Negotiation 2004; 9:79–109.

28. Rosenbloom B, Larsen T. Communication in business-to-business marketing channels: Does culture matter? Industrial marketing management 2003; 32:309–15.

29. Nakanishi M. Perceptions of self-disclosure in initial interaction: a Japanese sample. Human Communication Research 1986; 13:167–90.

30. Mushakoji K. (1976) The cultural premises of Japanese diplomacy. In Japan Center for the International Exchange,

ed. *The silent power. Japan's identity and world role.* Tokyo: Sumul Press, pp. 35–49.

31. Strauss A, Corbin J. (1990) *Basics of qualitative research: grounded theory procedures and techniques.* London: Sage.

32. Weiss RS. (1995) *Learning from strangers: the art and method of qualitative interview studies.* New York: Free Press.

33. Whitty M, Gavin J. Age/sex/location: uncovering the social cues in the development of online relationships. CyberPsychology & Behavior 2002; 4:623–60.

34. Suler J. The online disinhibition effect. Cyber Psychology & Behavior 2004; 7:321–6.

35. Walther JB. Computer-mediated communication: impersonal, interpersonal, and hyperpersonal interaction. Communication Research 1996; 23:3–43.

SOURCE: Farrer, James and Jeff Gavin. 2009. "On-line Dating in Japan: A Test of Social Information Processing Theory." *CyberPsychology and Behavior*, 12(4):409–12.

60

ONLINE ORGANIZATION OF THE LGBT COMMUNITY IN SINGAPORE

JOE PHUA

Singapore is a nation state in Southeast Asia known for its economic development and high-tech industries. Since its independence from Malaysia in 1965, Singapore has become one of the world's most modern cities. However, the Singapore government's policies towards the LGBT community have been highly conservative. Singapore's penal code 377a is specifically related to homosexual acts between 2 men, stating that "any male person who, in public or private, commits or abets the commission of, or procures or attempts to procure the commission by any male person of, any act of gross indecency with another male person, shall be punished with imprisonment for a term which may extend to 2 years" (Chia, 2001). It has historically been applied to convicting homosexuals, with the average sentence between 2 to 3 months, but from 1993 onward, it has usually been 6 months or longer. While homosexual sex between 2 males in public or private is outlawed, sexual relations between females are not illegal as long as they are kept behind closed doors.

Comprising a population of 4.5 million people, with Chinese and Malays making up the dominant ethnic groups, the social and moral landscape in Singapore is steeped in conservative "Asian values," which are informed by traditional Confucianism, as well as some Christian and Muslim ideals, because of its proximity to Indonesia and Malaysia. These play equal parts in influencing government policies and laws. "Asian values" advocate obedience to higher authority for the sake of social stability. Traditional sexual and gender roles also include expectations of marriage, childbirth, and taking care of aged parents and other older family members. Collectivistic tendencies also privilege group cohesion and family harmony at the expense of individual interests and personal rights. However, starting in the 1980s, "Asian values" began to be challenged by the emergence of a prosperous middle class (Matzner, 2004). The younger generation's newly-acquired financial power, increased exposure to Western ideas and images via the media, travel and education at Western universities contributed to their questioning of government policies. For the LGBT population, it has meant pushing for community organization, desire for greater individual rights, and development of gay-friendly public venues. However, because of penal code 377a, and the government's prohibition of any gay-related activities in the public domain and the local media, the LGBT community has found it very hard to organize themselves in conventional, offline ways, leading to the formation of online communities.

Online Organization

While other major Asian cities like Taipei and Hong Kong have scrapped laws criminalizing homosexuality, Singapore remains one of the few not to do so (Jen, 2001). In the past, Singaporean LGBT organizations have been mostly passive in their resistance to government policies because many of them fear that outspoken protests will spark crackdowns by the police. For these Singaporean groups, online organization has become a more practical and safer alternative. The majority of LGBT organizations moved online after failure to be licensed by the government. Several of these are described in the following section:

People Like Us (PLU)

People Like Us (PLU) is the preeminent online organization for the Singapore LGBT population. It began as a small discussion group in 1993, in reaction to the arrest and shaming of 12 gay men at a raid in a gay disco. Monthly Sunday forums were held by a group of gay men, including activists Russell Heng and Alex Au, to address issues like coming out, the law, insurance for singles, housing and safe sex (Lo & Huang, 2003). PLU also began publishing its own newsletter *The Thing*, which was freely distributed at local gay hangouts. Membership in PLU increased rapidly during this time, and the group began to meet regularly in public venues (Lo & Huang, 2003). PLU attempted to register formally as a society in 1995 and 2004, but were rejected both times on the grounds that it was contrary to public interest (Lo & Huang 2003). In November 1996, the Sunday forums were discontinued, and in March 1997, PLU was re-launched as an email list called the Singapore Gay News List (SIGNEL) (Lo & Huang, 2003). In 1998, lesbians set up their own email list called Red Queen (Lo & Huang, 2003). The movement online of PLU has aided in its growth, leading to its current status as the largest Singaporean LGBT online organization.

Fridae

Fridae, started by entrepreneur Dr. Stuart Koe, is an interactive site with news, a calendar of events, bulletin boards, photos, chat rooms, dating services and feature articles about gay life in Asia. Besides Singaporeans, Fridae has members from many other countries around the world, including China, Japan, Korea, Australia, Philippines and the UK. None of its advertising, promotional material or website decorations, however, contain the word "gay" or "lesbian." This is done so as to not break the rules imposed by the government specifically banning homosexual-related material in the media (Ammon, 2006). Besides acting as an online forum for the LGBT community, Fridae has also been responsible for organizing many high-profile events, including the Nation Party and the Snow Ball, two prominent annual dance music festivals which attract international tourists and media coverage.

Besides PLU and Fridae, other gay and lesbian online organizations in Singapore include Adventurers Like Us, Friends Like Us, Heartlanders, Men After Work, Oogachaga and Pelangi Pride Center, all of which cater to different demographics, and have their own online forum, message board and resource centers. A 2003 *Time* magazine article proclaimed that in 5 years, the Internet has brought about the equivalent of 20 years of gay evolution in Singapore (Price, 2003).

Nation Party

The Nation party, inaugurated in 2001 by Fridae, was a widely advertised, open-air gay mega-party (Han, 2006). Dubbed by the foreign media as Singapore's "Coming Out" party, the inaugural Nation event was held on August 8, 2001, the night before Singapore's National Day. By 2003, Nation.03 expanded to a 3-day event, with a nationally-televised finale that marked the first time in history a local gay event had been portrayed in the media in a positive light, accompanied by snippets of bare-chested men dancing on podia (Han, 2006). 2004's Nation party attracted over 40% international visitors from countries like Australia, Japan, Taiwan and the United States, and generated tourist revenue of S$6 million. However, in 2005, the Licensing division of the Singapore police department rejected Fridae's application to hold Nation.05, citing the event to be contrary to public interest (Han, 2006).

The banning of Nation.05 by the Singapore government illustrates a society that is "rife with contradictions, with the influences of commerce, globalization and the mass media collided with conservative societal, familial and filial notions of propriety" (Matzner, 2004). The Singapore LGBT community gained significant ground in the early 2000s in building infrastructure, experiencing freedom and opportunities, and even positive media visibility, but it has had to contend with the government's contradictory attitude towards the enforcement of anti-gay laws, as well as cycles of tolerance and intolerance. Faced with increased globalization, the Singapore government has had to continually renegotiate its stance on "Asian values." In the middle of this uncertainty stands the LGBT community.

Conservative Singaporeans

The Singapore government has repeatedly maintained that most ordinary Singaporeans are conservative and unreceptive to LGBT lifestyles. The PAP government, led by Prime Minister Lee Hsien-Loong, is traditionally supported at the grassroots level by "heartlanders," families living in government-subsidized housing estates.

Singapore also has a large religious voting cohort opposing such "liberal" issues as abortion, gambling, pornography and LGBT lifestyles. The Chinese population in Singapore is mainly Buddhist and Taoist, with a significant number of fundamentalist Christians and Catholics. In recent years, Christian fundamentalism has gained popularity in the country, with mega-churches attracting large followings in arena-sized stadiums. In addition, Singapore is surrounded on all sides by Muslim countries Malaysia and Indonesia, which have even stricter anti-homosexual and anti-sex laws.

For decades, Malaysian capital Kuala Lumpur and Singapore have been vying for commercial leadership in Southeast Asia (Ho, 2003). Malaysia has been a democracy since 1957, and Singapore since 1965. The main difference, however, is the influence of religion. Both governments have been secular and independent of religious affiliation, but Malaysia is 50% Muslim, and under Islamic influence. Singapore, on the other hand, has been known to throw religious views to the wind for commerce and enterprise, and as such the LGBT community

has enjoyed more freedom than its Malaysian counterpart.

One of the first surveys to test Singaporeans' tolerance of LGBT lifestyles was conducted by the PLU in 2000 (PlanetOut News, 2000). In April and May of 2000, volunteers surveyed 241 Singaporeans on the streets of several districts around the country, and a further 240 surveys were conducted online. Respondents' distribution among Singapore's major ethnic groups, Chinese, Malay and Indian, matched the national profile, and were at least 16 years of age. With a margin of error of 4% to 6%, the group described their findings as "an important threshold providing a sense of where Singaporeans stand with respect to such issues, and can be seen as leading indicators to the way Singapore social opinion is likely to evolve in the years ahead" (PlanetOut News, 2000). The poll first tested acceptance of gay and lesbian family members by respondents. Among respondents on the street, 46% said they would accept a gay sibling, 26% said they never could, 41% would accept a gay child, while 35% could not. Among Internet respondents, 74% would accept a gay sibling, 9% could not, while 66% would accept a gay child, and 13% could not (PlanetOut News, 2000). The survey also polled attitudes toward employment discrimination against gays and lesbians, with 74% of street respondents and 83% of online respondents opposing discrimination. Finally, respondents were also asked about whether oral sex between homosexual adults in private should be restricted; 39% of street respondents and 78% of online respondents opposed restriction, while 29% and 16% respectively supported restriction (PlanetOut News, 2000).

The researchers concluded that the survey, while "not entirely scientific," served to show that Singaporeans demonstrated a higher level of tolerance toward gays and lesbians than previously thought, and was "ahead of the government in judging which could be considered acceptable" (PlanetOut News, 2000). More recently, Detenber, Cenite, Ku, Ong, Tong and Yeow (2007) conducted telephone interviews of 1000 respondents, and found that 68.6% of Singaporeans held a negative attitude towards gay men and lesbians, 22.9% held a positive attitude, while 8.5% were neutral. As can be seen, the PLU poll and the Detenber et al. (2007) interviews revealed contradictory results. It is possible that, because the PLU poll was mainly conducted online, respondents tended to be younger, more educated, and had more exposure to international LGBT issues. As such, they reported greater tolerance of the Singapore LGBT community than those from the telephone interviews by Detenber et al. (2007).

The Current Study

The online organization of the LGBT community in Singapore has led to a bevy of political and social activities aimed at combating anti-homosexual legislation, raising social awareness of issues pertaining to the community, and most importantly, creating a sense of belonging and social support. The current study seeks to answer the following research questions:

RQ1: How do these websites create greater social awareness of LGBT issues?

RQ2: What part do these websites play in lobbying of the government to repeal anti-homosexual laws?

RQ3: What part does the government play in monitoring or censoring these websites?

RQ4: What are the reasons for organizing online?

RQ5: What are the benefits and costs of organizing online?

RQ6: Has the Singapore media and the public become more tolerant of the LGBT community?

Method

Semi-structured interviews were conducted from June to August 2007, with moderators and owners of popular websites catering to the Singapore LGBT community. These websites are, in most cases, the online versions of active LGBT organizations. They include news, message boards/forums, email lists, classifieds and other information relevant to the community. An Internet search using the terms "Singapore," "Gay," "Lesbian," "LGBT" and "Organizations" was utilized to find the websites and their contact persons. Each potential interviewee was sent an email requesting for an interview in May 2007.

After initial contact was made, the primary researcher traveled to Singapore in June 2007 and began the first round of interviews. Each interview (N = 36) lasted approximately 1 hour, and was tape-recorded. Interviewees were granted anonymity, and asked to speak freely about any issues pertaining to the LGBT community. The primary researcher returned to Los Angeles in late August 2007, and interviews were transcribed. General themes were identified in the data gathered, and answers to research questions are provided in the following section. To protect their identities, all interviewees quoted in this article have been given fictitious names.

Social Awareness

All of the interviewees (N = 36) indicated that their websites try to create greater social awareness of the LGBT community. This is achieved through encouraging a wide readership which also includes the general Singapore public, and people from other countries (N = 30). An interviewee, Mr. Tan, who manages one of the sites, explains:

> When we were offline, our newsletter was only read by other local gay men and lesbians. However, the Internet has given us a much larger readership, as we are able to reach people from all over the world, many of whom send us letters telling us how much they empathize with us in the Singapore LGBT community. (Personal Communication, June 28, 2007)

Several LGBT websites (N = 10), like Mr. Tan's, have a majority overseas readership, and receive regular emails and feedback from foreign subscribers. Another strategy to increase social awareness is for the websites (N = 12) to have databases with archival material, including news stories and media coverage of the LGBT community. These, according to several interviewees (N = 7), act as a resource for the community, as well as for researchers, government officials and other interested parties. Moreover, websites which include archival material and have majority overseas readership (N = 12) report that the feedback received indicates that readers gained the ability to understand Singapore's cultural nuances better and also expressed less stereotypical views of the LGBT community. Ms. Yap, who founded a popular LGBT social forum, explains:

One of the most gratifying and fulfilling aspects of starting the website is that we have many readers who write to us thanking us for putting all the articles on the site. We have researchers from overseas who find our site to be a useful resource. That is the ultimate aim for us: to have our voices heard and let people everywhere know that the LGBT community in Singapore is loud and proud. (Personal Communication, August 7, 2007)

Some interviewees (N = 5) indicated that they do not receive any feedback from readers other than members of the LGBT community, and therefore cannot attest to any increased social awareness among the heterosexual community. In general, interviewees agreed that social awareness is achieved through appealing to members of the Singapore public and overseas community, and posting of archival material on the sites.

Political Lobbying

In terms of political lobbying, particularly to repeal section 377a of the penal code, the majority of interviewees (N = 33) expressed that their websites employ indirect strategies. These are similar to creating greater social awareness: by reaching out to the heterosexual community in Singapore and overseas (N = 15), to change the attitudes and opinions among intellectuals (N = 15), encourage research (N = 12), encourage local and overseas news coverage of LGBT events and issues (N = 18), and create dialogue with government officials in order to influence policy development (N = 6). Mr. Lee, whose site offers safe sex advice and health tips for HIV patients, says:

As a marginalized community within a conservative country, we cannot afford to be too aggressive in pushing our agenda. God knows what the government may decide to do next. As much as we dislike the fact that penal code 377a prohibits 2 men from having consensual sex, we do not need the government to actually start raiding our bars and arresting our people again. We have suffered enough. (Personal Communication, July 19, 2007)

The general consensus among the majority of interviewees is that political lobbying must take place using a "soft" approach, in which the government is "pressured" into changing their policies toward the LGBT community through local and, particularly, overseas coverage of LGBT issues and problems. Also, interviewees (N = 5) expressed that their websites are able to indirectly influence policy development by creating dialogue and debate among intellectuals in the heterosexual community, including researchers, journalists and government officials. Mr. Lim, an active political lobbyist, argues:

We always try to take small steps toward progress. Particularly, we have been more successful at influencing the government's policies through getting people to debate the issue in the news media overseas. When CNN reports about us, the Singapore government cannot ignore the issue. (Personal Communication, July 12, 2007)

Government Monitoring

All interviewees (N = 36) agreed that the Singapore government currently does not crack down on LGBT websites, unless the websites include pornographic material. In the past, websites like "fluffboy.com" have been shut down due to some nude images posted. Because of this, most websites (N = 25) practice self-censorship, in which all messages posted by members on public message boards and forums are monitored and all pornographic and inappropriate material is removed immediately upon detection. Mr. Singh, who is part-owner of a dating site for gay men, explains:

It is important for us to screen our site for what can be considered as pornographic. You know, pictures of naked men, exposed penises, anal sex, all that good stuff. We make sure to remove all that, otherwise the next day we find that we ourselves have been removed by the powers that be. (Personal Communication, June 29, 2007)

Most websites (N = 29) only allow registered members to post messages. However, some sites also try to push the envelope on the type of material that is allowed online. Mr. Ong, who moderates a popular online forum for LGBT Singaporeans, says:

Let's face it! Sex, talking about sex, having sex, is part and parcel of the gay community. It is only human to be sexual. It is no fun if we cannot discuss sex in our forums. As a general rule, I will only remove any material that is considered inappropriate if we receive complaints from other users. (Personal Communication, August 2, 2007)

Reasons for Online Organization

Interviewees gave several reasons for organizing online. First, there are fewer restrictions online (N = 36). LGBT issues are more freely discussed and debated online rather than in print and broadcast media, where the topic is still taboo. Ms. Pereira, who works in the local television industry and operates a mailing list for lesbians, says:

I have yet to see any portrayals of lesbianism in the Singapore media. It's like we don't exist at all! I think producers of shows, they are afraid to offend their audience, so gays and lesbians, they don't exist in the media. But in cyberspace, that's where we can really be ourselves, where we find people like us. (Personal Communication, August 2, 2007)

The majority of organizations (N = 28) also migrated online due to their failure to receive governmental approval to register as societies offline. Several interviewees also indicated that their groups had grown too large (N = 12), and that a website was easier for members to keep in touch and find information about what is going on within the groups and also in the LGBT community, especially electronic mailing lists (N = 16) and message boards (N = 13). Mr. Thomas, owner of a hobby-based LGBT mailing list, states:

When our group used to meet at neighborhood community centers, we could only accommodate 15 to 20 people max. Ever since we started the mailing list, we have been able to expand our membership exponentially; we currently have more than 1000 members, including many from other parts of the world. (Personal Communication, July 4, 2007)

Benefits and Costs of Online Organization

All interviewees (N = 36) indicated that online is the only legal form of organization for the gay and lesbian community. Most of these websites (N = 28) have arisen from offline organizations

which have failed to be recognized by the governments as official, registered societies. Furthermore, a few interviewees (N = 8) talked about previous attempts by undercover police officers to infiltrate their unofficial group meetings, and shut them down. Mr. Chan, who started an online version of an organization which initially met offline, has this to say:

Back in the 1980s, we were afraid to meet in public places because there was always a possibility of being shut down, or worst, being arrested and taken away in handcuffs. On the Internet, we can have a safe meeting place where we will not get harassed. I think the Internet really helps groups like us. (Personal Communication, June 27, 2007)

Compared to offline organization, online organization is considered safer, easier and less controlled. Nearly half of all interviewees (N = 17) said there is no downside to online organization, while a few (N = 5) talked about the impersonal nature of the Internet, and how face-to-face contact among members has been reduced after their groups' migration online. Ms. Shankar, who manages the website for a LGBT HIV/AIDS group, says:

Even though the Internet has allowed us to more freely express our views, liberated us in a sense, I believe that it has also made the LGBT community less cohesive. I think it is easy to just stay at home and chat with people online, than to actually go out and make things happen. There are pros and cons, I guess. (Personal Communication, August 1, 2007)

A minority (N = 4) also indicated that online organization leads to complacency within their groups, as there is less of a push to engage in activities like public protests.

Tolerance of the Gay and Lesbian Community

As for tolerance, most interviewees (N = 28) expressed optimism that both the Singapore government and the public have become more tolerant of the LGBT community over the past 5 years, and will continue to do so, at a rapidly accelerating pace. Mr. Joseph, a teacher who also operates a LGBT online news resource, says:

I definitely think Singaporeans in general have become more accepting of gays and lesbians. I walk around town, and I see young guys holding hands, dancing together, kissing at the gay clubs. People don't even blink at this anymore. (Personal Communication, August 8, 2007)

Many (N = 18) characterized the Singapore media as having become more receptive towards LGBT issues and given the LGBT community greater and more positive coverage (N = 12), and more representative portrayals (N = 10). Interviewees also agreed that the LGBT community has become more visible in the media (N = 22), with greater media coverage of relevant issues. Many also attested to the greater number of gay-owned and operated businesses (N = 16), and positive public reception to the coming out of local celebrities (N = 15) as indicative of the public's greater tolerance of the LGBT community. Mr. Ray, an attorney and LGBT site operator, says:

More and more, we see a lot of people in the public spotlight, who have been afraid to identify as gay or lesbian, come out in the media. I think that being LGBT no longer holds the stigma it used to have. I definitely think the next step is for the government to repeal 377a. It is only a matter of time, I feel. (Personal Communication, August 14, 2007)

Limitations

There are some limitations associated with this study. First, the small sample size (N = 36) and its restriction to website owners and moderators did not allow the data collected to be generalized to the larger Singaporean population. Second, the short study period (3 months) did not give the primary researcher enough time to immerse himself in the Singapore LGBT community, and as such, he did not get to interact with many members of the community other than interviewees. Third, the need to give confidentiality to all data collected, and anonymity for all interviewees, meant that the researcher could only identify general themes and trends to answer the research questions, without revealing the real names of websites and persons interviewed.

Future studies, if undertaken, should include a larger sample size, a more varied group of interviewees (which include, other than moderators and owners of websites, general members of the LGBT community, activists, government officials, broadcasters, journalists and others), a longer study period (in order for more interviews to be conducted and for the researcher to become more familiar with local culture), utilize other research methods, including ethnography, surveys and/or focus groups, so as to acquire more varied datasets, including whether Singaporeans in general have become more tolerant of LGBT issues and community, and examine coverage of the gay and lesbian community in local media to find out whether the community has become more visible and more positively portrayed.

Conclusion

Through 40 years of nation-building, Singapore has transformed from a former British colony with no discernable natural resources to one of the most developed cities in the world. Despite tough laws against homosexual sex, Singapore has become one of Asia's premier gay capitals. The Singapore government is well aware that in order to attract foreign talent and foreign investors, it needs to be more permissive toward the LGBT community. However, due to pressure from heartlanders and the religious right, the main voting bloc, the Singapore government has been reluctant to repeal the anti-homosexual laws. This pressure has resulted in inconsistent actions by the government, with periods of LGBT tolerance marred by instances of intolerance and police action. "Homosexuality represents the last frontier of diversity in our society, and thus a place that welcomes the gay community welcomes all kinds of people" (Florida, 2003). With infrastructure for the LGBT community firmly in place on the Internet, the final battle will be for the repeal of penal codes 377 and 377(a).

On November 9, 2006, when the Singapore government revealed its amendments to the penal code to the public, oral and anal sex for heterosexuals was legalized, but gay sex remains illegal (Wockner, 2006). A statement released by the Home Affairs Ministry stated that "the government will not be proactive in enforcing the remaining ban on male-male sex" (Wockner, 2006). This latest development aptly illustrates Singapore's love-hate affair with its gay capital image. On one hand, the vibrant LGBT-friendly economy has attracted much-needed foreign creative investments and tourists to the country. On the other hand, the Singapore government continues to bow down to pressures exerted by its conservative voting bloc, stubbornly refusing to repeal its anti-homosexuality laws. With increasing globalization and the influx of foreign creative talent and investments over the next few decades, and the liberalization of values among Singapore's younger population, the country's socio-economical and political landscapes look set to undergo further transformation. Perhaps at that time, the Singapore LGBT community will finally be able to achieve equality in the eyes of the law. Until then, online organization is the LGBT community's only option.

REFERENCES

Advocate (2004, August 7). *Singapore to host Asia's biggest gay party.* Retrieved from: http://www.sodomylaws.org/world/singapore/sinews032.htm

Agence France Presse (2003, September 14). *Singapore is Asia's new gay capital.* Retrieved from: http://www.singapore-window.org/sw03/030914af.htm

Agence France Presse (2005, June 12). *Singapore's Pink capital image fades after gay festival ban.* Retrieved from: http://www.singapore-window.sg/sw05/050612af.htm

Ammon, R. (2006, May 1). *The New Gay Singapore '02–'06.* Retrieved from: http://www.globalgayz.com/g-sing02–06.html

Asian Week (2004, August 6). *Thailand, Singapore woo gays.* Retrieved from: http://news.asianweek.com/news/view_article.html?article_id=01518718d8c57b248cfd0a53dac1623f

Baker, M. (1998, September 26). Power without glory. *The Age, Melbourne.* Retrieved from: http://www.ilga.info/information/legal_survey/Asia-Pacific

BBC News (2003, July 4). *Singapore eases gay ban.* Retrieved from: http://news.bbc.co.uk/go/pr/fr/-/2/hi/americas/3044688.stm

BBC News (2006, May 26). *Vegas Sands wins Singapore casino.* Retrieved from: http://news.bbc.co.uk/1/hi/business/5019488.stm

Channel News Asia (2006, December 5). *Singapore slated to be entertainment capital of Asia: Lim Hng Kiang.* Retrieved from: http://sg.news.yahoo.com/051206/5/singapore182095.html

Chia, D. (2001). The offence of unnatural sex in Singapore. *Singapore Academy of Law Journal,* vol. 13, p. 406.

Detenber, B.H., Cenite, M., Ku, M., Ong, C., Tong, H. & Yeow, M. (2007). Singaporeans' Attitudes toward Lesbians and Gay Men and their Tolerance of Media Portrayals of Homosexuality. *International Journal of Public Opinion Research, 19*(3):367–379.

Florida, R. (2003). *The rise of the creative class.* New York, NY: Basic Books.

Hares, S. (2004, March 13). *Gay culture comes out in conservative Singapore.* Retrieved from: http://www.boston.com/news/world/asia/articles/2004/03/13

Han, B. (2006, July 30). *Singapore gays prepare to show their indignation.* Retrieved from: http://www.aegis.com/news/afp/2006/AF060761.html

Ho, K.L. (2003). *Shared responsibilities, Unshared power: The politics of policy-making in Singapore.* London, England: Eastern University Press.

I-S Magazine (2004, December 20). *Gay Singapore: A brief history.* Retrieved from: http://sodomylaws.org/world/singapore/sinews041.htm

Jen, W.T. (2001, October 17). *Boys' night out: we're here, we're queer. Get used to it.* Retrieved from: http://www.time/com/time/asia/features/sex/sexgay.htm

Kaiser Family Foundation (2005, May 11). *Number of new AIDS cases increase in 2004 in Singapore, especially among MSM, Health Minister says.* Retrieved from: http://www.kaisernetwork.org/daily_reports

Koh, L. (2005, March 13). Gay parties may have led to the sharp increases in AIDS cases. *The Straits Times.* Retrieved from: http://www.yawningbread.org/apdx_2005/imp-184.htm

Landow, G.P. (2006, July 18). *Singapore harbor from its founding to the present: A brief chronology.* Retrieved from: http://www.scholars.nus.edu.sg/post/singapore/economics/harborchron.html

Lim, E.B. (2005). The Mardi Gras boys of Singapore's English language theater. *Asian Theater Journal,* vol. 22, no. 2.

Loh, J. & Huang, G.W. (2003) (Eds.). *People Like Us: Sexual Minorities in Singapore.* Singapore: Select Publishing.

Matzner, A. (2004). *Singapore.* Retrieved from GLBTQ: An encyclopedia of gay, lesbian, bisexual, transgender and queer culture: http://www.glbtq.com/social-sciences/singapore.html

Nadarajan, B. (2004, December 11). Former Tatler editor gets two years for cocaine use. *The Straits Times.* Retrieved from: http://www.asiamedia.ucla.edu/article.asp?parentid=18515

Offord, B. (2003). *Homosexual rights as human rights: Activism in Indonesia, Singapore and Australia.* New York, NY: Peter Lang.

Peterson, W. (2003). The Queer Stage in Singapore. Lo, J. & Huang, G.Q. (eds.). *People Like Us: Sexual Minorities in Singapore.* Singapore: Select Publishing.

PlanetOut News. (2000, May 23). *Singapore poll finds tolerance.* Retrieved from: http://www.planetout.com/news/article.html?2000/05/23/2

Price, D.C. (2003, August 10). Singapore: It's in to be out. *Time Asia,* v. 162, no. 6.

Sayoni.com (2006, July 18). *August is Singapore gay pride season again.* Retrieved from: http://blog.saynoi.com/2006/07/18/press-release

Tan, K.P. (2003). Sexing Up Singapore. *International Journal of Cultural Studies,* 6(4), 403–423.

Utopia Asia (2006, October 3). *Singapore gay resources and travel tips by utopia.* Retrieved from: http://www.utopia-asia.com/tipssing.htm

Wockner, R. (2006, November 20). *Singapore will continue to ban gay sex.* Retrieved from: http://www.gaytravelnews.com/news06.cfm?id=58

SOURCE: Phua, Joe. 2008. *Online Organization of the LGBT Community in Singapore.* Paper presented at the International Communication Association Conference, Montreal, Canada, May.

INDEX

Achieving styles, 280–282, 285–289
Action
    masculine premium on, 502
    theories of, in decision-making research, 598–600
Adaptability, 432
Additive total, 127
Adler, Paul, 76, 129
Administration by notables, versus bureaucratic
    organization, 80–83
Administrator as integrator, 12–13
Affective states, 428
Affect theory of social exchange, 60–61, 63–68
Affirmative action, backlash against, 449
Ahistorical individual, rethinking, 451–452
Alderfer, Clayton, 452, 454
Alienation, 440–447
Allied Shipping Control (Salter), 136
American Dilemma, The (Myrdal), 530
Amoral familialism, 45
Analytical descriptive approach, 311
Antecedent conditions, 428
Anticipation of response, 423
Aoki, Masahiko, 229
Approach to Business Problems (Shaw), 422
Aquino, Corazon, 286, 290
Archibald, W. Peter, 412
Argote, Linda, 129
Argyris, Chris, 588
Ashcraft, Karen, 76
Assessments
    negative, 108
    positive, 109–110
Assimilation theory, 530
Associability, 45–46
Augmented Social Networks (ASNs), 683
Autarky, to collaboration, 677–681
Authority, 228, 230, 250–253, 259, 287

basis of, 241–247
hierarchy of, 149
structure, 151–153, 159 (figure)
See also Control
Autonomy, 227–232, 261, 269–270, 272.
    See also Empowerment

Bach, Jonathan, 662
Bailyn, Lotte, 591
Bargaining model, of organizational conflict, 427, 434–435
Baritz, Loren, 453
Batt, Rosemary, 230
Bauman, Zygmunt, 661
Beard, Stacy, 591
Bechky, Beth, 130
Beck, Ulrich, 339
Biculturalism, 539
Black studies, 538
Blanton, Hart, 231
Blumer, Herbert, xvi
Boisjoly, Roger, 500
Bolsin, Stephen, 383
Borys, Brian, 76, 129
Bots, in virtual reality, 672–674
Boundary spanners, 209, 213
Bounded rationality, 589
Bristol Royal Infirmary (BRI), 381–389
Brush, Candida, 378n2
Bureaucracy, 19–29, 79–83
    badly managed, 98–99
    coercive, 107–118
    enabling, 107–118
    feminist, 119–126
    formalization, 108–111
    horizontal dimension in, 87–93
    limits of, 98–104
    representative, 349–363, 390–407

theory, 698–699
types of, 107–118, 708 (table)
universalism and, 55–56
See also Organization(s)
Bureaucratic model, of organizational conflict, 427, 435–436
Bureaucratic organizational form, 73–78, 80–83
Bureaucratic perpetuity, objective and subjective bases of, 83
Bureaucratic segmentation, fundamental problem of, 99–101
Burns, Tom, 2
Bush, George, 287
Business, as an integrative unit, 7–13

Calculable rules, 81
Capital, 415–416
Capital (Marx), 410
Carson, Jay, 230
Challenger, 492–509
Change
    institutional, 651–652
    institutional isomorphic, 605–615
    microinstitutional, in surgery, 649–660
    See also Organizational change
Channels of appeal, 79
Christie-Luce-Macy experiments, 142
Clans, 19–29. *See also* Relational organizational form
Clegg, Stewart R., 489
CMS (critical management studies), 448–456
Coase, Ronald, 30
Coercive bureaucracy, 107–118
Coercive formalization, 111–115
Coercive isomorphism, 608–609
Cognitive presence, 693
Cognitive processes, 94–97
Cognitive states, 428
Collaborative achieving style, 288–289
Collective mind, in organizations, 173–185
Collective rationality, 605–615
Collective self-control, 136
Collins, Patricia Hill, 512
Collins, Randall, xix, 304
Colonizing consciousness, 546–562
Columbus, Christopher, 560n26
Combat, trust and influence in, 294–301
"Coming out" at work, 563–576
Commitment, 63
Communication
    channel usage, 144–145
    coordination and, 141–143
    cross-cultural differences in styles, 712–713
    e-mail as, 702
    formal and informal, 702–703
    hierarchy, 699 (figure), 704
    network, 144–145
Communities, emerging, 661–665

Communities of practice (COP), 188, 194–195
Community, in virtual worlds, 672–674
Competency traps, 618
Computer mediated communication (CMC), 711–713
Conceptualization of practice, 182–183
Conceptualization of topics, in organizational theory, 181–183
Conceptual sharing, and culture, 312
Conflict, constructive, 417–426.
        See also Organizational conflict
Conflictful behavior, 428
Conflict paradigm, xvii-xix
Connectedness, 606, 612n1
Connectionism, 174–175
Connective leadership, 279–293
Constructive conflict, 417–426
Contingency theory, contribution and limits, 110–111
Contributory achieving style, 288–289
Control, xx
    in organizations, 227–232
    process of, 133–138
    See also Authority
Control variables, 215–216
Cook, Richard, 498, 505–506
Cooperative systems, creating and sustaining, 289–290
Coordination, xx, 84–86, 135–144, 151, 173, 175
    communication and, 141–143
    in hospital emergency units, 163–172
    in trauma centers, 186–204
    of work, 127–131
    relational. *See* Relational coordination
COP. *See* Communities of practice
Corporate masculinity, dysfunctions of, 492–509
Coser, Lewis, xviii
Counterbureaucratic empowerment, 120
Creative Experience (Follett), 422
Critical management studies (CMS), 448–456
Cross-boundary intervention, 199
Cross-position collective, 655
Cultural entrepreneurship, 342–344
Cultural industries research, neglect of morality in, 338–339
Culturalization, 337, 346n1
Cultural researchers, the revolutionary vanguard, 315–316
Cultural work, 337–348
Culture, 311–314. *See also* Organizational culture
Culture contact, 530
Cultures of entrapment, hospitals as, 381–389
Customer service and sales, and work organization, 267–278

Dalton, Melville, 88
Dating, online, in Japan, 711–719
Davis, Kingsley, xx
Decision making, research on, 595–604
de Laval, Marc, 387
Delegation of authority, 246

Democratic leadership, 230
Demoralization, of cultural work, 339–340
Departments, integrating, 157
De-territorialization, 678
Dhasmana, Janardan, 383
Dialogic coordination practices, 190, 196–200
Differentiation perspective, 317–321
Diffusion, 622–624
DiMaggio, Paul, 588
Direct achiever, and the American ego-ideal, 282–284
Direct exchange, 66
Disabilities, hiring and accommodating people with, 577–586
Disciplinary measures, as policy tools, 394–395
Disclosure dilemma, 563–576
Discourse of oil, postcolonial critique of, 546–562
Discursive space, in organizational narratives, 641–648
Dissonance, organized, 119–126
Diversity, within organizations, 471–476
Diversity industry, rise of, 449
Division of labor, 25, 73, 75, 87–88, 91, 96–97, 227–228, 268, 409, 445, 495, 516, 528, 537, 655. *See also* Division of work; Specialization
Division of work, 139–145, 482, 485–486. *See also* Division of labor; Specialization
Double consciousness, 539
Double-loop models, in research on decision making, 595–604
Duality principle, 259, 261–262
Dunlap, Joanna C., 662
Durkheim, Emile, 307, 366
Dutton, Jane, 130
Dyadic trust, 46
Dynamic networks, 485–487
Dynamics, and culture, 313

Eccles, Bob, 38n9
Economic model, of the Japanese firm, 254–266
Economic organization, forms of, 30–37
Economy, political, 415–416
Economy and Society (Weber), xii, 112
Edmondson, Amy, 590
Education, entrepreneurship, for low-income women, 364–380
Efficiency outcomes, 219
Ego-ideal, and institutional needs, 285
Elemental Forms of Religious Life (Durkheim), 366
E-mail, in government, 696–710
Emerging communities, 661–665
Emotions, 62, 64 (table), 67
Empirical research, 701
Employee involvement (EI), 107
Employer characteristics, and people with disabilities, 580–583
Employment practices, and organizational social capital, 41–52
Employment relationships, stability in, 47–48
Empowerment, 268–273, 503, 508
    counterbureaucratic, 120–123

worker, 229–230
    See also Autonomy
Enabling formalization, 111–115
Enabling bureaucracy, 107–118
Entrapment, culture of, 381–389
Entrepreneurial ideas, gendering of, 466–467
Entrepreneurial studies, ideology-critique of, 457–469
Entrepreneurship, cultural, 342–344
Entrepreneurship education, for low-income women, 364–380
Entrusting instrumental achieving style, 287
Epistemic contestation, 198
Equilibrium, and conflict, 432–434
Erikson, Erik, 671
Ethical business, 341
Ethical relativism, 329
Ethical work, 337
Ethic of care, and relationships, 54, 57–58
Ethic of liberation, 338
Ethic of rights, 496
Ethics, as part of organizational culture, 303, 308, 309
Ethics, Law Enforcement Code of, 353
Ethnicity, in public schools, 390–407
Ethnicity paradigm, 530–534
Ethnic profiling, the Latino experience, 354–356
Ethnocentrism, and the legitimating of the dominant ideology, 464–466
Ethnographic approach, to defining and studying organizational culture, 311
Evocative objects, in virtual reality, 672–674
Exchange, forms of, 61, 66
Exchange, relational dimensions of, 62–63
Exchange network, 61
Exchange-to-emotion-to-cohesion chain, 63
Experience
    conservation of, 621–622
    interpretation of, 618–620
    language and the social construction of, 642
    structure of, improving, 625–626
Expertise coordination practices, 190, 192–196

False consciousness, xviii, xix, xxii, 340, 411, 458
Faraj, Samer, 129
Farrer, James, 663
Fast-response organizations, coordination in, 186–204
Faulty generalization, 528
Feedback, as intervention, 644–645
Felt conflict, 429–430
Female leadership styles, 279–293
Female-to-male transsexuals (FTM). *See* Transmen
Feminist bureaucracy, 119–126
Feminist organization, as counterbureaucratic empowerment, 120–121
Feminist poststructural lens, 641–642
Feynman, Richard, 498

Field of desire, 421
Finley, Moses, 32
Fletcher, Joyce, 231, 591
Flight decks, heedful interrelating on, 173–185
Follett, Mary Parker, xii, xvi, xix, 1, 74, 122, 127, 228,
    305, 411, 474, 591
Formalization, 108–115, 699, 701–703, 706
Formal legality, xiii
Fragile trust, 46
Frames, in organizational learning, 619
Freeman, John, 588
Free spaces, 652–653
Function, redistribution of, 9–10
Functionalist paradigm, xix-xx
Functional rationality, xiv
Functional specialization, 73–75, 83, 90, 127, 149, 152–153.
    See also Division of labor; Division of work;
    Specialization
Functional unity, underlying factors and
    relationships, 10–12

Galbraith, Jay, 129
Gallon, Michel, 684n1
Gandhi, Mohandas, 282, 286
Gans, Herbert, xix
Gavin, Jeff, 663
Gay men, disclosure dilemma for, 563–576
Gender
    authority, 373–374
    differences, 572
    discrimination, theories of, 511–512
    organization and, 478–481, 486
    political system, 479, 486
    swapping, in virtual reality, 672
    transmen and, 510–530
    See also Gay men; Lesbians; LGBT community (Singapore);
        Masculinity; Women
Gendered organization theory, 511–512
Gender socialization theory, 511
Generalization, faulty, 528
Generalized exchange, 66
Generalized trust, 46
Giamatti, A. Bartlett, 284
Giddens, Anthony, 661
Gift, The (Mauss), 36
Gilligan, Carol, 4, 54
Gittell, Jody Hoffer, 3, 129, 130, 205, 729
Globalization, 440–447
Goals, integration of individual and organizational, 248–253
Godwyn, Mary, 309, 364, 729
Goffman, Erving, xi
Golden Rule, 8
Government, e-mail in, 696–710
Granovetter, Mark, 38n9, 54

Greene, Patricia, 378n2
Greider, William, 684
Grounded theory, study methodology, 578
Group, as interrelated activity, 177–178
Group life, and culture, 313
Group mind, 174–176. See also Collective mind

Habermas, Jürgen, xv
Haldane, J. B. S., 134
Hammond, Phillip, 383
Hamper, Ben, 410
Handel, Michael, 304
Hannan, Michael, 588
Hardy, George, 499
Heckscher, Charles, 75
Heedful interrelating, on flight decks, 173-185
Heimer, Carol, 4
Hierarchies, 33–37
    office, 79
    static, 485, 487–489
    See also Organization(s)
High-performance work practices, 208–220
High-performance work systems, relational
    model of, 205–226. See also Relational coordination
H-mode, 254–255
Hoffman, Hans, 433
Horizontal dimension, in bureaucracy, 88–92
Hospitals
    as cultures of entrapment, 381–389
    emergency units in, 163–172
    See also Operating rooms
Howard, Earl, 422
Hsien-Loong, Lee, 722
Human capital theory, 511
Human Nature, Class, and Ethnicity (Gordon), 532
Hybridization thesis, 548

Iacocca, Lee, 289
Ideology, xviii, xix, xxii, 304, 320, 410, 411,
    441,451,457, 507, 523, 528, 537, 556, 626
    concept of, and its role in social science research, 458–461
    legitimating the dominant, 464–467
Inclusion, importance of, 653–655
Individualization, and a moral economy, 340–342
Inequality, racial, in the workplace, 448–456
Influence, in combat, 294–301
Informal formalization, 706
Information processing, model of organization, 146–162
Information systems, vertical, 153–154
Information technology, and individual autonomy, 270–271
Informed consensus, 102
Input uncertainty, 164–165, 191–192
    hypotheses, 167
    in hospital emergency units, 163–172

In Search of Excellence (Peters and Waterman), 316
Institutional change, in response to regulation, 651–652
Institutional isomorphism, 605–615
Institutional needs, and the ego-ideal, 285
Instrumental achieving styles, 282
Instrumental knowledge and skill, repositories of, 287–289
Integration
    bases of, 420–424
    obstacles to, 424–426
    of individual and organizational goals, 248–253
    principle of, 250–251
Integration perspective, and value engineering, 316–317
Intellectual dominance, struggle for, 315–336
Intelligence
    of learning, 626–627
    waste of, 99
Interactionist paradigm, xv–xvii
Interaction Ritual (Goffman), xi
Interactive technology, co-evolution of, with non-governmental organizations (NGOs), 676–686
Interactive type. *See* Post-bureaucratic type
Interdependence model, 294–301
Interdependent global order, and achieving styles, 285–287
Interrelating, heedful, 173–185
Intervention, feedback as, 644–645
"Iron cage," 605
Isomorphism, institutional, 605–615

Japan, online dating in, 711–719
Japanese firms, economic model of, 254–266
J-mode, 255–257
Johnson, Brenda, 412
Johnson, Lyndon, 288
Joint sensemaking, 198–199
Jurisdictional areas, 79

Kanter, Rosebeth Moss, xv, 471, 479, 489
Kellogg, Katherine, 591
Kelly and Thibaut model, for trust development, 296–297
Kennedy, John F., 506
Kilminster, Joe, 499–500, 502
Kimmel, Michael, 369
King, Martin Luther, 286
Knowledge
    power and, 642, 681–683
    sharing, 195–196, 256
Koe, Stuart, 721
Koike, Kazuo, 257
Kontor, 80
Kunda, Gideon, 304

Labor. *See* Division of labor
Labor markets, 94–97
Latent conflict, 428–429

Lateral politics, 100–101
Lateral relationships, 154–160
Latino community, racial profiling in the, 349–363
Latour, Bruno, 684n1
Lawler, Edward, 4
Lawrence, Paul, 587
Leadership
    connective, 279–293
    democratic, 230
    female styles, 279–293
    participatory, 230
    transformative, 230
    See also Management
Leana, Carrie, 5
Learning, organizational, 587–594, 616–630, 631–640
Learning management system (LMS), 687
Legitimate domination, xiii
Lesbians, disclosure dilemma for, 563–576. *See also* Gender; LGBT community (Singapore)
Levin, William, xvii
Levitt, Barbara, 589
LGBT community (Singapore), online organization of, 720–728. *See also* Gender
Liaison roles, 154
Lipman-Blumen, Jean, 230
Lipsky, Michael, 228
Lorsch, Jay, 587
Lowenthal, Patrick R., 662
Lucas, William, 501–503
Lund, Robert, 498, 500, 504
Lye, John, 410

Macneil, Ian, 31
Madonna, 670
Mailath, George, 260
Male identity, and work, 505. *See also* Masculinity
Management
    decisions, 259–262, 498–500
    feminist critique of, 493–498
    mechanistic system of, 14–18
    organic system of, 14–18
    scientific, 233–240, 493
    women and men in, 483, 484
    See also Leadership
Management of Innovation, The (Burns and Stalker), 2
Manifest conflict, 430–431
Mannhein, Karl, xiv
March, James, 589
Market failures framework, 21–25
Markets, 19–29, 32, 33–37. *See also* Organization(s)
Marrone, Jennifer, 230
Marx, Karl, xviii, xxi, 73, 227, 409, 440–447
Masculine ego-ideal, 280–282
Masculine ethic, 473, 494

Masculinity, central dimensions of, 500–507
Mason, Jerry, 499, 502, 504
Matrix organization, 157–160
Maume, David, 449
Mauss, Marcel, 36
Maximum prosperity, 233
Mayo, Elton, 432
McClelland, David, 463
McGregor, Douglas, 228
Mead, George Herbert, xii
Mechanistic management system, 14–18
Mediating processes, 67–68
Meijer, Albert Jacob, 663
Melting pot concept, 530
Men and Women of the Corporation (Kanter), 479
Men Who Manage (Dalton), 88
Merton, Robert, 307
Meyer, John, 610
Meyer, Marshall, 607
Microinstitutional change, 649–660
Micro social order, 60–71
Middle group minorities, 366
Middleman minorities, 366
Milkman, Ruth, 368
Mimetic processes, 609–610
Mind, as disposition to heed, 176–178
Minorities, middle group and middleman, 366
MLQ (Multifactor Leadership Questionnaire), 296
Monocratically organized, 79
Moore, Jesse, 498
Moore, Wilbert, xx
Moral economy, 337–348
Morality, neglect of, in cultural industrial research, 338–339
MUDs (Multi-User Dungeons), 667–674
Mulloy, Larry, 499, 503
Multifactor Leadership Questionnaire (MLQ), 296
Multiple advocacy model, 601–602
Multi-User Dungeons (MUDs), 667–674
Munch, Richard, xiv
Murray, Gilbert, 418
Myrdal, Gunnar, 530

Nadler, David, 129
Narrative skills, 181
Nasser, Gamal Abdel, 553
Negative assessments, 108
Negotiated exchange, 66
Nemeth, Charlan, 471
Network organizational form, 30–40, 53–59. *See also* Organization(s); Relational organizational form
New ethnicity, 530, 532–533, 536
New Palgrave, The (Archibald), 262
New State, The (Follett), xvi
Non-governmental organizations (NGOs), co-evolution with

interactive technology, 676–686
Nonseparability, 64
Normative pressures, 610–612
Northern Quarter Association, 342
"Norwegian Women's Revolution," 477
NUMMI (New United Motor Manufacturing, Inc.), 112–115

OBE (overcome by events), 183n3
Obligations, to others in networks, 53–59
Office hierarchy, 79
Oil, discourse of, 546–562
Oil Producing and Exporting Countries (OPEC), 552–554
Online dating, in Japan, 711–719
Online organization, of the LGBT community in Singapore, 720–728
Operating rooms, 649–660
Oppositional frames, 653
Organic management system, 14–18
Organizational change, 101, 587–593, 596, 601, 605–607, 612n2, 617–619, 624–627. *See also* Change
Organizational conflict, 409–414, 427–439. *See also* Conflict, constructive
Organizational coordination, xx, 84–86
   in hospital emergency units, 163–172
   in trauma centers, 186–204
Organizational culture, 303–310, 315–336. *See also* Culture
Organizational diversity, and organizational theory, 606–612
Organizational effectiveness, 166–167
Organizational failures framework, 25 (table)
Organizational fields, institutional isomorphism and collective rationality in, 605–615
Organizational forms
   bureaucratic, 73–78
   relational, 1–5
Organizational learning, 587–594, 616–630, 631–640
Organizational memory, 620–622
Organizational model, of social capital, 44
Organizational narratives, creating discursive space in, 641–648
Organizational networks, and particularism, 56–57
Organizational reciprocity norms, 48–49
Organizational social capital, 41–52
Organizational socialization, research on, 350–352
Organizational supportiveness, importance of, 564–565
Organizational teams, and learning goals, 635 (table)
Organizational theory, 699
   conceptualization of topics in, 181–183
   organizational diversity and, 606–612
Organization(s)
   challenges for, xx–xxiii
   collective mind in, 173–185
   design, 146–162
   diversity within, 471–476
   economic, forms of, 30–37
   fast-response, coordination in, 186–204

gender and, 478–481, 486, 493–498
information processing model of, 148–160
late-bureaucratic, 696–710
nature of, 19–20
network forms of, 30–40
non-governmental (NGOs), 676–686
race in, 527–545
typology of, 113–115
uncertainty in, 164
women's careers in, 477–491
See also Bureaucracy; Bureaucratic organizational form;
    Work; Workplace, the
Organized dissonance, 119–126
Orientalism (Said), 548
Other (the), representations of, 546–562
Ouchi, William, 2, 4, 306
Overcome by events (OBE), 183n3

Paradigms, in organizational learning, 619
Parsons, Talcott, 53, 89, 303
Participatory leadership, 230
Particularism, 53–58
Patterning, and culture, 312–313
People like us (PLU), 721
Perceived conflict, 429
Performance
    in customer service and sales, 267–278
    measurement, 209
    power versus, 120
    problems, and the feminist-bureaucratic hybrid, 121
Personal instrumental achieving style, 286–287
Personnel, integrating, 156
Pfeffer, Jeffrey, 588
Phua, Joe, 663
Piore, Michael, 75
Plug-and-play teaming, 194
Police socialization, 352–354
Policy feedbacks, 392
Policy tools, and representative bureaucracy, 390–407
Political economy, critique of, 415–416
Politics, exclusionary, 504–505
Pondy, Louis, 411
Pooled interdependence, 147
Popular will, 82–83
Positive assessments, 109–110
Postbureaucratic hybrid, 120
Post-bureaucratic type, 98–106
Postcolonial theory, overview, 547–549
Postlewaite, Andrew, 260
Postmodern analysis, 326–328
Poststructuralist inquiry, features of, 642
Powell, Walter, 2, 588
Power
    culture and, 304–306

knowledge and, 642
    performance versus, 120
Practical pushing, 641–648
Practice, conceptualization of, 182–183
Presentation of Self in Everyday Life, The (Goffman), xi
Private goods model, 43
Procedure, primacy of, 503
Process of control, 133–138
Productive exchange, 65
Productivity, 432
Profiling, racial, 349–363
Prosperity, maximum, 233
*Protestant Ethic and the Spirit of Capitalism,
    The* (Weber), 366, 605
Protocol breaking, 199–200
Public goods model, 43
Public schools, representation in, 390–407
Pyramidal politics, 503

Qgbor, John O., 413
Qualitative cultural studies, 321, 323
Quality Circles, 99
Quality improvement teams, 269
Quality outcomes, 217–219
Quinn, Ryan, 130

Race, in organizations, 527–545
Race relations cycle, 530
Racial inequality, in the workplace, 448–456
Racial profiling, in the Latino community, 349–363
Racism, everyday, 538
Raison d'état, 82–83
Rank, significance of, 504–505
Ranks, hierarchy of, 256–259
Rationalism, beyond, 306–307
Rationality, collective, 605–615
Rational paradigm, in organizational culture, 306–309
Reciprocal exchange, 66
Reciprocity, 36
Red Sheikh (Abdullah Tariki), 550–552
Reinartz, Stanley, 499, 503
Relational achieving styles, 281–282, 288–289
Relational coordination, 128–130, 206–212, 214–223.
    See also High-performance work systems, relational
    model of, 205–226
Relational mobilization, 650, 655
Relational model, of high-performance work systems, 205–226
Relational ontology, xvi
Relational organizational form, 1–5
Relational paradigm, xii–xv
Relational spaces, and microinstitutional change
    in surgery, 649–660
Relational total, 127
Relational trust. *See* Resilient trust

Relationships, and the ethic of care, 57–58
Representation, in public schools, 390–407
Representations of the other, 546–562
Representative bureaucracy
    Latino community and, 349–363
    policy tools and, 390–407
Resilient trust, 46, 50n2
Resistance, 642
Resource dependence, 588
Responsibility, 57–58
Roberts, Karlene, 129
Rockefeller, John D., 550
Role playing games, 669
Roosevelt, Franklin D., 433
Roylance, John, 382
Ruggie, John, 678
Russell, Brian, 504

SAFE, 123
Said, Edward, 547
Salancik, Gerald, 588
Salter, Arthur, 136
Sassen, Saskia, 677
Schein, Edgar, 303
Schools. *See* Public schools
Scientific management, 233–240, 493
Scientific Taylorism, 268–270
Sedlak, Michael, 608
Seidner, Rob, 130
Self, constructions and reconstructions of, in
    virtual reality, 667–675
Self-acceptance, degree of, 566
Self-actualization, 253n
Self-concept, and sexual orientation, 566
Self-managed team, 269
Servants of Power (Baritz), 453
Seven Sisters, 550, 551
Sexual orientation, and self-concept, 566
Shared responsibility, 64
Shaw, A. W., 422
Sine ira et studio, 81
Singapore, LGBT community in, 720–728
Single-loop models, in research on decision making, 595–604
Slack resources, 151
Smith, Adam, 346n3
Social awareness, 723–724
Social capital, organizational, 41–52
Social embeddedness, of labor markets and
    cognitive processes, 94–97
Social exchange, 60–71
Social information processing theory (SIPT), 711–719
Social instrumental achieving style, 287
Socialization, 352–354
Social loafing, 45

Social media, 661–665
Social order, micro, 60–71
Social presence, enhancing with Twitter, 687–695
Social process, 180
Social science research, and the concept of
    ideology, 458–461
Societal myths, and discourse on entrepreneurship, 461–464
Sociological paradigms, xii-xxii
Socio-Technical Systems (STS) theory, 268–270
Soldiering, systematic, 237
Solidarity ratings, 372
Sørensen, Jesper, 587
Spaces, relational, in surgery, 649–660
Specialization, 88, 107, 139–145, 591, 618, 698
    economies of, 255, 260
    functional, 73–75, 83, 90, 127, 149, 152–153
    See also Division of labor; Division of work
Stability, and culture, 312
Stalker, G. M., 2
Stark, David, 662
Static hierarchies, 485, 487–489.
    See also Organization(s)
Steele, Claude, 367–369, 375, 472
Stephens, John Paul, 130
Stereotype threat, 367–369
Stories, in organizational learning, 619
Strangers, 366
Street Corner Society (Whyte), 368
Structural equation model, 299 (figure)
Structural equivalence, 606
Structuration theory and new medium studies, 697–698
Student discipline, in public schools, 390–407
Substantive justice, 82
Substantive rationality, xiv
Success, ambiguity of, 619–620
Superstitious learning, 620
Surgery, spaces and change in, 649–660
Survey research approach, to defining and studying
    organizational culture, 311
Sweeney, Patrick, 231
Swope, Gerard, 246
Symbolic Interactionism (Blumer), xvii
Systematic soldiering, 237
Systems model, of organizational conflict, 427, 436–437

Tariki, Abdullah, 550–551
Task forces, 155
Task jointness, 63
Task predictability, and information processing, 146–148
Task uncertainty, alternative organization responses to, 150
    (figure)
Taylor, Frederick Winslow, 73, 493
Teaching presence, 693
Teaming, plug-and-play, 194

Teams, 155–156
    learning, 633–634, 636 (table).
            See also Organizational learning
    performance, dimensions of, 271
Teamwork, 284–285
Technology
    in customer service and sales, 267–278
    interactive, co-evolution with NGOs, 676–686
    new, 661–665
Tesluk, Paul, 230
Theory building, 208–210
Theory of relational cohesion, 63
Theory X, 248, 250
Theory Y, 248–253
Thompson, Arnie, 500
Thompson, E. P., 32
Thompson, James, 128
Thompson, Vaida, 231
Thye, Shane, 4
Total quality management (TQM), 107, 268–269
Total relativity, 133
Total situation, 134
Transacting, 46
Transsexuals, female-to-male. *See* Transmen
Transformational leadership, 230
Transition, and workplace gender advantages, 516–522
Transitional model, 600–601
Transmen, workplace experiences of, 510–526
Trauma centers, coordination in, 186–204
Treatment trajectory, in trauma centers, 189
Trump, Ivana, 670
Trust, 46–47, 63
    development, Kelly and Thibaut
            model for, 296–297
    dyadic versus generalized, 46–47
    fragile versus resilient, 46
    in combat, 294–301
    interdependence model for
            building, 295–296
Turkle, Sherry, 661
Tushman, Michael, 129
Twitter, and social presence, 687–695

Uncertainty
    absorption of, 143–144
    in hospital emergency units, 164–167
Universalism, 53–56

Valentine, Robert, 8
Value engineering, and the integration
        perspective, 316–317

Van Buren, Harry, 5
Vaughan, Diane, 386
Vicarious achieving style, 288–289
Viner, Katherine, 680
Virtual reality, constructions and reconstructions of self in,
        667–675

Warner, Lloyd, xi
Wayne, John, 283
Weber, Max, xii, 3, 55, 88, 366, 493, 605, 699
Weick, Karl, 4, 129
Weiss, Leigh, 3
Weitzman, Martin, 261
White, Harrison, 433
White Male System, 497, 507
Whyte, William, 368
Wimbush, Julian, 130
Wisheart, James, 382
Women
    careers of, in static and dynamic organizations, 477–491
    connective leadership and, 279–293
    entrepreneurship education for, 364–380
Women in Management (WIM) research, 478–481
Women's Business Centers (WBCs), 364–365
Work
    coordination of, 127–131
    cultural, 337–348
    division of, 139–145
    inefficiency, causes of, 235–240
    male identity and, 505
    organization, in customer service and sales, 267–278
    systems, high-performance, 205–226
    See also Organization; Workplawce, the
Workplace, the
    "coming out" disclosures in, 563–576
    female leadership styles in, 279–293
    racial inequality in, 448–456
    diversity in, and the colonizing consciousness, 556–558
    gender advantages in, 516–523
    progressive identities in, 344–346
    See also Organization; Work

Xiao, Yin, 129

Yoon, Jeongkoo, 4

ABOUT THE EDITORS

Mary Godwyn is an associate professor in the History and Society Division at Babson College. She holds a BA in philosophy from Wellesley College and a PhD in sociology from Brandeis University. She has lectured at Harvard University and taught at Brandeis University and Lasell College, where she was also the director of the Donahue Institute for Values and Public Life. Godwyn focuses on social theory as it applies to issues of inequality in formal and informal organizations. She studies entrepreneurship as a vehicle for the economic and political advancement of marginalized populations, especially women and minorities. In addition to publishing in journals such as *Symbolic Interaction, Research in Social Stratification and Mobility,* and the *Journal of Small Business and Entrepreneurship*, Godwyn has coauthored a book (with Donna Stoddard, DBA), *Minority Women Entrepreneurs: How Outsider Status Can Lead to Better Business Practices* (2011), published by Greenleaf Publishing and Stanford University Press. Godwyn served on the executive committee of the Critical Management Studies Division of the Academy of Management from 2008 to 2011, and was also the 2008 winner of the Dark Side Case Competition for her case "Hugh Connerty and Hooters: What Is Successful Entrepreneurship?" Her research has been funded by the Coleman Foundation, the Ewing Marion Kauffman Foundation, the Harold S. Geneen Charitable Trust, and the Babson College Board of Research Fund. In addition to scholarship and teaching, Godwyn consults to colleges and universities about how to integrate entrepreneurship into liberal arts programs.

Jody Hoffer Gittell is professor of management at Brandeis University's Heller School for Social Policy and Management, director of the Relational Coordination Research Collaborative, and acting director of the MIT Leadership Center. Before joining Brandeis, Gittell received her MA in political economy from The New School for Social Research and her PhD in management from the MIT Sloan School of Management, and served as assistant professor at the Harvard Business School. To complement Godwyn's expertise in sociology, Gittell brings to this project her knowledge of organization studies. She has developed a theory of relational coordination, proposing that work is most effectively coordinated through relationships of shared goals, shared knowledge, and mutual respect. Gittell has authored dozens of articles and chapters, as well as three books including *The Southwest Airlines Way: Using the Power of Relationships to Achieve High Performance* (McGraw-Hill, 2003); *Up in the Air: How Airlines Can Improve Performance by Engaging Their Employees* (Cornell University Press, 2009); and *High Performance Healthcare: Using the Power of Relationships to Achieve Quality, Efficiency and Resilience* (McGraw-Hill, 2009). Gittell has contributed to the *Handbook of Human Resource Management* (Sage, 2010) and the *Handbook of Positive Organizational Scholarship* (Oxford University Press, 2011). She won the Outstanding Young Scholar of the Year Award in 2004 from the

Labor and Employment Relations Association, the Best Book Award for Industry Studies in 2005 from the Alfred P. Sloan Foundation, a Best Paper Award in 2008 from the Academy of Management, and the Douglas McGregor Memorial Award for Best Paper of the Year in 2008 in the *Journal of Applied Behavioral Science.*

SAGE Research Methods Online

The essential tool for researchers

Sign up now at www.sagepub.com/srmo for more information.

An expert research tool

- An **expertly designed taxonomy** with more than 1,400 unique terms for social and behavioral science research methods

- **Visual and hierarchical search tools** to help you discover material and link to related methods

- Easy-to-use navigation tools
- Content organized by complexity
- Tools for citing, printing, and downloading content with ease
- Regularly updated content and features

A wealth of essential content

- The most comprehensive picture of quantitative, qualitative, and mixed methods available today

- More than **100,000 pages of SAGE book and reference material** on research methods as well as editorially selected material from SAGE journals

- More than **600 books** available in their entirety online

Launching 2011!

$SAGE research methods online